Math Expressions

Teacher Edition • Volume 1

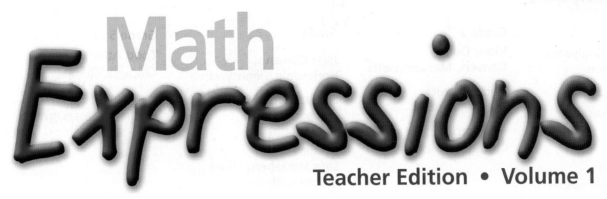

Developed by
The Children's Math Worlds Research Project

PROJECT DIRECTOR AND AUTHOR
Dr. Karen C. Fuson

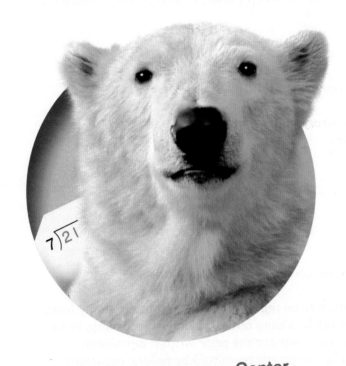

This material is based upon work supported by the
National Science Foundation
under Grant Numbers
ESI-9816320, REC-9806020, and RED-935373.

Any opinions, findings, and conclusions, or recommendations expressed in this material
are those of the author and do not necessarily reflect the views of the National Science Foundation.

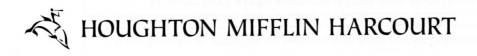

HOUGHTON MIFFLIN HARCOURT

Teacher Reviewers

Kindergarten
Patricia Stroh Sugiyama
Wilmette, Illinois

Barbara Wahle
Evanston, Illinois

Grade 1
Sandra Budson
Newton, Massachusetts

Janet Pecci
Chicago, Illinois

Megan Rees
Chicago, Illinois

Grade 2
Molly Dunn
Danvers, Massachusetts

Agnes Lesnick
Hillside, Illinois

Rita Soto
Chicago, Illinois

Grade 3
Jane Curran
Honesdale, Pennsylvania

Sandra Tucker
Chicago, Illinois

Grade 4
Sara Stoneberg Llibre
Chicago, Illinois

Sheri Roedel
Chicago, Illinois

Grade 5
Todd Atler
Chicago, Illinois

Leah Barry
Norfolk, Massachusetts

Special Thanks

Special thanks to the many teachers, students, parents, principals, writers, researchers, and work-study students who participated in the Children's Math Worlds Research Project over the years.

Credits

(t) © Superstock/Alamy, (b) © Steve Bloom Images/Alamy.

Illustrative art: Dave Klug, Eli Nicolosi, Geoff Smith, John Kurtz, Tim Johnson.
Technical art: Morgan-Cain & Associates

Introducing

Math Expressions

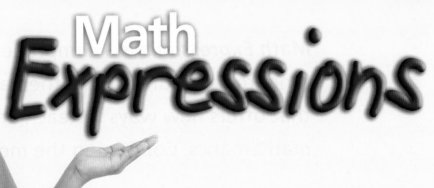

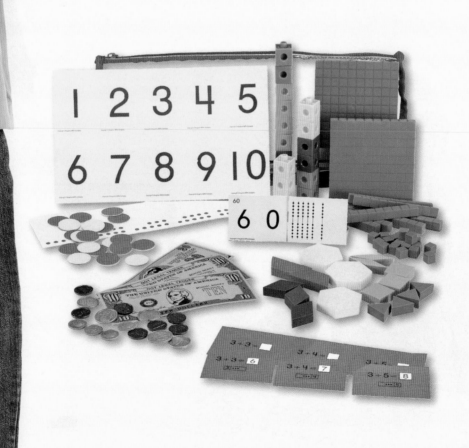

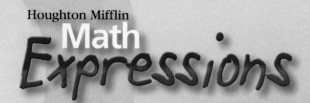

A Fresh Approach to

Math Expressions is a comprehensive Kindergarten–Grade 5 mathematics curriculum that offers new ways to teach and learn mathematics. Combining the most powerful

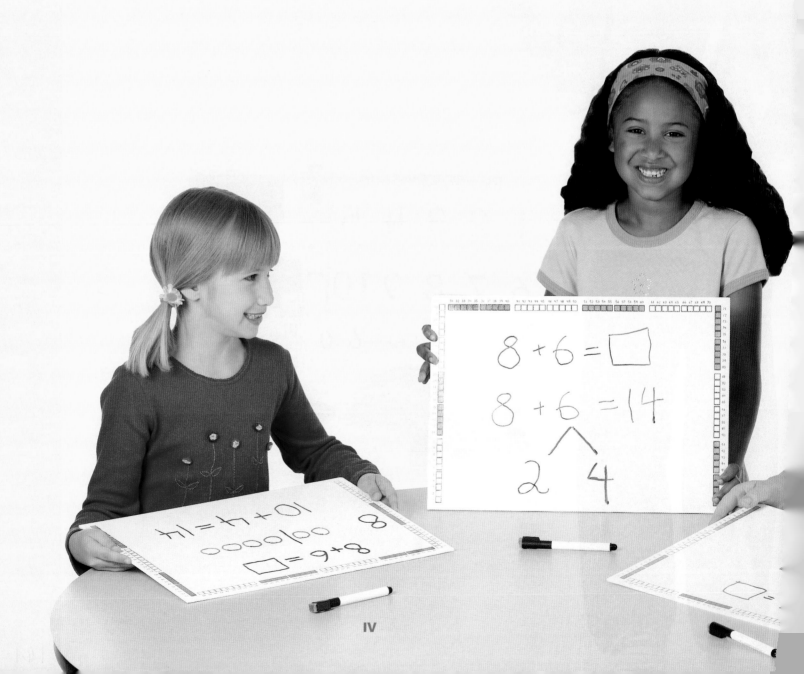

IV

Standards-Based Instruction

elements of standards-based instruction with the best of traditional approaches, *Math Expressions* uses objects, drawings, conceptual language, and real-world situations to help students build mathematical ideas that make sense to them.

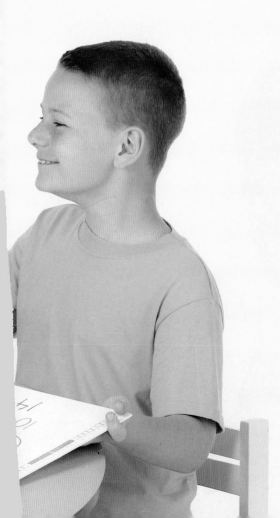

Math Expressions implements state standards as well as the recommendations and findings from recent reports on math learning:

Curriculum Focal Points (NCTM, 2007)

Principles and Standards for School Mathematics (NCTM, 2000)

Adding It Up
(National Research Council, 2001)

How Students Learn Mathematics in the Classroom
(National Research Council, 2005)

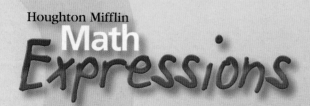

Houghton Mifflin
Math Expressions

Focused on Understanding

In **Math Expressions**, teachers create an inquiry environment and encourage constructive discussion. Students invent, question, and explore, but also learn

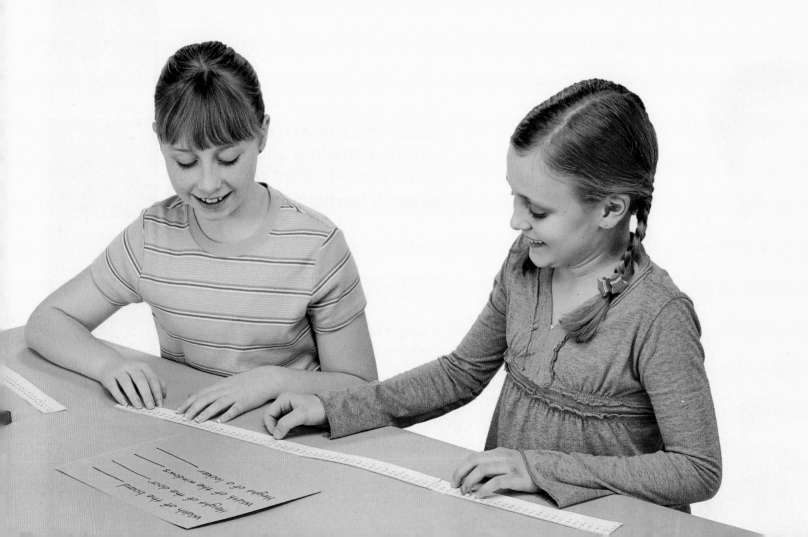

and Fluency

and practice important math strategies. Through daily Math Talk, students explain their methods and, in turn, become more fluent in them.

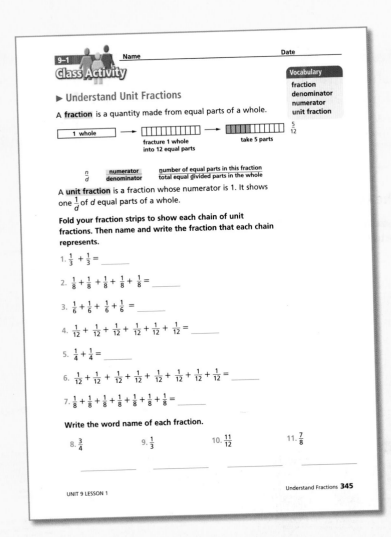

> "As Students are asked to communicate about the mathematics they are studying ... they gain insights into their thinking to others, students naturally reflect on their learning and organize and consolidate their thinking about mathematics"
>
> *- Principles and Standards for School Mathematics*, National Council of Teachers of Mathematics (2000), p. 120

Organized for

Math Expressions is organized around five crucial classroom structures that allow children to develop deep conceptual

Quick Practice
Routines involve whole-class responses or individual partner practice

Math Talk
Students share strategies and solutions orally and through proof drawings

Building Concepts
Objects, drawings, conceptual language, and real-world situations strengthen mathematical ideas and understanding

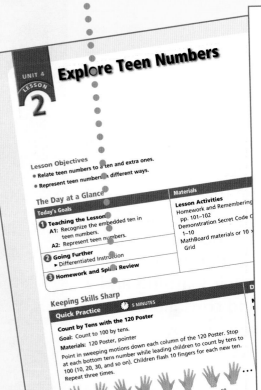

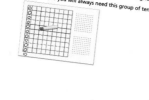

Classroom Success

understanding, and then practice, apply, and discuss
what they know with skill and confidence.

Helping Community

A classroom in which everyone is both
a teacher and a learner enhances
mathematical understanding,
competence, and confidence

Student Leaders

Teachers facilitate students' growth by
helping them learn to lead practice and
discussion routines

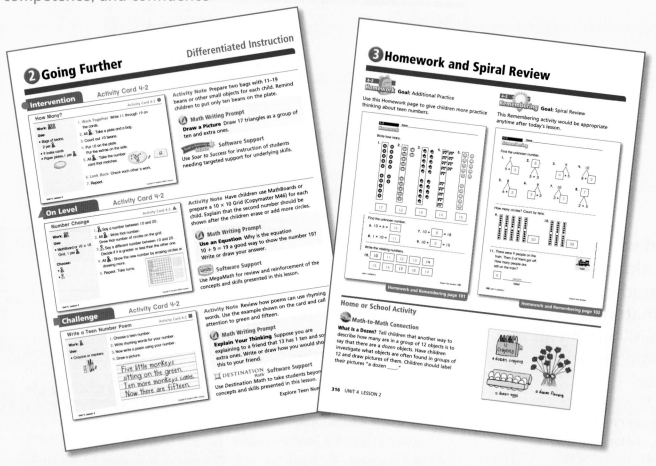

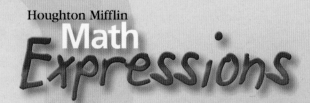

Differentiated for

Every *Math Expressions* lesson includes intervention, on level, and challenge differentiation to support classroom needs. Leveled Math Writing Prompts provide opportunities for in–depth thinking and analysis, and help prepare students for high-stakes tests.

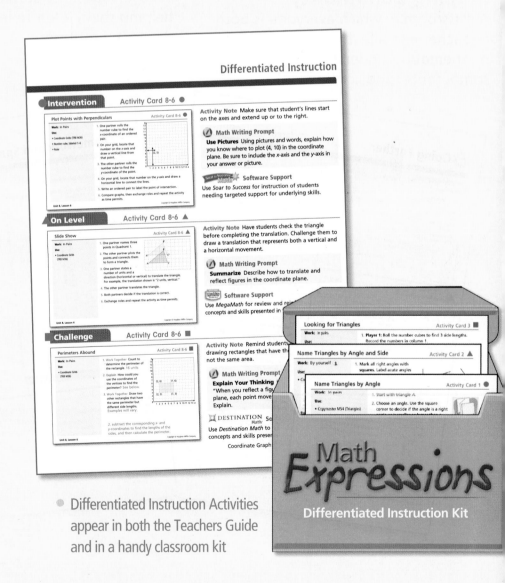

Differentiated Instruction Activities appear in both the Teachers Guide and in a handy classroom kit

Quick Practic
Community Quick
Helping Concepts
Building Concepts
Student Leaders
Math Talk

All Learners

Support for English Language Learners is included in each lesson. A special Challenge Math Center Easel, with activities, projects, and puzzlers, helps the highest math achievers reach their potential.

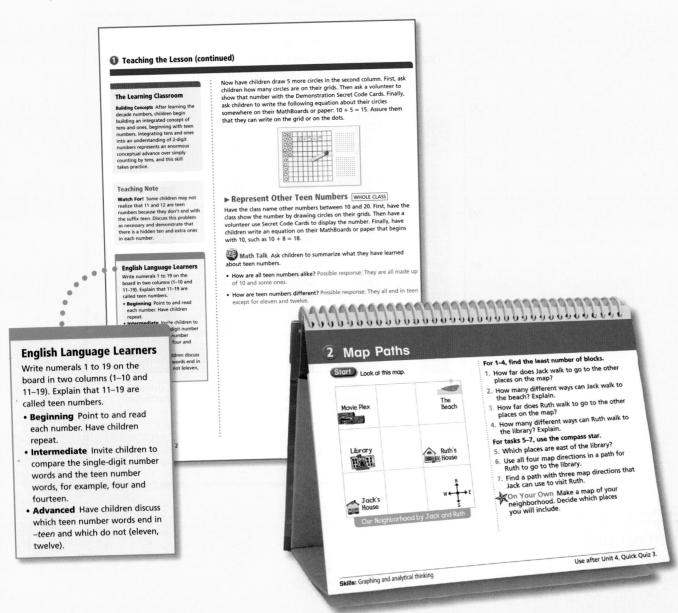

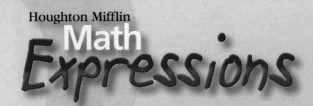

Validated Through Ten

For twenty-five years, Dr. Karen Fuson, Professor Emeritus of Education and Psychology at Northwestern University, researched effective methods of teaching and learning mathematics.

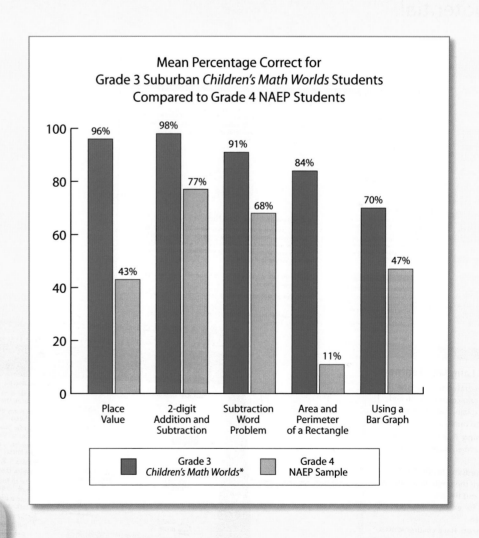

Mean Percentage Correct for Grade 3 Suburban *Children's Math Worlds* Students Compared to Grade 4 NAEP Students

"I have many children who cheer when it's math time"
- Grade 2 Teacher

Years of Research

During the last ten years, with the support of the National Science Foundation for the Children's Math Worlds research Project, Dr. Fuson began development of what is now the *Math Expressions* curriculum in real classrooms across the country.

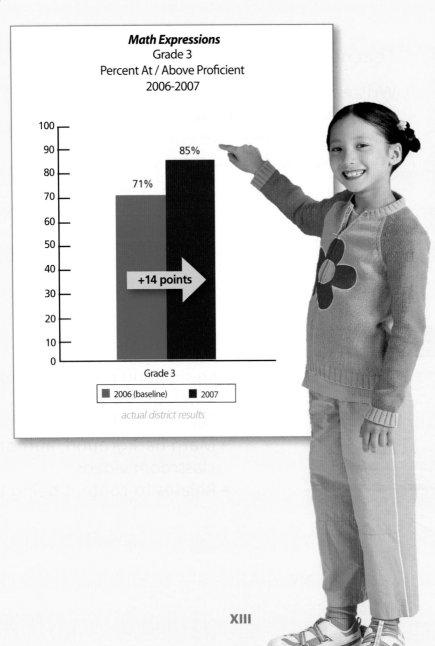

Math Expressions
Grade 3
Percent At / Above Proficient
2006-2007

71%

85%

+14 points

Grade 3

■ 2006 (baseline) ■ 2007

actual district results

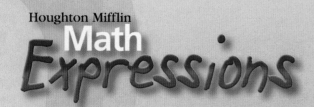

Powered by

Math Expressions is highly accessible by all teachers. To ensure the program gets off to the right start, our educational consultants are available to support districts implementing *Math Expressions.* Unique Teacher's Guide support and professional development options are also provided.

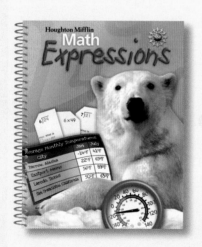

Teacher's Guide

Written in a learn while teaching style, math background and learning in the classroom resources are embedded at point of use in the Teachers Guide

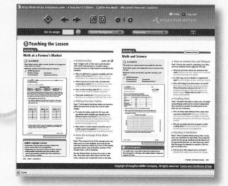

eTeacher's Guide

Offers on-demand professional development
- Available 24-7
- Direct links in the eTG
- Math background, author talks, and classroom videos
- Relates to content being taught

Professional Development

Special, in depth *Math Expressions* seminars
are also available.

- **Administrator Institute**
  For administrators with school-based
  curriculum responsibilities

- **Level I Institute**
  For teachers who are new to
  Math Expressions

- **Level II Institute**
  For teachers who have at least 6
  months' experience teaching
  Math Expressions

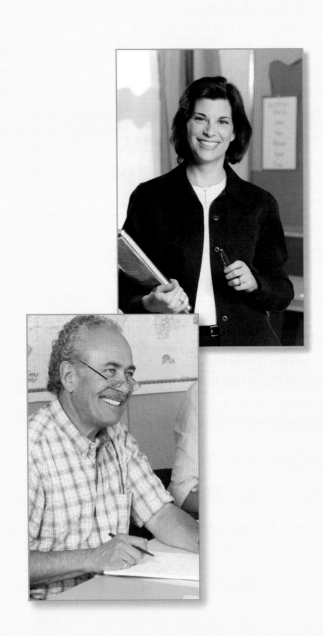

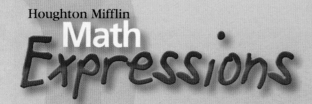

Components

	K	1	2	3	4	5
Core Components						
Teacher's Guide	•	•	•	•	•	•
Student Activity Book*	•	•	•	•	•	•
Homework and Remembering Book	•	•	•	•	•	•
Assessment Guide	•	•	•	•	•	•
Teacher Resource Book	•	•	•	•	•	•
MathBoards		•	•	•	•	•
Ready-Made Classroom Resources						
Individual Student Manipulatives Kit	•	•	•	•	•	•
Materials and Manipulatives Kit	•	•	•	•	•	•
Custom Manipulatives Kit	•	•	•	•	•	•
Challenge Math Center Easel	•	•	•	•	•	•
Hands-On Activity Workbook 3–5				•	•	•
Differentiated Instruction Activity Card Kit	•	•	•	•	•	•
Literature Library	•	•	•	•	•	•
Anno's Counting Book Big Book	•					
Technology						
eTeacher's Guide	•	•	•	•	•	•
eStudent Activity Book	•	•	•	•	•	•
Lesson Planner CD-ROM	•	•	•	•	•	•
ExamView Ways to Assess	•	•	•	•	•	•
Houghton Mifflin Online Assessment System	•	•	•	•	•	•
Mega Math	•	•	•	•	•	•
Destination Math	•	•	•	•	•	•
Soar to Success Math	•	•	•	•	•	•

*Grades K–5 available as consumable workbook; Grades 3–5 available as hardbound text

New hardcover version Grades 3–5

Materials and Manipulatives for Grade 4

The essential materials needed for teaching *Math Expressions* are provided in the Student Activity Book and/or can be made from Copymasters in the Teacher's Resource Book. However, many teachers prefer to use the more sturdy materials from the Materials and Manipulatives kits. This allows the students to take home the paper materials (from the Student Activity Book) or the cardstock materials (made from the Copymasters) to facilitate the connection between home and school.

Material or Manipulative in Grade 4	Pages in Student Activity Book	Copymasters in Teacher's Resource Book
Class Multiplication Table Poster*		
Product Cards: 2s, 5s, 9s*	11–12	M6–M7
Product Cards: 2s, 5s, 9s*	13–14	M8–M9
Product Cards: 3s, 4s*	25–26	M11–M12
Product Cards: 6s, 7s, 8s*	49–50	M20–M21
Product Cards: 6s, 7s, 8s*	51–52	M22–M23
Five in a Line Cards*		M33–M39
Target*	2	M1
Geometry and Measurement Poster (Gr 4)		
Telescoping Pointer		
Demonstration Whole Number Secret Code Cards		
Whole Number Secret Code Cards (1–100)	144A	M145
Whole Number Secret Code Cards (200–1,000)	144B	M146
Demonstration Decimal Secret Code Cards		
Decimal Secret Code Cards: Tenths and Hundredths	428A–428B	M135–M136
Decimal Secret Code Cards: Hundreds, Tens, and Ones	434A–434B	M137–M138
Decimal Secret Code Cards: Thousands and Thousandths	436A–436B	M139–M140
Base Ten Blocks (units, rods, flats)		
2-Color Counters		
Number Cubes (blank)		
Pattern Blocks		M77
Play Coins (pennies, nickels, dimes)		
Play Bills* (1-dollar, 10-dollar, 100-dollar)		

* These materials were developed specifically for this program during the Children's Math Worlds Research Project.

Using the Materials and Manipulatives for Each Unit

Material or Manipulative in Grade 4	Fluency Plan	Unit 1	Unit 2	Unit 3	Unit 4	Unit 5	Unit 6	Unit 7	Unit 8	Unit 9	Unit 10	Unit 11	Unit 12
Class Multiplication Table poster	•												
Product Cards: 2s, 5s, 9s	•												
Product Cards: 3s, 4s	•												
Product Cards: 6s, 7s, 8s	•												
Five in a Line Cards	•												
Targets	•	•											
Geometry and Measurement poster (Gr 4)			•		•		•						
Telescoping Pointer								•					
Demonstration Whole Number Secret Code Cards				•									
Whole Number Secret Code Cards (1–100)				•									
Whole Number Secret Code Cards (200–1,000)				•									
Demonstration Decimal Secret Code Cards												•	
Decimal Secret Code Cards: Tenths and Hundredths												•	
Decimal Secret Code Cards: Hundreds, Tens, and Ones												•	
Decimal Secret Code Cards: Thousands and Thousandths												•	
Base Ten Blocks (units, rods, flats)			•	•		•		•					
2-Color Counters	•	•		•		•		•		•			
Number Cubes (blank)			•	•		•		•		•		•	
Play Coins (pennies, nickels, dimes)	•		•	•		•			•	•		•	
Play Bills (1-dollar, 10-dollar, 100-dollar)			•	•				•	•	•		•	

All materials for each unit (including those not in the kits) are listed in the planning chart for that unit.

Introduction

History and Development

Math Expressions is a K–5 mathematics program, developed from the Children's Math Worlds (CMW) Research Project conducted by Dr. Karen Fuson, Professor Emeritus at Northwestern University. This project was funded in part by the National Science Foundation.

The Research Project

The project studied the ways children around the world understand mathematical concepts, approach problem solving, and learn to do computation; it included ten years of classroom research and incorporated the ideas of participating students and teachers into the developing curriculum.

The research focused on building conceptual supports that include special language, drawings, manipulatives, and classroom communication methods that facilitate mathematical competence.

Curriculum Design

Within the curriculum, a series of learning progressions reflect recent research regarding children's natural stages when mastering concepts such as addition, subtraction, multiplication, and problem solving. These learning stages help determine the order of concepts, the sequence of units, and the positioning of topics.

The curriculum is designed to help teachers apply the most effective conceptual supports so that each child progresses as rapidly as possible.

During the research, students showed increases in standardized test scores as well as in broader measures of student understanding. These results were found for a wide range of both urban and suburban students from a variety of socio-economic groups.

Philosophy

Math Expressions incorporates the best practices of both traditional and reform mathematics curricula. The program strikes a balance between promoting children's natural solution methods and introducing effective procedures.

Building on Children's Knowledge

Because research has demonstrated that premature instruction in formalized procedures can lead to mechanical, unthinking behavior, established procedures for solving problems are not introduced until students have developed a solid conceptual foundation. Children begin by using their own knowledge to solve problems and then are introduced to research-based accessible methods.

In order to promote children's natural solution methods, as well as to encourage students to become reflective and resourceful problem solvers, teachers need to develop a helping and explaining culture in their classrooms.

Student Interactions

Collaboration and peer helping deepen children's commitment to values such as responsibility and respect for others. *Math Expressions* offers opportunities for students to interact in pairs, small groups, whole-class activities, and special scenarios.

As students collaboratively investigate math situations, they develop communication skills, sharpen their mathematical reasoning, and enhance their social awareness. Integrating students' social and cultural worlds into their emerging math worlds helps them to find their own voices and to connect real-world experiences to math concepts.

Main Concept Streams

Math Expressions focuses on crucially important core concepts. These core topics are placed at grade levels that enable students to do well on standardized tests. The main related concept streams at all grade levels are number concepts and an algebraic approach to word problems.

Breaking apart numbers, or finding the embedded numbers, is a key concept running through the number concept units.

- Kindergartners and first-graders find the numbers embedded within single-digit numbers and find the tens and ones in multi-digit numbers.

- Second- and third-graders continue breaking apart multi-digit numbers into ones and groups of tens, hundreds, and thousands. This activity facilitates their understanding of multi-digit addition and subtraction as well as solving word problems.

- Second-, third-, and fourth-graders work on seeing the repeated groups within numbers, and this awareness helps them to master multiplication and division.

- Fourth- and fifth-graders approach fractions as sums of unit fractions using length models. This permits them to see and comprehend operations on fractions.

Students work with story problems early in kindergarten and continue throughout the other grades. They not only solve but also construct word problems. As a result, they become comfortable and flexible with mathematical language and can connect concepts and terminology with meaningful referents from their own lives. As part of this process, students learn to make math drawings that enable teachers to see student thinking and facilitate communication.

Concepts and skills in algebra, geometry, measurement, and graphing are woven in between these two main streams throughout the grades. In grades two through five, geometry and measurement mini-units follow each regular unit.

Program Features

Many special features and approaches contribute to the effectiveness of *Math Expressions*.

Quick Practice

The opening 5 minutes of each math period are dedicated to activities (often student-led) that allow students to practice newly acquired knowledge. These *consolidating activities* help students to become faster and more accurate with the concepts. Occasionally, *leading activities* prepare the ground for new concepts before they are introduced. Quick Practice activities are repeated so that they become familiar routines that students can do quickly and confidently.

Drawn Models

Special manipulatives are used at key points. However, students move toward math drawings as rapidly as possible.

These drawn models help students relate to the math situation, facilitate students' explanations of the steps they took to solve the problem, and help listeners comprehend these explanations.

The drawings also give teachers insight into students' mathematical thinking, and leave a durable record of student work.

Language Development

Math Expressions offers a wealth of learning activities that directly support language development. In addition to verbalizing procedures and explanations, students are encouraged to write their own problems and describe their problem-solving strategies in writing as soon as they are able.

Homework Assignments

To help students achieve a high level of mathematical performance, students complete homework assignments every night. Families are expected to identify a homework helper to be responsible for monitoring the student's homework completion and to help if necessary.

Remembering Activities

Remembering Activities provide practice with the important concepts covered in all the units to date. They are ideal for spare classroom moments when students need a quick refresher of what they have learned so far. These pages are also valuable as extra homework pages that promote cumulative review as an ongoing synthesis of concepts.

Student Leaders

Student Leaders lead Quick Practice activities and can help as needed during the solving phase of Solve and Discuss. Such experiences build independence and confidence.

Math Talk

A significant part of the collaborative classroom culture is the frequent exchange of mathematical ideas and problem-solving strategies, or Math Talk. There are multiple benefits of Math Talk:

- Describing one's methods to another person can clarify one's own thinking as well as clarify the matter for others.

- Another person's approach can supply a new perspective, and frequent exposure to different approaches tends to engender flexible thinking.

- In the collaborative Math Talk classroom, students can ask for and receive help, and errors can be identified, discussed, and corrected.

- Student math drawings accompany early explanations in all domains, so that all students can understand and participate in the discussion.

- Math Talk permits teachers to assess students' understanding on an ongoing basis. It encourages students to develop their language skills, both in math and in everyday English.

- Math Talk enables students to become active helpers and questioners, creating student-to-student talk that stimulates engagement and community.

The key supports for Math Talk are the various participant structures, or ways of organizing class members as they interact. The teacher always guides the activity to help students to work both as a community and also independently. Descriptions of the most common participant structures follow.

Participant Structures

Solve and Discuss (Solve, Explain, Question, and Justify) at the Board

The teacher selects 4 to 5 students (or as many as space allows) to go to the classroom board and solve a problem, using any method they choose. Their classmates work on the same problem at their desks. Then the teacher picks 2 or 3 students to explain their methods. Students at their desks are encouraged to ask questions and to assist their classmates in understanding.

> **Benefits:** Board work reveals multiple methods of solving a problem, making comparisons possible and communicating to students that different methods are acceptable. The teacher can select methods to highlight in subsequent discussions. Spontaneous helping occurs frequently by students working next to each other at the board. Time is used efficiently because everyone in the class is working. In addition, errors can be identified in a supportive way and corrected and understood by students.

Student Pairs

Two students work together to solve a problem, to explain a solution method to each other, to role play within a mathematical situation (for example, buying and selling), to play a math game, or to help a partner having difficulties. They are called helping pairs when more advanced students are matched with students who are struggling. Pairs may be organized formally, or they may occur spontaneously as help is needed. Initially, it is useful to model pair activities, contrasting effective and ineffective helping.

> **Benefits:** Pair work supports students in learning from each other, particularly in applying and practicing concepts introduced

Participant Structures (continued)

Student Pairs (continued)

in whole-class discussion. Helping pairs often foster learning by both students as the helper strives to adopt the perspective of the novice. Helping almost always enables the helper to understand more deeply.

Whole-Class Practice and Student Leaders

This structure can be either teacher-led or student-led. When students lead it, it is usually at the consolidation stage, when children understand the concept and are beginning to achieve speed and automaticity. It is an excellent way for students to work together and learn from each other.

> **Benefits:** Whole-class practice lets the less advanced students benefit from the knowledge of the more advanced students without having to ask for help directly. It also provides the teacher with a quick and easy means of assessing the progress of the class as a whole.

Scenarios

The main purpose of scenarios is to demonstrate mathematical relationships in a visual and memorable way. In scenario-based activities, a group of students is called to the front of the classroom to act out a particular situation. Scenarios are useful when a new concept is being introduced for the first time. They are especially valuable for demonstrating the physical reality that underlies such math concepts as embedded numbers (break-aparts) and regrouping.

> **Benefits:** Because of its active and dramatic nature, the scenario structure often fosters a sense of intense involvement among children. In addition, scenarios create meaningful contexts in which students can reason about numbers and relate math to their everyday lives.

Step-by-Step at the Board

This is a variation of the Solve and Discuss structure. Again, several children go to the board to solve a problem. This time, however, a different student performs each step of the problem, describing the step before everyone does it. Everyone else at the board and at their desks carries out that step. This approach is particularly useful in learning multi-digit addition, subtraction, multiplication, and division. It assists the least-advanced students the most, providing them with accessible, systematic methods.

> **Benefits:** This structure is especially effective when students are having trouble solving certain kinds of problems. The step-by-step structure allows students to grasp a method more easily than doing the whole method at once. It also helps students learn to verbalize their methods more clearly, as they can focus on describing just their own step.

Small Groups

Unstructured groups can form spontaneously if physical arrangements allow (for example, desks arranged in groups of four or children working at tables). Spontaneous helping between and among students as they work on problems individually can be encouraged.

For more structured projects, assign students to specific groups. It is usually a good idea to include a range of students and to have a strong reader in each group. Explain the problem or project and guide the groups as necessary. When students have finished, call a pair from each group to present and explain the results of their work or have the entire group present the results, with each member explaining one part of the solution or project. Having lower-performing students present first allows them to contribute, while higher-performing students expand on their efforts and give the fuller presentation.

> **Benefits:** Students learn different strategies from each other for approaching a problem or task. They are invested in their classmates' learning because the presentation will be on behalf of the whole group.

Volume 1 Contents

Unit 1   Solve Multiplication and Division Word Problems

Unit 2   Quadrilaterals

Unit 3   Place Value and Multi-Digit Addition and Subtraction

Big Idea Addition and Subtraction Problems

MINI UNIT Unit 4 Angles and Polygons

Unit 5 Multi-Digit Multiplication

Big Idea Multiplication by One-Digit Numbers

Big Idea Multiplication by Two-Digit Numbers

MINI UNIT

Unit 6   The Metric Measurement System

🌐 REAL WORLD Problem Solving

Volume 2 Contents

Unit 7 Multi-Digit Division

Big Idea Discover Long Division

Big Idea Problem Solving and Division

Unit 8 **Patterns, Functions, and Graphs**

Volume 2 Contents (Continued)

Big Idea Fractions With Unlike Denominators

Big Idea Data and Probability

Unit 10 **Three-Dimensional Figures**

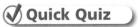

Unit 11 Decimal Numbers

Unit 12 **The U.S. Customary System**

 REAL WORLD Problem Solving

Big Idea Use Whole-Number and Fractional Customary Units of Measure

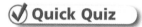
Extension Lessons

Big Idea Ratio and Rates

Pacing Guide

This grade level begins with a Basic Fact Fluency Plan for basic addition, subtraction, multiplication, and division. Depending on the needs of your students, these fluency lessons may take approximately one week at the beginning of the school year. For those students who need extra support with basic facts, you may need to spend two weeks on the fluency lessons. Unit 9 and Unit 11 build the kind of strong conceptual development and skill fluency with fractions and decimals that is often seen in the curricula of other countries that rank high in math performance. In the first year many classes may not cover all of the content of the later units. But as more students experience *Math Expressions* in previous grades, movement through the earlier units is more rapid and classes are able to do more of the later material in greater depth. Some lessons in every unit can be omitted if they do not focus on important state or district goals. Be sure to do the Quick Practice activities that begin each lesson, as they provide needed practice on core grade-level skills as well as support the growth of students as they lead these activities.

Unit	First Year Pacing Suggestions	Days	Later Years Pacing Suggestions	Days
1	This is a core Grade 4 mastery unit. Students master long division, apply division skills to problem solving, and understand what to do with remainders. They also write expressions, equations, and inequalities.	11	This unit will provide a strong foundation for division skills and applying division to word problems.	9
2	These are important Grade 4 geometry concepts.	6	These are important Grade 4 geometry concepts.	8
3	Generalize earlier student ideas about whole number place value and multi-digit addition and subtraction methods. Elicit student ideas and focus on word problem solving to develop Math Talk.	37	This unit will go more quickly for students who had *Math Expressions* in Grade 3. Elicit student ideas and focus on word problem solving to develop Math Talk.	28
4	These are important Grade 4 geometry concepts.	8	These are important Grade 4 geometry concepts.	7
5	This unit is a core Grade 4 mastery unit. Students need to master and explain one multiplication method, but many will master and explain two or more methods. Extend multiplication situations from Unit 1 single-digit cases to these multi-digit numbers.	25	Because this is a core Grade 4 mastery unit, be sure to spend enough time for students to master and explain at least one multiplication method. Elicit multiplication situations for numerical problems to deepen Math Talk.	23
6	Do only important district and state goals.	2	Do only important district and state goals.	5
7	This unit is a core Grade 4 mastery unit. Students need to master and explain one division method and understand remainders. Continue in depth Math Talk.	20	Math Talk will deepen as students explain their division method and remainders and relate division to multiplication.	24
8	Do only important district and state goals.	5	Extend knowledge of figures to polygons and circles.	6
9	Introduce basic fraction ideas in the first 8 lessons. Grade 5 will work in depth on fraction ideas and computation.	26	Doing this unit will provide a strong basis for completing the ambitious Grade 5 fractions units that develop fractions in depth and include fraction division.	30
10	Good for building students' spatial visualization.	2	Good for building students' spatial visualization.	4
11	Explore decimal numbers in Lessons 1 through 3.	9	This unit will enable students to move easily through Grade 5 Unit 2, thereby getting to the final units more rapidly.	12
12	Do only important district and state goals.	2	Do only important district and state goals.	4
All Units		**Total Days 153**		**Total Days 160**

Correlation to NCTM Curriculum Focal Points and Connections for Grade 4

Grade 4 Curriculum Focal Points

1 *Number and Operations* and *Algebra*: Developing quick recall of multiplication facts and related division facts and fluency with whole number multiplication

Students use understandings of multiplication to develop quick recall of the basic multiplication facts and related division facts. They apply their understanding of models for multiplication (i.e., equal-sized groups, arrays, area models, equal intervals on the number line), place value, and properties of operations (in particular, the distributive property) as they develop, discuss, and use efficient, accurate, and generalizable methods to multiply multidigit whole numbers. They select appropriate methods and apply them accurately to estimate products or calculate them mentally, depending on the context and numbers involved. They develop fluency with efficient procedures, including the standard algorithm, for multiplying whole numbers, understand why the procedures work (on the basis of place value and properties of operations), and use them to solve problems.

1.1 develop quick recall of the basic multiplication facts and related division facts	Fluency Plan L2–15, L17; U1 L1; U5 L1, L2; U7 L3
1.2 use models, place value, and properties of operations (in particular, the distributive property) to multiply multidigit whole numbers	U5 L1, L3, L5–8, L11–13, L15, L16
1.3 select and apply appropriate methods to estimate products or calculate them mentally	U5 L2, L4, L8, L13
1.4 develop fluency with efficient procedures, including the standard algorithm, for multiplying whole numbers and use them to solve problems	U5 L1, L3, L5–8, L10–16

2 *Number and Operations*: Developing an understanding of decimals, including the connections between fractions and decimals

Students understand decimal notation as an extension of the base-ten system of writing whole numbers that is useful for representing more numbers, including numbers between 0 and 1, between 1 and 2, and so on. Students relate their understanding of fractions to reading and writing decimals that are greater than or less than 1, identifying equivalent decimals, comparing and ordering decimals, and estimating decimal or fractional amounts in problem solving. They connect equivalent fractions and decimals by comparing models to symbols and locating equivalent symbols on the number line.

2.1 understand decimal notation as an extension of the base-ten system of writing whole numbers	U11 L1–8
2.2 relate fractions to reading and writing decimals that are greater than or less than 1	U11 L1–6, L9, L10
2.3 identify equivalent decimals	U11 L1, L5
2.4 compare and order decimals	U11 L3, L5, L8, L10
2.5 estimate decimal amounts in problem solving	U11 L6, L7, L12, L14
2.6 estimate fractional amounts in problem solving	U9 L2; U11 L14
2.7 compare decimal and fraction models to symbols	U9 L1–3, L6–9, L11–13, L17–20; U11 L1, L2, L6, L7, L9, L10
2.8 locate equivalent decimal and fraction symbols on the number line	U9 L20; U11 L6, L7, L14

3 *Measurement:* Developing an understanding of area and determining the areas of two-dimensional shapes
Students recognize area as an attribute of two-dimensional regions. They learn that they can quantify area by finding the total number of same-sized units of area that cover the shape without gaps or overlaps. They understand that a square that is 1 unit on a side is the standard unit for measuring area. They select appropriate units, strategies (e.g., decomposing shapes), and tools for solving problems that involve estimating or measuring area. Students connect area measure to the area model that they have used to represent multiplication, and they use this connection to justify the formula for the area of a rectangle.

3.1 recognize area as an attribute of two-dimensional regions	U2 L4–6; U4 L4; U6 L2
3.2 find the total number of same-sized units of area that cover the shape without gaps or overlaps	U2 L4, L6; U4 L4; U6 L2
3.3 understand that a square that is 1 unit on a side is the standard unit for measuring area	U2 L4–6; U4 L4; U6 L2
3.4 select appropriate units, strategies (e.g., decomposing shapes), and tools for solving problems that involve estimating or measuring area	U2 L4–6; U4 L4; U6 L2
3.5 connect area measure to an area model that represents multiplication	U2 L4, L5; U4 L4; U5 L1, L3, L5
3.6 justify the formula for the area of a rectangle	U2 L4

Connections to the Focal Points

4 *Algebra:* Students continue identifying, describing, and extending numeric patterns involving all operations and nonnumeric growing or repeating patterns. Through these experiences, they develop an understanding of the use of a rule to describe a sequence of numbers or objects.

4.1 identify, describe, and extend numeric patterns and nonnumeric growing or repeating patterns	Fluency Plan L2, L5–7, L11, L12, L14; U8 L1–3; U9 L1; U11 L11
4.2 use a rule to describe a sequence of numbers or objects	Fluency Plan L11; U1 L1; U4 L7; U8 L3

5 *Geometry:* Students extend their understanding of properties of two-dimensional shapes as they find the areas of polygons. They build on their earlier work with symmetry and congruence in grade 3 to encompass transformations, including those that produce line and rotational symmetry. By using transformations to design and analyze simple tilings and tessellations, students deepen their understanding of two-dimensional space.

5.1 find area of polygons	U2 L4–6; U4 L4; U6 L2
5.2 understand transformations, including those that produce line and rotational symmetry	U2 L1, L7; U4 L2; U8 L4
5.3 use transformations to design and analyze simple tilings and tessellations	U4 L7; U9 L22

Correlation to NCTM Curriculum Focal Points and Connections for Grade 4 (cont.)

Connections to the Focal Points (cont.)

6 *Measurement:* As part of understanding two-dimensional shapes, students measure and classify angles.

6.1 measure angles	U4 L1
6.2 classify angles	U4 L1, L3

7 *Data Analysis:* Students continue to use tools from grade 3, solving problems by making frequency tables, bar graphs, picture graphs, and line plots. They apply their understanding of place value to develop and use stem-and-leaf plots.

7.1 solve problems by making frequency tables	U1 L5, L6; U3 L21; U9 L16
7.2 solve problems by making bar graphs	U1 L5, L6; U7 L14
7.3 solve problems by making picture graphs	Fluency Plan L17; U1 L5
7.4 solve problems by making line plots	U7 L14; U9 L16
7.5 use stem-and-leaf plots	U1 L5

8 *Number and Operations:* Building on their work in grade 3, students extend their understanding of place value and ways of representing numbers to 100,000 in various contexts. They use estimation in determining the relative sizes of amounts or distances. Students develop understandings of strategies for multidigit division by using models that represent division as the inverse of multiplication, as partitioning, or as successive subtraction. By working with decimals, students extend their ability to recognize equivalent fractions. Students' earlier work in grade 3 with models of fractions and multiplication and division facts supports their understanding of techniques for generating equivalent fractions and simplifying fractions.

8.1 understand place value and ways of representing numbers to 100,000	U3 L7–10
8.2 use estimation in determining the relative sizes of amounts or distances	U3 L8, L13, L19; U12 L1
8.3 use models that represent division as the inverse of multiplication	Fluency Plan L5, L6, L9, L13
8.4 use models that represent division as partitioning and successive subtraction	Fluency Plan L6; U1 L4
8.5 use decimals to recognize equivalent fractions	U11 L1, L2
8.6 generate equivalent fractions	U9 L11–14, L20, L21
8.7 simplify fractions	U9 L11–14; L17, L21

NCTM Standards and Expectations
Correlation for Grade 4

Number and Operations Standard	
Understand numbers, ways of representing numbers, relationships among numbers, and number systems	
• understand the place-value structure of the base-ten number system and be able to represent and compare whole numbers and decimals;	U3 L7–L18; U5 L6, L12, L15–L16; U7 L5; U9 L3, L19, L21; U11 L1–L6
• recognize equivalent representations for the same number and generate them by decomposing and composing numbers;	U3 L1, L7–L8, L10, L14; U5 L1–8, L11–L16; U7 L1, L3; U9 L2, L8, L7–L9, L17; U11 L2, L4, L5
• develop understanding of fractions as parts of unit wholes, as parts of a collection, as locations on number lines, and as divisions of whole numbers;	U7 L6; U9 L1–L6, L8, L12, L16, L18–L19; U11 L7
• use models, benchmarks, and equivalent forms to judge the size of fractions;	U9 L1, L3–L4, L7–L14, L17–L19; U11 L5, L7
• recognize and generate equivalent forms of commonly used fractions, decimals, and percents;	U9 L8, L10–L13, L14, L21; U11 L1–L2
• explore numbers less than 0 by extending the number line and through familiar applications;	U6 L5; U12 L5
• describe classes of numbers according to characteristics such as the nature of their factors.	Fluency Plan L9, L14
Understand meanings of operations and how they relate to one another	
• understand various meanings of multiplication and division;	Fluency Plan L1, L3, L6–L7, L9, L14, L16; U1 L5, L8; U3 L6; U5 L1, L3–L16; U7 L1, L4–L7; U9 L18–L19, L21
• understand the effects of multiplying and dividing whole numbers;	Fluency Plan L7, L9, L11–L12, L13; U1 L5, L8; U5 L1, L3, L4, L7–L16; U7 L2–L4, L8–L9
• identify and use relationships between operations, such as division as the inverse of multiplication, to solve problems;	Fluency Plan L9, L11–L13, L15; U1 L4, L8; U3 L6, L15, L18; U5 L9, L10; U7 L7, L8
• understand and use properties of operations, such as the distributivity of multiplication over addition.	Fluency Plan L16; U5 L1, L3, L4, L11–L16
Compute fluently and make reasonable estimates	
• develop fluency with basic number combinations for multiplication and division and use these combinations to mentally compute related problems, such as 30 x 50;	U3 L20; U5 L1, L2, L4–L8, L11, L13–L16; U7 L1–L3
• develop fluency in adding, subtracting, multiplying, and dividing whole numbers;	Fluency Plan L1–L17; U1 L4, L8; U3 L1, L3–L6, L14; U5 L2–L3, L7, L13–L16; U7 L3–L4, L7; U11 L9–L10

Number and Operations Standard (cont.)	
Compute fluently and make reasonable estimates (cont.)	
• develop and use strategies to estimate the results of whole-number computations and to judge the reasonableness of such results;	U3 L13, L18–L20; U4 L5; U5 L4
• develop and use strategies to estimate computations involving fractions and decimals in situations relevant to students' experiences;	U3 L19; U11 L12, L14
• use visual models, benchmarks, and equivalent forms to add and subtract commonly used fractions and decimals;	U9 L2, L7, L9–L10, L12–L14, L19, L21; U11 L9, L10–L12
• select appropriate methods and tools for computing with whole numbers from among mental computation, estimation, calculators, and paper and pencil according to the context and nature of the computation and use the selected method or tools.	Fluency Plan L5, L14; U1 L2, L4–L5; U3 L3– L6, L11–L17, L19–20; U5 L1–L8, L11–L16; U7 L1–L6, L8, L10
Algebra Standard	
Understand patterns, relations, and functions	
• describe, extend, and make generalizations about geometric and numeric patterns;	Fluency Plan L2–L9, L11–L12, L14–L15; U1 L4; U7 L3; U8 L1–L2
• represent and analyze patterns and functions, using words, tables, and graphs.	Fluency Plan L6, L9; U1 L5–L6; U11 L9; U8 L3, L5–L6
Represent and analyze mathematical situations and structures using algebraic symbols	
• identify such properties as commutativity, associativity, and distributivity and use them to compute with whole numbers;	Fluency Plan L3, L16; U3 L1; U5 L8, L12, L15, L16
• represent the idea of a variable as an unknown quantity using a letter or a symbol;	U1 L4–L5; U3 L2–L5, L15
• express mathematical relationships using equations.	U1 L4–L5, L8; U3 L2–L5, L11; U3 L2–L19; U5 L8, L12, L15, L16; U8 L5
Use mathematical models to represent and understand quantitative relationships	
• model problem situations with objects and use representations such as graphs, tables, and equations to draw conclusions.	Fluency Plan L14; U1 L5–L6; U3 L3–L5, L7, L10, L14–L18; L21; U5 L8, L12, L15, L16; U7 L10
Analyze change in various contexts	
• investigate how a change in one variable relates to a change in a second variable;	Fluency Plan L11; U1 L1; U3 L2; U8 L3
• identify and describe situations with constant or varying rates of change and compare them.	U5 L15

NCTM Standards and Expectations Correlation for Grade 4 (cont.)

Geometry Standard	
Analyze characteristics and properties of two- and three-dimensional geometric shapes and develop mathematical arguments about geometric relationships	
• identify, compare, and analyze attributes of two- and three-dimensional shapes and develop vocabulary to describe the attributes;	U2 L1–L3, L5–L6; U4 L1, L3
• classify two- and three-dimensional shapes according to their properties and develop definitions of classes of shapes such as triangles and pyramids;	U4 L4; U10 L1–L3
• investigate, describe, and reason about the results of subdividing, combining, and transforming shapes	U2 L1–L3, L5–L6; U4 L1, L5
• explore congruence and similarity;	U2 L1; U4 L4; U10 L1-L3
• make and test conjectures about geometric properties and relationships and develop logical arguments to justify conclusions.	U2 L5; U4 L4
Specify locations and describe spatial relationships using coordinate geometry and other representational systems	
• describe location and movement using common language and geometric vocabulary;	U2 L1; U4 L4; U4 L6; U8 L4
• make and use coordinate systems to specify locations and to describe paths;	U2 L1–L3, L5–L6; U8 L4
• find the distance between points along horizontal and vertical lines of a coordinate system.	U4 L1; U8 L4
Apply transformations and use symmetry to analyze mathematical situations	
• predict and describe the results of sliding, flipping, and turning two-dimensional shapes;	U2 L1, L6–L7; U4 L1, L4; U8 L4
• describe a motion or a series of motions that will show that two shapes are congruent;	U2 L1
• identify and describe line and rotational symmetry in two- and three-dimensional shapes and designs.	U2 L1, L6–L7; U7 L14

Geometry Standard (cont.)	
Use visualization, spatial reasoning, and geometric modeling to solve problems	
• build and draw geometric objects;	U2 L1–L2, L5–L6; U4 L1, L3–L5; U10 L1–L3
• create and describe mental images of objects, patterns, and paths;	U4 L4; U10 L2
• identify and build a three-dimensional object from two-dimensional representations of that object;	U10 L1
• identify and draw a two-dimensional representation of a three-dimensional object;	U10 L1–L3
• use geometric models to solve problems in other areas of mathematics, such as number and measurement;	U2 L3, L5–L6; U4 L5; U6 L1; U10 L2
• recognize geometric ideas and relationships and apply them to other disciplines and to problems that arise in the classroom or in everyday life.	U4 L1
Measurement Standard	
Understand measurable attributes of objects and the units, systems, and processes of measurement	
• understand such attributes as length, area, weight, volume, and size of angle and select the appropriate type of unit for measuring each attribute;	U2 L4–L6; U6 L1–L5; U12 L1–L5
• understand the need for measuring with standard units and become familiar with standard units in the customary and metric systems;	U2 L4; U6 L1–L5; U12 L1–L5
• carry out simple unit conversions, such as from centimeters to meters, within a system of measurement;	U6 L1–L5; U4 L4; U12 L1–L5
• understand that measurements are approximations and how differences in units affect precision;	U6 L1; U12 L1, L3
• explore what happens to measurements of a two-dimensional shape such as its perimeter and area when the shape is changed in some way.	U2 L4–L6
Apply appropriate techniques, tools, and formulas to determine measurements	
• develop strategies for estimating the perimeters, areas, and volumes of irregular shapes;	U2 L5–L6; U6 L2; U12 L1–L2

NCTM Standards and Expectations Correlation for Grade 4 (cont.)

Measurement Standard (cont.)	
Apply appropriate techniques, tools, and formulas to determine measurements (cont.)	
• select and apply appropriate standard units and tools to measure length, area, volume, weight, time, temperature, and the size of angles;	U2 L4–L6; U6 L1–L5; U4 L1; U7 L10; U9 L6; U12 L1–L5
• select and use benchmarks to estimate measurements;	U2 L4; U6 L1, L5; U12 L1, L3
• develop, understand, and use formulas to find the area of rectangles and related triangles and parallelograms;	U2 L4; U6 L2; U12 L2
• develop strategies to determine the surface areas and volumes of rectangular solids.	U6 L2, L3; U12 L2
Data Analysis and Probability Standard	
Formulate questions that can be addressed with data and collect, organize, and display relevant data to answer them	
• design investigations to address a question and consider how data-collection methods affect the nature of the data set;	U1 L5; U9 L6
• collect data using observations, surveys, and experiments;	U1 L5; U6 L4
• represent data using tables and graphs such as line plots, bar graphs, and line graphs;	Fluency Plan L5, L17; U1 L1–L2, L5–L6, L19–L20; U2 L3; U3 L21; U6 L4; U7 L8; U8 L5–L6; U9 L16, L17, L19
• recognize the differences in representing categorical and numerical data.	U9 L6
Select and use appropriate statistical methods to analyze data	
• describe the shape and important features of a set of data and compare related data sets, with an emphasis on how the data are distributed;	U6 L4; U9 L6
• use measures of center, focusing on the median, and understand what each does and does not indicate about the data set;	U1 L6; U7 L8
• compare different representations of the same data and evaluate how well each representation shows important aspects of the data.	U1 L6; U7 L8
Develop and evaluate inferences and predictions that are based on data	
• propose and justify conclusions and predictions that are based on data and design studies to further investigate the conclusions or predictions.	U1 L5, L19; U3 L21; U9 L22

Data Analysis and Probability Standard (cont.)	
Understand and apply basic concepts of probability	
• describe events as likely or unlikely and discuss the degree of likelihood using such words as certain, equally likely, and impossible;	U5 L12–L13
• predict the probability of outcomes of simple experiments and test the predictions;	U5 L12–L13; U9 L15
• understand that the measure of the likelihood of an event can be represented by a number from 0 to 1.	U5 L12–L13
Problem Solving Standard	
• build new mathematical knowledge through problem solving;	Fluency Plan L3; U1 L19; U3 L5, L10, L13, L21; U2 L4, L6; U5 L3, L4, L6, L9–L11, L13, L14, L17; U6 L2; U7 L7, L8, L14; U9 L4, L11, L14–L15, L22; U11 L3, L12, L17; U12 L1, L4
• solve problems that arise in mathematics and in other contexts;	Fluency Plan L17; U1 L19; U2 L4, L6; U3 L2, L5–L6, L16, L18–L20, L21; U5 L9–L11, L13, L14, L17; U6 L2; U7 L2–L4, L7–L8, L14; U9 L13, L15, L17–L19, L22; U11 L2–L3, L8–L10, L13, L17; U12 L1, L4
• apply and adapt a variety of appropriate strategies to solve problems;	Fluency Plan L3, L10, L17; U1 L19; U3 L2, L5–L6, L10, L13, L16, L18, L19–L20, L21; U3 L3, L4, L6, L9–L11, L13, L14, L21; U6 L2; U7 L2–L4, L6–L8, L14; U9 L4, L11, L13, L15, L17–L19, L22; U11 L6, L10, L12–13, L17; U12 L1, L4
• monitor and reflect on the process of mathematical problem solving.	Fluency Plan L10; U3 L5, L18, L20, L21; U5 L17; U6 L2; U7 L4, L14; U9 L8, L17, L19, L22; U11 L8, L10, L17
Reasoning and Proof Standard	
• recognize reasoning and proof as fundamental aspects of mathematics;	Fluency Plan L16; U1 L19; U3 L2, L21; U5 L17; U7 L14; U9 L22; U11 L17
• make and investigate mathematical conjectures;	U1 L19; U2 L1, 3, 5, 6; U3 L8, L9, L21; U5 L17; U6 L1; U7 L14; U9 L22; U11 L17
• develop and evaluate mathematical arguments and proofs;	Fluency Plan L10, L14, L16; U1 L19; U3 L21; U5 L3, L17; U7 L14; U9 L22; U11 L17
• select and use various types of reasoning and methods of proof.	Fluency Plan L10, L14; U1 L19; U3 L8, L9, L21; U5 L3, L17; U7 L14; U9 L22; U11 L17
Communication Standard	
• organize and consolidate their mathematical thinking through communication;	U1 L19; U2 L4; U3 L1, L3, L4, L6–L8, L11–L16, L21; U5 L17; U7 L14; U9 L2–L3, L17, L19, L21, L22; U11 L4, L5, L9, L12, L17

NCTM Standards and Expectations Correlation for Grade 4 (cont.)

Communication Standard (cont.)	
• communicate their mathematical thinking coherently and clearly to peers, teachers, and others;	Fluency Plan L7, L9–L10, L16; U1 L19; U2 L4; U3 L2–L3, L10–L19, L21; U5 L1, L3–L8, L11–L16, L17; U7 L14; U9 L2–L19, L22; U11 L17; U12 L4, L5–L6, L9, L12
• analyze and evaluate the mathematical thinking and strategies of others;	U1 L19; U3 L2–L3, L11, L14, L18, L21; U5 L4–L8, L11–L16, L17; U7 L14; U9 L12–L13, L22; U11 L5, L8–L9, L17
• use the language of mathematics to express mathematical ideas precisely.	Fluency Plan L9; U1 L19; U3 L3, L9–L13, L15–L17, L19–20, L21; U5 L1, L3–L8, L11–L16, L17; U7 L14; U9 L22; U11 L4, L5, L8–L9, L17

Connections Standard	
• recognize and use connections among mathematical ideas;	Fluency Plan L11; U1 L8, L19; U3 L19, L21; U5 L17; U7 L14; U9 L11, L22; U11 L2, L4, L5, L9, L17
• understand how mathematical ideas interconnect and build on one another to produce a coherent whole;	Fluency Plan L11; U1 L8, L19; U3 L19, L21; U5 L17; U7 L14; U9 L11, L22; U11 L2, L4, L9, L17
• recognize and apply mathematics in contexts outside of mathematics.	U1 L19; U3 L19, L21; U5 L17; U7 L14; U9 L22; U11 L2–L3, L8, L10–L13, L17

Representation Standard	
• create and use representations to organize, record, and communicate mathematical ideas;	Fluency Plan L7, L13; U1 L2, L4, L6, L19; U3 L4, L7–L8, L10–L11, L12, L21; U5 L5–L8, L11–L16, L17; U6 L1; U7 L14; U9 L22; U11 L2, L5, L8–L10, L17
• select, apply, and translate among mathematical representations to solve problems;	Fluency Plan L10; U1 L1–L2, L4, L19; U2 L5; U3 L12, L17, L21; U5 L5–L8, L11–L16, L17; U7 L14; U9 L22; U11 L17
• use representations to model and interpret physical, social, and mathematical phenomena.	Fluency Plan L7, L10, L13; U1 L1, L19; U3 L4, L7–L8, L10, L16–L17, L21; U5 L6, L12, L13, L15, L17; U7 L14; U9 L22; U11 L8, L10, L17

Basic Facts Fluency Plan

THESE FLUENCY LESSONS build upon the concepts of patterns in count-bys, arrays, and equal groups. When students are successful using patterns to help them with multiplication and division, they may keep looking for patterns in mind as a strategy when learning new mathematical concepts and skills. The activities in this unit help students gain a conceptual understanding of basic multiplication and division and the inverse relationship between the two operations. This Fluency Plan is designed to meet the needs of all students.

Skills Trace

Grade 3	Grade 4	Grade 5
• Identify patterns in basic multiplication and division facts.	• Identify patterns in basic multiplication and division facts.	• Use strategies for basic multiplication and division facts.
• Model equal groups and array word problems.	• Model multiplication and division word problems.	• Solve multiplication and division word problems.
• Understand properties of multiplication.	• Understand and apply properties of multiplication.	• Understand and apply properties of multiplication.
• Develop fluency with addition, subtraction, multiplication, and division facts.	• Develop fluency with addition, subtraction, multiplication, and division facts.	• Develop fluency with multiplication, and division facts.

Fluency Plan Contents

Fluency Plan Assessment

✓ Fluency Plan Objectives	Assessment	Fluency Lessons
FP.1 Diagnosing Addition and Subtraction	Diagnostic Checkups p. 16–17	1
FP.2 Diagnosing Multiplication and Division	Diagnostic Checkups p. 16–17	2
FP.3 Fluency Days	Checkup A, B, D, E	4, 8, 17
	Target Practice A, B	13
	Write-On and Check Sheets	9, 15

Assessment and Review Resources

Formal Assessment

Assessment Guide
- Checkup A: 2s, 5s, 9s, 10s
- Checkup B: 2s, 5s, 9s, 3s, 4s, 1s, 0s
- Checkup C: 3s, 4s, 6s, 7s, 8s
- Checkup D: all facts
- Checkup E: 6s, 7s, 8s

Test Generator CD–ROM
- Open Response Test
- Multiple Choice Test
- Test Bank Items

Informal Assessment

Teacher Edition
- Ongoing Assessment (in every lesson)
- Quick Practice (in every lesson)
- Math Talk (in every lesson)
- Portfolio Suggestions (pp. 14, 104, 126, 142)

⟨123⟩ Math Talk
- ▸ The Learning Classroom (pp. 5, 18, 28, 32, 38, 54, 55, 68, 69, 84, 89, 91, 96, 101, 106, 107, 115, 118, 131)
- ▸ Activities (pp. 4, 9, 18, 32, 39, 47, 55, 61, 62, 64, 75, 77, 84, 89, 92, 96, 98, 99, 101, 102, 117, 118, 124, 133, 134, 140)
- ▸ Solve and Discuss (pp. 32, 34, 47, 48, 60, 62, 63, 74, 76, 83, 90, 102, 131, 134)
- ▸ Student Pairs (pp. 68, 83, 115, 140)
- ▸ Student Leaders (pp. 1, 15, 27, 28, 37, 38, 43, 51, 54, 59, 67, 73, 81, 87, 91, 95, 98, 101, 105, 113, 118, 121, 139)
- ▸ Small Groups (p. 83)
- ▸ Helping Partners (pp. 128, 134)

Review Opportunities

Homework and Remembering
- Review of recently taught topics
- Cumulative Review

Teacher Edition
- Checkup A (p. 38, TRB M119)
- Checkup B (p. 68, TRB M120)
- Checkup C (p. 138, TRB M121)
- Checkup D (TRB M122)
- Checkup E (TRB M123)

Test Generator CD-ROM
- Custom review sheets

Planning for Fluency Lessons

Lesson/NCTM Standards	Resources	Materials for Lesson Activities	Materials for Other Activities
FL–1 **Addition and Subtraction Methods** NCTM Standards: 1, 2, 6, 8	TE pp. 1–14 SAB pp. 1–4 H&R pp. 1–2 AC FP-1		Math Journals
FL–2 **Patterns in 2s, 5s, 10s, and 9s** NCTM Standards: 1, 2, 8	TE pp. 15–26 SAB pp. 5–10 H&R pp. 3–4 AC FP-2	✓ Targets (Manipulative Kit or TRB M1) Class MathBoard MathBoard Dry-erase markers, dry-erase material Division Digits: Sets 1–2 (TRB M3–M4) Sheet protector ✓ Class Multiplication Table	Comparing Numbers (TRB M50) ✓ Counters (2 colors) Math Journals
FL–3 **Arrays and Commutativity** NCTM Standards: 1, 2, 6	TE pp. 27–36 SAB pp. 11–14 H&R pp. 5–6 AC FP-3	Division Digits Materials	✓ Counters Math Journals
FL–4 **Fluency Day: 2s, 5s, 9s, and 10s** NCTM Standards: 1, 2	TE pp. 37–42 SAB pp. 15–16; 15A–16D H&R pp. 7–12 (includes Product Cards) AC FP-4	Checkup A Answer Key (TRB M5) ✓ Product Cards: 2s, 5s, 9s (TRB M6–M9) Paper clips or plastic sandwich bags Division Digits Materials ✓ Targets Multiplication Tables	Index cards (2 colors) Math Journals
FL–5 **Multiply and Divide With 3** NCTM Standards: 1, 2, 5	TE pp. 43–50 SAB pp. 17–18 H&R pp. 13–14 AC FP-5	MathBoard Materials ✓ Class Multiplication Table Division Digits Materials ✓ Product Cards: 5s, 9s	✓ Pennies Calendar page Markers (2 colors) Math Journals
FL–6 **Multiply and Divide With 4** NCTM Standards: 1, 2	TE pp. 51–58 SAB pp. 19–20 H&R pp. 15–16 AC FP-6	MathBoard Materials ✓ Class Multiplication Table Division Digits Materials Product Cards: 3s	✓ Counters Math Journals
FL–7 **Multiply and Divide With 1 and 0** NCTM Standards: 1, 2, 8, 10	TE pp. 59–66 SAB pp. 21–23 H&R pp. 17–18 AC FP-7	Division Digits Materials ✓ Product Cards: 2s, 5s, 9s	Index cards Math Journals
FL–8 **Fluency Day: 2s, 3s, 4s, 5s, 9s, and 10s** NCTM Standards: 1, 2	TE pp. 67–72 SAB pp. 25–26; 25A–26B H&R pp. 19–22 AC FP-8	Checkup B Answer Key (TRB M10) ✓ Product Cards: 2s, 3s, 4s, 5s, 9s (TRB M6–M9, M11–M12) Division Digits Materials	✓ Product cards: 3s and 4s ✓ Counters Multiplication Table Math Journals
FL–9 **Related Equations** NCTM Standards: 1, 2, 8	TE pp. 73–80 SAB pp. 27–32 H&R pp. 23–28 AC FP-9	Sheet protectors Dry-erase markers Division Digits Materials ✓ Product Cards: 2s, 3s, 4s, 5s, 9s	Index cards Math Journals

Resources/Materials Key: TE: Teacher Edition   SAB: Student Activity Book   H&R: Homework and Remembering
AC: Activity Cards   MCC: Math Center Challenge   AG: Assessment Guide   ✓: Grade 4 Kit   TRB: Teacher's Resource Book

Lesson/NCTM Standards	Resources	Materials for Lesson Activities	Materials for Other Activities
FL–10 **Group and Array Word Problems** NCTM Standards: 6, 7, 8, 10	TE pp. 81–86 SAB pp. 33–34 H&R pp. 29–30 AC FP-10	Student-created word problems from previous lessons Division Digits Materials ✓ Product Cards: 2s, 3s, 4s, 5s, 9s	5-part spinner Math Journals
FL–11 **Multiply and Divide With 6** NCTM Standards: 1, 2, 5, 9	TE pp. 87–94 SAB pp. 35–38 H&R pp. 31–32 AC FP-11	✓ Class Multiplication Table MathBoard Materials Division Digits Materials ✓ Product Cards: 2s, 3s, 4s, 5s, 9s	Math Journals
FL–12 **Multiply and Divide With 8 and 7** NCTM Standards: 1, 2	TE pp. 95–104 SAB pp. 39–40 H&R pp. 33–34 AC FP-12	MathBoard Materials ✓ Class Multiplication Table Division Digits Materials ✓ Product Cards: 2s, 3s, 4s, 5s, 6s, 9s	Index cards Math Journals
FL–13 **Fluency Day** NCTM Standards: 1, 2, 10	TE pp. 105–112 SAB pp. 41–44; 43A–43D H&R pp. 35–42 AC FP-13	*Blackout* Game (TRB M24–M25) ✓ Targets ✓ Product Cards: 6s, 7s, 8s (TRB M20–M23) Class MathBoard	✓ Counters Math Journals
FL–14 **Square Numbers, 11s and 12s** NCTM Standards: 1, 2, 7	TE pp. 113–120 SAB p. 46 H&R pp. 43–44 AC FP-14	Transparency of Student Book p. 46 Overhead projector Class MathBoard Target Practice Materials	Centimeter-Grid Paper (TRB M60) Math Journals
FL–15 **Fluency Day** NCTM Standards: 1, 2, 10	TE pp. 121–126 SAB pp. 47–52 H&R pp. 45–50 AC FP-15	Product Cards: 6s, 7s, 8s (TRB M20–M23) Sheet protectors Dry-erase markers Division Digits Materials	✓ Counters Student Book p.15 Index cards Math Journals
FL–16 **Properties of Multiplication** NCTM Standards: 1, 2, 7, 8	TE pp. 127–136 SAB pp. 53–56 H&R pp. 51–52 AC FP-16	Class MathBoard Target Practice Materials	Index cards ✓ Counters Math Journal
FL–17 **Fluency Day** NCTM Standards: 1, 5, 10	TE pp. 137–142 H&R pp. 53–54 Checkup D (TRB M122) Checkup E (TRB M123) AC FP-17	Checkup D Answer Key (TRB M40) Checkup E Answer Key (TRB M113) ✓ Product Cards: All *Five in a Line* Call List (TRB M31–M32) ✓ *Five in a Line* Cards (TRB M33–M39) Sheet protectors, dry-erase markers ✓ Counters, Class MathBoard	Make a Pictograph (TRB M124) Index cards Math Journals

Hardcover Student Book

- Together, the hardcover student book and its companion Activity Workbook contain all the pages in the consumable Student Activity Workbook.

Manipulatives and Materials

- Essential materials for teaching Math Expressions are available in the Grade 4 Kit. These materials are indicated by a ✓ in these lists. At the front of this Teacher Edition is more information about kit contents, alternatives for the materials, and use of the materials.

Independent Learning Activities

Ready-Made Math Challenge Centers

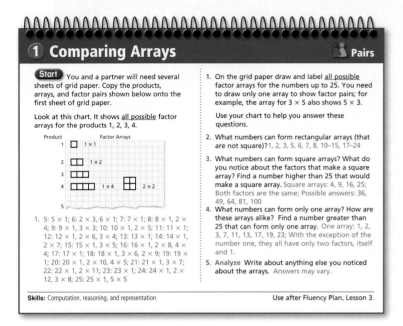

Grouping Pairs

Materials Centimeter grid paper (TRB M60), straightedge

Objective Students draw and analyze factor arrays.

Connections Computation and Representation

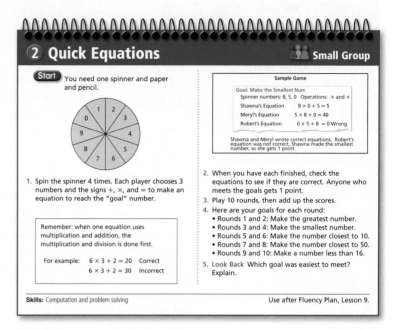

Grouping Small Groups

Materials Spinner labeled 0–9, paper clip and pencil

Objective Students practice writing two operation equations and learn about the order of operations.

Connections Computation and Problem Solving

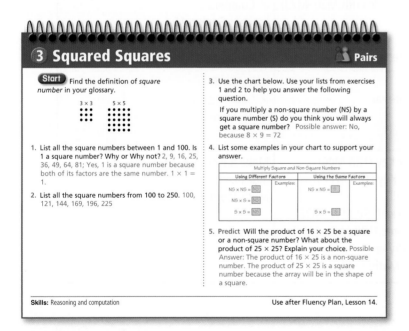

Grouping Pairs

Objective Students use their knowledge of square numbers to generate more and learn about combining square and non-square numbers.

Connections Number and Reasoning

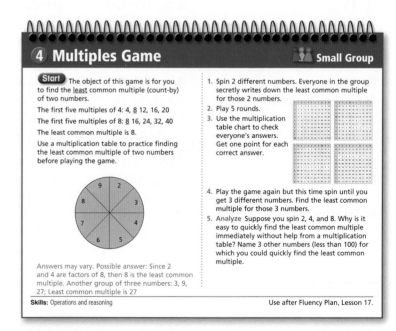

Grouping Small Groups

Materials Spinner labeled 2–9, paper clip and pencil, Multiplication Table (TRB M2)

Objective Students use their knowledge of least common multiples to generate the least common multiple of two and three different numbers.

Connections Number and Reasoning

Ready-Made Math Resources

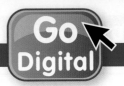

Technology — Tutorials, Practice, and Intervention

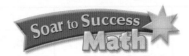

Use activity masters and online, individualized intervention and support to bring students to proficiency.

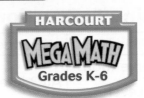

Help students practice skills and apply concepts through exciting math adventures.

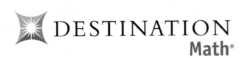

Extend and enrich students' understanding of skills and concepts through engaging, interactive lessons and activities.

Visit **Education Place**®
www.eduplace.com

Visit www.eduplace.com/mx2t/ and find family, teacher, and student materials, activities, games, and more.

Literature Links

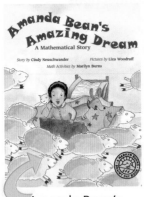

Amanda Bean's Amazing Dream: A Mathematical Story

Amanda Bean's Amazing Dream: A Mathematical Story
This imaginative story, about a girl who loves math, by Cindy Newschwander introduces basic addition and subtraction through adding like sets of objects.

Fluency Plan Teaching Resources

Differentiated Instruction

Individualizing Instruction

Activities	Level	Frequency
	• Intervention • On Level • Challenge	All 3 in every lesson.
Math Writing Prompts	Level	Frequency
	• Intervention • On Level • Challenge	All 3 in every lesson.
Math Center Challenges	For advanced students	
	4 for every unit	

Reaching All Learners

	Lessons	Pages
English Language Learners	1, 2, 3, 4, 5, 6, 7, 8, 9, 10, 11, 12, 13, 14, 15, 16, 17	5, 18, 29, 30, 38, 46, 56, 62, 68, 76, 82, 91, 100, 110, 114, 124, 129, 140
	Lessons	Pages
Extra Help	1, 3, 5, 10, 13	9, 31, 33, 45, 83, 108

Strategies for English Language Learners

Present this problem and activity to all students. Offer different levels of support to meet the student's levels of language proficiency.

Objective Help students visualize multiplication through skip counting.

Problem Write the problems 2×4, 5×4, 9×4 and 10×4 on the board. Divide the class into four groups. Have 1 group stand next to the board. Give each member two cards.

Newcomer

• As you give each student 2 cards say: One student, two cards... Two students, four cards... Have students repeat.

Beginning

• Gesture to the first student in the line with two cards. Say: **Two cards.** Have students repeat.

• Continue with the other group members then have students count the total number of cards.

Intermediate

• Ask: How many cards does each student have? 2 How many students are there? 4

• Have students count the cards in the group by 2.

Advanced

• Ask students to skip count the cards in a group.

• Have them multiply to find the number of cards and compare the answers.

Connections

Art Connection
Lesson 16, page 136

Music Connection
Lesson 15, page 126

Social Studies Connections
Lesson 3, page 36
Lesson 8, page 72
Lesson 12, page 104

Science Connection
Lesson 13, page 112

Real-World Connections
Lesson 1, page 14
Lesson 5, page 50
Lesson 6, page 58
Lesson 7, page 66
Lesson 10, page 86
Lesson 17, page 142

Math Connections
Lesson 9, page 80
Lesson 14, page 120

Literature Connection
Lesson 4, page 42

Math Background

Putting Research Into Practice for Basic Fact Fluency

From Our Curriculum Research Project: Multiplication and Division Consolidation

A core concept at the heart of student fluency is that multiplication and division are inverse operations. Students begin their study of division as soon as they learn the concept of multiplication. By studying the two operations together, the process of learning both operations is accelerated and solidified because students see that doing division is the same as finding an unknown factor in a multiplication situation.

Students build understanding by using language to describe the underlying concepts and situations of multiplication and division, such as equal groups and arrays.

As students study the count-bys (multiples) of the numbers from 1 through 12, they look for patterns that form the basis for learning these count-bys. They also learn to use products they know to find products they don't know or can't recall.

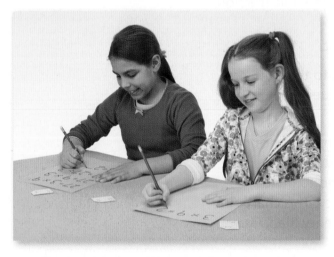

Through their daily in-class work and goal setting, students build fluency with multiplication and division and begin to accept responsibility for their own learning.

—Karen Fuson, Author
  Math Expressions

From Current Research: Multiplication

Children learn to skip-count lists for different multipliers (for example, they count 4, 8, 12, 16, 20, ... to multiply by four). They then count on and count down these lists, using their fingers to keep track of different products. They invent thinking strategies in which they derive related products from products they know.

As with addition and subtraction, children invent many of the procedures they use for multiplication. They find patterns and use skip counting (for example, multiplying 4 × 3 by counting 3, 6, 9, 12). Finding and using patterns and other thinking strategies greatly simplify the task of learning multiplication tables. Moreover, finding and describing patterns is a hallmark of mathematics. Thus, treating multiplication learning as pattern-finding both simplifies the task and uses a core mathematical idea.

National Research Council. "Developing Proficiency with Whole Numbers." *Adding It Up: Helping Students Learn Mathematics.* Washington D.C.: National Academy Press, 2001, pp. 191–192.

Other Useful References: Multiplication

Sherin, B. & Fuson, K., "Multiplication strategies and the appropriation of computational resources." *Journal for Research in Mathematics Education*, 36 (4), (2005) pp. 347–395.

This paper outlines student strategies for learning single-digit multiplication and division. *Math Expressions* Grades 3, 4, and 5 use approaches based on this research.

Mulligan, J., and Mitchelmore, M. C., "Young children's intuitive models of multiplication and division." *Journal for Research in Mathematics Education*, 28, (1997) pp. 309–330.

Lemaire, P., and Siegler, R. S., "Four aspects of strategic change: Contributions to children's learning of multiplication." *Journal of Experimental Psychology: General*, 124, (1995) pp. 83–97.

Getting Ready to Teach Basic Fact Fluency

As you teach these lessons,
emphasize understanding
of these terms.

• equation

• expression

• inverse operations

• order of operations

Why Teach Basic Fact Fluency?

As a Grade 4 teacher, you are aware of how entering students vary widely in their knowledge and fluency with multiplication and division facts. Unless you bring all your students to a competent level of fluency, your teaching of multiplication and division algorithms as well as fraction concepts and operations will be hampered by those students who are struggling to remember facts rather than concentrate on learning new mathematics.

Meeting the Needs of All Students

Before you begin Unit 1, use this Fluency Plan to help you bring all students to a competent level of fluency. The students will fall into three categories: those who need strategy teaching, those who need fluency practice, and those who have achieved fluency. This section provides support for all three.

Fluency Plan Structure

The Fluency Plan begins with Diagnostic Checkups followed by appropriate intervention.

Addition and Subtraction Facts

Entering fourth-graders should do well on addition and subtraction checkups, but if they do not, Lesson 1 is a comprehensive addition and subtraction intervention lesson with teaching activities, practice, differentiated instruction, and homework.

Multiplication and Division Facts

After this diagnostic checkup, group your students according to their fluency levels with the multiplication and division facts: developing fluency, building fluency, and having fluency.

Lessons 2 through 17 are a carefully structured series of lessons that include focused learning strategies for those who need to develop fluency, independent practice with progress checks for those who need to build fluency, and independent activities for those who have fluency. This chart shows how to pace these groups of students through the Fluency Plan.

Fluency Plan Lesson Pacing																
Lesson	2	3	4	5	6	7	8	9	10	11	12	13	14	15	16	17
Develop Fluency	T	T	T	T	T	T	T	T	T	T	T	T	T	T	T	T
Build Fluency	IP	T	T	IP	IP	T	T	T	T	IP	IP	T	IP	T	T	T
Achieved Fluency	IA	T	HP	IA	IA	T	HP	T	T	MC	IA	MC	IA	HP	T	HP

Key T: Teaching Activities   IP: Independent Practice   IA: Independent Activities   HP: Helping Partners

⬜ Fact Strategies   ⬜ Fluency Day   ⬜ Multiplication/Division Concepts

Basic Addition and Subtraction Fluency

Addition and Subtraction Checkups
Lesson 1

In Lesson 1 give all students the Diagnostic Checkups for addition and subtraction. Use the lesson to provide instruction for students who do not perform well on the checkups or to quickly review addition and subtraction facts, concepts, and methods with all students. The lesson ties basic fact strategies to work with greater numbers.

Diagnostic Addition Checkup

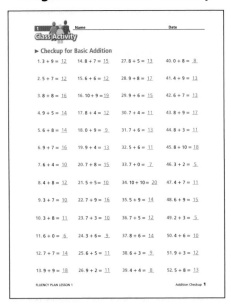

Diagnostic Subtraction Checkup

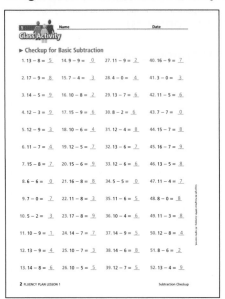

Addition and Subtraction Facts Study Plan Have students make a Study Plan for the facts they do not know. To do this, they list any addition and subtraction facts they missed in the Checkups. They then study them and review them at home with a family member. After they carry out their plan, you may reuse the Diagnostic Checkup to reassess their progress.

Connecting Addition and Subtraction
Lesson 1

Throughout *Math Expressions* understanding of the inverse nature of addition and subtraction is emphasized. A conceptual support for this idea is a break-apart drawing (called a Math Mountain in earlier grades). A break-apart drawing shows a total at the top and two addends at the bottom. Students see that they can add the two addends to get the total or subtract either addend for the total to get the other addend. They also see that eight related equations can be written for every break-apart drawing.

Break-Apart Drawing

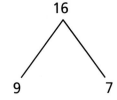

Related Equations

$$9 + 7 = 16 \qquad 16 = 9 + 7$$
$$7 + 9 = 16 \qquad 16 = 7 + 9$$
$$16 - 9 = 7 \qquad 7 = 16 - 9$$
$$16 - 7 = 9 \qquad 9 = 16 - 7$$

Multiplication and Division Fact Fluency Plan

Multiplication and Division Checkups
Lesson 2

Begin Lesson 2 by giving the Diagnostic Checkups for basic multiplication and related division. Use student performance on the checkups to group your students according to fluency:

- Developing Fluency (students who need to learn facts and concepts)
- Building Fluency (need to practice facts and understand concepts)
- Having Fluency (need to extend facts and concepts).

Diagnostic Multiplication Checkup   Diagnostic Division Checkup   Study Plan

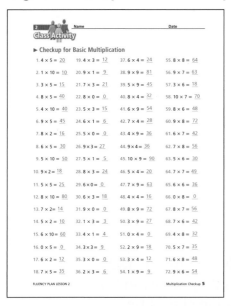

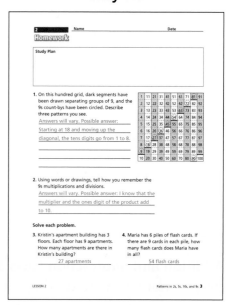

Multiplication and Division Facts Study Plan Students who are developing or building fluency should use the Study Plan section on their Homework pages to list any multiplication and division facts they missed in the Checkups. Have them study these facts and review them at home. As students complete further Checkups, they will update their Study Plans to include only those multiplication and division facts they still need to study.

Using the Fluency Plan Lessons Your goal is to move students from *developing* to *building* to *having* basic fact *fluency*.

- Teach the strategy lessons (Lessons 2, 5, 6, 11, 12, and 14) to the students developing fluency and to any building-fluency students who have difficulty with particular groups of facts.

- Use the Fluency Day lessons (Lessons 4, 8, 13, 15, and 17) to assess progress of developing-fluency students and to provide practice for building-fluency students.

- Present the conceptual lessons (Lessons 3, 7, 9, 10, and 16) that focus on the inverse multiplication-division relationship to the whole class.

The next pages describe fact strategies and learning tools, independent practice materials, and independent activity resources for the needs of your students.

Helping Students Who Need to Learn Strategies

The *Math Expressions* approach for helping students learn their basic multiplication and division facts is to teach learning strategies based on patterns and the inverse relationship between multiplication and division and to offer a variety of structured practice.

Learning Strategies

Strategies for learning the facts build on visual supports and patterns. Among the tools used in the Fluency Plan are the Class Multiplication Table, the Number Path (on the MathBoards), Targets, Count-bys, and drawings that relate multiplication and division.

Multiplication Table and Patterns
Lessons 2, 5, 6, 11, 12, and 14

Students find patterns first as they work together to see patterns in the Class Multiplication Table and then by circling groups on the Number Path on their MathBoards. They observe the visual patterns and analyze them to build understanding of the relationship between count-bys and products.

Count by 7s   Count by 8s

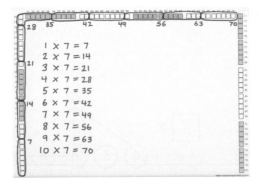
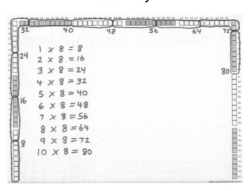

Targets
Lessons 2 and 14

In Lesson 2, students begin using their Targets with a Multiplication Table to learn related facts. By covering the Target circle, students can check on whether they know the product for two factors. By covering one end of the Target, they can check on a related division. In Lesson 14, students begin using the Target with Scrambled Multiplication Tables to check on their recall of the facts.

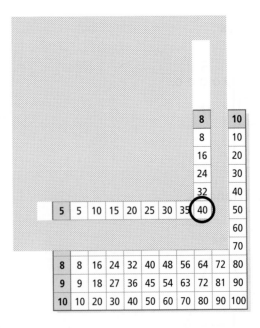

Count-bys and Close Count-bys
Lessons 4, 5, 6, 11, and 12

Students work with a multiplication they know to find a product they don't know or can't recall.

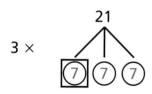

6s	7s	8s
1 x 6 = 6	1 x 7 = 7	1 x 8 = 8
2 x 6 = 12	2 x 7 = 14	2 x 8 = 16
3 x 6 = 18 ⌐ + 6	3 x 7 = 21 ⌐ + 7	3 x 8 = 24
4 x 6 = 24 ⌐ − 6	4 x 7 = 28 ⌐ − 7	4 x 8 = 32 ⌐ − 8
5 x 6 = 30 ⌐ + 12	5 x 7 = 35	5 x 8 = 40 ⌐ + 16
6 x 6 = 36 * ⌐ + 6	6 x 7 = 42 ⌐ + 7	6 x 8 = 48 ⌐ + 8
7 x 6 = 42 ⌐ + 6 ⌐ − 6	7 x 7 = 49 * ⌐ + 7	7 x 8 = 56 ⌐ + 8
8 x 6 = 48 ⌐ − 6	8 x 7 = 56	8 x 8 = 64 *
9 x 6 = 54	9 x 7 = 63	9 x 8 = 72

Relating Multiplication and Division With Drawings
Lessons 6, 9, 11, 13, 15

Students draw equal shares, fast arrays, and factor triangles to represent known and unknown factors and products in a conceptual format.

Equal Shares

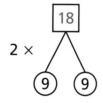

Fast Arrays

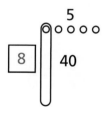

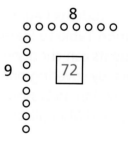

Factor Triangles.

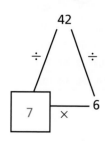

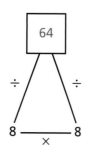

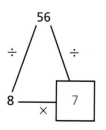

Related Equations
Lessons 2, 5, 6, 9, 11, and 12

Students write two related division equations for a multiplication equation. They may use their drawings or the Number Path.

Count by 7s

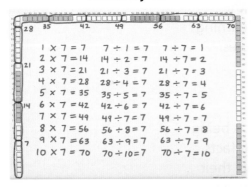

$$1 \times 7 = 7 \qquad 7 \div 1 = 7 \qquad 7 \div 7 = 1$$
$$2 \times 7 = 14 \qquad 14 \div 2 = 7 \qquad 14 \div 7 = 2$$
$$3 \times 7 = 21 \qquad 21 \div 3 = 7 \qquad 21 \div 7 = 3$$
$$4 \times 7 = 28 \qquad 28 \div 4 = 7 \qquad 28 \div 7 = 4$$
$$5 \times 7 = 35 \qquad 35 \div 5 = 7 \qquad 35 \div 7 = 5$$
$$6 \times 7 = 42 \qquad 42 \div 6 = 7 \qquad 42 \div 7 = 6$$
$$7 \times 7 = 49 \qquad 49 \div 7 = 7 \qquad 49 \div 7 = 7$$
$$8 \times 7 = 56 \qquad 56 \div 8 = 7 \qquad 56 \div 7 = 8$$
$$9 \times 7 = 63 \qquad 63 \div 9 = 7 \qquad 63 \div 7 = 9$$
$$10 \times 7 = 70 \qquad 70 \div 10 = 7 \qquad 70 \div 7 = 10$$

Count by 8s

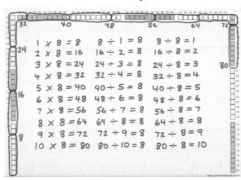

$$1 \times 8 = 8 \qquad 8 \div 1 = 8 \qquad 8 \div 8 = 1$$
$$2 \times 8 = 16 \qquad 16 \div 2 = 8 \qquad 16 \div 8 = 2$$
$$3 \times 8 = 24 \qquad 24 \div 3 = 8 \qquad 24 \div 8 = 3$$
$$4 \times 8 = 32 \qquad 32 \div 4 = 8 \qquad 32 \div 8 = 4$$
$$5 \times 8 = 40 \qquad 40 \div 5 = 8 \qquad 40 \div 8 = 5$$
$$6 \times 8 = 48 \qquad 48 \div 6 = 8 \qquad 48 \div 8 = 6$$
$$7 \times 8 = 56 \qquad 56 \div 7 = 8 \qquad 56 \div 8 = 7$$
$$8 \times 8 = 64 \qquad 64 \div 8 = 8 \qquad 64 \div 8 = 8$$
$$9 \times 8 = 72 \qquad 72 \div 9 = 8 \qquad 72 \div 8 = 9$$
$$10 \times 8 = 80 \qquad 80 \div 10 = 8 \qquad 80 \div 8 = 10$$

Hundred Grids
Homework and Remembering for Lessons 5, 6, 11, 12, and 13

Some homework and remembering activities reinforce using patterns to build fluency.

6s Patterns

1	11	21	31	41	51
2	(12)	22	32	(42)	52
3	13	23	33	43	53
4	14	(24)	34	44	(54)
5	15	25	35	45	55
(6)	16	26	(36)	46	56
7	17	27	37	47	57
8	(18)	28	38	(48)	58
9	19	29	39	49	59
10	20	(30)	40	50	(60)

7s Patterns

1	11	(21)	31	41	51	61
2	12	22	32	(42)	52	62
3	13	23	33	43	53	(63)
4	(14)	24	34	44	54	64
5	15	25	(35)	45	55	65
6	16	26	36	46	(56)	66
(7)	17	27	37	47	57	67
8	18	(28)	38	48	58	68
9	19	29	39	(49)	59	69
10	20	30	40	50	60	(70)

8s Patterns

1	11	21	31	41	51	61	71
2	12	22	(32)	42	52	62	(72)
3	13	23	33	43	53	63	73
4	14	(24)	34	44	54	(64)	74
5	15	25	35	45	55	65	75
6	(16)	26	36	46	(56)	66	76
7	17	27	37	47	57	67	77
(8)	18	28	38	(48)	58	68	78
9	19	29	39	49	59	69	79
10	20	30	(40)	50	60	70	(80)

Helping Students Who Need Practice

Math Expressions helps students build their fluency with the multiplication and division facts by providing practice materials that can be used independently.

Independent Practice

Have students who know the facts but are not completely fluent use the following materials for independent practice, along with any of the learning tools described above in Helping Students Who Need to Learn Strategies.

Product Cards
Lessons 4, 8, 13, 15, and 17

You will distribute Product Cards to students in sets related to the facts being studied. These cards provide visual and numeric cues for remembering facts. Multiplication is on the front, and division is on the back. Students sort their cards into *Fast, Slow,* and *Don't Know* piles to help prioritize their practice.

Product Cards (Front)

Product Cards (Back)

Checkups and Answer Keys
Lessons 4, 8, 17 and Lesson 1 of Unit 2

Checkups can be used as both assessment tools and fluency tools and are found in the Fluency Day student pages and in the Teacher Resource Book. Answer sheets are also provided so students can check their own work individually or with a partner. The Checkups are structured to emphasize different facts as listed below. They can be used over and over again throughout the year.

- **Checkup A:** 2s, 5s, 9s, 10s
- **Checkup B:** 2s, 5s, 9s, 3s, 4s, 1s, 0s
- **Checkup C:** 3s, 4s, 6s, 7s, 8s
- **Checkup D:** 2s, 5s, 9s, 3s, 4s, 6s, 7s, 8s, 1s, 0s
- **Checkup E:** 6s ,7s, 8s

Class Write-On Sheets and Check Sheets
Lessons 9 and 15

These reusable practice sheets are designed for use with a clear plastic sleeve and dry-erase markers. Check Sheets are provided so students can check their work individually or with a partner.

Class Write-On Sheet 1A

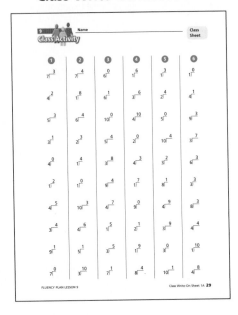

Check Write-On Sheet 1A

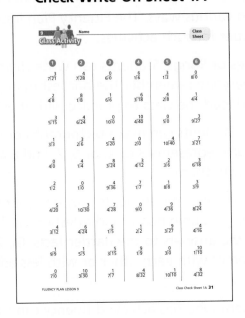

Games
Lessons 4, 8, 13, and 17

Games that provide fact practice in an engaging format are included in Fluency Day lessons. The first three games all use the Product Cards, and the last one is a bingo-like game based on knowing the multiplication facts.

- **Quotient Match**
- **High Card Wins**
- **Blackout**
- **Five in a Line**

Activities for Students Who Have Fluency

Some students entering Grade 4 may be able to recall basic multiplication and division facts accurately and quickly. However, they should not move forward without the rest of the class but should instead use the activities described below until the whole class is ready to start Unit 1 together.

Independent Activities

The independent activities described below are for those students who do not need extra teaching or practice for fluency.

Math Center Challenges Four extended activities are provided for every unit. These activities are projects or investigations that will engage your more able students. You will find a description of the Math Center Challenges for the Fluency Plan for on page 1F.

Challenge Activities Student Activity Cards describe independent activities related to the lesson content at three different ability levels. The Challenge Activity Card is facsimiled in the Differentiated Instruction section of each lesson.

Helping Partners

More able students often enhance their own understanding by helping others in various ways. The Fluency Plan lessons include many opportunities for such activities.

Inventing Rhymes or Songs Students can write rhymes or songs that will help everyone remember the hardest multiplication and division facts and lead the class to practice with them.

Creating Posters Students can make pictographs or function tables where each picture represents 3 or 4, or 6, 7, and 8 and lead the class to practice with them.

Building Board Games Some students may enjoy working in a group and creating a game board and question cards that require students to give the answers to the harder facts: 6s, 7, 8s. Students can play these games with each other or with less advanced students.

Coaching A student who has achieved fluency can function as a coach to help a less advanced student practice and plan effective practice methods. They can help students use different strategies. This individualized help and encouragement can be very helpful to a student in need of both.

Writing Word Problems Students can write word problems for each other. Type the problems into a class booklet with an answer key at the end, or have a separate answer booklet with all the different solutions for the problems. The problems can be mixed single-step problems and multistep problems. Save the booklets to use with Unit 1.

Conceptual Lessons

Lessons 3, 7, 9, 10, and 16 should be taught to the whole class because even your more fact-fluent students will benefit from the focus on the inverse relationship between multiplication and division.

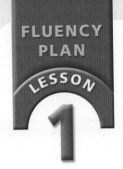

Addition and Subtraction Methods

Lesson Objectives

- Share different solution methods for adding and subtracting.
- Demonstrate an understanding of the Associative Property of Addition.

The Day at a Glance

Today's Goals	Materials
1 Teaching the Lesson A1: Assess recall for basic addition and subtraction. A2: Explain solution methods for addition problems. A3: Explain solution methods for subtraction problems. A4: Use the Associative Property to add, and prove it works for any numbers. **2 Going Further** ▶ Differentiated Instruction **3 Homework and Spiral Review**	**Lesson Activities** Student Activity Book pp. 1–4 or Student Hardcover Book pp. 1–3 and Activity Workbook pp. 1–2 (includes Checkups) Homework and Remembering pp. 1–2 **Going Further** Activity Cards FP-1 Math Journals 123 *Use* **Math Talk** *today!*

Keeping Skills Sharp

Quick Practice	Daily Routines
Having **Student Leaders** lead Quick Practice activities is a key element of *Math Expressions*. Help Student Leaders take over leading Quick Practices as soon as possible. Ask for volunteers initially, and choose socially confident students to begin. In the beginning, pair shy students with more confident students. After several months, almost all students will be ready to lead alone. For some Quick Practices, you may need to lead for a time or two, while for others you can lead initially by helping the Student Leader carry out the activity under your direction.	**Extend a Pattern** The numbers in a pattern increase by 6. If the first three numbers are 0, 6, and 12, what's the tenth number? 54

① Teaching the Lesson

Basic Addition and Subtraction

 10 MINUTES

Goal: Assess recall for basic addition and subtraction.

Materials: Student Activity Book pp. 1–2 or Hardcover Book pp. 1–2 and Activity Workbook pp. 1–2

✓ **NCTM Standards:**
Number and Operations
Algebra
Communication

Teaching Note

Common Error If students answer problems 11, 18, 33, and 40 incorrectly, you should review the Identity Property of Addition. Remind students "when you add any number and zero, the sum is that number."

Ask students to write the definition of the property in their own words and to then provide three number sentences that illustrate the property.

1
Class Activity

Name _____ Date _____

▶ **Checkup for Basic Addition**

1. 3 + 9 = 12	14. 8 + 7 = 15	27. 8 + 5 = 13	40. 0 + 8 = 8
2. 5 + 7 = 12	15. 6 + 6 = 12	28. 9 + 8 = 17	41. 4 + 9 = 13
3. 8 + 8 = 16	16. 10 + 9 = 19	29. 9 + 6 = 15	42. 6 + 7 = 13
4. 9 + 5 = 14	17. 8 + 4 = 12	30. 7 + 4 = 11	43. 8 + 9 = 17
5. 6 + 8 = 14	18. 0 + 9 = 9	31. 7 + 6 = 13	44. 8 + 3 = 11
6. 9 + 7 = 16	19. 9 + 4 = 13	32. 5 + 6 = 11	45. 8 + 10 = 18
7. 6 + 4 = 10	20. 7 + 8 = 15	33. 7 + 0 = 7	46. 3 + 2 = 5
8. 4 + 8 = 12	21. 5 + 5 = 10	34. 10 + 10 = 20	47. 4 + 7 = 11
9. 3 + 7 = 10	22. 7 + 9 = 16	35. 5 + 9 = 14	48. 6 + 9 = 15
10. 3 + 8 = 11	23. 7 + 3 = 10	36. 7 + 5 = 12	49. 2 + 3 = 5
11. 6 + 0 = 6	24. 3 + 6 = 9	37. 8 + 6 = 14	50. 4 + 6 = 10
12. 7 + 7 = 14	25. 6 + 5 = 11	38. 6 + 3 = 9	51. 9 + 3 = 12
13. 9 + 9 = 18	26. 9 + 2 = 11	39. 4 + 4 = 8	52. 5 + 8 = 13

FLUENCY PLAN LESSON 1   Addition Checkup **1**

Student Activity Book page 1

▶ Checkups for Basic Addition and Subtraction

As students arrive in fourth grade, they should be fluent with basic addition and subtraction. Use Student Book pages 1 and 2 to assess their ability to recall the more difficult additions and subtractions. Help students create a Study Plan for those additions and subtractions they may need to work on.

1

Name _____ Date _____

▶ **Checkup for Basic Subtraction**

1. 13 − 8 = 5	14. 9 − 9 = 0	27. 11 − 9 = 2	40. 16 − 9 = 7
2. 17 − 9 = 8	15. 7 − 4 = 3	28. 4 − 0 = 4	41. 3 − 0 = 3
3. 14 − 5 = 9	16. 10 − 8 = 2	29. 13 − 7 = 6	42. 11 − 5 = 6
4. 12 − 3 = 9	17. 15 − 9 = 6	30. 8 − 2 = 6	43. 7 − 7 = 0
5. 12 − 9 = 3	18. 10 − 6 = 4	31. 12 − 4 = 8	44. 15 − 7 = 8
6. 11 − 7 = 4	19. 12 − 5 = 7	32. 13 − 6 = 7	45. 16 − 7 = 9
7. 15 − 8 = 7	20. 15 − 6 = 9	33. 12 − 6 = 6	46. 13 − 5 = 8
8. 6 − 6 = 0	21. 16 − 8 = 8	34. 5 − 5 = 0	47. 11 − 4 = 7
9. 7 − 0 = 7	22. 11 − 8 = 3	35. 11 − 6 = 5	48. 8 − 0 = 8
10. 5 − 2 = 3	23. 17 − 8 = 9	36. 10 − 4 = 6	49. 11 − 3 = 8
11. 10 − 9 = 1	24. 14 − 7 = 7	37. 14 − 9 = 5	50. 12 − 8 = 4
12. 13 − 9 = 4	25. 10 − 7 = 3	38. 14 − 6 = 8	51. 8 − 6 = 2
13. 14 − 8 = 6	26. 10 − 5 = 5	39. 12 − 7 = 5	52. 13 − 4 = 9

2 FLUENCY PLAN LESSON 1   Subtraction Checkup

Student Activity Book page 2

Teaching Note

Common Errors Some students may need a reminder of the rules for subtraction involving zero.

If students answer problems 9, 28, 41, and 48 incorrectly, remind them, "when you subtract zero from any number, the difference is that number."

If students answer problems 8, 14, 34, and 43 incorrectly, remind them, "when you subtract a number from itself, the difference is zero."

Ask students to write each rule in their own words and then provide three number sentences that illustrate the rule.

① Teaching the Lesson

Activity 2

Different Ways to Add

 20 MINUTES

Goal: Explain solution methods for addition problems.

Materials: Student Activity Book or Hardcover Book p. 3

 NCTM Standards:
Number and Operations
Problem Solving
Communication

Teaching Note

Language and Vocabulary
Students often confuse the words *sum* in math and *some* in English. This confusion can create a problem in understanding the operation of addition because *sum* means "all" while *some* means "part." This program has emphasized using the word *total* to represent the sum of two addends. This word also relates well to the Spanish word *total*.

If students are not having any difficulty distinguishing between *sum* and *some*, allow them to use the math vocabulary word *sum* when they talk about an answer for addition. Work with your class to balance their need to know standard math vocabulary and the confusion *sum* can introduce into classroom Math Talk.

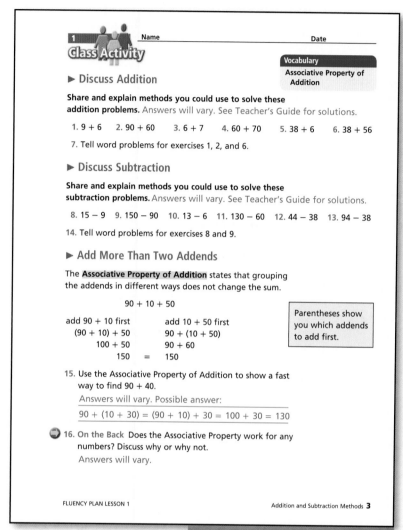

Student Activity Book page 3

▶ Discuss Addition

WHOLE CLASS   Math Talk

Ask for Ideas Give students an opportunity to share what they remember about addition. If students don't know how to begin, introduce some of the vocabulary for addition: addend, sum, total, joining, and so on.

Share Methods Work through the addition exercises on Student Book page 3, and have students share their solution methods. If there are not many methods shared, ask students to think of different ways to find the answers. Encourage students to share methods that use fingers. (They may be reluctant to share such methods unless you affirm that they are acceptable.)

Be sure that students notice and discuss how their methods are alike and different for exercises 1 and 2. Elicit similar comparisons for numbers 3 and 4, and for 5 and 6. (Note: This day may take longer than usual because many examples of student addition and subtraction methods should be discussed.)

Some possible student responses are:

1. 9 + 6

Count On
"Start at 9. Count on 6 more: 10, 11, 12, 13, 14, 15. I started at 9 and counted on 6 more to get to 15. So 9 + 6 = 15."

When students count on more than 3, they will often use their fingers to keep track of how many times they counted on. Allow them to do so. This is a powerful general method.

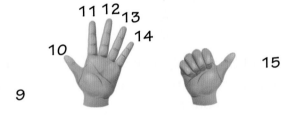

Make a 10
"9 and how many more make 10? Take 1 from the 6, leaving 5 and 10 + 5 = 15."

$$9 + 6 = 9 + 1 + 5 = 10 + 5 = 15$$
$$\overset{/\backslash}{} \\ 1 + 5$$

2. 90 + 60

As you discuss methods for 90 + 60, relate them to methods you used for 9 + 6. Students can use related methods by thinking about tens instead of ones.

Count On
"Start at 90. Count on 6 more tens: 100, 110, 120, 130, 140, 150. I started at 90 and counted on 6 more tens to get to 150. So 90 + 60 = 150."

Activity continued ▶

Activity 2

Teaching Note

What to Expect From Students
Some students may still be using finger methods for addition and subtraction with sums in the teens. Research has found that these methods are good enough for all problem solving if students are counting on and are accurate and rapid. Students who are still making little marks for addition and counting them all (or trying to count all of both numbers on their fingers) should be encouraged to count on from the larger number.

Make a 100
"90 and how many more make 100? Take 10 from the 60, leaving 50 and 100 + 50 = 150."

$$90 + 60 = 90 + 10 + 50 = 100 + 50 = 150$$
$$\overset{\displaystyle /\backslash}{10 + 50}$$

Make 10 Tens
"9 tens and how many more make 10 tens? Take 1 ten from the 6 tens, leaving 5 tens and 10 tens + 5 tens = 15 tens = 150."

$$9 \text{ tens} + 6 \text{ tens} = 9 \text{ tens} + 1 \text{ ten} + 5 \text{ tens} = 15 \text{ tens} = 150$$
$$\overset{\displaystyle /\backslash}{1 \text{ ten} + 5 \text{ tens}}$$

Using either of the above two methods will help students when they have to add multidigit numbers.

3. 6 + 7

Count On
"Start at 7. Count on 6 more: 8, 9, 10, 11, 12, 13. I started at 7 and counted on 6 more to get to 13. So 7 + 6 = 13." (Students may also start with 6 and count on 7.)

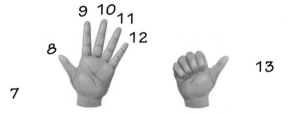

Make a 10
"6 and how many more make 10? Take 4 from the 7, leaving 3, and 6 + 4 + 3 = 10 + 3 = 13." Or, "7 and how many more make 10? Take 3 from the 6, leaving 3 and 7 + 3 + 3 = 10 + 3 = 13."

Doubles Plus 1	**Doubles Minus 1**
6 + 6 = 12 so	7 + 7 = 14 so
6 + 7 = 12 + 1 = 13	7 + 6 = 14 − 1 = 13

4. 60 + 70

As you discuss methods for 60 + 70, relate them to the methods
you used for 6 + 7. Students can use related methods by thinking
about tens instead of ones.

Count On
"Start at 70. Count on 6 more tens: 70, 80, 90, 100, 110, 120, 130.
I started at 60 and counted on 7 more tens to get to 130.
So 60 + 70 = 130."

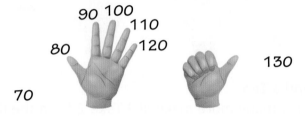

Make a 100
"60 and how many more make 100? Take 40 from the 70, leaving 30
and 100 + 30 = 130."

$$60 + 70 = 60 + 40 + 30 = 100 + 30 = 130$$
$$/\backslash$$
$$40 + 30$$

Make 10 Tens
"6 tens and how many more make 10 tens? Take 4 tens from the
7 tens, leaving 3 tens and 10 tens + 3 tens = 13 tens = 130."

$$6\ tens + 7\ tens = 6\ tens + 4\ tens + 3\ tens = 13\ tens = 130$$
$$/\backslash$$
$$4\ tens + 3\ tens$$

Using either of the above two methods will help students when
they have to add multi-digit numbers.

Activity continued ▶

5. 38 + 6

Count On

"Start at 38. Count on 6 more: 39, 40, 41, 42, 43, 44. I started at 38 and counted on 6 more to get to 44. So 38 + 6 = 44."

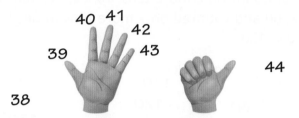

40 41
42
39 43
44
38

Add Around a Ten

"38 and how many more make 40? Take 2 from the 6, leaving 4 and 40 + 4 = 44."

$$38 + 6 = 38 + 2 + 4 = 40 + 4 = 44$$
$$\underset{2+4}{\wedge}$$

Add with Grouping

```
   38        ¹38        38         38
  + 6       + 6       + 6        + 6
  ----      ----      ----       ----
   44        44        30         14
                       14         30
                      ----       ----
                       44         44
```

6. 38 + 56

Add with Grouping

```
   38        ¹38        38         38
  +56       +56       +56        +56
  ----      ----      ----       ----
   94        94        80         14
                       14         80
                      ----       ----
                       94         94
```

Have students tell word problems for exercises 1, 2, and 6. This will give you some idea about the meanings your students have for addition before you begin the later days on types of addition word problems.

Different Ways to Subtract

▶ Discuss Subtraction

WHOLE CLASS   Math Talk

Ask for Ideas Ask students to share what they remember about subtraction. If students don't know how to begin, introduce some of the vocabulary that is associated with subtraction, such as difference, take away, compare, separating, and so on.

Share Methods Work through the subtraction exercises and have students share their solution methods. For each exercise, relate subtraction methods to the methods used for addition in the related exercise. If there are not many subtraction methods shared, ask students to think of different ways to find the answers. Encourage students to share methods that use an unknown addend (such as counting on—see below) and methods that use fingers. (Students may be reluctant to share such methods unless you affirm that they are acceptable.)

Some possible students responses are:

8. 15 − 9 or 9 + ? = 15

> **Count On**
> "Start at 9. Count on up to 15: 10, 11, 12, 13, 14, 15. I started at 9 and counted on 6 more to get to 15. So 15 − 9 = 6."

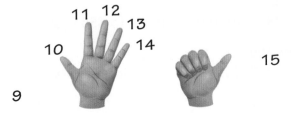

> **Take from 10**
> "15 is made from 10 and 5. I take 9 from the 10 and have 1 left to put with the 5, making 6."
>
> Or:
> 15 = 10 + 5
>   −9
>   1 + 5 = 6

> **Up Over 10**
> "9 up to 10 is 1, plus 5 more up to 15 is 6."

> **Down Over 10**
> "15 down to 10 is 5, plus 1 more down to 9 is 6."

Activity continued ▶

 20 MINUTES

Goal: Explain solution methods for subtraction problems.

Materials: Student Activity Book or Hardcover Book p. 3

✔ **NCTM Standards:**
Number and Operations
Problem Solving
Communication

 Differentiated Instruction

Extra Help Students who are still making little marks for subtraction and crossing out some of them should be helped towards counting on from the larger number up to the sum to find the unknown addend. For most students, the forward methods shown in this lesson are much easier than the counting down methods some students invent.

Activity 3

Teaching Note

Language and Vocabulary
In the lower grades, we emphasized relationships between addition and subtraction by using the addition vocabulary *total*, *addend*, *addend* in subtraction situations. Students learn that an answer to a subtraction is an unknown addend. They also learn that an answer to a subtraction is called a *difference*. One use of a difference is to describe how much larger or smaller one quantity is than another quantity. If you wish, you can introduce these two vocabulary words for subtraction which are not as common as the words mentioned above:

• The *subtrahend* is the number you are subtracting.

• The *minuend* is the number from which you are subtracting.

9. $150 - 90$, or $90 + ? = 150$

As you discuss methods for $150 - 90$, relate them to methods you used for $15 - 9$. Students can use related methods by thinking about tens instead of ones.

Count On
"Start at 90. Count on by tens: 100, 110, 120, 130, 140, 150. I started at 90 and counted on 6 more tens to get to 150. So $90 + 60 = 150$ and $150 - 90 = 60$."

Or, start at 9 tens. "Count on tens: 10, 11, 12, 13, 14, 15 tens. So 9 tens + 6 tens = 15 tens and 15 tens − 9 tens = 6 tens = 60."

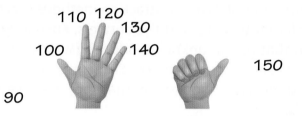

Take from 100
$150 = 100 + 50$
$\underline{-90}$
$10 + 50 = 60$
Or: "$100 - 90$ is 10 plus 50 more is 60."

Up Over 100
"90 up to 100 is 10, plus 50 more to 150 is 60."

Down Over 100
"150 down to 100 is 50, plus 10 more down to 90 is 60."

10. $13 - 6$ or $6 + ? = 13$

Doubles Plus 1
"$6 + 6 = 12$, so 1 more to make 13 instead of 12 is 7."

Take from 10
"$10 - 6$ is 4 plus 3 more in 13 is 7."

Up Over 10
"6 up to 10 is 4, plus 3 more up to 13 is 7."

Down Over 10
"13 down to 10 is 3, plus 4 more down to 6 is 7."

11. $130 - 60$ or $60 + ? = 130$

Doubles for Tens
"$60 + 60 = 120$, so 10 more to make 130 instead of 120 is 70."

Take from 100
"$100 - 60$ is 40 plus 30 more in 130 is 70."

Up Over 100
"60 up to 100 is 40, plus 30 more up to 130 is 70."

Down Over 100
"130 down to 100 is 30, plus 40 more down to 60 is 70."

12. $44 - 38$ or $38 + ? = 44$

Count On
"Start at 38. Then count on up to 44: 39, 40, 41, 42, 43, 44.
I counted on 6 more. So $38 + 6 = 44$ and $44 - 38 = 6$."

Add Around a Ten
"$38 + 2$ is 40, plus 4 more is 44, and $2 + 4 = 6$, so $38 + 6 = 44$ and
$44 - 38 = 6$."

Or:
$38 + 2 = 40$

$40 + \underline{4} = 44$

6

Subtract by Ungrouping

$$\begin{array}{r} \overset{3\ 14}{\cancel{4}\cancel{4}} \\ -\ 38 \\ \hline 6 \end{array}$$

13. $94 - 38$ or $38 + ? = 94$

Add Around a Ten
"$38 + 2$ is 40, plus 54 more is 94 and $54 + 2 = 56$, so $38 + 56 = 94$
and $94 - 38 = 56$."

Subtract by Ungrouping

$$\begin{array}{r} \overset{8\ 14}{\cancel{9}\cancel{4}} \\ -\ 38 \\ \hline 56 \end{array}$$

Elicit word problems for 8 and 9. Again, this will show you what your
students know about the meanings of subtraction.

Teaching Note

What to Expect from Students
Some students may subtract from left
to right after they have ungrouped.
That is acceptable, and we will discuss
it in Unit 1.

Teaching Note

Math Background Notice that
counting on to add or to subtract
(find the unknown addend) looks
exactly the same to an observer. But
subtracting is actually easier than
adding because you stop when you
say the sum. For adding, you have to
keep monitoring your fingers and
stop when your fingers show the
addend added on.

Make a 10 subtraction is also easier
than Make a 10 addition. They both
start the same way: find how many
more to 10. For subtraction you then
just add the ones from the teen total.
For addition you have to separate the
addend added on into that number
plus the rest and then add the rest
to 10.

Activity 4

The Associative Property of Addition

 20 MINUTES

Goal: Use the Associative Property to add, and prove it works for any numbers.

Materials: Student Activity Book pp. 3–4 or Hardcover Book p. 3

 NCTM Standards:
Number and Operations
Algebra
Communication

Teaching Note

Common Error Some students may confuse the Commutative Property and the Associative Property. Explain that the Commutative Property of Addition (or Multiplication) is used for two addends (or factors) and describes the order in which you write the numbers. The Associative Property of Addition (or Multiplication) is used for three or more addends (or factors) and describes the order in which you carry out (do) the operations.

 Ongoing Assessment

Ask questions such as:

▶ How can you find 8 + 5 by counting on?

▶ How can you find 14 − 5 by counting on?

▶ **Add More Than Two Addends** ⬛WHOLE CLASS

Read the definition of the Associative Property of Addition on page 3 of the Student Book. Discuss the example of 90 + 10 + 50 and check that students understand that parentheses mean, "Add these numbers first."

Ask:

● **Why is the sum for each expression the same?** You are adding the same numbers. They are just grouped differently.

Explain to students that we use parentheses to show which addends to add first. Students will use parentheses throughout the school year.

Also point out that this example shows an easy way to add 90 + 60. That is, you can add 90 + 60 by separating 60 into 10 + 50: 90 + 60 = 90 + 10 + 50.

Send as many students as will fit to the board to work on exercise 15 while the rest of the class solves it at their seats. This will let you see which students understand the pattern of parentheses in the Associative Property for adding around 100: 90 + (10 + 30) = (90 + 10) + 30. Do a few more examples if students seem to need them.

For example: 90 + 70 = 90 + (10 + 60) = (90 + 10) + 60
80 + 60 = 80 + (20 + 40) = (80 + 20) + 40

Discuss exercise 16. Students should understand that the Associative Property of Addition works for any numbers. Their explanations will vary, but should include the idea that everything is getting counted, even if different groups are counted first.

②Going Further

Intervention Activity Card FP-1

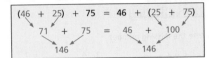

Group to Add Mentally   Activity Card FP-1 ●

Work: By Yourself

1. The Associative Property of Addition lets you change the way addends are grouped without changing the total. The addends in this equation are grouped so that you can add mentally. The parentheses tell you which addends to add first.

$$(46 + 25) + 75 = 46 + (25 + 75)$$
$$71 + 75 = 46 + 100$$
$$146 \qquad\qquad 146$$

2. Group the addends so that you can add mentally. Then find the sum.

   a. 57 + 92 + 8   **b.** 95 + 5 + 21   **c.** 25 + 75 + 50 + 50

3. Write two more expressions to show how the Associative Property of Addition can be used to add mentally.

Fluency Plan, Lesson 1   Copyright © Houghton Mifflin Company

Activity Note Review the Associative Property of Addition with students. Then ask students to explain the property in their own words.

✓ Math Writing Prompt

Explain Your Thinking How can you use the Associative Property of Addition to help you add mentally? Explain your thinking.

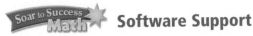 **Software Support**

Use *Soar to Success* for instruction of students needing targeted support for underlying skills.

▲ On Level Activity Card FP-1

Addition Properties   Activity Card FP-1 ▲

Work: In Pairs

1. The Associative Property of Addition tells you that the total stays the same when you change the grouping of the addends.

2. **Work Together** Work with your partner to prove whether or not the Associative Property is true for subtraction. Use these numbers.

   | $(10 + 5) + 4 = 10 + (5 + 4)$ | $(10 - 5) - 4 \bigcirc 10 - (5 - 4)$ |

3. The Commutative Property of Addition tells you that the total stays the same when you change the order of the addends.

4. **Work Together** Work with your partner to prove whether or not the Commutative Property is true for subtraction. Use these numbers.

   | $32 + 16 = 16 + 32$ | $32 - 16 \bigcirc 16 - 32$ |

Fluency Plan, Lesson 1   Copyright © Houghton Mifflin Company

Activity Note To extend the activity, have students explain how they could use the Commutative Property to solve 96 + 15 + 4 mentally.

✓ Math Writing Prompt

Explain Your Thinking How are the *Associative Property of Addition* and the *Commutative Property of Addition* alike? How are they different?

 Software Support

Use *MegaMath* for review and reinforcement of the concepts and skills presented in this lesson.

Challenge Activity Card FP-1

The Associative Property   Activity Card FP-1 ■

Work: In Pairs

1. Answer the following questions and explain your answers. Provide examples to support your answers.

2. Does the Associative Property work for subtraction?
   No, the order of the numbers changes the difference; example: 8 − 5 ≠ 5 − 8.

3. Does the Associative Property work for multiplication?
   Yes, the order of the factors does not change the product; $4 \times (3 \times 2) = (4 \times 3) \times 2$.

4. Does the Associative Property work for division?
   No, the order of the numbers changes the difference; example: 40 ÷ 10 = 4, 10 ÷ 40 = 0.25.

Fluency Plan, Lesson 1   Copyright © Houghton Mifflin Company

Activity Note Ask students why the name *Associative Property* makes sense.

✓ Math Writing Prompt

Explain Your Thinking Explain how the Associative Property can help you easily find $(89 + 94) + 6$.

 Software Support

Use *Destination Math* to take students beyond the concepts and skills presented in this lesson.

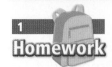

③ Homework and Spiral Review

Homework **Goal:** Additional Practice

✓ Include students' work for page 1 as part of their portfolios.

Remembering **Goal:** Spiral Review

This Remembering activity would be appropriate anytime after today's lesson.

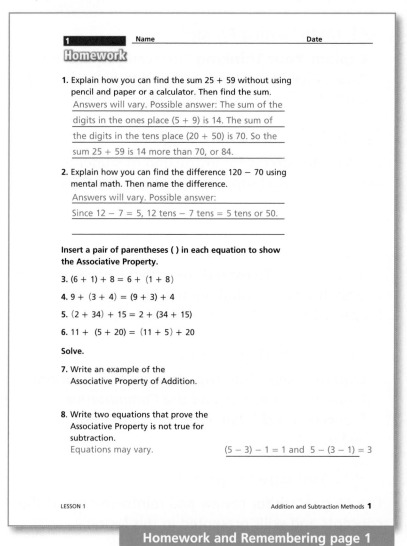

1 **Name** _____ **Date** _____
Homework

1. Explain how you can find the sum 25 + 59 without using pencil and paper or a calculator. Then find the sum.
   Answers will vary. Possible answer: The sum of the digits in the ones place (5 + 9) is 14. The sum of the digits in the tens place (20 + 50) is 70. So the sum 25 + 59 is 14 more than 70, or 84.

2. Explain how you can find the difference 120 − 70 using mental math. Then name the difference.
   Answers will vary. Possible answer:
   Since 12 − 7 = 5, 12 tens − 7 tens = 5 tens or 50.

Insert a pair of parentheses ( ) in each equation to show the Associative Property.

3. (6 + 1) + 8 = 6 + (1 + 8)
4. 9 + (3 + 4) = (9 + 3) + 4
5. (2 + 34) + 15 = 2 + (34 + 15)
6. 11 + (5 + 20) = (11 + 5) + 20

Solve.

7. Write an example of the Associative Property of Addition.

8. Write two equations that prove the Associative Property is not true for subtraction.
   Equations may vary.   (5 − 3) − 1 = 1 and 5 − (3 − 1) = 3

LESSON 1   Addition and Subtraction Methods **1**

Homework and Remembering page 1

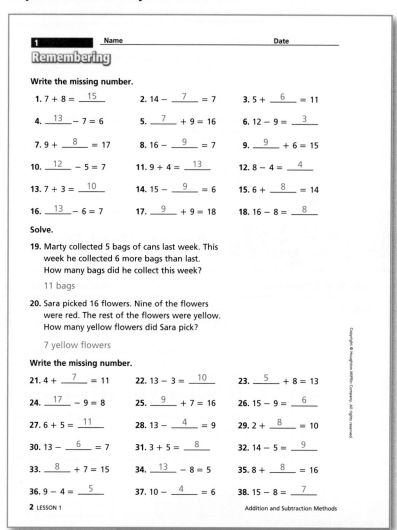

1 **Name** _____ **Date** _____
Remembering

Write the missing number.

1. 7 + 8 = __15__   2. 14 − __7__ = 7   3. 5 + __6__ = 11
4. __13__ − 7 = 6   5. __7__ + 9 = 16   6. 12 − 9 = __3__
7. 9 + __8__ = 17   8. 16 − __9__ = 7   9. __9__ + 6 = 15
10. __12__ − 5 = 7   11. 9 + 4 = __13__   12. 8 − 4 = __4__
13. 7 + 3 = __10__   14. 15 − __9__ = 6   15. 6 + __8__ = 14
16. __13__ − 6 = 7   17. __9__ + 9 = 18   18. 16 − 8 = __8__

Solve.

19. Marty collected 5 bags of cans last week. This week he collected 6 more bags than last. How many bags did he collect this week?
    11 bags

20. Sara picked 16 flowers. Nine of the flowers were red. The rest of the flowers were yellow. How many yellow flowers did Sara pick?
    7 yellow flowers

Write the missing number.

21. 4 + __7__ = 11   22. 13 − 3 = __10__   23. __5__ + 8 = 13
24. __17__ − 9 = 8   25. __9__ + 7 = 16   26. 15 − 9 = __6__
27. 6 + 5 = __11__   28. 13 − __4__ = 9   29. 2 + __8__ = 10
30. 13 − __6__ = 7   31. 3 + 5 = __8__   32. 14 − 5 = __9__
33. __8__ + 7 = 15   34. __13__ − 8 = 5   35. 8 + __8__ = 16
36. 9 − 4 = __5__   37. 10 − __4__ = 6   38. 15 − 8 = __7__

2 LESSON 1   Addition and Subtraction Methods

Homework and Remembering page 2

Home or School Activity

 Real-World Connection

Using Money Have students make lists of different items or activities that cost whole number dollar amounts. For example, a movie ticket might cost $6, or an item on a restaurant menu might cost $14. For each money amount, students write equations to show different ways to pay for the item. For example, you can pay for a $14 item with a ten-dollar bill and four one-dollar bills:

$$\$10 + \$1 + \$1 + \$1 + \$1 = \$14$$

Or, you can pay for a $14 item with a twenty-dollar bill and get $6 change:

$$\$20 - \$6 = \$14$$

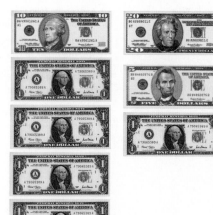

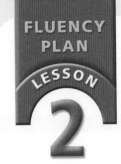

Patterns in 2s, 5s, 10s, and 9s

Vocabulary

Quick 9s
count-bys
10s-minus-1s
multiplier
product

Lesson Objectives

● Use the Target to practice multiplication and division.

● Explore patterns in count-bys and multiplications.

The Day at a Glance

Today's Goals	Materials	
1 Teaching the Lesson **A1:** Assess recall of basic multiplication and division. **A2:** Discuss how to use the Target to practice multiplication and division. **A3:** Describe patterns in 2s and 5s multiplications and count-bys. **A4:** Describe patterns in 10s and 9s multiplications and count-bys. **A5:** Learn a shortcut for finding 9s multiplications and divisions.	**Lesson Activities** Student Activity Book pp. 5–10 or Student Hardcover Book pp. 5–10 and Activity Workbook pp. 3–6 (includes Checkups and Family Letters) Homework and Remembering pp. 3–4 Targets (Manipulative Kit or TRB M1) Transparency sheet (optional) Class MathBoard MathBoard Dry-erase markers Dry-erase material	**Going Further** Activity Cards FP-2 Comparing Numbers (TRB M50) Counters (2 colors) Math Journals
2 Going Further ▶ Differentiated Instruction		
3 Homework and Spiral Review		

123 *Use* **Math Talk** *today!*

Keeping Skills Sharp

Quick Practice 🕐 5 MINUTES	Daily Routines
Goal: Practice divisions for 2s. **Materials:** Division Digits: Set 1 and Set 2 (TRB M3–M4), sheet protector, dry-erase marker See Lesson 1 for information about **Student Leaders.** **Division Digits for 2s** Place copies of Division Digits: Set 1 and Set 2 back-to-back in a sheet protector. The **Student Leader** reads problems from the 2s section of Set 1 aloud in any order. When the leader gives a signal, students raise the number of fingers for the answer. For example, if the leader reads 12 ÷ 2, students raise 6 fingers. The leader marks each problem with a dry-erase marker so that it is not repeated. For future lessons, the Division Digits pages, sheet protector, and dry-erase marker will be called Division Digits materials.	**Homework Review** Have students discuss the problems from their homework. Encourage students to help each other resolve any misunderstandings. **Extend a Pattern** The numbers in a pattern are each multiplied by 2. If the first three numbers are 3, 6, and 12, what's the sixth number? 96

Activity 1

Basic Multiplication and Division

 10 MINUTES

Goal: Assess recall of basic multiplication and division.

Materials: Student Activity Book pp. 5–6 or Hardcover Book pp. 5–6 and Activity Workbook pp. 3–4.

✔ **NCTM Standards:**
Number and Operations
Algebra
Communication

Teaching Note

Common Errors On Student Book page 5, if students answer problems 6 and 21 incorrectly, you should review the Identity Property of Multiplication. Remind students "when you multiply any number and 1, the product is that number."

If students answer problems 33 and 48 incorrectly, you should review the Property of Zero for Multiplication. Remind students "when you multiply any number and 0, the product is 0."

Ask students to write the definition of each property in their own words and then to provide three number sentences that illustrate the property.

The Learning Classroom

Student Leaders The **Quick Practice** activities are very important to do every day because they provide crucial practice and enable you to interact with students who may need guidance while **Student Leaders** lead or students practice individually. Many teachers do the Quick Practice at some time other than in math class.

---

2 Class Activity	Name		Date

▶ Checkup for Basic Multiplication

1. 4 × 5 = 20	19. 4 × 3 = 12	37. 6 × 4 = 24	55. 8 × 8 = 64
2. 1 × 10 = 10	20. 9 × 1 = 9	38. 9 × 9 = 81	56. 9 × 7 = 63
3. 3 × 5 = 15	21. 7 × 3 = 21	39. 5 × 9 = 45	57. 3 × 6 = 18
4. 8 × 5 = 40	22. 8 × 0 = 0	40. 8 × 4 = 32	58. 10 × 7 = 70
5. 4 × 10 = 40	23. 5 × 3 = 15	41. 6 × 9 = 54	59. 8 × 6 = 48
6. 9 × 5 = 45	24. 6 × 1 = 6	42. 7 × 4 = 28	60. 9 × 8 = 72
7. 8 × 2 = 16	25. 5 × 0 = 0	43. 4 × 9 = 36	61. 6 × 7 = 42
8. 6 × 5 = 30	26. 9 × 3 = 27	44. 9 × 4 = 36	62. 7 × 8 = 56
9. 5 × 10 = 50	27. 5 × 1 = 5	45. 10 × 9 = 90	63. 5 × 6 = 30
10. 9 × 2 = 18	28. 8 × 3 = 24	46. 5 × 4 = 20	64. 7 × 7 = 49
11. 5 × 5 = 25	29. 6 × 0 = 0	47. 7 × 9 = 63	65. 6 × 6 = 36
12. 8 × 10 = 80	30. 6 × 3 = 18	48. 4 × 4 = 16	66. 0 × 8 = 0
13. 7 × 2 = 14	31. 9 × 0 = 0	49. 8 × 9 = 72	67. 8 × 7 = 56
14. 5 × 2 = 10	32. 1 × 3 = 3	50. 3 × 9 = 27	68. 7 × 6 = 42
15. 6 × 10 = 60	33. 4 × 1 = 4	51. 0 × 4 = 0	69. 4 × 8 = 32
16. 0 × 5 = 0	34. 3 × 3 = 9	52. 2 × 9 = 18	70. 5 × 7 = 35
17. 6 × 2 = 12	35. 3 × 0 = 0	53. 3 × 4 = 12	71. 6 × 8 = 48
18. 7 × 5 = 35	36. 2 × 3 = 6	54. 1 × 9 = 9	72. 9 × 6 = 54

FLUENCY PLAN LESSON 2   Multiplication Checkup **5**

Student Activity Book page 5

▶ Checkups for Multiplication and Division

A goal of fourth grade students is to become fluent with basic multiplication and division. Use Student Book pages 5 and 6 to assess their ability to recall the more difficult multiplications and divisions. The Fluency Plan, described in the overview, provides appropriate support for students of all abilities.

The Checkup for Multiplication can be used to diagnose where students need more work.

Students Who Miss	Need to Practice Multiplications
Items 1–18	2s, 5s, and 10s
Items 19–36	0s, 1s, and 3s
Items 37–54	4s and 9s
Items 55–72	6s, 7s, and 8s

2 Class Activity

Name _____ Date _____

▶ **Checkup for Basic Division**

1. 35 ÷ 5 = 7	19. 27 ÷ 3 = 9	37. 72 ÷ 9 = 8	55. 42 ÷ 6 = 7
2. 40 ÷ 10 = 4	20. 10 ÷ 1 = 10	38. 24 ÷ 4 = 6	56. 18 ÷ 6 = 3
3. 30 ÷ 5 = 6	21. 12 ÷ 3 = 4	39. 27 ÷ 9 = 3	57. 42 ÷ 7 = 6
4. 16 ÷ 2 = 8	22. 21 ÷ 3 = 7	40. 81 ÷ 9 = 9	58. 64 ÷ 8 = 8
5. 15 ÷ 5 = 3	23. 0 ÷ 3 = 0	41. 28 ÷ 4 = 7	59. 30 ÷ 6 = 5
6. 45 ÷ 5 = 9	24. 6 ÷ 1 = 6	42. 20 ÷ 4 = 5	60. 49 ÷ 7 = 7
7. 90 ÷ 10 = 9	25. 18 ÷ 3 = 6	43. 63 ÷ 9 = 7	61. 54 ÷ 6 = 9
8. 25 ÷ 5 = 5	26. 15 ÷ 3 = 5	44. 32 ÷ 4 = 8	62. 24 ÷ 8 = 3
9. 10 ÷ 2 = 5	27. 1 ÷ 1 = 1	45. 54 ÷ 9 = 6	63. 21 ÷ 7 = 3
10. 5 ÷ 5 = 1	28. 30 ÷ 3 = 10	46. 16 ÷ 4 = 4	64. 72 ÷ 8 = 9
11. 80 ÷ 10 = 8	29. 7 ÷ 1 = 7	47. 45 ÷ 9 = 5	65. 48 ÷ 6 = 8
12. 40 ÷ 5 = 8	30. 9 ÷ 3 = 3	48. 36 ÷ 4 = 9	66. 56 ÷ 8 = 7
13. 8 ÷ 2 = 4	31. 9 ÷ 1 = 9	49. 9 ÷ 9 = 1	67. 56 ÷ 7 = 8
14. 18 ÷ 2 = 9	32. 6 ÷ 3 = 2	50. 8 ÷ 4 = 2	68. 36 ÷ 6 = 6
15. 20 ÷ 10 = 2	33. 0 ÷ 1 = 0	51. 40 ÷ 4 = 10	69. 48 ÷ 8 = 6
16. 6 ÷ 2 = 3	34. 3 ÷ 3 = 1	52. 18 ÷ 9 = 2	70. 63 ÷ 7 = 9
17. 20 ÷ 5 = 4	35. 24 ÷ 3 = 8	53. 12 ÷ 4 = 3	71. 6 ÷ 6 = 1
18. 12 ÷ 2 = 6	36. 8 ÷ 1 = 8	54. 36 ÷ 9 = 4	72. 35 ÷ 7 = 5

6 FLUENCY PLAN LESSON 2   Division Checkup

Student Activity Book page 6

The Checkup for Division can be used to diagnose where students need more work.

Students Who Miss	Need to Practice Divisions
Items 1–18	2s, 5s, and 10s
Items 19–36	1s and 3s
Items 37–54	4s and 9s
Items 55–72	6s, 7s, and 8s

Teaching Note

Common Error On Student Book page 6, if students answer problems 39 and 50 incorrectly, remind them, "when you divide any number by itself, the quotient is 1."

Ask students to write the rule in their own words and then provide three number sentences that illustrate the rule.

Activity 2

Target Check

 10 MINUTES

Goal: Discuss how to use the Target to practice multiplication and division.

Materials: Class Multiplication Table; Student Activity Book pp. 7–8 or Hardcover Book p. 7; Targets (Manipulative Kit or TRB M1) and transparency sheet (optional)

 NCTM Standard:
Number and Operations

The Learning Classroom

Math Talk You must direct student math talk for it to be productive. Over time, as students become more skilled at discussing their thinking and talking directly with each other, you will fade into the background more. But you will always monitor, clarify, extend, and ultimately make the decisions about how to direct the math conversation so that it is pro–ductive for your students.

English Language Learners

Help students visualize multiplication patterns. Draw a number line from 0 to 30. Draw arcs to show the jumps between 2s count-bys. Model how to label the arcs.

• **Beginning** Point to the first arc. Say: **This is 1 × 2 = 2.** Have students repeat.
• **Intermediate** Say: **This arc is 1 × 2 = ____.** Ask: **What is the next arc?** 2 × 2 = 4. Continue with the other arcs.
• **Advanced** Ask: **What is 1 × 2?** 2 Have students work in pairs to label the arcs.

▶ Use the Class Multiplication Table WHOLE CLASS

Display the Class Multiplication Table where all students can see it. Leave the poster in place as you work on this unit. Make sure students understand that the *rows* of a table go across, and the *columns* go up and down. To practice finding rows and columns, have them read the numbers and symbols they see in row 4. Next, have them choose a column and have them read the numbers. Then have students choose a different row and repeat the process.

Explain that the shaded row at the top of the table and shaded column on the left side of the table show the factors. In the shaded row, point to the column with the factor 5 at the top.

Math Talk Ask students to describe what they see down the column. Make sure the following points are discussed:

● The column shows the 5s multiplications from $1 \cdot 5 = 5$ to $12 \cdot 5 = 60$.

● In all the multiplications in the column, the 5 is the second factor.

● The large, bold numbers are the products, which are also the "5s count-bys" (the numbers we say when we count by 5.)

Explain to students that there are several ways to show multiplication using different symbols (×, •, *). For example, 5 × 2 is the same as 5 • 2 and 5 * 2. Each shows the product 10.

Multiplication Table

X	1	2	3	4	5	6	7	8	9
1	$1 \cdot 1 = 1$	$1 \cdot 2 = 2$	$1 \cdot 3 = 3$	$1 \cdot 4 = 4$	$1 \cdot 5 = 5$	$1 \cdot 6 = 6$	$1 \cdot 7 = 7$	$1 \cdot 8 = 8$	$1 \cdot 9 = 9$
2	$2 \times 1 = 2$	$2 \times 2 = 4$	$2 \times 3 = 6$	$2 \times 4 = 8$	$2 \times 5 = 10$	$2 \times 6 = 12$	$2 \times 7 = 14$	$2 \times 8 = 16$	$2 \times 9 = 18$
3	$3 \cdot 1 = 3$	$3 \cdot 2 = 6$	$3 \cdot 3 = 9$	$3 \cdot 4 = 12$	$3 \cdot 5 = 15$	$3 \cdot 6 = 18$	$3 \cdot 7 = 21$	$3 \cdot 8 = 24$	$3 \cdot 9 = 27$
4	$4 \cdot 1 = 4$	$4 \cdot 2 = 8$	$4 \cdot 3 = 12$	$4 \cdot 4 = 16$	$4 \cdot 5 = 20$	$4 \cdot 6 = 24$	$4 \cdot 7 = 28$	$4 \cdot 8 = 32$	$4 \cdot 9 = 36$
5	$5 \times 1 = 5$	$5 \times 2 = 10$	$5 \times 3 = 15$	$5 \times 4 = 20$	$5 \times 5 = 25$	$5 \times 6 = 30$	$5 \times 7 = 35$	$5 \times 8 = 40$	$5 \times 9 = 45$
6	$6 \cdot 1 = 6$	$6 \cdot 2 = 12$	$6 \cdot 3 = 18$	$6 \cdot 4 = 24$	$6 \cdot 5 = 30$	$6 \cdot 6 = 36$	$6 \cdot 7 = 42$	$6 \cdot 8 = 48$	$6 \cdot 9 = 54$
7	$7 \cdot 1 = 7$	$7 \cdot 2 = 14$	$7 \cdot 3 = 21$	$7 \cdot 4 = 28$	$7 \cdot 5 = 35$	$7 \cdot 6 = 42$	$7 \cdot 7 = 49$	$7 \cdot 8 = 56$	$7 \cdot 9 = 63$
8	$8 \times 1 = 8$	$8 \times 2 = 16$	$8 \times 3 = 24$	$8 \times 4 = 32$	$8 \times 5 = 40$	$8 \times 6 = 48$	$8 \times 7 = 56$	$8 \times 8 = 64$	$8 \times 9 = 72$
9	$9 \cdot 1 = 9$	$9 \cdot 2 = 18$	$9 \cdot 3 = 27$	$9 \cdot 4 = 36$	$9 \cdot 5 = 45$	$9 \cdot 6 = 54$	$9 \cdot 7 = 63$	$9 \cdot 8 = 72$	$9 \cdot 9 = 81$
10	$10 \cdot 1 = 10$	$10 \cdot 2 = 20$	$10 \cdot 3 = 30$	$10 \cdot 4 = 40$	$10 \cdot 5 = 50$	$10 \cdot 6 = 60$	$10 \cdot 7 = 70$	$10 \cdot 8 = 80$	$10 \cdot 9 = 90$
11	$11 \times 1 = 11$	$11 \times 2 = 22$	$11 \times 3 = 33$	$11 \times 4 = 44$	$11 \times 5 = 55$	$11 \times 6 = 66$	$11 \times 7 = 77$	$11 \times 8 = 88$	$11 \times 9 = 99$
12	$12 \cdot 1 = 12$	$12 \cdot 2 = 24$	$12 \cdot 3 = 36$	$12 \cdot 4 = 48$	$12 \cdot 5 = 60$	$12 \cdot 6 = 72$	$12 \cdot 7 = 84$	$12 \cdot 8 = 96$	$12 \cdot 9 = 108$

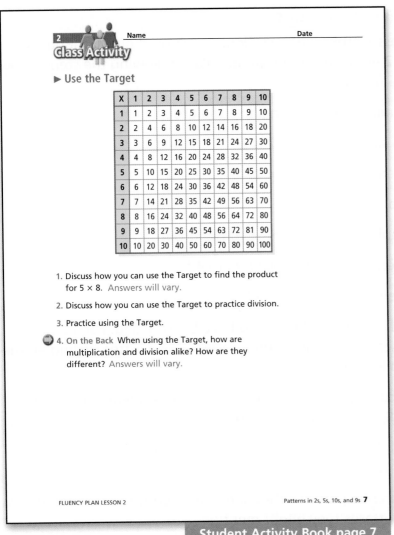

Name _____ Date _____

▶ Use the Target

X	1	2	3	4	5	6	7	8	9	10
1	1	2	3	4	5	6	7	8	9	10
2	2	4	6	8	10	12	14	16	18	20
3	3	6	9	12	15	18	21	24	27	30
4	4	8	12	16	20	24	28	32	36	40
5	5	10	15	20	25	30	35	40	45	50
6	6	12	18	24	30	36	42	48	54	60
7	7	14	21	28	35	42	49	56	63	70
8	8	16	24	32	40	48	56	64	72	80
9	9	18	27	36	45	54	63	72	81	90
10	10	20	30	40	50	60	70	80	90	100

1. Discuss how you can use the Target to find the product for 5 × 8. Answers will vary.

2. Discuss how you can use the Target to practice division.

3. Practice using the Target.

4. On the Back When using the Target, how are multiplication and division alike? How are they different? Answers will vary.

FLUENCY PLAN LESSON 2

Patterns in 2s, 5s, 10s, and 9s **7**

Student Activity Book page 7

Class Management

Preparing Materials If you have access to the *Math Expressions* Materials Kit, the Targets are included, so you will not have to prepare these materials.

If you do not have the kit, the Targets are on TRB M1. Make sure to copy this page onto a transparency sheet.

Teaching Note

Study Plans Throughout this unit each student will make a brief Study Plan for what multiplications and divisions to study. They can use a Target to take home and use it on the inside back cover of the Homework and Remembering book. If they will not take home the book, give each student a copy of TRB M2 to keep with their Target at home.

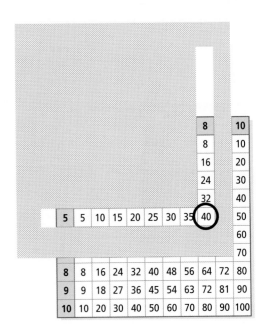

▶ Use the Target WHOLE CLASS

Have students turn to Student Book page 7, and give a Target to each student. Have students figure out how to use the Target to find 5 × 8 on the multiplication table. Select a student to describe the method. Students should overlay the Target as shown on the right, so the "legs" show the 5s row and the 8s column. The number in the circle, 40, is the product.

Have students practice their multiplications by covering the target circle with their finger and moving the legs to highlight different factors. They can say each product to themselves, and then uncover the circle to check their answer.

Students can also use the Targets to solve a division problem. Students should discover that the product divided by one of the factors is the other factor. So they can cover a factor to set up a division problem.

Patterns in 2s, 5s, 10s, and 9s **19**

Activity 3

2s and 5s on the Number Path

 15 MINUTES

Goal: Describe patterns in 2s and 5s multiplications and count-bys.

Materials: Class MathBoard, MathBoards, dry-erase markers, dry-erase material

 NCTM Standards:
Number and Operations
Algebra

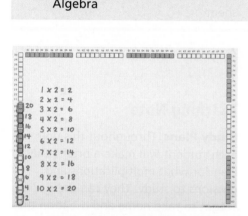

Class Management

MathBoard Materials For future lessons, the Class MathBoard, MathBoards, dry-erase markers, and dry-erase materials will be called MathBoard Materials.

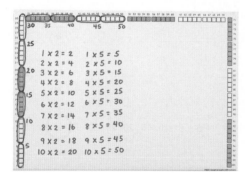

▶ 2s Patterns WHOLE CLASS

Work on the Class MathBoard as students work on their MathBoards. Circle groups of 2 up to 20 on the Number Path following the steps below after circling the first group:

- Write the cumulative total (2) next to the group.
- Have students say,"1 group of 2 is 2."
- Then, have them write "1 × 2 = 2."

After circling the second group:

- Write the cumulative total (4) next to the group.
- Have the students say "2 groups of 2 are 4."
- Then, have them write "2 × 2 = 4."

Continue until all groups of 2 up to 20 have been circled. Each time a group is circled repeat the three-step process above. After circling all the groups do the following:

- Point to each cumulative total in turn and have students say them aloud: 2, 4, 6, 8, 10, 12, 14, 16, 18, 20.
- Read the multiplication equations starting with 1 × 2 = 2 and ending with 10 × 2 = 20.

Have students describe patterns they see in the count-bys and equations. Here are a few patterns they might mention:

- All the products are even numbers.
- The ones digits follow the pattern 2, 4, 6, 8, 0, 2, 4, 6, 8, 0.
- The count-bys skip a number between them.

▶ 5s Patterns WHOLE CLASS

Erase the circles and count-bys on the Number Path, but leave the equations. Then repeat the above steps for the 5s on the Number Path. Have students describe patterns they see in the 5s count-bys and equations. Here are some examples:

- The numbers in the tens place of the 5s count-bys follow the pattern 0, 1, 1, 2, 2, 3, 3, 4, 4, 5.
- The ones digits of the 5s count-bys alternate between 0 and 5.
- The product of an even number and 5 ends in 0; the product of an odd number and 5 ends in 5.

Leave everything on the board for the next activity.

10s and 9s on the Number Path

▶ 10s Patterns WHOLE CLASS

Mark off groups of 10 by drawing line segments on the Number Path as shown. Write the cumulative total next to each mark. Have students write a multiplication equation for each 10s count-by as shown and take turns reading each equation for the class as they write. Have students describe patterns they see in the 10s and 5s count-bys and equations. Here are a few patterns they might mention:

- All of the 10s count-bys end in 0.

- The tens digit of each 10s product is the multiplier, and the ones digit is zero.

- The 10s count-bys are just the 1s count-bys (1, 2, 3, 4, and so on) with 0s on the ends.

- Every 10s count-by is also a 5s count-by. Every other 5s count-by is also a 10s count-by.

- Two 5s (2 × 5) are half of two 10s (2 × 10), three 5s are half of three 10s, and so on. (Or, equivalently, two 10s are twice two 5s, three 10s are twice three 5s, and so on.)

▶ 9s Patterns WHOLE CLASS

Erase the 5s circles and count-bys on the Number Path, and erase the 2s and 5s equations. Draw short segments separating sequential groups of 9 up to 90 on the Number Path and write the totals so far next to each group. After drawing the first segment, say, "1 group of 9 is 9." After drawing the second segment, say, "2 groups of 9 are 18," and so on. Have students write and say the 9s equations. Have students describe any patterns they see on the Number Path and in the equations. For example:

- On the Number Path, 1 square is between 9 and 10, 2 squares are between 18 and 20, 3 squares between 27 and 30, and so on. These differences correspond to the multipliers: 1 × 9 = 9, 2 × 9 = 18, 3 × 9 = 27, and so on.

- As you move down the column of 9s products, the tens digits increase by 1 and the ones digits decrease by 1.

- The digits of the larger products are the reverse of the digits of the smaller products. For example, the digits of 81 are the reverse of the digits of 18, and the digits of 72 are the reverse of the digits of 27.

- The digits in each 9s product have a sum of 9. For example, 3 × 9 = 27 and 2 + 7 = 9.

 15 MINUTES

Goal: Describe patterns in 10s and 9s multiplications and count-bys.

Materials: MathBoard Materials

 NCTM Standards:
Number and Operations
Algebra

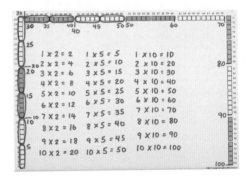

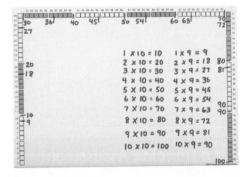

Teaching Note

Break Aparts Students who have used *Math Expressions* in earlier grades may know the term *break-apart partner* for the addends in addition. The digits that make up all of the 9s products to 9 × 10 are addends of 9. Your students should know the term *addend*, and you can discuss it here.

Activity continued ▶

Activity 4

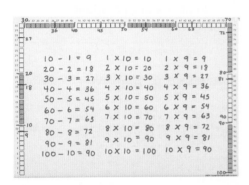

▶ How 10s Minus 1s Make 9s WHOLE CLASS

Have students look at each 10s equation and the corresponding
9s equation. As students follow along on their MathBoards, write the
10s-minus-1s equations to show the relationship between the products.
As you write each equation, describe the relationship between the 9s
and 10s multiplications in words. For example:

Write:	Say:
$10 - 1 = 9$	1×9 is 1 less than 1×10
$20 - 2 = 18$	2×9 is 2 less than 2×10

Ask questions about the relationship between the multipliers in the 9s
equations and the digits of the products. First, review the terms
multiplier and *product*. Point to the equation $2 \times 9 = 18$. Remind
students that 2 is the multiplier and 18 is the product. Repeat by
pointing to other equations, if necessary.

● In each of the 9s equations, look at the multiplier and look at the tens
digit of the product. What do you notice? The tens digit of the product
is 1 less than the multiplier.

● In each of the 9s equations, look at the multiplier and the ones digit
of the product. What do you notice? The multiplier and the ones
digit of the product add to 10.

Have students turn their MathBoards over, and hide the Class MathBoard.
Write 7×9 on the board and ask students to explain how to use the
9s patterns the class has just discussed to solve it.

Make sure these strategies are mentioned:

● 7×9 is 7 less than 7×10. So, $7 \times 9 = 70 - 7 = 63$.

● The tens digit of the answer is 1 less than 7. The ones digit is the number
you add to 7 to get 10. So, $7 \times 9 = 63$.

Give students two or three more 9s multiplications to solve.

✓ Ongoing Assessment

Ask students:

▶ How can you find 6×9, using the
10s-minus-1 strategy?

▶ What strategy would you use to
find 4×5?

Finger Patterns for 9s

▶ Quick 9s WHOLE CLASS

Now, show students a method called Quick 9s that will help them learn and remember their 9s multiplications.

To model this process, ask for a student volunteer. Have the student come to the front of the class and stand next to you with his or her back to the class.

Tell students to hold their hands with their palms facing them and their fingers extended.

● To find 1 × 9, bend down your left thumb, which is the first finger as you go from left to right. The fingers to the right of your thumb represent 9 ones. This is the answer: 1 × 9 = 9.

● To find 2 × 9, bend down the second finger. Leave the rest of your fingers up.

Be sure students can see the volunteer's hands. You can walk around the room to make sure students are doing this correctly.

● We know that 2 × 9 is 18. Can you see how your fingers show 18?

Help students see that the one finger to the left of the bent finger represents 1 ten, and the 8 fingers to the right represent 8 ones.

● How do you think we find 3 × 9? Bend down the third finger.

Have students show 3 × 9 using Quick 9s.

● Explain how your fingers show the answer. There are 2 fingers to the left of the bent finger and 7 fingers to the right. This shows 2 tens and 7 ones. So the answer is 27.

 20 MINUTES

Goal: Learn a shortcut for finding 9s multiplications and divisions.

 NCTM Standards:
Number and Operations
Algebra

Pattern:
1 × 9 is 1 ten − 1, so the answer has 9 ones and 1 ten − 1 ten = 0 tens.

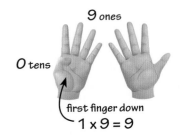

9 ones
0 tens
first finger down
1 x 9 = 9

Pattern:
2 × 9 is 2 tens − 2, so the answer has 8 ones and 2 tens − 1 ten = 1 ten.

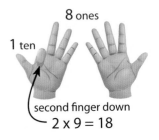

8 ones
1 ten
second finger down
2 x 9 = 18

Pattern:
3 × 9 is 3 tens − 3, so the answer has 7 ones and 3 tens − 1 ten = 2 tens.

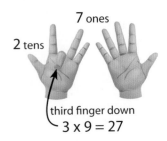

7 ones
2 tens
third finger down
3 x 9 = 27

Activity continued ▶

Activity 5

Teaching Note

Language and Vocabulary Mention that we can call the bent finger the *multiplier finger* because it shows the number we are multiplying 9 by.

Have students use Quick 9s to find the remaining 9s products in order. Provide help to students who need it. Then ask:

● As you did each multiplication in order, how did the number of fingers to the left of your bent finger change? It increased by 1.

● How did the number of fingers to the right of your bent finger change? It decreased by 1.

● For all the 9s multiplications, how many fingers did you have up? 9 Why? Because only one finger was bent.

Relate these observations to the patterns in the count-bys. With each count-by, the tens digit increased by 1, while the ones digit decreased by 1, and the sum of the digits of each count-by is 9.

Give students some 9s multiplication problems in mixed order, and have them find the products by using Quick 9s or the 10s-minus-1s pattern they discovered earlier.

▶ Solve Division Problems WHOLE CLASS

Write this division problem on the board:

63 ÷ 9

Ask students to think of solution strategies involving 9s patterns or Quick 9s. Make sure these strategies are discussed:

● 63 = 70 − 7. So, using the 10s-minus-1s patterns, we know 63 = 7 × 9, or equivalently 63 ÷ 9 = 7.

● The tens digit of 63 is 1 less than 7, and 7 plus the ones digit equals 10, so 63 = 7 × 9, or equivalently 63 ÷ 9 = 7.

● Bend down a finger so there are 6 fingers (6 tens) to the left of the bent finger and 3 fingers (3 ones) to the right. The seventh finger is down, so 63 ÷ 9 = 7.

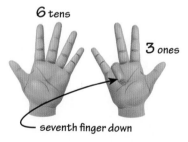

6 tens

3 ones

seventh finger down

Give students two or three more division problems to solve, such as 81 ÷ 9, 54 ÷ 9, and so on.

②Going Further

Differentiated Instruction

Intervention — Activity Card FP-2

Use a Number Line
Activity Card FP-2 ●

Work: By Yourself

Use:
- Comparing Numbers (TRB M50)

1. Look at the 0 to 10 number line shown below. The arcs show the jumps between 2s count-bys.

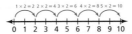

2. Make a 0 to 30 number line. Use arcs to show jumps between 5s count-bys.

3. Label each arc with the correct multiplication equation.

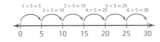

Fluency Plan, Lesson 2   Copyright © Houghton Mifflin Company

Activity Note Help students understand that the first factor in each equation is the number of arcs or jumps.

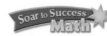 **Math Writing Prompt**

Patterns in the 9s There are many patterns in the 9s count-bys. Use words or drawings to describe as many patterns as you can.

Soar to Success Math ★ **Software Support**

Use *Soar to Success* for instruction of students needing targeted support for underlying skills.

On Level — Activity Card FP-2

Tic-Tac-Toe
Activity Card FP-2 ▲

Work: In Pairs

Use:
- 20 Counters, 10 each of two different colors

1. Each partner writes five multiplication equations each for the factors 2, 5, 9, and 10. For example, 2×1, 2×2, 2×3, and so on. Each of you will have 20 equations.

2. Each partner uses the products of any nine of their 20 equations to make a tic-tac-toe board like the one below.

3. Partners each select a color of counters and take turns reading one of the equations. If the product is on either card, cover it with a counter.

4. Repeat until one partner gets three in a row—across, down, or diagonally.

Fluency Plan, Lesson 2   Copyright © Houghton Mifflin Company

Activity Note Remind students of the definitions of *factors* and *products*.

 Math Writing Prompt

Explain a Strategy Explain how knowing the 10s count-bys can help you find the 9s count-bys. Give an example.

MegaMath **Software Support**

Use *MegaMath* for review and reinforcement of the concepts and skills presented in this lesson.

Challenge — Activity Card FP-2

Missing Factors
Activity Card FP-2 ■

Work: By Yourself

1. Look at the equations below. The value of the star is always the same, and the value of the smiley face is always the same.

$$\bigstar \times 8 = 72$$
$$\smiley \times \bigstar = 27$$
$$\diamond \times \smiley = 30$$

2. Find the value of each symbol.

$\bigstar = 9$ $\smiley = 3$ $\diamond = 10$

3. **Look Back** How can you determine if your answers are correct? Substitute the values into the equations and solve.

Fluency Plan, Lesson 2   Copyright © Houghton Mifflin Company

Activity Note Be sure students understand that whatever number is used for the star in the first equation has to be used for the star in the second equation, and so on.

 Math Writing Prompt

5s and 10s Explain why the products of 10 are also products of 5. Explain why the products of 5 are only sometimes the products of 10.

DESTINATION Math **Software Support**

Use *Destination Math* to take students beyond the concepts and skills presented in this lesson.

Patterns in 2s, 5s, 10s, and 9s   **25**

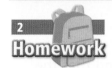

Homework and Spiral Review

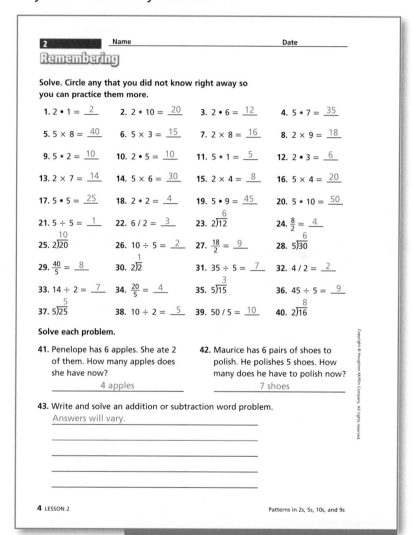

2 Homework **Goal:** Additional Practice

Remind students to include in their Study Plans the multiplications and divisions they need to practice.

---

2 Homework

Name _____ Date _____

Study Plan

1. On this hundred grid, dark segments have been drawn separating groups of 9, and the 9s count-bys have been circled. Describe three patterns you see.

Answers will vary. Possible answer:

Starting at 18 and moving up the

diagonal, the tens digits go from 1 to 8.

1	11	21	31	41	51	61	71	81	91
2	12	22	32	42	52	62	72	82	92
3	13	23	33	43	53	63	73	83	93
4	14	24	34	44	54	64	74	84	94
5	15	25	35	45	55	65	75	85	95
6	16	26	36	46	56	66	76	86	96
7	17	27	37	47	57	67	77	87	97
8	18	28	38	48	58	68	78	88	98
9	19	29	39	49	59	69	79	89	99
10	20	30	40	50	60	70	80	90	100

2. Using words or drawings, tell how you remember the 9s multiplications and divisions.

Answers will vary. Possible answer: I know that the

multiplier and the ones digit of the product add

to 10.

Solve each problem.

3. Kristin's apartment building has 3 floors. Each floor has 9 apartments. How many apartments are there in Kristin's building?

27 apartments

4. Maria has 6 piles of flash cards. If there are 9 cards in each pile, how many flash cards does Maria have in all?

54 flash cards

LESSON 2   Patterns in 2s, 5s, 10s, and 9s **3**

Homework and Remembering page 3

---

2 Remembering **Goal:** Spiral Review

This Remembering activity would be appropriate anytime after today's lesson.

---

2 Remembering

Name _____ Date _____

Solve. Circle any that you did not know right away so you can practice them more.

1. $2 \cdot 1 = $ 2
2. $2 * 10 = $ 20
3. $2 \cdot 6 = $ 12
4. $5 * 7 = $ 35
5. $5 \times 8 = $ 40
6. $5 \times 3 = $ 15
7. $2 \times 8 = $ 16
8. $2 \times 9 = $ 18
9. $5 * 2 = $ 10
10. $2 \cdot 5 = $ 10
11. $5 * 1 = $ 5
12. $2 \cdot 3 = $ 6
13. $2 \times 7 = $ 14
14. $5 \times 6 = $ 30
15. $2 \times 4 = $ 8
16. $5 \times 4 = $ 20
17. $5 \cdot 5 = $ 25
18. $2 * 2 = $ 4
19. $5 \cdot 9 = $ 45
20. $5 * 10 = $ 50
21. $5 \div 5 = $ 1
22. $6 / 2 = $ 3
23. $2\overline{)12}$ 6
24. $\frac{8}{2} = $ 4
25. $2\overline{)20}$ 10
26. $10 \div 5 = $ 2
27. $\frac{18}{2} = $ 9
28. $5\overline{)30}$ 6
29. $\frac{40}{5} = $ 8
30. $2\overline{)2}$ 1
31. $35 \div 5 = $ 7
32. $4 / 2 = $ 2
33. $14 \div 2 = $ 7
34. $\frac{20}{5} = $ 4
35. $5\overline{)15}$ 3
36. $45 \div 5 = $ 9
37. $5\overline{)25}$ 5
38. $10 \div 2 = $ 5
39. $50 / 5 = $ 10
40. $2\overline{)16}$ 8

Solve each problem.

41. Penelope has 6 apples. She ate 2 of them. How many apples does she have now?

4 apples

42. Maurice has 6 pairs of shoes to polish. He polishes 5 shoes. How many does he have to polish now?

7 shoes

43. Write and solve an addition or subtraction word problem.

Answers will vary.

4 LESSON 2   Patterns in 2s, 5s, 10s, and 9s

Homework and Remembering page 4

Home and School Connection

Family Letter Have children take home the Family Letter on Student Book page 9 or Activity Workbook page 5. This letter explains how the concept of multiplication and division is developed in *Math Expressions*. It gives parents and guardians a better understanding of the learning that goes on in math class and creates a bridge between school and home. A Spanish translation of this letter is on Student Book page 10 and Activity Workbook page 6.

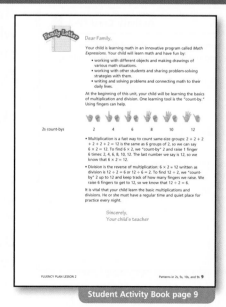

Student Activity Book page 9

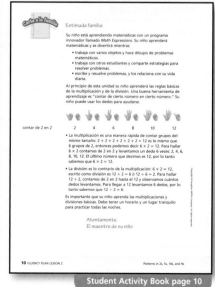

Student Activity Book page 10

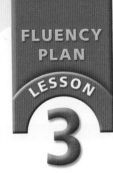

Arrays and Commutativity

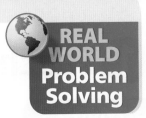

REAL WORLD Problem Solving

Vocabulary

array
Commutative Property of Multiplication
equation

Lesson Objectives

- Understand and apply the array model for multiplication.
- Understand and use the Commutative Property of Multiplication.

The Day at a Glance

Today's Goals	Materials	
1 Teaching the Lesson **A1:** Use multiplication to represent arrays. **A2:** Learn the Commutative Property of Multiplication. **A3:** Solve and write array word problems. **2 Going Further** ▶ Differentiated Instruction **3 Homework and Spiral Review**	**Lesson Activities** Student Activity Book pp. 11–14 or Student Hardcover Book pp. 11–14 Homework and Remembering pp. 5–6	**Going Further** Activity Cards FP-3 Counters Math Journals 123 Use **Math Talk** today!

Keeping Skills Sharp

Quick Practice ⏱ 5 MINUTES	Daily Routines	
Goal: Practice divisions for 2s and 5s. **Materials:** Division Digits materials **Division Digits for 2s** Have a **Student Leader** lead the activity, using problems from the 2s and 5s sections of Set 1. (See Lesson 2) **Division Digits for 5s** Repeat the activity, using problems from the 5s section of Set 1.	**Homework Review** Ask students to work with partners to review the multiplications and divisions in their Study Plans.	**Elapsed Time** On Saturday, Payat's family arrived at a street fair at 1:15 in the afternoon. They left the fair at 5:15 the same afternoon. How many hours did they spend at the fair? 4 hours

Teaching the Lesson

Multiplication and Arrays

 10 MINUTES

Goal: Use multiplication to represent arrays.

Materials: Student Activity Book or Hardcover Book pp. 11–12

✓ **NCTM Standards:**
Number and Operations
Algebra
Problem Solving

The Learning Classroom

Student Leaders Perhaps the top students are beginning to explain more details about their problem-solving strategies, but it is not the case for all of the students. You may want to have these top students do more explaining. They will model for other students how to explain their thinking, and the student-friendly language may connect with some students more successfully than your own way of talking about a concept.

Teaching Note

Vocabulary Some students may continue to use the language *number sentence* instead of *equation*. However, they will see the math vocabulary word, **equation**, on the student book page. Point out to students that an equation is a number sentence that has an equals sign.

$3 + 4 = 12$ is a number sentence.

$3 + 4 = 12$ is also called an equation.

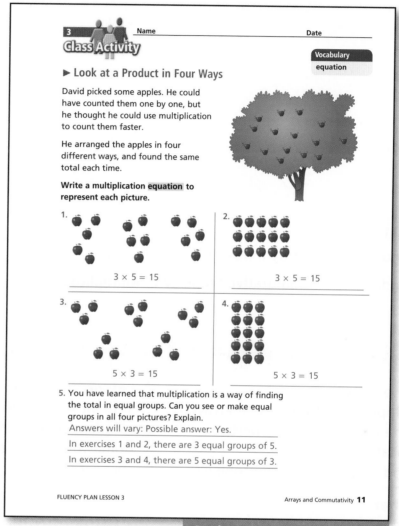

Student Activity Book page 11

▶ Look at a Product in Four Ways [INDIVIDUALS]

Read the text about David's apples on the top of page 11 of the Student Book. Give students a minute or two to examine the pictures and write the equations. Then have them share their equations and explain how they thought about the situations.

For exercises 1 and 3, some students will circle the group size in their equations, while others will not. Some students will write the multiplier first, while others will write the group size first. All of these variations are acceptable. Most students will think of exercises 2 and 4 as repeated-group situations, with the rows or columns as the groups.

In exercise 5, students should see that they can consider either the rows or columns to be equal groups.

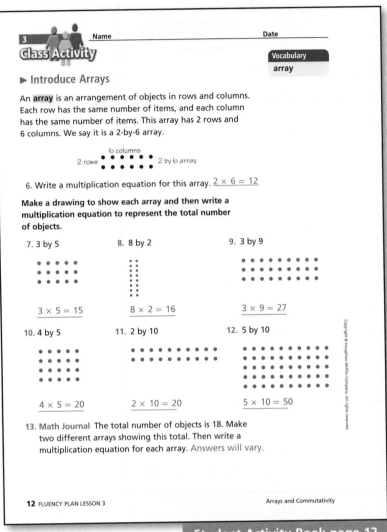

Student Activity Book page 12

Teaching Note

Language and Vocabulary Explain to students that *rows* are horizontal (go across) and *columns* are vertical (up or down). Have students list objects that are arranged in rows and columns. For example, stadium seats, packaged cookies, desks, and so on. Allow **English Language Learners** to draw their responses.

English Language Learners

Draw stars in a 2 by 5 array. Help students verbally identify the columns and rows.

- **Beginning** Say: This is an array. Ask: Is this a row? yes How many rows are there? 2 Is this a column? yes How many columns are there? 5
- **Intermediate** Ask: How many rows does the array have? Columns? How many stars are in each row? In each column? Total?
- **Advanced** Have students use short sentences to describe the array. Then have them rearrange the rows and columns. Have them describe the new array.

▶ Introduce Arrays WHOLE CLASS

Discuss exercise 6 on Student Book page 12.

- We can describe the array in exercise 6 as a 2-by-6 array because it has 2 rows and 6 columns.

Return to Student Book page 11. Discuss the example as a class:

- How would you describe the array in exercise 2 on page 11? It is a 3-by-5 array because it has 3 rows and 5 columns.

- How would you describe the array in exercise 4 on page 11? It is a 5-by-3 array because it has 5 rows and 3 columns.

Have students write a multiplication equation that represents the array for exercise 6. Then, explain that, although $2 \times 6 = 12$ and $6 \times 2 = 12$ are both correct, we usually write the number of rows first.

Have students complete exercises 7–13.

Activity 2

The Commutative Property

 15 MINUTES

Goal: Learn the Commutative Property of Multiplication.

Materials: MathBoard Materials, Student Activity Book or Hardcover Book p. 13

✔ **NCTM Standards:**
Number and Operations
Algebra
Problem Solving

The Learning Classroom

Building Concepts To further show how the Commutative Property of Multiplication works, show:

2 × 3 = 6	3 × 2 = 6
4 × 2 = 8	2 × 4 = 8

Emphasize to students that the Commutative Property of Multiplication states that the order in which numbers are multiplied does not change the product.

Teaching Note

Language and Vocabulary To help students make a meaningful connection to the word *commutative*, tell them to think of the meaning of *commute*. When people commute to work, they go back and forth between home and work.

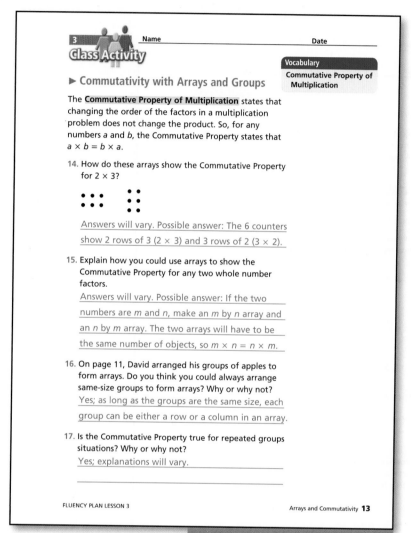

Student Activity Book page 13

▶ Commutativity with Arrays and Groups WHOLE CLASS

Read aloud the description of the Commutative Property of Multiplication on Student Book page 13. Then, have a student read exercise 14 aloud. Next, select students to share their ideas about exercise 14 with the class.

● The 2-by-3 array can be rotated to be a 3-by-2 array. (Students will also probably say that both arrays have 6 dots; accept this answer because it works for these specific arrays. But it cannot be the basis for a general argument for all arrays asked for next in exercise 15.)

Read and discuss exercise 15.

● Any *a*-by-*b* array can be rotated to become a *b*-by-*a* array. Rotating is a general argument that works for all arrays.

You might find it helpful, especially with **English Language Learners**, to work through two more examples with numbers to help students see or build a general argument that will work for any numbers (see 4 × 5 and 3 × 6 at the top of the next page).

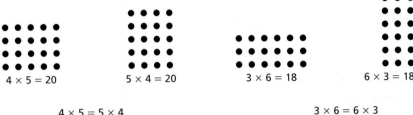

$4 \times 5 = 20$ $5 \times 4 = 20$ $3 \times 6 = 18$ $6 \times 3 = 18$

$4 \times 5 = 5 \times 4$ $3 \times 6 = 6 \times 3$

Students should begin to see that no matter which two whole numbers *a* and *b* you give them, they can always make two arrays: *a*-by-*b* and *b*-by-*a*. So $a \times b = b \times a$ for any two whole numbers.

Discuss exercise 16. Again, you might have students first work with specific examples. For example, have them make a math drawing to show 4 groups of 3, and then rearrange the groups to form the rows of an array.

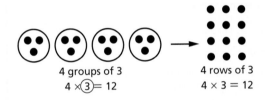

4 groups of 3   4 rows of 3
$4 \times ③ = 12$ $4 \times 3 = 12$

Students should see that they can rearrange any number of repeated groups in this way.

Read exercise 17 and ask students to share their thoughts. The key idea is that, once repeated groups are rearranged to form an array, the array can be rotated so the rows become columns and columns become rows. The array can then be rearranged again to form repeated groups from the rows. Therefore, switching the factors in a repeated groups situation does not change the product.

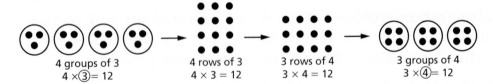

4 groups of 3   4 rows of 3   3 rows of 4   3 groups of 4
$4 \times ③ = 12$ $4 \times 3 = 12$ $3 \times 4 = 12$ $3 \times ④ = 12$

Activity 3

Array Word Problems

 35 MINUTES

Goal: Solve and write array word problems.

Materials: MathBoard Materials, Student Activity Book or Hardcover Book p.14

 NCTM Standards:
Number and Operations
Algebra
Problem Solving

📁 Class Management

Students will be making drawings to help them solve problems. Remind them that their drawings do not need to show lots of detail. For example, for problem 18, students can use circles to show bottle caps.

The Learning Classroom

Math Talk The **Solve and Discuss** structure of conversation is used throughout the *Math Expressions* program. The teacher selects four or five students to go to the board and solve a problem, using any method they choose. The other students work on the same problem at their desks. Then the teacher asks the students at the board to explain their methods. Students at their desks are encouraged to ask questions and to assist each other in understanding the problem. Thus, students actually solve, explain, question, and justify. Usually ask only 2 or 3 students to explain because classes do not like to sit through more explanations and time is better spent on the next issue.

---

3 **Class Activity**

Name _____ Date _____

▶ **Discuss Array Problems**

Make a math drawing for each problem and then solve. *Show your work.*

18. Avi arranged her bottle cap collection into an array. The array had 4 rows with 9 bottle caps in each row. How many bottle caps are in her collection?
__36 bottle caps__

19. On one wall of an art gallery, photographs were arranged in 2 rows with 7 photographs in each row. How many total photographs were on the wall?
__14 photographs__

On a separate sheet of paper, write the answers to exercises 20–22.

20. In Lesson 1, you explored the relationship between division and multiplication. You saw that dividing means finding an unknown factor. Use this idea to explain what division is in an array situation.
Answers will vary. See the discussion in the fourth paragraph on page 33 of this Teacher Guide.

▶ **Write Division Problems**

21. Write and solve two division word problems that are related to the multiplication word problem in problem 18. Answers will vary.

22. Write and solve two division word problems that are related to the multiplication word problem in problem 19. Answers will vary.

14 FLUENCY PLAN LESSON 3   Arrays and Commutativity

Student Activity Book page 14

▶ Discuss Array Problems

WHOLE CLASS   **Math Talk**

Multiplication Problems If you prefer, have students work on their MathBoards, rather than in their books. Use the **Solve and Discuss** structure for problems 18 and 19 on Student Book page 14.

Relating Multiplication and Division Discuss problem 20. Make sure the following points are made:

● There are three numbers involved in a repeated-groups situation: the group size (number in each group), the multiplier (or number of groups), and the total number of items. The group size and the multiplier are factors. The total number of items is the product.

● In a repeated-groups multiplication problem, you are given both factors (the group size and the multiplier), and you need to find the total, or product.

- In a repeated-groups division problem, you are given the product and one factor (either the group size or the multiplier), and you need to find the other factor.

- There are three numbers involved in an array situation: the number of rows, the number of columns, and the total number of items. The number of rows and the number of columns are the factors, and the total number of items is the product.

- In an array multiplication problem, you are given the two factors (the number of rows and number of columns), and you need to find the total, or product.

- In an array division problem, you are given the product (the total number of items) and one factor (either the number of rows or the number of columns), and you need to find the other factor.

▶ Write Division Problems WHOLE CLASS

Get students started on problem 21, which asks them to write two division word problems related to problem 18. Elicit from students the three key pieces of information for the situation. Write this information on the board:

Number of rows (factor): 4

Number of columns (factor): 9

Total (product): 36

Make sure students understand that, because they are writing a division problem, one of the factors, either the number of rows or the number of columns, must be the unknown. Suggest that, for the first problem, they assume the number of rows is unknown. Erase the 4, and replace it with a question mark.

Number of rows (factor): ?

Number of columns (factor): 9

Total (product): 36

Activity continued ▶

① Teaching the Lesson (continued)

Activity 3

Give students a minute or two to write their problems, and then have some students share what they wrote. Here is one possible correct problem:

● Avi has 36 bottle caps. She arranges them into 9 columns with the same number in each column. How many bottle caps are in each row?

Tell students that, even though they already know the solution, you would like them to go through the step of solving the problem. Use **Solve and Discuss** for this. Here are some possible methods:

● Write the multiplication problem _____ × 9 = 36, and think, "I know that 4 times 9 equals 36, so there must be 4 rows."

● Write the division problem 36 ÷ 9 = _____ and use Quick 9s or other 9s patterns to find the solution.

● Say the 9s count-bys until you reach 36: 9, 18, 27, 36. You said 4 count-bys so there are four 9s in 36.

● Make a math drawing. Draw rows of 9, counting by 9 for each row you draw, until you reach 36. There are 4 rows.

Draw one row of 9 at a time   Count:
● ● ● ● ● ● ● ● ●   9
● ● ● ● ● ● ● ● ●   18
● ● ● ● ● ● ● ● ●   27
● ● ● ● ● ● ● ● ●   36

Explain that, for the other problem the number of columns should be the unknown factor. Change the text on the board:

Number of rows (factor): 4

Number of columns (factor): ?

Total (product): 36

Again, have them write their problems and have some students share what they wrote. Then, use **Solve and Discuss** for problem 22.

② Going Further

Intervention   Activity Card FP-3

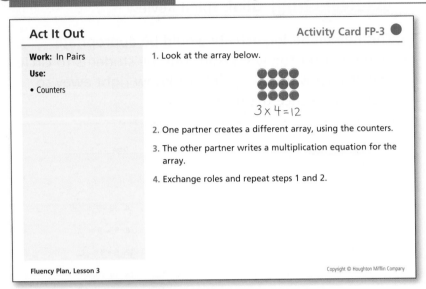

Act It Out   Activity Card FP-3 ●

Work: In Pairs

Use:
• Counters

1. Look at the array below.

$3 \times 4 = 12$

2. One partner creates a different array, using the counters.

3. The other partner writes a multiplication equation for the array.

4. Exchange roles and repeat steps 1 and 2.

Fluency Plan, Lesson 3   Copyright © Houghton Mifflin Company

Activity Note Remind students that the number of counters in each row and in each column of the array are the factors in the multiplication equation.

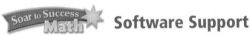 **Math Writing Prompt**

Draw a Picture Draw a picture that shows 4×6. Then write the multiplication equation.

Soar to Success Math ★ **Software Support**

Use *Soar to Success* for instruction of students needing targeted support for underlying skills.

On Level   Activity Card FP-3

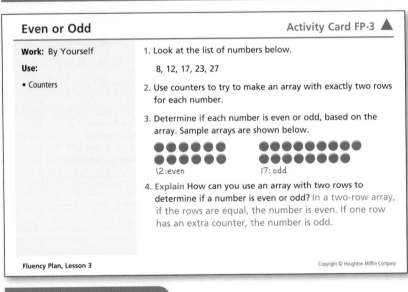

Even or Odd   Activity Card FP-3 ▲

Work: By Yourself

Use:
• Counters

1. Look at the list of numbers below.

   8, 12, 17, 23, 27

2. Use counters to try to make an array with exactly two rows for each number.

3. Determine if each number is even or odd, based on the array. Sample arrays are shown below.

12: even   17: odd

4. **Explain** How can you use an array with two rows to determine if a number is even or odd? *In a two-row array, if the rows are equal, the number is even. If one row has an extra counter, the number is odd.*

Fluency Plan, Lesson 3   Copyright © Houghton Mifflin Company

Activity Note Students' explanations should indicate that either odd numbers have only 1 counter in the last *column* of the array, or that one *row* has an extra counter.

 Math Writing Prompt

Explain Your Thinking Explain why 2×4 is the same as 4×2. Use drawings if needed.

MegaMath Grades K-6 **Software Support**

Use *MegaMath* for review and reinforcement of the concepts and skills presented in this lesson.

Challenge   Activity Card FP-3

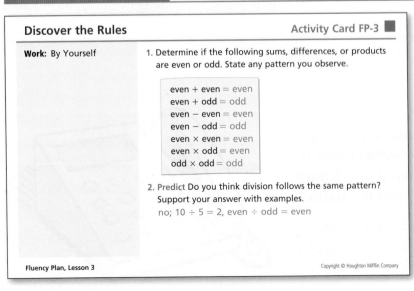

Discover the Rules   Activity Card FP-3 ■

Work: By Yourself

1. Determine if the following sums, differences, or products are even or odd. State any pattern you observe.

even + even = even
even + odd = odd
even − even = even
even − odd = odd
even × even = even
even × odd = even
odd × odd = odd

2. **Predict** Do you think division follows the same pattern? Support your answer with examples.
   no; 10 ÷ 5 = 2, even ÷ odd = even

Fluency Plan, Lesson 3   Copyright © Houghton Mifflin Company

Activity Note Remind students that it takes only one example to disprove a statement.

 Math Writing Prompt

Justify Your Reasoning Explain whether or not addition is commutative. Give an example to support your answer.

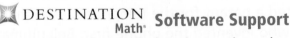 **DESTINATION Math® Software Support**

Use *Destination Math* to take students beyond the concepts and skills presented in this lesson.

③ Homework and Spiral Review

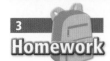

Homework **Goal:** Additional Practice

Use this Homework page to provide students with more practice with multiplication problems and the Commutative Property of Multiplication.

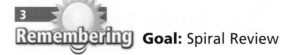

Remembering **Goal:** Spiral Review

This Remembering activity would be appropriate anytime after today's lesson. Tell the students to circle any problems that they did not know right away so they can practice them some more.

---

3   Name _____ Date _____

Homework

Study Plan

1. Write two multiplication equations to represent this array.

   $5 \times 7 = 35$
   _____
   $7 \times 5 = 35$
   _____

   * * * * * * *
   * * * * * * *
   * * * * * * *
   * * * * * * *
   * * * * * * *

Make a math drawing for each problem and then solve.

2. Mr. Jones has a small orchard in his backyard. His orchard has 8 rows of apple trees. Each row has 5 trees. How many apple trees are in his orchard?

3. The teachers' parking lot has 3 rows of parking spaces with the same number of spaces in each row. If 27 cars can park in the lot, many spaces are in each row?

   _____40 trees_____   _____9 spaces_____

4. On a separate sheet of paper, write and solve an array multiplication problem. **Answers will vary.**

5. **Math Journal** Explain how you know that multiplication is commutative. **Explanations will vary.**

Use your Target to practice. Focus on the multiplications and divisions in your Study Plan.

LESSON 3   Arrays and Commutativity **5**

Homework and Remembering page 5

---

3   Name _____ Date _____

Remembering

Solve.

1. $9 \cdot 1 = \underline{9}$ 2. $9 * 10 = \underline{90}$ 3. $9 \cdot 6 = \underline{54}$ 4. $10 * 7 = \underline{70}$

5. $10 \times 8 = \underline{80}$ 6. $10 \times 3 = \underline{30}$ 7. $9 \times 8 = \underline{72}$ 8. $9 \times 9 = \underline{81}$

9. $10 * 2 = \underline{20}$ 10. $9 \cdot 5 = \underline{45}$ 11. $10 * 1 = \underline{10}$ 12. $9 \cdot 3 = \underline{27}$

13. $9 \times 7 = \underline{63}$ 14. $10 \times 6 = \underline{60}$ 15. $9 \times 4 = \underline{36}$ 16. $10 \times 4 = \underline{40}$

17. $10 \cdot 5 = \underline{50}$ 18. $9 \cdot 2 = \underline{18}$ 19. $10 \cdot 9 = \underline{90}$ 20. $10 * 10 = \underline{100}$

21. $10 \div 10 = \underline{1}$ 22. $\frac{27}{9} = \underline{3}$ 23. $9\overline{)54}$ ^{6} 24. $36 \div 9 = \underline{4}$

25. $9\overline{)90}$ ^{10} 26. $20 \div 10 = \underline{2}$ 27. $70 / 10 = \underline{7}$ 28. $10\overline{)60}$ ^{6}

29. $\frac{40}{10} = \underline{4}$ 30. $9\overline{)9}$ ^{1} 31. $81 \div 9 = \underline{9}$ 32. $\frac{18}{9} = \underline{2}$

33. $63 \div 9 = \underline{7}$ 34. $80 \div 10 = \underline{8}$ 35. $10\overline{)30}$ ^{3} 36. $90 \div 10 = \underline{9}$

37. $10\overline{)50}$ ^{5} 38. $45 \div 9 = \underline{5}$ 39. $100 / 10 = \underline{10}$ 40. $9\overline{)72}$ ^{8}

Solve each problem.

41. One day at the pond, Allie caught 12 tadpoles. Mark only caught 6 tadpoles. How many more tadpoles did Allie catch?
    _____6 tadpoles_____

42. Jasper knew how to cook 9 recipes. Then he learned 3 more. How many recipes does Jasper know how to cook now?
    _____12 recipes_____

43. Write and solve an addition or subtraction word problem.
    _____Answers will vary._____
    _____
    _____
    _____
    _____

6 LESSON 3   Arrays and Commutativity

Homework and Remembering page 6

Home or School Activity

 Social Studies Connection

Everyday Array The telephone was invented in 1876 by Alexander Graham Bell. But what students may not know is that Elisha Gray, within hours of Bell, also submitted a patent for the telephone. Both men entered into a legal battle over who invented the phone first; Bell ultimately won the battle.

Have students write an array that shows the numbers on a telephone. Then have them make a list of other real-world items that are arranged in arrays.

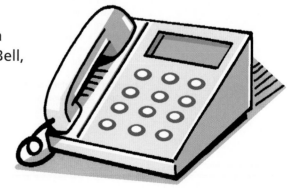

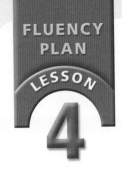

Fluency Day: 2s, 5s, 9s, and 10s

Lesson Objective

● Practice multiplications and divisions for 2s, 5s, 9s, and 10s in a variety of ways.

The Day at a Glance

Today's Goals	Materials
1 Teaching the Lesson **A1:** Take Checkup A on the multiplications and divisions covered so far. **A2:** Use Product Cards to practice 2s, 5s, and 9s. **2 Going Further** ▶ Differentiated Instruction **3 Homework and Spiral Review**	**Lesson Activities** Student Activity Book pp. 15–16, 16A–16D or Student Hardcover Book pp. 15–16 and Activity Workbook pp. 7–12 (includes Product Cards) Homework and Remembering 7–12 (includes Product Cards) Checkup A Answer Key (TRB M5) Product Cards: 2s, 5s, 9s (Manipulative Kit or TRB M6–M9) Paper clips or plastic sandwich bags (optional) **Going Further** Activity Cards FP-4 Index Cards (2 colors) Math Journals

123 Use **Math Talk** today!

Keeping Skills Sharp

Quick Practice   5 MINUTES

Goal: Practice multiplications and divisions for 2s, 5s, 9s, and 10s.

Materials: Division Digits materials, Targets, multiplication tables (Student Activity Book inside back cover)

Division Digits for 9s and 10s Have a **Student Leader** run the activity, using problems from the 9s and 10s section of the Set 1 prompt page. (See Lesson 2)

Target Practice Students use their Targets and the multiplication tables to practice multiplications and divisions for 2s, 5s, 9s, and 10s. Circulate around the room and make sure students are using their Targets correctly. Students should fill out their Study Plans on Homework page 7.

Daily Routines

Homework Review The Study Plans of some students may indicate a need for more practice with specific multiplications and divisions. Suggest that students work with Product Cards for those problems.

Skip Count Have students skip count by 9s from 9 to 108.

① Teaching the Lesson

Checkup A

 15 MINUTES

Goal: Take Checkup A on the multiplications and divisions covered so far.

Materials: Student Activity Book p. 15 or Hardcover Book p. 15 and Activity Workbook p. 7; Checkup A Answer Key (TRB M5)

✔ **NCTM Standards:**
Number and Operations
Algebra

 Class Management

You can give students a set amount of time to take the checkup, or you can let them work until most students have finished.

English Language Learners

Give students more practice saying and solving multiplications aloud. Write 1 × 5 =, 1 • 5 =, and 1 * 5 = on the board. Have students read them aloud. Continue with expressions for 2s, 9s, and 10s multiplications.

• **Beginning** Point to each expression. Say: **This says 1 times 5 equals ____.** 5 Ask: **Are they the same?** yes.

• **Intermediate and Advanced** Say: **These all mean the same thing.** Point each expression. Have students read them aloud and solve them.

---

4 Class Activity

Name _____   Date _____

▶ Checkup A: 2s, 5s, 9s, 10s

1. 3 × 2 = 6	19. 9 × 5 = 45	37. 4 / 2 = 2	55. $2\overline{)6}$ = 3
2. 1 • 5 = 5	20. 2 × 2 = 4	38. $\frac{5}{5}$ = 1	56. 10 ÷ 5 = 2
3. 8 * 5 = 40	21. 5 * 3 = 15	39. 8 ÷ 2 = 4	57. $9\overline{)27}$ = 3
4. 9 × 3 = 27	22. 10 × 2 = 20	40. 9 ÷ 9 = 1	58. 40 ÷ 5 = 8
5. 5 • 2 = 10	23. 5 • 5 = 25	41. 50 / 5 = 10	59. 18 / 9 = 2
6. 9 * 9 = 81	24. 1 * 9 = 9	42. $2\overline{)20}$ = 10	60. 2 ÷ 2 = 1
7. 8 × 2 = 16	25. 8 * 9 = 72	43. 54 ÷ 9 = 6	61. 36 / 9 = 4
8. 10 • 4 = 40	26. 2 * 4 = 8	44. $10\overline{)10}$ = 1	62. 16 ÷ 2 = 8
9. 7 * 5 = 35	27. 5 • 10 = 50	45. $\frac{10}{2}$ = 5	63. $5\overline{)15}$ = 3
10. 1 × 10 = 10	28. 4 × 9 = 36	46. 81 / 9 = 9	64. 63 / 9 = 7
11. 10 • 6 = 60	29. 7 • 2 = 14	47. 20 ÷ 10 = 2	65. 90 ÷ 9 = 10
12. 5 * 4 = 20	30. 10 * 3 = 30	48. $\frac{70}{10}$ = 7	66. 12 / 2 = 6
13. 9 × 7 = 63	31. 7 × 10 = 70	49. $5\overline{)30}$ = 6	67. 35 ÷ 5 = 7
14. 5 • 6 = 30	32. 9 • 6 = 54	50. 80 / 10 = 8	68. 100 / 10 = 10
15. 2 • 1 = 2	33. 2 * 9 = 18	51. $\frac{45}{9}$ = 5	69. $\frac{45}{5}$ = 9
16. 6 × 9 = 54	34. 10 • 9 = 90	52. 20 / 5 = 4	70. 18 / 2 = 9
17. 10 • 8 = 80	35. 10 × 10 = 100	53. $2\overline{)14}$ = 7	71. $9\overline{)72}$ = 8
18. 2 * 6 = 12	36. 7 * 9 = 63	54. 60 ÷ 10 = 6	72. 25 ÷ 5 = 5

FLUENCY PLAN LESSON 4   Checkup A **15**

Student Activity Book page 15

▶ Checkup A [INDIVIDUALS]

Tell students that today they will take Checkup A. The checkup will help them see which 2s, 5s, 9s, and 10s multiplications and divisions they need to practice. Emphasize that the checkup will not be graded. Also, there is no need for students to do the problems in numeric order. Have students turn to Student Book page 15 and start the checkup on your signal.

▶ Check the Answers [INDIVIDUALS]

Have students check their own answers or exchange papers with another student. TRB M5 is the answer key for the checkup. You can make copies of this for students to use, display it as an overhead, or simply read the answers aloud. Students should write the multiplications and divisions they missed on their Study Plans. Remind students of how important it is to practice at home to get really fast.

► Study Missed Exercises INDIVIDUALS

Give students a minute or two to study the exercises they missed. Tell students they will take another checkup again in a few days to see how much they have improved.

Activity 2

Product Cards for 2s, 5s, and 9s

► Discuss the Product Cards

WHOLE CLASS   Math Talk

Give a set of Product Cards for the 2s, 5s, and 9s to each student or have students cut out the cards on pages 16A–16D. Ask students to describe the cards and to discuss how the two sides of each card are related.

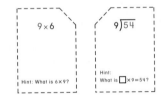

Make sure the following points are discussed:

● One side of each card has a multiplication problem; the other side has a division problem.

● The multiplication and division problems on a card involve the same factor-factor-product combination. The multiplication side shows one factor times the other factor; the division side shows the product divided by the first factor from the multiplication side.

Hold up the 5 × 6 card and say:

● Suppose I want to practice my multiplications. The multiplication exercise on this card is 5 × 6. I think the answer is 30. How can I check whether I am right? Turn the card over. The product is the number under the division bar.

● Now, what if I want to practice my divisions. The division exercise on this card is 30 ÷ 5. I think the answer is 6. How can I check my answers? Turn the card over. The answer is the factor 5 is being multiplied by.

► Practice With the Product Cards INDIVIDUALS

Give students a few minutes to practice their multiplications and divisions with the Product Cards.

Activity continued ▶

---

 30 MINUTES

Goal: Use Product Cards to practice 2s, 5s, 9s.

Materials: Product Cards: 2s, 5s, 9s (Manipulative Kit or TRB); Student Activity Book pp. 16, 16A–16D or Hardcover Book p. 16 and Activity Workbook pp. 8–12; paper clips or plastic sandwich bags (optional)

 NCTM Standard:
Number and Operations

The Learning Classroom

Building Concepts Product Cards are a quick and creative way to help students learn their multiplications and divisions. Since the two sides of each card are related, they will help students understand the relationship between multiplication and division. The cards can be used at any time for individual or partner practice with a friend or helper at home.

 Class Management

Product Cards at Home If you have the Product Cards from the Manipulative Kit, you can have students use the cards on the student pages as a home practice set. Black and white versions of the cards also appear on the Homework pages 19–12 and on TRB M6–M9. Copy M6 and M7 back to back and M8 and M9 back to back.

① Teaching the Lesson (continued)

Activity 2

The Learning Classroom

Helping Community Create a classroom where students are not competing, but desire to collaborate and help one another. Communicate often that your goal as a class is that everyone understands the math you are studying. Tell students that this will require everyone working together to help each other.

Class Management

Looking Ahead Students may need additional support for the table on Homework page 7, problem 5. Discuss with students the first 3 blank cells. Stress that they need to notice which number they know and whether that is the product or a factor. If they think about the function situation, they can fill in the table correctly.

Problem 6 of tonight's homework asks students to write and solve a division word problem. Tomorrow, collect these problem and save them. In Lesson 10, students will solve problems their classmates have written.

Ongoing Assessment

Ask students to:

▶ Write a division equation related to $6 \times 5 = 30$.

▶ Explain how to find the answer to $14 \div 2$ by using a related multiplication.

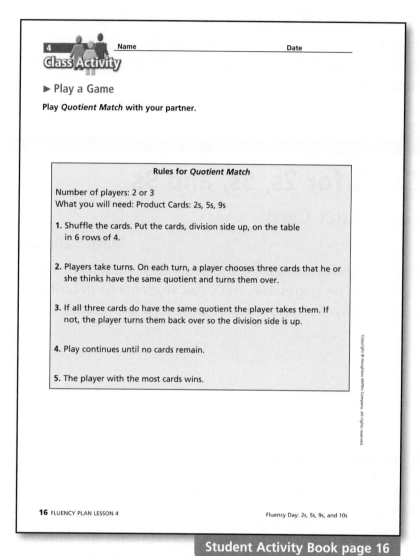

Student Activity Book page 16

▶ Play a Game [SMALL GROUPS]

Have students read the rules for *Quotient Match* on Student Book page 16 and answer any questions they have about how to play. Then, allow students to play for several minutes.

▶ Sort the Cards [INDIVIDUALS]

Have students sort their Product Cards into three piles, according to how quickly they can solve the division problems.

● *Fast*: Division problems they can solve quickly.

● *Slow*: Division problems that take them a little time to solve.

● *Don't Know*: Division problems they don't know.

Tell students that, as they practice over the next several days, they will be able to move cards from the *Slow* and *Don't Know* piles to the *Fast* pile. Give each student three paper clips or plastic sandwich bags to keep their piles separated.

②Going Further

Intervention — Activity Card FP-4

Multiplications — Activity Card FP-4

Work: In Pairs

1. Look at the multiplication equations below.

$$2 \times 1 = 2 \quad 5 \times 1 = 5$$
$$2 \times 2 = 4 \quad 5 \times 2 = 10$$
$$2 \times 3 = 6 \quad 5 \times 3 = 15$$
$$2 \times 4 = 8 \quad 5 \times 4 = 20$$

2. Each partner writes out multiplication and division equations for 2s, 5s, 9s, and 10s on a sheet of paper.

3. Partners compare their work.

4. Make any corrections necessary to your paper.

Fluency Plan, Lesson 4 — Copyright © Houghton Mifflin Company

Activity Note Students can use Product Cards or Targets to help check their equations.

✐ Math Writing Prompt

Math Vocabulary Describe how you can use multiplication to check the answer to a division problem. Use math vocabulary in your answer.

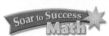 **Software Support**

Use *Soar to Success* for instruction of students needing targeted support for underlying skills.

On Level — Activity Card FP-4

Solve a Problem — Activity Card FP-4 ▲

Work: In Pairs

Use:
• Index cards, 4 of one color and 10 of another

1. Use the 4 index cards for Set A. Number the Set A cards 2, 5, 9, and 10.

2. Use the 10 index cards for Set B. Number the Set B cards 1, 2, 3, 4, 5, 6, 7, 8, 9, and 10.

3. Shuffle each set of cards separately. Then layout the cards as shown below. Turn over one card from each set.

Set A   Set B
(card showing 9) (card showing 6)

4. **Work Together** Work with your partner to write and solve a multiplication word problem, using the upturned cards.

5. Repeat steps 3 and 4.

Fluency Plan, Lesson 4 — Copyright © Houghton Mifflin Company

Activity Note Remind students that the two cards they turn up will be the factors of the multiplication in the word problem.

✐ Math Writing Prompt

Word Problems Write a word problem that uses multiplication. Solve the problem. Then change the problem to make it a division word problem.

 Software Support

Use *MegaMath* for review and reinforcement of the concepts and skills presented in this lesson.

Challenge — Activity Card FP-4

Discover the Pattern — Activity Card FP-4 ■

Work: In Pairs

1. One partner writes the multiplications for 5s with products to 50.

2. The other partner writes the multiplications for 10s with products to 50.

3. Partners identify any multiplications of 5s and 10s that have the same product.

4. Partners explain any patterns in the factors of the multiplications with the same products. The factor of 5 is two times the factor of the 10.

5. **Look Back** Explain why this pattern is logical. Use examples in the explanation. $5 \times 6 = 30$; $10 \times 3 = 30$. Five is half of 10, so the factor with 5 has to be two times the factor with 10 to get the same product.

Fluency Plan, Lesson 4 — Copyright © Houghton Mifflin Company

Activity Note Help students see that the Commutative Property of Multiplication can be applied:
$$10 \times 3 = (5 \times 3) \times 2$$
$$10 \times 3 = 5 \times (3 \times 2)$$
$$10 \times 3 = 5 \times 6$$

✐ Math Writing Prompt

Common Quotients Write four division equations that have the same quotient.

 Software Support

Use *Destination Math* to take students beyond the concepts and skills presented in this lesson.

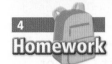

③ Homework and Spiral Review

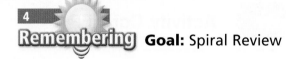

Homework **Goal:** Additional Practice

Use this Homework page to provide students with more practice with patterns in 2s, 5s, 9s, and 10s.

Remembering **Goal:** Spiral Review

This Remembering activity would be appropriate anytime after today's lesson. Have students circle problems that they did not know right away so they can practice them some more.

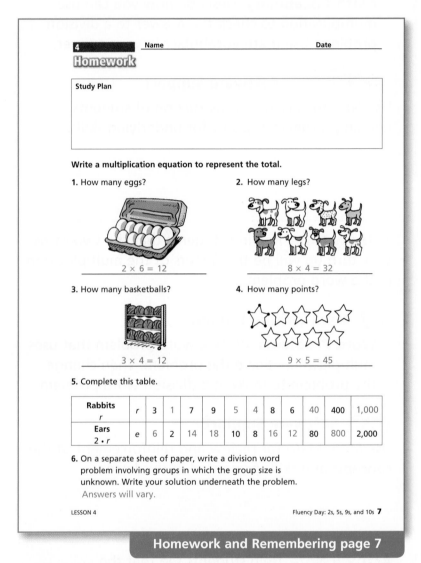

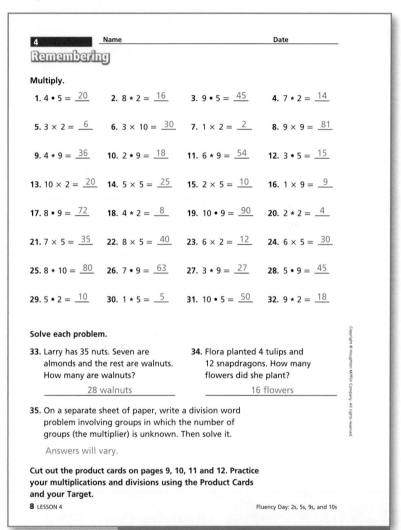

Home or School Activity

 Literature Connection

The Best of Times Read this book by Greg Tang, illustrated by Harry Briggs (Scholastic, January 2002) to the class. This book makes multiplication tables into rhymes.

Give students the opportunity to act out math situations in this book. Then have students make up their own rhymes or poems to help them remember the multiplications that are hard for them. Then, have students read or perform for someone else.

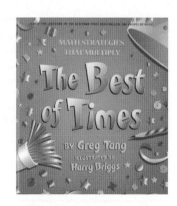

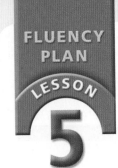
Multiply and Divide With 3

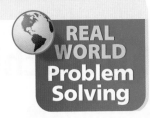

REAL WORLD Problem Solving

Lesson Objectives

- Explore patterns in 3s count-bys, multiplications, and divisions.
- Develop shortcuts for finding answers to multiplications and divisions.
- Practice multiplication for 2s and 5s, using pictographs.

Vocabulary

5s shortcut
Close Count-By shortcut
pictograph

The Day at a Glance

Today's Goals	Materials
① Teaching the Lesson **A1:** Discuss patterns in 3s count-bys, multiplications, and divisions. **A2:** Explore shortcuts for finding answers to 3s multiplications and divisions. **A3:** Develop and apply strategies for solving multiplication and division word problems. **A4:** Interpret pictographs in which each symbol represents 2 or 5. **② Going Further** ▸ Differentiated Instruction **③ Homework and Spiral Review**	**Lesson Activities** Student Activity Book pp. 17–18 or Student Hardcover Book pp. 17–18 Homework and Remembering pp. 13–14 MathBoard Materials Class Multiplication Table **Going Further** Activity Cards FP-5 Pennies Calendar page Markers (2 colors) Math Journals 123 Use Math Talk today!

Keeping Skills Sharp

Quick Practice · 5 MINUTES

Goal: Practice multiplications and divisions.

Materials: Division Digits materials, Product Cards: 5s, 9s

Division Digits for 5s and 9s Have a **Student Leader** run the activity, using problems from the 5s and 9s sections of Set 1. (See Lesson 2)

Practice Division with Product Cards Have students practice their divisions independently, using their Product Cards. Students should focus on the cards in their *Slow* and *Don't Know* piles, and should move cards to the *Fast* pile once they can solve the problems quickly and accurately. Students should then fill out their Study Plans.

Daily Routines

Homework Review Ask a student volunteer to share a word problem. Invite several students to solve it at the board, while others work at their seats. Collect student homework problems to use in Lesson 10.

Skip Count Have students skip count:

- ▸ by 2s from 37 to 65
- ▸ by 5s from 15 to 90

1 Teaching the Lesson

Activity 1

3s Patterns

 15 MINUTES

Goal: Discuss patterns in 3s count-bys, multiplications, and divisions.

Materials: MathBoard Materials

 NCTM Standards:
Number and Operations
Algebra

```
27   1 x 3 = 3
24   2 x 3 = 6
21   3 x 3 = 9
     4 x 3 = 12
18   5 x 3 = 15
     6 x 3 = 18
15   7 x 3 = 21
12   8 x 3 = 24
     9 x 3 = 27
9   10 x 3 = 30
6
3
```

```
27   1 x 3 = 3
24   2 x 3 = 6    6 ÷ 2 = 3
21   3 x 3 = 9
     4 x 3 = 12
18   5 x 3 = 15
     6 x 3 = 18
15   7 x 3 = 21
12   8 x 3 = 24
     9 x 3 = 27
9   10 x 3 = 30
6
3
```

```
27   1 x 3 = 3
24   2 x 3 = 6    6 ÷ 2 = 3    6 ÷ 3 = 2
21   3 x 3 = 9
     4 x 3 = 12
18   5 x 3 = 15
     6 x 3 = 18
15   7 x 3 = 21
12   8 x 3 = 24
     9 x 3 = 27
9   10 x 3 = 30
6
3
```

```
27   1 x 3 = 3    3 ÷ 1 = 3     3 ÷ 3 = 1
24   2 x 3 = 6    6 ÷ 2 = 3     6 ÷ 3 = 2
21   3 x 3 = 9    9 ÷ 3 = 3     9 ÷ 3 = 3
     4 x 3 = 12   12 ÷ 4 = 3    12 ÷ 3 = 4
18   5 x 3 = 15   15 ÷ 5 = 3    15 ÷ 3 = 5
     6 x 3 = 18   18 ÷ 6 = 3    18 ÷ 3 = 6
15   7 x 3 = 21   21 ÷ 7 = 3    21 ÷ 3 = 7
12   8 x 3 = 24   24 ÷ 8 = 3    24 ÷ 3 = 8
     9 x 3 = 27   27 ÷ 9 = 3    27 ÷ 3 = 9
9   10 x 3 = 30   30 ÷ 10 = 3   30 ÷ 3 = 10
6
3
```

▶ Patterns in Count-bys and Multiplications

WHOLE CLASS

Model these steps on the Class MathBoard as students work on their MathBoards.

One at a time, circle groups of 3 up to 30 on the Number Path and write the cumulative total next to each group. After students circle the first group, have them say in unison, "1 group of 3 is 3." Then, have them write and say, "1 × 3 = 3." Repeat this for the remaining multiplication equations.

Point to each cumulative total in turn and have students say them aloud: 3, 6, 9, 12, 15, 18, 21, 24, 27, 30.

Emphasize that the count-bys and the products in the multiplications are the same. Have students discuss the patterns they see in the count-bys and products.

● The sums of the digits of the products follow the pattern 3, 6, 9, 3, 6, 9, …

● The tens digits of the products follow the pattern 0, 0, 0, 1, 1, 1, 2, 2, 2, …

● The products alternate between odd and even.

▶ Write Division Equations WHOLE CLASS

On the Number Path, next to 2 × 3 = 6, write 6 ÷ 2 = _____. Then ask:

● What multiplication problem can we think of to help us solve this equation? 2 times what number equals 6?

● What is the value of the unknown factor? 3

Write a 3 after the equals sign.

Ask students what other division problem they can make from the multiplication equation 2 × 3 = 6. Write 6 ÷ 3 = _____ on the board. Again, ask students to share and solve the related multiplication problem, and write the answer, 2, after the equals sign.

Work with students to write a few more pairs of division equations, and then have them write the rest themselves.

Multiplication and division with 1 is difficult for some students, but they will understand it better after they have seen the rest of the number patterns.

Multiplication Shortcuts

▶ The 5s Shortcut [WHOLE CLASS]

Present the multiplications below and have students use 3s count-bys to find the answers. For example, to find 4 × 3, students count by 3s, raising a finger for each count-by until 4 fingers are raised.

4 × 3   2 × 3   5 × 3   8 × 3

Introduce students to the 5s shortcut. If students know their 5s multiplications, they can use a shortcut to find other multiplications.

Write 7 × 3 on the board.

- We could find 7 × 3 by saying seven 3s count-bys and raising 7 fingers. However, it is faster to start with 5 × 3 and count from there.

- Who can tell me what 5 × 3 equals? 15

- Put all the fingers on one hand up. We'll pretend that we already said the count-bys up to 15, and we'll count from there. We have counted five 3s. How many more 3s do we need to count to find 7 × 3? 2

As students follow along, raise all five fingers on one hand and say, "15." Then raise two fingers, one at a time, on your other hand as you say, "18, 21." Then, say "3 times 7 equals 21."

15   18   21

Tell students that this method is called the 5s shortcut. Have a student demonstrate how to use the 5s shortcut to find 8 × 3. Then, have the whole class use the 5s shortcut, counting in unison, to solve the problems below.

6 × 3   9 × 3   10 × 3

Next, write 21 ÷ 3 on the board. Ask a student to demonstrate how to use the 5s shortcut to find the answer. The student should raise all 5 fingers on one hand and say, "15," and then count by 3s from there, raising a finger for each count-by, until reaching 21. Seven fingers will be raised, indicating that 21 ÷ 3 = 7.

Have the whole class use the 5s shortcut, counting in unison, to solve the problems below.

18 ÷ 3   27 ÷ 3   30 ÷ 3   24 ÷ 3

Activity continued ▶

---

 15 MINUTES

Goal: Explore shortcuts for finding answers to 3s multiplications and divisions.

Materials: Class Multiplication Table

✓ **NCTM Standard:**
Number and Operations

Teaching Note

Multiplying and Dividing The finger action is the same for division and multiplication, but the mental process is different. Emphasize to students that when you multiply, you stop counting when your fingers show the correct number of groups (the multiplier); the last count-by you say is the answer. When you divide, you stop counting groups when you say the product; the number of fingers that are raised is the answer.

Differentiated Instruction

Extra Help Help students see the 5s Shortcut within the multiplication table. Indicate the 5 × 3 in the 3s column. Then use fingers as shown at the left to show the 5s Shortcut, touching the fingers to that product in the 3s column (for 8 × 3, the whole hand touches 5 × 3 = 15,

6 fingers raised touch 6 × 3 = 8,

7 fingers raised touch 7 × 3 = 21, and 8 fingers raised touch 8 × 3 = 24). Link the 5s Shortcut to the multiplication table on later days.

① Teaching the Lesson (continued)

Activity 2

The Learning Classroom

Helping Community By discussing multiple strategies for math problems, students become aware of other students' thinking. As students better understand other students' thinking, they become better "helpers." Instead of showing how they would solve problems, they are able to look at another student's work and in turn find problems in their own methods.

English Language Learners

Write 7 × 4 = ____. Say: **I don't know the answer. Let's use the Close Count-By shortcut.**

• **Beginning** Ask: **What numbers are close to 4?** 3, 5 Ask: **7 × 3 = ____?** 21 **21 + 7 = ____.** 28 **How many 7's did we use?** 4 **7 × 4 = ____?** 28

• **Intermediate** Say: **7 × 3 = ____.** 21 **Now add 7. Is that the same as 7 × 4?** yes Model how to work backward, using the shortcut.

• **Advanced** Ask: **What is 7 × 3?** 21 **21 + 7?** 28 **So 7 × 4 = ____?** 28 Help students solve 6 × 9 by starting with 6 × 10 and working backward.

▶ The Close Count-By Shortcut `WHOLE CLASS`

Ask for Ideas Ask students if they know any other shortcuts for finding multiplication and division answers. The Close Count-By shortcut is a variation of the 5s shortcut. It involves working forward or backward from any known product to find an unknown product. If no one suggests this method, lead a discussion to bring it out. For example:

● Suppose I don't know what 8 × 3 equals, but I do know that 9 × 3 = 27. What could I do? Start with 27, and count back one group of 3.

● Suppose I know that 3 × 3 = 9, but I can't remember what 4 × 3 is. What could I do? Start with 9, and count forward one group of 3.

● Suppose I know that 18 ÷ 3 = 6, but I don't know 24 ÷ 3. What could I do? Start with 6 fingers raised and think, "18." Then, count by 3s from there until you get to 24. The number of fingers you have up is the answer.

Emphasize that, whenever students don't know or are unsure of an answer, they can always work from a multiplication or division they know and count forward or backward.

▶ Use the Class Multiplication Table `WHOLE CLASS`

Ask students to find the 3s multiplications on the Class Multiplication Table. They should see that the 3s column has the 3s multiplications with the factor 3 given second, and the 3s row has the 3s multiplications with the factor 3 given first.

Point to the multiplication equations in the 3s column (up to 10 × 3 = 30) in order, as students say the equations in unison: "1 times 3 equals 3," "2 times 3 equals 6" and so on. Tell students they may raise their fingers to keep track of the count-bys, if needed.

Point to each equation in the 3s column (up to 10 × 3 = 30) once again, but, this time, have students say the 3s divisions in order: "3 divided by 3 equals 1," "6 divided by 3 equals 2," and so on. Tell students they may raise their fingers to keep track of the count-bys, if needed.

Have students close their eyes. Say 3s multiplications and divisions in mixed order. Give students a few seconds to think of the answer. Then say, "Answer," and have students say the answer in unison.

Word Problems

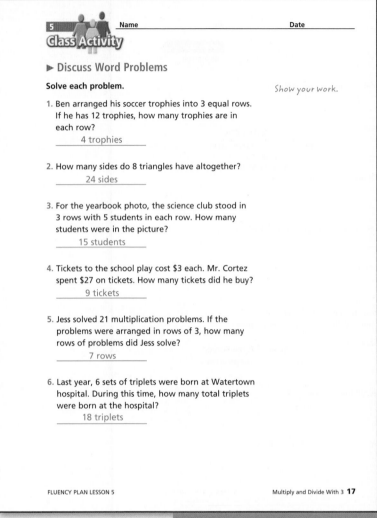

Student Activity Book page 17

▶ Discuss Word Problems

INDIVIDUALS

Math Talk

Have students use **Solve and Discuss** for problems 1–6 on Student Book page 17. You may prefer to have students work on their MathBoards, rather than in their books.

Most students should be using numeric solution methods.

Encourage students to make quick math drawings, rather than detailed pictures.

Teaching the Lesson (continued)

Interpret Pictographs

 15 MINUTES

Goal: Interpret pictographs in which each symbol represents 2 or 5.

Materials: Student Activity Book or Hardcover Book p. 18

✓ **NCTM Standards:**
Number and Operations
Data Analysis and Probability

✓ **Ongoing Assessment**

To help students understand pictographs have them:

▶ list the parts of a pictograph. Be sure they include the title, labels, symbols, and key.

▶ explain the purpose of each part of a pictograph.

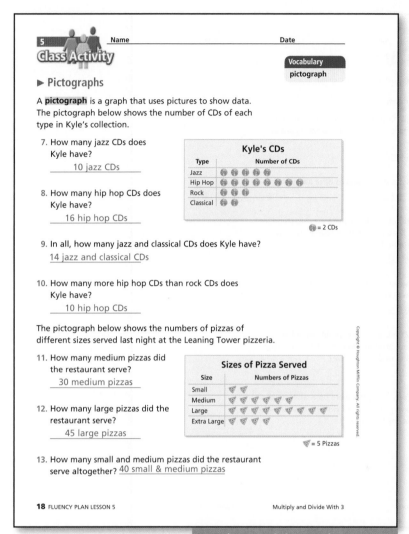

Student Activity Book page 18

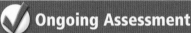 ▶ **Pictographs** INDIVIDUALS

2s Pictographs Have students look at the first pictograph on Student Book page 18. Ask if anyone can explain what the pictograph shows. Make sure students understand that each symbol represents two CDs. Have students solve exercise 7, and then ask students to share how they found the answer. Make sure both of these methods are discussed:

● Use the 2s count-bys, saying one count-by for each symbol: 2, 4, 6, 8, 10.

● There are 5 CD symbols and each one represents 2 CDs, so the number of jazz CDs is 5 × 2, or 10.

Use **Solve and Discuss** for exercises 8–10.

5s Pictographs Have students look at the second pictograph, and make sure they understand what it shows. Use **Solve and Discuss** for exercises 11–13.

② Going Further

Differentiated Instruction

Intervention | Activity Card FP-5

Practice Dividing | Activity Card FP-5

Work: In Groups of Three

Use:
• 30 Pennies

1. Each group member copies the chart below.

Total Number of Pennies	Number of Students	Equation
30	3	$30 \div 3 = 10$
21	3	
3	3	
15	3	
24	3	

$21 \div 3 = 7; 3 \div 3 = 1; 15 \div 3 = 5; 24 \div 3 = 8$

2. For each row, count out the number of pennies in the first column; for example, 30.

3. Each group member takes one penny at a time, in turn, until there are no pennies left.

4. Once all the pennies are taken, group members write a division equation in the last column to show how many pennies each student has.

Fluency Plan, Lesson 5

Copyright © Houghton Mifflin Company

Activity Note If everyone in the group has the same amount of pennies, no mistakes were made.

Math Writing Prompt

Draw a Picture Write a multiplication or a division word problem for a 3s multiplication. Draw equal groups to show the answer to your word problem.

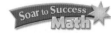 **Software Support**

Use *Soar to Success* for instruction of students needing targeted support for underlying skills.

On Level | Activity Card FP-5

Look for Patterns | Activity Card FP-5 ▲

Work: By Yourself

Use:
• Calendar page
• Markers, one dark and one light

1. On the calendar page, use a dark color to make an X on dates that are 3s count-bys.

2. Use a lighter color to shade in the dates that are 2s count-bys. An example is shown below.

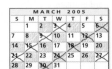

3. Look for as many patterns as you can.

4. Compare Work with three other students, and compare the patterns you found. Why might the patterns be different? Some patterns depend on what day of the week the month starts.

Fluency Plan, Lesson 5

Copyright © Houghton Mifflin Company

Activity Note Students should have calendar pages for different months or years so that the patterns they find will vary.

Math Writing Prompt

Explain Your Thinking Explain how you can find the answer to $18 \div 3$ if you already know that $12 \div 3 = 4$.

 Software Support

Use *MegaMath* for review and reinforcement of the concepts and skills presented in this lesson.

Challenge | Activity Card FP-5

Critical Thinking | Activity Card FP-5 ■

Work: In Small Groups

1. Read the statements below.
   • A whistle blows every 2 minutes.
   • A clock chimes every 3 minutes.
   • A bell rings every 5 minutes.
   • They all sound at 12:00 noon.

2. At what time will all three sound together again? 12:30

3. Look Back How can you check your answer?

Fluency Plan, Lesson 5

Copyright © Houghton Mifflin Company

Activity Note Recommend that students draw a picture if they need help visualizing the problem.

Math Writing Prompt

Compare and Contrast Explain how using your fingers for count-bys is the same for multiplication and division. Explain how it is different.

 DESTINATION Math **Software Support**

Use *Destination Math* to take students beyond the concepts and skills presented in this lesson.

Multiply and Divide With 3 **49**

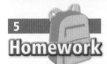

3 Homework and Spiral Review

Homework Goal: Additional Practice

Use this Homework page to provide students with more practice with patterns in 3s.

Remembering Goal: Spiral Review

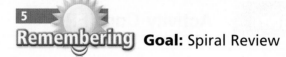

This Remembering activity would be appropriate anytime after today's lesson. Have students circle problems that they did not know right away so they can practice them some more.

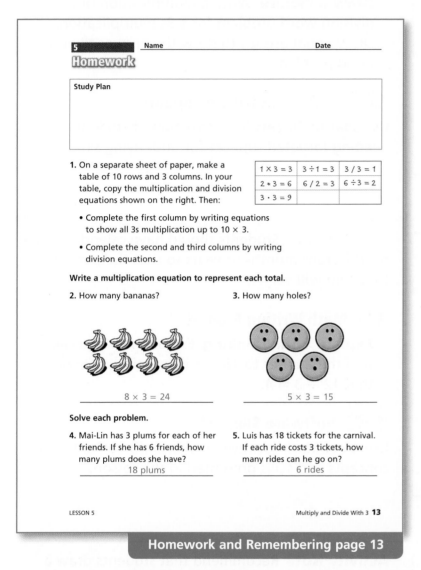

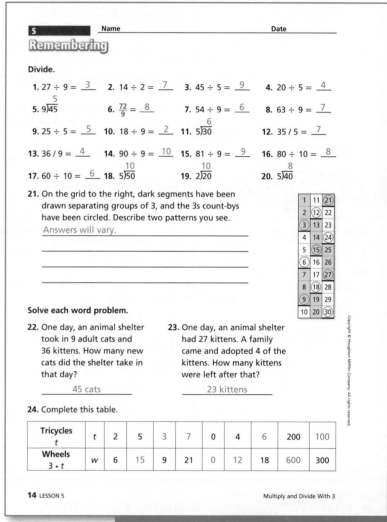

Homework and Remembering page 13

Homework and Remembering page 14

Home or School Activity

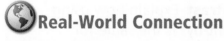

Real-World Connection

Change a Recipe Discuss with students how a recipe tells how much of each ingredient is needed. Sometimes you might want to double or even triple a recipe. The recipe for one Lime Pie is shown. Have students determine how much of each ingredient they would need to make 3 pies.

Have students bring in their favorite recipe to share with the class. They should be prepared to talk about how to double or triple the recipe.

Lime Pie
8 ounces cream cheese, softened
1 can sweetened condensed milk
6 ounces limeade concentrate
4 drops green food coloring
8 ounces frozen whipped topping
1 graham cracker crust
1 kiwifruit, peeled and sliced

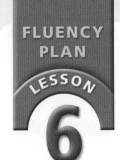

Multiply and Divide With 4

Vocabulary

Equal-Shares
 Drawing
Fast Array
5s shortcut
Close Count-By

Lesson Objectives

● Explore patterns in 4s count-bys, multiplications, and divisions.

● Practice shortcuts for finding multiplications and divisions.

The Day at a Glance

Today's Goals	Materials	
① Teaching the Lesson **A1:** Discuss patterns in 4s count-bys, multiplications, and divisions. **A2:** Use shortcuts to find and solve 4s multiplications and division problems. **A3:** Complete and interpret Equal-Shares Drawings and Fast Arrays. **② Going Further** ▶ Differentiated Instruction **③ Homework and Spiral Review**	**Lesson Activities** Student Activity Book pp. 19–20 or Student Hardcover Book pp. 19–20 Homework and Remembering pp. 15–16 MathBoard Materials Class Multiplication Table	**Going Further** Activity Cards FP-7 Counters Math Journals

123 *Use* **Math Talk** *today!*

Keeping Skills Sharp

Quick Practice 🕐 5 MINUTES	Daily Routines	
Goal: Practice multiplications and divisions. **Materials:** Division Digits materials, Product Cards: 3s **Division Digits for 3s** Have a **Student Leader** run the activity, using problems from the 3s section of Set 2. (See Lesson 2) **Practice Multiplications with Product Cards** Have students practice their multiplications independently, using their Product Cards. (See Lesson 5)	**Homework Review** Let students work together to check their work. Initially, pair less able students with more able students. Remind students to use what they know about helping others.	**Strategy Problem** Seth had some marbles that he shared equally with Josh. Then Josh gave half his marbles to his sister Elaine. If Elaine received 4 marbles, how many marbles did Seth start with? 16 marbles

① Teaching the Lesson

Activity 1

4s Patterns

 20 MINUTES

Goal: Discuss patterns in 4s count-bys, multiplications, and divisions.

Materials: MathBoard Materials

 NCTM Standards:
Number and Operations
Algebra

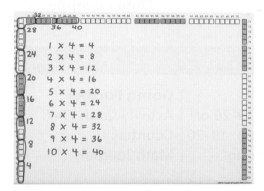

▶ Patterns in Count-bys and Multiplications

WHOLE CLASS

Model these steps on the Class MathBoard as students work on their MathBoards.

One at a time, circle groups of 4 up to 40 on the Number Path and write the cumulative total next to each group. After students circle the first group, have them say, "1 group of 4 is 4." Then, have them write and say, "$1 \times 4 = 4$." After students circle the second group, have them say, "2 groups of 4 are 8." Then, have them write and say "$2 \times 4 = 8$." Have students write and say the remaining multiplication equations.

Point to each cumulative total in turn and have students say them aloud: 4, 8, 12, 16, 20, 24, 28, 32, 36, 40.

Have students discuss the patterns they see in the count-bys and equations. For example:

● The ones digits of the count-bys follow the pattern
4, 8, 2, 6, 0, 4, 8, 2, 6, 0.

● The products are all even because 4 is an even number.

● If you ignore 40, and then start with the outside pair of products, 4 and 36, and move in, the ones digit of each pair of products (4 and 36, 8 and 32, 12 and 28, and 16 and 24) add to 10.

Point out to students that because multiplication is commutative they might already know some of these multiplication facts. For example, 2×4 has the same product as 4×2.

▶ Write Division Equations INDIVIDUALS

Have students write two division equations for each multiplication equation. Write the first two or three pairs as a class. Then discuss with students the patterns in the division equations.

Count-by Shortcuts

▶ 5s Shortcuts WHOLE CLASS

Write 7 × 4 on the board. Then ask a volunteer to explain how to use the 5s shortcut to find the answer. If necessary, remind students that the 5s shortcut involves starting with the fifth count-by—in this case, 5 × 4, or 20—and then counting up from there. To find 7 × 4, hold up all the fingers on one hand and say, "20," and then count up by two more 4s, raising two fingers on the other hand.

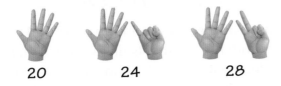

20   24   28

Next, write 32 ÷ 4 on the board, and have a student explain how to use the 5s shortcut to solve it.

The student should raise 5 fingers on one hand and say, "20," and then count up by 4s, raising a finger for each count-by, until reaching 32. The number of fingers raised, 8, is the answer.

Pose the multiplication and division problems below, and have the class use the 5s shortcut, counting in unison, to solve them.

6 × 4   36 ÷ 4   8 × 4   28 ÷ 4   9 × 4

▶ Close Count-bys WHOLE CLASS

Remind students that the Close Count-By strategy involves working forward or backward from any known product to find an unknown product. Pose the following questions to the students:

- Suppose I don't know what 8 × 4 equals, but I do know that 9 × 4 = 36. What could I do? Start with 36, and count back one group of 4.

- Suppose I know that 2 × 4 = 8, but I can't remember what 3 × 4 is. What could I do? Start with 8, and count forward one group of 4.

- Suppose I know that 24 ÷ 4 = 6, but I don't know 32 ÷ 4. What could I do? Start with 6 fingers raised and think, "24." Then, count by 4s from there until you get to 32. The number of fingers you have up is the answer.

  15 MINUTES

Goal: Use shortcuts to solve 4s multiplication and division problems.

Materials: Class Multiplication Table

  NCTM Standards:
Number and Operations
Algebra

  Class Management

Are your students still "aiming" their explanations to you rather than the other students? Remember to move to the side or the back of the room and direct the class from there. Also, are you remembering not to answer right away so you won't do all of the talking about math? Try to keep from telling answers and filling in explanations so that the students will learn to do this themselves.

The Learning Classroom

Helping Community It will be important to take some class time to discuss what *good helping* is all about. Students may come up with a list that can be posted in the classroom. It is important that they understand that good helping does not mean telling answers, but it means taking other students through steps so that they come up with the answer themselves.

Activity continued ▶

▶ Use the Class Multiplication Table [WHOLE CLASS]

Ask students to find the 4s multiplications on the Class Multiplication Table. They should see that the 4s column has the 4s multiplications with the factor 4 given second, and the 4s row has the 4s multiplications with the factor 4 given first.

Point to the multiplication equations in the 4s column (up to $10 \times 4 = 40$) in order as students say the equations in unison: "1 times 4 equals 4," "2 times 4 equals 8," and so on. Tell students they may raise their fingers to keep track of the count-bys if they need to.

Point to each equation in the 4s column (up to $10 \times 4 = 40$) once again, but, this time, have students say the 4s divisions in order: "4 divided by 4 equals 1," "8 divided by 4 equals 2," and so on. Tell students they may raise their fingers to keep track of the count-bys, if they need to.

▶ Multiplication and Division Practice [WHOLE CLASS]

Have students close their eyes. Have a **Student Leader** say the 4s multiplication and division problems in mixed order. The leader should give students a few seconds to think of the answer. Then, the leader should say, "Answer," and have students say the answer in unison.

> **Leader:** six times four
>
> (5 second pause)
>
> **Leader:** answer
>
> **Whole class:** twenty-four
>
> **Leader:** thirty-six divided by four
>
> (5 second pause)
>
> **Leader:** answer
>
> **Whole class:** nine
>
> **Leader:** three times four
>
> (5 second pause)
>
> **Leader:** answer
>
> **Whole class:** twelve

The Learning Classroom

Student Leaders Select different student leaders for different tasks. Take time to help students get used to being leaders. Support them for the first few times, and encourage classmates to be supportive. Most students gain confidence themselves when they help others learn.

Use Shortcuts

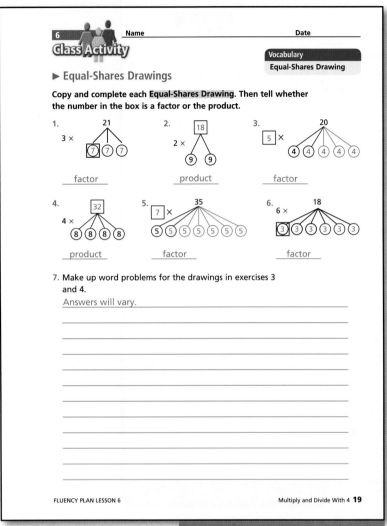

▶ Discuss Equal-Shares Drawings

INDIVIDUALS

Math Talk

Have students discuss Equal-Shares Drawings. Elicit from students that the number inside the circles tells the group size. The number of circles is the multiplier (the number of groups). The circles are connected by line segments to the total, or product.

Have students look at exercises 1–6 on Student Book page 19. Read the directions aloud and make sure students know what to do. Give students a few minutes to solve the problems, and then discuss their answers.

Have students complete exercise 7. For each drawing, choose one or two students to share their word problems. Discuss as a class whether the word problem fits the drawing. If not, have students suggest ways to fix it.

 20 MINUTES

Goal: Complete and interpret Equal-Shares Drawings and Fast Arrays.

Materials: Student Activity Book or Hardcover Book pp. 19–20

 NCTM Standards:
Number and Operations
Algebra

 Ongoing Assessment

Ask students questions such as:

▶ If you know what 3 x 4 equals, how could you use that to find out what 4 x 4 equals?

▶ How many division equations could you find for one multiplication equation?

The Learning Classroom

Math Talk This may be a good day to talk with the class for a few minutes about what makes a good explanation. Students may want to produce a list that can be posted on the wall of the classroom on a poster board for later reference. They may make suggestions such as:

1) Write your work so everyone can see it.

2) Talk loud enough for other students to hear.

3) Use a pointer to point at your work.

4) Say how you arrived at the answer, not just the answer.

5) Stand to the side of your work when you talk.

Activity continued ▶

① Teaching the Lesson (continued)

Activity 3

 Class Management

Introduce Pictographs Discuss the pictograph on Homework page 15 so that students understand that each dish of food represents 10 animals. For problem 7, they need to count the number of bowls for the dogs and multiply by 10 ($8 \times 10 = 80$).

Teaching Note

Fast Arrays Encourage students to draw open circles rather than closed circles when making these drawings so they can complete exercises more quickly.

 Class Management

Looking Ahead Problem 21 of today's Remembering page asks students to write and solve word problems. Tomorrow, collect these problems and save them. In Lesson 10, students will solve problems their classmates have written.

English Language Learners

Draw a 3 × 8 fast array on the board. Make sure students understand *fast array, factor,* and *product.*

- **Beginning** Say: **This is a fast array. 3 and 8 are factors.** Have students repeat. Ask: **What is 3 × 8?** 24 Say: **24 is the product.**
- **Intermediate** Ask: **Is this an array or a fast array?** fast array **What do we multiply?** 3, 8 Say: **They are the factors. 3 × 8 = ____.** 24 **24 is the product.**
- **Advanced** Have students draw a regular array and describe the differences using the terms *factors* and *product.*

> **6**
> **Class Activity**   Name ____ Date ____
>
> Vocabulary
> Fast Array
>
> ► Fast Arrays
>
> Copy and complete each **Fast Array**.
>
> 8. 8 / 3 / 24
> 9. 9 / 5 / 45
> 10. 7 / 2 / 14
> 11. 5 / 8 / 40
> 12. 4 / 6 / 24
> 13. 8 / 9 / 72
>
> 14. Write word problems for the drawings in exercises 8 and 12.
>   Answers will vary.
> _____
> _____
> _____
>
> **20** FLUENCY PLAN LESSON 6   Multiply and Divide With 4
>

Student Activity Book page 20

► Fast Arrays [INDIVIDUALS]

Have students look at exercises 8–13 on Student Book page 20. Explain that the diagrams in these exercises are Fast Arrays. Tell students that the numbers above and to the left of the dots are factors. The numbers below the dots are the products. Read the directions aloud and make sure students know what to do. Give students a few minutes to solve the problems, and then discuss their answers.

Have students complete exercise 14. For each drawing, choose one or two students to share their word problems. Discuss as a class whether the word problem fits the drawing. If not, have students suggest ways to fix it.

Discuss with students how these Fast Arrays and the Equal-Shares Drawings were introduced so that they do not have to draw out all the objects for any problem. Their drawings should start using numbers instead of drawing out everything.

② Going Further

● Intervention   Activity Card FP-6

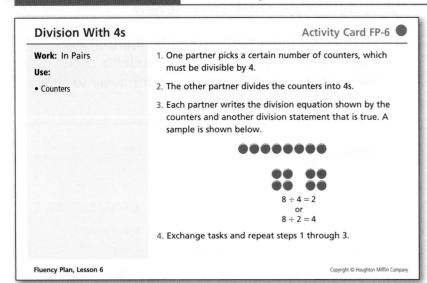

Division With 4s   Activity Card FP-6 ●

Work: In Pairs

Use:

• Counters

1. One partner picks a certain number of counters, which must be divisible by 4.

2. The other partner divides the counters into 4s.

3. Each partner writes the division equation shown by the counters and another division statement that is true. A sample is shown below.

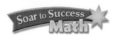

8 ÷ 4 = 2
or
8 ÷ 2 = 4

4. Exchange tasks and repeat steps 1 through 3.

Fluency Plan, Lesson 6   Copyright © Houghton Mifflin Company

Activity Note Remind students that if the counters cannot be separated into groups of 4, the number they chose is not divisible by 4.

✎ Math Writing Prompt

Explain Your Thinking Explain how knowing that 5 × 4 = 20 can help you find 4 × 4.

Soar to Success Math ☆ Software Support

Use *Soar to Success* for instruction of students needing targeted support for underlying skills.

▲ On Level   Activity Card FP-6

Sign It   Activity Card FP-6 ▲

Work: In Pairs

1. Each partner copies the equations below.

40 ◯ 4 = 10 ÷

2 ◯ 4 = 8 ×

28 ◯ 4 = 7 ÷

5 ◯ 4 = 20 ×

2. Partners write the correct operation symbol in each circle.

3. Each partner writes four more 4s problems with missing operation symbols.

4. Partners exchange problems and add the missing symbols to their partner's problems.

Fluency Plan, Lesson 6   Copyright © Houghton Mifflin Company

Activity Note Check that the new problems being written are practicing multiplying and dividing by 4.

✎ Math Writing Prompt

Word Problems Write a division word problem for a 4s multiplication.

MegaMath Grades K–6 Software Support

Use *MegaMath* for review and reinforcement of the concepts and skills presented in this lesson.

■ Challenge   Activity Card FP-6

Find a Pattern   Activity Card FP-6 ■

Work: In Pairs

1. The patterns below use 4s. Describe and extend each pattern.

5, 9, 13, 17, __, __, __, __
+4: 21, 25, 29, 33
5, 9, 17, 29, __, __, __, __
Add multiples of 4: 45, 65, 89, 117.

2. Each partner makes three different patterns using 4s.

3. Partners exchange papers.

4. Describe each number pattern. Extend each pattern by four numbers.

Fluency Plan, Lesson 6   Copyright © Houghton Mifflin Company

Activity Note Allow students to use number lines or multiplication charts to assist them in identifying the patterns.

✎ Math Writing Prompt

Even Mixes Explain why the 4s count-bys are all even numbers. Find other numbers that have count-bys that are all even.

✵ DESTINATION Math· Software Support

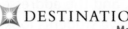

Use *Destination Math* to take students beyond the concepts and skills presented in this lesson.

③ Homework and Spiral Review

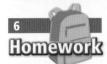

Homework Goal: Additional Practice

Use this Homework page to provide students with more practice with multiplying and dividing with 4.

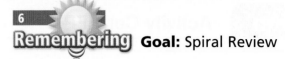

Remembering Goal: Spiral Review

This Remembering activity would be appropriate anytime after today's lesson. Have students circle problems that they did not know right away so they can practice them some more.

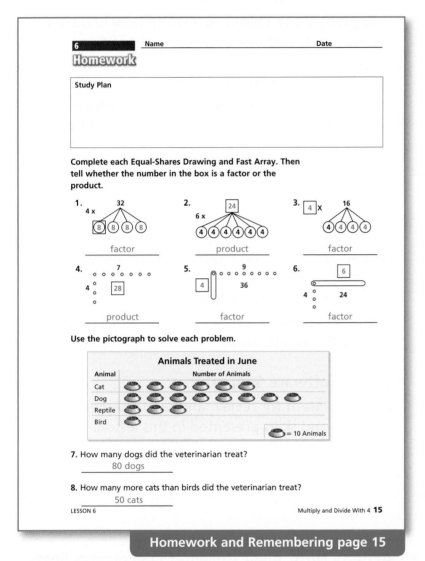

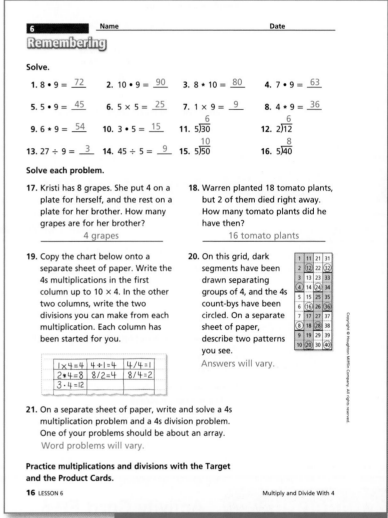

Homework and Remembering page 15

Homework and Remembering page 16

Home or School Activity

Real-World Connection

Find a Pattern Emphasize to students that they see many mathematical patterns every day. For example, the tiles on a floor or the bricks on a patio are arranged in geometric patterns, and the addresses of houses on a street follow a regular numeric pattern. Have students look for patterns over the course of a day and write about what they find.

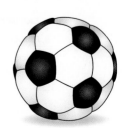

58 FLUENCY PLAN LESSON 6

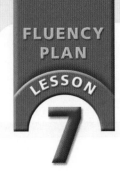
Multiply and Divide With 1 and 0

Lesson Objective
- Understand the rules for multiplying and dividing with 1 and 0.

Vocabulary
Identity Property of Multiplication

The Day at a Glance

Today's Goals	Materials
1 Teaching the Lesson **A1:** Observe and generalize patterns in multiplication and division with 1 and 0. **A2:** Compare patterns for adding 1 and 0 to patterns for multiplying with 1 and 0. **2 Going Further** ▶ Differentiated Instruction **3 Homework and Spiral Review**	**Lesson Activities** Student Activity Book pp. 21–23 or Student Hardcover Book pp. 21–23 Homework and Remembering pp. 17–18 **Going Further** Activity Cards FP-7 Index cards Math Journals

Use Math Talk today!

Keeping Skills Sharp

Quick Practice 5 MINUTES	Daily Routines
Goal: Practice multiplications and divisions. **Materials:** Division Digits materials, Product Cards: 2s, 5s, 9s **Division Digits for 3s** Have a **Student Leader** run the activity, using problems from the 3s section of Set 2. (See Lesson 2) **Practice Multiplications with Product Cards** Have students practice their multiplications independently, using their Product Cards. (See Lesson 5)	**Homework Review** If students need help with pictograph symbols, ask them to find the number each symbol stands for and skip count, using the symbols in each row. Then they can write the total. Collect student word problems from Remembering for use in Lesson 10. **Money** Beatriz has 79 cents. She has 10 coins. How many of each kind of coin does Beatriz have? *Possible answer:* 2 quarters, 1 dime, 3 nickels, 4 pennies

Teaching the Lesson

Multiply and Divide With 1 and 0

 20 MINUTES

Goal: Observe and generalize patterns in multiplication and division with 1 and 0.

Materials: Student Activity Book or Hardcover Book pp. 21–23

✔ **NCTM Standards:**
Communication
Number and Operations
Algebra
Representation

The Learning Classroom

Building Concepts Your students may already know rules for multiplying and dividing with 1 and 0. The goal of this lesson is for students to develop a conceptual understanding of the rules and to begin effective practice of the rules.

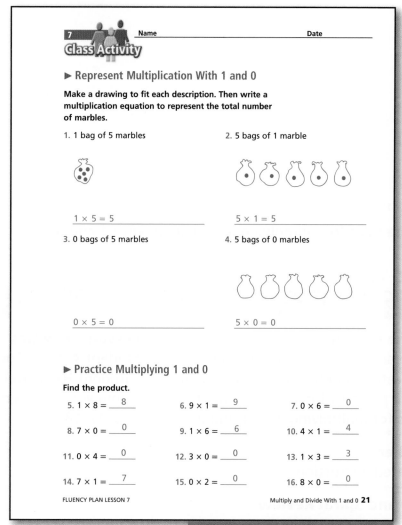

Student Activity Book page 21

▶ Represent Multiplication With 1 and 0 [INDIVIDUALS]

Use **Solve and Discuss** for exercises 1 and 2 on Student Book page 21. Then, as students look back at the problems, elicit the following information:

● In exercise 1, 1 is the multiplier and 5 is the group size.

● In exercise 2, 1 is the group size and 5 is the multiplier (the number in each group).

The product in each case is 5. That is, 1 group of 5 and 5 groups of 1 are both equal to 5.

● In exercise 3, 0 is the multiplier and 5 is the group size.

● In exercise 4, 0 is the group size and 5 is the multiplier.

The product in each case is 0. That is, 0 groups of 5 and 5 groups of 0 are both equal to 0.

▶ Generalize Results PAIRS

On Student Book page 21, ask students to look at exercises 1 and 2. Tell them to replace the number 5 with other numbers. Then have them draw pictures and write equations to fit their descriptions. The students should conclude that, no matter which number they choose, the total, or product is that number.

Tell students that if we use the letter n to represent "any number," we can write equations to generalize what they have discovered. Work with students to generate these four equations.

1 group of $n = n$ n groups of $1 = n$

$1 \times n = n$ $n \times 1 = n$

You might tell students that in mathematics the idea that 1 times any number or any number times 1 is that number, is called the Identity Property of Multiplication.

Repeat a similar process with exercises 3 and 4. Students should find that, no matter which number they choose, the total, or product is 0.

Math Talk Ask if anyone can generalize the results by writing equations in which n stands for "any number." Discuss all four of these equations.

0 groups of $n = 0$ n groups of $0 = 0$

$0 \times n = 0$ $n \times 0 = 0$

▶ Practice Multiplying 1 and 0 WHOLE CLASS

You can have students take turns reading the problems and giving the answers to exercises 5–16 aloud. All students should record the answers in the blanks.

Teaching Note

Language and Vocabulary Some *Math Expressions* students call a 1 in multiplication a "copier" because it makes 1 copy of the original number. They also call 0 a "zapper" because it zaps, or erases, the other factor.

 Class Management

Hearing students read and answer the numerical problems, exercises 5–16, will let you know which students need help in understanding these operations with 0 and 1. Depending on the class progress, you can either complete the multiplications with ones first, then move to the multiplications with zeros, or mix them up as students make progress.

Activity continued ▶

① Teaching the Lesson (continued)

Activity 1

📁 Class Management

One part of making everyone responsible for listening to one another is to make sure that the explainers are talking loudly enough and that they are talking to the whole class, not just you. Move to the side or the back of the class so that students have to look at their classmates to see you. (You can direct things from the side or the back and you have an interesting new view of your class.)

To encourage students to speak, you might ask them to:

- use pretend microphones which frees them to talk more loudly.

- pretend a family member is sitting in the back of the class and they need to speak loudly enough for them to hear.

- wiggle their fingers if they cannot hear the speaker.

English Language Learners

Model how to draw a picture to help solve a division-with-1 problem. Say: 3 people have 3 cars. Draw 3 stick figures and 3 cars on the board. Draw a line connecting each person to a car.

- **Beginning** Say: Each person drives 1 car. This is the same as $3 \div 3 = 1$.
- **Intermediate** Ask: Can 1 person drive 2 cars? no Say: Each person drives 1 car. $3 \div 3 = ?$ 1
- **Advanced** Ask: How many cars can each person drive? 1

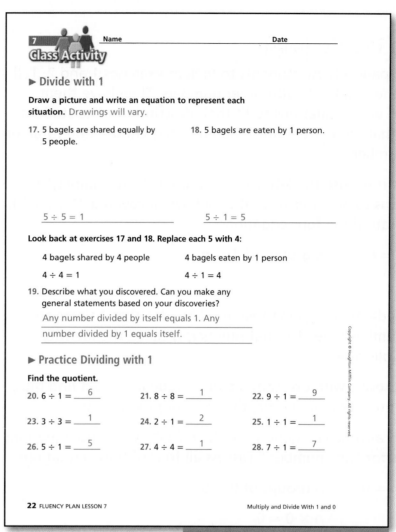

Student Activity Book page 22

▶ Divide With 1

WHOLE CLASS

Math Talk 123

Use **Solve and Discuss** for exercises 17–19 on Student Book page 22. In excercise 19, encourage students to use symbols to generalize. Students should observe the following:

- Dividing a number into that number of equal groups, gives each group a size of 1. In symbols, $n \div n = 1$.

- Dividing a number into 1 group, gives a group size equal to the number. In symbols, $n \div 1 = n$.

▶ Practice Dividing With 1   WHOLE CLASS

You can have students take turns reading the problems and giving the answers to exercises 20–28. All students should record the answers in the blank.

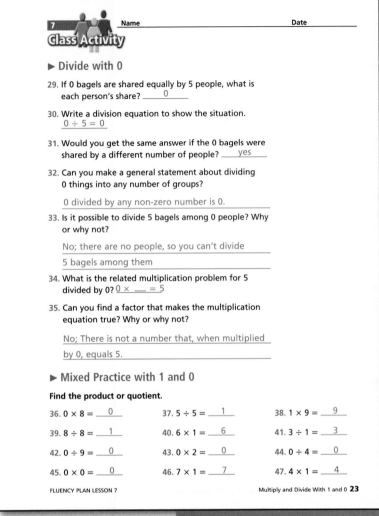

Student Activity Book page 23

The worksheet shows:

7 Class Activity

Name _____ Date _____

▶ Divide with 0

29. If 0 bagels are shared equally by 5 people, what is each person's share? ____0____

30. Write a division equation to show the situation.
    $0 \div 5 = 0$

31. Would you get the same answer if the 0 bagels were shared by a different number of people? ____yes____

32. Can you make a general statement about dividing 0 things into any number of groups?

    0 divided by any non-zero number is 0.

33. Is it possible to divide 5 bagels among 0 people? Why or why not?

    No; there are no people, so you can't divide
    5 bagels among them

34. What is the related multiplication problem for 5 divided by 0? $0 \times \_\_\_ = 5$

35. Can you find a factor that makes the multiplication equation true? Why or why not?

    No; There is not a number that, when multiplied
    by 0, equals 5.

▶ Mixed Practice with 1 and 0

Find the product or quotient.

36. $0 \times 8 = \_\_0\_\_$ 37. $5 \div 5 = \_\_1\_\_$ 38. $1 \times 9 = \_\_9\_\_$

39. $8 \div 8 = \_\_1\_\_$ 40. $6 \times 1 = \_\_6\_\_$ 41. $3 \div 1 = \_\_3\_\_$

42. $0 \div 9 = \_\_0\_\_$ 43. $0 \times 2 = \_\_0\_\_$ 44. $0 \div 4 = \_\_0\_\_$

45. $0 \times 0 = \_\_0\_\_$ 46. $7 \times 1 = \_\_7\_\_$ 47. $4 \times 1 = \_\_4\_\_$

FLUENCY PLAN LESSON 7   Multiply and Divide With 1 and 0 **23**

▶ Divide With 0

INDIVIDUALS   Math Talk

Using **Solve and Discuss**, have students solve exercises 29–32 on Student Book page 23. Students should see that dividing 0 into any number of groups gives each group 0. Ask:

• If we use the letter *n* to stand for "any number," what equation can we write to show what we learned in this problem? $0 \div n = 0$

Write the general equation on the board. Read it aloud as, "Zero divided by any number equals 0."

Next, use **Solve and Discuss** to have students solve exercises 33–35.

▶ Mixed Practice With 1 and 0   WHOLE CLASS

You can have students take turns reading the problems and giving the answers to exercises 36–47 on Student Book page 23. All students should record the answers in the blank.

Teaching Note

Dividing by Zero Dividing a number by 0 is not possible. Exercises 33–35 present two ways of understanding why dividing by 0 is impossible:

• In 33, students should see that it does not make sense to share a group of things among 0 people, so $5 \div 0$ has no meaning when 0 is the number of shares.

• In 34 and 35, students should write the multiplication equation $0 \times _____ = 0$ and reason that, because 0 times any number is 0, there is no number that can be put in the blank to make the equation true.

Activity 2

Multiplication and Addition Patterns

 15 MINUTES

Goal: Compare patterns for adding 1 and 0 to patterns for multiplying 1 and 0.

Materials: Student Activity Book or Hardcover Book p. 24

✔ **NCTM Standards:**
Communication
Number and Operations
Algebra
Representation

 Class Management

Looking Ahead Problem 27 of today's Remembering page asks students to write and solve a word problem. Tomorrow, collect these problems and save them. In Lesson 10, students will solve problems their classmates have written.

 Ongoing Assessment

Ask students questions such as:

▶ If $1 \times 0 = 0$, does $1 + 0 = 0$? Why?

▶ Write an equation to show that zero divided by any number is always zero.

7
Class Activity
Name _____ Date _____

▶ **Add and Multiply with 1 and 0**

Solve each problem.

48. $5 + 0 =$ __5__   49. $0 + 1 =$ __1__   50. $7 + 0 =$ __7__
51. $5 \times 0 =$ __0__   52. $0 \times 1 =$ __0__   53. $7 \times 0 =$ __0__

54. Describe how you can remember the patterns for adding 0 and for multiplying by 0 so you won't get confused.
Answers will vary. _____
_____
_____

55. $5 + 1 =$ __6__   56. $1 + 2 =$ __3__   57. $7 + 1 =$ __8__
58. $5 \times 1 =$ __5__   59. $1 \times 2 =$ __2__   60. $7 \times 1 =$ __7__

61. Describe how you can remember the pattern for adding 1 and for multiplying by 1 so you won't get confused.
Answers will vary. _____
_____
_____

62. Write the two problems with the same answer.

(6 + 0)   6 + 1   6 × 0   (6 × 1)

Student Activity Book page 24

▶ Add and Multiply With 1 and 0 [WHOLE CLASS]

Students sometimes confuse the 1s and 0s patterns for multiplication with the 1s and 0s patterns for addition. Exercises 48–62 on Student Book page 24 will help students articulate and remember the differences in the patterns.

Math Talk Give students a few minutes to solve these problems and then allow them to share their answers.

When discussing exercise 54, ask students to make up situations that $5 + 0$ and 5×0 could represent. For exercise 61, have them make up situations for $5 + 1$ and 5×1. Point out that thinking of situations that a problem could represent is a good way to understand the problem and avoid errors. To help describe situations, encourage students to use pictures or models in their explanations.

② Going Further

Intervention   Activity Card FP-7

Identify Patterns   Activity Card FP-7 ●

Work: By Yourself

1. Copy the list below on your own paper.

$$5 \times 5 = \underline{}\,25 \quad 5 \times 2 = \underline{}\,10$$
$$5 \times 4 = \underline{}\,20 \quad 5 \times 1 = \underline{}\,5$$
$$5 \times 3 = \underline{}\,15 \quad 5 \times 0 = \underline{}\,0$$

2. Fill in the blanks for each multiplication equation.

3. Copy the following sentence and fill in the blank.

   The products keep decreasing by __five__.

4. Make and complete three similar lists of number sentences by changing the red 5s to another number of your choice.

Fluency Plan, Lesson 7   Copyright © Houghton Mifflin Company

Activity Note Have students identify any patterns, based on the number in red and the answer to the fill-in-the-blank sentence.

 Math Writing Prompt

Thinking About 0 Tell how multiplying by zero is different from adding zero. Use real-life examples in your explanation.

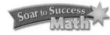 **Software Support**

Use *Soar to Success* for instruction of students needing targeted support for underlying skills.

▲ On Level   Activity Card FP-7

Adding Versus Multiplying   Activity Card FP-7 ▲

Work: In Pairs

Use:
• 10 Index cards

1. Label the index cards with the numbers 1 to 10.

2. Copy the equations below on a sheet of paper.

___ + 0 = ___	___ + 1 = ___
___ × 0 = ___	___ × 1 = ___
___ + 0 = ___	___ + 1 = ___
___ × 0 = ___	___ × 1 = ___
___ + 0 = ___	___ + 1 = ___

3. Shuffle the cards and place them face down in a stack.

4. Turn over the top card. Use the number on the card to fill in the first blank in the first equation. Then complete the equation.

5. Repeat steps 3 and 4 until the all the equations are completed.

Fluency Plan, Lesson 7   Copyright © Houghton Mifflin Company

Activity Note Remind students to carefully read each equation because there are two possible operations.

 Math Writing Prompt

Language Connections The Identity Property of Multiplication states that $1 \times n = n$. Explain how the name of the property can help you remember it.

 Software Support

Use *MegaMath* for review and reinforcement of the concepts and skills presented in this lesson.

■ Challenge   Activity Card FP-7

Letter Puzzles   Activity Card FP-7 ■

Work: In Small Groups

1. Copy the chart below on your own paper.

×	a	4	b
2	2	8	0
a	1	4	0
b	0	0	0

2. Study the chart to determine which letter represents 0. *b*

3. Study the chart to determine which letter represents 1. *a*

4. Math Talk What clues in the chart helped you determine the correct values for the variables?

Fluency Plan, Lesson 7   Copyright © Houghton Mifflin Company

Activity Note Extend the activity by having students create their own puzzles and exchange them to solve.

 Math Writing Prompt

Critical Thinking Explain why you can divide zero by any number but you cannot divide any number by zero.

 Software Support

Use *Destination Math* to take students beyond the concepts and skills presented in this lesson.

③ Homework and Spiral Review

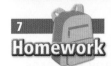

Homework **Goal:** Additional Practice

Use this Homework page to provide students with more practice with patterns in 0s and 1s. Have students circle any they did not know right away so they can practice them more.

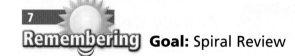

Remembering **Goal:** Spiral Review

This Remembering activity would be appropriate anytime after today's lesson.

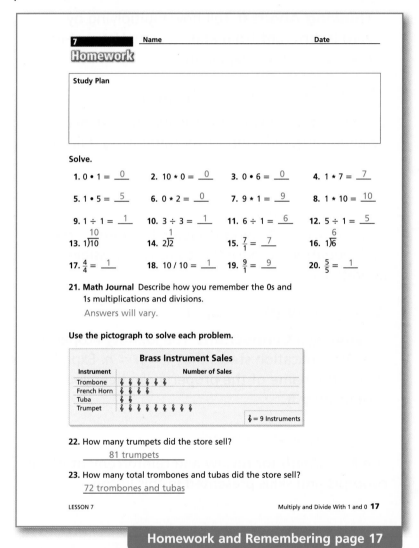

7   Name   Date

Homework

Study Plan

Solve.

1. $0 \cdot 1 = \underline{0}$ 2. $10 * 0 = \underline{0}$ 3. $0 \cdot 6 = \underline{0}$ 4. $1 * 7 = \underline{7}$

5. $1 \cdot 5 = \underline{5}$ 6. $0 * 2 = \underline{0}$ 7. $9 * 1 = \underline{9}$ 8. $1 * 10 = \underline{10}$

9. $1 \div 1 = \underline{1}$ 10. $3 \div 3 = \underline{1}$ 11. $6 \div 1 = \underline{6}$ 12. $5 \div 1 = \underline{5}$

13. $1\overline{)10}$ $\underline{10}$ 14. $2\overline{)2}$ $\underline{1}$ 15. $\frac{7}{1} = \underline{7}$ 16. $1\overline{)6}$ $\underline{6}$

17. $\frac{4}{4} = \underline{1}$ 18. $10 / 10 = \underline{1}$ 19. $\frac{9}{1} = \underline{9}$ 20. $\frac{5}{5} = \underline{1}$

21. **Math Journal** Describe how you remember the 0s and 1s multiplications and divisions.
    Answers will vary.

Use the pictograph to solve each problem.

Brass Instrument Sales

Instrument	Number of Sales
Trombone	🎼 🎼 🎼 🎼 🎼 🎼
French Horn	🎼 🎼 🎼
Tuba	🎼 🎼
Trumpet	🎼 🎼 🎼 🎼 🎼 🎼 🎼 🎼 🎼

🎼 = 9 Instruments

22. How many trumpets did the store sell?
    81 trumpets

23. How many total trombones and tubas did the store sell?
    72 trombones and tubas

LESSON 7   Multiply and Divide With 1 and 0 **17**

Homework and Remembering page 17

7   Name   Date

Remembering

Multiply.

1. $7 \cdot 5 = \underline{35}$ 2. $5 * 3 = \underline{15}$ 3. $1 \cdot 9 = \underline{9}$ 4. $9 * 3 = \underline{27}$

5. $1 \times 1 = \underline{1}$ 6. $1 \times 10 = \underline{10}$ 7. $6 \times 10 = \underline{60}$ 8. $8 \times 2 = \underline{16}$

9. $4 * 9 = \underline{36}$ 10. $2 \cdot 0 = \underline{0}$ 11. $8 * 9 = \underline{72}$ 12. $10 \cdot 9 = \underline{90}$

13. $3 \times 2 = \underline{6}$ 14. $10 \times 4 = \underline{40}$ 15. $5 \times 1 = \underline{5}$ 16. $6 \times 4 = \underline{24}$

17. $7 \cdot 10 = \underline{70}$ 18. $0 \cdot 3 = \underline{0}$ 19. $4 \cdot 5 = \underline{20}$ 20. $8 * 0 = \underline{0}$

21. $2 \times 4 = \underline{8}$ 22. $6 \times 2 = \underline{12}$ 23. $1 \times 3 = \underline{3}$ 24. $9 \times 1 = \underline{9}$

Solve each problem.

25. Jude had a package of 15 pencils. He gave 6 to his friend at school. How many pencils did he have left?
    9 pencils

26. Sam had 19 toy cars in his collection. Then he received 4 more toy cars for his birthday. How many toy cars does he have altogether?
    23 toy cars

27. Write and solve an addition or subtraction word problem.
    Answers will vary.

28. Complete the table.

Triangles t	t	6	9	1	0	4	5	20	300
Sides 3 · t	s	18	27	3	0	12	15	60	900

18 LESSON 7   Multiply and Divide With 1 and 0

Homework and Remembering page 18

Home or School Activity

 Real-World Connection

Sitting Around Tell students that to prepare for a large party, a restaurant manager is pushing small tables together. The final shape must be a square or a rectangle. Show students that eight people can sit around four small tables when they are pushed together as shown.

Ask students to draw an arrangement that allows 10 people to sit around the four tables and an arrangement that allows 14 people to sit around 6 small tables. Have students explain what these two arrangements have in common. **English Language Learners** would benefit from acting out this scenario.

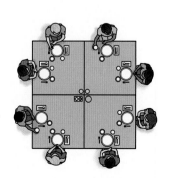

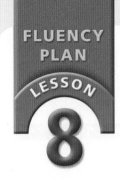

Fluency Day: 2s, 3s, 4s, 5s, 9s, and 10s

Lesson Objective

● Practice multiplications and divisions for 2s, 3s, 4s, 5s, 9s, and 10s in a variety of ways.

The Day at a Glance

Today's Goals	Materials
1 Teaching the Lesson A1: Use Checkup B to test the multiplications and divisions covered so far. A2: Use Product Cards to practice. **2 Going Further** ▶ Differentiated instruction **3 Homework and Spiral Review**	**Lesson Activities** Student Activity Book pp. 25–26, 26A–26B or Student Hardcover Book pp. 25–26 and Activity Workbook pp. 14–16 (includes Product Cards) Homework and Remembering pp. 19–22 (includes Product Cards) Checkup B Answer Key (TRB M10) Transparency of TRB M10 and overhead projector (optional) Product Cards: 2s, 3s, 4s, 5s, 9s (Manipulative Kit or TRB M6–M9 and M11–M12) **Going Further** Activity Cards FP-8 Product Cards: 3s and 4s (TRB M11–M12) Counters Multiplication table Math Journals

123 *Use* **Math Talk** *today!*

Keeping Skills Sharp

Quick Practice ⏱ 5 MINUTES	Daily Routines
Goal: Practice multiplications and divisions. **Materials:** Division Digits materials, Product Cards: 2s, 3s, 4s, 5s, 9s **Division Digits for 4s** Have a **Student Leader** run the activity, using problems from the 4s section of Set 2. (See Lesson 2) **Practice Multiplications with Product Cards** Have students practice their multiplications independently, using their Product Cards. (See Lesson 5)	**Homework Review** Ask students if they had difficulty with any part of the homework. Plan to set aside some time to work with students needing extra help. Save word problems from Remembering for use in Lesson 10. **Skip Count** Have students skip count: ▶ by 10s from 63 to 203 ▶ by 10s from 185 to 245

① Teaching the Lesson

Activity 1

Checkup B

 15 MINUTES

Goal: Use Checkup B to test the multiplications and divisions covered so far.

Materials: Student Activity Book p. 25 or Hardcover Book p. 25 and Activity Workbook p. 13; Checkup B Answer Key (TRB M10); transparency of Checkup B Answer Key and overhead projector (optional)

✔ **NCTM Standards:**
Number and Operations
Algebra

The Learning Classroom

Building Concepts The Checkup B Answer key on TRB M10 may be used by **Student Pairs** to quiz one another. One student can read the problems aloud, while the other says the answers.

English Language Learners

Read the game instructions aloud step by step and have a student volunteer help you model. Have students tell you what to do as you model each possibility in step 4.

- **Beginning** Ask: **Am I correct? Is student's name correct? Who has the higher card? Who gets the cards?**
- **Intermediate** Say: **(Student's name) is correct. I am wrong.** Ask: **Who gets the cards?** the student Say: **We are both correct. So, we see whose card is…?** higher
- **Advanced** Ask: **Who's correct? What happens?**

---

8 Class Activity

Name _____ Date _____

▶ Checkup B: 2s, 5s, 9s, 3s, 4s, 1s, 0s,

1. 5 * 3 = 15	19. 2)6̄ (3)	37. 9)27̄ (3)	55. 8 * 5 = 40
2. 1 • 5 = 5	20. 10 ÷ 5 = 2	38. 24/6 = 4	56. 4 × 3 = 12
3. 9 × 5 = 45	21. 4/2 = 2	39. 8 ÷ 2 = 4	57. 3 × 2 = 6
4. 9 × 3 = 27	22. 40 ÷ 5 = 8	40. 9 ÷ 9 = 1	58. 8 × 3 = 24
5. 4 • 8 = 32	23. 18/9 = 2	41. 50/5 = 10	59. 3 • 3 = 9
6. 8 * 3 = 24	24. 21 ÷ 7 = 3	42. 2)20̄ (10)	60. 7 * 3 = 21
7. 8 × 2 = 16	25. 36/9 = 4	43. 54 ÷ 9 = 6	61. 0 * 9 = 0
8. 10 • 4 = 40	26. 16 ÷ 2 = 8	44. 10)10̄ (1)	62. 2 * 4 = 8
9. 7 * 5 = 35	27. 5)15̄ (3)	45. 15/3 = 5	63. 5 • 10 = 50
10. 1 × 10 = 10	28. 90 ÷ 9 = 10	46. 10 • 6 = 60	64. 4 × 9 = 36
11. 81/9 = 9	29. 35 ÷ 5 = 7	47. 20 ÷ 10 = 2	65. 7 • 2 = 14
12. 5 * 4 = 20	30. 0/10 = 0	48. 70/10 = 7	66. 10 * 3 = 30
13. 9 × 7 = 63	31. 45/5 = 9	49. 5)30̄ (6)	67. 7 × 10 = 70
14. 5 • 6 = 30	32. 18/2 = 9	50. 80/10 = 8	68. 3 • 6 = 18
15. 7 * 4 = 28	33. 9)72̄ (8)	51. 72/9 = 8	69. 4 * 4 = 16
16. 6 × 9 = 54	34. 25 ÷ 5 = 5	52. 20/5 = 4	70. 2 • 0 = 0
17. 10 • 8 = 80	35. 63/9 = 7	53. 2)14̄ (7)	71. 7 * 4 = 28
18. 2 * 6 = 12	36. 12/2 = 6	54. 60 ÷ 10 = 6	72. 10 × 10 = 100

FLUENCY PLAN LESSON 8   Checkup B **25**

Student Activity Book page 25

▶ Checkup B   INDIVIDUALS

Tell students that today they will take Checkup B. This checkup tests the 2s, 5s, 9s, 3s, 4s, 1s, and 0s multiplications and divisions. This will allow them to see how much they have learned over the past few days. As before, the checkup will not be graded and students may work down rather than across.

Have students turn to Student Book page 25 and start the checkup on your signal.

▶ Check the Answers   INDIVIDUALS

Have students check their own answers or exchange papers with another student. TRB M10 is the answer key for the checkup. You can make copies of this for students to use, display it as an overhead, or simply read the answers aloud. Students should write the multiplications and divisions they missed on their Study Plans. Give students some time to study the problems they missed.

Activity 2

Product Cards for 3s and 4s

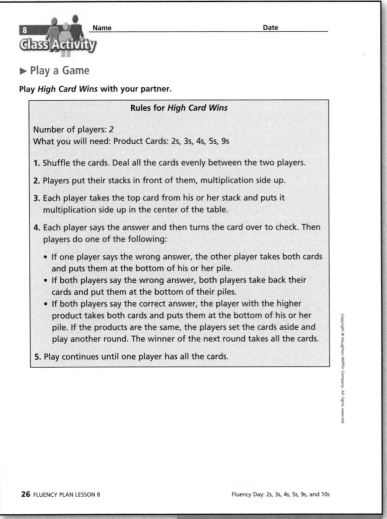

8
Class Activity

Name _____ Date _____

▶ Play a Game

Play *High Card Wins* with your partner.

Rules for *High Card Wins*

Number of players: *2*
What you will need: Product Cards: 2s, 3s, 4s, 5s, 9s

1. Shuffle the cards. Deal all the cards evenly between the two players.

2. Players put their stacks in front of them, multiplication side up.

3. Each player takes the top card from his or her stack and puts it multiplication side up in the center of the table.

4. Each player says the answer and then turns the card over to check. Then players do one of the following:

   • If one player says the wrong answer, the other player takes both cards and puts them at the bottom of his or her pile.
   • If both players say the wrong answer, both players take back their cards and put them at the bottom of their piles.
   • If both players say the correct answer, the player with the higher product takes both cards and puts them at the bottom of his or her pile. If the products are the same, the players set the cards aside and play another round. The winner of the next round takes all the cards.

5. Play continues until one player has all the cards.

26 FLUENCY PLAN LESSON 8   Fluency Day: 2s, 3s, 4s, 5s, 9s, and 10s

Student Activity Book page 26

▶ Play a Game [PAIRS]

Give each student a set of Product Cards for 3s and 4s or have them cut out the cards on pages 27 and 28. Have them combine all their cards—the old cards and these new cards—into a single pile. Have students read the rules for *High Card Wins* on page 26 and answer any questions they have about how to play the game. You might demonstrate by playing a round or two with a student. Some students may need a few minutes to practice the multiplications with Product Cards for 3s and 4s before playing the game with a partner.

▶ Sort the Cards [INDIVIDUALS]

Have students sort their Product Cards into *Fast*, *Slow*, and *Don't Know* piles. They can choose whether to sort by multiplication or by division. They should choose the operation that is most difficult for them.

Activity continued ▶

 30 MINUTES

Goal: Use Product Cards to practice.

Materials: Product Cards: 2s, 3s, 4s, 5s, 9s (Manipulative Kit or TRB); Student Activity Book pp. 26, 26A–26B or Hardcover Book p. 26 and Activity Workbook pp. 14–16; Homework and Remembering pp. 21–22

 NCTM Standards:
Number and Operations
Algebra

Teaching Note

Practice Product Cards Remind students of how important it is to practice at home to get really fast. Discuss how they will be able to take home Product Cards and sort them in these same ways. They can mix their 3s and 4s with their old 2s, 5s, and 9s Product Cards already at home or keep them separate.

Class Management

Product Cards at Home If you have the Product Cards from the Manipulative Kit, you can have students use the cards on the student pages as a home practice set. Black and white versions of the cards also appear on the Homework pages 21–22 and on pages M11–M12 in the Teacher's Resource Book.

The Learning Classroom

Math Talk As students play the game encourage them to let others finish their sentences before they speak. Also, remind students to keep their voices down so they do not disturb others.

Teaching the Lesson (continued)

 Ongoing Assessment

Ask students to:

▶ Pick one product card and say the related multiplication or division equation before looking at the answer.

▶ Say a sentence that suggests multiplication. For example, there are 4 rows of 5 desks in the classroom.

📁 **Class Management**

Looking Ahead Problems 6 and 7 of tonight's homework ask students to write and solve word problems. Tomorrow, collect these problems and save them. In Lesson 10, students will solve problems their classmates have written.

▶ **Product Cards for Home**

There is a set of Product Cards for 3s and 4s on Homework and Remembering pages 21–22. Students can cut out the cards and take them home to play the *High Card Wins* game or any other game.

At home, students may also use the Product Cards as flash cards to practice their multiplications and divisions with the aid of a family member.

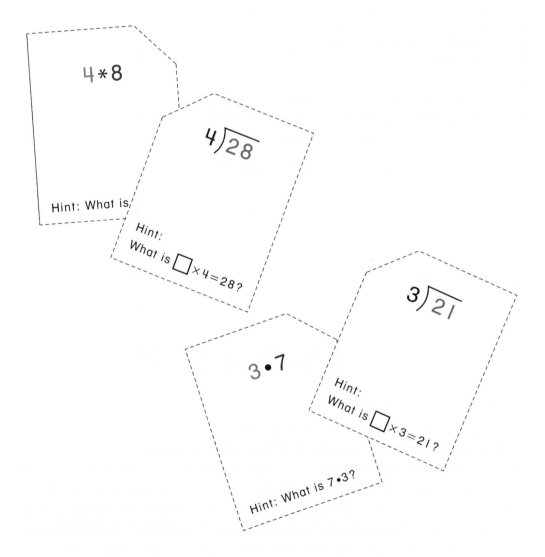

②Going Further

● Intervention — Activity Card FP-8

Make a Model
Activity Card FP-8 ●

Work: In Pairs

Use:
- Product Cards: 3s, 4s (TRB M11)
- Counters

1. Shuffle the product cards.

2. One partner selects a card and reads the multiplication problem.

3. The other partner models the problem, using counters. Two possible layouts for 3 × 5 are shown below.

3 Groups of 5   3-by-5 Array

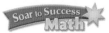

4. Exchange roles and repeat steps 2 and 3.

Fluency Plan, Lesson 8   Copyright © Houghton Mifflin Company

Activity Note Remind students that there are a variety of models they can use, but they only have to create one model.

 Math Writing Prompt

Draw a Picture Draw a picture that shows 4 × 6. Then write the equation.

Soar to Success Math **Software Support**

Use *Soar to Success* for instruction of students needing targeted support for underlying skills.

▲ On Level — Activity Card FP-8

Watch the Signs
Activity Card FP-8 ▲

Work: By Yourself

1. Copy the problems below.

$0 + 8 = \underline{8}$ $1 \times 9 = \underline{9}$
$3 \times 0 = \underline{0}$ $5 + 1 = \underline{6}$
$0 \div 4 = \underline{0}$ $9 \div 9 = \underline{1}$
$5 \times 0 = \underline{0}$ $3 - 3 = \underline{0}$
$7 \times 1 = \underline{7}$ $0 \div 3 = \underline{0}$

2. Answer the problems as quickly as you can.

3. Compare your answers with those of another student.

4. Math Talk Discuss how someone might get an incorrect answer.

Fluency Plan, Lesson 8   Copyright © Houghton Mifflin Company

Activity Note Extend the activity by having students create 10 of their own fluency problems and exchanging them with a partner.

 Math Writing Prompt

Write a Rhyme Create clever or humorous rhymes to match multiplications or divisions. For example: I know 3 times 2 is 6.
    So is 2 plus 2 plus 2 sticks.

MegaMath Grades K-6 **Software Support**

Use *MegaMath* for review and reinforcement of the concepts and skills presented in this lesson.

■ Challenge — Activity Card FP-8

Square Numbers
Activity Card FP-8 ■

Work: By Yourself

Use:
- Multiplication Table (TRB M2)

1. A square number is the product of a whole number and itself. For example, 3 × 3 = 9, so 9 is a square number.

2. Identify all of the square numbers on a multiplication table. 1, 4, 9, 16, 25, 36, 49, 64, 81, 100

3. Identify any pattern that is formed by the square numbers on the multiplication table. They form a diagonal on the multiplication table.

4. Add two rows and two columns to the multiplication table. Write the 11s and 12s multiples. What new square numbers did you add? 121 and 144

5. Write About It Why do you think a square number is called "square"? Answers will vary, but should refer to having an array of factors that is square.

Fluency Plan, Lesson 8   Copyright © Houghton Mifflin Company

Activity Note Have students make the array for 3 × 3 to reinforce the terminology *square number*.

 Math Writing Prompt

Explain Your Thinking Explain how adding 0 to a number differs from multiplying a number by 0.

✳ DESTINATION Math **Software Support**

Use *Destination Math* to take students beyond the concepts and skills presented in this lesson.

③ Homework and Spiral Review

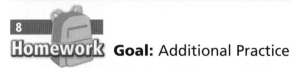

Homework **Goal:** Additional Practice

Use this Homework page to provide students more practice with multiplying and dividing by 2s, 3s, 4s, 5s, 9s, and 10s.

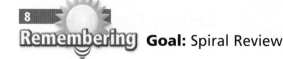

Remembering **Goal:** Spiral Review

This Remembering activity would be appropriate anytime after today's lesson.

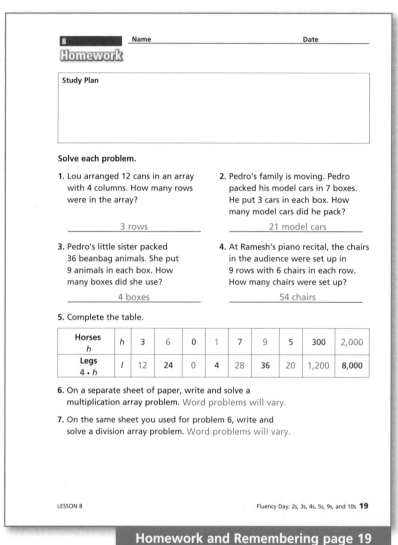

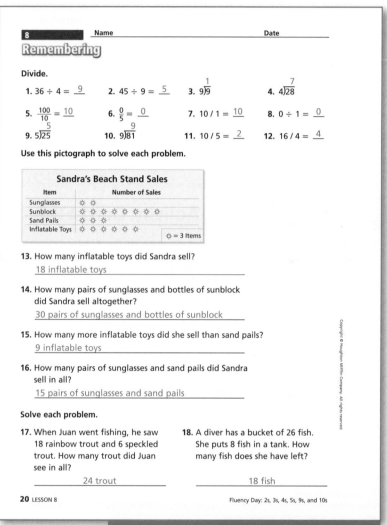

Homework and Remembering page 19

Homework and Remembering page 20

The detailed worksheet content:

Homework page 19

| 8 | Name _____ Date _____ |

Homework

Study Plan

Solve each problem.

1. Lou arranged 12 cans in an array with 4 columns. How many rows were in the array?
   _____ 3 rows _____

2. Pedro's family is moving. Pedro packed his model cars in 7 boxes. He put 3 cars in each box. How many model cars did he pack?
   _____ 21 model cars _____

3. Pedro's little sister packed 36 beanbag animals. She put 9 animals in each box. How many boxes did she use?
   _____ 4 boxes _____

4. At Ramesh's piano recital, the chairs in the audience were set up in 9 rows with 6 chairs in each row. How many chairs were set up?
   _____ 54 chairs _____

5. Complete the table.

Horses h	h	3	6	0	1	7	9	5	300	2,000
Legs $4 \cdot h$	l	12	24	0	4	28	36	20	1,200	8,000

6. On a separate sheet of paper, write and solve a multiplication array problem. Word problems will vary.

7. On the same sheet you used for problem 6, write and solve a division array problem. Word problems will vary.

LESSON 8 | Fluency Day: 2s, 3s, 4s, 5s, 9s, and 10s **19**

Remembering page 20

| 8 | Name _____ Date _____ |

Remembering

Divide.

1. $36 \div 4 = \underline{9}$
2. $45 \div 9 = \underline{5}$
3. $9)\overline{9}$ = 1
4. $4)\overline{28}$ = 7
5. $\frac{100}{10} = \underline{10}$
6. $\frac{0}{5} = \underline{0}$
7. $10 / 1 = \underline{10}$
8. $0 \div 1 = \underline{0}$
9. $5)\overline{25}$ = 5
10. $9)\overline{81}$ = 9
11. $10 / 5 = \underline{2}$
12. $16 / 4 = \underline{4}$

Use this pictograph to solve each problem.

Sandra's Beach Stand Sales

Item	Number of Sales
Sunglasses	☼ ☼
Sunblock	☼ ☼ ☼ ☼ ☼ ☼
Sand Pails	☼ ☼ ☼
Inflatable Toys	☼ ☼ ☼ ☼ ☼

☼ = 3 Items

13. How many inflatable toys did Sandra sell?
    18 inflatable toys

14. How many pairs of sunglasses and bottles of sunblock did Sandra sell altogether?
    30 pairs of sunglasses and bottles of sunblock

15. How many more inflatable toys did she sell than sand pails?
    9 inflatable toys

16. How many pairs of sunglasses and sand pails did Sandra sell in all?
    15 pairs of sunglasses and sand pails

Solve each problem.

17. When Juan went fishing, he saw 18 rainbow trout and 6 speckled trout. How many trout did Juan see in all?
    _____ 24 trout _____

18. A diver has a bucket of 26 fish. She puts 8 fish in a tank. How many fish does she have left?
    _____ 18 fish _____

20 LESSON 8 | Fluency Day: 2s, 3s, 4s, 5s, 9s, and 10s

Home or School Activity

 Social Studies Connection

I Spy 3s and 4s Ask students to find or think of food, clothing, and other items that are sold in packages of 3 or 4. For example, pairs of socks are often sold in packs of 3. Have students list as many items as they can, and then post the results on the bulletin board or create a class list with pictures of the packages of 3 or 4.

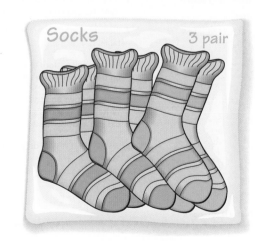

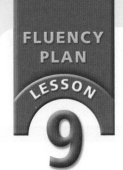

Related Equations

Vocabulary

inverse operations
Factor Triangle
Fast Array
Commutative Property
  of Multiplication

Lesson Objectives

● Understand the relationship between factors and their product.

● Understand the relationship between multiplication and division.

The Day at a Glance

Today's Goals	Materials	
1 Teaching the Lesson **A1:** Write and describe related equations based on a Factor Triangle and a Fast Array. **A2:** Write about the relationship between multiplication and division. **A3:** Use Write-On Sheets and Check Sheets to practice.	**Lesson Activities** Student Activity Book pp. 27–32 or Student Hardcover Book pp. 27–32 and Activity Workbook pp. 17–20 (includes Class Write-On Sheets and Check Sheets) Homework and Remembering pp. 23–28 (includes Home Write-On Sheets and Check Sheets) Sheet protectors Dry-erase markers	**Going Further** Activity Cards FP-9 Index cards Math Journals
2 Going Further ▸ Differentiated Instruction		
3 Homework and Spiral Review		

123 Use Math Talk today!

Keeping Skills Sharp

Quick Practice ⏱ 5 MINUTES	Daily Routines	
Goal: Practice multiplications and divisions. **Materials:** Division Digits materials, Product Cards: 2s, 3s, 4s, 5s, 9s **Division Digits for 4s** Have a **Student Leader** run the activity, using problems from the 4s section of Set 2. (See Lesson 2) **Practice Multiplications with Product Cards** Have students practice their multiplications independently using their Product Cards. (See Lesson 5)	**Homework Review** Ask several students to share the problems they wrote for homework. Have the class ask clarifying questions about each problem. Collect student homework problems.	**Draw a Picture** Mr. Kaku has 63 CDs. Each shelf of his CD storage unit holds 9 CDs. Draw a picture to show how many shelves Mr. Kaku's CDs will fill. *7 shelves*

① Teaching the Lesson

Eight Related Equations

 20 MINUTES

Goal: Write and describe related equations based on a Factor Triangle and a Fast Array.

Materials: Student Activity Book or Hardcover Book p. 27

 NCTM Standards:
Communication
Number and Operations
Algebra

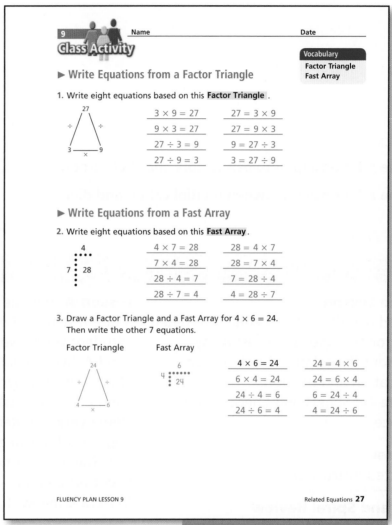

Student Activity Book page 27

► Write Equations from a Factor Triangle INDIVIDUALS

Have students look at the drawing in exercise 1 on Student Book page 27. Explain that the diagram is called a Factor Triangle. Ask:

● Which numbers in this triangle are the factors? 3 and 9

● Where are the factors located in the triangle? on the bottom

● Which number is the product? 27

● Where is the product located on the triangle? at the top

Explain that it is possible to write eight different equations—some multiplication and some division—based on one factor triangle. Use **Solve and Discuss** to challenge students to find all eight related equations for this triangle.

Some students may not realize that they can write an equation with the "answer" on the left side of the equals sign. For example, although they may write $3 \times 9 = 27$, they may not know that writing $27 = 3 \times 9$ is also correct. Explain that an equals (=) sign simply indicates that the expressions on both sides of an equation have the same value. It does not matter which expression goes on which side.

Here are the eight related equations for exercise 1. Students may write them in a different order.

$3 \times 9 = 27$	$27 = 3 \times 9$
$9 \times 3 = 27$	$27 = 9 \times 3$
$27 \div 3 = 9$	$9 = 27 \div 3$
$27 \div 9 = 3$	$3 = 27 \div 9$

123 Math Talk Discuss the relationships students might recognize among the equations. Make sure the following relationships are mentioned:

● For each multiplication equation, there is a corresponding multiplication equation with the factors in the reverse order. For example, $3 \times 9 = 27$ and $9 \times 3 = 27$. Name the property that tells us we can switch the order of the factors without changing the product.
Commutative Property of Multiplication

● For every division equation, there is a corresponding division equation with the quotient and divisor switched. For example, $9 = 27 \div 3$ and $3 = 27 \div 9$.

● Division undoes multiplication, and vice versa. We describe this relationship by saying that multiplication and division are **inverse operations**. For example, $3 \times 9 = 27$ and $27 \div 3 = 9$, and $27 \div 9 = 3$ and $3 \times 9 = 27$.

Activity continued ▶

Teaching Note

A Balanced Equation You might relate an equation to a balanced scale. If the weights in the pans are switched, the scale remains balanced. Likewise, equal values on both sides of an equation can be switched. If possible, use an actual balance scale with **English Learners**.

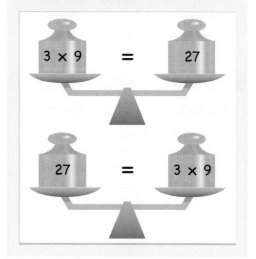

Teaching Note

Vocabulary Students have been using the language *related equations*. After this lesson, they should be able to explain that multiplication and division are inverse operations because one operation undoes the other. Ask them to illustrate this with two equations. Example: $4 \times 5 = 20$; $20 \div 5 = 4$

Activity 1

▶ Write Equations from a Fast Array INDIVIDUALS

Using **Solve and Discuss**, have students write eight related equations based on the Fast Array in exercise 2 on Student Book page 27.

Here are the eight related equations for exercise 2. Students may write them in a different order.

$$4 \times 7 = 28 \qquad 28 = 4 \times 7$$
$$7 \times 4 = 28 \qquad 28 = 7 \times 4$$
$$28 \div 4 = 7 \qquad 7 = 28 \div 4$$
$$28 \div 7 = 4 \qquad 4 = 28 \div 7$$

Select less advanced students to discuss the relationships they see among the equations. Invite other students to provide help and to make suggestions as needed. After students have expressed relationships among the equations in their own words, help them restate some of the relationships using math language. Encourage students to use mathematical terms like Commutative Property and inverse operations. Emphasize that it is important for students to be able to explain ideas in their own words because it shows they understand the ideas. However, it is also important to practice using math vocabulary.

Have students look at exercise 3. Only one multiplication equation is given. Ask students the following questions about the problem:

- Which numbers are the factors of this equation? 4 and 6
- Which number is the product? 24
- Which number will be the dividend in a related division equation? 24
- When you draw the Factor Triangle, which number goes on top? Which numbers go on the bottom? 24 goes on top; 4 and 6 go on the bottom
- When you draw the Fast Array, which numbers go on the left and on the top? 4 and 6

Write About Multiplication and Division

Name _____ Date _____

▶ **Discuss the Relationship Between Multiplication and Division**

4. Write your ideas about how multiplication and division are related.

   Answers will vary.

   _____
   _____
   _____
   _____
   _____
   _____
   _____
   _____

5. Explain how you can start with one multiplication or division equation and then write seven other equations.

   Answers will vary.

   _____
   _____
   _____
   _____
   _____
   _____
   _____
   _____
   _____

28 FLUENCY PLAN LESSON 9   Related Equations

Student Activity Book page 28

---

15 MINUTES

Goal: Write about the relationship between multiplication and division.

Materials: Student Activity Book or Hardcover Book p. 28

 NCTM Standards:
Communication
Number and Operations
Algebra

 Ongoing Assessment

Have students write:

▶ a related multiplication equation and a related division equation for $3 \times 5 = 15$.

▶ a related multiplication equation and a related division equation for $24 \div 6 = 4$.

▶ Discuss the Relationship Between Multiplication and Divison INDIVIDUALS   Math Talk

Read aloud exercises 4 and 5 on page 28 to make sure that students know what to do. Have students write their explanations on Student Activity Book page 28 or in their Math Journals. As you observe students, look for those who are writing clear, articulate statements. Then ask these students to read what they have written to the class. Encourage other students to comment on the statements and to ask questions. Guide the discussion so that students:

● Ask and answer clarifying questions.

● Restate statements made by others and explain why the statements are reasonable.

● Use reasoning to show that they understand the connection between multiplication and division.

Activity 3

Write-On and Check Sheets

 10 MINUTES

Goal: Use Write-On Sheets and Check Sheets to practice.

Materials: Student Activity Book pp. 29–32 or Hardcover Book pp. 29–32 and Activity Workbook pp. 17–20; sheet protectors, dry-erase markers; Homework and Remembering pp. 25–28

 NCTM Standards:
Number and Operations
Algebra

Class Management

Looking Ahead In Lesson 10, students will solve some of the word problems they have written for Homework in Lessons 4 and 8 and Remembering in Lessons 6 and 7. Before Lesson 10, select problems of a variety of types from those you have collected. Try to choose an equal number of multiplication and division problems. To save time in class, you may want to create a transparency or a handout of the problems, or write them on the board before you begin the lesson.

Teaching Note

What to Expect from Students

We are practicing multiplication in long-division format to help students relate multiplication and division.

Review with students the long-division format of the multiplication problems on Write-On Sheet 1A.

- The factors are the numbers to the left and on the top of the division symbol.

- The product is the number under the division symbol. It is also called the dividend.

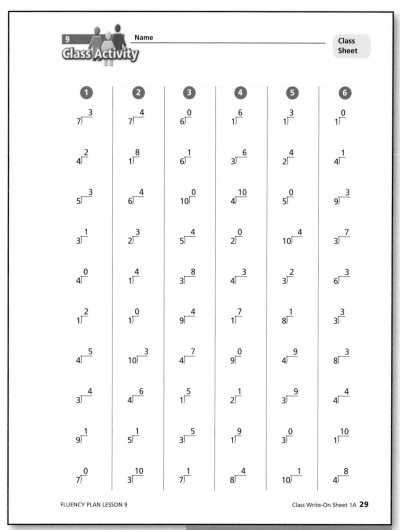

Student Activity Book page 29

▶ Write-On Sheets [INDIVIDUALS]

Give each student a sheet protector and a dry-erase marker. Have students tear out the Class Write-On Sheets 1A and 1B on pages 29–30. These class sheets can be found on TRB M13–M14. Ask students to put the sheets back-to-back in a sheet protector.

▶ Practice With Write-On and Check Sheets [PAIRS]

Give students a few minutes to practice with the Write-On Sheets. Have students check their answers and update their study plans. Tell students to use Check Sheets 1A and 1B on Student Book pages 31–32 (TRB M15–M16) to quiz one another or practice individually. (See page 123 for using Check Sheets to study alone.)

Have students use *Home* Write-On and Check Sheets on Homework and Remembering pages 25–28 for practice with their multiplications and divisions either by themselves or with a family member.

②Going Further

Intervention   Activity Card FP-9

Change-A-Round   Activity Card FP-9 ●

Work: In Pairs

Use:
• 5 Index cards

1. Write an equal sign (=) on one card.

2. On another card, write a multiplication sign (×) on one side and a division sign (÷) on the other side.

3. Write two factors and their product, each on one of the remaining three cards.

4. One partner uses the 5 cards to write a multiplication equation. A sample is shown below. The other partner records the equation.

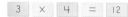

5. Switch tasks and continue until you have written and recorded all the multiplication and division equations possible using the three numbers.

Fluency Plan, Lesson 9   Copyright © Houghton Mifflin Company

Activity Note Have student pairs repeat the activity with a new set of factors and product.

 Math Writing Prompt

Draw a Picture Draw a picture that shows $3 \times 5 = 15$. Then draw a picture that shows $15 \div 3 = 5$. Tell what is the same and what is different about the pictures.

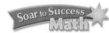 **Software Support**

Use *Soar to Success* for instruction of students needing targeted support for underlying skills.

On Level   Activity Card FP-9

Who's Related to 12?   Activity Card FP-9 ▲

Work: In Pairs

Use:
• Multiplication Table (TRB M2)

1. Identify the three factor pairs for 12.
   2×6; 3×4; 1×12

2. Write the eight related equations for each factor pair you found. See below.

3. Math Talk Add two rows and two columns to a multiplication table for 11s and 12s. Discuss how you can find all of the factor pairs of a number by using a multiplication table. Find all of the locations of the number inside the table. For each one, move to the top of the column and to the left to find the factors.

2. $2 \times 6 = 12$; $6 \times 2 = 12$; $12 = 2 \times 6$; $12 = 6 \times 2$; $12 \div 2 = 6$; $12 \div 6 = 2$; $2 = 12 \div 6$; $6 = 12 \div 2$

$3 \times 4 = 12$; $4 \times 3 = 12$; $12 = 3 \times 4$; $12 = 4 \times 3$; $12 \div 3 = 4$; $12 \div 4 = 3$; $3 = 12 \div 4$; $4 = 12 \div 3$

$12 \times 1 = 12$; $1 \times 12 = 12$; $12 = 12 \times 1$; $12 = 1 \times 12$; $12 \div 1 = 12$; $12 \div 12 = 1$; $1 = 12 \div 12$; $12 = 12 \div 1$

Fluency Plan, Lesson 9   Copyright © Houghton Mifflin Company

Activity Note Extend the activity by having students predict how many total equations will be written for the factor pairs of 10. 16

 Math Writing Prompt

Explain Why List all the related equations for $3 \times 3 = 9$. Explain why there are fewer than 8 related equations.

 Software Support

Use *MegaMath* for review and reinforcement of the concepts and skills presented in this lesson.

Challenge   Activity Card FP-9

It's a Race   Activity Card FP-9 ■

Work: In Pairs

Use:
• 10 Index cards

1. Label each of the index cards with the numbers 1 to 10.

2. Shuffle the cards and place them face down.

3. Randomly select 2 cards from the deck.

4. Race each other to see who can be the first to write all the related multiplication and division equations for those cards.

Fluency Plan, Lesson 9   Copyright © Houghton Mifflin Company

Activity Note Students can play best out of five and then switch partners with another pair of students.

 Math Writing Prompt

Summarize Explain how the Commutative Property and inverse operations help you write related equations.

 DESTINATION Math **Software Support**

Use *Destination Math* to take students beyond the concepts and skills presented in this lesson.

③ Homework and Spiral Review

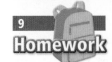

9
Homework **Goal:** Additional Practice

Use this Homework page to provide students with more practice with multiplying and dividing with 0s, 1s, 3s, and 4s.

9
Remembering **Goal:** Spiral Review

This Remembering activity would be appropriate anytime after today's lesson.

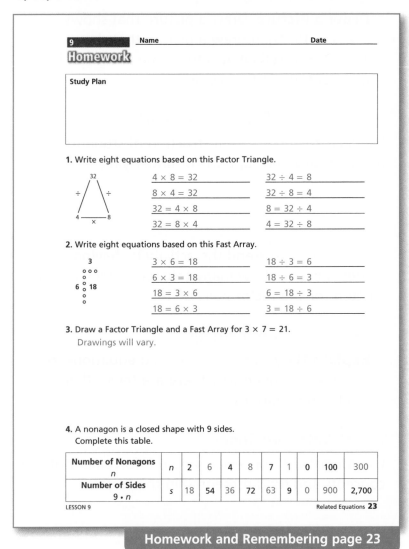

9   Name _____ Date _____

Homework

Study Plan

1. Write eight equations based on this Factor Triangle.

4 × 8 = 32	32 ÷ 4 = 8
8 × 4 = 32	32 ÷ 8 = 4
32 = 4 × 8	8 = 32 ÷ 4
32 = 8 × 4	4 = 32 ÷ 8

32
4 × 8

2. Write eight equations based on this Fast Array.

3 × 6 = 18	18 ÷ 3 = 6
6 × 3 = 18	18 ÷ 6 = 3
18 = 3 × 6	6 = 18 ÷ 3
18 = 6 × 3	3 = 18 ÷ 6

3. Draw a Factor Triangle and a Fast Array for 3 × 7 = 21.
Drawings will vary.

4. A nonagon is a closed shape with 9 sides. Complete this table.

Number of Nonagons n	n	2	6	4	8	7	1	0	100	300
Number of Sides $9 \cdot n$	s	18	54	36	72	63	9	0	900	2,700

LESSON 9   Related Equations **23**

Homework and Remembering page 23

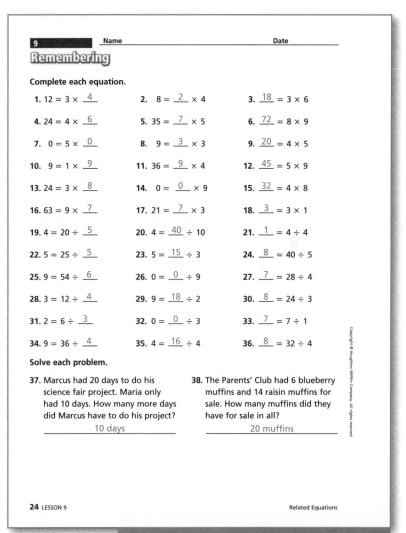

9   Name _____ Date _____

Remembering

Complete each equation.

1. 12 = 3 × _4_   **2.** 8 = _2_ × 4   **3.** _18_ = 3 × 6

4. 24 = 4 × _6_   **5.** 35 = _7_ × 5   **6.** _72_ = 8 × 9

7. 0 = 5 × _0_   **8.** 9 = _3_ × 3   **9.** _20_ = 4 × 5

10. 9 = 1 × _9_   **11.** 36 = _9_ × 4   **12.** _45_ = 5 × 9

13. 24 = 3 × _8_   **14.** 0 = _0_ × 9   **15.** _32_ = 4 × 8

16. 63 = 9 × _7_   **17.** 21 = _7_ × 3   **18.** _3_ = 3 × 1

19. 4 = 20 ÷ _5_   **20.** 4 = _40_ ÷ 10   **21.** _1_ = 4 ÷ 4

22. 5 = 25 ÷ _5_   **23.** 5 = _15_ ÷ 3   **24.** _8_ = 40 ÷ 5

25. 9 = 54 ÷ _6_   **26.** 0 = _0_ ÷ 9   **27.** _7_ = 28 ÷ 4

28. 3 = 12 ÷ _4_   **29.** 9 = _18_ ÷ 2   **30.** _8_ = 24 ÷ 3

31. 2 = 6 ÷ _3_   **32.** 0 = _0_ ÷ 3   **33.** _7_ = 7 ÷ 1

34. 9 = 36 ÷ _4_   **35.** 4 = _16_ ÷ 4   **36.** _8_ = 32 ÷ 4

Solve each problem.

37. Marcus had 20 days to do his science fair project. Maria only had 10 days. How many more days did Marcus have to do his project?
_____10 days_____

38. The Parents' Club had 6 blueberry muffins and 14 raisin muffins for sale. How many muffins did they have for sale in all?
_____20 muffins_____

24 LESSON 9   Related Equations

Homework and Remembering page 24

Home or School Activity

Math-to-Math Connection

Sharing Coins Put some real or play money—pennies and nickels—whose total is 40 cents or less in a bag. At each turn, a student or family member draws a handful of coins from the bag, counts the money, and then determines whether the amount of money can be shared evenly by 3 or 4 people. If the amount can be shared evenly, the player names a related multiplication or division fact for the situation.

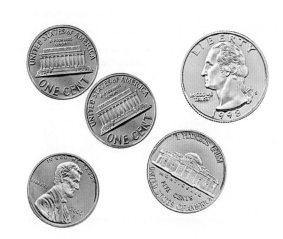

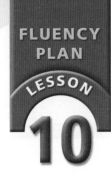

Group and Array Word Problems

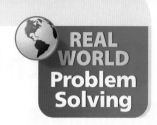

REAL WORLD Problem Solving

Lesson Objectives

- Apply understanding of repeated-groups and arrays to word problems.
- Relate repeated subtraction to division.

The Day at a Glance

Today's Goals	Materials	

1 Teaching the Lesson
A1: Identify the problem type for multiplication and division word problems.
A2: Develop and practice methods for solving multiplication and division word problems.
A3: Write word problems of given types.
A4: Connect the concept of repeated subtraction to division.
 	
2 Going Further
▶ Differentiated Instruction
 	
3 Homework and Spiral Review
	Lesson Activities
	Student Activity Book pp. 33–34 or
	  Student Hardcover Book pp. 33–34
	Homework and Remembering
	  pp. 29–30
	Student-created word problems
	  from previous lessons
		Going Further
		Activity Cards FP-10
		Student Book p. 33
		5-part spinner
		Math Journals

123 Use Math Talk today!

Keeping Skills Sharp

Quick Practice ⏱ 5 MINUTES	Daily Routines	
Goal: Practice multiplications and divisions. **Materials:** Division Digits materials, Product Cards: 2s, 3s, 4s, 5s, 9s **Division Digits for 3s and 4s** Have the **Student Leader** run the activity using problems from the 3s and 4s sections of Set 2. (See Lesson 2) **Practice Multiplications with Product Cards** Have students practice their multiplications independently, using their Product Cards. (See Lesson 5)	**Homework Review** Send two students to the board to show their solutions for problem 2. Have each student at the board explain the solution. Encourage the rest of the class to ask clarifying questions and make summary comments.	**Reasoning** Bella, Tom, Juan, and Katie are different heights. Their heights are 6 feet, 5 feet, 4 feet, and 3 feet. Bella is not 6 feet or 5 feet tall. Tom is not 6 feet or 4 feet tall. Katie is 3 feet tall. How tall is Juan? 6 feet tall

①Teaching the Lesson

Activity 1

Identify Problem Type

🕐 **20 MINUTES**

Goal: Identify the problem type for multiplication and division word problems.

Materials: Student Activity Book or Hardcover Book p. 33

✓ **NCTM Standards:**
Communication
Problem Solving
Representation

 Class Management

Looking Ahead In Activity 2, students will solve some of the problems they wrote for Homework in Lessons 4 and 8 and Remembring in Lessons 6 and 7. Before the lesson, select several problems. Try to choose an equal number of the various types of multiplication and division problems. To save time, you may want to create a transparency or a handout of the problems, or write them on the board before you begin the activity.

English Language Learners

Make sure students understand *group size* and *repeated groups*. Say: **There are 5 families. There are 4 people in each family.**

• **Beginning** Ask: **How many people are in each family?** 4 Say: **The *group size* is 4.** Ask: **How many groups are there?** 5 Say: **We repeat the group 5 times. 4 × 5 = ____.** 20

• **Intermediate and Advanced** Ask: **Which number is the *group size*?** 4 **How many times do we repeat it?** 5 **What kind of multiplication is this?** repeated groups

---

> 10 **Class Activity**
> Name _____ Date _____
>
> **Vocabulary**
> Array
> Repeated-Groups
>
> ▶ Identify the Problem Type
>
> **Identify the type for each problem. Choose from this list. (Write the letter, not the words.)**
>
>   **a.** **Array** Multiplication
>   **b.** Array Division
>   **c.** **Repeated-Groups** Multiplication
>   **d.** Repeated-Groups Division with Unknown Group Size
>   **e.** Repeated-Groups Division with Unknown Multiplier (number of groups)
>
> **For each multiplication problem, write a multiplication equation. For each division problem, write both a division equation and a multiplication equation.**
>
> 1. Latisha's uncle gave her 32 stamps and a new stamp book. The book has 8 pages, and she put the same number of stamps on each page. How many stamps did she put on each page?
>   Problem type: ___d___   Equation(s): $32 ÷ 8 = 4$, $8 × 4 = 32$
>
> 2. A parking lot has 7 rows of parking spaces. Each row has 7 spaces. How many cars can park in the lot?
>   Problem type: ___a___   Equation(s): $7 × 7 = 49$
>
> 3. Janine planted 5 rows of roses. If she planted a total of 40 roses, how many did she plant in each row?
>   Problem type: ___b___   Equation(s): $40 ÷ 5 = 8$, $5 × 8 = 40$
>
> 4. The produce market sells oranges in bags of 6. Santos bought 4 bags. How many oranges did he buy?
>   Problem type: ___c___   Equation(s): $4 × 6 = 24$
>
> ▶ Write Word Problems
>
> 5. Math Journal Write two word problems of different types.
> Word problems will vary.
>
> FLUENCY PLAN LESSON 10   Group and Array Word Problems **33**

Student Activity Book page 33

▶ Identify the Problem Type [INDIVIDUALS]

Read the instructions on Student Book page 33. Make sure students understand the following:

● They need only give the letter corresponding to the problem type.

● They need to write one equation for each multiplication problem and two equations for each division problem (a mystery multiplication equation and a division equation).

● They do not need to actually solve the problem.

For each problem, choose a student to share the problem type and equation(s) he or she wrote. Ask if everyone agrees. If not, have a class discussion about the problem and agree on the correct answers.

Student Word Problems

▶ Read and Solve Problems   INDIVIDUALS

If you made handouts of students' problems, distribute them. If you made an overhead, display it. Otherwise, write each problem on the board or read it aloud. Then use **Solve and Discuss** for each problem. Ask presenters to give the problem type before discussing their solutions.

This should be a summary activity. Most students should be able to differentiate multiplication problems from division problems and explain how they know which operation is needed. At this point, most students should be finding answers by writing and solving equations. Encourage those students who are still making drawings to try to use numerical methods. Suggest they try the 5s shortcut or Close Count-By shortcut.

 20 MINUTES

Goal: Develop and practice methods for solving multiplication and division word problems.

Materials: Student-created word problems from previous lessons

 NCTM Standards:
Communication
Problem Solving
Reasoning and Proof

Write Word Problems

▶ Write Word Problems   SMALL GROUPS

Have students work in **Student Pairs** or **Small Groups** to write one problem of each type listed on Student Book page 33.

Select students to read one of their problems, and have the other students identify the problem type.

- Array Multiplication
- Array Division
- Repeated-Groups Multiplication
- Repeated-Groups Division with Unknown Group Size
- Repeated-Groups Division with Unknown Multiplier (number of groups)

Writing word problems is much harder than solving them. Writing problems requires students to understand the situational structure of the problem. By this time of the year, some students may still be confusing problems with unknown group size partitive division and problems with unknown number of groups measurement division. This sometimes is just a confusion of the verbal labels. It is important that all students understand that both of these kinds of situations are division situations, but all students do not need to master writing specified types of word problems by name. It is important that they can use their own words and the words *multiplier* and *group size* to describe aspects of situations given visually or as word problems.

 20 MINUTES

Goal: Write word problems of given types.

Materials: Student Activity Book or Hardcover Book p. 33

 NCTM Standards:
Communication
Problem Solving
Representation

Differentiated Instruction

Extra Help Have students circle the numbers that they find in the word problem as they read the problem. Next, tell students to look for words in the problem that help them know what to do, such as "divided equally," or "same number of." Then, have students use the numbers to write a number sentence.

Teaching the Lesson (continued)

Repeated Subtraction

 30 MINUTES

Goal: Connect the concept of repeated subtraction to division.

Materials: Student Activity Book or Hardcover Book p. 34

✔ **NCTM Standards:**
Communication
Problem Solving
Representation

The Learning Classroom

Math Talk Have students practice explaining one another's work in their own words. Begin by having a volunteer write one of his or her problems on the board. Or, if you want to use a problem that you have preselected, identify the "author." Then as the students point to parts of the problem, another student identifies the parts, and tells the type of problem, and explains why.

 Ongoing Assessment

Have students:

▶ Write a related multiplication equation for 3 × 8.

▶ Write a related division equation for 24 ÷ 3.

▶ Show how 24 ÷ 3 can be solved by repeated subtraction.

10
Class Activity

Name _____ Date _____

▶ **Repeated Subtraction and Division**

Subtraction can be used to solve division word problems.

How many pieces of ribbon, each 5 centimeters long, can be cut from a ribbon that is 30 centimeters long?

6. What is the length of the ribbon?
   ___30 cm___

7. What length will be cut off each time the ribbon is cut?
   ___5 cm___

8. How many times did we subtract 5 cm from 30 cm?
   ___6 times___

9. How many pieces of ribbon, each 5 centimeters long, can be cut from a ribbon that is 30 centimeters long?
   ___6 pieces___

$$\begin{array}{r} 30 \\ -5 \\ \hline 25 \\ -5 \\ \hline 20 \\ -5 \\ \hline 15 \\ -5 \\ \hline 10 \\ -5 \\ \hline 5 \\ -5 \\ \hline 0 \end{array}$$

10. What division sentence can we write to represent this problem? ___30 ÷ 5 = 6___

Use any method to solve each problem. *Show your work.*

11. How many pieces of ribbon, each 6 centimeters long, can be cut from a ribbon that is 18 centimeters long?
    ___3 pieces___

12. How many groups of 4 students can be formed from a group of 20 students? ___5 groups___

13. How many pieces of string, each 4 centimeters long, can be cut from a string that is 36 centimeters long?
    ___9 pieces___

14. How many groups of 7 students can be formed from a group of 28 students? ___4 groups___

34 FLUENCY PLAN LESSON 10   Group and Array Word Problems

Student Activity Book page 34

▶ Repeated Subtraction and Division

WHOLE CLASS   **Math Talk**

Discuss this problem with students.

> **Alejandro needs 15 apples. Apples are sold with 5 apples in each bag. How many bags should Alejandro buy?**

Ask students to explain how they would solve this problem. Different solutions may include:

● Repeated addition: skip counting by fives from 5 to 15.

● Writing a multiplication equation: 5 × ▮ = 15.

● Writing a division equation. 15 ÷ 5 = ▮.

Point out that repeated subtraction can also be used by counting backward from 15. Write 15 − 5 − 5 − 5 = 0 on the board and point out that we can subtract 5 from 15 three times, so 3 × 5 = 15 or 15 ÷ 5 = 3.

Have students complete the exercises on Student Book page 34.

Intervention — Activity Card FP-10

Draw It
Activity Card FP-10 ●

Work: By Yourself

1. Look at the array below.

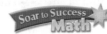
$3 \times 4 = 12 \quad 12 \div 3 = 4$

2. Draw the following arrays.
   • 4 rows by 3 columns
   • 5 rows of 9
   • 9 rows of 5

3. Write a multiplication and a division equation for each array. $4 \times 3 = 12$; $12 \div 4 = 3$; $5 \times 9 = 45$; $45 \div 5 = 9$; $9 \times 5 = 45$; $45 \div 9 = 5$

Fluency Plan, Lesson 10

Copyright © Houghton Mifflin Company

Activity Note Students may need to have counters to help them draw the arrays.

✎ Math Writing Prompt

Draw a Picture Draw a picture that shows 3 rows of 8. Describe something that this picture might represent.

Soar to Success Math ★ Software Support

Use *Soar to Success* for instruction of students needing targeted support for underlying skills.

On Level — Activity Card FP-10

Solve It
Activity Card FP-10 ▲

Work: By Yourself

1. Look at the problem below.

Randy has 35 CDs. She arranged them into 7 columns with the same number in each column.

How many CDs are in each row?

2. Make a drawing to model the situation.
   5 by 7 array or 35 grouped into 5s

3. Write a multiplication and a division problem to solve this problem. $5 \times 7 = 35$; $35 \div 7 = 5$

4. Answer the problem. 5 CDs in each row

Fluency Plan, Lesson 10

Copyright © Houghton Mifflin Company

Activity Note Extend the activity by having students create their own problem and write solution equations for it.

✎ Math Writing Prompt

Write a Problem Choose a two-digit number and a one-digit number. Then use them to create a multiplication or a division word problem.

MegaMath Grades K-6 Software Support

Use *MegaMath* for review and reinforcement of the concepts and skills presented in this lesson.

Challenge — Activity Card FP-10

Spin a Problem
Activity Card FP-10 ■

Work: In Pairs

Use:
• 5-part spinner or Circle Graph Helper (TRB M79)
• Student Book page 33

1. Make or label a spinner with five equal parts as shown below.

2. One partner writes two numbers from 1 to 10.

3. The other partner spins the spinner to choose a problem type. Refer to page 33 of the Student Book to identify the problem type.

4. **Work Together** Write and solve a word problem of that type, using the numbers from step 2.

5. Exchange roles and repeat steps 2 to 4.

Fluency Plan, Lesson 10

Copyright © Houghton Mifflin Company

Activity Note Copies of Circle Graph Helper (TRB M79) may be used to help students create 5-part spinners.

✎ Math Writing Prompt

Problem Solving Write and solve a repeated-groups division problem with an unknown group size.

✖ DESTINATION Math® Software Support

Use *Destination Math* to take students beyond the concepts and skills presented in this lesson.

③ Homework and Spiral Review

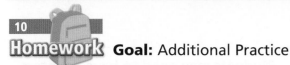

10 Homework **Goal:** Additional Practice

Use this Homework page to provide students with more practice with multiplication and division word problems that use groups and arrays.

10 Remembering **Goal:** Spiral Review

This Remembering activity would be appropriate anytime after today's lesson.

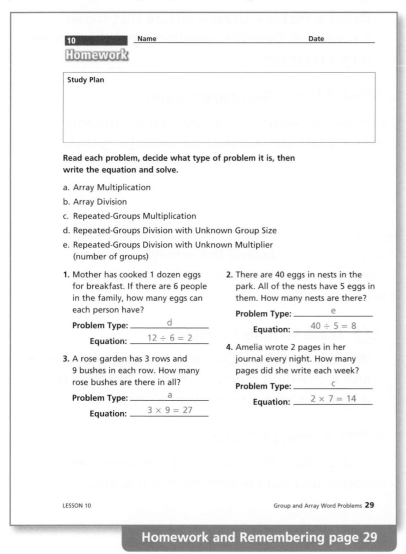

10 Homework

Name _____ Date _____

Study Plan

Read each problem, decide what type of problem it is, then write the equation and solve.

a. Array Multiplication

b. Array Division

c. Repeated-Groups Multiplication

d. Repeated-Groups Division with Unknown Group Size

e. Repeated-Groups Division with Unknown Multiplier (number of groups)

1. Mother has cooked 1 dozen eggs for breakfast. If there are 6 people in the family, how many eggs can each person have?

   Problem Type: _____d_____

   Equation: __$12 \div 6 = 2$__

2. There are 40 eggs in nests in the park. All of the nests have 5 eggs in them. How many nests are there?

   Problem Type: _____e_____

   Equation: __$40 \div 5 = 8$__

3. A rose garden has 3 rows and 9 bushes in each row. How many rose bushes are there in all?

   Problem Type: _____a_____

   Equation: __$3 \times 9 = 27$__

4. Amelia wrote 2 pages in her journal every night. How many pages did she write each week?

   Problem Type: _____c_____

   Equation: __$2 \times 7 = 14$__

LESSON 10   Group and Array Word Problems **29**

Homework and Remembering page 29

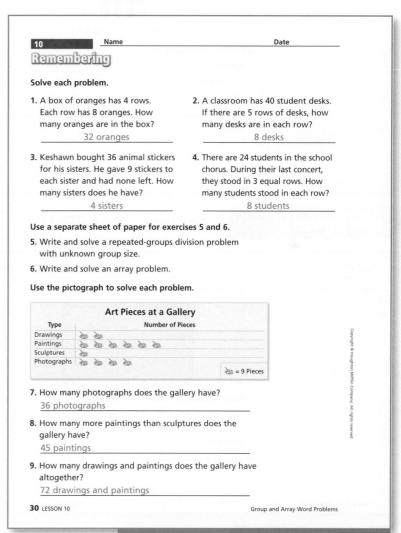

10 Remembering

Name _____ Date _____

Solve each problem.

1. A box of oranges has 4 rows. Each row has 8 oranges. How many oranges are in the box?

   _____32 oranges_____

2. A classroom has 40 student desks. If there are 5 rows of desks, how many desks are in each row?

   _____8 desks_____

3. Keshawn bought 36 animal stickers for his sisters. He gave 9 stickers to each sister and had none left. How many sisters does he have?

   _____4 sisters_____

4. There are 24 students in the school chorus. During their last concert, they stood in 3 equal rows. How many students stood in each row?

   _____8 students_____

Use a separate sheet of paper for exercises 5 and 6.

5. Write and solve a repeated-groups division problem with unknown group size.

6. Write and solve an array problem.

Use the pictograph to solve each problem.

Art Pieces at a Gallery	
Type	**Number of Pieces**
Drawings	🦢🦢
Paintings	🦢🦢🦢🦢🦢
Sculptures	🦢
Photographs	🦢🦢🦢🦢
	🦢 = 9 Pieces

7. How many photographs does the gallery have?

   _____36 photographs_____

8. How many more paintings than sculptures does the gallery have?

   _____45 paintings_____

9. How many drawings and paintings does the gallery have altogether?

   _____72 drawings and paintings_____

30 LESSON 10   Group and Array Word Problems

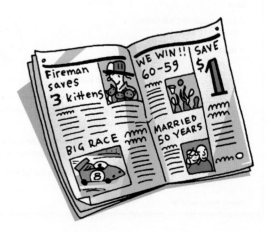

Homework and Remembering page 30

Home or School Activity

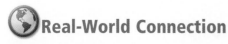

Real-World Connection

Write Problems Have students look for data or other information in a newspaper or magazine about which they can write one or more word problems. In class tomorrow, have students share their word problems and challenge others to solve them.

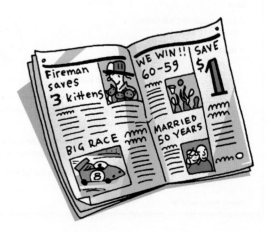

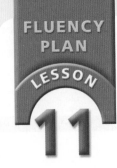

Multiply and Divide With 6

Lesson Objectives

- Explore patterns in 6s count-bys, multiplications, and divisions.
- Develop strategies for finding 6s multiplications.

The Day at a Glance

Today's Goals	Materials
1 Teaching the Lesson **A1:** Discuss patterns in 6s count-bys, multiplications, and divisions. **A2:** Develop strategies for multiplying with 6. **2 Going Further** ▶ Math Connection: Function Tables ▶ Differentiated Instruction **3 Homework and Spiral Review**	**Lesson Activities** Student Activity Book p. 35, 37–38 or Student Hardcover Book p. 35, 37–38 and Activity Workbook pp. 21–22 (includes Family Letters) Homework and Remembering pp. 31–32 Class Multiplication Table MathBoard Materials **Going Further** Student Activity Book page 36 or Student Hardcover Book p. 36 Activity Cards FP-11 Math Journals

123 *Use* **Math Talk** *today!*

Keeping Skills Sharp

Quick Practice ⏱ 5 MINUTES	Daily Routines
Goal: Practice multiplications and divisions. **Materials:** Division Digits materials, Product Cards: 2s, 3s, 4s, 5s, 9s **Division Digits for 3s and 4s** Have the Student Leader run the activity, using problems from the 3s and 4s sections of Set 2. (See Lesson 2) **Practice Multiplications with Product Cards** Have students practice their multiplications independently, using their Product Cards. (See Lesson 5)	**Homework Review** If students give incorrect answers, have them explain how they found the answers. This can help you determine whether the error is conceptual or procedural. **Reasoning** Mia has twice as many pens as Jenna. Jenna has twice as many pens as Kate. If Lu has 4 times as many pens as Kate, does she have the same number of pens as Mia? Why or why not? Yes; if k = Kate's pens, then $2k$ = Jenna's pens, and $2 \cdot 2k$ or $4k$ = Mia's pens; Lu's pens also equal $4k$. K ☐ k J ☐☐ $2k$ M ☐☐☐☐ $2 \cdot 2k$ or $4k$ L ☐☐☐☐ $4k$

Teaching the Lesson

6s Patterns

 30 MINUTES

Goal: Discuss patterns in 6s count-bys, multiplications, and divisions.

Materials: Class Multiplication Table, MathBoard Materials

✓ **NCTM Standards:**
Number and Operations
Algebra
Connection

Multiplication Table

X	1	2	3	4	5	6	7	8	9
1	1·1=1	1·2=2	1·3=3	1·4=4	1·5=5	1·6=6	1·7=7	1·8=8	1·9=9
2	2×1=2	2×2=4	2×3=6	2×4=8	2×5=10	2×6=12	2×7=14	2×8=16	2×9=18
3	3·1=3	3·2=6	3·3=9	3·4=12	3·5=15	3·6=18	3·7=21	3·8=24	3·9=27
4	4·1=4	4·2=8	4·3=12	4·4=16	4·5=20	4·6=24	4·7=28	4·8=32	4·9=36
5	5×1=5	5×2=10	5×3=15	5×4=20	5×5=25	5×6=30	5×7=35	5×8=40	5×9=45
6	6·1=6	6·2=12	6·3=18	6·4=24	6·5=30	6·6=36	6·7=42	6·8=48	6·9=54
7	7·1=7	7·2=14	7·3=21	7·4=28	7·5=35	7·6=42	7·7=49	7·8=56	7·9=63
8	8×1=8	8×2=16	8×3=24	8×4=32	8×5=40	8×6=48	8×7=56	8×8=64	8×9=72
9	9·1=9	9·2=18	9·3=27	9·4=36	9·5=45	9·6=54	9·7=63	9·8=72	9·9=81
10	10·1=10	10·2=20	10·3=30	10·4=40	10·5=50	10·6=60	10·7=70	10·8=80	10·9=90
11	11·1=11	11·2=22	11·3=33	11·4=44	11·5=55	11·6=66	11·7=77	11·8=88	11·9=99
12	12·1=12	12·2=24	12·3=36	12·4=48	12·5=60	12·6=72	12·7=84	12·8=96	12·9=108

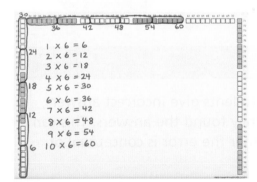

► Review What Students Have Learned WHOLE CLASS

Begin by reviewing the multiplications students have learned so far. You may want to cover up the last two rows, 11s and 12s, on the Class Multiplication Table.

● You've already learned lots of multiplications. Let's go through the table and circle those you have left to learn.

For each column, ask students which multiplications they have not yet studied. They should recognize that they have studied all the multiplications in the 1s, 2s, 3s, 4s, 5s, and 9s columns and most of those in the 6s, 7s, and 8s columns. When you are finished, the nine multiplications shown on the left should be circled.

● Look at all the multiplications you know! Today we will focus on the 6s column. We will look at all the multiplications in the column, but keep in mind that only three are new to you.

► Patterns in Count-bys and Multiplications

WHOLE CLASS

Model this activity on the Class MathBoard as students work on their MathBoards.

One at a time, circle groups of 6, up to 60, on the Number Path and write the cumulative total next to each group. After students circle the first group, have them say in unison "1 group of 6 is 6"; after they circle the second group, have them say "2 groups of 6 are 12"; and so on.

Point to each total in turn and have students say them aloud: "6, 12, 18, 24, 30, 36, 42, 48, 54, 60."

● When we said the 6s count-bys, did you hear any 3s count-bys? yes

● I'm going to write the 3s count-bys on the board. Who can tell me what to write? 3, 6, 9, 12, 15, 18, 21, 24, 27, 30

Then ask, "Which of these numbers are also 6s count-bys?" Underline the 6s count-bys as students say them.

3, <u>6</u>, 9, <u>12</u>, 15, <u>18</u>, 21, <u>24</u>, 27, <u>30</u>

● What pattern do you see? Every other 3s count-by is also a 6s count-by.

● Why does this make sense? Because there are two 3s in 6; if you put two groups of 3 together, you get a group of 6.

Next, write and read the multiplication equations as shown on the left. Remind students that the products in the equations are the same as the 6s count-bys.

Math Talk Have students discuss the patterns they see in the count-bys and products. For example:

- The 6s count-bys are all even numbers.

- The 6s count-bys are all 3s count-bys.

- Every third 6s count-by—18, 36, and 54—is a 9s count-by.

- The sum of the digits in each 6s count-by is a 3s count-by. (For 6, the sum is 6; for 12, the sum is $1 + 2 = 3$; for 18, the sum is $1 + 8 = 9$; and so on.)

- Ignoring 60, if you start with the outside pair of 6s count-bys (6 and 54) and move in, each pair (6 and 54, 12 and 48, and so on) adds to 60. Also, each pair of ones digits adds to 10.

- Each 6s product is twice the corresponding 3s product. (Write some of the corresponding products on the board as shown below to help students with this pattern.)

$1 \times 3 = 3$	$2 \times 3 = 6$	$3 \times 3 = 9$	$4 \times 3 = 12$
$1 \times 6 = 6$	$2 \times 6 = 12$	$3 \times 6 = 18$	$4 \times 6 = 24$

Have students draw a horizontal segment separating $5 \times 6 = 30$ and $6 \times 6 = 36$, as shown on the right. Ask them to compare the five products above the line to the five products below it and to describe any patterns or relationships they see. Make sure the following are mentioned:

- The ones digits in the top five products—6, 2, 8, 4, 0—are the same as the ones digits in the bottom five products.

- Each product below the line is 30 more than the corresponding product above the line. That is, 36 is 30 more than 6, 42 is 30 more than 12, and so on.

Ask how the last pattern is related to the 5s shortcut $5 \times 6 = 30$. Each product below the line is 30 plus some more 6s. For example, 6×6 is 30 plus 1 more 6, or 36; 7×6 is 30 plus 2 more 6s, or 42.

▶ Write Divisions INDIVIDUALS

Math Talk Have students write two division equations for each multiplication equation. Write the first two or three pairs as a class to help students.

Discuss patterns in the division equations. For example:

- Every division equation begins with a 6s count-by.

- In one column of division equations, all the quotients are 6s.

- In another column of division equations, all the divisors are 6s.

The Learning Classroom

Math Talk You can create math conversations by eliciting multiple strategies for solving problems. When you ask, "Did anyone do this problem differently?" your students will pay greater attention to the work on the board because they will be comparing and contrasting it with their own math strategies. The comparisons and contrasts that result can naturally springboard to significant math talk.

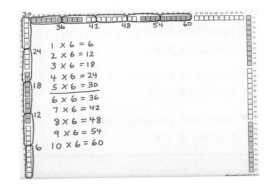

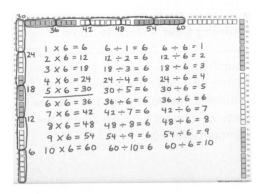

Activity 2

Practice Multiplying and Dividing With 6

 25 MINUTES

Goal: Develop strategies for multiplying with 6.

Materials: Student Activity Book or Hardcover Book p. 35, Class Multiplication Table

 NCTM Standards:
Number and Operations
Algebra

Ongoing Assessment

Have students look at Student Book page 35, and ask questions such as:

▶ How does Strategy 1 help you multiply 6 × 6?

▶ How does Strategy 2 help you multiply 6 × 6?

▶ How does Strategy 3 help you multiply 6 × 6?

Teaching Note

Adding Over a Decade Some students have difficulty adding larger numbers like 6, 7, 8 over a decade. Write 18 + 6 on the board and ask students if anyone splits the number into an amount to make 20 and the amount over 20.

18 + 6 = 18 + 2 + 4 = 20 + 4 = 24

After a student demonstrates this, go through the other two cases for the 6s that benefit from this strategy:

36 + 6 = 36 + 4 + __ = 40 + __ = 42
2; 2

48 + 6 = 48 + 2 + __ = 50 + __ = 54
4; 4

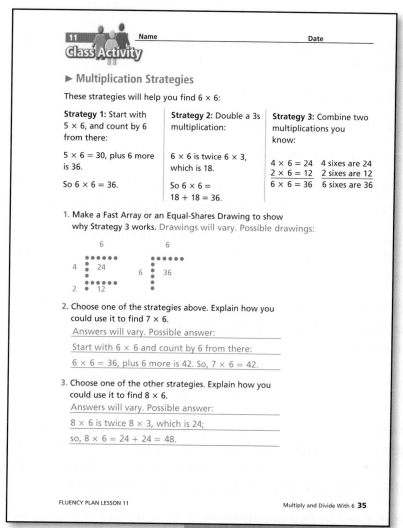

Student Activity Book page 35

▶ Multiplication Strategies WHOLE CLASS

Write these three multiplication problems on the board:

6 × 6   7 × 6   8 × 6

Remind students that these are the three 6s multiplications they need to learn today. Ask students to describe some strategies for finding 6 × 6. Then discuss the three strategies presented on Student Book page 35. (Some may be strategies students already mentioned.) Strategy 1 is the 5s shortcut that students have already learned in this unit.

Have students solve problem 1 on page 35. Make sure they understand that their drawings should show why 4 × 6 and 2 × 6 can be combined to get 6 × 6.

Then use **Solve and Discuss** for problems 2 and 3. Make sure all three strategies have been presented when this activity is finished.

▶ Use the Class Multiplication Table WHOLE CLASS

Ask students to find the 6s multiplications on the Class Multiplication Table.

Students should observe the following:

- The 6s column has the 6s multiplications with the factor 6 given second. For example, $1 \times 6 = 6$.

- The 6s row has the 6s multiplications with the factor 6 given first. For example, $6 \times 1 = 6$.

Point to the multiplication equations in the 6s column in order as students say the equations in unison: "1 times 6 equals 6," "2 times 6 equals 12," and so on, up to "10 times 6 equals 60". Tell students they may raise their fingers to keep track of the count-bys if they wish.

Point to each equation in the 6s column once again, but this time have students say the 6s divisions in order: "6 divided by 6 equals 1," "12 divided by 6 equals 2," and so on, up to "60 divided by 6 equals 10." Again, students may raise their fingers to keep track of the count-bys if they wish.

Have students close their eyes. Ask a **Student Leader** to say the 6s multiplication and division problems in mixed order. The leader should give students a few seconds to think of the answer. Then the leader should say "Answer" and have students say the answer in unison.

The Learning Classroon

Student Leaders Perhaps the top students are beginning to explain more details about their problem solving strategies, but it is not the case for all of the students. You may want to have these top students do more explaining. They will model for other students how to explain their thinking, and their explanations may connect with some students more successfully than your own way of talking about a concept.

English Language Learners
Teach students the game *ZIP* to practice 6s count-bys. Have students stand in a circle and count by 6s. Then have them count normally. Stop before the 6th student.

- **Beginning** Say: **When some says a 6s count-by everyone raises a hand.** Continue around the circle. Start again. Have students say *ZIP* instead of the number.
- **Intermediate** Say: **In this game you cannot say 6s count-bys. You say** *ZIP.*
- **Advanced** Tell students that this time they cannot say 6s count-bys. They have to say *ZIP.* If a student says a 6s count-by the counting starts again from 1.

Going Further

Math Connection: Function Tables

Goal: Complete a function table to show a relationship and use the relationship to make predictions.

Materials: Student Activity Book or Hardcover Book p. 36

✔ **NCTM Standards:**
Number and Operations
Algebra
Data Analysis and Probability

▶ Discuss Function Rules

| WHOLE CLASS |

Math Talk

In this lesson students will be connecting skip counting with the algebraic topic of patterns and functions.

Read the introduction at the top of Student Book page 36 aloud or read it together.

● How many legs does a ladybug have? 6

● What does the table show? the total number of legs for different numbers of ladybugs

Allow students to offer all the methods they can to decide how many legs 10 ladybugs have. Some students may say you can count by 6. Others will say you can add 6. A few students may say you can multiply the number of ladybugs by 6.

When students are asked to predict a term in a sequence, they will likely use addition to extend the pattern. However, if a prediction must be made for a significantly greater term of a sequence such as the 100th, addition is a very tedious way to determine the number. Help students recognize the relationship in each column. The numbers in each column of the table must share the same relationship for it to be a pattern.

Once that relationship is identified, it can be used to determine any term of the pattern. Because each ladybug has 6 legs, the number of legs for 100 ladybugs is 100 × 6 or 600 legs.

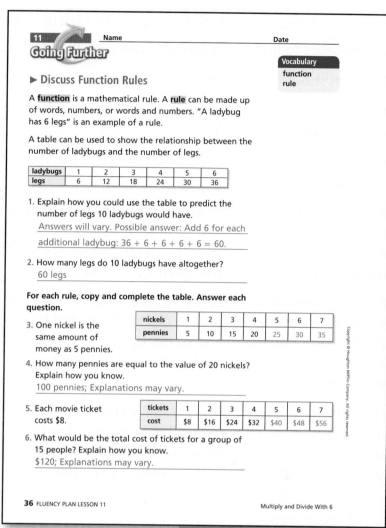

Student Activity Book page 36

▶ Critical Thinking | INDIVIDUALS |

Challenge students to write algebraic equations that describe the relationships in the tables.

n = the number of ladybugs, l = the number of legs; $l = 6 \cdot n$

n = the number of nickels, p = the number of pennies; $p = 5 \cdot n$

c = the cost in dollars, t = the number of tickets; $c = 8 \cdot t$

Differentiated Instruction

Intervention — Activity Card FP-11

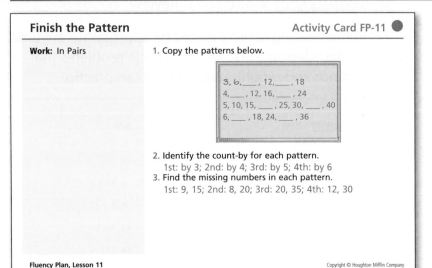

Finish the Pattern　　　Activity Card FP-11 ●

Work: In Pairs

1. Copy the patterns below.

   3, 6, ___, 12, ___, 18
   4, ___, 12, 16, ___, 24
   5, 10, 15, ___, 25, 30, ___, 40
   6, ___, 18, 24, ___, 36

2. Identify the count-by for each pattern.
   1st: by 3; 2nd: by 4; 3rd: by 5; 4th: by 6
3. Find the missing numbers in each pattern.
   1st: 9, 15; 2nd: 8, 20; 3rd: 20, 35; 4th: 12, 30

Fluency Plan, Lesson 11　　　Copyright © Houghton Mifflin Company

Activity Note Remind students to use their Number Paths or use their fingers to keep track of the count-bys.

 Math Writing Prompt

Related Equations Draw a Factor Triangle for $7 \times 6 = 42$. Write two division equations that are related to the drawing.

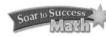 **Software Support**

Use *Soar to Success* for instruction of students needing targeted support for underlying skills.

On Level — Activity Card FP-11

How Many?　　　Activity Card FP-11 ▲

Work: By Yourself

1. Copy the following function tables onto your paper.

Cars	0	1	2	5	8		12
Wheels	0	4	8			40	

Drink Packs	1	3	4	5	7		
Drinks	6	18	24			66	72

Pints		6	8		18		24
Quarts	0	3		6	9	10	

2. Write a rule in words for each table. Cars × 4 = wheels; packs × 6 = drinks; pints ÷ 2 = quarts

3. Complete each table. Cars: 10; Wheels: 20, 32, 48; Drink Packs: 11, 12; Drinks: 30, 42; Pints: 0, 12, 20; Quarts: 4, 12

Fluency Plan, Lesson 11　　　Copyright © Houghton Mifflin Company

Activity Note Extend the activity by having students extend one function table with 4 different entries of their choice.

 Math Writing Prompt

Explain Your Thinking Explain how you know that 7×6 is twice 7×3. Find the products to check your work.

 Software Support

Use *MegaMath* for review and reinforcement of the concepts and skills presented in this lesson.

Challenge — Activity Card FP-11

Write the Rule　　　Activity Card FP-11 ■

Work: In Pairs

1. Each partner copies one of the tables.

Boxes	Crayons
1	5
4	20
5	
8	
b	

Packages	Eggs
2	12
5	30
	36
9	
p	

2. **Work Together** Complete the first four rows of each table.
   Crayons: 25, 40; Packages: 6; Eggs: 54

3. In the last row of each table, write a rule for using the variable given (*b* or *p*) $b \times 4$; $p \times 6$

Fluency Plan, Lesson 11　　　Copyright © Houghton Mifflin Company

Activity Note Have students write a rule in words to help them write the generic rule, if needed.

 Math Writing Prompt

Prove Your Point Explain why all 6s count-bys are also 3s count-bys, but not all 3s count-bys are also 6 count-bys. Give an example of a 3s count-by that is not a 6s count-by.

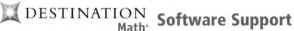 **Software Support**

Use *Destination Math* to take students beyond the concepts and skills presented in this lesson.

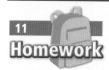

③ Homework and Spiral Review

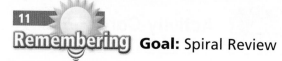

Homework **Goal:** Additional Practice

Use this Homework page to provide students with more practice with patterns in 6s.

Remembering **Goal:** Spiral Review

This Remembering activity would be appropriate anytime after today's lesson. Have students circle problems that they did not know right away so they can practice.

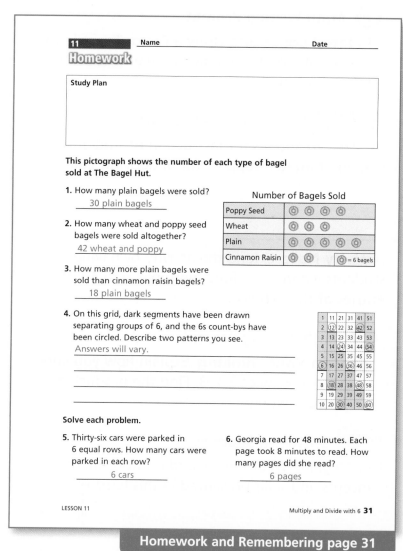

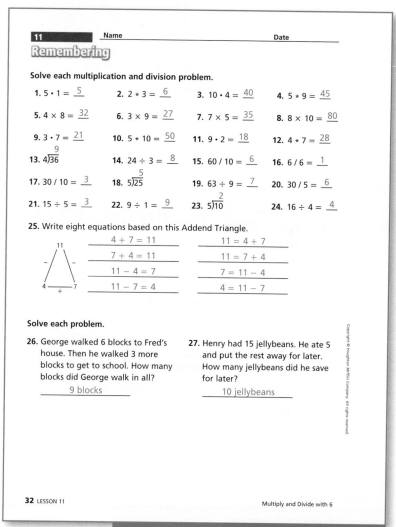

Home and School Connection

Family Letter Have children take home the Family Letter on Student Book page 37 or Activity Workbook page 21. This letter explains how the concepts of multiplication and division are developed in *Math Expressions*. It gives parents and guardians a better understanding of the learning that goes on in math class and creates a bridge between school and home. A Spanish translation of this letter is on Student Book page 38 and Activity Workbook page 22.

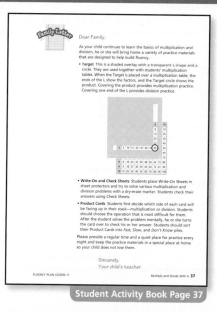

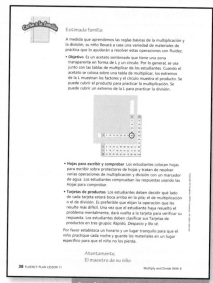

94 FLUENCY PLAN LESSON 11

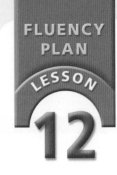

FLUENCY PLAN

LESSON 12

Multiply and Divide With 8 and 7

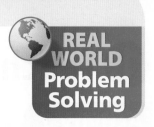

REAL WORLD Problem Solving

Lesson Objectives

- Explore patterns in 8s and 7s count-bys, multiplications, and divisions.
- Develop strategies for finding answers to multiplications.

The Day at a Glance

Today's Goals	Materials	
1 Teaching the Lesson **A1:** Discuss patterns in 8s count-bys, multiplications, and divisions. **A2:** Discuss patterns in 7s count-bys, multiplications, and divisions. **A2:** Solve word problems involving multiplication and division with 6s, 7s, and 8s.	**Lesson Activities** Student Activity Book pp. 39–40 or Student Hardcover Book pp. 39–40 Homework and Remembering pp. 33–34 MathBoard Materials Class Multiplication Table	**Going Further** Activity Cards FP-12 Index cards Math Journals
2 Going Further ▶ Differentiated Instruction		
3 Homework and Spiral Review		

123 Use Math Talk today!

Keeping Skills Sharp

Quick Practice ⏱ 5 MINUTES	Daily Routines	
Goal: Practice multiplications and divisions. **Materials:** Division Digits materials, Products Cards: 2s, 3s, 4s, 5s, 6s, 9s **Division Digits for 3s and 4s** Have a **Student Leader** run the activity, using problems from the 3s and 4s sections of Set 2. (See Lesson 2) **Practice Multiplications with Product Cards** Have students practice their multiplications independently, using their Product Cards. (See Lesson 5)	**Homework Review** If students need help with pictograph symbols, ask them to find the number each symbol stands for and skip count, using the symbols in each row. Then they can write the total.	**Write a Rule** If the pattern continues, what is the tenth number in this pattern? 1, 3, 5, 7, 9, . . . Explain the rule. 19; the pattern is Add 2.

1 Teaching the Lesson

Activity 1

8s Patterns

 20 MINUTES

Goal: Discuss patterns in 8s count-bys, multiplications, and divisions.

Materials: MathBoard Materials, Class Multiplication Table

 NCTM Standards:
Number and Operations
Algebra

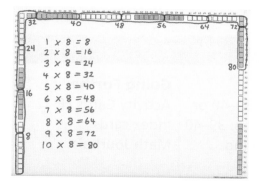

The Learning Classroom

Math Talk Aspire to make your classroom a place where all students listen to understand one another. Explain to students that this is different from just being quiet when someone else is talking. This involves thinking about what a person is saying so that you could explain it yourself. Also, students need to listen so that they can ask a question or help the explainer. Remind students that listening can also help you learn that concept better.

▶ Patterns in Count-bys and Multiplications WHOLE CLASS

Model this activity on the Class MathBoard as students work on their MathBoards.

Have students circle sequential groups of 8, up to 80, on the Number Path and write the cumulative totals next to each group. After they circle the first group, have them say in unison "1 group of 8 is 8." After they circle the second group, have them say "2 groups of 8 are 16," and so on.

Next, point to the totals on the class MathBoard as students say just the 8s count-bys aloud: "8, 16, 24, 32, 40, 48, 56, 64, 72, 80."

● When we said the 8s count-bys, did you hear any 4s count-bys?

● I'm going to write the 4s count-bys on the board. Who can tell me what to write?

Write the 4s count-bys on the board: 4, 8, 12, 16, 20, 24, 28, 32, 36, 40

● Which of these numbers are also 8s count-bys?

Underline the 8s count-bys as students say them. 4, <u>8</u>, 12, <u>16</u>, 20, <u>24</u>, 28, <u>32</u>, 36, <u>40</u>

● What pattern do you see? Every other 4s count-by is also an 8s count-by.

● Why does this make sense? Because there are two 4s in 8; if you put two groups of 4 together, you get a group of 8.

As students follow along, write and read a multiplication equation for each count-by, as shown on the left.

Math Talk Ask students to describe patterns they see in the count-bys and products. Here are some examples:

● The products are all even numbers.

● The products are all 4s count-bys *and* 2s count-bys.

● The ones digits of the products follow the pattern 8, 6, 4, 2, 0.

● Ignoring 80, if you start with the outside pair of products (8 and 72) and move in, each pair of products (8 and 72, 16 and 64, and so on) adds to 80. Also, the ones digits of each pair of products (8 and 72, 16 and 64, and so on) add to 10.

● Each 8s product is twice the corresponding 4s product. (Write some of the corresponding products on the board as shown below to help students with this pattern.)

$1 \times 4 = 4$	$2 \times 4 = 8$	$3 \times 4 = 12$	$4 \times 4 = 16$
$1 \times 8 = 8$	$2 \times 8 = 16$	$3 \times 8 = 24$	$4 \times 8 = 32$

Now have students draw a horizontal segment separating 5 × 8 = 40 and 6 × 8 = 48. Ask them to compare the five products above the line to the five products below it and to describe any patterns or relationships they see. Make sure the following are mentioned:

- The ones digits in the top five products—8, 6, 4, 2, 0—are the same as the ones digits in the bottom five products.

- Each product below the line is 40 more than the corresponding product above the line. That is, 48 is 40 more than 8, 56 is 40 more than 16, and so on.

- Each product below the line is 40 plus some more 8s. For example, 6 × 8 is 48, which is 40 plus 1 more 8; 7 × 8 is 56, which is 40 plus 2 more 8s.

Ask students how the last pattern is related to the 5s shortcut 5 × 8 = 40.

▶ Multiplication Strategies WHOLE CLASS

Ask students which of the 8s multiplications they haven't learned yet. There are only two: 7 × 8 = 56 and 8 × 8 = 64.

Have students describe strategies for finding 7 × 8. Allow them to come to the board to explain if necessary. Encourage other students to ask questions if they don't understand. Allow as many different methods as possible to be presented. If no one mentions the following methods, you might suggest them yourself:

- Start with 5 × 8 (or another 8s multiplication you know) and count by 8 from there: 5 × 8 = 40, plus 8 more is 48, plus 8 more is 56. So, 7 × 8 = 56.

- Combine two multiplications you know:

4 × 8 = 32	4 eights are 32.
3 × 8 = 24	3 eights are 24.
7 × 8 = 56	7 eights are 56.

- Double a 4s multiplication: 7 × 8 is twice 7 × 4, which is 28. So, 7 × 8 = 28 + 28 = 56.

For 8 × 8, repeat the process of having students describe their strategies. Again, consider suggesting the three bulleted methods above. Another method students may suggest for this product is starting at 9 × 8, or 72, and subtracting 8 to get 64.

Activity continued ▶

Activity 1

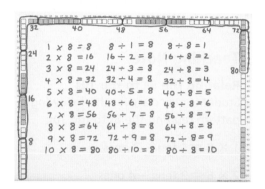

Teaching Note

What to Expect from Students
How did your students explain their math thinking today? Students are often unfamiliar with this process; they are accustomed to providing math answers only. Supporting students to talk about their thinking will take repeated efforts on your part. Expect this to be a building process that lasts for several weeks.

Early on, when a student provides an answer and then wants to sit down, try asking him or her to stay at the board and explain just one or two more things about the problem or his or her math thinking. For example, encourage a student to tell more about a drawing he or she made to solve a word problem and how he or she used the drawing to come up with an answer.

▶ Write Divisions [INDIVIDUALS]

Math Talk Have students write two division equations for each multiplication equation on their MathBoards, as shown at the left.

Discuss patterns in the division equations, and then have students erase everything on their boards.

▶ Use the Class Multiplication Table [WHOLE CLASS]

Ask students to find the 8s multiplications on the Class Multiplication Table. They should see that the 8s column has the 8s multiplications with the factor 8 given second, and that the 8s row has the 8s multiplications with the factor 8 given first.

Point to the multiplication equations in the 8s column (up to $10 \times 8 = 80$), in order, as students say them in unison: "1 times 8 equals 8," "2 times 8 equals 16," and so on. Tell students they may raise fingers to keep track of the count-bys if they wish.

Point to each equation in the 8s column (up to $10 \times 8 = 80$) once again, but this time have students say the 8s divisions in order: "8 divided by 8 equals 1," "16 divided by 8 equals 2," and so on. Again, students may raise fingers to keep track of the count-bys.

Now have students close their eyes. Have a **Student Leader** say the 8s multiplication and division problems in mixed order. The leader should give students a few seconds to think of the answer. Then the leader should say "Answer" and have students say the answer in unison.

7s Patterns

▶ Patterns in Count-bys and Multiplications

WHOLE CLASS

Model this activity on the Class MathBoard as students work on their MathBoards.

Have students circle sequential groups of 7, up to 70, on the Number Path and write the cumulative totals next to each group. After they circle the first group, have them say in unison "1 group of 7 is 7"; after they circle the second group, have them say "2 groups of 7 are 14"; and so on.

Next, point to the totals on the class MathBoard as students say just the 7s count-bys aloud: "7, 14, 21, 28, 35, 42, 49, 56, 63, 70."

As students follow along, write and read a multiplication equation for each count-by.

Math Talk Ask students to describe patterns they see in the count-bys and products. Here are some examples:

- Every other product is an even number; every other product is an odd number.

- Ignoring 70, if you start with the outside pair of products (7 and 63) and move in, each pair of products (7 and 63, 14 and 56, and so on) adds to 70. Also, each pair of ones digits adds to 10.

 20 MINUTES

Goal: Discuss patterns in 7s count-bys, multiplications, and divisions.

Materials: MathBoard Materials, Student Activity Book or Hardcover Book p. 39, Class Multiplication Table

✔ **NCTM Standards:**
Number and Operations
Algebra

Teaching Note

Adding Over a Decade Ask students to show how they can add over a decade when counting by 7s. Remind students that you are writing the steps, but that they can learn to do this mentally. Write $14 + 7$ on the board and ask students if anyone can split 7 into an amount to make 20 and the amount over 20.

$14 + 7 = 14 + 6 + 1 = 20 + 1 = 21$

After a student demonstrates this, go through the other cases for the 7s that benefit from this strategy:

$28 + 7 = 28 + 2 + \_ = 30 + \_ = 35$
5; 5

$35 + 7 = 35 + 5 + \_ = 40 + \_ = 42$
2; 2

$49 + 7 = 49 + 1 + \_ = 50 + \_ = 56$
6; 6

$56 + 7 = 56 + 4 + \_ = 60 + \_ = 63$
3; 3

Activity continued ▶

❶ Teaching the Lesson (continued)

Activity 2

English Language Learners

Help students understand *combining*. Draw a 4 by 7 array and a 2 by 7 array on the board. Have students describe the arrays. Say: **Let's *combine* them.** Draw a + between the arrays.

- **Beginning** Draw a 6 × 7 array. Ask: **What is this new array?** 6 × 7 = 42
- **Intermediate** Add the arrays. Ask: **What did I do?** added the arrays Say: **I *combined* 4 × 7 and 2 × 7 to get 6 × 7.**
- **Advanced** Model how to add the arrays. Emphasize the word *combine*. Have students work in pairs to combine other arrays and describe the steps.

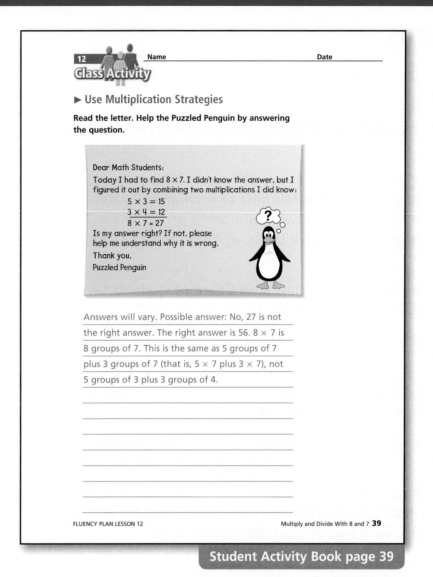

Student Activity Book page 39

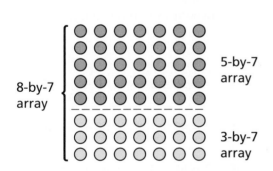
8-by-7 array
5-by-7 array
3-by-7 array

▶ Use Multiplication Strategies WHOLE CLASS

Have students read the letter on Student Book page 39. Allow several to share their ideas about what the Puzzled Penguin did wrong. Encourage them to make drawings on the board, such as the drawing on the left, if it helps them explain.

The penguin seems to think that combining multiplication equations involves adding the first factor to the first factor and adding the second factor to the second factor. Here are two ways to understand why this doesn't work:

- 8 × 7 is 8 groups of 7. This is the same as 5 groups of 7 plus 3 groups of 7 (that is, 5 × 7 plus 3 × 7) *not* 5 groups of 3 plus 3 groups of 4.
- 8 × 7 is the number of items in an 8-by-7 array. You can get an 8-by-7 array by putting together a 5-by-7 array and a 3-by-7 array, not by combining a 5-by-3 array and a 3-by-4 array.

Ask students which of the 7s multiplications they haven't learned yet. There is only one: 7 × 7 = 49.

Have students describe strategies for finding 7 × 7. Allow them to come to the board to explain if necessary. Encourage other students to ask questions if they don't understand. Allow as many different methods as possible to be presented. If no one mentions the following methods, you might suggest them yourself:

- Start with 5 × 7, and count by 7 from there: 5 × 7 = 35, plus 7 more is 42, plus 7 more is 49. So, 7 × 7 = 49.

- Combine two multiplications you know:

4 × 8 = 28	4 sevens are 28.
3 × 7 = 21	3 sevens are 21.
7 × 7 = 49	7 sevens are 49.

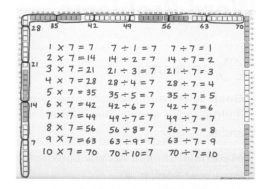

▶ Write Divisions INDIVIDUALS

Math Talk Have students write two division equations for each 7s multiplication equation, as shown on the right.

Discuss patterns in the division equations.

▶ Use the Class Multiplication Table WHOLE CLASS

Ask students to find the 7s multiplications on the Class Multiplication Table.

Students should see that:

- the 7s column has the 7s multiplications with the factor 7 given second. For example, 1 × 7 = 7.

- the 7s row has the 7s multiplications with the factor 7 given first. For example, 7 × 1 = 7.

Point to the multiplication equations in the 7s column (up to 10 × 7 = 70), in order, as students say them in unison: "1 times 7 equals 7," "2 times 7 equals 14," and so on. Students may raise fingers to keep track of the count-bys if they wish.

Point to each equation in the 7s column (up to 10 × 7 = 70) once again, but this time have students say the 7s divisions in order: "7 divided by 7 equals 1," "14 divided by 7 equals 2," and so on. Again, students may raise fingers to keep track of the count-bys.

Now have students close their eyes. Have a **Student Leader** say the 7s multiplication and division problems in mixed order. The leader should give students a few seconds to think of the answer. Then the leader should say "Answer" and have students say the answer in unison.

The Learning Classroom

Math Talk This may be a good day to talk with the class for a few minutes about what makes a good explanation. You may want to produce a list that can be posted on the wall of the classroom for later reference.

Suggestions for the list:

1) Write your work so everyone can see it.

2) Talk loud enough for other students to hear.

3) Use a pointer to point to the numbers as you talk.

4) Say how you arrived at the answer, not just the answer.

5) Stand to the side of your work when you talk.

Activity 3

Word Problems

 15 MINUTES

Goal: Solve word problems involving multiplication and division with 6s, 7s, and 8s.

Materials: Student Activity Book or Hardcover Book p. 40

 NCTM Standard:
Number and Operations

 Ongoing Assessment

Have students solve:

▶ Margaret volunteered to put books away at the library. She put the books on 5 shelves with 8 books on each shelf. How many books did she put away?

▶ Rachel has 63 bracelets and wants to divide them equally between her friends. If she has 7 friends, how many bracelets does each friend receive?

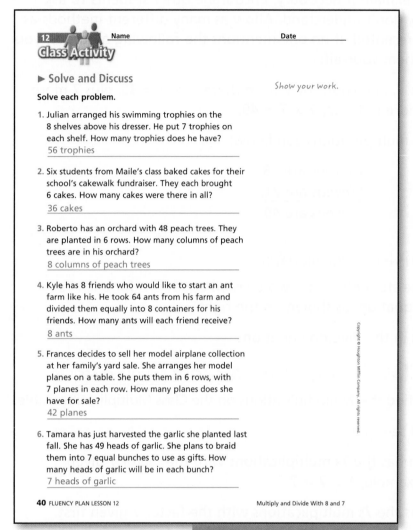

Student Activity Book page 40

▶ **Solve and Discuss**

| WHOLE CLASS |

Math Talk

Using **Solve and Discuss,** have students solve as many of the word problems on Student Book page 40 as time allows.

Intervention   Activity Card FP-12

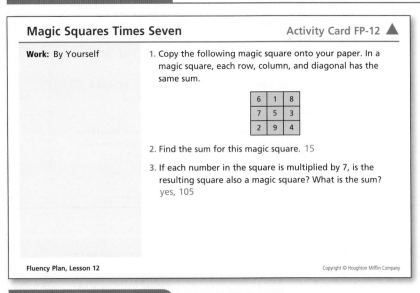

Pick Two   Activity Card FP-12 ●

Work: In Pairs

Use:
• 11 Index cards

1. Number nine of the cards 0 to 8 to create one set of cards. Write 7 and 8 on the other two cards.

2. Shuffle the first set of cards, and place them face down in a stack.

3. One partner selects the top card from the stack but does not show it. The other partner selects the 7 or 8 card.

4. Each partner writes the product of the two numbers, and then they compare answers.

5. Repeat steps 3 and 4 after exchanging roles.

Fluency Plan, Lesson 12   Copyright © Houghton Mifflin Company

Activity Note Students can use a multiplication table to check their products.

 Math Writing Prompt

Draw a Picture Draw a picture that shows 6 groups of 7. Then write the equation.

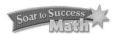 **Software Support**

Use *Soar to Success* for instruction of students needing targeted support for underlying skills.

On Level   Activity Card FP-12

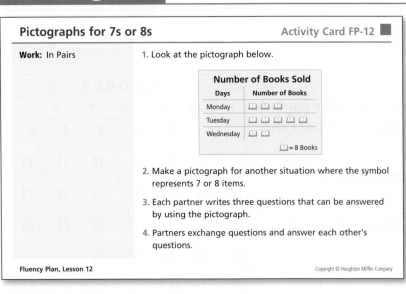

Magic Squares Times Seven   Activity Card FP-12 ▲

Work: By Yourself

1. Copy the following magic square onto your paper. In a magic square, each row, column, and diagonal has the same sum.

6	1	8
7	5	3
2	9	4

2. Find the sum for this magic square. 15

3. If each number in the square is multiplied by 7, is the resulting square also a magic square? What is the sum? yes, 105

Fluency Plan, Lesson 12   Copyright © Houghton Mifflin Company

Activity Note If students do not have a Magic Square after multiplying each number by 7, suggest that they recheck their computations.

 Math Writing Prompt

Create Your Own Write a multiplication and a division word problem, using a factor of 7 in one problem and a factor of 8 in the other problem. Exchange problems with a partner and solve.

 Software Support

Use *MegaMath* for review and reinforcement of the concepts and skills presented in this lesson.

Challenge   Activity Card FP-12

Pictographs for 7s or 8s   Activity Card FP-12 ■

Work: In Pairs

1. Look at the pictograph below.

Number of Books Sold

Days	Number of Books
Monday	▯ ▯ ▯
Tuesday	▯ ▯ ▯ ▯ ▯
Wednesday	▯ ▯

▯ = 8 Books

2. Make a pictograph for another situation where the symbol represents 7 or 8 items.

3. Each partner writes three questions that can be answered by using the pictograph.

4. Partners exchange questions and answer each other's questions.

Fluency Plan, Lesson 12   Copyright © Houghton Mifflin Company

Activity Note Have students write multiplication equations to find the total number of objects in each row on the pictographs they create.

 Math Writing Prompt

Explain Your Thinking Write a letter to the Puzzled Penguin to explain how to find the product of 8 × 14 if you already know the product of 8 × 7.

✳ **DESTINATION** **Software Support**
       Math

Use *Destination Math* to take students beyond the concepts and skills presented in this lesson.

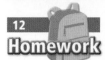 # 3 Homework and Spiral Review

12 Homework **Goal:** Additional Practice

✓ Include students' work for page 33 as part of their portfolios.

12 Remembering **Goal:** Spiral Review

This Remembering activity would be appropriate anytime after today's lesson.

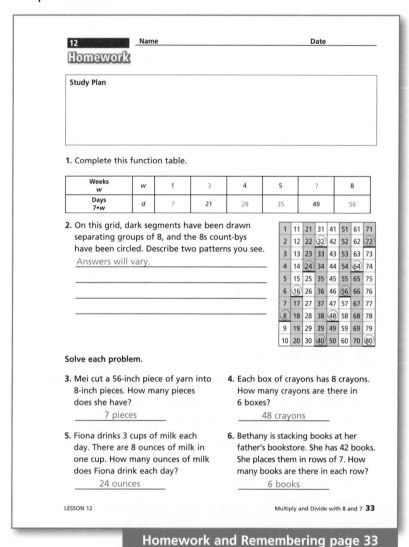

12 Homework	Name _____	Date _____

Study Plan

1. Complete this function table.

Weeks w	w	1	3	4	5	7	8
Days 7•w	d	7	21	28	35	49	56

2. On this grid, dark segments have been drawn separating groups of 8, and the 8s count-bys have been circled. Describe two patterns you see.
   Answers will vary.

Solve each problem.

3. Mei cut a 56-inch piece of yarn into 8-inch pieces. How many pieces does she have?
   7 pieces

4. Each box of crayons has 8 crayons. How many crayons are there in 6 boxes?
   48 crayons

5. Fiona drinks 3 cups of milk each day. There are 8 ounces of milk in one cup. How many ounces of milk does Fiona drink each day?
   24 ounces

6. Bethany is stacking books at her father's bookstore. She has 42 books. She places them in rows of 7. How many books are there in each row?
   6 books

LESSON 12   Multiply and Divide with 8 and 7 **33**

Homework and Remembering page 33

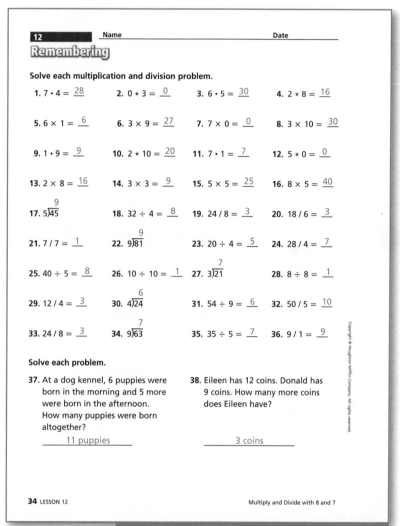

12 Remembering	Name _____	Date _____

Solve each multiplication and division problem.

1. $7 \cdot 4 = 28$
2. $0 * 3 = 0$
3. $6 \cdot 5 = 30$
4. $2 * 8 = 16$

5. $6 \times 1 = 6$
6. $3 \times 9 = 27$
7. $7 \times 0 = 0$
8. $3 \times 10 = 30$

9. $1 \cdot 9 = 9$
10. $2 * 10 = 20$
11. $7 \cdot 1 = 7$
12. $5 * 0 = 0$

13. $2 \times 8 = 16$
14. $3 \times 3 = 9$
15. $5 \times 5 = 25$
16. $8 \times 5 = 40$

17. $5\overline{)45} \; ^9$
18. $32 \div 4 = 8$
19. $24 / 8 = 3$
20. $18 / 6 = 3$

21. $7 / 7 = 1$
22. $9\overline{)81} \; ^9$
23. $20 \div 4 = 5$
24. $28 / 4 = 7$

25. $40 \div 5 = 8$
26. $10 \div 10 = 1$
27. $3\overline{)21} \; ^7$
28. $8 \div 8 = 1$

29. $12 / 4 = 3$
30. $4\overline{)24} \; ^6$
31. $54 \div 9 = 6$
32. $50 / 5 = 10$

33. $24 / 8 = 3$
34. $9\overline{)63} \; ^7$
35. $35 \div 5 = 7$
36. $9 / 1 = 9$

Solve each problem.

37. At a dog kennel, 6 puppies were born in the morning and 5 more were born in the afternoon. How many puppies were born altogether?
   11 puppies

38. Eileen has 12 coins. Donald has 9 coins. How many more coins does Eileen have?
   3 coins

34 LESSON 12   Multiply and Divide with 8 and 7

Homework and Remembering page 34

Home or School Activity

 ### Social Studies Connection

Calendar Sevens Tell students to list all the 7s count-bys on a calendar page and have them describe what day they all lie under. Have students repeat the activity with different calendar pages.

Ask students why the 7s count-bys will always be in a column under a particular day.

Ask students to explain why no other count-bys can be found in a column of a calendar.

OCTOBER						
S	M	T	W	T	F	S
		1	2	3	4	5
6	7	8	9	10	11	12
13	14	15	16	17	18	19
20	21	22	23	24	25	26
27	28	29	30	31		

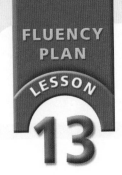

Fluency Day

Vocabulary

Factor Triangles
expression
number sentence
equation
inequality

Lesson Objective

● Practice multiplications and divisions for 6s, 7s, and 8s, in a variety of ways.

The Day at a Glance

Today's Goals	Materials	
1 Teaching the Lesson **A1:** Use Target with scrambled multiplication tables to practice. **A2:** Complete Factor Triangles to practice. **A3:** Use Product Cards to practice. **2 Going Further** ▶ Math Connection: Compare Expressions ▶ Differentiated Instruction **3 Homework and Spiral Review**	**Lesson Activities** Student Activity Book pp. 41–43, 43A–43D or Student Hardcover Book pp. 41–43 and Activity Workbook pp. 23–26 (includes Product Cards) Homework and Remembering pp. 35–42 (includes Product Cards) *Blackout* Game (TRB M24–M25) Targets Product Cards: 6s, 7s, 8s (Manipulative Kit or TRB M20–M23)	**Going Further** Student Activity Book p. 44 or Student Hardcover Book p. 44 Activity Cards FP-13 Counters Student Book p. 43 Math Journals

123 *Use* **Math Talk** *today!*

Keeping Skills Sharp

Quick Practice 🕐 5 MINUTES	Daily Routines
Goal: Practice multiplications and divisions. **Materials:** Class MathBoard **Practice with 6s, 7s, and 8s** On the Class MathBoard, write the nine multiplication problems and nine division problems for 6s, 7s, and 8s in a mixed order. $(8 \times 7, 6 \times 6, 7 \times 6, 7 \times 8, 8 \times 8, 6 \times 7, 6 \times 8, 7 \times 7, 8 \times 6, 7\overline{)56},$ $6\overline{)36}, 6\overline{)42}, 8\overline{)56}, 8\overline{)64}, 7\overline{)42}, 8\overline{)48}, 7\overline{)49}, 6\overline{)48})$ The **Student Leader** uses a pointer to point to each problem. On the leader's signal, the students say the answer in unison.	**Homework Review** Ask students if they had difficulty with any part of the homework. Plan to set aside some time to work with students needing extra help. **Skip Count** Have students skip count: ▶ by 5s from 55 to 110 ▶ by 8s from 16 to 56

① Teaching the Lesson

Activity 1

Target Practice

 15 MINUTES

Goal: Use Target with scrambled multiplication tables to practice.

Materials: Student Activity Book or Hardcover Book pp. 41–42; Targets

 NCTM Standard:
Number and Operations

The Learning Classroom

Math Talk You must direct student math talk for it to be productive. Over time, as students become more skilled at discussing their thinking and talking directly with each other, you will fade into the background more. But you will always monitor, clarify, extend, and ultimately make the decisions about how to direct the math conversation so that it is productive for your students.

Target Practice A

- The top left table has all numbers scrambled, so it is best for practicing all products or factors.

- The bottom left table just has the hard numbers, so it is best for practicing these hard numbers.

- The top right table has the 4 hardest numbers in order, so it is best for practicing these count-bys. (The 9s fingers and patterns make the 9s easier than the 4s.)

- The bottom right table has the same 4 hardest numbers but out of order, so it is best for practicing products and unknown factors.

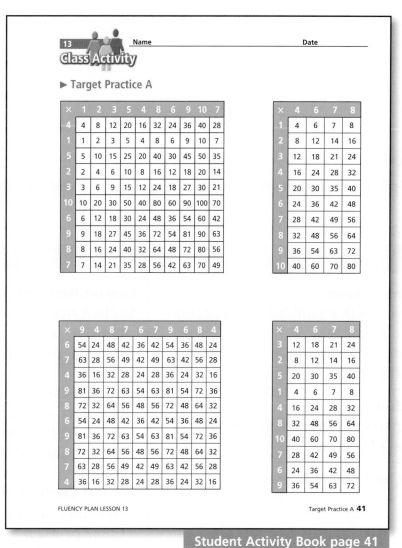

Student Activity Book page 41

▶ Target Practice WHOLE CLASS

Tell students they will practice their 6s, 7s, and 8s multiplications and divisions. Inform students that they will take a timed checkup tomorrow to see what they know and what they still need to study. The checkup will not be graded.

Have students turn to Student Book page 4l. Ask them to describe how the tables are different and say what each table would be best for practicing. See the side column for a description of the tables.

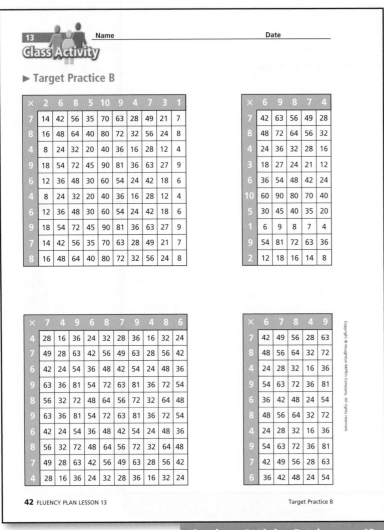

13
Class Activity

Name _____ Date _____

► Target Practice B

×	2	6	8	5	10	9	4	7	3	1
7	14	42	56	35	70	63	28	49	21	7
8	16	48	64	40	80	72	32	56	24	8
4	8	24	32	20	40	36	16	28	12	4
9	18	54	72	45	90	81	36	63	27	9
6	12	36	48	30	60	54	24	42	18	6
4	8	24	32	20	40	36	16	28	12	4
6	12	36	48	30	60	54	24	42	18	6
9	18	54	72	45	90	81	36	63	27	9
7	14	42	56	35	70	63	28	49	21	7
8	16	48	64	40	80	72	32	56	24	8

×	6	9	8	7	4
7	42	63	56	49	28
8	48	72	64	56	32
4	24	36	32	28	16
3	18	27	24	21	12
6	36	54	48	42	24
10	60	90	80	70	40
5	30	45	40	35	20
1	6	9	8	7	4
9	54	81	72	63	36
2	12	18	16	14	8

×	7	4	9	6	8	7	9	4	8	6
4	28	16	36	24	32	28	36	16	32	24
7	49	28	63	42	56	49	63	28	56	42
6	42	24	54	36	48	42	54	24	48	36
9	63	36	81	54	72	63	81	36	72	54
8	56	32	72	48	64	56	72	32	64	48
9	63	36	81	54	72	63	81	36	72	54
6	42	24	54	36	48	42	54	24	48	36
8	56	32	72	48	64	56	72	32	64	48
7	49	28	63	42	56	49	63	28	56	42
4	28	16	36	24	32	28	36	16	32	24

×	6	7	8	4	9
7	42	49	56	28	63
8	48	56	64	32	72
4	24	28	32	16	36
9	54	63	72	36	81
6	36	42	48	24	54
8	48	56	64	32	72
4	24	28	32	16	36
9	54	63	72	36	81
7	42	49	56	28	63
6	36	42	48	24	54

42 FLUENCY PLAN LESSON 13   Target Practice B

Student Activity Book page 42

The Learning Classroom

Math Talk In order to help students understand what you mean when you say, "explain your thinking," solve one of the problems at the board as if you were the student. Be sure to tell them about all parts of your problem and the thinking you used to solve it.

Class Management

For homework, have students continue their work with the new tables, using Homework and Remembering pages 37–38. Tell students to take them home and keep them in a safe place. Students should leave their school Target Practice A and B pages in their Student Books or in their desks.

► Practice With the New Tables [INDIVIDUALS]

Have students describe how the tables on Student Book page 42 are different and say what each table would be best for practicing, as they did for page 41. Students should find that the top left table practices all of the 5 hardest factors 4, 6, 7, 8, 9. The other 3 tables practice those 5 factors times each other. These are the hardest products and factors of all.

Give students a few minutes to practice with the different tables on Target Practice A and Target Practice B. Have students fill out their Study Plans once they determine what they need to practice.

Activity 2

Factor Triangles

 10 MINUTES

Goal: Complete Factor Triangles to practice.

Materials: Student Activity Book or Hardcover Book p. 43

 NCTM Standards:
Number and Operations
Algebra
Representation

Differentiated Instruction

Extra Help If students are having difficulty seeing how Factor Triangles work, show them that they can use the symbols and numbers to write an equation.

In exercise 1, start at the number 42. When you move to the box, you pass a division sign, so $42 \div \underline{\hspace{1cm}} = 6$. Because $7 \times 6 = 42$, the missing number is 7.

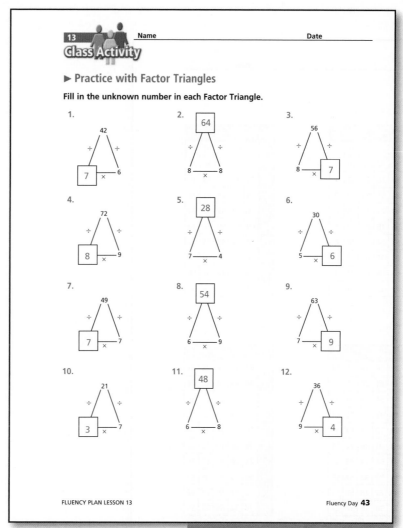

Student Activity Book page 43

▶ Practice With Factor Triangles INDIVIDUALS

Discuss with the class the exercises on Student Book page 43. Students should note that the problems are Factor Triangles like the ones they have seen before, only this time, one number is not shown.

Have students look at exercise 1. Ask:

● Where is the product located? at the top Do we know the product? yes, it is 42

● Where are the factors located? on the bottom Do we know both factors? no, one is not shown

● What is the unknown factor? 7

● How did you figure it out? I divided 42 by 6; I found the number you multiply 6 by to get 42.

Give students some time to finish the exercises. Let them discuss the answers with each other when they are done.

Product Cards for 6s, 7s, and 8s

▶ Product Cards   WHOLE CLASS

Pass out the Product Cards for 6s, 7s, and 8s or have students cut out the cards from the Student Activity Book or the Activity Workbook. Give students a few minutes to practice with the new cards.

Have students sort their new Product Cards into the three piles outlined below. They can choose whether to sort by multiplication or division. Students should sort by the operation that is most difficult for them.

- *Fast:* Problems they can solve quickly.

- *Slow:* Problems that take them a little time to solve.

- *Don't Know:* Problems they don't know.

▶ Play a Game   SMALL GROUPS

If time allows, have students read the rules for *Blackout* on TRB M24. Answer any questions they have about how to play. You might demonstrate by playing a round or two with a student.

 15 MINUTES

Goal: Use Product Cards to practice.

Materials: Product Cards: 6s, 7s, 8s (Manipulative Kit or TRB); Student Activity Book pp. 43A–43D or Activity Workbook pp. 23–26; *Blackout* Game (TRB M24–M25)

 NCTM Standard:
Number and Operations

 Ongoing Assessment

Ask students:

▶ How would you use your Target and multiplication table to practice your basic divisions?

▶ What is 36 ÷ 6 ?

 Class Management

Product Cards at Home If you have the Product Cards from the Manipulative Kit, you can have students use the cards on the student pages as a home practice set. Black and white versions of the cards also appear on the Homework pages 39–42 and on TRB M20–M23.

Going Further

Math Connection: Compare Expressions

Goal: Compare numerical expressions using symbols >, <, and =.

Materials: Student Activity Book or Hardcover Book p. 44.

✓ **NCTM Standards:**
Number and Operations
Algebra

▶ Expressions and Inequalities

WHOLE CLASS

This lesson connects operations with equations and inequalities. Two closely related terms that students often confuse with each other are defined on Student Book page 44: *expression* and *equation.* Make sure students understand the basic difference between an equation and an expression—an equation contains an equals sign and an expression does not. After discussing the different expressions for the number 6, ask students to give some expressions for the number 10. possible answers: 5×2, $13 - 3$, $30 \div 3$, $2 \times (4 + 1)$

Explain that a *number sentence* is a way of comparing two amounts. If the amounts are equal, the number sentence is an equation. If the amounts are not equal, the number sentence is an inequality.

Introduce the term *inequality.* Have students practice reading some simple inequalities aloud, such as:

$5 > 4$ 5 is greater than 4
$6 < 9$ 6 is less than 9

▶ Simplify and Compare

For exercises 1–15 on Student Book page 44, point out that students can start by simplifying the expressions.

Help students with the first exercise; show them how to write the simplified form of each expression to determine the correct symbol:

1. $5 + 8 \quad \underline{\ ?\ } \quad 14 - 4$
$\quad\ 13 \quad > \quad\ \ 10$
$\quad 5 + 8 \quad > \quad 14 - 4$

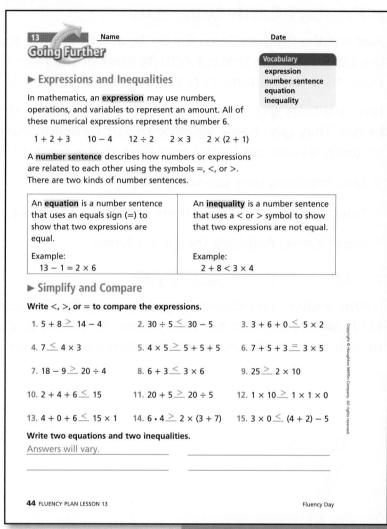

Student Activity Book page 44

English Language Learners

Have students practice reading and identifying equations, expressions and inequalities. Write an example of each on the board.

- **Beginning** Point to the equation. Ask: **Does this have an equals sign?** yes **Is it an equation?** yes Say: **Let's read it together.** Continue with other examples.
- **Intermediate** Ask: **Which one is an expression? How do you read it?** Say: **An expression is different from an equation. It doesn't have an _____?** equals sign
- **Advanced** Have students identify and read the examples. Help them compare the examples. Ask: **How are these the same? How are they different?**

Differentiated Instruction

Activity Card FP-13

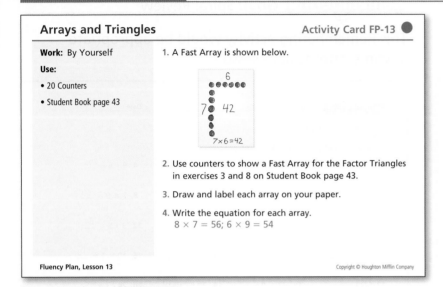

Arrays and Triangles   Activity Card FP-13

Work: By Yourself

Use:
- 20 Counters
- Student Book page 43

1. A Fast Array is shown below.

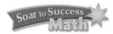

2. Use counters to show a Fast Array for the Factor Triangles in exercises 3 and 8 on Student Book page 43.

3. Draw and label each array on your paper.

4. Write the equation for each array.
   $8 \times 7 = 56; 6 \times 9 = 54$

Fluency Plan, Lesson 13   Copyright © Houghton Mifflin Company

Activity Note Students can use a multiplication table to check their products.

Math Writing Prompt

Draw a Multiplication Pick a multiplication you don't know well. Draw a Fast Array and a Factor Triangle for it.

Soar to Success Math — Software Support

Use *Soar to Success* for instruction of students needing targeted support for underlying skills.

On Level   **Activity Card FP-13**

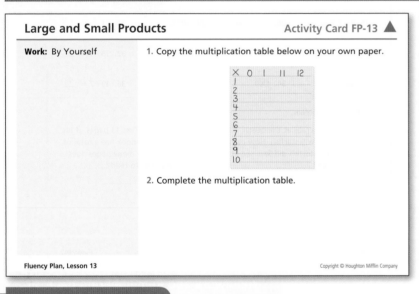

Large and Small Products   Activity Card FP-13

Work: By Yourself

1. Copy the multiplication table below on your own paper.

2. Complete the multiplication table.

Fluency Plan, Lesson 13   Copyright © Houghton Mifflin Company

Activity Note Ask students to identify any patterns they see in the table to extend the activity.

Math Writing Prompt

Explain Explain how to use a multiplication table to solve a Factor Triangle. Use an example.

MegaMath — Software Support

Use *MegaMath* for review and reinforcement of the concepts and skills presented in this lesson.

Challenge   **Activity Card FP-13**

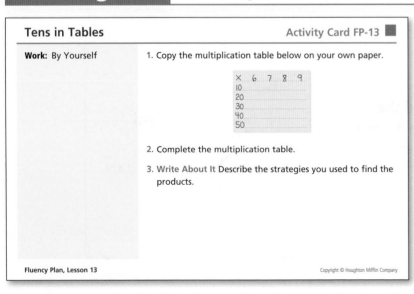

Tens in Tables   Activity Card FP-13

Work: By Yourself

1. Copy the multiplication table below on your own paper.

2. Complete the multiplication table.

3. Write About It Describe the strategies you used to find the products.

Fluency Plan, Lesson 13   Copyright © Houghton Mifflin Company

Activity Note To extend the activity, have students add rows to the multiplication table with other multiples of tens.

Math Writing Prompt

Create Your Own Make two Factor Triangles, using any numbers you want. Then write a multiplication or a division problem for each one.

DESTINATION Math — Software Support

Use *Destination Math* to take students beyond the concepts and skills presented in this lesson.

③ Homework and Spiral Review

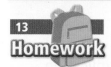

13 Homework **Goal:** Additional Practice

Use this Homework page to provide students with more practice with patterns in 6s, 7s, and 8s.

13 Remembering **Goal:** Spiral Review

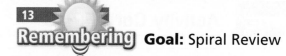

This Remembering activity would be appropriate anytime after today's lesson.

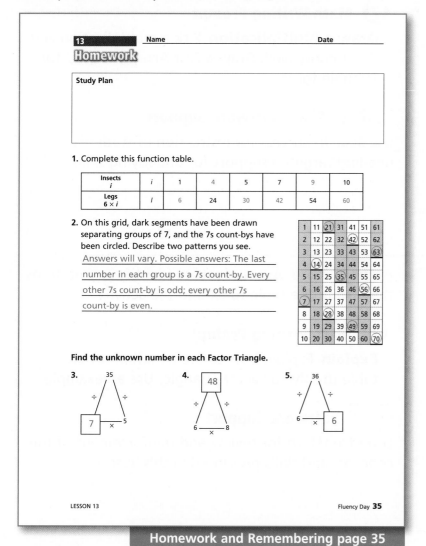

13 Homework Name _____ Date _____

Study Plan

1. Complete this function table.

Insects i	i	1	4	5	7	9	10
Legs $6 \times i$	l	6	24	30	42	54	60

2. On this grid, dark segments have been drawn separating groups of 7, and the 7s count-bys have been circled. Describe two patterns you see.
Answers will vary. Possible answers: The last number in each group is a 7s count-by. Every other 7s count-by is odd; every other 7s count-by is even.

1	11	21	31	41	51	61
2	12	22	32	42	52	62
3	13	23	33	43	53	63
4	14	24	34	44	54	64
5	15	25	35	45	55	65
6	16	26	36	46	56	66
7	17	27	37	47	57	67
8	18	28	38	48	58	68
9	19	29	39	49	59	69
10	20	30	40	50	60	70

Find the unknown number in each Factor Triangle.

3. 35, ÷ ÷, 7, × 5
4. 48, ÷ ÷, 6 × 8
5. 36, ÷ ÷, 6 × 6

LESSON 13   Fluency Day **35**

Homework and Remembering page 35

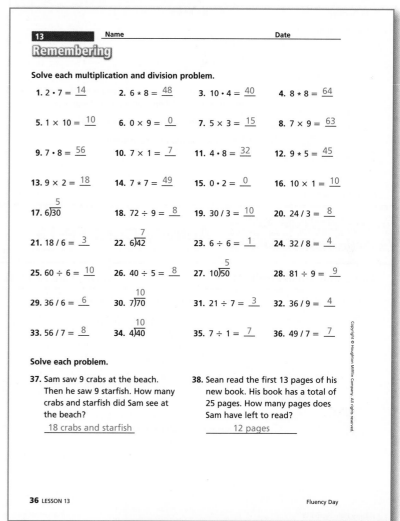

13 Remembering Name _____ Date _____

Solve each multiplication and division problem.

1. $2 \cdot 7 = \underline{14}$ 2. $6 * 8 = \underline{48}$ 3. $10 \cdot 4 = \underline{40}$ 4. $8 * 8 = \underline{64}$

5. $1 \times 10 = \underline{10}$ 6. $0 \times 9 = \underline{0}$ 7. $5 \times 3 = \underline{15}$ 8. $7 \times 9 = \underline{63}$

9. $7 \cdot 8 = \underline{56}$ 10. $7 \times 1 = \underline{7}$ 11. $4 \cdot 8 = \underline{32}$ 12. $9 * 5 = \underline{45}$

13. $9 \times 2 = \underline{18}$ 14. $7 * 7 = \underline{49}$ 15. $0 \cdot 2 = \underline{0}$ 16. $10 \times 1 = \underline{10}$

17. $6\overline{)30}$ (5)   18. $72 \div 9 = \underline{8}$ 19. $30 / 3 = \underline{10}$ 20. $24 / 3 = \underline{8}$

21. $18 / 6 = \underline{3}$ 22. $6\overline{)42}$ (7)   23. $6 \div 6 = \underline{1}$ 24. $32 / 8 = \underline{4}$

25. $60 \div 6 = \underline{10}$ 26. $40 \div 5 = \underline{8}$ 27. $10\overline{)50}$ (5)   28. $81 \div 9 = \underline{9}$

29. $36 / 6 = \underline{6}$ 30. $7\overline{)70}$ (10)   31. $21 \div 7 = \underline{3}$ 32. $36 / 9 = \underline{4}$

33. $56 / 7 = \underline{8}$ 34. $4\overline{)40}$ (10)   35. $7 \div 1 = \underline{7}$ 36. $49 / 7 = \underline{7}$

Solve each problem.

37. Sam saw 9 crabs at the beach. Then he saw 9 starfish. How many crabs and starfish did Sam see at the beach?
18 crabs and starfish

38. Sean read the first 13 pages of his new book. His book has a total of 25 pages. How many pages does Sam have left to read?
12 pages

36 LESSON 13   Fluency Day

Homework and Remembering page 36

Home or School Activity

Science Connection

Leggy Collections Have students do some research to find the differences between insects and spiders. Have them write a word problem about the number of legs in a group of spiders and insects.

> Ted collects bugs.
>
> He has 7 spiders and 9 beetles.
>
> How many legs do all these bugs have?

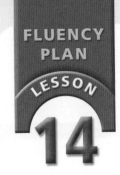
Square Numbers, 11s and 12s

Lesson Objectives

Vocabulary

square array
square number

- Explore patterns in square arrays and square numbers.
- Explore patterns in 11s and 12s multiplications and count-bys.

The Day at a Glance

Today's Goals	Materials
1 Teaching the Lesson **A1:** Write equations for square arrays, and explore patterns in square arrays and square numbers. **A2:** Explore patterns in 11s and 12s multiplications and count-bys. **2 Going Further** ▶ Differentiated Instruction **3 Homework and Spiral Review**	**Lesson Activities** Student Activity Book pp. 45–46 or Student Hardcover Book pp. 45–46 and Activity Workbook p. 27 Homework and Remembering pp. 43–44 Transparency of Student Book page 46 Overhead projector **Going Further** Activity Cards FP-14 Centimeter-Grid Paper (TRB M60) Math Journals 123 Use Math Talk today!

Keeping Skills Sharp

Quick Practice ⏱ 5 MINUTES	Daily Routines
Goal: Practice multiplications and divisions. **Materials:** Class MathBoard, Target Practice materials **Practice with 6s, 7s, and 8s** On the Class MathBoard, write the nine multiplication problems and nine division problems for 6s, 7s, and 8s in a mixed order. The **Student Leader** points to each problem on the board. On the leader's signal, the students say the answer in unison. (See Lesson 13) **Target Practice** Have students use the Target on Multiplication Table D to focus on the 6s, 7s, and 8s.	**Homework Review** The Study Plans of some students may indicate a need for more practice with specific multiplications and divisions. Suggest that they work with Product Cards for those problems. **Input/Output** When you put a number into a machine, it takes the number, reverses the digits, and divides it by 4. What number will the machine give when you input 23? 8

Teaching the Lesson

Patterns in Squares

 35 MINUTES

Goal: Write equations for square arrays, and explore patterns in square arrays and square numbers.

Materials: Student Activity Book pp. 45–46 or Hardcover Book pp. 45–46 and Activity Workbook p. 27; transparency of Student Book p. 46 and overhead projector (save transparency for reuse in Activity 2)

✓ **NCTM Standards:**
Number and Operations
Algebra

English Language Learners

Draw a 3 × 3 array on the board. Ask: **What array is this? What shape is it?** square. **What's the product?** 9 Say: **9 is a square number.**

• **Beginning** Draw 2 × 3 array. Ask: **What array is this? Is it a square?** no **What's the product?** 6 **Is 6 a square number?** no
• **Intermediate** Say: **When we multiply two numbers that are the same we get a square number.**
• **Advanced** Have students work in pairs to draw and describe other square arrays. Say: **We get a square number if we multiply two numbers that are _____.** the same

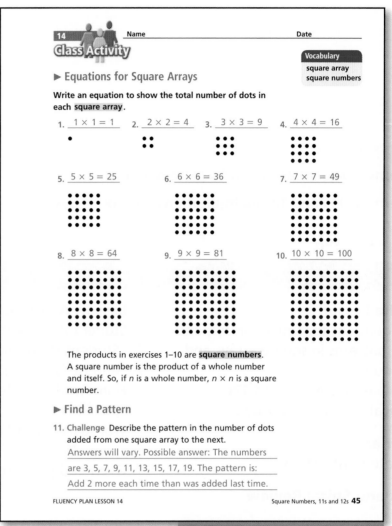

Student Activity Book page 45

▶ Equations for Square Arrays INDIVIDUALS

Have students look at the arrays on Student Book page 45. Ask,

● **How are all the arrays alike?** In each array, the number of rows of dots is the same as the number of columns of dots.

Explain that we call such arrays *square arrays*.

● **How do the arrays change as we move from one to the next?** The number of rows and the number of columns each increase by 1.

Give students a minute or two to write an equation for each array. Then have them list the products they found in exercises 1–10: 1, 4, 9, 16, 25, 36, 49, 64, 81, 100. Explain that these are called *square numbers*. A square number is the product of a whole number and itself. In other words, if *n* is a whole number, *n* × *n* is a square number.

▶ Find a Pattern PAIRS

On Student Book page 45, have students read problem 11, which challenges them to find a pattern in the number of dots added from one square array to the next. Have them work on the problem as **Student Pairs**.

They should discover that the number of dots added at each step follows the pattern 3, 5, 7, 9, 11, ..., which is a sequence of consecutive odd numbers.

A few students may be able to find a general rule for predicting how many dots are added from one array to the next: the number of dots added each time is equal to twice the previous factor plus 1. The new dots at each step are shown in red and blue in the art below. For example, the number of dots added to get from the fourth array (4×4) to the fifth (5×5) is $2 \times 4 + 1$, or 9. This is because you are adding 1 more column and 1 more row as you go, so you added to the 4×4 array a 4 column on the right and a 4 row at the bottom and then 1 more dot to make those both have 5 dots.

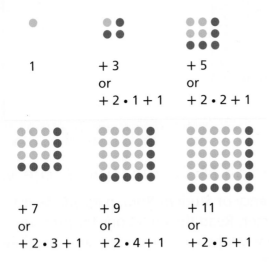

So in general you add to an $n \cdot n$ array 1 more column of n and 1 more row of n and then one dot at the bottom corner to make them both have $n + 1$. So you will always add $2 \cdot n + 1$ to the $n \cdot n$ array.

Activity continued ▶

The Learning Classroom

Helping Community Create a classroom where students are not competing, but desire to collaborate and help one another. Communicate often that your goal as a class is that everyone understands the math you are studying. Tell students that this will require everyone to work together to help each other.

The Learning Classroom

Math Talk Remember: Always start new topics by eliciting as much from students as possible. So even where the directions for a lesson are directing you to do the talking, remember to always ask for students' own ideas first.

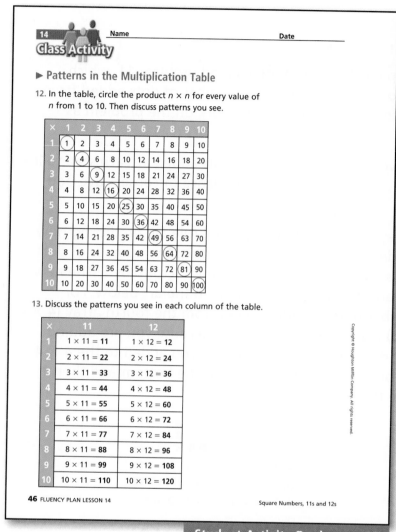

Student Activity Book page 46

×	1	2	3	4	5	6	7	8	9	10
1	①	2	3	4	5	6	7	8	9	10
2	2	④	6	8	10	12	14	16	18	20
3	3	6	⑨	12	15	18	21	24	27	30
4	4	8	12	⑯	20	24	28	32	36	40
5	5	10	15	20	㉕	30	35	40	45	50
6	6	12	18	24	30	㊱	42	48	54	60
7	7	14	21	28	35	42	㊾	56	63	70
8	8	16	24	32	40	48	56	㊍	72	80
9	9	18	27	36	45	54	63	72	㉛	90
10	10	20	30	40	50	60	70	80	90	⑩⓪

▶ Patterns in the Multiplication Table WHOLE CLASS

Display a transparency of Student Book page 46. Select a student to work at the projector. Read the directions for problem 12, and make sure students know what to do. When students are finished circling the numbers, ask them:

● **What do you notice about the numbers you circled?** They are the square numbers, and they form a diagonal from the upper left to the lower right.

● **The diagonal of square numbers divides the table in half. Look at the numbers below the diagonal and those above it. Do you notice anything interesting?** Each number on one side of the diagonal has a matching number on the other side.

● **The diagonal is like a line of symmetry for the table. If we were to fold the table along this diagonal, each number on one half would match with the same number on the other half.**

Ask students to draw an X through the number 21 in the bottom half of the table, as you do the same on the transparency.

- What multiplication equation goes with this 21? $7 \times 3 = 21$

Write $7 \times 3 = 21$ on the board. Then ask students to find and draw an X through the matching 21 on the top half of the table. Ask:

- What multiplication equation goes with this 21? $3 \times 7 = 21$

Write $3 \times 7 = 21$ on the board, next to the first equation.

$$7 \times 3 = 21 \qquad 3 \times 7 = 21$$

Repeat this for two or three more pairs of numbers. Then ask students what they notice about each pair of equations. The factors in one equation are the same as those in the other, but in a different order.

You might remind students that they learned that multiplication is *commutative*, meaning that the order of the factors can be switched without changing the product.

×	1	2	3	4	5	6	7	8	9	10
1	①	2	3	4	5	6	7	8	9	10
2	2	④	6	8	10	12	14	16	18	20
3	3	6	⑨	12	15	18	✗	24	27	30
4	4	8	12	⑯	20	24	28	32	36	40
5	5	10	15	20	㉕	30	35	40	45	50
6	6	12	18	24	30	㊱	42	48	54	60
7	7	14	✗	28	35	42	㊾	56	63	70
8	8	16	24	32	40	48	56	㉔	72	80
9	9	18	27	36	45	54	63	72	㈧	90
10	10	20	30	40	50	60	70	80	90	⑩

table square numbers 64, 81, 100 are circled in original

Activity 2

Patterns in 11s and 12s

▶ Patterns in 11s [WHOLE CLASS]

Show the transparency of Student Book page 46 again, and have students look at the multiplication table in problem 13. Ask what the columns show. the 11s multiplications up to 10×11 and the 12s multiplications up to 10×12

Math Talk Have students focus on the column of 11s multiplications. Ask,

- What patterns do you see in this column?

Most students will immediately notice that, for the multiplications up to 9×11, the tens and ones digits in the product are the same as the multiplier. Ask,

- Can anyone explain why this makes sense?

You may want to present the two ideas below, for 6×11, if no one mentions them. Similar reasoning will work for any 11s multiplication.

- 6×11 is equal to 11×6, which is eleven 6s. This is ten 6s, or 60, plus another 6, for a total of 66. This is similar to the 5s shortcut: we start with a multiplication we know, in this case 10×6, and count on from there.

Activity continued ▶

20 MINUTES

Goal: Explore patterns in 11s and 12s multiplications and count-bys.

Materials: Transparency of Student Book p. 46 and overhead projector

 NCTM Standards:
Number and Operations
Algebra
Reasoning and Proof

Activity 2

The Learning Classroom

Student Leaders When students explain their work, they need to stand beside their work and point to parts of it as they explain. Using a pointer that does not obscure any work enables all students to see the part of the drawing or math symbols that is being explained.

Class Management

Try using the "finger wiggle" to hold students accountable for really listening to one another. Rather than interrupting one another when they can't hear well, the student listeners wiggle their fingers in the air. The explaining student realizes that they need to talk louder or more clearly. This also helps students in their seats to begin to see their role as helping the explainer by listening and giving feedback.

Ongoing Assessment

Ask questions such as:

▶ How can you use what you know about square numbers to find 12 × 12?

▶ How can knowing 5 × 6 help you find 5 × 12?

● 11 = 1 ten + 1 one, so 6 × 11 is 6 tens + 6 ones, or 66. This follows a pattern similar to the one students used with 9s multiplications:

$$6 \times 9 = 6 \text{ tens} - 6 \text{ ones} \qquad 6 \times 11 = 6 \text{ tens} + 6 \text{ ones}$$

▶ Patterns in 12s WHOLE CLASS

Math Talk Continue to use the transparency on Student Book page 46 to show the multiplication table in problem 13. Ask students to describe any patterns they see in the column of 12s multiplications. For example,

● All the products are even.

● The products are 2s, 3s, 4s, and 6s count-bys.

● The sum of the digits in each product is a 3s count-by.

● Each 12s product is twice the corresponding 6s product. For example:

1 × 6 = 6	2 × 6 = 12	3 × 6 = 18	4 × 6 = 24
1 × 12 = 12	2 × 12 = 24	3 × 12 = 36	4 × 12 = 48

Say, "The 12s multiplications are not as easy to remember as the 11s multiplications, but you can use some of the strategies you already know to figure them out. Let's look at 7 × 12. Can anyone suggest a way to solve this problem?"

Here are a few possibilities students might mention:

● Use the 10s shortcut: 7 × 12 is equal to 12 × 7, which is twelve 7s. Start with ten 7s, or 70, and count on two more 7s: 70, 77, 84.

● Double a 6s multiplication: 7 × 12 is twice 7 × 6, which is 42. So 7 × 12 = 42 + 42 = 84.

● Combine multiplications. For example:

$$
\begin{array}{l}
7 \times 5 = 35 \\
7 \times 5 = 35 \\
\underline{7 \times 2 = 14} \\
7 \times 12 = 84
\end{array}
$$

Now have students close their books. Write two or three 12s multiplications on the board and give a **Student Leader** the opportunity to lead the **Solve and Discuss** to solve them.

Differentiated Instruction

Two Partners, One Array
Activity Card FP-14 ●

Work: In Pairs

1. The array below shows a square number.

$3 \times 3 = 9$

2. One partner draws a row of dots, using any number up to 12.

3. The other partner completes the array to show a square number and writes a multiplication equation for the array.

4. Partners exchange roles and repeat steps 2 and 3.

Fluency Plan, Lesson 14   Copyright © Houghton Mifflin Company

Activity Note Remind students that the arrays of the numbers should be squares, so the number of dots in the first row and in the first column is the same.

✎ Math Writing Prompt

Create Your Own Write a multiplication word problem, using the numbers 4 and 9.

Soar to Success Math ✦ Software Support

Use *Soar to Success* for instruction of students needing targeted support for underlying skills.

Correct It!
Activity Card FP-14 ▲

Work: By Yourself

1. The Puzzled Penguin multiplied mentally this way to find the product for 8×12.

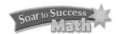

8 × 12 is 8 × 10 plus 20
So, 8 × 12 = 80 + 20 = 100

2. Identify the Puzzled Penguin's error. It should be 8×10 plus 16 because $8 \times 2 = 16$, not 20.

3. Show the correct way to find the product. 8×10 plus 16 is $80 + 16 = 96$.

Fluency Plan, Lesson 14   Copyright © Houghton Mifflin Company

Activity Note Have students draw an array for 8×12 to help demonstrate how the array can be correctly subdivided.

✎ Math Writing Prompt

Summarize Use your own words to write a definition of *square number.*

MegaMath Grades K-6 Software Support

Use *MegaMath* for review and reinforcement of the concepts and skills presented in this lesson.

Addition Patterns and Squares
Activity Card FP-14 ■

Work: By Yourself

Use:
• Centimeter-Grid Paper (TRB M60)

1. Copy the figures and numbers below onto grid paper.

2. Use drawings and numbers to continue the patterns to show the next two square numbers. 16, 25

3. Write About It Identify any patterns you can in the numbers and figures that are added to make the square numbers. The next odd number of squares is added to each figure. See Teacher Edition p. 115.

Fluency Plan, Lesson 14   Copyright © Houghton Mifflin Company

Activity Note Extend the problem by having students write only the addition pattern for the square numbers 36 and 49. $+ 11, + 13$

✎ Math Writing Prompt

Describe Patterns Describe the patterns in the products for the 11s multiplications. Describe the patterns in the products for the 12s multiplications.

✖ DESTINATION Math Software Support

Use *Destination Math* to take students beyond the concepts and skills presented in this lesson.

③ Homework and Spiral Review

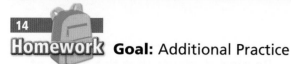

Goal: Additional Practice

Use this Homework page to provide students with more practice with 11s and 12s multiplications.

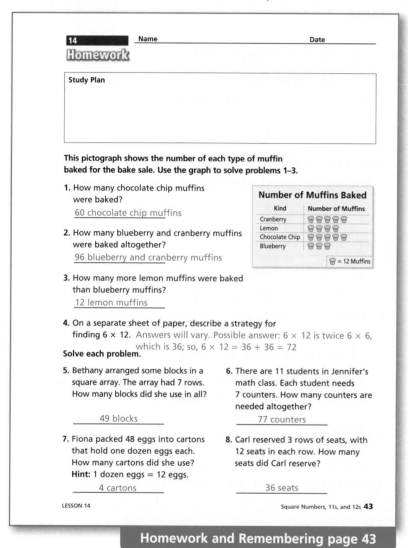

Homework and Remembering page 43

Remembering **Goal:** Spiral Review

This Remembering activity would be appropriate anytime after today's lesson.

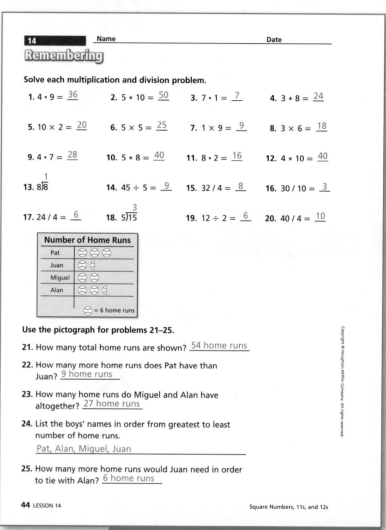

Homework and Remembering page 44

Home or School Activity

Math-to-Math Connection

What Kind of Rectangle Are You? Each student will work with a partner to measure each other's heights in feet and inches. Then they stand with their arms outstretched, measure their arm spans from the fingertips of their left hands to the fingertips of their right hands in feet and inches. Convert each measurement to inches. Students may measure several people and then make a table to record their heights and arm spans to see whether there are more "squares" or "rectangles that are not squares" in the classroom or family.

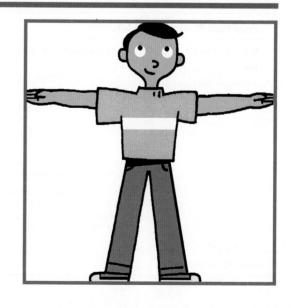

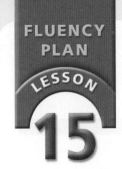

Fluency Day

Lesson Objective

● Practice multiplications and divisions for 6s, 7s, and 8s in a variety of ways.

The Day at a Glance

Today's Goals	Materials	

1 Teaching the Lesson
A1: Use Product Cards to practice.
A2: Use Write-On Sheets and Check Sheets to practice.
A3: Complete Factor Triangles and Fast Array problems to practice.
	Lesson Activities
	Student Activity Book pp. 47–52 or
	  Student Hardcover Book pp. 47–52
	  and Activity Workbook pp. 29–32
	  (includes Class Write-On Sheets
	  and Check Sheets)
	Homework and Remembering
	  pp. 45–50 (includes Home Write-
	  On Sheets and Check Sheets)
		Going Further
		Activity Cards FP-15
		Student Book p. 51
		Counters
		Index cards
		Math Journals

2 Going Further
▶ Differentiated Instruction
	Product Cards: 6s, 7s, 8s
	  (Manipulative Kit and
	  TRB M20–M23)	

3 Homework and Spiral Review	Sheet protectors Dry-erase markers	

123 Use Math Talk today!

Keeping Skills Sharp

Quick Practice 🕐 5 MINUTES	Daily Routines
Goal: Practice multiplications and divisions. **Materials:** Product Cards, Division Digits materials **Practice with Product Cards** Have students use their cards for independent practice. **Division Digits for 6s, 7s, 8s** The **Student Leader** uses problems from Set 3 (TRB M17). (See Lesson 2)	**Homework Review** Ask students to describe briefly some strategies they used in their homework. Sometimes you will find that students solve the problem correctly but use an inefficient strategy. **Calendar** Michael's soccer game will be in 5 days. If today is Monday, October 16, what will be the day and date of Michael's game? Saturday, October 21

① Teaching the Lesson

Activity 1

Product Cards

20 MINUTES

Goal: Use Product Cards to practice.

Materials: Product Cards: 6s, 7s, 8s

✔ **NCTM Standard:**
Number and Operations

▶ Sort Cards [INDIVIDUALS]

Give students a few minutes to sort their Product Cards for 6s, 7s, and 8s into *Fast*, *Slow*, and *Don't Know* piles. Have students sort the cards according to which operation is most difficult for them.

Activity 2

Write-On and Check Sheets

15 MINUTES

Goal: Use Write-On Sheets and Check Sheets to practice.

Materials: Student Activity Book pp. 47–50 or Hardcover Book pp. 47–50 and Activity Workbook pp. 29–32; sheet protectors; dry-erase markers

✔ **NCTM Standard:**
Number and Operations

Teaching Note

Long-Division Format The Write-On and Check sheets for both multiplication and division problems are shown in the long-division format. This practice format is intended to help students understand how division undoes multiplication and also how the factors and product are related to the divisor, quotient, and dividend in division.

▶ Write-On Sheets [WHOLE CLASS]

Give each student a sheet protector and a dry-erase marker. Have students tear out the Class Write-On Sheets on pages 47–48 of the Student Book. These class sheets can also be found on pages M27 and M28 in the Teacher's Resource Book. Ask them to put the Write-On Sheets back-to-back in the sheet protector.

15 **Class Activity**	Name _____				Class Sheet
①	**②**	**③**	**④**	**⑤**	**⑥**
$7)\overline{}5$	$5)\overline{}4$	$2)\overline{}4$	$4)\overline{}8$	$7)\overline{}4$	$6)\overline{}4$
$6)\overline{}2$	$10)\overline{}8$	$6)\overline{}5$	$1)\overline{}7$	$3)\overline{}7$	$1)\overline{}8$
$9)\overline{}8$	$8)\overline{}7$	$9)\overline{}6$	$6)\overline{}9$	$10)\overline{}6$	$4)\overline{}7$
$8)\overline{}1$	$4)\overline{}6$	$2)\overline{}6$	$8)\overline{}5$	$1)\overline{}6$	$7)\overline{}3$
$5)\overline{}6$	$7)\overline{}7$	$8)\overline{}9$	$5)\overline{}7$	$8)\overline{}8$	$5)\overline{}8$
$2)\overline{}8$	$9)\overline{}7$	$7)\overline{}2$	$3)\overline{}8$	$7)\overline{}0$	$10)\overline{}7$
$6)\overline{}1$	$6)\overline{}10$	$3)\overline{}6$	$10)\overline{}2$	$10)\overline{}4$	$6)\overline{}3$
$8)\overline{}6$	$9)\overline{}4$	$8)\overline{}3$	$6)\overline{}6$	$2)\overline{}7$	$8)\overline{}4$
$7)\overline{}9$	$6)\overline{}8$	$3)\overline{}4$	$7)\overline{}6$	$7)\overline{}8$	$7)\overline{}10$
$4)\overline{}4$	$7)\overline{}1$	$8)\overline{}0$	$8)\overline{}10$	$6)\overline{}0$	$6)\overline{}7$
FLUENCY PLAN LESSON 15					Class Write-On Sheet 2A **47**

Student Activity Book page 47

15 Class Activity

Name _____

Class Sheet

1	2	3	4	5	6
5 $7\overline{)35}$	4 $5\overline{)20}$	4 $2\overline{)8}$	8 $4\overline{)32}$	4 $7\overline{)28}$	4 $6\overline{)24}$
2 $6\overline{)12}$	8 $10\overline{)80}$	5 $6\overline{)30}$	7 $1\overline{)7}$	7 $3\overline{)21}$	8 $1\overline{)8}$
8 $9\overline{)72}$	7 $8\overline{)56}$	6 $9\overline{)54}$	9 $6\overline{)54}$	6 $10\overline{)60}$	7 $4\overline{)28}$
1 $8\overline{)8}$	6 $4\overline{)24}$	6 $2\overline{)12}$	5 $8\overline{)40}$	6 $1\overline{)6}$	3 $7\overline{)21}$
6 $5\overline{)30}$	7 $7\overline{)49}$	9 $8\overline{)72}$	7 $5\overline{)35}$	8 $8\overline{)64}$	8 $5\overline{)40}$
8 $2\overline{)16}$	7 $9\overline{)63}$	2 $7\overline{)14}$	8 $3\overline{)24}$	0 $7\overline{)0}$	7 $10\overline{)70}$
1 $6\overline{)6}$	10 $6\overline{)60}$	6 $3\overline{)18}$	2 $8\overline{)16}$	4 $10\overline{)40}$	3 $6\overline{)18}$
6 $8\overline{)48}$	4 $9\overline{)36}$	3 $8\overline{)24}$	6 $6\overline{)36}$	7 $2\overline{)14}$	4 $8\overline{)32}$
9 $7\overline{)63}$	8 $6\overline{)48}$	4 $3\overline{)12}$	6 $7\overline{)42}$	8 $7\overline{)56}$	10 $7\overline{)70}$
4 $4\overline{)16}$	1 $7\overline{)7}$	0 $8\overline{)0}$	10 $8\overline{)80}$	0 $6\overline{)0}$	7 $6\overline{)42}$

FLUENCY PLAN LESSON 15

Class Check Sheet 2A **49**

Student Activity Book page 49

▶ Practice With Check Sheets INDIVIDUALS

Give students a few minutes to practice with the Write-On Sheets. Have students check their answers and update their study plans using the Check sheets on Student Book pages 49–50 or Activity Workbook pages 31–32. Remind students that they can also use the Check sheets to quiz one another or practice individually. (See side column for ideas for individual practice.)

Individual Check Sheet Practice

Show students how to use Check Sheets for either multiplication or division. Fold a sheet of paper in half across the short way. To practice multiplication on Student Book page 49, you put the folded edge at the top with the top left corner covering the product 35 within the division box. The rest of the folded edge goes across to the right, also covering all of the other products within the division box but the numbers on the top are showing. You say the product of 7 times 5 to yourself ("35") and then slide the folded half sheet across to the right to check your answer. You then slide it far enough to the right to see the next divisor and the factor on the top (5 and 4) but keep the product covered. You say the product of 5 and 4 to yourself ("20") and slide to the right to check your answer. You continue across the row in this way. You can do the rows in any order to increase variation.

To practice division, you flip the folded edge to the bottom and put the sheet above the row of problems. It is better to start at the bottom and cover the whole row of problems and then carefully slide up the paper until you can see the divisor and product but not the factor on the top. Then slide the paper to the right as you answer (you can also do these right to left). At the end of the row, slide the sheet quickly back to cover that whole row and then carefully move it up so that you can see the division problems but not the answers for the next row up.

Class Management

Tell students to use the *Home* Write-On and Check Sheets 2A and 2B on Homework pages 47–50 for the rest of the unit.

① Teaching the Lesson (continued)

Activity 3

Factor Triangles and Fast Arrays

 10 MINUTES

Goal: Complete Factor Triangles and Fast Array problems to practice.

Materials: Student Activity Book or Hardcover Book pp. 51–52

 NCTM Standards:
Number and Operations
Algebra
Representation

✓ Ongoing Assessment

Ask students:

► What is 3 × 7?

► What is 54 ÷ 9?

► Write a multiplication sentence that has a product of 32.

Teaching Note

Fast Arrays Encourage students to draw open circles rather than closed circles when making these drawings so they can complete exercises more quickly.

English Language Learners

Make sure students understand how to complete the factor triangles and arrays. Draw an array for 7 × 5 = 35 without the 7.

• **Beginning** Say: **I know the product and one factor. I want to know the missing factor. I divide 35 by ____.** 5

• **Intermediate** Ask: **Can I divide to find the missing factor?** yes **What do I divide?** 35 by 5

• **Advanced** Have students work in pairs to brainstorm different strategies.

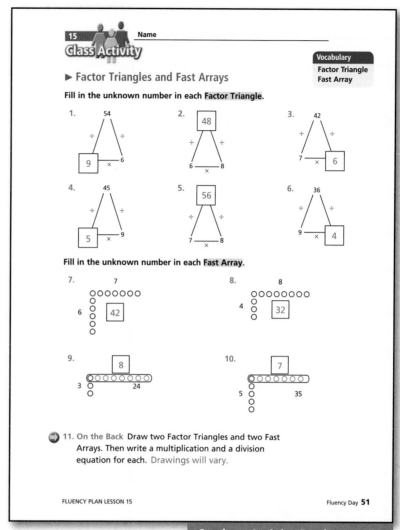

Student Activity Book page 51

► Factor Triangles and Fast Arrays INDIVIDUALS

Have students turn to Student Book page 51.

Math Talk Students should already be familiar with the Factor Triangle and Fast Array exercises. Have students complete the problems independently and then share their answers in class.

② Going Further

Differentiated Instruction on the right.

Differentiated Instruction

● Intervention — Activity Card FP-15

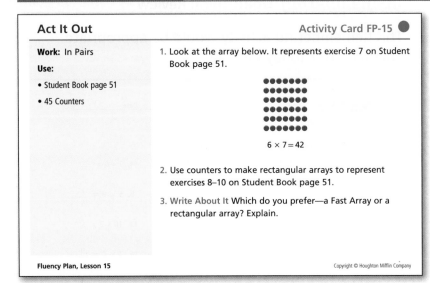

Act It Out — Activity Card FP-15 ●

Work: In Pairs

Use:
- Student Book page 51
- 45 Counters

1. Look at the array below. It represents exercise 7 on Student Book page 51.

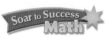

$6 \times 7 = 42$

2. Use counters to make rectangular arrays to represent exercises 8–10 on Student Book page 51.

3. **Write About It** Which do you prefer—a Fast Array or a rectangular array? Explain.

Fluency Plan, Lesson 15 — Copyright © Houghton Mifflin Company

Activity Note Point out that Student Book page 51 shows Fast Arrays, so students can duplicate the Fast Arrays and then complete them.

✎ Math Writing Prompt

Draw a Picture Draw a Fast Array for 7×8, and write the product. Explain your work.

Soar to Success Math ★ Software Support

Use *Soar to Success* for instruction of students needing targeted support for underlying skills.

▲ On Level — Activity Card FP-15

Division Fact Game — Activity Card FP-15 ▲

Work: In Small Groups

Use:
- 20 Index cards

1. Write the numbers below on index cards (1 per card).

12	14	16	18	21
24	28	30	32	35
36	40	42	48	49
54	56	63	64	72

2. Shuffle the cards and place them face down in a stack.

3. One person selects a card from the top of the stack and uses the number on the card to say a basic 6, 7, or 8 division.

4. If correct, that person keeps the card. If not, the card is returned to the bottom of the stack.

5. The next person selects a card and repeats steps 3 and 4.

6. Continue until there are no cards in the stack. The person with the most cards wins.

Fluency Plan, Lesson 15 — Copyright © Houghton Mifflin Company

Activity Note Other students in the group need to agree on the accuracy of the dividend.

✎ Math Writing Prompt

Make Connections Explain what the numbers in 36, 49, and 64 have in common.

MegaMath Grades K-6 Software Support

Use *MegaMath* for review and reinforcement of the concepts and skills presented in this lesson.

■ Challenge — Activity Card FP-15

Name That Change — Activity Card FP-15 ■

Work: By Yourself

1. Look at the function table below.

x	y
21	3
28	4
35	5
42	6
49	7

2. Write a division equation that shows the relationship between x and y. $y = x \div 7$

3. Use the equation to find the value of y when $x = 56$ and when $x = 63$. 8, 9

Fluency Plan, Lesson 15 — Copyright © Houghton Mifflin Company

Activity Note As an extension, students can make their own function tables for 6 and 8 division facts.

✎ Math Writing Prompt

Number Sense All numbers that are divisible by 6 are also divisible by 3 and 2. Explain why this is true.

✦ DESTINATION Math ® Software Support

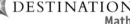

Use *Destination Math* to take students beyond the concepts and skills presented in this lesson.

3 Homework and Spiral Review

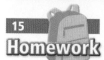

15 Homework **Goal:** Additional Practice

✓ Include students' work for page 45 as part of their portfolios.

15 Remembering **Goal:** Spiral Review

This Remembering activity would be appropriate anytime after today's lesson.

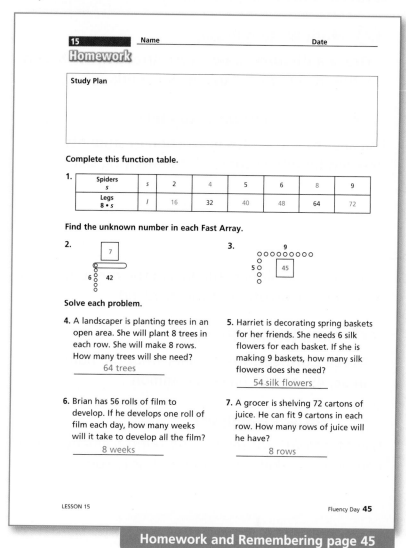

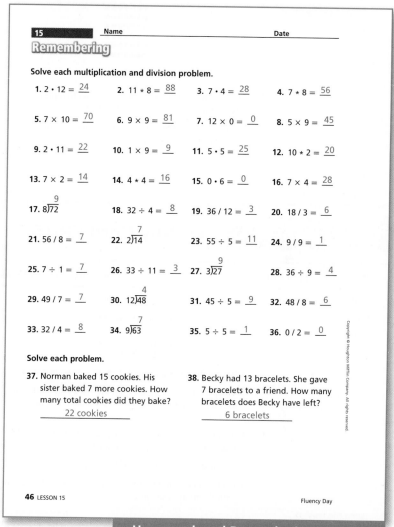

Home or School Activity

Music Connection

Multiplication Rap Rock N' Learn's *Multiplication Rap* CD can help students master their basic multiplications. Review the nines with students and listen to other multiplication raps as the unit progresses. Challenge students to write their own multiplication raps. You can use this CD in Unit 5 as well.

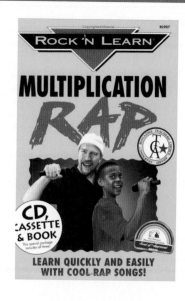

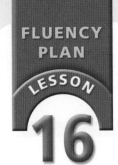
Properties of Multiplication

Lesson Objective

● Understand and apply the properties of multiplication and the Order
  of Operations.

The Day at a Glance

Today's Goals	Materials	
① Teaching the Lesson **A1:** Review the Commutative and Identity Properties of Multiplication. **A2:** Learn the Associative Property of Multiplication. **A3:** Learn the Distributive Property. **A4:** Use Order of Operations to simplify expressions. **② Going Further** ▶ Differentiated Instruction **③ Homework and Spiral Review**	**Lesson Activities** Student Activity Book pp. 53–56 or Hardcover Book pp. 53–56 Homework and Remembering pp. 51–52	**Going Further** Activity Cards FP-16 Index cards Counters Math Journals

Use **Math Talk** *today!*

Keeping Skills Sharp

Quick Practice · 5 MINUTES

Goal: Practice multiplications and divisions

Materials: Class MathBoard, Target Practice materials

Practice with 6s, 7s, and 8s On the Class MathBoard, write the nine multiplication problems and nine division problems for 6s, 7s, and 8s in a mixed order. (See Lesson 13)

Target Practice Have students use the Target on Multiplication Table D to focus on the 6s, 7s, and 8s.

Daily Routines

Homework Review Have students discuss the problems from their homework. Encourage students to help each other resolve any misunderstandings.

Reasoning A palindrome is a number, word, or sentence that reads the same way forward as backward. For example, *mom*, 303, and *Was it a cat I saw?* are palindromes.

Write a number with 4 digits and a word with 4 letters that are both palindromes. *Possible answers:* deed, noon, sees, peep, toot; 1221

Teaching the Lesson

Activity 1

Commutative and Identity Properties

 15 MINUTES

Goal: Review the Commutative and Identity Properties of Multiplication.

Materials: Student Activity Book or Hardcover Book p. 53

✓ **NCTM Standards:**
Number and Operations
Algebra
Reasoning and Proof

Teaching Note

Language and Vocabulary Explain that properties are qualities or characteristics—in this case, qualities or characteristics of multiplication. The Identity Property of Multiplication is so named because the product of 1 and any other number is *identical* to that number. For example, the product of 5 and 1 is 5: $5 \cdot 1 = 5$

The Commutative Property is so named because two factors can be commuted, or exchanged, without affecting the product. For example, $3 \times 2 = 2 \times 3$.

A *conjecture* is an educated guess, or hunch. Encourage students to make conjectures and then test them using mathematics.

 ## Class Management

Students may be confused because they have not solved multiplication problems with multidigit numbers. If so, point out that the directions say to use the Commutative Property of Multiplication. Ask students if they need to actually multiply the numbers to solve the problems.

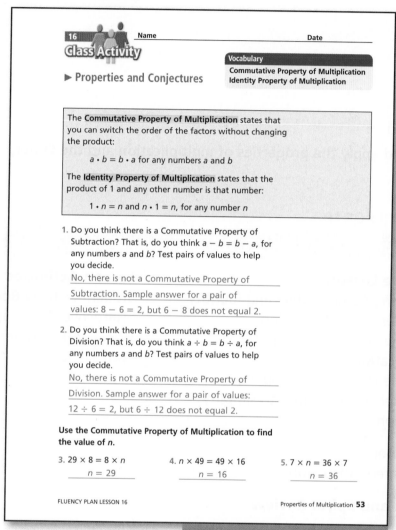

Student Activity Book page 53

► Properties and Conjectures WHOLE CLASS

Ask for Ideas Ask students what they remember about properties of multiplication. The box at the top of Student Book page 53 reviews the multiplication properties students have learned so far.
Go through the properties one at a time and discuss a few specific examples of each. This may be the first time your students have seen the formal name for the Identity Property of Multiplication.

Review with students the Commutative Property of Addition. Tell them that now they will determine whether there are commutative properties for subtraction and division as well. Have them work with a **Helping Partner** on problems 1 and 2, and then discuss the results as a class. Finally, have students solve exercises 3–5.

Associative Property

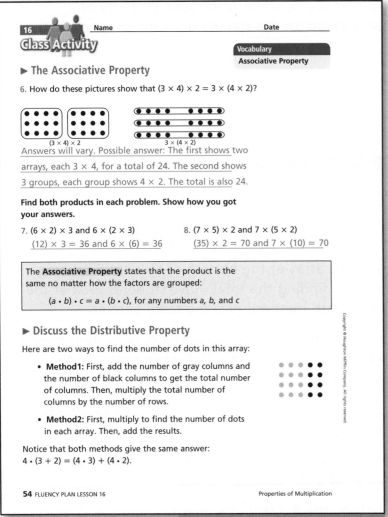

Student Activity Book page 54

▶ The Associative Property [WHOLE CLASS]

Ask students how each picture on Student Book page 54 represents the expression below it. Review the fact that parentheses in a mathematical expression mean, "Do this first." On the left, each of the two 3-by-4 arrays has 3 × 4 dots, so the total number of dots is (3 × 4) × 2. On the right, each row is 2 groups of 4, which is 2 × 4 or 4 × 2. There are 3 of these rows, for a total of 3 × (4 × 2).

Ask students how many dots are in each picture. 24 This shows that (3 × 4) × 2 = 3 × (4 × 2). Write the equation on the board. Then say:

● This equation shows that we get the same answer whether we multiply the first two factors and then multiply by the last factor or whether we multiply the last two factors and then multiply by the first factor.

For exercises 7 and 8, ask how the expressions in each are related. They have the same factors, but they are grouped differently.

Activity continued ▶

 20 MINUTES

Goal: Learn the Associative Property of Multiplication.

Materials: Student Activity Book or Hardcover Book p. 54

 NCTM Standards:
Number and Operations
Algebra

Teaching Note

Language and Vocabulary The word *associate* means "to bring together or join." The Associative Property is so named because when an expression has three factors, either the first two factors may be associated and multiplied first, or the last two factors may be associated and multiplied first. For example, 2 × (9 × 1) = (2 × 9) × 1.

English Language Learners

Help students visualize the Associative Property of Multiplication. Write (2 × 3) × 4 on the board. Say: **These are parentheses. We multiply the numbers inside first.** Draw arrays and model each step.

● **Beginning** Move the parentheses. Repeat the steps. Ask: **Is the answer different?** no

● **Intermediate** Move the parentheses. Have students work in pairs to solve the new problem. Ask: **What was different?** the order **What was the same?** the answer

● **Advanced** Have students work in pairs to draw arrays and solve the problem. Move the parentheses. Ask: **Did the order change the result?** no

Properties of Multiplication **129**

Activity 2

Ask how the products in each problem are related. They are equal.

Explain that these problems show the Associative Property of Multiplication. Read and discuss the statement of the property in the student book.

Activity 3

Distributive Property

 20 MINUTES

Goal: Learn the Distributive Property.

Materials: Student Activity Book or Hardcover Book pp. 54–55

 NCTM Standards:
Number and Operations
Algebra
Communication

Teaching Note

Language and Vocabulary One meaning of *distribute* is "to give out". If we apply the Distributive Property to 4 × (3 + 2), we *distribute* the 4 to each of the other numbers, 2 and 3:
4 × (3 + 2) = 4 × 3 + 4 + 2

▶ **Discuss the Distributive Property** WHOLE CLASS

Have students look at the array at the bottom of Student Book page 54. Discuss both methods for finding the total. Have students look at the equation showing that both methods give the same answer.

Write the equation on the board, underlining the 4s or writing them in a different color: **4 • (3 + 2) = (4 • 3) + (4 • 2)**. Explain that we say that the 4 *distributes* over the sum 3 + 2.

Work through problems 9–11 on Student Book page 55 as a class, eliciting the answers from students.

Write the equation from problem 11 on the board, again emphasizing the 4s: **(3 + 2) • 4 = 3 • 4 + 2 • 4**.

Point out that, as before, the 4 *distributes* over the sum 3 + 2, even though the order is different.

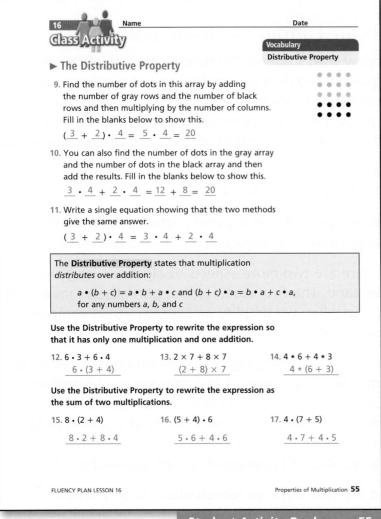

Student Activity Book page 55

Content of Student Activity Book page 55:

16 **Class Activity**
Name _____ Date _____

Vocabulary
Distributive Property

▶ **The Distributive Property**

9. Find the number of dots in this array by adding the number of gray rows and the number of black rows and then multiplying by the number of columns. Fill in the blanks below to show this.

   (_3_ + _2_) • _4_ = _5_ • _4_ = _20_

10. You can also find the number of dots in the gray array and the number of dots in the black array and then add the results. Fill in the blanks below to show this.

    _3_ • _4_ + _2_ • _4_ = _12_ + _8_ = _20_

11. Write a single equation showing that the two methods give the same answer.

    (_3_ + _2_) • _4_ = _3_ • _4_ + _2_ • _4_

    The **Distributive Property** states that multiplication *distributes* over addition:

    $a \cdot (b + c) = a \cdot b + a \cdot c$ and $(b + c) \cdot a = b \cdot a + c \cdot a$, for any numbers a, b, and c

Use the Distributive Property to rewrite the expression so that it has only one multiplication and one addition.

12. $6 \cdot 3 + 6 \cdot 4$ 13. $2 \times 7 + 8 \times 7$ 14. $4 * 6 + 4 * 3$
    _6 • (3 + 4)_   _(2 + 8) × 7_   _4 * (6 + 3)_

Use the Distributive Property to rewrite the expression as the sum of two multiplications.

15. $8 \cdot (2 + 4)$ 16. $(5 + 4) \cdot 6$ 17. $4 \cdot (7 + 5)$
    _8 • 2 + 8 • 4_   _5 • 6 + 4 • 6_   _4 • 7 + 4 • 5_

FLUENCY PLAN LESSON 16   Properties of Multiplication **55**

✓ **Ongoing Assessment**

Ask students:

What property is used in each equation?

$4 \times (8 \times 2) = (4 \times 8) \times 2$

$7 \times (6 + 4) = 7 \times 6 + 7 \times 4$

The Learning Classroom

Math Talk An effective way to verify that students understand a concept is to give them the opportunity to summarize what they have earned, using their own words and examples. For this lesson, ask students to explain and use examples to show the Commutative Property, the Identity Property, the Associative Property, and the Distributive Property of Multiplication. Invite a student to work at the board and record examples from the class discussion.

▶ The Distributive Property

Read the statement of the Distributive Property in the student book. Ask if anyone can explain the property in his or her own words. Here is one possible explanation: To find a number times a sum, multiply the number by each addend and then add the two products.

Remind students that, in earlier lessons, they learned to combine two multiplications to find another multiplication. Use the equation from problem 9 to show that combining multiplications is really using the distributive property:

$$(3 + 2) \cdot 4 = 3 \cdot 4 + 2 \cdot 4 \quad \begin{array}{l} 3 \cdot 4 = 12 \\ + 2 \cdot 4 = 8 \\ \hline 5 \cdot 4 = 20 \end{array} \left.\begin{array}{l} \\ \end{array}\right\} \begin{array}{l} \leftarrow 3 \cdot 4 + 2 \cdot 4 \\ \\ \leftarrow (3 + 2) \cdot 4 \end{array}$$

Use **Solve and Discuss** for exercises 12–17.

① Teaching the Lesson

Order of Operations

 60 MINUTES

Goal: Use Order of Operations to simplify expressions.

Materials: Student Activity Book or Hardcover Book p. 56

 NCTM Standards:
Number and Operations
Algebra
Reasoning and Proof

Teaching Note

Language and Vocabulary Explain to students that an **expression** is a number, a variable, or operations involving numbers or variables. Expressions include 4, b, $5a$, $2n + 1$, and $b \cdot c$. To **simplify** an expression (or equation) means to perform operations.

▶ **Using Algebraic Language** [WHOLE CLASS]

Ask for Ideas Review with students the concept that algebra is a mathematical language using its own notation. Algebraic language allows us to make statements about all numbers, as we have just seen in discussing properties in the previous activities. Ask students to summarize what they know about different ways to write multiplication.

- We can use a dot (•) instead of a times sign (×) to represent multiplication. For example, $2 \times 7 = 2 \cdot 7$.

- We can write two letters or a number and a letter next to each other to represent multiplication. For example, $a \cdot b = ab$ or $5 \cdot n = 5n$.

Tell students that there are two more aspects of algebraic language that they can now understand. The first aspect is that parentheses mean "do what is inside first." So when we simplify an expression, we compute inside the parentheses first.

The second aspect of algebraic language is a convention that allows us to use fewer parentheses. If we always knew that we would perform some operations before others, we could reduce the number of parentheses in some expressions, or eliminate them altogether. In other words, we can write expressions in a simpler way. So how can we decide whether it makes more sense to multiply/divide or add/subtract first?

Write on the board the two ways we represented the Distributive Property in Activities 2 and 3:

$$a \cdot (b + c) = a \cdot b + a \cdot c$$

$$a(b + c) = ab + ac$$

Ask students to name the equation that is easier to understand, and explain why. (The second equation is easier; we can see that the multiplications are performed first because a and b, and a and c, are next to each other.)

These two ways of writing the Distributive Property incorporate the next special convention of algebraic language, which is that we agree to perform the multiplications and divisions before we perform the additions and subtractions. This agreement eliminates the need to write a great number of parentheses.

$$a \cdot b + a \cdot c \text{ means } (a \cdot b) + (a \cdot c)$$

$$(a \cdot b) + (a \cdot c) \text{ means } (ab) + (ac)$$

$$(ab) + (ac) \text{ means } ab + ac$$

Share with students these two additional aspects of algebraic language.

- First, it is easier to operate on terms that use a letter and a number next to each other if they are always written in the same order. Since the algebraic convention is to write the number first, we write 5*a* to represent the product of 5 and *a*; we do not write *a*5.

- Second, it is also important to stress that parentheses can be used at any time to show something clearly. It is always acceptable to use parentheses to show a meaning. But we do not have to place parentheses around multiplications or divisions to show that we want them completed before additions or subtractions.

▶ Discuss the Order of Operations

| WHOLE CLASS |

Math Talk

Ask students to summarize what they know about different ways to write multiplication. (For example, use • instead of ×; $a • b = ab$; $5 • n = 5n$.)

Point out that when a numerical expression contains parentheses and/or more than one operation, the operations must be performed in an exact order.

Write the expression $10 + 6 ÷ 2$ on the board and ask students to add first and name the answer (8) and then divide first and name the answer (13). Point out that both answers cannot be correct, and lead students to understand that because expressions sometimes contain more than one operation, we need steps to follow to simplify those expressions.

After the completion of the activity, again write $10 + 6 ÷ 2$ on the board or overhead and ask students to explain why the expression simplifies to 13. More than one operation is present, and the Order of Operations states that we must divide before we add.

Activity continued ▶

Activity 4

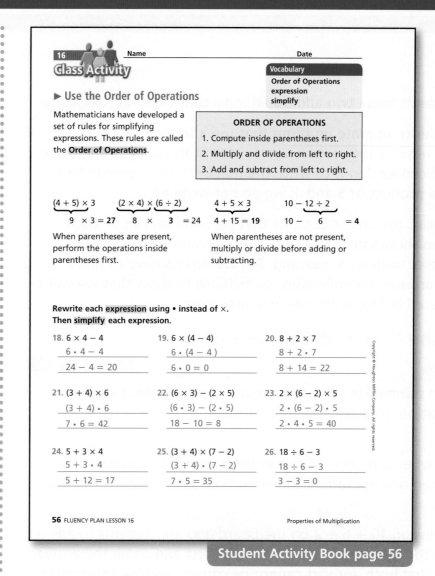

Student Activity Book page 56

▶ Use the Order of Operations WHOLE CLASS

Have students read the summary at the top of Student Book page 56 and work through the examples. Then use **Solve and Discuss** (or have each student with a **Helping Partner**) to complete exercises 18–26. These exercises provide an opportunity for students to practice writing multiplication with the more algebraic • symbol rather than the × sign.

Math Talk After the exercises have been completed, have students summarize the Order of Operations steps: parentheses, then multiplication/division, then addition/subtraction.

②Going Further

Differentiated Instruction

Intervention — Activity Card FP-16

Act It Out — Activity Card FP-16 ●

Work: In Pairs
Use:
- 10 Index cards
- Counters

1. Make two sets of cards, each numbered 1 to 5. Then shuffle the cards and place them face down in a stack.

2. One partner selects three cards and writes a multiplication expression, using one pair of parentheses around two of the numbers.

3. The other partner rewrites the expression, placing the parentheses in a different place.

4. Each partner uses counters to illustrate the expressions.

$(2 \times 3) \times 3 = 18$
$2 \times (3 \times 3) = 18$

Fluency Plan, Lesson 16   Copyright © Houghton Mifflin Company

Activity Note Have students identify groups in their models to reinforce that the products within parentheses are found first and shown as arrays.

 Math Writing Prompt

Draw a Picture Draw two arrays, one to show 2 × 5 and the other to show 5 × 2. Then write the name of the multiplication property shown by your drawing.

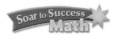 **Software Support**

Use *Soar to Success* for instruction of students needing targeted support for underlying skills.

On Level — Activity Card FP-16

Smart Moves — Activity Card FP-16 ▲

Work: By Yourself

1. Copy the following problems on your own paper.

   (23 × 5) × 2 = _____
   230; Associative Property
   8 • (105 + 2) = _____
   856; Distributive Property
   12 • 9 + 12 • 1 = _____
   120; Distributive Property

2. Rewrite the problems to make the computation easier. Then solve.

3. Identify the property of multiplication you used to rewrite each problem.

Fluency Plan, Lesson 16   Copyright © Houghton Mifflin Company

Activity Note As an extension, have students write their own problem that can be rewritten with the Associative Property of Multiplication to make solving easier.

 Math Writing Prompt

Explain Your Thinking Why is 2 • (5 + 3) the same as (2 • 5) + (2 • 3)? Use drawings, if needed.

 Software Support

Use *MegaMath* for review and reinforcement of the concepts and skills presented in this lesson.

Challenge — Activity Card FP-16

Multiply Bigger Numbers — Activity Card FP-16 ■

Work: By Yourself

1. Copy the following problems on your own paper.

   8 • 19 = _152_

   2 × 47 = _94_

   4 • (201) = _804_

2. Identify the property of multiplication you can use to rewrite all of the problems to make the computation easier. Distributive Property

3. Rewrite the problems and solve.

Fluency Plan, Lesson 16   Copyright © Houghton Mifflin Company

Activity Note As an extension, have students write their own problem that can be rewritten with the Distributive Property to make solving easier.

 Math Writing Prompt

Justify Your Reasoning Explain whether or not division is associative. Give at least one example.

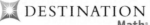 **Software Support**

Use *Destination Math* to take students beyond the concepts and skills presented in this lesson.

Properties of Multiplication   **135**

③ Homework and Spiral Review

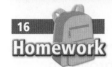

16 Homework — Goal: Additional Practice

Use this Homework page to provide students with more practice with properties of multiplication.

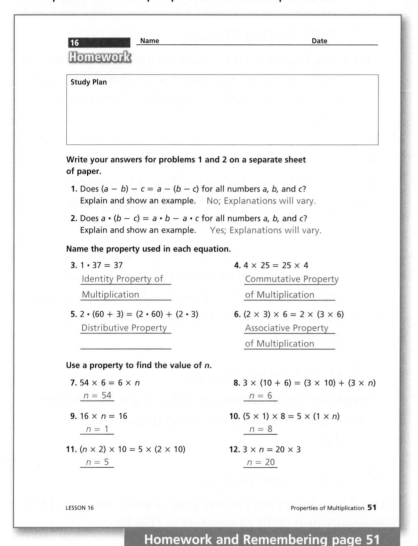

16 Homework

Name _____ **Date** _____

Study Plan

Write your answers for problems 1 and 2 on a separate sheet of paper.

1. Does $(a - b) - c = a - (b - c)$ for all numbers a, b, and c? Explain and show an example.   No; Explanations will vary.

2. Does $a \cdot (b - c) = a \cdot b - a \cdot c$ for all numbers a, b, and c? Explain and show an example.   Yes; Explanations will vary.

Name the property used in each equation.

3. $1 \cdot 37 = 37$
   Identity Property of Multiplication

4. $4 \times 25 = 25 \times 4$
   Commutative Property of Multiplication

5. $2 \cdot (60 + 3) = (2 \cdot 60) + (2 \cdot 3)$
   Distributive Property

6. $(2 \times 3) \times 6 = 2 \times (3 \times 6)$
   Associative Property of Multiplication

Use a property to find the value of n.

7. $54 \times 6 = 6 \times n$
   $n = 54$

8. $3 \times (10 + 6) = (3 \times 10) + (3 \times n)$
   $n = 6$

9. $16 \times n = 16$
   $n = 1$

10. $(5 \times 1) \times 8 = 5 \times (1 \times n)$
    $n = 8$

11. $(n \times 2) \times 10 = 5 \times (2 \times 10)$
    $n = 5$

12. $3 \times n = 20 \times 3$
    $n = 20$

LESSON 16   Properties of Multiplication **51**

Homework and Remembering page 51

16 Remembering — Goal: Spiral Review

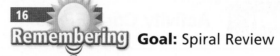

This Remembering activity would be appropriate anytime after today's lesson.

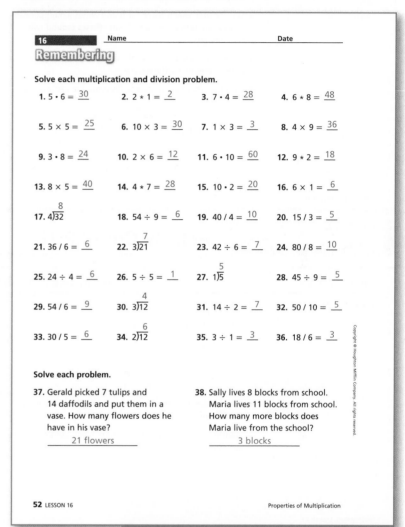

16 Remembering

Name _____ **Date** _____

Solve each multiplication and division problem.

1. $5 \cdot 6 = \underline{30}$
2. $2 * 1 = \underline{2}$
3. $7 \cdot 4 = \underline{28}$
4. $6 * 8 = \underline{48}$

5. $5 \times 5 = \underline{25}$
6. $10 \times 3 = \underline{30}$
7. $1 \times 3 = \underline{3}$
8. $4 \times 9 = \underline{36}$

9. $3 \cdot 8 = \underline{24}$
10. $2 \times 6 = \underline{12}$
11. $6 \cdot 10 = \underline{60}$
12. $9 * 2 = \underline{18}$

13. $8 \times 5 = \underline{40}$
14. $4 * 7 = \underline{28}$
15. $10 \cdot 2 = \underline{20}$
16. $6 \times 1 = \underline{6}$

17. $4\overline{)32}$ → 8
18. $54 \div 9 = \underline{6}$
19. $40 / 4 = \underline{10}$
20. $15 / 3 = \underline{5}$

21. $36 / 6 = \underline{6}$
22. $3\overline{)21}$ → 7
23. $42 \div 6 = \underline{7}$
24. $80 / 8 = \underline{10}$

25. $24 \div 4 = \underline{6}$
26. $5 \div 5 = \underline{1}$
27. $1\overline{)5}$ → 5
28. $45 \div 9 = \underline{5}$

29. $54 / 6 = \underline{9}$
30. $3\overline{)12}$ → 4
31. $14 \div 2 = \underline{7}$
32. $50 / 10 = \underline{5}$

33. $30 / 5 = \underline{6}$
34. $2\overline{)12}$ → 6
35. $3 \div 1 = \underline{3}$
36. $18 / 6 = \underline{3}$

Solve each problem.

37. Gerald picked 7 tulips and 14 daffodils and put them in a vase. How many flowers does he have in his vase?
    21 flowers

38. Sally lives 8 blocks from school. Maria lives 11 blocks from school. How many more blocks does Maria live from the school?
    3 blocks

52 LESSON 16   Properties of Multiplication

Homework and Remembering page 52

Home or School Activity

Art Connection

Comic Math Have students make a storyboard or comic strip consisting of three or more scenes to illustrate a multiplication property. For example, C-man might show the Commutative Property, Ashley the Great might rearrange things to show the Associative Property, and 1 Stick Person might represent the Identity Property.

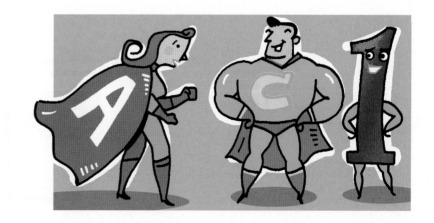

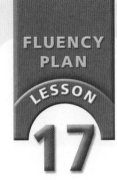

FLUENCY PLAN

LESSON

17

Fluency Day

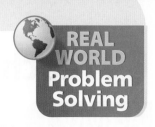

Lesson Objectives

● **Practice multiplications for 6s, 7s, and 8s in a variety of ways.**

● **Practice divisions for 0s, 1s, 3s, 4s, 6s, 7s, and 8s.**

The Day at a Glance

Today's Goals	Materials
1 Teaching the Lesson **A1:** Use Product Cards to practice multiplications and divisions. **A2:** Play Five in a Line to practice multiplications and divisions. **2 Going Further** ▶ Math Connection: Make a Pictograph ▶ Differentiated Instruction **3 Homework and Spiral Review**	**Lesson Activities** Homework and Remembering pp. 53–54 Checkup D (TRB M122) and Checkup D Answer Key (TRB M40) Checkup E (TRB M123) and Checkup E Answer Key (TRB M113) Product Cards: All (Manipulative Kit or TRB M6–M9, M11–M12, M20–M23) *Five in a Line* Call List (TRB M31–M32) *Five in a Line* Cards (Manipulative Kit or TRB M33–M39) Sheet protectors Dry-erase markers Counters **Going Further** Make a Pictograph (TRB M124) Activity Cards FP-17 Index cards Math Journals 123 Use Math Talk today!

Keeping Skills Sharp

Quick Practice ⏱ 5 MINUTES	Daily Routines
Goal: Practice multiplications and divisions. **Materials:** Class MathBoard, Product Cards **Practice with 6s, 7s, and 8s** On the Class MathBoard, write the nine multiplication problems and nine division problems for 6s, 7s, and 8s in a mixed order. (See Lesson 13) **Practice with Product Cards** Have students practice independently using their Product Cards. (See Lesson 5)	**Homework Review** Let students work together to check their work. Initially, pair less able students with more able students. Remind students to use what they know about helping others. **Find a Pattern** If this pattern continues, what are the next three numbers? 7, 11, 15, 19, 23, . . . 27, 31, 35

① Teaching the Lesson

Sort the Product Cards

 15 MINUTES

Goal: Use Product Cards to practice multiplications and divisions.

Materials: Checkup D (TRB M122); Checkup D Answer Key (TRB M40); Checkup E (TRB M123); Checkup E Answer Key (TRB M113); Product Cards: All (Manipulative Kit or TRB M6–M9, M11–M12, M20–M23)

 NCTM Standard:
Number and Operations

The Learning Classroom

Building Concepts Using Product Cards is a quick and creative way to help students learn their multiplications and divisions. Since the two sides of each card are related, they will help students understand the relationship between multiplication and division. The cards can be used at any time for individual or partner practice with a friend or helper at home.

▶ Checkup Practice

Provide additional multiplication and division practice, using Checkup D (TRB M122) or Checkup E (TRB M123). Checkup D tests all numbers students have learned so far. Checkup E is more challenging because it tests only 6s, 7s, and 8s. The Checkup D Answer Key is on TRB M40. The Checkup E Answer Key is on TRB M113.

▶ Sort the Product Cards [INDIVIDUALS]

Have students combine the Product Cards for 6s, 7s, and 8s with all of their other cards—new cards and old cards—into a single pile.

Have students sort the whole deck of cards into *Fast*, *Slow*, and *Don't Know* piles. Students may choose whether to sort them by multiplication or division. Tell students they will use the sorted cards to practice in the next unit.

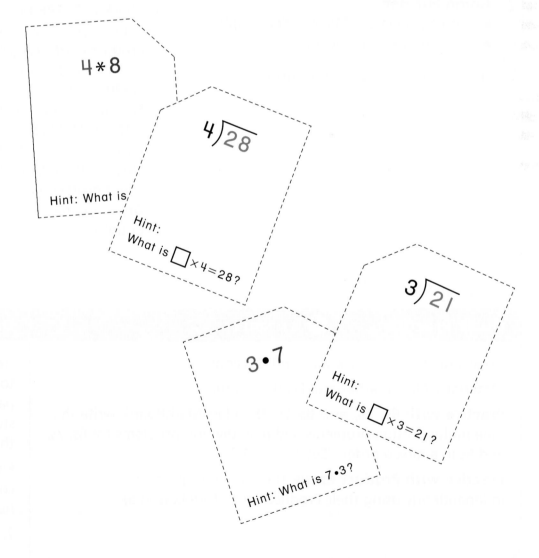

Five in a Line

▶ Play *Five in a Line* WHOLE CLASS

Choose a **Student Leader** to run the game. Put the *Five in a Line* Call List (TRB M31–M32) in a sheet protector and give it to the student leader.

Give a *Five in a Line* Card to each student. If you are using the TRB versions of the cards (M33–M39), and you have 28 students or more, you must make 2 or more copies of each card page. If you have the *Math Expressions* kit, 2 sets of the cards are already provided for you. If you are using 2 sets of cards, remember there will be two winners per game. Each student will also need about 10 counters or small pieces of paper to cover the numbers on the cards.

The student leader should read the problems (without answers) from the call list one at a time, starting with any problem and reading the problems in any order. The leader should mark each problem he or she reads. The leader should pause briefly after each problem to give students a chance to determine the answer. Students who have the answer on their cards should cover it.

When a student covers 5 numbers in a row—horizontally, vertically, or diagonally—he or she should shout, "Five in a Line!" The Student Leader should check the card to make sure that all the numbers the student covered are marked on the call list. If so, that student wins.

If time is limited, you can change the rules so that the first student to get 3 or 4 numbers in a row wins.

25 MINUTES

Goal: Play *Five in a Line* to practice multiplications and divisions.

Materials: *Five in a Line* Call List (TRB M31–M32); sheet protector; dry-erase marker; *Five in a Line* Cards (Manipulative Kit or TRB M33–M39); counters

 NCTM Standard:
Number and Operations

 Ongoing Assessment

Ask students to:

▶ Write a multiplication expression for each product on one of their Five in a Line cards.

▶ Write a division expression for each quotient on their other Five in a Line cards.

The Learning Classroom

Building Concepts Select different student leaders for different tasks. Take time to help students get used to being leaders. Support them for the first two times, and encourage classmates to be supportive. Most students gain confidence themselves when they help others.

② Going Further

Math Connection: Make a Pictograph

Goal: Organize data in a table and display the data in a pictograph.

Materials: Make a Pictograph (TRB M124)

✓ **NCTM Standards:**
Number and Operations
Representation
Data Analysis and Probability

▶ Discuss Pictographs WHOLE CLASS

In this lesson students will be connecting skip counting with representing data.

Ask for Ideas Ask students to describe what they remember about pictographs.

A pictograph uses symbols to represent data; each symbol represents the same number.

One of the more difficult aspects of constructing a pictograph is to identify common factors of the data, and to understand that these factors will affect the number of symbols that are required to display the data.

To help students practice this skill, distribute TRB M124, and then read the following data (or write it on the board or overhead) while students write the data in the table at the top of the copymaster.

Time	Number of Cars
6 A.M.	4
9 A.M.	20
Noon	16
3 P.M.	18
6 P.M.	8

 Math Talk Have students use their understanding of count-bys (such as count by 1s, count by 2s, and so on) to identify possible numbers of cars that each symbol may represent. Then ask students to discuss an advantage and/or disadvantage of each. Possible answers include:

Each symbol = 1 car: Many symbols would be needed. (disadvantage)

Each symbol = 2 cars: Fewer symbols would be needed. (advantage)

Each symbol = 4 cars: Fewer symbols would be needed than for 1 or 2 (advantage), but a half symbol would be needed to represent 18 cars because 4 is not a factor of 18. (disadvantage)

Working individually or in **Student Pairs**, ask students to choose a symbol, choose a number to represent that symbol, and make a pictograph of the data in the grid at the bottom of TRB M124.

Then have students compare and contrast the completed graphs, and lead them to conclude that the same data can be displayed in more than one way.

English Language Learners

Review *symbol* and *pictograph*. Draw baseball caps representing 12 players on Team A and 15 on Team B. Say: **This is a *pictograph*. The pictures equal numbers. They are *symbols*. 1 cap equals 3 players.**

• **Beginning** Say: There are 4 caps. 3 × 4 = ___. 12 There are 12 players on Team A. Continue with Team B.
• **Intermediate** Ask: How many caps are there for Team A? 4 What's 3 × 4? 12 How many players are on Team A? 12
• **Advanced** Have students describe the pictograph and find the number of players on each team.

Differentiated Instruction

Intervention — Activity Card FP-17

Pairs of Factors
Activity Card FP-17

Work: In Pairs

Use:
• 12 Index cards

1. Write the numbers 6, 7, 8 and 9 each on three different index cards.
2. Shuffle the cards and place them face down in any arrangement.
3. One partner selects any two cards and finds the product of the two numbers. The two cards are set aside.
4. The other partner repeats step 3.
5. Continue taking turns until all the cards are used.

Copyright © Houghton Mifflin Company

Activity Note Students can repeat the activity by adding cards with other numbers to practice fluency with other factors.

Math Writing Prompt
Explain Your Thinking Why is 6×9 the same as 9×6? Draw a picture, if needed.

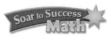 Software Support
Use *Soar to Success* for instruction of students needing targeted support for underlying skills.

On Level — Activity Card FP-17

What's the Product
Activity Card FP-17

Work: In Small Groups

Use:
• Index cards (1 for each student)

1. Look at the multiplication puzzle card below.

> What's the Product?
> One factor is 7.
> The product is between 60 and 70.
> The product is an odd number.

2. Each group member writes a multiplication puzzle on an index card and writes the solution on the back. Group members can work together, but the group must write a problem for every member.
3. The group then trades cards with another group and solves the other group's puzzles.

Copyright © Houghton Mifflin Company

Activity Note It may be helpful to give students a list of terms. For example: *factor, multiple, odd, even, prime, composite, between, greater,* or *less.*

Math Writing Prompt
Make a List Using the number 8 as a product or quotient, list as many different multiplication and division expressions as you can. Stop when your list has 25 expressions.

Software Support
Use *MegaMath* for review and reinforcement of the concepts and skills presented in this lesson.

Challenge — Activity Card FP-17

Create a Function Table
Activity Card FP-17

Work: By Yourself

1. This function table shows the total number of baseball players needed for baseball teams.

Baseball Teams

Number of Teams p	Number of Players $9 \cdot p$
2	18
5	45
10	90
30	270

2. Think of a multiplication or division situation that can be shown by using a function table.
3. Create a function table. Include a variable and rule for the table. Then complete the table for at least 10 numbers.

Copyright © Houghton Mifflin Company

Activity Note Remind students to use column heads to clearly identify what they are modeling in the table.

Math Writing Prompt
Create Your Own Write multiplication and division equations and inequalities, using at least three of the numbers 6, 7, 8, or 9 in each number sentence. You may use each number more than once in each number sentence.

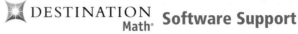 Software Support
Use *Destination Math* to take students beyond the concepts and skills presented in this lesson.

③ Homework and Spiral Review

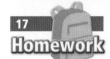

Homework **Goal:** Additional Practice

✓ Include students' work for page 53 as part of their portfolios.

Remembering **Goal:** Spiral Review

This Remembering activity would be appropriate anytime after today's lesson.

17	Name	Date

Homework

Study Plan

Complete this function table.

1.

Dozens of Eggs d	d	1	3	5	7	9	11
Number of Eggs $12 \cdot d$	n	12	36	60	84	108	132

Fill in the missing number in each Fast Array.

2. [7] 8 | 56

3. 11 ○○○○○○○○○○○ 7 [77]

Solve each problem.

4. Marisa's age is 4 times Sam's age. Marisa is 20 years old. How old is Sam?

_____5 years old_____

5. Raul and Rosa were playing basketball. Raul made 10 baskets. Rosa made half as many as Raul. How many baskets did Rosa make?

_____5 baskets_____

6. Jeff sold 12 cars on Friday. He sold 3 times as many cars on Saturday. How many cars did Jeff sell on Saturday?

_____36 cars_____

7. Danielle received $32 for her birthday. Three years ago, she received $\frac{1}{4}$ as much. How much did Danielle receive three years ago?

_____$8_____

LESSON 17

Fluency Day **53**

Homework and Remembering page 53

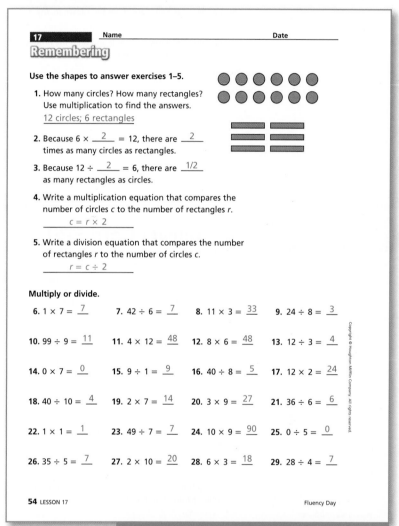

17	Name	Date

Remembering

Use the shapes to answer exercises 1–5.

1. How many circles? How many rectangles? Use multiplication to find the answers.
12 circles; 6 rectangles

2. Because $6 \times \underline{2} = 12$, there are _2_ times as many circles as rectangles.

3. Because $12 \div \underline{2} = 6$, there are _1/2_ as many rectangles as circles.

4. Write a multiplication equation that compares the number of circles c to the number of rectangles r.
$c = r \times 2$

5. Write a division equation that compares the number of rectangles r to the number of circles c.
$r = c \div 2$

Multiply or divide.

6. $1 \times 7 = \underline{7}$ **7.** $42 \div 6 = \underline{7}$ **8.** $11 \times 3 = \underline{33}$ **9.** $24 \div 8 = \underline{3}$

10. $99 \div 9 = \underline{11}$ **11.** $4 \times 12 = \underline{48}$ **12.** $8 \times 6 = \underline{48}$ **13.** $12 \div 3 = \underline{4}$

14. $0 \times 7 = \underline{0}$ **15.** $9 \div 1 = \underline{9}$ **16.** $40 \div 8 = \underline{5}$ **17.** $12 \times 2 = \underline{24}$

18. $40 \div 10 = \underline{4}$ **19.** $2 \times 7 = \underline{14}$ **20.** $3 \times 9 = \underline{27}$ **21.** $36 \div 6 = \underline{6}$

22. $1 \times 1 = \underline{1}$ **23.** $49 \div 7 = \underline{7}$ **24.** $10 \times 9 = \underline{90}$ **25.** $0 \div 5 = \underline{0}$

26. $35 \div 5 = \underline{7}$ **27.** $2 \times 10 = \underline{20}$ **28.** $6 \times 3 = \underline{18}$ **29.** $28 \div 4 = \underline{7}$

54 LESSON 17

Fluency Day

Homework and Remembering page 54

Home or School Activity

 Real-World Connection

Plan a Picnic Have students plan a picnic for 30 people. They should list the types of food they will serve at the picnic. Then they decide how many packages of food, plates, cups, napkins, and utensils they need to buy. Students may research how these items are packaged by visiting a store or checking with an adult at home.

Picnic for 30 People

Item	Quantity in Package	Packages Needed
Buns	8	4
Franks	10	6
Plates	24	2

Unit 1 Overview

Solve Multiplication and Division Word Problems

SOLVING WORD PROBLEMS is an essential part of the *Math Expressions* curriculum because these problems connect the outside world with the classroom. In their own lives, students encounter mathematical situations that require them to understand the relationships between known and unknown quantities. This unit encourages students to analyze the structure and language of different types of word problems and to discuss different models that can be used to solve the word problems. This unit builds literacy and communication skills for all students.

Skills Trace

Grade 3	Grade 4	Grade 5
• Solve comparison problems. • Interpret and make bar graphs. • Solve multistep problems.	• Solve comparison problems. • Interpret and make bar graphs. • Solve multistep problems. • Solve combination problems. • Write situation and solution equations. • Identify prime and composite numbers	• Solve combination and comparison problems. • Use graphs to solve comparison problems. • Solve multistep problems. • Write situation and solution equations. • Write prime factorization using exponents

Unit 1   Contents

Unit 1   Assessment

Unit Objectives Tested	Unit Test Items	Lessons
1.1 Solve comparison problems	5–8	4, 5, 6
1.2 Solve combination problems	1, 4	1, 2
1.3 Write an equation to solve multiplication and division problems.	2, 3	3
1.4 Solve multiple-step problems	10a	7, 9
1.5 Use factoring to determine whether a number is prime.	9, 10b	8, 9

Assessment and Review Resources

Formal Assessment

Student Activity Book
- Unit Review and Test (pp. 85–86)

Assessment Guide
- Quick Quiz 1
- Quick Quiz 2
- Test A–Open Response
- Test B–Multiple Choice
- Performance Assessment

Test Generator CD-ROM
- Open Response Test
- Multiple Choice Test
- Test Bank Items

Informal Assessment

Teacher Edition
- Ongoing Assessment (in every lesson)
- Quick Practice (in every lesson)
- Portfolio Suggestions (pp. 194, 210)

Math Talk
- ▸ The Learning Classroom (pp. 144, 145, 146, 152, 154, 167, 181, 182, 190, 197, 200)
- ▸ Math Talk in Action (p. 192)
- ▸ Activities (pp. 148, 152, 153, 154, 159, 167, 174, 181, 182, 184, 189, 206)
- ▸ Solve and Discuss (pp. 148, 152, 153, 154, 159, 167, 168, 172, 173, 189, 191, 200, 201)
- ▸ Student Pairs (pp. 144, 168, 174, 176, 192, 206)
- ▸ Student Leaders (pp. 143, 151, 157, 160, 165, 171, 179)
- ▸ Small Groups (pp. 147, 184)
- ▸ Helping Partners (pp. 176, 183, 191)

Review Opportunities

Homework and Remembering
- Review of recently taught Topics
- Cumulative Review

Teacher Edition
- Unit Review and Test (pp. 211–214)
- Checkup C (p. 144)
- Checkup D (p. 196)

Test Generator CD-ROM
- Custom review sheets

Planning Unit 1

Lesson/NCTM Standards	Resources	Materials for Lesson Activities	Materials for Other Activities
1–1 **Solve Word Problems With Tables** NCTM Standards: 1, 2, 5, 10	TE pp. 143–150 SAB pp. 57–62 H&R pp. 55–56 AC 1-1	Checkup C Answer Key (TRB M26)	✓ Counters Encyclopedias, almanacs, and Internet access Math Journals
1–2 **Tables of Combinations** NCTM Standards: 1, 5, 10	TE pp. 151–156 SAB pp. 63–64 H&R pp. 57–58 AC 1-2 MCC	Transparency of Student Book p. 63 and overhead projector (optional) MathBoard Materials Division Digits materials	Index cards Math Journals
1–3 **Situation and Solution Equations** NCTM Standards: 1, 2, 6	TE pp. 157–164 SAB pp. 65–66 H&R pp. 59–60 AG Quick Quiz 1 AC 1-3	Division Digits materials ✓ Targets Multiplication Table	Math Journals
1–4 **Multiplication Comparisons** NCTM Standards: 1, 2, 10	TE pp. 165–170 SAB pp. 67–68 H&R pp. 61–62 AC 1-4	Division Digits: Sets 2 and 3 (TRB M4 and M17) ✓ Product Cards: 6s, 7s, and 8s	Connecting cubes or Centimeter-Grid Paper (TRB M60) and colored pencils Math Journals
1–5 **Mixed Comparison Problems** NCTM Standards: 1, 2, 5, 10	TE pp. 171–178 SAB pp. 69–72 H&R pp. 63–64 AC 1-5 MCC	Division Digits: Sets 2 and 3 (TRB M4 and M17)	Centimeter-Grid Paper (TRB M60) Straightedge Colored pencils Math Journals

Resources/Materials Key: TE: Teacher Edition   SAB: Student Activity Book   H&R: Homework and Remembering
AC: Activity Cards   MCC: Math Center Challenge   AG: Assessment Guide   ✓: Grade 4 Kit   TRB: Teacher's Resource Book

Lesson/NCTM Standards	Resources	Materials for Lesson Activities	Materials for Other Activities
1–6 **Bar Graphs** NCTM Standards: 1, 2, 5, 8, 10	TE pp. 179–186 SAB pp. 73–76 H&R pp. 65–66 AC 1-6 MCC	Centimeter-Grid Paper (TRB M60) Ruler or straightedge Index cards Division Digits materials ✓ Product Cards	Centimeter-Grid Paper (TRB M60) Ruler or straightedge Colored pencils or markers Math Journals
1–7 **Solve Multistep Word Problems** NCTM Standards: 1, 2, 6	TE pp. 187–194 SAB pp. 77–78 H&R pp. 67–68 AC 1-7	✓ Product Cards	✓ Two-color counters Math Journals
1–8 **Factors and Prime Numbers** NCTM Standards: 1, 2, 7, 8	TE pp. 195–204 SAB pp. 79–82 H&R pp. 69–70 AC 1-8 AG Quick Quiz 2 MCC	Checkup D Answer Key (TRB M40) MathBoard Materials Division Digits materials ✓ Product Cards	✓ Counters Math Journals
1–9 **Use Mathematical Processes** NCTM Standards: 6, 7, 8, 9, 10	TE pp. 205–210 SAB pp. 83–84 H&R pp. 71–72 AC 1-9	Centimeter-Grid Paper (TRB M60) Make a Pictograph (TRB M124) Ruler or straightedge	✓ Number cubes Math Journals
Unit Review and Test	TE pp. 211–214 SAB pp. 85–86 AG Unit 1 tests		

Hardcover Student Book	Manipulatives and Materials
• Together, the hardcover student book and its companion Activity Workbook contain all the pages in the consumable Student Activity Workbook.	• Essential materials for teaching Math Expressions are available in the Grade 4 kit. These materials are indicated by a ✓ in these lists. At the front of this Teacher Edition is more information about kit contents, alternatives for the materials, and use of the materials.

Independent Learning Activities

Ready-Made Math Challenge Centers

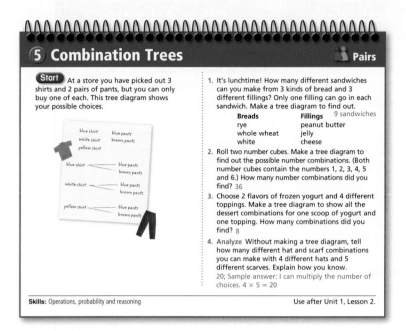

Grouping Pairs

Materials Number cubes (2 per pair)

Objective Students draw tree diagrams and generalize the number of outcomes.

Connections Probability and Reasoning

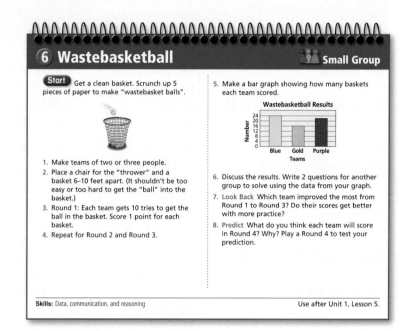

Grouping Small Groups

Materials Basket

Objective Students record and represent data in a bar graph and make predictions.

Connections Data and Communication

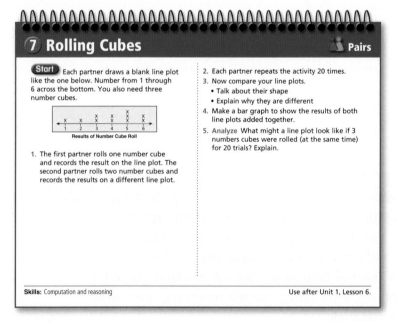

Grouping Pairs

Materials Number cubes (3 per pair)

Objective Students record results in line plots, combine results to create a bar graph, and analyze results.

Connections Data and Representation

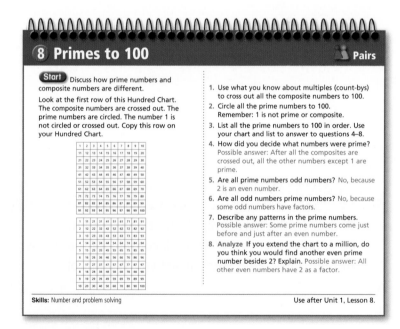

Grouping Pairs

Materials Hundred Chart (TRB M147)

Objective Students expand their understanding of numbers by investigating prime and composite numbers.

Connections Number and Reasoning

Ready-Made Math Resources

Technology — Tutorials, Practice, and Intervention

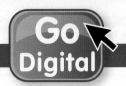

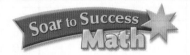

Use activity masters and online, individualized intervention and support to bring students to proficiency.

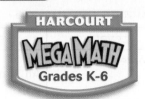

Help students practice skills and apply concepts through exciting math adventures.

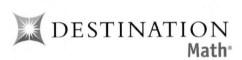

Extend and enrich students' understanding of skills and concepts through engaging, interactive lessons and activities.

Visit **Education Place®**
www.eduplace.com

Visit www.eduplace.com/mx2t/ and find family, teacher, and student materials, activities, games, and more.

Literature Links

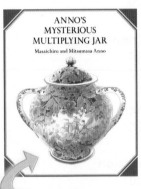

Anno's Mysterious Multiplying Jar

Anno's Mysterious Multiplying Jar
In this beautifully illustrated book by Masaichiro and Mitsumasa Anno, students will see how the concept of factorials is demonstrated in an imaginative story context.

Literature Connection

Arithme-Tickle: An Even Number of Odd Riddle-Rhymes by Patrick Lewis. Illustrated by Frank Remkiewicz. Voyager Books, Harcourt, Inc., 2002.

Unit 1   Teaching Resources

Differentiated Instruction

Individualizing Instruction

Activities	Level	Frequency
	• Intervention • On Level • Challenge	All 3 in every lesson
	Level	**Frequency**
Math Writing Prompts	• Intervention • On Level • Challenge	All 3 in every lesson
Math Center Challenges	For advanced students	
	4 in every unit	

Reaching All Learners

	Lessons	Pages
English Language Learners	1, 2, 3, 4, 5, 6, 7, 8, 9	146, 153, 158, 166, 175, 180, 188, 197, 207
	Lessons	**Pages**
Extra Help	1, 2, 6, 8	144, 153, 183, 196, 199
	Lesson	**Page**
Special Needs	6	182
	Lessons	**Pages**
Advanced Learners	2, 4	154, 168

Strategies for English Language Learners

Present this problem and activity to all students. Offer different levels of support to meet the students' levels of language proficiency.

Objective Help students organize data.

Problem Show three unequal groups of cubes: red, blue, and green. Say: **These cubes represent data.** Ask: **How can we organize these data into groups? How can we determine the number in each group?**

Newcomer

- Have students sort the cubes into color groups. Say: **Let's count the cubes.** Provide number words, and have students repeat.

Beginning

- Point and say: **There are 3 groups of cubes. One red, one green, one blue.** Have students repeat.

- Have students count the total number of cubes in each group.

Intermediate

- Ask: **How many groups of cubes are there?** 3 **What are the groups?** red, green, blue

- Guide students to record the data on paper.

Advanced

- Ask students to use short sentences to describe how to organize the cubes.

- Have students work in pairs to record their data on paper.

Connections

 Social Studies Connections
Lesson 3, page 164
Lesson 6, page 186

 Sports Connection
Lesson 2, page 156

 Science Connection
Lesson 4, page 170

 Math-to-Math Connections
Lesson 7, page 194
Lesson 8, page 204

 Physical Education Connection
Lesson 5, page 178

 Literature Connection
Lesson 9, page 210

Math Background

Putting Research Into Practice for Unit 1

From Our Curriculum Research Project: Analyzing the Structure and Language of Word Problems

In this unit, students analyze a variety of word-problem structures for real-world multiplication and division situations. Multiplication and division are taught together so students can see that one operation is the inverse of the other.

- Students relate these types of situations to each other and differentiate multiplication situations (unknown product) from division situations (unknown factor).

- Students use algebraic expressions and equations as well as drawings to represent and solve problems.

Different types of multiplication and division problems are presented:

Equal Groups problems involve objects that are separated into groups with the same number in each group.

Array problems involve objects organized in equal rows and columns that are not connected.

Area problems do not involve objects. They involve the number of square units that cover a shape.

Combination problems involve objects that can be organized in a table that has rows and columns of equal groups.

Comparison problems involve one quantity that is a number of times as many as or as much as another.

Throughout the unit, students discuss, draw, and/or model the relationships described in the problems.

—Karen Fuson, Author
  Math Expressions

From Current Research: Strategic Competence

Strategic Competence refers to the ability to formulate mathematical problems, represent them, and solve them.

Not only do students need to be able to build representations of individual situations, but they also need to see that some representations share common mathematical structures. Novice problem solvers are inclined to notice similarities in surface features of problems, such as the characters or situations described in the problem. More expert problem solvers focus more on the structural relationships within problems, relationships that provide the clues for how problems might be solved.

For example, one problem might ask students to determine how many different sacks of five blocks can be made using red and green blocks, and another might ask how many different ways hamburgers can be ordered with or without each of the following: catsup, onions, pickles, lettuce, and tomato. Novices would see these problems as unrelated; experts would see both as involving five choices between two things: red and green, or with and without.

National Research Council. "Strategic Competence." *Adding It Up: Helping Children Learn Mathematics.* Washington, D.C.: National Academy Press, 2001. pp. 124–125.

Other Useful References: Solving Problems

Carpenter, Thomas P., Fennena, E., Franks, M.L., Empson, S.B., & Levi, L.W. *Children's Mathematics: Cognitively Guided Instruction.* Portsmouth, NH: Heinemann, 1999.

Mulligan, Joanne T. and Mitchelmore, Michael C. Young children's intuitive models of multiplication and division. *Journal for Research in Mathematics Education,* May 1997, Vol. 28, Issue 3, pp. 309–330.

Getting Ready to Teach Unit 1

In this unit students learn about different problem types for multiplication and division. This builds on the introduction of multiplication and division problems types introduced in third grade.

Representing Word Problems

Writing Equations
Lesson 3

In this unit, students represent a word problem with a situation equation.

A *situation equation* shows the action or the relationships in a problem.

Then they may rewrite the situation equation as a solution equation.

A *solution equation* shows the operation that is performed to solve the problem.

Although these equations are the same for the simplest problems, they are different for the most difficult problems. When the numbers in a problem are small, students may be able to find the answer from a situation equation without having to write and solve a solution equation. When the numbers are greater (such as the multi-digit numbers in later units) or the situation is more complex, many students will find it helpful to use both equations. In Lesson 3, we discuss the distinction and, for this lesson only, students should write both equations so that they can experience the distinction.

Unknown Product
Lessons 2 and 3

The easiest problems for students to solve are the Equal Groups, Array, and Combination problems that involve an *unknown product*. For these problems, the situation equation is also the solution equation (multiply the two known factors to find the unknown product).

Equal Groups Problems

Situation and Solution Equation → Multiplier × Group Size = $\boxed{\text{Product}}$

Array and Combination Problems

Situation and Solution Equation → Row × Column = $\boxed{\text{Product}}$

As you teach this unit, emphasize understanding of these terms.
- factor
- product
- situation equation
- solution equation

Unknown First Factor
Lessons 2 and 3

Problems that are more difficult for students to solve are those with an **unknown first factor** in the situation equation. Although the solution equations for these problems involve division, students can find the unknown first factor from the situation equation if they count by the known second factor up to the product, or use a more advanced strategy. For multi-digit numbers, students will need to write or at least think of the solution equation that shows the division inverse operation, and then perform the multi-digit division.

Equal Groups Problems

Situation Equation → $\boxed{\text{Multiplier}} \times$ Group Size = Product

Solution Equation → Product $\div$ Group Size = $\boxed{\text{Multiplier}}$

Array, Area, and Combination Problems

Situation Equation → $\boxed{\text{Row}} \times$ Column = Product

Solution Equation → Product $\div$ Column = $\boxed{\text{Row}}$

Unknown Second Factor
Lessons 2 and 3

The most difficult problems for students to solve are those with an **unknown second factor** in the situation equation because these equations don't give the group size to use as a count-by number. But students can use the Commutative Property to write a multiplication solution equation with the unknown factor as the first number. Or as with the above problems, they can write a solution equation that is a division problem. For multi-digit numbers, students will need to write or at least think of the solution equation that shows the division inverse operation, and then perform the multi-digit division.

Equal Groups Problems

Situation Equation → Multiplier $\times$ $\boxed{\text{Group Size}}$ = Product

Solution Equation → $\boxed{\text{Group Size}} \times$ Multiplier = Product

Solution Equation → Product $\div$ Multiplier = $\boxed{\text{Group Size}}$

Array, Area, and Combination Problems

Situation Equation → Row $\times$ $\boxed{\text{Column}}$ = Product

Solution Equation → $\boxed{\text{Column}} \times$ Row = Product

Solution Equation → Product $\div$ Row = $\boxed{\text{Column}}$

What to Expect From Students The distinction between the unknown first factor and the unknown second factor may get blurred in actual use because in the real world there are two meanings for multiplication equations: 2 × 5 can mean 2 groups of 5 or 2 taken 5 times. Students may use either meaning, even though the more common meaning in this country is the former (2 × 5 means 2 groups of 5). Because some students in other countries have learned the latter meaning, *Math Expressions* allows students to be flexible. Therefore, for students who use the latter meaning, unknown first-factor problems will be the most difficult to solve because the group count-by number is not known. However, many students should be becoming facile in their use of the Commutative Property, so this distinction will become even less important as their facility increases.

Comparison Problems
Lessons 4, 5, and 6

Some comparisons involve multiplication and division. Students are encouraged to draw simple comparison bars to help them visualize the comparison. Students begin to use unit-fraction language (one third as many).

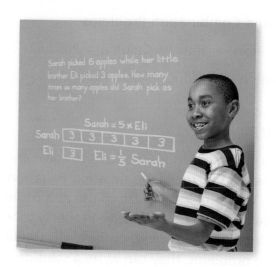

Sarah picked 15 apples while her little brother Eli picked 3 apples. How many times as many apples did Sarah pick as her brother?

Each comparison can be said two ways:

Multiplication Sarah picked 5 times as many as Eli.

Division Eli picked $\frac{1}{5}$ as many as Sarah.

Students learn that division involves a unit fraction.

Multistep Problems
Lesson 7

Solutions for multistep problems can be found in a variety of ways. Most students will use separate steps to find the answer, and that is fine. Some students may be able to write a single equation, using parentheses. As long as students can explain their thinking, and that thinking fits the problem situation, any equation that leads students to the correct answer is acceptable.

Problem Solving Summary

In *Math Expressions* a research-based, algebraic problem-solving approach that focuses on problem types is used: understand the situation, represent the situation with a math drawing or an equation, solve the problem, and see that the answer makes sense.

Representing Word Problems

Students using *Math Expressions* are taught a variety of ways to represent word problems. Some are conceptual in nature (making math drawings), while others are symbolic (writing equations). Students move from using math drawings to solving problems symbolically with equations. This table summarizes the representation methods taught in this unit.

Problem Type	Model	Equation
Equal Groups Seth had 5 bags with 2 apples in each bag.	$5 \times$ 10 — branching to (2) (2) (2) (2) (2)	Unknown Product $2 \times 5 = n$ Unknown Factors $n \times 5 = 10;\ 10 \div 5 = n$ $2 \times n = 10;\ 10 \div 2 = n$
Array Jenna has 2 rows of stamps with 5 stamps in each row.	5 across, 2 rows of ○ ○ ○ ○ ○	Unknown Product $2 \times 5 = n$ Unknown Factors $n \times 5 = 10;\ 10 \div 5 = n$ $2 \times n = 10;\ 10 \div 2 = n$
Area The floor of the kitchen is 2 meters by 5 meters.	5 by 2 grid rectangle	Unknown Product $2 \times 5 = n$ Unknown Factors $n \times 5 = 10;\ 10 \div 5 = n$ $2 \times n = 10;\ 10 \div 2 = n$
Combination Katone packed 2 pairs of pants and 5 shirts.	c t h p e W | Wc | Wt | Wh | Wp | We R | Rc | Rt | Rh | Rp | Re	Unknown Product $2 \times 5 = n$ Unknown Factors $n \times 5 = 10;\ 10 \div 5 = n$ $2 \times n = 10;\ 10 \div 2 = n$
Comparison Katie picked 5 times as many flowers as Benardo.	$B = \frac{1}{5} \times K$ B [2] K [2 | 2 | 2 | 2 | 2] $K = 5 \times B$	Unknown Product $2 \times 5 = n$ Unknown Factors $n \times 5 = 10;\ 10 \div 5 = n$ $2 \times n = 10;\ 10 \div 2 = n$

Use Mathematical Processes

The mathematical process skills of problem solving, reasoning and proof, communication, connections, and representation are pervasive in this program and underlie all the students' mathematical work. This table correlates the activities in Lesson 9 of this unit with the five process skills.

Process	Activity Number
Representation	1: Represent data in a table. 3: Draw a picture to represent and solve a problem. 5: Draw different representations.
Communication	1: Discuss the data. 4: Share reasoning.
Connections	1: Math and Science: Number Sense and Graphing
Reasoning and Proof	2: Make generalizations about adding, subtracting, and multiplying even and odd numbers. 3: Use reasoning to identify inverse operations.
Problem Solving	3: Draw a picture to represent and solve a problem. 5: Solve a problem involving remainders.

Basic Multiplication and Division Fluency

Students should continually work toward fluency for basic multiplication and division facts. Use checkups to assist students in monitoring their own learning. In this unit you will find Checkups C and D. In the Teacher's Resource Book (TRB) you will find copies of Checkups A–E.

Lesson 1-1: Checkup C Student Book p. 55, Answer Key for Checkup C (TRB M5)

Lesson 8-1: Checkup D Student Book p. 81, Answer Key for Checkup D (TRB M40)

See the Basic Facts Fluency Plan for information about practice materials.

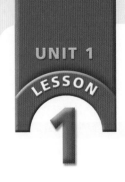

Solve Word Problems With Tables

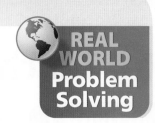

Vocabulary	
table	cell
data	function
row	rule
column	

Lesson Objectives

● Take a checkup on 6s, 7s, and 8s multiplications and divisions.

● Create tables and interpret data displayed in tables.

The Day at a Glance

Today's Goals	Materials	
1 Teaching the Lesson **A1:** Use Checkup C to test the multiplications and divisions for 6s, 7s, and 8s. **A2:** Interpret data displayed in a table. **A3:** Create a table of data and formulate questions about it. **2 Going Further** ▶ Extension: Function Tables ▶ Differentiated Instruction **3 Homework and Spiral Review**	**Lesson Activities** Student Activity Book pp. 57–59, 61–62 or Student Hardcover Book pp. 57–59, 61–62 and Activity Workbook pp. 33, 35–36 (includes Checkup C and Family Letter) Homework and Remembering pp. 55–56 Checkup C Answer Key (TRB M26) Transparency of Student Book p. 58 and overhead projector (optional)	**Going Further** Student Activity Book p. 60 or Student Hardcover Book p. 60 and Activity Workbook p. 34 Activity Cards 1-1 Counters Encyclopedias, almanacs, and Internet access Math Journals

123 *Use* **Math Talk** *today!*

Keeping Skills Sharp

Quick Practice	Daily Routines
Having **Student Leaders** lead Quick Practice activities is a key element of *Math Expressions*. Help Student Leaders take over leading Quick Practices as soon as possible. Ask for volunteers initially, and choose socially confident students to begin. In the beginning, pair shy students with more confident students. After several months, almost all students will be ready to lead alone. For some Quick Practices, you may need to lead for a time or two, while for others you can lead them initially by helping the Student Leader carry out the activity under your direction. Quick Practice begins in Lesson 2 of this unit.	**Elapsed Time** Mr. Jackson watched his daughter play in a soccer tournament. He arrived at 9:30 in the morning. He and his daughter went home at noon. How long was Mr. Jackson at the soccer tournament? 2 hours 30 minutes

① Teaching the Lesson

Checkup C

 15 MINUTES

Goal: Use Checkup C to test the multiplications and divisions for 6s, 7s, and 8s.

Materials: Student Activity Book p. 57 or Hardcover Book p. 57 and Activity Workbook p. 33; Checkup C Answer Key (TRB M26)

 NCTM Standard:
Number and Operations

Differentiated Instruction

Extra Help Remind students that they can skip the multiplications and divisions they don't know and come back to those when they have completed all the others. Sometimes they will remember the answer when they revisit the problem.

The Learning Classroom

Student Pairs The Checkup C Answer Key (TRB M26) may be used by pairs of students to quiz one another. One student can read the problems aloud, while the other says the answers.

1–1 Class Activity

Name _____ Date _____

▶ **Checkup C: 3s, 4s, 6s, 7s, 8s**

1. $8 \times 5 = \underline{40}$ 19. $4 \times 6 = \underline{24}$ 37. $80 / 10 = \underline{8}$ 55. $35 \div 5 = \underline{7}$

2. $7 \cdot 1 = \underline{7}$ 20. $7 \times 2 = \underline{14}$ 38. $\frac{9}{3} = \underline{3}$ 56. $32 / 4 = \underline{8}$

3. $4 * 8 = \underline{32}$ 21. $6 * 3 = \underline{18}$ 39. $27 \div 9 = \underline{3}$ 57. $2\overline{)8}^{\,4}$

4. $6 \times 2 = \underline{12}$ 22. $4 \times 7 = \underline{28}$ 40. $15 \div 5 = \underline{3}$ 58. $54 \div 9 = \underline{6}$

5. $7 \cdot 7 = \underline{49}$ 23. $6 \cdot 10 = \underline{60}$ 41. $24 / 4 = \underline{6}$ 59. $27 / 3 = \underline{9}$

6. $8 * 9 = \underline{72}$ 24. $8 * 4 = \underline{32}$ 42. $8\overline{)72}^{\,9}$ 60. $24 \div 6 = \underline{4}$

7. $4 \times 4 = \underline{16}$ 25. $7 * 6 = \underline{42}$ 43. $32 \div 4 = \underline{8}$ 61. $21 / 7 = \underline{3}$

8. $8 \cdot 9 = \underline{72}$ 26. $8 * 8 = \underline{64}$ 44. $7\overline{)35}^{\,5}$ 62. $42 \div 6 = \underline{7}$

9. $4 * 4 = \underline{16}$ 27. $4 \cdot 2 = \underline{8}$ 45. $\frac{12}{6} = \underline{2}$ 63. $8\overline{)40}^{\,5}$

10. $3 \times 8 = \underline{24}$ 28. $8 \times 7 = \underline{56}$ 46. $0 / 8 = \underline{0}$ 64. $15 / 3 = \underline{5}$

11. $4 \cdot 9 = \underline{36}$ 29. $6 \cdot 5 = \underline{30}$ 47. $70 \div 7 = \underline{10}$ 65. $36 \div 9 = \underline{4}$

12. $4 * 3 = \underline{12}$ 30. $8 * 2 = \underline{16}$ 48. $\frac{21}{3} = \underline{7}$ 66. $49 / 7 = \underline{7}$

13. $8 \times 6 = \underline{48}$ 31. $7 \times 9 = \underline{63}$ 49. $7\overline{)56}^{\,8}$ 67. $12 \div 2 = \underline{6}$

14. $7 \cdot 4 = \underline{28}$ 32. $6 * 6 = \underline{36}$ 50. $36 / 6 = \underline{6}$ 68. $48 / 6 = \underline{8}$

15. $7 * 8 = \underline{56}$ 33. $1 * 4 = \underline{4}$ 51. $\frac{24}{8} = \underline{3}$ 69. $\frac{16}{4} = \underline{4}$

16. $6 \times 4 = \underline{24}$ 34. $6 \cdot 8 = \underline{48}$ 52. $16 / 2 = \underline{8}$ 70. $63 / 7 = \underline{9}$

17. $7 \cdot 3 = \underline{21}$ 35. $4 \times 5 = \underline{20}$ 53. $4\overline{)40}^{\,10}$ 71. $8\overline{)56}^{\,7}$

18. $6 * 9 = \underline{54}$ 36. $6 * 7 = \underline{42}$ 54. $4 \div 1 = \underline{4}$ 72. $40 \div 5 = \underline{8}$

UNIT 1 LESSON 1   Checkup C **57**

Student Activity Book page 57

▶ Checkup C [INDIVIDUALS]

Tell students that today they will take a checkup to help them see which 3s, 4s, 6s, 7s, and 8s multiplications and divisions they need to practice. Emphasize that the checkup will not be graded.

Have students turn to Student Book page 57 and begin the checkup on your signal. Either give them a set amount of time to take it, or let them work until most students have finished.

▶ Check the Answers [INDIVIDUALS]

Have students exchange papers or check their own answers. TRB M26 is the answer key for the checkup. Make copies for students, display it as a transparency, or simply read the answers aloud. Have students write the multiplications and divisions they missed on their Study Plans.

Understand Tables

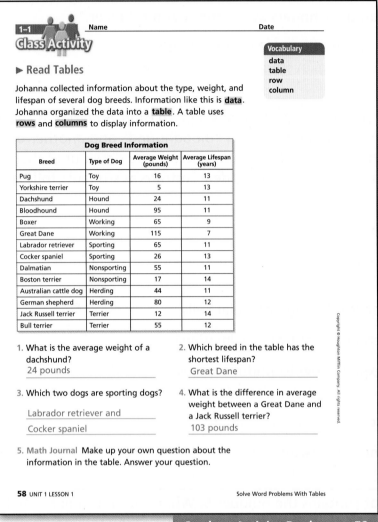

▶ Read Tables WHOLE CLASS

Ask for Ideas Discuss with students where they have seen tables and charts before. Possible response: newspapers, magazines, nutrition labels, textbooks You may want to display a transparency of Student Book page 58 to refer to during this discussion.

Read the text above the table aloud.

● Who can summarize what this table shows? the type, weight, and lifespan of different breeds of dog

Explain that tables display *data*, or sets of information. The data are arranged in rows and columns. Just as in an array, rows go across and columns go up and down.

 15 MINUTES

Goal: Interpret data displayed in a table.

Materials: Student Activity Book or Hardcover Book p. 58; Transparency of Student Book p. 58 and overhead projector (optional)

 NCTM Standards:
Number and Operations
Data Analysis and Probability
Representation

Teaching Note

Language and Vocabulary Students often have trouble remembering the distinction between *row* and *column*. To help them, you might gesture from left to right when talking about rows, and up and down when talking about columns. The tall straight "I" in the word *column* can remind us that this word means up and down.

The Learning Classroom

Math Talk Always start new topics by eliciting as much from students as possible. Students often know something about new topics. This builds feelings of competence and confidence and helps create the classroom community where everyone is a teacher and a learner. So even where the directions for a lesson are directing you to do the talking, remember to always ask for students' own ideas first.

Activity continued ▶

Activity 2

The Learning Classroom

Math Talk Aspire to make your classroom a place where all students listen to understand one another. Explain to students that this is different than just being quiet when someone else is talking. This involves thinking about what a person is saying so that you could explain it yourself. Also, students need to listen so that they can ask a question or help the explainer. Remind students that listening can also help you learn that concept better.

English Language Learners

Show a table. Discuss the data. Model how to identify rows and columns and locate data.

• **Beginning** Point to the data table. Say: **This is a table. It shows data. These are columns of data. These are rows of data.** Have students repeat.

• **Intermediate** Help students identify data, using rows and columns in the table. Ask: **What data is in the first column? The first row?**

• **Advanced** Have students work in pairs. One partner names a piece of data. The other finds the data, using the columns and rows.

Ask students to run their fingers down the "Average Weight" column.

● **What do the numbers in this column tell us?** the average weight of the different breeds

Ask students to run their fingers across the row for "Boxer."

● **What does the information in this row tell us?** information about boxers; the type of dog, average weight, and average lifespan of a boxer

Explain that each rectangle that contains a piece of information is called a *cell.* Have students put one finger on "Bloodhound" and another on "Average Lifespan" and slide their fingers across and down until they meet. If you are using a transparency, demonstrate as students follow along.

● **What number is in this cell?** 11

● **What does this number tell us?** that the average lifespan of a bloodhound is 11 years

Have students practice finding particular cells.

● **What is the average weight of a Dalmatian?** 55 pounds

● **Can someone explain how to find the answer?** Find the row for Dalmation, then move to the weight column.

● **What type of dog is a German shepherd?** herding

● **How did you find the answer?** Find the row for German shepherd and move to the type of dog column.

● **Find the cell that contains the number 5. What does this number tell us?** The average weight of a Yorkshire terrier is 5 pounds.

Give students several minutes to complete problems 1–5. Discuss the answers to problems 1–4. Then have several students share the questions they wrote for problem 5, and solve them as a class.

Make a Table

1–1
Class Activity

Name _____ Date _____

▶ **Make a Table**

6. Make a table with information about members of your group. One column should show information that is numbers. The other should show information that is words. Tables will vary.

Student's Name	Favorite Pet	Number of Pets
Adam	Dog	2
Bonnie	Dog	3
Frank	Cat	1
Hillary	Fish	3
Maya	Cat	0

7. Make up at least three questions about your table.
Answers will vary.

_____

_____

_____

_____

_____

_____

_____

_____

_____

_____

_____

_____

_____

_____

UNIT 1 LESSON 1   Solve Word Problems With Tables **59**

Student Activity Book page 59

---

15 MINUTES

Goal: Create a table of data and formulate questions about it.

Materials: Student Activity Book or Hardcover Book p. 59

 NCTM Standards:
Number and Operations
Data Analysis and Probability
Representation

 Ongoing Assessment

Ask students questions such as:

▶ How does a table help you organize information?

▶ What do the rows of your table show?

▶ What do the columns show?

▶ Make a Table SMALL GROUPS

Organize students into **Small Groups** of four or five. Tell them they will now make a table showing information about the people in their group. Have each student write the names of the group members in the first column of the table in problem 6 on Student Book page 59.

Tell students they need to decide what type of information to show in the other two columns. One column should show information that is expressed in numbers, such as height, shoe size, or number of siblings. The other should show information that is expressed in words, such as favorite band, favorite subject, or backpack color.

When groups are done making their tables, ask them to write at least three questions about them.

Have groups share their tables and at least one of their questions.

② Going Further

Extension: Function Tables

Goal: Write the rule and the equation of a function.

Materials: Student Activity Book p. 60 or Hardcover Book p. 60 and Activity Workbook p. 34

 NCTM Standards:
Number and Operations
Algebra
Representation

▶ Discuss Function Tables

| WHOLE CLASS | Math Talk |

Ask for Ideas Encourage students to share what they remember about functions or function tables. Then read the information at the top of Student Book page 60 together. Have students use their own words to describe the relationship shared by each input/output pair of numbers in the table.

Ask questions such as:

● What do you have to do to change 0 to 2? add 2

● What do you have to do to change 1 to 3? add 2

● Can you add 2 to each input in the table and get the correct output? yes

● What rule describes the relationship shared by all of the pairs of numbers in the table? add 2 to the x-value to find the y-value

● What equation describes the relationship shared by all of the pairs of numbers in the table? $y = x + 2$

▶ Write Function Rules | WHOLE CLASS |

Work through exercise 1 together as a class. Emphasize the importance of inspecting every pair of numbers in a table before identifying a rule.

Use **Solve and Discuss** for exercises 2–4.

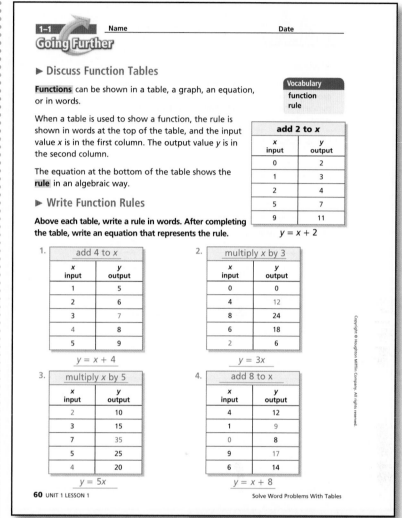

Student Activity Book page 60

Teaching Note

Math Symbols When working with functions, there are algebraic language conventions which describe the order of writing the expression involving x (or the input letter).

• The letter x is written before the added number (e.g., $x + 2$ not $2 + x$).

• Any multiplying number is written before x (or a different input letter), such as $8x$ or $10d$.

• The standard form for writing a function isolates y on the left side of the equation. For example, while $2x + 3 = y$ is correct, it is mathematical convention to write $y = 2x + 3$.

Differentiated Instruction

Intervention   Activity Card 1-1

Read Tables   Activity Card 1-1 ●

Work: In Pairs

Use:
- Student Book page 58
- 2 Counters

1. Decide which partner goes first.

2. The first partner selects a breed of dog and tells this to the other student and places a counter on that cell.

Dog Breed Information

Breed	Type of Dog	Average Weight (pounds)	Average Lifespan (years)
Pug	Toy	16	13
Yorkshire terrier	Toy	5	13

3. The second partner reads the information for the remaining cells in the row.

4. The second partner creates a question about the row where the counter is placed.

5. The first partner answers the question.

6. Trade tasks and repeat the process as time allows.

Unit 1, Lesson 1   Copyright © Houghton Mifflin Company

Activity Note Pair up less able readers with those who are more fluent. Encourage the more fluent student to help the other student pronounce words.

 Math Writing Prompt

Summarize Choose one dog breed from the table on the Student Book page 58. Write one or two sentences that summarize information about that dog.

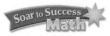 **Software Support**

Use *Soar to Success* for instruction of students needing targeted support for underlying skills.

On Level   Activity Card 1-1

Highs and Lows   Activity Card 1-1 ▲

Work: In Small Groups

Use:
- Encyclopedias
- Almanacs
- Computers with Internet access

1. Research record high and low temperatures for some cities around the United States.

City	Altitude	Low	High

2. Record your data in a table similar to the sample table above. Be sure to create an accurate title for the table.

3. Write two conclusions that can be made from your data.

Unit 1, Lesson 1   Copyright © Houghton Mifflin Company

Activity Note Students might want to include additional information about the cities they selected. For example, they could include the altitude of the city, the state it is located in, or the average annual rainfall.

 Math Writing Prompt

Summarize Why is it helpful to have data displayed in a table?

 Software Support

Use *MegaMath* for review and reinforcement of the concepts and skills presented in this lesson.

Challenge   Activity Card 1-1

Make Your Own   Activity Card 1-1 ■

Work: In Small Groups

Use:
- Encyclopedias
- Almanacs
- Computers with Internet access

1. Determine a topic the group wants to research and data about that topic that can be organized into a table.

2. Create a table similar to the sample table below that has at least 3 columns. Be sure to label the columns and provide a title for the table.

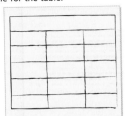

3. Write two conclusions that can be made from the data you collected.

Unit 1, Lesson 1   Copyright © Houghton Mifflin Company

Activity Note Extend the activity by having groups create three questions that can be answered using the table and provide correct answers.

 Math Writing Prompt

Explain Your Thinking Think of a situation in which you might use a table to display data. Explain why a table rather than a graph would be a good way to show the data.

 DESTINATION Math® **Software Support**

Use *Destination Math* to take students beyond the concepts and skills presented in this lesson.

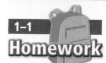

③ Homework and Spiral Review

Use this Homework page to provide students with more practice with tables.

This Remembering activity would be appropriate anytime after today's lesson.

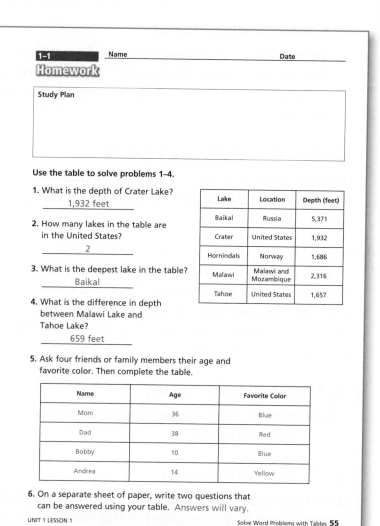

Homework and Remembering page 55

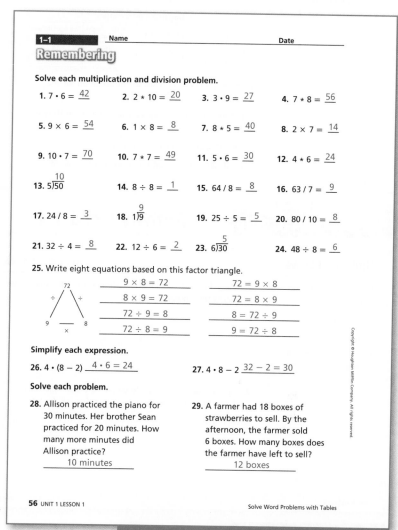

Homework and Remembering page 56

Home and School Connection

Family Letter Have children take home the family letter on Student Book page 61 or Activity Workbook page 35. The letter explains the different types of multiplication and division problems students will learn in this unit. It gives parents and guardians a better understanding of the learning that goes on in math class and creates a bridge between school and home. A Spanish translation of this letter is on Student Book page 62 and Activity Workbook page 36.

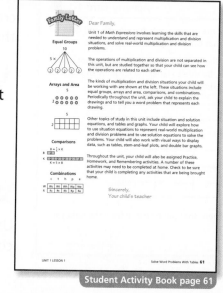

Student Activity Book page 61

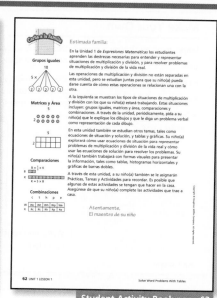

Student Activity Book page 62

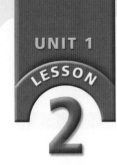
Tables of Combinations

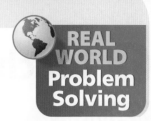
Lesson Objectives

- Make tables of data and use the entries to determine the total number of combinations.

- Use tables and other methods to solve problems involving combinations.

The Day at a Glance

Today's Goals	Materials	
1 Teaching the Lesson A1: Complete and use a data table to determine the total number of combinations. A2: Solve combination problems. **2 Going Further** ▶ Differentiated Instruction **3 Homework and Spiral Review**	**Lesson Activities** Student Activity Book pp. 63–64 or Student Hardcover Book pp. 63–64 Homework and Remembering pp. 57–58 Transparency of Student Book p. 63 and overhead projector (optional) MathBoard Materials	**Going Further** Activity Cards 1-2 Index cards Math Journals 123 Use Math Talk today!

Keeping Skills Sharp

Quick Practice ⏱ 5 MINUTES	Daily Routines
Goal: Practice divisions for 2s, 5s, and 10s. **Materials:** Division Digits: Sets 1 and 2 (TRB M3–M4), sheet protector, dry-erase marker **Division Digits for 2s, 5s, and 10s** Place copies of TRB M3–M4 back-to-back in a sheet protector. The **Student Leader** reads problems from the 2s, 5s, and 10s sections of Set 1 (TRB M3) aloud in any order. When the leader gives a signal, students raise the number of fingers for the answer. For example, if the leader reads 12 ÷ 2, students raise 6 fingers. The leader marks each problem with a dry-erase marker so that it is not repeated. For future lessons, the Division Digits pages, sheet protector, and dry-erase marker will be called Division Digits materials.	**Homework Review** Have students discuss the problems from their homework. Encourage students to help each other resolve any misunderstandings. **Find a Pattern** What is the rule for this pattern? 2, 4, 8, 16, 32, 64 Multiply by 2

Teaching the Lesson

Make a Table of Combinations

 25 MINUTES

Goal: Complete and use a data table to determine the total number of combinations.

Materials: Student Activity Book or Hardcover Book p. 63; transparency of Student Book p. 63 and overhead projector (optional)

✔ **NCTM Standards:**
Number and Operations
Data Analysis and Probability
Representation

The Learning Classroom

Helping Community By discussing multiple strategies for math problems, students become aware of other students' thinking. As students better understand each other's thinking, they become better "helpers." Instead of showing how they would solve problems, they are able to look at another student's work and help them to find mistakes in their own method.

The Learning Classroom

Math Talk You can create math conversations by eliciting multiple strategies for solving problems. When you ask, "Did anyone do this problem differently?" your students will pay greater attention to the work on the board because they will be comparing and contrasting it with their own math strategies. The comparisons and contrasts that result can provide a natural springboard to significant math talk.

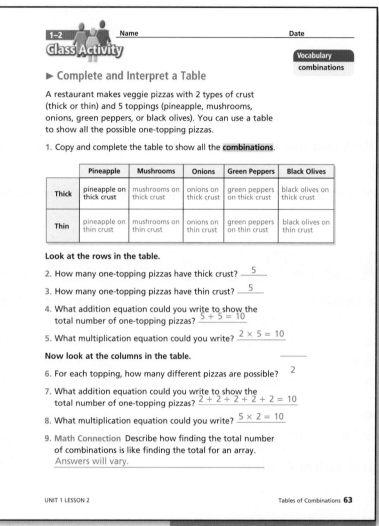

Student Activity Book page 63

▶ Complete and Interpret a Table [INDIVIDUALS]

It may help to display a transparency of Student Book page 63. Read the text above the table aloud. Make sure students understand how to fill in the table, and then give them a minute to do so. (Students can write the first letters for the toppings, rather than writing the full words.) Review the answers to make sure everyone filled in the table correctly. Using **Solve and Discuss**, have students complete problems 2–8.

Math Talk Read problem 9 aloud, and choose students to share their ideas. Students should observe that multiplying the number of rows and the number of columns to find the total combinations is like finding the total number of items in an array.

Activity 2

Solve Combination Problems

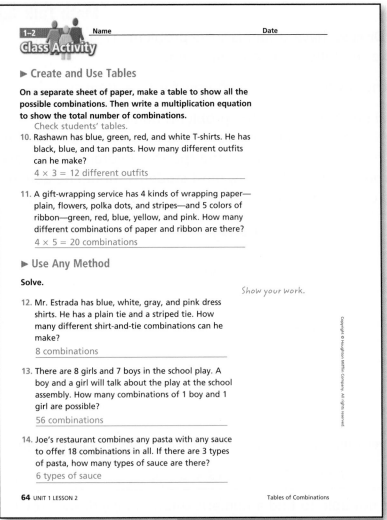

1-2
Class Activity

Name _____ Date _____

▶ **Create and Use Tables**

On a separate sheet of paper, make a table to show all the possible combinations. Then write a multiplication equation to show the total number of combinations.

Check students' tables.

10. Rashawn has blue, green, red, and white T-shirts. He has black, blue, and tan pants. How many different outfits can he make?

    $4 \times 3 = 12$ different outfits

11. A gift-wrapping service has 4 kinds of wrapping paper—plain, flowers, polka dots, and stripes—and 5 colors of ribbon—green, red, blue, yellow, and pink. How many different combinations of paper and ribbon are there?

    $4 \times 5 = 20$ combinations

▶ **Use Any Method**

Solve.

Show your work.

12. Mr. Estrada has blue, white, gray, and pink dress shirts. He has a plain tie and a striped tie. How many different shirt-and-tie combinations can he make?

    8 combinations

13. There are 8 girls and 7 boys in the school play. A boy and a girl will talk about the play at the school assembly. How many combinations of 1 boy and 1 girl are possible?

    56 combinations

14. Joe's restaurant combines any pasta with any sauce to offer 18 combinations in all. If there are 3 types of pasta, how many types of sauce are there?

    6 types of sauce

64 UNIT 1 LESSON 2   Tables of Combinations

Student Activity Book page 64

▶ Create and Use Tables [INDIVIDUALS]

 Math Talk Using **Solve and Discuss**, have students solve problems 10 and 11. These require students to solve combination problems, using tables. This will help students generalize the results they found when completing the first activity.

---

 30 MINUTES

Goal: Solve combination problems.

Materials: Student Activity Book or Hardcover Book p. 64; MathBoard Materials

✓ **NCTM Standards:**
Number and Operations
Data Analysis and Probability
Representation

Differentiated Instruction

Extra Help If a student needs help starting, ask the following questions:

• What type of combinations are we trying to find in problem 10?

• If each column is a T-shirt color; how many columns do we need?

• Suppose we make each row a pants color. How many rows do we need?

• What belongs in each cell?

English Language Learners

Make sure students can identify columns and rows in a table. Draw a sample table of combinations and point to the table.

• **Beginning** Say: This is a table of combinations. Ask: **Are the rows and columns the same?** (no) Point to a row. Say: **This is a row.** Point to a column. Ask: **Is this a row?** (no)

• **Intermediate** Ask: **What does this table show?** Have students identify rows and columns. Ask: **How many combinations are shown? How do you know?**

• **Advanced** Encourage students to use short sentences to compare rows and columns and identify combinations.

Activity continued ▶

Activity 2

✓ Ongoing Assessment

Ask students:

► How can you solve problem 12 without drawing a table?

► How is problem 14 different from the other problems? How would you solve it?

The Learning Classroom

Math Talk The **Solve and Discuss** structure of conversation is used throughout the *Math Expressions* program. The teacher selects four or five students to go to the board and solve a problem, using any method they choose. The other students work on the same problem at their desks. Then the teacher asks the students at the board to explain their methods. Students at their desks are encouraged to ask questions and to assist each other in understanding the problem. Thus, students actually solve, explain, question, and justify. Usually ask only two or three students to explain because classes do not like to sit through more explanations, and time is better spent on the next issue.

Differentiated Instruction

Advanced Learners Students can make up their own combinations and draw a tree diagram to represent the combinations. Then, they can write an equation.

► Discuss Different Methods

WHOLE CLASS   Math Talk

Using **Solve and Discuss**, have students solve problems 12–14. Many students will make the following generalization:

combinations = choices for 1st item × choices for Final item

Most students will be able to solve the problems numerically. Some students will need to make a table or diagram on their MathBoard. The numbers in problem 13 are fairly large, and specific children's names are not given. For larger problems like this, most students should be able to work numerically or make fast drawings without drawing everything.

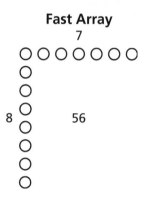

Fast Array

Problem 14 involves division. If s is the number of types of sauce, then,

$$3 \cdot s = 18 \quad \text{or} \quad 18 \div 3 = s.$$

Students who are not able to find a numeric solution may draw 3 rows of a table or an array and figure out how many columns they must make to get 18 cells or dots.

Use a Tree Diagram Some students may find it helpful to represent combination problems in a visual way. For example, the tree diagram below is a visual way to represent the combinations in exercise 12.

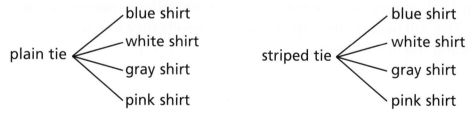

The tree diagram shows that there are 8 possible combinations. Ask students to identify the number of different ties 2 and the number of different shirts 4 that the diagram shows. Then students can write the equation that represents the number of combinations. $2 \times 4 = 8$

② Going Further

● Intervention   Activity Card I-2

Many Outfits
Activity Card 1-2 ●

Work: In Pairs

Use:
- Index cards
- Colored pencils or markers

1. With your partner draw four different T-shirts and two pairs of jeans, each on a separate card.

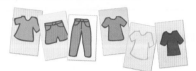

2. Create as many combinations of outfits as possible, writing each down. 8 outfits

3. Decide how to write an equation to find the total number of outfits. $2 \times 4 = 8$

4. Look Back How do your list of outfits and your equation compare? If they do not have the same results, make a table to represent the problem.

Unit 1, Lesson 2   Copyright © Houghton Mifflin Company

Activity Note Have students write all combinations for one shirt and then turn the card over to show that they are done with it.

 Math Writing Prompt

Draw a Picture Draw a picture to show all combinations you can make with 1 fruit and 1 drink. The fruit choices are apple, banana, and orange. The drink choices are milk or water.

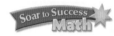 **Software Support**

Use *Soar to Success* for instruction of students needing targeted support for underlying skills.

▲ On Level   Activity Card I-2

Making a List
Activity Card 1-2 ▲

Work: By Yourself

1. Write the names of three different types of shoes, such as boots, shoes with buckles, and sneakers. Then write three different colors of socks, such as yellow, red, and green.

2. Make an organized list of all possible combinations of socks and shoes. 9 combinations

> boots and red socks
> boots and green socks
> boots and

3. Write a multiplication equation to show the number of possible combinations. $3 \times 3 = 9$

Unit 1, Lesson 2   Copyright © Houghton Mifflin Company

Activity Note If students have difficulty deciding how to start, suggest that they begin by making a table.

 Math Writing Prompt

Combinations Describe a situation with several combinations. Then make a table to show the combinations.

 Software Support

Use *MegaMath* for review and reinforcement of the concepts and skills presented in this lesson.

■ Challenge   Activity Card I-2

Lots of Choices
Activity Card 1-2 ■

Work: In Small Groups

1. Select 2 kinds of bread, 3 kinds of lunch meat, and 2 kinds of cheese for making sandwiches.

2. Make a tree diagram to show all the possible sandwich combinations.

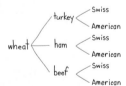

3. Write a multiplication equation to show the number of sandwich combinations. $2 \times 3 \times 2 = 12$

4. Math Talk Discuss each part of the tree diagram that matches each part of the equation.

Unit 1, Lesson 2   Copyright © Houghton Mifflin Company

Activity Note If students have difficulty reading the tree diagram, explain that the product is the last set of branches.

 Math Writing Prompt

Explain Your Reading Explain how to find all the combinations for 5 pairs of pants, 4 shirts, and 3 hats.

 DESTINATION Math· **Software Support**

Use *Destination Math* to take students beyond the concepts and skills presented in this lesson.

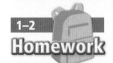

③ Homework and Spiral Review

Use this Homework page to provide students with more practice with combinations.

This Remembering activity would be appropriate anytime after today's lesson.

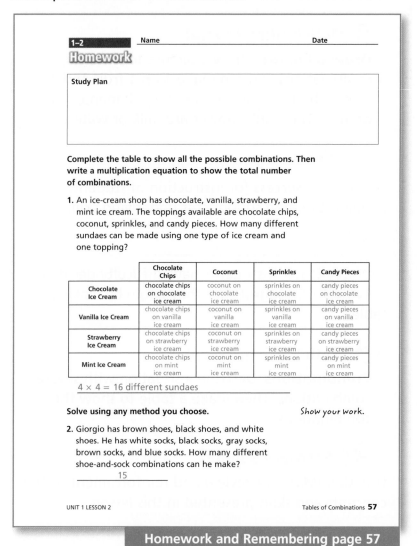

1–2
Homework   Name ___ Date ___

Study Plan

Complete the table to show all the possible combinations. Then write a multiplication equation to show the total number of combinations.

1. An ice-cream shop has chocolate, vanilla, strawberry, and mint ice cream. The toppings available are chocolate chips, coconut, sprinkles, and candy pieces. How many different sundaes can be made using one type of ice cream and one topping?

	Chocolate Chips	Coconut	Sprinkles	Candy Pieces
Chocolate Ice Cream	chocolate chips on chocolate ice cream	coconut on chocolate ice cream	sprinkles on chocolate ice cream	candy pieces on chocolate ice cream
Vanilla Ice Cream	chocolate chips on vanilla ice cream	coconut on vanilla ice cream	sprinkles on vanilla ice cream	candy pieces on vanilla ice cream
Strawberry Ice Cream	chocolate chips on strawberry ice cream	coconut on strawberry ice cream	sprinkles on strawberry ice cream	candy pieces on strawberry ice cream
Mint Ice Cream	chocolate chips on mint ice cream	coconut on mint ice cream	sprinkles on mint ice cream	candy pieces on mint ice cream

$4 \times 4 = 16$ different sundaes

Solve using any method you choose.   *Show your work.*

2. Giorgio has brown shoes, black shoes, and white shoes. He has white socks, black socks, gray socks, brown socks, and blue socks. How many different shoe-and-sock combinations can he make?
___ 15 ___

UNIT 1 LESSON 2   Tables of Combinations **57**

Homework and Remembering page 57

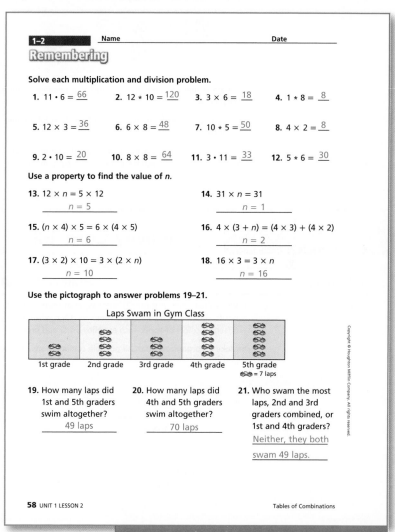

1–2
Remembering   Name ___ Date ___

Solve each multiplication and division problem.

1. $11 \cdot 6 = \underline{66}$ 2. $12 * 10 = \underline{120}$ 3. $3 \times 6 = \underline{18}$ 4. $1 * 8 = \underline{8}$

5. $12 \times 3 = \underline{36}$ 6. $6 \times 8 = \underline{48}$ 7. $10 * 5 = \underline{50}$ 8. $4 \times 2 = \underline{8}$

9. $2 \cdot 10 = \underline{20}$ 10. $8 \times 8 = \underline{64}$ 11. $3 \cdot 11 = \underline{33}$ 12. $5 * 6 = \underline{30}$

Use a property to find the value of n.

13. $12 \times n = 5 \times 12$ 14. $31 \times n = 31$
    ___ $n = 5$ ___   ___ $n = 1$ ___

15. $(n \times 4) \times 5 = 6 \times (4 \times 5)$ 16. $4 \times (3 + n) = (4 \times 3) + (4 \times 2)$
    ___ $n = 6$ ___   ___ $n = 2$ ___

17. $(3 \times 2) \times 10 = 3 \times (2 \times n)$ 18. $16 \times 3 = 3 \times n$
    ___ $n = 10$ ___   ___ $n = 16$ ___

Use the pictograph to answer problems 19–21.

Laps Swam in Gym Class

1st grade	2nd grade	3rd grade	4th grade	5th grade

🐟🐟 = 7 laps

19. How many laps did 1st and 5th graders swim altogether?
___ 49 laps ___

20. How many laps did 4th and 5th graders swim altogether?
___ 70 laps ___

21. Who swam the most laps, 2nd and 3rd graders combined, or 1st and 4th graders?
___ Neither, they both swam 49 laps. ___

58 UNIT 1 LESSON 2   Tables of Combinations

Homework and Remembering page 58

Home or School Activity

Sports Connection

Pitchers and Batters Tell students that a coach plans to have each of his three pitchers pitch one time to each of the 9 batters on the opposing team. Have students make a list or table to show all the combinations of pitchers and batters. Students should write an equation showing the number of pitcher-batter combinations. $3 \times 9 = 27$

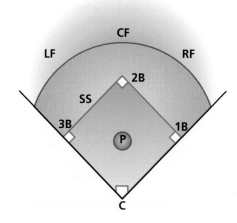

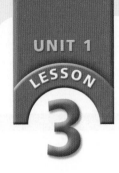

Situation and Solution Equations

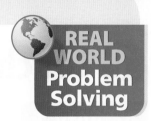

Lesson Objectives

● Write a situation equation to represent a problem.

● Write and solve a solution equation.

Vocabulary

situation equation
solution equation

The Day at a Glance

Today's Goals	Materials

1 Teaching the Lesson
A1: Discuss and write situation and solution equations.
A2: Write situation and solution equations; use inverse operations to solve problems.
 	
2 Going Further
▶ Differentiated Instruction
 	
3 Homework and Spiral Review
	Lesson Activities
	Student Activity Book pp. 65–66
	  or Student Hardcover Book
	  pp. 65–66
	Homework and Remembering
	  pp. 59–60
	Quick Quiz 1 (Assessment Guide) **Going Further**
	Activity Cards 1-3
	Math Journals

123 *Use* **Math Talk** *today!*

Keeping Skills Sharp

Quick Practice 🕐 5 MINUTES	Daily Routines
Goal: Practice multiplications and divisions for 3s, 4s, 9s, and 10s. **Materials:** Division Digits materials; Targets, multiplication tables (Student Activity Book inside back cover) **Division Digits for 3s, 4s, and 9s** Have a **Student Leader** run the activity, using problems from the 3s, 4s, and 9s sections of Set 1 and Set 2. (See Lesson 1-2) **Target Practice** Students use their targets and the multiplication tables to practice multiplications and divisions for the 3s, 4s, 9s, and 10s. Circulate around the room and make sure that students are using their targets correctly. Students should fill out their Study Plans on Homework page 59.	**Homework Review** The Study Plans of some students may indicate a need for more practice with specific multiplications and divisions. Suggest that students work with Product Cards for those problems. **Strategy Problem** Lashanna has 10 coins in her pocket. They have a value of 60¢. What coins does she have in her pocket? 1 quarter, 2 dimes, 2 nickels, and 5 pennies or 2 dimes, 8 nickels

① Teaching the Lesson

Relating and Writing Equations

 20 MINUTES

Goal: Discuss and write situation and solution equations.

Materials: Student Activity Book or Hardcover Book p. 65

 NCTM Standards:
Number and Operations
Algebra
Problem Solving

Teaching Note

Situation and Solution Equations: A *situation equation* shows the action or the relationships in a problem. A *solution equation* shows the operation that is performed to solve the problem.

In this lesson, students will write both equations. For additional information see the Unit 1 Overview.

English Language Learners

Review combination tables. Make sure students can identify rows, columns, and cells and find the total number of combinations.

- **Beginning** Draw a 4 × 3 fast array. Say: **This is a fast array. There are 4 columns and 3 rows. This shows all of the combinations.** Have students repeat the combinations after you name them.
- **Intermediate** Draw a 4 × 3 fast array. Ask: **What does this fast array represent? How many rows? How many columns?** Help students identify the combinations.
- **Advanced** Have students take turns to describe the steps to draw a 4 × 3 array and solve a combination problem.

▶ **Review Problem Types** WHOLE CLASS

Ask for Ideas Give students an opportunity to name or describe the types of multiplication and division problems they have solved. examples include Equal Groups, Arrays, Combination problems Also ask students to describe the types of math drawings that they have used to represent the problems. drawings include Equal Shares and Fast Arrays.

Review, if necessary, how to use a Fast Array drawing for a Combination problem that is put into a table. For example, the number of combinations that 3 pairs of shoes and 7 pairs of socks offer is 3 × 7 or 21.

The circles in a Fast Array drawing represent the cells in the table that show the combinations.

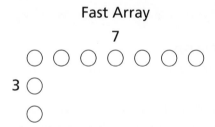

All of the multiplication and division problems students have seen thus far can be thought of as Equal Groups problems (using an Equal Shares drawing if necessary) or as Array/Combination problems (using a Fast Array drawing if necessary).

Encourage students who are still drawing all of the objects to use Equal Shares or Fast Array drawings to speed problem solving and abstraction of the problem.

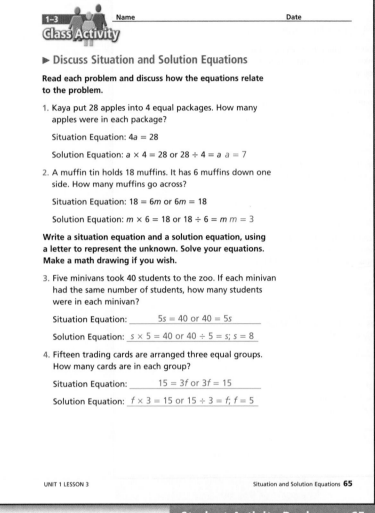

1-3
Class Activity

Name _____ Date _____

▶ Discuss Situation and Solution Equations

Read each problem and discuss how the equations relate
to the problem.

1. Kaya put 28 apples into 4 equal packages. How many
apples were in each package?

Situation Equation: $4a = 28$

Solution Equation: $a \times 4 = 28$ or $28 \div 4 = a$ $a = 7$

2. A muffin tin holds 18 muffins. It has 6 muffins down one
side. How many muffins go across?

Situation Equation: $18 = 6m$ or $6m = 18$

Solution Equation: $m \times 6 = 18$ or $18 \div 6 = m$ $m = 3$

Write a situation equation and a solution equation, using
a letter to represent the unknown. Solve your equations.
Make a math drawing if you wish.

3. Five minivans took 40 students to the zoo. If each minivan
had the same number of students, how many students
were in each minivan?

Situation Equation: _____ $5s = 40$ or $40 = 5s$ _____

Solution Equation: _$s \times 5 = 40$ or $40 \div 5 = s$; $s = 8$_

4. Fifteen trading cards are arranged three equal groups.
How many cards are in each group?

Situation Equation: _____ $15 = 3f$ or $3f = 15$ _____

Solution Equation: _$f \times 3 = 15$ or $15 \div 3 = f$; $f = 5$_

UNIT 1 LESSON 3   Situation and Solution Equations **65**

Student Activity Book page 65

Teaching Note

Math Symbols Throughout this
lesson, remind students to use a
letter to represent an unknown for
each problem. Relate using a letter
to methods students may have used
previously, such as

$6 + \square = 13$ or $6 + ? = 13$.

When choosing a letter, encourage
students to choose a letter that will
remind them of the meaning in the
problem situation. For example, a is
used in problem 1 to represent the
number of apples. In problem 3, s
is used to represent the number of
students.

▶ Discuss Situation and Solution Equations

WHOLE CLASS   Math Talk

Write Situation Equations and Solution Equations Have students
read problem 1, on Student Book page 65, and the situation and
solution equations. Discuss how the situation and solution equations
relate to the problem situation and to each other.

Use **Solve and Discuss** for students to write situation and solution
equations for problems 3 and 4. Although they are asked today to
write both equations, in later lessons and activities students may write
whichever equation they choose, or simply solve the problem using any
method.

Activity 2

Solving Mixed Problems

 20 MINUTES

Goal: Write situation and solution equations; use inverse operations to solve problems.

Materials: Student Activity Book or Hardcover Book p. 66

✓ **NCTM Standards:**
Number and Operations
Algebra
Problem Solving

The Learning Classroom

Student Leaders Although your top students may be beginning to explain their problem-solving strategies in more detail, the same may not be true for all students. You might want to have your top students do more explaining. Their explanations will serve as a model for how to explain one's thinking, and the student-friendly language may connect with some students more successfully than a different way of talking about a concept.

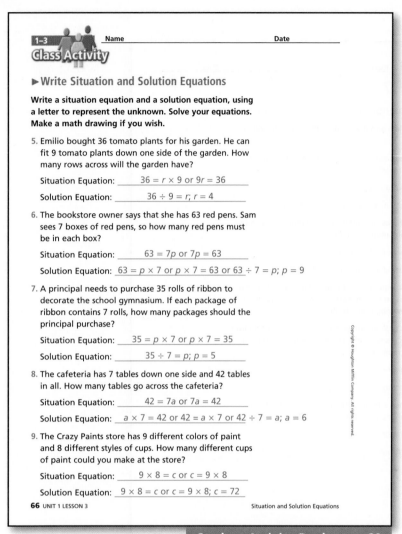

Student Activity Book page 66

► Write Situation and Solution Equations WHOLE CLASS

This activity contains mixed Equal Groups, Array, and Combination problems. For some problems, the situation and solution equations are the same. For other problems, a solution equation can be written that is different from the situation equation. The focus in solving these problems is writing the different kinds of equations and discussing how they relate to the problem situation.

The answers for Student Book page 66 give situation equations in two ways: with one number alone on the left and with one number alone on the right. If no students write equations with one number alone on the left for problem 1, ask how else the situation equation might have been written (36 is given first, so it is more natural to write $36 = r \times 9$). Remind students again that an equation with one number or letter alone on the left is a correct equation as long as the quantities on both sides are equal. Ask a related question for problems 5 and 6, where the product is given first.

Problem 5 Students need to understand that they can write the division equation $36 \div 9 = r$ as the solution equation. However, explain that it is not necessary to write this equation to solve the problem because they can solve for the unknown factor from the situation equations $36 = r \times 9$ or $r \times 9 = 36$ by:

- thinking "How many 9s equal 36?" or by using 9s count-bys up to 36.

- by using their 9s finger patterns and seeing that they put down the fourth finger to make 36.

- seeing that 36 is 4 less than 40, so the unknown factor must be 4 (because $40 - 4 = 36$ and $10 - 1 = 9$).

Problem 6 has an unknown second factor (which is the unknown group size in this Equal Groups problem), so the solution equation can use the Commutative Property to write a reversed multiplication problem ($63 = p \times 7$ or $p \times 7 = 63$), or the solution equation can be a division equation.

Activity continued ▶

Teaching Note

Writing Equations It is important for students to see equations with one number or variable alone on the left and one number or variable alone on the right to prepare them for flexible problem solving in algebra.

The Learning Classroom

Helping Community Students may be apprehensive about doing their math work in public because they are afraid to be incorrect. Emphasize that errors help us learn, and a comfortable culture develops in such a classroom because students do not fear criticism when they make mistakes. You can model this approach for students as you make, and fix, your own errors.

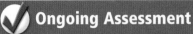 **Ongoing Assessment**

Ask students:

▶ Explain the difference between a situation equation and a solution equation.

① Teaching the Lesson (continued)

Activity 2

Teaching Note

Math Symbols When letters are used in an expression or equation to represent an unknown, we usually do not use an *x* because it looks so much like the multiplication times sign ×.

Teaching Note

Interpreting Equations Some states may require a specific order for writing multiplication equations. Unless you live in such a state, it is better to allow students to be flexible in how they write and interpret multiplication equations (e.g., 4×6 can be 4 sixes or fours taken 6 times).

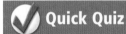

Quick Quiz

See Assessment Guide for Unit 1 Quick Quiz 1.

Problem 7 is like problem 5 because it has an unknown first factor. Therefore, students can solve directly from the situation equation ($35 = p \times 7$ or $p \times 7 = 35$). The division equation $35 \div 7 = p$ is not necessary as a solution equation, but it will be necessary in future lessons and activities that include greater numbers.

Problem 8 is like Problem 6 because it has an unknown second factor (an unknown number across in this Array problem), so the solution equation can use the Commutative Property to write a reversed multiplication problem ($a \times 7 = 42$ or $42 = a \times 7$), or the solution equation can be a division equation.

Problem 9 is an unknown product Equal Groups problem. The situation equation $9 \times 8 = c$ is also the solution equation because students simply need to multiply 9 times 8 (or 8 times 9) to find the value of c.

② Going Further

Differentiated Instruction

Intervention
Activity Card I-3

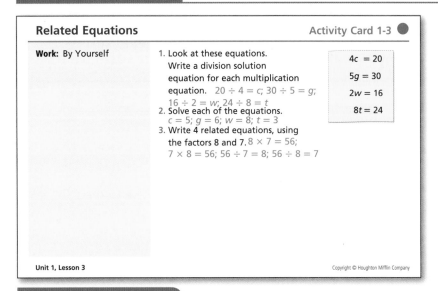

Related Equations   Activity Card 1-3

Work: By Yourself

1. Look at these equations.
   Write a division solution
   equation for each multiplication
   equation. $20 \div 4 = c$; $30 \div 5 = g$;
   $16 \div 2 = w$; $24 \div 8 = t$
2. Solve each of the equations.
   $c = 5$; $g = 6$; $w = 8$; $t = 3$
3. Write 4 related equations, using
   the factors 8 and 7. $8 \times 7 = 56$;
   $7 \times 8 = 56$; $56 \div 7 = 8$; $56 \div 8 = 7$

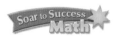

$4c = 20$
$5g = 30$
$2w = 16$
$8t = 24$

Unit 1, Lesson 3   Copyright © Houghton Mifflin Company

Activity Note It may be helpful to have students use a generic rule to help with writing related multiplication and division equations.
factor × factor = product
quotient = product ÷ factor

✎ Math Writing Prompt

Create Your Own Write a word problem for the situation equation $3p = 18$.

Soar to Success Math **Software Support**

Use *Soar to Success* for instruction of students needing targeted support for underlying skills.

On Level
Activity Card I-3

Situation or Solution?   Activity Card 1-3 ▲

Work: By Yourself

1. For each of the problems below define a variable and write an equation to solve the problem.

2. Decide if your equation is a situation equation or a solution equation.

3. Solve each problem
   • Walter bought 6 new notebooks for school. Each notebook cost $2. What is the total cost of the notebooks?
   t = total cost; solution equation: $6 \times 2 = t$; $t = \$12$
   • Josie bought 6 yards of fabric to make curtains for her room. She paid a total of $42 for the fabric. What is the cost of one yard of fabric? Let y = cost of one yard; situation equation: $6y = 42$; solution equation: $42 \div 6 = y$; $y = \$7$

Unit 1, Lesson 3   Copyright © Houghton Mifflin Company

Activity Note Explain to students that they define a variable by writing what the variable represents. Let t = the total cost

✎ Math Writing Prompt

Create Your Own Write a situation equation and a solution equation that are unrelated. Then write a word problem for each equation.

MegaMath **Software Support**

Use *MegaMath* for review and reinforcement of the concepts and skills presented in this lesson.

Challenge
Activity Card I-3

Which Is Which?   Activity Card 1-3 ■

Work: In Pairs

1. Write a word problem that can be represented by a solution equation.

2. Write a word problem can be represented by a situation equation.

3. Exchange your problems with your partner, and write the appropriate equations to represent the problems. Then solve the each problem. Word problems and solutions will vary.

Unit 1, Lesson 3   Copyright © Houghton Mifflin Company

Activity Note Extend the activity by having students create more word problems and save them for classmates to solve at a later date.

✎ Math Writing Prompt

Explain your Thinking Joy was working with the situation equation $3p = 27$. She wrote the related equation $p = 27 \times 3$. Explain what she did wrong.

DESTINATION Math **Software Support**

Use *Destination Math* to take students beyond the concepts and skills presented in this lesson.

Situations and Solution Equations   **163**

③ Homework and Spiral Review

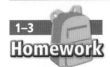

Homework **Goal:** Additional Practice

Use this Homework Page to provide more practice with solving multiplication and division problems.

Remembering **Goal:** Spiral Review

This Remembering activity would be appropriate anytime after today's lesson.

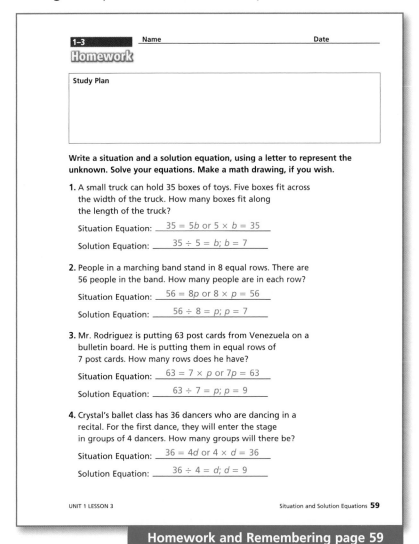

1–3   Name _____   Date _____

Homework

Study Plan

Write a situation and a solution equation, using a letter to represent the unknown. Solve your equations. Make a math drawing, if you wish.

1. A small truck can hold 35 boxes of toys. Five boxes fit across the width of the truck. How many boxes fit along the length of the truck?

Situation Equation: $35 = 5b$ or $5 \times b = 35$

Solution Equation: $35 \div 5 = b; b = 7$

2. People in a marching band stand in 8 equal rows. There are 56 people in the band. How many people are in each row?

Situation Equation: $56 = 8p$ or $8 \times p = 56$

Solution Equation: $56 \div 8 = p; p = 7$

3. Mr. Rodriguez is putting 63 post cards from Venezuela on a bulletin board. He is putting them in equal rows of 7 post cards. How many rows does he have?

Situation Equation: $63 = 7 \times p$ or $7p = 63$

Solution Equation: $63 \div 7 = p; p = 9$

4. Crystal's ballet class has 36 dancers who are dancing in a recital. For the first dance, they will enter the stage in groups of 4 dancers. How many groups will there be?

Situation Equation: $36 = 4d$ or $4 \times d = 36$

Solution Equation: $36 \div 4 = d; d = 9$

UNIT 1 LESSON 3   Situation and Solution Equations **59**

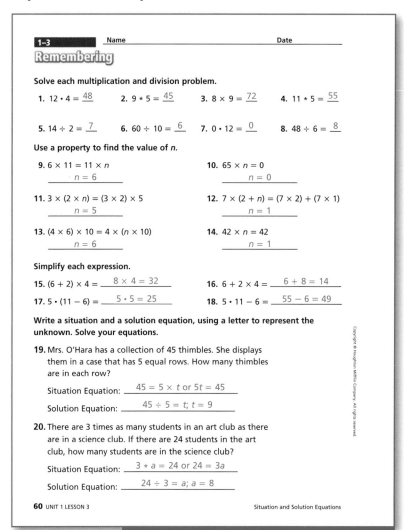

1–3   Name _____   Date _____

Remembering

Solve each multiplication and division problem.

1. $12 \cdot 4 = \underline{48}$ 2. $9 * 5 = \underline{45}$ 3. $8 \times 9 = \underline{72}$ 4. $11 * 5 = \underline{55}$

5. $14 \div 2 = \underline{7}$ 6. $60 \div 10 = \underline{6}$ 7. $0 \cdot 12 = \underline{0}$ 8. $48 \div 6 = \underline{8}$

Use a property to find the value of n.

9. $6 \times 11 = 11 \times n$
   $n = 6$

10. $65 \times n = 0$
   $n = 0$

11. $3 \times (2 \times n) = (3 \times 2) \times 5$
   $n = 5$

12. $7 \times (2 + n) = (7 \times 2) + (7 \times 1)$
   $n = 1$

13. $(4 \times 6) \times 10 = 4 \times (n \times 10)$
   $n = 6$

14. $42 \times n = 42$
   $n = 1$

Simplify each expression.

15. $(6 + 2) \times 4 = \underline{8 \times 4 = 32}$ 16. $6 + 2 \times 4 = \underline{6 + 8 = 14}$

17. $5 \cdot (11 - 6) = \underline{5 \cdot 5 = 25}$ 18. $5 \cdot 11 - 6 = \underline{55 - 6 = 49}$

Write a situation and a solution equation, using a letter to represent the unknown. Solve your equations.

19. Mrs. O'Hara has a collection of 45 thimbles. She displays them in a case that has 5 equal rows. How many thimbles are in each row?

Situation Equation: $45 = 5 \times t$ or $5t = 45$

Solution Equation: $45 \div 5 = t; t = 9$

20. There are 3 times as many students in an art club as there are in a science club. If there are 24 students in the art club, how many students are in the science club?

Situation Equation: $3 * a = 24$ or $24 = 3a$

Solution Equation: $24 \div 3 = a; a = 8$

60 UNIT 1 LESSON 3   Situation and Solution Equations

Homework and Remembering page 59   **Homework and Remembering page 60**

Home or School Activity

Social Studies Connection

U. S. Presidents Students can look up information about the first ten presidents of the United States. Ask them to find presidents' dates of birth and death and their ages when they became president. Students should record all the data in a table. Students may also include the presidents' occupations or the number of years lived after their presidencies.

Information about U.S. Presidents			
Name	Occupation	Age When Elected	Age at Death
George Washington	Soldier	57	67
John Adams	Lawyer	62	91

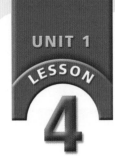

Multiplication Comparisons

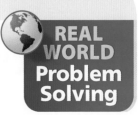

REAL WORLD Problem Solving

Lesson Objectives

- Write multiplication and division equations for comparison problems.
- Solve multiplication and division comparison word problems.

Vocabulary

compare
comparison bars

The Day at a Glance

Today's Goals	Materials	
1 Teaching the Lesson **A1:** Write multiplication and division equations for comparison problems. **A2:** Write equations for a variety of comparison problems.	**Lesson Activities** Student Activity Book pp. 67–68 or Student Hardcover Book pp. 67–68 Homework and Remembering pp. 61–62	**Going Further** Activity Cards 1-4 Connecting Cubes or grid paper and colored pencils Student Book pp. 67–68 Math Journals
2 Going Further ▶ Differentiated Instruction		
3 Homework and Spiral Review		

123 *Use* **Math Talk** *today!*

Keeping Skills Sharp

Quick Practice ⏱ 5 MINUTES	Daily Routines
Goal: Practice multiplications and divisions for 6s, 7s, and 8s. **Materials:** Division Digits Sets 2 and 3 (TRB M4 and M17); Product Cards **Division Digits** The **Student Leader** runs the Division Digits activity, mixing problems from the Set 2 and Set 3 prompt pages. (See Lesson 1–2) **Practice with Product Cards** Students practice independently, using their Product Cards for 6s, 7s, and 8s. They should focus on the cards in their *Slow* and *Don't know* piles moving them to the *Fast* pile once they solve them quickly and accurately. Then, they should fill out their Study Plans.	**Homework Review** If students give incorrect answers, have them explain how they found the answers. This can help you determine if the error is conceptual or procedural. **Money** Lian buys barrettes that cost a total of 59 cents. She gives the clerk three quarters. How much change should Lian receive? 16 cents

① Teaching the Lesson

Activity 1

Compare by Multiplying and Dividing

 25 MINUTES

Goal: Write multiplication and division equations for comparison problems.

Materials: Student Activity Book or Hardcover Book p. 67

 NCTM Standards:
Number and Operations
Algebra
Representation

The Learning Classroom

Helping Community Create a classroom where students are not competing, but desire to collaborate and help one another. Communicate often that your goal as a class is that everyone understands the math you are studying. Tell students that this will require everyone working together to help each other.

English Language Learners

Review comparison language. Review ways to compare quantities.

• **Beginning** Draw a row of 6 blocks and a row of 2 blocks. Say: **Jo had 6 blocks, while Lee had 2. Jo had 3 times the number of blocks Lee had.** Have students repeat.

• **Intermediate** Draw a row of 6 blocks and a row of 2 blocks. Say: **Jo had 6 blocks. How many did Lee have?** (2) **How many times as many blocks does Jo have as Lee?** (3)

• **Advanced** Have students brainstorm different ways to compare Jo's and Lee's blocks.

▶ **Discuss Comparison Language** WHOLE CLASS

Before students begin the activity, review with them the comparison language for multiplication and division that they learned in Grade 3. Write the following on the board:

Rashme picked 15 apples, while her little brother Eli picked 3 apples.

Explain that there are several ways to compare the two quantities in this problem. For example, we can use multiplication to describe the larger amount in terms of the smaller amount.

● How many times as many apples did Rashme pick as her brother?
5 times as many

Ask students how they know the answer is 5 times as many, and encourage them to discuss a variety of ways the answer can be found. Some students may say an unknown number times 3 equals 15 and write _____ × 3 = 15. Other students may say that 15 ÷ 3 = 5.

Comparison Bars In a comparison situation, the larger quantity represents repeated groups of the smaller quantity. Comparison bars can help provide this recognition.

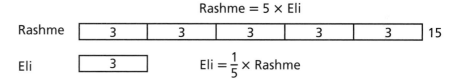

Explain that we can also describe the smaller amount in terms of the larger amount.

This requires a unit fraction. A unit fraction comes from "fracturing," or equally dividing, something. So if we divided Rashme's apples equally into groups of 3, we would get 5 equal parts. Each of these equal parts is called one-fifth written as $\frac{1}{5}$ (one of the 5 equal parts). So we can say two different comparing sentences:

Rashme picked 5 times as many apples as Eli picked.
15 is 5 times as many as 3, or $15 = 5 \times 3$.

Eli picked $\frac{1}{5}$ times as many apples as Rashme picked.
3 is $\frac{1}{5}$ as many as 15, or $3 = \frac{1}{5} \times 15$.

Because dividing gives equal shares, and a unit fraction $\frac{1}{d}$ is one of d equal shares, multiplying by a unit fraction $\frac{1}{d}$ (taking a $\frac{1}{d}$ part) is the same as dividing by d to get one of d equal shares.

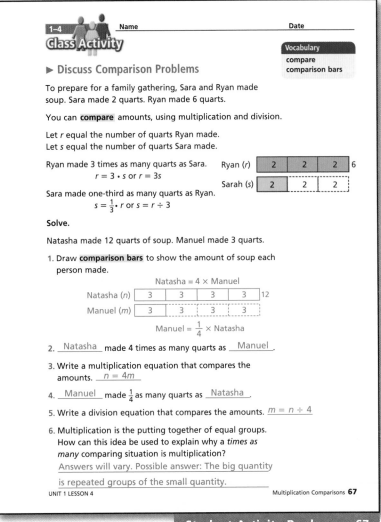

Student Activity Book page 67

Teaching Note

Math Background Multiplication Comparison situations involve the reciprocal of a number. For example, if one group is 5 times the size of the smaller group, the smaller group is the reciprocal of 5, or $\frac{1}{5}$, times the size of the larger group.

The Learning Classroom

Math Talk This may be a good day to talk with the class about what makes a good explanation. Students may want to produce a list on poster board that can be displayed in the classroom for later reference. Students may make suggestions such as these.

1) Write your work so that everyone can see it.

2) Talk loud enough for other students to hear.

3) Use a pointer to point at your work.

4) Say how you arrived at the answer, not just the answer.

5) Stand to the side of your work when you talk.

▶ Discuss Comparison Problems

| WHOLE CLASS |

Math Talk

Read the problem at the top of Student Book page 67. Point out that the situation is a comparison situation and that comparison bars can be drawn to represent it. Discuss the comparison bars and why they represent the situation. Then ask students to explain why the given equations correctly represent the situation.

Use **Solve and Discuss** for problems 1–6. Have students state the multiplication comparing sentence both ways (using a whole number multiplier and using a unit fraction multiplier).

Teaching the Lesson (continued)

Solve Comparison Problems

 30 MINUTES

Goal: Write equations for a variety of comparison problems.

Materials: Student Activity Book or Hardcover Book p. 68

 NCTM Standards:
Number and Operations
Algebra
Representation

 Ongoing Assessment

Natalie made 36 muffins. Samuel made 12 muffins. Tell students to complete the sentence.

▶ Natalie made _____ times as many muffins as Samuel.

Teaching Note

Encouraging Discussion While the students are in small groups, listen to the dialogue. Encourage students who are not sharing to contribute.

During **Solve and Discuss**, observe students as they solve problems on the board. If a student makes a mistake, ask a classmate to explain what the correct answer is. Have students who used a different method share it with the class.

Differentiated Instruction

Advanced Learners Ask students to create their own comparison problems. Then have them exchange problems with a partner and answer the problems.

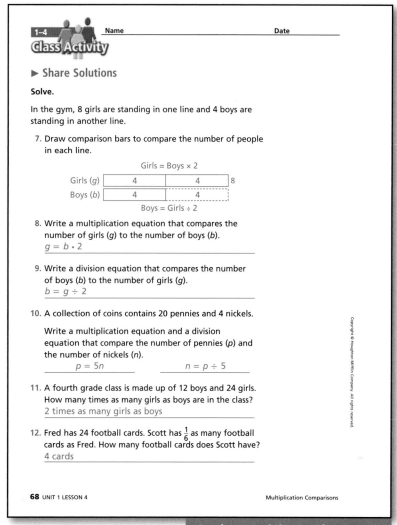

Student Activity Book page 68

▶ Share Solutions SMALL GROUPS

Have **Student Pairs** work together and complete exercises 7–9 as a class. As they work, suggest that students ask themselves the following questions to help them draw comparison bars:

● Who has more?

● Who has less?

● What is the unknown?

● What multiplier makes the smaller quantity equal the larger quantity?

Use **Solve and Discuss** for exercises 10–12. As they complete the exercises, remind students that they can draw comparison bars for each situation to help them solve the problems.

Intervention — Activity Card 1-4

Act It Out — Activity Card 1-4 ●

Work: In Pairs

Use:
- Connecting cubes of different colors, or grid paper and colored pencils
- Student Book pp. 67–68

1. Look at the sample problem at the top of Student Book page 67. You can model this problem by using connecting cubes or grid paper and colored pencils.

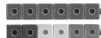

2. One partner should model Ryan's amount, while the other partner models Sara's amount.

3. **Math Talk** How many of Sara's amounts are needed to have the same number as Ryan's amount? Sample answer: You need 3 sets of Sara's amount to have the same number as Ryan's amount.

4. Use connecting cubes to model problems 7, 10, and 12 on Student Book page 68.

Unit 1, Lesson 4 — Copyright © Houghton Mifflin Company

Activity Note Suggest that students model Sara's amount with different colored connecting cubes or grid paper and colored pencils to help identify how many of her amounts are needed to equal Ryan's amount.

 Math Writing Prompt

Create Your Own Write a Comparison word problem, using the numbers 15 and 3.

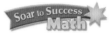 **Software Support**

Use *Soar to Success* for instruction of students needing targeted support for underlying skills.

On Level — Activity Card 1-4

Make Comparisons — Activity Card 1-4 ▲

Work: By Yourself

1. Look at the drawing below.

2. Write a multiplication equation that compares the number of squares s and the number of circles c. $s = c \cdot 5$ or $s = 5c$

3. Write a division equation that compares the number of circles to the number of squares. $c = s \div 5$

4. Write some comparisons of your own. Explain each equation.

Unit 1, Lesson 4 — Copyright © Houghton Mifflin Company

Activity Note Remind students that it may be helpful to identify the number of circles and squares first.

 Math Writing Prompt

Write Comparisons Write two comparison statements about this situation.
Mindy has 18 goldfish.
Raj has 3 goldfish.

 Software Support

Use *MegaMath* for review and reinforcement of the concepts and skills presented in this lesson.

Challenge — Activity Card 1-4

Comparison Problems — Activity Card 1-4 ■

Work: By Yourself

1. Define variables for the situation.

> Evan has 18 trading cards.
> Chloe has 9 trading cards.
> Amy has 3 trading cards.

Sample answer: e = Evan's amount, c = Chloe's amount, a = Amy's amount

2. Write at least 3 multiplication equations to represent the relationship between two of the quantities.
Sample answers: $e = 2c$; $e = 6a$; $c = 3a$

3. Write 3 sentences to describe a different problem situation. Then write at least 3 comparison equations that represent your situation.

Unit 1, Lesson 4 — Copyright © Houghton Mifflin Company

Activity Note Extend the activity by having students write all possible multiplication equations to describe the situations. Remind them that they can use whole numbers and fractions.

 Math Writing Prompt

Justify Your Thinking Explain how you can describe a smaller amount in terms of a larger amount. Give an example.

 DESTINATION Math **Software Support**

Use *Destination Math* to take students beyond the concepts and skills presented in this lesson.

Multiplication Comparisons   **169**

③ Homework and Spiral Review

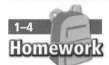

1-4 Homework   Goal: Additional Practice

Use this Homework page to provide students with more practice with multiplication comparisons.

1-4   Name _____   Date _____
Homework

Study Plan

Use the shapes to answer exercises 1–5.

1. How many squares? How many triangles? Use multiplication to find the answers.
<u>12 squares; 4 triangles</u>

2. Because 4 × <u>3</u> = 12, there are <u>3</u> times as many squares as triangles.

3. Because 12 ÷ <u>3</u> = 4, there are $\frac{1}{3}$ as many triangles as squares.

4. Write a multiplication equation that compares the number of squares *s* to the number of triangles *t*. <u>s = 3t</u>

5. Write a division equation that compares the number of triangles *t* to the number of squares *s*. <u>t = s ÷ 3</u>

Solve each problem.

6. Elena's age is 6 times Victor's age. Elena is 12 years old. How many years old is Victor?
<u>2 years old</u>

7. Megan walked 6 kilometers. This distance is 6 times as many kilometers as Marco walked. What distance did Marco walk?
<u>1 kilometer</u>

UNIT 1 LESSON 4   Multiplication Comparisons **61**

Homework and Remembering page 61

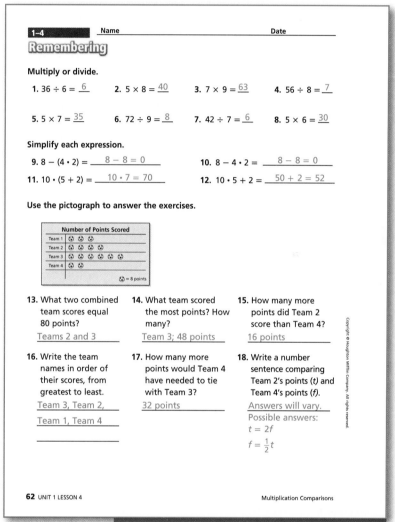

1-4 Remembering   Goal: Spiral Review

This Remembering activity would be appropriate anytime after today's lesson.

1-4   Name _____   Date _____
Remembering

Multiply or divide.

1. 36 ÷ 6 = <u>6</u>   **2.** 5 × 8 = <u>40</u>   **3.** 7 × 9 = <u>63</u>   **4.** 56 ÷ 8 = <u>7</u>

5. 5 × 7 = <u>35</u>   **6.** 72 ÷ 9 = <u>8</u>   **7.** 42 ÷ 7 = <u>6</u>   **8.** 5 × 6 = <u>30</u>

Simplify each expression.

9. 8 − (4 · 2) = <u>8 − 8 = 0</u>   **10.** 8 − 4 · 2 = <u>8 − 8 = 0</u>

11. 10 · (5 + 2) = <u>10 · 7 = 70</u>   **12.** 10 · 5 + 2 = <u>50 + 2 = 52</u>

Use the pictograph to answer the exercises.

Number of Points Scored	
Team 1	☺ ☺ ☺
Team 2	☺ ☺ ☺ ☺
Team 3	☺ ☺ ☺ ☺ ☺ ☺
Team 4	☺ ☺

☺ = 8 points

13. What two combined team scores equal 80 points?
<u>Teams 2 and 3</u>

14. What team scored the most points? How many?
<u>Team 3; 48 points</u>

15. How many more points did Team 2 score than Team 4?
<u>16 points</u>

16. Write the team names in order of their scores, from greatest to least.
<u>Team 3, Team 2,</u>
<u>Team 1, Team 4</u>

17. How many more points would Team 4 have needed to tie with Team 3?
<u>32 points</u>

18. Write a number sentence comparing Team 2's points (*t*) and Team 4's points (*f*).
<u>Answers will vary.</u>
Possible answers:
$t = 2f$
$f = \frac{1}{2}t$

62 UNIT 1 LESSON 4   Multiplication Comparisons

Homework and Remembering page 62

Home or School Activity

Science Connection

Animals Have students research, using books or the Internet, to find how fast some land animals can run. Then tell them to write a comparison problem about two of the animals based on their findings.

An antelope can run 60 mph. A zebra can run 40 mph. How much faster can an antelope run than a zebra?

Land Animals	
Animal	**Speed (mph)**
Cheetah	70
Antelope	60
Lion	50
Elk	45
Zebra	40

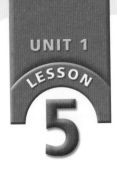
Mixed Comparison Problems

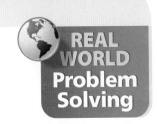
Lesson Objective

- Answer and write comparisons questions about a pictograph and a bar graph.

Vocabulary

pictograph
vertical bar graph
stem-and-leaf plot

The Day at a Glance

Today's Goals	Materials	
1 **Teaching the Lesson** **A1:** Write multiplication and division equations for comparison problems about a pictograph. **A2:** Write multiplication and division equations for comparison problems about a bar graph. **A3:** Conduct a survey and display the data in a bar graph. Use the graph to draw conclusions and make predictions. **2** **Going Further** ▶ Extension: Stem-and-Leaf Plots ▶ Differentiated Instruction **3** **Homework and Spiral Review**	**Lesson Activities** Student Activity Book pp. 69–71 or Student Hardcover Book pp. 69–71 and Activity Workbook p. 37 Homework and Remembering pp. 63–64	**Going Further** Student Activity Book p. 72 or Student Hardcover Book p. 72 and Activity Workbook p. 37 Blank transparency and overhead projector (optional) Activity Cards 1-5 Centimeter-grid paper Straightedge Colored pencils Math Journals

123 Use Math Talk today!

Keeping Skills Sharp

Quick Practice ⏱ 5 MINUTES	Daily Routines
Goal: Practice multiplications and divisions. **Materials:** Division Digits: Sets 2 and 3 (TRB M4 and M17); Product Cards **Division Digits** Place copies of TRB M4 and M17 back-to-back in a sheet protector. The **Student Leader** runs the activity, mixing problems from Sets 2 and 3. (See Lesson 1-2) **Practice with Product Cards** Have students practice independently, using their Product Cards. They should focus on the cards in their *Slow* and *Don't Know* piles, moving them to the *Fast* pile once they can solve the problems quickly and accurately. They should then fill out their Study Plans.	**Homework Review** Check that students completed the assignment, and see whether any problem caused difficulty for many students. **Logic Problems** Read these statements aloud. ▶ All of the numbers in a blue box are even. None of the numbers in a red box are even. In which box should you place the number 55? red box ▶ All of the numbers in a green box are even and 200 or less. None of the numbers in a yellow box are less than 500. In which box will you place the number 1,546? yellow box

Teaching the Lesson

Solve Mixed Comparison Problems

 20 MINUTES

Goal: Write multiplication and division equations for comparison problems about a pictograph.

Materials: Student Activity Book or Hardcover Book p. 69

✔ **NCTM Standards:**
Number and Operations
Algebra
Data Analysis and Probability

Teaching Note

Two Ways to Compare Amounts can be compared additively (how many more/less?) or multiplicatively (how many times as many?). The language in the comparing sentence tells which kind of comparison is needed.

For multiplicative comparisons, remind students that a multiplicative comparison can be said in two ways: using a whole number (the big amount is 4 times as many as the small amount) and using a unit fraction (the small amount is $\frac{1}{4}$ as many as the big amount). Also, the question can use misleading language as in problem 5 that says, "Jamarcus checked out three times as many books as Dawson." But you know Jamarcus checked out 15 books, and that is more than Dawson checked out. So you have to divide by 3 to find how many books Dawson checked out.

For all comparison problems, you must decide which amount is bigger and which is smaller. Drawing comparison bars can help.

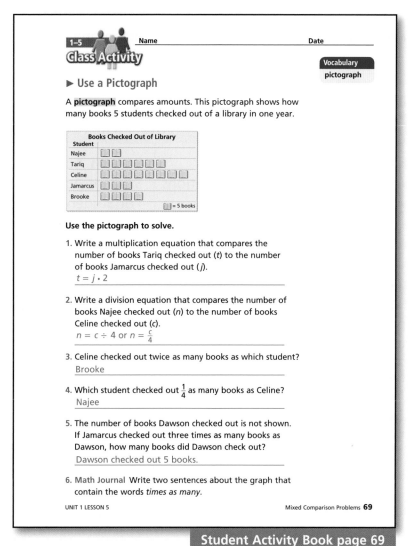

Student Activity Book page 69

▶ Use a Pictograph WHOLE CLASS

Discuss the pictograph on Student Book page 69 with the class. Encourage discussion of all aspects of the pictograph. For example, have students discuss the title, the categories, the symbols, and the key.

Explain that a graph is a display that helps us visually compare the data presented in it. Point out that multiplication and division are often used to answer questions about a graph.

● Use the words "times as many" to compare the number of books Najee and Tariq checked out. Tariq checked out *3 times as many* books as Najee.

● Use a fraction to compare how many books they checked out. Najee checked out $\frac{1}{3}$ as many books as Tariq.

Use **Solve and Discuss** to complete problems 1–6.

Bar Graphs and Comparison Questions

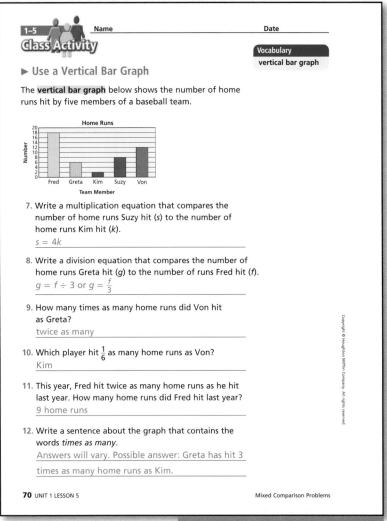

Student Activity Book page 70

Within the activity book image:

1-5
Class Activity
Name _____   Date _____

Vocabulary
vertical bar graph

▶ **Use a Vertical Bar Graph**

The **vertical bar graph** below shows the number of home runs hit by five members of a baseball team.

Home Runs
(bar graph with Number axis 0–20, Team Member axis: Fred, Greta, Kim, Suzy, Von)

7. Write a multiplication equation that compares the number of home runs Suzy hit (*s*) to the number of home runs Kim hit (*k*).
$s = 4k$

8. Write a division equation that compares the number of home runs Greta hit (*g*) to the number of runs Fred hit (*f*).
$g = f \div 3$ or $g = \frac{f}{3}$

9. How many times as many home runs did Von hit as Greta?
twice as many

10. Which player hit $\frac{1}{6}$ as many home runs as Von?
Kim

11. This year, Fred hit twice as many home runs as he hit last year. How many home runs did Fred hit last year?
9 home runs

12. Write a sentence about the graph that contains the words *times as many*.
Answers will vary. Possible answer: Greta has hit 3 times as many home runs as Kim.

70 UNIT 1 LESSON 5   Mixed Comparison Problems

▶ **Use a Vertical Bar Graph** WHOLE CLASS

Discuss the bar graph on Student Book page 70 with the class.

Explain that, like pictographs, bar graphs allow you to compare data visually. Point out that sometimes a visual comparison of data is all that is needed to solve a comparison problem.

● Who hit more home runs—Kim or Fred? Fred How do you know?
  The bar is longer than Kim's.

Help students recognize that comparing data may involve multiplication and division. Use the words "times as many" to compare the home runs made by two team members. Fred hit 9 times as many home runs as Kim. (Other possible answer: Fred hit 3 times as many home runs as Greta.) Then use a fraction to compare the same two team members' home runs. Kim hit $\frac{1}{9}$ as many home runs as Fred.

Use **Solve and Discuss** to complete problems 7–12.

20 MINUTES

Goal: Write multiplication and division equations for comparison problems about a bar graph.

Materials: Student Activity Book or Hardcover Book p. 70

 NCTM Standards:
Number and Operations
Algebra
Data Analysis and Probability

 Ongoing Assessment

Have students:

▶ explain in their own words what a pictograph is.

▶ explain how a pictograph and a bar graph are alike and how they are different.

The Learning Classroom

Helping Community It will be important to take some class time to discuss what *good helping* is all about. Students may come up with a list that can be posted in the classroom. It is important that they understand that good helping does not mean telling answers, but it means taking other students through steps so that they come up with the answers themselves.

Mixed Comparison Problems   **173**

Teaching the Lesson (continued)

Activity 3

Surveys and Data Displays

 40 MINUTES

Goal: Conduct a survey and display the data in a bar graph. Use the graph to draw conclusions and make predictions.

Materials: Student Activity Book p. 71 or Hardcover Book p. 71 and Activity Workbook p. 37

✔ **NCTM Standards:**
Data Analysis and Probability
Representation
Number and Operations

1–5
Class Activity   Name _____   Date _____

▶ Plan and Conduct a Survey

Choose a survey topic from the box or make up one of your own. Conduct your survey and record your results in the tally chart.

Topics
Favorite Fruit
Favorite Juice
Favorite Vegetable
Favorite Snack

Which _____ do you like best?	
Answer Choices	Tally

Use the tally chart to draw a horizontal bar graph.

_____

Check graphs to make sure they match tally charts.

UNIT 1 LESSON 5   Mixed Comparison Problems **71**

Student Activity Book page 71

▶ Plan and Conduct a Survey

PAIRS   **Math Talk**

Step 1: Choose a Question Have **Students Pairs** work together to choose a survey topic. Then ask them to predict four likely answer choices and write them in the tally chart.

Step 2: Collect the Data Pairs of students can meet with other pairs to conduct the surveys and record the results.

Step 3: Display the Data After students record a sufficient number of tallies, have them make a bar graph. Use questioning to help students transfer their data from the tally chart to the graph:

● What title and labels are needed for your graph?

● Where are the answer choices shown on the graph?

● How do you know how tall to draw each bar?

▶ Conclusions and Comparisons WHOLE CLASS

Step 4: Draw Conclusions and Write Comparison Statements

Ask students to draw conclusions from their graphs on Student Book page 71. For example:

- Apples were named more often than any other fruit.

- Since a fruit was named by each student, each student has at least one favorite fruit.

Remind students that the operations of addition, subtraction, multiplication, and division can be used to compare data. Then ask students to use each operation (if possible) and to write a comparison statement of the data. For example:

- Addition: Three more students chose apples than chose oranges.

- Subtraction: Four fewer students chose blueberries than chose strawberries.

- Multiplication: Three times as many students chose watermelon as chose cantaloupe.

- Division: One-half as many students chose peaches as chose cherries.

Challenge your advanced learners to write additional comparison statements that include more than one operation. For example:

- Addition and Multiplication: The number of students who chose raisins was 2 more than 3 times the number of students who chose prunes.

▶ Make Predictions WHOLE CLASS

Step 5: Make Predictions

Ask students to make predictions based on their graphs on Student Book page 71. For example:

- Suppose you were to conduct your survey with a different group of fourth-grade students. Do you think the results would be similar? Explain.

- If twice the number of students were surveyed, how many students would you expect to choose each type of fruit? Explain.

Class Management

Walk around the room and observe as pairs of students write the comparison statements. Watch for opportunities to show them additional ways to compare the data.

English Language Learners

Show a bar graph. Discuss the data. Model how to compare data in the graph.

- **Beginning** Point to the bar graph. Say: **We can compare the data in the graph.** Point to the data with the most. Say: **This has the most.** Point to the data with the least. Say: **This has the least.** Have the students repeat.

- **Intermediate** Point to the bar graph. Guide students to compare the data. Ask: **Which is the most? Which is least? How many more?**

- **Advanced** Have students take turns making a comparison statement of the data in the graph.

Going Further

Extension: Stem-and-Leaf Plots

 25 MINUTES

Goal: Apply understanding of place value to develop and use as stem-and-leaf plot.

Materials: Student Activity Book or Hardcover Book p. 72; blank transparency and overhead projector (optional)

✓ **NCTM Standards:**
Data Analysis and Probability
Representation
Number and Operations

▶ Introduce Stem-and-Leaf Plots

WHOLE CLASS

Write the following data table, and the incomplete stem-and-leaf plot, on the board or overhead as **Student Pairs** copy the information on a sheet of paper.

Quiz Scores (number correct)
15 13 14 15   14   14

Quiz Scores (number correct)	
Stem	Leaf

Legend:

Emphasize Place Value Use questioning to help students understand that data in a stem-and-leaf plot are displayed by place value.

● These quiz scores are two-digit numbers. In any two-digit number, which place does the digit farthest to the right represent? Ones Explain that the digits in the ones place represent leaves.

● Which place does the digit farthest to the left represent? Tens Explain that the digits in the tens place represent stems.

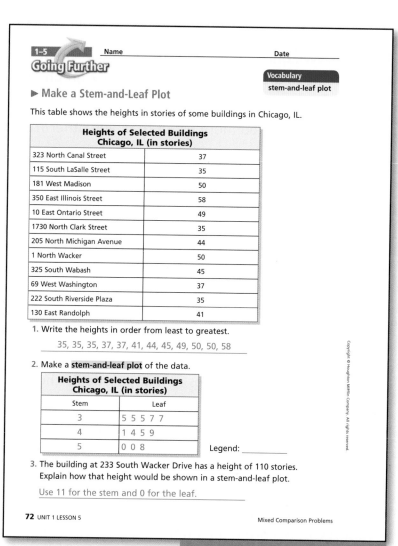

1–5
Going Further

Name _____ Date _____

Vocabulary
stem-and-leaf plot

▶ **Make a Stem-and-Leaf Plot**

This table shows the heights in stories of some buildings in Chicago, IL.

Heights of Selected Buildings Chicago, IL (in stories)	
323 North Canal Street	37
115 South LaSalle Street	35
181 West Madison	50
350 East Illinois Street	58
10 East Ontario Street	49
1730 North Clark Street	35
205 North Michigan Avenue	44
1 North Wacker	50
325 South Wabash	45
69 West Washington	37
222 South Riverside Plaza	35
130 East Randolph	41

1. Write the heights in order from least to greatest.
   35, 35, 35, 37, 37, 41, 44, 45, 49, 50, 50, 58

2. Make a **stem-and-leaf plot** of the data.

Heights of Selected Buildings Chicago, IL (in stories)	
Stem	Leaf
3	5 5 5 7 7
4	1 4 5 9
5	0 0 8

Legend: _____

3. The building at 233 South Wacker Drive has a height of 110 stories. Explain how that height would be shown in a stem-and-leaf plot.

Use 11 for the stem and 0 for the leaf.

72 UNIT 1 LESSON 5   Mixed Comparison Problems

Student Activity Book page 72

Have **Student Pairs** write the quiz scores in order from least to greatest, then complete the stem-and-leaf plot by writing a stem and a leaf for each score. Discuss with students a possible legend or key that can be written to help a reader make sense of the display.

Math Quiz (number correct)	
Stem	Leaf
1	3 4 4 4 5 5

Legend: 1|2 = 12

▶ Make a Stem-and-Leaf Plot PAIRS

Have students work with a **Helping Partner** to complete Student Book page 72.

Differentiated Instruction

Intervention — Activity Card I-5

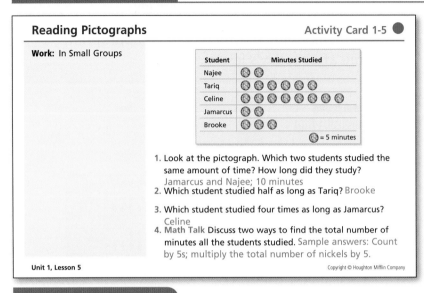

Reading Pictographs   Activity Card 1-5 ●

Work: In Small Groups

Student	Minutes Studied
Najee	
Tariq	
Celine	
Jamarcus	
Brooke	

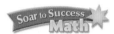 = 5 minutes

1. Look at the pictograph. Which two students studied the same amount of time? How long did they study?
   Jamarcus and Najee; 10 minutes
2. Which student studied half as long as Tariq? Brooke
3. Which student studied four times as long as Jamarcus? Celine
4. Math Talk Discuss two ways to find the total number of minutes all the students studied. Sample answers: Count by 5s; multiply the total number of nickels by 5.

Unit 1, Lesson 5   Copyright © Houghton Mifflin Company

Activity Note Extend the activity by having each student create their own comparison question, using the graph, and present it to the rest of the group to solve.

✎ Math Writing Prompt

Summarize Explain how the names *pictograph* and *bar graph* describe the way each graph shows data.

Soar to Success Math ★ Software Support

Use *Soar to Success* for instruction of students needing targeted support for underlying skills.

On Level — Activity Card I-5

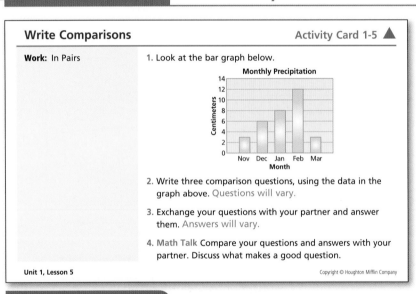

Write Comparisons   Activity Card 1-5 ▲

Work: In Pairs

1. Look at the bar graph below.

Monthly Precipitation

2. Write three comparison questions, using the data in the graph above. Questions will vary.
3. Exchange your questions with your partner and answer them. Answers will vary.
4. Math Talk Compare your questions and answers with your partner. Discuss what makes a good question.

Unit 1, Lesson 5   Copyright © Houghton Mifflin Company

Activity Note Check that students are correctly interpreting the heights of bars that are between the horizontal scale lines.

✎ Math Writing Prompt

Create Your Own Look at the Monthly Precipitation graph. Tell how to write equations that compare the centimeters of precipitation in December (*d*) and in February (*f*).

MegaMath Grades K-8 Software Support

Use *MegaMath* for review and reinforcement of the concepts and skills presented in this lesson.

Challenge — Activity Card I-5

Some Doubling   Activity Card 1-5 ■

Work: By Yourself

Use:
- Student Book page 70
- Centimeter-grid paper
- Straightedge
- Colored pencils

1. Use grid paper to draw the Home Runs bar graph that is on Student Book page 70. Change the scale to intervals of 4.

Home Runs

2. How are the graphs the same; how are they different? bars are shorter; number of home runs is the same
3. Now, adjust the graph so that the numbers of home runs for Greta, Kim, and Suzy are doubled. With these changes, are the answers to exercises 7 and 9 on the Student Book page the same or different? Explain your answer.
   The multiplication equation is the same for exercise 7 because the bars for both Kim and Suzy are doubled. For exercise 9, Greta now has the same number of runs as Von.

Unit 1, Lesson 5   Copyright © Houghton Mifflin Company

Activity Note Extend the activity by having students create their own questions and answer them based on the new bar graph they created.

✎ Math Writing Prompt

Justify Your Reasoning The sum of the lifespan of a mouse and a cow is 18 years. If a cow lives 5 times as long as a mouse what are the lifespans of the mouse and the cow? Explain. mouse 3 yr; cow 15 yr

DESTINATION Math® Software Support

Use *Destination Math* to take students beyond the concepts and skills presented in this lesson.

③ Homewok and Spiral Review

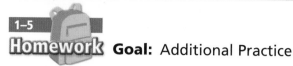

Homework **Goal:** Additional Practice

Use this Homework page to provide students with more practice with mixed comparison problems.

Remembering **Goal:** Spiral Review

This Remembering activity would be appropriate anytime after today's lesson.

1–5
Homework
Name _____ Date _____

Study Plan

The graph below shows the amount of snow recorded each month last winter. Use the graph for exercises 1–6.

1. During which month was the amount of snow recorded $\frac{1}{2}$ as much as was recorded during February?
   __December__

2. During which month was the amount of snow recorded 4 times greater than the amount recorded during November?
   __January__

Snowfall Last Winter

(bar graph: Inches vs Month — Nov., Dec., Jan., Feb., Mar.)

3. The total amount of snow shown in the graph is four times as much snow as was recorded during the winter of 2004. How much snow was recorded during the winter of 2004?
   __13 inches__

4. Write a multiplication equation that compares the number of inches recorded during December (d) to the number of inches recorded during March (m).
   $d = 2m$

5. Write a division equation that compares the number of inches recorded during November (n) to the number of inches recorded during February (f).
   $n = f \div 12$

6. On a separate sheet of paper, write a sentence about the graph that contains the words *times as much*.

UNIT 1 LESSON 5

Mixed Comparison Problems **63**

Homework and Remembering page 63

1–5
Remembering
Name _____ Date _____

Use the pictograph below for exercises 1–4.

1. During which hour did the fewest students visit the library?
   __9 A.M. to 10 A.M.__

   How many students visited the library during that hour?
   __3 students__

Library Visitors (Monday Morning)

Time	Number of Students
8 A.M. to 9 A.M.	🧍🧍🧍🧍
9 A.M. to 10 A.M.	🧍
10 A.M. to 11 A.M.	🧍🧍🧍
11 A.M. to 12 P.M.	🧍🧍🧍🧍🧍

🧍 = 3 Students

2. During which hour was the number of students 5 times greater than the number of students who visited from 9 A.M. to 10 A.M.?
   __8 A.M. to 9 A.M.__

3. During which 3-hour span did a total of 30 students visit the library?
   __9 A.M. to 12 P.M.__

4. Altogether that day, 75 students visited the school library. How many students visited the library during the afternoon hours?
   __30 students__

Multiply or divide.

5. $4 \times 7 = \underline{28}$ 6. $72 \div 9 = \underline{8}$ 7. $1 \times 2 = \underline{2}$ 8. $49 \div 7 = \underline{7}$

9. $54 \div 6 = \underline{9}$ 10. $9 \times 7 = \underline{63}$ 11. $3 \times 4 = \underline{12}$ 12. $45 \div 5 = \underline{9}$

Simplify each expression.

13. $(7 + 4) \cdot 3 = \underline{11 \cdot 3 = 33}$ 14. $7 + 4 \cdot 3 = \underline{84}$

15. $18 \div (6 - 3) = \underline{18 \div 3 = 6}$ 16. $18 \div 6 - 3 = \underline{3 - 3 = 0}$

64 UNIT 1 LESSON 5

Mixed Comparison Problems

Homework and Remembering page 64

Home or School Activity

 Physical Education Connection

Graph It Have your students survey classmates and family members to find out how much they walked for daily exercise. Students can make a pictograph or a bar graph to display the data. Then have students write a few comparison statements about the data shown in the graph.

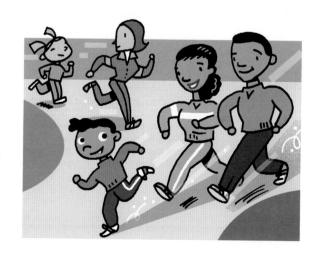

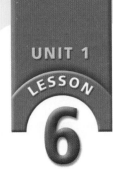

Bar Graphs

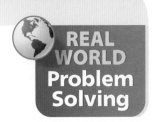

REAL WORLD **Problem Solving**

Vocabulary

horizontal bar graph
axes
scale
vertical bar graph
double bar graph

Lesson Objectives

● Understand horizontal and vertical bar graphs.

● Use a table to create horizontal and vertical bar graphs.

The Day at a Glance

Today's Goals	Materials
1 Teaching the Lesson **A1:** Interpret horizontal and vertical bar graphs and write and answer questions about bar graphs. **A2:** Make a bar graph to represent data in a table. **2 Going Further** ▶ Extension: Double Bar Graphs ▶ Differentiated Instruction **3 Homework and Spiral Review**	**Lesson Activities** Student Activity Book pp. 73–75 or Student Hardcover Book pp. 73–75 and Activity Workbook p. 38 Homework and Remembering pp. 65–66 Index cards Ruler or straightedge Centimeter-grid paper **Going Further** Student Activity Book p. 76 or Student Hardcover Book p. 76 Activity Cards 1-6 Centimeter-grid paper Ruler or straightedge Colored pencils or markers Math Journals 123 *Use* **Math Talk** *today!*

Keeping Skills Sharp

Quick Practice ⏱ 5 MINUTES	Daily Routines
Goal: Practice multiplications and divisions. **Materials:** Division Digits, Product Cards **Division Digits** The **Student Leader** runs the activity, mixing problems from Set 3 for 6s, 7s, 8s. (See Lesson 1-2) **Practice with Product Cards** Have students practice independently, using their Product Cards. (See Lesson 1-4)	**Homework Review** Allow time for students to share the sentences they wrote for exercise 6. Help students resolve any misunderstandings. **Skip Count** Have students skip count: ▶ by 5s from 450 to 485. ▶ by 2s from 315 to 335.

1 Teaching the Lesson

Interpret Bar Graphs

 20 MINUTES

Goal: Interpret horizontal and vertical bar graphs and write and answer questions about bar graphs.

Materials: Student Activity Book or Hardcover Book pp. 73–74; index cards

 NCTM Standards:
Algebra
Data Analysis and Probability

The Learning Classroom

Building Concepts To support building coherence, have students take turns briefly summarizing the previous day's lesson at the beginning or end of each math class. Either way, if you do this regularly, students will get used to making mental summaries of math concepts and making conceptual connections.

English Language Learners

Review ways to compare data, using comparison language.

- **Beginning** Point to the numbers along the bottom of the bar graph. Say: **This bar graph shows 0, 5, 10, 15, 20, 25, 30, 35, and 40. It counts by 5s. The scale on this bar graph counts by 5s.** Have students repeat.
- **Intermediate** Point to the numbers along the bottom of the bar graph. Say: **This bar graph starts with 0 and counts to 40.** Have students read the numbers from 0–40. Say: **It counts by 5s.** Ask: **What does the scale on this bar graph count by?** (fives)
- **Advanced** Have students identify the scale on the bar graph.

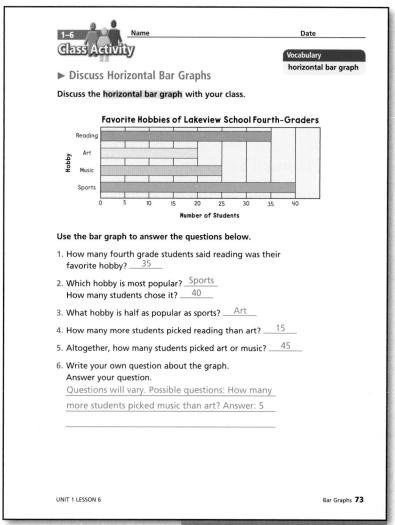

Student Activity Book page 73

▶ Discuss Horizontal Bar Graphs [WHOLE CLASS]

Have students examine the horizontal bar graph on Student Book page 73.

- **What is the title of the graph?** Favorite Hobbies of Lakeview School Fourth-Graders

- **What does the vertical axis show?** types of hobbies

- **What are the different hobbies shown?** sports, music, art, reading

- **What does the horizontal axis show?** the number of students who voted for each hobby

- **Where is the scale, and why is it important?** The row of numbers on the horizontal axis; it tells you how much each bar represents

- **How many students voted for music?** 25 **How can you tell?** The bar for music goes up to the number 25 on the scale.

▶ Interpret Horizontal Bar Graphs INDIVIDUALS

Give students a few minutes to work independently to answer the questions following the graph. When most students have finished, discuss the answers. Allow several students to share answers.

▶ Compare Types of Graphs WHOLE CLASS   Math Talk

Remind students that in earlier lessons, they worked with pictographs. Ask students how bar graphs and pictographs are alike and how they are different. Here are some possible responses:

● Both graphs organize information and show how many of something are in different groups or categories.

● Pictographs use a symbol to represent a given number of items. Bar graphs use bars and a scale.

Now ask:

● Could we show the information in this bar graph in a pictograph? yes

● What would we have to do? Possible answer: Use a symbol to stand for a certain number of students. Then list the hobbies and draw the correct number of symbols after each one.

Sketch a pictograph on the board as students tell you what to draw. Be sure to include a key for your graph. (See pictograph at right.)

▶ Discuss Vertical Bar Graphs WHOLE CLASS

After giving students some time to examine the vertical bar graph on Student Book page 74, ask:

● What does the graph show? the number of DVD movies of different types rented on Monday

Math Talk Discuss how this graph is similar to the horizontal bar graph students just looked at and how it is different:

● *Similarities*: It shows information. It has a title and a horizontal and vertical axis. It has a scale that shows how much each bar represents.

● *Differences*: The bars on this graph go up and down instead of across. The scale is on the vertical axis instead of along the horizontal axis. The labels for the bars are along the horizontal axis instead of on the vertical axis. Some bars don't exactly match numbers on the scale.

Activity continued ▶

Class Management

Sometimes a student will take a while to formulate and verbalize his or her thinking. Be sure to have a role for the students who are at their seats waiting. For example, suggest that students at their seats get ready to be the next explainers. They should think of how they will explain their strategies in two or three complete sentences. They can also be thinking of good questions to ask the explainers, which will help everyone learn. (One teacher calls these "good thinker questions.")

Favorite Hobbies of Lakeview School Fourth-Graders

Reading	● ● ● (
Art	● ●
Music	● ● (
Sports	● ● ● ●

Key: ● = 10 Students
     (= 5 Students

The Learning Classroom

Math Talk You must direct student math talk for it to be productive. Over time, as students become more skilled at discussing their thinking and talking directly with each other, you will fade into the background more. But you will always monitor, clarify, extend, and ultimately make the decisions about how to direct the math conversation so that it is productive for your students.

Teaching the Lesson (continued)

Tell students to look at the DVD graph, then ask:

▶ What does the vertical axis show?

▶ What does the horizontal axis show?

▶ What is the scale of the graph?

The Learning Classroom

Math Talk Have students practice explaining one another's work in their own words. Begin by having a volunteer write one of his or her problems on the board. Or, if you want to use a problem that you have preselected, identify the "author." Then as the students point to parts of the problem, another student identifies the parts, tells the type of problem, and explains why.

Differentiated Instruction

Special Needs For students who did not read the bar graph correctly, have them line up an index card with the top of each bar and read the value on the vertical axis. Then have them write the value at the top of each bar.

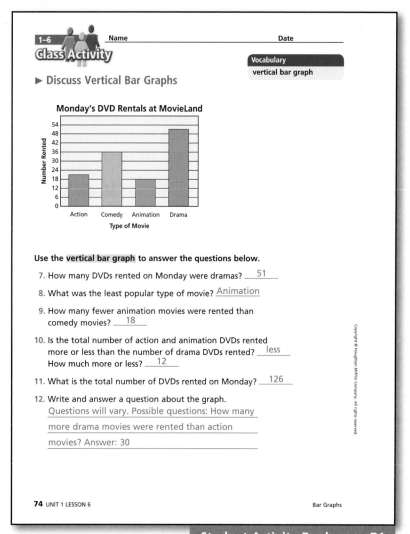

Student Activity Book page 74

Point out that the top of the bar for action movies is between two scale values. Give students a few seconds to figure out how many action DVDs were rented. Select a student to explain the answer.

Math Talk Then ask if anyone can think of another way to find the answer. Here are three possible methods:

● $24 = 18 + 6$, so the number halfway between 18 and 24 must be equal to $18 + 3$, which is 21.

● Each whole interval is equal to 6, so half an interval must be equal to 3. Therefore, the top of the bar is at $18 + 3$, or 21.

● List the numbers from 18 to 24: 18, 19, 20, 21, 22, 23, 24. The middle number is 21, so it is halfway between 18 and 24.

▶ Interpret Vertical Bar Graphs INDIVIDUALS

Give students a few minutes to work independently to answer the questions following the graph on Student Book page 74. When most students have finished, discuss the answers. Allow several students to share the questions they wrote for problem 12.

Create a Bar Graph

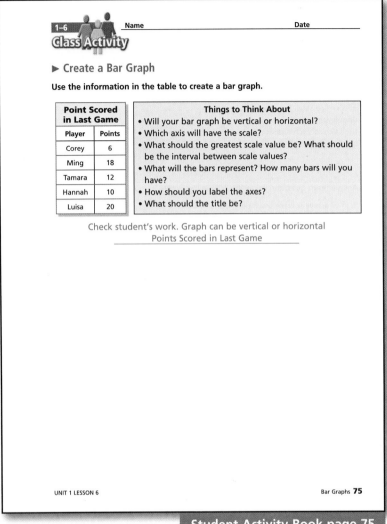

1–6

Class Activity

Name _____ Date _____

▶ Create a Bar Graph

Use the information in the table to create a bar graph.

Point Scored in Last Game	
Player	Points
Corey	6
Ming	18
Tamara	12
Hannah	10
Luisa	20

Things to Think About
- Will your bar graph be vertical or horizontal?
- Which axis will have the scale?
- What should the greatest scale value be? What should be the interval between scale values?
- What will the bars represent? How many bars will you have?
- How should you label the axes?
- What should the title be?

Check student's work. Graph can be vertical or horizontal
Points Scored in Last Game

UNIT 1 LESSON 6   Bar Graphs **75**

Student Activity Book page 75

 25 MINUTES

Goal: Make a bar graph to represent data in a table.

Materials: Student Activity Book p. 75 or Hardcover Book p. 75 and Activity Workbook p. 38; ruler or straightedge

 NCTM Standards:
Algebra
Data Analysis and Probability

Differentiated Instruction

Extra Help As students work, provide help as needed. You might suggest that students start by thinking about the scale.

- What should the largest value be?

- What should the interval between grid lines be? (Intervals of 2 or 4 work well. If students use an interval of 4, the bar for Hannah will be halfway between the grid lines for 8 and 12.)

▶ Make a Bar Graph PAIRS

Ask students to look at the table of data on Student Book page 75, and make sure students understand what the data show. Tell students that they will make a bar graph to show this information. Ask:

- What will each bar on your graph represent? one of the players

- How many bars will you need to make? 5

- What will the numbers on the scale represent? points

- Which bar will be the longest on your finished graph? the bar for Luisa

Tell students they will work with **Helping Partners,** but each student should make his or her own graph. When most students have finished, choose a few pairs of students to present and explain their work.

Bar Graphs   **183**

② Going Further

Extension: Double Bar Graphs

Goal: Read double bar graphs.

Materials: Student Activity Book; or Hardcover Book p. 76; centimeter-grid paper

 NCTM Standards:
Number and Operations
Representation
Communication

▶ Use Double Bar Graphs WHOLE CLASS

Have students look at the double bar graph at the top of Student Book page 76. Discuss the graph by asking the following questions:

- How is this double bar graph different than a single bar graph? There are two bars for each item on the horizontal axis.

- What do the bars show? the number of mountain bikes and road bikes sold

- Why is it good to have the two bars for each year side by side on the graph? You can compare the number of mountain bikes with the number of road bikes.

Then have **Student Pairs** work together to answer exercises 1–5.

Drawing a Double Bar Graph After discussing exercises 1–5, have students work in **Small Groups** to complete problem 6.

Suggest that they use the following table to organize their data.

Topic	Type 1	Type 2	Type 3
Boys			
Girls			
Total			

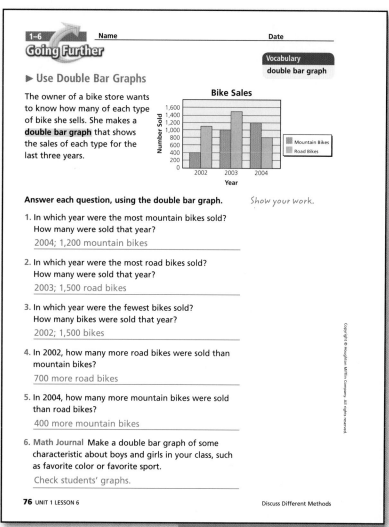

Student Activity Book page 76

Math Talk Discuss how students' tables can be used to create bar graphs.

- Give an example of characteristics you can write in for Type 1, Type 2, and Type 3. blue, green, red; soccer, softball, hockey

- Where would these colors show up on the graph? along the horizontal axis

- How would you use a double bar graph for this data? For each type, there would be one color bar for girls and a different color bar for boys.

- What would the numbers along the vertical axis represent? The number of students who chose each color.

Have groups present their bar graphs to the class.

Differentiated Instruction

Intervention — Activity Card 1-6

Change It!
Activity Card 1-6 ●

Work: By Yourself

Use:
- Centimeter-grid paper
- Ruler or straightedge
- Colored pencils or markers

1. Use grid paper to redraw the graph below as a vertical bar graph. Use a ruler or straightedge to draw the axes.

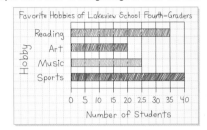

2. Look Back Are all the data included? Does the graph have a title, and are all parts correctly labeled?

Unit 1, Lesson 6 — Copyright © Houghton Mifflin Company

Activity Note Some students may find that turning the graph on its side may help them draw a vertical graph.

 Math Writing Prompt

You Decide Explain why you might make a vertical bar graph for one set of data and a horizontal bar graph for a different set of data. showing length vs. showing height

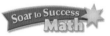 **Software Support**

Use *Soar to Success* for instruction of students needing targeted support for underlying skills.

On Level — Activity Card 1-6

How Many People?
Activity Card 1-6 ▲

Work: By Yourself

Puppet Show Attendance

1. Look at the bar graph. What show had an attendance of 20 more people than the attendance of the *Funny Forest* show? Happy Sea

2. What show had an attendance of two times as many people as *Mystery Island*? Happy Sea

3. Explain Estimate the total attendance of all the shows. Explain how you found your answer. About 300 people

Unit 1, Lesson 6 — Copyright © Houghton Mifflin Company

Activity Note Extend the activity by having students write their own questions based on the graph.

 Math Writing Prompt

Make a Table Explain why it might be necessary to change the scale of a bar graph. Give an example. when data include large numbers

 Software Support

Use *MegaMath* for review and reinforcement of the concepts and skills presented in this lesson.

Challenge — Activity Card 1-6

Seeing Double
Activity Card 1-6 ■

Work: By Yourself

Use:
- Centimeter-grid paper
- Ruler or straightedge
- Colored pencils or markers

1. Look at the table below. It shows the responses for two classes about the number of brothers and sisters they have.

Brothers and Sisters		
Number of Brothers or Sisters	4th Grade	5th Grade
None	16	20
1	18	9
2	15	18
3 or More	8	12

2. Make a double bar graph to show the responses for both grade levels. Make the bars for each grade a different color. Remember to include a key for the colors of the bars. Graphs may vary.

Unit 1, Lesson 6 — Copyright © Houghton Mifflin Company

Activity Note Extend the activity by having students identify any multiplication comparisons in the data. Have them indicate how to identify these on the bar graph.

 Math Writing Prompt

Explain Your Reasoning Explain why double bar graphs are helpful.

 Software Support

Use *Destination Math* to take students beyond the concepts and skills presented in this lesson.

3 Homework and Spiral Review

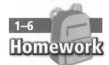 **Homework** **Goal:** Additional Practice

Use this Homework page to provide students with more practice with bar graphs.

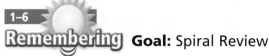 **Remembering** **Goal:** Spiral Review

This Remembering activity would be appropriate any time after today's lesson.

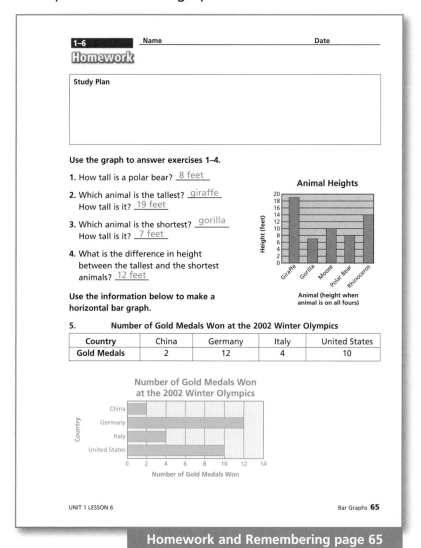

Homework and Remembering page 65

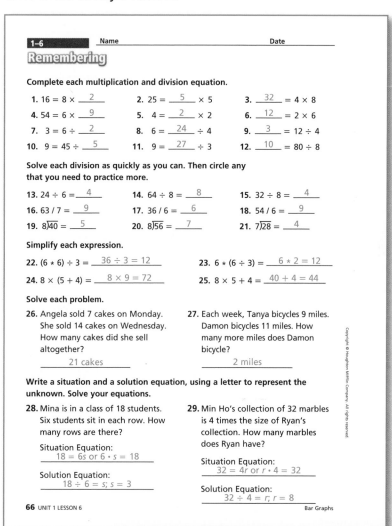

Homework and Remembering page 66

Home or School Activity

 Social Studies Connection

Graphs in the News Have students cut out or copy a bar graph from a newspaper or magazine. Then have them explain what the graph shows. Be sure they include the title, axes labels, and scale in their explanation.

Ask students to write five statements about the data in the bar graph, and to include at least two comparison statements.

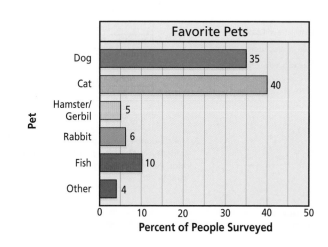

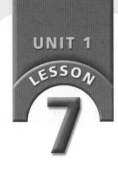

Solve Multistep Word Problems

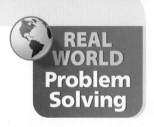

REAL
WORLD
**Problem
Solving**

Lesson Objective

● Use addition, subtraction, multiplication, and division
  to solve problems that involve more than one step.

The Day at a Glance

Today's Goals	Materials	
1 **Teaching the Lesson** **A1:** Solve problems that involve more than one step.	**Lesson Activities** Student Activity Book pp. 77–78 or Hardcover Book pp. 77–78 Homework and Remembering pp. 67–68	**Going Further** Activity Cards 1-7 Two-color counters Math Journals
2 **Going Further** ▶ Differentiated Instruction		
3 **Homework and Spiral Review**		

123 Use
Math Talk
today!

Keeping Skills Sharp

Quick Practice ⏱ 5 MINUTES	Daily Routines
Goal: Practice multiplications and divisions. **Materials:** Product Cards **Practice with Product Cards** Have students practice independently, using their Product Cards for the 6s, 7s, and 8s. (See Lesson 1-4)	**Homework Review** Let students work together to check their work. Initially, pair less able students with more able students. Remind students to use what they know about helping others. **Make a List** How many different ways can Juan, Isobel, Lashanna, and Tyler stand in line if Juan is always first. 6 ways

Teaching the Lesson

Multistep Word Problems

 45 MINUTES

Goal: Solve problems that involve more than one step.

Materials: Student Activity Book or Hardcover Book pp. 77–78

✔ **NCTM Standards:**
Number and Operations
Algebra
Problem Solving

Teaching Note

Vocabulary We are using the term *Hidden Questions* just to make the conceptual point that you may need to answer these questions even if they do not appear in the problem. Explain to students that *Hidden Questions* is not a technical math term. It is just an idea to help them solve multiple-step word problems.

English Language Learners

Review phrases that imply operations (sum, difference, product, quotient, more than, less than, etc.)

• **Beginning** Write and then read this Problem. **4 dogs have 3 collars each. How many collars in all?** Say: **We are trying to find the total number of collars if 4 dogs each have 3 collars.** Have students repeat.

• **Intermediate** Write and then read this problem. **4 dogs have 3 collars each. How many collars in all?** Ask: **What is another way to say what the problem asks for?** total number of collars if 4 dogs each have 3 collars

• **Advanced** Have students work in pairs. One student says a simple word problem and the other restates the given problem.

▶ **Identify the Hidden Questions** WHOLE CLASS

Share with students the following introduction to solving multistep word problems:

● We're going to solve some multistep problems today.

● For some problems, you might want to write equations using parentheses. Or you may solve them using separate steps. Either way is fine.

● Multistep problems give you opportunities to use the algebraic language and notation you have been learning.

● It is important to label your work with a letter or some other symbol so you know how your numbers relate to the problem.

● Some multistep problems have "Hidden Questions" that are not asked but need to be answered to solve the problem.

Class Activity

Name _____ Date _____

▶ **Discuss Multi-Step Word Problems**

Solve.   *Show your work.*

1. Eli reads 6 pages in a book each night. Shelby reads 8 pages each night. How many pages altogether will Eli and Shelby read in one week? _98 pages_

2. Min Soo is ordering 5 pizzas for a party. Each pizza will be cut into 8 slices. Three pizzas will have multiple toppings, and the others will be plain cheese. How many slices of plain cheese pizza is Min Soo ordering for the party? _16 slices_

3. Team A and Team B have 17 players each. Team A has 6 girls. Team B has twice as many girls as Team A. On both teams, how many players are girls? How many players are boys? _18 girls; 16 boys_

4. Jasmine and Mori each received the same number of party favor bags at a friend's party. Each bag contained 8 favors. If Jasmine and Mori received a total of 48 favors, how many party favor bags did they each receive? _3 bags_

5. In art class, Ernesto made some fruit bowls for his mother and brother. Nine apples can be placed in each bowl. Ernesto's brother placed 18 apples in the bowls he was given, and Ernesto's mother placed 36 apples in the bowls she was given. How many fruit bowls did Ernesto make? _6 bowls_

6. On Tuesday, a bicycle shop employee replaced all of the tires on 6 bicycles. On Wednesday, all of the tires on 5 tricycles were replaced. What is the total number of tires that were replaced on those days? _27 tires_

UNIT 1 LESSON 7   Solve Multistep Word Problems **77**

Student Activity Book page 77

▶ Discuss Multi-Step Word Problems

WHOLE CLASS   **Math Talk**

Use **Solve and Discuss** for problems 1–6 on Student Book page 77. Here are hidden questions, alternative solution methods, and issues for problems that the class discussion should be sure to address.

1. Hidden Question: How many nights in 1 week?

   Possible Solutions: $7 \bullet 6 + 7 \bullet 8 = 42 + 56 = 98$

   $7(6 + 8) = 7 \bullet 14 = 98$

Activity continued ▶

Teaching Note

Order of Operations If you did not teach Fluency Lesson 16 at the beginning of the book, you may need to explain the order of operations before starting this lesson.

1. Work inside parentheses first.

2. Multiply and divide from left to right.

3. Add and subtract from left to right.

✓ Ongoing Assessment

Ask questions such as: For problem 1:

▶ How can we find the number of pages Eli reads each week?

▶ Can you use the same method to find the number of pages Shelby reads each week?

▶ How can you find the number of pages read by both Eli and Shelby?

▶ When must you perform more than one operation to solve a problem?

▶ Is there a specific order in which those operations must be performed?

Activity 1

The Learning Classroom

Math Talk Are you giving your students time to respond? By waiting for students to respond and refraining from providing answers and explanations, the students will have an opportunity to think about and communicate answers and explanations. Many teachers tell us that this situation is their biggest challenge, but when they wait and encourage thoughtful student responses, there are beneficial results.

Teaching Note

What to Expect From Students: Sample ways to find the solutions are given. However, solutions for multi-step problems can often be found in a variety of ways; not all of those ways are shown here.

Also, students may use variations in their algebraic notation. For example, some may still use the × sign for multiplication while others may use a • or parentheses such as 3(2) or (3)2; each method is acceptable.

2. Hidden Question: How many pizzas are plain cheese?

   Possible Solutions: $5 - 3 = 2$, and $2 • 8 = 16$

   Subtract the number of multiple-topping slices from the total number of slices: $5 • 8 - 3 • 8 = 40 - 24 = 16$ slices; ask students why this equation does not need parentheses. In algebraic language (order of operations), multiplications are performed before subtractions.

3. Hidden Question: How many girls are on Team B?

   Possible Solutions: Twice as many girls are on Team B (Team A = 6), so there are $6 + 12 = 18$ girls altogether.

   Find the number of boys on both teams by answering the Hidden Question "*How many players are on both teams?*" and subtracting the number of girls.

   $2 • 17 - 18 = 34 - 18 = 16$ boys

   Use one equation: $2 • 17 - (6 + 12) = 34 - 18 = 16$ boys

4. Hidden Question: How many bags did they receive altogether?

   Possible Solutions: $48 ÷ 8 = 6$, and $6 ÷ 2 = 3$ bags each

   Use One Equation: $(48 ÷ 8) ÷ 2 = 6 ÷ 2 = 3$ bags each

5. Hidden Questions: How many bowls does his brother have? How many bowls does his mother have?

   Possible solutions: $18 ÷ 9 + 36 ÷ 9 = 2 + 4 = 6$ bowls

   $$(18 + 36) ÷ 9 = 54 ÷ 9 = 6 \text{ bowls}$$

   Notice that these two methods show the two sides of the Distributive Property.

6. Hidden Questions: How many bicycle tires? How many tricycle tires?

   Possible Solutions: 6 bicycles • 2 tires = 12 tires;

   5 tricycles • 3 tires = 15 tires; $12 + 15 = 27$ tires in all

   Use One Equation: $6 • 2 + 5 • 3 = 12 + 15 = 27$ tires

▶ **Solve Multi-Step Word Problems**

Solve.

Show your work.

7. Mrs. Luong bought 9 trees for $40 each. She paid for her purchase with four $100 bills. How much change did she receive? ____$40____

8. Erica is painting the floors of her front porch and her back porch. The front porch floor is 10 feet by 6 feet and the back porch floor is 6 feet by 4 feet. How many square feet will Erica paint altogether?
____84 square feet____

9. Chan Hee is carrying a box that weighs 37 pounds. In the box are five containers of equal weight, and a book that weighs 2 pounds. What is the weight of each container? ____7 pounds____

10. A pet shop is home to 6 cats, 10 birds, 3 dogs, and 18 tropical fish. Altogether, how many legs do those pets have? ____56 legs____

11. Dan has 7 fish in his aquarium. Marilyn has 4 times as many fish in her aquarium. How many fish do Dan and Marilyn have altogether? ____35 fish____

12. Write a problem that is solved using more than one step. Then show how the problem is solved.
____Problems and solutions will vary.____
_____
_____
_____
_____
_____
_____
_____

78 UNIT 1 LESSON 7   Solve Multistep Word Problems

Student Activity Book page 78

▶ **Solve Multi-Step Word Problems** | WHOLE CLASS |

Now solve problems 7 through 11 on Student Book page 78. Continue **Solve and Discuss** if students need such help, or have them solve the problems individually, using **Helping Partners** when necessary.

Give early finishers an opportunity to go to the board and write a variety of solutions for each problem. Then discuss the solutions, and ask students to note where properties are used.

The Learning Classroom

Helping Community When stronger math students finish their work early, give them an opportunity to help others who might be struggling. Many students enjoy the role of helping other students. In their "helper" role, students who might become bored challenge themselves as they explain math content to others.

Activity continued ▶

Activity 1

 Math Talk in Action

Students may be interested to learn how other students approach multi-step problem solving.

What are some good ideas to think about when you solve multi-step word problems?

Kenesha: Problems that have three or more numbers may be multi-step problems.

Joel: Sometimes I do not use all the information in a problem. For example, I do not need to know the number of tropical fish to solve problem 10.

Mieko: The most important thing about solving word problems is understanding the situation. Making a drawing and writing an equation are ways to help me understand problems.

7. Hidden Questions: How much did the trees cost?

   How much did Mrs. Luong pay?

   Possible Solutions: 9 • $40 = $360 and 4 • $100 = $400, so $400 − $360 = $40

   Use One Equation:

   4 × $100 − 9 × $40 = $400 − $360 = $40

8. Hidden Question: How many square feet for each floor?

   Possible solutions: 10 ft × 6 ft = 60 sq ft and

   6 ft × 4 ft = 24 sq ft, so 60 sq ft + 24 sq ft = 84 sq ft

   Use one equation: 10 • 6 + 6 • 4 = 60 + 24 = 84 sq ft

9. Hidden Question: What is the weight of all the containers?

   Possible Solution: (37 − 2) ÷ 5 = 35 ÷ 5 = 7 pounds

10. Hidden Questions: Which of the pets have legs? How many legs does each kind of pet have?

    Possible Solution:

    4 • 6 + 2 • 10 + 4 • 3 = 24 + 20 + 12 = 56 legs

11. Hidden Question: How many goldfish does Marilyn have?

    Possible Solutions: 4 • 7 = 28, so 7 + 28 = 35

    Use One Equation:

    7 + 4 • 7 = 1 • 7 + 4 • 7 = (1 + 4) • 7 = 5 • 7 = 35

(Using one equation is more complicated, but it shows an application of the Identity Property and gives students an opportunity to see that this property is actually used in problem solving.)

Let the class work in **Student Pairs** to discuss the problems they wrote for exercise 12.

Summarize this exploration of multi-step word problems by reiterating what is true for solving all word problems: The most important thing is to understand the situation. Once the situation has been understood, algebraic language can be used to represent and solve the problem.

②Going Further

Differentiated Instruction

● Intervention — Activity Card I-7

Act It Out — Activity Card 1-7 ●

Work: In Pairs
Use:
• 40 two-color counters

1. Use counters to make an array to show the total number of bicycle tires repaired.
Array should be 4 groups of 2.

 This is an array for 6 × 2 = 12.

Mike's Bike Shop repaired all of the tires on 4 bicycles on Friday. The shop repaired all of the tires on 8 tricycles on Saturday. How many total tires did Mike's Bike Shop repair on Friday and Saturday?

2. Use different counters to make a separate array that shows the total number of tricycle tires repaired.
Array should be 8 groups of 3.
3. Write an equation to show how to solve the problem.
8 + 24 = 32 tires or (4 × 2) + (8 × 3) = 32 tires

Unit 1, Lesson 7   Copyright © Houghton Mifflin Company

Activity Note Check that students are making two different arrays for each part of the problem. Recommend that they use different colors for each array.

 Math Writing Prompt

Explain Your Thinking Explain how to find (3 + 2) × 6.

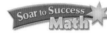 **Software Support**

Use *Soar to Success* for instruction of students needing targeted support for underlying skills.

▲ On Level — Activity Card I-7

Different Steps, Same Answer — Activity Card 1-7 ▲

Work: In Pairs

1. Read this problem. Jorge does 5 sit-ups every morning. He does 7 sit-ups every night. How many sit-ups does he do in one week?

There are two ways to solve this problem.
One Way   **Another Way**
5 × 7 = 35   5 + 7 = 12
7 × 7 = 49   12 × 7 = 84
35 + 49 = 84

2. Mrs. Glover is making tablecloths as gifts. She uses 3 yards of fabric for each tablecloth. Yesterday, she made 9 tablecloths. Today, she made 2 tablecloths. How many feet of fabric did she use? Solve this problem two ways.
99 feet
3. Work together to write a multi-step word problem. Then find two ways to solve your problem.

Unit 1, Lesson 7   Copyright © Houghton Mifflin Company

Activity Note Remind students that there can sometimes be more than two ways to solve a problem. Allow time for students to discuss this idea.

 Math Writing Prompt

Create Your Own Write a multistep problem for the equation 10 + 2 × 4 = *m*. Then solve the problem.

 Software Support

Use *MegaMath* for review and reinforcement of the concepts and skills presented in this lesson.

■ Challenge — Activity Card I-7

Three Operations — Activity Card 1-7 ■

Work: In Pairs

1. Read this problem. Mike has 8 marbles. Pat has half as many marbles as Mike. Ernesto has 4 times as many marbles as Mike. How many more marbles does Ernesto have than Pat?

This problem requires three operations to solve it.
Mike = 8   Pat = 8 ÷ 2   Ernesto = 4 × 8

4 × 8 − (8 ÷ 2) = 32 − 4 or 28

Ernesto has 28 more marbles than Pat.

2. Write a problem that requires three operations and Exchange the problem with your partner.
3. Solve your partner's problem by writing an equation.
Problems, equations, and answers will vary.
4. **Look Back** Is there more than one equation that can be used to solve the problem? If yes, try to write a different equation.

Unit 1, Lesson 7   Copyright © Houghton Mifflin Company

Activity Note Many multistep problems have questions within questions. Have students identify all the information they need to include before they begin to write their own problems.

 Math Writing Prompt

Create Your Own Write a comparison word problem for the equation (3 × 4) − (5 × 2) = *n*.

 Software Support

Use *Destination Math* to take students beyond the concepts and skills presented in this lesson.

③ Homework and Spiral Review

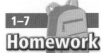

Homework **Goal:** Additional Practice

✓ Include students' work for page 67 as part of their portfolios.

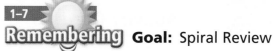

Remembering **Goal:** Spiral Review

This Remembering activity would be appropriate anytime after today's lesson.

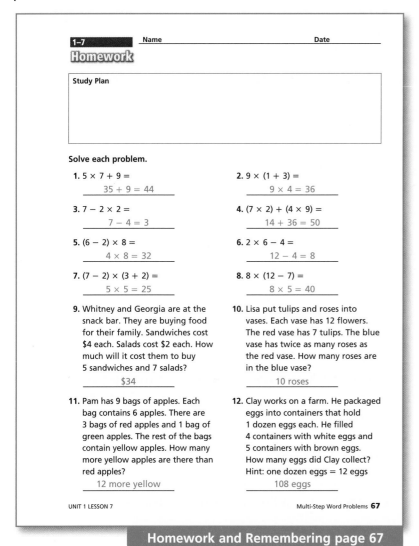

Homework and Remembering page 67

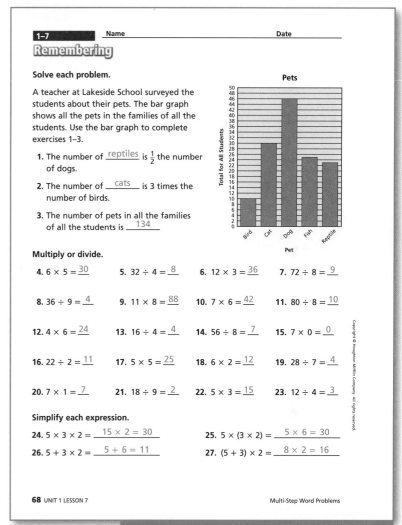

Homework and Remembering page 68

Home or School Activity

Math-to-Math Connection

Heights in Inches Have students ask at least three friends or family members what their heights are in feet and inches. Then students will write and solve an equation to find each height in inches. After they find each height in inches, ask them to put all of the heights in order from least to greatest.

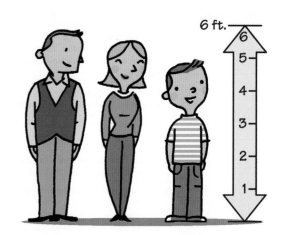

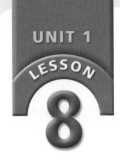

Factors and Prime Numbers

Vocabulary

factor pair
prime number
composite number
Factor Fireworks
multiple
factor tree

Lesson Objectives

● Find factor pairs for given numbers and use them to determine whether a number is prime or composite.

● Write numbers as products of prime factors and use prime factorizations to solve division problems.

The Day at a Glance

Today's Goals	Materials

1 Teaching the Lesson
A1: Take a checkup on multiplications and divisions.
A2: Find factor pairs for given numbers, and use them to determine whether a number is prime or composite.
A3: Write numbers as products of prime factors, and use prime factorizations to solve division problems.
A4: Compose and decompose numbers, using factors and multiples
 	
2 Going Further
▶ Differentiated Instruction
 	
3 Homework and Spiral Review
	Lesson Activities
	Student Activity Book pp. 79–82
	  or Student Hardcover Book
	  pp. 79–82 and Activity Workbook
	  p. 39 (includes Checkup D)
	Homework and Remembering
	  pp. 69–70
	Checkup D Answer Key (TRB M40)
	MathBoard Materials
	Transparency of TRB M40 and over-
	  head projector (optional)
	Quick Quiz 2 (Assessment Guide)
		Going Further
		Activity Cards 1-8
		Counters
		Math Journals

123 Use Math Talk today!

Keeping Skills Sharp

Quick Practice 5 MINUTES	Daily Routines
Goal: Practice multiplications and divisions. **Materials:** Class MathBoard, Division Digits materials, Product Cards **Practice with 6s, 7s, and 8s** On the Class MathBoard, write nine multiplication and nine division problems for the 6s, 7s, and 8s in a mixed order. (See Fluency Lesson 13) **Practice with Product Cards** Have students practice independently using their Product Cards. (See Lesson 1-4)	**Homework Review** If students have difficulty with word problems, encourage them to write situation equations and then change them to solution equations. **Money** Paul is buying 3 pennants for each of his 4 friends. If each pennant costs $2, how much will Paul spend? $24

①Teaching the Lesson

Checkup D

 15 MINUTES

Goal: Take a checkup on multiplications and divisions.

Materials: Student Activity Book p. 79 or Hardcover Book p. 79 and Activity Workbook p. 39; Checkup D Answer Key (TRB M40); transparency of TRB M40 and overhead projector (optional)

 NCTM Standard:
Number and Operations

Differentiated Instruction

Extra Help Circulate and check students' papers. Are some students still getting a lot of incorrect answers? Perhaps these students could benefit from a little extra help before moving to the next unit. Encourage these students to use their Product Cards, Homework and Remembering pages, and any other aids they might have to practice their multiplications and divisions.

| 1–8 | Name _____ | | Date _____ |

Class Activity

▶ Checkup D: 2s, 5s, 9s, 3s, 4s, 6s, 7s, 8s, 1s, 0s

1. 5 * 3 = 15	19. 1 × 8 = 8	37. 3 × 3 = 9	55. 24 / 4 = 6
2. 9 / 3 = 3	20. 7 * 4 = 28	38. 9 * 6 = 54	56. 7)21 (3)
3. 4)28 (7)	21. 16 ÷ 8 = 2	39. 63 / 7 = 9	57. 2 * 3 = 6
4. 6 • 6 = 36	22. 56 / 7 = 8	40. 6)18 (3)	58. $\frac{40}{8}$ = 5
5. $\frac{81}{9}$ = 9	23. 4)32 (8)	41. 8 • 4 = 32	59. 15 ÷ 3 = 5
6. 42 ÷ 6 = 7	24. 0 • 3 = 0	42. 6 × 3 = 18	60. 27 / 9 = 3
7. 7 × 9 = 63	25. 9 × 8 = 72	43. $\frac{63}{9}$ = 7	61. 8)24 (3)
8. 18 / 9 = 2	26. $\frac{12}{4}$ = 3	44. 2 * 6 = 12	62. 5 • 9 = 45
9. 6 * 7 = 42	27. 2 * 7 = 14	45. 8 ÷ 4 = 2	63. 6 × 4 = 24
10. 2 • 8 = 16	28. 8 • 6 = 48	46. 3 • 4 = 12	64. $\frac{18}{3}$ = 6
11. 8)32 (4)	29. 36 ÷ 9 = 4	47. 30 / 6 = 5	65. 64 ÷ 8 = 8
12. $\frac{6}{3}$ = 2	30. 3 × 8 = 24	48. 7 × 7 = 49	66. 24 / 6 = 4
13. 24 ÷ 3 = 8	31. 54 / 9 = 6	49. 7)42 (6)	67. 3 * 6 = 18
14. 4 × 7 = 28	32. 9 * 7 = 63	50. 4 * 6 = 24	68. 6)6 (1)
15. 2 * 9 = 18	33. 8 • 3 = 24	51. $\frac{36}{6}$ = 6	69. $\frac{20}{4}$ = 5
16. 12 / 3 = 4	34. 4)36 (9)	52. 6 • 8 = 48	70. 3 * 7 = 21
17. 9)45 (5)	35. $\frac{0}{7}$ = 0	53. 27 ÷ 3 = 9	71. 12 ÷ 6 = 2
18. 5 • 6 = 30	36. 48 ÷ 8 = 6	54. 4 × 3 = 12	72. 9 × 9 = 81

UNIT 1 LESSON 8   Checkup D **79**

Student Activity Book page 79

▶ Checkup D [INDIVIDUALS]

Tell students that today they will take a Checkup which tests all of the multiplications and divisions. Remind students that Checkup D will not be graded.

Have students turn to Student Book page 79 and begin the checkup on your signal. Either give students a set amount of time to take it or let them work until most students have finished.

▶ Check the Answers [INDIVIDUALS]

Have students exchange papers or check their own answers. TRB M40 is the answer key for the Checkup D. Make copies for students, display it as a transparency, or simply read the answers aloud. Have students write the multiplications and divisions they missed on their Study Plans.

Find Factor Pairs

▶ Find Factor Pairs WHOLE CLASS

Write the number 6 on the board. Then ask, "Can anyone name a pair of factors that has a product of 6?" The student who answers should say either "1 and 6" or "2 and 3." Write the student's answer on the board. Now ask if anyone can name another factor pair with a product of 6, and record it as well. Make sure students understand that the order of the factors does not matter; 2 and 3 is the same factor pair as 3 and 2.

Select several students to work at the board, while the rest work at their MathBoards. Explain that you will give them some numbers and they should try to find every possible factor pair for each number. Read each number aloud, giving students a minute to find the factor pairs for each:

> 7   12   13   24   29   30

For each number, have students compare their answers to make sure they have found all the factor pairs. If some students are finding the factor pairs easily, you might ask them to share their methods with the class.

You may need to remind students that 1 times any number is that number. So every number has at least one factor pair: 1 and itself.

Students may forget to list 2 and 12 for 24 and 2 and 15 for 30. If so, ask questions to try to elicit these factor pairs.

Finally, ask the following:

● Which of the numbers had only one factor pair? 7, 13, and 29

● For each of those numbers, what do you notice about that one factor pair? It is 1 and the number itself.

● Numbers greater than 1 that have 1 and themselves as their only factors have a special name. Does anyone know what they are called? prime numbers

Introduce the term *prime number.* Explain that numbers with more than one factor pair are called *composite numbers.* Tell students that the number 1 is neither prime nor composite.

15 MINUTES

Goal: Find factor pairs for given numbers, and use them to determine whether a number is prime or composite.

Materials: MathBoard Materials

✓ **NCTM Standard:**
Number and Operations

The Learning Classroom

Math Talk In order to help students understand what you mean when you say, "explain your thinking," solve one of the problems at the board as if you were the student. Be sure to tell them about all parts of your problem and the thinking you used to solve it.

English Language Learners

Review the word *factor.*

● **Beginning** Write the number 12. Say: **Let's list the factors that have a product of 12.** Write 2 and 6, 3 and 4, and 1 and 12. Say: **The factors of 12 are 2, 3, 4, 6, 1 and 12.** Have students repeat the factors.

● **Intermediate** Write the number 12. Say: **What factors have a product of 12?** Guide students to list the factors.

● **Advanced** Have students explain how to use multiplication and division to determine the **factors** of a number.

Teaching the Lesson (continued)

Factor Fireworks

 25 MINUTES

Goal: Write numbers as products of prime factors, and use prime factorizations to solve division problems.

Materials: Student Activity Book or Hardcover Book pp. 80–81; MathBoard Materials

✔ **NCTM Standards:**
Number and Operations
Algebra
Connection

Teaching Note

Math Background Every whole number greater than 1 is either prime, or capable of being expressed as a product of primes.

Teaching Note

Language and Vocabulary Discuss with students how the word *prime* has different meanings outside of mathematics. For example, it can mean "first quality" (*prime* real estate or *prime* cuts of meat). It can also refer to rank (*prime* minister).

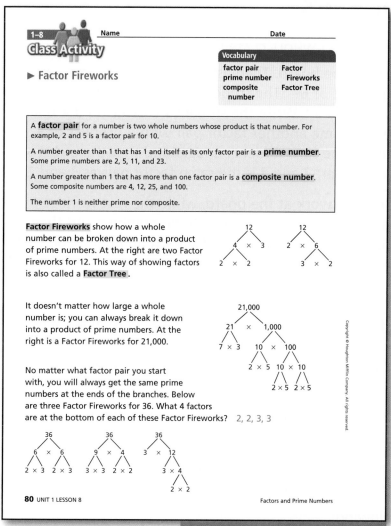

Student Activity Book page 80

▶ Factor Fireworks WHOLE CLASS

Write the number 12 on the board. Explain that you want to "break 12 down" as far as possible into factors, and you will start with the factor pair 3 and 4. Draw two branches coming from the 12, and label their ends 3 and 4, as shown by the diagram on the left.

Explain that you will now look at each of these factors to see if you can break it down further. Point to the 3 and ask:

● Can you think of two factors with a product of 3? 1 and 3

● That's correct, but I don't want to count this factor pair because it contains the number 3. It doesn't "break down" 3 into smaller factors.

● Is there a different pair of factors with a product of 3? no So we can't break down 3 any further.

Now point to the 4.

● Can you think of two factors with a product of 4? 1 and 4, 2 and 2

If students suggest 1 and 4, point out that this does not "break down" 4 into smaller factors. Draw two branches coming down from the 4, and write a 2 at the end of each, as shown by the diagram on the right.

Point to one of the 2s. Ask students if they can break it down further.

● Look at the numbers at the ends of the branches: 2, 2, and 3. What kinds of numbers are these—prime numbers, composite numbers, or neither? prime numbers

Ask what you would get if you multiplied the numbers at the ends of the branches. Then write 3 × 2 × 2 = 12 on the board.

Tell students that diagrams like the one you just made can be called Factor Fireworks. Factor Fireworks show how a number breaks down into a product of prime numbers.

● To make the Factor Fireworks for 12, I started with the factor pair 3 and 4. Let's see what would happen if I started with 2 and 6 instead.

Next to the first Factor Fireworks, begin a new one starting with 2 × 6. Have students tell you what to write at each step.

Draw the diagram to the right. When the diagram is complete, ask,

● Look at the factors at the ends of the branches. How do they compare to those in the first Factor Fireworks? They are the same.

Write 2 × 3 × 2 = 12 on the board, next to 3 × 2 × 2 = 12.

Point out that because the order of the factors in the equations does not matter, the products are the same.

▶ **Make Factor Fireworks** [INDIVIDUALS]

Choose students to work at the board while others work at their MathBoards. Read the numbers one at a time, giving students enough time to write them down.

24   30   36

Have students make Factor Fireworks for each number and then compare their work. Ask whether some students began with a different factor pair. Have students compare the prime factors at the ends of the branches. Make sure they see that, no matter which factor pair they start with, the prime factors are the same. Look at Student Book page 80 and find the factors in each Factor Fireworks (circling them helps).

Activity continued ▶

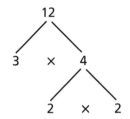

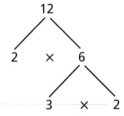

Teaching Note

What to Expect from Students
Many people have difficulty remembering that 2 is a prime number. It is the only even prime number. If students say 2 is not prime, ask them to list the factor pairs for 2. The only factor pair is 1 and 2. Therefore, 2 fits the definition of a prime number.

Differentiated Instruction

Extra Help Have students circle the numbers at the end of the branches. This will help them identify the numbers that are the prime factors.

Teaching the Lesson (continued)

Activity 3

 Ongoing Assessment

Ask questions such as:

▶ Is 14 a prime number or a composite number? How do you know?

▶ How do you know if you have completed a Factor Fireworks?

The Learning Classroom

Math Talk In problems 1–6, students use prime factorizations to solve divisions beyond the basic division problems they have studied. Problem 7 makes the point that even numbers always have 2 as a prime factor; odd numbers do not.

 Quick Quiz

See Assessment Guide for Unit 1 Quick Quiz 2.

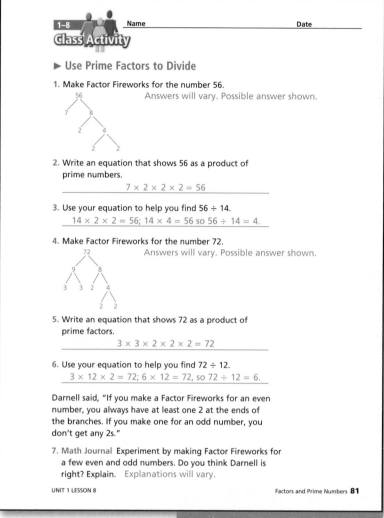

Student Activity Book page 81

▶ Use Prime Factors to Divide [WHOLE CLASS]

Tell students that you can use prime factors to divide larger numbers: Some of the prime factors will make the dividing number and the rest of the factors will make the answer (the factor you don't know yet). Ask students to tell you the prime factors of 36. $2 \times 2 \times 3 \times 3$ can be written in any order.

● What if I didn't know what $36 \div 12$ was? How could I use this list of prime factors to find out?

Elicit and discuss student ideas. They should include circling or otherwise finding the prime factors of $12 = 2 \times 2 \times 3$ (in any order), which leaves a 3 in the list of prime factors of 36 that has not been used. So $36 = (2 \times 2 \times 3) \times 3 = 12 \times 3$.

● Which property is being used to find the unknown factor? The Associative Property groups the prime factors into the factor pairs for the problem; the Commutative Property might be needed to rearrange the order of the prime factors.

Use **Solve and Discuss** to solve problems 1–7 on Student Book page 81.

Whole Number Factors and Multiples

▶ Factors and Multiples   WHOLE CLASS

Share the definition of a multiple with the students. (A **multiple** of a number is a product of that number and a counting number.)

Count-bys Explain to students that we can use count-bys to name multiples. Ask a student to use count-bys to name the first five multiples of 3. Write the numbers on the board as they are named. 3, 6, 9, 12, 15

Multiplication Explain that we can also use multiplication to find multiples—we can use the product of 3 and the first five counting numbers to find the first five multiples of 3.

Write $3 \times 1 = 3$ on the board. Let student volunteers write $3 \times 2 = 6$, $3 \times 3 = 9$, $3 \times 4 = 12$, and $3 \times 5 = 15$. Then ask: What do you notice about the products? The products are the same as the count-bys for 3.

Give students time to complete exercise 8 on Student Book page 82, and then ask them to share their methods.

Use **Solve and Discuss** to complete exercises 9–11.

25 MINUTES

Goal: Compose and decompose numbers, using factors and multiples.

Materials: Student Activity Book or Hardcover Book p. 82

  NCTM Standards:
Number and Operations
Reasoning and Proof

Teaching Note

Math Background As students find factors, factor pairs, and prime factorizations, they are engaged in decomposing numbers. They are engaged in composing numbers as they find products and multiples.

Activity continued ▶

Activity 4

Teaching Note

Math Background A *factor* of a whole number can never be greater than that number. For example, any number greater than 10 cannot be a factor of 10.

A *multiple* of a whole number can never be less than that number. For example, any number less than 10 cannot be a multiple of 10.

As students work with factors and multiples in this lesson, lead them to these generalizations:

• A factor of a whole number is always less than or equal to that number.

• A multiple of a whole number is always greater than or equal to that number.

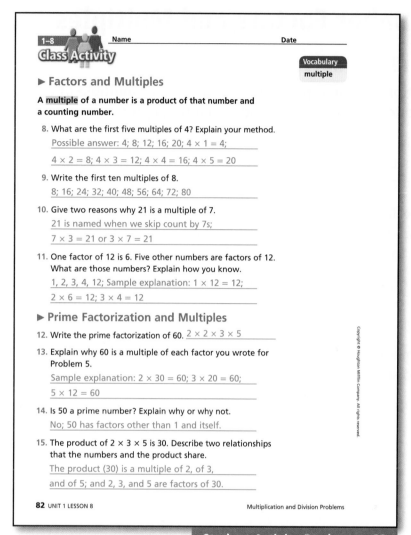

Student Activity Book page 82

▶ Prime Factorization and Multiples [WHOLE CLASS]

Write 2 × 3 × 5 = 30 on the board, then ask:

● **Why are 2, 3, and 5 factors of 30?** Possible answer: The product of 2 and 15, 3 and 10, and 5 and 6, is 30.

● **Why is 30 a multiple of 2, 3, and 5?** Possible answer: 30 is named when we skip count by 2s, by 3s, and by 5s.

Encourage those students who name division in one or both answers to explain how division can be used to decide if a number is a factor or a multiple of another number. If the remainder of a quotient is zero, the divisor is a factor of the dividend, and the dividend is a multiple of a divisor.

Have students complete exercises 12–15 on Student Book page 82. Give students an opportunity to share their answers.

② Going Further

Intervention   Activity Card I-8

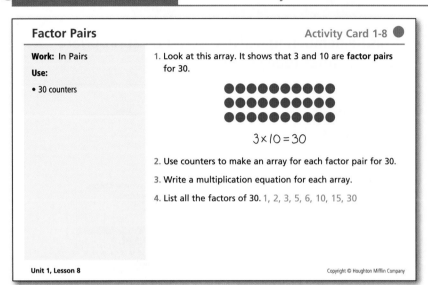

Factor Pairs   Activity Card 1-8 ●

Work: In Pairs
Use:
• 30 counters

1. Look at this array. It shows that 3 and 10 are **factor pairs** for 30.

$3 \times 10 = 30$

2. Use counters to make an array for each factor pair for 30.
3. Write a multiplication equation for each array.
4. List all the factors of 30. 1, 2, 3, 5, 6, 10, 15, 30

Unit 1, Lesson 8   Copyright © Houghton Mifflin Company

Activity Note Each array can be represented by two multiplication equations using the Commutative Property of Multiplication.

 Math Writing Prompt

Explain Your Thinking Explain how you know when a number can be divided by 2. Draw a picture if needed. it divides into 2 equal groups

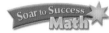 **Software Support**

Use *Soar to Success* for instruction of students needing targeted support for underlying skills.

▲ On Level   Activity Card I-8

Multiples   Activity Card 1-8 ▲

Work: By Yourself

1. Look at these count-bys for 5.
   5, 10, 15, 20

   They are also multiples of 5.
   $1 \times 5 = 5$
   $2 \times 5 = 10$ | Every **multiple** of 5 has 5 as a factor. |
   $3 \times 5 = 15$
   $4 \times 5 = 20$

2. Use the information above to find the first five multiples of each of these numbers:
   6   6, 12, 18, 24, 30
   8   8, 16, 24, 32, 40
   20   20, 40, 60, 80, 100
   25   25, 50, 75, 100, 125
   30   30, 60, 90, 120, 150

Unit 1, Lesson 8   Copyright © Houghton Mifflin Company

Activity Note Remind students that a multiple of any whole number, except zero, is the product of that number and a counting number.

 Math Writing Prompt

Is It Finished? Tell how you decide whether you have found all the prime factors for the prime factorization of a number. the product of the prime factors must equal the number

 Software Support

Use *MegaMath* for review and reinforcement of the concepts and skills presented in this lesson.

■ Challenge   Activity Card I-8

Prime Factorization   Activity Card 1-8 ■

Work: By Yourself

1. Read the following definition. The **prime factorization** of a whole number is that number expressed as the product of its prime factors.

   For example,
   $24 = 2 \times 2 \times 2 \times 3$.

2. Copy the table on the right onto paper.

3. For **prime** numbers write the word prime.

4. Write the prime factorization for **composite** numbers.

Number	Prime Factors
12	$2 \times 2 \times 3$
13	Prime
14	2×7
15	3×5
16	$2 \times 2 \times 2 \times 2$
17	prime
18	$2 \times 3 \times 3$
19	prime
20	$2 \times 2 \times 5$
40	$2 \times 2 \times 2 \times 5$

Unit 1, Lesson 8   Copyright © Houghton Mifflin Company

Activity Note Remind students that a prime number has exactly two factors, 1 and itself. The number 1 is not a prime number. The number 2 is the only even prime number.

 Math Writing Prompt

Justify Your Reasoning Explain how knowing the prime factorization of 84 can help you find 84 ÷ 14. $84 = 2 \times 2 \times 3 \times 7; 2 \times 7 = 14; 2 \times 3 = 6; 6 \times 14 = 84$

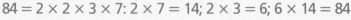 **Software Support**

Use *Destination Math* to take students beyond the concepts and skills presented in this lesson.

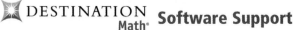

③ Homework and Spiral Review

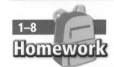

1-8
Homework **Goal:** Additional Practice

Use this Homework page to provide students with more practice with factoring and prime numbers.

1-8
Remembering **Goal:** Spiral Review

This Remembering activity would be appropriate anytime after today's lesson.

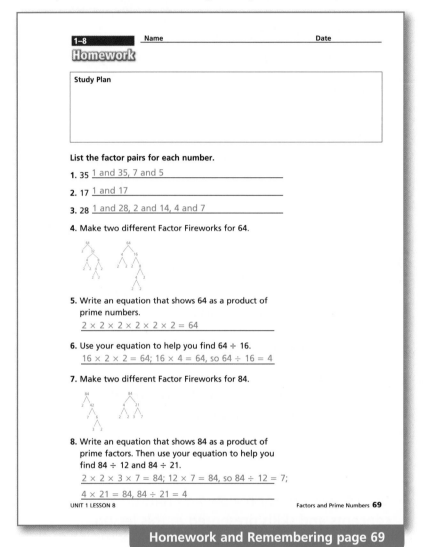

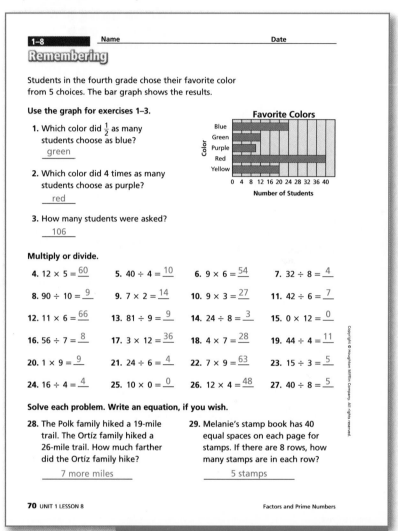

Homework and Remembering page 69

Homework and Remembering page 70

Home or School Activity

Math-to-Math Connection

Prime or Composite Pay Ask students to pretend that they have won a prize for the best math project done in October. But to get the prize, they have to choose between getting $2 for each prime number date or $1 for each composite number date in October. Ask them to decide which option they would choose and to write a paragraph explaining why. Have students find or make a calendar for October. Students may use the calendar to help them find the answer.

OCTOBER						
S	M	T	W	T	F	S
						1
2	3	4	5	6	7	8
9	10	11	12	13	14	15
16	17	18	19	20	21	22
23	24	25	26	27	28	29
30	31					

204 UNIT 1 LESSON 8

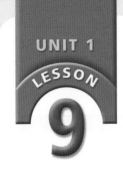

Use Mathematical Processes

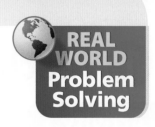

Lesson Objectives

• Solve a variety of problems, using mathematical processes and skills.

• Use the mathematical processes of problem solving, connections, reasoning and proof, communication, and representation.

The Day at a Glance

Today's Goals	Materials	
1 Teaching the Lesson **A1: Science Connection** Connect science data to the skill of representing and comparing data. **A2: Reasoning and Proof** Use logical reasoning to decide if an answer is even or odd, and use examples or nonexamples to support an answer. **A3: Representation** Draw a picture to represent a mathematical situation. **A4: Communication** Explain why a set of steps provides a correct answer. Write a set of steps that will result in a given number. **A5: Problem Solving** Interpret a remainder and demonstrate that there is more than one solution to a problem.	**Lesson Activities** Student Activity Book pp. 83–84 or Student Hardcover Book pp. 83–84 Homework and Remembering pp. 71–72 Centimeter-Grid Paper (TRB M60) Make a Pictograph (TRB M124) Straightedge or ruler	**Going Further** Activity Cards 1-9 Number cubes Math Journals
2 Going Further ▶ Differentiated Instruction		
3 Homework and Spiral Review		

123 *Use* **Math Talk** *today!*

Keeping Skills Sharp

Quick Practice/Daily Routines	
No Quick Practice or Daily Routines are recommended. If you choose to do some, use activities that meet the needs of your class.	**Class Management** Use this lesson to provide more understanding of the NCTM process standards. Depending upon how you choose to carry out the activities, this lesson may take two or more days of teaching.

1 Teaching the Lesson

Math and Science

 30 MINUTES

Goal: Interpret information from bar graphs or pictographs.

Materials: Student Activity Book or Hardcover Book p. 83; Centimeter-Grid Paper (TRB M60); Make a Pictograph (TRB M124); ruler or straightedge

✔ **NCTM Standards:**
Connections   Representation
Problem Solving

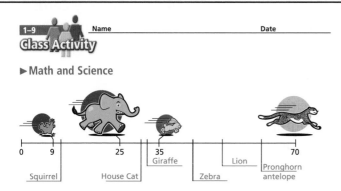

► Math and Science

The fastest recorded running speed for a human is about 27 miles per hour over $\frac{1}{4}$ mile. The table below shows data for the estimated fastest running speeds for ten animals over the same distance.

Running Speeds	
Animal	**Estimated Speed**
Cheetah	70 mph
Pronghorn antelope	61 mph
Lion	50 mph
Zebra	40 mph
Rabbit	35 mph
Giraffe	32 mph
House cat	30 mph
Elephant	25 mph
Squirrel	12 mph
Chicken	9 mph

1. A human can run about how many times as fast as a chicken?
   about 3 times

2. Which animal can run closest to the fastest recorded human speed?
   elephant

3. Name an animal that can run faster than a squirrel but slower than a zebra.
   Accept elephant, house cat, giraffe, or rabbit.

4. Copy the number line at the top of the page. Write the missing animal names in the correct positions.
   From left to right: squirrel, house cat, giraffe, zebra, lion, pronghorn

UNIT 1 LESSON 9   Using Mathematical Processes **83**

Student Activity Book page 83

► **Discuss the Data**   Math Talk

Task 1 Look at the table on Student Book page 83. Tell students that the data represents a sustained speed over a quarter mile and that the speed is the greatest speed recorded, not an average speed. Discuss the data as a whole class and ask questions such as:

► Which animal can run twice as fast as a rabbit? cheetah, $35 \times 2 = 70$

► Which animal runs at half the speed of a lion? elephant, $50 \div 2 = 25$

► Which animal is more likely to beat a house cat in a quarter-mile race, a giraffe or an elephant? giraffe

Have students work individually to answer exercises 1–4.

► **Graph the Data**

Task 2 Have **Student Pairs** choose four or five of the animals. Have one student present the data for the animals they choose on a bar graph and the other student present the data on a pictograph. (If necessary, refer students to Student Book pages 18 and 75 to review graphs.)

Compare Data Displays Represented in Different Ways Have students compare the two ways they graphed the data. Discuss if one type of graph is better than the other for presenting this type of data. Ask questions such as:

► Which graph is easier to read?

► On which graph is it easier to compare speeds?

Make Conclusions Have students write two or more questions that others can answer by drawing a conclusion from the graph. For example, is there a connection between an animal's size and its speed. Support your answer. No, a rabbit is much smaller than an elephant but it is faster.

Even and Odd Numbers

🕐 **30 MINUTES**

Goal: Make generalizations about even and odd numbers.

Materials: Student Activity Book or Hardcover Book p. 84

✓ **NCTM Standards:**
Reasoning and Proof   Problem Solving

| 1–9 | Name _____ | Date _____ |

Class Activity

▶ **Even and Odd Numbers**

Decide if the answer to each operation will be even or odd. Write *even* or *odd*. Then give two examples to prove your answer is correct. Examples will vary.

5. even + even = ___even___ _____

6. even + odd = ___odd___ _____

7. odd + odd = ___even___ _____

8. even − even = ___even___ _____

9. even − odd = ___odd___ _____

10. odd − odd = ___even___ _____

11. even × even = ___even___ _____

12. even × odd = ___even___ _____

13. odd × odd = ___odd___ _____

14. When you divide 2 even whole numbers will the answer always be even? Use examples to support your answer.
No. 40 ÷ 4 = 10, but 40 ÷ 8 = 5

Use the process of elimination to identify the product. Explain your choice.

15. 22 × 15

  A. 230   **B.** 233   **C.** 330   **D.** 333

The product of an even number and an odd number is even, so B and D cannot be correct.
20 × 15 = 300. Since 22 > 20, A cannot be correct. The answer is C.

84 UNIT 1 LESSON 9   Using Mathematical Processes

Student Activity Book page 84

▶ **Sums**

Task 1 As a class, discuss whole-number sums. Decide if the sum will be even or odd in each of the following cases. Students should apply reasoning to answer the questions. Once they decide on an answer, they should use examples to support their position.

▶ sum of two even whole numbers
   even; 4 + 4 = 8, 6 + 10 = 16

▶ sum of two odd whole numbers
   even; 5 + 5 = 10, 7 + 9 = 16

▶ sum of an even and an odd whole number
   odd; 5 + 4 = 9, 7 + 8 = 15

▶ **Differences**

Task 2 Follow the same procedure to answer these questions about differences.

▶ difference between two even whole numbers
   even; 10 − 2 = 8, 12 − 10 = 2

▶ difference between two odd whole numbers
   even; 7 − 5 = 2, 9 − 5 = 4

▶ difference between an even and an odd whole number odd; 10 − 7 = 3, 6 − 1 = 5, 11 − 8 = 3, 15 − 4 = 9

▶ **Products**

Task 3 Follow the same procedure to answer these questions about products.

▶ product of two even whole numbers
   even; 6 × 6 = 36, 4 × 8 = 32

▶ product of two odd whole numbers
   odd; 5 × 7 = 35, 3 × 9 = 27

▶ product of an even and an odd whole number
   even; 4 × 5 = 20, 2 × 9 = 18

Have students work individually to answer exercises 5–15.

Activity 3

Muffins in Boxes

 15 MINUTES

Goal: Use a drawing to solve a problem.

 NCTM Standards:
Representation
Problem Solving

Write this problem on the board: Cora has 30 muffins. She has 5 boxes. She puts the same number of muffins in each box. How many muffins go in each box?

Ask students to draw a picture or diagram of the situation in the problem and then give the answer. Check students' drawings. 6 muffins go in each box.

Help students see that a model can help them represent the problem situation.

▶ **What do your pictures look like?** Have students show and describe their pictures. Invite other students to ask clarifying questions about the pictures.

▶ **What would a picture look like if Cora only had 2 boxes?** Allow students to draw their pictures on the chalkboard. The pictures should show that there are 2 boxes with 15 muffins in each box.

Activity 4

What's Your Age?

 15 MINUTES

Goals: Follow a set of steps and analyze why they work. Write a set of steps that someone can follow.

 NCTM Standards:
Communication
Problem Solving

Students write down their ages and then follow these steps: Multiply your age by 2. Subtract 4. Add 10. Subtract 6. Divide by 2. Is the result your age? Yes. Try the steps for a different age. Do the steps yield the original age again? Yes.

Hold a whole-class discussion of the problem.

▶ **Will the steps always work?** Allow students to show examples that they think support or disprove.

▶ **Discuss why the steps work.** Allow students to share their ideas. Help students see that the operations used "undo" each other for a gain or loss of 0.

▶ Encourage students to write their own sets of rules to perform operations that "undo" each other and arrive at the original number. See student's work.

Activity 5

How Many Cars?

 15 MINUTES

Goal: Explain what to do with a remainder when solving a problem, and model a situation that more than one solution.

 NCTM Standards:
Problem Solving   Communication
Represent

Chen's class is going on a field trip. There are 26 students in the class. Each car can carry 4 students. How many cars will be needed? 7

Discuss what to do with the remainder in this problem.

▶ **Why is 6 or 6 ½ not the answer to this problem?** 6 cars hold only 24 students, so the class needs 7 cars.

More Than One Correct Answer Ask **Student Pairs** to work together to make drawings or diagrams that show two different arrangements of 26 students in 7 cars. 6 cars with 4 students, 1 car with 2 students; and 5 cars with 4 students. 2 cars with 3 students.

② Going Further

Intervention Activity Card 1-9

Draw a Multiplication Picture
Activity Card 1-9 ●

Work: By Yourself

Use:
• 1–6 number cubes
• 4–9 number cubes (optional)

1. Roll two number cubes.

2. Use the numbers you roll to write a multiplication sentence.

3. Draw a picture that represents the multiplication sentence. Be sure to include the product in you drawing.

4. Roll two more numbers. Write a multiplication sentence for the numbers on the back of a piece of paper. On the front, draw a picture to represent the number sentence.

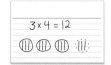

Unit 1, Lesson 9   Copyright © Houghton Mifflin Company

Activity Note If write-one cubes are available, have students repeat the activity using one 1–6 cube and one 4–9 cube.

 Math Writing Prompt

Write a Multiplication Story Pedro draws a picture of 2 groups of crayons. There are 3 crayons in each group. Write a multiplication story for this picture.

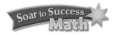 **Software Support**

Use *Soar to Success* for instruction of students needing targeted support for underlying skills.

On Level Activity Card 1-9

Write a Multiplication Word Problem
Activity Card 1-9 ▲

Work: By Yourself

Use:
• 1–6 number cubes
• Number cubes with other combinations of 1-digit numbers (optional)

1. Roll two number cubes.

2. Use the numbers you roll to write a multiplication word problem. Use words and numbers to show the solution to your word problem.

3. Repeat the activity but this time roll the number cubes twice. Use the first roll to make a 2-digit number. Choose one of the numbers from the second roll as the 1-digit number, but do not choose the number 1.

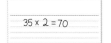

Unit 1, Lesson 9   Copyright © Houghton Mifflin Company

Activity Note Review how to form the 2-digit and 1-digit numbers. For the rolls $\frac{3}{6}$ and $\frac{4}{2}$, students could make 36×4, 36×2, 63×4, and 63×2.

 Math Writing Prompt

Write a Different Word Problem Choose one of your word problems. Write a different multiplication word problem that uses the same numbers.

 Software Support

Use *MegaMath* for review and reinforcement of the concepts and skills presented in this lesson.

Challenge Activity Card 1-9

Support or Disprove
Activity Card 1-9 ■

Work: In Pairs

1. Support or disprove the following statements using examples.
   • If a number is divisible by 2 and by 3, then it is divisible by 6. Yes. Sample: 12, 18, and 24 are all divisible by 2, 3, and 6.
   • If a number is a multiple of 2 and 4, then it is a multiple of 8. No. Sample: 20 is a multiple of 2 and 4, but is not a multiple of 8.
   • If a number ends in 2 or 4, it is divisible by 6. No. Sample: 12 and 24 are divisible by 6 but 14 isn't.

2. Make a statement that includes the numbers 2, 5, and 10. Support or disprove the statement with examples. Sample: If a number is divisible by 2 and 5, then it is divisible by 10. Some numbers that support this are: 20, 30, 40.

Unit 1, Lesson 9   Copyright © Houghton Mifflin Company

Activity Note Remind students that it takes only one example to disprove a statement. Have students compare the statements they wrote for exercise 2.

 Math Writing Prompt

Tell Why Look back at all of the statements. If any of the statements are not true, use the concept of multiples to explain why they are not true.

✳ **DESTINATION** Math® **Software Support**

Use *Destination Math* to take students beyond the concepts and skills presented in this lesson.

③ Homework and Spiral Review

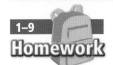

Homework **Goal:** Additional Practice

✔ Include student's completed Homework page as part of their portfolios.

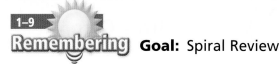

Remembering **Goal:** Spiral Review

This Remembering page would be appropriate anytime after today's lesson.

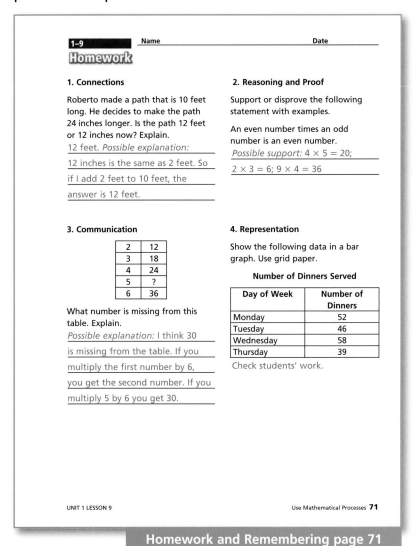

1–9 Name _____ Date _____
Homework

1. Connections

Roberto made a path that is 10 feet long. He decides to make the path 24 inches longer. Is the path 12 feet or 12 inches now? Explain.

12 feet. Possible explanation:
12 inches is the same as 2 feet. So
if I add 2 feet to 10 feet, the
answer is 12 feet.

2. Reasoning and Proof

Support or disprove the following statement with examples.

An even number times an odd number is an even number.

Possible support: 4 × 5 = 20;
2 × 3 = 6; 9 × 4 = 36

3. Communication

2	12
3	18
4	24
5	?
6	36

What number is missing from this table. Explain.

Possible explanation: I think 30
is missing from the table. If you
multiply the first number by 6,
you get the second number. If you
multiply 5 by 6 you get 30.

4. Representation

Show the following data in a bar graph. Use grid paper.

Number of Dinners Served

Day of Week	Number of Dinners
Monday	52
Tuesday	46
Wednesday	58
Thursday	39

Check students' work.

UNIT 1 LESSON 9 — Use Mathematical Processes **71**

Homework and Remembering page 71

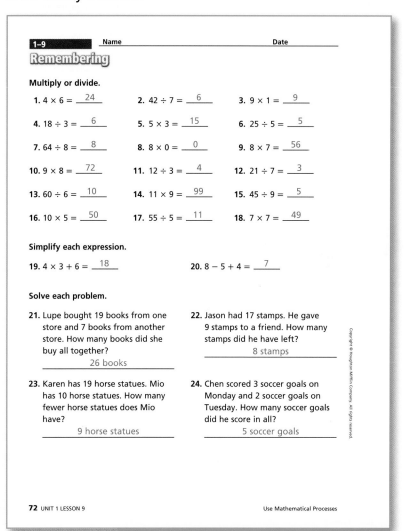

1–9 Name _____ Date _____
Remembering

Multiply or divide.

1. 4 × 6 = __24__   2. 42 ÷ 7 = __6__   3. 9 × 1 = __9__

4. 18 ÷ 3 = __6__   5. 5 × 3 = __15__   6. 25 ÷ 5 = __5__

7. 64 ÷ 8 = __8__   8. 8 × 0 = __0__   9. 8 × 7 = __56__

10. 9 × 8 = __72__   11. 12 ÷ 3 = __4__   12. 21 ÷ 7 = __3__

13. 60 ÷ 6 = __10__   14. 11 × 9 = __99__   15. 45 ÷ 9 = __5__

16. 10 × 5 = __50__   17. 55 ÷ 5 = __11__   18. 7 × 7 = __49__

Simplify each expression.

19. 4 × 3 + 6 = __18__   20. 8 − 5 + 4 = __7__

Solve each problem.

21. Lupe bought 19 books from one store and 7 books from another store. How many books did she buy all together?
    26 books

22. Jason had 17 stamps. He gave 9 stamps to a friend. How many stamps did he have left?
    8 stamps

23. Karen has 19 horse statues. Mio has 10 horse statues. How many fewer horse statues does Mio have?
    9 horse statues

24. Chen scored 3 soccer goals on Monday and 2 soccer goals on Tuesday. How many soccer goals did he score in all?
    5 soccer goals

72 UNIT 1 LESSON 9 — Use Mathematical Processes

Homework and Remembering page 72

Home or School Activity

 Literature Connection

Arithme-Tickle: An Even Number of Odd Riddle-Rhymes Have students read "Jumping on the Moon" on page 15 of this book of rhyming riddles by Patrick Lewis (Voyager Books, Harcourt, Inc., 2002, Illustrator Frank Remkiewicz). After they have answered the riddle, students should act out how high Earth jumps of various lengths, such as 4 inches, would be on the Moon. For longer Earth jumps, students can use unit cubes to compare pairs of Earth/Moon jumps.

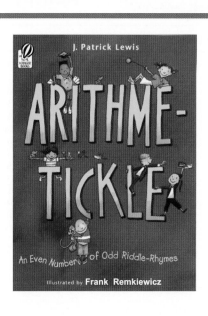

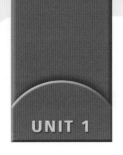

Unit Review and Test

Lesson Objective
● **Assess student progress on unit objectives.**

The Day at a Glance

Today's Goals	Materials
1 Assessing the Unit ► Assess student progress on unit objectives. ► Use activities from unit lessons to reteach content. **2 Extending the Assessment** ► Use remediation for common errors. There is no homework assignment on a test day.	Unit 1 Test, Student Activity Book or Student Hardcover Book pp. 85–86 Unit 1 Test, Form A or B, Assessment Guide (optional) Unit 1 Performance Assessment, Assessment Guide (optional) Multiplication and Division Assessment (TRB M114) (optional)

Keeping Skills Sharp

Quick Practice ⏱ 5 MINUTES	
Goal: Review any skills you choose to meet the needs of your class. If you are doing a unit review day, use any of the Quick Practice activities that provide support for your class. If this is a test day, omit Quick Practice.	**Review and Test Day** You may want to choose a quiet game or other activity (reading a book or working on homework for another subject) for students who finish early.

Assess Unit Objectives

🕐 **45 MINUTES** (more if schedule permits)

Goal: Assess student progress on unit objectives.

Materials: Student Activity Book or Hardcover Book pp. 85–86, Assessment Guide (optional), Multiplication and Division Assessment (TRB M114) (optional)

▶ Review and Assessment

If your students are ready for assessment of the unit objectives, you may use either the test on the Student Book pages or one of the forms of the Unit 1 Test in the Assessment Guide to assess student progress.

If you feel that students need some review first, you may use the test on the Student Book pages as a review of unit content, and then one of the forms of the Unit 1 Test in the Assessment Guide to assess student progress.

You may also choose to use the Unit 1 Performance Assessment. Scoring for that assessment may be found in its rubric in the Assessment Guide.

▶ Reteaching Resources

The chart at the right lists the test items, the unit objectives they cover, and the lesson activities in which the unit objective is covered in this unit. You may revisit these activities with students who do not show mastery of the objectives.

▶ Unit 1 Assessment and Scoring

To assign a numerical score for this unit test, use 10 points for each item 1–9. For item 10, use 5 points for part a and 5 points for part b.

If you wish to assess basic multiplication and division problems, Multiplication and Division Assessment (TRB M114) can be used. Assign 2 points for each item 1–50.

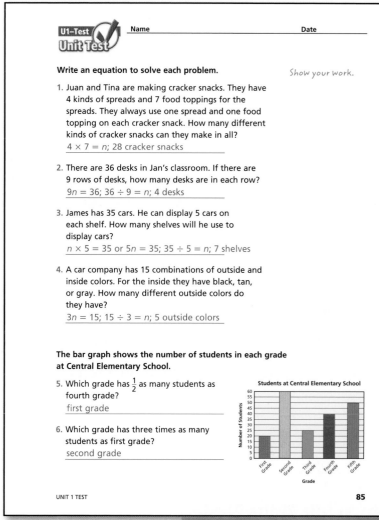

Student Activity Book page 85

Unit Test Items	Unit Objectives Tested	Activities to Use for Reteaching
5–8	**1.1** Solve comparison problems; interpret a pictograph and a bar graph.	Lesson 4, Activities 1–2 Lesson 5, Activities 1–2 Lesson 6, Activities 1–2
1, 4	**1.2** Solve combination problems.	Lesson 1, Activities 1–3 Lesson 2, Activities 1–2
1–4	**1.3** Write an equation to solve multiplication and division problems.	Lesson 3, Activities 1–2

Student Activity Book page 86

The pictograph shows the number of pounds of fruits sold at a fruit stand.

7. Which fruit was sold twice as much as bananas?

   pears

8. Which fruit was sold $\frac{1}{4}$ as much as apples?

   oranges

9. Write the factors for each number and then identify the prime numbers.

   a. 63   b. 17 1, 17; prime factor: 17
   1, 3, 7, 9, 21, 63; prime factors: 3, 7

*10. Solve the word problem.

   a. Extended Response Sam bought 7 hats for $6 each. He paid with a $50 bill. How much change did he receive? Explain how you found your answer.
   $8; Possible answer: I multiplied to find the
   total cost of the hats, then subtracted the
   product from $50 to find the change.

   b. If you multiply two prime numbers will the product always be prime? Explain your reasoning.
   No; the prime numbers themselves will be factors of
   the product, as well as 1 and the product. Example:
   $3 \times 7 = 21$; factors of 21 are 1, 3, 7, and 21

Pounds of Fruits Sold	
Fruit	Pounds of Fruit
Apples	🍎🍎🍎🍎🍎🍎🍎🍎
Bananas	🍌🍌
Oranges	🍊🍊
Pears	🍐🍐🍐🍐🍐
Strawberries	🍓🍓🍓🍓🍓

🍎 = 2 pounds of fruit sold

*Item 10 also assesses the processes skills of problem solving, connections, reasoning and proof, and communication

86 UNIT 1 TEST

Unit Test Items	Unit Objectives Tested	Activities to Use for Reteaching
10a	**1.4** Solve multistep problems.	Lesson 7, Activity 1
9, 10b	**1.5** Use factoring to determine if a number is prime.	Lesson 8, Activities 1–3 Lesson 9, Activities 1–3

► Assessment Guide Resources

Free Response Tests
Unit 1 Test, Student Activity Book or Hardcover Book pp. 85–86
Unit 1 Test, Form A, Assessment Guide

Extended Response Item
The last item in the Student Activity Book test and in the Form A test will require an extended response as an answer.

Multiple Choice Test
Unit 1 Test, Form B, Assessment Guide

Performance Assessment
Unit 1 Performance Assessment, Assessment Guide
Unit 1 Performance Assessment Rubric, Assessment Guide

► Portfolio Assessment

Teacher-selected Items for Student Portfolios:

- Homework, Lessons 7 and 9
- Class Activity work, Lessons 4 and 6

Student-selected Items for Student Portfolios:

- Favorite Home or School Activity
- Best Writing Prompt

② Extending the Assessment

Unit Objective 1.1

Solve comparison problems; interpret a pictograph and a bar graph.

Common Error: Misreads a Graph

Students may not correctly read the value on a graph.

Remediation Review the scales on a bar graph. Tell students to use a sheet of paper to help them visually line up the top of the bar and the scale on the left. Remind students to first check the key of a pictograph. Students should touch each picture as they skip count.

Unit Objective 1.2

Solve combination problems.

Common Error: Solves Combination Problems Incorrectly

Students may have difficulty solving combination problems.

Remediation Students should make a table listing one group along the side and one group along the top. Then they should fill in the cells of the table and count.

Unit Objective 1.3

Write an equation to solve multiplication and division problems.

Common Error: Cannot Distinguish Between Multiplication and Division Problems.

Students may not understand the underlying situation as multiplication or division.

Remediation Have students work in pairs to analyze a variety of multiplication and division problems. Have them list the similarities and differences of each problem. For example:

- Both problems involve equal groups.
- When you need to find the total, you use multiplication.
- When you are looking for an unknown factor, you use division.

Common Error: Solves the Problem in the Incorrect Order.

Students may not know which step to solve first in a two-step word problem.

Remediation Have students try to tell a question that can help them with a middle step.

Unit Objective 1.4

Solve multistep problems.

Common Error: Solves Multistep Problems Incorrectly

Students may not solve all the steps of the problem.

Remediation Work with students to re-read the problem. Take each part of the problem and ask the student to translate it into numbers. Then discuss why one step may need to be computed before another.

Unit Objective 1.5

Use factoring to determine if a number is prime.

Common Error: Factors Incorrectly

Students may find all the factors of a number.

Remediation Remind students to write 1 and the number as factors. Then have students decide if a number is divisible by 2 (even or odd); divisible by 10 (ends with 0), divisible by 5 (ends with 5 or 0), and so on, to help them decide if a number has more than 1 and itself as factors.

Unit 2   Overview

Quadrilaterals

THIS UNIT EXPLORES congruence, similarity, and symmetry; parallel and perpendicular lines; and the differences among some quadrilaterals.

In addition, activities in this unit help students understand what perimeter and area are and how they are measured. A Big Idea is that perimeter and area are two different measurements of the same shape and that each has its own kind of measurement unit: linear units for perimeter and square units for area.

Students will use what they learn in this unit about area again in Unit 5, where area is used as a graphic model for multi-digit multiplication.

Skills Trace

Grade 3	Grade 4	Grade 5
• Identify congruent figures. • Draw lines of symmetry. • Identify lines, line segments, and quadrilaterals. • Find perimeter and area of rectangles and squares.	• Identify congruent and similar figures. • Draw lines of symmetry. • Identify and draw lines, line segments, and quadrilaterals. • Find perimeter and area of quadrilaterals and complex figures.	• Identify and draw similar figures: find a missing measurement. • Draw lines of symmetry. • Identify and draw lines, lines segments, and angles. • Determine the missing angle of a quadrilateral. • Find perimeter and area of regular polygons and complex figures.

Unit 2   Contents

Unit 2 Assessment

✓ Unit Objectives Tested	Unit Test Items	Lessons
2.1 Identify congruent and similar figures.	1, 7	1
2.2 Identify figures that have lines of symmetry.	2	1
2.3 Identify lines, line segments, and quadrilaterals.	3–6	2, 3
2.4 Find perimeter and area of quadrilaterals and complex figures.	8–10	4, 5, 6

Assessment and Review Resources

Formal Assessment	Informal Assessment	Review Opportunities
Student Activity Book • Unit Review and Test (pp. 117–118) **Assessment Guide** • Quick Quiz 1 • Quick Quiz 2 • Test A–Open Response • Test B–Multiple Choice • Performance Assessment **Test Generator CD-ROM** • Open Response Test • Multiple Choice Test • Test Bank Items	**Teacher Edition** • Ongoing Assessment (in every lesson) • Math Talk (in every lesson) • Portfolio Suggestions (pp. 238, 250, 258, 266) **📟 Math Talk** ▸ The Learning Classroom (pp. 217, 220) ▸ Math Talk in Action (pp. 216, 234, 236) ▸ Activities (pp. 217, 218, 241, 242, 256, 260, 262, 264) ▸ Solve and Discuss (pp. 245, 246) ▸ Student Pairs (pp. 222, 226, 227, 248, 264) ▸ Student Leaders (p. 220) ▸ Small Groups (pp. 217, 226, 227, 228, 236, 242, 243, 244, 255, 256, 261, 262, 263) ▸ Helping Partners (pp. 218, 222, 246)	**Homework and Remembering** • Review of recently taught topics • Cumulative Review **Teacher Edition** • Unit Review and Test (pp. 267–270) **Test Generator CD-ROM** • Custom review sheets

Planning Unit 2

NCTM Standards Key: **1.** Number and Operations **2.** Algebra **3.** Geometry **4.** Measurement **5.** Data Analysis and Probability **6.** Problem Solving **7.** Reasoning and Proof **8.** Communication **9.** Connections **10.** Representation

Lesson/NCTM Standards	Resources	Materials for Lesson Activities	Materials for Going Further
2–1 **Congruence, Similarity, and Symmetry** NCTM Standards: 3, 7, 10	TE pp. 215–224 SAB pp. 87–94 H&R pp. 73–74 AC 2-1	Drawing Figures (TRB M41) Congruency and Symmetry (TRB M42) Transparency of Centimeter-Grid Paper (TRB M60) Sheet protectors, dry-erase markers Scrap paper Scissors Transparent mirror (optional) ✓Geometry and Measurement Poster	Geoboard/Dot Paper (TRB M56) Transparency of TRB M56 Overhead projector Congruence Match-up Cards (TRB M43) Grid paper, dot paper or MathBoard materials Math Journals
2–2 **Lines, Line Segments, and Rays** NCTM Standards: 3, 10	TE pp. 225–230 SAB pp. 95–98 H&R pp. 75–76 AC 2-2	Index cards	Centimeter ruler Math Journals
2–3 **Kinds of Quadrilaterals** NCTM Standards: 3, 7	TE pp. 231–238 SAB pp. 99–100, 100A H&R pp. 77–78 AG Quick Quiz 1 AC 2-3		Scissors Large sheet of paper or poster board Math Journals
2–4 **Perimeter and Area of Rectangles** NCTM Standards: 1, 3, 4, 6, 7, 8	TE pp. 239–250 SAB pp. 101–108 H&R pp. 79–80 AC 2-4	Transparency of Units of Perimeter and Area (TRB M44), overhead projector Stringing Perimeters (TRB M45) Centimeter-Grid Paper (TRB M60) Tack or pushpin board, tacks or pushpins String, pens or markers	Stringing Perimeters (TRB M45) Tack or pushpin boards Tacks or pushpins String Pens or markers Centimeter rulers Math Journals
2–5 **Perimeter and Area of Parallelograms** NCTM Standards: 3, 4, 7, 10	TE pp. 251–258 SAB pp. 109–112 H&R pp. 81–82 AC 2-5	Parallelograms (TRB M46) Scissors Centimeter rulers	Drawing Figures (TRB M41) Scissors Centimeter rulers Math Journals
2–6 **Perimeter and Area of Complex Figures** NCTM Standards: 3, 4, 6, 7, 10	TE pp. 259–266 SAB pp. 113–116 H&R pp. 83–84 AG Quick Quiz 2 AC 2-6	Drawing Figures (TRB M41) Centimeter rulers (optional)	Centimeter-Grid Paper (TRB M60) Transparency of TRB M60 Overhead projector Math Journals
Unit Review and Test	TE pp. 267–270 SAB pp. 117–118 AG Unit 2 tests		

Resources/Materials Key: TE: Teacher Edition SAB: Student Activity Book H&R: Homework and Remembering
AC: Activity Cards MCC: Math Center Challenge AG: Assessment Guide ✓: Grade 4 kits TRB: Teacher's Resource Book

Hardcover Student Book/Activity Workbook

- Together, the hardcover student book and its companion Activity Workbook contain all the pages in the consumable Student Activity Workbook.

Manipulatives and Materials

- Essential materials for teaching Math Expressions are available in the Grade 4 kit. These materials are indicated by a ✓ in these lists. At the front of this Teacher Edition is more information about kit contents, alternatives for the materials, and use of the materials.

Unit 2　Teaching Resources

Differentiated Instruction

<table>
<tr><th colspan="3">Individualizing Instruction</th></tr>
<tr><td rowspan="2" colspan="2">Activities</td><td>Level</td><td>Frequency</td></tr>
<tr><td>• Intervention
• On Level
• Challenge</td><td>All 3 in every lesson</td></tr>
<tr><td rowspan="2" colspan="2">Math Writing Prompts</td><td>Level</td><td>Frequency</td></tr>
<tr><td>• Intervention
• On Level
• Challenge</td><td>All 3 in every lesson</td></tr>
<tr><td colspan="2" rowspan="2">Math Center Challenges</td><td colspan="2">For advanced students</td></tr>
<tr><td colspan="2">4 in every unit</td></tr>
</table>

<table>
<tr><th colspan="3">Reaching All Learners</th></tr>
<tr><td rowspan="2">English Language Learners</td><td>Lessons</td><td>Pages</td></tr>
<tr><td>1, 2, 3, 4, 5, 6</td><td>215, 225, 231, 239, 251, 259</td></tr>
<tr><td rowspan="2">Extra Help</td><td>Lesson</td><td>Page</td></tr>
<tr><td>1</td><td>221</td></tr>
<tr><td rowspan="2">Advanced Learners</td><td>Lessons</td><td>Pages</td></tr>
<tr><td>2, 4</td><td>228, 246</td></tr>
</table>

Strategies for English Language Learners

Present this problem to all students. Offer the different levels of support to meet students' levels of language proficiency.

Objective Classify triangle, square, and rectangle.

Problem Show a triangle. Ask: **How many sides are there?** 3 **How many angles?** 3 **Are there other shapes with the same number of sides and angles?** no Continue with other shapes.

Newcomer

- Have students hold a shape. Say: **This is a ____.** triangle, square and so on **Let's count the sides.** Have students repeat the name of the shape and touch each side as they count. Provide the number words as needed.

Beginning

- Point and say: **This is a ____.** triangle, square, and so on **It has ___ sides.** Have students repeat.

- Write the name of the shape and the number of sides. Have students repeat.

Intermediate

- Ask: **What is the name of this shape? How many sides are there? How many angles?** Invite students to point to the sides and the angles in the shape.

Advanced

- Have students describe sides and angles in a shape. Ask them to name different shapes with the same number of sides and angles.

Connections

 Art Connection
Lesson 2, page 230

 Social Studies Connection
Lesson 6, page 266

 Language Arts Connection
Lesson 4, page 250

 Physical Education Connection
Lesson 5, page 258

 Technology Connection
Lesson 3, page 238

Independent Learning Activities

Ready-Made Math Challenge Centers

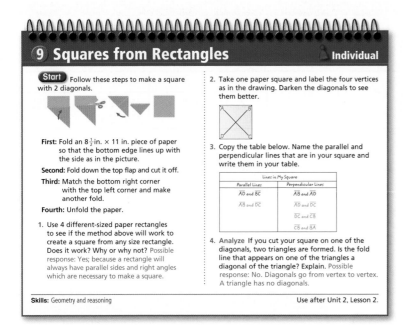

9 Squares from Rectangles   Individual

Start Follow these steps to make a square with 2 diagonals.

First: Fold an $8\frac{1}{2}$-in. × 11 in. piece of paper so that the bottom edge lines up with the side as in the picture.

Second: Fold down the top flap and cut it off.

Third: Match the bottom right corner with the top left corner and make another fold.

Fourth: Unfold the paper.

1. Use 4 different-sized paper rectangles to see if the method above will work to create a square from any size rectangle. Does it work? Why or why not? Possible response: Yes; because a rectangle will always have parallel sides and right angles which are necessary to make a square.

2. Take one paper square and label the four vertices as in the drawing. Darken the diagonals to see them better.

3. Copy the table below. Name the parallel and perpendicular lines that are in your square and write them in your table.

Lines in My Square	
Parallel Lines	Perpendicular Lines
$\overline{AD}$ and $\overline{BC}$	$\overline{AB}$ and $\overline{AD}$
$\overline{AB}$ and $\overline{DC}$	$\overline{AD}$ and $\overline{DC}$
	$\overline{DC}$ and $\overline{CB}$
	$\overline{CB}$ and $\overline{BA}$

4. **Analyze** If you cut your square on one of the diagonals, two triangles are formed. Is the fold line that appears on one of the triangles a diagonal of the triangle? Explain. Possible response: No. Diagonals go from vertex to vertex. A triangle has no diagonals.

Skills: Geometry and reasoning   Use after Unit 2, Lesson 2.

Grouping Individual

Materials Paper rectangles (nonsquare) of different sizes, e.g., construction paper and notebook paper, ruler, and scissors

Objective Students make squares from rectangles and analyze some parallel and perpendicular lines in a square.

Connections Geometry and Reasoning

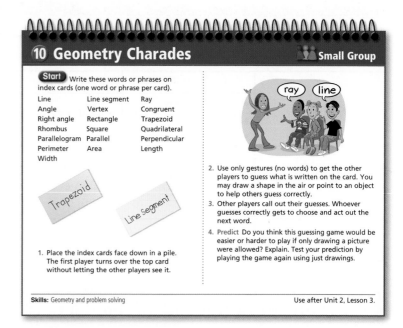

10 Geometry Charades   Small Group

Start Write these words or phrases on index cards (one word or phrase per card).

Line   Line segment   Ray
Angle   Vertex   Congruent
Right angle   Rectangle   Trapezoid
Rhombus   Square   Quadrilateral
Parallelogram   Parallel   Perpendicular
Perimeter   Area   Length
Width

1. Place the index cards face down in a pile. The first player turns over the top card without letting the other players see it.

2. Use only gestures (no words) to get the other players to guess what is written on the card. You may draw a shape in the air or point to an object to help others guess correctly.

3. Other players call out their guesses. Whoever guesses correctly gets to choose and act out the next word.

4. **Predict** Do you think this guessing game would be easier or harder to play if only drawing a picture were allowed? Explain. Test your prediction by playing the game again using just drawings.

Skills: Geometry and problem solving   Use after Unit 2, Lesson 3.

Grouping Small Groups

Materials Index cards (20 per group)

Objective Students try to convey geometric figures and terms without words.

Connections Geometry and Communication

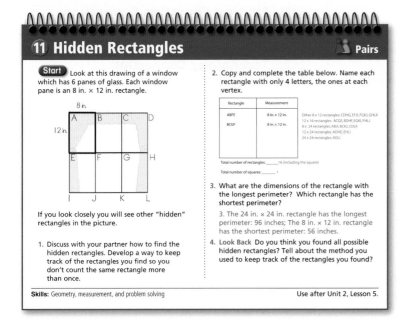

11 Hidden Rectangles   Pairs

Start Look at this drawing of a window which has 6 panes of glass. Each window pane is an 8 in. × 12 in. rectangle.

If you look closely you will see other "hidden" rectangles in the picture.

1. Discuss with your partner how to find the hidden rectangles. Develop a way to keep track of the rectangles you find so you don't count the same rectangle more than once.

2. Copy and complete the table below. Name each rectangle with only 4 letters, the ones at each vertex.

Rectangle	Measurement
ABFE	8 in. × 12 in.
BCGF	8 in. × 12 in.

Other 8 x 12 rectangles: CDHG, EFJI, FGKJ, GHLK
12 x 16 rectangles: ACGE, BDHF, EGKI, FHLJ
8 x 24 rectangles: ABJI, BCKJ, CDLK
12 x 24 rectangles: ADHE, EHLI
24 x 24 rectangles: ADLI

Total number of rectangles: _____ 16 (including the square)

Total number of squares: _____ 1

3. What are the dimensions of the rectangle with the longest perimeter? Which rectangle has the shortest perimeter?

3. The 24 in. × 24 in. rectangle has the longest perimeter: 96 inches; The 8 in. × 12 in. rectangle has the shortest perimeter: 56 inches.

4. **Look Back** Do you think you found all possible hidden rectangles? Tell about the method you used to keep track of the rectangles you found?

Skills: Geometry, measurement, and problem solving   Use after Unit 2, Lesson 5.

Grouping Pairs

Objective Students expand understanding of rectangles, and develop visualization skills.

Connections Problem Solving and Geometry

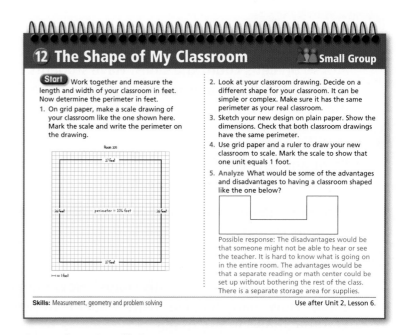

12 The Shape of My Classroom   Small Group

Start Work together and measure the length and width of your classroom in feet. Now determine the perimeter in feet.

1. On grid paper, make a scale drawing of your classroom like the one shown here. Mark the scale and write the perimeter on the drawing.

Room 205

27 feet

26 feet   perimeter = 106 feet   26 feet

27 feet

⊢—⊣ = 1 foot

2. Look at your classroom drawing. Decide on a different shape for your classroom. It can be simple or complex. Make sure it has the same perimeter as your real classroom.

3. Sketch your new design on plain paper. Show the dimensions. Check that both classroom drawings have the same perimeter.

4. Use grid paper and a ruler to draw your new classroom to scale. Mark the scale to show that one unit equals 1 foot.

5. **Analyze** What would be some of the advantages and disadvantages to having a classroom shaped like the one below?

Possible response: The disadvantages would be that someone might not be able to hear or see the teacher. It is hard to know what is going on in the entire room. The advantages would be that a separate reading or math center could be set up without bothering the rest of the class. There is a separate storage area for supplies.

Skills: Measurement, geometry and problem solving   Use after Unit 2, Lesson 6.

Grouping Small Groups

Materials Grid paper, yardsticks or tape measures

Objective Students take initial steps to understand scale and practice measuring large objects.

Connections Measurement and Real World

Ready-Made Math Resources

Technology — Tutorials, Practice, and Intervention

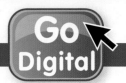

Go Digital

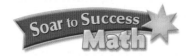

Use activity masters and online, individualized intervention and support to bring students to proficiency.

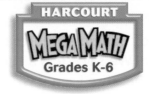

HARCOURT MEGA MATH Grades K-6

Help students practice skills and apply concepts through exciting math adventures.

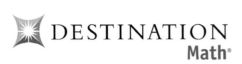

DESTINATION Math

Extend and enrich students' understanding of skills and concepts through engaging, interactive lessons and activities.

Visit **Education Place**
www.eduplace.com

Visit **www.eduplace.com/mx2t/** and find family, teacher, and student materials, activities, games, and more.

Literature Links

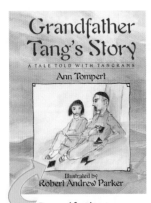

Grandfather Tang's Story: A Tale Told with Tangrams

Grandfather Tang's Story: A Tale Told with Tangrams

Children will be asked to think creatively as Ann Tompert and Robert Andrew Parker's tangram story unfolds, a story a grandfather tells his granddaughter about two shape changing fox fairies.

Math Background

Putting Research Into Practice for Unit 2

From Current Research: How Geometric Thinking Develops

At the **visual level** of thinking, figures are judged by their appearance. We say, "It is a square. I know that it is one because I see it is." Children might say, "It is a rectangle because it looks like a box."

At the next level, the **descriptive level,** figures are the bearers of their properties. A figure is no longer judged because "it looks like one" but rather because it has certain properties. For example, an equilateral triangle has such properties as three sides; all sides equal; three equal angles; and symmetry, both about a line and rotational.

At this level, language is important for describing shapes. However, at the descriptive level, properties are not yet logically ordered, so a triangle with equal sides is not necessarily one with equal angles.

At the next level, the **informal deduction level,** properties are logically ordered. They are deduced from one another; one property precedes or follows from another property. Students use properties that they already know to formulate definitions—for example, for squares, rectangles, and equilateral triangles—and use them to justify relationships, such as explaining why all squares are rectangles or why the sum of the angle measures of any triangle must be 180°. However, at this level, the intrinsic meaning of deduction, that is, the role of axioms, definitions, theorems, and their converses, is not understood.

My experience as a teacher of geometry convinces me that all too often, students have not yet achieved this level of informal deduction. Consequently, they are not successful in their study of the kind of Geometry that Euclid created, which involves formal deduction.

van Hiele, Pierre M. "Developing Geometric Thinking Through Activities That Begin with Play." *Teaching Children Mathematics* 5.6 (Feb. 1999).

Other Useful References: Quadrilaterals

Ferrer, Bellasanta B., Bobbie Hunter, Kathryn C. Irwin, Maureen J. Sheldon, Charles S. Thompson, and Catherine P. Vistro-Yu. "By the Unit or Square Unit?" *Mathematics Teaching in the Middle School* 7.3 (Nov. 2001).

Learning Math: Geometry. Annenberg/CPB Learner.org. 1997–2004. <www.learner.org/resources/series167.html>.

Learning Math: Measurement. Annenberg/CPB Learner.org. 1997–2004. <www.learner.org/resources/series184.html>.

National Council of Teachers of Mathematics, *Mathematics Teaching in the Middle School* (Focus Issue: Measurement) 9.8 (Apr. 2004).

National Council of Teachers of Mathematics, *Principles and Standards for School Mathematics.* Reston: NCTM, 2000.

National Council of Teachers of Mathematics, *Teaching Children Mathematics* (Focus Issue: Geometry and Geometric Thinking) 5.6 (Feb. 1999).

Getting Ready to Teach Unit 2

Analyzing Geometric Figures

Symmetry and Congruence
Lesson 1

In Unit 2, students revisit lines of symmetry that they first encountered in Grade 3. The will see that a line of symmetry divides a figure in half so that, if you fold the figure along the line, the two halves will match exactly. Each half of the figure formed by a line of symmetry is a congruent half.

Similar Figures
Lesson 1

Congruent figures have exactly the same measurements. Similar figures can be different sizes, but they have sides in the same proportion. At this grade, students learn that congruent figures are also similar. These rectangles are similar.

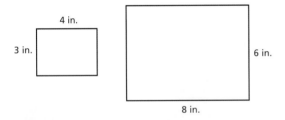

Properties of Quadrilaterals
Lessons 1, 2, 3, 4, and 5

In Unit 2, students explore the attributes of quadrilaterals in a mathematical way. They learn to use specialized vocabulary for the line segments that make up each quadrilateral (for example, *parallel*, *perpendicular*, *opposite*, and *adjacent*), and they discover properties, such as *congruence* and *symmetry*. They also gain an understanding of the classification of the various quadrilaterals. (For example, squares are special kinds of rectangles, which are special kinds of parallelograms.)

This basic knowledge about quadrilaterals lays the conceptual foundation for simple formula development. If students know that the opposite sides of a parallelogram or rectangle are equal, for example, they can simplify the perimeter formula ($l + w + l + w$) to ($l \times 2$) + ($w \times 2$). They can also develop a formula for area, knowing that we only need two measurements (length and width) and not all four.

Area and Multiplication Practice
Lessons 4 and 5

In *Math Expressions*, the geometry mini-units that follow each regular unit facilitate connections and enable students to review what they have recently learned. In this mini-unit, students use the multiplication and division skills they learned in the Fluency Plan to find the area of rectangles. In turn, their knowledge of area will prepare them to use rectangular area models for multi-digit multiplication in later units.

As students work with the area of rectangles in Unit 2, links are drawn between arrays, which they already know, and area.

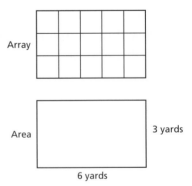

Rearranging Shapes
Lessons 5 and 6

After this fundamental work with the area and perimeter of rectangles, students will develop strategies for finding the area and perimeter of other shapes. For example, students discover that a parallelogram can be cut and reassembled as a rectangle.

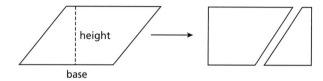

Its area is therefore found by multiplying the length of the *base* times the *height*, which is the same as the width of the corresponding rectangle.

Complex shapes can be understood by applying what we already know about quadrilaterals to find the unknown dimensions. In the figure shown here, we can find the missing dimensions because we know that the opposite sides of the embedded rectangles are equal.

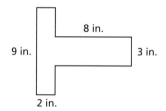

In Unit 4, students will use similar strategies to deconstruct rectangles and parallelograms into triangles.

Basic Multiplication and Division Fluency

Students should continually work toward fluency for basic multiplication and division facts. Use checkups to assist students in monitoring their own learning. For this unit, you can use

- Checkup D: 2s, 5s, 9s, 3s, 4s, 6s, 7s, 8s, 1s, 0s (TRB M122) and Checkup D Answer Sheet (TRB M40).

- Checkup E: 6s, 7s, 8s (TRB M123) and Checkup E Answer Sheet (TRB M113).

If students have some multiplications and divisions they need to work on, have them make a Study Plan and work toward proficiency.

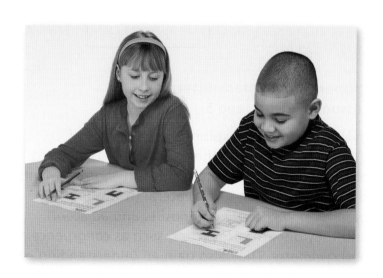

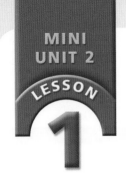

Congruence, Similarity, and Symmetry

Vocabulary

plane
congruent
congruence
similar
line symmetry
line of symmetry
reflection
line of reflection

Lesson Objectives

- Identify congruent figures.
- Determine similarity.
- Explore line symmetry and congruence.

The Day at a Glance

Today's Goals	Materials	
① Teaching the Lesson **A1:** Identify and draw congruent figures. **A2:** Determine similarity by inspection. **A3:** Demonstrate understanding of line symmetry. **A4:** Compare congruence and line symmetry. **② Going Further** ▶ Math Connections: Line Symmetry and Reflections ▶ Differentiated Instruction **③ Homework and Spiral Review**	**Lesson Activities** Student Activity Book pp. 87–91, 93–94 or Student Hardcover Book pp. 87–91, 93–94 and Activity Workbook pp. 40–41, 43–44 (includes Family Letters) Homework and Remembering pp. 73–74 Drawing Figures (TRB M41) Congruency and Symmetry (TRB M42) Transparency of Centimeter-Grid Paper (TRB M60) Sheet protectors Dry-erase markers Transparent mirror (optional) Scrap paper Scissors Overhead projector Geometry and Measurement Poster	**Going Further** Student Activity Book p. 92 or Student Hardcover Book p. 92 and Activity Workbook p. 42 Geoboard/Dot Paper (TRB M56) Transparency of TRB M56 Overhead projector Activity Cards 2-1 Congruence Match-up Cards (TRB M43) Grid paper, dot paper, or MathBoard materials Math Journals

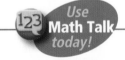

Keeping Skills Sharp

Daily Routines	English Language Learners
Reasoning Chen, Wendy, Lourdes, and Rick have bikes. Each bike is a different color: red, green, black, or white. Wendy's bike is white. Chen's bike is not red. Rick's bike is not green. Lourdes's bike is not black or red. What color is each person's bike? Chen's bike is black. Wendy's bike is white. Lourdes's bike is green. Rick's bike is red.	Use squares to help students understand congruence. • **Beginning** Draw 2 congruent squares. Say: **These two squares are the same size and shape. They are congruent.** Have students repeat. • **Intermediate** Draw 2 congruent squares. Ask: **Are these two squares the same size and shape?** yes Say: **When two figures have the same size and shape, they are congruent.** Ask: **Are these congruent?** yes • **Advanced** Have students draw 2 congruent squares. Have them use short sentences to explain how they know their squares are congruent.

Teaching the Lesson

Explore Congruent Figures

 20 MINUTES

Goal: Identify and draw congruent figures.

Materials: Student Activity Book or Hardcover Book pp. 87–88, Drawing Figures 1 (TRB M41) (1 per small group of students), sheet protectors, dry-erase markers, dry-erase materials, Geometry and Measurement Poster (optional)

✔ **NCTM Standards:**
Geometry
Reasoning and Proof

📁 Class Management

You may want to display the Geometry and Measurement Poster while students study this unit.

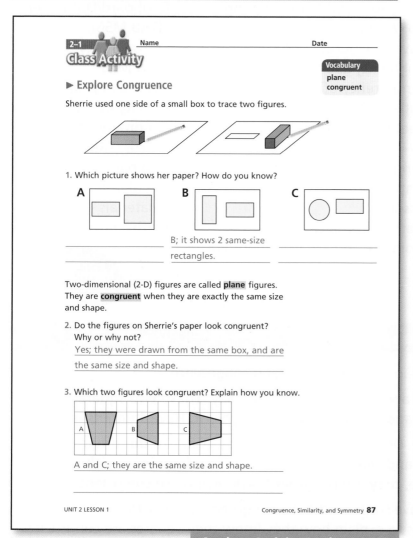

Student Activity Book page 87

▶ **Explore Congruence** WHOLE CLASS

Have students read and discuss problem 1 on Student Book page 87. Sample dialogue follows:

 Math Talk in Action

Why does each drawing match or not match the problem situation?

Marc: Sherrie only used one face of the box. But the drawing shows two different rectangles, or one square and one rectangle—so that doesn't match the problem.

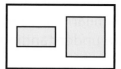

Graciela: These two rectangles are the same size and shape but in different positions on the page. They match the problem, so this picture looks like it matches Sherrie's paper.

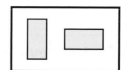

Anita: This is a drawing of two different figures, a circle and a rectangle. That doesn't match the problem situation, so this can't be Sherrie's paper.

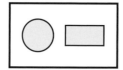

Graciela: Picture **B** must be Sherrie's paper. One rectangle is turned, but the problem just says she traced the face two times. It doesn't say she traced the face in exactly the same position.

Summarizing Congruence Write on the classroom board the words *congruent* and *congruence*. Invite students to discuss what they already know about congruence.

● What makes geometric figures congruent? They are the same shape and size.

● Are figures still congruent if they are turned or flipped? yes

Have students then discuss exercise 2: whether the figures on Sherrie's paper are congruent or not congruent and how they know. They are congruent; they are the same size and shape even though they are turned different ways.

Encourage students to explain their answers to exercise 3.

● How do you know **B** is not congruent to **A**? Even if **B** is turned, it is not the same size and shape.

▶ Identify Congruent Figures WHOLE CLASS

Have students discuss which pairs or groups of figures are congruent in exercises 4–11 on Student Book page 88. Encourage them to explain their decisions in their own words.

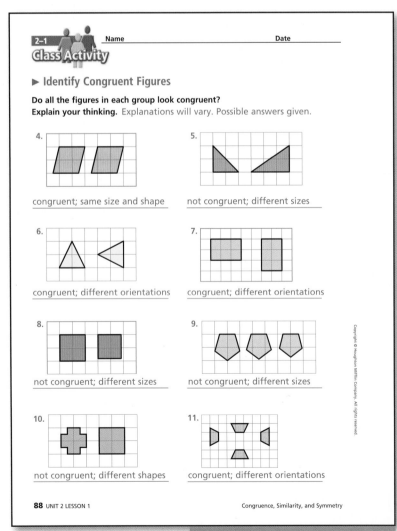

▶ Draw Congruent Figures SMALL GROUPS

Give each **Small Group** of students Drawing Figures 1 (TRB M41) inside a sheet protector and dry-erase materials.

Have students take turns drawing pairs or groups of figures that are or are not congruent. The rest of the students in the group name the figures as congruent or not congruent.

The grid on TRB M41 is provided as a general guide only. Encourage students to draw as many different kinds of figures as they can.

Math Talk If students draw an interesting pair or group of figures, invite them to share their figures and their thinking with the rest of the class. This opportunity will encourage student-to-student math talk.

Define Congruence Have students work independently to draw at least two different sets of congruent figures.

The Learning Classroom

Math Talk Always start new topics by eliciting as much from students as possible. Students often know some things about new topics. This builds feelings of competence and confidence and helps create the classroom community where everyone is a teacher and a learner. So even where the directions for a lesson are directing you to do the talking, remember to ask for students' own ideas first.

Activity 2

Explore Similar Figures

 20 MINUTES

Goal: Determine similarity by inspection.

Materials: Transparency of Centimeter-Grid Paper (TRB M60); overhead projector; Student Activity Book pp. 89–90 or Hardcover Book pp. 89–90 and Activity Workbook p. 40

 NCTM Standards:
Geometry
Representation
Reasoning and Proof

▶ Discuss Similar Figures

WHOLE CLASS   **Math Talk**

Make a transparency of Centimeter-Grid Paper (TRB M60) and place it on the overhead. Introduce the concept of similarity by drawing and labeling a 1-by-3 rectangle. Next to it, draw and label a 4-by-12 rectangle.

Have students discuss the relationship shared by the corresponding sides of the figures. Each measure of the larger rectangle is four times the corresponding measure of the smaller rectangle. Explain that because the lengths of the corresponding sides of the rectangles share the same relationship, the rectangles are similar. Then draw, or invite volunteers to draw, other similar figures on the transparency.

Before students complete the activity, give them an opportunity to observe their classroom and identify any figures in it that appear to be similar.

▶ Identify Similar Figures WHOLE CLASS

Before students complete exercise 12 on Student Book page 89, ask them to compare the base of the larger triangle to the base of the smaller triangle, and compare the height of the larger triangle to the height of the smaller triangle, and describe the relationship. Make sure students can conclude that because the bases and heights share the *same* relationship (the larger is four times the smaller), the triangles are similar.

On Student Book pages 89–90, have students complete exercises 13–18 individually or with a **Helping Partner.**

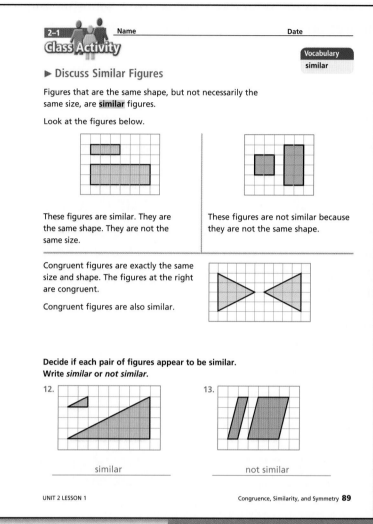

Student Activity Book page 89

2-1	Name		Date

Class Activity

▶ **Identify Similar Figures**

Decide if each pair of figures appear to be similar. Write
similar **or** *not similar*. **Then decide if the figures appear**
to be congruent. Write *congruent* **or** *not congruent*.

14.

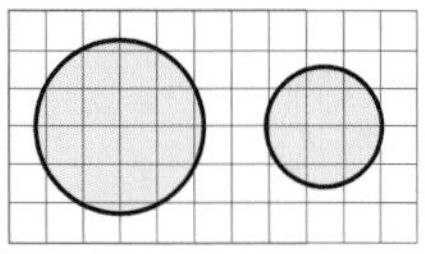

similar; not congruent

15.

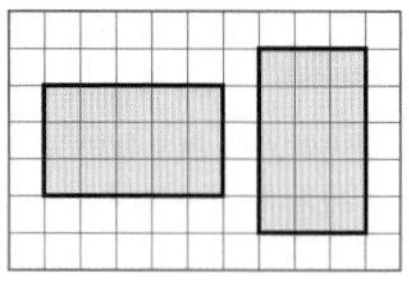

similar; congruent

Write *true* **or** *false* **for each sentence. Draw an example.** Check students' examples.

16. All squares are similar. ___true___

17. All right triangles are similar. ___false___

18. Draw two similar figures that are not congruent.
Describe the measures of the figures, and explain
why they are similar.

Check students' drawings and explanations.

90 UNIT 2 LESSON 1

Congruence, Similarity, and Symmetry

Student Activity Book page 90

Teaching Note

Watch For! Students may decide that the circles in exercise 3 are not similar. Help these students recognize that all circles are similar because they are the same shape, and the circumferences share the same relationship with the diameters (or radii). Point out that for any circle, the circumference is *approximately* three times the length of the diameter. Emphasize that this relationship is true for *all* circles. Therefore, all circles are similar, regardless of their size.

Teaching the Lesson (continued)

Explore Line Symmetry

 20 MINUTES

Goal: Demonstrate understanding of line symmetry.

Materials: Student Activity Book p. 91 or Hardcover Book p. 91 and Activity Workbook p. 41; transparent mirror (optional)

✓ **NCTM Standards:**
Geometry
Reasoning and Proof

▶ Review Symmetry WHOLE CLASS

Some students may already know about line symmetry and lines of symmetry. Invite them to be **Student Leaders** as the class reviews these concepts.

Write on the classroom board the words *line symmetry* and *line of symmetry*.

Have students discuss what they already know about symmetry. Lines of symmetry have exact mirror images on each side.

▶ Identify Lines of Symmetry WHOLE CLASS

Elicit a discussion about the figures in exercises 19–24 on Student Book page 90.

Ask students to complete exercises 25–27.

Define Symmetry Invite students to draw at least two different figures with line symmetry. Students then draw the line(s) of symmetry for each figure. Have them define *line symmetry* and *line of symmetry* in their own words.

✓ Ongoing Assessment

Ask students questions such as the following:

▶ How can you tell if a figure has line symmetry?

▶ Describe a design or logo that has line symmetry.

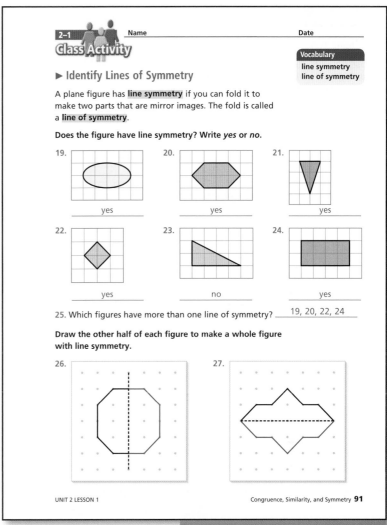

Student Activity Book page 91

✋ Alternate Approach

Mirror Image Students can use a transparent mirror to test for line symmetry. The image in the mirror is congruent to the part of the figure that we can see through the mirror.

The Learning Classroom

Student Leaders Select different student leaders for different tasks. Take time to help students get used to being leaders. Support them for the first few times, and encourage classmates to be supportive. Most students gain confidence themselves when they help others learn.

Symmetry and Congruent Parts

 20 MINUTES

Goal: Compare congruence and line symmetry.

Materials: scrap paper (1 square and 1 rectangle per student), scissors (1 per student), Congruence and Symmetry (TRB M42)

 NCTM Standards:
Geometry
Reasoning and Proof

▶ Parts of a Square WHOLE CLASS

Give each student a square of scrap paper. Have students fold their square in half on a diagonal.

The halves are congruent.

Ask these questions to encourage discussion.

● **Are the halves congruent?** Yes; they are clearly the same size and shape.

● **Is the fold line a line of symmetry?** Yes; the halves are mirror images.

▶ Halves of a Rectangle WHOLE CLASS

Give each student a rectangle of scrap paper. Have students fold their paper in half on a diagonal.

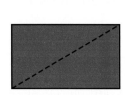 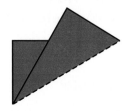

The diagonal is not a line of symmetry.

Ask these questions to encourage discussion.

● **Are the halves congruent?** They look as if they might be congruent, but it's hard to tell by just looking.

● **How can we find out if the halves are congruent?** We can find out by cutting on the fold line and turning one half.

● **Is the fold line a line of symmetry?** No. The halves are not mirror images.

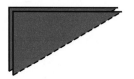

The parts are congruent.

Summarize Symmetry and Congruent Parts Ask students to write and draw to explain the difference between line symmetry and congruent halves of plane figures.

The parts on each side of a line of symmetry are always congruent.

Figures that can be divided into two congruent parts do not always have a line of symmetry.

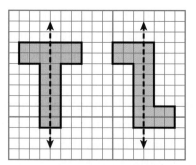

Differentiated Instruction

Extra Help Students may need more experience with congruence and line symmetry. They can use Congruence and Symmetry (TRB M42) to practice finding lines of symmetry and to identify which figures have congruent parts but do not have line symmetry.

② Going Further

Math Connection: Line Symmetry and Reflections

 20 MINUTES

Goal: Relate reflections to lines of symmetry.

Materials: Geoboard/Dot Paper (TRB M56) and a transparency of TRB M56; overhead projector; Student Activity Book p. 92 or Hardcover Book p. 92 and Activity Workbook p. 42

 NCTM Standard:
Geometry

▶ Discuss Line Symmetry | WHOLE CLASS |

In this activity, students will connect what they know about line symmetry with reflections of a figure across a line.

Distribute Geoboard/Dot Paper (TRB M56) to each student and make an overhead transparency of it.

Ask for Ideas Have students share what they already know about line symmetry and lines of symmetry.

Discuss the definitions and examples at the top of Student Book page 92. Duplicate the drawings on your overhead transparency as students duplicate them on the Geoboard/Dot Paper. Then have students fold each figure along the dashed lines to see that both halves match exactly.

Point out that every point on both figures has a corresponding point that is the same distance from the line of symmetry, but on the opposite side of the figure.

Ask **Student Pairs** to work together where one student draws one-half of a shape and a horizontal or vertical line of symmetry that touches the shape. The other student draws the reflection of the shape. After students switch roles, ask one student to draw a whole shape and a horizontal or vertical line of reflection outside the shape. The other student draws the reflection, and then students switch roles.

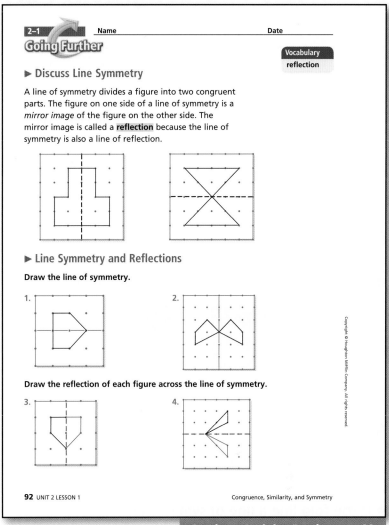

Student Activity Book page 92

▶ Line Symmetry and Reflections | INDIVIDUALS |

Have students work individually (or with a **Helping Partner**) to complete exercises 1–4 on Student Book page 92.

Teaching Note

Watch For! Students who may have difficulty visualizing symmetry and reflections will find it helpful to trace the given figures (or duplicate them on dot paper) and then fold them to help find the correct answers.

Intervention Activity Card 2-1

Congruence Match-Up Activity Card 2-1 ●

Work: In Pairs

Use:
• Congruence Match-Up Cards (TRB M43)

1. Cut out the Congruence Match-Up Cards. Then place the cards face down and mix them up.

2. Keep the cards face down and place them in four rows of four cards each.

3. Partners take turns turning over two cards at a time. If the two cards show congruent figures, like the sample below, the partner keeps the cards. If the figures are not congruent, the partner turns the cards face down again.

4. A partner can challenge a match by explaining why the figures on two cards are not congruent.

Unit 2, Lesson 1 Copyright © Houghton Mifflin Company

Activity Note Use Congruence Match-up Cards (TRB M43) to make one copy for each pair of students. Note that if the cards in the sample are rotated it is easier to identify the congruent figures.

 Math Writing Prompt

Understand Congruence Explain why all the matching sides in two congruent figures must be equal in length.

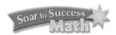 **Software Support**

Use *Soar to Success* for instruction of students needing targeted support for underlying skills.

On Level Activity Card 2-1

The Other Half Activity Card 2-1 ▲

Work: In Pairs

Use:
• Grid paper or dot paper

1. The drawing below shows half a figure. If you use line symmetry to draw the other half of the figure, the completed figure is a square.

2. Each partner draws half a figure on grid paper or dot paper. The figure can be simple, as the square above, or more complex.

3. Partners exchange figures and draw the other half of the figure to make a whole figure with line symmetry.

Unit 2, Lesson 1 Copyright © Houghton Mifflin Company

Activity Note Students may find it helpful to fold the drawing along the line of symmetry and trace its shape on the back of the paper. Students then unfold the paper to reveal the whole figure.

 Math Writing Prompt

Explain Your Thinking Draw half a figure. Explain how to draw the other half so that the whole figure has line symmetry.

 Software Support

Use *MegaMath* for review and reinforcement of the concepts and skills presented in this lesson.

Challenge Activity Card 2-1

Symmetry in the Alphabet Activity Card 2-1 ■

Work: By Yourself

Use:
• Grid paper, dot paper, or MathBoard materials

1. Print the 26 letters of the alphabet as capital letters in block-letter style on grid paper, dot paper, or on the MathBoard.

2. Identify the letters of the alphabet that show line symmetry, and draw at least one line of symmetry on the letter. See below.

3. Cross out the letters of the alphabet that do not show line symmetry. F, G, J, L, N, P, Q, R, S, Z
2. A, B, C, D, E, H, I, K, M, O, T, U, V, W, X, Y; Answers may vary depending on how some letters, such as B, are drawn. See students' lines of symmetry.

Unit 2, Lesson 1 Copyright © Houghton Mifflin Company

Activity Note Have students compare their answers and discuss possible differences.

 Math Writing Prompt

Investigate Math Which of the capital letters do not have line symmetry, but can be cut into two congruent halves? Explain your thinking. N, S, Z

 DESTINATION Math· Software Support

Use *Destination Math* to take students beyond the concepts and skills presented in this lesson.

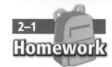 Homework and Spiral Review

Homework **Goal:** Additional Practice

For homework, students identify congruent figures and lines of symmetry.

Remembering **Goal:** Spiral Review

This Remembering activity would be appropriate anytime after today's lesson.

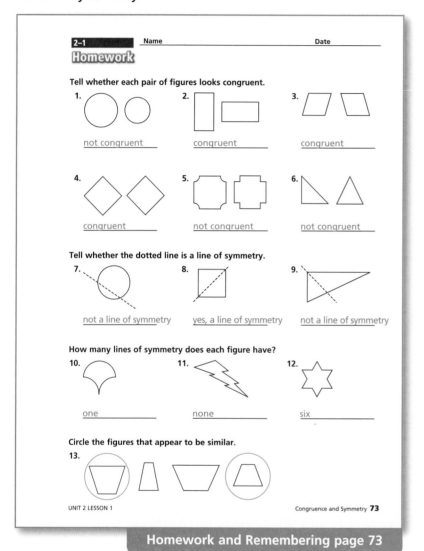

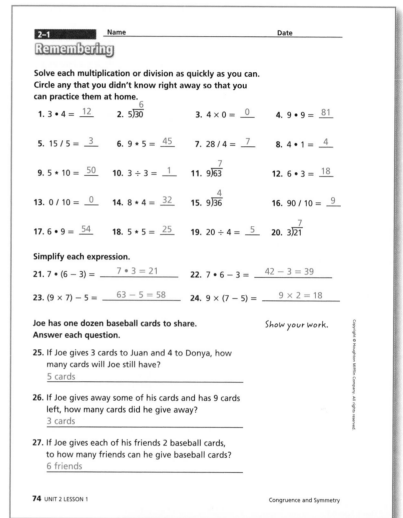

Home and School Connection

Family Letter Have students take home the Family Letter on Student Book page 93 or Activity Workbook page 43. The letter explains how the concept of quadrilaterals is developed in *Math Expressions*. It gives parents and guardians a better understanding of the learning that goes on in math class and creates a bridge between school and home. A Spanish translation of this letter is on the Student Book page 94 and Activity Workbook page 44.

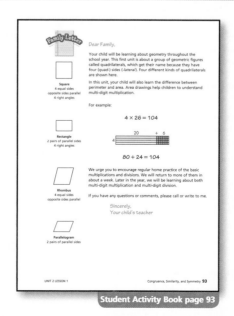

Student Activity Book page 93

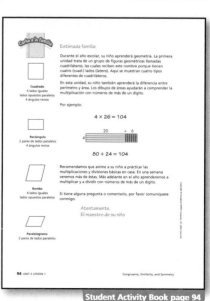

Student Activity Book page 94

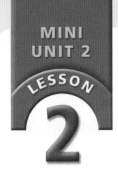

Lines, Line Segments, and Rays

Vocabulary

line
line segment
ray
angle
vertex
oblique
perpendicular
right angle
parallel

Lesson Objectives

- Identify lines, line segments, and rays.
- Demonstrate understanding of perpendicular and parallel.
- Draw, label, and name geometric figures.

The Day at a Glance

Today's Goals	Materials	

① Teaching the Lesson
A1: Sort and name geometric figures.
A2: Use letters to label geometric figures.
A3: Draw and name geometric figures.
	Lesson Activities
	Student Activity Book pp. 95–98 or
	  Student Hardcover Book
	  pp. 95–98 and Activity Workbook
	  p. 45
	Homework and Remembering
	  pp. 75–76
	Index cards
		Going Further
		Activity Cards 2-2
		Centimeter ruler
		Math Journals

② Going Further ▶ Differentiated Instruction		
③ Homework and Spiral Review		

123 *Use* **Math Talk** *today!*

Keeping Skills Sharp

Daily Routines	English Language Learners
Homework Review Have students discuss the problems from their homework. Encourage students to help each other resolve any misunderstandings. **Find a Pattern** Use triangles, squares, and circles to make a pattern that matches the pattern A, A, B, B, C, C, A, A, B, B, C, C. If the pattern continues, what shape will the fifteenth figure be? *Possible answer:* ▲▲■■●●▲▲■■●●; in this pattern, the fifteenth figure will be a square.	Write the word *line* on the board. Ask students to name different types of lines they know of (lunch line, fishing line, line of symmetry, lines in movies, songs, or poems, and so on). Explain to students that the kind of line in geometry is different from these others. • **Beginning** Draw a line. Say: **This is a line in geometry. It has arrows on both ends. The arrows mean that the line goes on forever in both directions.** Have students repeat. • **Intermediate** Draw a line. Point to the arrows on each end. Ask: **What are these?** arrows **What do the arrows mean?** the line goes on forever in each direction Cover one of the arrows on the line. Ask: **Is it a line if it has one arrow?** no • **Advanced** Ask students to draw a line. Have them use short sentences or phrases to explain how they know their drawing is a line.

1 Teaching the Lesson

Activity 1

Identify Geometric Figures

 20 MINUTES

Goal: Sort and name geometric figures.

Materials: Student Activity Book or Hardcover Book pp. 95–96

✓ **NCTM Standards:**
Geometry
Representation

▶ **Sort and Name Figures** WHOLE CLASS

Have students discuss what they know about lines. Explain to them that they will learn the special meaning of the word *line* in geometry. A line goes forever in both directions.

Invite students to describe figure B on Student Book page 95. Descriptions will vary; students should recognize that the lines do not form four right angles. Explain that when two lines intersect and they are not perpendicular, the lines are *oblique*.

Invite students to explore the similarities and differences among figures A–P. Encourage them to identify figures that share some common feature. Responses can vary; students should be able to defend their thinking.

Students can complete exercises 1–8 on Student Book pages 95–96 individually, in **Small Groups**, or in **Student Pairs**. Ensure that after completing the exercises students are able to name each kind of figure.

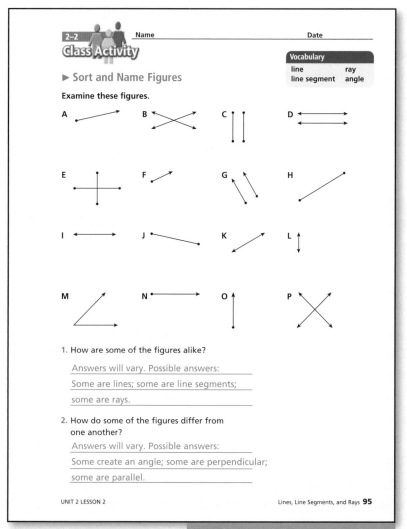

Student Activity Book page 95

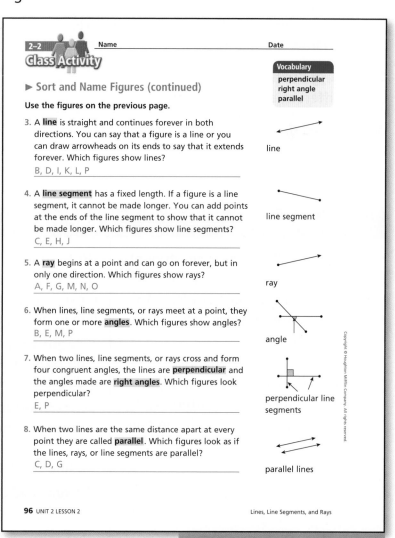

Student Activity Book page 96

Use Letters to Name Figures

 20 MINUTES

Goal: Use letters to label geometric figures.

Materials: Student Activity Book or Hardcover Book pp. 97–98

 NCTM Standards:
Geometry
Representation

▶ Label Lines, Line Segments, Rays, and Angles SMALL GROUPS

On Student Book page 97, students can discuss exercises 9–14 in **Small Groups** or **Student Pairs**.

After completing the exercises, they should understand:

- Lines, line segments, and rays are named with two letters.

- Angles are named with three letters, and the middle letter represents the vertex or the common or shared endpoint of the rays.

▶ Label the Parts of Plane Figures

INDIVIDUALS

Invite students to work individually to complete exercises 15–20 on Student Book page 98. Students will practice using letters to name sides and angles.

Student Activity Book page 97

2–2
Class Activity

Name _____ Date _____

Vocabulary
vertex
angle

▶ Label Lines, Line Segments, Rays, and Angles

You can name figures by labeling them with letters. Possible answers given.

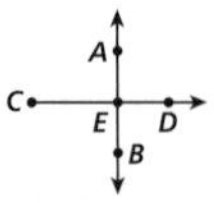

9. The letters *AB* name the line in this figure.
   Which letters name the ray in the figure? _____ *CD*

10. A **vertex** is a point that is common to the two sides of an angle. One **angle** in this figure is ∠AEC. The middle letter of an angle's name indicates its vertex.

    Name three other angles in this figure. ∠CEB, ∠BED, and ∠DEA

Name the line segments, vertex points, and angles in each figure below. Answers for angles may vary.

11. 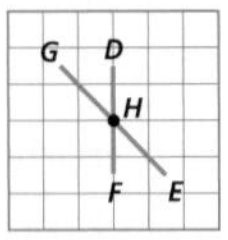 Line segments: *GE, DF*
    Vertex point: *H*
    Angles: ∠GHD, ∠DHE, ∠EHF, ∠FHG

12. 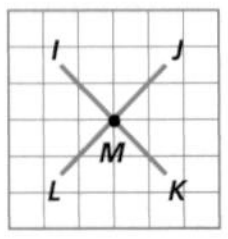 Line segments: *IK, LJ*
    Vertex point: *M*
    Angles: ∠IMJ, ∠JMK, ∠KML, ∠LMI

13. 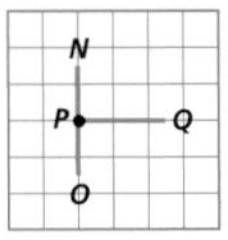 Line segments: *NO, PQ*
    Vertex point: *P*
    Angles: ∠NPQ, ∠QPO

14. Choose one of figures 11–13 and name the line segments and angles that look congruent.

    Answers will vary. _____

UNIT 2 LESSON 2   Lines, Line Segments, and Rays **97**

Student Activity Book page 98

2–2
Class Activity

Name _____ Date _____

▶ Label the Parts of Plane Figures

For each figure, name the sides that look parallel and those that look perpendicular. Not every example has both.
Name at least one angle. Answers for angles will vary. Possible answers are given.

15. 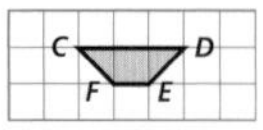 Parallel: *CD and FE*
    Perpendicular: _____
    Angle: ∠CFE

16. 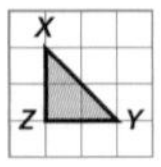 Parallel: _____
    Perpendicular: *XZ and ZY*
    Angle: ∠XZY

17. 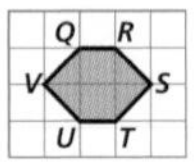 Parallel: *QR and UT; QV and ST; RS and UV and QV and VU;*
    Perpendicular: *RS and ST*
    Angle: ∠TUV

18. 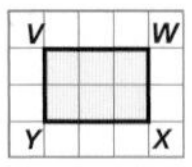 Parallel: *VW and YX; VY and WX*
    Perpendicular: _____
    Angle: ∠XYV

19. 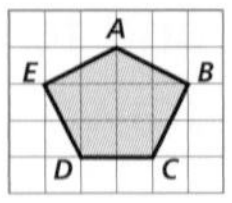 Parallel: _____
    Perpendicular: *AB and BC; AE and ED*
    Angle: ∠ABC

20. 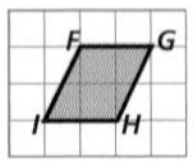 Parallel: *FG and IH; FI and GH*
    Perpendicular: _____
    Angle: ∠FGH

▶ Draw Figures

21. Draw and label a figure with one pair of parallel line segments.

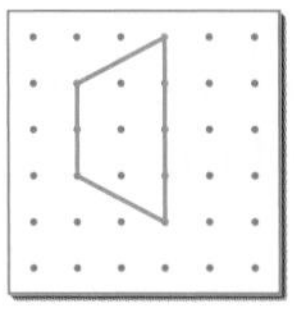

22. Draw and label a figure with one pair of perpendicular line segments.

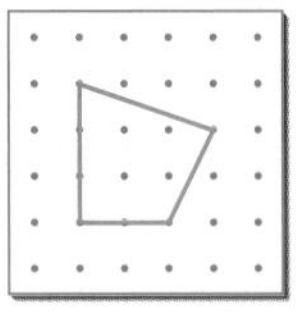

    Drawings will vary.

98 UNIT 2 LESSON 2   Lines, Line Segments, and Rays

Lines, Line Segments, and Rays   **227**

Activity 3

Draw and Name Figures

 20 MINUTES

Goal: Draw and name geometric figures.

Materials: Student Activity Book p. 98 or Hardcover Book p. 98 and Activity Workbook p. 45, index cards

 NCTM Standards:
Geometry
Representation

▶ Practice With a Group SMALL GROUPS

Write the following words on the classroom board:

> line
> line segment
> ray
> angle
> vertex
> parallel lines
> perpendicular lines
> right angle
> oblique lines

Working in **Small Groups,** students practice drawing each figure from the list, labeling it with letters, and naming its various parts. Encourage each group to discuss the representations and to decide which figures are and are not accurately drawn and labeled.

Allow time for each student to have an opportunity to select a figure for others to draw.

▶ Draw Figures SMALL GROUPS

In **Small Groups,** students can share their answers to exercises 21 and 22 on Student Book page 98.

Next, invite students to define the terms *line*, *line segment*, *ray*, *parallel*, *perpendicular,* and *oblique*.

Ongoing Assessment

Ask students to write their first name, using only line segments. Have them answer the following questions:

▶ Which letters have perpendicular line segments?

▶ Which letters have parallel line segments?

▶ Which letters have both?

▶ Which letters have neither?

Teaching Note

Math Symbols The special symbols for a line, a line segment, or a ray are omitted when the figure is specifically named. That is, we write either segment *AB* or $\overline{AB}$, but not segment $\overline{AB}$, which is redundant.

Many sources will omit the symbols when the meaning is clear from the context. When we say *AB* is parallel to *CD*, this statement will be true whether we are representing lines, segments, or rays. In this series, we will use the special symbols so that students become familiar with them and use them correctly.

Differentiated Instruction

Materials: 3" × 5" index cards

Advanced Learners Two-dimensional geometric figures are called *plane figures* because they are a part of a *plane*. A **plane** is a flat surface that extends forever in all directions.

To help students visualize a plane, provide each student with an index card. Confirm that the card is a rectangle. Explain that the rectangle is only a part of a flat plane that extends out from the top, bottom, and sides of the rectangle. Even though the index card has depth, you can use it to demonstrate how to look at the index card with one eye closed while turning it sideways until it appears to be a line. The line represents the plane the rectangle is in.

② Going Further

Intervention   Activity Card 2-2

Draw Lines
Activity Card 2-2 ●

Work: By Yourself

Use:
• Centimeter ruler

1. Mark and label two points on a piece of paper.

2. Join the points, using a ruler to form a line segment. Then name and label the figure.

3. Change the line segment to make it a ray. Name the new figure.

4. Change the ray to make it a line. Name the new figure.

5. **Explain** What change to the figure did you make for Steps 3 and 4? What do those changes tell you about the figure? 3. added an arrow at one end, shows that ray extends forever in one direction; 4. added an arrow at the other end, shows that figure extends forever in both directions.

Unit 2, Lesson 2   Copyright © Houghton Mifflin Company

Activity Note If necessary, remind students that an arrow indicates that a line segment extends forever in the direction the arrow is pointing.

📝 **Math Writing Prompt**

Understand Parallel Lines Explain why two parallel lines can never share a common point.

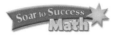 **Software Support**

Use *Soar to Success* for instruction of students needing targeted support for underlying skills.

▲ On Level   Activity Card 2-2

How Many Segments?
Activity Card 2-2 ▲

Work: By Yourself

1. Copy the drawing below onto your own paper.

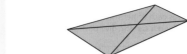

2. Use letters to label the figure's 4 vertices. Labels will vary.

3. Name all the possible line segments in the figure. Answers will vary; there are 6 possible line segments.

4. Identify at least two pairs of oblique line segments. Any lines that intersect without forming right angles.

5. **Look Back** How many line segments were you able to name? Are there line segments you cannot name? Explain your reasoning. 6; Yes. It is not possible to name the line segments from the vertices to the center of the figure unless you name the point at the center.

Unit 2, Lesson 2   Copyright © Houghton Mifflin Company

Activity Note While there are 10 line segments, students can name only 6 of them. It is possible to name 10 line segments only if the point at the intersection of the diagonals is labeled.

📝 **Math Writing Prompt**

Explain Your Thinking A ray goes from point *A* through point *B*. Are ray *AB* and ray *BA* both names for the ray? Explain your thinking.

 Software Support

Use *MegaMath* for review and reinforcement of the concepts and skills presented in this lesson.

■ Challenge   Activity Card 2-2

Intersecting Lines
Activity Card 2-2 ■

Work: By Yourself

1. Use the diagram below to answer questions 2 and 3.

2. Which pair of lines are perpendicular? How do you know? right pair; They intersect at a 90° angle.

3. Which pair of lines are oblique? How do you know? left pair; They do not intersect at a 90° angle.

4. On your own paper, draw 3 sets of intersecting lines that are oblique and 3 sets of intersecting lines that are perpendicular. Drawings will vary.

Unit 2, Lesson 2   Copyright © Houghton Mifflin Company

Activity Note Point out that perpendicular lines form 4 congruent angles while oblique lines form two different pairs of congruent angles.

📝 **Math Writing Prompt**

Investigate Math How many different lines can you draw through one point? How many different lines can you draw through two points? Explain your thinking.

 DESTINATION Math **Software Support**

Use *Destination Math* to take students beyond the concepts and skills presented in this lesson.

3 Homework and Spiral Review

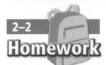

2-2 Homework **Goal:** Additional Practice

For homework, students identify and draw parallel and perpendicular lines.

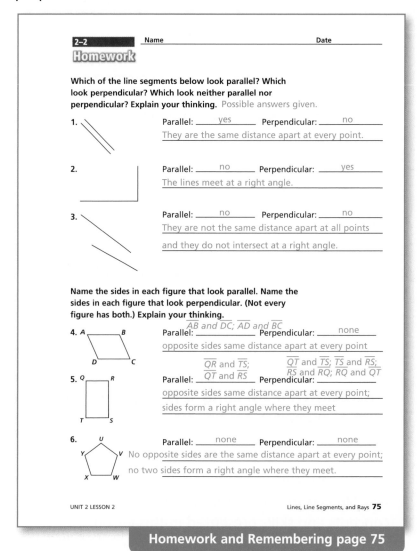

2-2 Homework

Name _____ Date _____

Which of the line segments below look parallel? Which look perpendicular? Which look neither parallel nor perpendicular? Explain your thinking. Possible answers given.

1. Parallel: ___yes___ Perpendicular: ___no___
They are the same distance apart at every point.

2. Parallel: ___no___ Perpendicular: ___yes___
The lines meet at a right angle.

3. Parallel: ___no___ Perpendicular: ___no___
They are not the same distance apart at all points
and they do not intersect at a right angle.

Name the sides in each figure that look parallel. Name the sides in each figure that look perpendicular. (Not every figure has both.) Explain your thinking.

4. A   B   Parallel: $\overline{AB}$ and $\overline{DC}$; $\overline{AD}$ and $\overline{BC}$ Perpendicular: ___none___
   D   C   opposite sides same distance apart at every point

5. Q   R   Parallel: $\overline{QR}$ and $\overline{TS}$;   Perpendicular: $\overline{QT}$ and $\overline{TS}$; $\overline{TS}$ and $\overline{RS}$;
                 $\overline{QT}$ and $\overline{RS}$ $\overline{RS}$ and $\overline{RQ}$; $\overline{RQ}$ and $\overline{QT}$
   T   S   opposite sides same distance apart at every point;
                 sides form a right angle where they meet

6. U   Parallel: ___none___ Perpendicular: ___none___
   Y   V   No opposite sides are the same distance apart at every point;
   X   W   no two sides form a right angle where they meet.

UNIT 2 LESSON 2   Lines, Line Segments, and Rays **75**

Homework and Remembering page 75

2-2 Remembering **Goal:** Spiral Review

This Remembering activity would be appropriate anytime after today's lesson.

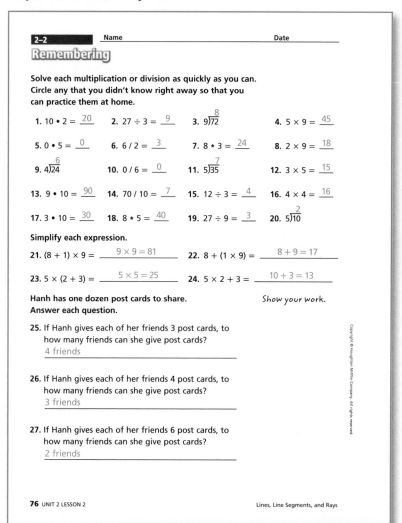

2-2 Remembering

Name _____ Date _____

Solve each multiplication or division as quickly as you can. Circle any that you didn't know right away so that you can practice them at home.

1. $10 \cdot 2 =$ ___20___   2. $27 \div 3 =$ ___9___   3. $9\overline{)72}$ = 8   4. $5 \times 9 =$ ___45___

5. $0 \cdot 5 =$ ___0___   6. $6 / 2 =$ ___3___   7. $8 * 3 =$ ___24___   8. $2 \times 9 =$ ___18___

9. $4\overline{)24}$ = 6   10. $0 / 6 =$ ___0___   11. $5\overline{)35}$ = 7   12. $3 \times 5 =$ ___15___

13. $9 \cdot 10 =$ ___90___   14. $70 / 10 =$ ___7___   15. $12 \div 3 =$ ___4___   16. $4 \times 4 =$ ___16___

17. $3 \cdot 10 =$ ___30___   18. $8 * 5 =$ ___40___   19. $27 \div 9 =$ ___3___   20. $5\overline{)10}$ = 2

Simplify each expression.

21. $(8 + 1) \times 9 =$ ___$9 \times 9 = 81$___   22. $8 + (1 \times 9) =$ ___$8 + 9 = 17$___

23. $5 \times (2 + 3) =$ ___$5 \times 5 = 25$___   24. $5 \times 2 + 3 =$ ___$10 + 3 = 13$___

Hanh has one dozen post cards to share. Answer each question.   *Show your work.*

25. If Hanh gives each of her friends 3 post cards, to how many friends can she give post cards?
    4 friends

26. If Hanh gives each of her friends 4 post cards, to how many friends can she give post cards?
    3 friends

27. If Hanh gives each of her friends 6 post cards, to how many friends can she give post cards?
    2 friends

76 UNIT 2 LESSON 2   Lines, Line Segments, and Rays

Homework and Remembering page 76

Home or School Activity

Art Connection

Find Angles Have students describe and sketch three objects that have angles that are not right angles.

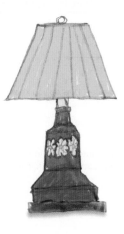

The top and bottom of the shade and some of the angles in the base of the lamp are angles, but they are not right angles.

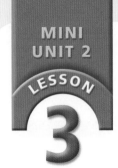

Kinds of Quadrilaterals

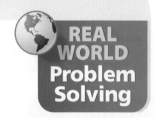

REAL
WORLD
**Problem
Solving**

Vocabulary

quadrilateral
trapezoid
isosceles trapezoid
parallelogram
rhombus
rectangle
square

Lesson Objective

● Recognize and apply characteristics of different types of quadrilaterals.

The Day at a Glance

Today's Goals	Materials

① Teaching the Lesson
  A1: Recognize and describe quadrilaterals.
  A2: Classify quadrilaterals.
  A3: Name and draw quadrilaterals.

② Going Further
  ▶ Math Connection: Use Venn Diagrams
  ▶ Differentiated Instruction

③ Homework and Spiral Review

Lesson Activities
Student Activity Book pp. 99–100
  or Student Hardcover Book
  pp. 99–100
Homework and Remembering
  pp. 77–78
Quick Quiz 1 (Assessment Guide)

Going Further
Student Activity Book
  p. 100A or Activity
  Workbook p. 47
Scissors
Large sheets of paper
  or poster board
Activity Cards 2-3
Math Journals

123 *Use* **Math Talk** *today!*

Keeping Skills Sharp

Daily Routines	English Language Learners

Homework Review Ask students to place their homework at the corner of their desks. As you circulate, check that students completed the assignment, and see whether any problem caused difficulty for many students.

Skip Count Have students skip count:

▶ by 2s from 475 to 499.
▶ by 4s from 126 to 170.

Write the words *parallel, perpendicular,* and *congruent* on the board. Name something in the classroom that is an example of parallel (desks in rows, lines in tile, and so on). Say: **Parallel lines go on in the same direction without intersecting.** Name something in the classroom that is an example of perpendicular (window panes, corners of board, and so on). Say: **Perpendicular lines intersect to form a right angle.** Name something in the room that is an example of congruent (desks). Say: **Congruent means things are the same size and shape.**

• **Beginning** Draw 2 parallel lines. Say: **These two lines go in the same direction without intersecting. They are parallel.** Have students repeat.

• **Intermediate** Draw 2 parallel lines. Ask: **What are these?** lines **Do they intersect?** no **What type of lines go on in the same direction without intersecting?** parallel

• **Advanced** Have students work in pairs. One partner names *parallel, perpendicular,* or *congruent.* The other partner draws an example and explains how they know their drawing is correct.

① Teaching the Lesson

Activity 1

Sort 4-Sided Figures

 20 MINUTES

Goal: Recognize and describe quadrilaterals.

Materials: Student Activity Book or Hardcover Book p. 99

 NCTM Standard:
Geometry

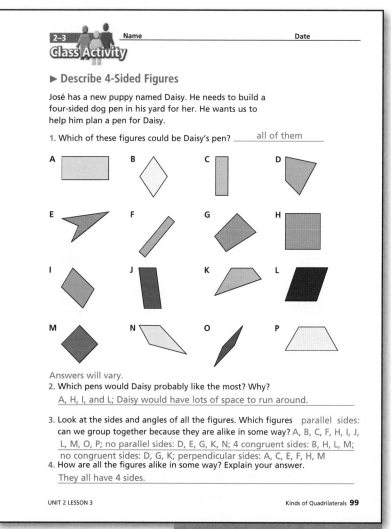

▶ Describe 4-Sided Figures [WHOLE CLASS]

Read with students the problem at the top of Student Book page 99 about José and his puppy, Daisy.

Invite several students to go to the classroom board and draw a possible 4-sided pen for Daisy.

Leave the figures on the classroom board and ask a different group of students to go to the classroom board and add their ideas for a possible pen for Daisy. Invite enough students so that you have a variety of 4-sided figures to consider.

Discuss the Figures Have students discuss the similarities and differences among the figures on the classroom board. They can also compare their drawings to the figures shown in question 1.

Prompt students as necessary to discuss sides and angles, and encourage them to consider which elements of the pen designs make the designs alike or different.

● Which figures have perpendicular sides? A, C, F, H, M

● Which figures have parallel sides? A, B, C, F, H, I, J, L, M, O, P

● Which figures have at least two congruent sides? A, B, C, E, F, H, I, J, L, M, N, O, P

If possible, leave students' drawings on the classroom board so you can refer to them in Activity 3.

Teaching Note

Language and Vocabulary Before moving on to the following activities, students must understand *perpendicular, parallel*, and *congruent*. Spend as much time as necessary for mastery of the terms.

Classify Quadrilaterals

 20 MINUTES

Goal: Classify quadrilaterals.

Materials: Student Activity Book or Hardcover Book p. 100

 NCTM Standards:
Geometry
Reasoning and Proof

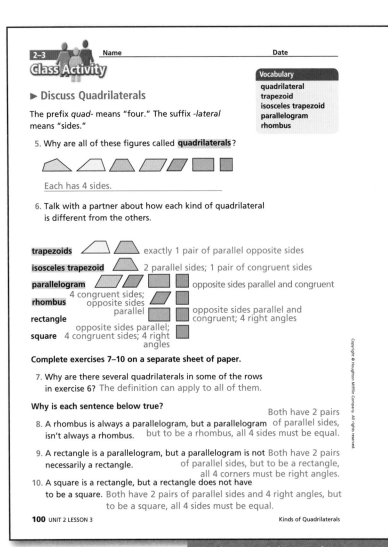

Student Activity Book page 100

▶ Discuss Quadrilaterals   WHOLE CLASS

Elicit a step-by-step discussion about the figures on Student Book page 100 to ensure that students understand the essential differences among the basic quadrilaterals.

Begin the discussion by drawing these closed and not closed figures on the classroom board. Explain that you can trace a closed figure from a starting point, and back to the same starting point, without crossing or retracing any part of the figure.

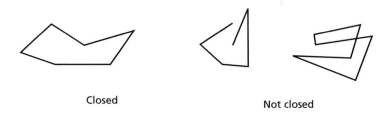

Closed   Not closed

Clarify for students that a quadrilateral is any closed figure with four sides.

Have students complete exercises 5–10.

Guide them in a discussion about each set of figures in exercise 6.

Continue with a discussion such as the Math Talk in Action on the next page.

Activity continued ▶

Activity 2

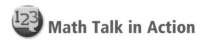 **Math Talk in Action**

Tell me about the trapezoids.

Damaris: They have a pair of opposite parallel sides; the other pair of sides is not parallel.

What do you notice about the isosceles trapezoid?

Eva: It has a pair of opposite parallel sides.

Jordan: Yes, and its other pair of opposite sides is congruent.

There are four parallelograms. Tell me about them.

Dmitri: Each pair of opposite sides is parallel.

The rhombus has two sets of sides that are parallel, too. What can you tell me about the rhombus that makes it different from a parallelogram?

Ella: All of its sides are the same length—they're congruent.

Tell me about the rectangle.

Nia: It's a parallelogram, too, but all the angles are right angles.

What about the square?

Otis: It's a rectangle with four equal sides.

Name Quadrilaterals

 20 MINUTES

Goal: Name and draw quadrilaterals.

Materials: Student Activity Book or Hardcover Book p. 99

 NCTM Standards:
Geometry
Reasoning and Proof

▶ Name Quadrilaterals WHOLE CLASS

Redirect students' attention to the ideas for Daisy's dog pen on the board or on Student Book page 99. Have them name as many of the quadrilaterals as they can and share their reasons for choosing the name they did in each case.

▶ Draw and Write About Quadrilaterals
WHOLE CLASS

Have students draw three different examples for each kind of quadrilateral. Challenge them to write in their own words a definition for each kind of quadrilateral that tells how it is different from the others.

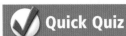 **Quick Quiz**

See Assessment Guide for Unit 2 Quick Quiz 1.

Ongoing Assessment

Ask students the following questions:

▶ How is a parallelogram like a trapezoid? How are the two figures different?

▶ How is a rhombus like a square? How are the two figures different?

Teaching Note

Math Background The trapezoid is an anomaly in the hierarchy of quadrilaterals.

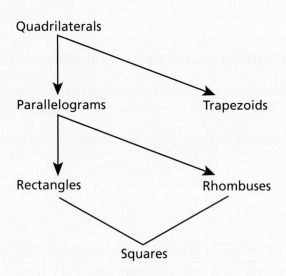

Other than the isosceles trapezoid, there is no subgroup of quadrilaterals under the trapezoid.

Going Further

Math Connection: Use Venn Diagrams

 40 MINUTES

Goal: Use a Venn diagram to sort and classify quadrilaterals.

Materials: Student Activity Book p. 100A or Activity Workbook p. 47; scissors (1 per student); large sheets of paper or poster board (1 per group)

✔ **NCTM Standards:**
Geometry
Reasoning and Proof

▶ Sort and Classify Quadrilaterals
SMALL GROUPS

In this activity, students will connect what they know about classifying quadrilaterals with Venn diagrams.

Have students arrange themselves in **Small Groups** of three or four and cut out the sixteen quadrilaterals.

Sketch the Venn diagram shown below on the board.

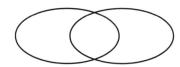

On a large sheet of paper or poster board, have students duplicate the diagram. Ask each group to create a variety of sorting rules that can be used to sort the quadrilaterals, and then classify the figures by arranging them on the Venn diagram.

Tell students to write their sorting rules directly on the diagrams so that the rules are easy to remember. They should use pencils so that they can erase the rules and write new rules if you have time for more than one sorting and classifying activity.

Discuss possible sorting rules that may be used. Sample answers shown.

● How can angles be used to sort the quadrilaterals? figures with at least one right angle; figures with at least one obtuse angle

● How can sides be used to sort the figures? figures with no congruent sides; figures with two or more congruent sides

If students sort and classify the figures into two exclusive groups (for example, rectangles, not rectangles), challenge them to change their sorting rules so that some figures will be placed in the intersection (or middle) of the Venn diagram.

 Math Talk in Action

Upon completion of the activity, encourage representatives from each group to identify their sorting rules and explain how those rules were used to classify the quadrilaterals.

Kuri: We used "at least one right angle" and "at least one pair of parallel sides" as our sorting rules.

Greg: Quadrilateral *G* has at least one right angle, but no parallel sides. We placed it in the left oval.

Kuri: Quadrilaterals *B, D, F, I,* and *P* have parallel sides, but no right angles. We placed them in the right oval.

Greg: Quadrilaterals that fit both sorting rules are *A, H, J, M,* and *N*. We placed them in the middle of the Venn diagram.

Kuri: The other quadrilaterals do not fit the rules, so they do not go on the Venn diagram. They are Quadrilaterals *C, E, K, L,* and *Q*.

Right Angles
G

Right Angles and Parallel Sides
A, H, J, M, N

Parallel Sides
B, D, F, I, P

Differentiated Instruction

Intervention   Activity Card 2-3

Other Names for Quadrilaterals   Activity Card 2-3 ●

Work: Small Groups

1. Look at the drawing of a rectangle below.

2. Discuss with your group whether any of the names below also describe the rectangle. Explain your reasoning.

   trapezoid No, because it must have only one set of parallel sides.

   parallelogram Yes, because the opposite sides are parallel.

   rhombus No, it must have 4 congruent sides.

   square No, it must have 4 congruent sides.

Unit 2, Lesson 3   Copyright © Houghton Mifflin Company

Activity Note Encourage a small-group discussion among the students. Remind them that they are considering only the rectangle shown on the card, not any rectangle.

✓ Math Writing Prompt

Understand Quadrilaterals Explain why every square is a rhombus, but not every rhombus is a square.

Soar to Success Math ✦ Software Support

Use *Soar to Success* for instruction of students needing targeted support for underlying skills.

On Level   Activity Card 2-3

Draw a Picture   Activity Card 2-3 ▲

Work: By Yourself

Use:
• Ruler or straightedge

1. Draw a quadrilateral with two right angles that is not a rectangle. Then label your figure. See sample below.

2. Draw a trapezoid with two congruent sides that is NOT an isosceles trapezoid. Mark the congruent sides. See sample below.

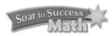

1. 2.

Unit 2, Lesson 3   Copyright © Houghton Mifflin Company

Activity Note For a quadrilateral to have two right angles and not be a rectangle, the angles must have a common side. For a trapezoid to have two congruent sides and not be isosceles, the congruent segments must be adjacent.

✓ Math Writing Prompt

Explain Your Thinking Explain why a trapezoid can never be a rectangle, a rhombus, a square, or a parallelogram.

MegaMath Grades K-6 Software Support

Use *MegaMath* for review and reinforcement of the concepts and skills presented in this lesson.

Challenge   Activity Card 2-3

Problems With More Than One Solution   Activity Card 2-3 ■

Work: By Yourself

1. As shown below, there are many types of quadrilaterals other than squares and rectangles. Some have specific names and others can only be called a quadrilateral. Which ones have specific names? Blue: parallelogram; red, purple, pink and green: trapezoids

2. Draw as many quadrilaterals as you can think of that have no right angles and only two congruent sides.

3. Name the quadrilaterals as specifically as you can, and classify your drawings. Sample drawings

trapezoid   isosceles trapezoid   quadrilateral

Unit 2, Lesson 3   Copyright © Houghton Mifflin Company

Activity Note Review with students what is meant by *specifically*. There are two special classifications for trapezoids. Isosceles trapezoids have non-parallel sides that are congruent. Right trapezoids have two consecutive right angles.

✓ Math Writing Prompt

Investigate Math If a trapezoid has three congruent sides, explain why it must be an isosceles trapezoid.

 DESTINATION Math® Software Support

Use *Destination Math* to take students beyond the concepts and skills presented in this lesson.

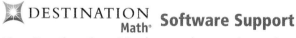

③ Homework and Spiral Review

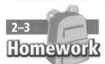

2–3
Homework **Goal:** Additional Practice

✓ Include students' work for page 77 as part of their portfolios.

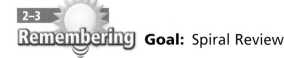

2–3
Remembering **Goal:** Spiral Review

This Remembering activity would be appropriate anytime after today's lesson.

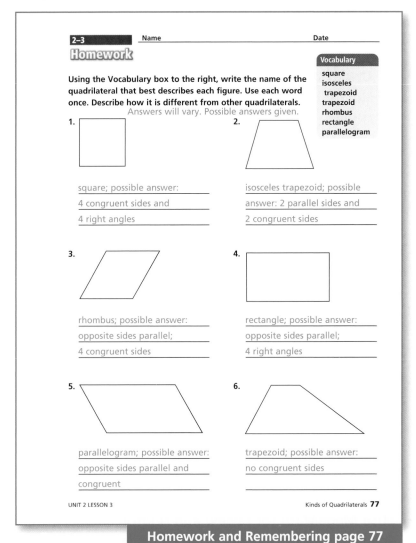

Homework and Remembering page 77

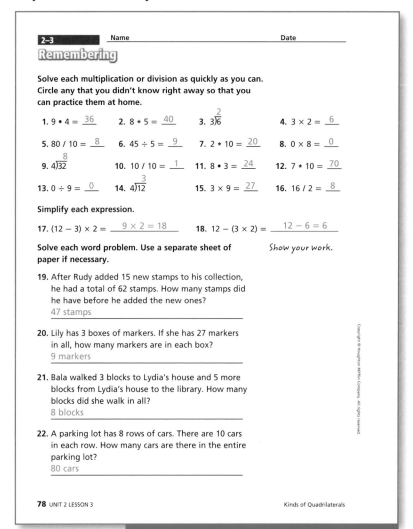

Homework and Remembering page 78

Home or School Activity

 Technology Connection

Draw Quadrilaterals Have students use graphic arts software to draw an example of each type of quadrilateral.

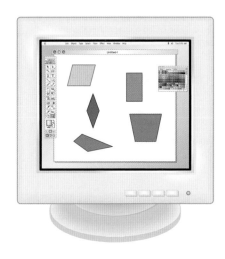

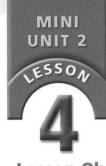

Perimeter and Area of Rectangles

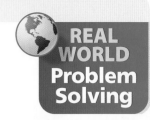

Lesson Objectives

- Demonstrate understanding of perimeter and area.
- Explore general methods for finding perimeter and area of rectangles.

Vocabulary

unit
perimeter
length
width
area
square unit

The Day at a Glance

Today's Goals	Materials

Today's Goals

1 Teaching the Lesson
  A1: Investigate units for measuring perimeter and area.
  A2: Multiply to calculate area.
  A3: Calculate perimeter and area.
  A4: Compare perimeter and area.

2 Going Further
  ▶ Problem Solving Strategy: Guess and Check
  ▶ Differentiated Instruction

3 Homework and Spiral Review

Materials

Lesson Activities
Student Activity Book pp. 101–107
  or Student Hardcover Book
  pp. 101–107 and Activity
  Workbook p. 49
Homework and Remembering
  pp. 79–80
Transparency of Units of Perimeter
  and Area (TRB M44)
Stringing Perimeters (TRB M45)
Centimeter-Grid Paper (TRB M60)
Tack or pushpin boards
Tacks or pushpins (4 per student)
String
Pens or markers
Overhead projector

Going Further
Student Activity Book
  p. 108 or Student
  Hardcover Book
  p. 108
Activity Cards 2-4
Stringing Perimeters
  (TRB M45)
Tack or pushpin
  boards
Tacks or pushpins
String
Pens or markers
Centimeter rulers
Math Journals

123 *Use* **Math Talk** *today!*

Keeping Skills Sharp

Daily Routines	English Language Learners

Daily Routines

Homework Review Have students who need more practice identifying figures make flash cards to practice.

Reasoning Draw this diagram, which shows how many people used paint and/or glitter to decorate shirts. Have students interpret it.

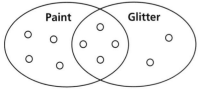

4 used paint only, 2 used glitter only, 4 used both

English Language Learners

Ask the class to brainstorm a list of units they know. Have students explain what each unit on the list is (length, weight, and so on). Say: **These are different units. We use them to measure different things.** Ask students to name things that could be measured using each of the units on the list.

- **Beginning** Cover a student desktop with sheets of paper. Say: **I covered the area of this desktop with paper. Area tells us how much space is on the desktop.**

- **Intermediate** Cover a student desktop with sheets of paper. Ask: **What did I do?** covered the desktop with paper Say: **I covered the area with paper.** Ask: **What did I cover?** area

- **Advanced** Have students use short sentences to explain how to find the area of a desktop and how this information can be used.

Teaching the Lesson

Units of Perimeter and Area

 15 MINUTES

Goal: Investigate units for measuring perimeter and area.

Materials: Student Activity Book or Hardcover Book pp. 101–102, overhead projector, transparency of Units of Perimeter and Area (TRB M44), Stringing Perimeters (TRB M45), tack or pushpin boards (1 per student), tacks or pushpins (4 per student), string about 1 yard long (1 per student), pens or markers (1 per student)

✔ **NCTM Standards:**
Measurement
Communication

▶ Measurement Units WHOLE CLASS

Ask for Ideas Ask students what they already know about measurement units.

Have students make a list of measurement units they know and how they are used.

If students don't mention centimeters as a unit, show them what a centimeter is on a standard centimeter ruler.

Define a measurement unit for the class.

● A measurement unit is always the same size. One inch is always the same length. One square inch is always the same size. It is one inch on each side.

Discuss different measurement units and their uses with the class. As you discuss, elicit from students the importance of standard units.

▶ Units of Perimeter WHOLE CLASS

Ask for Ideas Ask students what they already know about perimeter. It is the distance around the outside of a figure.

Have them discuss how they can find the perimeter of rectangle X on Student Book page 101. Guide the discussion so they understand that perimeter is measured in units of distance; centimeters in the case of these rectangles.

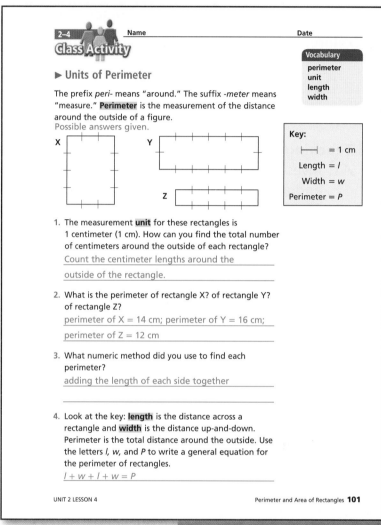

Student Activity Book page 101

Direct students' attention to the key at the right of the rectangles and the 1-cm measure provided. Use the top half of the Units of Perimeter and Area transparency to work along with students as they count the number of 1-cm measurements around the outside of the rectangle.

Use Numeric Methods to Find Perimeter Invite students to think about numeric methods for finding the perimeter that are easier than counting each individual distance unit. Continue to use Student Book page 101 for this discussion.

- How many units are on the left side? 4

- On the top? 3 on the right side? 4 on the bottom? 3

- What numeric method does this suggest?
  $l + w + l + w = P$

- What do you notice about the number of units on the two long sides (length)? on the two short sides (width)? Lengths are both 4 cm; widths are both 3 cm.

- Does this help you to write a shorter expression for the perimeter? $(l \times 2) + (w \times 2) = P$ or $(l + w) \times 2 = P$

Have students discuss how they can find the perimeter of rectangles Y and Z with a numeric method.

Note: All students should be able to do at least the first numeric method, adding the four side dimensions.

Use exercises 1–4 to summarize the discussion. Make sure the students understand the concepts of length and width as well as perimeter.

▶ Units of Area

| WHOLE CLASS |

Math Talk

Ask for Ideas Ask students what they already know about area. The discussion should include following concepts.

- Area is determined by counting the total number of same-sized units that cover a shape.

- Area is determined by counting the square units that will cover a shape without gaps or overlaps.

Discuss how they can find the area of rectangles X, Y, and Z on Student Book page 102. Ask questions to help them understand that area is measured in square units; square centimeters in the case of these rectangles.

2-4

Class Activity

Name _____ Date _____

Vocabulary
area
square units

▶ Units of Area

Area is the total number of **square units** inside a figure. Each square unit inside these rectangles is 1 cm long and 1 cm wide, so it is 1 square centimeter (1 sq cm).

X   Y

Z

Key:
☐ = 1 sq cm
Length = *l*
Width = *w*
Area = *A*

5. How can you find the total number of square centimeters inside each rectangle?
   Possible answers: count each square; multiply length × width

6. What is the area of rectangle X? of rectangle Y? of rectangle Z?
   area of X = 12 sq cm; area of Y = 12 sq cm; area of Z = 5 sq cm

7. Using *l* to stand for length, *w* to stand for width, and *A* to stand for area, what general equation can you write for finding the area of any rectangle?
   $l \times w = A$; $A = l \times w$

8. Why does the same general equation work for all rectangles?
   Answers will vary.

102 UNIT 2 LESSON 4   Perimeter and Area of Rectangles

Student Activity Book page 102

Count and Calculate Area Call attention to the key on Student Book page 102. Use the bottom half of the Units of Perimeter and Area transparency to work along with students.

Then have them discuss numeric methods.

- We know there are 12 squares. What numeric methods will give us that answer?

Adding rows: $3 + 3 + 3 + 3 = 12$ or 4 groups of $3 = 12$

Adding columns: $4 + 4 + 4 = 12$ or 3 groups of $4 = 12$

What faster numeric method do these addition methods suggest? Multiplication is a fast way to add same-size groups: $3 \times 4 = 12$ or $4 \times 3 = 12$. Both work.

Activity continued ▶
Perimeter and Area of Rectangles   **241**

Activity 1

▶ Visualize Perimeter and Area

WHOLE GROUPS

Use exercises 5–8 on Student Book page 102 to summarize the discussion.

If some of your students are having trouble understanding the difference between perimeter and area, this activity might make the difference more tangible for them.

Have students tack Stringing Perimeters (TRB M45) to a board with four tacks to show the four corners of a rectangle.

Ask students to wrap a string around the outside of the four tacks. Then have them use a pen or a marker to mark each unit on the string.

Invite students to discuss their rectangle.

● What kind of measurement do the unit squares inside your rectangle represent? area How many unit squares are inside your rectangle? Answers will vary.

● What does the string represent? perimeter Unwrap the string and count the units of perimeter on the string. How many are there? Answers will vary.

Have students reposition their pins and make a different rectangle by rewrapping their string. Ask the same questions again.

The Learning Classroom

Building Concepts Using hands-on materials can help students to construct their own knowledge and understanding of perimeter and area.

Activity 2

Area and Arrays

 10 MINUTES

Goal: Multiply to calculate area.

Materials: Student Activity Book or Hardcover Book p. 103

 NCTM Standards:
Measurement
Problem Solving

▶ Discuss Real-World Situations

SMALL GROUPS   Math Talk

Invite students to discuss problem 9 on Student Book page 103. Make sure they remember how to use multiplication to find an array total and that they see the arrangement of square tiles as an array.

Then have them discuss problem 10. They should see that pushing the squares together doesn't change the number of squares in the array, but it does turn the array into a rectangle.

Ask students to discuss the remaining problems on Student Book page 103 in **Small Groups**.

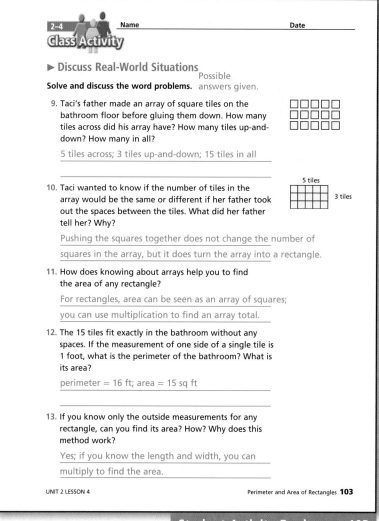

Student Activity Book page 103

Calculate Perimeter and Area

 20 MINUTES

Goal: Calculate perimeter and area.

Materials: Student Activity Book pp. 104–106 or Hardcover Book pp. 104–106 and Activity Workbook p. 49

✔ **NCTM Standard:**
Measurement

▶ Review Perimeter and Area WHOLE CLASS

Have students discuss the information about the perimeter and area formulas on Student Book page 104.

2-4
Class Activity

Name _____ Date _____

▶ Review Perimeter and Area

Perimeter and Area

Perimeter and area are measured with different kinds of units: units of distance or length for perimeter and square units for area.

Perimeter is the total distance around the outside of a figure.

This rectangle has 4 units along its length and 3 units along its width. To find the perimeter, you add the distances of all of the sides:

$$l + w + l + w = P$$

Area is the total number of square units inside a figure.

For rectangles, area can be seen as an array of squares. This rectangle is an array of 4 squares across (length) and 3 squares down (width). To find its area, you can multiply length times width:

$$l \times w = A$$

▶ Adapt the Formulas

How can you change the equations for the area and perimeter of rectangles to apply to squares? *Possible answers given.*

$4 \times s = P; s \times s = A$

_____
_____
_____
_____
_____
_____

104 UNIT 2 LESSON 4   Perimeter and Area of Rectangles

Student Activity Book page 104

▶ Explore Real-World Applications of Perimeter and Area SMALL GROUPS

Ask students to work in **Small Groups** to brainstorm real-world examples of perimeter and area, such as:

● Carpeting a room = area

● How far you run when you run around the block = perimeter

● The glass in the window = area

● The molding around the window = perimeter

▶ Adapt the Formulas SMALL GROUPS

Challenge students to work in **Small Groups** to adapt the equations for perimeter and area of rectangles to squares.

Read the problem on Student Book page 104 aloud and invite discussion.

Have students tell what they remember about squares. Be sure they mention that a square has four congruent sides.

● How can you apply the numeric method for perimeter to a figure with four congruent sides? $4 \times s = P$

Then have students discuss how to apply the numeric method for area to rectangles with four congruent sides. If necessary, remind them about the square numbers. $s \times s = A$

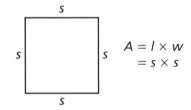

Activity continued ▶

Perimeter and Area of Rectangles **243**

▶ Practice with Perimeter and Area

WHOLE CLASS

Point out the pairs of rectangles on Student Book page 105. Encourage students to use what they have learned about perimeter and area to complete this page.

When students finish, discuss why, in exercise 14, the perimeter and area have the same number. It just happened this time that the total number of units of distance around is the same as the total number of square units of area; it doesn't happen very often.

▶ Calculate Perimeter and Area

SMALL GROUPS

Have students work in **Small Groups** to find the perimeter and area of the rectangles on Student Book page 106.

✓ Ongoing Assessment

This exercise provides a good opportunity to informally assess students' understanding of perimeter and area. Circulate as students talk among themselves. Take notes on individuals needing extra support and concepts that need revisiting.

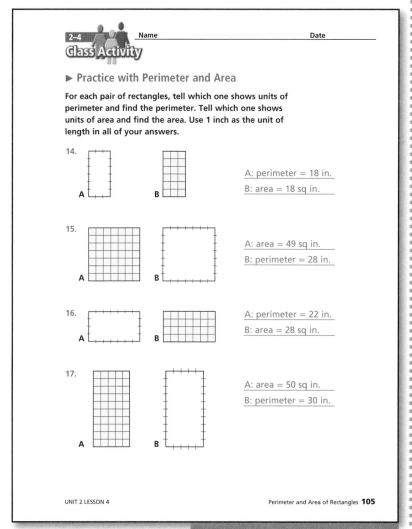

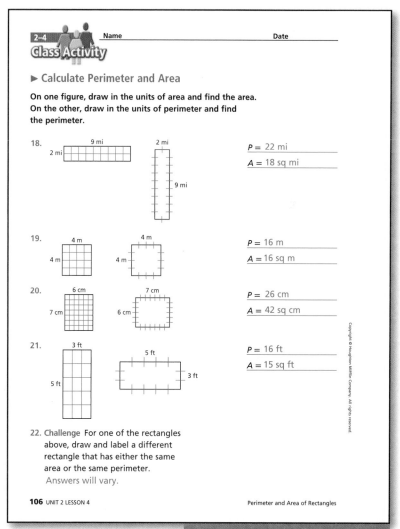

Activity 4

Exploring Perimeter and Area

 30 MINUTES

Goal: Compare perimeter and area.

Materials: Student Activity Book or Hardcover Book p. 107; Centimeter-Grid Paper (TRB M60)

✓ **NCTM Standards:**
Geometry
Reasoning and Proof

▶ Compare Perimeter and Area

WHOLE CLASS

Ask for Ideas Invite students to summarize what they remember about the perimeter and the area of a rectangle. *Perimeter is the distance around a rectangle. Area is the number of square units that are needed to cover a rectangle.* Ask them to describe the kinds of units that are used to measure perimeter *linear units* and area *square units*, and to explain how to find perimeter and area if they know the lengths of two adjacent sides. $P = l + w + l + w$ or $P = 2(l + w)$ and $A = l \cdot w$

Use **Solve and Discuss** to complete exercises 23 and 24 on Student Book page 107. Ask students to draw their rectangles for exercise 23 near the top of the grid. They will then have room at the bottom of the grid to complete exercise 26.

- Ask students to explain how their knowledge of factor pairs and prime numbers can be used to help solve these exercises. *The factor pairs of 20 can be the lengths of two adjacent sides of the rectangles because the area of a rectangle is the product of those sides.*

- Discuss different ways to find the perimeter, and emphasize how easy it is to simply add the lengths of two adjacent sides and then double that sum.

2-4
Class Activity

Name _____ Date _____

▶ **Compare Perimeter and Area**

Copy and complete each table.

23. On centimeter-grid paper, draw every possible rectangle that has an area of 20 square centimeters and sides whose lengths are whole centimeters. Label the lengths of two adjacent sides of each rectangle.

| Rectangles with an Area of 20 sq cm | |
Lengths in cm of Two Adjacent Sides	Perimeter
1 and 20	42 cm
2 and 10	24 cm
4 and 5	18 cm

24. Find and label the perimeter of each rectangle. Then complete the table.

25. Rectangles that have the same ___area___ can have different _perimeters_.

26. On centimeter-grid paper, draw every possible rectangle that has a perimeter of 18 centimeters and sides whose lengths are whole centimeters. Label the lengths of two adjacent sides of each rectangle.

| Rectangles with a Perimeter of 18 cm | |
Lengths in cm of Two Adjacent Sides	Area
1 and 8	8 sq cm
2 and 7	14 sq cm
3 and 6	18 sq cm
4 and 5	20 sq cm

27. Find and label the area of each rectangle. Then complete the table at the right.

28. Rectangles that have the same _perimeter_ can have different _areas_.

UNIT 2 LESSON 4   Perimeter and Area of Rectangles **107**

Student Activity Book page 107

Teaching Note

What to Expect from Students In the activities of the past several days, students have sometimes needed to write a factor pair of a number as 1 and that number. Make sure your discussions during today's activity help clarify the concept that if the *only* factor pair of a number greater than 1 is 1 and that number, the number is prime. Remind students that composite numbers have *more than two* factors.

Activity continued ▶

Perimeter and Area of Rectangles **245**

Activity 4

● Ask students to describe how the rectangles they drew can be broken apart to show that they have the same area (e.g., if they move one column of the 2 by 10 rectangle and place it under the other column, they will make a 1 by 20 rectangle; if they move two columns of the 4 by 5 rectangle and place them under the other two columns, they will make a 2 by 10 rectangle; and so on).

Possible drawings are shown below.

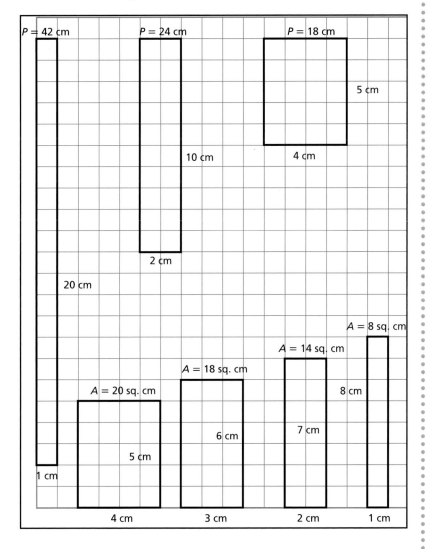

Use **Solve and Discuss** or **Helping Partners** for the related exercises 26 and 27 on Student Book page 107. Repeat the talking points that were used for exercises 23 and 24.

Ask students to explain when they need to remember, and when they do not need to remember, to use the factor pair 1 and another number. Students should understand that it is used for the equation chain of all ways to write a number as two or more factors, and to make a rectangle with the area of a given number; it is not used to make factor trees because it is just an extra step that does not help break down the number into factors.

Teaching Note

What to Expect From Students When asked to find the perimeter of a rectangle when only the measures of two adjacent sides of the rectangle are given, some students may forget to account for the two lengths that are not given. Have students brainstorm ways to remember that they need to add four lengths, or double the lengths of two adjacent sides, to find the perimeter of a rectangle.

Differentiated Instruction

Advanced Learners Challenge your advanced learners to describe a formula that can be used to find the perimeter of a rectangle that is different from $P = l + w + l + w$ or $P = 2(l + w)$. Possible answer: A square is a rectangle. The formula $P = 4 \cdot s$ (where s is the length of a side) can be used to find the perimeter of a square because a square has four sides of equal length.

▶ Critical Thinking

● Can the number that is used to describe the perimeter of a rectangle also be used to describe the area of that rectangle? Give an example to support your answer. Yes; examples will vary. Possible answer: A square whose sides each measure 4 inches has a perimeter of 4 + 4 + 4 + 4 or 16 inches and an area of 4 × 4 or 16 square inches.

● If you know the area of a square, how could you find the length of one of its sides? Name the number that when multiplied by itself equals the area of the square.

● If you know the perimeter of a square, how could you find the length of one of its sides? Name the number that when added four times equals the perimeter of the square; or divide by 4.

● A rectangle is longer than it is wide. If you know its length and its area, how could you find its width? Name the number that when multiplied by the length equals the area.

● A rectangle is longer than it is wide. If you know its length and its perimeter, how could you find its width? Double the length and subtract that number from the perimeter, and then name one-half of the result.

② Going Further

Problem Solving Strategy: Guess and Check

Goal: Use the Guess and Check strategy to solve problems.

Materials: Student Activity Book or Hardcover Book p. 108

✔ **NCTM Standards:**
Number and Operations
Problem Solving

▶ Introduce the Strategy WHOLE CLASS

Say, "I am thinking of two digits that have a sum of 10. What are they?" Encourage students to guess digits. List them on the board, adding to check each guess. Now say, "The digits have a difference of 4. What are they?" Lead students to see that this fact narrows down the listed guesses, so that the only possible digits are 7 and 3. Explain that the strategy students just used to identify the two digits is called Guess and Check.

▶ Guess and Check WHOLE CLASS

Have students read the text at the top of Student Book page 108. Then read the example problem. Ask:

● What do we need to know to solve this problem?

● What do we know about all of their books?

● Who bought more books?

● What do we know about the number of books Tim bought compared to the number Sarah bought?

Lead students to understand that the answers to these questions are used to guess and check the answers in the table.

Ask these questions to help students understand how the strategy was used in the example:

● Why do we multiply our guess for Sara's books by 3 to find our guess for Tim's books?

● Why do we add the two guesses to check?

● Why is 7 a reasonable second guess for Sara's books?

● How do we know that the answer is right?

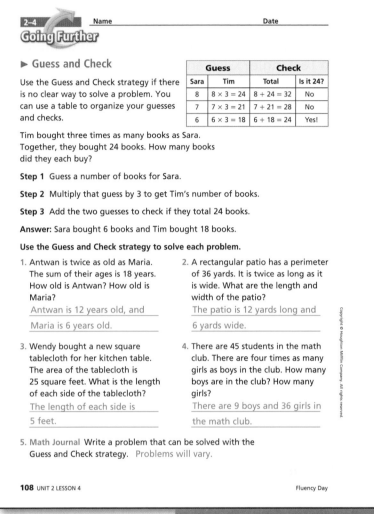

Student Activity Book page 108

Have **Student Pairs** work together to solve problems 1–4. Suggest that they make a table to organize their guesses. Remind students to check their answers.

▶ Critical Thinking WHOLE CLASS

Review the answers together as a class. Ask the following questions about each problem:

● How did you choose and check your first guess?

● How did you use that check to choose your second guess?

● How did you know when you had the right answer?

Differentiated Instruction

Make a Rectangle   Activity Card 2-4 ●

Work: In Pairs

Use:
- Stringing Perimeters (TRB M45)
- Tack or pushpin board
- Tacks or pushpins
- 1-yard string
- Pen or marker
- Grid paper

1. One partner creates a rectangle, using tacks and string on a tack board.

2. Work together to determine the perimeter and the area of the rectangle.

3. The other partner draws the same rectangle on a piece of grid paper. A sample is shown below.

4. Determine if the perimeter and area of the string rectangle and the drawing of the rectangle are the same.

Unit 2, Lesson 4   Copyright © Houghton Mifflin Company

Activity Note Make sure that the rectangle made on the tack board has dimensions that are whole units.

 Math Writing Prompt

You Decide The principal wants to cover the floor of her office with carpet. She knows the perimeter of her office. Does she need to know any other measure? Explain your thinking.

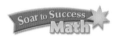 **Software Support**

Use *Soar to Success* for instruction of students needing targeted support for underlying skills.

Draw a Picture   Activity Card 2-4 ▲

Work: By Yourself

1. Look at the rectangles below.

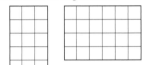

2. Write a formula to find the perimeter and the area of rectangles. $P = l + w + l + w$ or $P = (l \times 2) + (w \times 2)$; $A = l \times w$

3. Use the formulas to find the perimeter and area of each figure. See below.
   Left rectangle: $P = 3 + 5 + 3 + 5 = 16$ units, $A = 3 \times 5 = 15$ sq units; Middle rectangle: $P = 6 + 4 + 6 + 4 = 20$ units, $A = 6 \times 4 = 24$ sq units; right rectangle: $P = 4 + 4 + 4 + 4 = 16$ units, $A = 4 \times 4 = 16$ sq units

Unit 2, Lesson 4   Copyright © Houghton Mifflin Company

Activity Note Check that students are using correct formulas for both perimeter and area. Some students may use the formula $P = 4s$ for a square.

 Math Writing Prompt

Exploring Formulas Is $l + w + l + w$ the formula for the area or the perimeter of a rectangle? Explain how you know.

 Software Support

Use *MegaMath* for review and reinforcement of the concepts and skills presented in this lesson.

Investigate Area   Activity Card 2-4 ■

Work: By Yourself

Use:
- Centimeter ruler
- Grid paper

1. The table below shows some measures of four rectangles.

Rectangle	Length (units)	Width (units)	Perimeter (units)	Area (sq units)
A	5	3	16	15
B	10	4	28	40
C	6	6	24	36
D	8	5	26	40

Use the given information to make a drawing to help you find the missing side measure. This drawing shows rectangle A.

Rectangle A
5 Units

A = 15 square units

2. **Explain** How does the drawing help you identify the width?

3. Complete the table.

Unit 2, Lesson 4   Copyright © Houghton Mifflin Company

Activity Note Have students discuss how to find the perimeter.

 Math Writing Prompt

Problem Solving With Area A school wants to carpet six classrooms. Four classrooms are the same size rectangle. The other two classrooms are the same size square. What must the school do to figure out how much carpet to buy?

 DESTINATION Math **Software Support**

Use *Destination Math* to take students beyond the concepts and skills presented in this lesson.

Perimeter and Area of Rectangles   **249**

③ Homework and Spiral Review

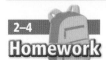

Homework **Goal:** Additional Practice

✓ Include students' work for page 79 as part of their portfolios.

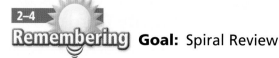
Remembering **Goal:** Spiral Review

This Remembering activity would be appropriate anytime after today's lesson.

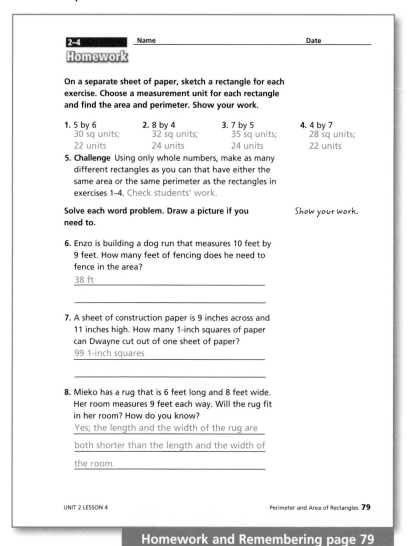

2-4 Name _____ Date _____
Homework

On a separate sheet of paper, sketch a rectangle for each exercise. Choose a measurement unit for each rectangle and find the area and perimeter. Show your work.

1. 5 by 6
30 sq units;
22 units

2. 8 by 4
32 sq units;
24 units

3. 7 by 5
35 sq units;
24 units

4. 4 by 7
28 sq units;
22 units

5. **Challenge** Using only whole numbers, make as many different rectangles as you can that have either the same area or the same perimeter as the rectangles in exercises 1–4. Check students' work.

Solve each word problem. Draw a picture if you need to. *Show your work.*

6. Enzo is building a dog run that measures 10 feet by 9 feet. How many feet of fencing does he need to fence in the area?
   38 ft

7. A sheet of construction paper is 9 inches across and 11 inches high. How many 1-inch squares of paper can Dwayne cut out of one sheet of paper?
   99 1-inch squares

8. Mieko has a rug that is 6 feet long and 8 feet wide. Her room measures 9 feet each way. Will the rug fit in her room? How do you know?
   Yes; the length and the width of the rug are
   both shorter than the length and the width of
   the room.

UNIT 2 LESSON 4   Perimeter and Area of Rectangles **79**

Homework and Remembering page 79

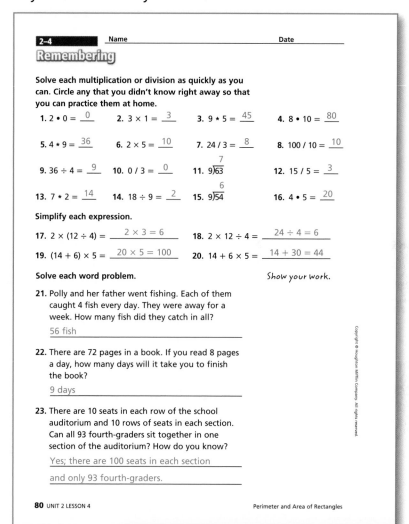

2-4 Name _____ Date _____
Remembering

Solve each multiplication or division as quickly as you can. Circle any that you didn't know right away so that you can practice them at home.

1. 2 • 0 = 0
2. 3 × 1 = 3
3. 9 * 5 = 45
4. 8 • 10 = 80

5. 4 * 9 = 36
6. 2 × 5 = 10
7. 24 / 3 = 8
8. 100 / 10 = 10

9. 36 ÷ 4 = 9
10. 0 / 3 = 0
11. 9)63̄ → 7
12. 15 / 5 = 3

13. 7 * 2 = 14
14. 18 ÷ 9 = 2
15. 9)54̄ → 6
16. 4 • 5 = 20

Simplify each expression.

17. 2 × (12 ÷ 4) = 2 × 3 = 6
18. 2 × 12 ÷ 4 = 24 ÷ 4 = 6
19. (14 + 6) × 5 = 20 × 5 = 100
20. 14 + 6 × 5 = 14 + 30 = 44

Solve each word problem. *Show your work.*

21. Polly and her father went fishing. Each of them caught 4 fish every day. They were away for a week. How many fish did they catch in all?
   56 fish

22. There are 72 pages in a book. If you read 8 pages a day, how many days will it take you to finish the book?
   9 days

23. There are 10 seats in each row of the school auditorium and 10 rows of seats in each section. Can all 93 fourth-graders sit together in one section of the auditorium? How do you know?
   Yes; there are 100 seats in each section
   and only 93 fourth-graders.

80 UNIT 2 LESSON 4   Perimeter and Area of Rectangles

Homework and Remembering page 80

Home or School Activity

 Language Arts Connection

Prefixes and Suffixes Prefixes can be added to the beginning of a word. Suffixes can be added to the end of a word.

The prefix *peri-* means "around." The suffix *–meter* means "measure." Perimeter is the measurement of the distance around.

Have students list other math prefixes and suffixes and words that have these prefixes and suffixes.

Prefix	word	Suffix	word
peri-	**peri**meter	-meter	peri**meter**
centi-	**centi**meter	-meter	centi**meter**
hexa-	**hexa**gon	-meter	deci**meter**
octa-	**octa**gon	-gon	penta**gon**
deci-	**deci**meter	-angle	rect**angle**
tri-	**tri**angle		

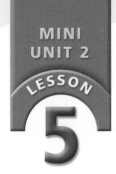

Perimeter and Area of Parallelograms

Vocabulary

parallelogram
base
height
slant
rhombus
perpendicular
height

Lesson Objectives

● Relate the formulas for the perimeter and area of rectangles to the formulas for the perimeter and area of parallelograms.

● Calculate the perimeter and area of parallelograms.

The Day at a Glance

Today's Goals	Materials
1 Teaching the Lesson **A1:** Add the lengths of sides to calculate the perimeter of a parallelogram. **A2:** Identify base and height of a parallelogram; use the formula to calculate the area of a parallelogram. **A3:** Calculate the area of parallelograms. **2 Going Further** ▶ Extension: Change Dimensions ▶ Differentiated Instruction **3 Homework and Spiral Review**	**Lesson Activities** Student Activity Book pp. 109–111 or Student Hardcover Book pp. 109–111 Homework and Remembering pp. 81–82 Parallelograms (TRB M46) Scissors Centimeter rulers	**Going Further** Student Activity Book p. 112 or Student Hardcover Book p. 112 and Activity Workbook p. 50 MathBoard Materials Activity Cards 2-5 Drawing Figures (TRB M41) Scissors Centimeter rulers Math Journals

123 Use Math Talk today!

Keeping Skills Sharp

Daily Routines	English Language Learners
Homework Review Send students to the board to show their solutions for problems 5 and 7. Encourage the rest of the class to ask clarifying questions and make comments. Add students' Homework to their portfolios. **Reasoning** A rectangle has a perimeter of 20 centimeters. One side of the rectangle is 6 centimeters long. What are the lengths of the other three sides of the rectangle? 6 cm, 4 cm, and 4 cm	Review quadrilaterals. Draw examples of a rectangle, square, parallelogram, trapezoid, and rhombus on the board. Have volunteers classify the shapes based on their sides, angles, parallel and perpendicular sides, and so on. • **Beginning** Point to a parallelogram. Say: **This quadrilateral is a parallelogram. It has 2 pairs of parallel sides.** Point to the pairs of parallel sides. Have students repeat. • **Intermediate** Point to a parallelogram. Ask: **What type of quadrilateral is this?** parallelogram Say: **These 2 sides are parallel.** Point to 2 parallel sides. Ask: **Are there any other parallel sides?** yes • **Advanced** Have students explain how to tell whether a quadrilateral is a parallelogram.

① Teaching the Lesson

Activity 1

Perimeter of Parallelograms

 15 MINUTES

Goal: Add the lengths of sides to calculate the perimeter of a parallelogram.

Materials: Student Activity Book or Hardcover Book p. 109

✓ **NCTM Standards:**
Geometry
Measurement

▶ Perimeter of a Parallelogram

WHOLE CLASS

Draw a parallelogram on the classroom board.

● How can you find the perimeter of this parallelogram? Add the measurements of all the sides like we did for rectangles.

Together, look at Student Book page 109 to see how to apply the same numeric methods for the perimeter of rectangles to parallelograms. Ask students to answer questions 1–4.

● Why doesn't the perimeter of the figure change when only the angles change? The perimeter doesn't change because the sides don't change, and perimeter is the distance around the outside of the figure.

Keep the parallelogram that you drew on the board for later reference.

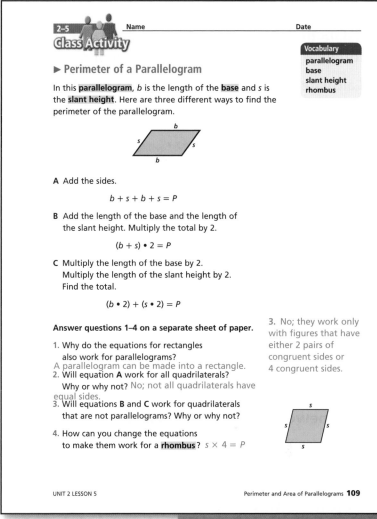

Student Activity Book page 109

Teaching Note

Math Background Parallelograms are useful to reinforce the difference between perimeter and area. Students will learn that all parallelograms with the same base and height have equal areas.

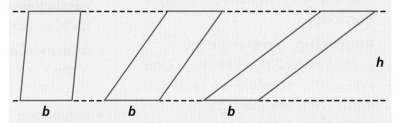

Two non-congruent parallelograms with the same base and height will always have different perimeters. The greater the "slant," the greater the perimeter, and vice versa.

Activity 2

Area of a Parallelogram

 20 MINUTES

Goal: Identify base and height of a parallelogram; use the formula to calculate the area of a parallelogram.

Materials: Parallelograms (TRB M46), scissors (1 per student), centimeter rulers (1 per student)

 NCTM Standards:
Geometry
Measurement
Representation

▶ Dimensions of a Parallelogram

WHOLE CLASS

Distribute Parallelograms (TRB M46) and invite students to examine parallelograms A and B.

● **Do parallelograms A and B look as if they are the same size? Why or why not?** They don't appear to be the same size because the angles are different measures.

Explain to students that they will prove that parallelograms A and B have exactly the same area. Sketch parallelogram A on the board.

Find the Height Ask half of the class to cut out parallelogram A and the other half to cut out parallelogram B.

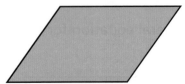

Have students fold their parallelograms in half and align the top and bottom sides. Ask them to then measure the distance along the fold (5 cm).

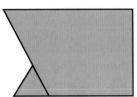

 Class Management

Students can use whole centimeters for all of the measurements in this activity. However, keep in mind that photocopying can distort images, so the figures on their copies may no longer be entirely accurate.

Explain to students that the measurement along the fold line is called the height. Add a line showing height to the parallelogram on the classroom board and write the word beside it.

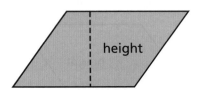

● **What do you know about the position of the fold line?** It is perpendicular to the bottom side. **How do you know this?** I know it is perpendicular because it looks like the corner of a rectangle or a square.

Deconstruct the Parallelogram Have students cut their parallelograms along the fold line.

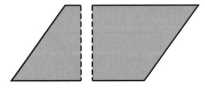

Ask them to think about how cutting along the fold line might help them find the area. As a hint, suggest that they consider what they already know about finding the area of a rectangle.

● **How can you rearrange the two pieces to form a rectangle?** The slanted sides fit together to make a rectangle.

● **Why are you able to fit these two pieces together?** The sides are congruent and parallel to each other.

Activity continued ▶

Activity 2

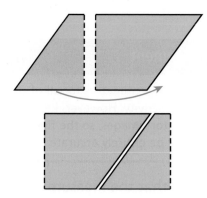

Measure the Base Label the base on the parallelogram on the classroom board and explain to students that the bottom of a parallelogram is called its base.

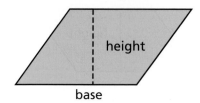

Students can now measure the base (both A and B are 10 cm) and the height (both A and B are 5 cm) of their rectangles.

Find the Area Engage students in a discussion of how finding the area of a parallelogram is like finding the area of a rectangle: 10 cm × 5 cm = 50 sq cm

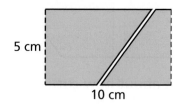

Invite students to compare their rectangles with parallelograms A and B.

● Did the area of parallelograms A and B change in any way as rectangles? No; we just cut them into two pieces and put the pieces together in a new way.

● Are parallelograms A and B the same size? yes

● How do you know? If we place the rectangles that we made on top of each other, we can see that they are congruent.

● Why do the two parallelograms have the same area? They have the same base and height measurements.

● What measurements do you need in order to find the area of a parallelogram? base and height

● Why don't you need to know the length of the slanted sides to find the area? The slanted sides can be different lengths, as they are for parallelograms A and B, without changing the area.

Parallelograms and Rectangles Draw a rectangle on the classroom board near your parallelogram and label the length and width.

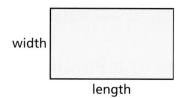

A rectangle is a kind of parallelogram.

● Which side of this rectangle is the base? length

● Which side is the height? width

● What is the general equation for the area of a rectangle? $A = l \times w$

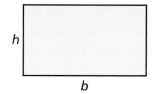

● Rewrite the equation using b instead of l and h instead of w. $A = b \times h$

● What is the general equation for the area of a parallelogram? $A = b \times h$

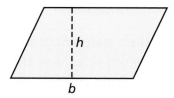

✓ Ongoing Assessment

Ask students to do the following: Draw a parallelogram. Cut your parallelogram into two pieces that will fit together without overlapping, to make a rectangle.

Practice with Parallelograms

 20 MINUTES

Goal: Calculate the area of parallelograms.

Materials: Student Activity Book or Hardcover Book pp. 110–111; Parallelograms (TRB M46); centimeter rulers (1 per student)

 NCTM Standards:
Geometry
Measurement

▶ Parallelograms and Rectangles

SMALL GROUPS

Refer to Student Book pages 110–111 as necessary to promote discussion about finding the area of parallelograms. Have students answer questions 5–12.

Practice Have students work independently or in **Small Groups** to find the area of parallelograms C, D, and E on TRB M46. Encourage them to use a method of their choice; they can cut out and rearrange each figure, or measure and calculate the area while leaving the parallelograms intact.

parallelogram C: $8 \times 3 = 24$ sq cm

parallelogram D: $5 \times 4 = 20$ sq cm

parallelogram E: $2 \times 9 = 18$ sq cm

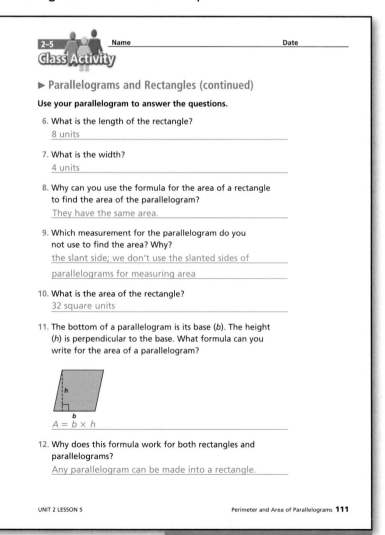

Student Activity Book page 110

Student Activity Book page 111

② Going Further

Extension: Change Dimensions

Goal: Explore how area and perimeter change when the base and height change.

Materials: MathBoard Materials, Student Activity Book p. 112 or Hardcover Book p. 112 and Activity Workbook p. 50

 NCTM Standards:
Geometry
Measurement
Reasoning and Proof

▶ Change Rectangle Dimensions

INDIVIDUALS

Have students draw three rectangles on their MathBoards and record the area of each. Then ask students to draw three rectangles that are twice as wide as the first rectangles and to record the area of each.

● **What pattern do you see?** Each rectangle in the second group is double the area of its original in the first group.

Students can then draw three rectangles twice as high as the second set of rectangles and record the area of each.

● **What pattern do you see now?** Each rectangle's area is double its previous area and four times its original area.

● **Why does this happen?** When you double one side, you double the rectangle's area; when you double the other side, you double its area again: 2 × 2 = 4.

Ask students to complete exercises 1–5 individually or in **Small Groups** for more practice with this concept.

Compare Perimeter and Area To help students compare change in area with change in perimeter, ask:

● **What do you need to do to the sides of a rectangle to double its perimeter?** double both sides

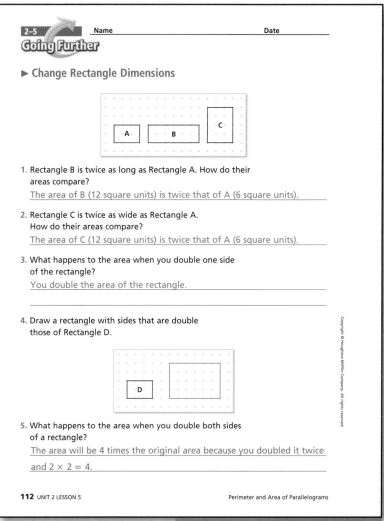

2-5
Going Further

▶ **Change Rectangle Dimensions**

1. Rectangle B is twice as long as Rectangle A. How do their areas compare?
   The area of B (12 square units) is twice that of A (6 square units).

2. Rectangle C is twice as wide as Rectangle A. How do their areas compare?
   The area of C (12 square units) is twice that of A (6 square units).

3. What happens to the area when you double one side of the rectangle?
   You double the area of the rectangle.

4. Draw a rectangle with sides that are double those of Rectangle D.

5. What happens to the area when you double both sides of a rectangle?
   The area will be 4 times the original area because you doubled it twice and 2 × 2 = 4.

112 UNIT 2 LESSON 5   Perimeter and Area of Parallelograms

Student Activity Book page 112

▶ Discuss These Situations

WHOLE CLASS   Math Talk

Have students give an example to support each of their answers to these questions:

● A rectangle measures 4 units by 5 units. How could you change the dimensions of the rectangle to double its area? double the length or double the width

● Each side of a square is 1 unit long. In order for the area of the square to be four times greater, how must the lengths of the sides change? each length must double

Differentiated Instruction

Intervention   Activity Card 2-5

Model Area   Activity Card 2-5

Work: By Yourself

Use:
• Drawing Figures (TRB M41)
• Scissors

1. Draw a rectangle on the Drawing Figures grid.

2. Determine the area of your rectangle.

3. Draw a slanted line on your rectangle as shown below. First, cut out the rectangle. Then cut it into two pieces along the slanted line.

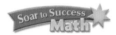

4. Rearrange the pieces without overlapping to create a parallelogram.

5. **Explain** Why is the area of the parallelogram formed exactly the same as that of the rectangle? Sample: Because the area did not change; it only changed positions.

Unit 2, Lesson 5   Copyright © Houghton Mifflin Company

Activity Note Students may experiment with cutting the same sized rectangle several different ways and comparing the results.

 Math Writing Prompt

Understand Area A rectangle has length 5 cm and width 3 cm. A parallelogram has base 5 cm and height 3 cm. Will the two figures have the same area? Explain your reasoning.

Soar to Success Math **Software Support**

Use *Soar to Success* for instruction of students needing targeted support for underlying skills.

On Level   Activity Card 2-5

Use Logic   Activity Card 2-5 ▲

Work: By Yourself

1. The figures below have the same height, and their bases are the same width.

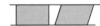

Do the figures have the same area? Explain your answer. See below.

2. Do the figures have the same perimeter? Explain your answer. See below.

1. Yes; Sample: A rectangle and a parallelogram with the same base and the same height have the same area.

2. No; Sample: The length of the side of the parallelogram is greater than the width of the rectangle, so the perimeter of the parallelogram will be greater.

Unit 2, Lesson 5   Copyright © Houghton Mifflin Company

Activity Note Be certain students can identify the base and the height of each figure.

 Math Writing Prompt

Compare How does the area of a square rhombus with 10-cm sides compare with the area of a non-square rhombus with 10-cm sides? Explain your thinking.

 Software Support

Use *MegaMath* for review and reinforcement of the concepts and skills presented in this lesson.

Challenge   Activity Card 2-5

Estimate Area   Activity Card 2-5 ■

Work: By Yourself

Use:
• Centimeter ruler

1. Select 3 flat objects in the classroom. Try to find at least one item that has a parallelogram shape.

2. Estimate the area of each object in square centimeters.

3. Measure the objects to the nearest centimeter, and use the measurements to calculate the approximate area.

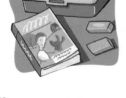

4. **Compare** How close are your estimates and your calculated areas? How could you make better estimates in the future?

Unit 2, Lesson 5   Copyright © Houghton Mifflin Company

Activity Note Remind students that, because they are measuring to the nearest centimeter, the areas they calculate are approximate rather than exact.

 Math Writing Prompt

Investigate Math Draw a parallelogram. Show the height. Why must the height be perpendicular to the base?

 DESTINATION Math **Software Support**

Use *Destination Math* to take students beyond the concepts and skills presented in this lesson.

③ Homework and Spiral Review

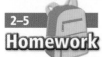

2–5

Homework **Goal:** Additional Practice

✔ Include students' work for page 81 as part of their portfolios.

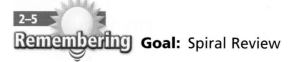

2–5

Remembering **Goal:** Spiral Review

This Remembering activity would be appropriate anytime after today's lesson.

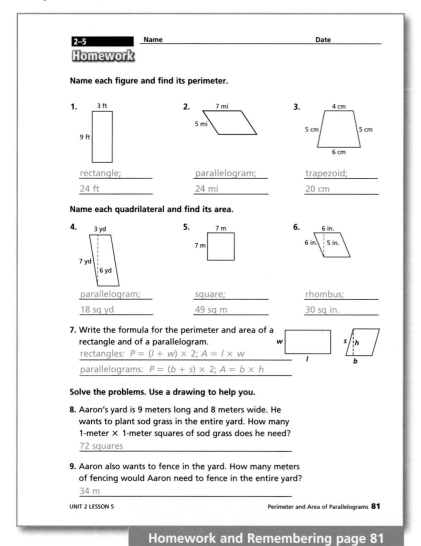

2–5 Name _____ Date _____
Homework

Name each figure and find its perimeter.

1. 3 ft / 9 ft
2. 7 mi / 5 mi
3. 4 cm / 5 cm / 5 cm / 6 cm

rectangle; 24 ft

parallelogram; 24 mi

trapezoid; 20 cm

Name each quadrilateral and find its area.

4. 3 yd / 7 yd / 6 yd
5. 7 m / 7 m
6. 6 in. / 6 in. / 5 in.

parallelogram; 18 sq yd

square; 49 sq m

rhombus; 30 sq in.

7. Write the formula for the perimeter and area of a rectangle and of a parallelogram.

rectangles: $P = (l + w) \times 2; A = l \times w$

parallelograms: $P = (b + s) \times 2; A = b \times h$

Solve the problems. Use a drawing to help you.

8. Aaron's yard is 9 meters long and 8 meters wide. He wants to plant sod grass in the entire yard. How many 1-meter × 1-meter squares of sod grass does he need?
72 squares

9. Aaron also wants to fence in the yard. How many meters of fencing would Aaron need to fence in the entire yard?
34 m

UNIT 2 LESSON 5   Perimeter and Area of Parallelograms **81**

Homework and Remembering page 81

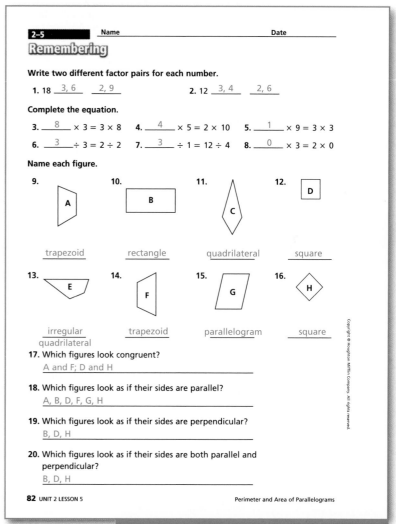

2–5 Name _____ Date _____
Remembering

Write two different factor pairs for each number.

1. 18 3, 6   2, 9   2. 12 3, 4   2, 6

Complete the equation.

3. __8__ × 3 = 3 × 8   4. __4__ × 5 = 2 × 10   5. __1__ × 9 = 3 × 3

6. __3__ ÷ 3 = 2 ÷ 2   7. __3__ ÷ 1 = 12 ÷ 4   8. __0__ × 3 = 2 × 0

Name each figure.

9. A
10. B
11. C
12. D

trapezoid   rectangle   quadrilateral   square

13. E
14. F
15. G
16. H

irregular quadrilateral   trapezoid   parallelogram   square

17. Which figures look congruent?
A and F; D and H

18. Which figures look as if their sides are parallel?
A, B, D, F, G, H

19. Which figures look as if their sides are perpendicular?
B, D, H

20. Which figures look as if their sides are both parallel and perpendicular?
B, D, H

82 UNIT 2 LESSON 5   Perimeter and Area of Parallelograms

Homework and Remembering page 82

Home or School Activity

Physical Education Connection

Quadrilaterals and Sports Ask students to list as many sports as possible that use quadrilaterals in some form (for example, in equipment or venue).

Ask students to select one item from the list and write a paragraph to describe why a quadrilateral is a good choice for that item.

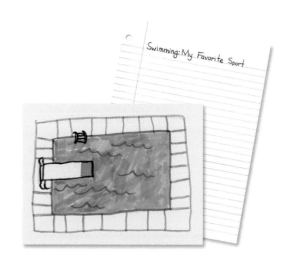

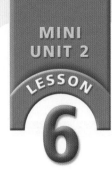

Perimeter and Area of Complex Figures

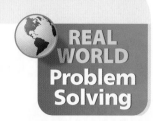

REAL WORLD Problem Solving

Vocabulary

rectangle
area
complex figure
perimeter
dimension

Lesson Objectives

● Compose and decompose complex figures.

● Find the perimeter and area of complex figures.

The Day at a Glance

Today's Goals	Materials
① Teaching the Lesson **A1:** Analyze the composition of complex figures and demonstrate how to find their perimeter and area. **A2:** Decompose complex figures. **A3:** Find the missing dimensions of complex figures. **② Going Further** ▸ Math Connection: Estimating Perimeter and Area ▸ Differentiated Instruction **③ Homework and Spiral Review**	**Lesson Activities** Student Activity Book pp. 113–116 or Student Hardcover Book pp. 113–116 and Activity Workbook pp. 51–52 Homework and Remembering pp. 83–84 Drawing Figures (TRB M41) Centimeter rulers (optional) Quick Quiz 2 (Assessment Guide) **Going Further** Centimeter-Grid Paper (TRB M60) Transparency of TRB M60 Overhead projector Activity Cards 2-6 Grid paper Math Journals

123 Use Math Talk today!

Keeping Skills Sharp

Daily Routines	English Language Learners
Homework Review If students give incorrect answers, have them explain how they found the answers. This can help you determine whether the error is conceptual or procedural. Add students' Homework to their portfolios. **Reasoning** A farmer is building a rectangular pen on one side of his barn. A 35-foot wall of the barn will form one side of the pen. A fence will form the other three sides of the pen. If the area of the pen will be 350 sq ft, how much fencing will the farmer need? 55 feet	Draw a rectangle, square, parallelogram, and trapezoid on the board. Ask students to name each of the quadrilaterals. Have students identify right angles, perpendicular and parallel lines in the quadrilaterals. • **Beginning** Point to a square. Say: **This quadrilateral is a square. It has 4 sides and 4 angles. Each of the angles is a right angle.** Have students repeat. • **Intermediate** Point to a square. Ask: **What type of quadrilateral is this?** square **How many sides are there?** 4 **How many angles?** 4 **What kind of angles are they?** right **How do you know?** line segments are perpendicular in a square • **Advanced** Have students say what type of angles are in a square. Make sure they understand that the perpendicular lines make the right angles. Have them explain which other quadrilaterals contain right angles.

① Teaching the Lesson

Activity 1

Explore Complex Figures

 15 MINUTES

Goal: Analyze the composition of complex figures and demonstrate how to find their perimeter and area.

Materials: Student Activity Book or Hardcover Book p. 113

✓ **NCTM Standards:**
Geometry
Measurement
Problem Solving

▶ Explore Complex Figures `WHOLE CLASS`

Invite students to read and discuss the problem about City Park's new wading pool at the top of Student Book page 113.

● What kinds of angles do you see in the figure of the new pool? right angles

● What shapes make up the new pool? rectangles

Be sure that students understand that a quadrilateral with right angles is made up of rectangles.

Next, examine questions 1–6 and have students answer them.

 Math Talk Together, discuss the answers to questions 7 and 8. Encourage students to explain how they know that the area of a complex figure is equal to the total of the areas of the figures that compose it, but that the perimeter of a complex figure is not equal to the total of the perimeters of the figures that compose it. They may offer such responses as:

● For area, you just add the area of the wading pool and the deep pool. You're adding the whole inside of the figure.

● But you can't do it the same way for perimeter. This time you're going all the way around the outside of the new figure. So you don't add the sides of the figures that are on the inside.

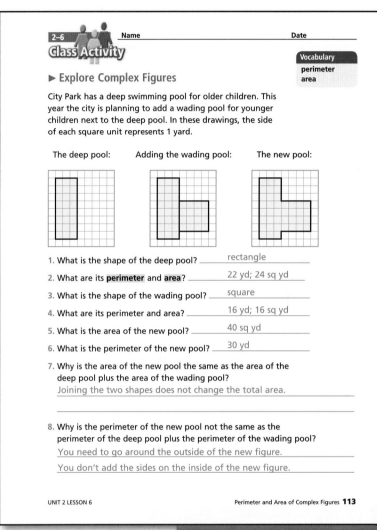

> **2–6**
> **Class Activity**
> Name _____ Date _____
> Vocabulary
> perimeter
> area
>
> ▶ Explore Complex Figures
>
> City Park has a deep swimming pool for older children. This year the city is planning to add a wading pool for younger children next to the deep pool. In these drawings, the side of each square unit represents 1 yard.
>
> The deep pool: Adding the wading pool: The new pool:
>
> 1. What is the shape of the deep pool? ___ rectangle ___
> 2. What are its **perimeter** and **area**? ___ 22 yd; 24 sq yd ___
> 3. What is the shape of the wading pool? ___ square ___
> 4. What are its perimeter and area? ___ 16 yd; 16 sq yd ___
> 5. What is the area of the new pool? ___ 40 sq yd ___
> 6. What is the perimeter of the new pool? ___ 30 yd ___
> 7. Why is the area of the new pool the same as the area of the deep pool plus the area of the wading pool?
>   Joining the two shapes does not change the total area.
>
> 8. Why is the perimeter of the new pool not the same as the perimeter of the deep pool plus the perimeter of the wading pool?
>   You need to go around the outside of the new figure.
>   You don't add the sides on the inside of the new figure.
>
> UNIT 2 LESSON 6   Perimeter and Area of Complex Figures **113**

Student Activity Book page 113

Activity 2

Decompose Complex Figures

20 MINUTES

Goal: Decompose complex figures.

Materials: Student Activity Book pp. 114–115 or Hardcover Book pp. 114–115 and Activity Workbook p. 51; centimeter rulers (optional)

 NCTM Standards:
Geometry
Measurement

▶ Perimeter and Area of Complex Figures [WHOLE CLASS]

Ask students to measure the sides of figure 9 on Student Book page 114. Each unit square of the grid is 1 cm × 1 cm, so students can either count the units of perimeter or use their centimeter rulers and measure whole units.

● **How can you find the perimeter?** I can find the perimeter by adding all of the sides.

● **How can you find the area?** I can find the area by finding the rectangles inside the shape, finding the area of each rectangle, and adding the areas together.

There is more than one way to decompose any complex figure. Invite students to share their different solutions.

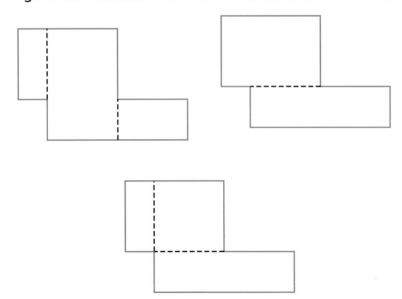

Have students work independently or in **Small Groups** with figures 10 and 11. When they are finished, invite them to share their solutions.

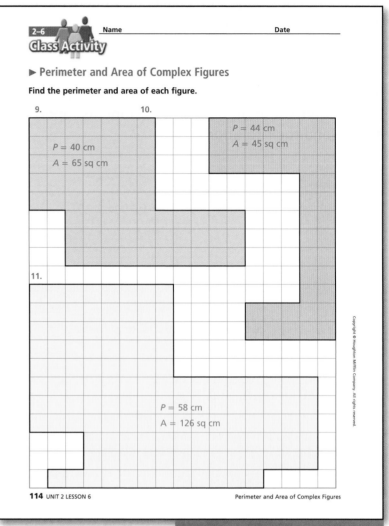

2–6
Class Activity
Name _____ Date _____

▶ Perimeter and Area of Complex Figures

Find the perimeter and area of each figure.

9.   10.

$P = 40$ cm
$A = 65$ sq cm

$P = 44$ cm
$A = 45$ sq cm

11.

$P = 58$ cm
$A = 126$ sq cm

114 UNIT 2 LESSON 6   Perimeter and Area of Complex Figures

Student Activity Book page 114

Teaching Note

Watch For! Students may say that they can figure out the area simply by counting squares. Ask them if they can think of another way and encourage discussion of which way is faster and why.

Activity continued ▶

Perimeter and Area of Complex Figures **261**

Activity 2

In **Small Groups**, have students work on exercises 12–16 on Student Book page 115. Challenge students to find the perimeter and area of each figure.

 Math Talk Invite each group to share with the rest of the class its solutions to one of the figures. Encourage the use of math talk as students report on and defend their solutions.

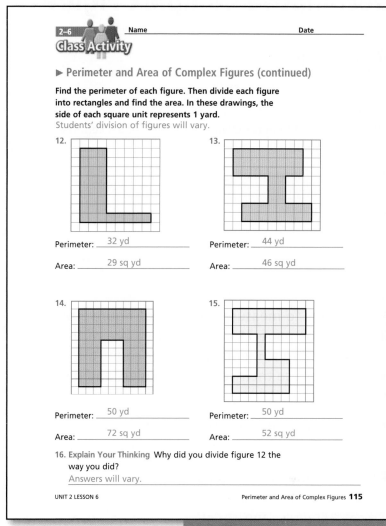

2–6
Class Activity
Name _____ Date _____

▶ **Perimeter and Area of Complex Figures** (continued)

Find the perimeter of each figure. Then divide each figure into rectangles and find the area. In these drawings, the side of each square unit represents 1 yard.
Students' division of figures will vary.

12.

Perimeter: ____32 yd____

Area: ____29 sq yd____

13.

Perimeter: ____44 yd____

Area: ____46 sq yd____

14.

Perimeter: ____50 yd____

Area: ____72 sq yd____

15.

Perimeter: ____50 yd____

Area: ____52 sq yd____

16. **Explain Your Thinking** Why did you divide figure 12 the way you did?
Answers will vary.

UNIT 2 LESSON 6   Perimeter and Area of Complex Figures **115**

Student Activity Book page 115

✓ Ongoing Assessment

Ask students to draw two rectangles and to find the area and perimeter of each. Then have students cut out the rectangles and join them along one side. Finally, have students find the area and perimeter of the new complex figure.

Practice with Complex Figures

 20 MINUTES

Goal: Find the missing dimensions of complex figures.

Materials: Student Activity Book p. 116 or Hardcover Book p. 116 and Activity Workbook p. 52; Drawing Figures 1 (TRB M41)

 NCTM Standards:
Geometry
Measurement
Representation

▶ Find the Missing Dimensions
WHOLE CLASS

Have the students discuss how to find, and then find, the missing dimensions of the figures in exercise 17 on Student Book page 116.

● **What do you know about all the angles in the figures?** They are all right angles.

● **What does the information about the angles tell you about the smaller figures that make up the larger figure?** The larger figure is made of rectangles.

● **What do you know about opposite sides of rectangles?** They are parallel and congruent.

Students may respond:

● In figure A, the long side up and down the left is 9 inches. The other three up-and-down sides must add up to 9 inches.

● That means the length of the missing up-and-down side must be 9 − 6 = 3 inches.

● The short side at the very top is 2 inches, so the short side exactly opposite it must be 2 inches, too.

● That's true for the last missing side. It has to be congruent to the 5-inch side above it.

Ask students to complete exercises 18 and 19.

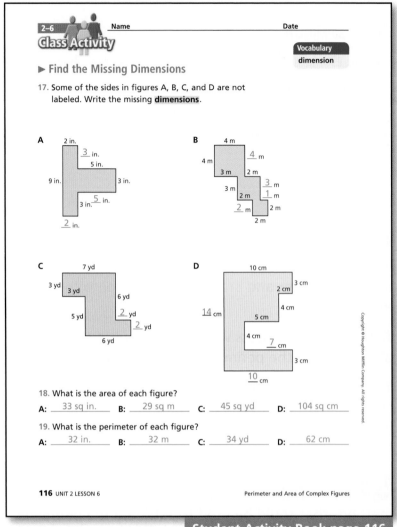

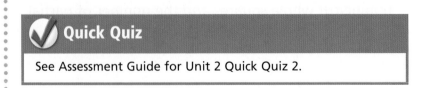

Student Activity Book page 116

▶ Draw and Find the Perimeter and Area of Complex Figures SMALL GROUPS

Students can work independently or in **Small Groups**.

Distribute Drawing Figures 1 (TRB M41) and challenge students to draw several different complex figures on the grid. Then ask them to find the perimeter and area of their figures. Invite as many students as possible to share their figures and solutions with the rest of the class.

✓ **Quick Quiz**

See Assessment Guide for Unit 2 Quick Quiz 2.

② Going Further

Math Connection: Estimating Perimeter and Area

 30 MINUTES

Goal: Estimate the perimeter and area of irregular shapes.

Materials: Centimeter-Grid Paper (TRB M60), transparency of TRB M60 and overhead projector

✓ **NCTM Standards:**
  Geometry
  Measurement
  Reasoning and Proof

▶ Discuss Different Methods | WHOLE CLASS |

In this activity, students will connect what they know about perimeter and area with estimation of perimeter and area.

Ask for Ideas Discuss with students what they recall about finding the perimeter and the area of a figure.

Then place a transparency of Centimeter-Grid Paper (TRB M60) on the overhead. Point out that the grid is a centimeter grid. Draw a closed curve on the transparency.

Math Talk Have students describe different methods that could be used to estimate the perimeter and the area of the shape. The following questions can be used to prompt the discussion.

● An estimate is an approximation, not an exact answer. Why is it difficult to estimate the perimeter of this shape? The edge of the shape is not always on a grid line.

● If we estimate the area of this shape by counting the number of whole squares that are inside the shape, will our answer be greater or less the actual area? Explain why. less; partial squares were not counted

● If we estimate the area of this shape by counting the number of whole squares *and* the number of partial squares, will our answer be greater or less the actual area? Explain why. greater; partial squares were counted as whole squares

Draw a rectangle around the entire shape. Ask students to name the perimeter and the area of the rectangle.

● Drawing one rectangle around the shape is a way to estimate its perimeter and its area. How could we use more than one rectangle to make more accurate estimates? Cover the shape with a number of smaller, non-overlapping rectangles; add the perimeters and areas of the rectangles to estimate the perimeter and area of the entire shape.

Distribute Centimeter-Grid Paper (TRB M60).

▶ Make Estimates | PAIRS |

Have one member of each pair place a hand (with fingers touching) on the copymaster while the partner traces its outline. **Student Pairs** work together to make an estimate of the perimeter and an estimate of the area.

Repeat the activity by having the other member of the pair place the Centimeter-Grid Paper on the floor and place a foot on the copymaster. The partner traces the outline, and **Student Pairs** again work together to estimate the perimeter and the area.

After the activities have been completed, have students share their estimates.

Intervention   Activity Card 2-6

Draw a Picture   Activity Card 2-6 ●

Work: By Yourself

Use:
• Grid paper

1. Look at this complex figure. The top rectangle measures 3 units by 5 units and the bottom rectangle measures 4 units by 2 units.

2. Draw the two rectangles on your grid paper to form the complex figure shown.

3. Determine the perimeter and the area of the figure. *P* = 22 units; *A* = 23 sq units

4. Use the same two rectangles to draw a different complex figure. Determine its perimeter and area. Check students' work.

5. **Compare** How do the perimeter and area of the figures in step 3 relate to those you drew in step 4? Areas are equal. Perimeters may vary.

Unit 2, Lesson 6   Copyright © Houghton Mifflin Company

Activity Note Point out that there are many ways to make a complex figure with two rectangles.

✎ Math Writing Prompt

Understand Complex Figures When you join two or more rectangles to make a complex figure, you add the areas of the rectangles. Why is it important that the rectangles do not overlap when they are joined?

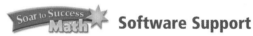 **Software Support**

Use *Soar to Success* for instruction of students needing targeted support for underlying skills.

On Level   Activity Card 2-6

The Smallest Perimeter   Activity Card 2-6 ▲

Work: By Yourself

Use:
• Grid paper

1. In this complex figure one rectangle measures 3 units by 5 units and the other measures 2 units by 4 units.

2. Use the same two rectangles to draw another complex figure. Be sure that the rectangles do not overlap. What is the perimeter of your complex figure?

3. Use the same two rectangles to draw the complex figure with the smallest possible perimeter. 20 units,

4 units

Unit 2, Lesson 6   Copyright © Houghton Mifflin Company

Activity Note The greater the number of units along the segment where the rectangles are joined, the smaller the perimeter.

✎ Math Writing Prompt

Explain Your Thinking Draw two complex figures with the same area and different perimeters. Explain why the perimeters are different.

MegaMath **Software Support**

Use *MegaMath* for review and reinforcement of the concepts and skills presented in this lesson.

Challenge   Activity Card 2-6

Estimate Area   Activity Card 2-6 ■

Work: In Pairs

Use:
• Centimeter-grid paper

1. Look at this closed curve. If you count the squares within the curve you will see that its area is about 65 sq units. Draw a different closed curve on your own grid paper, and make an estimate of its area.

2. Exchange drawings with your partner, and estimate the area of your partner's drawing.

3. Compare the estimates for both drawings.

4. **Math Talk** Discuss the methods you used to make each estimate. Decide which method is most accurate.

Unit 2, Lesson 6   Copyright © Houghton Mifflin Company

Activity Note A simple method for estimating the area is to count the whole squares. A more precise method is to count the whole and partial squares.

✎ Math Writing Prompt

Investigate Math Sketch three non-congruent rectangles, each with a perimeter of 12 cm and a whole-number length. Describe the rectangle that has the greatest area.

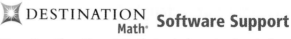 **Software Support**

Use *Destination Math* to take students beyond the concepts and skills presented in this lesson.

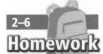

③ Homework and Spiral Review

Homework **Goal:** Additional Practice

✓ Include students' work for page 83 as part of their portfolios.

Remembering **Goal:** Spiral Review

This Remembering activity would be appropriate anytime after today's lesson.

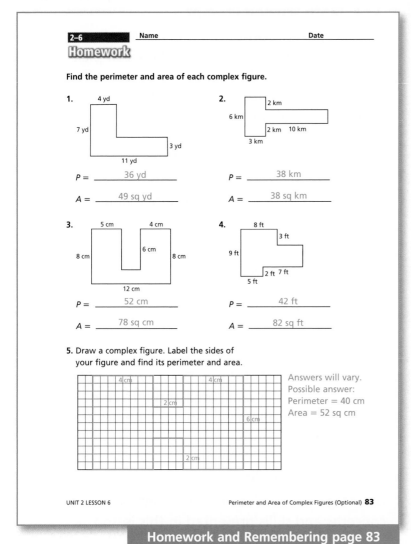

2–6　Name _____ Date _____
Homework

Find the perimeter and area of each complex figure.

1.
4 yd
7 yd
3 yd
11 yd
P = ____36 yd____
A = ____49 sq yd____

2.
2 km
6 km
2 km　10 km
3 km
P = ____38 km____
A = ____38 sq km____

3.
5 cm　4 cm
8 cm　6 cm　8 cm
12 cm
P = ____52 cm____
A = ____78 sq cm____

4.
8 ft
3 ft
9 ft
2 ft　7 ft
5 ft
P = ____42 ft____
A = ____82 sq ft____

5. Draw a complex figure. Label the sides of your figure and find its perimeter and area.

4 cm　4 cm
2 cm
6 cm
2 cm

Answers will vary. Possible answer: Perimeter = 40 cm Area = 52 sq cm

UNIT 2 LESSON 6　　Perimeter and Area of Complex Figures (Optional) **83**

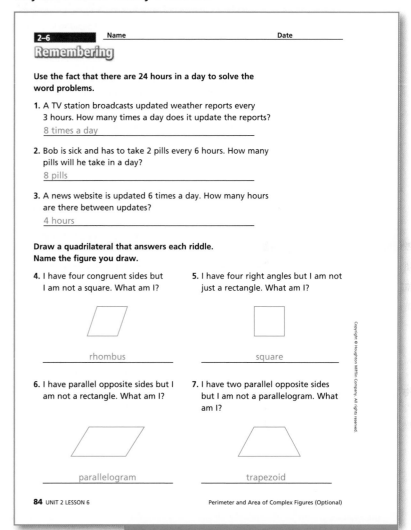

2–6　Name _____ Date _____
Remembering

Use the fact that there are 24 hours in a day to solve the word problems.

1. A TV station broadcasts updated weather reports every 3 hours. How many times a day does it update the reports?
____8 times a day____

2. Bob is sick and has to take 2 pills every 6 hours. How many pills will he take in a day?
____8 pills____

3. A news website is updated 6 times a day. How many hours are there between updates?
____4 hours____

Draw a quadrilateral that answers each riddle. Name the figure you draw.

4. I have four congruent sides but I am not a square. What am I?
____rhombus____

5. I have four right angles but I am not just a rectangle. What am I?
____square____

6. I have parallel opposite sides but I am not a rectangle. What am I?
____parallelogram____

7. I have two parallel opposite sides but I am not a parallelogram. What am I?
____trapezoid____

84 UNIT 2 LESSON 6　　Perimeter and Area of Complex Figures (Optional)

Homework and Remembering page 83

Homework and Remembering page 84

Home or School Activity

 Social Studies Connection

Maps Have students locate and examine a map of the United States. Have them answer the following questions: Which states are in the shape of a rectangle? If you straighten out the borders, which states look like complex figures made of rectangles?

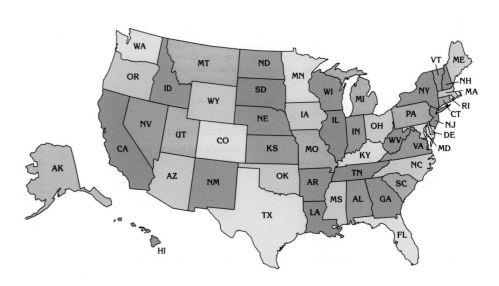

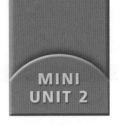

Unit Review and Test

Lesson Objective
● **Assess student progress on unit objectives.**

The Day at a Glance

Today's Goals	Materials
① **Assessing the Unit** ▶ Assess student progress on unit objectives. ▶ Use activities from unit lessons to reteach content. ② **Extending the Assessment** ▶ Use remediation for common errors. There is no homework assignment on a test day.	Unit 2 Test, Student Activity Book pp. 117–118 or Student Hardcover Book pp. 117–118 and Activity Workbook p. 53 Unit 2 Test, Form A or B, Assessment Guide (optional) Unit 2 Performance Assessment, Assessment Guide (optional)

Keeping Skills Sharp

Daily Routines 🕐 5 MINUTES	
If you are doing a unit review day, go over the homework. If this is a test day, omit the homework review.	**Review and Test Day** You may want to choose a quiet game or other activity (reading a book or working on homework for another subject) for students who finish early.

Assessing the Unit

Assess Unit Objectives

🕐 **45 MINUTES** (more if schedule permits)

Goal: Assess student progress on unit objectives.

Materials: Student Activity Book pp. 117–118 or Hardcover Book pp. 117–118 and Activity Workbook p. 53; Assessment Guide (optional)

▶ Review and Assessment

If your students are ready for assessment on the unit objectives, you may use either the test on the Student Book pages or one of the forms of the Unit 2 Test in the Assessment Guide to assess student progress.

If you feel that students need some review first, you may use the test on the Student Book pages as a review of unit content, and then use one of the forms of the Unit 2 Test in the Assessment Guide to assess student progress.

To assign a numerical score for all of these test forms, use 10 points for each question.

You may also choose to use the Unit 2 Performance Assessment. Scoring for that assessment can be found in its rubric in the Assessment Guide.

▶ Reteaching Resources

The chart at the right lists the test items, the unit objectives they cover, and the lesson activities in which the objective is covered in this unit. You may revisit these activities with students who do not show mastery of the objectives.

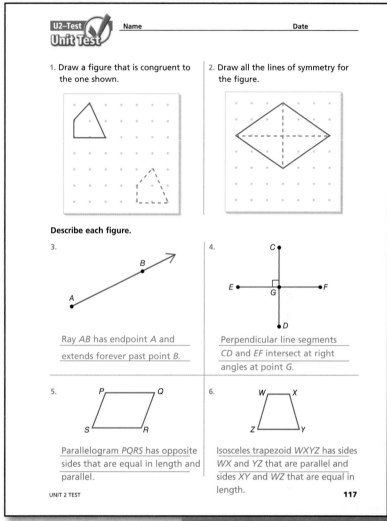

Student Activity Book page 117

Unit Test Items	Unit Objectives Tested	Activities to Use for Reteaching
1, 7	**2.1** Identify congruent and similar figures.	Lesson 1, Activities 1–2
2	**2.2** Identify figures that have lines of symmetry.	Lesson 1, Activity 3
3–6	**2.3** Identify lines, line segments, rays, and quadrilaterals.	Lesson 2, Activity 3 Lesson 3, Activity 2
8–10	**2.4** Find perimeter and area of quadrilaterals and complex figures.	Lesson 4, Activity 3 Lesson 5, Activities 1–2 Lesson 6, Activity 2

U2–Test
Unit Test

Name _____ Date _____

Circle two shapes that appear to be similar.

7.

Find the perimeter and area of each figure. Show your work.

8.

2 ft
10 ft
3 ft
6 ft
8 ft

Perimeter _42 ft_____

Area _74 sq ft_____

Solve each problem.

Show your work.

9. A parallelogram has a base of 10 cm. Its perimeter is 30 cm. What are the lengths of the other three sides?

Answer _5 cm, 10 cm, 5 cm_____

10. **Extended Response** A square has an area of 25 sq ft. What is the length of one side? Sketch a picture and explain your reasoning.

The sides of a square are the same length.

Let the length of each side equal s. Then

$s \times s = 25$ is my equation. I know that

$5 \times 5 = 25$, so $s = 5$. The sides are 5 ft long.

_____

_____

* Item 10 also assesses the process skills of Communication and Reasoning and Proof.

118 UNIT 2 TEST

Student Activity Book page 118

▶ Assessment Resources

Free Response Tests
Unit 2 Test, Student Activity Book pp. 117–118 or Hardcover Book pp. 117–118 and Activity Workbook p. 53
Unit 2 Test, Form A, Assessment Guide

Extended Response Item
The last item in the Student Book test and in the Form A test will require an extended response as an answer.

Multiple Choice Test
Unit 2 Test, Form B, Assessment Guide

Performance Assessment
Unit 2 Performance Assessment, Assessment Guide
Unit 2 Performance Assessment Rubric, Assessment Guide

▶ Portfolio Assessment

Teacher-selected Items for Student Portfolios:

- Homework, Lessons 3, 4, 5, and 6

- Class Activity work, Lessons 1, 4, and 6

Student-selected Items for Student Portfolios

- Favorite Home or School Activity

- Best Writing Prompt

② Extending the Assessment

Unit Objective 2.1
Identify congruent and similar figures.

Common Error: Inability to Determine Congruence

Students may fail to recognize congruence, or lack of congruence, of two figures, especially if they are flipped or turned.

Remediation Encourage such students to trace one figure on tracing paper and to slide or turn the traced figure to see if it fits exactly on the other figure. Remind students that all congruent figures are also similar. But not all similar figures are congruent.

Unit Objective 2.2
Identify figures that have lines of symmetry.

Common Error: Identifies Too Few Lines of Symmetry

Students may identify some, but not all, of the lines of symmetry of a figure. For example, they may recognize the vertical and horizontal symmetry lines of a square, but not the symmetry lines along the diagonals.

Remediation Suggest that they draw a vertical line and position their figure so the line goes down the middle of it. Then they can turn their figures and recognize when the parts on each side of the line look exactly the same.

Unit Objective 2.3
Identify lines, line segments, rays, and quadrilaterals.

Common Error: Misidentifies Perpendicular Lines

Students may not recognize a right angle unless two line segments cross to form four right angles.

Remediation Demonstrate that the intersection of a ray and a line may create only two right angles. Have students use an index card or a protractor to help decide if an angle is a right angle. Remind students that a right-angle symbol should be used to show perpendicularity.

Common Error: Doesn't Differentiate Kinds of Quadrilaterals

Students may fail to see a difference between two types of quadrilaterals. For example, a square may be identified only as a rhombus unless it is positioned horizontally on a side.

Remediation Make side-by-side lists comparing the properties of the different figures, including the kinds of angles and lines used to make each one. Position figures in various ways to help recognize their properties.

Unit Objective 2.4
Find perimeter and area of quadrilaterals and complex figures.

Common Error: Does Not Label Answers Correctly

Some students do not remember to label their answers with the correct units, such as square units for area.

Remediation Remind students that answers must show the units used. For example, an answer of 3 might mean 3 cm or 3 dm, and this is especially important if dimensions are given in different units. They should also check their answers by looking back at the problem to verify that they have used the correct unit.

Common Error: Includes Part of the Area More Than Once

When decomposing a complex figure, students may include part of the area more than once.

Remediation Remind students that they first separate the figure into smaller parts for which they can find the area. Suggest that they shade or mark each part of the complex figure as they find its area to prevent including it in another part. They might even write in the area for each part of the figure.

Place Value and Multi-Digit Addition and Subtraction

UNIT 3 DEVELOPS the concepts of grouping and ungrouping numbers as a key step in performing multi-digit addition and subtraction. The activities in this unit help students gain practical understanding of addition and subtraction and the relationship between the two operations. Estimation and mental math provide students with a method to validate their answers.

Skills Trace

Grade 3	Grade 4	Grade 5
• Understand place value through ten thousands.	• Understand place value through millions.	• Understand place value through billions.
• Compare and order whole numbers through ten thousands.	• Compare and order whole numbers through millions.	• Compare and order whole numbers through billions.
• Round whole numbers to estimate.	• Round whole numbers to estimate.	• Round whole numbers to estimate.
• Use the Commutative Property and the Associative Property of Addition.	• Use the Commutative Property and the Associative Property of Addition.	• Use the Commutative Property and the Associative Property of Addition.
• Solve two-step problems.	• Solve multistep problems.	• Solve multistep problems.
• Add and subtract whole numbers to ten thousands.	• Add and subtract whole numbers to millions.	• Add and subtract whole numbers to billions.
• Write equations and inequalities.	• Write equations and inequalities.	• Write equations and inequalities.

Unit 3   Contents

Unit 3   Assessment

✓ Unit Objectives Tested	Unit Test Items	Lessons
3.1 Solve a variety of problems involving addition and subtraction.	1–6	1–6, 20–21
3.2 Read, write, and identify the place value of numbers to millions.	7–10	7, 10
3.3 Compare, order, and round numbers; estimate sums and differences.	11–14	8–9, 13, 18–19
3.4 Add and subtract whole numbers.	15–20	11–12, 14–18

Assessment and Review Resources

Formal Assessment	Informal Assessment	Review Opportunities

Formal Assessment

Student Activity Book
- Unit Review and Test (pp. 179–180)

Assessment Guide
- Quick Quiz 1
- Quick Quiz 2
- Quick Quiz 3
- Quick Quiz 4
- Test A–Open Response
- Test B–Multiple Choice
- Performance Assessment

Test Generator CD–ROM
- Open Response Test
- Multiple Choice Test
- Test Bank Items

Informal Assessment

Teacher Edition
- Ongoing Assessment (in every lesson)
- Quick Practice (in every lesson)
- Math Talk (in every lesson)
- Portfolio Suggestions (pp. 286, 300, 324, 350, 388, 432)

📱 Math Talk
- ▸ The Learning Classroom (pp. 273, 284, 288, 302, 304, 308, 327, 348, 357, 372, 391, 409, 416, 423)
- ▸ Math Talk in Action (pp. 281, 282, 337, 371)
- ▸ Activities (pp. 272, 273, 274, 280, 288, 294, 297, 298, 302, 304, 317, 326, 332, 345, 347, 352, 363, 368, 378, 385, 390, 394, 398, 401, 406, 416, 418, 424)
- ▸ Solve and Discuss (pp. 272, 275, 283, 289, 295, 298, 302, 303, 304, 312, 317, 321, 332, 363, 369, 378, 390, 393, 414, 418)
- ▸ Student Pairs (pp. 358, 418, 424)
- ▸ Student Leaders (pp. 287, 293, 301, 303, 307, 315, 325, 335)
- ▸ Small Groups (p. 328, 386)
- ▸ Helping Partners (pp. 298, 378, 386, 424)
- ▸ Scenarios (pp. 348, 358)

Review Opportunities

Homework and Remembering
- Review of recently taught topics
- Cumulative Review

Teacher Edition
- Unit Review and Test (pp. 433–436)

Test Generator CD-ROM
- Custom review sheets

Planning Unit 3

Lesson/NCTM Standards	Resources	Materials for Lesson Activities	Materials for Other Activities
3–1 **Understand Equality** NCTM Standards: 1, 2, 8	TE pp. 271–278 SAB pp.119–124 H&R pp. 85–86 AC 3-1		✓Counters Math Journals
3–2 **Addition and Subtraction Change Problems** NCTM Standards: 2, 6, 8	TE pp. 279–286 SAB pp. 125–126 H&R pp. 87–88 AC 3-2		✓Counters Math Journals
3–3 **Addition and Subtraction Collection Problems** NCTM Standards: 1, 2, 8,10	TE pp. 287–292 SAB pp. 127–130 H&R pp. 89–90 AC 3-3		✓Counters Math Journals
3–4 **Addition and Subtraction Comparison Problems** NCTM Standards: 1, 2, 10	TE pp. 293–300 SAB pp. 131–134 H&R pp. 91–92 AC 3-4		Math Journals
3–5 **Two-Step Problems Using Addition and Subtraction** NCTM Standards: 1, 2, 6	TE pp. 301–306 SAB pp. 135–136 H&R pp. 93–94 AC 3-5		Markers (2-colors) Number Lines Encyclopedia Almanac Computer with Internet access Math Journals
3–6 **Mixed Word Problems** NCTM Standards: 1, 6, 7	TE pp. 307–314 SAB pp. 137–138 H&R pp. 95–96 AG Quick Quiz 1 AC 3-6		Math Journals
3–7 **Place Value to Thousands** NCTM Standards: 1, 2, 10	TE pp. 315–324 SAB pp. 139–144 H&R pp. 97–98 AC 3-7	MathBoard or MathBoard Dot Array (TRB M47) Dry-erase markers Dry-erase materials ✓Base-ten blocks (optional)	✓Number cubes Math Journals
3–8 **Read, Write, and Round Numbers** NCTM Standards: 1, 2, 10	TE pp. 325–334 SAB pp. 144A–146 H&R pp. 99–100 AC 3-8	Secret Code Cards (TRB M145–M146) Place Value to Thousands transparency (TRB M49) Rounding Concepts (TRB M53) MathBoard Dot Array (TRB M47) Envelope or plastic bag Scissors MathBoard Materials	Index cards Math Journals

Resources/Materials Key: TE: Teacher Edition   SAB: Student Activity Book   H&R: Homework and Remembering
AC: Activity Cards   MCC: Math Center Challenge   AG: Assessment Guide   ✓: Grade 4 Kit   TRB: Teacher's Resource Book

Planning Unit 3 (Continued)

NCTM Standards Key: **1.** Number and Operations **2.** Algebra **3.** Geometry **4.** Measurement **5.** Data Analysis and Probability **6.** Problem Solving **7.** Reasoning and Proof **8.** Communication **9.** Connections **10.** Representation

Lesson/NCTM Standards	Resources	Materials for Lesson Activities	Materials for Other Activities
3–9 **Compare Whole Numbers** NCTM Standards: 1, 2, 7, 8	TE pp. 335–342 SAB pp. 147–150 H&R pp. 101–102 AC 3-9	Comparing Numbers transparency (TRB M50) MathBoard Materials Overhead projector	Number Lines (TRB M51) Math Journals
3–10 **Numbers to Millions** NCTM Standards: 1, 2, 6, 8, 10	TE pp. 343–350 SAB pp. 151–152A H&R pp. 103–104 AG Quick Quiz 2 AC 3-10	Reading and Writing Millions (TRB M146) (optional) Secret Code Cards (TRB M48) MathBoard Materials	Scissors Math Journals
3–11 **Make New Groups for Addition** NCTM Standards: 1, 2, 6, 8, 10	TE pp. 351–360 SAB p. 153–154 H&R pp. 105–106 AC 3-11	MathBoard Materials ✓Base-ten blocks (optional)	✓Play money ✓Base-ten blocks Math Journals
3–12 **Addition to Millions** NCTM Standards: 1, 8	TE pp. 361–366 SAB pp. 155–156 H&R pp. 107–108 AC 3-12		Grid paper ✓Number cubes Math Journals
3–13 **Estimation and Mental Math** NCTM Standards: 1, 6, 8,	TE pp. 367–374 SAB pp. 157–158 H&R pp. 109–110 AG Quick Quiz 3 AC 3-13	Calculators (optional)	✓Number cubes Math Journals
3–14 **Subtract From Hundreds** NCTM Standards: 1, 2, 8	TE pp. 375–380 SAB pp. 159–162 H&R pp. 111–112 AC 3-14	MathBoard Materials	✓Base-ten blocks MathBoard Materials Math Journals
3–15 **Subtraction Undoes Addition** NCTM Standards: 1, 2, 8	TE pp. 381–388 SAB pp. 163–164 H&R pp. 113–114 AC 3-15	MathBoard Materials ✓Base-ten blocks (optional)	Index cards Math Journals
3–16 **Ungroup for Any Subtraction** NCTM Standards: 1, 2, 6, 8, 10	TE pp. 389–396 SAB p. 165–166 H&R pp. 115–116 AC 3-16	MathBoard Materials ✓Base-ten blocks (optional)	✓Play money ✓Counters ✓Number cubes MathBoard Materials Math Journals

Lesson/NCTM Standards	Resources	Materials for Lesson Activities	Materials for Other Activities
3–17 **Subtract From Thousands** NCTM Standards: 1, 2, 8, 10	TE pp. 397–404 SAB pp. 167–168 H&R pp. 117–118 AC 3-17	MathBoard Materials	MathBoard Materials Grid paper Math Journals
3–18 **Subtract Larger Numbers** NCTM Standards: 1, 6, 8	TE pp. 405–412 SAB p. 169–170 H&R pp. 119–120 AC 3-18	MathBoard Materials	MathBoard Materials ✓Number cubes Math Journals
3–19 **Estimate With Real-World Situations** NCTM Standards: 1, 6, 8, 9	TE pp. 413–420 SAB pp. 171–174 H&R pp. 121–122 AC 3-19	Calculators (optional)	Index cards Math Journals
3–20 **Problem Solving With Larger Numbers** NCTM Standards: 1, 2, 6, 8	TE pp. 421–426 SAB pp. 175–176 H&R pp. 123–124 AG Quick Quiz 4 AC 3-20		Math Journals
3–21 **Use Mathematical Processes** NCTM Standards: 6, 7, 8, 9, 10	TE pp. 427–432 SAB pp. 177–178 H&R pp. 125–126 AC 3-21	Centimeter-Grid Paper (TRB M60)	Centimeter-Grid Paper (TRB M60) Paper bag Small blocks or other small objects Math Journals
Unit Review and Test	TE pp. 433–436 SAB pp. 179–180 AG Unit 3 tests		

Hardcover Student Book/Activity Workbook	Manipulatives and Materials
• Together, the hardcover student book and its companion Activity Workbook contain all of the pages in the consumable Student Activity Workbook.	• Essential materials for teaching Math Expressions are available in the Grade 4 Kit. These materials are indicated by a ✓ in these lists. At the front of this Teacher Edition is more information about kit contents, alternatives for the materials, and use of the materials.

Independent Learning Activities

Ready-Made Math Challenge Centers

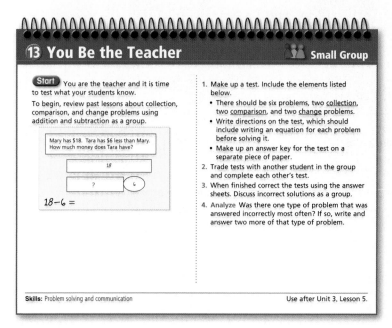

13 You Be the Teacher — Small Group

Start You are the teacher and it is time to test what your students know.

To begin, review past lessons about collection, comparison, and change problems using addition and subtraction as a group.

Mary has $18. Tara has $6 less than Mary. How much money does Tara have?

18

? 6

18 − 6 =

1. Make up a test. Include the elements listed below.
   • There should be six problems, two collection, two comparison, and two change problems.
   • Write directions on the test, which should include writing an equation for each problem before solving it.
   • Make up an answer key for the test on a separate piece of paper.
2. Trade tests with another student in the group and complete each other's test.
3. When finished correct the tests using the answer sheets. Discuss incorrect solutions as a group.
4. Analyze Was there one type of problem that was answered incorrectly most often? If so, write and answer two more of that type of problem.

Skills: Problem solving and communication Use after Unit 3, Lesson 5.

Grouping Small Groups

Materials Textbook

Objective Students deepen their understanding of collection, change, and compare situations by making up problems.

Connections Communications and Problem Solving

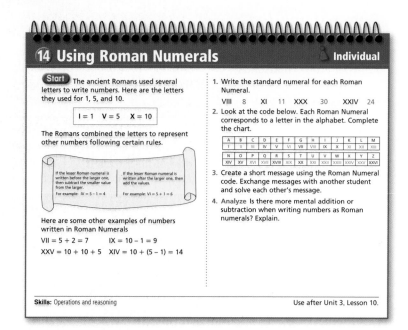

14 Using Roman Numerals — Individual

Start The ancient Romans used several letters to write numbers. Here are the letters they used for 1, 5, and 10.

I = 1   V = 5   X = 10

The Romans combined the letters to represent other numbers following certain rules.

If the lesser Roman numeral is written before the larger one, then subtract the smaller value from the larger.
For example: IV = 5 − 1 = 4

If the lesser Roman numeral is written after the larger one, then add the values.
For example: VI = 5 + 1 = 6

Here are some other examples of numbers written in Roman Numerals

VII = 5 + 2 = 7   IX = 10 − 1 = 9
XXV = 10 + 10 + 5   XIV = 10 + (5 − 1) = 14

1. Write the standard numeral for each Roman Numeral.
   VIII 8   XI 11   XXX 30   XXIV 24
2. Look at the code below. Each Roman Numeral corresponds to a letter in the alphabet. Complete the chart.

A	B	C	D	E	F	G	H	I	J	K	L	M
I	II	III	IV	V	VI	VII	VIII	IX	X	XI	XII	XIII

N	O	P	Q	R	S	T	U	V	W	X	Y	Z
XIV	XV	XVI	XVII	XVIII	XIX	XX	XXI	XXII	XXIII	XXIV	XXV	XXVI

3. Create a short message using the Roman Numeral code. Exchange messages with another student and solve each other's message.
4. Analyze Is there more mental addition or subtraction when writing numbers as Roman numerals? Explain.

Skills: Operations and reasoning Use after Unit 3, Lesson 10.

Grouping Individual

Objective Students investigate Roman numerals and their relationship to standard numbers.

Connections Number and Social Studies

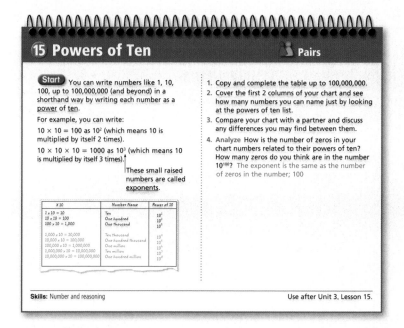

15 Powers of Ten — Pairs

Start You can write numbers like 1, 10, 100, up to 100,000,000 (and beyond) in a shorthand way by writing each number as a power of ten.

For example, you can write:

$10 \times 10 = 100$ as 10^2 (which means 10 is multiplied by itself 2 times).

$10 \times 10 \times 10 = 1000$ as 10^3 (which means 10 is multiplied by itself 3 times).

These small raised numbers are called exponents.

X 10	Number Name	Power of 10
1 × 10 = 10	Ten	10^1
10 × 10 = 100	One hundred	10^2
100 × 10 = 1,000	One thousand	10^3
1,000 × 10 = 10,000	Ten thousand	10^4
10,000 × 10 = 100,000	One hundred thousand	10^5
100,000 × 10 = 1,000,000	One million	10^6
1,000,000 × 10 = 10,000,000	Ten million	10^7
10,000,000 × 10 = 100,000,000	One hundred million	10^8

1. Copy and complete the table up to 100,000,000.
2. Cover the first 2 columns of your chart and see how many numbers you can name just by looking at the powers of ten list.
3. Compare your chart with a partner and discuss any differences you may find between them.
4. Analyze How is the number of zeros in your chart numbers related to their powers of ten? How many zeros do you think are in the number 10^{100}? The exponent is the same as the number of zeros in the number; 100

Skills: Number and reasoning Use after Unit 3, Lesson 15.

Grouping Pairs

Objective Use powers of ten to write numbers and see the relationship between the exponent and the number of zeros.

Connections Reasoning and Number

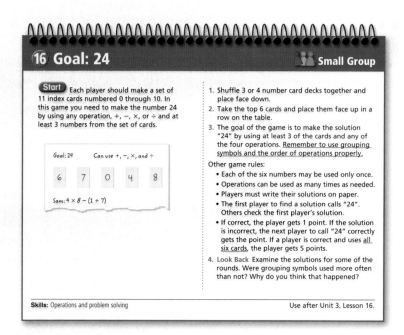

16 Goal: 24 — Small Group

Start Each player should make a set of 11 index cards numbered 0 through 10. In this game you need to make the number 24 by using any operation, +, −, ×, or ÷ and at least 3 numbers from the set of cards.

Goal: 24   Can use +, −, ×, and ÷

6   7   0   4   8

Sam: 4 × 8 − (1 + 7)

1. Shuffle 3 or 4 number card decks together and place face down.
2. Take the top 6 cards and place them face up in a row on the table.
3. The goal of the game is to make the solution "24" by using at least 3 of the cards and any of the four operations. Remember to use grouping symbols and the order of operations properly.

Other game rules:
   • Each of the six numbers may be used only once.
   • Operations can be used as many times as needed.
   • Players must write their solutions on paper.
   • The first player to find a solution calls "24". Others check the first player's solution.
   • If correct, the player gets 1 point. If the solution is incorrect, the next player to call "24" correctly gets the point. If a player is correct and uses all six cards, the player gets 5 points.
4. Look Back Examine the solutions for some of the rounds. Were grouping symbols used more often than not? Why do you think that happened?

Skills: Operations and problem solving Use after Unit 3, Lesson 16.

Grouping Small Groups

Materials Index cards (11 per student)

Objective Students write equations and use grouping symbols.

Connections Computation and Problem Solving

Ready-Made Math Resources

Technology — Tutorials, Practice, and Intervention

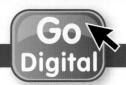

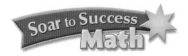

Use activity masters and online, individualized intervention and support to bring students to proficiency.

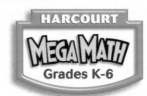

Help students practice skills and apply concepts through exciting math adventures.

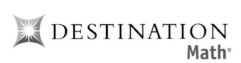

Extend and enrich students' understanding of skills and concepts through engaging, interactive lessons and activities.

Visit **Education Place**
www.eduplace.com

Visit www.eduplace.com/mx2t/ and find family, teacher, and student materials, activities, games, and more.

Literature Links

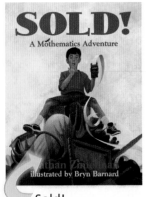

Sold!
A Mathematics
Adventure

Sold! A Mathematics Adventure

Find out how a pesky moth causes a boy to spend far more than he had intended at an auction in this book by Nathan Zimeiman. In the end, it turns out this mistake is worth a fortune!

Differentiated Instruction

Individualizing Instruction

Activities	Level	Frequency
	• Intervention • On Level • Challenge	All 3 in every lesson

Math Writing Prompts	Level	Frequency
	• Intervention • On Level • Challenge	All 3 in every lesson

Math Center Challenges	For advanced students
	4 in every unit

Reaching All Learners

English Language Learners	Lessons	Pages
	1, 2, 3, 4, 5, 6, 7, 8, 9, 10, 11, 12, 13, 14, 15, 16, 17, 18, 19, 20, 21	272, 282, 289, 297 302, 308, 317, 329, 336, 344, 358, 364, 369, 377, 385, 390, 401, 408, 414, 423

Extra Help	Lessons	Pages
	10, 15, 17, 19	344, 345, 383, 401, 402, 418

Advanced Learners	Lessons	Pages
	12, 19	363, 415

Strategies for English Language Learners

Present this problem to all students. Offer the different levels of support to meet students' levels of language proficiency.

Objective Identify *greater than, less than,* and *equal to.*

Problem Draw a table showing the number of stickers for Jake (14), Helio (9), Min (14), and Anna (11). Have students describe the table, using *greater than, less than,* and *equal to.*

Newcomer

• Point to the table. Say the names and number of stickers. Have students repeat. Then point to the numbers. Have students repeat *greater than, less than,* and *equal to.*

Beginning

• Have students read the names and numbers of stickers aloud. Say: 14 is greater than 9. Jake has a greater number than Helio. 9 is less than 11. Helio has less than Anna. 14 is equal to 14. Min has a number equal to Jake.

Intermediate

• Have students read the names and numbers of stickers aloud. Ask: Who has a number greater than Helio? Jake Who has less than Anna? Helio Who has a number equal to Jake? Min

Advanced

• Ask students to explain greater than, less than, or equal amounts. Then ask students to list the steps they followed in ordering the numbers.

Connections

Music Connection
Lesson 4, page 300

Social Studies Connections
Lesson 6, page 314
Lesson 10, page 350
Lesson 18, page 412
Lesson 19, page 420

Science Connections
Lesson 9, page 342
Lesson 11, page 360

Sports Connections
Lesson 2, page 286
Lesson 12, page 366

Language Arts Connections
Lesson 8, page 334
Lesson 15, page 388
Lesson 20, page 426
Lesson 21, page 432

Real-World Connections
Lesson 13, page 374
Lesson 17, page 404

Math-to-Math Connections
Lesson 5, page 306
Lesson 16, page 396

Literature Connection
Lesson 3, page 292

Math Background

Putting Research Into Practice for Unit 3

From Our Curriculum Research Project: Multi-Digit Addition and Subtraction Methods

We show three methods for multi-digit addition: the common algorithm (New Groups Above), plus two methods found to be effective during the research project, New Groups Below and Show Subtotals. These methods are introduced to help students see and discuss core mathematical ideas about addition and subtraction. When using the New Groups Below method, students record a regrouped digit on the line below the addition exercise, instead of above the addition exercise. This New Groups Below method allows students to see the tens and ones, or hundreds and tens, more closely together than in the New Groups Above method. In the Show Subtotals method, students add in each place, record the total for each place, then add these totals to find the sum.

To subtract multi-digit numbers, we teach students to ungroup all the places before they subtract. This approach reduces errors and helps develop conceptual understanding of multi-digit subtraction. Some students make the common error of consistently subtracting the smaller digit in a place-value column from the larger digit, even if the smaller digit is on top. To help students remember to ungroup in subtraction, they are encouraged to draw a "magnifying glass" around the top number to prepare for ungrouping. They "look inside" the magnifying glass to see which places need to be ungrouped.

—Karen Fuson, Author
   Math Expressions

From Current Research: Accessible Methods for Multi-Digit Addition

Method B [New Groups Below] is taught in China and has been invented by students in the United States. In this method the new 1 or regrouped 10 (or new hundred) is recorded on the line separating the problem from the answer . . . [it] requires that children understand what to do when they get 10 or more in a given column. . . . Method C [Show Subtotals], reflecting more closely many students' invented procedures, reduces the problem [of carrying] by writing the total for each kind of unit on a new line. The carrying-regrouping-trading is done as part of the adding of each kind of unit. Also, Method C can be done in either direction.

Method A: New Groups Above	Method B: New Groups Below
The new →1 1← The new hundred 186 ten +749 935	186 +749 The new →11← The new hundred 935 ten

Method C: Show Subtotals

$$
\begin{array}{r}
186 \\
+749 \\
\hline
800 \\
\text{The new hundred} \rightarrow 120 \\
\text{The new ten} \rightarrow \ \ 15 \\
\hline
935
\end{array}
$$

National Research Council. "Developing Proficiency with Whole Numbers." *Adding It Up: Helping Children Learn Mathematics*. Washington, D.C.: National Academy Press, 2001. 203.

Other Useful References: Addition and Subtraction

Number and Operations Standard for Grades 3–5. *Principles and Standards for School Mathematics*. Reston, VA: National Council of Teachers of Mathematics, 2000. 148–155.

Van de Walle, John A., *Elementary and Middle School Mathematics: Teaching Developmentally*. 3rd ed. New York: Longman, 1998. 213–221.

Carpenter, Thomas P., Fennena, E., Franks, M.L., Empson, S.B., & Levi, L.W. *Children's Mathematics: Cognitively Guided Instruction*. Portsmouth, NH: Heinemann, 1999

Getting Ready to Teach Unit 3

This unit includes three major groups of lessons: addition and subtraction problems, reading and writing numbers to millions, and adding and subtracting multi-digit numbers. Students using *Math Expressions* are taught a variety of ways to represent word problems. Students move from using math drawings to solving problems symbolically with equations.

As you teach these lessons, emphasize understanding these terms.
- Commutative Property of Addition
- equality
- inequality
- place value

Problem Solving

Representing Word Problems
Lessons 2, 3, and 6

When students read and represent problems, they often translate the words in the order they appear in a problem. This literal translation may result in an equation that represents the problem but is not in a form that students can use to find the solution. This unit emphasizes using a break-apart model to represent addition and subtraction problems. Students use the model to write a situation equation and a solution equation to solve word problems.

Break-Apart Model

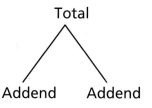

Change Problems
Lessons 2 and 6

Some addition and subtraction situations involve change, where the starting number, the change, or the result will be unknown. Most students can solve problems in their heads when they involve basic addition and subtraction. When word problems involve larger numbers, it is important for students to understand how to set up situation and solution equations to represent them.

Change Plus	Change Minus
Unknown Total (sum)	**Unknown Result (difference)**
Six children were playing tag in the yard. Three more children came to play.	Jake has 10 trading cards. He gave 3 to his brother.
How many children are playing in the yard now?	How many trading cards does he have left?
Solution Equation: $6 + 3 = n$	*Solution Equation*: $10 - 3 = n$
Unknown Start	**Unknown Start**
Some children were playing tag in the yard. Three more children came to play. Now there are 9 children in the yard. How many children were in the yard originally?	Jake has some trading cards. He gave 3 to his brother. Now Jake has 7 trading cards left. How many cards did he start with?
Situation Equation: $n + 3 = 9$	*Situation Equation*: $n - 3 = 7$
Solution Equation: $9 - 3 = n$	*Solution Equation*: $7 + 3 = n$
Unknown Change	**Unknown Change**
Six children were playing tag in the yard. Some more children came to play. Now there are 9 children in the yard. How many children came to play?	Jake has 10 trading cards. He gave some to his brother. Now Jake has 7 trading cards left. How many cards did he give to his brother?
Situation Equation: $6 + n = 9$	*Situation Equation*: $10 - n = 7$
Solution Equation: $9 - 6 = n$	*Solution Equation*: $10 - 7 = n$

Collection Problems
Lessons 3 and 6

Collection problems involve putting together (joining) or taking apart (separating) groups physically or conceptually. All of the objects in the groups are there from the beginning, and in many problems, there is no action at all.

Put Together: Two addends are put together to make the total.

Take Apart: The total is taken apart to make the two addends.

No Action: The problem describes the total and the addends.

Break-Apart Model

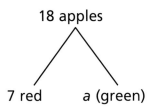

18 apples

7 red   a (green)

Put Together	Take Apart	No Action
Unknown Total (sum) Ana put 9 dimes and 4 nickels in her pocket. How many coins did she put in her pocket?	**Unknown Total** (sum) Jenna has 26 flowers. She put 14 flowers in a red vase and 12 flowers in a blue vase. How many flowers did she start with?	**Unknown Total** (sum) There are 11 red and 7 green apples in a bowl. How many apples are in the bowl?
Solution Equation: $9 + 4 = c$	*Solution Equation*: $14 + 12 = f$	*Solution Equation*: $11 + 7 = a$
Unknown Addend (partner) Ana put 13 coins in her pocket. Nine coins are dimes and the rest are nickels. How many are nickels?	**Unknown Addend** (partner) Jenna has 26 flowers. She put 14 flowers in a red vase and the rest of the flowers in a blue vase. How many flowers are in the blue vase?	**Unknown Partner** (addend) There are 18 red and green apples in a bowl. Seven apples are red. The rest of the apples are green. How many apples are green?
Situation Equation: $13 = 9 + c$ *Solution Equation*: $13 - 9 = c$	*Situation Equation*: $26 = 14 + f$ *Solution Equation*: $26 - 14 = f$	*Situation Equation*: $18 = 7 + a$ *Solution Equation*: $18 - 7 = a$
Unknown Addend (partner) Ana put 13 coins in her pocket. Some coins are dimes and 4 coins are nickels. How many coins are dimes?	**Unknown Addend** (partner) Jenna has 26 flowers. She put some flowers in a red vase and 12 flowers in a blue vase. How many flowers are in the red vase?	**Unknown Partner** (addend) There are 18 red and green apples in a bowl. Some apples are red and 11 apples are green. How many apples are red?
Situation Equation: $13 = c + 4$ *Solution Equation*: $13 - 4 = c$	*Situation Equation*: $26 = f + 12$ *Solution Equation*: $26 - 12 = f$	*Situation Equation*: $18 = a + 11$ *Solution Equation*: $18 - 11 = a$

Comparison Problems
Lessons 4 and 6

Two amounts can be compared by multiplication and division as we did in Unit 1, or they can be compared by addition and subtraction, as we will do in this unit. When working with comparison problems, focus the instruction on helping students understand the language.

Questions Students always need to decide which amount is larger and which is smaller. For additive comparisons, the comparing question can be asked in two ways, with either amount as the subject of the sentence.

• Who has more? (or Who has fewer?)

• How many more? (or How many fewer?)

Models In both kinds of situations, comparison bars can help with the solution. With addition comparison bars, the difference is shown by an oval so that the two compared amounts in the rectangle can be clearly seen. The unknown may be the smaller quantity, the larger quantity, or the difference between the quantities.

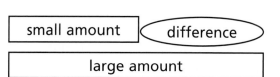

Language Emphasize that students must read word problems carefully—more than once, if necessary. Sometimes a word or phrase in a problem may suggest subtraction, but one must add to find the answer. Other times a word or phrase may suggest addition, but subtraction is used to find the answer. Students must understand the situation, not just look at the numbers and a key word.

Leading Language	**Misleading Language**
Language suggests subtraction; use subtraction	Language suggests subtraction; use addition
Problem The nursery has 83 rose bushes and 66 lilac bushes. How many fewer lilac bushes than rose bushes are in the garden?	**Problem** There are 10 dogs at the kennel. There are 6 fewer dogs than cats. How many cats are at the kennel?
Question Are there more rose bushes or lilac bushes?	**Question** Are there more dogs or cats?
Model There are more rose bushes, so the number of rose bushes is the larger number.	**Model** There are more cats, so the number of cats is the larger number.
Rose: 83 rose bushes Lilac: 66 lilac bushes d	Cats: c (cats) Dogs: 10 dogs 6
Solution Equation $83 - 66 = d$	**Solution Equation** $10 + 6 = c$
There are 17 fewer lilac bushes in the nursery.	There are 16 cats at the kennel.

Two-Step Problems
Lessons 5 and 6

The equations that students write for multistep problems may include more than one operation. Sometimes the order in which these operations are completed is not important. In other problems, students must find the answer to a *hidden question* and use that answer to answer the question of the problem. We use the term *hidden questions* just to make the conceptual point that students may need to answer these questions even if they do not appear in the problem.

Use Mathematical Processes
Lesson 21

The mathematical process skills of problem solving, reasoning and proof, communication, connections, and representation are pervasive in this program and underlie all the students' mathematical work. This table correlates the activities in Lesson 21 of this unit with the five process skills.

Process	Activity Number
Representation	1: Represent data in a graph. 4: Make a graph.
Communication	1: Discuss the data in a graph 2, 4: Share reasoning.
Connections	1: Math and Science: Number Sense and Data
Reasoning and Proof	3: Use reasoning to make a true equation. 4: Use reasoning to interpret a graph.
Problem Solving	2: Develop a survey and analyze the results 5: Solve an open-ended problem with multiple solutions

Place-Value Concepts

Place-Value Drawings
Lesson 7

Unit 3 broadens and deepens students' experiences with numbers through millions. Students read and write these numbers, build representations of these numbers, compare these numbers and visualize their comparative size and location within the place-value system.

In *Math Expressions*, students use place-value drawings to help them conceptualize numbers and understand the relative sizes of place values. In the early lessons of this unit, students make these drawings on the dot-array side of their MathBoards. The drawing below represents the number 456. It shows

- 4 hundred boxes (2 squares that each contain 100 dots) = 400.

- 5 quick tens (5 line segments that each connect 10 dots) = 50.

- 6 ones (6 circles that each contain 1 dot) = 6.

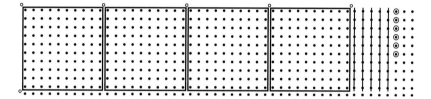

The place-value drawing helps students understand, for example, that the 4 in the hundreds place actually represents 400.

Once students have a conceptual understanding of the number of 1s contained inside each place, they move to drawings without dots. For example, the drawing below shows 2,697. Because these types of drawings do not need to be perfectly scaled, students can make them quickly. (Grouping the shapes by fives, as in this drawing, makes them easier to count.)

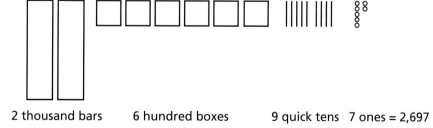

2 thousand bars   6 hundred boxes   9 quick tens 7 ones = 2,697

Whole Number Secret Code Cards
Lesson 8

Students explore place value by assembling Secret Code Cards to form multi-digit numbers. The cards show place values and are also used to show larger numbers. To make the number 2,745, students select the cards representing 2 thousands, 7 hundreds, 4 tens, and 5 ones.

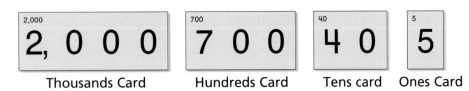

| Thousands Card | Hundreds Card | Tens card | Ones Card |

Standard Form Students place the cards on top of each other to represent a number in standard form.

Expanded Form Students can use their MathBoards and Secret Code Cards to model the expanded form of numbers. You might wish to have students make "plus sign" cards so they can easily represent several numbers in expanded form on their desks.

Word Form The backs of the cards show the values in word form. The word form of a number (when we read it or write it) uses the singular form of the place names. For example, two thousand, seven hundred forty-five. A hyphen is used for all two-digit numbers from twenty-one to ninety-nine.

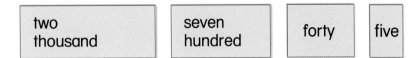

Read and Write Large Numbers
Lesson 10

Students explore large numbers by representing them both visually with dot arrays and numerically with Secret Code Cards.

Dot Arrays Students build large numbers, using dots array in the student book.

Each square =
1 hundred box

Each row =
1 thousand bar

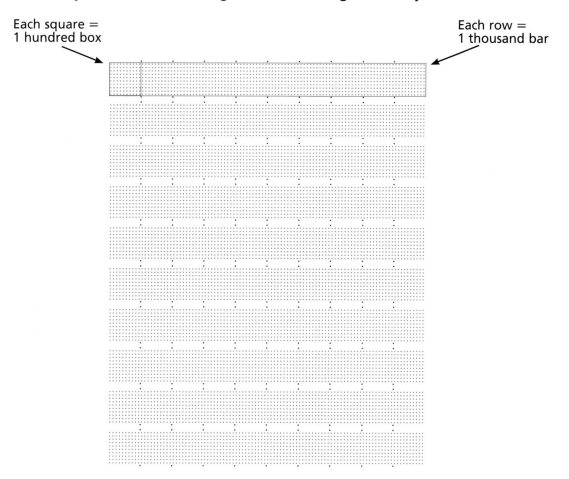

Secret Code Cards Students can build large numbers, using Secret Code Cards and the Reading and Writing Millions Frame (TRB M144).

Reading Millions Frame

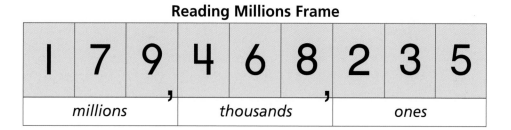

Methods for Addition and Subtraction

Most students entering Grade 4 know how to add and subtract ones and tens and perhaps also hundreds. However, some students go through the motions without understanding why they do what they do. In this unit, students explore the conceptual bases for multi-digit addition and subtraction.

Drawings for Addition
Lessons 11 and 12

Students use place-value drawings to help them understand grouping. To model 197 + 246, make place-value drawings for the two addends. Then group 10 ones to make a new ten, and group 10 tens to make a new hundred. The drawing shows 4 hundreds, 4 tens, and 3 ones, or 443.

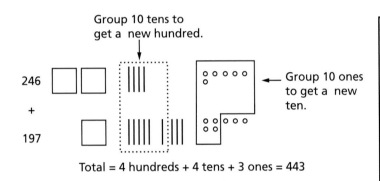

Group 10 tens to get a new hundred.

Group 10 ones to get a new ten.

Total = 4 hundreds + 4 tens + 3 ones = 443

> **Language and Vocabulary**
>
> For addition, *Math Expressions* uses the term *grouping* to refer to the process of combining 10 ones to make a new ten or 10 tens to make a new hundred.
>
> The opposite process in subtraction is referred to as *ungrouping*. Ungrouping involves breaking apart 1 unit of a place value to get 10 units of the next smaller place value (for example, breaking apart 1 hundred to get 10 tens).

Numeric Addition Methods
Lessons 11 and 12

Students connect the place-value drawings with numeric methods. The examples below show three numeric methods for adding 246 and 197.

New Groups Above	New Groups Below	Show Subtotals
1 1 246 +197 — 443	246 +197 1 1 — 443	246 +197 — 300 130 13 — 443

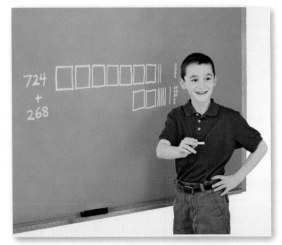

Drawings for Subtraction
Lesson 14

Start With the Larger Number To make place-value drawings for subtraction, draw the number you are subtracting from and take away the number you are subtracting. For example, to find 325 − 176 start with the drawing for 325.

Take Away the Smaller Number You must take away 1 hundred, 7 tens, 6 ones. There are not enough tens or ones in the drawing to do this, so you must ungroup a ten to get more ones and ungroup a hundred to get more tens.

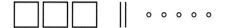

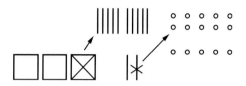

Identify the Difference After crossing out 1 hundred, 7 tens, 6 ones, you are left with 1 hundred, 4 tens, and 9 ones, or 149.

We encourage you to allow students to use any addition and subtraction methods that work. However, research shows that the methods in this unit are helpful to students having trouble with addition and subtraction.

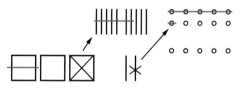

1 hundred + 4 tens + 9 ones = 149

Numeric Subtraction Methods
Lessons 15, 16, 17, and 18

Students are encouraged to do all the ungrouping before subtracting. Students can ungroup either from left to right or from right to left. Once everything is ungrouped, students can subtract the places in any order.

Ungroup from Left to Right

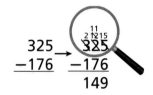

$$\begin{array}{r}325 \\ -176 \\ \hline \end{array} \rightarrow \begin{array}{r}325 \\ -176 \\ \hline 149\end{array}$$

Ungroup from Right to Left

$$\begin{array}{r}325 \\ -176 \\ \hline \end{array} \rightarrow \begin{array}{r}325 \\ -176 \\ \hline 149\end{array}$$

Basic Multiplication and Division Fluency
Students should continually work toward fluency for basic multiplication and division facts. Use checkups to assist students in monitoring their own learning. For this unit, you can use

- Checkup D: 2s, 5s, 9s, 3s, 4s, 6s, 7s, 8s, 1s, 0s (TRB M122) and Checkup D Answer Sheet (TRB M40).

- Checkup E: 6s, 7s, 8s (TRB M123) and Checkup E Answer Sheet (TRB M113).

If students have some multiplications and divisions they need to work on, have them make a Study Plan and work toward proficiency. See the Basic Facts Fluency Plan at the beginning of this Teacher Edition.

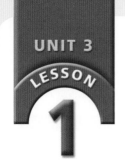

UNIT 3

LESSON

1

Understand Equality

Vocabulary
equation
sum
difference
Commutative Property of Addition
break-apart drawing
inverse operation
addend
inequality

Lesson Objectives

● Read and write related addition and subtraction equations.

● Demonstrate an understanding of the Commutative Property of Addition.

The Day at a Glance

Today's Goals	Materials	
1 Teaching the Lesson **A1:** Use = and ≠ to make true statements. **A2:** Explore the Commutative Property of Addition. **A3:** Explore inverse operations through reading and writing related equations. **2 Going Further** ▶ Extension: Inequalities ▶ Differentiated Instruction **3 Homework and Spiral Review**	**Lesson Activities** Student Activity Book pp. 119–121, 123–124 or Student Hardcover Book pp. 119–121, 123–124 and Activity Workbook pp. 55–56 (includes Family Letters) Homework and Remembering pp. 85–86	**Going Further** Student Activity Book p. 122 or Student Hardcover Book p. 122 Activity Cards 3-1 Counters Math Journals

123 *Use* **Math Talk** *today!*

Keeping Skills Sharp

Quick Practice	Daily Routines
This section provides repetitive, short activities that either help students become faster and more accurate at a skill or help them prepare for new concepts. Quick Practice for this unit will start with Lesson 2.	**Equations** Write these equations on the board. Have students copy the equations and write >, <, or = for each circle. $3 + 5 \ominus 8$ $7 + 4 \oslash 12$ $9 \oslash 4 + 3$ $2 + 9 \oslash 13$ $11 \oslash 9 + 1$ $8 + 5 \ominus 13$ $14 \oslash 6 + 7$ $9 + 6 \ominus 15$ $12 \oslash 4 + 9$

Understand Equality **271**

Teaching the Lesson

The = and ≠ Signs

 20 MINUTES

Goal: Use = and ≠ to make true statements.

Materials: Student Activity Book or Hardcover Book p. 119

 NCTM Standards:
Number and Operations
Algebra

Class Management

You can use these exercises as an opportunity for students to practice going to the board quickly and quietly. Emphasize how important it is to save time by doing this quickly and that if students learn to do so, more students can have turns to go to the board.

English Language Learners

Write addition number sentences to review = and ≠ symbols.

• **Beginning** Point to the =. Say: **This is the equals sign. It means values are the same.** Point to the ≠. Say: **This is the unequal sign. It means values are different.** Have students repeat.

• **Intermediate** Ask: **Which is the equals sign? Does it mean that values are the same?** yes Point to the unequal sign. Ask: **What sign is this?** unequal Say: **It means that values are _____.** different

• **Advanced** Have students make cards with both signs. One partner names two quantities. 6 apples, 4 bananas The other holds up the correct sign. ≠

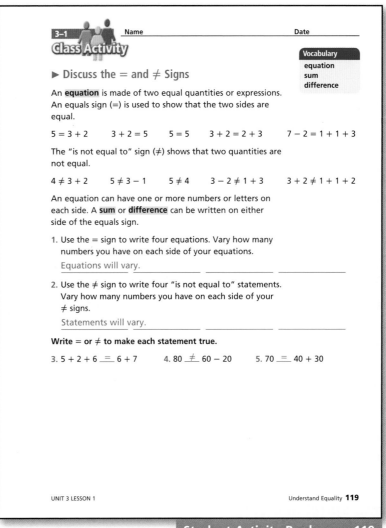

Student Activity Book page 119

▶ Discuss the = and ≠ Signs

WHOLE CLASS   Math Talk

Have students look at the definitions and examples using the "equals" sign and the "is not equal to" sign on Student Book page 119.

Point out and discuss the examples with the "answer" on the left (5 = 3 + 2, 5 ≠ 3 − 1). This equation form may be new to some students. It is important for algebraic understanding.

Use **Solve and Discuss** for exercises 1–5. Have students do exercise 1. As a class, quickly examine the equations the students wrote at the board. Have students at their seats ask any questions they have of the students at the board. Then ask all students who did not write at least one equation with only one number on the left side to write such an equation.

Send different students to the board and repeat for exercise 2, using the "is not equal to" sign. Repeat the process for exercises 3–5, using = or ≠.

Activity 2

Commutative Property

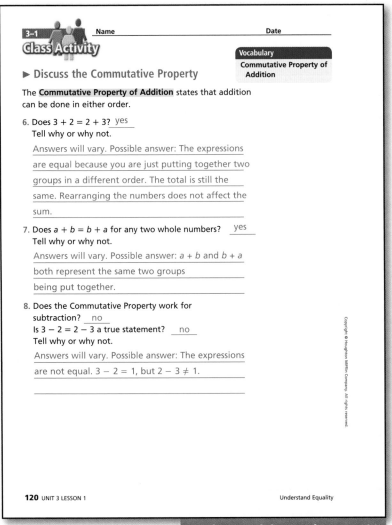

Student Activity Book page 120

The content of the student activity book page:

3–1 Class Activity

Name _____ Date _____

► Discuss the Commutative Property

Vocabulary
Commutative Property of Addition

The **Commutative Property of Addition** states that addition can be done in either order.

6. Does 3 + 2 = 2 + 3? _yes_
Tell why or why not.

Answers will vary. Possible answer: The expressions are equal because you are just putting together two groups in a different order. The total is still the same. Rearranging the numbers does not affect the sum.

7. Does $a + b = b + a$ for any two whole numbers? _yes_
Tell why or why not.

Answers will vary. Possible answer: $a + b$ and $b + a$ both represent the same two groups being put together.

8. Does the Commutative Property work for subtraction? _no_
Is 3 − 2 = 2 − 3 a true statement? _no_
Tell why or why not.

Answers will vary. Possible answer: The expressions are not equal. 3 − 2 = 1, but 2 − 3 ≠ 1.

120 UNIT 3 LESSON 1   Understand Equality

► Discuss the Commutative Property

WHOLE CLASS   Math Talk

Have students read and discuss in their own words the Commutative Property of Addition. Elicit any related meanings students might think of such as a *commuter*, who goes back and forth from home to work and from work to home in the opposite order.

Briefly discuss exercises 6–8 on Student Book page 120. Some students may know about negative numbers and discuss them here: 2 − 3 = −1. You can discuss subtracting $3 from a bank account that only has $2 in it. That person would owe the bank $1 (one interpretation of negative numbers is owing the amount of the negative number).

15 MINUTES

Goal: Explore the Commutative Property of Addition.

Materials: Student Activity Book or Hardcover Book p. 120

 NCTM Standards:
Number and Operations
Algebra

The Learning Classroom

Math Talk This may be a good day to review what makes a good explanation. Refer to a classroom list if one was posted earlier.

1) Write your work so everyone can see it.

2) Talk loud enough for other students to hear.

3) Use a pointer to point at your work.

4) Say how you arrived at the answer, not just the answer.

5) Stand to the side of your work when you talk.

Understand Equality   **273**

Activity 3

Relate Addition and Subtraction

 20 MINUTES

Goal: Explore inverse operations through reading and writing related equations.

Materials: Student Activity Book or Hardcover Book p. 121

 NCTM Standards:
Number and Operations
Algebra
Communication

Teaching Note

Math Background In many programs, students study groups of four related equations called *fact families*. For example, $2 + 3 = 5$, $3 + 2 = 5$, $5 - 3 = 2$, and $5 - 2 = 3$ form a fact family. In this program, students also consider the four related equations with the single number on the left—for example, $5 = 2 + 3$, $5 = 3 + 2$, $2 = 5 - 3$, and $3 = 5 - 2$—for a total of eight related equations.

Teaching Note

What To Expect From Students Students who have had *Math Expressions* before may call the break-apart drawings *Math Mountains*. They are called that in Kindergarten through Grade 3. Allow students to use whatever language they find most comfortable.

In earlier grades, students use *partner* rather than *addend*. At this grade, students should be making the transition from *partner* to *addend*.

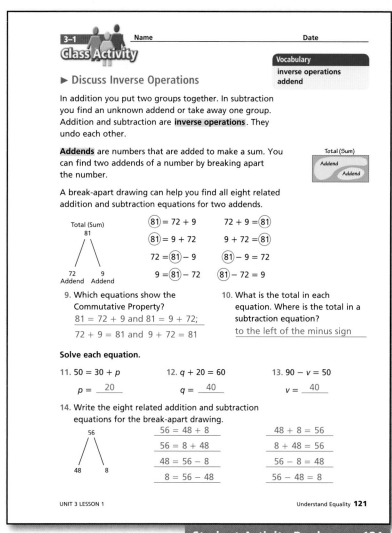

Student Activity Book page 121

▶ Discuss Inverse Operations

WHOLE CLASS

Math Talk

On Student Book page 121, have students look at the definitions of addition and subtraction. Briefly discuss how addition and subtraction are inverse operations. For example, $4 + 2 = 6$ (4 and 2 put together gives 6) and $6 - 2 = 4$ (2 taken from 6 gives 4).

Have students read and discuss in their own words the definition of *addends* and the *total* (the sum). Write the words *sum* (total) and *some* (part of the total) on the board and discuss these homophones: *sum* and *some* sound alike but have different meanings. To avoid confusion in class discussions, we will often use total instead of sum, but students do need to know the meanings and spellings of both these words.

Discuss exercise 9.

● The first two pairs of equations in each column show the Commutative Property. For example, $81 = 72 + 9$ and $81 = 9 + 72$. Some students may think that the bottom two pairs in each column also show the Commutative Property. Remind students that the Commutative Property does not hold true for subtraction. By switching the order of the numbers in the bottom two pairs of equations you've created two equations with different differences.

Discuss exercise 10.

● Understanding these patterns can be very helpful in solving equations with an unknown, such as exercises 11–13.

It may be helpful to circle the total, especially in subtraction equations. It may help some students to make a *break-apart drawing* for each equation (the total goes at the top and the addends at the bottom of the branches). You can do exercises 11–13 together as a class or quickly send students to the board to **Solve and Discuss** (only two students should explain their thinking so that you can move along quickly). Ask the students at the board to make a break-apart drawing with the total at the top and the addends at the bottom to help everyone understand these problems.

11. $50 = 30 + p$ 30 and 20 make 50, so $p = 20$.

Send as many students as possible to the board to write the eight related equations for exercise 14. Students will write these equations in different orders, providing a good opportunity to discuss different relationships and to check that all eight equations are there.

Do not worry if this is new to students. They will get much better at finding the unknown as they **Solve and Discuss** different kinds of addition and subtraction situations in Lessons 3, 4, and 5. We introduce in those lessons other visual tools that can help students understand those situations. Focusing on which number is the total in the equation can always help students solve for the unknown.

Teaching Note

What To Expect From Students
For exercises 11–14, we do not expect students to know or use any formal algebraic methods of solving for the unknown. Students should use their understanding of which numbers are the addends and which is the total to find the unknown.

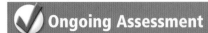 **Class Management**

Looking Ahead There are several different kinds of addition and subtraction situations. These will be discussed in Lessons 3, 4, and 5. Each situation will show how addition and subtraction are inverses because they undo each other. This can be discussed in each lesson.

Ongoing Assessment

Ask questions such as:

▶ How can you use inverse operations to solve exercise 13?

▶ How can you use the Commutative Property of Addition to find the related equations for exercise 14?

② Going Further

Extension: Inequalities

Goal: Compare numbers and expressions using > and <.

Materials: Student Activity Book or Hardcover Book p. 122

✔ **NCTM Standard:**
Number and Operations

▶ Use Inequality Symbols WHOLE CLASS

Explain to the class that >, <, and ≠ are all symbols of inequality.

Write the following inequalities on the board:

$$8 > 5 \qquad\qquad 2 < 4$$

Draw a number line on the board to show that the greater number is farther to the right on the number line and the lesser number is farther to the left on the number line.

Tell students that all of the statements on the page can be made true with ≠, but > and < are more specific. These symbols show which is the greater number or expression.

Circle two numbers on the number line you drew on the board. Write a statement using those two numbers and ≠. Then ask the students for a more specific statement using > or <.

▶ Inequalities WHOLE CLASS

Have students read the top of Student Book page 122. Write all the example problems on the board, and ask the students why each is true.

The students may be confused as to which inequality symbol is which. To help students remember what the symbols > and < mean, tell them that the smaller part of each symbol "points" (is next to) the smaller number.

Have students work independently on exercises 1–12. Encourage students to create challenging numerical expressions for partners to compare.

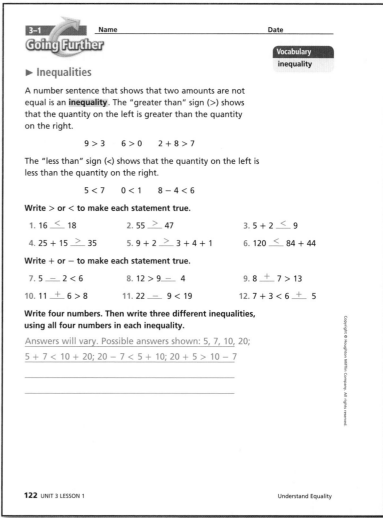

Student Activity Book page 122

 Class Management

Walk around the room to observe how students are completing the exercises. This will enable you to catch students who are confusing the inequality symbols. You can then remind them that each symbol points to the smaller number.

Students will have the opportunity to compare numbers later in this book. In Lesson 9, they will compare whole numbers and expressions. In Unit 9, they will compare fractions. In Unit 11, they will compare decimals.

Differentiated Instruction

Intervention — Activity Card 3-1

Count It Out!

Activity Card 3-1

Work: In Pairs

Use:
• 20 counters

1. One partner makes two groups of counters and writes an addition expression as shown below.

●●● ●●●●
3 + 4

2. The second partner makes another group of counters and writes the number for that group as shown below.

●●●●●●
6

3. Compare the two sets of counters, and write a statement using either = or ≠.

●●● ●●●● ●●●●●●
3 + 4 ≠ 6

4. Exchange roles and repeat the activity.

Unit 3, Lesson 1 — Copyright © Houghton Mifflin Company

Activity Note To extend the activity, have students use =, <, or >.

Math Writing Prompt

Draw a Picture Write two numbers. Draw that many stars under each number. Write a statement about your numbers, using = or ≠. Then write a sentence about your drawing.

Soar to Success Math — Software Support

Use *Soar to Success* for instruction of students needing targeted support for underlying skills.

On Level — Activity Card 3-1

Number Line Equations

Activity Card 3-1 ▲

Work: By Yourself

1. Draw a number line from 0 to 10. Circle 3 different numbers on the number line.

2. Count on from the least number circled to the greatest number circled. Write an addition expression describing what you did.

3. Repeat step 2, beginning with the middle number circled. Write an equation using the two addition expressions

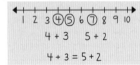

1 2 3 ④⑤ 6 ⑦ 8 9 10
4 + 3   5 + 2
4 + 3 = 5 + 2

4. Explain Why is the equation that you wrote correct?
The sums are equal.

Unit 3, Lesson 1 — Copyright © Houghton Mifflin Company

Activity Note It may be helpful for students to draw arcs on their number lines when counting forward. Note that the sums must be equal because they are counting on to the same number both times.

Math Writing Prompt

Create Your Own Which sum is easier to find by counting on, 4 + 39 or 39 + 4? Explain your thinking.

MegaMath Grades K-6 — Software Support

Use *MegaMath* for review and reinforcement of the concepts and skills presented in this lesson.

Challenge — Activity Card 3-1

Compare Expressions

Activity Card 3-1 ■

Work: In Pairs

1. One partner says an expression using addition, subtraction, or multiplication, such as 3 + 8. Both partners write the expression on a sheet of paper.

2. The other partner says another expression, such as 2 × 7 + 6. Again, both partners write the expression.

3. On your own, find the value for both expressions that you wrote. Then write a statement, using the two expressions and one of the symbols <, >, or =.

3 + 8 < 2 × 7 + 6
11 < 20

4. Compare Is your statement the same as your partner's? If not, justify your result.

Unit 3, Lesson 1 — Copyright © Houghton Mifflin Company

Activity Note Students can create expressions with one or more operations. For expressions with multiple operations, students must apply the order of operations to simplify the expressions.

Math Writing Prompt

Explain Your Thinking Explain why 4 × 7 > 6 + 6 + 6 + 6.

DESTINATION Math — Software Support

Use *Destination Math* to take students beyond the concepts and skills presented in this lesson.

Understand Equality   **277**

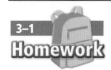 # Homework and Spiral Review

3-1

Homework **Goal:** Additional Practice

Use this Homework page to provide students with more practice with addition and subtraction methods.

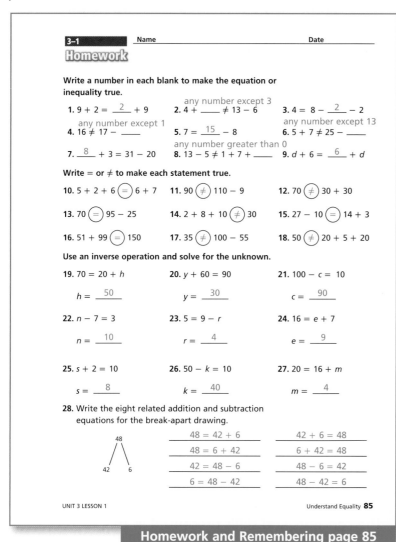

Homework and Remembering page 85

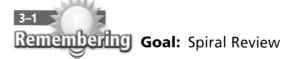 **Remembering** **Goal:** Spiral Review

This Remembering activity would be appropriate anytime after today's lesson.

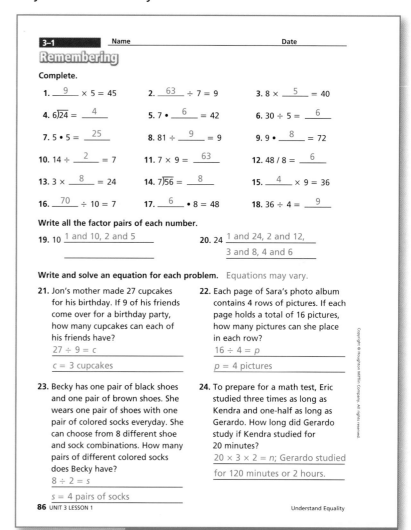

Homework and Remembering page 86

Home and School Connection

Family Letter Have children take home the Family Letter on Student Book page 123 or Activity Workbook page 55. This letter explains how the concept of addition and subtraction is developed in *Math Expressions*. It gives parents and guardians a better understanding of the learning that goes on in math class and creates a bridge between school and home. A Spanish translation of this letter is on page 124 in the Student Book and page 56 in the Activity Workbook.

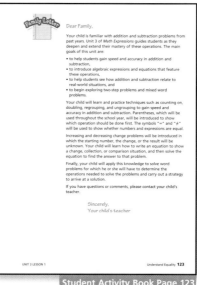

Student Activity Book Page 123

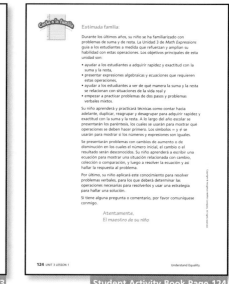

Student Activity Book Page 124

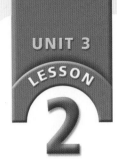

Addition and Subtraction Change Problems

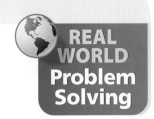

REAL WORLD Problem Solving

Vocabulary

start
change
result
change plus
change minus
situation equation
solution equation

Lesson Objectives

- Solve equations with an unknown by thinking of the relationship among the addend, addend, and total.
- Write and solve addition and subtraction problems.

The Day at a Glance

Today's Goals	Materials	
1 Teaching the Lesson **A1:** Identify the unknown and the known quantities in a word problem. **A2:** Write a problem for an equation. **2 Going Further** ▶ Differentiated Instruction **3 Homework and Spiral Review**	**Lesson Activities** Student Activity Book pp. 125–126 or Student Hardcover Book pp. 125–126 Homework and Remembering pp. 87–88	**Going Further** Activity Cards 3-2 Counters Math Journals

123 *Use* **Math Talk** *today!*

Keeping Skills Sharp

Quick Practice ⏱ 5 MINUTES

Goal: Add and subtract tens.

Equation Chains Have students create addition chains that have the same sum. $100 = 40 + 60 = 20 + 80 = 70 + 30 = 10 + 90$, and so on.

Have students create subtraction chains that have the same difference. $20 = 120 - 100 = 80 - 60 = 90 - 70 = 130 - 110 = 75 - 55 = 25 - 5$, and so on.

Daily Routines

Homework Review Ask students to place their homework at the corner of their desks. As you circulate during Quick Practice, check that students completed the assignment, and see whether any problem caused difficulty for many students.

Elapsed Time Ms. Ryan and Mrs. Taylor ran the same distance in a race. They had different starting times. Ms. Ryan started at 8:20 in the morning and finished at 9:50. Mrs. Taylor started at 8:45 in the morning and finished at 10:15. What were the times for each runner? Which woman had the faster time? Ms. Ryan's time: 1 hour 30 minutes; Mrs. Taylor's time: 1 hour 30 minutes; both women had the same time.

Teaching the Lesson

Represent Change Problems With Situation Equations

 30 MINUTES

Goal: Identify the unknown and the known quantities in a word problem.

Materials: Student Activity Book or Hardcover Book p. 125

✔ **NCTM Standards:**
Algebra
Problem Solving

Teaching Note

Math Background Some addition and subtraction situations involve a change. The change can be an increase or a decrease. In a change problem, the starting number, the change, or the result will be unknown. An equation with a letter can be used to show a change situation.

Change Plus Situations

Unknown Start	Unknown Change	Unknown Result
$n + 2 = 5$	$3 + n = 5$	$3 + 2 = n$

Change Minus Situations

Unknown Start	Unknown Change	Unknown Result
$n - 2 = 3$	$5 - n = 3$	$5 - 2 = n$

Situation and Solution Equations
- A *situation equation* shows the action or the relationships in a problem.
- A *solution equation* shows the operation you perform to solve the problem.

For simple numbers, students may find the answer from a situation equation. They do not always need to write a solution equation.

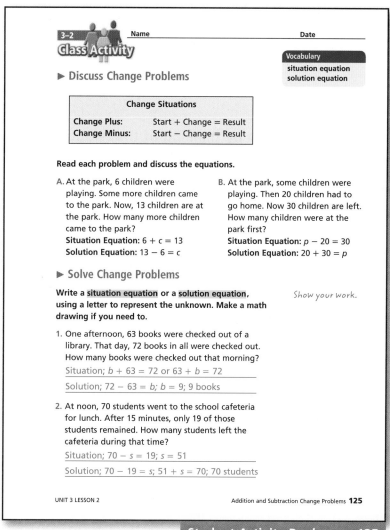

3–2
Class Activity

Name _____ Date _____

Vocabulary
situation equation
solution equation

▶ Discuss Change Problems

Change Situations	
Change Plus:	Start + Change = Result
Change Minus:	Start − Change = Result

Read each problem and discuss the equations.

A. At the park, 6 children were playing. Some more children came to the park. Now, 13 children are at the park. How many more children came to the park?
Situation Equation: $6 + c = 13$
Solution Equation: $13 - 6 = c$

B. At the park, some children were playing. Then 20 children had to go home. Now 30 children are left. How many children were at the park first?
Situation Equation: $p - 20 = 30$
Solution Equation: $20 + 30 = p$

▶ Solve Change Problems

Write a situation equation or a solution equation, using a letter to represent the unknown. Make a math drawing if you need to.

Show your work.

1. One afternoon, 63 books were checked out of a library. That day, 72 books in all were checked out. How many books were checked out that morning?
Situation; $b + 63 = 72$ or $63 + b = 72$
Solution; $72 - 63 = b$; $b = 9$; 9 books

2. At noon, 70 students went to the school cafeteria for lunch. After 15 minutes, only 19 of those students remained. How many students left the cafeteria during that time?
Situation; $70 - s = 19$; $s = 51$
Solution; $70 - 19 = s$; $51 + s = 70$; 70 students

UNIT 3 LESSON 2   Addition and Subtraction Change Problems **125**

Student Activity Book page 125

▶ Discuss Change Problems

WHOLE CLASS   **Math Talk**

In this lesson students analyze addition and subtraction change situations to determine which value is unknown. Equations are the representations that will help students express these relationships.

On Student Book page 125, discuss which problem (A or B) is a change plus situation and which is a change minus situation. Have students identify the start, change, and result quantity in each situation. You may need to discuss the meanings of these words.

Read problem A together.

Write *Start + Change = Result* on the board.

Math Talk in Action

Teacher Notes	Classroom Dialogue
Clarify and extend student's points as necessary so that start, change, and result are related clearly to the specifics in the problem.	**Where are the start, change, and result quantities in problem A?** *Jason:* There were 6 children in the beginning, so 6 is the start number. *Amy:* Some more children came to the park, so we don't know the change. *Zach:* There are 13 children at the end, so the result is 13.
Identify the unknown quantity.	**What is unknown?** *Erica:* We don't know how many "some" is, so the change is the unknown.
While any letter can be used to represent the unknown, it is often easier for students to use the first letter of the word.	**How can we represent the unknown?** *Pedro:* We can use a box. *Kayla:* We can use a letter. *Curtis:* We can use a c for children.

Teaching Note

Math Symbols Throughout this lesson, encourage students to use a letter to represent an unknown for each problem. Relate using a letter to methods students may have used previously, such as $6 + \square = 13$ or $6 + ? = 13$.

Discuss the equations below problem A.

- Which equation matches the action that the words describe?
  $6 + c = 13$

- Since $6 + c = 13$ matches the situation in the problem, we call it a *situation equation*.

- Why can you use $13 - 6 = c$ to find the answer? Because addition and subtraction are related operations. The 6 and the *c* are addends.

- When we rewrite the equation to find the answer, we call the new equation a *solution equation*.

Explain to students that when the numbers are small, it is easy to use mental math to find the solution. But when the numbers are too large to compute mentally, they will need to rewrite the equation as a related solution equation. See possible solutions to problem A in the sidebar Teaching Note.

Teaching Note

Possible solutions for problem A include:

- Think, "6 plus what number equals 13?" or "What number plus 6 equals 13?" Count on to find the answer: Start with 6, count on 7, 8, 9, 10, 11, 12, 13. I counted 7 more so $c = 7$.

- Mentally add up to 13: $6 + 7$ equals 13, so $c = 7$.

- Use an inverse operation to isolate the unknown. This gives the related equation $13 - 6 = c$. So $c = 7$.

Activity continued ▶

Activity 1

Teaching Note

Possible solutions for Problem B include:

- 30 plus 20 equals 50.

- 3 tens + 2 tens = 5 tens.

- Start with 20, then count on 10 three times to get 50.

This is using a forward solution to solve a subtraction equation. This solution method works because addition and subtraction are inverse operations. Any solution is fine as long as a student can explain it. Forward solution methods are usually easier.

English Language Learners

Write *situation* and *solution*, and an equation for each. Model how to tell them apart.

- **Beginning** Point to each word. Say: **A situation shows us the action and the result. We can use it to solve any problem. A solution shows us how to find the answer.** Have students repeat.
- **Intermediate** Say: **We can use a situation for any problem-solving activity.** Point to solution. Ask: **Is solution the same as situation?** no **What is a solution?** how you find an answer to a problem
- **Advanced** Have students write a situation and a solution equation and explain how they are different.

Read problem B together.

Write *Start − Change = Result* on the board.

 Math Talk in Action

Teacher Notes	Classroom Dialogue
Encourage students to use start, change, and result to describe the problem.	**Use *start*, *change*, and *result* to describe this problem.**
	Jason: 20 is the start number.
	How do you know?
	Jason: Because 20 children went home.
Ask questions to clarify the information in the problem.	**What else do we know about the problem?**
	Amy: 20 is the change; they went home.
	Curtis: We need to find how many children are left in the park.
	Zach: We don't know the result, so that is our unknown. I think they used *p* for park.
Help students understand that any letter could be used to represent the unknown.	**Could we use a different letter?**
	Zach: We could use *s* for "still there."
	Kayla: We can use *c* for "children."

Discuss the equations below problem B.

- Which equation matches the action of the words?
  $p - 20 = 30$

- Since $p - 20 = 30$ matches the words, it is the situation equation. For this problem, the solution equation is $20 + 30 = p$.

Although most students naturally and easily write situation equations, a variety of methods will be used to find the solutions. For this reason, always invite students to share and explain their methods. See possible solutions for problem B in the sidebar Teaching Note.

▶ Solve Change Problems WHOLE CLASS

On Student Book page 125, have students use **Solve and Discuss** to complete problems 1 and 2. Students need to say whether they wrote a situation equation or a solution equation. They can write either. Remind students that in some problems, the situation equation is the solution equation. In other problems, they are two different equations.

Possible solutions for problems 1 and 2 include:

1. $63 + 7 = 70$ plus 2 more is 72, so $7 + 2 = 9$ or
63 is 7×9 and 72 is 8×9,
so the difference is 9.

2. $70 - 19$ is one more than $70 - 20 = 50$, so $50 + 1 = 51$ or
$19 + 1 = 20$ and $20 + 50 = 70$,
so $1 + 50 = 51$ or
$70 - 20 = 50$, so 51 is one more.

Teaching Note

Language and Vocabulary Explain to students that *change plus* means an addition situation with an action that suggests addition. The original group increases to a greater number after the action takes place.

Explain to students that *change minus* means a subtraction situation with an action that suggests subtraction. The original group decreases to a smaller number after the action takes place.

① Teaching the Lesson (continued)

Activity 2

Write Change Problems

 20 MINUTES

Goal: Write a problem for an equation.

Materials: Student Activity Book or Hardcover Book p. 126

✓ **NCTM Standards:**
Problem Solving
Communication

The Learning Classroom

Math Talk Depending on your class, work through some or all of the equations together. The focus here is on linking equations and situations. These problems do not need to be solved.

Be sure that students vary the language in their problems. If they consistently use phrases such as "in the beginning" or "at the end," or other words or phrases, provide some models of how the language can be varied.

 Ongoing Assessment

Have students:

▶ say a sentence that suggests addition. For example, 6 girls joined a group of students watching a chess game.

▶ say a sentence that suggests subtraction. For example, 4 bees flew away from the bees in the hive.

3–2
Class Activity

Name _____ Date _____

Vocabulary
change plus
change minus

▶ Write Change Problems

Choose 2 equations. Write a **change plus** or a **change minus** word problem to represent each situation equation.

| $35 + n = 40$ | $n - 20 = 5$ | $5 + 40 = n$ |
| $n + 40 = 45$ | $45 - n = 20$ | $50 - 5 = n$ |

3. Change plus
   Answers will vary.
   _____
   _____
   _____
   _____
   _____
   _____
   _____

4. Change minus
   Answers will vary.
   _____
   _____
   _____
   _____
   _____
   _____
   _____

126 UNIT 3 LESSON 2   Addition and Subtraction Change Problems

Student Activity Book page 126

▶ Write Change Problems WHOLE CLASS

For exercises 3 and 4 on Student Book page 126, students are asked to write a problem that the given equation might represent. Because some students may find this difficult, you might first choose to invite the whole class to suggest and discuss possible situations for one or more of the equations.

Below is a list with each equation identified as a change plus or change minus problem.

Situation Equation	Problem Type
$35 + n = 40$	change plus, unknown change
$n - 20 = 5$	change minus, unknown start
$5 + 40 = n$	change plus, unknown result
$n + 40 = 45$	change plus, unknown start
$45 - n = 20$	change minus, unknown change
$50 - 5 = n$	change minus, unknown result

②Going Further

Intervention   Activity Card 3-2

Translate Words Into Equations	Activity Card 3-2 ●

Work: By Yourself

Use:
• 30 counters

1. Write an equation describing the problem, using only operations and words. red beads + blue beads = total beads

> Janelle has 16 red beads on a string. She puts 10 blue beads on the string. How many beads are on the string now?

2. Replace the words in your equation with the numbers from the problem. $16 + 10 = ?$

3. Use counters to model the equation, and then solve the problem. Models should have 16 counters and 10 counters for a total of 26.

Unit 3, Lesson 2   Copyright © Houghton Mifflin Company

Activity Note It may be helpful to remind students of the basic word form of a change plus equation, *start + change = result*.

 Math Writing Prompt

Representing Operations Write two sentences, one that suggests addition and one that suggests subtraction.

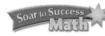 **Software Support**

Use *Soar to Success* for instruction of students needing targeted support for underlying skills.

On Level   Activity Card 3-2

Write Problems	Activity Card 3-2 ▲

Work: In Pairs

1. Situation equations describe a situation, and solution equations isolate a variable to make it easy to solve the problem.

1. **Math Talk** Discuss how situation equations are different from solution equations. See left.

2. Read the change plus word problem below.

> The Math Club had 8 members at the beginning of the school year and 10 members at the end of the school year. How many members joined the club during the school year?

3. Write a situation equation and a solution equation for the word problem. $8 + n = 10; n = 10 - 8$

4. Work together to create two change plus problems. Then write a situation equation and a solution equation for each problem.

Unit 3, Lesson 2   Copyright © Houghton Mifflin Company

Activity Note Check that students correctly recall the distinctions between situation and solution equations. Have them create their own samples if needed.

 Math Writing Prompt

Explain Your Thinking Write a change problem and describe the relationship of the words in the problem to the words *start*, *change*, and *result*.

 Software Support

Use *MegaMath* for review and reinforcement of the concepts and skills presented in this lesson.

Challenge   Activity Card 3-2

Make a Display	Activity Card 3-2 ■

Work: In Small Groups

1. Read the table of data below for Hank Aaron's runs batted in (RBI's) for the last 4 years of his career.

Year	RBI's
1973	96
1974	69
1975	60
1976	35

2. On your own, write a change plus word problem and a change minus word problem, using the data in the table.

3. Work together to solve all the word problems. Write *Situation* or *Solution* for each equation that you use to solve the problems.

Unit 3, Lesson 2   Copyright © Houghton Mifflin Company

Activity Note Have students discuss other methods of presenting the data. Ask students if a bar graph would have been easier to use for these problems.

 Math Writing Prompt

Create Your Own Write a change plus equation and a word problem that the equation might represent. Next, write a change minus equation and a word problem for that equation.

 DESTINATION Math **Software Support**

Use *Destination Math* to take students beyond the concepts and skills presented in this lesson.

Addition and Subtraction Change Problems   **285**

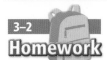

③ Homework and Spiral Review

Homework **Goal:** Additional Practice

✓ Include students' work for page 87 in their portfolios.

Remembering **Goal:** Spiral Review

This Remembering activity would be appropriate anytime after today's lesson.

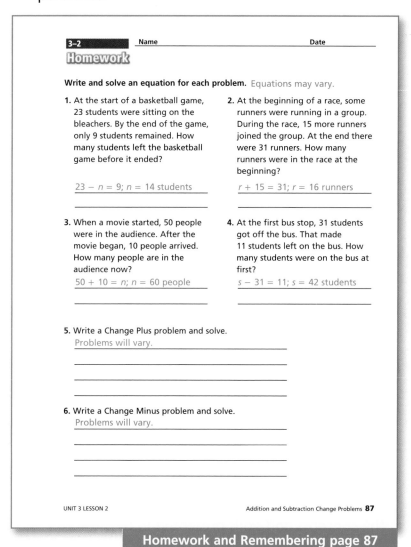

3–2 Name _____ Date _____
Homework

Write and solve an equation for each problem. Equations may vary.

1. At the start of a basketball game, 23 students were sitting on the bleachers. By the end of the game, only 9 students remained. How many students left the basketball game before it ended?

   $23 - n = 9$; $n = 14$ students

2. At the beginning of a race, some runners were running in a group. During the race, 15 more runners joined the group. At the end there were 31 runners. How many runners were in the race at the beginning?

   $r + 15 = 31$; $r = 16$ runners

3. When a movie started, 50 people were in the audience. After the movie began, 10 people arrived. How many people are in the audience now?

   $50 + 10 = n$; $n = 60$ people

4. At the first bus stop, 31 students got off the bus. That made 11 students left on the bus. How many students were on the bus at first?

   $s - 31 = 11$; $s = 42$ students

5. Write a Change Plus problem and solve.
   Problems will vary.

6. Write a Change Minus problem and solve.
   Problems will vary.

UNIT 3 LESSON 2   Addition and Subtraction Change Problems **87**

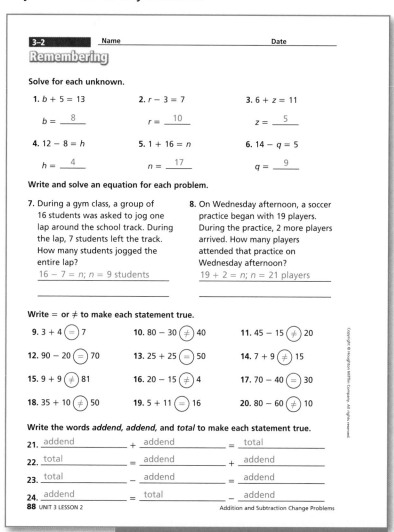

3–2 Name _____ Date _____
Remembering

Solve for each unknown.

1. $b + 5 = 13$
   $b =$ ___8___

2. $r - 3 = 7$
   $r =$ ___10___

3. $6 + z = 11$
   $z =$ ___5___

4. $12 - 8 = h$
   $h =$ ___4___

5. $1 + 16 = n$
   $n =$ ___17___

6. $14 - q = 5$
   $q =$ ___9___

Write and solve an equation for each problem.

7. During a gym class, a group of 16 students was asked to jog one lap around the school track. During the lap, 7 students left the track. How many students jogged the entire lap?
   $16 - 7 = n$; $n = 9$ students

8. On Wednesday afternoon, a soccer practice began with 19 players. During the practice, 2 more players arrived. How many players attended that practice on Wednesday afternoon?
   $19 + 2 = n$; $n = 21$ players

Write = or ≠ to make each statement true.

9. $3 + 4 \,(=)\, 7$
10. $80 - 30 \,(\neq)\, 40$
11. $45 - 15 \,(\neq)\, 20$
12. $90 - 20 \,(=)\, 70$
13. $25 + 25 \,(=)\, 50$
14. $7 + 9 \,(\neq)\, 15$
15. $9 + 9 \,(\neq)\, 81$
16. $20 - 15 \,(\neq)\, 4$
17. $70 - 40 \,(=)\, 30$
18. $35 + 10 \,(\neq)\, 50$
19. $5 + 11 \,(=)\, 16$
20. $80 - 60 \,(\neq)\, 10$

Write the words *addend*, *addend*, and *total* to make each statement true.

21. _addend_ + _addend_ = _total_
22. _total_ = _addend_ + _addend_
23. _total_ − _addend_ = _addend_
24. _addend_ = _total_ − _addend_

88 UNIT 3 LESSON 2   Addition and Subtraction Change Problems

Homework and Remembering page 87

Homework and Remembering page 88

Home or School Activity

Sports Connection

Data About Sports Students can research and compile data about sports. Then ask them to write 2 word problems about the data they collected and share them with their classmates.

For example, the number of players on the field at any given time depends primarily on the sport being played, and occasionally depends on the gender of the players. Women's lacrosse allows 12 players on the field at one time, while men's lacrosse allows only 10. Other examples are shown at the right.

Type of Sport	Number of Players on Field
Baseball	9
Soccer	11
Basketball	5
Water Polo	7
Volleyball	6

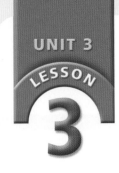

Addition and Subtraction Collection Problems

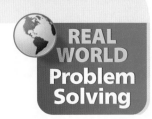
Vocabulary

collection situation
no action
put together
take apart
unknown total
situation equation
solution equation

Lesson Objectives

● Write and solve equations for collection problems.

● Use a letter to represent the unknown.

The Day at a Glance

Today's Goals	Materials	

1 Teaching the Lesson
A1: Write and solve equations for collection problems.
A2: Write a label for a given situation.
A3: Write a collection word problem.
 	
2 Going Further
▶ Differentiated Instruction
 	
3 Homework and Spiral Review
	Lesson Activities
	Student Activity Book pp. 127–130
	  or Student Hardcover Book
	  pp. 127–130
	Homework and Remembering
	  pp. 89–90
		Going Further
		Activity Cards 3-3
		Counters
		Math Journals
		
		123 Use Math Talk today!

Keeping Skills Sharp

Quick Practice ⏱ 5 MINUTES

Goal: Solve simple addition and subtraction equations.

Finding Unknown Values A **Student Leader** writes these eight equations on the board:

$7 = 2 + e$ $12 = h + 10$ $r + 10 = 13$ $16 - a = 10$

$5 = 8 - f$ $b = 13 - 3$ $4 = q - 4$ $17 = 10 + r$

The leader uses a pointer to point to each equation and, on a signal, the whole class says the answer (for example, "e equals 5."). If a substantial portion of the class says the wrong answer, the Student Leader (or someone helping the Student Leader) gives the correct answer and explains why it is correct.

Daily Routines

Homework Review Ask several students to share the problems they wrote for homework. Have the class ask clarifying questions about each problem. If necessary, model asking questions.

Strategy Problem Anwar sold tickets for a school fair. Adult tickets cost $8, and student tickets cost $5. Anwar sold 12 tickets for $87. How many student tickets did he sell? 3 student tickets

Teaching the Lesson

Represent Collection Problems

 30 MINUTES

Goal: Write and solve equations for collection problems.

Materials: Student Activity Book or Hardcover Book pp. 127–128

✓ **NCTM Standards:**
Number and Operations
Algebra
Representation

The Learning Classroom

Math Talk Having students use their own words and examples to discuss what they have learned is an effective way to be sure that they understand a concept. Invite a student to go to the board and summarize the class discussion. For this lesson, ask students to summarize what they know about addition and subtraction collection problems.

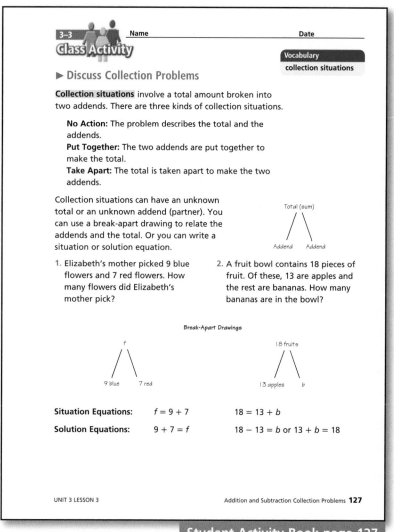

3-3
Class Activity

Name _____ Date _____

Vocabulary
collection situations

▶ **Discuss Collection Problems**

Collection situations involve a total amount broken into two addends. There are three kinds of collection situations.

　No Action: The problem describes the total and the addends.
　Put Together: The two addends are put together to make the total.
　Take Apart: The total is taken apart to make the two addends.

Collection situations can have an unknown total or an unknown addend (partner). You can use a break-apart drawing to relate the addends and the total. Or you can write a situation or solution equation.

1. Elizabeth's mother picked 9 blue flowers and 7 red flowers. How many flowers did Elizabeth's mother pick?

2. A fruit bowl contains 18 pieces of fruit. Of these, 13 are apples and the rest are bananas. How many bananas are in the bowl?

Break-Apart Drawings

f / 9 blue / 7 red

18 fruits / 13 apples / b

Situation Equations: $f = 9 + 7$　　$18 = 13 + b$

Solution Equations: $9 + 7 = f$　　$18 - 13 = b$ or $13 + b = 18$

UNIT 3 LESSON 3　　　　　Addition and Subtraction Collection Problems **127**

Student Activity Book page 127

▶ Discuss Collection Problems

WHOLE CLASS　　　　　　　　　　　　　Math Talk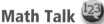

Collection situations involve putting together (joining) or taking apart (separating) groups physically or conceptually. All objects in the groups are there from the beginning, and in many problems there is no action.

On Student Book page 127, read the introduction with the class. Then discuss problem 1. Ask the students if the situation involves putting together or taking apart. taking apart On the board, make a break-apart drawing for the unknown total. Then write the situation equation and solution equation under it. Discuss how these relate to problem 1.

The equation $f = 9 + 7$ is the situation equation because mother picked all of the flowers and then separated them into groups of 9 and 7. Some students may write $9 + 7 = f$ because it is a more familiar form to them.

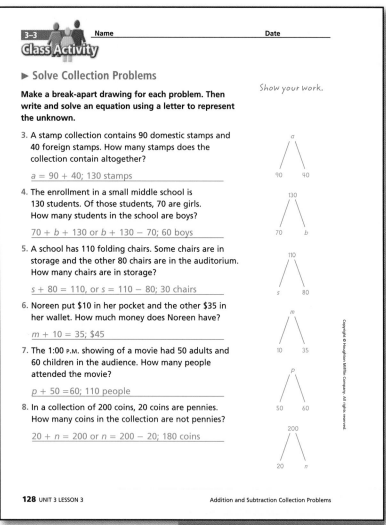

Discuss problem 2. Ask the students whether the situation can be viewed as no action, putting together, or taking apart. It is no action because the fruit does not move. We describe the total as fruit and the addends as apples and bananas: fruit = apples + bananas.

▶ Solve Collection Problems INDIVIDUALS

Use **Solve and Discuss** as students complete problems 3–8 on Student Book page 128. Focus the discussion on whether the problem situation has an unknown total or addend. Labeling the equations or break-apart drawings can be helpful.

Teaching Note

Math Background In today's lesson, students will learn about addition and subtraction situations in which the number in each group remains the same; the total and the addends do not increase or decrease. It may be beneficial to students to discuss the similarities and differences between change problems and collection problems.

Identifying the subcategories of addition and subtraction problems is not important. It is important for students to recognize that the solution to all of these problems involves addition or subtraction, and to identify the total and the addends.

The distinction between situation equations and solution equations is much more subtle and less important for collection situations than for change situations. Do not worry about this distinction. Any true equation that makes sense for the problem is fine. Often students prefer to make a break-apart drawing and do not even need to write an equation. That is also acceptable.

English Language Learners

Write a change and a collection problem. Model how to recognize the correct label in exercise 3.

- **Beginning** Say: **This problem is about ___.** stamps **Stamps is the label.** Have students repeat.
- **Intermediate** Ask: **What is the problem about?** stamps Ask: **What is the label?** stamps
- **Advanced** Have students work in pairs. One reads a collection problem and the other identifies the correct label.

Activity 2

Write Labels

 10 MINUTES

Goal: Write a label for a given situation.

Materials: Student Activity Book or Hardcover Book p. 129

 NCTM Standards:
Number and Operations
Communication

 Ongoing Assessment

Ask students to:

▶ give a problem in which we know the two addends.

▶ say a sentence that has a total and one addend.

Teaching Note

Math Background For exercises 9–12 on page 129, students are asked to write labels that are appropriate for the given totals. In some collection situations, a special class name may be used for the total, and members of the class are used for the addends.

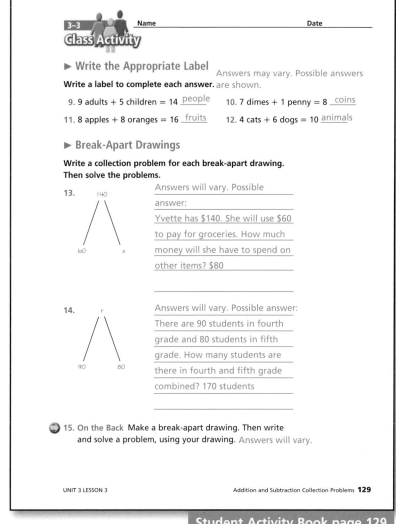

Student Activity Book page 129

▶ **Write the Appropriate Label** WHOLE CLASS

On Student Book page 129, discuss exercises 9–12 together and then brainstorm examples of classes of objects that might be in a problem.

Activity 3

Write Collection Problems

 15 MINUTES

Goal: Write a collection word problem.

Materials: Student Activity Book or Hardcover Book pp. 129–130

NCTM Standards:
Number and Operations

▶ **Break-Apart Drawings** INDIVIDUALS

For exercises 13 and 14 on Student Book page 129, students are asked to write problems to match break-apart drawings. Because some students may find this difficult, you might first invite the whole class to discuss possible situations.

② Going Further

Intervention — Activity Card 3-3

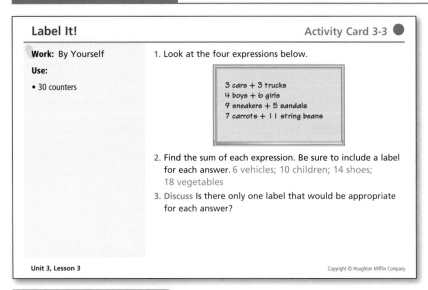

Label It!   Activity Card 3-3 ●

Work: By Yourself
Use:
• 30 counters

1. Look at the four expressions below.

> 3 cars + 3 trucks
> 4 boys + 6 girls
> 9 sneakers + 5 sandals
> 7 carrots + 11 string beans

2. Find the sum of each expression. Be sure to include a label for each answer. 6 vehicles; 10 children; 14 shoes; 18 vegetables

3. Discuss Is there only one label that would be appropriate for each answer?

Unit 3, Lesson 3   Copyright © Houghton Mifflin Company

Activity Note If students are having trouble identifying appropriate labels, ask questions such as *What category word describes both cars and trucks?*

✎ Math Writing Prompt

Use Labels Write an addition problem about numbers of different objects. Make sure to label your answer.

Soar to Success Math — Software Support

Use *Soar to Success* for instruction of students needing targeted support for underlying skills.

On Level — Activity Card 3-3

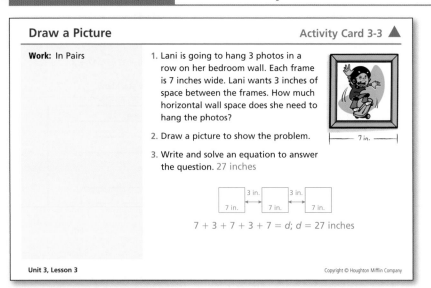

Draw a Picture   Activity Card 3-3 ▲

Work: In Pairs

1. Lani is going to hang 3 photos in a row on her bedroom wall. Each frame is 7 inches wide. Lani wants 3 inches of space between the frames. How much horizontal wall space does she need to hang the photos?

⊢— 7 in. —⊣

2. Draw a picture to show the problem.

3. Write and solve an equation to answer the question. 27 inches

$7 + 3 + 7 + 3 + 7 = d$; $d = 27$ inches

Unit 3, Lesson 3   Copyright © Houghton Mifflin Company

Activity Note Be sure students understand that the total linear measure required to hang the photos includes only the horizontal distances between the photos and the lengths of the photos themselves.

✎ Math Writing Prompt

Draw a Picture Write a problem that can be solved by drawing a picture. Exchange problems with your partner and solve.

MegaMath — Software Support

Use *MegaMath* for review and reinforcement of the concepts and skills presented in this lesson.

Challenge — Activity Card 3-3

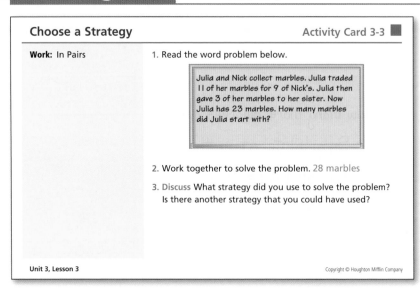

Choose a Strategy   Activity Card 3-3 ■

Work: In Pairs

1. Read the word problem below.

> Julia and Nick collect marbles. Julia traded 11 of her marbles for 9 of Nick's. Julia then gave 3 of her marbles to her sister. Now Julia has 23 marbles. How many marbles did Julia start with?

2. Work together to solve the problem. 28 marbles

3. Discuss What strategy did you use to solve the problem? Is there another strategy that you could have used?

Unit 3, Lesson 3   Copyright © Houghton Mifflin Company

Activity Note Suggest that students brainstorm a list of strategies before solving the problem. Work Backward and Draw a Picture may be useful.

✎ Math Writing Prompt

Create Your Own Write a word problem that you could solve by drawing a picture. Can you think of any other ways to solve your problem? Explain your thinking.

✖ DESTINATION Math — Software Support

Use *Destination Math* to take students beyond the concepts and skills presented in this lesson.

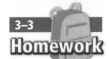

③ Homework and Spiral Review

3–3 Homework **Goal:** Additional Practice

Use this Homework page to provide students with more practice with addition and subtraction collection problems.

3–3 Remembering **Goal:** Spiral Review

This Remembering activity would be appropriate anytime after today's lesson.

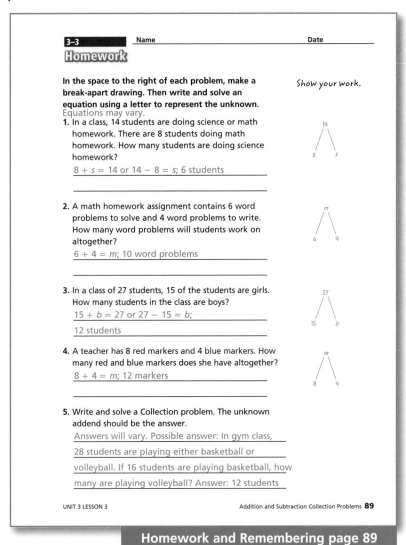

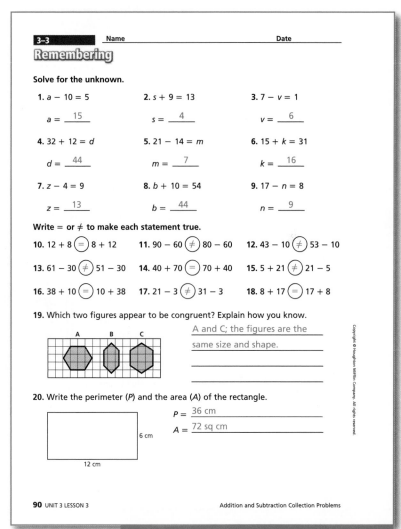

Homework and Remembering page 89

Homework and Remembering page 90

Home or School Activity

Literature Connection

Numbers in Fairy Tales Ask students to talk with friends or family about the fairy tales and nursery rhymes they heard when they were younger and how numbers were used in these. Then have students make up and solve word problems about fairy-tale or nursery-rhyme characters. Students may enjoy acting out the math situations.

How many more dwarves are in the Snow White story than the number of bears in the Goldilocks story?

$7 - 3 = 4$

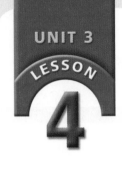

Addition and Subtraction Comparison Problems

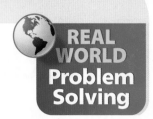

REAL WORLD Problem Solving

Vocabulary

comparison situation
fewer
difference
comparison bars
leading
misleading

Lesson Objectives

● Write and solve addition and subtraction comparison problems.

● Use a letter to represent the unknown.

The Day at a Glance

Today's Goals	Materials	
1 Teaching the Lesson **A1:** Solve comparison problems with leading language. **A2:** Solve comparison problems with misleading language. **2 Going Further** ▶ Differentiated Instruction **3 Homework and Spiral Review**	**Lesson Activities** Student Activity Book pp. 131–134 or Student Hardcover Book pp. 131–134 Homework and Remembering pp. 91–92	**Going Further** Activity Cards 3-4 Math Journals

123 Use Math Talk today!

Keeping Skills Sharp

Quick Practice ⏱ 5 MINUTES

Goal: Solve simple addition and subtraction equations.

Finding Unknown Values A **Student Leader** writes these eight equations on the board:

$r + 6 = 9$	$8 = 3 + e$	$10 = h + 3$	$14 = 10 + h$
$3 = 7 - f$	$b = 15 - 5$	$6 = q - 4$	$11 - a = 10$

The leader uses a pointer to point to each equation and, on a signal, the whole class says the answer (for example, "*r* equals 3."). If a substantial portion of the class says the wrong answer, the Student Leader (or someone helping the Student Leader) gives the correct answer and explains why it is correct.

Daily Routines

Homework Review Ask a student volunteer to share a word problem. Invite several students to solve it at the board, while others work at their seats.

Strategy Problem Draw two rectangles with the same area but different perimeters. *Possible answer:*

$p = 8$ units $p = 10$ units
$A = 4$ units² $A = 4$ units²

Teaching the Lesson

Comparison Problems with an Unknown Difference

 20 MINUTES

Goal: Solve comparison problems with leading language.

Materials: Student Activity Book or Hardcover Book p. 131

✓ **NCTM Standards:**
Number and Operations
Algebra
Representation

Teaching Note

Math Background Two amounts can be compared by multiplication and division as we did in Unit 1, or they can be compared by addition and subtraction, as we are doing here. In both kinds of situations, comparison bars can help with the solution. You always need to decide which amount is bigger and which is smaller. But for multiplicative comparisons the comparing question asks, "How many times a is b?" and for additive comparisons the comparing question asks, "How much more is a than b?" Both kinds of comparing situations can ask the comparing sentence in 2 ways, with either amount the subject of the sentence. With additive comparison bars, the difference is shown by an oval so that the two compared amounts in the rectangle can be clearly seen.

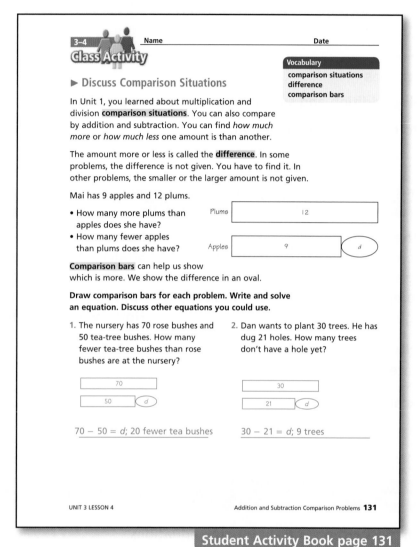

Student Activity Book page 131

▶ Discuss Comparison Situations

WHOLE CLASS   Math Talk

When working with comparison problems, focus the instruction on helping students understand the language. Comparison problems involve one quantity that is more or less than another quantity; the quantities can be compared by multiplication or by addition.

For additive comparing situations, the comparing statement or question has two key pieces of information:

● Who has more? (or Who has fewer?)

● How many more? (or How many fewer?)

Asking themselves these two key questions and recording the information in the comparison bars will help students understand the situation. Begin this lesson by asking students to summarize comparing situations by multiplication and division.

For all problems, have students say the alternative comparing sentence by switching the order of the two compared quantities. (They will also have to change the words *more* and *fewer* or change the sentence in another way.) This helps them learn this difficult comparing language.

Read the introduction and the problem on Student Book page 131. Discuss how the comparison bars show the problem situation.

Have students tell how to find the difference. Students may write many different equations to solve comparison problems, so discuss and explain all of the possible equations for the example.

- $12 = 9 + d$
- $12 = d + 9$
- $9 = 12 - d$
- $d = 12 - 9$

Emphasize that students may write any true equation that comes from the situation or the comparison bars.

Brainstorm other ways students might ask comparing questions about the fruits. For example,

Equalizing questions:

- How many more apples does Mai need in order to have as many apples as plums?

- How many plums should she eat in order to have as many plums as apples?

Matching questions:

- If we matched the plums and apples 1-to-1, how many plums wouldn't be paired with an apple?

- If we matched the plums and apples 1-to-1, how many extra plums would we have? (Emphasize that the difference is the extra amount left in the large quantity when the items are matched 1-to-1.)

Tests use many different forms of comparing language, so it is important to brainstorm and facilitate students' learning of this difficult language.

Use **Solve and Discuss** to solve problems 1 and 2. Practice saying different comparing questions. Discuss different equations students may write and how these are all true and come from the same comparison bars.

Activity continued ▶

Teaching Note

What to Expect From Students
Students may draw comparison bars different ways. Allow students to draw the bars in a way that makes sense to them. It does help if students consistently draw the larger amount first, but if a different method is working for students, let them use it.

This variation with the difference inside the larger amount is also acceptable. Students may draw this for particular problems or for all problems.

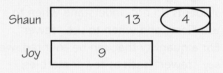

Teaching Note

Watch For! Some students might believe that comparison bars must always be drawn proportionally. Make sure these students understand that this is not the case. For example, a bar representing 10 does not have to be twice as long as a bar representing 5. These are only rough sketches in which it is important only that the bar representing the greater amount is longer than the bar representing the lesser amount.

Activity 1

For problem 1, other questions might be:

● How many more rose bushes are there than tea-tree bushes?

● How many tea-tree bushes would the nursery need to have the same number of tea-tree bushes and rose bushes?

● How many rose bushes would the nursery need to sell to have the same number of tea-tree bushes and rose bushes?

● If we lined up the tea-tree bushes and the rose bushes so that each had a partner, which type of bush would be left over? How many left over bushes would there be?

● If we lined up the tea-tree bushes and the rose bushes so that each had a partner, which bush would we need more of so that each bush had a partner? How many more would we need?

Students should write 70 in the longer bar and 50 in the shorter bar. Possible true equations students may write to show this problem are:
$50 + d = 70$ $\qquad 70 = 50 + d$ $\qquad 50 = 70 - d$ $\qquad 70 - 50 = d$

For problem 2, other questions might be:

● How many more holes does Dan need to dig to plant the rest of the trees?

● How many fewer holes are there than trees?

● If we tried to match each tree to a hole, how any trees would be left over?

Students should write 30 in the longer bar and 21 in the shorter bar. Possible true equations students may write to show this problem are:
$21 + d = 30$ $\qquad 30 = 21 + d$ $\qquad 21 = 30 - d$ $\qquad 30 - 21 = d$

Ask students to discuss how comparing amounts by addition/subtraction is like and different from comparing amounts by multiplication/division. Then ask students to review leading and misleading language in comparing situations by multiplication. The misleading question directed you to do the wrong operation, so you have to carefully think about which amount was more. This leads into the discussion on the following page. As necessary, continue to relate additive comparing to multiplicative comparing so that students can see how the problem-solving processes are similar (decide which is more and put that into the comparison bar) even though the language and operations are different.

Leading or Misleading Language?

Student Activity Book page 132

3–4
Class Activity
Name _____ Date _____

Vocabulary
leading
misleading

▶ **Discuss the Language**

The large amount or the small amount can be the unknown. Some comparing sentences have **leading** language that suggests what to do. Other comparing sentences have **misleading** language that may trick you into doing the wrong operation.

Copy and label the comparison bars and solve. Say the reverse comparing sentence to see if it helps you.

3. There are 10 dogs at the kennel. There are 6 fewer dogs than cats. How many cats are at the kennel?

cats | c |
dogs | 10 | 6 |
10 + 6 = c; 16 cats

4. There are 15 girls in Ms. Roedel's fourth-grade class. There are 3 more girls than boys. How many boys are there?

girls | 15 |
boys | b | 3 |
15 = b + 3 or b = 15 − 3; 12 boys

132 UNIT 3 LESSON 4   Addition and Subtraction Comparison Problems

---

▶ # Discuss the Language

WHOLE CLASS   **Math Talk**

Explain to students that they must carefully read a word problem, more than once if necessary, before they solve it. Sometimes a word or phrase in a problem may suggest subtraction, but they must add to find the answer. Or a word or phrase may suggest addition, but subtraction is used to find the answer. Have a student read the paragraph and problem at the top of page 132, and then solve problem 3 together.

● **What question do we need to answer?** How many cats are at the kennel?

● **What do we know?** There are 10 dogs and 6 fewer dogs than cats.

● **Are there more dogs or more cats?** cats

● **How do you know?** The problem says 6 fewer dogs than cats.

Work through problem 4 in a similar way.

Activity continued ▶

---

 25 MINUTES

Goal: Solve comparison problems with misleading language.

Materials: Student Activity Book or Hardcover Book pp. 132–134

✔ **NCTM Standards:**
Number and Operations
Algebra
Representation

Teaching Note

Watch For! In problem 3, some students may put dogs in the longer bar because the problem says 10 dogs. Remind students that the most important thing is to decide which is more and which is less.

English Language Learners

Show how *fewer* can be *misleading*. Write on the board: There are 8 red marbles. There are 3 fewer red marbles than blue. Read the problem aloud.

● **Beginning** Point to the word *fewer*. Ask: **Does *fewer* mean "more" or "less"?** less Say: **Be careful. There are 3 fewer red marbles than blue marbles. This means there are more blue marbles than red marbles.**

● **Intermediate** Ask: **Are there more blue or red marbles?** blue Say: **Be careful. *Fewer* makes us think "less", but there are more blue. *Fewer* is *misleading*.**

● **Advanced** Have students tell what word is misleading in the problem and explain whether there are more blue or red marbles.

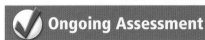

Teaching Note

Math Background Remind students that when working with problems that have misleading language, they should reverse the comparing statement. Reversing the comparing statement can help students decide whether to add or subtract to solve the problem. Also, drawing comparison bars is the key to helping students decide which operation to choose.

✓ Ongoing Assessment

While working through problem 3 on Student Book page 132, ask questions such as:

▶ How do the bars show the number of dogs and the number of cats?

▶ What do you think the oval represents?

▶ What equations would you write to solve the problem? Why?

3–4	Name	Date

Class Activity

▶ Share Solutions

Draw comparison bars for each problem. Write and solve an equation. Don't let misleading language trick you!

Show your work.

5. At the zoo there are 7 monkeys. There are 6 more kangaroos than monkeys. How many kangaroos are at the zoo?

$7 + 6 = k$; $k = 13$; 13 kangaroos

```
| k |
| 7 | 6 |
```

6. The soccer team drilled for 50 minutes. It drilled 10 minutes longer than it scrimmaged. How long did the soccer team scrimmage?

$50 - 10 = s$; $s = 40$; 40 min

```
| 50 |
| s | 10 |
```

7. Avery is 13 years old. He is 4 years older than Marisa. How old is Marisa?

$13 - 4 = m$; $m = 9$; 9 years old.

```
| 13 |
| m | 4 |
```

8. Sabrina studied 15 more minutes than Sean. How long did Sean study if Sabrina studied for 45 minutes?

$45 - 15 = n$; $n = 30$; 30 minutes.

```
| 45 |
| n | 15 |
```

9. On the last day of school, 10 more students wore shorts than wore jeans. If 13 students wore jeans, how many students wore shorts?

$13 + 10 = s$; $s = 23$; 23 students

```
| s |
| 13 | 10 |
```

10. **On the Back** Write a comparison problem. Show comparison bars and an equation to solve your problem. Answers will vary.

UNIT 3 LESSON 4   Addition and Subtraction Comparison Problems **133**

Student Activity Book page 133

▶ Share Solutions

| WHOLE CLASS | **Math Talk**
|---|

Direct students to solve problems 5–9 on Student Book page 133. Use **Solve and Discuss** if you think your class needs to work through more examples together. Otherwise, allow students to work alone or with a **Helping Partner**. You might want to work with struggling students at the board or practice the language with English language learners.

② Going Further

Intervention   Activity Card 3-4

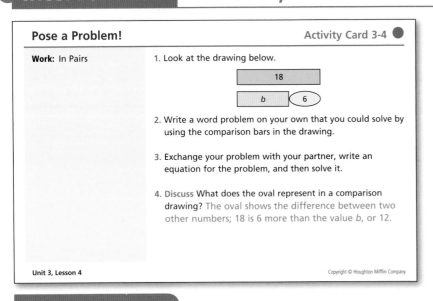

Pose a Problem!   Activity Card 3-4 ●

Work: In Pairs

1. Look at the drawing below.

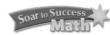

2. Write a word problem on your own that you could solve by using the comparison bars in the drawing.

3. Exchange your problem with your partner, write an equation for the problem, and then solve it.

4. **Discuss** What does the oval represent in a comparison drawing? *The oval shows the difference between two other numbers; 18 is 6 more than the value b, or 12.*

Unit 3, Lesson 4   Copyright © Houghton Mifflin Company

Activity Note Have students identify whether their equation is a situation or a solution equation before they begin solving it. Extend the activity by having students think of some **Scenarios** for the diagram.

✐ Math Writing Prompt

Draw a Picture Write your own comparison problem. Draw comparison bars to represent your problem.

Soar to Success Math ★ Software Support

Use *Soar to Success* for instruction of students needing targeted support for underlying skills.

On Level   Activity Card 3-4

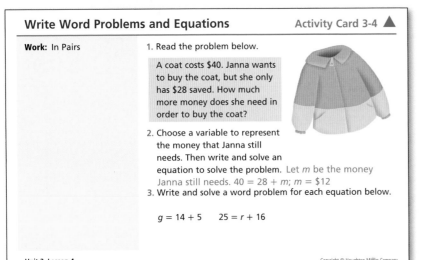

Write Word Problems and Equations   Activity Card 3-4 ▲

Work: In Pairs

1. Read the problem below.

A coat costs $40. Janna wants to buy the coat, but she only has $28 saved. How much more money does she need in order to buy the coat?

2. Choose a variable to represent the money that Janna still needs. Then write and solve an equation to solve the problem. *Let m be the money Janna still needs. 40 = 28 + m; m = $12*

3. Write and solve a word problem for each equation below.

$g = 14 + 5$ $25 = r + 16$

Unit 3, Lesson 4   Copyright © Houghton Mifflin Company

Activity Note Remind students that they should select a variable that has meaning for the problem and then identify what the variable represents.

✐ Math Writing Prompt

Create Your Own Create a comparison-bar diagram showing an unknown difference. Write a word problem for the diagram, and exchange with a partner to solve.

MegaMath Grades K-6 Software Support

Use *MegaMath* for review and reinforcement of the concepts and skills presented in this lesson.

Challenge   Activity Card 3-4

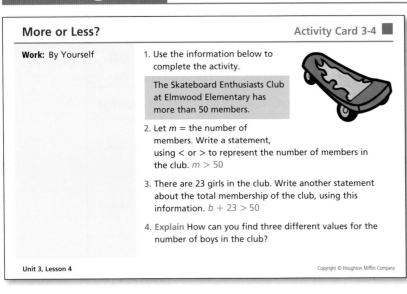

More or Less?   Activity Card 3-4 ■

Work: By Yourself

1. Use the information below to complete the activity.

The Skateboard Enthusiasts Club at Elmwood Elementary has more than 50 members.

2. Let m = the number of members. Write a statement, using < or > to represent the number of members in the club. *m > 50*

3. There are 23 girls in the club. Write another statement about the total membership of the club, using this information. *b + 23 > 50*

4. **Explain** How can you find three different values for the number of boys in the club?

Unit 3, Lesson 4   Copyright © Houghton Mifflin Company

Activity Note Point out that the statements $m > 50$ and $50 < m$ are equivalent. Both indicate that the variable value is greater than 50.

✐ Math Writing Prompt

Explain Your Thinking Marcy says she has more than 40 basketball trading cards. She says 18 of them are rookie cards, and that less than 23 are from non-rookie years. Is this possible? Explain.

✴ DESTINATION Math® Software Support

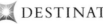

Use *Destination Math* to take students beyond the concepts and skills presented in this lesson.

Addition and Subtraction Comparison Problems   **299**

③ Homework and Spiral Review

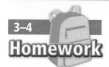

3-4
Homework **Goal:** Additional Practice

✓ Include students' work for page 91 in their portfolios.

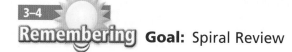

3-4
Remembering **Goal:** Spiral Review

This Remembering activity would be appropriate anytime after today's lesson.

3-4 Name _____ Date _____
Homework

In the space to the right of each problem, draw comparison bars. Then write and solve an equation.

Show your work. Comparison bars may vary.

1. Terrell has 3 brothers. This is 2 fewer brothers than James has. How many brothers does James have?
$3 + 2 = j; j = 5$; James has 5 brothers.

| j |
| 3 | 2 |

2. During the first lunch period, 54 students ate hot lunch. This is 9 fewer students than ate hot lunch during the second lunch period. How many students ate hot lunch during the second lunch period?
$54 + 9 = s; s = 63$; 63 students

| s |
| 54 | 9 |

3. A zoo cares for 15 tigers and 9 lions. How many fewer lions than tigers are at the zoo?
$15 - 9 = d ; d = 6$; 6 fewer lions

| 15 |
| 9 | d |

4. A game is being watched by 60 adults and some children. If there are 20 more adults than children, how many children are watching the game?
$60 - 20 = h; h = 40$; 40 children

| 60 |
| h | 20 |

5. At the park there are 15 more bushes than trees. There are 50 bushes. How many trees are at the park?
$50 - 15 = n; n = 35$; 35 trees

| 50 |
| n | 15 |

6. Erika and Spencer play the piano. Last month, Erika practiced 4 fewer times than Spencer. If Erika practiced 14 times last month, how many times did Spencer practice?
$14 + 4 = n; n = 18$; Spencer practiced 18 times.

| n |
| 14 | 4 |

7. Write a comparison problem. Show a comparison bar and an equation to solve your problem.
Answers will vary.

UNIT 3 LESSON 4

Addition and Subtraction Comparison Problems **91**

Homework and Remembering page 91

3-4 Name _____ Date _____
Remembering

Complete.

1. $8 \times \underline{4} = 32$ 2. $4)\overline{28} = \underline{7}$ 3. $\underline{72} \div 9 = 8$

4. $\underline{6} \cdot 9 = 54$ 5. $18 \div 3 = \underline{6}$ 6. $4 \cdot 6 = \underline{24}$

7. $40 \div \underline{5} = 8$ 8. $6 \cdot \underline{8} = 48$ 9. $36 \div \underline{6} = 6$

10. $9 \times 3 = \underline{27}$ 11. $25 / 5 = \underline{5}$ 12. $\underline{56} \div 7 = 8$

13. $6)\overline{42} = \underline{7}$ 14. $9 \cdot \underline{4} = 36$ 15. $18 \div 2 = \underline{9}$

Simplify each expression.
$5 + 20 = 25$ $10 \times 4 = 40$ $5 + 20 = 25$
16. $5 + (5 \times 4) = $ _____   17. $(5 + 5) \times 4 = $ _____   18. $5 + 5 \times 4 = $ _____

Solve each equation. Label the addends and total if it will help you.

19. $2 + h = 8$ 20. $m - 6 = 6$ 21. $c + 7 = 15$
$h = \underline{6}$ $m = \underline{12}$ $c = \underline{8}$

22. $r - 50 = 90$ 23. $60 + x = 110$ 24. $13 - a = 4$
$r = \underline{140}$ $x = \underline{50}$ $a = \underline{9}$

Solve.

25. Write an Unknown Start problem and solve it.
Answers will vary. Possible answer: Margo planted some flowers this morning. She planted 18 more flowers this afternoon. She planted 30 flowers altogether. How many flowers did she plant this morning? Answer: 12 flowers

26. Write an Unknown Change problem and solve it.
Answers will vary. Possible answer: Geoff entered a hiking trail at mile marker 3. He left the hiking trail at mile marker 7. How many miles of the trail did Geoff hike? Answer: 4 miles

92 UNIT 3 LESSON 4

Addition and Subtraction Comparison Problems

Homework and Remembering page 92

Home or School Activity

Music Connection

Stringed Instruments Have students do some research to find out how many strings different stringed musical instruments have. Some examples are shown in the table. Have students write a paragraph about stringed instruments, using the data they find. Suggest that they compare numbers of strings or group instruments that have the same number of strings.

Number of Strings on Musical Instruments	
Instrument	**Number of Strings**
Banjo	5
Guitar	6
Koto	13
Sitar	17
Violin	4
Zither	34

Two-Step Problems Using Addition and Subtraction

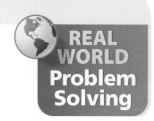

REAL WORLD Problem Solving

Lesson Objective

● Solve two-step problems using a variety of approaches including equations, drawings, and mental math.

The Day at a Glance

Today's Goals	Materials

1 Teaching the Lesson
A1: Discuss the steps of a two-step problem.
A2: Solve two-step problems.
 	
2 Going Further
▶ Differentiated Instruction
 	
3 Homework and Spiral Review
	Lesson Activities
	Student Activity Book pp. 135–136
	  or Student Hardcover Book
	  pp. 135–136
	Homework and Remembering
	  pp. 93–94
		Going Further
		Activity Cards 3-5
		Markers (2 colors)
		Number lines
		Encyclopedias
		Almanecs
		Computers with
		  Internet access
		Math Journals

123 *Use* **Math Talk** *today!*

Keeping Skills Sharp

Quick Practice ⏱ 5 MINUTES	Daily Routines

Goal: Solve simple addition and subtraction equations.

Finding Unknown Values A **Student Leader** writes these eight equations on the board:

$t + 8 = 10$ $4 = 3 + e$ $19 = 10 + h$ $10 = r + 5$

$4 = 7 - f$ $3 = q - 7$ $b = 18 - 8$ $12 - a = 10$

The leader uses a pointer to point to each equation and, on a signal, the whole class says the answer (for example, "*t* equals 2."). If a substantial portion of the class says the wrong answer, the Student Leader (or someone helping the Student Leader) gives the correct answer and explains why it is is correct.

Homework Review Send students to the board to show their solutions for problems 5 and 6. Have each student at the board explain his/her solution. Encourage the rest of the class to ask clarifying questions and make comments.

Strategy Problem Together two DVD's cost $32. One DVD cost $4 more than the other. How much did each DVD cost? $18 and $14; algebraic solution: Let $x =$ the price of one DVD. $x + (x + 4) = \$32$; $2x + 4 = 32$; $2x = \$28$; $x = \$14$; $x + 4 = \$18$

$32		
x	x	$4

Teaching the Lesson

Discuss Two-Step Problems

 20 MINUTES

Goal: Discuss the steps of a two-step problem.

Materials: Student Activity Book or Hardcover Book p. 135

✔ **NCTM Standards:**
Number and Operations
Algebra
Problem Solving

The Learning Classroom

Math Talk Always start by eliciting student ideas about a new topic. Students will increase their engagement in classes if they believe that their contributions will be heard. This may involve allowing for interruptions from students during teacher explanations of content. The teacher continues to decide what is important to explore further, but allows students to "own" new ideas or strategies. Often students come up with and explain strategies that the teacher was about to teach.

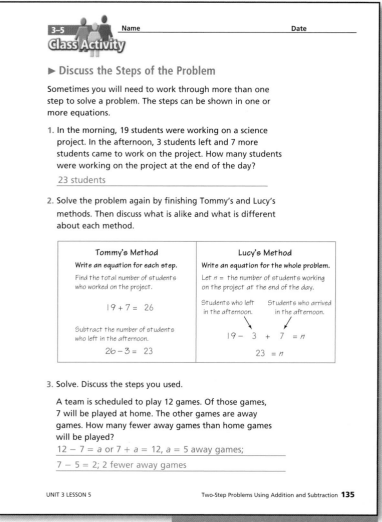

Student Activity Book page 135

▶ Discuss the Steps of the Problem

WHOLE CLASS   **Math Talk**

Ask a student to read the problem at the top of page 135 of the Student Book, or read it together.

● **What is the problem about?** Students working together on a science project.

● **What do you need to find?** The number of students working on the project at the end of the day.

Use **Solve and Discuss** to solve the problem. Discuss methods used at the board and any other methods used by students at their seats.

In problem 2, have students finish Tommy's and Lucy's methods and then have a **Student Leader** lead a discussion in how these methods are alike and different. The methods differ in the order in which Tommy and Lucy did the operations. Lucy did the operations in the order in which events happened. Tommy found the total number of students who worked on the project and then subtracted the 3 who left.

Use **Solve and Discuss** to solve problem 3. For this problem, students do not have to write equations but they may do so. Some students may find it helpful to draw comparison bars.

Discuss any different methods used at the board and any other methods used by students at their seats.

Make sure students understand that the overall problem is to find how many fewer away games than home games will be played. Ask the students to identify the question that is a helping question and not the final question. How many games are away games? Tell students that in some two-step problems, there will only be one question; students will have to think of another question on their own, answer it, and then use the answer to solve the overall problem.

Teaching Note

Math Background The equations that students write for multi-step problems may include more than one operation. Because those operations are limited to addition and subtraction for this activity, the order in which the operations are completed is not important. Students should complete any addition and subtraction operations they find in an equation as they work from left to right.

Later, students will work with expressions that require the operations to be completed in a particular order. At that time, students will learn and apply the order of operations to simplify expressions.

English Language Learners

Write a word problem on the board. Model the different ways to find a solution.

- **Beginning** Show a word problem. Read it aloud and have students repeat. Say: **This problem is about ___.** apples **We need to find the total number of apples.** Have students repeat.
- **Intermediate** Show a word problem. Read the problem together. Ask: **What is this problem about?** apples Ask: **What do we need to find?** the total number of apples
- **Advanced** Show a word problem. Have volunteers read the problem aloud and identify what the problem is about and what needs to be found.

Teaching the Lesson (continued)

Solve Two-Step Problems

 25 MINUTES

Goal: Solve two-step problems.

Materials: Student Activity Book or Hardcover Book p. 136

✓ **NCTM Standards:**
Number and Operations
Algebra
Problem Solving

The Learning Classroom

Math Talk As students finish solving each problem, provide an opportunity for them to describe the drawings or equations they may have used to represent and solve the problems. Encourage questioning by other students about the equations that are described.

 Ongoing Assessment

Present students with this problem:

Jack has 4 baseball, 9 basketball, 7 hockey, and 15 soccer posters. How many more soccer posters than baseball and hockey posters does he have?

Then ask students to:

▶ Write an equation for the problem.

▶ Solve the equation.

▶ Answer the question.

▶ Identify extra or missing information.

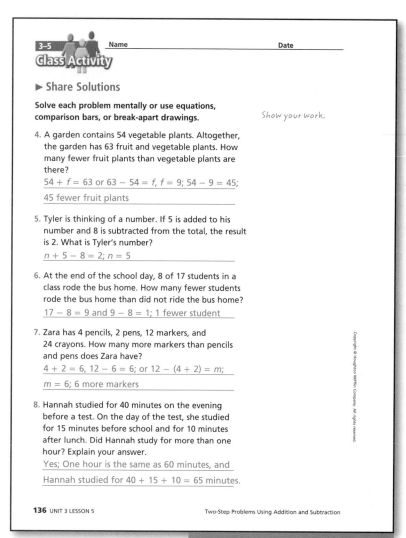

The class activity page shows:

3–5 Class Activity   Name _____   Date _____

▶ **Share Solutions**

Solve each problem mentally or use equations, comparison bars, or break-apart drawings.   *Show your work.*

4. A garden contains 54 vegetable plants. Altogether, the garden has 63 fruit and vegetable plants. How many fewer fruit plants than vegetable plants are there?
$54 + f = 63$ or $63 - 54 = f$, $f = 9$; $54 - 9 = 45$; 45 fewer fruit plants

5. Tyler is thinking of a number. If 5 is added to his number and 8 is subtracted from the total, the result is 2. What is Tyler's number?
$n + 5 - 8 = 2$; $n = 5$

6. At the end of the school day, 8 of 17 students in a class rode the bus home. How many fewer students rode the bus home than did not ride the bus home?
$17 - 8 = 9$ and $9 - 8 = 1$; 1 fewer student

7. Zara has 4 pencils, 2 pens, 12 markers, and 24 crayons. How many more markers than pencils and pens does Zara have?
$4 + 2 = 6$, $12 - 6 = 6$; or $12 - (4 + 2) = m$; $m = 6$; 6 more markers

8. Hannah studied for 40 minutes on the evening before a test. On the day of the test, she studied for 15 minutes before school and for 10 minutes after lunch. Did Hannah study for more than one hour? Explain your answer.
Yes; One hour is the same as 60 minutes, and Hannah studied for $40 + 15 + 10 = 65$ minutes.

136 UNIT 3 LESSON 5   Two-Step Problems Using Addition and Subtraction

Student Activity Book page 136

▶ Share Solutions

WHOLE CLASS   **Math Talk**

Use **Solve and Discuss** to solve problems 4–8 on Student Book page 136. Help students identify intermediate questions they can ask themselves to get to the final question. For example, in problem 4, they need to find how many fruit plants before they can compare fruit plants to vegetable plants. Some problems can be easily represented by equations while others cannot; comparison bars or break-apart addend drawings may be helpful in such cases.

Close with a summary discussion about solving two-step problems. Problems that have three or more numbers in them may be two-step problems. But as in problem 7, some numbers might not be used in the solution (you do not need the number of crayons to solve the problem).

② Going Further

● Intervention   Activity Card 3-5

From Here to There   Activity Card 3-5 ●

Work: By Yourself

Use:
- Comparing Numbers (TRB M50)
- Two-color markers

1. Choose a starting number and an ending number. Sample numbers are given below.

   | START: 7 | END: 15 |

2. Write a two-step arithmetic problem, using addition and subtraction to get from the starting number to the ending number.

   SAMPLE: $7 + 10 - 2 = 15$

3. Model the problem on a number line

4. **Analyze** Does the order of the steps you choose make a difference in the result? Why or why not? No, because of the order of operations rules.

Unit 3, Lesson 5   Copyright © Houghton Mifflin Company

Activity Note Recommend that students use different color markers to show addition and subtraction on their number lines.

 Math Writing Prompt

Create Your Own Write a two-step word problem, using addition and/or subtraction. Exchange papers with a partner, and solve each other's problems.

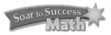 **Software Support**

Use *Soar to Success* for instruction of students needing targeted support for underlying skills.

▲ On Level   Activity Card 3-5

Write Word Problems   Activity Card 3-5 ▲

Work: In Pairs

1. Write a two-step word problem about objects in your classroom. Use both the operations of addition and subtraction.

2. Write and solve an equation to solve the problem.

3. Exchange your problem with another student to solve, and exchange again to check the results.

4. **Discuss** Is there more than one equation that you could use to solve your problem? Justify your answer.

Unit 3, Lesson 5   Copyright © Houghton Mifflin Company

Activity Note Remind students that they should always define the variable before writing an equation for a word problem.

 Math Writing Prompt

Explain Your Thinking Are addition and subtraction the only operations you can use in a two-step problem? Give an example.

 Software Support

Use *MegaMath* for review and reinforcement of the concepts and skills presented in this lesson.

■ Challenge   Activity Card 3-5

Create Your Own   Activity Card 3-5 ■

Work: In Small Groups

Use:
- Encyclopedias
- Almanacs
- Computers with Internet access

1. Work together to research data about the land area of counties in your state. Make a table of the data that you find.

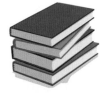

2. On your own, write a two-step word problem about adding or subtracting the data.

3. Work together to solve each of the problems. Exchange problems with other groups to solve, and then exchange again to compare results.

Unit 3, Lesson 5   Copyright © Houghton Mifflin Company

Activity Note Remind students that they need to be careful to align place values when adding and subtracting large numbers. Have them use estimation to see if their answers are reasonable.

 Math Writing Prompt

Explain Your Thinking Do word problems always give you enough information to solve them? Give an example.

 DESTINATION Math® **Software Support**

Use *Destination Math* to take students beyond the concepts and skills presented in this lesson.

Two-Step Problems Using Addition and Subtraction   **305**

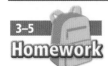

③ Homework and Spiral Review

3-5 Homework **Goal:** Additional Practice

Use this Homework page to provide students with more practice with estimating with two-step problems for addition and subtraction.

3-5 Remembering **Goal:** Spiral Review

This Remembering activity would be appropriate anytime after today's lesson.

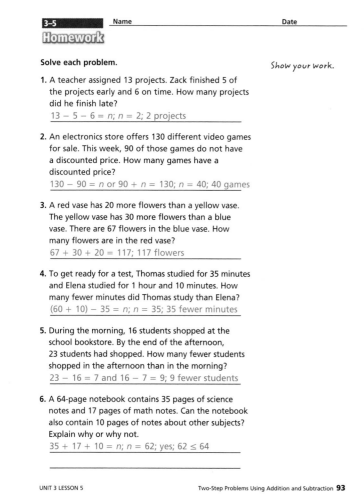

3-5 Homework
Name _____ Date _____

Solve each problem. *Show your work.*

1. A teacher assigned 13 projects. Zack finished 5 of the projects early and 6 on time. How many projects did he finish late?
   13 − 5 − 6 = n; n = 2; 2 projects

2. An electronics store offers 130 different video games for sale. This week, 90 of those games do not have a discounted price. How many games have a discounted price?
   130 − 90 = n or 90 + n = 130; n = 40; 40 games

3. A red vase has 20 more flowers than a yellow vase. The yellow vase has 30 more flowers than a blue vase. There are 67 flowers in the blue vase. How many flowers are in the red vase?
   67 + 30 + 20 = 117; 117 flowers

4. To get ready for a test, Thomas studied for 35 minutes and Elena studied for 1 hour and 10 minutes. How many fewer minutes did Thomas study than Elena?
   (60 + 10) − 35 = n; n = 35; 35 fewer minutes

5. During the morning, 16 students shopped at the school bookstore. By the end of the afternoon, 23 students had shopped. How many fewer students shopped in the afternoon than in the morning?
   23 − 16 = 7 and 16 − 7 = 9; 9 fewer students

6. A 64-page notebook contains 35 pages of science notes and 17 pages of math notes. Can the notebook also contain 10 pages of notes about other subjects? Explain why or why not.
   35 + 17 + 10 = n; n = 62; yes; 62 ≤ 64

UNIT 3 LESSON 5   Two-Step Problems Using Addition and Subtraction **93**

Homework and Remembering page 93

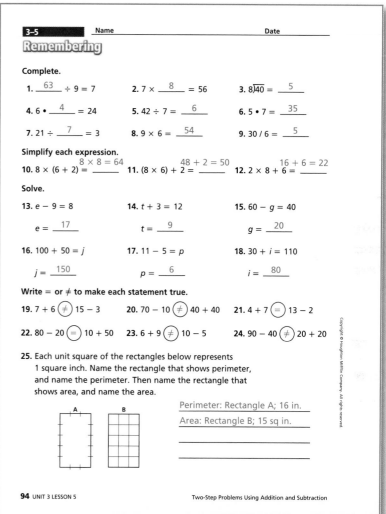

3-5 Remembering
Name _____ Date _____

Complete.

1. $\underline{63} \div 9 = 7$ 2. $7 \times \underline{8} = 56$ 3. $8\overline{)40} = \underline{5}$

4. $6 \cdot \underline{4} = 24$ 5. $42 \div 7 = \underline{6}$ 6. $5 \cdot 7 = \underline{35}$

7. $21 \div \underline{7} = 3$ 8. $9 \times 6 = \underline{54}$ 9. $30 / 6 = \underline{5}$

Simplify each expression.
                         $8 \times 8 = 64$ $48 + 2 = 50$ $16 + 6 = 22$
10. $8 \times (6 + 2) = \underline{\quad}$ 11. $(8 \times 6) + 2 = \underline{\quad}$ 12. $2 \times 8 + 6 = \underline{\quad}$

Solve.

13. $e − 9 = 8$ 14. $t + 3 = 12$ 15. $60 − g = 40$

    $e = \underline{17}$ $t = \underline{9}$ $g = \underline{20}$

16. $100 + 50 = j$ 17. $11 − 5 = p$ 18. $30 + i = 110$

    $j = \underline{150}$ $p = \underline{6}$ $i = \underline{80}$

Write = or ≠ to make each statement true.

19. $7 + 6 (\neq) 15 − 3$ 20. $70 − 10 (\neq) 40 + 40$ 21. $4 + 7 (=) 13 − 2$

22. $80 − 20 (=) 10 + 50$ 23. $6 + 9 (\neq) 10 − 5$ 24. $90 − 40 (\neq) 20 + 20$

25. Each unit square of the rectangles below represents 1 square inch. Name the rectangle that shows perimeter, and name the perimeter. Then name the rectangle that shows area, and name the area.

    Perimeter: Rectangle A; 16 in.
    Area: Rectangle B; 15 sq in.
    _____
    _____

94 UNIT 3 LESSON 5   Two-Step Problems Using Addition and Subtraction

Homework and Remembering page 94

Home or School Activity

Math-to-Math Connection

Roman Numerals The table shows some Roman numerals and their equivalent Arabic numerals. In Roman numerals, if a smaller value follows a larger value, the values are added. For example, VIII = 5 + 1 + 1 + 1 = 8. If a larger value follows a smaller value, the smaller is subtracted from the larger. For example, IX = 10 − 1 = 9. No more than three of the same Roman numeral can appear "in a row." So 32 is represented as XXXII, but 42 is represented as XLII.

Have students talk with friends or family about where Roman numerals are used. Then have them write the year they were born and this year in Roman numerals.

Arabic Numeral	Roman Numeral
1	I
5	V
10	X
50	L
100	C
500	D
1,000	M

306 UNIT 3 LESSON 5

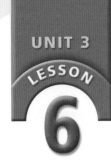

Mixed Word Problems

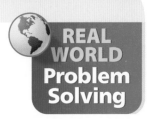

REAL WORLD
Problem Solving

Vocabulary

addend
total
operation
equal groups
factor
product

Lesson Objective

• Solve a variety of problems involving addition, subtraction, multiplication, and division.

The Day at a Glance

Today's Goals	Materials	
1 **Teaching the Lesson** **A1:** Discuss how the information in a problem helps determine the operation you will use. **A2:** Solve a variety of word problems. **2** **Going Further** ▶ Differentiated Instruction **3** **Homework and Spiral Review**	**Lesson Activities** Student Activity Book pp. 137–138 or Student Hardcover Book pp. 137–138 Homework and Remembering pp. 95–96 Quick Quiz 1 (Assessment Guide)	**Going Further** Activity Cards 3-6 Math Journals

123 Use Math Talk today!

Keeping Skills Sharp

Quick Practice ⏱ 5 MINUTES	Daily Routines
Goal: Solve simple addition and subtraction equations. **Finding Unknown Values** A **Student Leader** writes these eight equations on the board: $m + 3 = 10$ $16 = 10 + r$ $10 = h + 1$ $2 = 7 - f$ $17 - a = 10$ $6 = 3 + e$ $7 = q - 3$ $b = 14 - 4$ The leader uses a pointer to point to each equation and, on a signal, the whole class says the answer (for example, "m equals 7."). If a substantial portion of the class says the wrong answer, the Student Leader (or someone helping the Student Leader) gives the correct answer and explains why it is correct.	**Homework Review** Have students discuss the problems from their homework. Encourage students to help each other resolve any misunderstandings. **Estimation** A school picnic committee has a budget of $25 for paper and plastic products. One package of paper plates costs $6.79. A package of napkins costs $3.29. A package of cups costs $3.25. A box of plastic forks costs $2.59. If the committee needs two packages each of plates and cups, one package of napkins, and one box of forks, will they stay within their budget? Estimate to find your answer. No; the estimate is $26.00.

Teaching the Lesson

Discuss Mixed Word Problems

 30 MINUTES

Goal: Discuss how the information in a problem helps determine the operation you will use.

Materials: Student Activity Book or Hardcover Book p. 137

✓ **NCTM Standards:**
Number and Operations
Reasoning and Proof

The Learning Classroom

Math Talk Aspire to make your classroom a place where all students listen to understand one another. Explain to students that this is different from just being quiet when someone else is talking; it involves thinking about what a person is saying so that you could explain it yourself or help them explain it more clearly. Also, they need to listen so that they can ask a question or help the explainer.

English Language Learners

Write an addition word problem and solution. Review *addend* and *total*.

• **Beginning** Point to the word *addend*. Say: **The numbers we add are called addends.** Point to the word *total*. Say: **Total is the answer to an addition problem.** Have students repeat.

• **Intermediate** Ask: **What is an addend?** a number that is added Ask: **What is a total?** the answer to an addition problem

• **Advanced** Have students use short sentences to describe how to use addends to get a total amount in an addition problem.

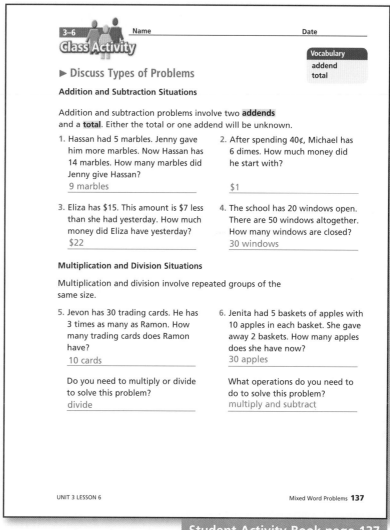

Student Activity Book page 137

▶ Discuss Types of Problems [WHOLE CLASS]

Addition and Subtraction Situations Read the introductory sentence or Student Book page 137 with the class. Students are likely to know that addition involves addends. To help them recognize and understand that subtraction also involves addends, write the following phrases and related equations on the board.

addend + addend = total   5 + 6 = 11

total − addend = addend   11 − 6 = 5

Invite students to suggest other related number sentences that show that both addition and subtraction involve addends. Ask students to summarize their work with 8 related equations for addition and subtraction.

As they share their suggestions, remind students that addition and subtraction are inverse operations.

Read problem 1 together. For this problem, the students should decide who has more and what needs to be done to find the missing amount. Have students look at the word "more" in the problem.

- Does this word "more" in this problem suggest addition or subtraction? addition **Why?** Jenny gave Hassan more marbles so it means addition.

- Is 5 an addend or the total? addend

- Is 14 an addend or the total? total

- Do you need to add or subtract to solve the problem? subtract

- Tell a problem that contains the word "more" and requires addition to find the answer. Possible answer: John has 5 dollars. Mary give him 9 more dollars. How many dollars does he have now?

Emphasize to students that before they choose an operation to solve a problem, they must read the problem carefully. They must understand the situation. Then they can solve the problem.

Discuss problem 2. This is a two-step problem. Students should identify the missing question as "What is the value of 6 dimes?"

Activity continued ▶

Teaching Note

Language and Vocabulary Some students assume that the word "more" means subtract because of problems that contain the phrase "how many more." Other students assume that "more" means add because it suggests receiving additional items. Students make similar assumptions when the word "less" is present in a problem. Remind students that rather than relying on these key words to choose an operation, they should carefully consider the entire problem and understand the situation before solving.

Activity 1

Teaching Note

Math Background The research says that word-problem solving is more complex than "read and choose the operation." Successful solvers build a mental and/or drawn/represented model of the situation. They might not consciously "choose an operation." The solution method may arise more organically from the situation.

Discuss problem 3. In this problem, students may see the word "less" and think they should subtract. Have students explain why they should add to solve the problem. If they are having difficulty, ask:

● Does Eliza have more money today than she had yesterday? no

● Does Eliza have less money today than she had yesterday? yes

● Did Eliza have more money yesterday than today? yes

● How can we find out how much more? add $7 to $15

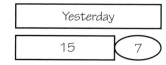

Discuss problem 4. This problem has an unknown addend.

Explain to students how all of the types of addition and subtraction situations—change, collection, and comparison—involve two addends that make the total. Any of these can be unknown.

Multiplication and Division Situations Read the introductory sentence with the class. Emphasize to students that multiplication and division situations can be thought of as involving equal groups. On the board, write the following phrases and related equations.

factor × factor = product 5 × 6 = 30

product ÷ factor = factor 30 ÷ 6 = 5

Remind students that multiplication and division are inverse operations and that division involves finding an unknown factor.

Discuss problem 5. For this problem, the students should decide who has more and what needs to be done to find the missing amount.

● Who has more trading cards, Jevon or Ramon? Jevon

● How can you find out how many Jevon has? divide 30 by 3

- Tell a problem that contains the phrase "times as many" and you need to multiply. Possible answer: Jake has 5 dimes. Ali has 3 times as many. How many dimes does Ali have?

Discuss problem 6. This is a two-step problem. See if your students come up with at least two ways to solve it. Two methods are:

- 5 baskets − 2 baskets = 3 baskets; 3 baskets × 10 = 30 apples
- 5 × 10 = 50; 2 × 10 = 20; 50 − 20 = 30 apples

So we see that all of these multiplication/division situations involve an unknown product or an unknown factor. These were comparison and equal grouping situations, but array, area, and combination situations also involve an unknown product or an unknown factor.

Teaching the Lesson (continued)

Solve Mixed Word Problems

 25 MINUTES

Goal: Solve a variety of word problems.

Materials: Student Activity Book or Hardcover Book p. 138

 NCTM Standards:
Number and Operations
Problem Solving

 Ongoing Assessment

Ask students:

▶ Does subtraction involve addends? Give two related number sentences to support your answer.

▶ What are inverse operations? Give an example.

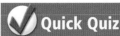 **Quick Quiz**

See Assessment Guide for Unit 3 Quick Quiz 1.

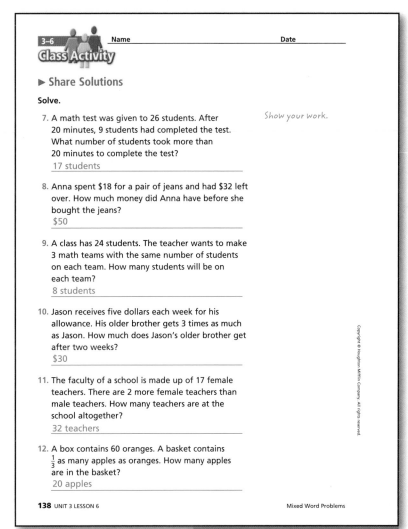

Student Activity Book page 138

▶ **Share Solutions** WHOLE CLASS

Use **Solve and Discuss** to solve problems 7–12 on page 138 of the Student Book. Have students especially focus on why the problem is addition/ subtraction or multiplication/division. Have students state each problem in different ways to review the kinds of language for each kind of problem.

② Going Further

Intervention   Activity Card 3-6

Guess and Check   Activity Card 3-6 ●

Work: In Pairs

1. Read the problem below.

> Jess has 50 toy cars. Some are black and the rest are
> yellow. She has 12 more black cars than yellow cars.
> How many of each color does she have?

2. Copy the table below. Use it to help you solve the problem.

Guess for Yellow	Number of Black	Total Number	High/Low
19	31	50	

3. **Analyze** How did the table help you to find the solution?
   If the total number was too high, the guess needed to
   be lowered. If the total was too low, the guess needed
   to be raised.

Unit 3, Lesson 6   Copyright © Houghton Mifflin Company

Activity Note Let interested students work on
writing Guess and Check problems of their own.

 Math Writing Prompt

Explain Your Thinking Explain how you decide
what number to use for your first guess in a
Guess and Check problem.

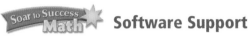 **Software Support**

Use *Soar to Success* for instruction of students
needing targeted support for underlying skills.

▲ On Level   Activity Card 3-6

Too Much Information   Activity Card 3-6 ▲

Work: In Pairs

1. Read the problem below.

> Joshua bought paint and brushes to complete a mural.
> He bought 24 tubes of paint and 6 packets of brushes.
> Each packet of brushes has 5 brushes. How many total
> brushes did he buy?

2. Work with your partner to decide what information in the
   problem is needed and what is extra. See below.

3. Solve the problem. Joshua bought 30 brushes.

4. Now create your own problem with too much information.
   Then exchange with your partner to solve.

   2. needed: number of packets of brushes and number
   of brushes in each packet; extra: number of tubes of
   paint

Unit 3, Lesson 6   Copyright © Houghton Mifflin Company

Activity Note Remind students that they can use
labels in the question to help identify necessary
information. If the question only asks about brushes,
the information about paint can be disregarded.

 Math Writing Prompt

Too Much Information Have you ever been in
a situation where too much information is given
to solve a problem? Give an example.

MEGAMATH Grades K-6 **Software Support**

Use *MegaMath* for review and reinforcement of
the concepts and skills presented in this lesson.

■ Challenge   Activity Card 3-6

What's Missing?   Activity Card 3-6 ■

Work: In Pairs

1. Read the problem below.

> Mr. Lopez gave each of his students 6 sheets of paper.
> How many packs of paper did he use?

2. Work with your partner to decide if you have enough
   information to solve the problem. If not, what information
   is needed? no; how many sheets are in a pack; how
   many students Mr. Lopez has

3. Make up any missing information, and solve the problem.

Unit 3, Lesson 6   Copyright © Houghton Mifflin Company

Activity Note Make sure that students realize that
more than one piece of information can be missing
in a problem-solving situation.

 Math Writing Prompt

Explain Your Thinking Write a word problem
with at least one piece of information missing.
Exchange papers with a partner, and have your
partner identify what is missing.

✖ **DESTINATION Math·** **Software Support**

Use *Destination Math* to take students beyond
the concepts and skills presented in this lesson.

③ Homework and Spiral Review

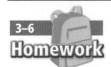

Homework **Goal:** Additional Practice

Use this Homework page to provide students with more practice with mixed word problems.

Remembering **Goal:** Spiral Review

This Remembering activity would be appropriate anytime after today's lesson.

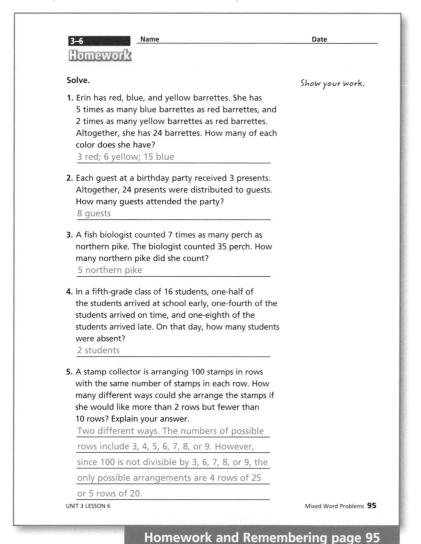

3-6 Name _____ Date _____
Homework

Solve.   *Show your work.*

1. Erin has red, blue, and yellow barrettes. She has 5 times as many blue barrettes as red barrettes, and 2 times as many yellow barrettes as red barrettes. Altogether, she has 24 barrettes. How many of each color does she have?
   3 red; 6 yellow; 15 blue

2. Each guest at a birthday party received 3 presents. Altogether, 24 presents were distributed to guests. How many guests attended the party?
   8 guests

3. A fish biologist counted 7 times as many perch as northern pike. The biologist counted 35 perch. How many northern pike did she count?
   5 northern pike

4. In a fifth-grade class of 16 students, one-half of the students arrived at school early, one-fourth of the students arrived on time, and one-eighth of the students arrived late. On that day, how many students were absent?
   2 students

5. A stamp collector is arranging 100 stamps in rows with the same number of stamps in each row. How many different ways could she arrange the stamps if she would like more than 2 rows but fewer than 10 rows? Explain your answer.
   Two different ways. The numbers of possible rows include 3, 4, 5, 6, 7, 8, or 9. However, since 100 is not divisible by 3, 6, 7, 8, or 9, the only possible arrangements are 4 rows of 25 or 5 rows of 20.

UNIT 3 LESSON 6   Mixed Word Problems **95**

Homework and Remembering page 95

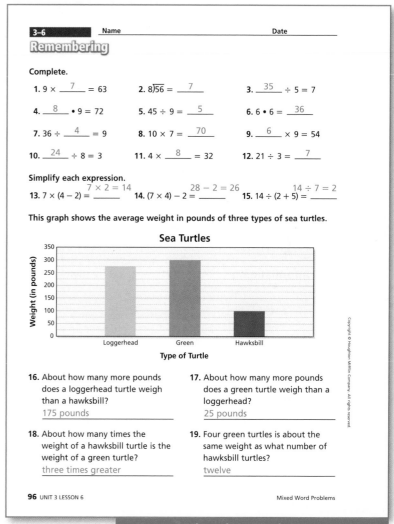

3-6 Name _____ Date _____
Remembering

Complete.

1. $9 \times \underline{7} = 63$ 2. $8\overline{)56} = \underline{7}$ 3. $\underline{35} \div 5 = 7$

4. $\underline{8} \cdot 9 = 72$ 5. $45 \div 9 = \underline{5}$ 6. $6 \cdot 6 = \underline{36}$

7. $36 \div \underline{4} = 9$ 8. $10 \times 7 = \underline{70}$ 9. $\underline{6} \times 9 = 54$

10. $\underline{24} \div 8 = 3$ 11. $4 \times \underline{8} = 32$ 12. $21 \div 3 = \underline{7}$

Simplify each expression.

13. $7 \times (4 - 2) = \underline{\quad}$ ($7 \times 2 = 14$)
14. $(7 \times 4) - 2 = \underline{\quad}$ ($28 - 2 = 26$)
15. $14 \div (2 + 5) = \underline{\quad}$ ($14 \div 7 = 2$)

This graph shows the average weight in pounds of three types of sea turtles.

Sea Turtles

Weight (in pounds) — vertical axis: 0, 50, 100, 150, 200, 250, 300, 350
Type of Turtle — Loggerhead, Green, Hawksbill

16. About how many more pounds does a loggerhead turtle weigh than a hawksbill?
    175 pounds

17. About how many more pounds does a green turtle weigh than a loggerhead?
    25 pounds

18. About how many times the weight of a hawksbill turtle is the weight of a green turtle?
    three times greater

19. Four green turtles is about the same weight as what number of hawksbill turtles?
    twelve

96 UNIT 3 LESSON 6   Mixed Word Problems

Homework and Remembering page 96

Home or School Activity

Social Studies Connection

My Community Have students make a map of their community. Be sure they include their homes and some important places, such as school, the library, the park, and so on.

Have students describe what information they need to make the map. For example, how many blocks is it from the town hall to the library? How many stop lights are there between my house and school?

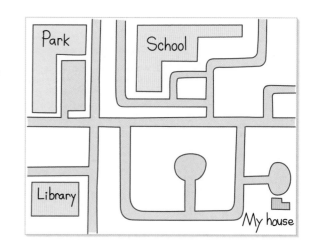

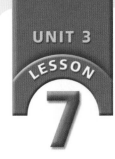

Place Value to Thousands

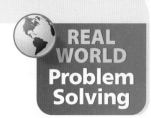
REAL WORLD Problem Solving

Lesson Objective

• Identify the place value of numbers through thousands.

Vocabulary
place-value drawings
dot array

The Day at a Glance

Today's Goals	Materials
1 Teaching the Lesson **A1:** Connect a dot array to the ones, tens, and hundreds places. **A2:** Represent larger numbers with dot arrays. **A3:** Represent numbers without a dot array. **2 Going Further** ▶ Math Connection: Place Value and Money ▶ Differentiated Instruction **3 Homework and Spiral Review**	**Lesson Activities** Student Activity Book pp. 139–141, 143–144 or Student Hardcover Book pp. 139–141, 143–144 and Activity Workbook pp. 57–58 (includes Family Letters) Homework and Remembering pp. 97–98 MathBoards or MathBoard Dot Array (TRB M47) Dry-erase markers Dry-erase materials Base-ten blocks (optional) **Going Further** Student Activity Book p. 142 or Student Hardcover Book p. 142 Activity Cards 3-7 Number cubes Math Journals

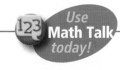
123 Use Math Talk today!

Keeping Skills Sharp

Quick Practice 5 MINUTES	Daily Routines
Goal: Solve simple addition and subtraction equations. **Finding Unknown Values** Have a **Student Leader** write the eight equations on the board: $9 = 4 + e$ $10 = 6 + h$ $r + 7 = 13$ $16 = 10 + r$ $13 = 18 - f$ $b = 17 - 6$ $8 = q - 3$ $14 - a = 7$ Then have the Student Leader use a pointer to point to the first equation and, on a signal, the whole class says, "e equals 5." If a substantial portion of the class gets it wrong, the Student Leader (or someone helping the Student Leader) explains why it is 5. Repeat this process for the remaining seven equations.	**Homework Review** If students give incorrect answers, have them explain how they found the answers. This can help you determine whether the error is conceptual or procedural. **Representation** Write the number 1,403 in five different ways. *Possible answers:* 1,000 + 400 + 3; 1,400 + 3; 1,410 – 7; 1,406 – 3; 1 thousand 4 hundred 3; 1,300 + 103; 1,000 + 100 + 100 + 100 + 100 + 3; one thousand, four hundred, three

① Teaching the Lesson

Activity 1

Draw Ones, Tens, and Hundreds

 20 MINUTES

Goal: Connect a dot array to the ones, tens, and hundreds places.

Materials: Student Activity Book or Hardcover Book p. 139, MathBoards or MathBoard Dot Array (TRB M47), dry-erase markers, dry-erase materials

 NCTM Standards:
Number and Operations
Algebra
Representation

Teaching Note

Fluency During this unit, it is important that students maintain and improve their knowledge of the basic multiplications and divisions. You will find suggestions for games and practice at the end of the Unit 3 Overview.

📁 Class Management

In future lessons we will use MathBoard Materials to refer to the following materials:

MathBoards
Dry-erase markers
Dry-erase materials

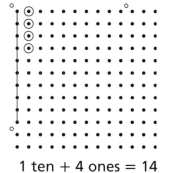

1 ten + 4 ones = 14

▶ **Represent Ones and Tens** | WHOLE CLASS |

Use a Dot Array Have students work on their MathBoards or give each student a copy of MathBoard Dot Array (TRB M47). Have students look at the dots and the open circles along the left and top sides of the paper.

Tell students the dots form an array. Have students count the dots between the open circles. There are 10 dots between open circles. Discuss with students how the open circles can help them count 20 dots across and 20 dots down.

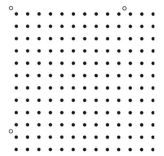

Represent Ones Have students draw a circle around 1 dot. Ask students what number that dot represents. 1 Then discuss how they could show a bigger number, such as 4 or 7.

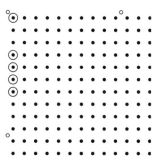

Quick Tens Write the number 14 on the board. Discuss the place value of each digit in the number.

● What does the 4 represent? 4 ones

● What does the 1 represent? 10 ones; 1 group of ten

Students should discuss how they could show 14 on the dot array. Circle 14 dots or circle 1 group of 10 dots plus 4 single dots.

Introduce the idea of a *quick ten* to represent 1 ten. A quick ten is shown by drawing a line through ten dots. Now show students how they can represent 14 with 1 quick ten and 4 circles. (See drawing at left.)

Student Activity Book page 139

3-7
Class Activity

Name _____   Date _____

Vocabulary
place-value drawings
dot array

▶ Represent Hundreds

You can represent numbers by making **place-value drawings**
on a **dot array**.

1. What number does this drawing show? __537__
   Explain your thinking.
   Each box represents 100, each line represents 10,
   and each circle represents 1. 500 + 30 + 7 = 537.

▶ Represent Thousands

**Discuss this place-value drawing. Write the number
of each.**

2. ones: __8__

3. quick tens: __6__

4. hundred boxes: __4__

5. thousand bars: __3__

6. How many hundred boxes could we draw
   inside each thousand bar? Explain.
   10; There are 10 hundreds in
   1 thousand.

7. What number does this drawing show?
   3,468

UNIT 3 LESSON 7   Place Value to Thousands **139**

Teaching Note

Student MathBoards Dry-erase
boards will be used in grade 4 in a
variety of ways. Students should write
on them only with dry-erase markers.
Any other kind of writing utensil can
permanently ruin the surface of the
boards. Each student will also need
some kind of dry-eraser material. A
dry, soft cloth, such as a clean cotton
sock, works well. A paper towel or
tissue also works. You may wish to
devise some easy system of
distributing the dry-erase materials.

English Language Learners

Draw a place-value drawing for
537. Model how to count the
hundreds, tens, and ones.

- **Beginning** Say: **The drawing
  shows the place value of digits
  in a number. 537 is 5 hundreds, 3
  tens, and 7 ones.** Have students
  repeat.

- **Intermediate** Ask: **What number
  does the drawing show?** 537 Ask:
  How many hundreds? 5 **Tens?** 3
  Ones? 7

- **Advanced** Have students explain
  how a place-value drawing shows
  the value of digits.

▶ Represent Hundreds

WHOLE CLASS

Math Talk

Write the number 126 on the board. Discuss the value of each digit.
Have students explain how they can show 100 on the dot array. Draw 10
quick tens. Ask students for another way to show 100. Elicit from
students that they can draw a box around the dots that would be in the
10 quick tens. Tell students that they can call a box with 100 dots inside
of it a *hundred box*. (See drawing at right.)

Ask students to show 126 on the dot array.

Solve and Discuss exercise 1 on page 139 of the Student Book.

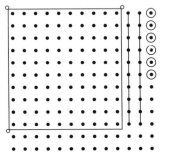

Activity 2

Draw Thousands

 20 MINUTES

Goal: Represent larger numbers with dot arrays.

Materials: MathBoard Materials, Student Activity Book or Hardcover Book p. 139

 NCTM Standards:
Number and Operations
Algebra
Representation

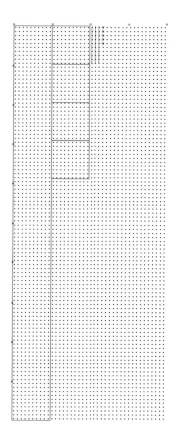

1 thousand + 4 hundreds + 3 tens + 5 ones = 1,435

▶ **Use MathBoards** WHOLE CLASS

Have students hold their boards the long way with the white space at the right side.

Discuss the array of dots on the board and the spacing of the open circles down the left side and across the bottom

● How many dots are there between open circles? 10 going across and 10 going down

● How many dots are there in all going across? 10 groups of 10 = 100

● How many dots are there in all going down? 5 groups of 10 = 50

▶ **Represent Thousands** WHOLE CLASS

Write the number 1,435 on the board. Have students discuss how they could show 1,000 on the dot array. 10 groups of 100 or 10 hundred boxes

If necessary, students may count by 100s up to 1,000, keeping track of the hundreds on their fingers, to demonstrate to themselves that 10 hundreds = 1,000.

Have students discuss how they can make 1 thousand without drawing 10 boxes. Tell them that they can call a box with 1,000 dots inside of it a *thousand bar*. Have them show 1,435 on their boards. See the example shown on the left.

Discuss briefly the purpose of place-value notation. Tell students it is an easy way to write large numbers, using only the ten numerals 0 through 9. Place value tells whether a 2, for example, is 2 ones, 2 tens, 2 hundreds, and so on.

Use exercises 2–7 on page 139 of the Student Book as needed to make sure everyone understands ones, tens, hundreds, and thousands places.

Quick-Draw Place Value

▶ Discuss MathBoards WHOLE CLASS

Have students discuss the greatest number they can show on their
boards. 100 dots across by 50 dots down = 5 thousand bars or 5,000

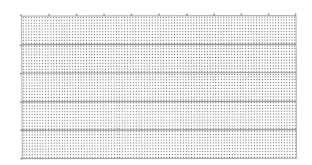

Have students show numbers that are smaller than 5,000 on their
boards. The class can choose numbers, or have partners work together,
to give each other numbers to draw.

▶ Zero as a Place Holder WHOLE CLASS

Write the number 803 on the board, then have students show the place
value on their boards. 8 hundred boxes + 3 ones

Make sure they understand why they don't need to show any quick tens.

Write the number 2,041 on the board and have students show it. Again
discuss what happens in a drawing when there is a zero that is holding a
place. No value in the hundreds place means no hundred boxes in the
drawing.

 15 MINUTES

Goal: Represent numbers without a
dot array.

Materials: Student Activity Book
or Hardcover Book pp. 140–141,
MathBoard Materials, base-ten blocks
(optional)

 NCTM Standards:
Number and Operations
Algebra
Representation

Teaching Note

What to Expect From Students
Have students summarize their
understanding of the magnitudes of
the place values.

- There are 10 ones in 1 ten:
  $10 \times 1 = 10$

- There are 10 tens in 1 hundred:
  $10 \times 10 = 100$

- There are 10 hundreds in
  1 thousand:
  $10 \times 100 = 1,000$

Activity continued ▶

1 Teaching the Lesson (continued)

Activity 3

Teaching Note

Research The human eye can visualize groups of up to 5 items without counting. For this reason, you should encourage the students to group the parts of their place-value drawings in 5s.

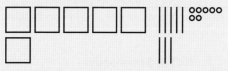

6 hundreds + 8 tens + 7 ones = 687

This will reduce errors, make explaining easier, and facilitate describing make-a-ten methods for adding and subtracting as you make a new group of ten in adding and take from a group of ten in subtracting.

The Learning Classroom

Helping Community When stronger math students finish their work early, let them help others who might be struggling. Many students enjoy the role of helping other students. In their "helper" roles, students who might become bored challenge themselves as they explain math content to others.

3–7
Class Activity

Name _____ Date _____

▶ **Draw Larger Numbers**

Place value can also be shown without using a dot array.

8. What number does this drawing represent? Explain your thinking.
   1,279. The drawing shows
   1 thousand bar,
   2 hundred boxes, 7 quick tens,
   and 9 ones.

What would the drawing represent if it had:

9. 3 more hundred boxes? _1,579_
10. 0 hundred boxes? _1,079_
11. 2 fewer quick tens? _1,259_
12. 2 more quick tens? _1,299_
13. 0 quick tens? _1,209_
14. 5 fewer ones? _1,274_
15. 0 ones? _1,270_
16. 4 more thousand bars? _5,279_
17. On your MathBoard, make a place-value drawing for a different number that has the digits 1, 2, 7, and 9.
    Drawings will vary.
18. Explain how your drawing is similar to and different from the drawing for 1,279.
    Explanations will vary.

140 UNIT 3 LESSON 7   Place Value to Thousands

Student Activity Book page 140

▶ Draw Larger Numbers WHOLE CLASS

Write the number 6,487 on the board. Ask students:

● Can 6,487 be shown on one MathBoard? No; there are not enough dots.

● Can two boards be used to show 6,487? Yes

Ask students to turn their boards to the white side, then have them think about how they could draw place value without showing the dots inside. by drawing the place-value shapes: ones dots or circles, quick tens, hundred boxes, and thousand bars. Then they should consider what they would have to include in a place-value drawing of 6,487. 6 thousand bars, 4 hundred boxes, 8 quick tens, and 7 circles or dots

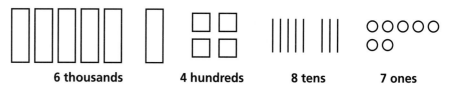

6 thousands   4 hundreds   8 tens   7 ones

Have students complete exercises 8–18 on page 140 of the Student Book.

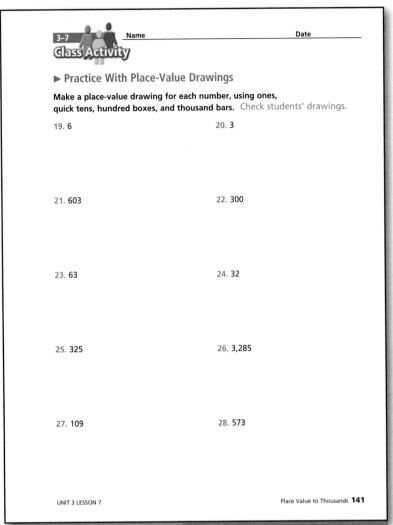

3-7 Class Activity

Name _____ Date _____

▶ Practice With Place-Value Drawings

Make a place-value drawing for each number, using ones, quick tens, hundred boxes, and thousand bars. Check students' drawings.

19. 6

20. 3

21. 603

22. 300

23. 63

24. 32

25. 325

26. 3,285

27. 109

28. 573

UNIT 3 LESSON 7

Place Value to Thousands **141**

Student Activity Book page 141

▶ **Practice With Place-Value Drawings** WHOLE CLASS

Use **Solve and Discuss** to do exercises 19–24 on page 141 of the Student Book. Be sure to discuss how zeros work in place value. Have students make up more numbers until you are sure that students understand. Then have students make drawings independently for exercises 25–28, and give more numbers if necessary.

 Alternate Approach

Base-ten blocks Some students may need to use concrete materials to represent numbers. This may help them more easily make the connection between models and numbers.

Provide students with base-ten materials for modeling the numbers in the lesson.

235
2 hundreds 3 tens   5 ones

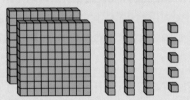

Ask students to relate the ten hundreds-flats in the thousands cube to the ten hundreds-squares on the MathBoard drawings. Some students have difficulty seeing the ten hundreds-flats in a cube. They only see the 6 flats on the cube's surfaces.

 Ongoing Assessment

Ask questions such as:

▶ How many quick tens will you need to show 75?

▶ How many ones will you need to show 53?

▶ How many quick tens will you need to show 308?

▶ Explain how to show 218.

② Going Further

Math Connection: Place Value and Money

Goal: Connect place value and money.

Materials: Student Activity Book or Hardcover Book p. 142

✓ **NCTM Standard:**
Number and Operations

▶ Place Value and Money WHOLE CLASS

In this lesson, students will connect place value with money. Explain to the class that our system of money has the same base-ten relationship as our place-value system.

Write $462 on the board. Tell the class that the 4 represents four hundred dollars, the 6 represents sixty dollars, and the 2 represents two dollars. Ask the class how many hundred-dollar bills, ten-dollar bills, and one-dollar bills can be used to represent the number.

Then draw a place-value chart and write the numbers in the place-value chart.

$462

Hundreds	Tens	Ones
4	6	2

Read the top of Student Book page 142 with the class. Work through the problem together. Draw a place-value chart on the board for the number 214. Ask the students if there are any other ways Mr. Jansen could have paid for the television.

Discuss exercise 1 by asking a student to say the number and type of bills aloud. Then, have students work independently on exercises 2–5.

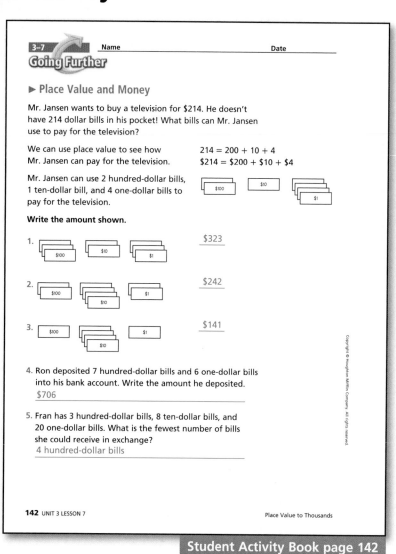

Student Activity Book page 142

📁 Class Management

Walk around the room to observe how students are completing the exercises. This will enable you to determine any students who do not yet understand how place-value relates to money. You can then suggest that they use a place-value chart to help them.

Differentiated Instruction

Intervention   Activity Card 3-7

Order Numbers	Activity Card 3-7

Work: In Small Groups

Use:
- Number cube

1. On your own, copy the places for a four-digit number on a sheet of paper as shown below.

   ____ , ____ ____ ____

2. Take turns rolling the number cube. Each member of the group records the number in any place in the four-digit number.

3. Continue until 4 rolls have been completed.

4. List the numbers written by each member of your group. Then work together to order the numbers from least to greatest.

Unit 3, Lesson 7   Copyright © Houghton Mifflin Company

Activity Note Students can repeat the activity as time permits. Have students make a list of the four numbers, aligning place values, to compare and order their numbers after each round.

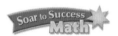 **Math Writing Prompt**

Use Place Value Write the greatest number possible, using the digits 3, 6, 1, and 4. Make a place-value drawing for your number.

Soar to Success Math **Software Support**

Use *Soar to Success* for instruction of students needing targeted support for underlying skills.

On Level   Activity Card 3-7

Interpret Data	Activity Card 3-7

Work: In Pairs

1. Use the information in the table to answer the questions below.

August Profits	
Business	**Profits**
Card Store	$7,228
Coffee Shop	$5,985
Shoe Store	$7,822
Video Store	$9,575

2. Which business had a profit that was less than the Card Store's profit? Coffee Shop

3. How many businesses had a profit greater than the Shoe Store's profit? one

4. On your own, write three questions comparing the data in the table. Then exchange with your partner, and find the answers.

Unit 3, Lesson 7   Copyright © Houghton Mifflin Company

Activity Note Students may find it easier to write all the profits in order from least to greatest and then label the numbers with the names of the stores.

 Math Writing Prompt

Predict Is it likely that the Shoe Shop will make more profit than the Card Store every month? Explain your reasoning.

 Software Support

Use *MegaMath* for review and reinforcement of the concepts and skills presented in this lesson.

Challenge   Activity Card 3-7

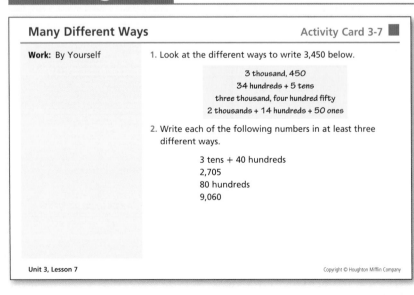

Many Different Ways	Activity Card 3-7

Work: By Yourself

1. Look at the different ways to write 3,450 below.

> 3 thousand, 450
> 34 hundreds + 5 tens
> three thousand, four hundred fifty
> 2 thousands + 14 hundreds + 50 ones

2. Write each of the following numbers in at least three different ways.

> 3 tens + 40 hundreds
> 2,705
> 80 hundreds
> 9,060

Unit 3, Lesson 7   Copyright © Houghton Mifflin Company

Activity Note Remind students that standard form, word form, and place-value form are all different ways to write the same number.

 Math Writing Prompt

Find the Error Elaina wrote 12 hundreds + 14 tens as 1,214. Is she correct? Explain your answer.

 DESTINATION Math **Software Support**

Use *Destination Math* to take students beyond the concepts and skills presented in this lesson.

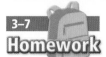 # ③ Homework and Spiral Review

✔ Include students' work for page 97 as part of their portfolios.

This Remembering activity would be appropriate anytime after today's lesson.

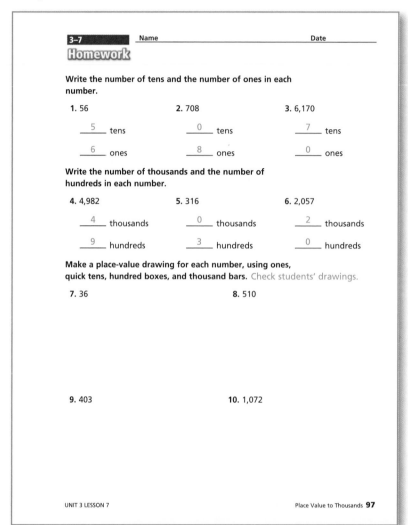

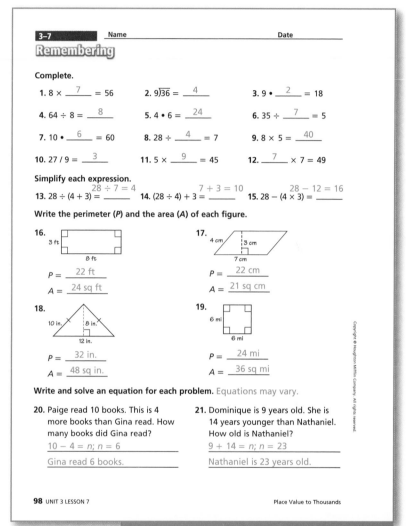

Homework and Remembering page 97

Homework and Remembering page 98

Home and School Connection

Family Letter Have children take home the Family Letter on Student Book page 143 or Activity Workbook page 57. This letter explains how the concepts of place value and addition of greater numbers are developed in *Math Expressions.* It gives parents and guardians a better understanding of the learning that goes on in math class. A Spanish translation of this letter is on page 144 in the Student Book and page 58 in the Activity Workbook.

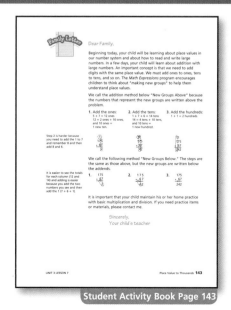

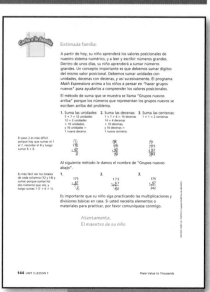

Student Activity Book Page 143

Student Activity Book Page 144

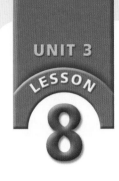

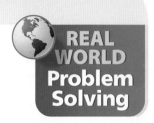

REAL WORLD Problem Solving

UNIT 3 LESSON 8

Read, Write, and Round Numbers

Vocabulary

standard form
word form
place value
expanded form

Lesson Objectives

● Read and write numbers to thousands.

● Round numbers to the nearest ten, hundred, or thousand.

The Day at a Glance

Today's Goals	Materials
1 Teaching the Lesson **A1:** Read and round numbers, and write numbers different ways. **A2:** Discuss rounding rules. **A3:** Round numbers to the nearest ten, hundred, and thousand. **2 Going Further** ▶ Differentiated Instruction **3 Homework and Spiral Review**	**Lesson Activities** Student Activity Book pp. 144A–146 or Student Hardcover Book pp. 145–146 and Activity Workbook pp. 59–60 (includes Whole Number Secret Code Cards) Homework and Remembering pp. 99–100 Secret Code Cards (TRB 145–146) Rounding Concepts (TRB M53) MathBoard Dot Array (TRB M47) MathBoard materials Scissors, envelope or plastic bag **Going Further** Activity Cards 3-8 Index Cards Math Journals

Use 123 **Math Talk** *today!*

Keeping Skills Sharp

Quick Practice ⏱ 5 MINUTES	Daily Routines
Goal: Solve simple addition and subtraction equations. **Finding Unknown Values** Have a **Student Leader** write these eight equations on the board: $b + 8 = 18$ $13 = 7 + q$ $12 = 4 + n$ $13 = 4 + t$ $2 = p - 8$ $12 - r = 6$ $c = 15 - 8$ $7 = 14 - h$ Then have the Student Leader use a pointer to point to the first equation and, on a signal, the whole class says, "*b* equals 10." If a substantial portion of the class gets it wrong, the Student Leader (or someone helping the Student Leader) explains why it is 10. Repeat this process for the remaining seven equations.	**Homework Review** Ask students if they had difficulty with any part of the homework. Plan to set aside some time to work with students needing extra help. **Skip Count** Have students skip count by thousands from 1,000 to 12,000.

① Teaching the Lesson

Read, Write, and Round Numbers

 25 MINUTES

Goal: Read and round numbers, and write numbers in different ways.

Materials: Student Activity Book pp. 144A–146 or Hardcover Book pp. 145–146 and Activity Workbook pp. 59–60; MathBoards materials, scissors

✔ **NCTM Standards:**
Number and Operations
Representation

Teaching Note

Language and Vocabulary
In our number system, there are irregularities in the way some numbers are read and written. To demonstrate this fact, ask students to find their 10, 40, and 6 Whole Number Secret Code Cards. Have them use the backs of the cards to make the numbers *sixteen* and *forty-six*. Then ask them to say each number aloud and to describe how the spoken forms of the numbers are different. For 16, we say the digit in the ones place first; for 46, we say the digit in the tens place first.

▶ **Secret Code Cards** WHOLE CLASS

Have students look at the Whole Number Secret Code Cards before they cut them out. Ask students to describe the patterns they see on the fronts and the backs of the cards. Make sure the discussion includes the following points.

● The fronts of the cards show the first four places in order from the thousands place to the ones place.

● Each column shows all of the possible numbers for that place.

● The backs of the cards show the value, and the values are not shown in order (thousands is on the right) because the cards are flipped over.

● The backs of the tens column cards show the decade (for example, fifty) and the value in tens (for example, five tens) of the numbers on the front of the cards.

 Math Talk Discuss the English language irregularities in the column of tens words. Be sure to include these ideas in the discussion.

● If our word names for numbers were consistent, the word names for numbers in tens would be written and spoken in the same way as word names for numbers in hundreds and in thousands.

● The suffix *–ty* at the end of our tens words means ten, but this is not clear. It would be clearer if we said ten instead of *–ty*.

● The decade words *sixty*, *seventy*, *eighty*, and *ninety* have a consistent pattern: the ones word followed by the suffix *–ty*. However, all of the other decade words are irregular in their sound (*twenty*, *thirty*, *fifty*) or in their spelling (*forty* instead of *fourty*).

Point out that the place names for the tens are written on the Secret Code Cards to remind students of the values of those words and what they mean.

Review Place Value Write the names of the first four whole-number places on the board (as shown below), and leave them visible for the remainder of the lesson. Under each place name, make the corresponding drawing from the MathBoard. Under each drawing write the numerals for that place. Review the words and drawings as needed (or draw them on the Class MathBoard if necessary).

thousands	hundreds	tens	ones
thousands bar	hundreds square	tens stick	ones circle
1,000	100	10	1

Have students cut along the dotted lines of the Secret Code Cards and cut out all of the cards. Ask them to arrange the cards from left to right in groups of thousands, hundreds, tens, and ones, and arrange the values of each place in order from least to greatest. Doing this will ensure that individual cards can be easily located.

Model Numbers Write 3,678 on the board, and draw it on the Class MathBoard, as shown at the right.

Ask students to use their Secret Code Cards to make 3,678 and to arrange the cards so that they show the same value as in the drawing on the MathBoard. (To make the number, students must use the cards that correspond to each of the place values in the number.)

- Invite volunteers to explain how they made the number and to explain how the cards show the value of each place in the number. (Possible explanations can be found in the Math Talk feature on the previous page.)

- Have students discuss the order of the cards and explain why the order is, or is not, important.

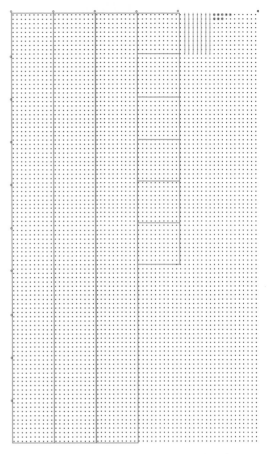

3 thousands + 6 hundreds + 7 tens + 8 ones = 3,678

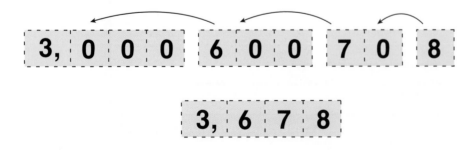

Activity continued ▶

Activity 2

Teaching Note

Language and Vocabulary Review the use of commas and hyphens in our number system.

- A comma is used after the thousands place to make it easier to recognize that the number is a four-, five-, or six-digit number in thousands.

- A hyphen is used when the word name of a two-digit number contains more than one word. For example, the word name for 70 is only one word, so it has no hyphen; the word name for 71 is two words, so it has a hyphen.

- The word form of a number (when we read it or write it) uses the singular form of the place names. For example, eight thousand or five hundred.

- When place value words are used to represent a number, the place-value words are plural and include an "s" at the end of the words. For example, eight thousands or five hundreds.

▶ Write Numbers Different Ways SMALL GROUPS

At the top of Student Book page 145, discuss the different representations of 8,562.

Expanded Form Write the expanded form of 3,678 on the board (3,678 = 3,000 + 600 + 70 + 8) and explain that expanded form is a way to write numbers by showing the place value of each digit. Then arrange students in **Small Groups** and ask them to use their MathBoards and Secret Code Cards to model both the standard form and the expanded form of the numbers shown below.

2,819   4,035   1,708

Again working in Small Groups, have students complete exercises 1–23 on Student Book page 145.

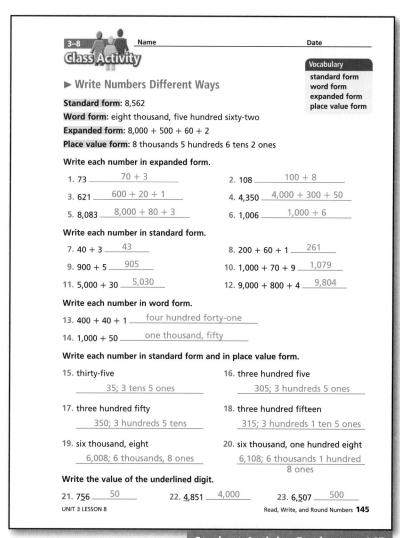

Student Activity Book page 145

▶ Other Representations [WHOLE GROUP] (Optional)

Write 150 = 75 + 25 + 50 on the board, and explain that the equation shows one way to write 150 by using addition.

Invite as many volunteers as possible to the board. Ask each volunteer to write 150 a different way, using one operation (+, −, ×, or ÷) or more than one operation.

Discuss the different representations and lead students to conclude that there are an infinite (too many to count) number of ways to express any number.

Use **Solve and Discuss** to complete exercises 24–31 on Student Book page 146.

Now have students put page 146 aside. They will complete exercises 32–49 after they have discussed rounding.

3-8
Class Activity

Name _____ Date _____

▶ Other Representations

Any number can be represented in many different ways.

100 = 90 + 6 + 4   100 = 110 − 10   100 = 10 × 10   100 = 200 ÷ 2

Represent each number a different way.

24. 1,200 _____   25. 3,456 _____

26. 675 _____   27. 287 _____

28. 149 _____   29. 500 _____

30. 1,000 _____   31. 9,001 _____

▶ Discuss Rounding Numbers

Round to the nearest ten. Make a rounding frame for the first number.

32. 87 __90__   33. 16 __20__   34. 71 __70__

35. 65 __70__   36. 14 __10__   37. 98 __100__

Round to the nearest hundred. Make a rounding frame for the first number.

38. 734 __700__   39. 363 __400__   40. 178 __200__

41. 249 __200__   42. 251 __300__   43. 992 __1,000__

Round to the nearest thousand. Make a rounding frame for the first number.

44. 1,275 __1,000__   45. 8,655 __9,000__   46. 5,482 __5,000__

47. 3,804 __4,000__   48. 1,501 __2,000__   49. 9,702 __10,000__

146 UNIT 3 LESSON 8   Read, Write, and Round Numbers

Student Activity Book page 146

Teaching Note

An Infinite Number of Ways Using only one operation, there are an infinite number of ways to write any number. For example, subtraction can be used to make the whole number 6 by continuing the pattern of subtracting 1 from 7, 2 from 8, 3 from 9, and so on.

$6 = 7 − 1 = 8 − 2 = 9 − 3 \ldots$

Division can be used to make the whole number 6 by using consecutive multiples of 6 and increasing the divisor by 1. For example:

$6 = 6 ÷ 1 = 12 ÷ 2 = 18 ÷ 3 =$

Share these patterns with students, and then encourage them to create patterns of their own design and share them with the class.

English Language Learners

Write *standard form* and *word form* on the board. Give examples of each, using 261.

- **Beginning** Point to 261. Say: **This is the standard form. Standard form uses numbers.** Point to *two hundred sixty-one.* Say: **This is the word form. Word form uses words.** Have students repeat.

- **Intermediate** Write 261. Say: **This is standard form. What does *standard form* mean?** It uses numbers. Point to *word form.* Ask: **What do we use to write numbers in word form?** words

- **Advanced** Have students work in pairs. One partner names a number and says "standard form" or "word form". The other partner writes the number in the form requested.

Activity 2

Discuss Rounding

 20 MINUTES

Goal: Discuss rounding rules.

Materials: Rounding Concepts (TRB M53) MathBoard materials

 NCTM Standards:
Number and Operations
Algebra
Representation

Teaching Activity

Rounding and Secret Code Cards Students use the cards to make the number, then lift off the card(s) to the right of the place to which they are rounding. For example, to round the number 9,559, to the nearest hundred, students would lift off 59 and see 9,500. Then they decide if they should keep the 500 card or replace it with the 600 card. In this case, they would use the 600 card since 9,559 rounded to the nearest hundred is 9,600.

▶ Discuss Why We Round WHOLE CLASS

Write this problem on the board. Read it with the class.

> Maury has $3.00 to buy 3 pens for school. Each pen costs 98 cents. Does Maury have enough money? How do you know?

To get a better idea of what students already know about rounding, ask:

● Why do we sometimes round numbers? We round to make numbers easier to use mentally, or to estimate their size.

● What do we do when we round? We find the nearest tens, hundreds, or thousands number.

● What is a rounded number? an approximate value

● How can rounding make the problem on the board easier to solve? 98 cents is very close to $1.00; $1.00 is an easier number to work with than 98 cents; so rounding up makes sense for this problem.

▶ Find the Nearest Ten WHOLE CLASS

Give students a copy of Rounding Concepts (TRB M53). Direct their attention to the three boxes at the top of the page. Point out that when we round to the nearest 10, the answer will be one of the "count-by-ten" numbers. What if we round to the nearest 100? To the nearest 1,000?

Have students do the first 6 exercises. The middle number in each group is the one to be rounded to the nearest 10. The tens place is underlined. For example, students should determine whether 27 in exercise 1, is closer to 20 or to 30.

When they reach exercise 5, students may wonder what to do with a number that is right in the middle between 30 and 40. Explain that we usually round these numbers up because in most cases it is safer to have a higher estimate. In real-life situations, you do what makes the most sense.

When students have finished the first 6 exercises, elicit the rules for rounding to the nearest 10. Which digit tells us whether to go up or down? the digit in the ones place Discuss the various possibilities with the class.

● 6, 7, 8, and 9 are rounded up to 10 because they are nearer to 10 than to 0.

● 1, 2, 3, and 4 are rounded down to 0 because they are nearer to 0 than to 10.

● 5 is rounded up (although, for real-world problems, it is best to consider the situation when rounding with 5).

Round to Tens, Hundreds, and Thousands

▶ Use Rounding Rules   WHOLE CLASS

Represent Numbers Have students use their MathBoards or a copy of MathBoard Dot Array (TRB M47).

Tell students to show the numbers 40, 37, and 30 and then to write the numbers next to each.

Find the Nearest Ten As a class, discuss whether 37 is nearer to 40 or to 30 and why. Nearer to 40; because 7 is nearer to 10 than to 0.

● What do all three drawings share? 3 quick tens

● What does this mean? 40, 37, and 30 all contain 3 tens.

● What makes the three drawings different? What comes after the 3 quick tens: 1 more quick tens for 40, 7 ones for 37, and nothing for 30.

● Which place in the number 37 tells us which way to round? the ones place

● What will happen to the ones place in 37 after we round? changes to a 0

● What will happen to the 7 ones after we round 37? Why? 7 is nearer to 10 than to 0, so we will make a ten.

● What happens in the tens place to show that we have made a new ten? Why? It becomes 4. 7 becomes a 10 and gets added to 30.

 30 MINUTES

Goal: Round numbers to the nearest ten, hundred, and thousand.

Materials: Student Activity Book or Hardcover Book p. 146, MathBoard materials or MathBoard Dot Array (TRB M47) (optional), envelope or plastic bag

✓ **NCTM Standards:**
Number and Operations
Algebra
Representation

📁 Class Management

Secret Code Cards Students will use these cards in subsequent lessons, so they need to store them at the end of the day. Ask students to have their cards all arranged in stacks and to place the ones on top of the tens on top of the hundreds on top of the thousands before they put them in an envelope or plastic bag.

Activity continued ▶

Activity 3

✓ **Ongoing Assessment**

Ask questions such as:

▶ What is 582 rounded to the nearest hundred? Did you round up or down? How did you decide?

▶ What is 1,370 rounded to the nearest thousand? Did you round up or down? How did you decide?

▶ **Discuss Rounding Numbers**

WHOLE CLASS   Math Talk

Round to the Nearest Ten Have students discuss how they can remember which place to look at when they round to the nearest ten.

● Which place determines the way to round? the ones

● Which place is increased if the ones tell us to round up? the tens

● What happens if the ones tell us to round down? The value in the ones place changes to 0 and the value in the tens place stays the same.

Exercises 32–37 on Student Book page 146 can be used as needed to give students practice in rounding to the nearest ten.

Round to the Nearest Hundred Write the numbers 300, 246, and 200 on the board. Draw these numbers on the Class MathBoard.

● Which place could be made greater or stay the same if we are rounding to the nearest hundred? the hundreds place

● Which places tell us the way to round? the tens and ones places

● What question do we need to ask about 46 to find out which way to round? Is 46 nearer to 100 or nearer to 0?

● Why do we round 246 to 200? Because 46 is nearer to 0 than to 100.

Use exercises 38–43 on page 146 of the Student Book for discussion and practice as needed. Use the MathBoards as necessary to show the size of the numbers.

Round to the Nearest Thousand Ask students to tell you a four-digit number. Then have them discuss how they could round it to the nearest thousand by asking and answering similar questions to the ones we asked when rounding to the nearest hundred.

● Which place will either be made greater or stay the same if we are rounding to the nearest thousand? the thousands place

● Which places tell us the way to round? all of the places to the right of the thousands place

● What question do we need to ask and answer? Is the value in those places nearer to 1,000 or nearer to 0?

Use exercises 44–49 on page 146 of the Student Book as a discussion tool and for practice as needed.

● **Intervention**   Activity Card 3-8

Round, Round, Round!	Activity Card 3-8 ●

Work: In Small Groups

Use:
• Index cards

Decide:
Who will be the translator and who will be the rounder for the first round.

1. On your own, create a four-digit number, and write it in standard form on an index card. Collect the cards and shuffle them. Place them face down in a pile.

2. Select a card from the pile. The translator writes the number in word form. The rounder rounds the number to the nearest thousand.

3. Change roles, and repeat the activity four times.

4. **Discuss** Which was easier to do, writing the number in word form or rounding to the nearest thousand? Why?

Unit 3, Lesson 8   Copyright © Houghton Mifflin Company

Activity Note Students may find it helpful to use a place-value chart to write numbers in word form and round to the nearest thousand.

📝 **Math Writing Prompt**

Investigate Rounding Make a list of 10 numbers that round to 600 when rounding to the nearest hundred. Include 5 numbers that are less than 600 and 5 numbers that are greater than 600.

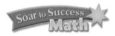 **Software Support**

Use *Soar to Success* for instruction of students needing targeted support for underlying skills.

▲ **On Level**   Activity Card 3-8

What's the Difference?	Activity Card 3-8 ▲

Work: In Small Groups

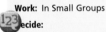 **Decide:**
Who will start the activity.

1. Sit in a circle with your group. Begin by having one member of the group write 2 four-digit numbers less than 9,000 on a sheet of paper. Pass the paper to the left.

2. The next person in the circle rounds both numbers up to the next thousand. Find the sum of the two rounded numbers, and record the result. Pass the paper to the left again.

3. Continue the activity by rounding both numbers down to the next thousand. Find and record the new sum.

4. **Explain** What is the range for the estimated sum of the first two numbers? The range is the difference between the two estimated sums.

Unit 3, Lesson 8   Copyright © Houghton Mifflin Company

Activity Note Be sure that students recall the meaning of a range before beginning the activity. Discuss situations, such as calculating needed supplies, in which finding a range might be useful.

 Math Writing Prompt

Explain Your Thinking Explain how to round a five-digit number to the nearest thousand, and give an example.

 Software Support

Use *MegaMath* for review and reinforcement of the concepts and skills presented in this lesson.

■ **Challenge**   Activity Card 3-8

Enough's Enough	Activity Card 3-8 ■

Work: By Yourself

1. Use the information below to answer the questions below.

   Arthur needs 1,440 small tiles for a wall design. The tiles are sold in boxes of 100 each. Arthur needs to decide how many boxes to buy.

2. What is 1,440 rounded to the nearest hundred? 1,400

3. Will Arthur be able to complete his design with 14 boxes of tiles? Why or why not? No, he will be 40 tiles short if he buys 14 boxes.

4. **Decide** How many boxes should Arthur buy to complete his design? Explain your reasoning. 15 boxes; 14 boxes only have 1400 tiles, and he needs 1440.

Unit 3, Lesson 8   Copyright © Houghton Mifflin Company

Activity Note Ask students to suggest other situations in which an overestimate of a needed quantity would be useful.

 Math Writing Prompt

More Estimating Suppose Arthur needs 1,488 tiles for a design. He knows that he can return a full, unopened box for a refund. Why might he decide to buy 16 instead of 15 boxes?

 DESTINATION Math **Software Support**

Use *Destination Math* to take students beyond the concepts and skills presented in this lesson.

Read, Write, and Round Numbers   **333**

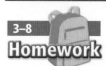

③ Homework and Spiral Review

Use this Homework page to provide students with more practice with naming and rounding numbers.

This Remembering activity would be appropriate anytime after today's lesson.

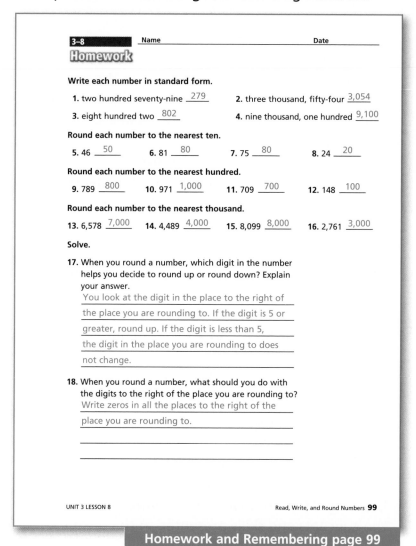

3–8   Name _____ Date _____

Homework

Write each number in standard form.

1. two hundred seventy-nine _279_   2. three thousand, fifty-four _3,054_

3. eight hundred two _802_   4. nine thousand, one hundred _9,100_

Round each number to the nearest ten.

5. 46 _50_   6. 81 _80_   7. 75 _80_   8. 24 _20_

Round each number to the nearest hundred.

9. 789 _800_   10. 971 _1,000_   11. 709 _700_   12. 148 _100_

Round each number to the nearest thousand.

13. 6,578 _7,000_   14. 4,489 _4,000_   15. 8,099 _8,000_   16. 2,761 _3,000_

Solve.

17. When you round a number, which digit in the number helps you decide to round up or round down? Explain your answer.
You look at the digit in the place to the right of the place you are rounding to. If the digit is 5 or greater, round up. If the digit is less than 5, the digit in the place you are rounding to does not change.

18. When you round a number, what should you do with the digits to the right of the place you are rounding to?
Write zeros in all the places to the right of the place you are rounding to.

UNIT 3 LESSON 8   Read, Write, and Round Numbers **99**

Homework and Remembering page 99

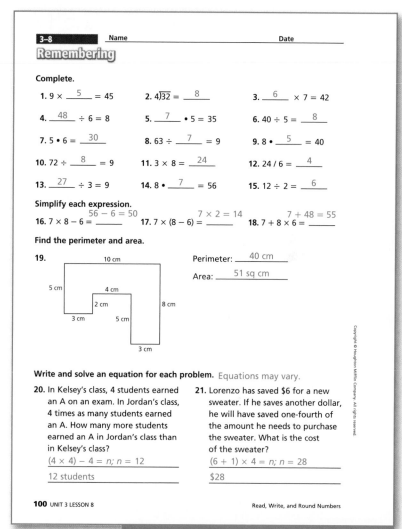

3–8   Name _____ Date _____

Remembering

Complete.

1. $9 \times$ _5_ $= 45$ 2. $4\overline{)32} =$ _8_   3. _6_ $\times 7 = 42$

4. _48_ $\div 6 = 8$ 5. _7_ $\bullet 5 = 35$ 6. $40 \div 5 =$ _8_

7. $5 \bullet 6 =$ _30_   8. $63 \div$ _7_ $= 9$ 9. $8 \bullet$ _5_ $= 40$

10. $72 \div$ _8_ $= 9$ 11. $3 \times 8 =$ _24_   12. $24 / 6 =$ _4_

13. _27_ $\div 3 = 9$ 14. $8 \bullet$ _7_ $= 56$ 15. $12 \div 2 =$ _6_

Simplify each expression.

16. $7 \times 8 - 6 =$ _56 − 6 = 50_   17. $7 \times (8 - 6) =$ _7 × 2 = 14_   18. $7 + 8 \times 6 =$ _7 + 48 = 55_

Find the perimeter and area.

19.
Perimeter: _40 cm_

Area: _51 sq cm_

Write and solve an equation for each problem. Equations may vary.

20. In Kelsey's class, 4 students earned an A on an exam. In Jordan's class, 4 times as many students earned an A. How many more students earned an A in Jordan's class than in Kelsey's class?
$(4 \times 4) - 4 = n; n = 12$
12 students

21. Lorenzo has saved $6 for a new sweater. If he saves another dollar, he will have saved one-fourth of the amount he needs to purchase the sweater. What is the cost of the sweater?
$(6 + 1) \times 4 = n; n = 28$
$28

100 UNIT 3 LESSON 8   Read, Write, and Round Numbers

Homework and Remembering page 100

Home or School Activity

 Language Arts Connection

Writing Numbers Review with students these rules for writing numbers in word form, and give examples:

● If the number is between 20 and 100, and you need two words, use a hyphen. (68 is sixty-eight.)

● Do not use the word *and* when writing whole numbers as words. (3,249 is three thousand, two hundred forty-nine; 6,007 is six thousand, seven.)

Ask students to write some numbers in word form.

Number	Words
25	twenty-five
186	one hundred eighty-six
1,615	one thousand, six hundred fifteen
4,609	four thousand, six hundred nine
8,030	eight thousand, thirty

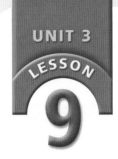

Compare Whole Numbers

Vocabulary

greater than >
less than <
digit
greatest
least
range
expression
equality
inequality

Lesson Objective

● Understand greater than and less than comparisons, and use the >
and < signs.

The Day at a Glance

Today's Goals	Materials	

1 Teaching the Lesson
A1: Compare and order numbers.
A2: Make the greatest and least numbers from given digits.
A3: Compare numbers, using a number line.
 	
2 Going Further
▶ Math Connection: Working with Expressions
▶ Differentiated Instruction
 	
3 Homework and Spiral Review
	Lesson Activities
	Student Activity Book pp. 147–149
	  or Student Hardcover Book
	  pp. 147–149 and Activity
	  Workbook pp. 61–62
	Homework and Remembering
	  pp. 101–102
	Comparing Numbers transparency
	  (TRB M50)
	MathBoard Materials
	Overhead projector
		Going Further
		Student Activity Book
		  p. 150 or Student
		  Hardcover Book
		  p. 150
		Activity Cards 3-9
		Number Lines
		  (TRB M51)
		Math Journals

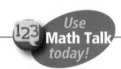

Keeping Skills Sharp

Quick Practice 5 MINUTES

Goal: Solve simple addition and subtraction equations.

Finding Unknown Values Have a **Student Leader** write these
eight equations on the board:

$5 = h - 4$ $13 - s = 5$ $4 = 14 - t$ $k = 11 - 4$

$12 = 5 + m$ $17 = 8 + c$ $p + 5 = 13$ $11 = 6 + d$

Then have the Student Leader use a pointer to point to the first
equation and, on a signal, the whole class says, "*h* equals 9." If a
substantial portion of the class gets it wrong, the Student Leader
(or someone helping the Student Leader) explains why it is 9.
Repeat this process for the remaining seven equations.

Daily Routines

Homework Review Let students work
together to check their work. Initially,
pair less able students with more able
students. Remind students to use what
they know about helping others.

Nonroutine Problem Name three
consecutive numbers that have a sum of
30. 9, 10, and 11; algebraic solution: Let
x = the lowest number. $x + (x + 1) +$
$(x + 2) = 30; 3x + 3 = 30; 3x = 27; x = 9$

30		
x	$x + 1$	$x + 2$

Teaching the Lesson

Greater Than and Less Than

 20 MINUTES

Goal: Compare and order numbers

Materials: Student Activity Book or Hardcover Book p. 147, MathBoard Materials

✓ **NCTM Standards:**
Number and Operations
Communication

Differentiated Instruction

Math Drawings Have students who need to do so make math drawings of numbers for Activity 1 and Activity 2. As students discover that the best way to compare numbers is to start with the largest places by underlining them, they also can learn to put a small check under those places if they are the same, underline the next places to the right, and compare those, etc., until they find places with numbers that are different.

English Language Learners

Make sure students understand the > and < symbols. Write 42 > 24 on the board. Say: **42 is greater than 24.** Point to the >.

• **Beginning** Say: **This means "greater than".** Have students repeat. Write 24 < 42. Say: **24 is less than 42.** Point to the <. Say: **This means "less than".**

• **Intermediate** Ask: **What does this mean?** greater than Write 24 < 42. Ask: **How do I say this?** 24 is less than 42.

• **Advanced** Have students read a *less than* phrase off the board. Then have them work in pairs to say and write other phrases.

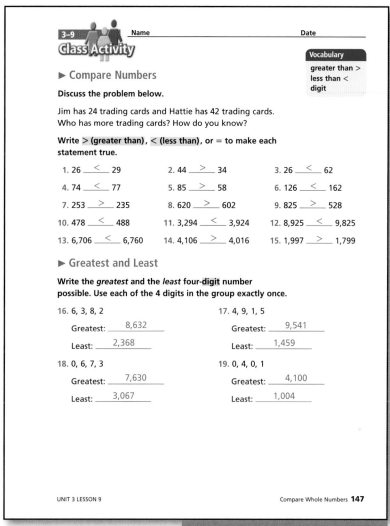

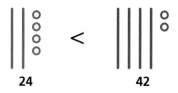 **Student Activity Book page 147**

▶ Compare Numbers WHOLE CLASS

Discuss the problem at the top of Student Book page 147. Students can use their MathBoards to draw place-value models of 24 and 42. They should discuss which number is greater and how they know.

● **What makes 2 larger in 24 than it is in 42?** In 24, the 2 stands for 2 tens, or 20. In 42, it stands for just 2 ones.

● **What makes 4 smaller in 24 than it is in 42?** In 24, the 4 stands for just 4. In 42, it stands for 4 tens, or 40.

Use Inequality Symbols With the students, review the notation for greater than and less than.

- The smaller number is always at the closed (smaller) end of the symbol: 24 < 42, or 24 is less than 42.

- The larger number is always at the open (larger) end of the symbol: 42 > 24, or 42 is greater than 24.

Exercises 1–15 may be used for discussion and practice as needed.

Activity 2

Reasoning and Place Value

▶ Greatest and Least ┃WHOLE CLASS┃

Have as many students as possible work at the board while the others work at their seats.

Tell students to write four different numerals from 0 to 9. For example, 5, 7, 3, and 9. Next, instruct them to make the greatest number they can from their numerals. 9,753 Then, instruct them to make the least number they can from the same numerals. 3,579 Finally, have them write an inequality statement comparing their numbers. 3,579 < 9,753

Ask students to explain how they found:

- the greatest number? arranging the numerals in order from greatest to least

- the least number? arranging the numerals in order from least to greatest

Exercises 16–19 on page 147 of the Student Book may be used for discussion and practice as needed.

20 MINUTES

Goal: Make the greatest and least numbers from given digits.

Materials: Student Activity Book or Hardcover Book p. 147

NCTM Standards:
Number and Operations
Communication
Reasoning and Proof

Math Talk in Action

Students may reason different ways as they work on these numbers.

Trisha: I just put the numbers in order from least to greatest to make the least number.

Matt: I put the least number with the least place value.

Teaching the Lesson *(continued)*

Activity 3

Compare Numbers on a Number Line

 15 MINUTES

Goal: Compare numbers, using a number line.

Materials: Student Activity Book pp. 148–149 or Hardcover Book pp. 148–149 and Activity Workbook pp. 61–62, Comparing Numbers transparency (TRB M50), overhead projector

✔ **NCTM Standards:**
Number and Operations
Algebra
Communication

Teaching Note

Math Background Students should understand that a number line can have any equal-sized divisions and the labeling can start and end at any point.

 Class Management

You can use a transparency of Number Lines (TRB M51) for additional discussion and practice.

▶ **Use a Number Line** [WHOLE CLASS]

Understand a Number Line Have the students look at Number Line A on page 148 of the Student Book. You may find it helpful to make a transparency of Comparing Numbers (TRB M50) to aid in the discussion. Then ask the questions below.

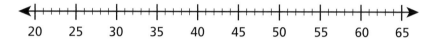

- What do the numbers under the longer marks on the number line mean? Each long mark represents every fifth number on the number line.

- What do the shorter marks between the longer ones stand for? Each shorter mark represents a whole number.

- Why do the number lines have arrows on both ends? They can be extended in either direction.

- What whole numbers come before 20? 19, 18, 17, and so on

- What whole numbers come after 65? 66, 67, 68, and so on

Ask students to explain how number lines A, B, and C are different. A: each mark represents 1 unit; B: each mark represents 2 units; C: each mark represents 100 units

- What numbers do the shorter lines on B stand for? 102, 104, 106, 108, and so on

- What about for C? 1,600; 1,700; 1,800; 1,900; and so on

- What numbers could we use for the D and E number lines? any numbers that represent equal divisions of the line

Identify Numbers On number line A, have the students find 25, 35, and 50. Instruct the students to compare the size of the numbers in as many ways as they can.

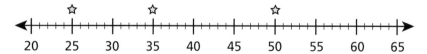

They should be able to explain their answers with place-value words. For example, 25 < 35 because 25 has only 2 tens and 35 has 3 tens. 25 is also smaller because it is closer to zero on the number line.

▶ **Compare Numbers Within a Range** [WHOLE CLASS]

On the number line on Student Book page 149, have the students mark off the part of the line that starts with 25 and ends with 55. Tell them that any portion of the number line is called a *range* of numbers.

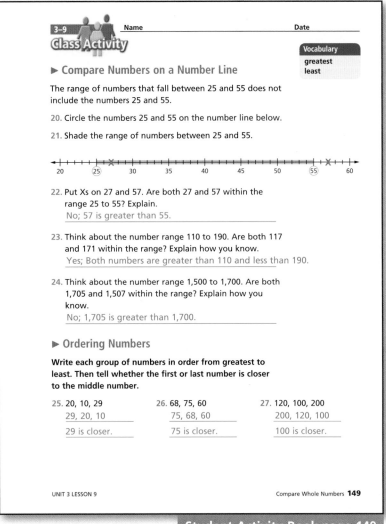

Instruct the students to find 38 on the line and discuss whether 25 or 55 is closer to 38. Then tell students they can subtract to find the distance between the numbers.

$$38 - 25 = 13$$
$$55 - 38 = 17$$
$$13 < 17$$

This means, 38 is closer to 25 than 55.

▶ Compare Numbers on a Number Line WHOLE CLASS

Have students use the number line on page 149 to discuss exercises 22–24 as a class. Use the number lines on page 148 to solve exercises 23 and 24. Use the blank number lines D and E to do more problems as necessary.

▶ Ordering Numbers WHOLE CLASS

Exercises 25–27 involve putting three numbers in order from greatest to least.

Teaching Note

Language and Vocabulary The common usage of the word *range* is an amount or extent of variation. The mathematical use is a set of all values a given function may take on. The statistical use is the difference between the largest and smallest number in a frequency distribution.

Closer to: For exercises 25, 26, and 27, some students may count up from the smaller to the larger number while others may subtract or use other strategies.

 Ongoing Assessment

Ask students to:

▶ find the range of the number line on page 149 of the Student Book.

▶ tell if 37 is closer to 32 or 48. Have them explain their reasoning.

② Going Further

Math Connection: Working with Expressions

 20 MINUTES

Goal: Use inequality symbols and variables to make true statements.

Materials: Student Activity Book or Hardcover Book p. 150

✓ **NCTM Standard:**
Number and Operations

▶ Compare Expressions ┌WHOLE CLASS┐

In this lesson, students will connect what they know about comparing numbers to using inequality symbols with expressions.

Ask for Ideas Explain to the class that expressions can be compared using >, <, and = symbols. Ask several students to describe how they remember using > (greater than) and < (less than).

Write this comparison on the board:

$$8 + 5 \quad \bigcirc \quad 3 \times 5$$

Point out that that before we can write an inequality symbol (< or >) or an equality symbol (=) to complete the comparison, we must first simplify the expressions.

Ask students to name the sum of 8 and 5 (13) and the product of 3 and 5 (15). At the board, invite a volunteer to write a symbol to complete the comparison and explain why that symbol was used. A less than symbol (<) is used because 13 < 15.

Reverse the order of the expressions and have students note that a > symbol makes the statement true.

$$3 \times 5 \quad \bigcirc \quad 8 + 5$$

On Student Book page 50, have students complete exercises 1–13 individually.

▶ Properties

If necessary, review the properties of addition and multiplication prior to having students complete exercises 14–19. Since the properties in these exercises are presented symbolically with variables instead of with whole numbers, some students may find it helpful to make simple substitutions (such as replace b with 1 and a with 2 in exercise 14) to help recognize the properties.

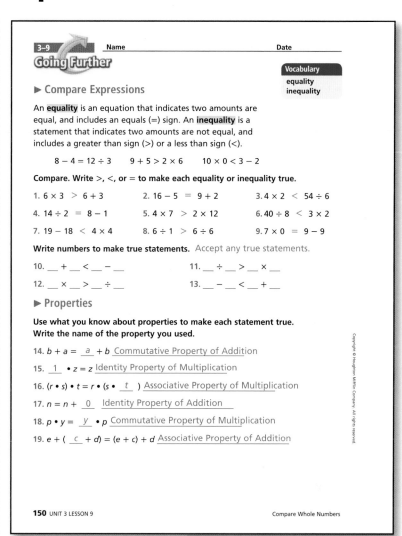

3–9 Name _____ Date _____
Going Further

Vocabulary
equality
inequality

▶ **Compare Expressions**

An **equality** is an equation that indicates two amounts are equal, and includes an equals (=) sign. An **inequality** is a statement that indicates two amounts are not equal, and includes a greater than sign (>) or a less than sign (<).

$8 - 4 = 12 \div 3$ $9 + 5 > 2 \times 6$ $10 \times 0 < 3 - 2$

Compare. Write >, <, or = to make each equality or inequality true.

1. $6 \times 3 \; > \; 6 + 3$ 2. $16 - 5 \; = \; 9 + 2$ 3. $4 \times 2 \; < \; 54 \div 6$

4. $14 \div 2 \; = \; 8 - 1$ 5. $4 \times 7 \; > \; 2 \times 12$ 6. $40 \div 8 \; < \; 3 \times 2$

7. $19 - 18 \; < \; 4 \times 4$ 8. $6 \div 1 \; > \; 6 \div 6$ 9. $7 \times 0 \; = \; 9 - 9$

Write numbers to make true statements. Accept any true statements.

10. __ + __ < __ − __   11. __ ÷ __ > __ × __

12. __ × __ > __ ÷ __   13. __ − __ < __ + __

▶ **Properties**

Use what you know about properties to make each statement true. Write the name of the property you used.

14. $b + a = \underline{\;a\;} + b$ Commutative Property of Addition

15. $\underline{\;1\;} \cdot z = z$ Identity Property of Multiplication

16. $(r \cdot s) \cdot t = r \cdot (s \cdot \underline{\;t\;})$ Associative Property of Multiplication

17. $n = n + \underline{\;0\;}$ Identity Property of Addition

18. $p \cdot y = \underline{\;y\;} \cdot p$ Commutative Property of Multiplication

19. $e + (\underline{\;c\;} + d) = (e + c) + d$ Associative Property of Addition

150 UNIT 3 LESSON 9   Compare Whole Numbers

Copyright © Houghton Mifflin Company. All rights reserved.

Student Activity Book page 150

Teaching Note

Math Background An expression is a number, a letter, or a combination of both. Usually an expression is written with an operation sign.

Examples of expressions include:

n 4 $3a$ $4 - 1$ $y + 6$

An equation is a statement which indicates that two expressions are equal.

$3 + 4 = 7$ $5n = 25$ $6 + 4 = 20 - b$

An inequality is a statement which indicates that two expressions are not equal.

$2 < 5$ $8 + 9 > 6$ $12 \div 4 \neq 1 + 5$

Differentiated Instruction

Intervention Activity Card 3-9

In the Range
Activity Card 3-9 ●

Work: In Pairs

Use:
• Number Lines (TRB M51)

1. Use a number line labeled with multiples of 10.

0 10 20 30 40 50 60 70 80 90 100 110 120

2. On a separate sheet of paper, write six numbers between 0 and 120 that are not multiples of 10.

3. Exchange papers with your partner, and locate the numbers on the number line.

4. Work together to write 5 statements, using > or < to compare the 12 numbers that you located on the number line.

5. Analyze How does the number line help you to write comparison statements? The number to the right is always the greater number.

Unit 3, Lesson 9   Copyright © Houghton Mifflin Company

Activity Note Remind students that, regardless of the inequality symbol used (< or >), the arrow always points to the lesser number.

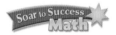 **Math Writing Prompt**

Explain Your Thinking Write two statements comparing 563 and 365. Use < and > to write your statements.

Soar to Success Math ★ **Software Support**

Use *Soar to Success* for instruction of students needing targeted support for underlying skills.

On Level Activity Card 3-9

Compare Expressions
Activity Card 3-9 ▲

Work: By Yourself

1. Copy each statement below on your paper.

   15 − 0 ○ 15 − 15 >

   6 + 3 ○ 3 + 6 =, Commutative Property of Addition

   9 + 6 + 4 ○ 4 + 6 + 9 =, Associative Property of Addition

   4 • (3 + 5) ○ 12 + 20 =, Distributive Property

   24 − 8 ○ 24 − 0 <

2. Complete each statement by writing the symbol <, >, or = in the circle to make a true statement.

3. Identify any property or rule of operations you used to complete each statement.

Unit 3, Lesson 9   Copyright © Houghton Mifflin Company

Activity Note Have students list the identities and operation properties that they have learned before beginning the activity.

 Math Writing Prompt

Explain Your Thinking Explain how you can group addends to help you complete the statement 4 + 5 + 9 ○ 9 + 3 + 4 mentally.

MegaMath Grades K-6 **Software Support**

Use *MegaMath* for review and reinforcement of the concepts and skills presented in this lesson.

Challenge Activity Card 3-9

More or Less?
Activity Card 3-9 ■

Work: In Pairs

1. Look at the bar graph below about the number of stamps in each person's collection.

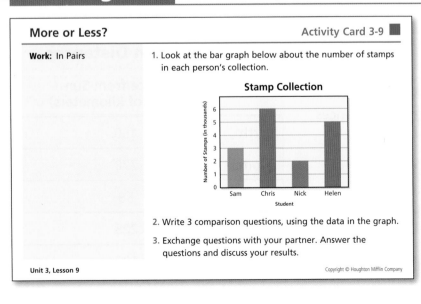

Stamp Collection

2. Write 3 comparison questions, using the data in the graph.

3. Exchange questions with your partner. Answer the questions and discuss your results.

Unit 3, Lesson 9   Copyright © Houghton Mifflin Company

Activity Note Remind students that they do not need to use an operation to answer a comparison question unless the question asks for a comparison in terms of the difference.

 Math Writing Prompt

Using Data Is it easier to compare data from a table or a bar graph? Explain your reasoning.

 DESTINATION Math· **Software Support**

Use *Destination Math* to take students beyond the concepts and skills presented in this lesson.

③ Homework and Spiral Review

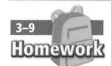

3–9 Homework Goal: Additional Practice

Use this Homework page to provide students with more practice with comparing numbers.

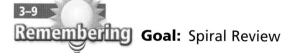

3–9 Remembering Goal: Spiral Review

This Remembering activity would be appropriate anytime after today's lesson.

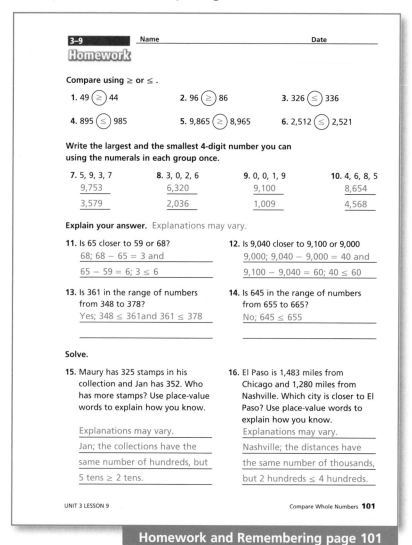

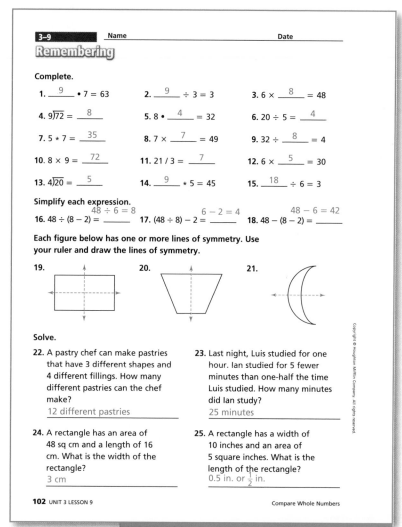

Home or School Activity

Science Connection

Planet Distances From the Sun Give your students a table like the one shown. Either provide the distances or have them research the distances with a family member. Ask your students to write comparison questions, such as:

- Which planet is closer to the Sun, Mars or Venus? Venus
- Which planet is farther from the Sun, Earth or Mercury? Earth
- Name a planet that is farther from the Sun than Mars. Jupiter

Some answers will vary if additional planets are included in the table.

Solar System Distances	
Planet	Distance from Sun (millions of kilometers)
Earth	150
Jupiter	778
Mercury	58
Mars	228
Venus	108

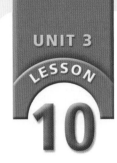
Numbers to Millions

Lesson Objectives

- Identify place value for numbers up to millions.
- Understand the magnitude of one million.

Vocabulary

place value

The Day at a Glance

Today's Goals	Materials	
1 Teaching the Lesson **A1:** Read and write numbers in the thousands and millions. **A2:** Construct and visualize large numbers up to one million. **2 Going Further** ▶ Differentiated Instruction **3 Homework and Spiral Review**	**Lesson Activities** Student Activity Book pp. 151–152A or Student Hardcover Book pp. 151–152 and Activity Workbook p. 63 Homework and Remembering pp. 103–104 Quick Quiz 2 (Assessment Guide) Reading and Writing Millions (TRB M146) (optional) (optional) Secret Code Cards (TRB M48) MathBoard Materials Building a Million (TRB M52) (optional)	**Going Further** Activity Cards 3-10 Scissors Math Journals

123 Use Math Talk today!

Keeping Skills Sharp

Quick Practice ⏱ 5 MINUTES	Daily Routines
Goal: Compare three-digit and four-digit numbers. **Say, Write, and Compare** Have several students work at the board. Dictate a pair of numbers to each student, giving only the numerals (for example, "4, 8, 9"). 489 498 651 561 3,210 2,310 5,298 5,098 Have students use place-value words to tell which number in each pair is greater. Have the students at the board write > or < between the numbers in each pair. Then have the whole class say the inequalities both ways for each pair: "498 is greater than 489" and "489 is less than 498," and so on.	**Homework Review** Ask students if they had difficulty with any part of the homework. Plan to set aside some time to work with students needing extra help. **Money** Ms. Delgado has four $10 bills, three $100 bills, and six $1 bills. How much money does she have? Write your answer. $346

Teaching the Lesson

Read and Write Millions

 20 MINUTES

Goal: Read and write numbers in the thousands and millions.

Materials: Student Activity Book or Hardcover Book pp. 151–152, MathBoard Materials, Secret Code Cards (TRB M48), Reading and Writing Millions (TRB M146) (optional).

✓ **NCTM Standards:**
Number and Operations
Algebra
Communication

Teaching Note

Watch For! Some students might incorrectly use the word *and* when saying a number. If this happens, explain that when we get to decimal numbers (write 25.37 on the board), we will use "and" to say the decimal point (twenty-five *and* thirty-seven hundredths). So it is better not to say "and" when saying a whole number.

Teaching Note

Reading and Writing Millions (TRB M146) makes the distinction between how we read and say large numbers and how we say the place-value names. You may want to use it before working through Student Book page 151.

Students will use their Secret Code Cards to make the large numbers by making groups of three cards and placing them on a Reading Millions Frame that shows them how to read these large numbers.

In Activity 2, students will use Student Activity Book page 152A or Activity Workbook page 63 to see the large numbers they have been discussing so they will understand these large quantities.

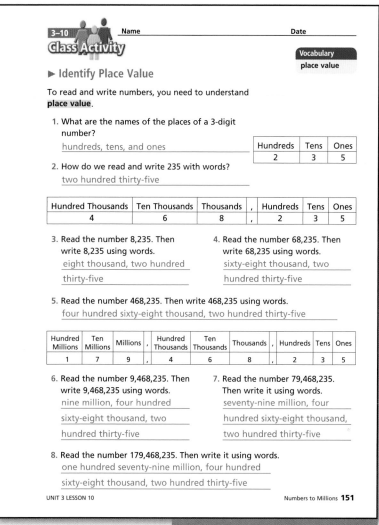

Student Activity Book page 151

▶ Identify Place Value WHOLE CLASS

Hundreds, Tens, and Ones Write the number 235 on the board.

Ask a student to make a place–value drawing at the board.

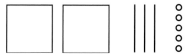

Have students answer exercise 1 on Student Book page 151, and then discuss what each digit in the number 235 represents. 2 represents 2 hundreds; 3 represents 3 tens; 5 represents 5 ones.

Have students read the number 235 aloud. *"Two hundred thirty-five"*

Then have a student write the words for 235 on the board as the rest of the class answers exercise 2.

Thousands and Hundred Thousands Write the number 468,235 on the board. Have the students read and discuss problems 3–5. [Note that problem 3 asks how to read and write 8,235. If students look at the place-value chart in their Student Book, remind them that we are not considering the numerals 4 and 6; suggest that they cover those numerals with a finger.]

(123) **Math Talk** After discussing problems 3–5, discuss how students might make a place-value drawing for a number as large as 468,235 and how much space it would take if they were to draw it.

● How many thousand bars would we need to draw? 8

● What shape could represent ten thousand? a square that is made of 10 thousand bars side by side

● How many of these would we need? 6

● What shape could represent one hundred thousand? a rectangle that is made of 10 ten-thousand squares side by side

● How many would we need? 4

Ask students to discuss how the thousands were read (as if they were hundreds, tens, and ones but you then add "thousands" to the words). We do not say "four hundred thousands six ten thousands 8 thousands" because it would take too long. We make a group of 3 and separate it by a comma. Tell them that millions will work the same way.

Millions Write the number 179,468,235 on the board. With the students, read and discuss problems 6–8.

Write *million* under the 179 and *thousand* under the 468 and read the whole number again. Ask a student to summarize how the comma makes groups of 3 numbers and how we read them. Then write several more big numbers on the board and ask volunteers to read them. Then write *million* under the first group of 3 numbers and *thousand* under the second group of 3 numbers and have the class read the number together 3 times.

Place-value names versus saying a big number Have students look at the names of the places on page 151 and tell all the patterns they see. Then point to a particular number in the big numbers you have written on the board and ask what its place value name is. Then have students discuss the differences between knowing and saying the names of particular place values and saying a big number. You use the 3 groups and do not say all of the place values. When reading a big number, you only say million and thousand at the end of their group of 3 numbers.

Activity continued ▶

The Learning Classroom

Building Concepts The guide for discussion provided here addresses concepts in terms that are understandable to students. It is not necessary to use these exact words. You may think of other ways to explain the material.

Differentiated Instruction

Extra Help If students need more help to see the pattern of how to read numbers, you can have individuals or groups use the Secret Code Cards on TRB M48 or Student Activity Book page 144 or Activity Workbook page 58 in Lesson 8. Make groups of 3 numbers with the Secret Code Cards, and place a group on the millions, a group on the thousands, and a group on the right. Read each group of 3 numbers and use the word below each group to say the special name of that group.

English Language Learners

Review 2, 3, and 4 digit numbers. Write an example of each. Have students identify digits in the ones, tens, hundreds, and thousands places. Write 732. Point to the 7, then 3, then 2.

● **Beginning** Say: This is 732. Is 7 in the hundreds or thousands place? hundreds Continue with the other digits.

● **Intermediate** Ask: What is the place value of the 7? hundreds Continue with the other digits.

● **Advanced** Have students work in pairs to write 4-digit numbers and identify the place value for each digit.

① Teaching the Lesson (continued)

Activity 1

The Learning Classroom

Building Concepts For exercises 9–16, students will read the numbers aloud. To reinforce reading and writing skills, have a student volunteer write these numbers in standard form and in word form on the board.

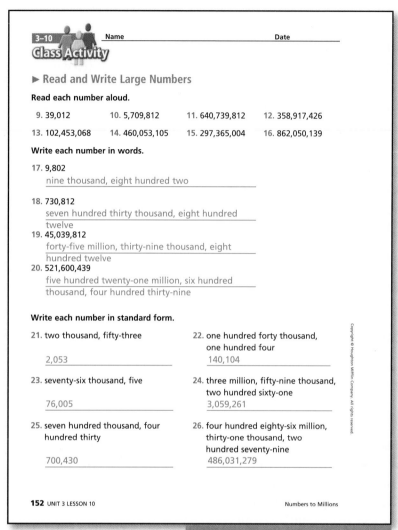

Student Activity Book page 152

▶ Read and Write Large Numbers WHOLE CLASS

For exercise 9 on Student Book page 152, have several volunteers read the number aloud, and then have the entire class read it in unison. Follow the same procedure for exercises 10–16.

After students complete exercises 17–20, have volunteers read their written answers aloud.

After students complete exercises 21–26, you can also have volunteers read the numbers aloud.

Use whatever time remains to have students practice reading the numbers in the exercises already discussed. Also, question them about place value:

● In exercise 11, what is the value of the numeral 9? nine thousand

● In exercise 14, what is the value of the numeral 6? sixty million

Build Dot Arrays

▶ Discuss and Construct Large Numbers

WHOLE CLASS

Math Talk

Ask for Ideas Discuss where students have used large numbers in real life or where they have seen them used. Situations might include:

- local, state, or national budgets.

- human population figures.

- distances and numbers of stars and other objects in outer space.

Build Hundreds and Thousands Have each student use Student Activity Book page 152A or Activity Workbook page 63 and draw a hundred box in the top bar as shown below, and then count the hundreds in the entire bar. 10 hundreds

Ask what name we use for 10 hundreds. one thousand

Elicit from the students that each bar represents 1,000, and the whole page represents 10,000. Have them draw rules to make a thousands bar.

Each square = 1 hundred box

Each row = 1 thousand bar

 15 MINUTES

Goal: Construct and visualize large numbers up to one million.

Materials: Student Activity Book page 152A or Activity Workbook p. 63, Building a Million (TRB M52) (optional)

 NCTM Standards:
Number and Operations
Representation
Problem Solving
Algebra

Activity continued ▶

Activity 2

The Learning Classroom

Scenario The main purpose of a scenario is to demonstrate mathematical relationships in a visual and memorable way. A group of students is called to the front of the room to act out a situation. Because of its active and dramatic nature, the scenario structure fosters a sense of intense involvement among children. Scenarios create meaningful contexts in which students relate math to their everyday lives.

 Ongoing Assessment

Ask questions such as:

▶ How do you write seventy-six thousand, five, using numbers?

▶ How do you write four hundred three million, twenty-eight thousand, five, using numbers?

▶ How do you write 700,430, using words?

 Quick Quiz

See Assessment Guide for Unit 3 Quick Quiz 2.

Build by Ten Thousands Use the **Scenario** structure as students pin or tape one page at a time to a wall, counting the total each time by 10,000s.

1 page = 10,000

2 pages = 20,000

3 pages = 30,000, and so on

Students should calculate how many dots they would have on the wall after every student hangs his or her page. For example, with 30 students in the class, there would be 30 × 10,000 = 300,000 dots.

They should also figure out how many more pages they would need to have a total of 1 million dots. For 30 students: 1,000,000 − 300,000 = 700,000, so they would need 70 more pages.

▶ **Build a Million (Optional)** WHOLE CLASS

Construct Dot Arrays If possible, you may want to make a total of 100 copies of Build A Million (TRB M52). Over the next several days, students can hang more pages, always figuring out the total and also figuring out how many more pages they need to make 1,000,000.

Students should count or calculate the number of thousands it took to make 1 million. 1,000 thousands

Also, students should calculate other combinations of hundreds, ten thousands, and hundred thousands that make up 1 million. 10,000 hundreds; 100 ten thousands; 10 hundred thousands

Identify Numbers During the time the one-million dot array is posted, label in the display the quantities for each place value up to 1,000,000: 1; 10; 100; 1,000; 10,000; 100,000.

You could have students locate and mark on the paper where other large numbers would be situated on the array. For example, 101,035 would be after 101 of the thousand bars plus 35 more ones.

②Going Further

● Intervention   Activity Card 3-10

Words and Numbers	Activity Card 3-10 ●
Work: In Pairs **Use:** • Scissors **Decide:** Who will be Student 1 and who will be Student 2.	1. On your own, fold a piece of paper to make 6 equal sections, and then cut them out. 2. **Student 1:** Write these words, one on each section: *two, six, nine, ten, thirteen, sixty.* 3. **Student 2:** Write these words, one on each section: *twenty-, fifty-, seventy-, hundred, thousand, million.* 4. Shuffle all 12 sections and place them face down. 5. **Work Together** Pick 5 or more sections. Use the words to form a name for a number, and write the number in standard form.

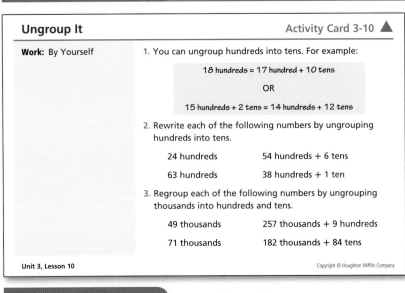

Unit 3, Lesson 10   Copyright © Houghton Mifflin Company

Activity Note Students should pick enough sections to include at least one period name. The goal is to use all the words they choose to make one number.

 Math Writing Prompt

Explain Your Thinking If you have two different numbers, does the greater number always have the longer word name? Explain.

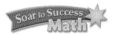 **Software Support**

Use *Soar to Success* for instruction of students needing targeted support for underlying skills.

▲ On Level   Activity Card 3-10

Ungroup It	Activity Card 3-10 ▲
Work: By Yourself	1. You can ungroup hundreds into tens. For example: 18 hundreds = 17 hundred + 10 tens OR 15 hundreds + 2 tens = 14 hundreds + 12 tens 2. Rewrite each of the following numbers by ungrouping hundreds into tens. 24 hundreds 54 hundreds + 6 tens 63 hundreds 38 hundreds + 1 ten 3. Regroup each of the following numbers by ungrouping thousands into hundreds and tens. 49 thousands 257 thousands + 9 hundreds 71 thousands 182 thousands + 84 tens

Unit 3, Lesson 10   Copyright © Houghton Mifflin Company

Activity Note Some students may find using base-ten blocks helpful to ungroup hundreds into tens or thousands into hundreds and tens.

 Math Writing Prompt

Rhyme Time Create your own rhyme to help recall how to ungroup one thousand into hundreds and tens.

 Software Support

Use *MegaMath* for review and reinforcement of the concepts and skills presented in this lesson.

■ Challenge   Activity Card 3-10

Short Word Form	Activity Card 3-10 ■
Work: By Yourself **2.** 5 million + 147 thousand; 47 million + 256 thousand + 804; 62 million + 578 thousand + 235; 514 million + 200 thousand; 398 million + 125 thousand; 6 million + 257 thousand + 320; 42 million; 1 million + 857 thousand + 365	1. Another way to write numbers is the short word form. 32,350,000 can be written as 32 million + 350 thousand. 2. Write each of the following in short word form. 5,147,000 47,256,804 62,578,235 514,200,000 398,125,000 6,257,320 42,000,000 1,857,365 See left.

Unit 3, Lesson 10   Copyright © Houghton Mifflin Company

Activity Note Note that the short word form groups numbers by using periods. Suggest that students write the period names in order before beginning the activity.

 Math Writing Prompt

Explain Your Reasoning Explain why writing a number in short word form might help you to write it in standard form.

DESTINATION Math® Software Support

Use *Destination Math* to take students beyond the concepts and skills presented in this lesson.

③ Homework and Spiral Review

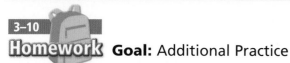

✓ Include students' work for page 103 in their portfolios.

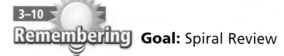

This Remembering activity would be appropriate anytime after today's lesson.

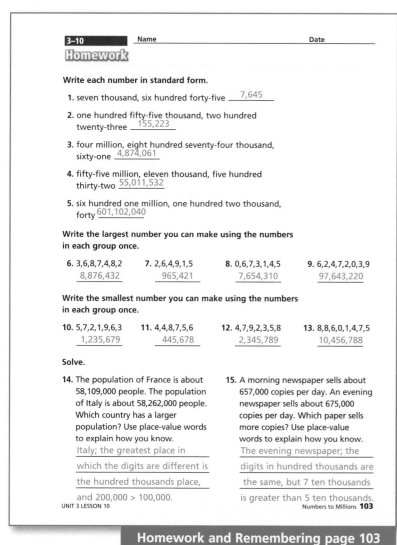

3–10	Name _____	Date _____

Homework

Write each number in standard form.

1. seven thousand, six hundred forty-five ___7,645___

2. one hundred fifty-five thousand, two hundred twenty-three ___155,223___

3. four million, eight hundred seventy-four thousand, sixty-one ___4,874,061___

4. fifty-five million, eleven thousand, five hundred thirty-two ___55,011,532___

5. six hundred one million, one hundred two thousand, forty ___601,102,040___

Write the largest number you can make using the numbers in each group once.

6. 3,6,8,7,4,8,2
___8,876,432___

7. 2,6,4,9,1,5
___965,421___

8. 0,6,7,3,1,4,5
___7,654,310___

9. 6,2,4,7,2,0,3,9
___97,643,220___

Write the smallest number you can make using the numbers in each group once.

10. 5,7,2,1,9,6,3
___1,235,679___

11. 4,4,8,7,5,6
___445,678___

12. 4,7,9,2,3,5,8
___2,345,789___

13. 8,8,6,0,1,4,7,5
___10,456,788___

Solve.

14. The population of France is about 58,109,000 people. The population of Italy is about 58,262,000 people. Which country has a larger population? Use place-value words to explain how you know.
___Italy; the greatest place in___ ___which the digits are different is___ ___the hundred thousands place,___ ___and 200,000 > 100,000.___

15. A morning newspaper sells about 657,000 copies per day. An evening newspaper sells about 675,000 copies per day. Which paper sells more copies? Use place-value words to explain how you know.
___The evening newspaper; the___ ___digits in hundred thousands are___ ___the same, but 7 ten thousands___ ___is greater than 5 ten thousands.___

UNIT 3 LESSON 10

Numbers to Millions **103**

Homework and Remembering page 103

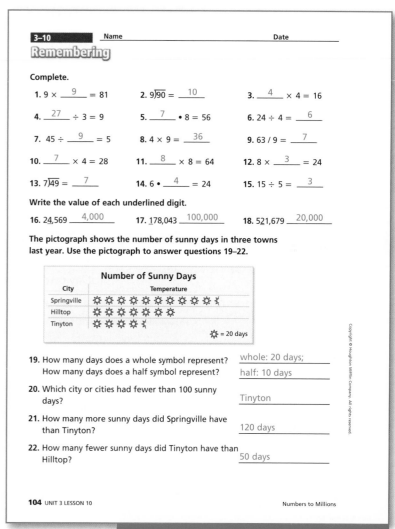

3–10	Name _____	Date _____

Remembering

Complete.

1. 9 × ___9___ = 81
2. 9)‾90‾ = ___10___
3. ___4___ × 4 = 16

4. ___27___ ÷ 3 = 9
5. ___7___ • 8 = 56
6. 24 ÷ 4 = ___6___

7. 45 ÷ ___9___ = 5
8. 4 × 9 = ___36___
9. 63 / 9 = ___7___

10. ___7___ × 4 = 28
11. ___8___ × 8 = 64
12. 8 × ___3___ = 24

13. 7)‾49‾ = ___7___
14. 6 • ___4___ = 24
15. 15 ÷ 5 = ___3___

Write the value of each underlined digit.

16. 24,569 ___4,000___
17. 178,043 ___100,000___
18. 521,679 ___20,000___

The pictograph shows the number of sunny days in three towns last year. Use the pictograph to answer questions 19–22.

Number of Sunny Days	
City	**Temperature**
Springville	☼ ☼ ☼ ☼ ☼ ☼ ☼ ☼ ☼ ☽
Hilltop	☼ ☼ ☼ ☼ ☼ ☼
Tinyton	☼ ☼ ☼ ☼ ☽

☼ = 20 days

19. How many days does a whole symbol represent? How many days does a half symbol represent?
whole: 20 days; half: 10 days

20. Which city or cities had fewer than 100 sunny days?
Tinyton

21. How many more sunny days did Springville have than Tinyton?
120 days

22. How many fewer sunny days did Tinyton have than Hilltop?
50 days

104 UNIT 3 LESSON 10

Numbers to Millions

Homework and Remembering page 104

Home or School Activity

Social Studies Connection

Population of States Students should make a table of the population of 4 or 5 states. Then tell them to write 3 conclusions based on the data. They can share their thinking with their classmates.

Sample conclusions might be:

- California has more than twice the population of Florida.

- Arizona has the fewest residents.

- An estimate of the population in all 5 states is about 90,000,000 people.

Populations of States in 2004	
State	**Population**
Arizona	5,743,834
California	35,893,799
Florida	17,397,161
New Jersey	8,698,879
Texas	22,490,022

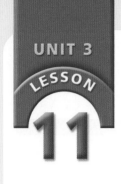

Make New Groups for Addition

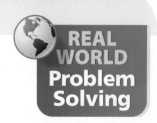

Lesson Objectives

● **Understand when new groups are needed in addition and why.**

● **Analyze different ways of keeping track of new groups.**

The Day at a Glance

Today's Goals	Materials	
① Teaching the Lesson **A1:** Explore and share methods for multi-digit addition. **A2:** Discover and discuss different addition methods. **A3:** Discuss special addition situations. **② Going Further** ▶ Math Connection: Addition and Money ▶ Differentiated Instruction **③ Homework and Spiral Review**	**Lesson Activities** Student Activity Book p. 153 or Student Hardcover Book p. 153 Homework and Remembering pp. 105–106 MathBoard Materials Base-ten blocks (optional)	**Lesson Activities** Student Activity Book p. 154 or Student Hardcover Book p. 154 Activity Cards 3-11 Play money Base-ten blocks Math Journals

Use Math Talk today!

Keeping Skills Sharp

Quick Practice ⏱ 5 MINUTES

Goal: Compare multi-digit numbers.

Say, Write, and Compare Have several students work at the board while other students work in pairs at their seats. Write two numbers for each student at the board (see top row). Have the students write the numbers in reverse order (see bottom row). Students at their seats choose one set of numbers to compare in both directions.

7,643 6,743	10,502 10,250	202,356 202,653
6,743 7,643	10,250 10,502	202,653 202,356

All students put a > or < between each pair of numbers. Then have the class read aloud some of the inequalities together.

Daily Routines

Homework Review Send students to the board to show their solutions and explanations for problems 14 and 15. Have each student at the board explain his/her solution. Encourage the rest of the class to ask clarifying questions and make comments.

Place Value Name a number 1,000 more than each these numbers.

6,740 7,740   3,216 4,216

1,085 2,085   8,988 9,988

① Teaching the Lesson

Activity 1

Explore Addition Methods

 20 MINUTES

Goal: Explore and share methods for multi-digit addition.

Materials: MathBoard Materials

 NCTM Standards:
Number and Operations
Algebra
Communication

$$
\begin{array}{r}
\overset{1\ 1}{2\ 7\ 8} \\
+\ 1\ 5\ 6 \\
\hline
4\ 3\ 4
\end{array}
\qquad
\begin{array}{r}
2\ 7\ 8 \\
+\ 1\ 5\ 6 \\
\hline
\underset{1\ 1}{4\ 3\ 4}
\end{array}
\qquad
\begin{array}{r}
2\ 7\ 8 \\
+\ 1\ 5\ 6 \\
\hline
3\ 0\ 0 \\
1\ 2\ 0 \\
+\ \ \ 1\ 4 \\
\hline
4\ 3\ 4
\end{array}
\qquad
\begin{array}{r}
2\ 7\ 8 \\
+\ 1\ 5\ 6 \\
\hline
1\ 4 \\
1\ 2\ 0 \\
+\ 3\ 0\ 0 \\
\hline
4\ 3\ 4
\end{array}
$$

▶ **Share Addition Methods** WHOLE CLASS

Read the following problem to the students. Write the numbers 278 and 156 on the board as you read them.

> Jerry and Martha collected seashells at the beach. Jerry found 278 shells and Martha found 156. How many seashells did Jerry and Martha find altogether?

Have some students make place-value drawings at the board while the others draw on their MathBoards. Then have students share their different solution methods.

Your students may use the methods shown on the left, or other methods. Any method is acceptable as long as it is accurate and the student can explain it. Students will discuss each of these methods in the next activity.

Activity 2

Keep Track of New Groups

 20 MINUTES

Goal: Discover and discuss different addition methods.

Materials: Student Activity Book or Hardcover Book p. 153

 NCTM Standards:
Number and Operations
Communication
Representation

▶ **Discuss Different Methods**

WHOLE CLASS   Math Talk

Page 153 of the Student Book illustrates three different addition methods, each of which shows the new place-value groups differently. Have the students describe as many of the features of each method as they can and relate each step in the numeric solution to parts of the drawing. Also have them discuss the advantages and disadvantages of each method.

3-11

Class Activity

Name _____ Date _____

▶ Discuss Different Methods

Discuss how each part of the place-value drawing is related
to each addition method.

879

+

754

1. New Groups Above Method

Step 1	Step 2	Step 3
1	1 1	1 1
879	879	879
+ 754	+ 754	+ 754
3	33	1,633

2. New Groups Below Method

Step 1	Step 2	Step 3
879	879	879
+ 754	+ 754	+ 754
1	1 1	1 1
3	33	1,633

3. Show Subtotals Method   Left-to-Right   Right-to-Left

Step 1	Step 2	Step 3	Step 4		
879	879	879	879		879
+ 754	+ 754	+ 754	+ 754		+ 754
1,500	1,500	1,500	1,500		13
	120	120	120		120
		13	+ 13		+ 1,500
			1,633		1,633

4. Discuss how each method above shows new groups.

5. On a separate sheet of paper, describe how the
Left-to-Right solution and the Right-to-Left solution are
alike and how they are different.

UNIT 3 LESSON 11   Make New Groups for Addition **153**

Student Activity Book page 153

Teaching Note

What to Expect From Students
Students may make the ones by using
horizontal rows of 5 or a vertical
column of ten with a space to show
the 5-group. Any method that clearly
shows the 5-groups is fine. Remind
students to show 5-groups for tens
and hundreds to reduce errors and
so that other people can understand
their drawing.

New Groups Above Method By grade 4, many students may already
know how to do multi-digit addition. Some may use the first method
shown below. We call it the New Groups Above Method because the
notation for the new groups is written above the top numbers of the
example. The steps are given below.

1. Add the ones:
  9 ones + 4 ones = 13 ones
  13 ones = 10 ones + 3 ones
  Group 10 ones as 1 ten.

Write "1" (the new ten made from 10 ones)
above the tens column and "3" at the bottom of
the ones column.

$$\begin{array}{r} \overset{1}{8}\ 7\ 9 \\ +\ 7\ 5\ 4 \\ \hline 3 \end{array}$$

Teaching Note

Math Background This discussion is
not intended to change the way
students add, but rather to help them
understand why their methods work.
We discuss these methods so students
can see place value in action in
different ways. After today, they
should be allowed to use whatever
method they choose.

Activity continued ▶

Activity 2

Teaching Note

Watch For! In multi-digit addition, students sometimes forget to add the digit that represents the new group. Students also tend to forget that the new-group digit is directly related to the old-group digit. The method shown on this page may help these students. Writing the new-group digit at the *bottom* of a column has two advantages:

▶ It is easier to add the two numbers you see in the problem and then increase that total by one (7 + 5 + 1 = 12 + 1 = 13) than to add as in New Groups Above (1 + 7 + 5 = 8 (remember it even though you can't see it) + 5 = 13).

▶ It is closer to the old-group digit, providing visual reinforcement of its relationship to the old-group digit. The 1 and 3 that are circled in step 1 at the right are the new-group digit and old-group digit, respectively. It is easy to see that they represent 1 ten and 3 ones, or 13.

2. Add the tens:

   1 ten + 7 tens + 5 tens = 13 tens

   13 tens = 10 tens + 3 tens

   Group 10 tens as 1 hundred.

$$\begin{array}{r} \overset{1}{8}\,\overset{1}{7}\,9 \\ +\,7\,5\,4 \\ \hline 3\,3 \end{array}$$

Write "1" (the new hundred from 10 tens) at the top of the hundreds column. Write the "3" at the bottom of the tens column.

3. Add the hundreds:

   1 hundred + 8 hundreds + 7 hundreds = 16 hundreds

   16 hundreds = 10 hundreds + 6 hundreds

   Group 10 hundreds as 1 thousand.

$$\begin{array}{r} \overset{1}{8}\,\overset{1}{7}\,\overset{1}{9} \\ +\,7\,5\,4 \\ \hline 1,6\,3\,3 \end{array}$$

Write "1" (the new thousand from 10 hundreds) in the thousands column of the answer and "6" in the hundreds column.

There are two other methods, both of which are easier for some students to understand. We call them "New Groups Below" and "Show Subtotals."

New Groups Below Method The three steps below are nearly the same as for New Groups Above. The only difference is where the new-group digit is written. This is a minor modification, but it can be conceptually and procedurally simpler.

1. Add the ones.

$$\begin{array}{r} 8\,7\,9 \\ +7\,5\,4 \\ \hline 3 \end{array}$$

2. Add the tens.

$$\begin{array}{r} 8\,7\,9 \\ +\,7\,5\,4 \\ \hline 3\,3 \end{array}$$

3. Add the hundreds.

$$\begin{array}{r} 8\,7\,9 \\ +\,7\,5\,4 \\ \hline 1,6\,3\,3 \end{array}$$

Show Subtotals Method Because this method does not depend on making new groups one place at a time, addition can start at either the left or the right. On this page, the hundreds are added first, but the process could start with the ones, or with any other column.

1. Add the hundreds.

8 hundreds + 7 hundreds = 15 hundreds

800 + 700 = 1500

```
    8 7 9
  + 7 5 4
  1, 5 0 0
```

2. Add the tens.

7 tens + 5 tens = 12 tens

70 + 50 = 120

```
      8 7 9
    + 7 5 4
    1, 5 0 0
      1 2 0
```

3. Add the ones.

9 + 4 = 13

```
      8 7 9
    + 7 5 4
    1, 5 0 0
      1 2 0
        1 3
```

4. Add the subtotals for the hundreds, tens, and ones.

```
      8 7 9
    + 7 5 4
    1, 5 0 0
      1 2 0
  +     1 3
  1, 6 3 3
```

Now have the students return to page 153 of the Student Book. Ask them to repeat the task of explaining each of the three methods as they refer to the place-value drawing. Ask them again to discuss advantages and disadvantages of each method. Finally, have them look at the Right-to-Left Show Subtotals Method. Ask them to describe how it is like and how it is different from the Left-to-Right Show Subtotals Method.

Conclude the activity by giving some students an opportunity to describe their favorite method and why it works for them. In the following days, give other students a chance to explain their method.

Teaching Note

Math Background The Show Subtotals method is convenient for numbers up to about 5 digits, and it shows in full the numbers that are being added. It is not so convenient for larger numbers. For example, adding 72,835,726 and 36,799,355 would require using 8 subtotals, one for each place value.

Activity 3

Grouping Decisions

 15 MINUTES

Goal: Discuss special addition situations.

Materials: Base-ten blocks (optional)

 NCTM Standards:
Number and Operations
Communication

Teaching Note

What to Expect from Students
Some students prefer to add from left to right. This method is taught in many European countries. Students learn to either go back and change a number if they have made a new group or look ahead to see where they might need a new group before they write the total. In cases where the total in the next-right column is 9, students will need to look ahead more than one column to make sure they add in all of the new groups they make.

 Alternate Approach

Base-Ten Blocks Some students may need to work through the examples, using concrete materials. You can have them use base-ten blocks or some other hands-on base-ten materials.

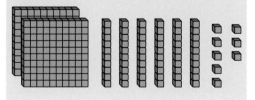

▶ **Are New Groups Necessary?** WHOLE CLASS

Write this addition example on the board:

$$724 + 268$$

Have students go to the board to show the example with a place-value drawing.

724

+

268

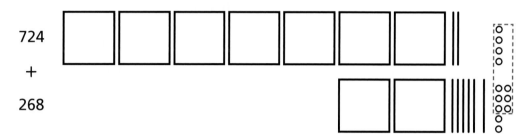

Have students describe the addition, including where new groups are needed and why. Tell them to add ones, then tens, then hundreds. Elicit the following:

- 4 ones + 8 ones = 12 ones, so 1 new ten is needed.
- 2 tens + 6 tens + 1 new ten = 9 tens, so a new hundred is *not* needed.
- 7 hundreds + 2 hundreds = 9 hundreds, so a new thousand is *not* needed.

Now guide a summary discussion about when new groups are needed or not needed for addition.

- When do you need to make a new group? when the total in a place is greater than or equal to 10
- When do you *not* need to make a new group? when the total in a place is less than or equal to 9

▶ Adding from Left to Right WHOLE CLASS

Write this addition on the board:

338 + 565

Have students solve the problem, using a place-value drawing.

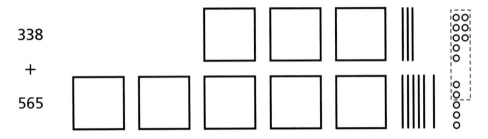

338

+

565

Have the students add the hundreds, then the tens, and then the ones.

● 3 hundreds + 5 hundreds = 8 hundreds

● 3 tens + 6 tens = 9 tens

● 8 ones + 5 ones = 13 ones, so 1 new ten is needed.

Ask students to discuss what needs to be done now that they know a new ten is needed.

● The new ten must be added to the tens column.
  1 new ten + 9 tens = 10 tens, making 1 new hundred.

● The new hundred must be added to the hundreds column.
  1 new hundred + 8 hundreds = 9 hundreds.

```
  338
+565
─────
  903
```

Note that in this example, a new group is needed in a column because a new group is created in the next column to the right. A student adding from left to right might have difficulty foreseeing the need for a new group in a particular column. However, if students adding from left to right do not have difficulty with cases such as this, allow them to continue to use their method. Encourage them to explain what they are doing as they work.

✓ Ongoing Assessment

Have students:

▶ explain how to add 48 + 75.

▶ find the sum of 276 + 438.

The Learning Classroom

Math Talk How did your students explain their math thinking today? Early on, when a student provides an answer and then wants to sit down, try asking him or her to stay at the board and explain just one or two more things about the problem or math thinking. For example, a student may be encouraged to tell more about a drawing they drew to solve a word problem or how they used the drawing to come up with an answer.

Going Further

Math Connection: Addition and Money

Goal: Use money to solve problems involving addition with money.

Materials: Student Activity Book or Hardcover Book p. 154, play money (one-dollar bills, ten-dollar bills, and hundred-dollar bills)

✔ **NCTM Standards:**
Number and Operations
Communication
Representation
Problem Solving

▶ Addition and Money PAIRS

In this lesson, students connect what they know about adding with adding money amounts.

Have the class discuss the introductory problem on Student Book page 154. Ask the class to describe how the model for Carlos' addition is like a place-value drawing. The ten-dollar bills are like tens and the one-dollar bills are like ones. Discuss how a group of 11 one-dollar bills can be made into a group of 1 ten-dollar bill and 1 one-dollar bill.

Tell the class that in this activity, they will be acting out with only one-dollar bills, ten-dollar bills, and hundred-dollar bills (no five-dollar bills or twenty-dollar bills).

Use the **Scenario** structure as **Student Pairs** complete problems 1–3, using play money. Students can also use drawings instead of play money. They can draw rectangles that have $1, $10, or $100 inside them to show the money values.

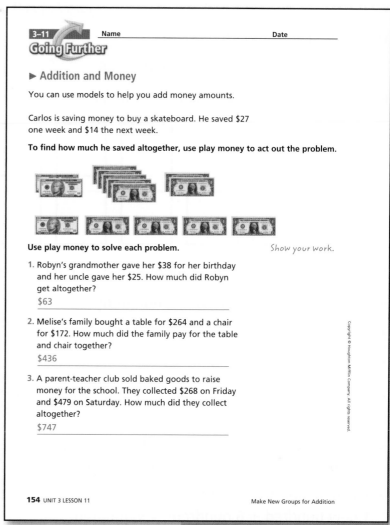

Student Activity Book page 154

English Language Learners

Draw a $1, $10, and $100 bill on the board. Review the values.

- **Beginning** Point to each bill. Say: **A $1 bill is the same as 1 one.** Ask: **Is $10 the same as 10 ones?** yes **How many ones is a $100 bill?** 100 ones
- **Intermediate** Point to the $1. Ask: **How many ones is this?** 1 Point to the $10. Ask: **Is this 1 one?** no **How many ones is this?** 10 Point to the $100. Ask: **How many ones is this?** 100
- **Advanced** Have students use short sentences to describe the difference between the values of a $1, $10, and $100 bill.

Differentiated Instruction

Intervention — Activity Card 3-11

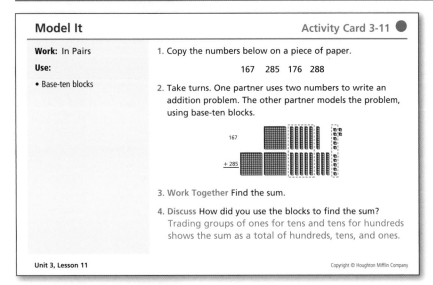

Model It — Activity Card 3-11 ●

Work: In Pairs

Use:
• Base-ten blocks

1. Copy the numbers below on a piece of paper.

167   285   176   288

2. Take turns. One partner uses two numbers to write an addition problem. The other partner models the problem, using base-ten blocks.

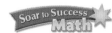

167

+ 285

3. **Work Together** Find the sum.

4. **Discuss** How did you use the blocks to find the sum? Trading groups of ones for tens and tens for hundreds shows the sum as a total of hundreds, tens, and ones.

Unit 3, Lesson 11   Copyright © Houghton Mifflin Company

Activity Note Remind students to start the addition process by regrouping.

 Math Writing Prompt

Model Addition Draw a picture that shows 150 + 162.

Soar to Success Math **Software Support**

Use *Soar to Success* for instruction of students needing targeted support for underlying skills.

On Level — Activity Card 3-11

Mental Math — Activity Card 3-11 ▲

Work: In Pairs

1. Work together to decide how to use mental math to find the sum below. Describe the steps you would follow.

507 + 745

2. On your own, write 5 addition problems that can be solved by using mental math.

3. Exchange papers with your partner. Use mental math to solve the problems.

4. **Discuss** What methods did you use to solve the problems?

Unit 3, Lesson 11   Copyright © Houghton Mifflin Company

Activity Note Discuss real-world situations where using mental math is helpful because pencil and paper or calculators are not available.

 Math Writing Prompt

Explain Your Thinking Choose your favorite method of addition, and explain why it is your favorite.

MegaMath Grades K-6 **Software Support**

Use *MegaMath* for review and reinforcement of the concepts and skills presented in this lesson.

Challenge — Activity Card 3-11

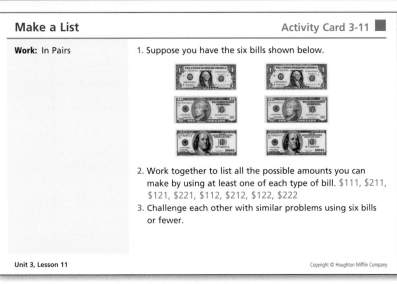

Make a List — Activity Card 3-11 ■

Work: In Pairs

1. Suppose you have the six bills shown below.

2. Work together to list all the possible amounts you can make by using at least one of each type of bill. $111, $211, $121, $221, $112, $212, $122, $222

3. Challenge each other with similar problems using six bills or fewer.

Unit 3, Lesson 11   Copyright © Houghton Mifflin Company

Activity Note Suggest that students organize a list of the different amounts of money they can make by listing the number of each type of bill they use under the headings 100s, 10s, and 1s.

 Math Writing Prompt

Investigate Math Write an addition word problem that would require more than one new ten group and more than one new hundred group.

DESTINATION Math **Software Support**

Use *Destination Math* to take students beyond the concepts and skills presented in this lesson.

③ Homework and Spiral Review

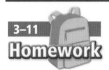

Homework Goal: Additional Practice

Use this Homework page to provide students with more practice with addition.

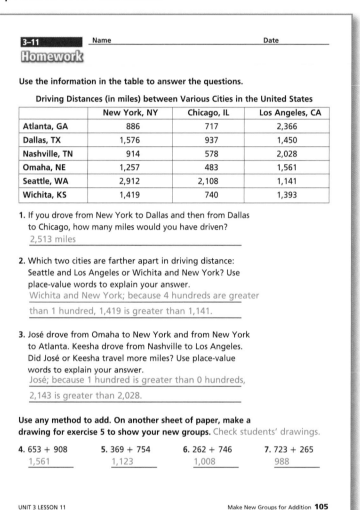

Name _____ **Date** _____

Homework

Use the information in the table to answer the questions.

Driving Distances (in miles) between Various Cities in the United States

	New York, NY	Chicago, IL	Los Angeles, CA
Atlanta, GA	886	717	2,366
Dallas, TX	1,576	937	1,450
Nashville, TN	914	578	2,028
Omaha, NE	1,257	483	1,561
Seattle, WA	2,912	2,108	1,141
Wichita, KS	1,419	740	1,393

1. If you drove from New York to Dallas and then from Dallas to Chicago, how many miles would you have driven?
   2,513 miles

2. Which two cities are farther apart in driving distance: Seattle and Los Angeles or Wichita and New York? Use place-value words to explain your answer.
   Wichita and New York; because 4 hundreds are greater than 1 hundred, 1,419 is greater than 1,141.

3. José drove from Omaha to New York and from New York to Atlanta. Keesha drove from Nashville to Los Angeles. Did José or Keesha travel more miles? Use place-value words to explain your answer.
   José; because 1 hundred is greater than 0 hundreds, 2,143 is greater than 2,028.

Use any method to add. On another sheet of paper, make a drawing for exercise 5 to show your new groups. Check students' drawings.

4. 653 + 908   5. 369 + 754   6. 262 + 746   7. 723 + 265
   1,561   1,123   1,008   988

UNIT 3 LESSON 11   Make New Groups for Addition **105**

Homework and Remembering page 105

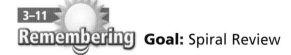

Remembering Goal: Spiral Review

This Remembering activity would be appropriate anytime after today's lesson.

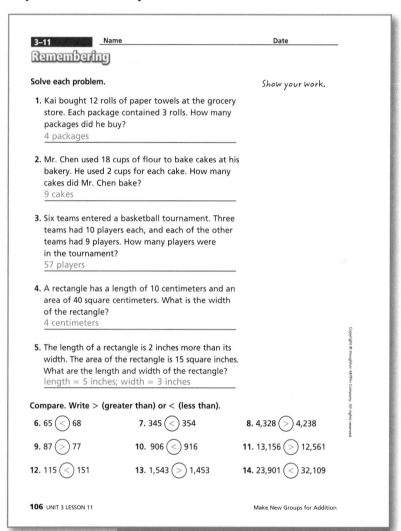

Name _____ **Date** _____

Remembering

Solve each problem.   *Show your work.*

1. Kai bought 12 rolls of paper towels at the grocery store. Each package contained 3 rolls. How many packages did he buy?
   4 packages

2. Mr. Chen used 18 cups of flour to bake cakes at his bakery. He used 2 cups for each cake. How many cakes did Mr. Chen bake?
   9 cakes

3. Six teams entered a basketball tournament. Three teams had 10 players each, and each of the other teams had 9 players. How many players were in the tournament?
   57 players

4. A rectangle has a length of 10 centimeters and an area of 40 square centimeters. What is the width of the rectangle?
   4 centimeters

5. The length of a rectangle is 2 inches more than its width. The area of the rectangle is 15 square inches. What are the length and width of the rectangle?
   length = 5 inches; width = 3 inches

Compare. Write > (greater than) or < (less than).

6. 65 $<$ 68   7. 345 $<$ 354   8. 4,328 $>$ 4,238

9. 87 $>$ 77   10. 906 $<$ 916   11. 13,156 $>$ 12,561

12. 115 $<$ 151   13. 1,543 $>$ 1,453   14. 23,901 $<$ 32,109

106 UNIT 3 LESSON 11   Make New Groups for Addition

Homework and Remembering page 106

Home or School Activity

Science Connection

Dinnertime Have students make a dinner menu, including the number of calories for a serving of each item. They can research in a library or on the Internet to find calorie amounts. Have them find the total number of calories in the dinner.

Dinner Food	Calories
Chicken Nuggets (10)	530
Brown Rice (1 cup)	217
Carrots (1 cup)	53
Corn on the Cob	123
Total Calories	923

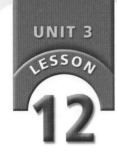

UNIT 3
LESSON
12

Addition to Millions

Lesson Objective

• Understand different addition methods.

Vocabulary
digit

The Day at a Glance

Today's Goals	Materials	
1 Teaching the Lesson **A1:** Extend knowledge of regrouping and adding to larger place values. **A2:** Identify incorrect alignment of place values and use correct alignment to add. **2 Going Further** ▸ Differentiated Instruction **3 Homework and Spiral Review**	**Lesson Activities** Student Activity Book pp. 155–156 or Student Hardcover Book pp. 155–156 Homework and Remembering pp. 107–108	**Going Further** Activity Cards 3-12 Student Activity Book p. 156 or Student Hardcover Book p. 156 Grid paper Number cubes Math Journals

123 Use **Math Talk** today!

Keeping Skills Sharp

Quick Practice ⏱ 5 MINUTES	Daily Routines
Goal: Add and subtract tens **Equation Chains** Have students create addition chains that have the same sum. $100 = 40 + 60 = 20 + 80 = 70 + 30 = 10 + 90$, and so on. Have students create subtraction chains that have the same difference. $20 = 120 - 100 = 80 - 60 = 90 - 70 = 130 - 110 = 75 - 55 = 25 - 5$, and so on.	**Homework Review** Ask students to place their homework at the corner of their desks. As you circulate during Quick Practice, check that students completed the assignment, and see whether any problem cause difficulty for many students. **Estimation** Round each of these numbers. ▸ to the nearest ten: 96; 14; 566 100; 10; 570 ▸ to the nearest hundred: 434; 1,073; 5,250 400; 1,100; 5,300 ▸ to the nearest thousand: 3,881; 5,499; 2,950 4,000; 5,000; 3,000

Teaching the Lesson

Add Larger Numbers

 30 MINUTES

Goal: Extend knowledge of regrouping and adding to larger place values.

Materials: Student Activity Book or Hardcover Book p. 155

✔ **NCTM Standards:**
Number and Operations
Communication

The Learning Classroom

Helping Community By discussing multiple strategies for math examples, students become aware of other students' thinking, which leads them to become better "helpers." Instead of showing how they would solve problems, they are able to look at other students' work and help them to find mistakes in their methods.

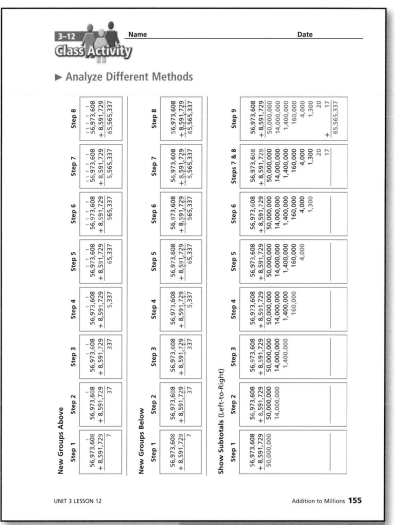

Student Activity Book page 155

▶ Analyze Different Methods WHOLE CLASS

Write on the classroom board: 56,973,608 + 8,591,729.

Ask for 3 volunteers to go to the board and solve the problem for each method discussed in Lesson 11: One student does New Groups Above, another does New Groups Below, and another does Show Subtotals. Students at their seats choose which method they will do, but challenge students who feel comfortable to try a different method just for this problem. Have each student explain his/her solution, with help from the class or you as necessary (be sure place-value language is used). Leave the problems on the board to use in the next discussion.

Now direct the students' attention to page 155 in the Student Book. Ask them to look at the three methods for a couple of minutes to prepare to discuss how the methods are alike and how they are different. Have students also identify the advantages and disadvantages of the methods. Carry out the discussion using the problems on the board as needed.

Similarly, if students are comfortable with the New Groups Below method, ask them to differentiate between where there is and is not a new group and to explain why. If the New Groups Below method is new to most of your students, ask for a volunteer to **Solve and Discuss**, using that method.

Math Talk For the Show Subtotals method, students should discuss how they would get the same result if they worked right-to-left. They should also be able to explain where the ending zeros come from at each step.

- In what place is the 5 in the first subtotal row? the ten millions place
- What does the 5 represent? 5 ten millions or 50 million
- How do you write that number? 50,000,000

If any students have chosen to use another method they know, have them write their method on the board and describe each step as they go.

Ask students to summarize the big ideas about adding multi-digit numbers. They should mention at least these points:

- You add like places to each other.
- When you get ten or more of a given place value, you make a group of ten and add it in as 1 group of the next larger place value in the column to the left.
- All three methods we discussed will get the same total because all of them do these steps.

Differentiated Instruction

Advanced Learners Encourage students to describe the same numbers different ways. For example, 500,000 can be thought of as:
5 hundred thousands or 5 × 100,000
50 ten thousands or 50 × 10,000
500 thousands or 500 × 1,000
5,000 hundreds or 5,000 × 100
50,000 tens or 50,000 × 10
500,000 ones or 500,000 × 1

Teaching the Lesson (continued)

Activity 2

Align Places

 25 MINUTES

Goal: Identify incorrect alignment of place values and use correct alignment to add.

Materials: Student Activity Book or Hardcover Book p. 156

 NCTM Standards:
Number and Operations
Communication

Ongoing Assessment

Ask:

▶ What is 4,060,001 + 50,002?

▶ If Mya uses New Groups Above and Jim uses New Groups Below, will their totals be the same? Explain.

English Language Learners

Review how to *align*. Write 15,324 + 8,109 in vertical form on the board. Have students identify the digits and places values in each number. Say: **We align the digits to add.**

- **Beginning** Ask: **Are the hundreds digits in the same column?** yes **How many digits are in the ten thousands column?** 1
- **Intermediate** Ask: **How many digits are in 15,324?** 5 **In 8,109?** 4 **Can we put the 8 under the 1 to add?** no Say: **We have to ___.** align the digits
- **Advanced** Write the problem vertically. Don't align it. Ask: **Is this correct?** no **What do we have to do?** align the digits

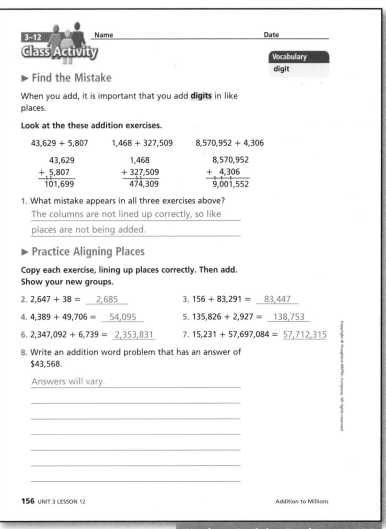

Student Activity Book page 156

[Student Activity Book page 156 content:]

3–12
Class Activity   Name _____ Date _____

Vocabulary: digit

▶ **Find the Mistake**

When you add, it is important that you add **digits** in like places.

Look at the these addition exercises.

43,629 + 5,807	1,468 + 327,509	8,570,952 + 4,306
43,629	1,468	8,570,952
+ 5,807	+ 327,509	+ 4,306
101,699	474,309	9,001,552

1. What mistake appears in all three exercises above?
The columns are not lined up correctly, so like places are not being added.

▶ **Practice Aligning Places**

Copy each exercise, lining up places correctly. Then add. Show your new groups.

2. 2,647 + 38 = __2,685__   3. 156 + 83,291 = __83,447__

4. 4,389 + 49,706 = __54,095__   5. 135,826 + 2,927 = __138,753__

6. 2,347,092 + 6,739 = __2,353,831__   7. 15,231 + 57,697,084 = __57,712,315__

8. Write an addition word problem that has an answer of $43,568.
Answers will vary.
_____
_____
_____
_____
_____
_____

156 UNIT 3 LESSON 12   Addition to Millions

▶ Find the Mistake WHOLE CLASS

Have students answer exercise 1 on page 156 of the Student Book. Then ask them to share and discuss answers. The answers they write may vary somewhat. Guide a discussion to elicit these related concepts:

- The mistake is that columns are not properly aligned.

- This is a mistake because you need to add ones and ones, tens and tens, and so on.

▶ Practice Aligning Places WHOLE CLASS

Have as many students as possible work at the classroom board to write and solve exercises 2–7. Students can use any method they wish. The rest of the class can ask these students about their methods. Then have students individually answer problem 8. Allow students to share their problems if time permits.

② Going Further

Differentiated Instruction

● Intervention   Activity Card 3-12

Grid It   Activity Card 3-12 ●

Work: In Pairs

Use:
- Centimeter-Grid Paper (TRB M60)
- Student Book page 156

1. Choose one of the exercises from Student Book page 156, and write it on grid paper in vertical form. Use the columns to help you line up place values.

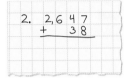

2. Add the numbers to find the sum.
3. **Compare** Exchange answers with your partner and compare. If answers differ, justify or correct your answer.
4. Repeat the activity for the rest of the problems.

Unit 3, Lesson 12   Copyright © Houghton Mifflin Company

Activity Note Remind students to right align all numbers so that the same place values are in the same column.

 Math Writing Prompt

Understanding Place Value Explain how you can tell that you will need to make a new ten when you add two numbers.

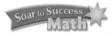 **Software Support**

Use *Soar to Success* for instruction of students needing targeted support for underlying skills.

▲ On Level   Activity Card 3-12

Roll Addends   Activity Card 3-12 ▲

Work: In Pairs

Use:
- Number cube

1. One partner rolls the number cube.
2. The other partner rolls the cube that many times to find and record the digits for the addend.
3. Exchange roles, and repeat to find and record a second addend.
4. On your own, calculate the sum and compare answers with your partner.
5. Repeat the activity to create and solve four more problems.

Unit 3, Lesson 12   Copyright © Houghton Mifflin Company

Activity Note Variations of the activity can include finding three or more addends or allowing students to use a calculator to check answers.

 Math Writing Prompt

Explain Your Thinking Write a word problem that requires adding two five-digit numbers and has a six-digit answer. Explain how you chose your numbers.

 Software Support

Use *MegaMath* for review and reinforcement of the concepts and skills presented in this lesson.

■ Challenge   Activity Card 3-12

Speed Addition   Activity Card 3-12 ■

Work: In Small Groups

Decide:
Who will be the Leader for the first round.

1. **Leader:** Write an addition problem in column form with three addends that each have 7 digits and exactly 3 zeros. Calculate the sum without showing it to your group.
2. Show the addition problem to everyone in your group at once. The first person to find the correct sum earns one point.

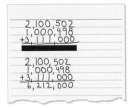

3. Repeat the activity, taking turns as leader, until every member has taken a turn. The highest score wins.

Unit 3, Lesson 12   Copyright © Houghton Mifflin Company

Activity Note Note that the three zeros do not have to be consecutive. Have groups discuss methods they used to complete the addition.

 Math Writing Prompt

Explain Your Thinking If you add two *different* six-digit numbers, what is the greatest possible total? What is the least possible total? Explain your answers.

 DESTINATION Math® **Software Support**

Use *Destination Math* to take students beyond the concepts and skills presented in this lesson.

Addition to Millions   **365**

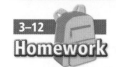
③ Homework and Spiral Review

Homework **Goal:** Additional Practice

Use this Homework page to provide students with more practice with addition to millions.

Remembering **Goal:** Spiral Review

This Remembering activity would be appropriate anytime after today's lesson.

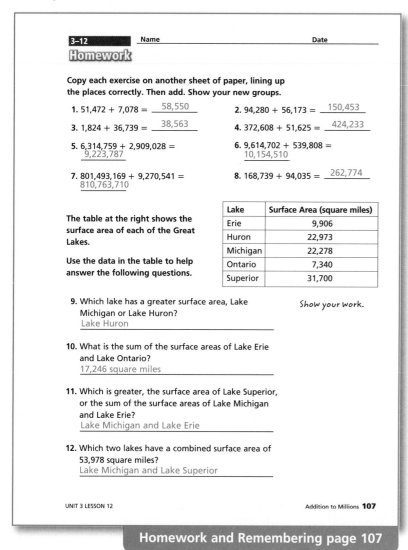

3–12	Name		Date
Homework

Copy each exercise on another sheet of paper, lining up the places correctly. Then add. Show your new groups.

1. 51,472 + 7,078 = __58,550__
2. 94,280 + 56,173 = __150,453__
3. 1,824 + 36,739 = __38,563__
4. 372,608 + 51,625 = __424,233__
5. 6,314,759 + 2,909,028 = __9,223,787__
6. 9,614,702 + 539,808 = __10,154,510__
7. 801,493,169 + 9,270,541 = __810,763,710__
8. 168,739 + 94,035 = __262,774__

The table at the right shows the surface area of each of the Great Lakes.

Use the data in the table to help answer the following questions.

Lake	Surface Area (square miles)
Erie	9,906
Huron	22,973
Michigan	22,278
Ontario	7,340
Superior	31,700

9. Which lake has a greater surface area, Lake Michigan or Lake Huron?
   Lake Huron

Show your work.

10. What is the sum of the surface areas of Lake Erie and Lake Ontario?
    17,246 square miles

11. Which is greater, the surface area of Lake Superior, or the sum of the surface areas of Lake Michigan and Lake Erie?
    Lake Michigan and Lake Erie

12. Which two lakes have a combined surface area of 53,978 square miles?
    Lake Michigan and Lake Superior

UNIT 3 LESSON 12

Addition to Millions **107**

Homework and Remembering page 107

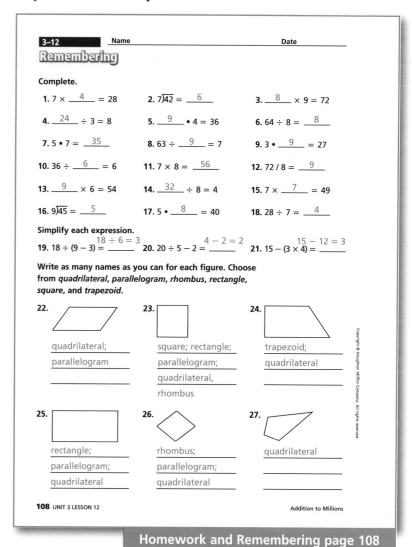

3–12	Name		Date
Remembering

Complete.

1. 7 × __4__ = 28
2. 7)42̄ = __6__
3. __8__ × 9 = 72
4. __24__ ÷ 3 = 8
5. __9__ • 4 = 36
6. 64 ÷ 8 = __8__
7. 5 • 7 = __35__
8. 63 ÷ __9__ = 7
9. 3 • __9__ = 27
10. 36 ÷ __6__ = 6
11. 7 × 8 = __56__
12. 72 / 8 = __9__
13. __9__ × 6 = 54
14. __32__ ÷ 8 = 4
15. 7 × __7__ = 49
16. 9)45̄ = __5__
17. 5 • __8__ = 40
18. 28 ÷ 7 = __4__

Simplify each expression.

19. 18 ÷ (9 − 3) = _18 ÷ 6 = 3_
20. 20 ÷ 5 − 2 = _4 − 2 = 2_
21. 15 − (3 × 4) = _15 − 12 = 3_

Write as many names as you can for each figure. Choose from *quadrilateral*, *parallelogram*, *rhombus*, *rectangle*, *square*, and *trapezoid*.

22. quadrilateral; parallelogram

23. square; rectangle; parallelogram; quadrilateral, rhombus

24. trapezoid; quadrilateral

25. rectangle; parallelogram; quadrilateral

26. rhombus; parallelogram; quadrilateral

27. quadrilateral

108 UNIT 3 LESSON 12

Addition to Millions

Homework and Remembering page 108

Home or School Activity

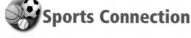
Sports Connection

Find an Attendance Total Have students choose a professional sports team. Have them find the total number of tickets sold for several home games for that team.

Stallions	Attendance
July 5	30,896
July 6	34,736
July 7	36,004
July 8	28,990
Total	130,626

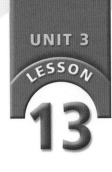

UNIT 3
LESSON
13

Estimation and Mental Math

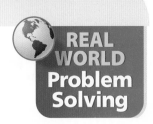

REAL WORLD Problem Solving

Lesson Objectives

- **Add using mental math.**
- **Use rounding and estimation to check addition.**

The Day at a Glance

Today's Goals	Materials
① Teaching the Lesson **A1:** Explore adjusting an estimated total to find an exact total. **A2:** Add numbers mentally. **A2:** Use rounding and estimation to check answers to addition problems.	**Lesson Activities** Student Activity Book pp. 157–158 or Student Hardcover Book pp. 157–158 Homework and Remembering pp. 109–110 Quick Quiz 3 (Assessment Guide) Calculators (optional)
② Going Further ▶ Differentiated Instruction	**Going Further** Activity Cards 3-13 Number cubes Math Journals
③ Homework and Spiral Review	

123 Use Math Talk today!

Keeping Skills Sharp

Quick Practice ⏱ 5 MINUTES	Daily Routines
Goal: Add multi-digit numbers. **Find the Sum** Write this problem on the board. Have the students write the problem in their Math Journals and solve it. 649,392 + 8,718 If any students do not get the correct solution, write the incorrect solution(s) on the board. The class can discuss why each solution is wrong, and how to fix it.	**Homework Review** Have students discuss the problems from their homework. Encourage students to help each other resolve any misunderstandings. **Place Value** Name a number 10,000 more than each of these numbers. 56,347 10,921 624,088 66,347 20,921 634,088 98,159 861,976 245,635 108,159 871,976 255,635

1 Teaching the Lesson

Activity 1

Round and Adjust

 15 MINUTES

Goal: Explore adjusting an estimated total to find an exact total.

Materials: Student Activity Book or Hardcover Book pp. 157–158

✓ **NCTM Standards:**
Number and Operations
Problem Solving
Communication

Teaching Note

What to Expect from Students The prices for the fruit at the top of Student Book page 157 are not needed to solve the problem. Guide students to recognize that the prices represent extra information.

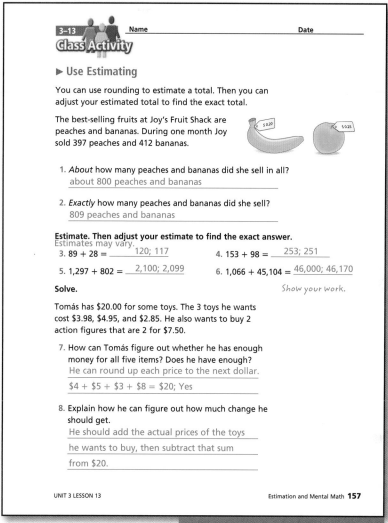

Student Activity Book page 157

3-13
Class Activity   Name _____   Date _____

▶ **Use Estimating**

You can use rounding to estimate a total. Then you can adjust your estimated total to find the exact total.

The best-selling fruits at Joy's Fruit Shack are peaches and bananas. During one month Joy sold 397 peaches and 412 bananas.

1. *About* how many peaches and bananas did she sell in all?
   about 800 peaches and bananas

2. *Exactly* how many peaches and bananas did she sell?
   809 peaches and bananas

Estimate. Then adjust your estimate to find the exact answer.
Estimates may vary.
3. 89 + 28 = ___120; 117___   4. 153 + 98 = ___253; 251___
5. 1,297 + 802 = ___2,100; 2,099___   6. 1,066 + 45,104 = ___46,000; 46,170___

Solve.   *Show your work.*

Tomás has $20.00 for some toys. The 3 toys he wants cost $3.98, $4.95, and $2.85. He also wants to buy 2 action figures that are 2 for $7.50.

7. How can Tomás figure out whether he has enough money for all five items? Does he have enough?
   He can round up each price to the next dollar.
   $4 + $5 + $3 + $8 = $20; Yes

8. Explain how he can figure out how much change he should get.
   He should add the actual prices of the toys
   he wants to buy, then subtract that sum
   from $20.

UNIT 3 LESSON 13   Estimation and Mental Math **157**

▶ **Use Estimating** WHOLE CLASS

Use **Solve and Discuss** for problems 1 and 2 on Student Book page 157. Elicit the following:

● For problem 1, 400 peaches + 400 bananas = 800 peaches and bananas.

● For problem 2, 400 peaches is 3 extra and 400 bananas is 12 too few, so the exact answer is 800 − 3 + 12 = 809.

Math Talk Have students discuss the estimating and adjusting strategies that they used for exercises 3–6. Strategies can vary, as long as students can explain how they found the answer and why it is correct.

Problem 3 $89 + 28 =$

Round and estimate: Round 89 up to 90 and 28 up to 30. $90 + 30 = 120$

Adjust to find the exact answer: Subtract 1 from the total because rounding 89 to 90 added 1. Subtract 2 from the total because rounding 28 to 30 added 2. $120 - 1 - 2 = 117$.

Problem 4 $153 + 98 =$

Round and estimate: Round 98 up to 100. $153 + 100 = 253$.

Adjust to find the exact answer: Subtract 2 from the total because rounding 98 to 100 added 2. $253 - 2 = 251$.

Some students may have rounded 153 down to 150. Ask why it is not necessary to round 153. Rounding 98 to 100 makes the problem easy enough to handle. Rounding 153 would make the problem more difficult.

Problem 5 $1,297 + 802 =$

Round and estimate: Round 1,297 up to 1,300 and 802 down to 800. $1,300 + 800 = 2,100$.

Adjust to find the exact answer: Subtract 1 from the total because rounding 802 to 800 subtracted 2 and rounding 1,297 to 1,300 added 3. $2,100 - 1 = 2,099$.

Problem 6 $1,066 1 45,104 =$

Round and estimate: Round 45,104 down to 45,100: $1,066 + 45,100 = 46,166$.

Adjust to find the exact answer: Add 4 to the total because rounding 45,104 to 45,100 subtracted 4. $46,166 + 4 = 46,170$.

Ask why this adjustment is easy. $6 + 4 = 10$, so $166 + 4 = 170$ is easy.

Use **Solve and Discuss** for problems 7–8 on page 157 and problems 9–10 on page 158 of the Student Book.

Use **Solve and Discuss** for problems 7–8 on page 157 and problems 9–10 on page 158 of the Student Book.

English Language Learners

Write the word *cook* two times on the board. Discuss its noun form and verb form. Write the word *estimate* two times on the board.

- **Beginning** Say: An estimate (EHS-tuh-mit) is a close value. Estimate (EHS-tuh-mate) is what you do to find that value. Have students repeat, practicing different pronunciations of the word.
- **Intermediate** Ask: What is an estimate (EHS-tuh-mit)? a close value Ask: What does it mean to estimate (EHS-tuh-mate)? to find that value Give students practice saying sentences with each form of the word.
- **Advanced** Have students make up short sentences, using the different forms and pronunciations of *estimate*.

Teaching Note

Language and Vocabulary The guide for the lesson provided here expresses concepts in terms that are understandable to students. Do not feel compelled to use these exact words. You may think of other ways to explain the material.

Teaching Note

Math Background Remind students that overestimating is important for money because you must have enough to pay for the items you want to buy. Items are often priced just under whole dollar amounts, so overestimating by rounding up is often appropriate.

Teaching the Lesson (continued)

Activity 2

Mental Math

 15 MINUTES

Goal: Add numbers mentally.

Materials: Student Activity Book or Hardcover Book p. 158

✔ **NCTM Standards:**
Number and Operations
Problem Solving
Communication

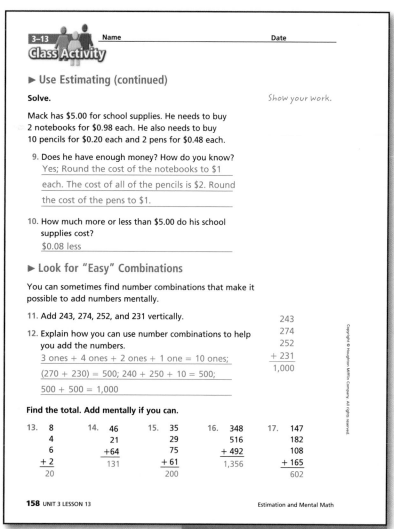

Student Activity Book page 158

▶ Look for "Easy" Combinations WHOLE CLASS

Tell students they can sometimes find number combinations that make addition problems easier.

The students should read and discuss problems 11 and 12.

Remind students to write the numbers so that the digits with the same place value line up.

$$\begin{array}{r} 243 \\ 274 \\ 252 \\ + 231 \end{array}$$

Students should see that the digits in the ones column add up to 10; tell them to remember that 10. Now the numbers to be added are 240, 270, 250, and 230 (that is, 24 tens, 27 tens, 25 tens, and 23 tens). Group 270 and 230 because they add up to 500. Now add:
(270 + 230) + 240 + 250 + 10 = 1,000

370 UNIT 3 LESSON 13

▶ Share Solutions

The students should discuss how this method can help them do each of the column additions in exercises 13–17. Again, strategies can vary, as long as students can explain how they found their answers and why they are correct. In the suggested methods below, the parentheses show how to group numbers for mental math.

13.
```
   8 ⌐
   4 ⌐
   6 ⌐
 + 2 ⌐
 ─────
  20
```
$8 + 2 = 10$
$4 + 6 = 10$
$10 + 10 = 20$

14.
```
 ⌐46⌐
  21 
+ 64⌐
 ─────
 131
```
$(6 + 4) + 1 = 11$
$(60 + 40) + 20 = 120$
$11 + 120 = 131$

15.
```
 ⌐35⌐
 ⌐29⌐
 ⌐75⌐
+ 61⌐
 ─────
 200
```
$5 + 5 = 10$
$9 + 1 = 10$
$(30 + 70) + (20 + 60) = 100 + 80 = 180$
$10 + 10 + 180 = 200$

16.
```
  348⌐
 ⌐516
 ⌐492⌐
 ──────
 1,356
```
$(8 + 2) + 6 = 16$
$(510 + 490) + 340 = 1,000 + 340 = 1,340$
$16 + 1,340 = 1,356$

17.
```
 ⌐147⌐
 ⌐182⌐
 ⌐108⌐
+ 165⌐
 ──────
  602
```
$2 + 8 = 10$
$7 + 5 = 12$
$(140 + 160) + (180 + 100) = 300 + 280 = 580$
$10 + 12 + 580 = 602$

Math Talk in Action

Have students discuss estimating as a way of checking to see if answers are reasonable.

Trinh: For exercise 11, all four numbers are about 250, so I thought $250 + 250 + 250 + 250 = 1,000$.

Ben: For exercise 17, 147 and 165 are both close to 150, so their sum is about 300. 182 is about 200 and 108 is about 100 so their sum is about 300. $300 + 300$ is about 600.

✔ Ongoing Assessment

Have students estimate each total and then adjust their estimated total to find the exact total.

▶ $78 + 19$

▶ $2,403 + 296$

Activity 3

Check Addition (optional)

 15 MINUTES

Goal: Use rounding and estimation to check answers to addition problems.

Materials: calculators (optional)

 NCTM Standards:
Number and Operations
Communication

The Learning Classroom

Math Talk Have students discuss how they might get a wrong answer by using a calculator. Elicit these possible reasons if students do not think of them:

▶ pressing a wrong key

▶ pressing the wrong number of keys

Emphasize that incorrect keystrokes can produce incorrect answers and that estimating is important for catching errors.

 Quick Quiz

See Assessment Guide for Unit 3 Quick Quiz 3.

▶ **Estimate to Check a Sum** WHOLE CLASS

Have students solve the addition problem below. They may use calculators if you have them available.

$3{,}642 + 7{,}693 = 11{,}335$

Now discuss how to estimate to check that the answer is reasonable. Rounding each addend to its greatest place, we have:

$4{,}000 + 8{,}000 = 12{,}000$

So 11,335 is reasonable.

Have students solve these addition problems and then use estimation to check that each answer is reasonable.

$10{,}672 + 61{,}829 = 72{,}501$

$10{,}000 + 60{,}000 = 70{,}000$

$7{,}390 + 79{,}036 = 86{,}426$

$7{,}000 + 80{,}000 = 87{,}000$

$56{,}293 + 86{,}910 = 143{,}203$

$60{,}000 + 90{,}000 = 150{,}000$

$9{,}482{,}504 + 8{,}691{,}046 = 18{,}173{,}550$

$9{,}000{,}000 + 9{,}000{,}000 = 18{,}000{,}000$

$68{,}493{,}025 + 8{,}409{,}182 = 76{,}902{,}207$

$70{,}000{,}000 + 8{,}000{,}000 = 78{,}000{,}000$

② Going Further

Intervention — Activity Card 3-13

Let's Roll
Activity Card 3-13 ●

Work: In Pairs

Use:
• Number cube

1. One partner rolls the number cube.

2. The second partner predicts how many more rolls it will take to have a sum of 10.

3. The second partner rolls the cube to complete the prediction and gets one point for a correct prediction. Examples are shown below.

First roll: 5	First Roll: 3
Prediction: 1 roll	Prediction: 2 rolls
Next Roll: 3	Next Rolls: 6, 1
Sum: 5 + 3 = 8	Sum: 3 + 6 + 1 = 10
Result: no point	Result: 1 point

4. Take turns. Repeat the activity until both partners have made three predictions.

Unit 3, Lesson 13   Copyright © Houghton Mifflin Company

Activity Note To make the game easier, you can change the goal to be any sum equal to or greater than 10. The first player to earn 5 points wins.

 Math Writing Prompt

Make a Drawing How can you solve 12 + 15 + 13 by making tens? Make a drawing to show how.

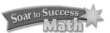 **Software Support**

Use *Soar to Success* for instruction of students needing targeted support for underlying skills.

On Level — Activity Card 3-13

Clustering
Activity Card 3-13 ▲

Work: In Pairs

1. One method of estimating sums is called clustering. You can use clustering when all the addends in an addition problem are close to the same number. Look at the example below.

253	+ 3	All of the numbers are close to 250, so a good estimate of the sum is: 250 + 250 + 250 + 250, or 1,000.
247	− 3	
262	+ 12	
+ 240	− 10	

2. On your own, choose a cluster number. Then write 3 addition problems with addends near the cluster number. Each problem should have 2 to 4 addends.

3. Exchange papers. Estimate each sum, using clustering. Then calculate the actual sums.

Unit 3, Lesson 13   Copyright © Houghton Mifflin Company

Activity Note Have students discuss solution methods and other estimation strategies they could use for each sum.

 Math Writing Prompt

Explain Your Thinking Explain how you can solve this addition problem by using mental math: 102 + 126 + 98 + 74.

 Software Support

Use *MegaMath* for review and reinforcement of the concepts and skills presented in this lesson.

Challenge — Activity Card 3-13

Make It Easy
Activity Card 3-13 ■

Work: By Yourself

1. Can you think of an easy way to add the numbers 1 though 10? The diagram at the right may give you a hint.

2. What is the sum of each set of numbers connected by a bracket? Write a multiplication to find the sum of the digits. Then find the sum to check your answer. 11; 5 × 11 = 55

3. Find a multiplication that will help you add all the whole numbers from 1 though 20. Then write a multiplication to find the sum of all the whole numbers from 1 through 100. 10 × 21 = 210; 50 × 101 = 5,050

Unit 3, Lesson 13   Copyright © Houghton Mifflin Company

Activity Note Challenge students to develop a formula for the sum of all the whole numbers from 1 to any even number, *n*. (n ÷ 2) × (n + 1)

 Math Writing Prompt

Explain Your Thinking Explain the difference between rounding 1,389 to the nearest ten and rounding to the greatest place.

 DESTINATION Math· **Software Support**

Use *Destination Math* to take students beyond the concepts and skills presented in this lesson.

③ Homework and Spiral Review

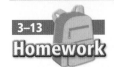

Homework **Goal:** Additional Practice

Use this Homework page to provide students with more practice with addition.

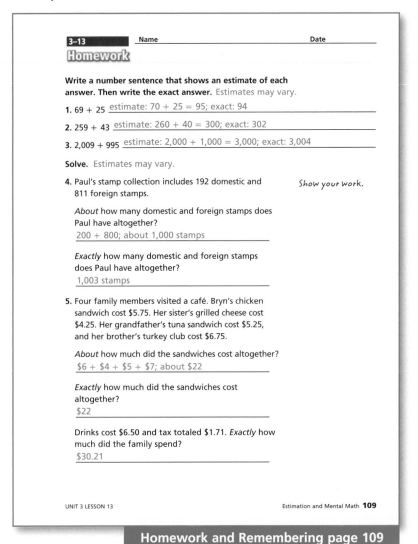

Remembering **Goal:** Spiral Review

This Remembering activity would be appropriate anytime after today's lesson.

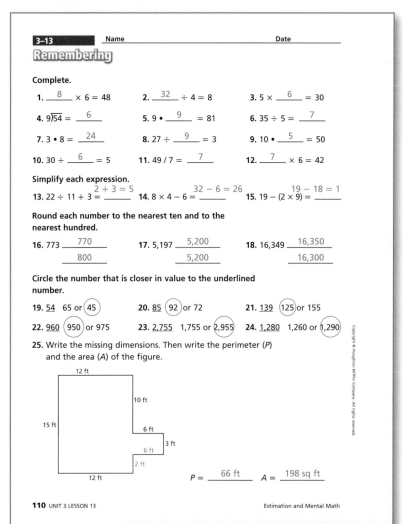

The homework page (left) shows:

3–13   Name   Date

Homework

Write a number sentence that shows an estimate of each answer. Then write the exact answer. *Estimates may vary.*

1. 69 + 25 estimate: 70 + 25 = 95; exact: 94
2. 259 + 43 estimate: 260 + 40 = 300; exact: 302
3. 2,009 + 995 estimate: 2,000 + 1,000 = 3,000; exact: 3,004

Solve. *Estimates may vary.*

Show your work.

4. Paul's stamp collection includes 192 domestic and 811 foreign stamps.

   About how many domestic and foreign stamps does Paul have altogether?
   200 + 800; about 1,000 stamps

   Exactly how many domestic and foreign stamps does Paul have altogether?
   1,003 stamps

5. Four family members visited a café. Bryn's chicken sandwich cost $5.75. Her sister's grilled cheese cost $4.25. Her grandfather's tuna sandwich cost $5.25, and her brother's turkey club cost $6.75.

   About how much did the sandwiches cost altogether?
   $6 + $4 + $5 + $7; about $22

   Exactly how much did the sandwiches cost altogether?
   $22

   Drinks cost $6.50 and tax totaled $1.71. *Exactly* how much did the family spend?
   $30.21

UNIT 3 LESSON 13   Estimation and Mental Math **109**

Homework and Remembering page 109

The remembering page (right) shows:

3–13   Name   Date

Remembering

Complete.

1. $\underline{8} \times 6 = 48$ 2. $\underline{32} \div 4 = 8$ 3. $5 \times \underline{6} = 30$
4. $9\overline{)54} = \underline{6}$ 5. $9 \cdot \underline{9} = 81$ 6. $35 \div 5 = \underline{7}$
7. $3 \cdot 8 = \underline{24}$ 8. $27 \div \underline{9} = 3$ 9. $10 \cdot \underline{5} = 50$
10. $30 \div \underline{6} = 5$ 11. $49 / 7 = \underline{7}$ 12. $\underline{7} \times 6 = 42$

Simplify each expression.
13. $22 \div 11 + 3 = \underline{\ \ }$ (2 + 3 = 5)   14. $8 \times 4 - 6 = \underline{\ \ }$ (32 − 6 = 26)   15. $19 - (2 \times 9) = \underline{\ \ }$ (19 − 18 = 1)

Round each number to the nearest ten and to the nearest hundred.
16. 773 770 / 800   17. 5,197 5,200 / 5,200   18. 16,349 16,350 / 16,300

Circle the number that is closer in value to the underlined number.
19. 54 65 or (45)   20. 85 (92) or 72   21. 139 (125) or 155
22. 960 (950) or 975   23. 2,755 1,755 or (2,955)   24. 1,280 1,260 or (1,290)

25. Write the missing dimensions. Then write the perimeter (*P*) and the area (*A*) of the figure.

12 ft, 10 ft, 15 ft, 6 ft, 6 ft, 3 ft, 2 ft, 12 ft

$P = \underline{66 \text{ ft}}$ $A = \underline{198 \text{ sq ft}}$

110 UNIT 3 LESSON 13   Estimation and Mental Math

Homework and Remembering page 110

Home or School Activity

 Real-World Connection

Plan Your Trip Have students choose another town, city, or state they have visited or would like to visit. Tell them to use a road map to find the distance in miles. Have them apply their skills of estimating and finding tens if possible.

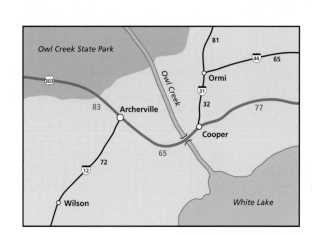

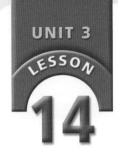

UNIT 3

LESSON 14

Subtract From Hundreds

Lesson Objectives

- Understand how to make new groups for subtraction.
- Subtract from hundreds.

The Day at a Glance

Today's Goals	Materials	
① Teaching the Lesson **A1:** Draw and discuss ungrouping for subtraction. **A2:** Practice subtraction from hundreds. **② Going Further** ▶ Differentiated Instruction **③ Homework and Spiral Review**	**Lesson Activities** Student Activity Book pp. 159–162 or Student Hardcover Book pp. 159–162 and Activity Workbook pp. 65–66 (includes Family Letters) Homework and Remembering pp. 111–112 MathBoard Materials	**Going Further** Activity Cards 3-14 Base-ten blocks MathBoard Materials Math Journals

123 Use **Math Talk** today!

Keeping Skills Sharp

Quick Practice ⏱ 5 MINUTES	Daily Routines
Goal: Compare multi-digit numbers. **Say, Write, and Compare** Use these numbers to have students compare multi-digit numbers. See Lesson 11. 11,828 11,288 236,800 263,008 11,288 11,828 263,008 236,800 101,965 110,569 526,923 625,329 110,569 101,965 625,329 526,923	**Homework Review** Ask students to describe briefly some strategies they used in their homework. Sometimes you will find that students solve the problem correctly but use an inefficient strategy. **Mental Math** Write an explanation of how you can add 15 + 8 + 5 in your head. *Possible answer:* Think 15 + 5 + 8 or 15 + 5 + 5 + 3.

Teaching the Lesson

Draw Multi-Digit Subtraction

 25 MINUTES

Goal: Draw and discuss ungrouping for subtraction.

Materials: Student Activity Book or Hardcover Book p. 159, MathBoard Materials

✓ **NCTM Standards:**
Number and Operations
Algebra
Communication

Teaching Note

Lesson Sequence This program starts multi-digit subtraction with examples that have zeros in the top number because students often struggle with such exercises. Also, numbers with zeros on top ensure that students will have to ungroup every place, so they offer the best example of the ungroup-everything-first method.

Teaching Note

Watch For! We ask students to draw a big circle (like a magnifying glass) around the top number, leaving enough space to write ungrouped numbers as needed. With the magnifying glass, the students can "look inside" each place of the top number to make sure there are enough to subtract.

We also ask students to check that *every* top number is bigger and ungroup as needed *before* they do any subtracting. This helps them avoid the top-from-bottom error. Doing all necessary ungrouping first also helps students understand subtraction conceptually. They can see that they are just writing a new form of the top number to give them enough to subtract in each place.

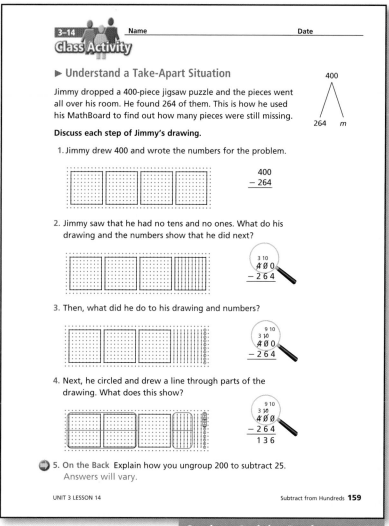

Student Activity Book page 159

▶ Understand a Take-Apart Situation WHOLE CLASS

Have the students read the problem on page 159 of the Student Book.

Have the students discuss the problem and decide what operation is needed to solve it. subtraction

When ungrouping, students should start with the place-value drawing of the top number in the numeric example. A magnifying glass (or circle) is drawn around the top number. This will help students remember that they need to check each place-value column to see if they need to ungroup.

Make a Break-Apart Drawing Have students begin the break-apart drawing about Jimmy's puzzle. Have them discuss how they could find the missing number.

Break Apart a Place-Value Drawing Have students discuss the steps in Jimmy's drawing and relate them to the numeric steps.

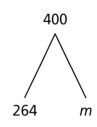

Step 1 Discuss why Jimmy drew only the top number. This is the number we start with. Then we take away the bottom number.

Step 2 Have students discuss how the drawing and the numbers show the ungrouping of 1 hundred to make 10 tens. 4 hundreds become 3 hundreds and 10 tens.

Step 3 Have students explain how the drawing and numbers show ungrouping of 1 ten to make 10 ones. 10 tens becomes 9 tens and 10 ones. Remind students to show these steps on their MathBoards.

Step 4 Have students discuss the parts of the drawing that were not crossed out and how this relates to the word problem situation and to the numeric solution. 1 hundred, 3 tens, and 6 ones are not lined out in the drawing, so the answer is 136. Jimmy must find 136 more pieces before he can complete his puzzle.

Finish the Break-Apart Drawing Have students finish the break-apart drawing for this problem and write both subtraction equations.

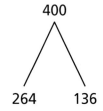

$$400 - 264 = 136$$
$$400 - 136 = 264$$

Have students create new word problems about Jimmy's puzzle that would relate to the second subtraction equation, such as:

● Jimmy has a favorite 400-piece jigsaw puzzle. One day he and his friend put together 136 pieces of the puzzle. How many pieces do they still have to put together?

● Jimmy and his friend were putting together a 400-piece jigsaw puzzle. They made 2 piles of puzzle pieces. One pile had 136 pieces. How many were in the other pile?

Teaching Note

What to Expect from Students
Some students might prefer to solve a problem like Jimmy's by adding on. They may do it mentally or write various steps. For example:

264 +   6 is 270   or   264 +   36 is 300
      + 30 is 300   + 100 is 400
      + 100 is 400   136
          136

Teaching Note

Watch For! When modeling take-away subtraction situations, some students might begin by drawing both numbers, just as they did for addition. Emphasize that in take-away subtraction situations, you should only *start with the larger number*. This number is then separated into the amount that is taken away and the amount left over.

English Language Learners
Write 369 + 548 on the board. Review how to regroup to solve the problem. Write *ungroup* on the board.

● **Beginning** Say: *Ungroup* means "break apart". You can ungroup 1 ten into 10 ones. You can ungroup 1 hundred into 10 tens. Have students repeat.

● **Intermediate** Ask: Does *ungroup* mean "break apart" or "put together"? break apart Ask: **How can you ungroup 1 ten?** into 10 ones Ask: **How can you ungroup 1 hundred?** into 10 tens

● **Advanced** Have students work in pairs. One partner names a quantity (10, 100, 1000, etc). The other partner ungroups the quantity.

Activity 2

Practice Multi-Digit Subtraction

 30 MINUTES

Goal: Practice subtraction from hundreds.

Materials: MathBoard Materials

✔ **NCTM Standards:**
Number and Operations
Algebra
Communication

Teaching Note

Language and Vocabulary
Ungrouping, regrouping, trading, unpacking, or *borrowing*—any language that is meaningful and familiar to students can be used in the lesson. Elicit terms that students have used before. *Math Expressions* uses *grouping* for addition and *ungrouping* for subtraction because these words capture the inverse actions involved. We use *regrouping* to describe the overall process done in addition and subtraction. You should introduce this language, but feel free to use whatever language best fits your students' needs.

 Ongoing Assessment

▶ What is 500 - 138?

▶ Give a word problem that you could solve by finding 300 – 176.

▶ ## Practice Subtraction
WHOLE CLASS

Math Talk

Use **Solve and Discuss** to provide practice in subtracting from other hundred numbers with zeros in the tens and ones places. Students at their seats can work independently or with **Helping Partners**. Some suggested exercises are listed below.

1. 300 − 176 = 124   **2.** 500 − 385 = 115   **3.** 600 − 438 = 162

For each exercise, have students give a word problem situation and draw the hundred number on either the dot side or the white side of their MathBoards.

Students should show and discuss the ungrouping in their drawings and numeric solutions.

▶ ## Estimate to Check   WHOLE CLASS

Ask for Ideas Ask students what they remember about rounding rules. Review rounding rules with the class.

For exercise 1 above, discuss how students can estimate to check their answer. Ask them to decide if they want to round to the nearest hundred or the nearest ten?

Ask two students to work at the board to show each method.
nearest ten: 300 − 180 = 220; nearest hundred: 300 − 200 = 100

Which way is easier?
Since rounding to the nearest ten still requires ungrouping, students will probably say rounding to the nearest hundred is easier.

Now ask students to use estimation to check exercises 2 and 3.

2. Rounded to the nearest hundred: 500 − 400 = 100

3. Rounded to the nearest hundred: 600 − 400 = 200

②Going Further

Differentiated Instruction

Intervention   Activity Card 3-14

Model It   Activity Card 3-14 ●

Work: In Pairs

Use:
• Base-ten blocks

1. You can model subtraction problems by using base-ten blocks. Look at the problem and its model below.

$$300 - 144 = 156$$

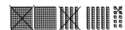

2. **Work Together** Model a three-digit number with base-ten blocks, and then choose a second number to subtract from that value.

3. Model the subtraction to find the difference.

4. **Analyze** How did you decide how to model the subtraction? Is there another way that you could have used the model to find the difference?

Unit 3, Lesson 14   Copyright © Houghton Mifflin Company

Activity Note Before students begin the activity, review the process of breaking apart the hundreds block, if needed.

🖊 Math Writing Prompt

Draw a Picture Draw a picture to solve the problem 400 − 216. Explain the parts of your picture.

Soar to Success Math ★ Software Support

Use *Soar to Success* for instruction of students needing targeted support for underlying skills.

On Level   Activity Card 3-14

What's Missing?   Activity Card 3-14 ▲

Work: In Pairs

Use:
• MathBoard materials

1. Copy the problem below onto your MathBoard.

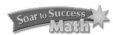

2. **Work Together** Find the values of the missing digits.

3. On your own, create four missing-digit subtraction problems, and exchange them with your partner to solve.

4. **Discuss** What strategy did you use to solve the problem? Is there another strategy that you could have used?

Unit 3, Lesson 14   Copyright © Houghton Mifflin Company

Activity Note Remind students that they have to ungroup the 700 in order to be able to subtract from it.

🖊 Math Writing Prompt

Explain Your Thinking Explain what you would do to find the missing digit in 300 − 1 ☐ 8 = 172.

MegaMath Grades K-6 Software Support

Use *MegaMath* for review and reinforcement of the concepts and skills presented in this lesson.

Challenge   Activity Card 3-14

Many Ways   Activity Card 3-14 ■

Work: In Pairs

1. Look at the three methods to complete the subtraction problem 500 − 294 shown to the right.

2. On your own, create four subtraction problems, and exchange them with your partner.

3. Show as many ways as you can think of to solve each problem. Then exchange with your partner again to check your answers.

Activity Note Students may also use models, such as number lines or base-ten blocks, to solve subtraction problems.

🖊 Math Writing Prompt

Explain Your Thinking Explain two ways to solve 600 − 367.

✖ DESTINATION Math® Software Support

Use *Destination Math* to take students beyond the concepts and skills presented in this lesson.

Subtract From Hundreds   **379**

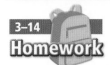

③ Homework and Spiral Review

Use this Homework page to provide students with more practice with subtracting from hundreds.

This Remembering activity would be appropriate anytime after today's lesson.

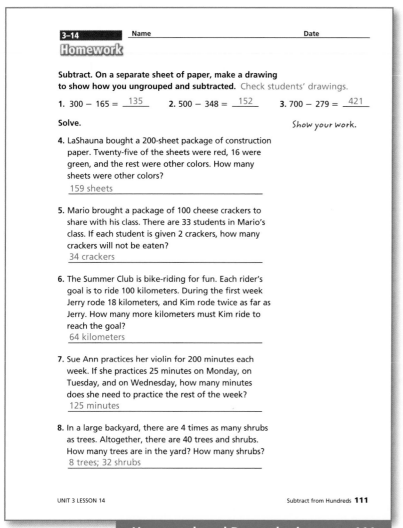

3–14   Name   Date
Homework

Subtract. On a separate sheet of paper, make a drawing to show how you ungrouped and subtracted. Check students' drawings.

1. $300 - 165 =$ _135_   2. $500 - 348 =$ _152_   3. $700 - 279 =$ _421_

Solve.   *Show your work.*

4. LaShauna bought a 200-sheet package of construction paper. Twenty-five of the sheets were red, 16 were green, and the rest were other colors. How many sheets were other colors?
159 sheets

5. Mario brought a package of 100 cheese crackers to share with his class. There are 33 students in Mario's class. If each student is given 2 crackers, how many crackers will not be eaten?
34 crackers

6. The Summer Club is bike-riding for fun. Each rider's goal is to ride 100 kilometers. During the first week Jerry rode 18 kilometers, and Kim rode twice as far as Jerry. How many more kilometers must Kim ride to reach the goal?
64 kilometers

7. Sue Ann practices her violin for 200 minutes each week. If she practices 25 minutes on Monday, on Tuesday, and on Wednesday, how many minutes does she need to practice the rest of the week?
125 minutes

8. In a large backyard, there are 4 times as many shrubs as trees. Altogether, there are 40 trees and shrubs. How many trees are in the yard? How many shrubs?
8 trees; 32 shrubs

UNIT 3 LESSON 14   Subtract from Hundreds **111**

Homework and Remembering page 111

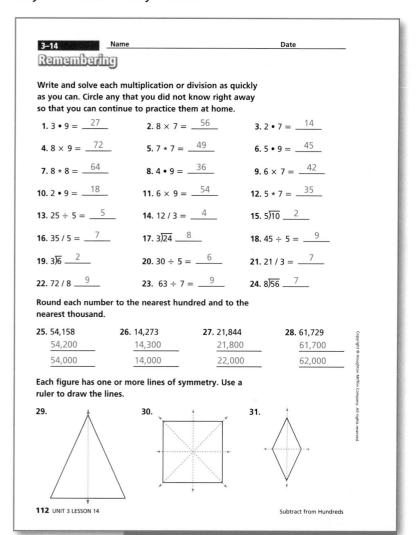

3–14   Name   Date
Remembering

Write and solve each multiplication or division as quickly as you can. Circle any that you did not know right away so that you can continue to practice them at home.

1. $3 \cdot 9 =$ _27_   2. $8 \times 7 =$ _56_   3. $2 \cdot 7 =$ _14_

4. $8 \times 9 =$ _72_   5. $7 * 7 =$ _49_   6. $5 \cdot 9 =$ _45_

7. $8 * 8 =$ _64_   8. $4 \cdot 9 =$ _36_   9. $6 \times 7 =$ _42_

10. $2 \cdot 9 =$ _18_   11. $6 \times 9 =$ _54_   12. $5 * 7 =$ _35_

13. $25 \div 5 =$ _5_   14. $12 / 3 =$ _4_   15. $5\overline{)10}$ _2_

16. $35 / 5 =$ _7_   17. $3\overline{)24}$ _8_   18. $45 \div 5 =$ _9_

19. $3\overline{)6}$ _2_   20. $30 \div 5 =$ _6_   21. $21 / 3 =$ _7_

22. $72 / 8$ _9_   23. $63 \div 7 =$ _9_   24. $8\overline{)56}$ _7_

Round each number to the nearest hundred and to the nearest thousand.

25. 54,158   26. 14,273   27. 21,844   28. 61,729
54,200   14,300   21,800   61,700
54,000   14,000   22,000   62,000

Each figure has one or more lines of symmetry. Use a ruler to draw the lines.

29.   30.   31.

112 UNIT 3 LESSON 14   Subtract from Hundreds

Homework and Remembering page 112

Home and School Connection

Family Letter Have children take home the Family Letter on Student Book page 161 or Activity Workbook page 65. This letter explains how the concept of "ungrouping" to subtract is developed in *Math Expressions*. It gives parents and guardians a better understanding of the learning that goes on in math class and creates a bridge between school and home. A Spanish translation of this letter is on Student Book page 162 and Activity Workbook page 66.

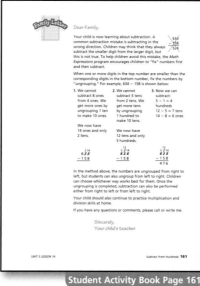

Student Activity Book Page 161

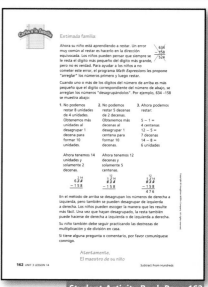

Student Activity Book Page 162

380   UNIT 3 LESSON 14

Subtraction Undoes Addition

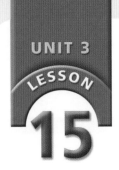

Lesson Objectives

- Understand subtraction as the inverse of addition.
- Understand how grouping and ungrouping are related.

The Day at a Glance

Today's Goals	Materials	

1 Teaching the Lesson
A1: Discuss and apply the inverse relationship of subtraction to addition.
A2: Discuss the relationiship between grouping for addition and ungrouping for subtraction.
	Lesson Activities
	Student Activity Book pp. 163–164
	  or Student Hardcover Book
	  pp. 163–164
	Homework and Remembering
	  pp. 113–114
	MathBoard Materials
	Base-ten blocks (optional)
		Going Further
		Activity Cards 3-15
		Index cards
		Math Journals

2 Going Further ▶ Differentiated Instruction		
3 Homework and Spiral Review		

123 Use Math Talk today!

Keeping Skills Sharp

Quick Practice ⏱ 5 MINUTES	Daily Routines
Goal: Compare multi-digit numbers. **Say, Write, and Compare** Use these numbers to have students compare multi-digit numbers. See Lesson 11.	**Homework Review** If students have difficulty with word problems, encourage them to write situation equations and then change them to solution equations. **Estimation** What is the sum of 13 + 245 rounded to the nearest ten? 260

1,925,603	1,952,603	88,926,437	89,862,247
1,952,603	1,925,603	89,862,247	88,926,437
329,835,209	329,835,902	562,453,910	562,435,910
329,835,902	329,835,209	562,435,910	562,453,910

Teaching the Lesson

Addition and Subtraction as Inverse Operations

 15 MINUTES

Goal: Discuss and apply the inverse relationship of subtraction to addition.

Materials: Student Activity Book or Hardcover Book pp. 163–164, MathBoard Materials, base-ten blocks (optional)

✔ **NCTM Standards:**
Number and Operations
Algebra

Teaching Note

MathBoards If your students are proficient in addition and subtraction, they may not need to make place-value drawings. However, they should follow along with the discussion, using the drawings on the student pages.

Students who need the concepts emphasized should use the white side of their MathBoards to sketch place-value drawings. The *addition* drawing should be sketched on the *left* side of the board and the *subtraction* on the *right* side. Then students can compare the drawings for addition and subtraction.

The Learning Classroom

Helping Community Students may fear doing their math work in public because they are afraid to be incorrect. Emphasize that errors help us learn. A safe culture develops in this type of classroom because students do not fear criticism when they make mistakes. You can model this for students as you make your own errors. Fixing your errors models a healthy approach for students.

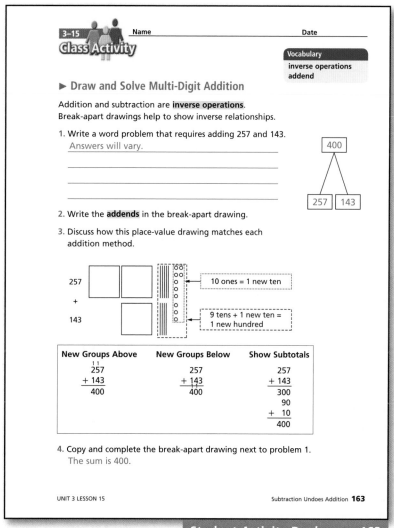

Student Activity Book page 163

▶ Draw and Solve Multi-Digit Addition WHOLE CLASS

Draw this break-apart diagram on the board.

For exercise 1 on Student Book page 163, ask students to write and discuss situations that this drawing could represent. For example, "An after-school program has 257 boys and 143 girls enrolled. How many total students are enrolled?"

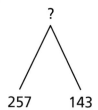

Next, have the students explain how they could solve their problem and find the number that goes at the top of the break-apart drawing. by adding 257 and 143

Tell students that making a break-apart drawing using the numbers in the problem can help them to find the solution.

At the Board Have as many students as possible work at the board while the rest of the class works on the left half of their MathBoards.

Tell students to sketch place-value drawings to show their addition. Have different students describe different parts of the place-value drawings on the board and how the parts relate to different addition methods.

New Groups Above Method	New Groups Below Method	Show Subtotals Method
$\overset{1\ 1}{257}$ +143 ——— 400	257 +143 $\underset{1\ 1}{———}$ 400	257 +143 ——— 300 90 + 10 ——— 400

In the ones place, 7 + 3 = 10, and 10 ones makes 1 new ten.

- For the New Groups Above Method, the new group is written above the 5 in the tens column.

- For the New Groups Below Method, the new group is written under the 4 in the tens column.

- For the Show Subtotals Method, the new group is the subtotal 10.

In the tens place, 5 tens + 4 tens + 1 new ten = 10 tens, and 10 tens are the same as 1 hundred.

- For the New Groups Above Method, the new group is written above the 2 in the hundreds column.

- For the New Groups Below Method, the new group is written under the 1 in the hundreds column.

- For the Show Subtotals Method, the new group is the subtotal 90.

Once students have the answer to their addition, tell them to complete the break-apart drawing in exercise 1.

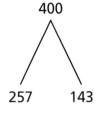

400 / 257 143

Activity continued ▶

 Alternate Approach

Base-ten blocks If some students need a hands-on approach to place-value concepts as they relate to addition, you can use base-ten blocks to represent the examples in this lesson.

257 + 143

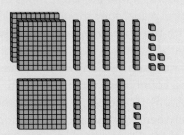

Differentiated Instruction

Extra Help If you believe some students need more practice with dots, have them work on the dot side of their MathBoards. Other students should mostly work on the white side.

 Class Management

Looking Ahead Keep at least one of the addition place-value drawings on the board for the next part of the lesson.

① Teaching the Lesson (continued)

Activity 1

Teaching Note

Math Background Lessons 14, 15, and 16 focus on 3-digit subtraction. This is to ensure that all students are introduced to *Math Expressions* methods and can use place-value meanings to understand ungrouping (borrowing). In Lesson 14 you may have had some students who were not able to explain ungrouping or were still making subtract top-from-bottom errors. However, if your students had *Math Expressions* in third grade, they should be familiar with the ungroup-everything-first method and have an understanding of how subtraction works. In this case you could move rapidly through Lessons 15 and 16. The relationships between addition and subtraction should still be discussed during this lesson though, as this was not covered in depth in *Math Expressions* grade 3.

Teaching Note

Watch For! The most common error in multi-digit subtraction is subtracting the smaller digit from the larger, even if the top digit is smaller. Students just look at each column and subtract. Two examples of this mistake are shown.

$$\begin{array}{r} 400 \\ -163 \\ \hline 363 \end{array} \qquad \begin{array}{r} 639 \\ -584 \\ \hline 155 \end{array}$$

Student Activity Book page 164

> ## ► Draw and Solve Multi-Digit Subtraction WHOLE CLASS

Draw this break-apart drawing on the board.

Elicit a real-world problem situation that is a counterpart for the addition problem that students wrote. For example, "There are 400 students enrolled in an after-school program. Of these, 257 are boys. How many are girls?"

Have the students discuss how they could find the missing number in this diagram. by subtracting 257 from 400

Refer students to the addition place-value drawing on the board. Remind them that place-value drawings can help them to solve addition *and* subtraction problems. Invite several students to draw and solve the subtraction problem 400 − 257 on the board. All other students should work on the right half of their MathBoards. Have students begin by drawing 4 hundred boxes to represent 400.

Ungroup Everything First Have the students discuss how to show ungrouping in all of the place values. Encourage them to use place-value language. Have them check to be sure that the steps in the drawing and in the numeric solution are related, both for ungrouping and for subtracting. Ask:

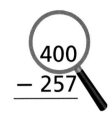

- Can we subtract 2 hundreds from 4 hundreds? yes Why? 2 is less than 4

- Can we subtract 5 tens from 0 tens? no Why not? 5 is more than 0

- What do we need to do to fix the tens place so we can subtract? ungroup 1 hundred to make 10 tens

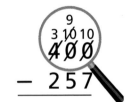

- How do the drawing and the numbers (exercise 6) show ungrouping for 1 hundred? One hundred box becomes 10 quick tens, leaving 3 hundred boxes; the 4 in 400 is changed to a 3; the ungrouped 10 is written as a 10 above the tens place.

- Can we subtract 7 ones from 0 ones? no Why not? 7 is more than 0

- How do the drawing and the numbers (exercise 7) show ungrouping for 1 ten? One quick ten is changed to 10 ones, leaving 9 quick tens; the 10 written in the tens place is crossed out and replaced with a 9, and 10 ones are written in the ones place.

(123) **Math Talk** Tell students to look at the place-value drawings on Student Book page 164. Have the students discuss subtracting from right-to-left and left-to-right. (The order of the questions shown below assumes right-to-left subtraction. For left-to-right subtraction, the order of the questions would be reversed.)

- How do the drawing and the numbers show subtraction of the ones? 7 of the ones in the drawing have been subtracted (crossed out), showing 3 ones left over; the numeric solution shows $10 - 7 = 3$.

- How do the drawing and the numbers show subtraction of the tens? 5 of the quick tens have been crossed out, showing 4 quick tens sticks left over; the numeric solution shows 9 tens − 5 tens = 4 tens.

- How do the drawing and the numbers show subtraction of the hundreds? 2 of the hundred boxes in the drawing have been crossed out, showing 1 hundred box left over; the numeric solution shows 3 hundreds − 2 hundreds = 1 hundred.

Have the students discuss how to use the relationship between addition and subtraction to check their answers.

Teaching Note

Subtraction with Zeros We start subtraction with a problem with multiple zeros on the top so that we have to ungroup all places first and then subtract everywhere. We will then suggest using this method on all subtraction problems because it is so clear conceptually and it avoids the common error of subtracting the top from the bottom number. Also, when we start with these problems that are usually viewed as difficult, we find that students can do them easily.

English Language Learners

Review +, −, ×, and ÷ key words (sum, total, difference, product, equal parts, and so on). Write the word *inverse* on the board.

- **Beginning** Say: *Inverse* means "opposite". Addition and subtraction are opposite actions. They undo each other. They are opposite or inverse operations. Have students repeat.

- **Intermediate** Say: *Inverse* means "opposite". Ask: What is the inverse of addition? subtraction What is the inverse of multiplication? division How do you know? they undo each other

- **Advanced** Have students use short sentences to tell which operations are the inverse of each other.

Activity 2

Relate Grouping and Ungrouping

 15 MINUTES

Goal: Discuss the relationship between grouping for addition and ungrouping for subtraction.

Materials: Base-ten blocks (optional)

 NCTM Standards:
Number and Operations
Communication

Teaching Note

Language and Vocabulary
If students have difficulty with the words "grouping" and "ungrouping", demonstrate by tying and untying shoelaces, or wrapping and unwrapping a package. Then use base-ten blocks or connecting cubes to demonstrate grouping and ungrouping.

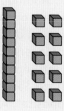

 Ongoing Assessment

▶ How can you use addition to check 900 − 574?

▶ How can you use subtraction to check 326 + 574?

▶ **Practice Addition and Subtraction** [WHOLE CLASS]

Have the students work individually, as **Helping Partners**, or in **Small Groups** to solve these subtraction exercises. Students should also write the related addition equation to check.

Exercise:	Check with:
900 − 574 = 326	574 + 326 = 900
800 − 216 = 584	216 + 584 = 800
500 − 161 = 339	339 + 161 = 500

▶ **Compare Addition and Subtraction** [WHOLE CLASS]

Lead a discussion with the students concerning relationships between addition and subtraction. In particular, discuss how grouping in addition is similar to or different from ungrouping in subtraction. Be sure that the discussion covers these points:

● Both kinds of regrouping use the 1-for-10 relationship between adjacent place values in the number system: 10 ones = 1 ten; 10 tens = 1 hundred, and so on.

● When adding in a smaller place gives us a total of 10 or more, we take 10 out of the total and make a new group for the next larger place.

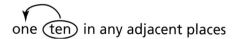

one (ten) in any adjacent places

● When a subtraction does not contain enough in the top digit of a smaller place, we undo 1 group in the next larger place to give 10 more to the smaller place.

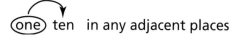

(one) ten in any adjacent places

● The bottom totals in the addition (before grouping) match the top numbers in the subtraction (after ungrouping). See the 3, 9, and 10 in the addition and subtraction below.

$$
\begin{array}{r}
257 \\
+ 143 \\
\hline
400
\end{array}
\qquad
\begin{array}{r}
\overset{9}{\overset{3\ \cancel{10}\ 10}{4\ \cancel{0}\ \cancel{0}}} \\
- 257 \\
\hline
1\ 4\ 3
\end{array}
$$

➁ Going Further

● Intervention   Activity Card 3-15

Related Equations   Activity Card 3-15 ●

Work: In Pairs

1. **Work Together** Make a break-apart drawing, using the following numbers.

   | 53 | 78 | 25 |

2. Write two addition equations and two subtraction equations, using the numbers and the drawing.
   $25 + 53 = 78$; $53 + 25 = 78$; $78 - 53 = 25$; $78 - 25 = 53$

3. Repeat the activity, using the numbers below.

   | 114 | 68 | 46 | $68 + 46 = 114$;
   $46 + 68 = 114$; $114 - 68 = 46$; $114 - 46 = 68$

4. **Discuss** How are the addition and subtraction equations related? Subtracting each addend from the sum gives the other addend as the difference.

Unit 3, Lesson 15   Copyright © Houghton Mifflin Company

Activity Note The easiest way to create an addition equation is to add the two numbers of lesser value. The greatest number in each set must be the sum.

 Math Writing Prompt

Draw a Diagram Explain how to make a break-apart drawing by using 7, 13, and 20. Make a drawing to illustrate your explanation.

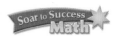 **Software Support**

Use *Soar to Success* for instruction of students needing targeted support for underlying skills.

▲ On Level   Activity Card 3-15

Checking Subtraction with Addition   Activity Card 3-15 ▲

Work: In Pairs
Use:
• Index cards

1. On your own, write a subtraction problem on an index card. Do not include the answer.

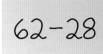

2. Trade cards with your partner, and find the missing difference.

3. Then write two addition equations that can be used to check your answer to the problem.

4. **Discuss** Why is it possible to check your answer to a subtraction problem by using addition? Addition and subtraction are opposite operations.

Unit 3, Lesson 15   Copyright © Houghton Mifflin Company

Activity Note Students can extend the activity by creating a word problem for their subtraction equations.

 Math Writing Prompt

Explain Your Thinking Explain why the three numbers in a break-apart drawing can be used in either an addition or a subtraction equation.

 Software Support

Use *MegaMath* for review and reinforcement of the concepts and skills presented in this lesson.

■ Challenge   Activity Card 3-15

Inverses and Equations   Activity Card 3-15 ■

Work: In Pairs
Use:
• Index cards

1. Write each of the following equations on a separate index card.

$3 + n = 9$	$n = 6$
$b + 12 = 20$	$b = 8$
$a + 36 = 200$	$a = 164$
$k - 2 = 6$	$k = 8$
$p - 5 = 17$	$p = 22$
$c - 15 = 260$	$c = 275$

2. Work with your partner to solve each equation.

3. Then choose two equations, and write a word problem for each equation on two new index cards. Exchange word problems with other pairs of students, and solve the problems.

Unit 3, Lesson 15   Copyright © Houghton Mifflin Company

Activity Note Addition and subtraction are inverse operations. Suggest using inverse operations, a break-apart drawing, or mental math to solve each equation.

 Math Writing Prompt

Explain Your Thinking In your own words, explain how the operations of subtraction and addition are related.

 Software Support

Use *Destination Math* to take students beyond the concepts and skills presented in this lesson.

Subtraction Undoes Addition   **387**

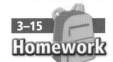# ③ Homework and Spiral Review

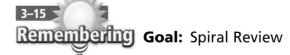

3-15 Homework **Goal:** Additional Practice

✓ Include students' work on page 113 in their portfolios.

3-15 Remembering **Goal:** Spiral Review

This Remembering activity would be appropriate anytime after today's lesson.

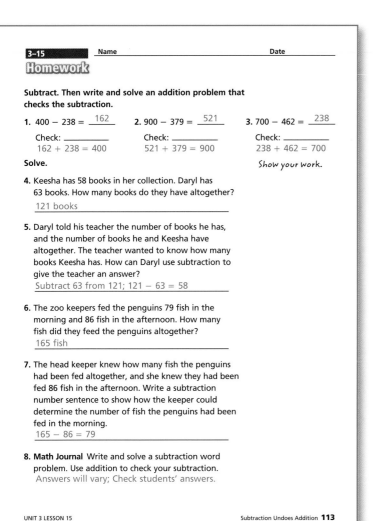

3-15	Name	Date

Homework

Subtract. Then write and solve an addition problem that checks the subtraction.

1. $400 - 238 = \underline{162}$ 2. $900 - 379 = \underline{521}$ 3. $700 - 462 = \underline{238}$

Check: _____   Check: _____   Check: _____
162 + 238 = 400   521 + 379 = 900   238 + 462 = 700

Solve.   *Show your work.*

4. Keesha has 58 books in her collection. Daryl has 63 books. How many books do they have altogether?
   121 books

5. Daryl told his teacher the number of books he has, and the number of books he and Keesha have altogether. The teacher wanted to know how many books Keesha has. How can Daryl use subtraction to give the teacher an answer?
   Subtract 63 from 121; 121 − 63 = 58

6. The zoo keepers fed the penguins 79 fish in the morning and 86 fish in the afternoon. How many fish did they feed the penguins altogether?
   165 fish

7. The head keeper knew how many fish the penguins had been fed altogether, and she knew they had been fed 86 fish in the afternoon. Write a subtraction number sentence to show how the keeper could determine the number of fish the penguins had been fed in the morning.
   165 − 86 = 79

8. **Math Journal** Write and solve a subtraction word problem. Use addition to check your subtraction.
   Answers will vary; Check students' answers.

UNIT 3 LESSON 15   Subtraction Undoes Addition **113**

Homework and Remembering page 113

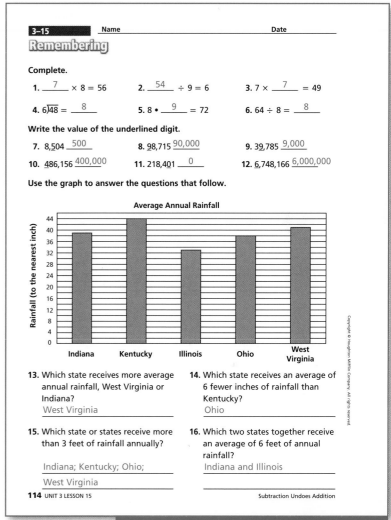

3-15	Name	Date

Remembering

Complete.

1. $\underline{7} \times 8 = 56$ 2. $\underline{54} \div 9 = 6$ 3. $7 \times \underline{7} = 49$

4. $6\overline{)48} = \underline{8}$ 5. $8 \bullet \underline{9} = 72$ 6. $64 \div 8 = \underline{8}$

Write the value of the underlined digit.

7. 8,504 _500_   8. 98,715 _90,000_   9. 39,785 _9,000_

10. 486,156 _400,000_   11. 218,401 _0_   12. 6,748,166 _6,000,000_

Use the graph to answer the questions that follow.

Average Annual Rainfall

Rainfall (to the nearest inch)

Indiana   Kentucky   Illinois   Ohio   West Virginia

13. Which state receives more average annual rainfall, West Virginia or Indiana?
    West Virginia

14. Which state receives an average of 6 fewer inches of rainfall than Kentucky?
    Ohio

15. Which state or states receive more than 3 feet of rainfall annually?
    Indiana; Kentucky; Ohio; West Virginia

16. Which two states together receive an average of 6 feet of annual rainfall?
    Indiana and Illinois

114 UNIT 3 LESSON 15   Subtraction Undoes Addition

Homework and Remembering page 114

Home or School Activity

Language Arts Connection

Opposites in Our Daily Lives Addition and subtraction are "opposites." That is, they "undo" each other. Ask students to think about opposite actions in their daily lives, such as making a mess and cleaning it up, writing on the board and erasing it, and so on.

Ask students to make a list of pairs of opposite actions that "undo" each other.

Opposite Actions	
open	close
spill	clean up
tie	untie

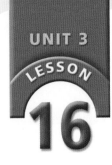

Ungroup for Any Subtraction

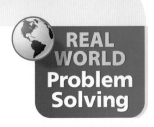
Lesson Objective

● Understand general methods for subtraction.

The Day at a Glance

Today's Goals	Materials	
① Teaching the Lesson **A1:** Discuss ungrouping to subtract from top numbers other than zero. **A2:** Practice ungrouping and subtraction. **② Going Further** ► Math Connection: Subtraction and Money ► Differentiated Instruction **③ Homework and Spiral Review**	**Lesson Activities** Student Activity Book p. 165 or Student Hardcover Book p. 165 Homework and Remembering pp. 115–116 MathBoard Materials Base-ten blocks (optional)	**Going Further** Student Activity Book p. 166 or Student Hardcover Book p. 166 Play money Activity Cards 3-16 Colored counters Number cubes MathBoard Materials Math Journals 123 *Use* **Math Talk** *today!*

Keeping Skills Sharp

Quick Practice ⏱ 5 MINUTES

Goal: Subtract from hundreds.

Find the Difference Write both problems below on the board. Have students write them in their Math Journals and solve.

500 − 274
900 − 639

If any students get incorrect solutions, write the incorrect solutions on the board and have the class discuss why each solution is wrong and how to fix it.

Daily Routines

Homework Review Ask several students to share the problems they wrote for homework. Have the class ask clarifying questions about each problem. If necessary, model asking questions.

Mental Math Explain how to subtract 395 from 500 in your head. *Possible answer:* Count up 5 to 400; 500 − 400 = 100; 100 + 5 = 105. Have students explain why they added 5 instead of subtracting 5.

Teaching the Lesson

Subtract From Numbers Other Than Zero

 25 MINUTES

Goal: Discuss ungrouping to subtract from top numbers other than zero.

Materials: MathBoard Materials, base-ten blocks (optional)

✔ **NCTM Standards:**
Number and Operations
Algebra
Communication

English Language Learners

Write 352 – 167 on the board. Write the word *ungroup*. Have students tell whether to ungroup in hundreds, tens, and ones columns.

- **Beginning** Point to the tens. Say: **We cannot subtract 5 – 6. We need to ungroup.** Point to the ones. Say: **We cannot subtract 2 – 7. We need to ungroup.** Have students repeat.
- **Intermediate** Point to the tens. Ask: **Can we subtract 5 – 6?** no **What do we need to do?** ungroup Point to the ones. Ask: **Can we subtract 2 – 7?** no **Do we need to ungroup?** yes
- **Advanced** Have students tell which columns need to be ungrouped.

▶ **Ungroup Different Ways** WHOLE CLASS

Have several students work at the board while the remaining students work on their MathBoards.

Write this example on the board and ask students for possible word problem situations that match the numbers.

$$\begin{array}{r} 352 \\ -167 \\ \hline \end{array}$$

Have the students draw the top number. Students working on MathBoards can use either the dot side or the white side.

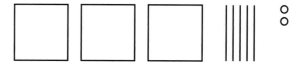

Students may solve the problem using any method that they have learned.

123 Math Talk Use **Solve and Discuss** to examine methods students used. Be sure that the points below are covered and that students use place-value language in describing ungrouping from left to right and ungrouping from right to left.

- Can we subtract 1 hundred from 3 hundreds? yes

- Can we subtract 6 tens from 5 tens? No, we need more tens.

- Can we subtract 7 ones from 2 ones? No, we need more ones.

Ungroup Left to Right Start with the place-value drawing of the top number and the numeric example. Draw the magnifying glass (or circle) around the top number. Remember that many students may still make the small-from-large subtraction error. The magnifying glass helps them remember that they need to check each place-value column to see if they need to ungroup.

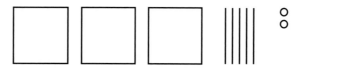

Here we can see that the 2 is less than the 7 in the ones column so we'll need more ones to be able to subtract 7. And we can see that the 5 is less than the 6 in the tens column, so we'll need more tens to be able to subtract 6 tens.

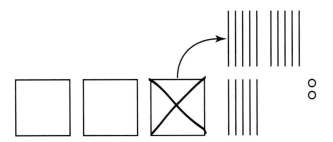 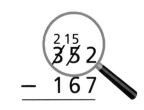

Seven ones are more than 2 ones, so we cross out 1 ten and replace it with 10 ones. There are now 14 tens and a new total of 12 ones.

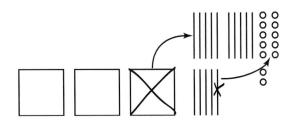 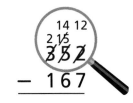

Ungroup Right to Left To show right-to-left ungrouping, start with the top number as we did above. Again, use the magnifying glass (circle) to isolate the top number.

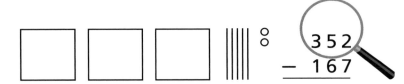

There are not enough ones on top to subtract 7, so 10 ones have been drawn on top of 1 quick ten. There are now 12 ones, with 4 tens remaining.

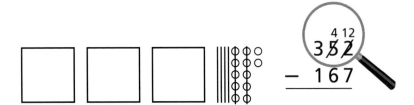

Activity continued ▶

Teaching Note

Another Method Students can also show ungrouping by drawing ones on top of a quick ten and quick tens inside a hundred box. This drawing method is shown in the section for right-to-left ungrouping. Either drawing method can be used for either left-to-right or right-to-left ungrouping.

The Learning Classroom

Math Talk You should note how the students at the board are solving the subtraction problem and ask one student who ungrouped left-to-right and one who ungrouped right-to-left to explain their solutions. If only one ungrouping direction is represented at the board, ask another student to explain the other direction. Be sure students use place-value language when explaining.

Activity 1

Alternate Approach

Base-ten Blocks Some students may need hands-on experience to understand ungrouping. These students can use base-ten materials to act out the examples in this lesson.

352 − 167

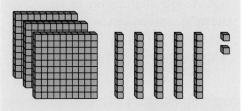

Teaching Note

Subtraction Strategies Remember that some students may be drawing ones by using horizontal rows of 5 or other methods. Also note how the subtraction to the right was done by taking from the ungrouped ten. This facilitates learning the mental take-from-ten method. For example, in the ones place 7 ones were subtracted from the ten, leaving 3 ones to be put with the 2 ones that were already there.

There are not enough tens on top to subtract 6, so 10 quick tens have been drawn inside 1 hundred box. Now there are 14 tens, with 2 hundreds remaining.

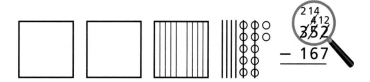

Subtract Right to Left or Left to Right Because each column now has a larger top number than bottom number, students can subtract each column independently. They may subtract either in the same order they used for ungrouping, or in the opposite order.

On the place-value drawings, using either ungrouping direction, if students subtract (cross out) 1 hundred, 6 tens, and 7 ones, they have 1 hundred, 8 tens, and 5 ones left: 352 − 167 = 185.

Ungroup Left-to-Right

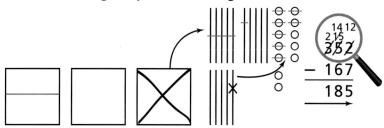

Ungroup Right-to-Left

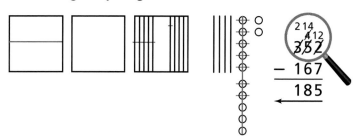

The results of ungrouping in either direction are the same because ungrouping in all columns first makes each column independent for subtraction.

Activity 2

Practice Ungrouping for Subtraction

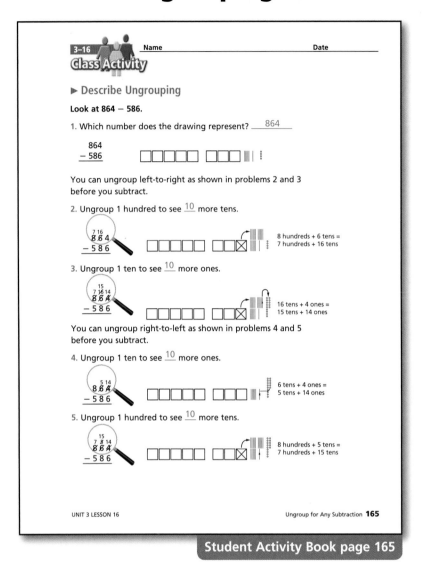

Student Activity Book page 165

 20 MINUTES

Goal: Practice ungrouping and subtraction.

Materials: Student Activity Book or Hardcover Book p. 165

 NCTM Standards:
Number and Operations
Communication

Teaching Note

What to Expect from Students

If any of your students are using the method that alternates between ungrouping and subtracting, discuss this method with them. The sketches of ungrouping are the same. Students need to understand that this method has the same steps as what you are doing in class, but the steps are in a different order.

 Ongoing Assessment

▶ Explain the ungrouping steps needed to find 943 − 575.

▶ Why is ungrouping needed?

▶ Describe Ungrouping WHOLE CLASS

Direct the students' attention to the subtraction and place-value drawing at the top of Student Book page 165. Ask students why the place-value drawing represents 864 only. It is the number we are subtracting from. As students complete exercises 1–5, have them describe each ungrouping step. Their verbal descriptions should relate each ungrouping step to both the numbers and the place-value drawing.

Practice Ungrouping Have students use **Solve and Discuss** to complete some or all of the following exercises.

943 − 575 = 368   558 − 389 = 169   493 − 287 = 206
869 − 286 = 583   782 − 451 = 331   615 − 236 = 379

Estimate to Check Have students use the rounding method to check the answers to the exercises above.

Going Further

Math Connection: Subtraction and Money

Goal: Use money to solve problems involving subtraction with money.

Materials: Student Activity Book or Hardcover Book p. 166, play money (one-dollar bills, ten-dollar bills, and hundred-dollar bills)

✓ **NCTM Standards:**
Number and Operations
Communication
Representation
Problem Solving

▶ Subtraction and Money [PAIRS]

In this lesson, students will connect what they know about subtracting with subtracting money amounts.

Have the class read the introduction on Student Book page 166. Ask the class to describe how the model for Sondra's subtraction is like a place-value drawing. The hundred-dollar bill is like a hundred box and the ten-dollar bills are like quick tens. Discuss how they can exchange a hundred-dollar bill for 10 ten-dollar bills.

Tell the class that in this activity, they will be acting out with only one-dollar bills, ten-dollar bills, and hundred-dollar bills.

Have the class complete problems 1–4, using play money.

As in Lesson 12, students can use drawings instead of play money. They can draw rectangles that have $1, $10, or $100 inside them to show the money values.

▶ Determine Reasonable Answers

Students may have different methods for determining reasonable answers. Give students an opportunity to share different methods.

For example in problem 2, students may decide to subtract $50 from $250 because it is easy to take away $50, $250 − 50 = $200 and then take $25 more, $200 − $25 = $175.

Ask students to explain how they know their answers are reasonable. Give several students the opportunity to share their reasoning to the class.

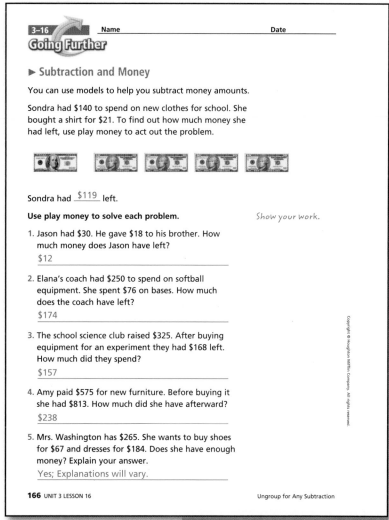

Student Activity Book page 166

Problem 5 Students might round $184 to $200 and $67 to $70 and say there is not enough money. Suggest that these students round to the nearest ten and then decide if there is enough money. Other students may reason that $67 is 2 dollars more than $65 and $184 is less than $200, so there is enough money.

Math Talk Encourage students to explain how they decided that Mrs. Washington did or did not have enough money. Encourage students to share different ways to estimate.

Differentiated Instruction

Intervention · Activity Card 3-16

Ungrouping
Activity Card 3-16

Work: In Pairs

Use:
- 10 red counters
- 20 blue counters
- 20 yellow counters

1. Copy the following problem onto your paper.

    235 – 156

2. **Work Together** Use the counters to model the problem.

3. First, model 235, using the following color assignments for place value.

red	hundreds
blue	tens
yellow	ones

4. Trade counters to ungroup and then complete the subtraction. Record the difference on your paper.

Unit 3, Lesson 16   Copyright © Houghton Mifflin Company

Activity Note Check that students understand that 1 red equals 10 blues and 1 blue equals 10 yellows. Tell students to make new expressions for their partners to solve with the same modeling method.

 Math Writing Prompt

Draw a Picture Make a drawing that shows how to use ungrouping for 543 – 218.

Soar to Success Math ★ **Software Support**

Use *Soar to Success* for instruction of students needing targeted support for underlying skills.

On Level · Activity Card 3-16

The Greatest Difference
Activity Card 3-16 ▲

Work: In Pairs

Use:
- 6 Number cubes

1. Each partner rolls 3 number cubes and arranges the cubes to make a three-digit number.

2. Each partner calculates the difference and then compares answers.

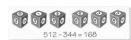

512 – 344 = 168

3. **Work Together** Rearrange one set of cubes to create a new number. Then find the new difference. Continue rearranging the same set of number cubes until you find the greatest possible difference.

4. **Discuss** What strategy did you use to find the greatest possible difference?

Unit 3, Lesson 16   Copyright © Houghton Mifflin Company

Activity Note One variation of the game is to find the least difference. Have students discuss strategies for finding the least or greatest difference.

 Math Writing Prompt

Explain Your Method Do you prefer to do all ungrouping first, or alternate between ungrouping and subtracting? Explain your preference.

MegaMath Grades K-6 **Software Support**

Use *MegaMath* for review and reinforcement of the concepts and skills presented in this lesson.

Challenge · Activity Card 3-16

European Subtraction
Activity Card 3-16 ■

Work: In Pairs

Use:
- MathBoard materials

1. On your MathBoard, copy the subtraction problem at the right. This method of subtraction is sometimes used in Europe and Latin America.

$$\begin{array}{r} {}^{1}976 \\ -\,248 \\ \hline 728 \end{array}$$

2. **Analyze** Describe how the method works.

3. **Work Together** Write three more subtraction problems. Be sure to include problems that require regrouping in the tens and the hundreds places. Use this method of regrouping to solve the problems.

Unit 3, Lesson 16   Copyright © Houghton Mifflin Company

Activity Note Make sure students realize that this regrouping method involves both the top number and the bottom number. Ten was added to the top ones place and also the bottom tens place.

 Math Writing Prompt

Write a Problem Write a subtraction word problem where ungrouping is required and the answer is 734.

 DESTINATION Math **Software Support**

Use *Destination Math* to take students beyond the concepts and skills presented in this lesson.

Ungroup for Any Subtraction   **395**

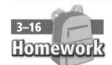

③ Homework and Spiral Review

Use this Homework page to provide students with more practice with ungrouping for subtraction.

This Remembering activity would be appropriate anytime after today's lesson.

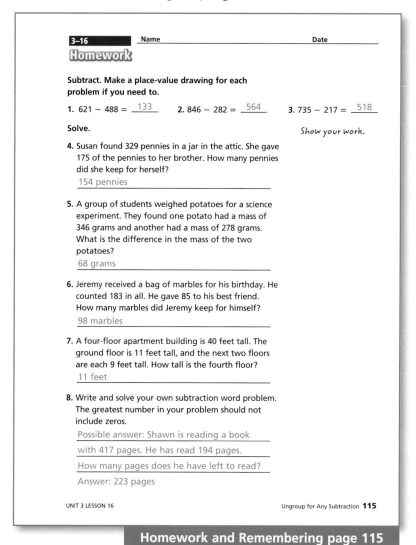

3–16 Name _____ Date _____
Homework

Subtract. Make a place-value drawing for each problem if you need to.

1. $621 - 488 =$ __133__   2. $846 - 282 =$ __564__   3. $735 - 217 =$ __518__

Solve.   *Show your work.*

4. Susan found 329 pennies in a jar in the attic. She gave 175 of the pennies to her brother. How many pennies did she keep for herself?
   __154 pennies__

5. A group of students weighed potatoes for a science experiment. They found one potato had a mass of 346 grams and another had a mass of 278 grams. What is the difference in the mass of the two potatoes?
   __68 grams__

6. Jeremy received a bag of marbles for his birthday. He counted 183 in all. He gave 85 to his best friend. How many marbles did Jeremy keep for himself?
   __98 marbles__

7. A four-floor apartment building is 40 feet tall. The ground floor is 11 feet tall, and the next two floors are each 9 feet tall. How tall is the fourth floor?
   __11 feet__

8. Write and solve your own subtraction word problem. The greatest number in your problem should not include zeros.
   Possible answer: Shawn is reading a book
   with 417 pages. He has read 194 pages.
   How many pages does he have left to read?
   Answer: 223 pages

UNIT 3 LESSON 16   Ungroup for Any Subtraction **115**

Homework and Remembering page 115

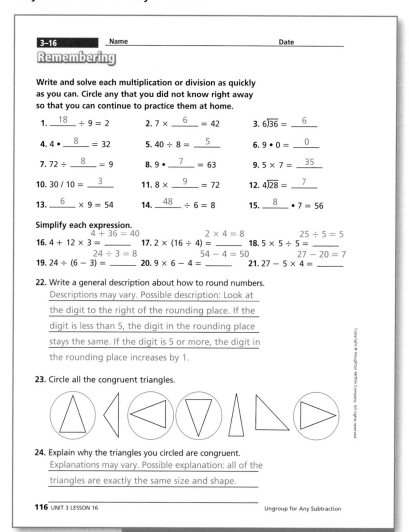

3–16 Name _____ Date _____
Remembering

Write and solve each multiplication or division as quickly as you can. Circle any that you did not know right away so that you can continue to practice them at home.

1. $\underline{18} \div 9 = 2$ 2. $7 \times \underline{6} = 42$ 3. $6\overline{)36} = \underline{6}$

4. $4 \bullet \underline{8} = 32$ 5. $40 \div 8 = \underline{5}$ 6. $9 \bullet 0 = \underline{0}$

7. $72 \div \underline{8} = 9$ 8. $9 \bullet \underline{7} = 63$ 9. $5 \times 7 = \underline{35}$

10. $30 / 10 = \underline{3}$ 11. $8 \times \underline{9} = 72$ 12. $4\overline{)28} = \underline{7}$

13. $\underline{6} \times 9 = 54$ 14. $\underline{48} \div 6 = 8$ 15. $\underline{8} \bullet 7 = 56$

Simplify each expression.

       $4 + 36 = 40$ $2 \times 4 = 8$ $25 \div 5 = 5$

16. $4 + 12 \times 3 =$ ____   17. $2 \times (16 \div 4) =$ ____   18. $5 \times 5 \div 5 =$ ____

       $24 \div 3 = 8$ $54 - 4 = 50$ $27 - 20 = 7$

19. $24 \div (6 - 3) =$ ____   20. $9 \times 6 - 4 =$ ____   21. $27 - 5 \times 4 =$ ____

22. Write a general description about how to round numbers.
   Descriptions may vary. Possible description: Look at
   the digit to the right of the rounding place. If the
   digit is less than 5, the digit in the rounding place
   stays the same. If the digit is 5 or more, the digit in
   the rounding place increases by 1.

23. Circle all the congruent triangles.

24. Explain why the triangles you circled are congruent.
   Explanations may vary. Possible explanation: all of the
   triangles are exactly the same size and shape.

116 UNIT 3 LESSON 16   Ungroup for Any Subtraction

Homework and Remembering page 116

Home or School Activity

Math-to-Math Connection

Ungrouping in Measurement Suppose you have 1 quart of milk and use 3 cups for a recipe. You can "ungroup" 1 quart and represent it as 4 cups to find out how much you have left.

1 quart − 3 cups = 4 cups − 3 cups = 1 cup

Ask students to find examples for which they can use "ungrouping" to solve measurement problems (capacity, length, weight, time, and so on.)

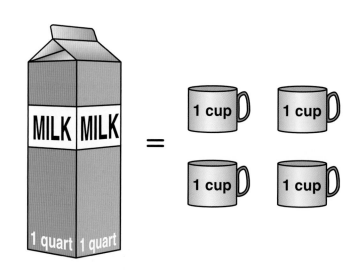

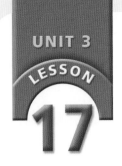

Subtract From Thousands

Lesson Objective

● Subtract from numbers with up to four digits.

The Day at a Glance

Today's Goals	Materials

① Teaching the Lesson
A1: Subtract from thousands with top-number zeros.
A2: Subtract from thousands with top-numbers other than zero.
A2: Explore special ungrouping situations.
 	
② Going Further
▶ Differentiated Instruction
 	
③ Homework and Spiral Review
	Lesson Activities
	Student Activity Book pp. 167–168
	  or Student Hardcover Book
	  pp. 167–168
	Homework and Remembering
	  pp. 117–118
	MathBoard Materials
	
	Going Further
	Activity Cards 3-17
	MathBoard Materials
	Grid paper
	Math Journals

123 *Use* **Math Talk** *today!*

Keeping Skills Sharp

Quick Practice ⏱ 5 MINUTES	Daily Routines
Goal: Compare multi-digit numbers. **Say, Write, and Compare** Use these numbers to have students compare multi-digit numbers. See Lesson 11. 63,714,258　63,417,285　　74,035,026　74,026,035 63,417,285　63,714,258　　74,026,035　74,035,026 176,402,503　176,204,503　　196,234,578　186,243,578 176,204,503　176,402,503　　186,243,578　196,234,578	**Homework Review** Ask a student volunteer to share a word problem. Invite several students to solve it at the board, while others work at their seats. **Logic** Use *some, all,* or *none* to complete these sentences. 1) If all isosceles triangles have at least two equal sides, then ____ equilateral triangles are isosceles triangles. all 2) If all squares have four equal sides and four equal angles, then ____ rhombuses are squares. some

① Teaching the Lesson

Subtract From Zeros

 25 MINUTES

Goal: Subtract from thousands with top-number zeros.

Materials: Student Activity Book or Hardcover Book p. 167, MathBoard Materials

 NCTM Standards:
Number and Operations
Algebra
Representation
Communication

Teaching Note

Reminder The magnifying glass image is to remind students to "look inside" the top number to know what ungrouping they need to do. It also makes the top-from-bottom error less likely.

▶ Discuss Ungrouping With Zeros

WHOLE CLASS   Math Talk

Write 4,000 − 2,345 on the board. Invite as many students as possible to work the solution at the board. The remaining students should work on their MathBoards.

Ask students for possible real-world situations that will match these numbers. Then have them make the break-apart drawing.

Have the students write the problem vertically and make the place-value drawing of 4,000. If necessary, remind them to draw the magnifying glass around and above the top number.

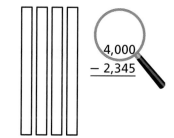

Next, have the students discuss each step of the ungrouping they need to do. They should note any changes that occur in the drawing or the numbers, and explain how the drawing and numbers are related at each step.

● We do not have enough hundreds to subtract 3 hundreds, so we ungroup 1 thousand to get 10 more hundreds. 4 thousands = 3 thousands + 10 hundreds.

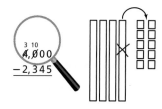

● We cannot subtract 4 tens from 0 tens, so we ungroup 1 hundred to get 10 more tens. 4 thousands = 3 thousands + 9 hundreds + 10 tens

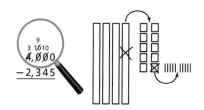

- We cannot subtract 5 ones from 0 ones, so we ungroup 1 ten to get 10 more ones. 4 thousands = 3 thousands + 9 hundreds + 9 tens + 10 ones

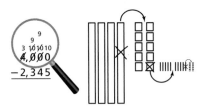

- Now that all ungrouping is done, we can subtract either right-to-left or left-to-right.

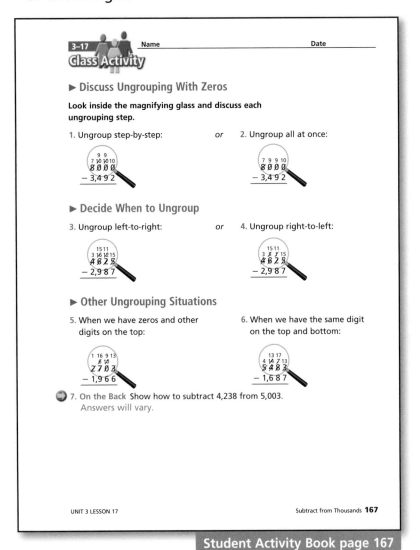

Activity continued ▶

Activity 1

Teaching Note

Math Background The pattern in this section can be described as:

n thousands, 9 hundreds, 9 tens, 10 ones

You can see that if you add these amounts, you have *n* + 1 thousands since 9 hundreds + 9 tens + 10 ones = 1 thousand.

Look at Patterns Ask for the numbers that appear at the tops of all columns after ungrouping in the subtraction example on the previous page. 3, 9, 9, 10

Have the students discuss all the necessary steps for exercises 1 and 2 on Student Book page 167. Ask for the numbers that appear at the tops of all columns after ungrouping. 7, 9, 9, 10

● What pattern appears after ungrouping when subtracting from thousands with three zeros? One less thousand, 9 hundreds, 9 tens, 10 ones

Practice Write on the board: 8,000 − 6,917.

Have 3 or 4 students solve the example at the board while the others work on their MathBoards. Have the students draw the place values if they still need graphic support. Use the "magnifying glass" to remind students to look inside the top numbers.

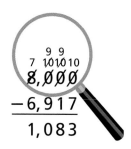

Have students explain ungrouping all-at-once. Instead of ungrouping step-by-step, ungroup 1 thousand all at once into 9 hundreds, 9 tens, and 10 ones.

Discuss any other solutions on the board. Refer questions to the group for answers whenever possible.

Subtract From Numbers Other Than Zeros

▶ Decide When to Ungroup WHOLE CLASS

Have as many students as possible work at the board. Have the remaining students work on their MathBoards.

Write on the board: 4,625 − 2,987. Elicit real-world situations that may represent the problem.

 Math Talk Have one student at the classroom board explain ungrouping left-to-right.

- Ungroup 1 thousand:
  4 thousands + 6 hundreds =
  3 thousands + 16 hundreds

- Ungroup 1 hundred:
  16 hundreds + 2 tens =
  15 hundreds + 12 tens

- Ungroup 1 ten:
  12 tens + 5 ones = 11 tens + 15 ones

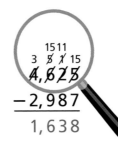

Have another student explain ungrouping right-to-left.

- Ungroup 1 ten:
  2 tens + 5 ones = 1 ten + 15 ones

- Ungroup 1 hundred:
  6 hundreds + 1 ten = 5 hundreds + 11 tens

- Ungroup 1 thousand:
  4 thousands + 5 hundreds =
  3 thousands + 15 hundreds

Have the students discuss exercises 3 and 4 on Student Book page 167 to ensure that they understand that ungrouping in either direction gives the same answer. The steps are the same in both methods but are performed in a different order.

Practice Write on the board: 9,462 − 5,678 = 3,784.

Have some of the students ungroup right-to-left and others ungroup left-to-right, or let students choose which way they will ungroup. Some students may still need to make a place-value drawing of the top number.

🕐 **15 MINUTES**

Goal: Subtract from thousands with top-numbers other than zero.

Materials: Student Activity Book or Hardcover Book p. 167, MathBoard Materials

✓ **NCTM Standards:**
Number and Operations
Communication

Differentiated Instruction

Extra Help Encourage students to make a place-value drawing for the top number when they need to. For students who can do the ungrouping and the subtraction by working only with the numbers, make sure they use place-value language to explain their ungrouping.

English Language Learners

Write 8,148 − 6,259 on the board vertically. Review the term *ungroup*.

- **Beginning** Say: Ungroup the thousands to 7 thousands + 11 hundreds. Ungroup the hundreds to 10 hundreds + 15 tens. Ungroup the tens to 14 tens + 18 ones. Have students repeat.
- **Intermediate** Say: Ungroup. Ask: **What are the thousands?** 7 thousands + 11 hundreds **The hundreds?** 10 hundreds + 15 tens **The tens?** 14 tens + 18 ones
- **Advanced** Have students work in pairs. One partner names a 4-digit number. The other ungroups it to an equal number. 8,100 = 7 thousands, 11 hundreds

Activity 3

Special Ungrouping Situations

 15 MINUTES

Goal: Explore special ungrouping situations.

Materials: Student Activity Book or Hardcover Book p. 167, MathBoard Materials

✓ **NCTM Standards:**
Number and Operations
Communication

Differentiated Instruction

Extra Help If your students need more practice making place-value drawings to show ungrouping for 4-digit subtraction and connecting the parts of the drawings to numeric solutions, you should spend another day on these activities. Below are some exercises that you can use for Solve and Discuss in class.

$4,000 - 2,945 = 1,055$
$9,040 - 5,712 = 3,328$
$6,000 - 5,036 = 964$
$8,006 - 4,692 = 3,314$
$8,531 - 7,624 = 907$
$7,180 - 4,385 = 2,795$
$7,919 - 3,846 = 4,073$
$4,221 - 2,805 = 1,416$

 Ongoing Assessment

Ask students:

▶ What numbers will be at the tops of the place columns after you do all the ungrouping for $7,000 - 572$?

▶ Subtract: $4,605 - 1,711$

▶ **Other Ungrouping Situations** WHOLE CLASS

Moving Over Two Columns to Ungroup Have the students look at the magnifying glass in exercise 5 on Student Book page 167. Have them discuss the situation. The student discussion should be similar to the steps outlined below:

● The top number contains a zero and other numbers.

● You choose to ungroup right-to-left.

● You try to get more ones, but the tens column is zero.

● So, you have to ungroup 1 hundred to get 10 tens.

● Then you can do the rest of the ungrouping.

● You need to look into the place to the left of the zero to get what you need to ungroup.

Practice Have 3 students work at the board while the others work on their MathBoards. Give each student at the board one of the following exercises. Either assign an exercise or have the students at their seats pick one of the exercises to solve.

$6,034 - 2,756 = 3,278$ $8,502 - 3,749 = 4,753$ $4,650 - 2,793 = 1,857$

When most students have finished, discuss how the zeros are handled in the various place-value positions.

A Special Ungrouping Situation A special ungrouping situation is shown in exercise 6 of Student page 167. It occurs only in left-to right ungrouping, and it is only a problem when both the top and bottom digits in a place-value column are the same and the next lower place needs to be ungrouped.

Step 1	Step 2	Step 3
Ungrouping the thousands and hundreds is easy.	The tens seem to be ready for subtraction, but the ones need to be ungrouped.	After you ungroup the ones, it turns out that you have to ungroup the tens after all.

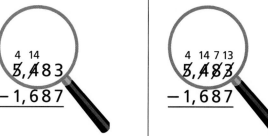 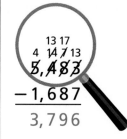

② Going Further

Intervention — Activity Card 3-17

Practice Subtraction
Activity Card 3-17

Work: In Pairs

Use:
• MathBoard materials

Decide:
Who will be Student 1 and who will be Student 2 for the first round.

1. Copy the following problem onto your MathBoard.

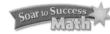
4,000
− 840

2. **Student 1:** Make a place-value model of the problem on the board. Ungroup and subtract, using that model.

3. **Student 2:** Complete the subtraction by working with the numbers.

4. Exchange roles and repeat the activity, using 3,000 − 1,476.

5. **Discuss** Which method do you prefer? Why?

Unit 3, Lesson 17   Copyright © Houghton Mifflin Company

Activity Note Encourage students to continue to practice by making up their own subtraction problems.

🖊 Math Writing Prompt

Explain a Drawing Which problem requires more steps to model with base-ten blocks: 6,000 − 560 or 6,000 − 2,476? Explain your answer with a drawing.

Soar to Success Math ⭐ Software Support

Use *Soar to Success* for instruction of students needing targeted support for underlying skills.

On Level — Activity Card 3-17

Zero Tac Toe
Activity Card 3-17 ▲

Work: In Pairs

Use:
• Centimeter-Grid Paper (TRB M60)

1. Mark a grid as shown.

2. Take turns writing one digit at a time in the squares in any order to make a subtraction problem. Put at least two zeros in the top number.

4,007
− 909
3,098

3. Work together to calculate the difference. Then repeat the activity.

Unit 3, Lesson 17   Copyright © Houghton Mifflin Company

Activity Note Remind students that to create a four-digit number, the number in the thousands place must be a non-zero digit.

🖊 Math Writing Prompt

I Need to Remember Write about one thing you need to remember when subtracting from numbers that have one or more zeros.

MegaMath Grades K-6 Software Support

Use *MegaMath* for review and reinforcement of the concepts and skills presented in this lesson.

Challenge — Activity Card 3-17

Digit Jumble
Activity Card 3-17 ■

Work: In Pairs

Use:
• MathBoard materials

1. On your own MathBoard, write a subtraction problem with 2 four-digit numbers. Use the digits 0, 7, 2, 0, 0, 2, 0, 3.

7,300
− 2,020

2. Exchange boards with your partner to solve the problem. The partner with the smaller difference wins that round.

3. Repeat the activity to see who wins the best of five rounds. No four-digit number may be used twice.

Unit 3, Lesson 17   Copyright © Houghton Mifflin Company

Activity Note Have students discuss strategies that they used to create problems with the least possible difference.

🖊 Math Writing Prompt

Digit Pattern Suppose you need to subtract a five-digit number that has no zeros from 40,000. What numbers will appear at the tops of all the columns after you ungroup? Explain.

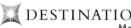 **DESTINATION Math® Software Support**

Use *Destination Math* to take students beyond the concepts and skills presented in this lesson.

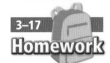

3 Homework and Spiral Review

3–17
Homework **Goal:** Additional Practice

Use this Homework page to provide students with more practice with subtraction methods.

3–17
Remembering **Goal:** Spiral Review

This Remembering activity would be appropriate anytime after today's lesson.

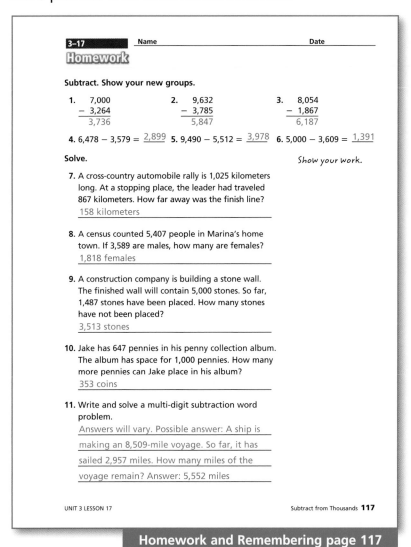

3–17 Name _____ Date _____

Homework

Subtract. Show your new groups.

1.
```
   7,000
 − 3,264
   3,736
```
2.
```
   9,632
 − 3,785
   5,847
```
3.
```
   8,054
 − 1,867
   6,187
```

4. $6,478 − 3,579 = \underline{2,899}$ 5. $9,490 − 5,512 = \underline{3,978}$ 6. $5,000 − 3,609 = \underline{1,391}$

Solve.   *Show your work.*

7. A cross-country automobile rally is 1,025 kilometers long. At a stopping place, the leader had traveled 867 kilometers. How far away was the finish line?
   158 kilometers

8. A census counted 5,407 people in Marina's home town. If 3,589 are males, how many are females?
   1,818 females

9. A construction company is building a stone wall. The finished wall will contain 5,000 stones. So far, 1,487 stones have been placed. How many stones have not been placed?
   3,513 stones

10. Jake has 647 pennies in his penny collection album. The album has space for 1,000 pennies. How many more pennies can Jake place in his album?
    353 coins

11. Write and solve a multi-digit subtraction word problem.
    Answers will vary. Possible answer: A ship is
    making an 8,509-mile voyage. So far, it has
    sailed 2,957 miles. How many miles of the
    voyage remain? Answer: 5,552 miles

UNIT 3 LESSON 17   Subtract from Thousands **117**

Homework and Remembering page 117

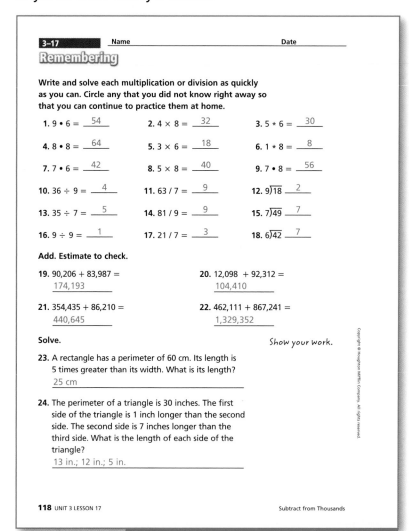

3–17 Name _____ Date _____

Remembering

Write and solve each multiplication or division as quickly as you can. Circle any that you did not know right away so that you can continue to practice them at home.

1. $9 \cdot 6 = \underline{54}$ 2. $4 \times 8 = \underline{32}$ 3. $5 * 6 = \underline{30}$

4. $8 \cdot 8 = \underline{64}$ 5. $3 \times 6 = \underline{18}$ 6. $1 * 8 = \underline{8}$

7. $7 \cdot 6 = \underline{42}$ 8. $5 \times 8 = \underline{40}$ 9. $7 \cdot 8 = \underline{56}$

10. $36 ÷ 9 = \underline{4}$ 11. $63 / 7 = \underline{9}$ 12. $9\overline{)18}$ $\underline{2}$

13. $35 ÷ 7 = \underline{5}$ 14. $81 / 9 = \underline{9}$ 15. $7\overline{)49}$ $\underline{7}$

16. $9 ÷ 9 = \underline{1}$ 17. $21 / 7 = \underline{3}$ 18. $6\overline{)42}$ $\underline{7}$

Add. Estimate to check.

19. $90,206 + 83,987 =$ 20. $12,098 + 92,312 =$
    174,193   104,410

21. $354,435 + 86,210 =$ 22. $462,111 + 867,241 =$
    440,645   1,329,352

Solve.   *Show your work.*

23. A rectangle has a perimeter of 60 cm. Its length is 5 times greater than its width. What is its length?
    25 cm

24. The perimeter of a triangle is 30 inches. The first side of the triangle is 1 inch longer than the second side. The second side is 7 inches longer than the third side. What is the length of each side of the triangle?
    13 in.; 12 in.; 5 in.

118 UNIT 3 LESSON 17   Subtract from Thousands

Homework and Remembering page 118

Home or School Activity

Real-World Connection

Metric Height Have students find the heights of several friends or family members in millimeters, and then find how much taller one person is than another.

Name	Height
Aunt Alice	1,651 mm
Mr. Smith	1,829 mm
Amy	1,270 mm
Miguel	1,372 mm
Tran	1,321 mm

```
  1,829
− 1,270
    559
```
Mr. Smith is 559 millimeters taller than Amy.

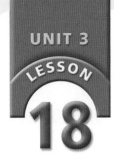

Subtract Larger Numbers

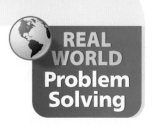
REAL WORLD Problem Solving

Lesson Objectives

- Understand how methods for ungrouping apply to subtraction for any size numbers.

- Understand how to use addition to check subtraction.

The Day at a Glance

Today's Goals	Materials
1 Teaching the Lesson A1: Subtract from greater numbers and discuss when ungrouping is necessary. A2: Explore ways to check subtraction. **2 Going Further** ▶ Math Connection: Estimate Differences ▶ Differentiated Instruction **3 Homework and Spiral Review**	**Lesson Activities** Student Activity Book p. 169 or Student Hardcover Book p. 169 Homework and Remembering pp. 119–120 MathBoard Materials **Going Further** Student Activity Book p. 170 or Student Hardcover Book p. 170 Activity Cards 3-18 MathBoard Materials Number cubes Math Journals

123 *Use Math Talk today!*

Keeping Skills Sharp

Quick Practice 🕐 5 MINUTES	Daily Routines
Goal: Subtract thousands. **Find the Difference** Write both examples below on the board. Have students write them in their Math Journals and solve. 4,058 − 1,774 3,672 − 1,479 If any students get an incorrect solution, write the incorrect solution on the board and have the class discuss where the error occurred and how to fix it.	**Homework Review** Ask students if they had difficulty with any part of the homework. Plan to set aside some time to work with students needing extra help. **Making Change** Carmen buys a swimsuit that costs $39.05. She gives the salesclerk a $50 bill and one nickel. How much change should Carmen receive? Why did she give the clerk the nickel? $11; to avoid coins equaling 95¢

Teaching the Lesson

Subtract from Millions

 25 MINUTES

Goal: Subtract from greater numbers and discuss when ungrouping is necessary.

Materials: MathBoard Materials

✓ **NCTM Standards:**
Number and Operations
Communication

Teaching Note

Math Background This activity should reinforce students' understanding that any two adjacent places are related by the same 1-for-10 relationship.

▶ Ungroup With Greater Numbers

| WHOLE CLASS |

Math Talk

Have several students work at the board while the remaining students work at their seats.

Write on the board: 2,856,402 − 780,169.

Have the students rewrite the example vertically. Check to make sure that the place values are aligned. Have a student explain why place values must be aligned. We can only subtract like place values.

Have the students discuss where ungrouping is needed and explain why it is needed. Ungrouping is needed where the top digit is smaller than the bottom digit. The top number needs to be large enough to subtract from.

Direct students to do all necessary ungrouping first.

$$
\begin{array}{r}
\overset{\overset{9}{}}{}\\[-4pt]
\overset{7\ 15\quad 3\ 10\ 12}{2,8\,\cancel{5}\,6,\cancel{4}\,\cancel{0}\,\cancel{2}}\\
-\ \ \ 7\,8\,0,1\,6\,9\\
\hline
2,0\,7\,6,2\,3\,3
\end{array}
$$

● Have one student explain ungrouping left-to-right.

● Have a different student explain ungrouping right-to-left.

● Have the class do the subtractions either left-to-right or right-to-left.

When finished, have the students compare their solutions. Confirm any methods that yield the correct solution. Discuss any methods that do not give the correct solution to find out why.

Write on the board: 8,507,216 − 3,192,567.

Have the students solve this example independently. Some students should work at the board while the others work at their seats. Right-to-left ungrouping is shown below:

$$
\begin{array}{r}
\overset{\quad\quad\ 11\ 10}{}\\[-4pt]
\overset{4\ 10\ 6\quad \cancel{7}\ \cancel{0}\ 16}{8,\cancel{5}\,\cancel{0}\,\cancel{7},2\,\cancel{1}\,\cancel{6}}\\
-\ 3,1\,9\,2,5\,6\,7\\
\hline
5,3\,1\,4,6\,4\,9
\end{array}
$$

When most have finished, discuss the results.

📁 Class Management

Looking Ahead Keep one correct version of the example on the board for the next activity.

Check Subtraction

3–18
Class Activity

Name _____   Date _____

▶ **Find and Correct Mistakes**

Always check your work. Many mistakes can be easily fixed.

What is the mistake in each problem? How can you fix the mistake and find the correct answer?
Answers will vary. Possible answers given.

1. 67,308 − 5,497

```
        12
     6 1810
   6 7,3 0 8
  −  5,4 9 7
   1 2,3 3 8
```

The numbers are not aligned correctly. To fix the mistake, rewrite the problem so that ones line up with ones, tens line up with tens, and so on.

2. 134,865 − 5,294

```
   134,865
  −  5,294
   131,631
```

The student subtracted the smaller digit from the larger digit when the larger digit was on the bottom. To fix the mistake, ungroup so that a larger number is always on top.

▶ **Check Subtraction by "Adding Up"**

"Add up" to find any places where there is a subtraction mistake. Discuss how each mistake might have been made and correct the subtraction if necessary.

3. 163,406	4. 526,741	5. 2,380,043	6. 5,472,639
− 84,357	− 139,268	− 678,145	− 2,375,841
79,159	413,473	1,701,908	3,096,798
79,049	387,473	1,701,898	no mistakes
subtracted top from bottom	subtracted top from bottom	ungrouped incorrectly	

7. Write and solve a subtraction problem with numbers in the millions.

Answers will vary.
_____
_____

UNIT 3 LESSON 18   Subtract Larger Numbers **169**

Student Activity Book page 169

---

 30 MINUTES

Goal: Explore ways to check subtraction.

Materials: Student Activity Book or Hardcover Book p. 169, MathBoard Materials

 NCTM Standards:
Number and Operations
Problem Solving
Communication

The Learning Classroom

Helping Community Some students are initially reluctant to explain their thinking. As you respond positively to student efforts to talk about their thinking, your class will realize that there is an expectation in the math community to respond positively to one another. More students will then desire to make their math thinking the center of discussion.

▶ Find and Correct Mistakes   WHOLE CLASS

Have the students find and discuss the conceptual mistakes shown in exercises 1 and 2 on Student Book page 169.

● In exercise 1 the places are not properly aligned. Ones must be subtracted from ones, and so on. Have one or more students work at the board while the others work at their seats to rewrite the exercise with correct alignment and find the correct answer. 61,811

● In exercise 2 no ungrouping has been done. One hundred should have been ungrouped to make more tens. Instead the smaller digit was subtracted from the larger digit. The same mistake was made in the thousands place. Again, have one or more students work at the board while the others work at their seats. They should ungroup as needed and find the correct answer. 129,571

Activity continued ▶

Activity 2

Teaching Note

Language and Vocabulary
The mathematical word for the relationship between addition and subtraction is *inverse*. Students may also use *opposite, reverse, undoing,* or some other description.

Break-Apart Drawing

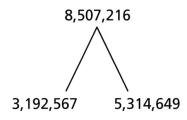

8,507,216

3,192,567   5,314,649

English Language Learners

Write the word *inverse* on the board. Review the meaning and inverse operations.

- **Beginning** Ask: **Does *inverse* mean "opposite"?** yes Say: **Addition is the inverse of ___.** subtraction **We can use addition to check ___.** subtraction
- **Intermediate** Ask: **What does *inverse* mean?** opposite **What is the inverse of subtraction?** addition **What can we check with addition?** the answer to a subtraction problem
- **Advanced** Have students work in pairs. One partner names a +, −, × or ÷ problem. The other names the inverse operation that could be used to check the answer.

► Check Subtraction by "Adding Up" WHOLE CLASS

To review the relationship between addition and subtraction, use the break-apart drawing shown on the left of a previous practice example.

Have the students discuss how the diagram shows both subtraction and addition. If you subtract either bottom number from the top number, you get the other bottom number as the answer. If you add the two bottom numbers, you get the top number as the answer.

Have students discuss how they could use this knowledge to check subtraction. Try to elicit the following method: You can check subtraction by "adding up." Add the answer and the bottom number (the addends in an addition) to get the top number (the total in an addition).

The "adding up" method is shown below. The new groups are shown as 1s in the appropriate columns just below the answer in the subtraction.

$$
\begin{array}{r}
8{,}507{,}216 \\
-\ 3{,}192{,}567 \\
\hline
5{,}314{,}649 \\
{\scriptstyle 1\ \ 1\ 1}
\end{array}
$$

Have the students take turns adding place values, beginning with the ones place.

- Add the ones bottom to top: $9 + 7 = 16$. The 16 is consistent with the 6 that is already at the top of the ones column. Write a 1 for the regrouped ten at the bottom of the tens column.

- Add the tens bottom to top: $1 + 4 + 6 = 11$. The 11 is consistent with the 1 that is already at the top of the tens column. Write a 1 for the regrouped hundred at the bottom of the hundreds column.

- Continue "adding up" in the other places.

- The total is 8,507,216.

Practice Have several students work at the board while the others work at their seats to check exercise 3 on Student page 169. Remind students to check by "adding up."

Have the students discuss their findings. Refer student questions to the class for resolution whenever possible.

Then have them work through exercises 4–6 by themselves while you walk around and check for understanding.

After students have written problems for exercise 7, have them exchange papers, solve the problem, and add up to check.

Have different students discuss the errors they found. Explanations for the errors are listed below:

3.
```
    163,406
  -  84,357
    ─────────
     79,159
```
Subtracted top-from-bottom in tens.
Correct Answer: 79,049

4.
```
    526,741
  - 139,268
    ─────────
    413,473
```
Subtracted top-from-bottom in ten thousands and thousands. Correct Answer: 387,473

5.
```
  2,380,043
  -  678,145
    ─────────
  1,701,908
```
Ungrouped incorrectly in tens column.
Correct Answer: 1,701,898

6.
```
  5,472,639
  - 2,375,841
    ─────────
  3,096,798
```
No mistakes

▶ Estimate to Check WHOLE CLASS

Discuss how to round larger numbers to check the exercises above.

Rounding to the Nearest Ten Thousand In exercise 1, ask students questions that will help them decide how to round.

- Which place will stay the same or change if we are rounding to the nearest ten thousand? ten thousands place

- Which place tell us which way to round? the place to the right of the ten thousands place, the thousands place

- How do we round 84,357 to the nearest ten thousand? 80,000

- How do we round 164,406 to the nearest thousand? 160,000

- Ask students to estimate the difference. 80,000

Rounding to the Nearest Hundred Thousand For exercises 2 and 3, students should round to the nearest hundred thousand to check. Use questions similar to those above.

Rounding to the Nearest Million Remind students that rounding rules remain the same for any number of digits. Since both numbers in exercise 4 are in the millions, students should round to the nearest millions to check for reasonableness. Use questions similar to those above.

The Learning Classroom

Math Talk Encourage students to respond before you do, especially to other students' questions. Allow time for students to make comments or ask questions about each other's work before you begin to speak. If you tend to speak first, the students will not take ownership of their role as crucial participants in the discourse; they will look to you instead.

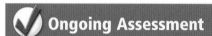 **Ongoing Assessment**

▶ Describe any ungrouping you would need to do for:
```
  1,256,844
  -  117,012
```

▶ Explain how you look for mistakes in a subtraction problem.

Going Further

Math Connection: Estimate Differences

Goal: Estimate differences by rounding and determine if answers are reasonable.

Materials: Student Activity Book or Hardcover Book p. 170, MathBoard Materials

✔ **NCTM Standards:**
Number and Operations
Communication
Problem Solving

▶ Estimate Differences [WHOLE CLASS]

In this lesson, students connect what they know about subtraction and estimation to determine whether differences are reasonable.

Have the class read the introduction about Dan's estimate on Student Book page 170.

- How do we decide if Dan's answer is reasonable? Round to the nearest thousand. 8,000 − 6,000 = 2,000

- Is Dan's answer reasonable? probably not

Write the subtraction with Dan's incorrect answer vertically on the board and tell students to do the same on their MathBoards.

$$\begin{array}{r} 8{,}196 \\ -\ 5{,}980 \\ \hline 3{,}816 \end{array}$$

Tell the students to find the mistake and describe how to fix it. Dan subtracted the top digit from the bottom digit in the hundreds place. He should have regrouped 8 thousands to make 7 thousands and 10 hundreds.

- What is the correct answer? 2,216

Have students discuss problems 1–2.

To prepare students for some of the remaining exercises, ask how to estimate 601,107 − 297,965. Round to the nearest hundred thousand.

600,000 − 300,000 = 300,000

Have students work independently on exercises 3–5.

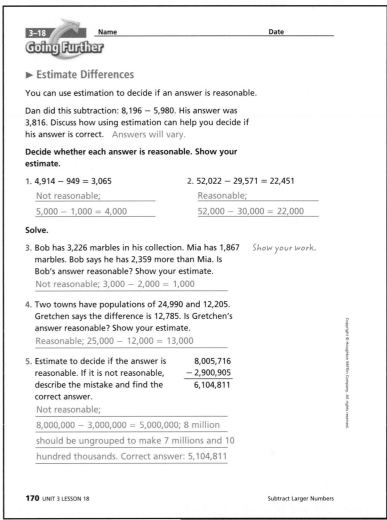

3-18
Going Further
Name _____ Date _____

▶ **Estimate Differences**

You can use estimation to decide if an answer is reasonable.

Dan did this subtraction: 8,196 − 5,980. His answer was 3,816. Discuss how using estimation can help you decide if his answer is correct.   Answers will vary.

Decide whether each answer is reasonable. Show your estimate.

1. 4,914 − 949 = 3,065
   Not reasonable;
   5,000 − 1,000 = 4,000

2. 52,022 − 29,571 = 22,451
   Reasonable;
   52,000 − 30,000 = 22,000

Solve.

3. Bob has 3,226 marbles in his collection. Mia has 1,867 marbles. Bob says he has 2,359 more than Mia. Is Bob's answer reasonable? Show your estimate.   *Show your work.*
   Not reasonable; 3,000 − 2,000 = 1,000

4. Two towns have populations of 24,990 and 12,205. Gretchen says the difference is 12,785. Is Gretchen's answer reasonable? Show your estimate.
   Reasonable; 25,000 − 12,000 = 13,000

5. Estimate to decide if the answer is reasonable. If it is not reasonable, describe the mistake and find the correct answer.
   $$\begin{array}{r} 8{,}005{,}716 \\ -\ 2{,}900{,}905 \\ \hline 6{,}104{,}811 \end{array}$$
   Not reasonable;
   8,000,000 − 3,000,000 = 5,000,000; 8 million should be ungrouped to make 7 millions and 10 hundred thousands. Correct answer: 5,104,811

170 UNIT 3 LESSON 18   Subtract Larger Numbers

Student Activity Book page 170

Teaching Note

Math Background In many situations, there is no "right way" to estimate. Estimating is often a matter of judgment, and it can vary depending on the numbers involved and the purpose of the estimate. In problem 4, a student might estimate by rounding to the nearest ten thousand: 20,000 − 10,000 = 10,000. This is acceptable, but may not be "the best way."

Emphasize the main purpose of this activity—to determine whether answers are reasonable. This is a habit that should be strongly encouraged.

Differentiated Instruction

Intervention   Activity Card 3-18

When to Ungroup?   Activity Card 3-18

Work: In Pairs

Use:
• MathBoard materials
• 3 Number cubes

Decide:
Who will be Student 1 and who will be Student 2 for the first round.

1. **Student 1:** Roll the 3 number cubes, and use the digits to form a subtraction problem. For example, if 2, 5, and 6 are rolled, a problem like the one below can be written.

$$\begin{array}{r} 52 \\ -6 \\ \hline \end{array}$$

2. **Student 2:** Subtract, using ungrouping as needed.

3. **Discuss** Is the difference correct? How do you know? You can check subtraction by using addition.

4. **Exchange** roles and repeat the activity.

Unit 3, Lesson 18   Copyright © Houghton Mifflin Company

Activity Note Extend the activity by having students roll the number cube more than 3 times for each problem to make greater numbers.

✓ Math Writing Prompt

Define Your Work Break the word *ungroup* into "un" and "group." Define each part of the word. Give another example of a word that starts with *un* and define it.

Soar to Success Math ★ Software Support

Use *Soar to Success* for instruction of students needing targeted support for underlying skills.

On Level   Activity Card 3-18

Cover Up   Activity Card 3-18 ▲

Work: By Yourself

Use:
• MathBoard materials

1. Copy the problem at the right on your MathBoard.

2. Use paper to cover all of the digits except 60 and 28.

3. Decide if ungrouping is needed and then perform the steps. Move the paper to the right one column at a time. Ungroup as needed, and subtract to solve the problem.

4. **Analyze** Why you think this method does or does not work? Explain.

Unit 3, Lesson 18   Copyright © Houghton Mifflin Company

Activity Note To extend the activity, have students work left to right and compare the results to the results of the right-to-left method.

✓ Math Writing Prompt

Investigate Math Explain how subtracting 56,000 from 84,000 is similar to subtracting 56 from 84. Compare the answers.

MegaMath Grades K-6 Software Supports

Use *MegaMath* for review and reinforcement of the concepts and skills presented in this lesson.

Challenge   Activity Card 3-18

Missing Digits   Activity Card 3-18 ■

Work: In Pairs

Use:
• MathBoard materials

1. Copy the example below on your MathBoard.

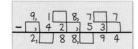

2. **Work Together** Find the missing digits.
   9,108,727 − 6,420,533 = 2,688,194

3. On your own, write another missing-digits problem on your MathBoard.

4. Exchange boards with your partner, and solve the problem. Then check your answer, using addition.

Unit 3, Lesson 18   Copyright © Houghton Mifflin Company

Activity Note Have students discuss their methods for deciding if they need to regroup or ungroup to find the missing digits.

✓ Math Writing Prompt

Explain Your Thinking You buy 4 items at a store, but the receipt is smudged and you cannot read one of the item costs. Explain how you can find the missing cost.

✹ DESTINATION Math® Software Support

Use *Destination Math* to take students beyond the concepts and skills presented in this lesson.

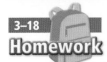

③ Homework and Spiral Review

3–18
Homework **Goal:** Additional Practice

Use this Homework page to provide students with more practice with subtraction and ungrouping.

3–18
Remembering **Goal:** Spiral Review

This Remembering activity would be appropriate anytime after today's lesson.

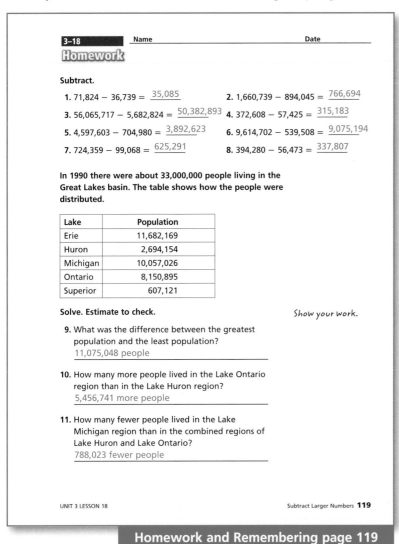

3–18 Name _____ Date _____

Homework

Subtract.

1. $71,824 - 36,739 =$ __35,085__
2. $1,660,739 - 894,045 =$ __766,694__
3. $56,065,717 - 5,682,824 =$ __50,382,893__
4. $372,608 - 57,425 =$ __315,183__
5. $4,597,603 - 704,980 =$ __3,892,623__
6. $9,614,702 - 539,508 =$ __9,075,194__
7. $724,359 - 99,068 =$ __625,291__
8. $394,280 - 56,473 =$ __337,807__

In 1990 there were about 33,000,000 people living in the Great Lakes basin. The table shows how the people were distributed.

Lake	Population
Erie	11,682,169
Huron	2,694,154
Michigan	10,057,026
Ontario	8,150,895
Superior	607,121

Solve. Estimate to check.   *Show your work.*

9. What was the difference between the greatest population and the least population?
   11,075,048 people

10. How many more people lived in the Lake Ontario region than in the Lake Huron region?
    5,456,741 more people

11. How many fewer people lived in the Lake Michigan region than in the combined regions of Lake Huron and Lake Ontario?
    788,023 fewer people

UNIT 3 LESSON 18   Subtract Larger Numbers **119**

Homework and Remembering page 119

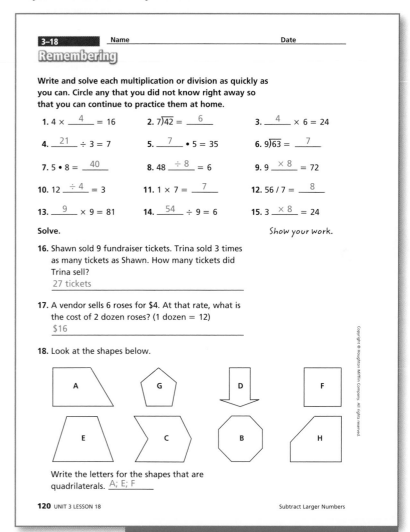

3–18 Name _____ Date _____

Remembering

Write and solve each multiplication or division as quickly as you can. Circle any that you did not know right away so that you can continue to practice them at home.

1. $4 \times$ __4__ $= 16$
2. $7\overline{)42} =$ __6__
3. __4__ $\times 6 = 24$
4. __21__ $\div 3 = 7$
5. __7__ $\bullet 5 = 35$
6. $9\overline{)63} =$ __7__
7. $5 \bullet 8 =$ __40__
8. $48 \div 8 = 6$
9. 9 __$\times 8$__ $= 72$
10. 12 __$\div 4$__ $= 3$
11. $1 \times 7 =$ __7__
12. $56 / 7 =$ __8__
13. __9__ $\times 9 = 81$
14. __54__ $\div 9 = 6$
15. 3 __$\times 8$__ $= 24$

Solve.   *Show your work.*

16. Shawn sold 9 fundraiser tickets. Trina sold 3 times as many tickets as Shawn. How many tickets did Trina sell?
    27 tickets

17. A vendor sells 6 roses for $4. At that rate, what is the cost of 2 dozen roses? (1 dozen = 12)
    $16

18. Look at the shapes below.

    [shapes labeled A, G, D, F, E, C, B, H]

    Write the letters for the shapes that are quadrilaterals. A; E; F

120 UNIT 3 LESSON 18   Subtract Larger Numbers

Homework and Remembering page 120

Home or School Activity

 Social Studies Connection

Numbers in the News Have students find articles in newspapers, magazines, or on the Internet that contain large numbers. Ask them to bring in the articles. Have the class use them as a basis for practice with adding, subtracting, and using one operation to check an answer for the other operation.

> CENTERVILLE – The mayor reported that next year's budget will be $5,670,000. That will be an increase of $1,250,000 over this year's budget. . . .

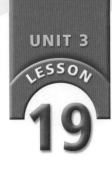

Estimate With Real-World Situations

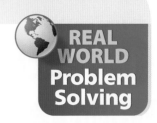

REAL WORLD **Problem Solving**

Lesson Objectives

- Solve money problems involving estimation and mental math.
- Solve multistep estimation problems, using data in a table.
- Write and solve addition and subtraction word problems with numbers to the millions.

Vocabulary
acre
estimate

The Day at a Glance

Today's Goals	Materials

1 Teaching the Lesson
A1: Use information in a table to solve money problems by estimation and mental math.
A2: Solve multistep word problems involving estimation, using the data in a table.
A3: Find and organize real-world data to use for word problems.
A4: Check large-number subtractions with and without a calculator.
 	
2 Going Further
▶ Problem Solving: Estimate or Exact Answer
▶ Differentiated Instruction
 	
3 Homework and Spiral Review
	Lesson Activities
	Student Activity Book pp. 171–173
	  or Student Hardcover Book
	  pp. 171–173
	Homework and Remembering
	  pp. 121–122
	Calculators (optional)
		Going Further
		Student Activity Book
		  p. 174 or Student
		  Hardcover Book
		  p. 174
		Activity Cards 3-19
		Index cards
		Math Journals

123 Use **Math Talk** today!

Keeping Skills Sharp

Quick Practice 5 MINUTES	Daily Routines
Goal: Subtract multi-digit numbers. **Find the Difference** Have the students write and solve this problem. 6,004,328 − 327,029 Note any students who have the wrong answer. Have the class discuss errors, how they might have been made, and how they could be fixed.	**Homework Review** Let students work together to check their work. Initially, pair less able students with more able students. Remind students to use what they know about helping others. **Place Value** Name a number 1,000 less than each of these numbers. 56,420 55,420 81,233 80,233 341,688 340,688 760,721 759,721

Teaching the Lesson

Estimate With Money

 15 MINUTES

Goal: Use information in a table to solve money problems by estimation and mental math.

Materials: Student Activity Book or Hardcover Book p. 171

✓ **NCTM Standards:**
Number and Operations
Communication
Problem Solving

English Language Learners

Write the word *supplies* on the board. Have students tell what they know about supplies.

- **Beginning** Say: **Supplies are things people need for something. People need these supplies for school.** Read each of the supplies, having students repeat after you.
- **Intermediate** Say: **Supplies are things people need for something.** Ask: **What do people need these supplies for?** school Ask students to identify some of the supplies listed.
- **Advanced** Have students work in pairs. One partner names a job or task. The other partner names supplies that someone might need in order to do it.

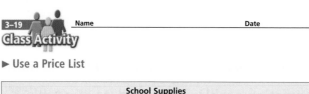

3–19 **Class Activity** Name ___ Date ___

▶ Use a Price List

School Supplies			
Pen	$0.19	Spiral notebook	$0.89
Pencil	$0.15	Loose-leaf paper (50 sheets)	$0.69
Colored markers (box of 8)	$1.49	Computer disk	$0.75
Pencil box	$0.70	Gym T-shirt	$3.50
Eraser	$0.15	Combination lock	$2.89

Answer each question. Explain your thinking.   *Show your work.*

1. Sylvia has $5.00 to buy a T-shirt. Will she have enough left to buy a box of markers?
   $5.00 − $3.50 = $1.50, and $1.50 is more than $1.49. She will have enough money left.

2. Bo has $4.00. How many computer disks can he buy?
   5 computer disks; Each disk costs less than $0.80.
   5 × $0.80 = $4.00, so 5 × $0.75 is less than $4.00.

3. Bilana has $4.00. She wants to buy a combination lock, pencil box, and a notebook. Does she have enough?
   no; $2.89 + $0.70 + $0.89 is more than $4.00.
   $2.89 is only $0.11 less than $3.00 and $0.70 + $0.89 is more than $1.50.

4. Joseph has $2.00. He wants to buy a pack of paper and 2 erasers. Can he also buy 5 ball-point pens?
   yes; Round $0.69 up to $0.70. The paper and erasers cost less than $1.00. Round $0.19 up to $0.20. Five pens cost less than $1.00.

5. Math Journal Use the price list to write two word problems.
   Word problems will vary.

UNIT 3 LESSON 19   Estimate With Real-World Situations **171**

Student Activity Book page 171

▶ Use a Price List WHOLE CLASS

Have the students examine and discuss the table at the top of Student Book page 171. Encourage students to make comparisons by asking questions such as:

- **What supplies cost the same or close to the same?** pencils and erasers are both $0.15; pencil boxes, loose-leaf paper, and computer disks are almost the same price

- **What costs the most?** gym T-shirt

- **What costs the least?** pencils and erasers

Use **Solve and Discuss** for problems 1–4.

Next, ask students to write one or more new problems based on the table that can be solved using mental math or estimation.

Activity 2

Estimate With Larger Numbers

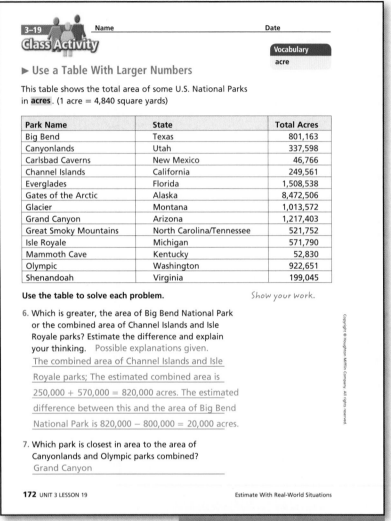

3–19

Class Activity

Name _____ Date _____

Vocabulary
acre

► **Use a Table With Larger Numbers**

This table shows the total area of some U.S. National Parks in **acres**. (1 acre = 4,840 square yards)

Park Name	State	Total Acres
Big Bend	Texas	801,163
Canyonlands	Utah	337,598
Carlsbad Caverns	New Mexico	46,766
Channel Islands	California	249,561
Everglades	Florida	1,508,538
Gates of the Arctic	Alaska	8,472,506
Glacier	Montana	1,013,572
Grand Canyon	Arizona	1,217,403
Great Smoky Mountains	North Carolina/Tennessee	521,752
Isle Royale	Michigan	571,790
Mammoth Cave	Kentucky	52,830
Olympic	Washington	922,651
Shenandoah	Virginia	199,045

Use the table to solve each problem.   *Show your work.*

6. Which is greater, the area of Big Bend National Park or the combined area of Channel Islands and Isle Royale parks? Estimate the difference and explain your thinking.   Possible explanations given.

   The combined area of Channel Islands and Isle
   Royale parks; The estimated combined area is
   250,000 + 570,000 = 820,000 acres. The estimated
   difference between this and the area of Big Bend
   National Park is 820,000 − 800,000 = 20,000 acres.

7. Which park is closest in area to the area of Canyonlands and Olympic parks combined?
   Grand Canyon

172 UNIT 3 LESSON 19   Estimate With Real-World Situations

Student Activity Book page 172

► Use a Table With Larger Numbers WHOLE CLASS

Direct students' attention to the table at the top of Student Book page 172. Discuss the listed information about U.S. National Parks. If some students have experiences visiting one or more of the parks, ask them to describe the size of the park as they remember it. If a U.S. map showing parks is available, you can point out the size of each park on the map. Encourage discussion by asking:

● What is the largest park in the table? Gates of the Arctic

● What is the smallest? Carlsbad Caverns

● An acre is 4,840 square yards. Can you describe a rectangle whose area is one acre? Possible answer: 10 yards wide and 484 yards long

Have the students discuss their strategies for solving problems 6–10.

15 MINUTES

Goal: Solve multistep word problems involving estimation, using the data in a table.

Materials: Student Activity Book or Hardcover Book pp. 172–173

 NCTM Standards:
Number and Operations
Communication

Teaching Note

Language and Vocabulary To give students an idea of the size of an acre, relate it to a football field or soccer field. The "in bounds" portion of a football field is 100 yards long and about 50 yards wide, so the area is about 5,000 square yards, or slightly more than one acre.

Differentiated Instruction

Advanced Learners If some students are seeking a challenge, pose the following problem: The area of an average house lot is about $\frac{1}{4}$ acre. About how many house lots this size would fit into the Gates of the Arctic National Park? Explain your answer.

Estimate With Real-World Situations **415**

Activity 3

Write Word Problems (optional)

 15 MINUTES

Goal: Find and organize real-world data to use for word problems.

Materials: Student Activity Book or Hardcover Book p. 173

 NCTM Standards:
Number and Operations
Communication
Connections
Problem Solving

Teaching Note

Math Background Students need to understand that mathematics is not an isolated subject. Whenever possible, use real-world connections to demonstrate to students the importance of using mathematics in various situations.

The Learning Classroom

Math Talk Aspire to make your classroom a place where all students listen to understand one another. Explain to students that this is different than just being quiet when someone else is talking. This involves thinking about what a person is saying so that you can contribute to the discussion and help with explanations.

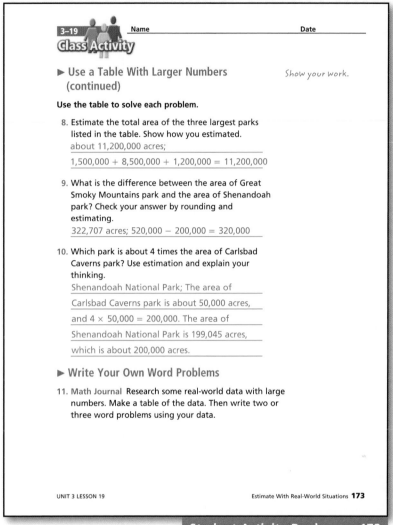

3–19
Class Activity
Name _____ Date _____

▶ Use a Table With Larger Numbers (continued)   *Show your work.*

Use the table to solve each problem.

8. Estimate the total area of the three largest parks listed in the table. Show how you estimated.
about 11,200,000 acres;
1,500,000 + 8,500,000 + 1,200,000 = 11,200,000

9. What is the difference between the area of Great Smoky Mountains park and the area of Shenandoah park? Check your answer by rounding and estimating.
322,707 acres; 520,000 − 200,000 = 320,000

10. Which park is about 4 times the area of Carlsbad Caverns park? Use estimation and explain your thinking.
Shenandoah National Park; The area of
Carlsbad Caverns park is about 50,000 acres,
and 4 × 50,000 = 200,000. The area of
Shenandoah National Park is 199,045 acres,
which is about 200,000 acres.

▶ Write Your Own Word Problems

11. Math Journal Research some real-world data with large numbers. Make a table of the data. Then write two or three word problems using your data.

UNIT 3 LESSON 19   Estimate With Real-World Situations **173**

Student Activity Book page 173

▶ Write Your Own Word Problems

WHOLE CLASS   **Math Talk**

To help students make a connection between this lesson and the real world, have them do the following:

● Find real-world data with large numbers, using any available reference sources.

● Make a table of their data and write several addition and subtraction problems using the data.

● Share their problems and solutions with the class.

Use Different Methods to Check for Reasonableness (optional)

▶ Use a Calculator to Check [WHOLE CLASS]

Select one or more of the large-number exercises listed below and write them on the board. Have the students solve the problems and check their answers, using a calculator.

53,642,198 − 7,693,258 = 45,948,940

61,672,849 − 6,829,364 = 54,843,485

79,390,426 − 7,036,824 = 72,353,602

25,756,293 − 486,910 = 25,269,383

69,482,504 − 8,691,046 = 60,791,458

68,493,025 − 8,409,182 = 60,083,843

Ask students how they could check if their answers are reasonable without using a calculator. Round and estimate.

Have students re-check their answers, without a calculator, using rounding and estimating.

▶ Use Estimation to Check

Discuss how to round larger numbers to check the exercises above.

Rounding to the Nearest Million Explain to students that when one number in an exercise is rounded to the nearest million, both numbers should be rounded to the nearest million.

● Which place will stay the same or change if we are rounding to the nearest million? millions place

● Which place tells us which way to round? the place to the right of the millions place, the hundred thousands place

● How do we round 7,693,258 to the nearest million? 8,000,000

● How do we round 53,642,198 to the nearest million? 54,000,000

● Ask students to estimate the difference. 46,000,000

Continue to estimate to check, using questions similar to those above. For exercise 4 above, some students may need help rounding 486,910 to the nearest million. Show that because 4 is less than 5, the number rounds to 0, and 26,000,000 − 0 = 26,000,000. Ask students if for this exercise the estimate would be more accurate if they round to hundred thousands. yes; 25,800,000 − 500,000 = 25,300,000

 15 MINUTES

Goal: Check large-number subtractions with and without a calculator.

Materials: calculators

 NCTM Standards:
Number and Operations
Communication
Connections

Teaching Note

Watch For! Calculators do not provide commas. Encourage students to write calculator results on paper and use commas to help them read what the number is.

 Ongoing Assessment

▶ What place value would you need to round to estimate the difference between 53,642,198 and 7,693,258?

▶ Explain why you chose that place value.

Going Further

Problem Solving: Estimate or Exact Answer?

Goal: Decide whether an exact or estimated answer is needed to solve a problem.

Materials: Student Activity Book or Hardcover Book p. 174

✔ **NCTM Standards:**
Number and Operations
Communication
Problem Solving

▶ Estimate or Exact Answer? WHOLE CLASS

Explain to the class that some problems require an exact answer, while other problems only need an estimate.

Ask students to give examples of real-world situations for which an estimate is useful. Ask students to give a problem example for each situation.

● time

● money

● distances

● shopping

Math Talk Have students look at Student Book page 174. Ask a student to read the directions aloud, and then read problem 1 together.

Give several students the opportunity to explain how they would decide the amount of change Miguel would receive. See if students can find different ways to solve this problem. Then work through the rest of the problems together as a class or with **Student Pairs** and **Solve and Discuss.**

As an extension, you may want to have students create challenging problems for partners to solve. Remind them that their problems can require either an estimate or an exact answer.

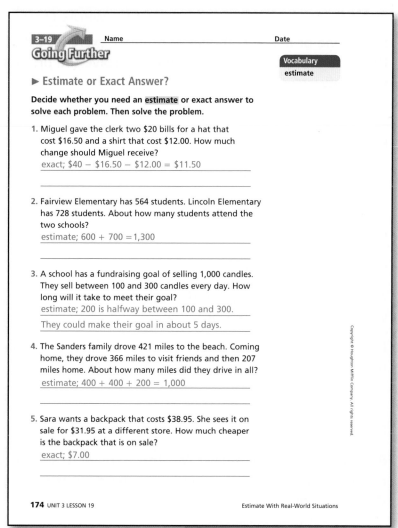

3-19
Going Further

Name _____ Date _____

Vocabulary
estimate

▶ **Estimate or Exact Answer?**

Decide whether you need an **estimate** or exact answer to solve each problem. Then solve the problem.

1. Miguel gave the clerk two $20 bills for a hat that cost $16.50 and a shirt that cost $12.00. How much change should Miguel receive?
   exact; $40 − $16.50 − $12.00 = $11.50

2. Fairview Elementary has 564 students. Lincoln Elementary has 728 students. About how many students attend the two schools?
   estimate; 600 + 700 = 1,300

3. A school has a fundraising goal of selling 1,000 candles. They sell between 100 and 300 candles every day. How long will it take to meet their goal?
   estimate; 200 is halfway between 100 and 300.
   They could make their goal in about 5 days.

4. The Sanders family drove 421 miles to the beach. Coming home, they drove 366 miles to visit friends and then 207 miles home. About how many miles did they drive in all?
   estimate; 400 + 400 + 200 = 1,000

5. Sara wants a backpack that costs $38.95. She sees it on sale for $31.95 at a different store. How much cheaper is the backpack that is on sale?
   exact; $7.00

174 UNIT 3 LESSON 19   Estimate With Real-World Situations

Student Activity Book page 174

Differentiated Instruction

Extra Help Some students may have difficulty determining whether an exact or estimated answer is required for problems that do not use the word *about.* Ask questions such as:

● Do you need to count the items, minutes, or money?

● If you estimate, will you have answered the question?

Differentiated Instruction

Intervention Activity Card 3-19

Round It! Activity Card 3-19 ●

Work: In Pairs

Use:
• 10 Index cards

1. Label a set of cards with the digits 0 to 9, using one digit on each card.

2. Shuffle the cards and place them face down. Choose 4 or 5 cards. Arrange them face up to make a number.

Caller says "hundreds."
Partner rounds number to 3,100.

3. Take turns. One partner calls out a place value. The other partner chooses the correct place value on the cards and then rounds to that place.

4. Repeat the activity for 10 numbers.

Unit 3, Lesson 19   Copyright © Houghton Mifflin Company

Activity Note If students are having difficulty with place value, have them create an oversized place-value chart to position the index cards.

 Math Writing Prompt

Explain Your Thinking Explain how to round a five-digit number to the hundreds place. Give an example.

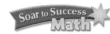 **Software Support**

Use *Soar to Success* for instruction of students needing targeted support for underlying skills.

On Level Activity Card 3-19

Find a Range Activity Card 3-19 ▲

Work: By Yourself

1. There is only one location in the United States where 4 states meet. It is called Four Corners. Data about the population of each state are given in the table below. Use the table to make estimates.

State	Estimated 2007 Population
Arizona	6,338,755
Colorado	4,861,515
New Mexico	1,969,915
Utah	3,645,330

2. Underestimate each population by rounding down to the millions place. Overestimate each population by rounding up to the next million.

3. The total population of the Four Corners states will fall within the range of estimates. What is the range of estimates? 14,000,000 to 18,000,000

Unit 3, Lesson 19   Copyright © Houghton Mifflin Company

Activity Note To make an underestimate, round the number in the rounding place down, regardless of the digit in the following place. To make an overestimate, round the same number up.

 Math Writing Prompt

Explain Your Reasoning Explain why estimating is helpful in real-world situations. Give an example.

 Software Support

Use *MegaMath* for review and reinforcement of the concepts and skills presented in this lesson.

Challenge Activity Card 3-19

Guess and Check Activity Card 3-19 ■

Work: In Pairs

Ticket	Price
Senior	$7.50
Other Adult	$11.25
Child	$6.50

1. On your own, use the information in the table to calculate the cost of 3 combinations of tickets. Then write a problem for each combination. An example is shown below.

> Adam bought 8 tickets for a total price of $73.00. How many of each ticket did Adam buy?   2 Senior, 4 Other Adult, 2 Child

2. Exchange problems with your partner, and use guess and check to solve each problem.

Unit 3, Lesson 19   Copyright © Houghton Mifflin Company

Activity Note Have students make an organized list with the following headings: *Number of Senior Tickets, Total Cost of Senior Tickets, Number of Other Adult Tickets, Total Cost of Other Adult Tickets, Number of Child Tickets,* and *Total Cost of Child Tickets.*

 Math Writing Prompt

Write a Problem Write your own Guess and Check problem. Exchange with another student.

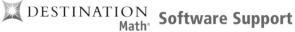 **Software Support**

Use *Destination Math* to take students beyond the concepts and skills presented in this lesson.

③ Homework and Spiral Review

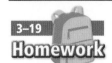

3-19
Homework **Goal:** Additional Practice

Use this Homework page to provide students with more practice, using data in tables to estimate and subtract.

3-19
Remembering **Goal:** Spiral Review

This Remembering activity would be appropriate anytime after today's lesson.

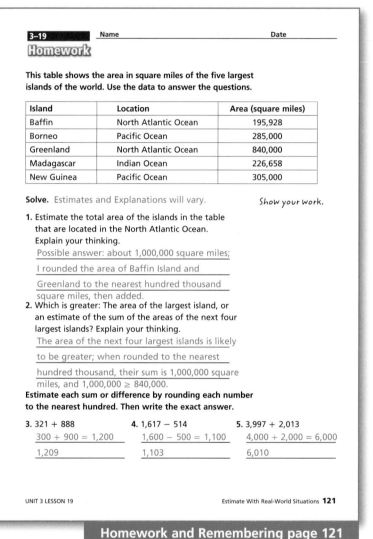

Homework and Remembering page 121

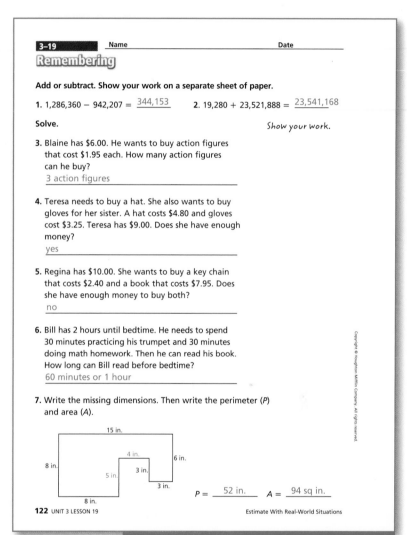

Homework and Remembering page 122

Home or School Activity

Social Studies Connection

Estimate Areas Have students find the land area (in square miles) of any 5 states of their choice. Tell students to organize the information in a list, and then write and answer comparison questions.

Sample questions:
- Which state has the greatest area when rounded to the nearest ten thousand?

- About how much more land area does Georgia have than Virginia?

Land Area of Some States	
State	Land Area (square miles)
Alaska	571,951
California	155,959
Georgia	57,906
Michigan	56,804
Virginia	39,594

420 UNIT 3 LESSON 19

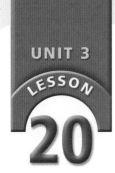

UNIT 3

LESSON

20

Problem Solving With Larger Numbers

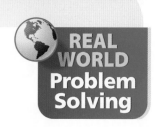

REAL WORLD **Problem Solving**

Lesson Objective

● Solve addition and subtraction word problems with larger numbers.

The Day at a Glance

Today's Goals	Materials	
① Teaching the Lesson **A1:** Using math drawings, devise and solve word problems. **A2:** Solve addition and subtraction word problems. **② Going Further** ▶ Differentiated Instruction **③ Homework and Spiral Review**	**Lesson Activities** Student Activity Book pp. 175–176 or Student Hardcover Book pp. 175–176 Homework and Remembering pp. 123–124 Quick Quiz 4 (Assessment Guide)	**Going Further** Activity Cards 3-20 Math Journals

123 *Use* **Math Talk** *today!*

Keeping Skills Sharp

Quick Practice ⏱ 5 MINUTES	Daily Routines
Goal: Compare multi-digit numbers. **Say, Write, and Compare** Use these numbers to have students compare multi-digit numbers. See Lesson 11. 1,438,419 1,483,419 64,583,684 64,583,791 1,483,419 1,438,419 64,583,791 64,583,684 482,661,787 428,661,787 687,156,866 687,165,866 428,661,787 482,661,787 687,165,866 687,156,866	**Homework Review** Send students to the board to show their solutions for problem 2. Have each student at the board explain his/her solution. Encourage the rest of the class to ask clarifying questions and make comments. **Strategy Problem** Gwen has 7 more tropical fish than Ramon has. Together they have 35 tropical fish. How many fish does each child have? Ramon 14 fish; Gwen 21 fish; $r + (r + 7) = 35$; $2r + 7 = 35$; $2r = 28$; $r = 14$; so $r = 7 = 21$.

35 fish		
r	r	7

Gwen's fish

Teaching the Lesson

Compose Word Problems

 15 MINUTES

Goal: Using math drawings, devise and solve word problems.

Materials: Student Activity Book or Hardcover Book p. 175

✔ **NCTM Standards:**
Number and Operations
Algebra
Communication

The Learning Classroom

Building Concepts To help students build coherence from one lesson to the next, remember to have students review and summarize concepts that they have learned in previous lessons. In this lesson, students may benefit from a review of the different kinds of addition and subtraction word problems with smaller numbers.

As an ongoing process, have students take turns summarizing the previous day's lesson at the beginning of math class. They can do this in one or two sentences. An alternative may be to have a student summarize at the end of the lesson. Either way, if you do this regularly, students will get used to making mental summaries of the math concepts discussed and will make the needed conceptual connections.

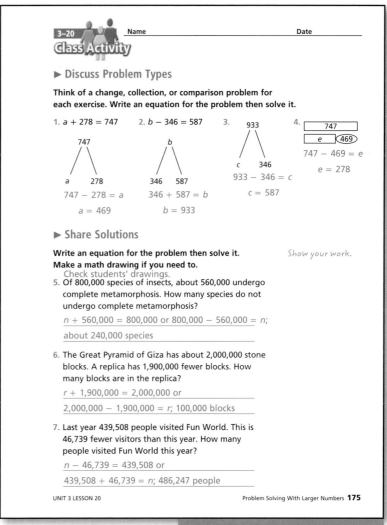

Student Activity Book page 175

▶ Discuss Problem Types WHOLE CLASS

Have the class devise word problems for exercises 1 and 2 on Student Book page 175. Review change problems for addition and subtraction if necessary.

Change Plus Problems involve a situation with an action that suggests addition. The original number increases to a larger number after the action takes place.

Change Minus Problems involve a situation with an action that suggests subtraction. The original number decreases to a smaller number after the action takes place.

On the board make break-apart addend drawings for exercises 1 and 2. Write solution equations for each one. Stress to the students the relationship between the total and the two addends. Students should write the equations on Student Book page 175.

Ask students to devise a collection and comparison problem for exercises 3 and 4. Next write and discuss the solution equations.

Collection Problems involve putting together (joining) or taking apart (separating) physically or conceptually. All of the objects are there from the beginning and in many cases, there is no action at all. The addends and the total are described in different ways.

Comparison Problems involve one quantity that is more or less than another quantity. The comparing statement has two key pieces of information. Who has *more*? (or Who has *fewer*?) and How many *more*? (or How many *fewer*?)

Situation Equations and Solution Equations Ask students to review the difference between situation equations and solution equations. With smaller numbers they might have been able to solve some difficult situation equations such as $a + 8 = 17$ by knowing the addends that make 17. But with the situation equations for exercises 1, 2, and 3, they now probably need to write solution equations or make a break-apart drawing to know what operation to do. Students do not have to write solution equations, but they can sometimes be helpful.

The Learning Classroom

Math Talk For lessons that require student interaction and discussion, take some time to review with the class about what makes a good explanation. You may want to refer to any class lists that the class previously developed. Items to be reviewed might include:

- Talk loud enough for others to hear.
- Explain your thinking.
- Say how you arrived at the answer, not just the answer.
- Allow other students to question your work.
- Have partners or group members help with the explanation.

English Language Learners

Write the words increase and decrease. Draw a diagram to illustrate the terms.

- **Beginning** Say: Increase means "get larger." When you add, you increase. Say: *Decrease* means "get smaller." When you subtract, you decrease. Have students repeat.
- **Intermediate** Ask: What does increase mean? get larger Do you increase when you add? yes What does decrease mean? get smaller. Do you decrease when you add? no
- **Advanced** Have students use short sentences to tell which operations are associated with *increase* and *decrease*.

Teaching the Lesson (continued)

Solve Word Problems

 20 MINUTES

Goal: Solve addition and subtraction word problems.

Materials: Student Activity Book or Hardcover Book pp. 175–176

 NCTM Standards:
Number and Operations
Algebra
Problem Solving

 Ongoing Assessment

Have students:

▶ describe the difference between a break-apart drawing and a comparison drawing.

▶ explain when you would use each type of drawing.

Quick Quiz

See Assessment Guide for Unit 3 Quick Quiz 4.

The Learning Classroom

Student Pairs Initially, it is useful to model pair activities for students by contrasting effective and ineffective helping. For example, students need to help partners solve a problem their way, rather than doing the work for the partner. **Helping Pairs** often foster learning in both students as the helper strives to adopt the perspective of the novice.

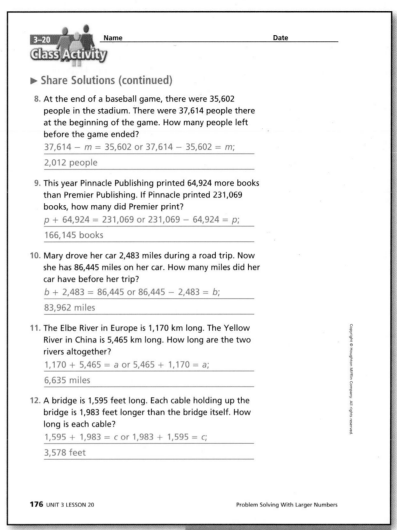

3–20 Class Activity Name _____ Date _____

▶ **Share Solutions** (continued)

8. At the end of a baseball game, there were 35,602 people in the stadium. There were 37,614 people there at the beginning of the game. How many people left before the game ended?

   $37{,}614 - m = 35{,}602$ or $37{,}614 - 35{,}602 = m;$

   2,012 people

9. This year Pinnacle Publishing printed 64,924 more books than Premier Publishing. If Pinnacle printed 231,069 books, how many did Premier print?

   $p + 64{,}924 = 231{,}069$ or $231{,}069 - 64{,}924 = p;$

   166,145 books

10. Mary drove her car 2,483 miles during a road trip. Now she has 86,445 miles on her car. How many miles did her car have before her trip?

    $b + 2{,}483 = 86{,}445$ or $86{,}445 - 2{,}483 = b;$

    83,962 miles

11. The Elbe River in Europe is 1,170 km long. The Yellow River in China is 5,465 km long. How long are the two rivers altogether?

    $1{,}170 + 5{,}465 = a$ or $5{,}465 + 1{,}170 = a;$

    6,635 miles

12. A bridge is 1,595 feet long. Each cable holding up the bridge is 1,983 feet longer than the bridge itself. How long is each cable?

    $1{,}595 + 1{,}983 = c$ or $1{,}983 + 1{,}595 = c;$

    3,578 feet

176 UNIT 3 LESSON 20   Problem Solving With Larger Numbers

Student Activity Book page 176

▶ **Share Solutions** SMALL GROUPS   Math Talk

Have students work in **Small Groups** or **Student Pairs** to solve problems 5–12 on Student Book pages 175–176.

● Ask students to retell the word problem in their own words and make a math drawing if they need to.

● They should discuss whether they need to find a total or an addend.

● Then have students write a solution equation and solve the problem.

● Finally, have students explain how they decided on their solution equations and share any math drawings they made.

After the groups have discussed the exercises, have several students explain why their answers make sense. Discuss different ways to check their computaton.

② Going Further

Intervention — Activity Card 3-20

Draw It! Say It! Solve It! Activity Card 3-20 ●

Work: By Yourself

1. Create a break-apart drawing with one part missing. An example is shown at the right.
2. Find the missing part of the drawing, and write 2 addition and 2 subtraction equations for the drawing.
3. Write a story about your drawing.

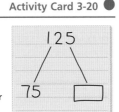

Unit 3, Lesson 20   Copyright © Houghton Mifflin Company

Activity Note Create a variation of the activity by having students create a comparison drawing with a blank and repeating the steps.

✎ Math Writing Prompt

Explain a Drawing Draw a diagram to show an addition or subtraction problem. Explain how the picture shows the problem.

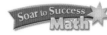 **Software Support**

Use *Soar to Success* for instruction of students needing targeted support for underlying skills.

On Level — Activity Card 3-20

Fill in the Blanks Activity Card 3-20 ▲

Work: In Small Groups

Decide:

Who will be Student 1 for the first round.

1. Copy the following break-apart drawing on a sheet of paper.
2. **Student 1:** Fill in the blanks to create a correct drawing without sharing it with your group.
3. Take turns asking one question at a time about the digits and their location in the drawing. Continue until someone recreates the same drawing.
4. Change roles, and repeat the activity with another drawing.

Unit 3, Lesson 20   Copyright © Houghton Mifflin Company

Activity Note Have students record how many questions they needed to solve each round of the game. Have them discuss what information is most helpful to solve the puzzle.

✎ Math Writing Prompt

Which Is Easier? Make a math drawing or write a situation equation. Then write a problem for the drawing or equation.

 Software Support

Use *MegaMath* for review and reinforcement of the concepts and skills presented in this lesson.

Challenge — Activity Card 3-20

What Did You Say? Activity Card 3-20 ■

Work: In Pairs

1. Write one addition word problem and one subtraction word problem, using the limited information given below.

   Yesterday 4,905 radio listeners called in to win a prize. Today ___,4___3 called in.

2. **Work Together** Find several possible answers by placing different digits in the blanks.
3. **Analyze** How many possible answers are there for each problem? Explain your answer. 90; there are 9 possible digits for the first blank and 10 possible digits for the second blank. 9 × 10 = 90.

Unit 3, Lesson 20   Copyright © Houghton Mifflin Company

Activity Note Students may repeat the activity by using their own incomplete word problem and sharing it with other pairs of students.

✎ Math Writing Prompt

Explain Another Way Explain subtraction, using the term *break-apart* or *ungrouping*. Then explain it without these words.

  Software Support

Use *Destination Math* to take students beyond the concepts and skills presented in this lesson.

③ Homework and Spiral Review

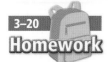
Use this Homework page to provide students with more practice with ungrouping with subtraction.

3–20
Remembering **Goal:** Spiral Review

This Remembering activity would be appropriate anytime after today's lesson.

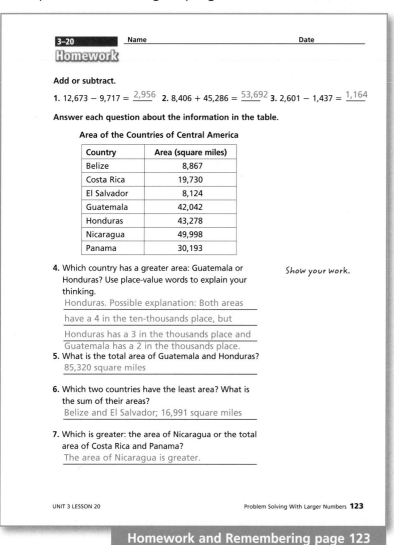

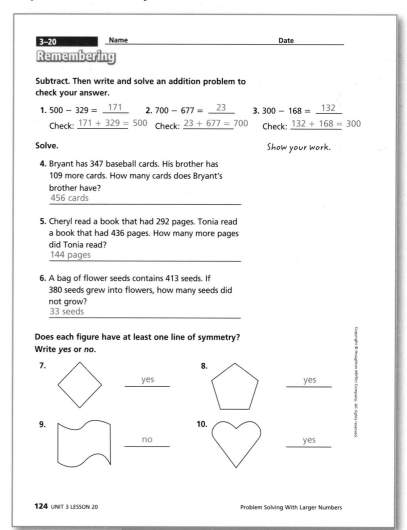

Home or School Activity

 Language Arts Connection

Comparisons Tell students the word *comparison* comes from the word *compare*. Have students explain what *comparison* means. They should use the word in three different sentences. Encourage them to use it in the context of math as well as other subjects.

Before I buy something, I always make a comparison between the prices at two different stores.

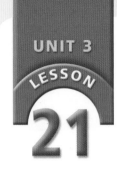

Use Mathematical Processes

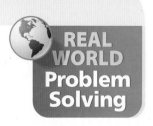

REAL WORLD Problem Solving

Lesson Objectives

• Solve a variety of problems, using mathematical processes and skills.

• Use the mathematical processes of problem solving, connections, reasoning and proof, communication, and representation.

The Day at a Glance

Today's Goals	Materials	

1 Teaching the Lesson
A1: Science Connections Use data from a table to make comparisons and draw conclusions.
A2: Representation Compare data from two bar graphs. Pose a question, and design a survey.
A3: Reasoning and Proof Use logical reasoning to solve a problem.
A4: Communication Suggest a scenario, and develop labels for a bar graph.
A5: Problem Solving Answer an open-ended question that has more than one correct response.
 	
2 Going Further
▶ Differentiated Instruction
 	
3 Homework and Spiral Review
	Lesson Activities
	Student Activity Book
	  pp. 177–178 or Student
	  Hardcover Book pp. 177–178
	Homework and Remembering
	  pp. 125–126
	Centimeter-Grid Paper
	  (TRB M60)
		Going Further
		Activity Cards 1-9
		Centimeter-Grid
		  Paper (TRB M60)
		Paper bag
		Small blocks or other
		  small obojects
		Math Journals

Use Math Talk today! 123

Keeping Skills Sharp

Quick Practice/Daily Routines	
No Quick Practice or Daily Routines are recommended. If you choose to do some, use activities that meet the needs of your class.	**Class Management** Use this lesson to provide more understanding of the NCTM process standards. Depending on how you choose to carry out the activities, this lesson may take two or more days of teaching.

Teaching the Lesson

Math and Science

 30 MINUTES

Goals: Use data from a table to make comparisons and draw conclusions.

Materials: Student Activity Book or Hardcover Book p. 177

✔ **NCTM Standards:**
Connections
Problem Solving
Communication

Name   Date

Class Activity

▶ **Math and Science**

T. rex "Sue" is the largest *T. rex* dinosaur skeleton ever found. You can see Sue at The Field Museum in Chicago. The table below shows data about Sue and some animals that live on Earth today.

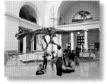

Name	Approximate Weight	Number of Teeth
T. Rex Sue	7 tons	58
Humpback whale	35–50 tons	0
African elephant	3–6 tons	24
Giant anteater	50–100 lb	0
Opossum	8–13 lb	50

1. Look at the data in the table. Is there is a relationship between the weight of the animals and the number of teeth they have? Use the data to support your answer.
No. Sample: The humpback whale weighs the most and has no teeth. Sue and an opossum are very different in size, but they have almost the same number of teeth.

2. Suppose you had a giant balance scale with a 35-ton humpback whale on one side. About how many dinosaurs the size of Sue would you have to put on the other side to balance the scale? Explain how you got your answer.
5 dinosaurs; Sample: I divided the whale's weight by Sue's weight. 35 ÷ 7 = 5.

3. Write a question that can be answered by using the data in the table. Provide the answer to the question.
Sample: An opossum has about twice as many teeth as which animal? Answer: an elephant; 50 ÷ 2 = 25

UNIT 3 LESSON 21   Use Mathematical Processes **177**

Student Activity Book page 177

Teaching Note

Technology Students may want to do research on the Internet to find the weight and number of teeth for different animals. Have students tell if their findings support or refute their original opinion.

▶ **Discuss the Data**   Math Talk

Task 1 Begin this activity with a whole-class discussion of the introductory information on Student Book page 177. Make sure students understand that the weights shown are in different units and that 1 U. S. ton = 2,000 pounds. Have students answer the question independently. Then ask:

▶ How did you support your answer about the relationship between the weight of the animals and the number of teeth they have? Answers will vary. Allow students to share their arguments.

▶ Tell students that the average weight for an adult person in the United States is 163–190 pounds, and that adults have 28 teeth, excluding wisdom teeth. Does this information support or contradict your answer to exercise 1? Supports because this is close to the number of teeth an elephant has.

▶ Use the Data to Answer a Question

Task 2 Be certain that students understand the concept of a balance scale before answering exercise 2.

▶ How did you figure out how many *T. Rex* dinosaurs it would take to balance the humpback whale? Allow students to share their ideas.

▶ Use the Data to Formulate a Question

Task 3 As a whole class, write a question that can be answered by using the data from the table. Then have **Student Pairs** work together to write two more questions.

Have pairs share their questions with the class, or have pairs exchange and answer each other's questions.

Comparing Sets of Data From a Survey

 45 MINUTES

Goals: Compare data from two bar graphs. Design a survey.

Materials: Student Activity Book or Hardcover Book p. 178, Centimeter-Grid Paper (TRB M60)

 NCTM Standards:
Communication   Representation

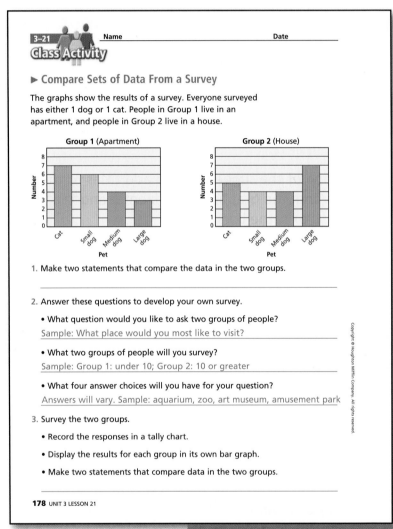

Student Activity Book page 178

▶ Compare Sets of Data From a Survey

Task 1 Begin with a whole-class discussion of the bar graphs shown on Student Book page 178. Ask questions to be certain that students understand the situation represented.

▶ **How many groups and how many people were surveyed?** 2 groups of 20 people each

▶ **What is the difference between the 2 groups?** Group 1 live in an apartment; Group 2 live in a house.

▶ **What do you think the question could have been?** Possible answer: Which of the following do you have: cat, small dog, medium dog, large dog?

As a class, develop one statement that compares the data in the two groups. Then have **Student Pairs** work together to answer question 1.

▶ Develop a Survey

Task 2 Conduct a whole-class discussion that focuses on developing a survey question and answer choices that can be asked of two different groups of people at school.

▶ **What question would you like to ask in a survey?** Discuss various questions posed.

▶ **What answer choices will you include?** Brainstorm answers to a suggested question.

Have **Student Pairs** work together on exercise 2.

▶ Make a Survey and Graph the Data

Task 3 Have the same pairs make their survey. Then have each student graph the data for one group. Discussion could include the following:

▶ Was the answer chosen most (or least) frequently the same for both groups?

▶ Were you surprised at the results? Explain why or why not.

English Language Learners

Write *survey* on the board. Say: **When we do a *survey* we ask a group of people the same questions as on page 178.**

• **Beginning** Ask: **Do all the people live in a house?** no **Do they all have a pet?** yes

• **Intermediate and Advanced** Ask: **What do all the people in the *survey* have?** a pet

Activity 3

Mystery Numbers

 15 MINUTES

Goal: Use logical reasoning to solve a problem.

 NCTM Standards:
Reasoning and Proof   Problem Solving

Place the numbers 3, 4, and 8 in the shapes below so that the number sentence is true. The same number goes in both squares. square = 4, triangle = 8, circle = 3

$$\frac{\square + \triangle}{\square} = \bigcirc$$

Reasoning and Proof

On the board, write the numbers and draw the equation. Be certain that students understand that one number will be used twice and that it goes in both squares.

▶ What number is least likely to go in the square? Lead students to see that since division is involved, it is unlikely that 8 goes in the square.

Have students work with a **Helping Partner** to place the numbers and prove the answer.

▶ Have students use the same equation but place the numbers 2, 8, and 5. $(2 + 8) \div 2 = 5$

Activity 4

What Could this Graph Communicate?

 15 MINUTES

Goal: Suggest a scenario, and develop labels for a bar graph.

 NCTM Standards:
Communication   Representation

Draw a bar graph with a scale of 0, 5, 10, 15, 20 and 25 on the board. Include bars that measure 15, 5, and 20. Do not include any labels on the graph. Ask students what the graph might represent.

Communication

Discuss the scale on the graph with the class.

▶ What might you communicate to someone by using this graph? Possible answer: The value of different numbers of nickels, anything that is in sets of five

Use one of the suggestions to add titles to the following: the graph, the horizontal and the vertical axis, the bars.

Activity 5

How Many Ways Can You Spend $8.00?

 15 MINUTES

Goal: Answer an open-ended question that has more than one correct response.

 NCTM Standards:
Problem Solving   Communication

Bring in a menu from a restaurant. Have **Student Pairs** decide what they can order if they have $8.00 to spend. Students should list the items and the prices and show the total amount they will spend.

Problem Solving

Have students share their lists and permit others to ask clarifying questions. Make a list of all the "correct" answers.

Then try the following.

▶ Find the greatest number of items you can order and still spend only $8.00. Constraint: You cannot order more than two of any item. Allow pairs of students to develop a new list of items.

Have students share their second list.

② Going Further

Intervention — Activity Card 3-21

Make a Bar Graph   Activity Card 3-21 ●

Work: By Yourself

Use:
• Centimeter-Grid Paper (TRB M60)

1. The graph shows the number of four different shapes that Janet used to make a design.

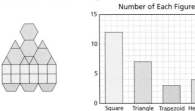

Number of Each Figure

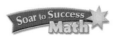

2. Ramon made a design that used 6 squares, 14 triangles, 2 trapezoids, and 2 hexagons.

3. Make a bar graph that shows the figures that Ramon used. Use Janet's bar graph as a model.

Unit 3, Lesson 21   Copyright © Houghton Mifflin Company

Activity Note Be sure students understand how to read the heights of the bars on the graph. Check that students graphs of the shapes Ramon used have the same scale as the graph shown.

 Math Writing Prompt

Write a Comparison Did Ramon use more or fewer squares than Janet used? Write a sentence that compares the number of squares.

Soar to Success Math ★ **Software Support**

Use *Soar to Success* for instruction of students needing targeted support for underlying skills.

On Level — Activity Card 3-21

Pick 15   Activity Card 3-21 ▲

Work: In Pairs

Use:
• Centimeter-Grid Paper (TRB M60)
• Paper bag with 4 colors of small blocks (or other small objects), about 5 of each color

1. One partner takes 15 blocks from the bag without looking and records the colors picked. Then the partner returns the blocks to the bag.

2. The second partner repeats step 1.

3. **Work Together** Plan a bar graph to display the colors taken from the bag.

4. Each partner makes a bar graph that shows the number of blocks of each color he or she picked.

Unit 3, Lesson 21   Copyright © Houghton Mifflin Company

Activity Note Be certain that students understand that their graphs should be the same except for the data.

 Math Writing Prompt

Explain the Scale What scale did you use on your graph? Explain how you decided on what scale to use.

MegaMath Grades K-6 **Software Support**

Use *MegaMath* for review and reinforcement of the concepts and skills presented in this lesson.

Challenge — Activity Card 3-21

Favorite Muffins   Activity Card 3-21 ■

Work: In Pairs

Use:
• Centimeter-Grid Paper (TRB M60)

1. The table shows the results of a survey about favorite muffins.

Flavor	Banana	Blueberry	Carrot-Raisin	Oatmeal
Number of People	4	6	8	2

2. Display the data on a bar graph.

3. Make up a new set of data for the same survey. Be certain to include the same number of entries in your new data set.

4. On a second graph, graph the new data set.

Unit 3, Lesson 21   Copyright © Houghton Mifflin Company

Activity Note Be certain that students understand that their graphs should be the same except for the data and should reflect 20 people surveyed.

 Math Writing Prompt

What's the Question What question might the people in the survey have been asked? Write a question that someone can answer by using the information in *both* graphs.

 DESTINATION Math **Software Support**

Use *Destination Math* to take students beyond the concepts and skills presented in this lesson.

③ Homework and Spiral Review

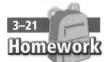

3–21 Homework **Goal:** Additional Practice

Include student's completed Homework page 125 as part of their portfolios.

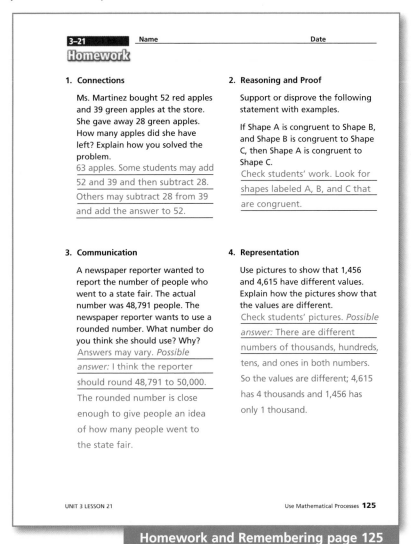

3–21 **Homework**   Name   Date

1. Connections

Ms. Martinez bought 52 red apples and 39 green apples at the store. She gave away 28 green apples. How many apples did she have left? Explain how you solved the problem.

63 apples. Some students may add 52 and 39 and then subtract 28. Others may subtract 28 from 39 and add the answer to 52.

2. Reasoning and Proof

Support or disprove the following statement with examples.

If Shape A is congruent to Shape B, and Shape B is congruent to Shape C, then Shape A is congruent to Shape C.

Check students' work. Look for shapes labeled A, B, and C that are congruent.

3. Communication

A newspaper reporter wanted to report the number of people who went to a state fair. The actual number was 48,791 people. The newspaper reporter wants to use a rounded number. What number do you think she should use? Why?

Answers may vary. *Possible answer:* I think the reporter should round 48,791 to 50,000. The rounded number is close enough to give people an idea of how many people went to the state fair.

4. Representation

Use pictures to show that 1,456 and 4,615 have different values. Explain how the pictures show that the values are different.

Check students' pictures. *Possible answer:* There are different numbers of thousands, hundreds, tens, and ones in both numbers. So the values are different; 4,615 has 4 thousands and 1,456 has only 1 thousand.

UNIT 3 LESSON 21   Use Mathematical Processes **125**

Homework and Remembering page 125

3–21 Remembering **Goal:** Spiral Review

This Remembering page would be appropriate anytime after today's lesson.

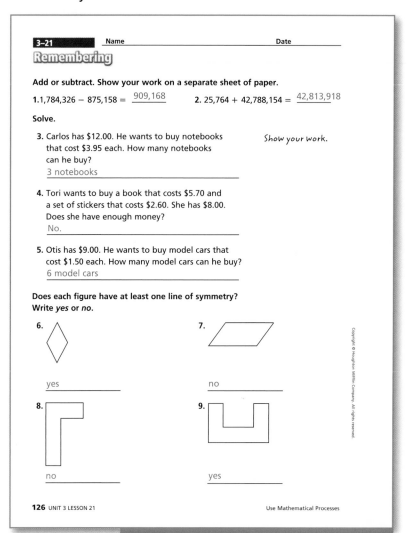

3–21 **Remembering**   Name   Date

Add or subtract. Show your work on a separate sheet of paper.

1. $1,784,326 - 875,158 =$ ___909,168___   2. $25,764 + 42,788,154 =$ ___42,813,918___

Solve.

3. Carlos has $12.00. He wants to buy notebooks that cost $3.95 each. How many notebooks can he buy?

    3 notebooks   *Show your work.*

4. Tori wants to buy a book that costs $5.70 and a set of stickers that costs $2.60. She has $8.00. Does she have enough money?

    No.

5. Otis has $9.00. He wants to buy model cars that cost $1.50 each. How many model cars can he buy?

    6 model cars

Does each figure have at least one line of symmetry? Write *yes* or *no*.

6.   7.

   yes   no

8.   9.

   no   yes

126 UNIT 3 LESSON 21   Use Mathematical Processes

Homework and Remembering page 126

Home or School Activity

Language Arts Connection

Graphs With Large Numbers Show students how the scale on a bar graph, such as the one on the right, can reflect a large number without writing out all of the digits in the number. For example, the number 15 on the scale of this graph means 15,000,000.

Have students find examples of this type of scale in a magazine, the newspaper or on the Internet. Ask students to show what quantity the numbers actually represent.

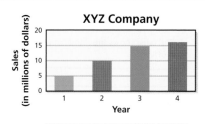

Number	Quantity
5	5,000,000
10	10,000,000
15	15,000,000
20	20,000,000

Each number means millions

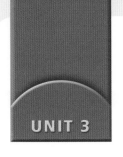

Unit Review and Test

Lesson Objective

● **Assess student progress on unit objectives.**

The Day at a Glance

Today's Goals	Materials
1 **Assessing the Unit** ► Assess student progress on unit objectives. ► Use activities from unit lessons to reteach content. **2** **Extending the Assessment** ► Use remediation for common errors. There is no homework assignment on a test day.	Unit 3 Test, Student Activity Book or Student Hardcover Book pp. 179–180 Unit 3 Test, Form A or B, Assessment Guide (optional) Unit 3 Performance Assessment, Assessment Guide (optional)

Keeping Skills Sharp

Quick Practice ⏱ 5 MINUTES	
Goal: Review any skills you choose to meet the needs of your class. If you are doing a unit review day, use any of the Quick Practice activities that provide support for your class. If this is a test day, omit Quick Practice.	**Review and Test Day** You may want to choose a quiet game or other activity (reading a book or working on homework for another subject) for students who finish early.

Assess Unit Objectives

⏱ **45 MINUTES** (more if schedule permits)

Goal: Assess student progress on unit objectives.

Materials: Student Activity Book or Hardcover Book pp. 179–180; Assessment Guide (optional)

▶ Review and Assessment

If your students are ready for assessment on the unit objectives, you may use either the test on the Student Book pages or one of the forms of the Unit 3 Test in the Assessment Guide to assess student progress.

If you feel that students need some review first, you may use the test on the Student Book pages as a review of unit content, and then use one of the forms of the Unit 3 Test in the Assessment Guide to assess student progress.

To assign a numerical score for all of these test forms, use 5 points for each question.

You may also choose to use the Unit 3 Performance Assessment. Scoring for that assessment can be found in its rubric in the Assessment Guide.

▶ Reteaching Resources

The chart at the right lists the test items, the unit objectives they cover, and the lesson activities in which the objective is covered in this unit. You may revisit these activities with students who do not show mastery of the objectives.

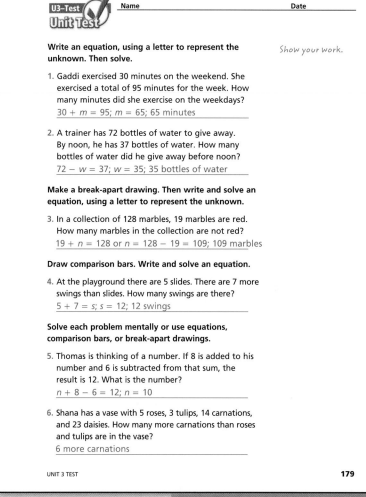

Student Activity Book page 179

Unit Test Items	Unit Objectives Tested	Activities to Use for Reteaching
1–6	**3.1** Solve a variety of problems involving addition and subtraction.	Lesson 1, Activity 3 Lesson 2, Activities 1–2 Lesson 3, Activities 1–2 Lesson 4, Activities 1–2 Lesson 5, Activities 1–2 Lesson 6, Activity 2 Lesson 20, Activities 1–2 Lesson 21, Activity 5
7–10	**3.2** Read, write, and identify the place value of numbers to millions.	Lesson 7, Activities 1–3 Lesson 10, Activities 1–2

Student Activity Book page 180

U3–Test
Unit Test

Name _____ Date _____

Write the value of the underlined digit.

7. 59,803 _8 hundreds_

8. 8,774,002 _7 ten thousands_

Write each number in standard form.

9. seventy-five thousand, four hundred eight
   75,408

10. five million, sixty-nine thousand, seven hundred thirty-six
    5,069,736

Write >, <, or = to make each statement true.

11. 45,907 _>_ 45,799   12. 728,925 _<_ 729,825

Round to the nearest hundred.

13. 8,659 _8,700_

Round to the nearest thousand.

14. 37,808 _38,000_

Copy each exercise, lining up the places correctly. Then add or subtract.

15. 1,472 + 5,178 = _6,650_   16. 25,097 + 57,336 = _82,433_

17. 6,824 − 3,731 = _3,093_   18. 57,875 − 43,088 = _14,787_

19. 50,000 − 31,602 = _18,398_

20. **Extended Response** Determine whether the following statement is true or false. Explain your thinking.

    6,421 − (284 + 653) = (6,421 − 284) + 653
    false; 6,421 − (284 + 653) = 5,484;
    (6,421 − 284) + 653 = 6,790; 5,484 ≠ 6,790

    * Item 20 also assesses the process skills of Communication and Reasoning and Proof.

180 UNIT 3 TEST

Unit Test Items	Unit Objectives Tested	Activities to Use for Reteaching
11–14	**3.3** Compare, order, and round numbers and estimate sums and differences.	Lesson 8, Activity 2 Lesson 9, Activity 1 Lesson 13, Activity 1 Lesson 18, Activity 2 Lesson 19, Activity 1
15–20	**3.4** Add and subtract whole numbers.	Lesson 11, Activity 1 Lesson 12, Activity 1 Lesson 14, Activities 1–2 Lesson 15, Activity 1 Lesson 16, Activity 1 Lesson 17, Activity 1 Lesson 18, Activity 1

▶ Assessment Guide Resources

Free Response Tests
Unit 3 Test, Student Activity Book or Hardcover Book pp. 179–180
Unit 3 Test, Form A, Assessment Guide

Extended Response Item
The last item in the Student Book test and in the Form A test will require an extended response as an answer.

Multiple Choice Test
Unit 3 Test, Form B, Assessment Guide

Performance Assessment
Unit 3 Performance Assessment, Assessment Guide
Unit 3 Performance Assessment Rubric, Assessment Guide

▶ Portfolio Assessment

Teacher-selected Items for Student Portfolios:

- Homework, Lessons 2, 4, 7, 10, 15, and 21

- Class Activity work, Lessons 3, 4, 10, 14, 18, and 21.

Student-selected Items for Student Portfolios:

- Favorite Home or School Activity

- Best Writing Prompt

② Extending the Assessment

Unit Objective 3.1

Solve a variety of problems involving addition and subtraction.

Common Error: Does Not Regroup Correctly

Remediation Give students an opportunity to act out the operation in each place by using place-value drawings. Working in pairs, have one student draw and explain each ungrouping step and then the **Helping Partner** writes and explains the numeric ungrouping.

If needed, introduce alternative algorithms such as decomposing and composing numbers.

$$43 = 40 + 3 \qquad 43 = 30 + 13$$
$$-16 = 10 + 6 \qquad -16 = 10 + 6$$

Unit Objective 3.2

Read, write, and identify the place value of numbers to millions.

Common Error: Omits Zeros

Remediation When students are asked to change the word form of a number to standard form, they may sometimes omit one or more zeros. Use the Secret Code Cards from TRB M145–M146 to help students see how zeros work.

Unit Objective 3.3

Compare, order, and round numbers and estimate sums and differences.

Common Error: Rounds to an Incorrect Place

Remediation Students may confuse the place to be rounded with the place that is used to decide which number to round. Have students underline the place to be rounded. Then have them look to the right of the place and decide whether to round up or down.

For example, to round 7,359 to the nearest hundred:

Underline the hundreds place.

Look at the place to the right of the hundreds place.

Then follow conventional rounding rules.

Unit Objective 3.4

Add and subtract whole numbers.

Common Error: Incorrect Alignment

Remediation Ascertain whether a student's alignment errors are careless or conceptual. Remediate the former by asking the student to be more careful. With special-needs students, have them work on paper with vertical lines to help them make columns. Or have them use grid paper, which provides rows and columns. Remediate lack of conceptual understanding by having the students make math drawings for the problems to see which numbers they need to add to which.

Unit 4   Overview

Angles and Polygons

THIS UNIT INTRODUCES measuring angles, using a protractor. Students use these concepts to sort and classify angles and triangles. Concepts involving angles are applied in rotations and in rotational symmetry. Concepts involving perimeter and area are extended to include perimeter of any polygon and area of triangles. Concepts involving patterns and congruence are applied as students explore transformations.

Skills Trace

Grade 3	Grade 4	Grade 5
• Use reasoning to determine the measure of an angle that is a multiple of 10°.	• Use protractor to determine the measure of an angle that is a multiple of 10°.	• Use a protractor to determine the measure of any angle.
• Classify triangles by their angles and sides.	• Classify triangles by their angles and sides.	• Classify triangles by their angles and sides.
• Identify two-dimensional figures with line symmetry.	• Identify two-dimensional figures with line and rotational symmetry.	• Identify two- and three-dimensional figures with line and rotational symmetry.
• Derive formulas and find the perimeter of quadrilaterals and triangles.	• Use formulas to find the perimeter of polygons.	• Use formulas to find the perimeter of polygons; find the circumference of a circle.
• Derive formulas and find the area of rectangles and squares.	• Derive formulas and find the area of rectangles, parallelograms, and triangles.	• Derive formulas and find the area of polygons and circles.
• Identify and use translations, reflections, and rotations to extend patterns.	• Identify and use translations, reflections, and rotations to verify congruence and extend patterns.	• Identify and draw translations, reflections, and rotations on a coordinate grid.

Angles and Polygons   **437A**

Unit 4 Contents

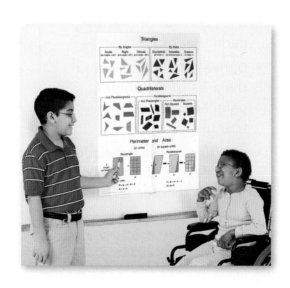

Unit 4   Assessment

Unit Objectives Tested	Unit Test Items	Lessons
4.1 Classify triangles by their angles and sides.	1–5	1, 3, 4
4.2 Identify figures with rotational symmetry.	6	2
4.3 Find the perimeter and area of polygons.	7, 9–10	5, 6
4.4 Identify translations, reflections, and rotations.	8	7

Assessment and Review Resources

Formal Assessment

Student Activity Book
- Unit Review and Test (pp. 215–216)

Assessment Guide
- Quick Quiz 1
- Quick Quiz 2
- Quick Quiz 3
- Test A–Open Response
- Test B–Multiple Choice
- Performance Assessment

Test Generator CD-ROM
- Open Response Test
- Multiple Choice Test
- Test Bank Items

Informal Assessment

Teacher Edition
- Ongoing Assessment (in every lesson)
- Quick Practice (in every lesson)
- Math Talk (in every lesson)
- Portfolio Suggestions (pp. 454, 462, 470, 478, 486, 494)

Math Talk
- ▸ Math Talk in Action (pp. 459, 475)
- ▸ Activities (pp. 440, 444, 450, 451, 456, 465, 480, 492)
- ▸ Solve and Discuss (p. 451)
- ▸ Small Groups (pp. 439, 442, 443, 452, 458, 459, 460, 467, 475, 476, 484, 491, 492)
- ▸ Helping Partners (pp. 449, 467, 488, 492)
- ▸ Student Pairs (pp. 439, 481, 490, 491)
- ▸ Scenarios (p. 448)

Review Opportunities

Homework and Remembering
- Review of recently taught topics
- Cumulative Review

Teacher Edition
- Unit Review and Test (pp. 495–498)

Test Generator CD-ROM
- Custom review sheets

Planning Unit 4

NCTM Standards Key: 1. Number and Operations 2. Algebra 3. Geometry
4. Measurement 5. Data Analysis and Probability 6. Problem Solving
7. Reasoning and Proof 8. Communication 9. Connections 10. Representation

Lesson/NCTM Standards	Resources	Materials for Lesson Activities	Materials for Going Further
4–1 **Naming and Measuring Angles** NCTM Standards: 3, 4, 7	TE pp. 437–446 SAB pp. 181–188 H&R pp. 127–128 AC 4-1	Protractor (TRB M125) Naming and Measuring Angles (TRB M126) Pencils, scissors, scrap paper 8 1/2-inch square of paper ✓ Geometry and Measurement Poster	Math Journals
4–2 **Rotations and Rotational Symmetry** NCTM Standard: 3	TE pp. 447–454 SAB pp. 189–190 H&R pp. 129–130 AG Quick Quiz 1 AC 4-2	Rotations and Rotational Symmetry (TRB M127) Large sheet of paper or poster board (optional) Scissors (optional)	Grid paper Protractor Math Journals
4–3 **Name Triangles** NCTM Standard: 3	TE pp. 455–462 SAB pp. 191–196 H&R pp. 131–132 AC 4-3		Scissors, glue Triangles (TRB M54) Centimeter ruler Strips of paper Math Journals
4–4 **Triangles and Diagonals** NCTM Standards: 3, 6, 7	TE pp. 463–470 SAB pp. 197–200 H&R pp. 133–134 AC 4-4	Triangles and Diagonals (TRB M55) Transparency of Triangles and Diagonals (TRB M55) and overhead projector (optional) Scissors Glue	Dots and Paths (TRB M128) transparency Geoboards or Geoboard/Dot Paper (TRB M56) Colored rubber bands Grid paper Math Journals
4–5 **Perimeter and Area of Triangles** NCTM Standard: 3	TE pp. 471–478 SAB pp. 201–204 H&R pp. 135–136 AC 4-5	Perimeter and Area of Triangles (TRB M57) Centimeter rulers	Grid paper Scissors Centimeter rulers Math Journals
4–6 **Polygons** NCTM Standards: 3, 4	TE pp. 479–486 SAB pp. 205–208 H&R pp. 137–138 AG Quick Quiz 2 AC 4-6	Make Polygons (TRB M75) Find the Perimeter of Regular Polygons (TRB M76) Scissors	Pattern blocks or Pattern Blocks (TRB M77) Straightedge or ruler Math Journals
4–7 **Transformations** NCTM Standards: 3, 6, 7	TE pp. 487–494 SAB pp. 209–214 H&R pp. 139–140 AG Quick Quiz 3 AC 4-7	Exploring Transformations (TRB M129) Mirror (optional)	Grid paper Pattern blocks or Pattern Blocks (TRB M77) Math Journals
Unit Review and Test	TE pp. 495–498 SAB pp. 215–216 AG Unit 4 test		

Resources/Materials Key: TE: Teacher Edition   SAB: Student Activity Book   H&R: Homework and Remembering
AC: Activity Cards   MCC: Math Center Challenge   AG: Assessment Guide   ✓: Grade 4 Kit   TRB: Teacher's Resource Book

Hardcover Student Book

- Together, the hardcover student book and its companion Activity Workbook contain all of the pages in the consumable Student Activity Workbook.

Manipulatives and Materials

- Essential materials for teaching Math Expressions are available in the Grade 4 kit. These materials are indicated by a ✓ in these lists. At the front of this Teacher Edition is more information about kit contents, alternatives for the materials, and use of the materials.

Unit 4 Teaching Resources

Differentiated Instruction

Individualizing Instruction		
	Level	Frequency
Activities	• Intervention • On Level • Challenge	All 3 in every lesson
	Level	Frequency
Math Writing Prompts	• Intervention • On Level • Challenge	All 3 in every lesson
Math Center Challenges	For advanced students	
	4 in every unit	

Reaching All Learners		
English Language Learners	Lessons	Pages
	1, 2, 3, 4, 5, 6, 7	437, 447, 455, 463, 471, 479, 487
Extra Help	Lessons	Pages
	2, 5, 6	451, 473, 480
Advanced Learners	Lessons	Pages
	1, 4, 7	442, 467, 491, 492

Strategies for English Language Learners

Present this problem to all students. Offer the different levels of support to meet students' levels of language proficiency.

Objective Identify quadrilaterals and their angles

Problem Show a square, rhombus, trapezoid, parallelogram, and rectangle. Ask: **How many sides are there? Angles? What figures have 4 sides and angles? What kind of figures are these?**

Newcomer

• Say the name of each figure, and have students repeat. Say: **These figures are quadrilaterals. Quadrilaterals have 4 sides and angles.** Have students repeat.

Beginning

• Guide students to name each figure. Say: **Each figure has 4 sides and 4 angles. Figures with 4 sides and 4 angles are quadrilaterals.** Have students repeat.

Intermediate

• Have students identify each figure. Ask: **How many sides and angles are in a quadrilateral?** 4 **Are these all quadrilaterals?** yes

Advanced

• Have students name the different types of quadrilaterals and describe how to tell whether a figure is a quadrilateral.

Connections

 Art Connection
Lesson 6, page 486

 Social Studies Connection
Lesson 4, page 470

 Math-to-Math Connection
Lesson 2, page 454

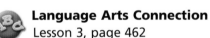 **Language Arts Connection**
Lesson 3, page 462

 Real-World Connections
Lesson 5, page 478
Lesson 7, page 494

Independent Learning Activities

Ready-Made Math Challenge Centers

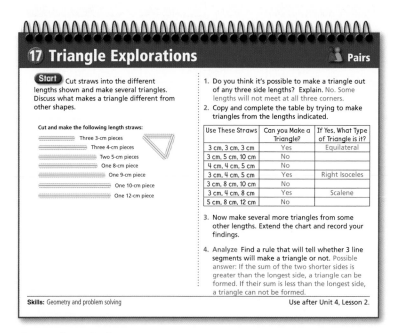

Grouping Pairs

Materials straws (or thin strips of paper), scissors

Objective Students learn that not just any three line segments can form a triangle.

Connections Geometry and Measurement

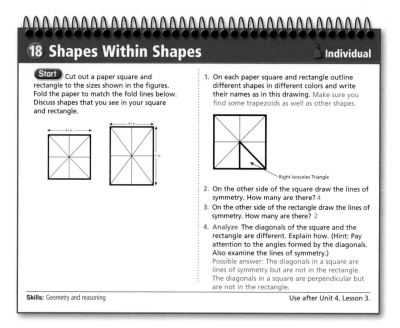

Grouping Individuals

Materials ruler, crayons or markers, scissors

Objective Students deepen their visualization skills and examine differences in squares and rectangles.

Connections Geometry and Reasoning

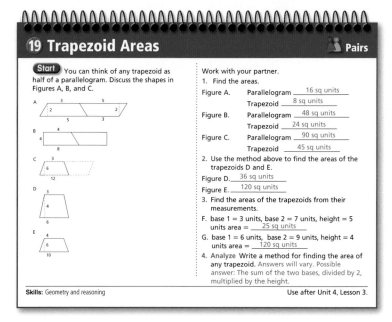

Grouping Pairs

Materials Grid paper (optional)

Objective Students use their knowledge of parallelogram and triangle areas to find the areas of trapezoids.

Connections Geometry and Reasoning

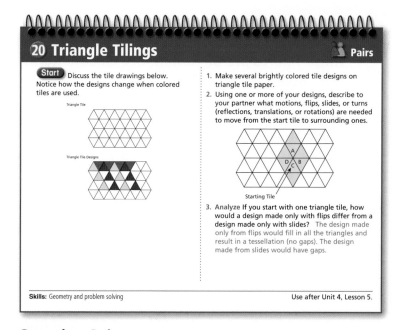

Grouping Pairs

Materials Paper and pencil, crayons or markers

Objective Students informally explore tessellations.

Connections Geometry, Real Word

Ready-Made Math Resources

Technology — Tutorials, Practice, and Intervention

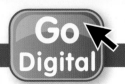

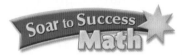

Use activity masters and online, individualized intervention and support to bring students to proficiency.

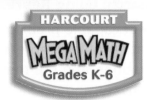

Help students practice skills and apply concepts through exciting math adventures.

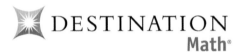

Extend and enrich students' understanding of skills and concepts through engaging, interactive lessons and activities.

Visit **Education Place**
www.eduplace.com

Visit www.eduplace.com/mx2t/ and find family, teacher, and student materials, activities, games, and more.

Literature Links

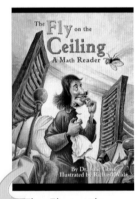

The Fly on the Ceiling

The Fly on the Ceiling
This story about a mathematics philosopher, René Descartes (father of analytic geometry), by Dr. Julie Glass explains how this French character uses coordinates to keep track of his worldly possessions.

Math Background

Putting Research Into Practice for Unit 4

From Current Research: Using Representations

Research suggests that capable problem solvers "construct appropriate problem representations in problem solving situations, and use these representations as aids for understanding the information and relationships of the situation" (Cifarelli 1998, p. 239).

If we want children to be successful in problem solving, we must give them many opportunities to solve problems in meaningful contexts. We must also give children strategies for making sense of the mathematics in these problem-solving situations to help them connect the situations with the appropriate computational processes.

This teaching strategy requires the appropriate use of representations that support such connections for children in meaningful problem contexts. Children also need opportunities to use both concrete and pictorial representations that support this sense-making process and to share their thinking strategies with peers.

Moyer, Patricia S. "Using Representations to Explore Perimeter and Area." *Teaching Children Mathematics* 8.1 (Sept. 2001): p. 52.

Expanding Mathematical Vocabulary

In the early grades, students will have classified and sorted geometric objects such as triangles or cylinders by noting general characteristics. In grades 3–5, they should develop more precise ways to describe shapes, focusing on identifying and describing the shape's properties and learning specialized vocabulary associated with these shapes and properties. To consolidate their ideas, students should draw and construct shapes, compare and discuss their attributes, classify them, and develop and consider definitions on the basis of a shape's properties.

When discussing shapes, students in grades 3–5 should be expanding their mathematical vocabulary by hearing terms used repeatedly in context. As they describe shapes, they should hear, understand, and use mathematical terms such as *parallel, perpendicular, face, edge, vertex, angle, trapezoid, prism,* and so forth, to communicate geometric ideas with greater precision. For example, as students develop a more sophisticated understanding of how geometric shapes can be the same or different, the everyday meaning of *same* is no longer sufficient, and they begin to need words such as *congruent* and *similar* to explain their thinking.

National Council of Teachers of Mathematics. *Principles and Standards for School Mathematics.* Reston: NCTM, 2000.

Other Useful References: Perimeter and Area

Cifarelli, V.V. "The Development of Mental Representations as a Problem Solving Activity." *Journal of Mathematical Behavior* 17 (1998): pp. 239–264.

Del Grande, John and Lorna J. Morrow. *Geometry and Spatial Sense: Addenda Series, Grades K–6.* Curriculum and Evaluation Standards Addenda Series. Reston: NCTM, 1993.

National Council of Teachers of Mathematics. *Principles and Standards for School Mathematics* (Measurement Standard for Grades 3–5). Reston: NCTM, 2000.

National Council of Teachers of Mathematics. *Principles and Standards for School Mathematics* (Reasoning and Proof Standard for Grades 3–5). Reston: NCTM, 2000.

Van de Walle, John A. "Measuring Area." *Elementary and Middle School Mathematics: Teaching Developmentally.* 4th ed. New York: Addison, 2001. pp. 284–287.

Getting Ready to Teach Unit 4

Building on Concepts from Earlier Units

Naming Triangles by Angles
Lessons 1 and 3

Math Expressions Vocabulary

As you teach this unit, emphasize understanding of these terms.

• acute

• right

• obtuse

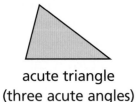

acute triangle
(three acute angles)

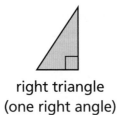

right triangle
(one right angle)

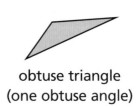

obtuse triangle
(one obtuse angle)

Naming Triangles by Sides
Lesson 3

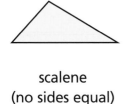

scalene
(no sides equal)

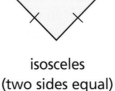

isosceles
(two sides equal)

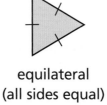

equilateral
(all sides equal)

Perimeter and Area of Rectangles, Parallelograms, and Triangles
Lessons 4 and 5

The concept of the area of special quadrilaterals was developed in Unit 2. This unit extends the concept to triangles, first by helping students to recognize that a diagonal always divides these quadrilaterals into two congruent triangles. Because they are congruent, they must have the same area.

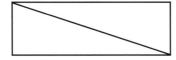
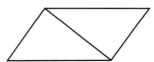

Then students work with pairs of congruent triangles to see that they can be joined together to make a parallelogram.

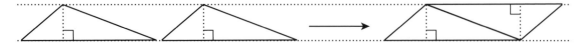

The parallelogram's base and height are the same as the triangle's base and height. From this, students can conclude that the area of any triangle is half of the area of the parallelogram.

Knowing that for a parallelogram $A = b \times h$, they can see that the area of a triangle is $\frac{1}{2} \times b \times h$.

Measuring Angles
Lesson 1

In this lesson students will use a protractor to measure angles that are multiples of 10 degrees. To use a protractor accurately, students need to align the vertex of the angle carefully with the center mark on the protractor and align one ray with the zero line. Most protractors are labeled clockwise and counterclockwise. Students should choose the scale depending on the orientation of the angle.

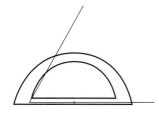

This protractor is not positioned correctly.

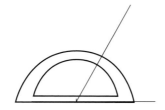

Does this angle measure 60° or 120°?

Rotations and Rotational Symmetry
Lesson 2

An exploration of rotational symmetry enables students to consolidate their understanding of angles, turns, and symmetry. If we can rotate (or turn) a figure around a center point in fewer than 360° and the figure appears unchanged, then the figure has rotational symmetry. The point around which you rotate is called the center of rotation, and the smallest angle you need to turn is called the angle of rotation.

We can describe a figure with rotational symmetry in two ways: either by its rotation angle or by its degree of rotational symmetry. A regular pentagon fits on itself 5 times in one full turn. Its degree of rotational symmetry is 5.

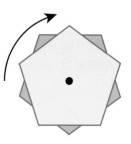

We can divide 360° by 5 to determine the rotation angle, 72°. This regular pentagon has 72° rotational symmetry.

Translations, Reflections, and Rotations
Lesson 7

Euclidean plane isometry is any way of transforming the plane without changing it. Suppose you translate, reflect, or rotate a paper triangle, the shape of the figure does not change, but its position does. In reflections, the figure's image becomes a mirror image of the original figure.

Performing these transformations allows students to verify congruence and identify patterns.

Translation

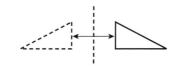

Reflection

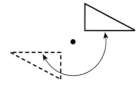

Rotation

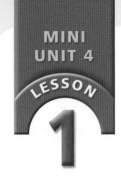

Naming and Measuring Angles

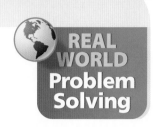

REAL WORLD **Problem Solving**

Lesson Objectives

- Make and describe right, acute, and obtuse angles.
- Measure angles.
- Apply knowledge of angles to real-world situations.

Vocabulary

right angle
acute angle
obtuse angle
protractor

The Day at a Glance

Today's Goals	Materials	
1 Teaching the Lesson **A1:** Discuss right, acute, and obtuse angles. **A2:** Use a protractor to measure angles. **A3:** Sort and classify angles. **2 Going Further** **3 Homework and Spiral Review**	**Lesson Activities** Student Activity Book pp. 181–188 or Student Hardcover Book pp.181–188 and Activity Workbook pp. 67–72 (includes Angle Cutouts and Family Letters) Homework and Remembering pp. 127–128 Geometry and Measurement Poster Protractor (TRB M125) Naming and Measuring Angles (TRB M126) Pencils, Scissors, Scrap paper $8\frac{1}{2}$-inch square of paper	**Going Further** Activity Cards 4-1 Math Journals

123 *Use* **Math Talk** *today!*

Keeping Skills Sharp

Daily Routines	English Language Learners
Elapsed Time Hannah has been asked to baby-sit her sisters from 9:30 in the morning until 2:15 in the afternoon. How many hours is that? 4 hours 45 minutes	Draw a triangle, a square, and a rectangle on the board. Say: **These are two-dimensional figures.** Have students identify each figure. • **Beginning** Point to the angles of the triangle. Say: **One, two, three angles. A triangle has 3 angles.** Then ask: **How many angles does a triangle have?** 3 Repeat with square and rectangle. • **Intermediate** Compare the triangle and the square. Ask: **Do these figures have the same number of angles?** no **How many angles does the triangle have?** 3 **How many angles does the rectangle have?** 4 **Which other shape has 4 angles?** square • **Advanced** Show the 3 figures. Say: **These figures contain angles.** Ask: **How many angles does each figure have?** triangle has 3, rectangle has 4, and square has 4. Ask: **Which figures have the same number of angles?** rectangle and square

① Teaching the Lesson

Activity 1

Right, Acute, and Obtuse Angles

 20 MINUTES

Goal: Discuss right, acute, and obtuse angles.

Materials: pencils (2 per student), Student Activity Book pp. 181–182 or Hardcover Book pp. 181–182 and Activity Workbook p. 67, Geometry and Measurement Poster (optional)

 NCTM Standard:
Geometry

▶ Make Right Angles WHOLE CLASS

Have the students make a right angle with their pencils.

● How can you remember what a right angle is? Rectangles have right angles; the prefix *rect-* and the word *right* sound a bit alike.

If some of the right angles have different orientations, ask the students to see how many different ways they can flip or reverse their angles without changing the angle size. Make sure that they understand that only the size of the angle counts.

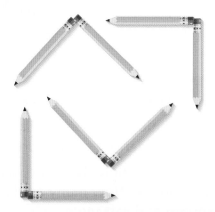

 Class Management

You may wish to display the Geometry and Measurement Poster while you are teaching this unit. The poster is included in the Class Manipulative Kit.

▶ Make Acute Angles WHOLE CLASS

Challenge students to make an angle that is smaller than a right angle.

● An angle that is smaller than a right angle is called *acute*. How can you remember what an acute angle is? The word acute has the word cut, and acute angles are sharp.

Have the students see how many different kinds of acute angles they can make using any orientation, as long as the size is smaller than a right angle.

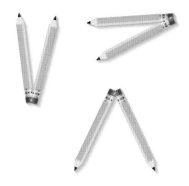

▶ Make Obtuse Angles WHOLE CLASS

Challenge students to make as many different angles as they can that are larger than a right angle, using any orientation and any size bigger than a right angle.

● An angle that is larger than a right angle is called *obtuse*. How can you remember what an obtuse angle is? The word obtuse means "dull," or not sharp, an obtuse angle isn't sharp the way an acute angle is.

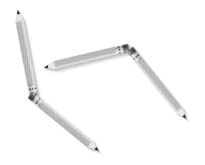

▶ **Discuss Angles** SMALL GROUPS

On Student Book page 181, have students work in **Small Groups** to complete exercises 1–5.

▶ **Classify Angles** INDIVIDUALS

On Student Book page 182, have students work individually or in **Student Pairs** to complete exercises 6–10. Note that students can read the angles in exercises 6–8 in two different ways, for example, ∠FGH or∠HGF.

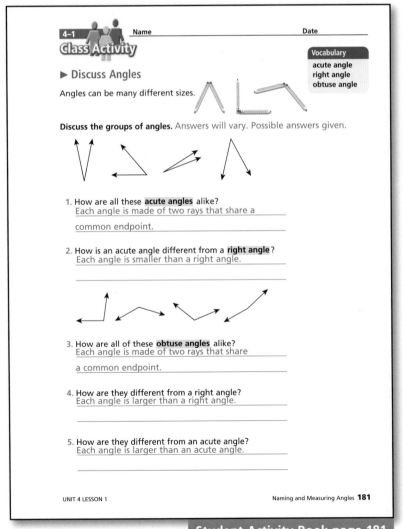

Activity 2

Use a Protractor to Measure Angles

 30 MINUTES

Goal: Use a protractor to measure angles.

Materials: Protractor (TRB M125); Student Activity Book pp. 183–184 or Hardcover Book pp. 183–184 and Activity Workbook p. 68; $8\frac{1}{2}$-inch square of paper

 NCTM Standards:
Geometry
Measurement

▶ Circles and Angles

WHOLE CLASS

Math Talk

Draw a circle on the board with perpendicular diameters, as shown below.

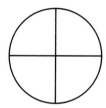

Ask for Ideas Explain that the diameters of the circle are perpendicular, and then ask students to describe what they know about perpendicular lines and segments. Students should be able to verbalize the concept that perpendicular lines and segments intersect and form congruent angles; each angle is a right angle.

Explain that we measure angles in degrees and the measure of a right angle is 90°. Write 90° on each of the right angles that are formed by the intersecting diameters of the circle.

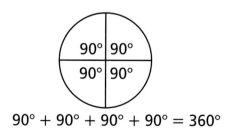

$$90° + 90° + 90° + 90° = 360°$$

- If one right angle is 90° what do you think the measure of a circle is? Students should conclude that the degree measure of a circle is 360° because $90° + 90° + 90° + 90° = 360°$.

Highlight the horizontal diameter of the circle.

- A circle is an angle with a measure of 360°. The diameter is a straight angle. What do you think the measure of a straight angle is? Lead students to conclude that it is 180°, and the measure of a straight angle is one-half the measure of a circle because $180° + 180° = 360°$.

Invite volunteers to summarize in their own words why the measure of a circle is 360° and the measure of a straight angle is 180°.

▶ Use a Protractor WHOLE CLASS

Discuss the protractor on Student Book page 183. Explain that some protractors have one scale while others have two; when a protractor has two scales, either scale may be used to measure.

Distribute Protractor (TRB M125) and have students cut out the protractor. Allow them time to find the 0° mark and align the base ray of the angle with the 0° mark of the scale. Then demonstrate how to read the scale where the remaining ray of the angle intersects the scale. You might want to do this at the overhead.

Ask students to work individually to complete exercises 11–14 on Student Book page 183, and encourage them to work with a helping partner if they so choose.

▶ Sketch Angles INDIVIDUALS

For exercises 15–18 on Student Page 184, it is sufficient for students to informally sketch each angle. Challenge your advanced learners to use a protractor and draw the angles with precision.

▶ Use Reasoning INDIVIDUALS

Before students complete exercises 19–23 on Student Book page 184, remind them that whenever possible, we use three letters to name an angle, and the middle letter always represents the vertex of the angle.

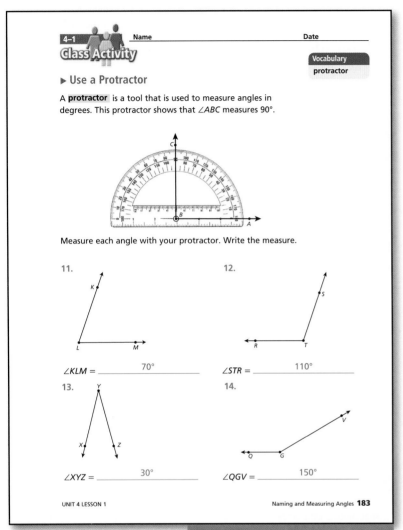

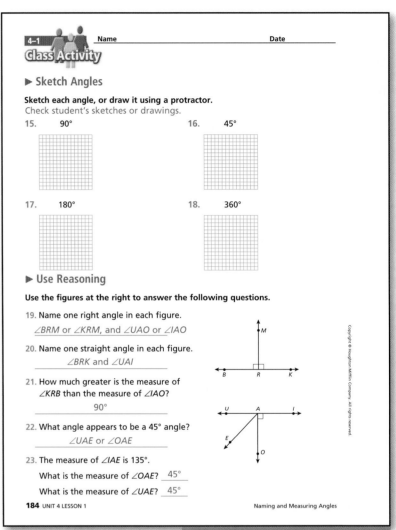

▶ Introduce 45° Angles

Make a paper square by cutting $2\frac{1}{2}$ inches off of the top of an $8\frac{1}{2}$-inch by 11-inch sheet of unlined paper. Then fold the square along one diagonal and cut along the fold line to form two isosceles right triangles.

Pass one triangle around the classroom while you display the other and explain that one angle of the triangle measures 90° and two angles each measure 45°.

Tear off the two non-right angle corners of the triangle and paste or clip them to the right angle to demonstrate that two 45° angles form a 90° right angle.

Summarize Ask students to say a key word or words to answer these questions.

● What is the measure of a right angle? 90°

● A right angle is double the measure of what angle? a 45° angle

● The measure of a straight angle is double the measure of what angle? a right or 90° angle

● The measure of a straight angle is one half the measure of what angle? a circle or a 360° angle

Naming and Measuring Angles **441**

Activity 3

Sort and Classify Angles

 30 MINUTES

Goal: Sort and classify angles.

Materials: Student Activity Book p. 184A or Activity Workbook p. 69; scissors (1 per student); scrap paper; Naming and Measuring Angles (TRB M126)

✔ **NCTM Standards:**
Geometry
Reasoning and Proof

 Compare Angles to 90° [SMALL GROUPS]

Ask for Ideas Begin the activity by asking students to recall what they know about 90° angles. Make sure the recollections include the following ideas.

● A 90° angle is a right angle and looks like a square corner.

● A 45° angle is half of a right angle.

● Perpendicular lines intersect to form four right angles.

● Two right angles can be arranged to form a straight angle. A straight angle has a measure of 180° and looks like a straight line.

● Four right angles can be arranged to form a circle. The measure of a circle is 360°.

Have students arrange themselves in **Small Groups** of three or four and cut out the sixteen Sort Angles cards. Make sure students cut along the dashed lines.

Explain that the angles will be used in sorting activities, and the first activity is to compare the angles to 90° and sort them into three groups: angles that appear to be less than 90° D, L, R, S, X, angles that appear to be about 90° F, N, and angles that appear to be greater than 90° B, C, K, M, P, Q, W, Y, Z.

▶ Compare Angles to 180° [SMALL GROUPS]

Ask for Ideas Begin the activity by asking students to give an example of a 180° angle. A straight line is a 180° angle.

Again have students arrange themselves in **Small Groups** of three or four and then sort the angles into three groups: those angles that appear to be less than 180° C, D, F, K, L, M, N, P, R, S, X, Y, those angles that appear to be about 180° Q, Z, and those angles that appear to be greater than 180° B, W.

Upon completion of the activity, encourage a representative from each group share their findings.

Teaching Note

Angles Greater than 180° When the measure of an angle is greater than 180° and less than 360°, the angle is called a *reflex* angle. In this activity, students have a card that shows a 270° angle. You may want to discuss this angle because students will see it again when students act out rotations in the next lesson.

Differentiated Instruction

Advanced Learners If time permits, you can extend the activity by pointing out that a 135° angle is halfway between a 90° angle and a 180° angle, and then challenge students to compare the angles to 135° by inspection.

▶ Compare Angles to 45° INDIVIDUALS

On a small piece of scrap paper, have students use a protractor to draw a 90° angle. The sides of the angle should extend to the edge of the scrap, as shown below.

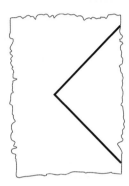

Have students use scissors to cut out the angle and then fold it in half. Ask:

● Before we folded the right angle in half, it had a measure of 90°. What is the measure of the angle now after it has been folded? How do you know? The angle measures 45° because 45° + 45° = 90°.

For this activity, students will use only those angles from the cut-out page that are acute; those angles are *D, L, R, S,* and *X.* Have students sort the angles by comparing them to the 45° paper angle. Upon completion of the sorting, students should have classified the angles in this way:

< 45°	45°	> 45°
L	S	D
X		R

▶ Two-Dimensional Shapes (Optional)
SMALL GROUPS

If time permits, invite students to work in **Small Groups** to classify the angles of quadrilaterals using Naming and Measuring Angles (TRB M126).

Point out that triangles, rectangles, squares, and parallelograms are some examples of two-dimensional shapes. Ask each group to develop sorting rules that will enable them to classify the angles of the figures.

Students are likely to begin by sorting the angles of the figures into two exclusive groups (for example, those with right angles and those with non-right angles). Encourage them to develop additional sorting rules that involve three conditions (such as acute angles, right angles, and obtuse angles) and identify figures (such as a right trapezoid) which have angles that meet all three classifications.

① Teaching the Lesson (continued)

Activity 4

Applications of Angles

 20 MINUTES

Goal: Name different angles on a map.

Materials: Student Activity Book or Hardcover Book pp. 185–186

✓ **NCTM Standard:**
Geometry

▶ Angles in the Real World [WHOLE CLASS]

As a class, discuss the map on Student Book page 185. Make sure students know how to find the directions on the map.

Math Talk Have students discuss and complete exercises 24–26.

▶ More Angles in the Real World

[SMALL GROUPS]

Encourage students to share ideas while completing exercises 27 and 28 on Student Book page 186.

Draw and Describe Angles Invite students to draw two different right angles, two different acute angles, and two different obtuse angles. Have them describe the essential differences in their own words.

✓ **Ongoing Assessment**

This activity provides an excellent opportunity to see how well students understand the concepts taught.

4–1
Class Activity
Name _____ Date _____

▶ Angles in the Real World

Here is a map of Jon's neighborhood. The east and west streets are named for presidents of the United States. The north and south streets are numbered. The avenues have letters. Jon's house is on the corner of Lincoln and First.

[Map of Jon's neighborhood showing streets Lincoln, Washington, Jefferson running east-west; First, Second, Third, Fourth, Fifth, Sixth running north-south; Avenues A, B, C. Compass showing N, E, S, W. Jon's house and Cora's house marked.]

24. What do the arrows to the left of the map tell you?
   the directions on the map

25. Jon leaves his house and rides his bike south on First. What kind of angle does he make for each turn in this route?
   • He turns southeast onto avenue A. obtuse
   • When he reaches Washington, he turns west. acute
   • When he gets back to First, he turns south. right

26. Jon's cousin Cora rides east on Lincoln from Jon's house to avenue C. What kind of angle will she make if she turns northeast? if she turns southwest?
   obtuse; acute

UNIT 4 LESSON 1   Naming and Measuring Angles **185**

Student Activity Book page 185

4–1
Class Activity
Name _____ Date _____

▶ More Angles in the Real World

Look at the map of Jon's neighborhood on page 185.

27. Cora lives at the corner of Jefferson and Sixth. Record three different routes she can use to get from her house to Jon's house. For each route, tell what kind of angle each turn makes.
   Answers will vary.

28. Write what you know about right, acute, and obtuse angles.
   Answers should describe the similarities and/or differences.

186 UNIT 4 LESSON 1   Naming and Measuring Angles

Student Activity Book page 186

Intervention — Activity Card 4-1

Testing Angles — Activity Card 4-1 ●

Work: In Pairs

Use:
• Straightedge or ruler

1. One partner draws an angle.

2. The other partner uses the corner of a sheet of paper to compare the angle drawn to a right angle.

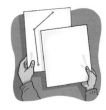

3. Then the first partner records the name of the angle type—acute, right, or obtuse.

4. Partners exchange tasks and repeat steps 1 through 3.

Unit 4, Lesson 1 — Copyright © Houghton Mifflin Company

Activity Note Check that students understand that the corner of the piece of paper they are using to identify angle is a right angle.

 Math Writing Prompt

Summarize Explain all the ways you can tell the difference between a right angle, an acute angle, and an obtuse angle.

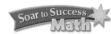 **Software Support**

Use *Soar to Success* for instruction of students needing targeted support for underlying skills.

On Level — Activity Card 4-1

Alphabet Angles — Activity Card 4-1 ▲

Work: By Yourself

1. Identify upper case letters which contain straight line segments that meet to form an angle. Write several of the letters, using block-letter style.

2. Classify each angle formed by line segments in the letter as acute, right, or obtuse.

acute
obtuse
acute

3. **Look Back** Did you list all the possible upper case letters that have angles? How many angles can you identify in the upper case letter R? Explain your answer. Answers may vary; none, there are no straight line segments that meet in the letter R.

Unit 4, Lesson 1 — Copyright © Houghton Mifflin Company

Activity Note Remind students that they should only measure angles when the lines forming the angle are straight lines. Identifying angles in letters like D and P is not appropriate.

 Math Writing Prompt

Memory Aid Explain how you remember what the terms *right angle*, *acute angles*, and *obtuse angle* mean. Draw examples of each kind of angle.

 Software Support

Use *MegaMath* for review and reinforcement of the concepts and skills presented in this lesson.

Challenge — Activity Card 4-1

Estimate Angle Measurements — Activity Card 4-1 ■

Work: By Yourself

Use:
• Protractor (TRB M125)

1. In the classroom, select 3 objects that have angles.

2. Identify all the angles in the object, and list them on your paper.

3. Estimate the measure of each angle. Then use your protractor to measure the angles.

4. **Look Back** Calculate how close your estimates were to the measures you found using a protractor.

Unit 4, Lesson 1 — Copyright © Houghton Mifflin Company

Activity Note Many protractors read with numbers from left to right and right to left. Make sure that students know to read the numbers that increase from the direction of the bottom side of the angle.

 Math Writing Prompt

You Decide Chin said that on his walk he made two acute angles, an obtuse angle, and he ended where he started. Can he be correct? Explain.

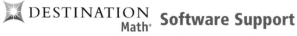 **DESTINATION Math· Software Support**

Use *Destination Math* to take students beyond the concepts and skills presented in this lesson.

③ Homework and Spiral Review

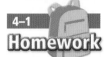
For homework, students identify, define, and draw one-dimensional figures.

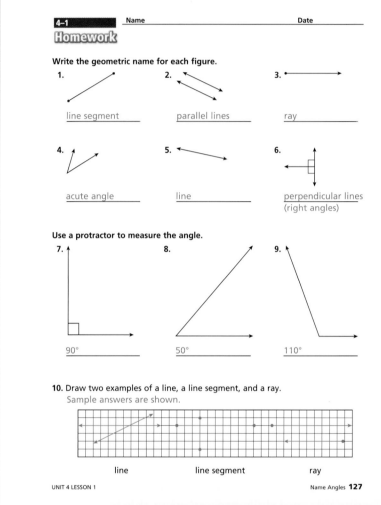

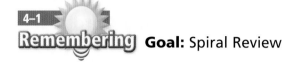
This Remembering activity would be appropriate anytime after today's lesson.

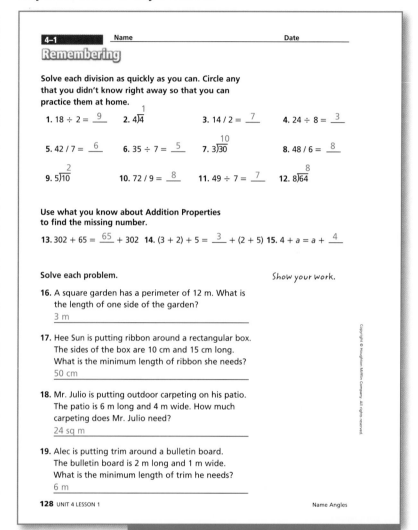

Home and School Connection

Family Letter Have students take home the Family Letter on Student Book page 187 or Activity Workbook page 71. This letter explains how the concepts of triangles and finding the area and perimeter of triangles are developed in *Math Expressions*. It gives parents and guardians a better understanding of the learning that goes on in math class and creates a bridge between school and home. A Spanish translation of this letter is on the following page in the Student Book page 188 and Activity Workbook page 72.

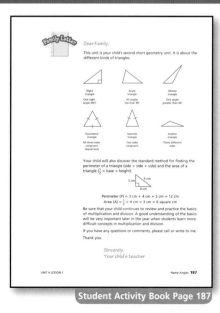

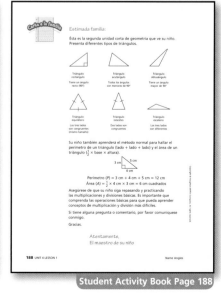

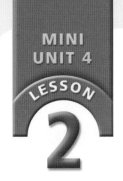

MINI UNIT 4
LESSON 2
Rotations and Rotational Symmetry

Lesson Objective

● Demonstrate an understanding of rotations and rotational symmetry.

The Day at a Glance

Today's Goals	Materials

① Teaching the Lesson
A1: Rotate plane figures.
A2: Identify rotational symmetry.
 	
② Going Further
▶ Differentiated Instruction
 	
③ Homework and Spiral Review
	Lesson Activities
	Student Activity Book pp. 189–190
	  or Student Hardcover Book
	  pp. 189–190
	Homework and Remembering
	  pp. 129–130
	Rotations and Rotational
	  Symmetry (TRB M127)
	Blank transparency and
	  overhead projector (optional)
	Scissors (optional)
	Large sheet of paper or poster
	  board (optional)
	Quick Quiz 1 (Assessment Guide)
		Going Further
		Activity Cards 4-2
		Grid paper
		Protractor
		Math Journals

123 Use Math Talk today!

Keeping Skills Sharp

Daily Routines	English Language Learners
Homework Review If students give incorrect answers, have them explain how they found the answers. This can help you determine whether the error is conceptual or procedural. **Logic** Use *sometimes, always,* or *never* to complete these sentences. 1) If a parallelogram has two sets of parallel sides, then triangles are ____ parallelograms. never 2) If two equilateral triangles share one side, they ____ form a rhombus. always	Make a paper triangle and put it on the board. Have students identify the figure and then close their eyes. Turn the triangle so that it points to the right. Have students identify what was done to the triangle. Move the triangle to its original position. • **Beginning** Point to the triangle. Say: **This was our triangle before a turn.** Turn the triangle so it points to the right. Say: **This is our triangle after a turn.** Have students repeat. • **Intermediate** Say: **This was our triangle before a turn.** Have students turn the triangle so that it points to the right. Ask: **Does the triangle look the same before and after a turn?** no **How is it different?** It points a different way. • **Advanced** Have students show a turn of the triangle. Have students describe how the triangle looks different after a turn.

Teaching the Lesson

Explore Rotations

 15 MINUTES

Goal: Rotate plane figures.

Materials: Student Activity Book or Hardcover Book p. 189; blank transparency and overhead projector (optional)

✔ **NCTM Standard:**
Geometry

▶ **Discuss Turns** | WHOLE CLASS |

Ask for Ideas Begin the activity by asking students to describe real-world examples of turns.

Write the terms *rotation, clockwise*, and *counter-clockwise* on the board. Explain that a rotation is a *turn*. Have students look at an analog clock or watch and use their own words to describe the clockwise movements of the hands. Then discuss movement in the opposite (or counter-clockwise) direction.

On the Board Point out that rotations or turns are measured in degrees. Sketch the following turns on the board or overhead.

A quarter turn is 90°.

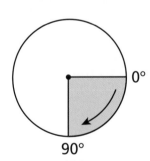
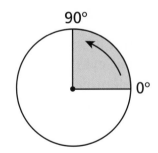

clockwise   **counter-clockwise**

A half turn is 180°.

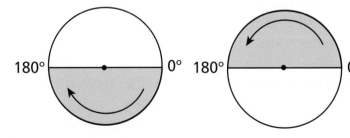

clockwise   **counter-clockwise**

A three-quarter turn is 270°.

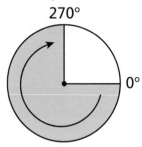
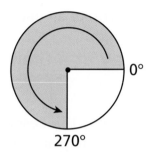

clockwise   **counter-clockwise**

A full turn is 360°.

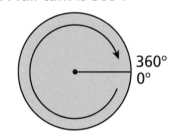
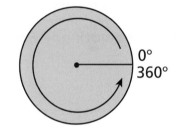

clockwise   **counter-clockwise**

▶ **Act It Out** | WHOLE CLASS |

Point out the North, South, East, and West walls of your classroom. Use the **Scenario** structure and ask students to stand facing the East wall and complete the turns described below. After each turn, have them name the direction they are facing.

● 90° clockwise south

● 90° counter-clockwise north

● 180° clockwise west

● 180° counter-clockwise west

● 270° clockwise north

● 270° counter-clockwise south

● 360° clockwise east

● 360° counter-clockwise east

Challenge volunteers to explain how they would show a 45° turn. half of a 90° turn is a 45° turn

Act out examples of 45° turns that result in students facing northeast, northwest, southwest, and southeast.

▶ Identify Rotations [INDIVIDUALS]

Have students work individually (or with a **Helping Partner**) to complete the activity on Student Book page 189. Students will use the process of elimination to determine the correct answer. Some students may find it helpful to trace the given figures, or rotate the activity page, to help identify the correct answers.

After the activity has been completed, have students look at the choices they eliminated for each exercise and identify the rotation(s) for those choices.

Exercise 1

Choice A: 90° clockwise or 270° counter-clockwise

Choice B: 180° clockwise or 180° counter-clockwise

Exercise 2

Choice A: 90° clockwise or 270° counter-clockwise

Choice C: 180° clockwise or 180° counter-clockwise

Exercise 3

Choice A: 270° clockwise or 90° counter-clockwise

Choice C: 180° clockwise or 180° counter-clockwise

Exercise 4

Choice A: 180° clockwise or 180° counter-clockwise

Choice B: 270° clockwise or 90° counter-clockwise

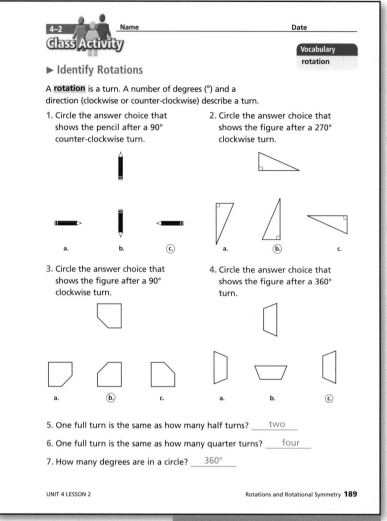

Student Activity Book page 189

The Learning Classroom

Helping Community When stronger math students finish their work early, let them help others who might be struggling. Many students enjoy the role of helping other students. In their "helper" role, students who might become bored challenge themselves as they explain math content to others.

Rotations and Rotational Symmetry **449**

Activity 2

Explore Rotational Symmetry

 30 MINUTES

Goal: Identify rotational symmetry.

Materials: Student Activity Book or Hardcover Book p. 190; Rotations and Rotational Symmetry (TRB M127) (optional); scissors (optional); large sheet of paper or poster board (optional)

 NCTM Standard:
Geometry

▶ **Discuss Rotational Symmetry**

 WHOLE CLASS   **Math Talk**

Model Stand under an analog clock and hold a blank sheet of square paper in front of you. Rotate the paper 90° clockwise and point out that the paper looks exactly as it did before the turn. Ask students to describe the turn in degrees and direction. 90° clockwise. Again turn the paper 90° clockwise three more times, ask students to count the number of full turns as you make them three, and name the number of times the square looked exactly like itself in that full turn four. Explain that you have just demonstrated *90° rotational symmetry*—the square looked exactly like itself after rotating 90°.

Have students close their books and place them face-up on their desks. Explain that they should ignore the art and design of the cover and turn the book to discover the number of times that the cover fits exactly on itself in one full turn. Ask students to identify the degree of rotational symmetry they just demonstrated. 180°

Point out that these examples of rotational symmetry involve rotating a shape around a point at the center of the shape.

Teaching Note

Math Background Rotational symmetry is also called *point symmetry.* When a figure has point symmetry, every point of the figure has a corresponding point that is opposite the point at the center of the figure. A square is an example of a figure with point symmetry. Each corner of a square has a corresponding corner that is on the opposite side of the point at the center of the square, and the same distance from that point. Since a square has four corners, it has 360° ÷ 4 or 90° rotational symmetry.

A simple test for students to help decide if a figure has point symmetry is to turn the figure upside-down. If the figure looks the same after the turn, it has point symmetry because a figure with point symmetry is unchanged by a 180° turn.

▶ Rotational Symmetry [WHOLE CLASS]

Math Talk Discuss the rotational symmetry example at the top of Student Book page 190. Make sure students can recognize that the square fits exactly on itself after a 90° or *quarter turn,* and then ask them to name other turns after which the square will fit exactly on itself. 180° or half turn, 270° or three-quarter turn, and 360° or a full turn Make sure students understand that although the square fits exactly on itself four times in one full turn, its rotational symmetry in degrees is the *first time* this happens, which is 90°. From this fact, lead students to generalize that the first time a figure is turned less than 360° and fits exactly on itself is the degree of rotational symmetry for that figure.

Have students complete exercises 8–10.

Use **Solve and Discuss** to complete exercise 11. If necessary, help steer the discussion toward these facts:

● The figure appears to be an equilateral triangle.

● When rotated, an equilateral triangle will fit exactly on itself three times in one full turn.

● The degree of rotational symmetry is the addend that has a sum of 360° when used three times. An equilateral triangle has 120° rotational symmetry because 120° + 120° + 120° = 360°.

Teaching Note

Generalize Before students begin the activity, it is important for them to understand that a figure does not have rotational symmetry if it must be turned 360° (one full turn) before it fits exactly on itself.

Differentiated Instruction

Extra Help Students who have difficulty visualizing a rotation can trace and cut out each figure, then use the tip of a pencil or pen to press down on each figure at its center while it is being rotated.

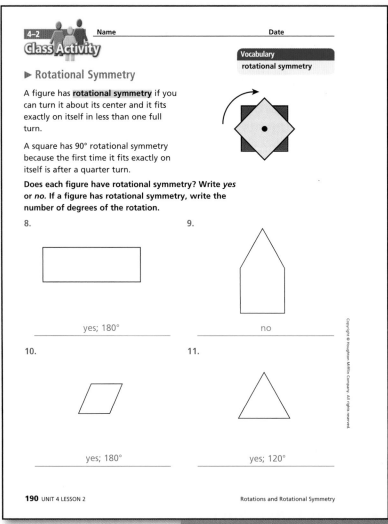

Student Activity Book page 190

✔ Ongoing Assessment

Ask students to draw a figure that has

▶ 90° rotational symmetry.

▶ 180° rotational symmetry.

Activity continued ▶

Activity 2

▶ **Line and Rotational Symmetry (Optional)** SMALL GROUPS

Distribute Rotations and Rotational Symmetry (TRB M127). Have students arrange themselves in **Small Groups** of three or four and cut (TRB M127) along the dashed lines.

Sketch the Venn diagram shown below on the board.

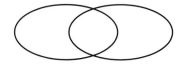

On a large sheet of paper or poster board, have students duplicate the Venn diagram. Ask each group to use the following sorting rules to classify the letters in the Venn diagram.

● Letters that have line symmetry. A, B, C, D, E, H, I, K, M, O, T, U, V, W, X, Y

● Letters that have rotational symmetry. H, I, N, O, S, X, Z

● Letters that have both line symmetry and rotational symmetry. H, I, O, X

After the activity has been completed, ask a volunteer from each group to name several letters of the alphabet, name the locations in the Venn diagram that the letters were placed, and explain why the letters were placed in those locations.

 Quick Quiz

See Assessment Guide for Unit 4 Quick Quiz 1.

Intervention — Activity Card 4-2

Make a Turn — Activity Card 4-2 ●

Work: In Pairs

Use:
• Centimeter-Grid Paper (TRB M60)

1. This rectangle shows rotational symmetry when turned a half turn.

2. Partners each draw a simple quadrilateral on grid paper.

3. Partners use a series of quarter turns to decide if their shapes have rotational symmetry.

4. Write About It Explain how you can decide if a shape has rotational symmetry. If you can turn it less than a full turn and it looks just the same, it has rotational symmetry.

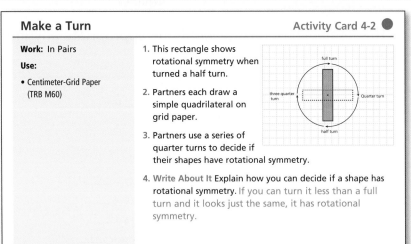

Unit 4, Lesson 2   Copyright © Houghton Mifflin Company

Activity Note There are shapes that have rotational symmetry with degrees that are not 90°. Just because their pattern or quarter turn does not show symmetry does not mean that there is none.

✍ Math Writing Prompt

Draw a Picture Draw an uppercase A. Then create a quarter-turn and a half-turn rotation of the letter.

Soar to Success Math ★ Software Support

Use *Soar to Success* for instruction of students needing targeted support for underlying skills.

On Level — Activity Card 4-2

Around and Around We Go — Activity Card 4-2 ▲

Work: By Yourself

Use:
• Centimeter-Grid Paper (TRB M60)
• Protractor (TRB M125)

1. Find three objects in your classroom that have rotational symmetry.

2. Sketch the objects on your paper and describe them.

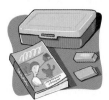

3. Sketch a rotation which proves that the object has rotational symmetry.

4. Identify the degree of rotational symmetry.

Unit 4, Lesson 2   Copyright © Houghton Mifflin Company

Activity Note Point out that the easiest way to find the degree of rotation is to determine how many times the figure is symmetric in one full rotation. Then divide 360° by that number.

✍ Math Writing Prompt

Explain Your Thinking Determine how many degrees are in a quarter turn, a half turn, and a full turn. Explain your answer.

MegaMath Grades K-6 Software Support

Use *MegaMath* for review and reinforcement of the concepts and skills presented in this lesson.

Challenge — Activity Card 4-2

Turn and Fold — Activity Card 4-2 ■

Work: By Yourself

1. The figure shown has both rotational symmetry and line symmetry.

2. Draw three different figures that have both rotational and line symmetry.

3. Determine the degree of rotational symmetry for each shape.

4. Write About It Explain how to prove that your shapes have rotational symmetry and line symmetry. They show the original figure when rotated less that a full turn around a point; can fold along a line of symmetry.

Unit 4, Lesson 2   Copyright © Houghton Mifflin Company

Activity Note Students may make shapes that are simple or complex. Check that they have identified all lines of symmetry and the correct degree of rotational symmetry.

✍ Math Writing Prompt

Explain Your Thinking Explain how you know if a shape has rotational symmetry.

✸ DESTINATION Math® Software Support

Use *Destination Math* to take students beyond the concepts and skills presented in this lesson.

③ Homework and Spiral Review

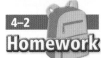

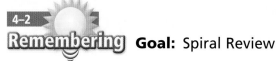

Homework **Goal:** Additional Practice

✔ Include students' completed Homework page 129 as part of their portfolios.

Remembering **Goal:** Spiral Review

This Remembering page would be appropriate anytime after today's lesson.

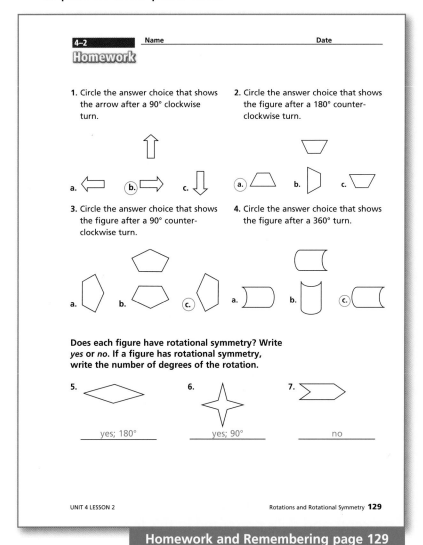

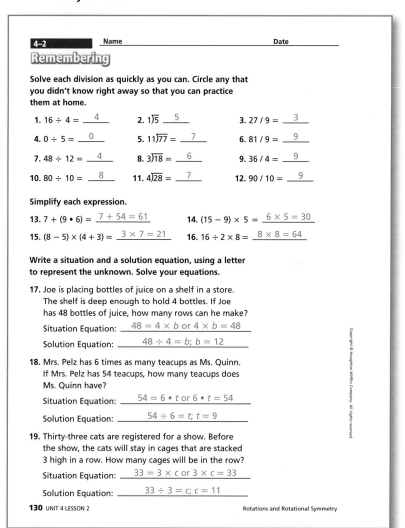

Homework and Remembering page 129

Homework and Remembering page 130

Home or School Activity

 Math-to-Math Connection

Have students draw a square and an equilateral triangle on a piece of paper and cut out a congruent square and an equilateral triangle. Students place a cutout on top of the corresponding figure and mark the top center of the cutout. Then they place the point of their pencil in the center of the cutout and rotate the cutout, recording the figure's rotational symmetry in degrees. Students can try this with other figures, such as a regular pentagon or hexagon.

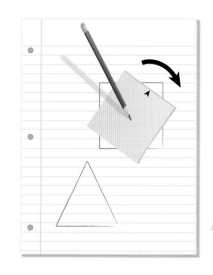

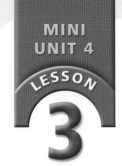

Name Triangles

Lesson Objectives

● Define, identify, and draw right, obtuse, and acute triangles.

● Define, identify, and draw scalene, isosceles, and equilateral triangles.

The Day at a Glance

Today's Goals	Materials
1 Teaching the Lesson **A1:** Make triangles and name them by their angles. **A2:** Identify triangles by their sides. **A3:** Name and draw triangles with various sides and angles. **2 Going Further** ▶ Math Connection: Sort and Classify Triangles ▶ Differentiated Instruction **3 Homework and Spiral Review**	**Lesson Activities** Student Activity Book pp. 191–195 or Student Hardcover Book pp. 191–195 and Activity Workbook pp. 73–75 Homework and Remembering pp. 131–132	**Going Further** Student Activity Book p. 196 or Student Hardcover Book p. 196 and Activity Workbook p. 76 Scissors Glue Activity Cards 4-3 Triangles (TRB M54) Centimeter ruler Strips of paper Math Journals

123 Use Math Talk today!

Keeping Skills Sharp

Daily Routines	English Language Learners
Homework Review Check that students completed the Homework assignment, and see whether any problem caused difficulty for many students. **Multistep Problem** Mitch has saved $13.00 so that he can buy a T-shirt. When he goes to the store, he finds a second T-shirt that he wants to get for his brother's birthday. If each T-shirt costs $8.50, how much more money does Mitch need to buy both T-shirts? $4.00	Draw an acute, a right, and an obtuse angle on the board. Have students identify them as angles. Help students describe the differences. ● **Beginning** Point to the right angle. Say: **This is a right angle.** Point to the acute angle. Ask: **Is this a right angle?** no **Is it bigger or smaller than a right angle?** smaller Say: **This is an acute angle.** Point to the obtuse angle. Ask: **Is this a right angle?** no **Is it bigger or smaller than a right angle?** bigger Say: **This is an obtuse angle.** ● **Intermediate** Ask: **Are the angles the same size?** no Point to the right angle. Ask: **What kind of angle is this?** right Continue with the other angles. ● **Advanced** Say: **These are different kinds of angles.** Ask: **Which is the right angle? Acute angle? Obtuse angle? How can you tell them apart?** their size

1 Teaching the Lesson

Activity 1

Name Triangles by Their Angles

 25 MINUTES

Goal: Make triangles and name them by their angles.

Materials: Student Activity Book pp. 191–192 or Hardcover Book pp. 191–192 and Activity Workbook p. 73

 NCTM Standard:
Geometry

▶ Make Right, Acute, and Obtuse Angles
WHOLE CLASS

Have as many students as possible work at the classroom board while the others work at their desks.

Ask one third of the students to draw a right angle, another third to draw an acute angle, and the last group to draw an obtuse angle.

● How can you turn your angle into a triangle? by drawing the third side to close the shape

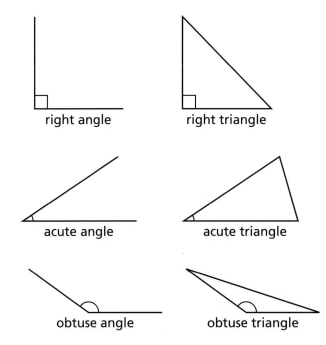

right angle   right triangle

acute angle   acute triangle

obtuse angle   obtuse triangle

Teaching Note

Watch For! Some students' acute triangles may contain either a right angle or an obtuse angle. Have students adjust the length of the sides so that all three angles are acute.

▶ Discuss Right, Acute, and Obtuse Triangles
WHOLE CLASS   Math Talk

Have students discuss the differences among the angles in their triangles. Responses might include:

● The right triangle has one right angle and two other angles (both acute, students will find when they explore the issue).

● The acute triangle has three acute angles.

● The obtuse triangle has one obtuse angle and two other angles (both acute, students will find when they explore the issue).

Teaching Note

Math Background Napoleon Bonaparte was an emperor of France about 200 years ago. He excelled at mathematics in school and was very interested in geometry. Napoleon's Theorem, a result in geometry attributed to Napoleon himself, is about equilateral triangles:

Start with any triangle. Draw an equilateral triangle on each of the triangle's sides, then join the center point of those triangles. You always get another equilateral triangle.

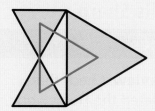

The Learning Classroom

Building Concepts To support building coherence, remember to have students take turns briefly summarizing the previous day's lesson at the beginning of each math class. Alternately, you may have a student summarize at the end of each lesson. Either way, if you do this regularly, students will get used to making mental summaries of math concepts and making conceptual connections.

▶Discuss Angles of a Triangle WHOLE CLASS

Together, read and discuss the information on Student Book page 191. Have students complete exercises 1–3.

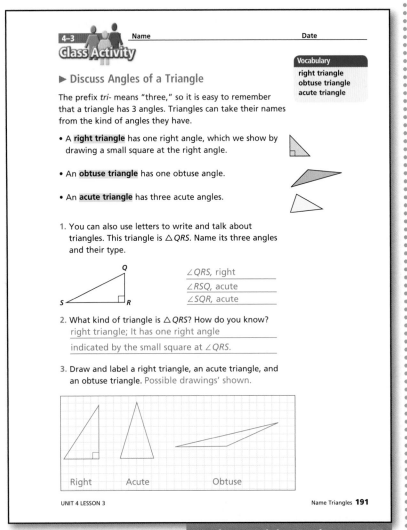

▶Identify Angles of a Triangle
INDIVIDUALS

Have students work individually to complete exercises 4–16 on Student Book page 192.

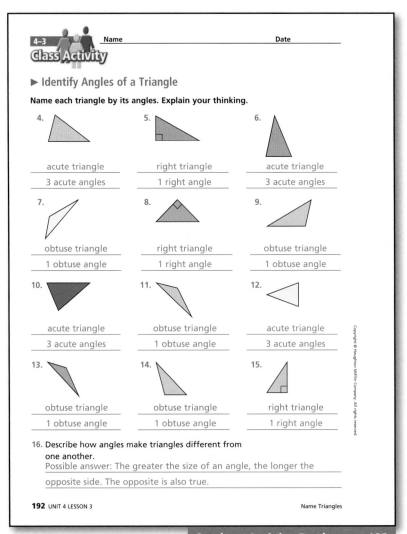

Teaching Note

Mathematical Notation You may wish to introduce the symbols that are used to represent congruency. The use of these symbols (tick marks) enables a student to keep track of equal measures and determine congruency.

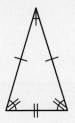 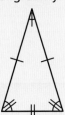

✓ Ongoing Assessment

As students complete exercises 4–16, note how they answer the questions. Encourage them to look at all the angles in a triangle (right triangles and obtuse triangles also have acute angles).

Teaching the Lesson (continued)

Activity 2

Name Triangles by Their Sides

 20 MINUTES

Goal: Identify triangles by their sides.

Materials: Student Activity Book or Hardcover Book pp. 193–194

✔ **NCTM Standard:**
Geometry

▶ Discuss Sides of a Triangle [WHOLE CLASS]

As a class, read and discuss the information at the top of Student Book page 193. Some students may recognize that an equilateral triangle is also an isosceles triangle because it has two congruent sides. Then have students complete exercises 17–19.

▶ Identify Sides of a Triangle [SMALL GROUPS]

Have students work in **Small Groups** to complete exercises 20–32. Encourage them to consult Student Book page 193 as needed.

Teaching Note

Language and Vocabulary Be sure to say the words *isosceles* and *scalene* clearly during the discussion to help the students learn the correct pronunciation.

Scalene = skay'–leen

Isosceles = I-saw'–sell-eez

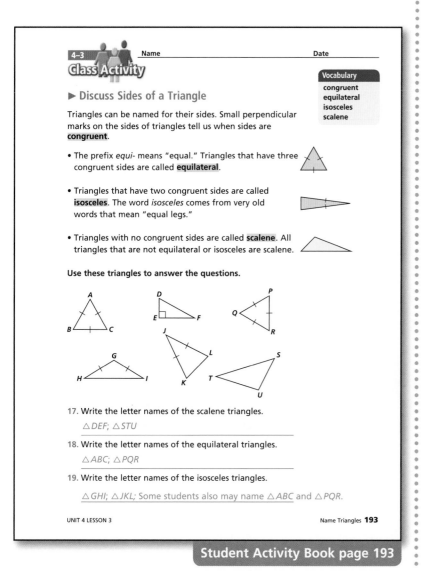

Student Activity Book page 193

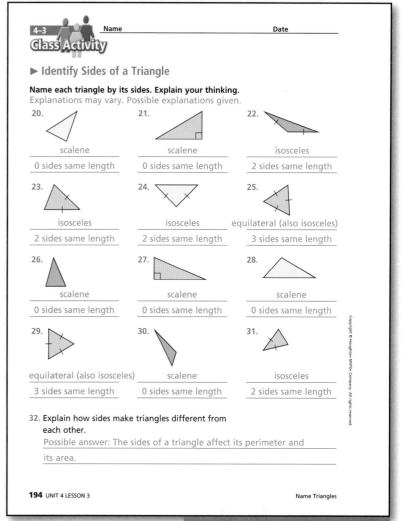

Student Activity Book page 194

Name Triangles by Their Angles and Sides

 15 MINUTES

Goal: Name and draw triangles with various sides and angles.

Materials: Student Activity Book p. 195 or Hardcover Book p. 195 and Activity Workbook p. 75

 NCTM Standard:
Geometry

▶ Possible Ways to Name Triangles

WHOLE CLASS

Have students discuss the various ways to name triangles. See a sample dialogue of Math Talk in Action on this page. As the discussion progresses, draw examples of the kinds of triangles on the board and have students draw them in their journals. Be sure to touch on the following:

● If a triangle has either a right angle or an obtuse angle, the other two angles have to be acute.

● An equilateral triangle can have only acute angles.

Have students work in **Small Groups** or independently to answer questions 33–39 on Student Book page 195.

 Math Talk in Action

Describe a way that you can name a triangle.

Daniel: You can name it by its sides. If the sides are all different, it's scalene. If two are the same, it's isosceles. If all three are the same, it's equilateral.

That's right. Is there another way to name a triangle?

Lourdes: By its angles. If it has a right angle, or an obtuse angle, or an acute angle, then it's a right triangle, an obtuse triangle, or an acute triangle.

That's a very good use of the names. Does anyone have anything to add to that answer?

Jung Mee: In an acute triangle all three angles have to be acute, not just one.

Yes. That's something to be careful about.

4–3
Class Activity
Name _____ Date _____

▶ **Possible Ways to Name Triangles**

33. Can triangles be named for both their sides and their angles? Explain your thinking.
    Yes; they can be named based on their sides and also on their angles because sides and angles are two different ways of classifying triangles.

Answers will vary. Possible
Draw each triangle. If you can't, explain why. answers given.

34. Draw a right scalene triangle.	35. Draw an obtuse scalene triangle.
36. Draw a right equilateral triangle. Not possible. You cannot make a right triangle with three sides equal in length.	37. Draw an acute isosceles triangle.
38. Draw an obtuse equilateral triangle. Not possible. You cannot make a triangle with an obtuse angle and three equal sides.	39. Draw a right isosceles triangle.

Student Activity Book page 195

Going Further

Math Connection: Sort and Classify Triangles

Goal: Use a Venn diagram to sort triangles in various ways.

Materials: Student Activity Book p. 196 or Hardcover Book p. 196 and Activity Workbook p. 76; scissors (1 per student); glue

✔ **NCTM Standard:**
Geometry

▶ Sort Triangles in Different Ways

WHOLE CLASS

In this lesson, students will connect sorting and classifying triangles with Venn diagrams.

Ask students how they might be able to tell if the triangles on Student Book page 196 are scalene (all sides different), isosceles (2 sides congruent), or equilateral (all sides congruent). They should realize that they must compare side lengths. Possible responses about how to compare the side lengths are:

● by looking at the sides

● by measuring the sides with a ruler

● by marking how long the sides are on a piece of paper

Next, discuss how students might be able to tell if the triangles are right, acute, or obtuse. They should realize that they have to identify one right angle in a right triangle, three acute angles in an acute triangle, and one obtuse angle in an obtuse triangle.

Have students work in **Small Groups** to complete Student Activity Book page 196.

Students can write in pencil on the lines the kinds of triangles in the two ovals. Ask students to figure out when they will have no triangles in the overlapping part of the ovals and when they will have triangles in the overlapping part. When we sort triangles only by sides or only by angles, there will not be any overlapping triangles. When we sort by sides and by angles, there will not be any equilateral obtuse or equilateral right angles.

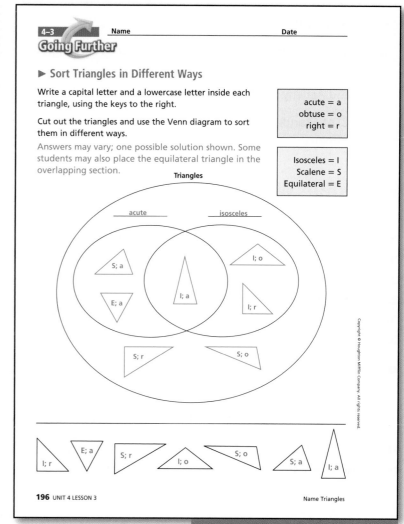

Student Activity Book page 196

At the end, you can have students glue one of their triangle sorts on their page and display them in the classroom. Be sure that students glue different kinds of sorts for the display.

Differentiated Instruction

Intervention   Activity Card 4-3

Name by Angles   Activity Card 4-3 ●

Work: In Pairs

Use:
• Triangles (TRB M54)

1. One partner uses the corner of a piece of paper to decide if the angles in triangles A, B, and C are less than, greater than, or equal to a right angle.

2. The other partner marks each right angle with a small square, each obtuse angle with an O, and each acute angle with an A, as shown below.

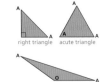
right triangle   acute triangle

obtuse triangle

3. Together, partners name the triangles by their angles.

4. Partners switch roles for triangles D, E, and F.

Unit 4, Lesson 3   Copyright © Houghton Mifflin Company

Activity Note Check that students understand that the corner of the piece of paper they are using to identify angles is a right angle.

🖉 Math Writing Prompt

Draw a Picture Draw and label a scalene triangle, an isosceles triangle, and an equilateral triangle.

Soar to Success Math ★ Software Support

Use *Soar to Success* for instruction of students needing targeted support for underlying skills.

On Level   Activity Card 4-3

Practice With Triangle Names   Activity Card 4-3 ▲

Work: By Yourself

Use:
• Triangles (TRB M54)

1. Use perpendicular marks to identify all congruent sides of each triangle.

2. Use squares to mark any right angles.

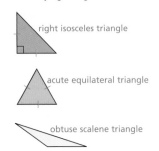
right isosceles triangle

acute equilateral triangle

obtuse scalene triangle

3. Name each triangle, using sides and angles.

Unit 4, Lesson 3   Copyright © Houghton Mifflin Company

Activity Note Students may find it helpful to list the number of equal sides, and the types of angles in each triangle, to make naming the triangles easier.

🖉 Math Writing Prompt

Summarize Use letters, angles, and sides to describe all the ways to name a triangle.

MegaMath Grades K-6   Software Support

Use *MegaMath* for review and reinforcement of the concepts and skills presented in this lesson.

Challenge   Activity Card 4-3

Make and Name a Triangle   Activity Card 4-3 ■

Work: By Yourself

Use:
• Centimeter ruler
• Three strips of paper
• Tape

1. Choose three side lengths between 1 and 10 cm.

2. Use a centimeter ruler to mark each length on a strip of paper.

3. Use the strips to make a triangle with those side lengths. Tape the pieces together.

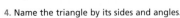
acute scalene triangle

4. Name the triangle by its sides and angles.

5. Decide What side lengths will form an equilateral triangle? Any three equal lengths will form an equilateral triangle.

Unit 4, Lesson 3   Copyright © Houghton Mifflin Company

Activity Note Students may want to use the corner of a piece of paper or a protractor to determine the angle measures in the triangle they form.

🖉 Math Writing Prompt

Impossible Triangles With words and pictures, explain why it is impossible to have a right triangle with an obtuse angle.

✦ DESTINATION Math®   Software Support

Use *Destination Math* to take students beyond the concepts and skills presented in this lesson.

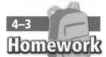

③ Homework and Spiral Review

Homework **Goal:** Additional Practice

✓ Include students' work for page 131 as part of their portfolios.

Remembering **Goal:** Spiral Review

This Remembering activity would be appropriate anytime after today's lesson.

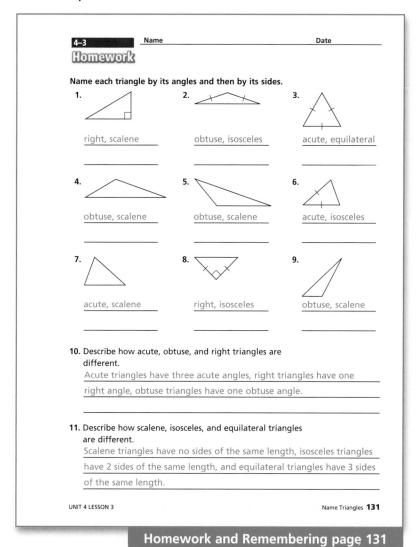

4-3 Name _____ Date _____

Homework

Name each triangle by its angles and then by its sides.

1. right, scalene
2. obtuse, isosceles
3. acute, equilateral
4. obtuse, scalene
5. obtuse, scalene
6. acute, isosceles
7. acute, scalene
8. right, isosceles
9. obtuse, scalene

10. Describe how acute, obtuse, and right triangles are different.
Acute triangles have three acute angles, right triangles have one right angle, obtuse triangles have one obtuse angle.

11. Describe how scalene, isosceles, and equilateral triangles are different.
Scalene triangles have no sides of the same length, isosceles triangles have 2 sides of the same length, and equilateral triangles have 3 sides of the same length.

UNIT 4 LESSON 3   Name Triangles **131**

Homework and Remembering page 131

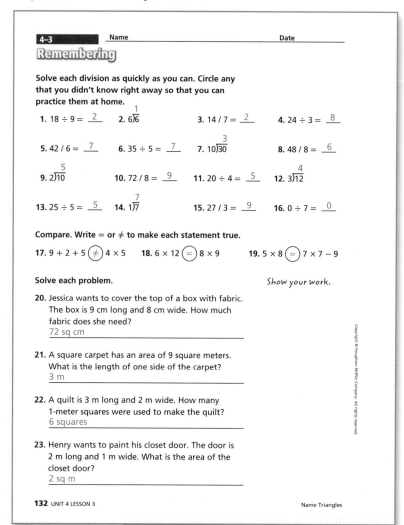

4-3 Name _____ Date _____

Remembering

Solve each division as quickly as you can. Circle any that you didn't know right away so that you can practice them at home.

1. $18 \div 9 = \underline{2}$ 2. $6\overline{)6}^{\,1}$ 3. $14 / 7 = \underline{2}$ 4. $24 \div 3 = \underline{8}$

5. $42 / 6 = \underline{7}$ 6. $35 \div 5 = \underline{7}$ 7. $10\overline{)30}^{\,3}$ 8. $48 / 8 = \underline{6}$

9. $2\overline{)10}^{\,5}$ 10. $72 / 8 = \underline{9}$ 11. $20 \div 4 = \underline{5}$ 12. $3\overline{)12}^{\,4}$

13. $25 \div 5 = \underline{5}$ 14. $1\overline{)7}^{\,7}$ 15. $27 / 3 = \underline{9}$ 16. $0 \div 7 = \underline{0}$

Compare. Write = or ≠ to make each statement true.

17. $9 + 2 + 5 \,(\neq)\, 4 \times 5$ 18. $6 \times 12 \,(=)\, 8 \times 9$ 19. $5 \times 8 \,(=)\, 7 \times 7 - 9$

Solve each problem.   *Show your work.*

20. Jessica wants to cover the top of a box with fabric. The box is 9 cm long and 8 cm wide. How much fabric does she need?
72 sq cm

21. A square carpet has an area of 9 square meters. What is the length of one side of the carpet?
3 m

22. A quilt is 3 m long and 2 m wide. How many 1-meter squares were used to make the quilt?
6 squares

23. Henry wants to paint his closet door. The door is 2 m long and 1 m wide. What is the area of the closet door?
2 sq m

132 UNIT 4 LESSON 3   Name Triangles

Homework and Remembering page 132

Home or School Activity

Language Arts Connection

Alphabet Angles Have students write a large upper-case letter that includes an angle—for example, A, K, L, M, V, T, and so on. Ask students to name the angle, add a side to make a triangle, then name the triangle by its angles and sides.

Acute angle
Acute isosceles triangle

Right angle
Right scalene triangle

Obtuse angle
Obtuse isosceles triangle

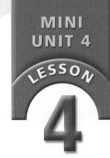

4

Triangles and Diagonals

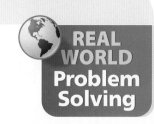

REAL
WORLD
**Problem
Solving**

Lesson Objectives

- Recognize how two congruent triangles make a parallelogram.
- Discover how the diagonal of a parallelogram splits the figure into two congruent triangles.

Vocabulary

triangle
quadrilateral
congruent
diagonal

The Day at a Glance

Today's Goals	Materials
1 **Teaching the Lesson** **A1:** Join congruent triangles to make a parallelogram. **A2:** Divide a parallelogram into two congruent triangles. **2** **Going Further** ▶ Extension: Explore Paths ▶ Differentiated Instruction **3** **Homework and Spiral Review**	**Lesson Activities** Student Activity Book pp. 197–199 or Student Hardcover Book pp. 197–199 and Activity Workbook p. 77 Homework and Remembering pp. 133–134 Triangles and Diagonals (TRB M55) Transparency of Triangles and Diagonals (TRB M55) (optional) Overhead projector (optional) Scissors Glue	**Going Further** Student Activity Book p. 200 or Student Hardcover Book p. 200 and Activity Workbook p. 79 Dots and Paths (TRB M128) transparency Overhead projector Activity Card 44 Geoboards or Geoboards/Dot Paper (TRB M56) Colored rubber bands Grid paper Math Journals

123 Use
Math Talk
today!

Keeping Skills Sharp

Daily Routines	English Language Learners
Homework Review Have students discuss their explanations for problems 10 and 11 on their Homework. Help them clarify any misunderstandings. **Skip Count** Have students skip count ▶ by 10s from 1,038 to 1,108. ▶ by 100s from 9,954 to 10,754.	Draw an acute triangle, an obtuse triangle, and a right triangle. Point to each triangle. Have students tell how they are alike and different. • **Beginning** Say: **This triangle has a right angle. It is a right triangle.** Point to the acute triangle. Ask: **Does this triangle have a right angle?** no Point to the obtuse triangle. Ask: **Does this triangle have a right angle?** no • **Intermediate** Ask: **Which triangle has a right angle? What do we call a triangle with a right angle?** a right triangle **Which is an acute triangle? Which is an obtuse triangle?** • **Advanced** Ask: **How do you tell if a triangle is right?** It has a right angle in it. **Acute?** It has acute angles in it. **Obtuse?** It has an obtuse angle in it. **What is the difference between acute, right, and obtuse triangles?** the size of the angles inside them

① Teaching the Lesson

Make Quadrilaterals With Triangles

 30 MINUTES

Goal: Join congruent triangles to make a parallelogram.

Materials: Triangles and Diagonals (TRB M55); scissors (1 per student); Student Activity Book pp. 197–198 or Hardcover Book pp. 197–198 and Activity Workbook p. 77; overhead projector and transparency of Triangles and Diagonals (optional); glue

 NCTM Standard:
Geometry

▶ Cut Out and Name Triangles WHOLE CLASS

Give each student Triangles and Diagonals (TRB M55). If possible, project a transparency of this page with an overhead projector.

Have the students cut out triangles Q, R, and S from Section II of TRB M55.

● Name the triangles by their angles and by their sides. Q is an acute triangle, R is an obtuse triangle, and S is a right triangle. All are scalene.

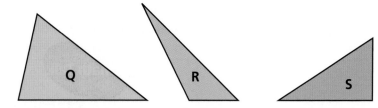

▶ Build a Parallelogram With Two Congruent Triangles WHOLE CLASS

Have the students find parallelogram A in Section I.

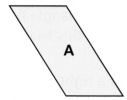

● One half of this parallelogram is exactly the same size and shape as either triangle Q, triangle R, or triangle S. How can you find out which triangle it is? You can put each triangle on top of the parallelogram.

● What is the first thing you need to see? 2 sides and 1 angle that exactly match

● What is the second thing? The empty part of the parallelogram is exactly the same size as the triangle.

● Which triangle is exactly one half of parallelogram A? triangle S

Sketch the parallelogram on the board and draw in the diagonal to show the congruent triangles, or draw the diagonal on the overhead transparency.

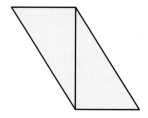

▶ Build More Parallelograms With Congruent Triangles SMALL GROUPS

Write this chart on the board:

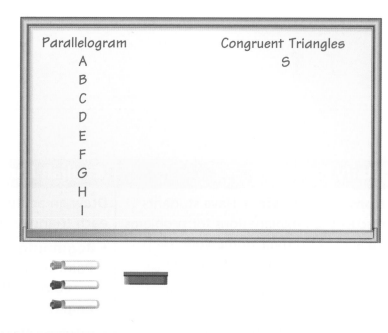

Have students find out which triangle makes each of the other parallelograms in Section I.

Invite students to complete the chart and to sketch the parallelogram with the diagonal, or to add the diagonal to the transparency, as you did for parallelogram A. Two of triangle Q make parallelograms C, E, and H. Two of R make B, G, and I. Two of S make A, D, and F.

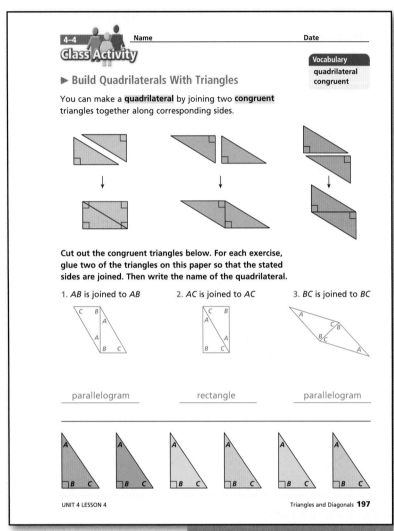

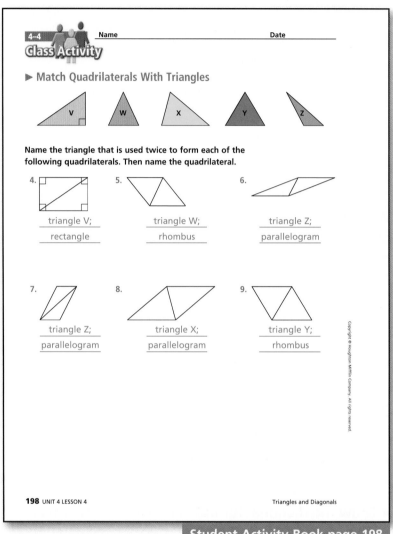

▶ Build Quadrilaterals With Triangles

INDIVIDUALS

Point out that congruent triangles can be joined along each of the three congruent sides, as shown on Student Book page 197.

Encourage students to use the diagrams as a guide as they complete exercises 1–3. Remind students to glue the triangles wallpaper-side down.

▶ Match Quadrilaterals With Triangles

SMALL GROUPS

Math Talk Have students discuss which congruent triangles make the parallelograms as they complete exercises 4–9 on Student Book page 198.

✓ Ongoing Assessment

Ask students to look at the triangles at the top of Student Book page 198.

▶ Which triangle has a right angle?

▶ Which triangle is equilateral?

▶ Which triangle is isosceles?

▶ How would you describe the two remaining triangles?

Then have students look at the triangles that make the quadrilaterals.

▶ How can you use the features of the triangles in each quadrilateral to help you find the matching triangle at the top of the page?

Triangles and Diagonals   **465**

Activity 2

Make Congruent Triangles From Parallelograms

 30 MINUTES

Goal: Divide a parallelogram into two congruent triangles.

Materials: Student Activity Book or Hardcover Book p. 199

 NCTM Standard:
Geometry

▶ Draw Diagonals to Make Triangles

WHOLE CLASS

Write the word *diagonal* on the board. Have students discuss what they already know about that word. Some may know the general meaning: "having a slanted direction."

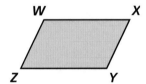

Draw a parallelogram (or a rectangle) on the board. Label the vertices with the letters *W, X, Y,* and *Z.*

● What does a diagonal to a parallelogram look like? a line joining opposite corners

● Draw the diagonal for me. Name it with its letters. *XZ* or *ZX*

● What figure does the diagonal create inside the parallelogram? 2 triangles

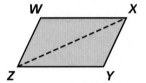

● What are the letter names of the triangles? Δ*ZWX* and Δ*XYZ*

● What do you know about the size and shape of the triangles? The triangles are congruent.

● How do you know? We made parallelograms by putting two congruent triangles together.

Draw the parallelogram again.

● Is there another way to draw a diagonal on the parallelogram? You can join the other two corners with a line.

● Draw the diagonal for me. Name it with its letters. *WY*

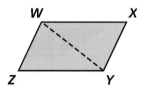

● What are the letter names of the triangles? Δ*WXY* and Δ*YZW*

Teaching Note

Math Background When you make congruent triangles by drawing a diagonal in a parallelogram, or when you make a parallelogram from congruent triangles, the triangles are related by a rotation of 180° and a translation.

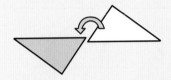 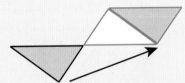

You can also make a quadrilateral if you reflect a triangle along any of its sides.

If you reflect an equilateral triangle along any of its sides, the quadrilateral you make will always be a rhombus.

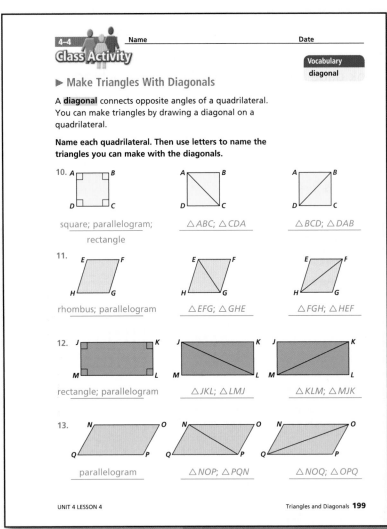

► Make Triangles With Diagonals

4–4

Class Activity

Name   Date

Vocabulary
diagonal

► Make Triangles With Diagonals

A **diagonal** connects opposite angles of a quadrilateral. You can make triangles by drawing a diagonal on a quadrilateral.

Name each quadrilateral. Then use letters to name the triangles you can make with the diagonals.

10.

square; parallelogram; rectangle   △ABC; △CDA   △BCD; △DAB

11.

rhombus; parallelogram   △EFG; △GHE   △FGH; △HEF

12.

rectangle; parallelogram   △JKL; △LMJ   △KLM; △MJK

13.

parallelogram   △NOP; △PQN   △NOQ; △OPQ

UNIT 4 LESSON 4   Triangles and Diagonals **199**

Student Activity Book page 199

► Make Triangles With Diagonals

SMALL GROUPS

Direct students' attention to the quadrilaterals in exercises 10–13 on Student Book page 199. Have students work in **Small Groups** or with **Helping Partners** to name the triangles made when the diagonals are added.

Practice Making Congruent Triangles For more practice opportunities, have students work in **Small Groups** to draw parallelograms, label the vertices, draw diagonals, and name the triangles.

Differentiated Instruction

Advanced Learners Ask students to classify the triangles according to sides and angles. Students should get the following answers:

10: right isosceles for both; 11: acute isosceles, obtuse isosceles; 12: right scalene for both; 13: acute scalene, obtuse scalene

The Learning Classroom

Helping Community Create a classroom where students are not competing but desire to collaborate and help one another. Communicate often that your goal for small groups (and the whole class) is that everyone understands the math you are studying. Tell students that this will require everyone to work together to help each other.

Going Further

Extension: Explore Paths

 20 MINUTES

Goal: Identify paths.

Materials: Transparency of Dots and Paths (TRB M128) and overhead projector; Student Activity Book p. 200 or Hardcover Book p. 200 and Activity Workbook p. 79

✔ **NCTM Standards:**
Geometry
Problem Solving
Reasoning and Proof

▶ Arrays and Paths WHOLE CLASS

Place Dots and Paths (TRB M128) on the overhead. Point out the 3-by-3 dot array and have students look at the array that is shown on the top of Student Book page 200. Explain that a goal of this activity is to connect all the dots in the array by a continuous path without crossing that path or picking up their pencils. Give students an opportunity to draw paths for all three arrays.

Use the transparency of TRB M128 to give students an opportunity to share the different paths they drew. After students have shared different paths, ask if there is one type of path that can be used on all three dot arrays.

If students suggest that such a path is not possible, point out that a spiral path can be used for any size dot array. (Shown as the answer for the 5-by-5 array)

▶ Maps and Paths INDIVIDUALS

Give students time to look at the map grid on Student Book page 200. The map grid shows the blocks of a community. Explain that the paths they choose must be along the lines of the grid. They cannot cross blocks on diagonals to find the shortest paths.

Lead a class discussion about the solutions for exercises 2–4.

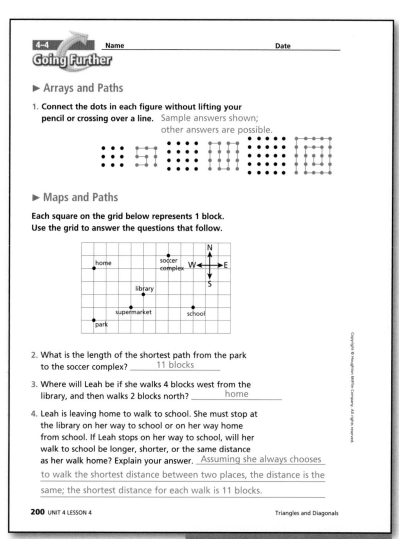

Student Activity Book page 200

Differentiated Instruction

Intervention Activity Card 4-4

Make Congruent Triangles — Activity Card 4-4 ●

Work: In Pairs

Use:
- Geoboard or Geoboard/Dot Paper (TRB M56)
- Colored rubber bands
- Centimeter-Grid Paper (TRB M60)

1. One partner makes a parallelogram on the geoboard and then adds a diagonal by joining opposite points with a rubber band. An example is shown below.

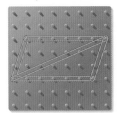

2. The other partner draws the parallelogram and the diagonal on grid paper.

3. Cut out the two triangles formed, and check that they are congruent.

Unit 4, Lesson 4 — Copyright © Houghton Mifflin Company

Activity Note Students can check congruence by placing the cutout triangles one on top of the other.

Math Writing Prompt

Show What You Know What is the diagonal of a quadrilateral? Use pictures and words to explain. How many diagonals can you draw in a quadrilateral?

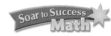 **Software Support**

Use *Soar to Success* for instruction of students needing targeted support for underlying skills.

On Level Activity Card 4-4

Build Parallelograms — Activity Card 4-4 ▲

Work: By Yourself

Use:
- Grid paper

1. Draw a right triangle on the grid paper.

2. Draw another congruent triangle. The second triangle should not touch or overlap the first one.

3. Join the matching vertices of the triangle with a line segment.

4. Name the quadrilaterals that are in the drawing.

Unit 4, Lesson 4 — Copyright © Houghton Mifflin Company

Activity Note Students should label vertices to help identify all the quadrilaterals.

Math Writing Prompt

Summarize In your own words, explain how congruent triangles can be used to make quadrilaterals.

Software Support

Use *MegaMath* for review and reinforcement of the concepts and skills presented in this lesson.

Challenge Activity Card 4-4

Diagonals in Other Quadrilaterals — Activity Card 4-4 ■

Work: By Yourself

Use:
- Centimeter-Grid Paper (TRB M60)

1. Draw two congruent isosceles trapezoids on grid paper. Then draw a different diagonal in each figure.

2. Write the names of the triangles you created.

3. Compare the triangles to determine which triangles are congruent.

4. **Explain** What is different about the triangles created with a diagonal in an isosceles trapezoid and a diagonal in a parallelogram? The triangles formed by a diagonal in a parallelogram are congruent; the triangles formed by a diagonal in an isosceles triangle are not congruent.

Unit 4, Lesson 4 — Copyright © Houghton Mifflin Company

Activity Note Have students label the vertices of the trapezoids to help identify corresponding parts of the congruent triangles.

Math Writing Prompt

Make a List Suppose you want to make a rhombus from two congruent triangles. Thinking of sides and angles, list all the kinds of triangles you can use. Explain your thinking.

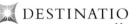 **Software Support**

Use *Destination Math* to take students beyond the concepts and skills presented in this lesson.

Triangles and Diagonals **469**

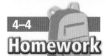 # Homework and Spiral Review

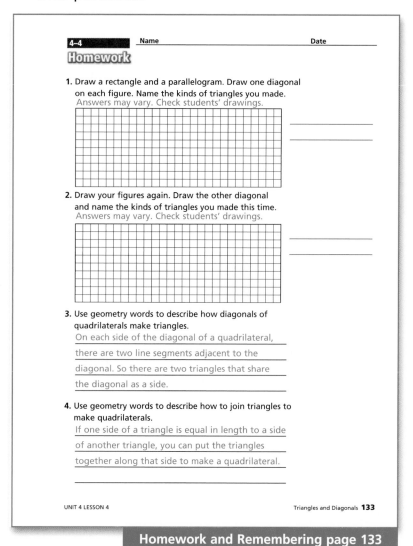
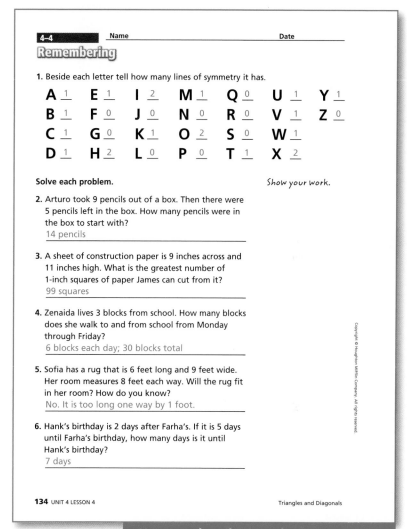

Homework and Remembering page 133

Homework and Remembering page 134

Home or School Activity

 ### Social Studies Connection

Pioneer Quilts Pioneers made quilts from scraps of fabric. Have students make a mixed-media quilt using a cardboard triangle (cut from a cereal box) as a template for each half of a parallelogram.

Students might use one or more of these materials to create their quilt:

- scraps of fabric
- gift wrap
- newspapers
- magazine ads
- tissue paper

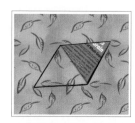
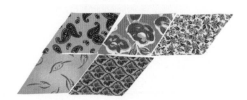

470 UNIT 4 LESSON 4

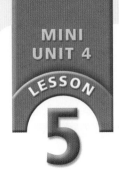

Perimeter and Area of Triangles

Lesson Objective
● Find the perimeter and area of triangles.

The Day at a Glance

Today's Goals	Materials
1 Teaching the Lesson **A1:** Find the perimeter of triangles and relate the method to finding the perimeter of quadrilaterals. **A2:** Find the area of different kinds of triangles and relate the method to finding the area of quadrilaterals. **A3:** Practice finding the perimeter and area of triangles. **2 Going Further** ▶ Differentiated Instruction **3 Homework and Spiral Review**	**Lesson Activities** Student Activity Book pp. 201–204 or Student Hardcover Book pp. 201–204 and Activity Workbook pp. 80–81 Homework and Remembering pp. 135–136 Perimeter and Area of Triangles (TRB M57) Centimeter rulers **Going Further** Activity Cards 4-5 Grid paper Scissors Centimeter rulers Math Journals

123 Use Math Talk today!

Keeping Skills Sharp

Daily Routines	English Language Learners
Homework Review Let students work together to check their work. Initially, pair less able students with more able students. Remind students to use what they know about helping others. **Strategy Problem** A region has 10 towns that are connected by roads. If each road connects only 2 towns, how many roads are there? 45 roads	Write *perimeter* and *area* on the board. Draw a rectangle. Label the sides 4, 5, 4, and 5. Have students identify the base and height. Say: **Perimeter is the distance around the figure. Area is the space inside the figure.** • **Beginning** Point to the word *perimeter*. **We add the sides for** *perimeter*. **4 + 5 + 4 + 5 = ___.** 18 **The** *perimeter* **is 18.** Point to the word *area*. Ask: **Is this** *perimeter*? no • **Intermediate** Say: **The** *perimeter* **is the distance around a figure.** Ask: **How do you find the** *perimeter* **of the rectangle?** Add all the side lengths. **What is 4 + 5 + 4 + 5?** 18 **Are** *perimeter* **and** *area* **the same thing?** no • **Advanced** Ask: **What is the perimeter of the rectangle?** 18 **How do you find the area of the rectangle?** base × height, or 5 × 4 **What is the area?** 20 square units

Teaching the Lesson

Perimeter of Triangles

 20 MINUTES

Goal: Find the perimeter of triangles and relate the method to finding the perimeter of quadrilaterals.

Materials: Student Activity Book or Hardcover Book p. 201

✔ **NCTM Standard:**
Geometry

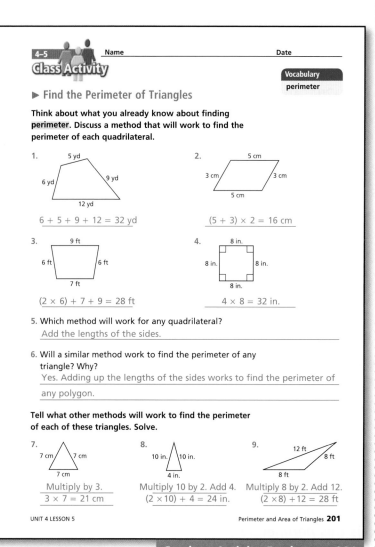

Student Activity Book page 201

▶ Find the Perimeter of Triangles

WHOLE CLASS

Ask students what they remember about the word *perimeter.* It's the distance around the outside of a figure.

On Student Book page 201, have the students discuss exercises 1–4.

● What is the general method for finding the perimeter of a quadrilateral? Add the lengths of all the sides.

● How else can you find the perimeter of a rectangle or parallelogram? Multiply the length of each different side by two and then add. Or, add the lengths of the two different sides and then multiply by two.

● How else can you find the perimeter of a square or rhombus? Multiply the length of a side by four.

Have students complete exercises 5–9.

 Ongoing Assessment

Circulate throughout the class and assess informally students' understanding of perimeter. If necessary, remind them that perimeter is the measure around a figure, like a fence. This may help them see that adding the side lengths is another way to find the perimeter of any triangle.

Activity 2

Area of Triangles

 20 MINUTES

Goal: Find the area of different kinds of triangles and relate the method to finding the area of quadrilaterals.

Materials: Student Activity Book pp. 202–203 or Hardcover Book pp. 202–203 and Activity Workbook pp. 80–81

 NCTM Standard:
Geometry

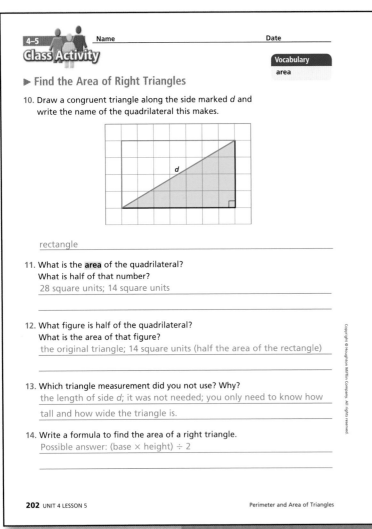

Student Activity Book page 202

► Find the Area of Right Triangles

WHOLE CLASS

Review with students how to join congruent triangles to make quadrilaterals.

● What do you know about finding the area of rectangles? *area = length × width*

On Student Book page 202, have students read and discuss exercises 10–14. They should recognize that because a right triangle is half of a rectangle, the area of a right triangle is half of the area of that rectangle: $\frac{1}{2} \times$ *length × width.*

Differentiated Instruction

Extra Help To reinforce the idea that the triangles are congruent and have the same area, students shade one square (or part square) in the bottom triangle; then they do the same for the matching square (or part square) in the top triangle. They continue until the entire rectangle is shaded.

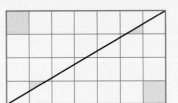

Activity continued ►

Perimeter and Area of Triangles **473**

Activity 2

▶ Find the Area of Other Triangles

WHOLE CLASS

● What do you know about finding the area of parallelograms? Multiply base times height.

On Student Book page 203, invite students to read and discuss questions 15–19. They should recognize that joining any two congruent triangles will make a parallelogram, so the general method for finding the area of any triangle is $\frac{1}{2} \times$ *base* $\times$ *height*.

Teaching Note

Language and Vocabulary Focus on the meaning of the words in the questions. Discuss various ways to help students remember them.

- triangle: *tri* = three, like the three wheels on a tricycle
- height: The height of a figure is how tall it is, just like your height is how tall you are.
- area: measured with square units, like an area rug
- quadrilateral: 4 sides like a square
- parallelogram: has sides that are parallel, like the letters *l* in the word

Name _____ Date _____

Class Activity

▶ Find the Area of Other Triangles
Possible answers given.

15. Draw a congruent triangle along the side marked *d*.
Write the name of the quadrilateral this makes.

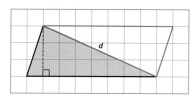

parallelogram _____

16. What measurement does the dotted line represent in the triangle above?
the height of the triangle

17. Why do you need the height to find the area of the quadrilateral?
You need the height of the parallelogram to find its area, because the area is base times height.

18. Why do you also need the height to find the area of the triangle?
The area of the triangle is half of the area of the parallelogram, so you use the height to find the area of the parallelogram, and then take half that number to get the area of the triangle.

19. Write a formula to find the area of any triangle.
Multiply the base by the height, then divide by 2; $\frac{1}{2} \times b \times h$

UNIT 4 LESSON 5   Perimeter and Area of Triangles **203**

Student Activity Book page 203

Activity 3

Practice With Triangles

 20 MINUTES

Goal: Practice finding the perimeter and area of triangles.

Materials: Student Activity Book or Hardcover Book p. 204; centimeter ruler (1 per student); Perimeter and Area of Triangles (TRB M57)

✔ **NCTM Standard:**
Geometry

▶ Find Perimeter and Area of Triangles

SMALL GROUPS

Draw students' attention to the triangles on Student Book page 204.

● What measurements do you need so that you can find the perimeter and area of a triangle? You need side lengths for perimeter. For area you also need the height, which may or may not be a side length.

Invite students to form **Small Groups** to discuss the different ways they can measure the base and height of a triangle. See sample dialogue below.

Ask students to complete exercises 20–23. Encourage them to look for a base and height that are easy to measure.

 Math Talk in Action

To find the area of a triangle, you need to know the base and the height. What are the base and height of a triangle?

Alvin: The base is the side on the bottom. The height is how tall it is up and down.

Good. Have a look at the triangles in your book. Will measuring side lengths tell you about the base or the height?

Mori: The base is a side, so measuring side length will tell you about the base. The height isn't always a side, though. It is in the right triangle, but not in the others.

If you turn a triangle so a different side is on the bottom, will the base or height change? Try turning your books to see.

Elisa: Yes. The base and height change when you turn these triangles.

Alvin: For some triangles it might not change. It would depend on the side lengths, I think.

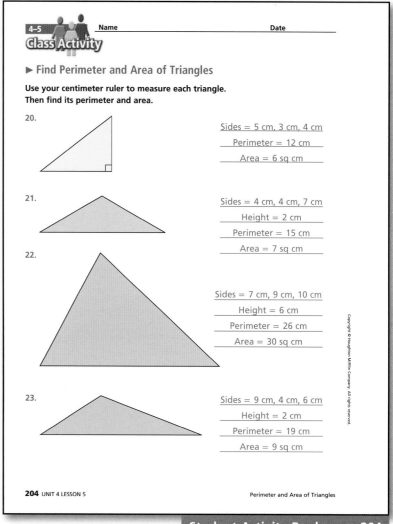

Student Activity Book page 204

That's right. Do you think the area of a triangle changes when you turn it?

Alvin: No. The area stays the same.

Correct. How many different ways could you find the base and height of a triangle to calculate its area?

Alvin: Three. Each side could be the base. They all have to give the same area.

Yes. Sometimes measuring will be easier if you choose a different side for the base.

Teaching Note

Math Background Height is measured at a right angle from the base. You can extend a base, if needed, to measure the height of a triangle.

Activity continued ▶

Perimeter and Area of Triangles **475**

Activity 3

▶ **More Practice** [SMALL GROUPS]

Students may need more practice measuring triangles and calculating perimeter or area. Others may not understand that the general method for calculating the area of triangles is $\frac{1}{2} \times base \times height$. Have students work with the figures on Perimeter and Area of Triangles (TRB M57).

In **Small Groups**, have students measure the sides of triangle *ABC*, using a centimeter ruler. *AB* = 8 cm, *AC* = 6 cm, *BC* = 12 cm

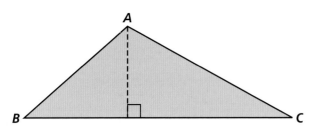

● What is the perimeter of triangle *ABC*? 8 + 12 + 6 = 26 cm

● What line do you need to add to parallelogram *ABCD* to show that the area of triangle *ABC* is $\frac{1}{2}$ of the area of the parallelogram? line *AC*

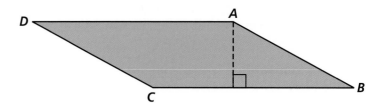

Have students discuss triangle *FGH* and parallelogram *EFGH* in similar ways. *FH* = 8 cm, *FG* = 6 cm, *GH* = 8 cm; perimeter = 8 + 6 + 8 = 22 cm; line *FH* needs to be added to the parallelogram

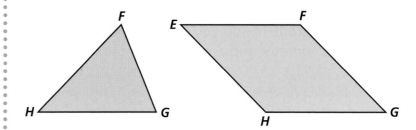

Have the students measure the height of triangle *ABC* and find the area. Height = 4 cm; $\frac{1}{2}$ of (4 × 12) = $\frac{1}{2}$ of 48 = 24 (Note that the area of triangle *FGH* is harder to compute because the height in centimeters is not a whole number.)

② Going Further

Intervention Activity Card 4-5

Match Triangles Activity Card 4-5 ●

Work: In Pairs

Use:
- Centimeter-Grid Paper (TRB M60)
- Scissors
- Tape

1. One partner draws a right triangle on grid paper.

2. The other partner draws a congruent triangle. An example is shown below.

3. Cut out the two triangles. Join them along the longest side to make a rectangle. Tape the triangles together.

4. Use the rectangle to determine the area of each triangle.

5. **Look Back** Explain how you know the two triangles are congruent. Answers will vary.

Unit 4, Lesson 5   Copyright © Houghton Mifflin Company

Activity Note Students can calculate the area of the rectangles. Then they can find the area of the triangle by taking half the area of the rectangle.

📝 Math Writing Prompt

You Decide You know both the perimeter and the area of a triangular garden. Explain which one will help you decide how much fertilizer to put on the garden.

Soar to Success Math **Software Support**

Use *Soar to Success* for instruction of students needing targeted support for underlying skills.

On Level Activity Card 4-5

Paper Triangles Activity Card 4-5 ▲

Work: In Pairs

Use:
- Centimeter ruler

1. Fold the corner of a sheet of paper to form a triangle as shown below.

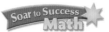

2. Fold another corner of the paper to form a different-sized triangle.

3. Name each triangle by its angles. Will this always be true? right; yes

4. Use the centimeter ruler to measure the side lengths. Round each length to the nearest centimeter.

5. Find the perimeter and the area of each triangle.

Unit 4, Lesson 5   Copyright © Houghton Mifflin Company

Activity Note Help students see that the triangle formed by the fold will always be a right triangle.

📝 Math Writing Prompt

Problem Solving Suppose you want to make a rectangular flag with a diagonal line. The part to the right of the diagonal will be red; the other part will be gray. If you know the flag's size, how can you find how much of each color to buy?

MegaMath Grades K-6 **Software Support**

Use *MegaMath* for review and reinforcement of the concepts and skills presented in this lesson.

Challenge Activity Card 4-5

More Than One Solution Activity Card 4-5 ■

Work: By Yourself

Use:
- Centimeter ruler

1. Look at the riddle below.

> I am a triangle. One of my sides is 4 centimeters long. My other two sides are whole numbers of centimeters. My perimeter is 12 centimeters. Sketch me.

2. Sketch all possible triangles.

3. How many different triangles can you draw? two

3 cm   5 cm   4 cm   4 cm

4 cm   4 cm

Unit 4, Lesson 5   Copyright © Houghton Mifflin Company

Activity Note Students may sketch triangles with sides that are 1-7-4 and 2-6-4. Have them draw these triangles on grid paper to see if they work.

📝 Math Writing Prompt

Explore Formulas Describe a method that will work to find the perimeter of any closed figure with straight sides. What formula or equations can you use to represent your method?

✠ DESTINATION Math® **Software Support**

Use *Destination Math* to take students beyond the concepts and skills presented in this lesson.

③ Homework and Spiral Review

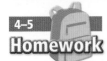

Homework **Goal:** Additional Practice

✓ Include students' work for page 135 as part of their portfolios.

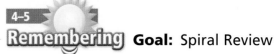

Remembering **Goal:** Spiral Review

This Remembering activity would be appropriate anytime after today's lesson.

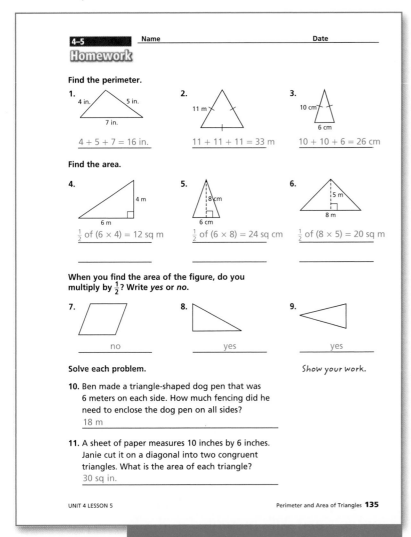

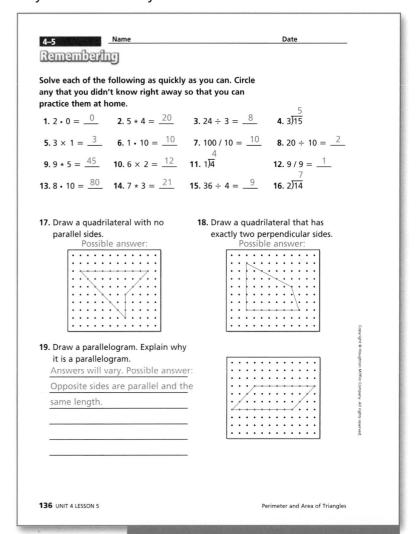

Homework and Remembering page 135

Homework and Remembering page 136

Home or School Activity

🌐 **Real-World Connection**

Triangle Safari Have students look in their environment for triangles such as paving stones, floor tiles, quilt sections, textile patterns, and so on. Ask them to sketch the figures and write where they found each one. Have students measure and calculate the perimeter and area of three of their examples.

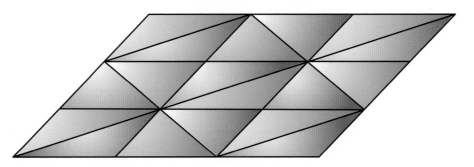

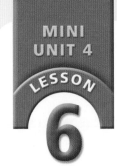

Polygons

Vocabulary

polygon
closed
regular
irregular
congruent
convex
concave
triangle
quadrilateral
pentagon

Lesson Objectives

● Identify the attributes of, and name, regular and irregular polygons.

● Construct a variety of polygons, including regular, irregular, convex, and concave.

● Find the perimeter of polygons.

The Day at a Glance

Today's Goals	Materials	

1 **Teaching the Lesson**
A1: Identify the attributes of regular and irregular polygons; name polygons.
A2: Construct a variety of polygons, including regular, irregular, convex, and concave.
A3: Find the perimeter of regular polygons.
 	
2 **Going Further**
▶ Differentiated Instruction
 	
3 **Homework and Spiral Review**
	Lesson Activities
	Student Activity Book pp. 205–208
	  or Student Hardcover Book
	  pp. 205–208
	Homework and Remembering
	  pp. 137–138
	Make Polygons (TRB M75)
	Find the Perimeter of Regular
	  Polygons (TRB M76)
	Scissors
	Quick Quiz 2 (Assessment Guide)
		Going Further
		Activity Cards 4-6
		Pattern blocks or
		  Pattern Blocks
		  (TRB M77)
		Straightedge or ruler
		Math Journals

123 Use Math Talk today!

Keeping Skills Sharp

Daily Routines	English Language Learners
Homework Review Ask students if they had difficulty with any part of the homework. Plan to set aside some time to work with students needing extra help. **Strategy Problem** Suppose that you cut a string in half. Then you cut each half in half. Then you cut each new half in half again. If you cut all the pieces in half two more times, how many pieces of string will you have? 32 pieces What is the pattern? Multiply by 2.	Draw the two figures below on the board. Have students identify which is open, closed, and which is a quadrilateral. • **Beginning** Point to the quadrilateral. Ask: **Is this open or closed?** closed Say: **It is a quadrilateral.** Point to the other figure. Ask: **Is this figure closed?** no Say: **This figure is open. It is NOT a quadrilateral.** • **Intermediate** Compare the two figures. Ask: **Which figure is closed? What is the figure?** quadrilateral, trapezoid Ask: **Which figure is open? Is this figure a quadrilateral?** no • **Advanced** Say: These figures both have 4 sides. Ask: **Are both figures quadrilaterals?** no **How do you know?** one is open, one is closed **Is a quadrilateral an open figure or a closed figure?** closed

① Teaching the Lesson

Activity 1

Explore Polygons

 15 MINUTES

Goal: Identify the attributes of regular and irregular polygons; name polygons.

Materials: Student Activity Book or Hardcover Book pp. 205–207

 NCTM Standard:
Geometry

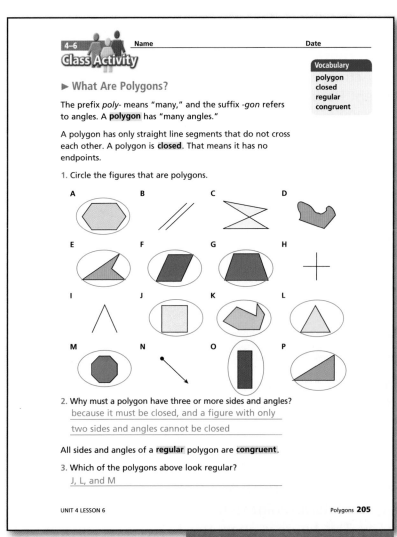

Student Activity Book page 205

▶ **What Are Polygons?** WHOLE CLASS

On Student Book page 205, discuss the figures in exercise 1.

● Is figure A a polygon? yes

● **How do you know?** It has straight line segments for sides. They are all connected, and they don't cross over each other.

● **What about figure B?** No; the line segments aren't connected.

● **How can you describe figure B?** a pair of parallel line segments

● **Is figure C a polygon?** No; the line segments cross each other.

● **What about figure D?** No; part of the edge (or perimeter) isn't straight.

Have students mark the other polygons in exercise 1, and ask them to name as many of the figures as they can.

Differentiated Instruction

Extra Help Students can make a checklist of features of a polygon and use it to classify the figures as polygons. This would be especially helpful for **English Learners**.

• Made up of straight line segments

• Segments don't cross

• Closed (no endpoints)

Math Talk Ask students to read and discuss exercises 2 and 3. When students' discuss exercise 3, point out that a polygon that is not regular is called *irregular*. These questions may help students' thinking.

● If there are only one or two sides in a figure, can it be a polygon? No; because it has to be closed.

● Do polygons F and J have congruent sides? yes

● Why isn't polygon F regular? It doesn't have all congruent angles.

● Does polygon J have congruent angles? yes

● Are all quadrilaterals polygons? Yes; they're closed figures with straight line segments that don't cross.

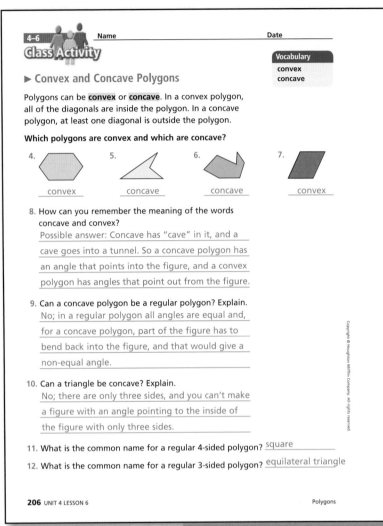

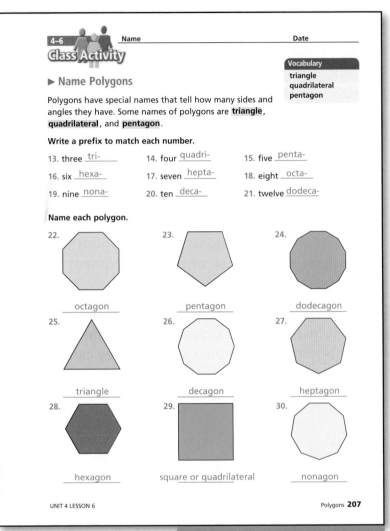

▶ Convex and Concave Polygons PAIRS

Ask for Ideas Have students tell what they remember about diagonals. A diagonal is drawn between two nonadjacent (opposite) angles (vertices).

Draw these polygons on the board without diagonals. Ask volunteers to draw the diagonals.

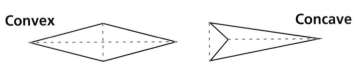

Convex **Concave**

Ask students how the convex and concave polygons are different. The diagonals of the convex polygon are all inside it; the diagonals of the concave polygon are not all inside it.

Have **Student Pairs** work to complete exercises 4–12.

▶ Name Polygons PAIRS

Write these prefixes in random order on the classroom board: *deca-, octa-, penta-, nona-, quadri-, hepta-, tri-, hexa-,* and *dodeca-.*

Invite the students to discuss what number might match each prefix. If a dictionary is available, students can check their predictions. Have the class work in **Student Pairs** to complete exercises 13–30 on Student Book page 207.

Teaching Note

Language and Vocabulary The prefix *deca-* means "10" and the prefix *dodeca-* means "12." *Do* sounds like *dos,* the Spanish word for "two," and two more than 10 is 12.

Polygons **481**

❶ Teaching the Lesson (continued)

Activity 2

Make Polygons

 25 MINUTES

Goal: Construct a variety of polygons, including regular, irregular, convex, and concave.

Materials: Make Polygons (TRB M75) (1 per small group), scissors (1 per student)

✔ **NCTM Standard:**
Geometry

▶ Make Convex and Concave Polygons

SMALL GROUPS

Give each group of students Make Polygons (TRB M75). Have students cut out all of the line-segment pieces along the dotted lines.

Invite students to experiment with using the different pieces to make various polygons and name them. Students might sketch their work so they can share what they have made.

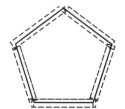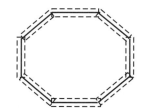

Concave: One or more angles point to the inside.

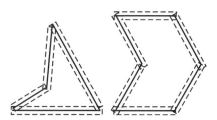

Convex: All angles point to the outside.

▶ Make Regular Polygons SMALL GROUPS

Have the students sort their pieces so that each student has 12 pieces of the same length. One copymaster has enough pieces for 6 students.

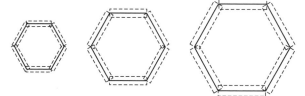

Ask each student in the group to make a regular hexagon.

● What happens to the inside angles of the hexagon as the length of the sides increases? nothing; the angles stay the same regardless of the length of the sides.

Then have each student in the group make a different regular polygon.

● What happens to the angles as the number of sides increases? the more sides, the bigger the inside angles

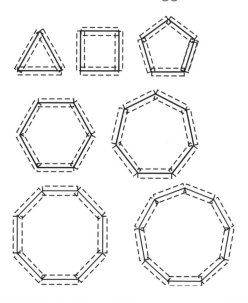

Teaching Note

Measure Angles Students can measure the angles in their polygons with a protractor and record the measurements on the board beside the name of each regular polygon.

 Ongoing Assessment

Ask students to sketch examples of polygons you describe.

▶ a concave pentagon

▶ an irregular quadrilateral with all sides congruent

▶ a regular hexagon

482 UNIT 4 LESSON 6

Find the Perimeter of a Polygon

 20 MINUTES

Goal: Find the perimeter of regular polygons.

Materials: Find the Perimeters of Regular Polygons (TRB M76)
(1 per small group); scissors (1 per student); Student Activity
Book or Hardcover Book p. 208

 NCTM Standards:
Geometry
Measurement

▶ Review Perimeter and Congruence

WHOLE CLASS

Ask for Ideas Discuss with students what they
remember about perimeter and congruence.

● What does it mean to say two figures are congruent?
  They are the same size and the same shape.

● What is the perimeter of a geometric figure? the
  distance around the outside of it

Have a student sketch a right triangle on the board.
Label the sides *a*, *b*, and *c* to stand for their lengths.

● Write the addition equation for the perimeter.
  $P = a + b + c$

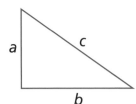

Have another student sketch a parallelogram. Label
the sides *b* and *s*.

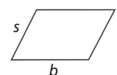

● What do you know about the opposite sides of the
  parallelogram? Their lengths are equal (or they are
  congruent).

● Write an equation for the perimeter. $P = b + s + b$
  $+ s$ or $P = (2 \bullet b) + (2 \bullet s)$ or $P = 2(b + s)$

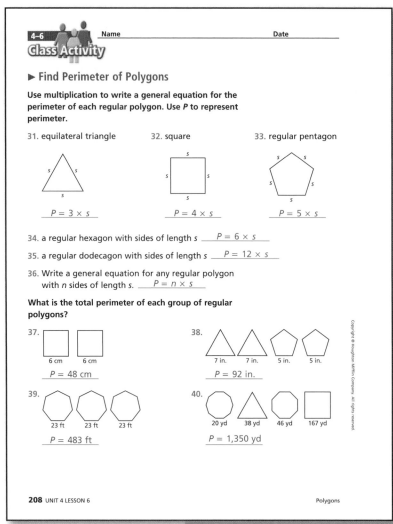

Activity continued ▶

Polygons **483**

Activity 3

▶ Find Perimeter of Polygons

SMALL GROUPS

Have the students work in **Small Groups**. Give each group Find the Perimeters of Regular Polygons (TRB M76). Ask students to cut on the dotted line to cut off the 25-centimeter ruler at the top of the page.

Invite students to "roll" each polygon along the ruler to get a sense of the perimeter of the figure. Students can place a mark in one corner of the polygon to track its movement. The example below shows a nonagon with 2-cm sides. (Note: Example shown is not drawn to scale.)

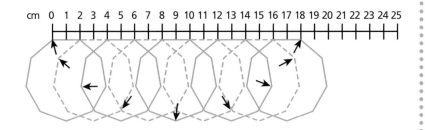

● What happens as you turn the polygon? Rolling along the ruler shows the total measure of the congruent sides.

● How can you use multiplication to find the perimeter of the polygons on the page? Multiply the number of sides by the length of one side.

● Why can you use multiplication? The sides are congruent, so you are always adding the same number.

● Why is multiplication a better method than addition? It's faster.

Ask students to complete exercises 31–36 on Student Book page 208.

Together, discuss exercise 37.

● How can you find the total perimeter of more than one congruent polygon? by multiplying $s \times n$ to find the perimeter of one of the polygons, then multiplying that number by the number of polygons or adding the perimeters of the individual polygons

● What is the perimeter of one square? 24 cm

● What is the total perimeter of the squares? 48 cm

Discuss exercise 38.

● What is the perimeter of one triangle? 21 in.

● What is the perimeter of one pentagon? 25 in.

● What is the total perimeter? 92 in.

Have students complete exercises 39 and 40 on their own.

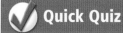 **Quick Quiz**

See Assessment Guide for Unit 4 Quick Quiz 2.

② Going Further

Intervention   Activity Card 4-6

Identify Polygons   Activity Card 4-6 ●

Work: In Pairs

Use:
• Pattern blocks or Pattern Blocks (TRB M77)

1. Trace each pattern block onto your paper.

2. Describe each pattern block in as many ways as possible.

regular hexagon

regular quadrilateral square, parallelogram rhombus

irregular quadrilateral rhombus

irregular quadrilateral isosceles trapezoid

regular triangle equilateral triangle

irregular quadrilateral rhombus

3. **Look Back** Review your descriptions. Are there any additional terms you could use for the polygons? Did you identify each polygon as regular or irregular? Answers will vary.

Unit 4, Lesson 6   Copyright © Houghton Mifflin Company

Activity Note Use Pattern Blocks (TRB M77) if pattern blocks are not available. It might be helpful to provide students with a list of all possible terms for polygons.

 Math Writing Prompt

Write About It Explain how a regular polygon is different from other polygons with the same number of sides.

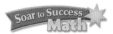 **Software Support**

Use *Soar to Success* for instruction of students needing targeted support for underlying skills.

On Level   Activity Card 4-6

Investigate Math   Activity Card 4-6 ▲

Work: In Pairs

Use:
• Pattern blocks or Pattern Blocks (TRB M77)
• Straightedge or ruler

1. Trace the equilateral triangle, the square, and the hexagon onto your own paper.

3

4

6

2. Draw all possible lines of symmetry for each polygon.

3. Describe the relationship between the number of sides of a regular polygon and the number of lines of symmetry you can draw. The number of sides of a regular polygon is equal to the number of lines of symmetry that polygon has.

Unit 4, Lesson 6   Copyright © Houghton Mifflin Company

Activity Note Use Pattern Blocks (TRB M77) if pattern blocks are not available. Students may want to use scissors to cut out and fold the shapes.

 Math Writing Prompt

Make a Drawing Draw a picture to help you explain why it is impossible for a polygon with three sides (triangle) to be concave.

 Software Support

Use *MegaMath* for review and reinforcement of the concepts and skills presented in this lesson.

Challenge   Activity Card 4-6

Plan It   Activity Card 4-6 ■

Work: By Yourself

1. Look at the riddle below.

> I am a square. If you could turn my sides to make one long line segment, my length would be 20 inches. What is my area?

2. What information do you know about the square? The sum of its sides is 20 in.

3. What do you know about the sides of a square? They are equal.

4. Solve the riddle. $20 \div 4 = 5$; $5 \times 5 = 25$; 25 sq in.

5. Create and solve your own riddle about a regular polygon. Exchange it with a partner.

Unit 4, Lesson 6   Copyright © Houghton Mifflin Company

Activity Note Check that students include the step of finding the length of one side before finding the area.

 Math Writing Prompt

Investigate Math If you know only the number of sides of a regular polygon, can you predict whether or not it has parallel sides? Explain your thinking.

 DESTINATION Math® **Software Support**

Use *Destination Math* to take students beyond the concepts and skills presented in this lesson.

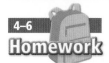

③ Homework and Spiral Review

4-6 Homework **Goal:** Additional Practice

✓ Include students' completed Homework page 137 as part of their portfolios.

4-6 Remembering **Goal:** Spiral Review

This Remembering page would be appropriate anytime after today's lesson.

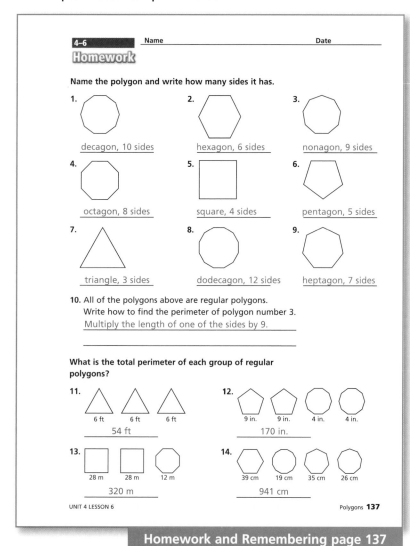

Homework and Remembering page 137

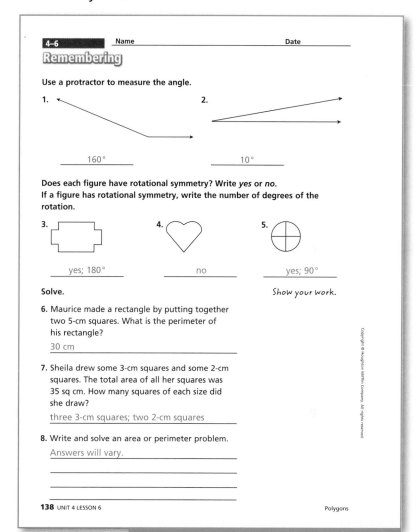

Homework and Remembering page 138

Home or School Activity

 Art Connection

Bas Relief Sculpture Show students an example of a bas-relief and explain that a small part of the art is raised. Suggest that they use this technique to create a wall sculpture with polygons.

Have students use wooden sticks, such as those used to stir coffee, to create a wall sculpture that includes both convex and concave polygons. The sculpture can be realistic or abstract and can include other media, such as paint.

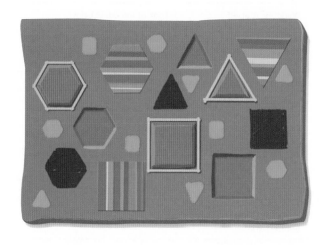

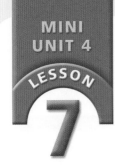

Transformations

Vocabulary

transformation
rotation
translation
reflection
congruent

Lesson Objectives

● **Rotate, translate, and reflect figures.**

● **Use transformations to prove congruence and extend patterns.**

The Day at a Glance

Today's Goals	Materials

① Teaching the Lesson

A1: Rotate a figure about a point, given a number of degrees and a direction.

A2: Translate a figure a given distance and direction.

A3: Reflect a figure across a vertical or horizontal line.

A4: Develop an understanding of transformations and congruence.

② Going Further
▶ Extension: Patterns and Transformations
▶ Differentiated Instruction

③ Homework and Spiral Review

Lesson Activities
Student Activity Book pp. 209–213
  or Student Hardcover Book
  pp. 209–213 and Activity
  Workbook pp. 82–85
Homework and Remembering
  pp. 139–140
Exploring Transformations
  (TRB M129)
Mirror (optional)
Quick Quiz 3 (Assessment Guide)

Going Further
Student Activity Book
  p. 214 or Student
  Hardcover Book
  p. 214
Activity Cards 4-7
Grid paper
Pattern blocks or
  Pattern Blocks
  (TRB M77)
Math Journals

123 *Use* **Math Talk** *today!*

Keeping Skills Sharp

Daily Routines	English Language Learners

Homework Review Have students discuss the problems from their homework. Encourage students to help each other resolve any misunderstandings.

Place Value Name 10,000 less than each number.

98,715 88,715   **32,786** 22,786

187,384 176,384   **418,667** 408,667

Have students brainstorm a list of things that turn. Write their answers on the board and discuss how each example turns. Write the word *rotate* on the board.

• **Beginning** Point to the word *rotate.* Say: ***Rotate* means "turn". These are things that *rotate*.** Read some of the examples from the list. Show a square on the table. Say: **Watch as I *rotate* the square.** Rotate the square on the table.

• **Intermediate** Ask: **What means the same as *rotate*?** turn Guide students to name some of the examples from the list. Show a square on the table. Ask students to show you how to *rotate* the square.

• **Advanced** Ask: **What does it mean to *rotate* a figure?** to turn it Have students name some examples of things that rotate. Ask: **What changes when we rotate a figure?** the direction

Teaching the Lesson

Rotations

 20 MINUTES

Goal: Rotate a figure around a point, given a number of degrees and a direction.

Materials: Exploring Transformations (TRB M129); Student Activity Book pp. 209 and 212 or Hardcover Book pp. 209 and 212 and Activity Workbook pp. 82 and 85

✓ **NCTM Standards:**
Geometry
Problem Solving

▶ Model Rotations [WHOLE CLASS]

Ask For Ideas Have students share what they recall about rotations, and encourage them to draw sketches at the board to support their recollections.

Discuss the examples at the top of Student Book page 209 with the class. Make sure students understand that the dashed lines show the original locations of the figures, and the solid lines show the positions of the figures after a 90° clockwise rotation.

All of the triangles in the example are identical. For this lesson students will only rotate figures about a point that is on the figure.

Have students cut out figure *R* from Exploring Transformations (TRB M129) and place it on the grid on Student Book page 212. Using pencils, ask them to trace the outline of the square. Then, after rotating it 90° clockwise, trace it a second time. Have students repeat the activity to practice other rotations.

Challenge students to name *pairs* of rotations that produce the same result. For example, a 90° counter-clockwise rotation and 270° clockwise rotation produce the same result.

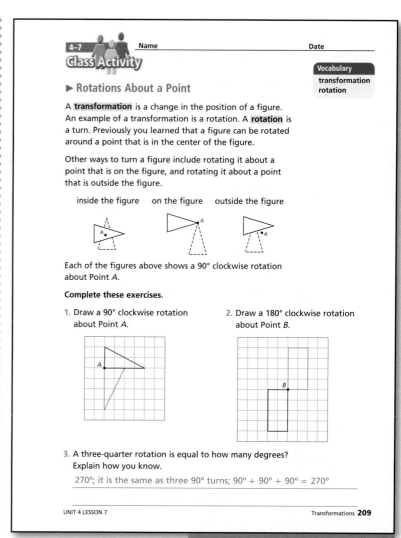

Student Activity Book page 209

▶ Rotations About a Point [INDIVIDUALS]

Have students complete exercises 1 and 2 on page 209 individually or with a **Helping Partner**. Then, discuss exercise 3.

Teaching Note

Watch For! If students have difficulty visualizing a rotation, have them trace the figure on a separate sheet of paper, and use a pen or pencil to press down on the tracing at the point of rotation. The tracing can then be rotated any number of degrees in either direction.

Translations

 15 MINUTES

Goal: Translate a figure a given distance and direction.

Materials: Student Activity Book pp. 210 and 212 or Hardcover Book pp. 210 and 212 and Activity Workbook pp. 83 and 85; Exploring Transformations (TRB M129)

 NCTM Standards:
Geometry
Problem Solving

▶ Model Translations WHOLE CLASS

Read the introduction at the top of Student Book page 210 or ask a volunteer to read it aloud. Invite the students to describe the different examples of translations, using their own words. Their descriptions should include the idea that after each translation, the figure is the same distance from the line as it was before the translation.

Have students cut out figure *S* from Exploring Transformations (TRB M129) and place it on or near the horizontal line on Student Book page 212. Using pencils, ask them to trace the outline of the rectangle. Then, after translating it a number of units to the left or to the right, trace it a second time. Ask students to repeat the activity by translating the rectangle along the vertical line.

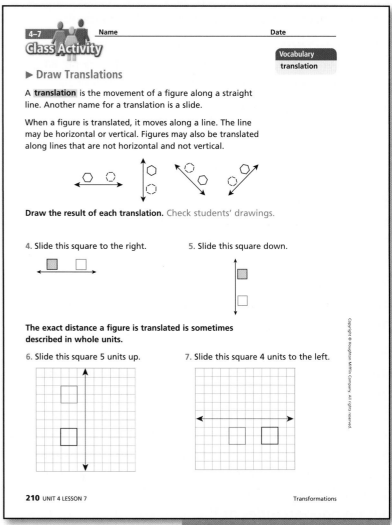

▶ Draw Translations INDIVIDUALS

Ask students to complete exercises 4 and 5 on Student Book page 210. Discuss the positions of the translations. Remind students that the distance of the figure from the line of translation must be the same after the translation as before.

For exercises 6 and 7, point out that the number of units and the direction are specified for each exercise.

Activity 3

Reflections Across a Line

 40 MINUTES

Goal: Reflect a figure across a vertical or horizontal line.

Materials: Mirror; Student Activity Book pp. 211–212 or Hardcover Book pp. 211–212 and Activity Workbook pp. 84–85; Exploring Transformations (TRB M129); mirror (optional)

✓ **NCTM Standards:**
Geometry
Problem Solving

▶ Model Reflections PAIRS

A reflection is sometimes called a *mirror image*. Demonstrate a reflection by inviting students to write their name on a piece of paper, hold the paper near a mirror, and read their name by looking in the mirror. Invite discussion as students discover the "opposite" nature of a reflection.

Have students discuss the examples of reflections shown on Student Book p. 211 and describe them, using their own words. Make sure students understand that every point on a reflected figure will be the same distance from the line of reflection as its corresponding point on the original figure, but on the opposite side of the line. For example, point out that the top vertex of each letter A is 1 unit from the line of reflection, but on opposite sides of the line. Encourage students to use the distance and direction relationship of corresponding points to check their work after a reflection has been drawn.

Have students cut out figures *P, X, Y,* and *Z* from TRB M129 and place the figures in different locations on the grid on Student Page 212. Working in **Student Pairs,** they can reflect each figure twice—once across the horizontal line and once across the vertical line.

Teaching Note

Watch For! Reflections can be the most difficult transformations for students to perform. Watch for students who slide a figure rather than reflect it. If possible, use a mirror to show them what the reflection should look like. Then assist them in flipping the figure to show the reflection.

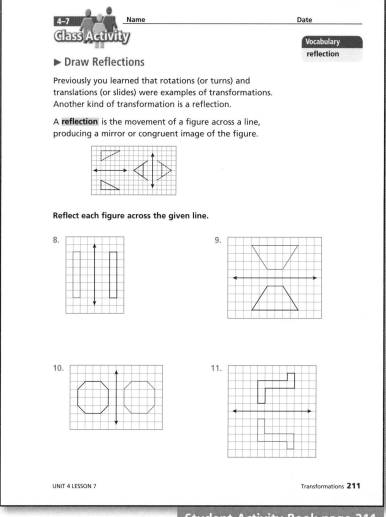

Student Activity Book page 211

▶ Draw Reflections PAIRS

On Student Book page 211, have students work individually to complete exercises 8–11, and work in **Student Pairs,** using the distance and direction relationship of corresponding points to check their work.

 Ongoing Assessment

Ask students to use a small book to demonstrate and explain a rotation about a point, a translation, and a reflection across a line.

Use Transformations to Prove Congruence

 20 MINUTES

Goal: Develop an understanding of transformations and congruence.

Materials: Student Activity Book or Hardcover Book p. 213

 NCTM Standards:
Geometry
Reasoning and Proof

▶ Discuss Congruence [WHOLE CLASS]

Ask for Ideas Have students share what they recall about congruent figures. Students should verbalize that, for two figures to be congruent, they must be *exactly* the same size and shape. In other words, identical in every way.

Give students an opportunity to observe their classroom and identify any congruent figures that can be seen.

▶ Transformations and Congruent Figures [SMALL GROUPS]

On Student Book page 213, have students work in **Small Groups** to complete exercises 12–15. For these exercises, more than one correct answer is sometimes possible (for example, the congruence in exercise 1 can be proved by a 90° clockwise rotation or by a 270° counter-clockwise rotation). Therefore, you might choose to challenge each group to provide more than one correct answer for each exercise, whenever possible.

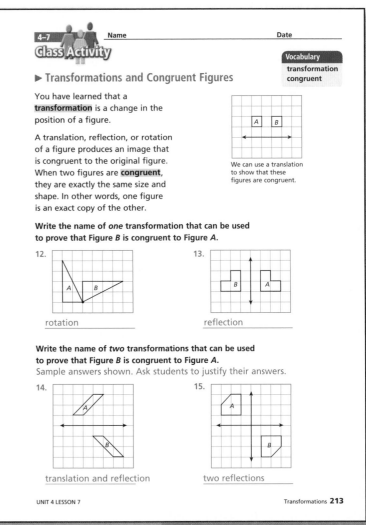

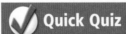
Student Activity Book page 213

Differentiated Instruction

Advanced Learners Ask students to draw a figure on grid paper, and then draw the image of the figure after all three transformations have been applied to it. **Student Pairs** can discuss whether changing the order in which the transformations are applied produces the same, or a different, result.

✓ Quick Quiz

See Assessment Guide for Unit 4 Quick Quiz 3.

② Going Further

Extension: Transformations and Patterns

 25 MINUTES

Goal: Identify transformations in a pattern of figures.

Materials: Student Activity Book or Hardcover Book p. 214

 NCTM Standards:
Geometry
Reasoning and Proof

▶ Discuss Patterns

SMALL GROUPS   **Math Talk**

Ask for Ideas Have students share what they recall about patterns, and invite volunteers to write patterns of numbers and patterns of shapes on the board. Ask the students to work in **Small Groups** and discuss each pattern, identify its rule, name or describe the next term in the pattern, and compare their findings to those of other groups.

▶ Extend Patterns   PAIRS

Pair students with a **Helping Partner** to complete the exercises on Student Book page 214. Point out that if a rotation is included in the rule of a pattern, students should include a number of degrees and a direction in their answer. Some pairs may find it helpful to trace the first figure in each pattern, and then move the tracing in different ways to help identify the rule.

Since some of the patterns can be described by more than one rule, you might choose to challenge each group to describe more than one rule, whenever possible. For example, the pattern in exercise 3 can be described as a continuous series of reflections across a vertical line, or as a continuous series of 180° rotations.

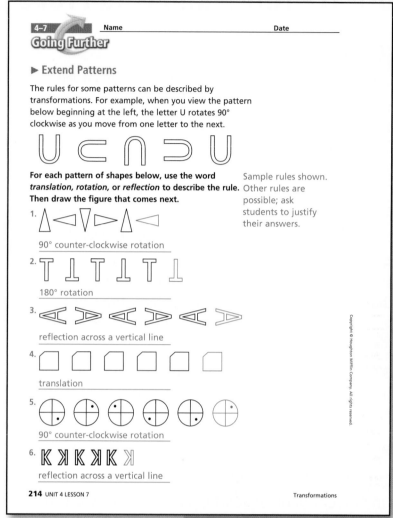

Student Activity Book page 214

Differentiated Instruction

Advanced Learners If time permits upon completion of the activity, encourage interested students to design their own patterns and challenge classmates to identify the rule of the pattern and describe the next term.

Differentiated Instruction

Intervention   Activity Card 4-7

Alphabet Transformations   Activity Card 4-7 ●

Work: By Yourself

Use:
- Centimeter-Grid Paper (TRB M60)

1. Copy the figures at the right.
2. Determine which transformation has occurred for each figure.
3. Draw an upper case C on your grid paper.
4. Create a translation, a reflection, and a rotation for the letter, and label each.
5. **Explain** How can you tell if a transformation is a translation?
   The object has the same orientation, but is in a different location.

 translation

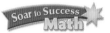 reflection

rotation

Unit 4, Lesson 7   Copyright © Houghton Mifflin Company

Activity Note Students may need scissors to cut out a letter P and repeat the transformations to correctly identify them.

✎ Math Writing Prompt

Summarize Describe a reflection in your own words. Draw an example if needed.

★ Soar to Success Math — Software Support

Use *Soar to Success* for instruction of students needing targeted support for underlying skills.

On Level   Activity Card 4-7

Combining Shapes   Activity Card 4-7 ▲

Work: By Yourself

Use:
- Pattern blocks or Pattern Blocks (TRB M77)
- Centimeter-Grid Paper (TRB M60)

1. Combine two pattern blocks to make a polygon.
2. Trace your polygon on grid paper.
3. Create a translation for your polygon, and trace it on the grid paper. Label it like the sample shown below.

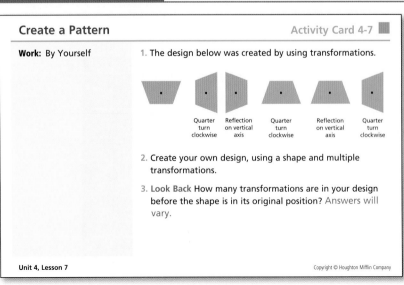

original → translation

4. Now create a reflection and a rotation of your polygon, and label them.

Unit 4, Lesson 7   Copyright © Houghton Mifflin Company

Activity Note Point out that for some shapes a reflection and a translation can look the same. Note that for rotations it is important to show the point of rotation.

✎ Math Writing Prompt

Explain Your Thinking Which pattern blocks look the same after a translation, a reflection, and a rotation? Explain your answer.

MEGAMATH Grades K-6 — Software Support

Use *MegaMath* for review and reinforcement of the concepts and skills presented in this lesson.

Challenge   Activity Card 4-7

Create a Pattern   Activity Card 4-7 ■

Work: By Yourself

1. The design below was created by using transformations.

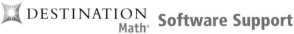

| Quarter turn clockwise | Reflection on vertical axis | Quarter turn clockwise | Reflection on vertical axis | Quarter turn clockwise |

2. Create your own design, using a shape and multiple transformations.
3. **Look Back** How many transformations are in your design before the shape is in its original position? Answers will vary.

Unit 4, Lesson 7   Copyright © Houghton Mifflin Company

Activity Note Students may make shapes that are simple or complex. For more complex figures, it may be easier to use grid paper.

✎ Math Writing Prompt

Draw a Picture Show a shape that looks the same after a reflection and a translation and one that does not look the same. Explain what things influence this.

✖ DESTINATION Math® — Software Support

Use *Destination Math* to take students beyond the concepts and skills presented in this lesson.

③ Homework and Spiral Review

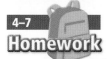

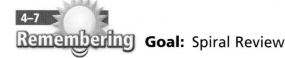

4–7 Homework Goal: Additional Practice

✔ Include students' completed Homework page 139 as part of their portfolios.

4–7 Remembering Goal: Spiral Review

This Remembering page would be appropriate anytime after today's lesson.

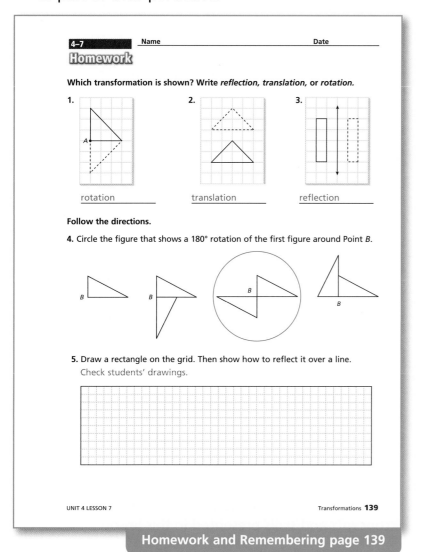

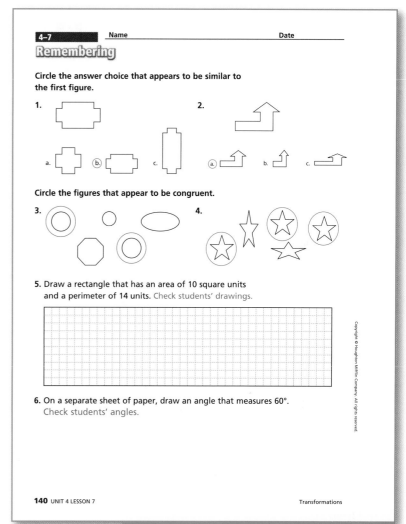

Homework and Remembering page 139

Homework and Remembering page 140

Home or School Activity

 Real-World Connection

Transformation Hunt Discuss the use of translations, reflections, and rotations in the design of practical objects, such as quilts, tiles in a floor, or bricks in a walkway. Have students look in their environment for examples of transformations and sketch each example. Students should label each sketch with the type of transformation it represents.

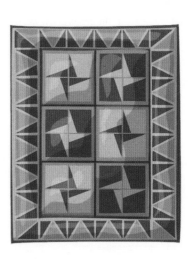

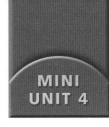

Unit Review and Test

Lesson Objective

● **Assess student progress on unit objectives.**

The Day at a Glance

Today's Goals	Materials
1 **Assessing the Unit** ▶ Assess student progress on unit objectives. ▶ Use activities from unit lessons to reteach content. **2** **Extending the Assessment** ▶ Use remediation for common errors. There is no homework assignment on a test day.	Unit 4 Test, Student Activity Book pp. 215–216 or Student Hardcover Book pp. 215–216 and Activity Workbook p. 86 Unit 4 Test, Form A or B, Assessment Guide (optional) Unit 4 Performance Assessment, Assessment Guide (optional)

Keeping Skills Sharp

Daily Routines 🕐 5 MINUTES	
If you are doing a unit review day, go over the homework. If this is a test day, omit the homework review.	**Review and Test Day** You may want to choose a quiet game or other activity (reading a book or working on homework for another subject) for students who finish early.

Assessing the Unit

Assess Unit Objectives

45 MINUTES (more if schedule permits)

Goal: Assess student progress on unit objectives.

Materials: Student Activity Book pp. 215–216 or Hardcover Book pp. 215–216 and Activity Workbook p. 86; Assessment Guide (optional)

▶ Review and Assessment

If your students are ready for assessment on the unit objectives, you may use either the test on the Student Book pages or one of the forms of the Unit 4 Test in the Assessment Guide to assess student progress.

If you feel that students need some review first, you may use the test on the Student Book pages as a review of unit content, and then use one of the forms of the Unit 4 Test in the Assessment Guide to assess student progress.

To assign a numerical score for all of these test forms, use 5 points for questions 4A and 4B and 10 points for each other question.

You may also choose to use the Unit 4 Performance Assessment. Scoring for that assessment can be found in its rubric in the Assessment Guide.

▶ Reteaching Resources

The chart lists the test items, the unit objectives they cover, and the lesson activities in which the objective is covered in this unit. You may revisit these activities with students who do not show mastery of the objectives.

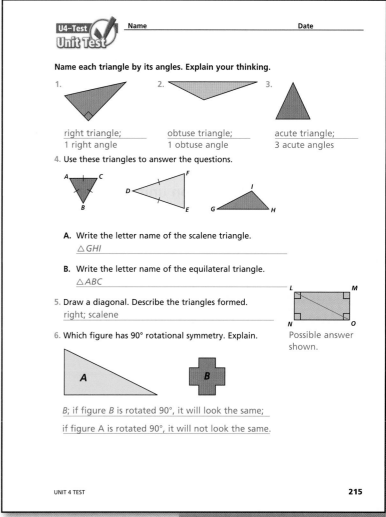

Student Activity Book page 215

Unit Test Items	Unit Objectives Tested	Activities to Use for Reteaching
1–5	**4.1** Classify triangles by their angles and sides.	Lesson 1, Activity 1 Lesson 3, Activities 1–2 Lesson 4, Activity 1
6	**4.2** Identify figures with rotational symmetry.	Lesson 2, Activity 1
7, 9–10	**4.3** Find the perimeter and area of polygons.	Lesson 5, Activities 1–2 Lesson 6, Activity 3
8	**4.4** Identify translations, reflections, and rotations.	Lesson 7, Activities 2–3

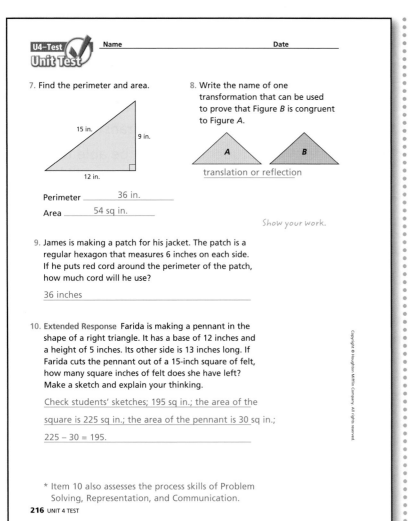

U4-Test
Unit Test ✓

Name _____ Date _____

7. Find the perimeter and area.

15 in.
9 in.
12 in.

Perimeter ____ 36 in. ____
Area ____ 54 sq in. ____

8. Write the name of one transformation that can be used to prove that Figure *B* is congruent to Figure *A*.

A   B

translation or reflection

Show your work.

9. James is making a patch for his jacket. The patch is a regular hexagon that measures 6 inches on each side. If he puts red cord around the perimeter of the patch, how much cord will he use?

36 inches

10. **Extended Response** Farida is making a pennant in the shape of a right triangle. It has a base of 12 inches and a height of 5 inches. Its other side is 13 inches long. If Farida cuts the pennant out of a 15-inch square of felt, how many square inches of felt does she have left? Make a sketch and explain your thinking.

Check students' sketches; 195 sq in.; the area of the

square is 225 sq in.; the area of the pennant is 30 sq in.;

225 − 30 = 195.

* Item 10 also assesses the process skills of Problem Solving, Representation, and Communication.

216 UNIT 4 TEST

Student Activity Book page 216

▶ Assessment Resources

Free Response Tests
Unit 4 Test, Student Activity Book pp. 215–216 or Hardcover Book pp. 215–216 and Activity Book p. 86
Unit 4 Test, Form A, Assessment Guide

Extended Response Item
The last item in the Student Book test and in the Form A test will require an extended response as an answer.

Multiple Choice Test
Unit 4 Test, Form B, Assessment Guide

Performance Assessment
Unit 4 Performance Assessment, Assessment Guide
Unit 4 Performance Assessment Rubric, Assessment Guide

▶ Portfolio Assessment

Teacher-selected Items for Student Portfolios:

- Homework, Lessons 2, 3, 4, 5, 6, and 7

- Class Activity work, Lesson 1

Student-selected Items for Student Portfolios:

- Favorite Home or School Activity

- Best Writing Prompt

② Extending the Assessment

Unit Objective 4.1
Classify triangles by their angles and sides.

Common Error: Misidentifies Right Angles

Students may fail to identify right angles, especially if the right angle is not in the bottom corner of the triangle.

Remediation Encourage such students to use an index card to help decide whether an angle is a right angle. Also have them look for the little square that denotes a right angle in the triangle.

Common Error: Does Not Differentiate Triangles

Students may fail to distinguish between types of triangles.

Remediation Suggest that students make side-by-side lists comparing the properties of the different triangles, including the kinds of angles and lines in each triangle.

Unit Objective 4.2
Identify figures with rotational symmetry.

Common Error: Cannot Visualize 90°, 180°, and 270° Rotations

Some students cannot easily visualize what an object will look like when it is rotated.

Remediation Have students use a book, chalkboard eraser, or other classroom object to act out rotational symmetry. Remind them that a 90° rotation forms a right angle to the original position, and a 180° rotation forms a straight line from its original position.

Unit Objective 4.3
Find the perimeter and area of polygons.

Common Error: Doesn't Use All Measurements

In finding perimeter, students may fail to use the lengths of all sides of a triangle.

Remediation Remind students that the number of addends used to find the perimeter must equal the number of sides of the triangle. It may help to count the sides and the addends as a check that all sides have been used.

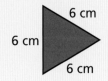

Unit Objective 4.4
Identify translations, reflections, and rotations.

Common Error: Cannot Visualize the Results of a Transformation

Students may not be able to visualize what a figure will look like after it is translated along a line, reflected across a line, or rotated around a point.

Remediation Have students trace a figure and cut it out. Then have them act out each transformation to see which one works. Some students may need to do this many times with different figures.

Multi-Digit Multiplication

UNIT 5 REVIEWS AND BUILDS upon the concepts of arrays, single-digit multiplication, place value, and area that the students discovered in earlier grades or lessons. The activities in this unit help students gain a conceptual understanding of multi-digit multiplication. They are expected to apply their understanding of multi-digit multiplication to numeric calculations and real-world problem solving situations, including multiplication combinations and comparisons.

Skills Trace

Grade 3	Grade 4	Grade 5
• Multiply a two- and three-digit number by a one-digit number. • Identify problems with too little information. • Solve problems with too much information. • Solve two-step problems.	• Multiply a two- and three-digit number by a one-digit number. • Multiply hundreds and thousands. • Multiply a two- and three-digit number by a two-digit number. • Estimate products. • Identify problems with too little information. • Solve problems with too much information. • Solve multistep problems.	• Multiply any whole numbers. • Estimate products. • Identify problems with too little information. • Solve problems with too much information. • Solve multistep problems.

Unit 5 Contents

Unit 5   Assessment

✓ Unit Objectives Tested	Unit Test Items	Lessons
5.1 Solve multiplication problems, using mental math.	1	2
5.2 Multiply by a one-digit number.	2–3	3, 5, 6, 7, 8
5.3 Estimate products.	4–5	4, 8, 13
5.4 Multiply by a two-digit number.	6–7, 10	11, 12, 15, 17
5.5 Solve multistep word problems with too much information.	8–9	9, 10

Assessment and Review Resources

Formal Assessment

Student Activity Book
- Unit Review and Test
  (pp. 259–260)

Assessment Guide
- Quick Quiz 1
- Quick Quiz 2
- Quick Quiz 3
- Quick Quiz 4
- Test A–Open Response
- Test B–Multiple Choice
- Performance Assessment

Test Generator CD-ROM
- Open Response Test
- Multiple Choice Test
- Test Bank Items

Informal Assessment

Teacher Edition
- Ongoing Assessment
  (in every lesson)
- Quick Practice (in every lesson)
- Math Talk (in every lesson)
- Portfolio Suggestions (pp. 520, 534, 560, 572, 622)

123 Math Talk
- ▸ The Learning Classroom (pp. 501, 510, 516, 526, 538, 551, 569, 592, 600)
- ▸ Math Talk in Action (pp. 509, 531, 545, 554, 563, 575, 590, 601, 608)
- ▸ Activities (pp. 515, 516, 526, 543, 544, 551, 569, 570, 576, 580, 581, 592, 600, 614, 618, 619)
- ▸ Solve and Discuss (pp. 516, 525, 538, 546, 552, 557, 563, 564, 576, 580, 581, 590, 593, 594, 601, 606, 607, 608, 613, 614)
- ▸ Student Leaders (pp. 507, 513, 521, 529, 535, 541, 549, 552, 561, 567, 573, 579, 580, 589, 597, 600, 605, 611)
- ▸ Small Groups (pp. 510, 602)
- ▸ Helping Partners (pp. 510, 515, 590)
- ▸ Student Pairs (pp. 510, 517, 518, 531, 537, 545, 554, 558, 569, 586, 594, 600, 602)
- ▸ Step by Step at the Board (p. 526)

Review Opportunities

Homework and Remembering
- Review of recently taught topics
- Cumulative Review

Teacher Edition
- Unit Review and Test
  (pp. 623–626)

Test Generator CD-ROM
- Custom review sheets

Planning Unit 5

Lesson/NCTM Standards	Resources	Materials for Lesson Activities	Materials for Other Activities
5–1 **Multiplication Arrays** NCTM Standards: 1, 8	TE pp. 449–506 SAB pp. 217–222 H&R pp. 141–142 AC 5-1	MathBoard Materials	Centimeter-Grid Paper (TRB M60) ✓ Counters Math Journals
5–2 **Mental Math and Multiplication With Tens** NCTM Standard: 1	TE pp. 507–512 SAB pp. 223–224 H&R pp. 143–144 AG Quick Quiz 1 AC 5-2		✓ Base-ten blocks Cross-Number Grid (TRB M61) Math Journals
5–3 **Model One-Digit by Two-Digit Multiplication** NCTM Standards: 1, 6, 7, 8	TE pp. 513–520 SAB pp. 225–228 H&R pp. 145–146 AC 5-3	✓ Base-ten blocks (optional) MathBoard Materials	*Match-Up* Game Cards (TRB M62–M63) Scissors Math Journals
5–4 **Estimate Products** NCTM Standards: 1, 6, 8	TE pp. 521–528 SAB pp. 229–230 H&R pp. 147–148 AC 5-4	MathBoard Materials Colored pencils or markers (optional)	Math Journals
5–5 **Methods of One-Digit by Two-Digit Multiplication** NCTM Standards: 1, 8, 10	TE pp. 529–534 SAB pp. 231–232 H&R pp. 149–150 AC 5-5		✓ Coins Math Journals
5–6 **Discuss Different Methods** NCTM Standards: 1, 6, 8	TE pp. 535–540 SAB pp. 233–234 H&R pp. 151–152 AC 5-6		Math Journals
5–7 **One-Digit by Three-Digit Multiplication** NCTM Standards: 1, 6, 8, 10	TE pp. 541–548 SAB p. 235–236 H&R pp. 153–154 AC 5-7	MathBoard Materials ✓ Base-ten blocks (optional)	*Go Fish* Game Cards (TRB M64) Scissors Math Journals
5–8 **Practice One-Digit by Three-Digit Multiplication** NCTM Standards: 1, 2, 8, 10	TE pp. 549–560 SAB pp. 237–240 H&R pp. 155–156 AC 5-8		Math Journals
5–9 **Too Much or Too Little Information** NCTM Standards: 1, 6	TE pp. 561–566 SAB pp. 241–242 H&R pp. 157–158 AC 5-9		✓ Number cubes Math Journals
5–10 **Solve Multi-Step Word Problems** NCTM Standards: 1, 6, 8	TE pp. 567–572 SAB pp. 243–244 H&R pp. 159–160 AG Quick Quiz 2 AC 5-10		Homework p. 159 Math Journals

Resources/Materials Key: TE: Teacher Edition   SAB: Student Activity Book   H&R: Homework and Remembering
AC: Activity Cards   MCC: Math Center Challenge   AG: Assessment Guide   ✓: Grade 4 Kits   TRB: Teacher's Resource Book

Lesson/NCTM Standards	Resources	Materials for Lesson Activities	Materials for Other Activities
5–11 **Two-Digit by Two-Digit Multiplication** NCTM Standards: 1, 6, 8, 10	TE pp. 573–578 SAB pp. 245–246 H&R pp. 161–162 AC 5-11	MathBoard Materials	Math Journals
5–12 **Different Methods for Two-Digit Multiplication** NCTM Standards: 1, 2, 8, 10	TE pp. 579–588 SAB pp. 247–248 H&R pp. 163–164 AC 5-12	MathBoard Materials	Multiplication Methods Cards (TRB M65) Multiplication Puzzle (TRB M66) Colored pencils or crayons Index cards Scissors Math Journals
5–13 **Check Products of Two-Digit Numbers** NCTM Standards: 1, 6, 8, 10	TE pp. 589–596 SAB pp. 249–250 H&R pp. 165–166 AC 5-13	MathBoard Materials	Math Journals
5–14 **Practice Multiplication** NCTM Standards: 1, 6, 8, 10	TE pp. 597–604 SAB pp. 251–252 H&R pp. 167–168 AG Quick Quiz 3 AC 5-14		Lattice Multiplication Grids (TRB M67) ✓ Number cubes Math Journals
5–15 **Multiplication With Hundreds** NCTM Standards: 1, 2, 8, 10	TE pp. 605–610 SAB pp. 253–254 H&R pp. 169–170 AC 5-15	MathBoard Materials	Index cards Math Journals
5–16 **Multiplication With Thousands** NCTM Standards: 1, 2, 8, 10	TE pp. 611–616 SAB pp. 255–256 H&R pp.171–172 AG Quick Quiz 4 AC 5-16	MathBoard Materials ✓ Base-ten blocks (optional)	Product Search (TRB M68) Math Journals
5–17 **Use Mathematical Processes** NCTM Standards: 6, 7, 8, 9, 10	TE pp. 617–622 SAB pp. 257–258 H&R pp. 173–174 AC 5-17		MathBoard Dot Array (TRB M47) ✓ Number cubes Math Journals
Unit Review and Test	TE pp. 623–626 SAB pp. 259–260 AG Unit 5 tests		

Hardcover Student Book

- Together, the hardcover student book and its companion Activity Workbook contain all of the pages in the consumable Student Activity Workbook.

Manipulatives and Materials

- Essential materials for teaching Math Expressions are available in the Grade 4 kits. These materials are indicated by a ✓ in these lists. At the front of this Teacher Edition is more information about kit contents, alternatives for the materials, and use of the materials.

Differentiated Instruction

Individualizing Instruction

	Level	Frequency
Activities	• Intervention • On Level • Challenge	All 3 in every lesson
	Level	Frequency
Math Writing Prompts	• Intervention • On Level • Challenge	All 3 in every lesson
Math Center Challenges	For advanced students	
	4 in every unit	

Reaching All Learners

	Lessons	Pages
English Language Learners	1, 2, 3, 4, 5, 6, 7, 8, 9, 10, 11, 12, 13, 14, 15, 16	500, 508, 514, 524, 530, 536, 544, 554, 562, 568, 576, 586, 591, 601, 606, 613, 618
Extra Help	Lessons	Pages
	9	563
Advanced Learners	Lessons	Pages
	3	516
Special Needs	Lessons	Pages
	13	593

Strategies for English Language Learners

Present this problem to all students. Offer the different levels of support to meet students' levels of language proficiency.

Objective Identify factors and products and solve a multiplication problem.

Problem On the board, draw 6 groups of triangles with 4 triangles in each group. Ask: **How many groups?** 6 **How many triangles in each group?** 4 **What is the total number of triangles?** 24

Newcomer

• Say: **Let's count the triangles.** Provide number words as needed.

Beginning

• Say: **There are 6 groups. Each group has 4 triangles. There are a total of 24 triangles.**

• Write 6 × 4 = 24 on the board. Say: **The factors are 6 and 4. The product is 24.**

Intermediate

• Point to 6 × 4 = 24 on the board. Have students identify the factors and the product.

Advanced

• Have students tell their own multiplication problem using factors and products.

Connections

Math-to-Math Connection
Lesson 4, page 528

Social Studies Connections
Lesson 3, page 520
Lesson 7, page 548
Lesson 10, page 572
Lesson 17, page 622

Science Connections
Lesson 2, page 512
Lesson 13, page 596

Sports Connection
Lesson 11, page 578

Language Arts Connection
Lesson 12, page 588

Real-World Connections
Lesson 6, page 540
Lesson 8, page 560
Lesson 9, page 566
Lesson 14, page 604
Lesson 15, page 610
Lesson 16, page 616

Literature Connection
Lesson 5, page 534

Independent Learning Activities

Ready-Made Math Challenge Centers

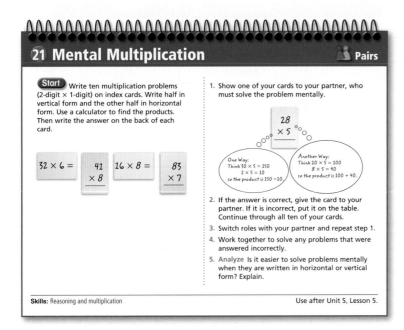

21 Mental Multiplication — Pairs

Start Write ten multiplication problems (2-digit × 1-digit) on index cards. Write half in vertical form and the other half in horizontal form. Use a calculator to find the products. Then write the answer on the back of each card.

$32 \times 6 =$ $41 \\ \times 8$ $16 \times 8 =$ $83 \\ \times 7$

1. Show one of your cards to your partner, who must solve the problem mentally.

    $28 \\ \times 5$

    One Way:
    Think $30 \times 5 = 150$
    $2 \times 5 = 10$
    so the product is $150 - 10$.

    Another Way:
    Think $10 \times 5 = 100$
    $8 \times 5 = 40$
    so the product is $100 + 40$.

2. If the answer is correct, give the card to your partner. If it is incorrect, put it on the table. Continue through all ten of your cards.
3. Switch roles with your partner and repeat step 1.
4. Work together to solve any problems that were answered incorrectly.
5. Analyze Is it easier to solve problems mentally when they are written in horizontal or vertical form? Explain.

Skills: Reasoning and multiplication   Use after Unit 5, Lesson 5.

Grouping Pairs

Materials Index cards, markers, calculators

Objective Students use mental calculation to solve 2-digit × 1-digit multiplication problems.

Connections Operations and Reasoning

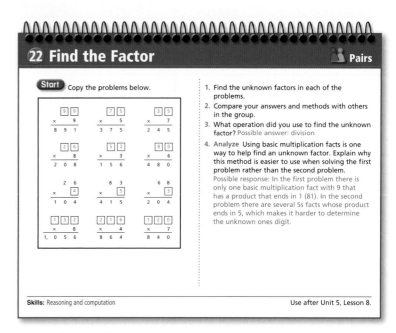

22 Find the Factor — Pairs

Start Copy the problems below.

1. Find the unknown factors in each of the problems.
2. Compare your answers and methods with others in the group.
3. What operation did you use to find the unknown factor? Possible answer: division
4. Analyze Using basic multiplication facts is one way to help find an unknown factor. Explain why this method is easier to use when solving the first problem rather than the second problem.
    Possible response: In the first problem there is only one basic multiplication fact with 9 that has a product that ends in 1 (81). In the second problem there are several 5s facts whose product ends in 5, which makes it harder to determine the unknown ones digit.

Skills: Reasoning and computation   Use after Unit 5, Lesson 8.

Grouping Pairs

Materials None

Objective Students solidify their understanding of the inverse relationship between multiplication and division.

Connections Operations and Reasoning

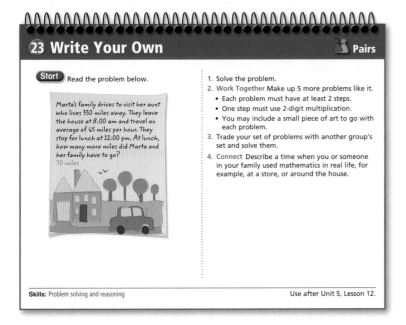

23 Write Your Own — Pairs

Start Read the problem below.

Marta's family drives to visit her aunt who lives 330 miles away. They leave the house at 8:00 am and travel an average of 65 miles per hour. They stop for lunch at 12:00 pm. At lunch, how many more miles did Marta and her family have to go?
70 miles

1. Solve the problem.
2. Work Together Make up 5 more problems like it.
    • Each problem must have at least 2 steps.
    • One step must use 2-digit multiplication.
    • You may include a small piece of art to go with each problem.
3. Trade your set of problems with another group's set and solve them.
4. Connect Describe a time when you or someone in your family used mathematics in real life, for example, at a store, or around the house.

Skills: Problem solving and reasoning   Use after Unit 5, Lesson 12.

Grouping Pairs

Materials None

Objective Students write multistep problems while practicing multi-digit multiplication.

Connections Problem Solving and Communication

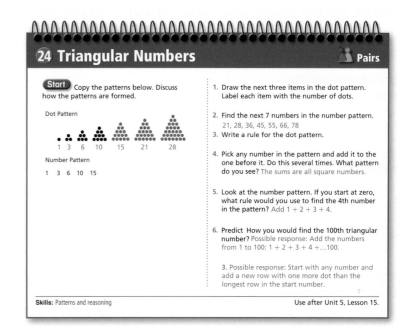

24 Triangular Numbers — Pairs

Start Copy the patterns below. Discuss how the patterns are formed.

Dot Pattern

1   3   6   10   15   21   28

Number Pattern

1   3   6   10   15

1. Draw the next three items in the dot pattern. Label each item with the number of dots.
2. Find the next 7 numbers in the number pattern. 21, 28, 36, 45, 55, 66, 78
3. Write a rule for the dot pattern.
4. Pick any number in the pattern and add it to the one before it. Do this several times. What pattern do you see? The sums are all square numbers.
5. Look at the number pattern. If you start at zero, what rule would you use to find the 4th number in the pattern? Add $1 + 2 + 3 + 4$.
6. Predict How you would find the 100th triangular number? Possible response: Add the numbers from 1 to 100: $1 + 2 + 3 + 4 + \ldots 100$.

    3. Possible response: Start with any number and add a new row with one more dot than the longest row in the start number.

Skills: Patterns and reasoning   Use after Unit 5, Lesson 15.

Grouping Pairs

Materials None

Objective Students further their study of number theory by investigating the triangular number patterns.

Connections Number and Reasoning

Ready-Made Math Resources

Technology — Tutorials, Practice, and Intervention

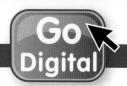

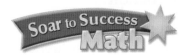

Use activity masters and online, individualized intervention and support to bring students to proficiency.

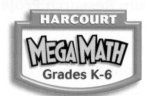

Help students practice skills and apply concepts through exciting math adventures.

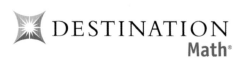

Extend and enrich students' understanding of skills and concepts through engaging, interactive lessons and activities.

Visit **Education Place®**
www.eduplace.com

Visit **www.eduplace.com/mx2t/** and find family, teacher, and student materials, activities, games, and more.

Literature Links

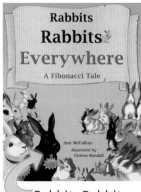

Rabbits Rabbits
Everywhere, a
Fibonacci Tale

Rabbits Rabbits Everywhere, a Fibonacci Tale

Yikes! Rabbits are becoming more plentiful by the minute, and rabbits are eating everything in their path in this tale by Ann McCallum. It is up to a young girl to figure out the pattern of how they are increasing.

Literature Connection
The King's Chessboard by David Birch, illustrated by Devis Grebu (Puffin, 1993)

Math Background

Putting Research Into Practice for Unit 5

From Our Curriculum Research Project: Multiplication Methods

We show three methods for multi-digit multiplication that we have found to be understood by students and that capture important mathematical ideas. Many less-advanced students prefer the area method because they sometimes get confused about which numbers to multiply by which in the numerical methods. In the area method, students find and write the products in the rectangle and add them up. In the algebraic method, students multiply horizontally.

Most students choose the expanded-notation method because they feel more comfortable seeing the tens and ones in each number and writing out the products they are finding. This method can be done from the right or from the left. Students often find it easier to start from the left because they get the largest product first and then they can align all of the other products under this number.

—Karen Fuson, Author
  Math Expressions

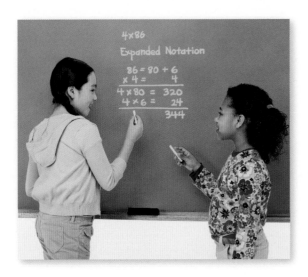

From Current Research: The Influence of Instruction

[An] observation is that proficiency with multi-digit computation is more heavily influenced by instruction than is single-digit computation. Many features of multi-digit procedures (for example, the base-10 elements and how they are represented by place-value notation) are not part of children's everyday experience and need to be learned in the classroom. In fact, many students are likely to need help learning efficient forms of multi-digit procedures.

Developing Proficiency with Whole Numbers
Adding It Up: Helping Children Learn Mathematics, p. 197.

Other Useful References: Multiplication

Number and Operations Standard for Grades 3–5 *Principles and Standards for School Mathematics.* Reston, VA: National Council of Teachers of Mathematics, 2000, pp. 148–180.

Ma, Liping. *Knowing and Teaching Elementary Mathematics*, pp. 28–54. Mahwah, NJ: Lawrence Eribaum Associates, Inc., 1999.

Van de Walle, John A. Models for Multiplication and Division. *Elementary and Middle School Mathematics: Teaching Developmentally*, (Fourth Edition). New York: Longman, 2001, pp. 120–122.

Getting Ready to Teach Unit 5

Concept Building Activities

Groups, Arrays, and Area

The concepts of multiplication as a fast way to count groups and as a way to find the total in arrays were reviewed in Unit 1. By turning an array 90°, the students discovered commutativity (for example, $5 \times 3 = 3 \times 5$). In geometry Unit 2, the students used arrays of pushed-together squares to represent areas of rectangles.

Arrays of Squares	**Arrays of Pushed-Together Squares**
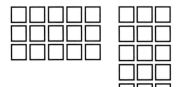	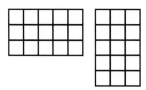
3 rows of 5 each *or* 5 rows of 3 each	5 rows of 3 each *or* 3 rows of 5 each
3×5 or 5×3	

This unit builds on the concept of area as pushed-together arrays of squares to help students understand multi-digit multiplication.

Place-Value Models
Lesson 1

Lessons on multi-digit addition and subtraction in Unit 3 used the MathBoard. These activities provided tangible, graphic support for the students' understanding of the relative sizes of the ones, tens, hundreds, and higher places. The students drew and described place-value diagrams of numbers, such as the one shown below for 356.

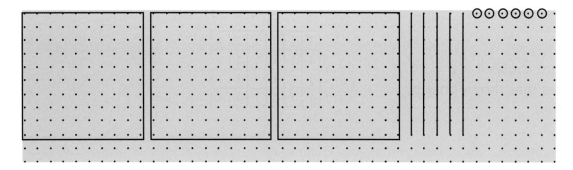

3 boxes that each contain 100 dots = 3 hundreds = 300
5 segments that each connect 10 dots = 5 tens = 50
6 circled single dots = 6 ones = 6

This activity helped the students understand that a 3 in the hundreds place is not just 3, but actually represents 300. It also helped prepare the way for the understanding of place value needed to conceptualize multi-digit multiplication.

Area Models
Lessons 3 and 4

In using place-value drawings, the students counted the dots. In Unit 5, students will be finding the number of unit "spaces" between the dots in order to find total areas of rectangles. Little crosses (+) every 10 spaces horizontally and vertically make it easier to count the units. The drawing below shows such a representation for the multiplication 23 × 4.

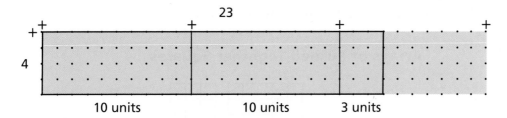

As students progress through the unit, usually they will be able to draw rectangles without using the dots. On the MathBoard, they should move from the side with the dots to the side without the dots. Their understanding will be approaching a higher level of abstraction.

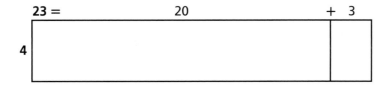

Multiplication Models
Lessons 5, 6, 7, and 8

Any multiplication can be drawn as a rectangle.

Single-digit times single-digit

The drawing at the right shows 4 × 6 = 24. It is a 4-by-6 array of ones that shows ones-by-ones place multiplication.

	6				
1	1	1	1	1	1
1	1	1	1	1	1
1	1	1	1	1	1
1	1	1	1	1	1

Single-digit times multi-digit
The drawing below shows $4 \times 36 = 144$.

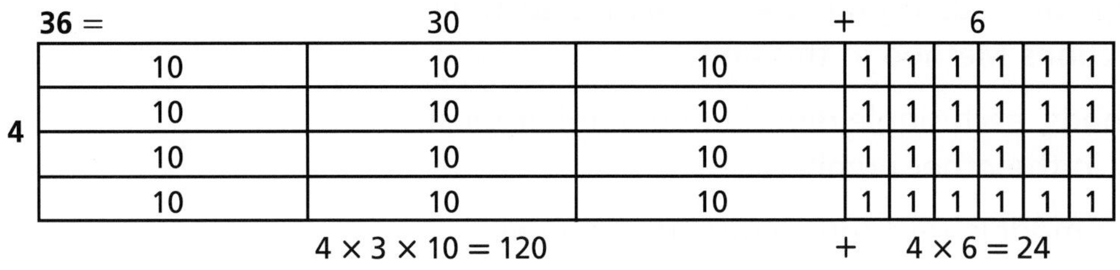

36 =	30			+	6					
4	10	10	10	1	1	1	1	1	1	
	10	10	10	1	1	1	1	1	1	
	10	10	10	1	1	1	1	1	1	
	10	10	10	1	1	1	1	1	1	

$$4 \times 3 \times 10 = 120 \qquad + \qquad 4 \times 6 = 24$$

The rectangle is made up of two arrays:

- A 4-by-3 array of groups of ten that shows the
  ones-by-tens place multiplication: $\qquad 4 \times 3 \times 10 = \quad 120$

- A 4-by-6 array of ones that shows the
  ones-by-ones place multiplication: $\qquad 4 \times 6 = \quad \underline{\quad 24}$

Adding the tens group product and the ones product $\qquad\qquad\qquad 144$
gives the total:

Multi-digit times multi-digit
The drawing below shows $23 \times 36 = 828$.

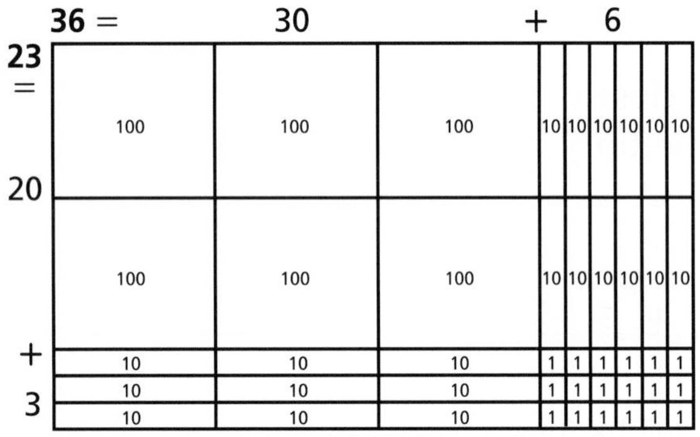

36 =	30			+	6
23 =					
20	100	100	100	10 10 10 10 10 10	
	100	100	100	10 10 10 10 10 10	
+ 3	10 10 10	10 10 10	10 10 10	1 1 1 1 1 1 / 1 1 1 1 1 1 / 1 1 1 1 1 1	

The rectangle is made up of four arrays:

- A 2-by-3 array of hundreds groups that shows the
  tens-by-tens place multiplication: $\qquad 2 \times 3 \times 100 = \quad 600$

- A 3-by-3 array of groups of tens that shows the
  ones-by-tens place multiplication: $\qquad 3 \times 3 \times 10 = \quad 90$

- A 2-by-6 array of groups of ten that shows the
  tens-by-ones place multiplication: $\qquad 2 \times 6 \times 10 = \quad 120$

- A 3-by-6 array of ones that shows the
  ones-by-ones place multiplication: $\qquad 3 \times 6 = \quad \underline{\quad 18}$

Adding the hundreds, tens, and ones groups gives the total: $\qquad\qquad 828$

Multiplication Methods
Lessons 11, 12, 13, 14, 15, and 16

The method of drawing a rectangle and adding the areas of all the sections is referred to as the **Rectangle Sections Method** in this unit.

In all numeric multiplication methods, each single digit in one number must be multiplied by each single digit in the other number.

For multi-digit multiplication, area models with connecting arcs can help students keep track of which numbers they need to multiply. This area model is related to the following numeric method. The colored arcs in the multiplication correspond to the like-colored arcs in the model.

$$36 = \quad (30 + 6)$$
$$\times\, 23 = \quad\; 20 + 3$$
$$20 \times 30 = 600$$
$$20 \times\; 6 = 120$$
$$3 \times 30 = \;\; 90$$
$$3 \times\; 6 = \;\; 18$$
$$= 828$$

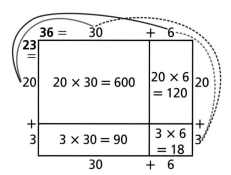

This method is referred to as the **Expanded Notation Method** in this unit.

Another numeric method, called the **Algebraic Notation Method**, is closely related to the Expanded Notation Method because students must multiply each digit in one number by each digit in the other number.

$$36 \cdot 23 = (30 + 6) \cdot (20 + 3)$$
$$= 600 + 90 + 120 + 18$$
$$= 828$$

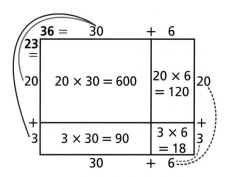

The discussion of numeric methods concludes with the **Shortcut Method**, the common algorithm taught in most U.S. schools. Not all students are expected to gain proficiency using this method in this unit. Rather, it is preferred that students are capable of understanding multiplication using one of the methods above.

$$\begin{array}{r} {}^{1}{}_{1}\,36 \\ \times\, 23 \\ \hline 108 \\ 72 \\ \hline 828 \end{array}$$

Patterns in Products
Lesson 2

In this unit, students look at patterns of products in which one of the numbers multiplied is a ten or a power of ten (such as 10, 100, and 1,000). Students examine groups of related multiplications such as:

$6 \times 3 = 6 \times 3 \times 1 = 18$

$6 \times 30 = 6 \times 3 \times 10 = 18 \times 10 = 180$

$6 \times 300 = 6 \times 3 \times 100 = 18 \times 100 = 1,800$

They rewrite each product so one factor is a power of ten. Then they see that the product is the product of the non-zero digits (in this case, 6×3), followed by the number of zeros in the power of 10.

Area models help students understand *why* they can "count the zeros" when multiplying by tens and tens groups. These patterns can also help students understand how to estimate products and round and multiply to check the accuracy of their calculations.

Real-World Problem Solving

Throughout the unit, real-world situations are used as the context for problem-solving situations, including problems that involve two or more different operations. Students are also expected to analyze problems to determine whether they have too little or too much information to solve. Students are encouraged to make mathematical connections to their content-area subjects, particularly social studies and science, as well as in their lives at home and school. Teachers are encouraged to talk about real-world math applications to help students attend to how they and others use mathematics in everyday life.

This program's strong and continuous focus on solving a wide range of word problems helps with language development. The Math Talk approach to discussing word problems facilitates language growth. Students have experienced substantial increases in vocabulary and in reasoning; such gains can be beneficial in areas other than math.

This systematic and research-based focus on word problems has changed the word-problem solving modes of many students: They no longer just look at the numbers and do something with them (for example, add or multiply all numbers they see). They think about the situation and try to understand it.

See the Overviews for Units 1 and 3 for problem types and models.

Use Mathematical Processes
Lesson 17

The mathematical process skills of problem solving, reasoning and proof, communication, connections, and representation are pervasive in this program and underlie all the students' mathematical work. This table correlates the activities in Lesson 17 of this unit with the five process skills.

Process	Activity Number
Representation	1: Represent data in a timeline.
	2: Collect data and make a double bar graph.
	4: Draw a picture to solve a problem.
Communication	2: Discuss the data in a graph. Defend a decision.
	5: Write directions for multiplying two two-digit numbers.
Connections	1: Math and Social Studies: Time and Data
Reasoning and Proof	2: Draw conclusions based on collected data. Defend a decision.
	3: Use reasoning to solve a problem.
Problem Solving	3: Choose an answer, using process of elimination.
	4: Solve a problem with multiple solutions.

Basic Multiplication and Division Fluency

Students should continually work toward fluency for basic multiplication and division facts. Use checkups to assist students in monitoring their own learning. For this unit, you can use

• Checkup D: 2s, 5s, 9s, 3s, 4s, 6s, 7s, 8s, 1s, 0s (TRB M122) and Checkup D Answer Sheet (TRB M40).

• Checkup E: 6s, 7s, 8s (TRB M123) and Checkup E Answer Sheet (TRB M113).

If students have some multiplications and divisions they need to work on, have them make a Study Plan and work toward proficiency. For detailed information, see the Basic Facts Fluency Plan at the beginning of this Teacher Edition.

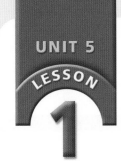

Multiplication Arrays

Lesson Objective

• Understand area models of multiplication for ones and tens.

Vocabulary

array
area

The Day at a Glance

Today's Goals	Materials	

1 Teaching the Lesson
A1: Model multiplication of ones and tens.
A2: Model multiplication of tens.
 	
2 Going Further
▶ Differentiated Instruction
 	
3 Homework and Spiral Review
	Lesson Activities
	Student Activity Book pp. 217–222
	  or Student Hardcover Book
	  pp. 217–222 and Activity
	  Workbook pp. 87–89 (includes
	  Family Letters)
	Homework and Remembering
	  pp. 141–142
	MathBoard Materials
		Going Further
		Activity Cards 5-1
		Centimeter-Grid
		  Paper (TRB M60)
		Counters
		Math Journals

123 **Use Math Talk today!**

Keeping Skills Sharp

Quick Practice	Daily Routines
This section provides repetitive, short activities that either help students become faster and more accurate at a skill or help them prepare for new concepts. Quick Practice for this unit will start in Lesson 2.	**Estimation** A museum holds two crafts days for children. They have enough supplies for 138 projects. On Saturday, 72 children make projects. On Sunday, 57 children make projects. If each child makes one project, does the museum have enough supplies for all the children? Explain how you can use estimation to answer the question. *Yes, there are enough supplies; possible explanation:* round 72 to 70 and round 57 to 60; then use mental math to add 70 + 60 = 130.

Teaching the Lesson

Arrays of Ones and Tens

 25 MINUTES

Goal: Model multiplication of ones and tens.

Materials: MathBoard Materials, Student Activity Book or Hardcover Book pp. 217–218

✓ **NCTM Standards:**
Number and Operations
Communication

Teaching Note

Watch For! Students often make rectangles 1 unit too short on the length and width. They do this because they are counting the dots rather than the lengths. Be sure to point out that 2 represents 2 unit lengths and 3 represents 3 unit lengths.

English Language Learners

Draw a 4 × 2 rectangle showing 4 unit squares across and 2 down. Write *array* and *area* on the board.

• **Beginning** Say: The array of unit squares is 4 across × 2 down. The area of the rectangle is 4 × 2. Ask: **What is 4 × 2?** 8

• **Intermediate** Ask: **What is the array of unit squares?** 4 × 2 **How do you find the area of the rectangle?** Multiply 4 × 2 **What is the area?** 8

• **Advanced** Have students work in pairs. One partner names an array of unit squares in a rectangle and the other names the area.

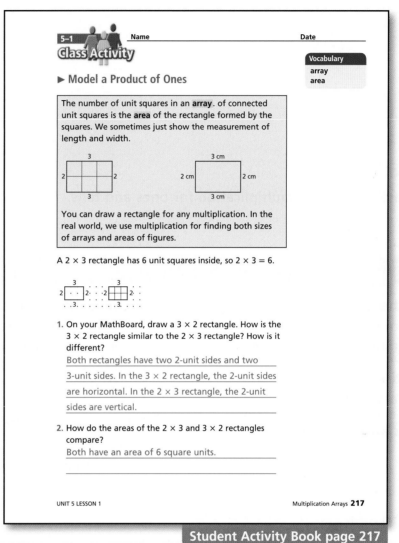

Student Activity Book page 217

▶ Model a Product of Ones WHOLE CLASS

On their MathBoards, have students draw a 2 × 3 rectangle, and label the sides. Have them draw the six unit squares inside.

Discuss how the rectangle shows that 2 × 3 = 6. To emphasize that this array is composed of units of 1, write the equation as 2 × 3 × 1 = 6.

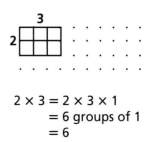

$$2 \times 3 = 2 \times 3 \times 1$$
$$= 6 \text{ groups of } 1$$
$$= 6$$

▶ Review the Commutative Property WHOLE CLASS

Have students draw a 3 × 2 rectangle. Discuss problems 1 and 2 on Student Book page 217.

- How is this rectangle similar to the 2 × 3 rectangle? Both have a 2-unit side and a 3-unit side. How is it different? It is turned, so the 2-unit side is on the bottom instead of the 3-unit side.
- How do the areas of the 2 × 3 and 3 × 2 rectangles compare? They are the same.

Write 2 × 3 = 3 × 2 on the board. Ask if anyone can remember which property tells us that the order of the factors in a multiplication does not matter. The Commutative Property

▶ Model a Product of Ones and Tens WHOLE CLASS

Have students draw a 2 × 30 rectangle and label its sides. Ask students how they could find the area of this rectangle. As each of the following possibilities arises, have students draw and label a new 2 × 30 rectangle.

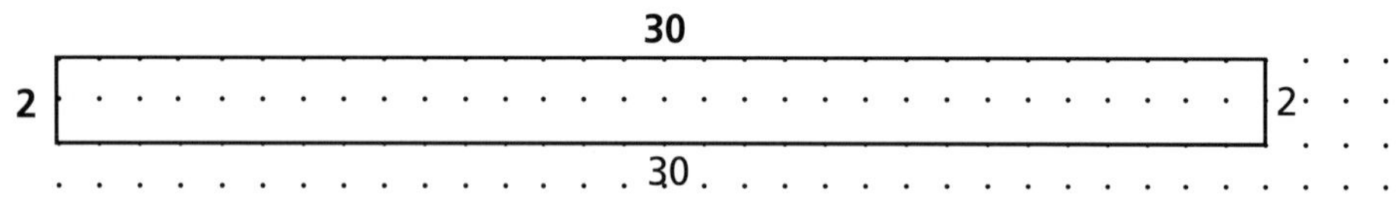

- Divide the rectangle *across* to show 2 groups of 30.

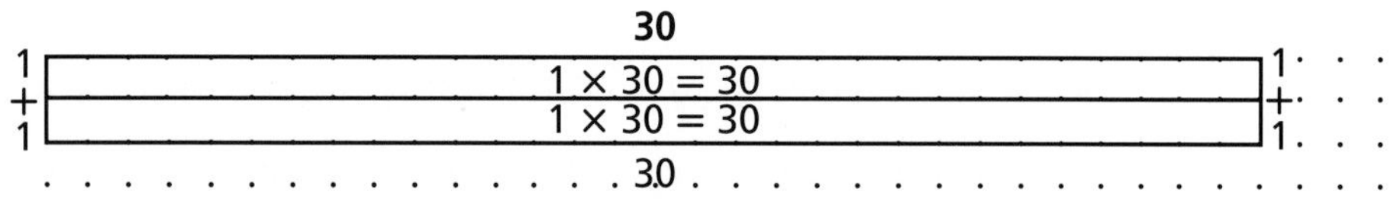

- Divide the rectangle *up-and-down* to show 3 groups of 20.

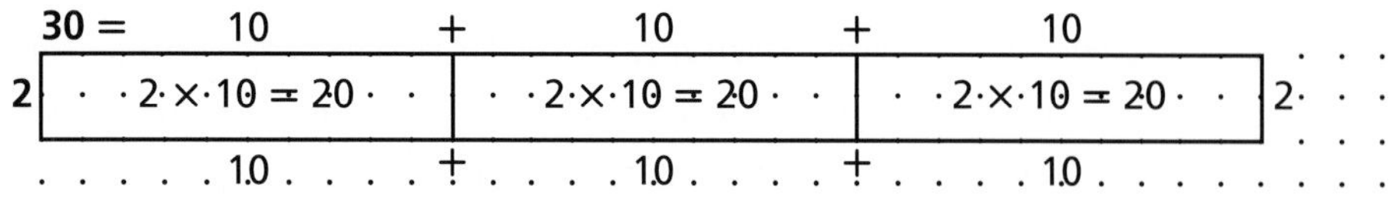

- Divide the rectangle both *across* and *up-and-down* to show 6 groups of 10. (Students need only label one of the inner rectangles.)

Activity continued ▶

The Learning Classroom

Math Talk Have students practice explaining one another's work in their own words. Begin by having a volunteer write his or her work on the board. Then as the students point to parts of the problem, another student identifies and explains the parts.

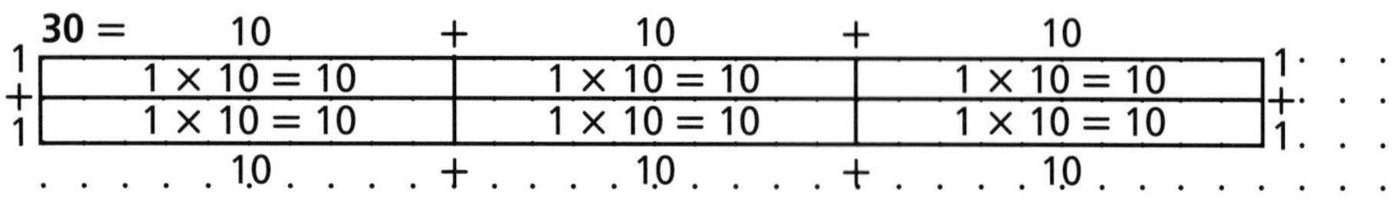

Activity 1

5–1 Class Activity

Name ______________________ Date __________

► Factor the Tens to Multiply Ones and Tens

This 2 × 30 rectangle contains 6 groups of 10 square units, so its area is 60 square units.

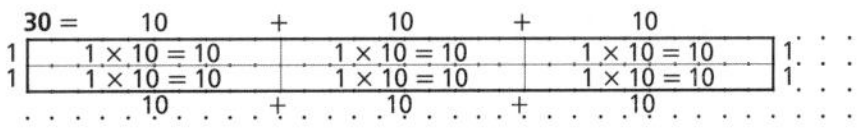
30 = 10 + 10 + 10
1 × 10 = 10
1 × 10 = 10
1 × 10 = 10
1 × 10 = 10
1 × 10 = 10
1 × 10 = 10
1
1
1
1
10 + 10 + 10

3. How can we show this numerically? Complete the steps.

$2 \times 30 = (2 \times 1) \times (\underline{3} \times 10)$

$= (\underline{2} \times \underline{3}) \times (1 \times 10)$

$= \underline{6} \times 10 = 60$

4. On your MathBoard, draw a 30 × 2 rectangle and find its area.

60 square units

5. How is the 30 × 2 rectangle similar to the 2 × 30 rectangle? How is it different?

Both rectangles have two 2-unit sides and two 30-unit sides. In the 30 × 2 rectangle, the 2-unit sides are horizontal. In the 2 × 30 rectangle, the 2-unit sides are vertical.

6. Write out the steps for finding 4 × 20 by factoring the tens. Use your MathBoard if you need to.

4 × 20 = (4 × 1) × (2 × 10) = (4 × 2) × (1 × 10) =
8 × 10 = 80

218 UNIT 5 LESSON 1 Multiplication Arrays

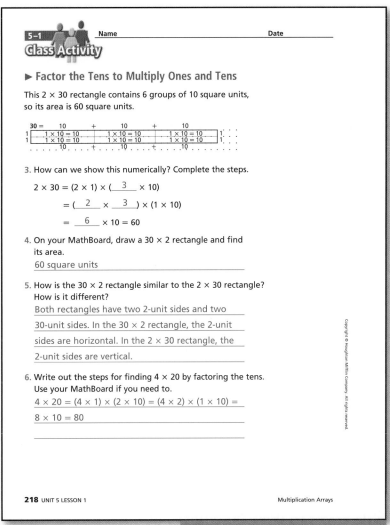

Student Activity Book page 218

Teaching Note

What to Expect From Students
Some students may find the process of rewriting 2 × 30 as (2 × 3) × (1 × 10) to be tedious and unnecessary. Tell them that understanding this process will give them a strategy for solving more difficult products.

► Factor the Tens to Multiply Ones and Tens INDIVIDUALS

Have students turn to Student Book page 218. Explain that factoring the tens can help them find products such as 2 × 30. Have students complete exercise 3 in their books and then discuss the steps. Students should see that 2 × 30 becomes (2 × 3) × (1 × 10), or 6 groups of 1 × 10 rectangles.

You might discuss the properties involved in writing the steps in exercise 3. As discussed above, the Commutative Property allows us to change the order of the factors. The Associative Property lets us group the factors in different ways.

Have students complete exercises 4–6. Exercises 4 and 5 review the Commutative Property. Exercise 6 gives students more practice factoring the tens.

Arrays of Hundreds

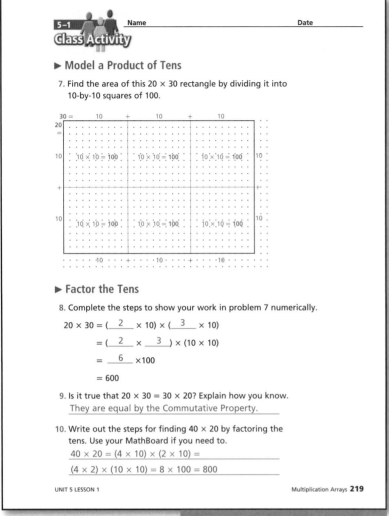

 25 MINUTES

Goal: Model multiplication of tens.

Materials: Student Activity Book pp. 219–220 or Hardcover Book pp. 219–220 and Activity Workbook p. 87, MathBoard Materials (optional)

 NCTM Standards:
Number and Operations
Communication

▶ Model a Product of Tens WHOLE CLASS

Refer students to the rectangle in exercise 7 on page 219 of their books or have them draw a 20 × 30 rectangle on their MathBoards.

Have students divide this rectangle into an array of 10-by-10 squares.

● What value does each of these squares represent? 100

● How many groups of 100 are there? 6 What is the total area? 600

▶ Factor the Tens INDIVIDUALS

Explain that factoring the tens can help students find 20 × 30. Have students complete exercise 8 of the Student Book. Then discuss the steps as a class.

Have students complete exercises 9 and 10.

Activity continued ▶

Activity 2

Ongoing Assessment

Have students draw a 4 × 7 rectangle and find its area. Then ask them to write out the steps for finding each of the following products:

$$4 \times 70$$

$$40 \times 70$$

▶ **Compare Equations** [INDIVIDUALS]

Exercises 11–13 on Student Book page 220 review the equations students studied in this lesson. Have students complete the problems, and then discuss the answers as a class. Make sure students see that the total number of zeros in the factors is the same as the number of zeros in the product.

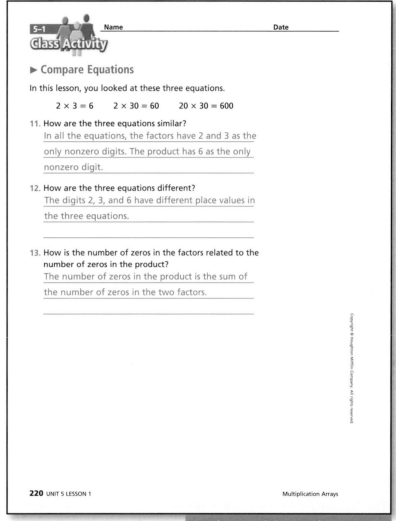

5-1   Name _____   Date _____

Class Activity

▶ Compare Equations

In this lesson, you looked at these three equations.

$$2 \times 3 = 6 \qquad 2 \times 30 = 60 \qquad 20 \times 30 = 600$$

11. How are the three equations similar?
    In all the equations, the factors have 2 and 3 as the
    only nonzero digits. The product has 6 as the only
    nonzero digit.

12. How are the three equations different?
    The digits 2, 3, and 6 have different place values in
    the three equations.

13. How is the number of zeros in the factors related to the
    number of zeros in the product?
    The number of zeros in the product is the sum of
    the number of zeros in the two factors.

220 UNIT 5 LESSON 1   Multiplication Arrays

Student Activity Book page 220

②Going Further

Differentiated Instruction

Intervention   Activity Card 5-1

| Make a Multiplication Chart | Activity Card 5-1 |

Work: By Yourself

Use:
- Centimeter-Grid Paper (TRB M60)

1. Copy the multiplication chart onto your grid paper.
2. Fill in as many products as you can from memory.
3. Draw a rectangle on the grid with a length and width equal to the factors of any product that you cannot remember.
4. **Think** How can you use the rectangle to find the product? Count squares inside the rectangle.

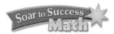

Unit 5, Lesson 1   Copyright © Houghton Mifflin Company

Activity Note Once students have completed their charts, have them work in pairs to check answers and discuss any discrepancies.

✐ Math Writing Prompt

Describe a Pattern Choose a one-digit number, and describe a pattern in the multiplication of that number by 10, 100, 1,000, and so on.

Soar to Success Math ★ Software Support

Use *Soar to Success* for instruction of students needing targeted support for underlying skills.

On Level   Activity Card 5-1

| Find Rectangles for Products | Activity Card 5-1 ▲ |

Work: By Yourself

Use:
- Centimeter-Grid Paper (TRB M60)

1. The diagram below shows two possible rectangles for the product 24. Copy them onto your grid paper.

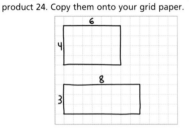

2. Find all other possible rectangles for 24.
3. Repeat the process to find all possible rectangles for 16 and 19.

Unit 5, Lesson 1   Copyright © Houghton Mifflin Company

Activity Note This and other hands-on activities can be helpful for **English Language Learners**. Point out that 16 is a square number, so one of the possible rectangles is a 4-by-4 square.

✐ Math Writing Prompt

Organization Skills How can you be sure that you have found all the rectangles for a number?

MegaMath Grades K-6 Software Support

Use *MegaMath* for review and reinforcement of the concepts and skills presented in this lesson.

Challenge   Activity Card 5-1

| Find Primes | Activity Card 5-1 ■ |

Work: By Yourself

Use:
- Counters

1. The drawing below shows the arrays for the prime number 7. A prime number has exactly two possible arrays because it has exactly two factors.

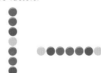

2. Find all the numbers less than 100 that have exactly two arrays. Use counters if necessary. 2, 3, 5, 7, 11, 13, 17, 19, 23, 29, 31, 37, 41, 43, 47, 53, 59, 61, 67, 71, 73, 79, 83, 89, 97

Unit 5, Lesson 1   Copyright © Houghton Mifflin Company

Activity Note Remind students that prime numbers have only two factors, 1 and the number itself. Therefore, there are only two possible rectangles.

✐ Math Writing Prompt

Reasoning Skills Do any numbers have an odd number of rectangular arrays? Explain.

✹ DESTINATION Math· Software Support

Use *Destination Math* to take students beyond the concepts and skills presented in this lesson.

③ Homework and Spiral Review

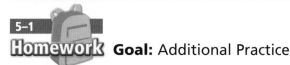

5–1 Homework Goal: Additional Practice

Use this Homework page to provide students with more practice finding the area of rectangles.

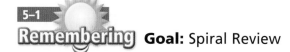

5–1 Remembering Goal: Spiral Review

This Remembering activity would be appropriate anytime after today's lesson.

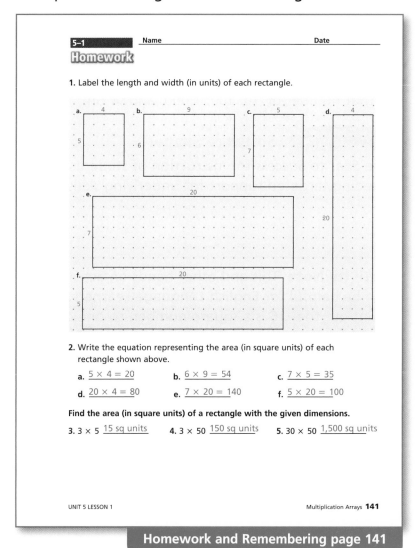

5–1 Homework Name _____ Date _____

1. Label the length and width (in units) of each rectangle.

2. Write the equation representing the area (in square units) of each rectangle shown above.

a. $5 \times 4 = 20$ b. $6 \times 9 = 54$ c. $7 \times 5 = 35$

d. $20 \times 4 = 80$ e. $7 \times 20 = 140$ f. $5 \times 20 = 100$

Find the area (in square units) of a rectangle with the given dimensions.

3. 3×5 15 sq units   4. 3×50 150 sq units   5. 30×50 1,500 sq units

UNIT 5 LESSON 1   Multiplication Arrays **141**

Homework and Remembering page 141

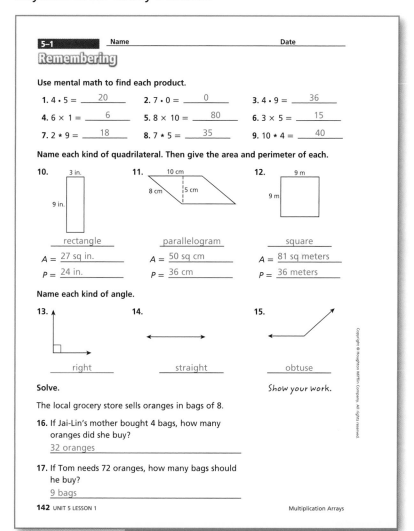

5–1 Remembering Name _____ Date _____

Use mental math to find each product.

1. $4 \cdot 5 =$ 20   2. $7 \cdot 0 =$ 0   3. $4 \times 9 =$ 36

4. $6 \times 1 =$ 6   5. $8 \times 10 =$ 80   6. $3 \times 5 =$ 15

7. $2 * 9 =$ 18   8. $7 * 5 =$ 35   9. $10 * 4 =$ 40

Name each kind of quadrilateral. Then give the area and perimeter of each.

10. 3 in. / 9 in.   11. 10 cm / 8 cm / 5 cm   12. 9 m / 9 m

rectangle   parallelogram   square

$A =$ 27 sq in. $A =$ 50 sq cm $A =$ 81 sq meters

$P =$ 24 in. $P =$ 36 cm $P =$ 36 meters

Name each kind of angle.

13.   14.   15.

right   straight   obtuse

Solve.   Show your work.

The local grocery store sells oranges in bags of 8.

16. If Jai-Lin's mother bought 4 bags, how many oranges did she buy?

32 oranges

17. If Tom needs 72 oranges, how many bags should he buy?

9 bags

142 UNIT 5 LESSON 1   Multiplication Arrays

Homework and Remembering page 142

Home and School Connection

Family Letter Have children take home the Family Letter on Student Book page 221 or Activity Workbook page 88. This letter explains how multi-digit multiplication is developed in *Math Expressions*. It gives parents and guardians a better understanding of the learning that goes on in math class and creates a bridge between school and home. A Spanish translation of this letter is on the Student Book page 222 and on Activity Workbook page 89.

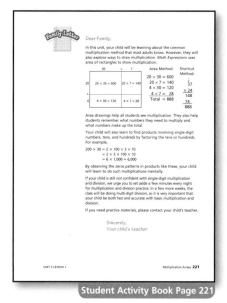

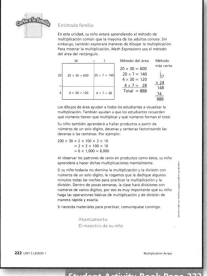

Student Activity Book Page 221

Student Activity Book Page 222

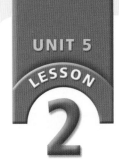

Mental Math and Multiplication With Tens

Lesson Objective
- Understand patterns of multiplication with ones, tens, and hundreds.

The Day at a Glance

Today's Goals	Materials
1 Teaching the Lesson **A1:** Find numeric patterns in multiplication with ones and tens. **A2:** Solve multiplication problems mentally by factoring the tens. **2 Going Further** ▶ Differentiated Instruction **3 Homework and Spiral Review**	**Lesson Activities** Student Activity Book pp. 223–224 or Student Hardcover Book pp. 223–224 Homework and Remembering pp. 143–144 Quick Quiz 1 (Assessment Guide) **Going Further** Activity Cards 5-2 Base-ten blocks Cross-Number Grid (TRB M61) Math Journals

123 *Use* **Math Talk** *today!*

Keeping Skills Sharp

Quick Practice ⏱ 5 MINUTES

Goal: Find the unknown addend in an equation involving multiplication and addition.

Unknown Addend Have four **Student Leaders** go to the board. Have each write five equations in which a multiplication is followed by an unknown addition (see examples below). Specify that three of their equations show the total on the left (for example, $51 = 10 \cdot 5 + y$). Each Student Leader, in turn, uses a pointer to point to each problem in his or her list. Students hold up fingers to show the unknown. Then, at a hand signal from the leader, the class says the equation with the answer.

Equation	Class Holds Up	Class Says
$105 = 10 \cdot 10 + d$	5 fingers	"One hundred five equals ten times ten plus five."
$4 \cdot 5 + n = 24$	4 fingers	"Four times five plus four equals twenty-four."

Daily Routines

Homework Review Ask students to place their homework at the corner of their desks. Check that students completed the assignment, and see whether any problem caused difficulty for many students.

Draw a Picture Draw two rectangles with different perimeters that have the area of 24 square units. *Possible answer:* 3×8 units with a perimeter of 22 units; 2×12 units with a perimeter of 28 units

Teaching the Lesson

Review Multiplication With Tens

 30 MINUTES

Goal: Find numeric patterns in multiplication with ones and tens.

Materials: Student Activity Book or Hardcover Book pp. 223–224

✔ **NCTM Standard:**
Number and Operations

English Language Learners

Write 8 × 4 = 32 on the board. Write the words *factor* and *product*. Have students help you label the 8, 4, and 32 with those words.

• **Beginning** Say: 32 is the product of 8 × 4. The numbers 8 and 4 are factors of 32. Have students repeat.

• **Intermediate** Ask: What is the product? 32 What are the factors? 8 and 4

• **Advanced** Have students tell how factors and products are related.

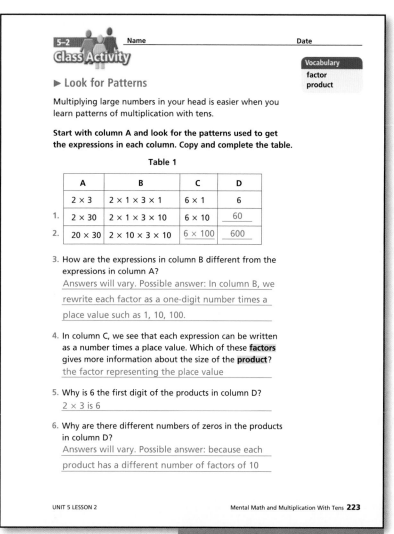

Student Activity Book page 223

▶ Look for Patterns WHOLE CLASS

Direct students to Table 1 on page 223 of the Student Book. Have students complete Table 1 on their own or by working with a partner.

When the class has completed the table, review the answers to exercises 1–2 and then use exercises 3–6 to discuss the table. Allow time for the students to record their answers to each exercise.

Ask a volunteer to show how to rearrange the factors in column B of the last row to get 6 × 100. 2 × 10 × 3 × 10 = (2 × 3) × (10 × 10) = 6 × 100

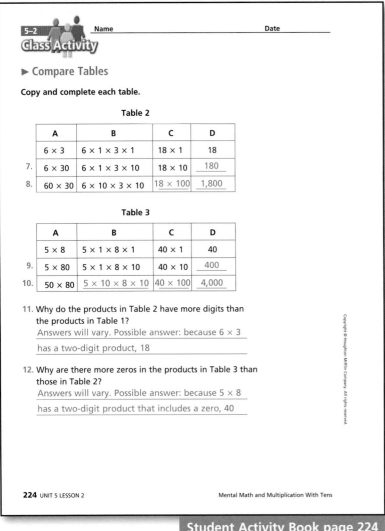

5-2
Class Activity

Name _____ Date _____

▶ **Compare Tables**

Copy and complete each table.

Table 2

	A	B	C	D
	6 × 3	6 × 1 × 3 × 1	18 × 1	18
7.	6 × 30	6 × 1 × 3 × 10	18 × 10	180
8.	60 × 30	6 × 10 × 3 × 10	18 × 100	1,800

Table 3

	A	B	C	D
	5 × 8	5 × 1 × 8 × 1	40 × 1	40
9.	5 × 80	5 × 1 × 8 × 10	40 × 10	400
10.	50 × 80	5 × 10 × 8 × 10	40 × 100	4,000

11. Why do the products in Table 2 have more digits than the products in Table 1?
Answers will vary. Possible answer: because 6 × 3 has a two-digit product, 18

12. Why are there more zeros in the products in Table 3 than those in Table 2?
Answers will vary. Possible answer: because 5 × 8 has a two-digit product that includes a zero, 40

224 UNIT 5 LESSON 2   Mental Math and Multiplication With Tens

Student Activity Book page 224

▶ Compare Tables [WHOLE CLASS]

Have students complete Tables 2 and 3 (exercises 7–10) and exercises 11 and 12 on Student Book page 224. Make sure students understand that the difference from Table 1 to Table 2 is that the product of the non-zero digits has two digits instead of one. For a sample of classroom dialogue for exercise 11, see Math Talk in Action in the side column.

Exercise 12 asks students why there are more zeros in the products of Table 3. Make sure students understand that the pattern is the same. The pattern with the zeros only looks different because the product of the non-zero digits (5 × 8) includes a zero.

Ask students when and why they would encounter the pattern variation found in Table 3. If necessary, explain that they would encounter the variation when the non-zero digits are 5 and an even number. The product of the non-zero digits will end in zero, so the final product will have an "extra" zero.

The Learning Classroom

Building Concepts Discuss with students how helpful it is to factor the tens when multiplying tens. Students should see that multiplying one-digit numbers is easier to do in their head.

 Math Talk in Action

How are Tables 1 and 2 different?

Kim: In Table 1, 2 is multiplied by 3. Then the product, 6, is multiplied by the product of the 10s. In Table 2, 6 is multiplied by 3. Then the product, 18, is multiplied by the product of the 10s.

Hannah: The answers in column D have one more digit in Table 2.

Jacob: The product of 2 × 3 has one digit but the product of 6 × 3 has two digits, so the answers in column D in Table 2 have one more digit than the answers in column D in Table 1.

Mental Math and Multiplication With Tens   **509**

Teaching the Lesson (continued)

Mental Multiplication

 25 MINUTES

Goal: Solve multiplication problems mentally by factoring the tens.

 NCTM Standard:
Number and Operations

 Ongoing Assessment

Have students:

▶ choose a two-digit number ending in zero and multiply it by a one-digit number of their choice.

▶ indicate whether their pair of numbers is like the pairs in Table 1, Table 2, or Table 3.

 Quick Quiz

See Assessment Guide for Unit 5 Quick Quiz 1.

The Learning Classroom

Student Pairs Initially, it is useful to model pair activities for students by contrasting effective and ineffective helping. For example, students need to help partners solve a problem their way, rather than doing the work for the partner. **Helping Partners** often foster learning in both students as the helper strives to adopt the perspective of the novice.

▶ **Practice Mental Math** | SMALL GROUPS |

Have the students work in **Small Groups** or **Student Pairs** to solve the problems below and then discuss the number patterns.

9 × 2 and 9 × 20 18; 180   6 × 5 and 60 × 5 30; 300

3 × 2 and 30 × 2 6; 60   4 × 9 and 4 × 90 36; 360

6 × 8 and 60 × 80 48; 4,800   7 × 3 and 70 × 30 21; 2,100

4 × 5 and 40 × 50 20; 2,000   8 × 2 and 80 × 20 16; 1,600

Ask volunteers to share their thought processes.

Encourage all students to ask questions that will help everyone understand the factoring-the-tens method presented in the lesson. Discussing this method out loud may help students internalize the process. Ask students how knowing their basic multiplications can help them find products involving tens numbers. I can multiply the non-zero digits and then multiply the tens. For example, in the first exercise, I know that 9 × 2 = 18. Then I just multiply the 10s.

Students who know their multiplications may be able to do these problems in their heads and will finish the activities very quickly. Challenge these students to write a table for the products in the exercises. Have them classify each exercise as the pattern type found in Table 1, Table 2, or Table 3 on Student Book pages 223–224.

②Going Further

Differentiated Instruction

● Intervention   Activity Card 5-2

Model It   Activity Card 5-2 ●

Work: By Yourself

Use:
• Base-ten blocks

1. Look at the models of the products below. The product of the non-zero digits tells how many of the place-value models you need to represent the problem.

$2 \times 3 = 6 \times 1$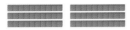
$3 \times 20 = 6 \times 10$

2. Now model the products for these multiplications.

5×3 3×4 7×2

40×3 70×2 5×30

3. **Think** Which factors can be paired to help you find each product?

Unit 5, Lesson 2   Copyright © Houghton Mifflin Company

Activity Note Be sure that students make the connection between having a factor that is a multiple of 10 and using tens blocks to model the product.

📝 Math Writing Prompt

Compare Products Describe how the products 2×4 and 20×4 are alike and how they are different.

Soar to Success Math ★ **Software Support**

Use *Soar to Success* for instruction of students needing targeted support for underlying skills.

▲ On Level   Activity Card 5-2

Number Puzzle   Activity Card 5-2 ▲

Work: In Pairs

Use:
• Cross-Number Grid (TRB M61)

1. Copy and solve the cross-number puzzle below.

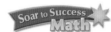

¹8	0	0		²3	
1			³4	5	
0		⁴1	2	0	
	⁵5	0	0		
⁶9	0	0	0	0	

Across	Down
1. 20×40	**1.** 9×90
3. 5×9	**2.** 7×50
4. 6×20	**3.** 60×70
5. 50×10	**4.** 5×20
6. 450×200	**5.** 25×2

2. **Explain** What strategies did you use?

Unit 5, Lesson 2   Copyright © Houghton Mifflin Company

Activity Note Students who finish early can create their own multiplication number puzzle and exchange with another pair to solve.

📝 Math Writing Prompt

Explain Your Thinking Explain how you would use the factor 10 to multiply 70×80 mentally.

MegaMath Grades K-6 **Software Support**

Use *MegaMath* for review and reinforcement of the concepts and skills presented in this lesson.

■ Challenge   Activity Card 5-2

Work Backward   Activity Card 5-2 ■

Work: By Yourself

1. Copy the table below. Then complete the table, using the directions below. Each row has three products that are equal.

Column A	Column B	Column C
2×60	$2 \times 6 \times 10$	12×10
6×600	$6 \times 6 \times 100$	36×100
3×6	$3 \times 6 \times 1$	18×1
$9 \times 6,000$	$9 \times 6 \times 1,000$	$54 \times 1,000$

2. In Column B, write the product with three factors, one of which is 1, 10, 100, or 1,000.

3. In Column A, write the product in Column B as the product of two factors, one of which is a multiple of 1, 10, 100, or 1,000.

Unit 5, Lesson 2   Copyright © Houghton Mifflin Company

Activity Note Students who finish early can extend the activity by finding alternative equivalent products for Columns A and B.

📝 Math Writing Prompt

Alternate Approaches Explain how you can rewrite the number 40,000 as a product of factors that include 10, 100, or 1,000. Explain a strategy for finding five different ways of doing this.

✶ DESTINATION Math® **Software Support**

Use *Destination Math* to take students beyond the concepts and skills presented in this lesson.

Mental Math and Multiplication With Tens   **511**

③ Homework and Spiral Review

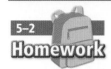 **Homework** **Goal:** Additional Practice

Use this Homework page to provide students with more practice with mental math and multiplication with tens.

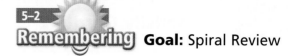 **Remembering** **Goal:** Spiral Review

This Remembering activity would be appropriate anytime after today's lesson.

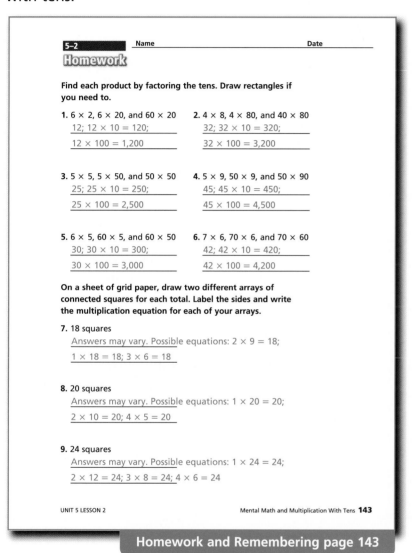

5-2 Homework Name _____ Date _____

Find each product by factoring the tens. Draw rectangles if you need to.

1. 6 × 2, 6 × 20, and 60 × 20
12; 12 × 10 = 120;
12 × 100 = 1,200

2. 4 × 8, 4 × 80, and 40 × 80
32; 32 × 10 = 320;
32 × 100 = 3,200

3. 5 × 5, 5 × 50, and 50 × 50
25; 25 × 10 = 250;
25 × 100 = 2,500

4. 5 × 9, 50 × 9, and 50 × 90
45; 45 × 10 = 450;
45 × 100 = 4,500

5. 6 × 5, 60 × 5, and 60 × 50
30; 30 × 10 = 300;
30 × 100 = 3,000

6. 7 × 6, 70 × 6, and 70 × 60
42; 42 × 10 = 420;
42 × 100 = 4,200

On a sheet of grid paper, draw two different arrays of connected squares for each total. Label the sides and write the multiplication equation for each of your arrays.

7. 18 squares
Answers may vary. Possible equations: 2 × 9 = 18;
1 × 18 = 18; 3 × 6 = 18

8. 20 squares
Answers may vary. Possible equations: 1 × 20 = 20;
2 × 10 = 20; 4 × 5 = 20

9. 24 squares
Answers may vary. Possible equations: 1 × 24 = 24;
2 × 12 = 24; 3 × 8 = 24; 4 × 6 = 24

UNIT 5 LESSON 2 — Mental Math and Multiplication With Tens **143**

Homework and Remembering page 143

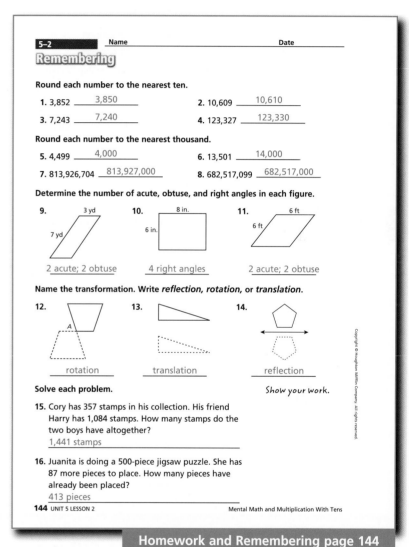

5-2 Remembering Name _____ Date _____

Round each number to the nearest ten.

1. 3,852 ___3,850___
2. 10,609 ___10,610___
3. 7,243 ___7,240___
4. 123,327 ___123,330___

Round each number to the nearest thousand.

5. 4,499 ___4,000___
6. 13,501 ___14,000___
7. 813,926,704 ___813,927,000___
8. 682,517,099 ___682,517,000___

Determine the number of acute, obtuse, and right angles in each figure.

9. 3 yd, 7 yd — 2 acute; 2 obtuse

10. 8 in., 6 in. — 4 right angles

11. 6 ft, 6 ft — 2 acute; 2 obtuse

Name the transformation. Write reflection, rotation, or translation.

12. rotation

13. translation

14. reflection

Solve each problem. *Show your work.*

15. Cory has 357 stamps in his collection. His friend Harry has 1,084 stamps. How many stamps do the two boys have altogether?
1,441 stamps

16. Juanita is doing a 500-piece jigsaw puzzle. She has 87 more pieces to place. How many pieces have already been placed?
413 pieces

144 UNIT 5 LESSON 2 — Mental Math and Multiplication With Tens

Homework and Remembering page 144

Home or School Activity

 ### Science Connection

Numbers in Astronomy Have students find the mass of Earth. Have them figure out how many factors of ten it contains. Then have them find another number from astronomy and have them figure out how many factors of ten this number contains.

> 6,000,000,000,000,000,000,000,000
> has 24 factors of 10.

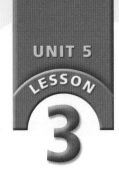

Model One-Digit by Two-Digit Multiplication

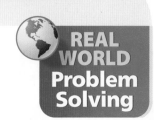

REAL WORLD Problem Solving

Lesson Objective

- Represent one-digit by two-digit multiplication, using area models.

Vocabulary

area
square units

The Day at a Glance

Today's Goals	Materials
1 Teaching the Lesson **A1:** Understand one-digit by two-digit multiplication. **A2:** Practice one-digit by two-digit multiplication. **2 Going Further** ▶ Math Connection: Multiplication With Dollars ▶ Differentiated Instruction **3 Homework and Spiral Review**	**Lesson Activities** Student Activity Book pp. 225–226 or Student Hardcover Book pp. 225–226 Homework and Remembering pp. 145–146 Base-ten blocks (optional) MathBoard Materials	**Going Further** Student Activity Book pp. 227–228 or Student Hardcover Book pp. 227–228 Activity Cards 5-3 *Match–Up* Game Cards (TRB M62–M63) Scissors Math Journals

123 *Use* **Math Talk** *today!*

Keeping Skills Sharp

Quick Practice ⏱ 5 MINUTES

Goal: Find the unknown addend in an equation involving multiplication and addition.

Unknown Addend Have four **Student Leaders** go to the board. Have each write five equations in which a multiplication is followed by an unknown addition (see examples below). See Lesson 2.

Equation	Class holds up	Class says
$82 = 8 \cdot 10 + d$	2 fingers	"Eighty-two equals eight times ten plus two."
$9 \cdot 4 + n = 42$	6 fingers	"Nine times four plus six equals forty-two."

Daily Routines

Homework Review Send students to the board to show their solutions for problems 7–9. Have each student at the board explain his/her solution. Encourage the rest of the class to ask clarifying questions and make comments.

Place Value Write these numbers on the board. Have students name a number that is 1,000 more than each given number.

14,700 15,700   19,048 20,048

156,234 157,234   281,005 282,005

1,320,000 1,321,000 6,054,169
                     6,055,169

Teaching the Lesson

Multiplication Modeling

 30 MINUTES

Goal: Understand one-digit by two-digit multiplication.

Materials: Student Activity Book or Hardcover Book p. 225, base-ten blocks (optional)

✔ **NCTM Standards:**
Number and Operations
Reasoning and Proof

The Learning Classroom

Building Concepts Why use the area method to teach multi-digit multiplication? The area method is the easiest method for students to use. By teaching it first, we build conceptual understanding for all students and provide a method that any student can use. We also encourage students to explore other methods. We then teach a research-based algorithm that is accessible to most students.

English Language Learners

Draw and label a 5 × 6 rectangle on the board. Write the words *area* and *square unit*.

- **Beginning** Say: The area of the rectangle is 5 × 6. There are 30 square units in the rectangle.
- **Intermediate** Ask: How do you find the area of the rectangle? 5 × 6 How many square units in the rectangle? 30
- **Advanced** Have students tell how area and square units are used with rectangles.

5–3

Class Activity

Name _____ Date _____

Vocabulary
area
square units

▶ Explore the Area Model

```
        20              +    6
  ┌──────────────────┬──────────┐
4 │· · · · · · · · · │· · · · · │
  │· · · · · · · · · │· · · · · │
  └──────────────────┴──────────┘
```

1. How many **square units** of **area** are there in the tens part of the drawing? ___80___

2. What multiplication equation gives the area of the tens part of the drawing? 4 × 20 = 80 Write this equation in its rectangle.

3. How many square units of area are there in the ones part? ___24___

4. What multiplication equation gives the area of the ones part? 4 × 6 = 24 Write this equation in its rectangle.

5. What is the total of the two areas? ___104___

6. How do you know that 104 is the correct product of 4 × 26?
   Answers will vary. _____

7. Read problems A and B.
   A. Al's photo album has 26 pages. Each page has 4 photos. How many photos are in Al's album?
   B. Nick took 4 photos. Henri took 26 photos. How many more photos did Henri take than Nick?

   Which problem could you solve using the multiplication you just did? Explain why.
   Problem A; In problem A we are finding the total
   in 26 groups of 4. We find this by calculating
   4 × 26.

UNIT 5 LESSON 3   Model One-Digit by Two-Digit Multiplication **225**

Student Activity Book page 225

▶ Explore the Area Model [WHOLE CLASS]

Refer students to the area model at the top of Student Book page 225. Use problems 1–6 to help students see that the model represents 4 × 26 = 104.

Here are some additional questions to help encourage discussion.

● How can you prove that there are 80 square units in the tens part of the drawing? Possible answers: Count 80 small squares or count 8 groups of 10 squares.

● How can you prove that there are 24 square units in the ones part of the drawing? Possible answer: Count the squares.

- **How can you prove that there are 104 squares units in the whole drawing?** The large rectangle is made up of the two smaller rectangles and 80 + 24 = 104.

- **How can you use repeated addition to check that 4 × 26 = 104?**
  26 + 26 + 26 + 26 = 104

If students are having difficulty visualizing the multiplication, you may want to use base-ten blocks. See the Alternate Approach section at the right.

 Math Talk Discuss problem 7. Encourage all students to ask questions so they understand that problem A can be solved by multiplying 26 by 4 and problem B can be solved by subtracting 4 from 26. Model questioning if needed.

- **What is the problem situation for each problem?** Problem A: Equal Groups; Problem B: Additive Comparison

- **How can you represent each problem?**

Encourage students to identify and discuss situations in which multiplication would help to solve a real-world problem. If time permits, have **Helping Partners** write and exchange multiplication problems about real situations (buying two or three of the same item, doubling a recipe, finding the area of a room, and so on).

Alternate Approach

Base-ten blocks Have students model each multiplication problem, using base-ten blocks.

4 × 26

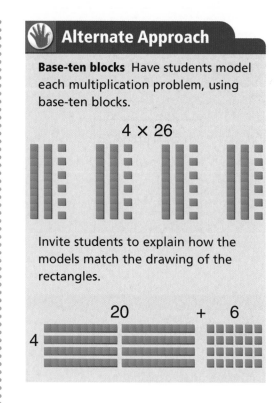

Invite students to explain how the models match the drawing of the rectangles.

20   +   6

4

Activity 2

Practice Multiplication

▶ Use Rectangles to Multiply [WHOLE CLASS]

Have students use their MathBoards (either side) to solve problems 8–15 on Student Book page 226. Ask volunteers to share their work. Encourage all students to ask questions that will help everyone understand the methods that were used. Model the questioning if needed.

- How did you label your rectangle?

- Why did you write 28 as 20 + 8?

- Why did you add the two products?

 25 MINUTES

Goal: Practice one-digit by two-digit multiplication.

Materials: MathBoard Materials, Student Book or Hardcover Book p. 226

✔ **NCTM Standards:**
   Number and Operations
   Problem Solving

Activity continued ▶

❶ Teaching the Lesson (continued)

Activity 2

The Learning Classroom

Math Talk Review with the class what makes a good explanation.

1) Write your work so everyone can see it.

2) Talk loud enough for other students to hear.

3) Use a pointer to point to your work.

4) Say how you arrived at the answer, not just the answer.

5) Stand to the side of your work when you talk.

✓ Ongoing Assessment

▶ Compare 2×30 and 2×37. How are they the same? How are they different?

▶ Describe in your own words how you would find the product of 2×31.

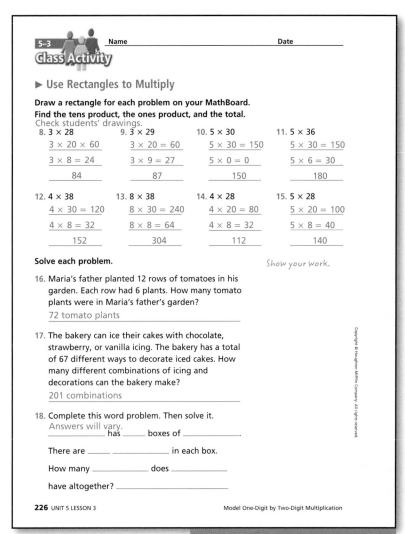

5-3 **Class Activity**   Name _____   Date _____

▶ **Use Rectangles to Multiply**

Draw a rectangle for each problem on your MathBoard.
Find the tens product, the ones product, and the total.
Check students' drawings.

8. 3×28	9. 3×29	10. 5×30	11. 5×36
$3 \times 20 \times 60$	$3 \times 20 = 60$	$5 \times 30 = 150$	$5 \times 30 = 150$
$3 \times 8 = 24$	$3 \times 9 = 27$	$5 \times 0 = 0$	$5 \times 6 = 30$
84	87	150	180

12. 4×38	13. 8×38	14. 4×28	15. 5×28
$4 \times 30 = 120$	$8 \times 30 = 240$	$4 \times 20 = 80$	$5 \times 20 = 100$
$4 \times 8 = 32$	$8 \times 8 = 64$	$4 \times 8 = 32$	$5 \times 8 = 40$
152	304	112	140

Solve each problem.   *Show your work.*

16. Maria's father planted 12 rows of tomatoes in his garden. Each row had 6 plants. How many tomato plants were in Maria's father's garden?
72 tomato plants

17. The bakery can ice their cakes with chocolate, strawberry, or vanilla icing. The bakery has a total of 67 different ways to decorate iced cakes. How many different combinations of icing and decorations can the bakery make?
201 combinations

18. Complete this word problem. Then solve it.
Answers will vary.
_____ has _____ boxes of _____.

There are _____ _____ in each box.

How many _____ does _____

have altogether? _____

226 UNIT 5 LESSON 3   Model One-Digit by Two-Digit Multiplication

Student Activity Book page 226

---

123 **Math Talk** Use problems 8–15 on Student Book page 226 to help students make connections.

● How might you find the product for exercise 9, using addition rather than multiplication? Why?
Add $29 + 29 + 29.$ $29 + 29 + 29$ is equal to $3 \times 29.$

● How would the rectangle for exercise 10 be different from the rectangle for exercise 11? The rectangle for exercise 10 would have only a tens part, not a ones part.

● How could you use your answer from exercise 14 to quickly find the answer to exercise 15? Add 28 to the answer to exercise 14.

Use **Solve and Discuss** for problems 16–18. Have students work independently, using whatever method they like. Encourage questioning by the other students to clarify different strategies. Model questions as needed.

Going Further

Math Connection: Multiplication With Dollars

Goal: Multiply with dollars.

Materials: Student Activity Book or Hardcover Book pp. 227–228

✔ **NCTM Standards:**
Number and Operations
Communication
Problem Solving

▶ Multiply One-Digit Dollar Amounts by Two-Digit Numbers [PAIRS]

In this activity, students will connect multiplication by two-digit numbers with multiplication of money.

Read the first problem on Student Book page 227 to the class.

● What do we need to find? the cost of 24 packages

● What do we know about the cost of one package? It is $2.

● How do we find the cost of 24 packages if we know that one package costs $2? Multiply 24 by 2.

● What is the answer? $48

Have the class work in **Student Pairs** to solve exercises 2–6.

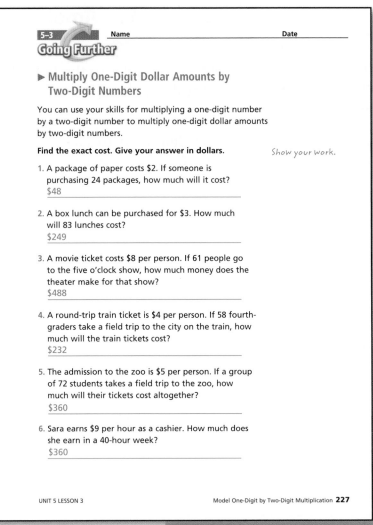

5-3 **Going Further**

Name _____ Date _____

▶ Multiply One-Digit Dollar Amounts by Two-Digit Numbers

You can use your skills for multiplying a one-digit number by a two-digit number to multiply one-digit dollar amounts by two-digit numbers.

Find the exact cost. Give your answer in dollars. *Show your work.*

1. A package of paper costs $2. If someone is purchasing 24 packages, how much will it cost?
$48

2. A box lunch can be purchased for $3. How much will 83 lunches cost?
$249

3. A movie ticket costs $8 per person. If 61 people go to the five o'clock show, how much money does the theater make for that show?
$488

4. A round-trip train ticket is $4 per person. If 58 fourth-graders take a field trip to the city on the train, how much will the train tickets cost?
$232

5. The admission to the zoo is $5 per person. If a group of 72 students takes a field trip to the zoo, how much will their tickets cost altogether?
$360

6. Sara earns $9 per hour as a cashier. How much does she earn in a 40-hour week?
$360

UNIT 5 LESSON 3   Model One-Digit by Two-Digit Multiplication **227**

Student Activity Book page 227

Activity continued ▶

▶ Multiply Two-Digit Dollar Amounts by One-Digit Numbers PAIRS

The next group of problems is similar to the last set. The only difference is that the dollar amount is the two-digit number.

Have the class work in **Student Pairs** to solve exercises 7–12 on Student Book page 228.

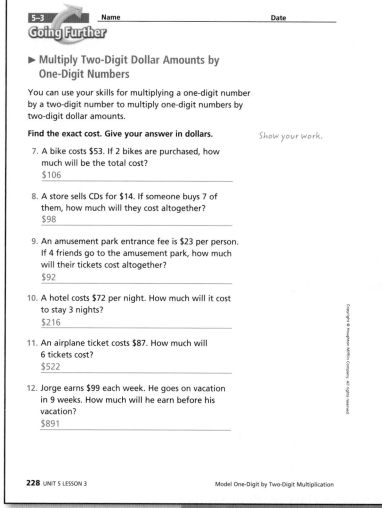

5–3
Going Further

Name _____ Date _____

▶ Multiply Two-Digit Dollar Amounts by One-Digit Numbers

You can use your skills for multiplying a one-digit number by a two-digit number to multiply one-digit numbers by two-digit dollar amounts.

Find the exact cost. Give your answer in dollars. *Show your work.*

7. A bike costs $53. If 2 bikes are purchased, how much will be the total cost?
$106

8. A store sells CDs for $14. If someone buys 7 of them, how much will they cost altogether?
$98

9. An amusement park entrance fee is $23 per person. If 4 friends go to the amusement park, how much will their tickets cost altogether?
$92

10. A hotel costs $72 per night. How much will it cost to stay 3 nights?
$216

11. An airplane ticket costs $87. How much will 6 tickets cost?
$522

12. Jorge earns $99 each week. He goes on vacation in 9 weeks. How much will he earn before his vacation?
$891

228 UNIT 5 LESSON 3

Model One-Digit by Two-Digit Multiplication

Student Activity Book page 228

Differentiated Instruction

Multiplication *Match-Up*   Activity Card 5-3 ●

Work: In Pairs

Use:
- *Match-Up* Game Cards (TRB M62–M63)
- Scissors

1. Cut out the 16 game cards, and place them face down in a rectangular array.

2. Take turns. Choose two cards. If the cards match a multiplication and a model, keep the cards. If the cards do not match, return them face down in the same positions.

     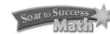

3. Continue playing until all cards are matched. The player with more cards wins the game.

Unit 5, Lesson 3   Copyright © Houghton Mifflin Company

Activity Note If time allows, students can repeat the game with the same cards or use index cards to make up their own multiplications and models for a new game.

 Math Writing Prompt

Understand Multiplication Explain how 3×47 and $47 + 47 + 47$ are related.

Soar to Success Math **Software Support**

Use *Soar to Success* for instruction of students needing targeted support for underlying skills.

Create Word Problems   Activity Card 5-3 ▲

Work: In Pairs

1. Write a word problem for each of the expressions below.

4×35 $35 - 4$ $4 + 35$

2. Exchange problems with your partner to solve.

3. **Discuss** Is there more than one way to solve any of the word problems? How could you check each solution?

Unit 5, Lesson 3   Copyright © Houghton Mifflin Company

Activity Note To reinforce multiplication concepts, select appropriate student problems to use for class discussion.

 Math Writing Prompt

Explain Your Thinking Write a multiplication word problem for 2×45. Show a way to find the product. Use pictures, words, or symbols to explain your answer.

MegaMath **Software Support**

Use *MegaMath* for review and reinforcement of the concepts and skills presented in this lesson.

Work Backward   Activity Card 5-3 ■

Work: By Yourself

1. Find the one-digit by two-digit multiplication example that you can solve by using this addition. 27×3

$$\begin{array}{r} 60 \\ +21 \\ \hline 81 \end{array}$$

2. Find three one-digit by two-digit multiplication examples that you can solve by using this addition. 24×4; 12×8; 48×2

$$\begin{array}{r} 80 \\ +16 \\ \hline 96 \end{array}$$

3. **Analyze** Why is there only one possible multiplication for the first product and three for the second? 21 has only 1 set of one-digit factors, 3 and 7, but 24 has 3 sets of one-digit factors.

Unit 5, Lesson 3   Copyright © Houghton Mifflin Company

Activity Note Extend the activity by having students write a word problem for each multiplication that they write.

 Math Writing Prompt

Investigate Math Suppose you know that $7 \times 34 = 238$. How does that help you to find 14×34? Explain your thinking.

DESTINATION Math **Software Support**

Use *Destination Math* to take students beyond the concepts and skills presented in this lesson.

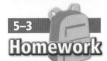 **Homework and Spiral Review**

5-3 Homework Goal: Additional Practice

✓ Include students' work for Homework page 145 in their portfolios.

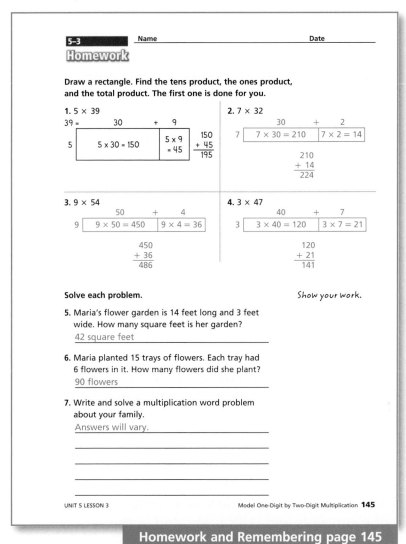

5-3 Homework

Name _____ Date _____

Draw a rectangle. Find the tens product, the ones product, and the total product. The first one is done for you.

1. 5 × 39

39 =   30   +   9

| 5 | 5 × 30 = 150 | 5 × 9 = 45 |

150
+ 45
195

2. 7 × 32

    30   +   2

| 7 | 7 × 30 = 210 | 7 × 2 = 14 |

210
+ 14
224

3. 9 × 54

    50   +   4

| 9 | 9 × 50 = 450 | 9 × 4 = 36 |

450
+ 36
486

4. 3 × 47

    40   +   7

| 3 | 3 × 40 = 120 | 3 × 7 = 21 |

120
+ 21
141

Solve each problem.   *Show your work.*

5. Maria's flower garden is 14 feet long and 3 feet wide. How many square feet is her garden?
   42 square feet

6. Maria planted 15 trays of flowers. Each tray had 6 flowers in it. How many flowers did she plant?
   90 flowers

7. Write and solve a multiplication word problem about your family.
   Answers will vary.

UNIT 5 LESSON 3   Model One-Digit by Two-Digit Multiplication **145**

Homework and Remembering page 145

5-3 Remembering Goal: Spiral Review

This Remembering activity would be appropriate anytime after today's lesson.

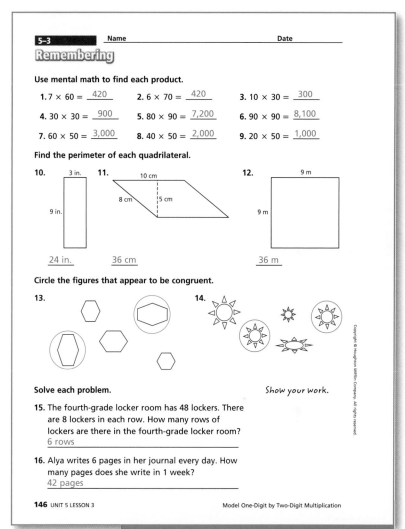

5-3 Remembering

Name _____ Date _____

Use mental math to find each product.

1. 7 × 60 = __420__   2. 6 × 70 = __420__   3. 10 × 30 = __300__

4. 30 × 30 = __900__   5. 80 × 90 = __7,200__   6. 90 × 90 = __8,100__

7. 60 × 50 = __3,000__   8. 40 × 50 = __2,000__   9. 20 × 50 = __1,000__

Find the perimeter of each quadrilateral.

10.   3 in.   9 in.   **24 in.**

11.   10 cm   8 cm   5 cm   **36 cm**

12.   9 m   9 m   **36 m**

Circle the figures that appear to be congruent.

13.

14.

Solve each problem.   *Show your work.*

15. The fourth-grade locker room has 48 lockers. There are 8 lockers in each row. How many rows of lockers are there in the fourth-grade locker room?
   6 rows

16. Alya writes 6 pages in her journal every day. How many pages does she write in 1 week?
   42 pages

146 UNIT 5 LESSON 3   Model One-Digit by Two-Digit Multiplication

Homework and Remembering page 146

Home or School Activity

 Social Studies Connection

Congress Have students research how the number of United States senators is determined. Have students describe how they could use their skills for multiplying a one-digit number by a two-digit number to find this number. Ask them what information is needed to make this calculation.

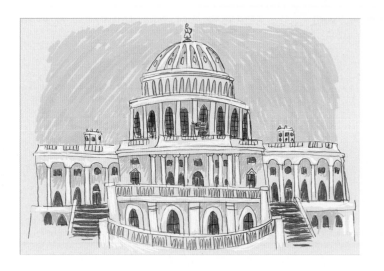

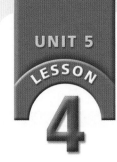

Estimate Products

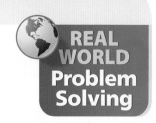
Lesson Objective

- Use estimation and multiplication with tens to check products and solve real-world problems.

Vocabulary

estimate
rounding

The Day at a Glance

Today's Goals	Materials	

1 Teaching the Lesson
A1: Use the area model to round numbers and estimate.
A2: Practice estimating products.
	Lesson Activities
	Student Activity Book pp. 229–230
	  or Student Hardcover Book
	  pp. 229–230
	Homework and Remembering
	  pp. 147–148
	MathBoard Materials
	Colored pencils or markers (optional)
		Going Further
		Activity Cards 5-4
		Math Journals

2 Going Further ▶ Differentiated Instruction		
3 Homework and Spiral Review		

123 Use Math Talk today!

Keeping Skills Sharp

Quick Practice ⏱ 5 MINUTES	Daily Routines
Goal: Fluency with zeros patterns. **Zeros Patterns** Select four **Student Leaders** to go to the board and write three products involving two non-zero digits. The first product should have no zeros in the factors, the second product should have a zero in one factor, and the third product should have a zero in both factors (see example below). Then have each Student Leader use a pointer to point to each problem in his or her list. Have the class respond with the product of the non-zero digits and the place-value name of this product and then give the answer. Then the Student Leader writes the answers.	**Homework Review** Ask several students to share the problems they wrote for homework. Have the class ask clarifying questions about each problem. If necessary, model asking questions. **Mental Math** Mr. Peña is buying some clothes to wear on a camping trip. He needs two shirts that each cost $25, one jacket that costs $75, and boots that cost $55. How can you use mental math to find out how much Mr. Peña's new clothes will cost? *Possible answer:* Add $25 + $75 = $100; add $25 + $50 + $5 = $75 + $5 = $80; $100 + $80 = $180.

Problem	Class Response	Student Leader Writes
3 × 8	"24 ones equals twenty-four."	= 24
3 × 80	"24 tens equals two hundred forty."	= 240
30 × 80	"24 hundreds equals two thousand, four hundred."	= 2,400

① Teaching the Lesson

Activity 1

Estimate Products

 20 MINUTES

Goal: Use the area model to round numbers and estimate.

Materials: Student Activity Book or Hardcover Book p. 229, MathBoard Materials, colored pencils or markers (optional)

 NCTM Standards:
Number and Operations
Problem Solving
Communication

Teaching Note

Math Background In this lesson students round two-digit factors to the nearest ten to estimate one-digit by two-digit multiplication.

▶ **Round to the Nearest Ten** WHOLE CLASS

Write 68 on the Class MathBoard.

Have students discuss what they remember about rounding by asking:

● Why do we sometimes round numbers? to make them easier to work with

● What do we do when we round a number to the nearest tens place? decide if the number is closer to the next higher ten or to the next lower ten

Write 70 above and 60 below 68. Underline the tens place to see the place to which we are rounding. Then ask:

```
70
68
60
```

● Which digit tells which way to round? the ones place

```
70
68
60
```

● How do we decide which way to round? 5 and more gets changed to the next higher ten; 4 and less gets changed to zero

● What is the value of 68 rounded to the nearest tens place? 70

Circle 70.

```
 70
 68
 60
```

Tell students that rounding can help them estimate products.

On the Class MathBoard, sketch four rectangles with a height of 4 and lengths of 70, 68, 63, and 60, and list the products they represent. Then have students draw these on their MathBoards.

```
            70
    ┌──────────────────────┐
  4 │                      │     4 × 70 = 280
    └──────────────────────┘

            68
    ┌─────────────────────┐
  4 │                     │      4 × 68 =
    └─────────────────────┘

            63
    ┌──────────────────┐
  4 │                  │         4 × 63 =
    └──────────────────┘

            60
    ┌─────────────────┐
  4 │                 │          4 × 60 = 240
    └─────────────────┘
```

Have students solve 4 × 70 and 4 × 60 first and write these equations in the rectangles. Tell students that the 4 × 70 and 4 × 60 rectangles are *rounding frames* for both 4 × 63 and 4 × 68. These rounding frames show the two tens products that the answers are between.

Next, show the lower rounding frame visually by breaking the 4 × 63 and 4 × 68 rectangles into two parts where one part is the lower frame (a 4 × 60 rectangle). Then extend each rectangle with a dashed line to show the upper frame (a 4 × 70 rectangle). Have students draw these frames on their MathBoard as well. Have them discuss how the products for 63 and 68 are between the product for the lower frame and the product for the upper frame.

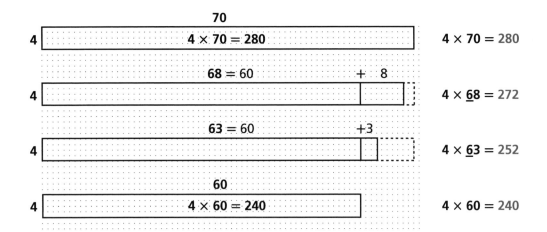

- Compare the 4 × 68 rectangle to the 4 × 70 and the 4 × 60 rectangles. Which one is it closer to? 4 × 70 So is 4 × 68 closer to 240 or 280? 280

- Compare the 4 × 63 rectangle to the 4 × 70 and the 4 × 60 rectangles. Which one is it closer to? 4 × 60 So is 4 × 63 closer to 240 or 280? 240

Have students find the products 4 × 63 and 4 × 68 to check their estimates. Discuss how both answers are between the frames of 240 and 280. Explain that rounding frames can be used to quickly check if an answer makes sense, but now we will just use numerical rounding frames instead of drawing the rectangles.

Activity continued ▶

Teaching Note

Language and Vocabulary In the area model, two-digit multiples of ten are called "rounding frames." The lower tens factor "frames" the number by creating a rectangle that is smaller than the number to be estimated. The higher tens factor "frames" the number by creating a rectangle larger than the number to be estimated.

The Learning Classroom

Helping Community Encourage dialogue between students about the purposes of estimation, past experience with estimation, and other estimation models they have found helpful.

Acknowledging students' past experience makes them feel that they are contributing members of the class.

Activity 1

Teaching Note

Quick Sketches Encourage students to move from drawing on the dot side of their MathBoards to making quick sketches on the white side. Some students may find it helpful to make sketches as shown. Students could also just show the number labels.

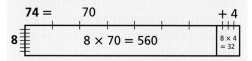

Ongoing Assessment

Have students estimate the following products:

▶ 53 × 7

▶ 57 × 3

Alternate Approach

 Color Suggest that students use colored pencils or markers to highlight the 4 × 70 and 4 × 60 rounding frames, making them easier to recognize.

English Language Learners

Have students look at the first example on the page (4 × 68). Write *rounding* and *estimate* on the board.

- **Beginning** Say: Round 68 to 70. Multiply 70 by 4. This gives an estimate of the area. Have students repeat.
- **Intermediate** Say: We can round 68 to ___ 70 What do we multiply to find an estimate of the area? 70 × 4
- **Advanced** Have students tell how rounding is used to find an estimate.

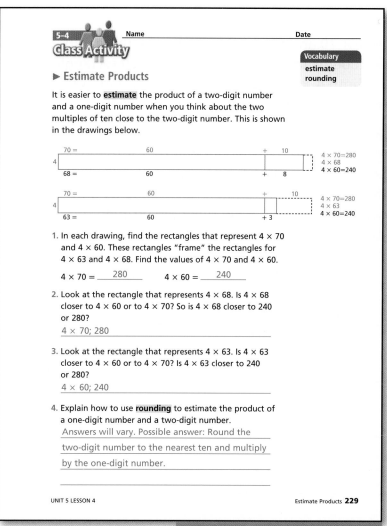

Student Activity Book page 229

▶ Estimate Products INDIVIDUALS

Have students answer problems 1–4 on Student Book page 229 individually. These problems review the previous discussion. Go over the answers with the class. For problem 4, have one student give his or her answer and then have other students ask questions.

Have students discuss how they use rounding and estimation to check answers to multiplication problems.

Activity 2

Practice Estimation

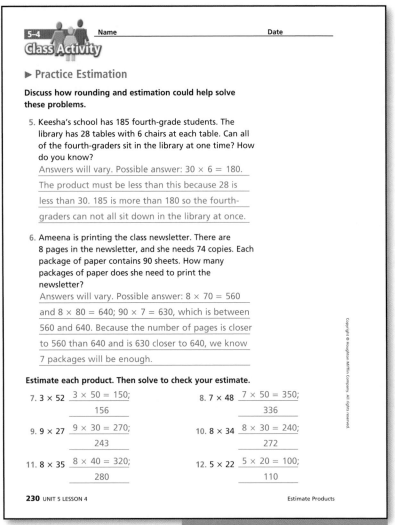

Student Activity Book page 230

---

 15 MINUTES

Goal: Practice estimating products.

Materials: Student Activity Book or Hardcover Book p. 230

✓ **NCTM Standards:**
Number and Operations
Problem Solving
Communication

Differentiated Instruction

Extra Help If students need more explanation, draw the rounding frame to show that 6 × 28 is smaller than 6 × 30.

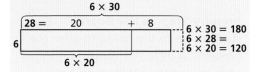

▶ Practice Estimation [WHOLE CLASS]

Apply Estimation to Real-World Situations Explain that problems 5 and 6 on Student Book page 230 will show how estimation can be used to find reasonable answers for real-world problems. Use **Solve and Discuss** for problem 5.

Here is one way students may reason about problem 5.

● We can round the number of tables up to 30 and multiply by 6 chairs per table. But even though we rounded 28 up to 30, 30 tables (30 × 6) still gives us only 180 chairs. We know there are not enough chairs for 185 students. We don't need to look any further. We don't need to multiply exactly to solve this problem.

Activity continued ▶

① Teaching the Lesson (continued)

Activity 2

Teaching Note

What to Expect from Students
Some students may prefer to draw sketches they feel represent the situations more realistically than the rectangles do. For example, for problem 5, some students might want to sketch 30 tables and write a 6 in each table to estimate the number of chairs. Explain to students that such drawings take a long time. We're using the rectangles to help us visualize general ways that will work with numbers so that we don't have to draw all of those things when we estimate.

The Learning Classroom

Step-by-Step at the Board Several students go to the board to solve the problem. A different student performs each step of the problem, using a pointer as he or she describes the step. In this case, let one student round the factor, another estimate the answer, and another find the exact solution.

Math Talk Have a student read problem 6 aloud. Then discuss the solution.

- **What do we need to find out?** how many packages of 90 sheets are needed to print the newsletter

- **What do we need to know before we can find the number of packages that are needed?** the number of sheets of paper she needs to do the printing

- **How do we find the number of sheets of paper needed?** 8×74

- **Estimate 8×74 with frames.** $8 \times 70 = 560$ and $8 \times 80 = 640$

- **Each package has 90 pages. How many packages would be needed for 560 pages? That is, what number times 90 gives at least 560, or how many 90s are in 560?** $90 \times 6 = 540$ and $90 \times 7 = 630$, so at least 7 packages are needed.

- **Is 7 packages enough?** Yes, from the estimation we know that the number needed is closer to 560 than 640. Because 630 is closer to 640, it is sure to be enough.

Use **Step-by-Step at the Board** (see The Learning Classroom) to have students complete exercises 7–8. Then have students complete 9–12 on their own.

② Going Further

Differentiated Instruction

Intervention   Activity Card 5-4

Lower and Higher
Activity Card 5-4 ●

Work: In Pairs

1. Copy the table below. Complete the columns for *Nearest Ten Below* and *Nearest Ten Above*.

Nearest Ten Below	Number	Nearest Ten Above	Rounded Value
50	56	60	60
30	31	40	30
80	88	90	90
70	74	80	70
20	29	30	30

2. Make a rectangle model as shown below for each of the numbers in the table. Use the model to round each number.

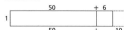

Unit 5, Lesson 4   Copyright © Houghton Mifflin Company

Activity Note Ask the students to explain how the rectangle model helps them see how to round the number.

 Math Writing Prompt

Explain Your Thinking Would 40 × 7 or 50 × 7 give you a better estimate of 47 × 7? Explain your answer.

Soar to Success Math ★ **Software Support**

Use *Soar to Success* for instruction of students needing targeted support for underlying skills.

On Level   Activity Card 5-4

Range of Estimates
Activity Card 5-4 ▲

Work: In Pairs

1. Look at the multiplication rectangles below.

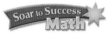

2. On your own, determine what product each model represents. Then decide what two products will show the range for the estimate. See below.

3. Explain your answers to your partner.
   2. 3 × 58, 3 × 50, 3 × 60; 6 × 42, 6 × 40, 6 × 50; 2 × 81, 2 × 80, 2 × 90

Unit 5, Lesson 4   Copyright © Houghton Mifflin Company

Activity Note Extend the activity by having students work together to choose multiplications and then draw estimate models for them.

 Math Writing Prompt

Use Estimation There are 128 students who each need 4 books. Estimate how many books are needed. Explain whether your estimate is too high or too low.

MegaMath Grades K-6 **Software Support**

Use *MegaMath* for review and reinforcement of the concepts and skills presented in this lesson.

Challenge   Activity Card 5-4

One-Digit Patterns
Activity Card 5-4 ■

Work: By Yourself

1. The model below shows the difference between 3 × 70 and 3 × 60.

2. Create models to the difference between each pair of products below.

   4 × 70 and 4 × 60 40

   5 × 70 and 5 × 60 50

3. **Analyze** What patterns do you see in the models? Use the patterns to find three pairs of products that have a difference of 20. Each difference is a multiple of 10 and the one-digit factor.

Unit 5, Lesson 4   Copyright © Houghton Mifflin Company

Activity Note Pairs of products, such as 2 × 70 and 2 × 60, have a difference of 20. Challenge students to write products that have a difference that is not a product of 10, such as 25. 5 × 60 and 5 × 65

 Math Writing Prompt

Write Your Own Write a word problem with an answer that could be estimated as 40 × 6.

✳ DESTINATION Math® **Software Support**

Use *Destination Math* to take students beyond the concepts and skills presented in this lesson.

Estimate Products   **527**

③ Homework and Spiral Review

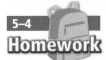

Homework **Goal:** Additional Practice

Use this Homework page to provide students with more practice estimating products.

Remembering **Goal:** Spiral Review

This Remembering activity would be appropriate anytime after today's lesson.

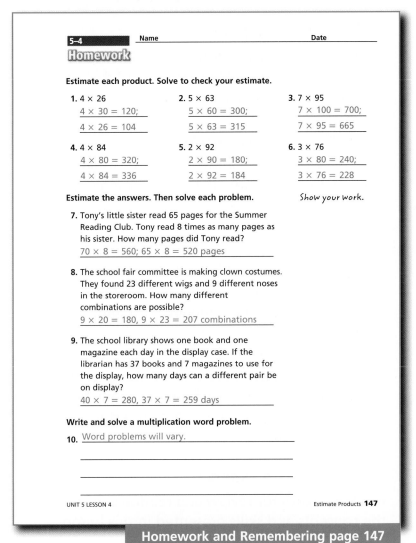

5–4 Name _____ Date _____
Homework

Estimate each product. Solve to check your estimate.

1. 4 × 26
   4 × 30 = 120;
   4 × 26 = 104

2. 5 × 63
   5 × 60 = 300;
   5 × 63 = 315

3. 7 × 95
   7 × 100 = 700;
   7 × 95 = 665

4. 4 × 84
   4 × 80 = 320;
   4 × 84 = 336

5. 2 × 92
   2 × 90 = 180;
   2 × 92 = 184

6. 3 × 76
   3 × 80 = 240;
   3 × 76 = 228

Estimate the answers. Then solve each problem. *Show your work.*

7. Tony's little sister read 65 pages for the Summer Reading Club. Tony read 8 times as many pages as his sister. How many pages did Tony read?
   70 × 8 = 560; 65 × 8 = 520 pages

8. The school fair committee is making clown costumes. They found 23 different wigs and 9 different noses in the storeroom. How many different combinations are possible?
   9 × 20 = 180, 9 × 23 = 207 combinations

9. The school library shows one book and one magazine each day in the display case. If the librarian has 37 books and 7 magazines to use for the display, how many days can a different pair be on display?
   40 × 7 = 280, 37 × 7 = 259 days

Write and solve a multiplication word problem.

10. Word problems will vary.
    _____
    _____
    _____

UNIT 5 LESSON 4   Estimate Products **147**

Homework and Remembering page 147

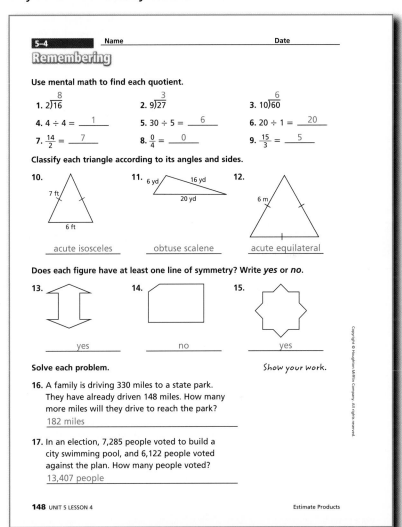

5–4 Name _____ Date _____
Remembering

Use mental math to find each quotient.

1. $2\overline{)16}$ → 8

2. $9\overline{)27}$ → 3

3. $10\overline{)60}$ → 6

4. 4 ÷ 4 = __1__

5. 30 ÷ 5 = __6__

6. 20 ÷ 1 = __20__

7. $\frac{14}{2}$ = __7__

8. $\frac{0}{4}$ = __0__

9. $\frac{15}{3}$ = __5__

Classify each triangle according to its angles and sides.

10. 7 ft / 6 ft
    acute isosceles

11. 6 yd, 16 yd, 20 yd
    obtuse scalene

12. 6 m
    acute equilateral

Does each figure have at least one line of symmetry? Write *yes* or *no*.

13. yes

14. no

15. yes

Solve each problem. *Show your work.*

16. A family is driving 330 miles to a state park. They have already driven 148 miles. How many more miles will they drive to reach the park?
    182 miles

17. In an election, 7,285 people voted to build a city swimming pool, and 6,122 people voted against the plan. How many people voted?
    13,407 people

148 UNIT 5 LESSON 4   Estimate Products

Homework and Remembering page 148

Home or School Activity

Math-to-Math Connection

Consumer Math Estimating can be a useful tool when shopping. Have students select an item in a newspaper ad or catalog that they want to buy. Have them estimate the cost of purchasing three of these items. Then have them calculate the exact price.

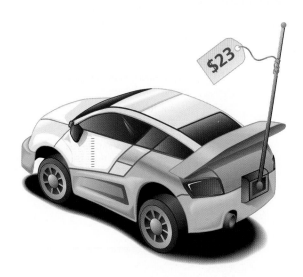

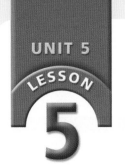

Methods of One-Digit by Two-Digit Multiplication

Lesson Objectives

● Relate the area model of multiplication to numeric methods of multiplication.

● Practice one-digit by two-digit multiplication.

The Day at a Glance

Today's Goals	Materials
① Teaching the Lesson **A1:** Relate the area model for multiplication to numeric methods for multiplication. **A2:** Use expanded or algebraic notation to multiply a one-digit number by a two-digit number. **② Going Further** ▶ Differentiated Instruction **③ Homework and Spiral Review**	**Lesson Activities** Student Activity Book pp. 231–232 or Student Hardcover Book 231–232 Homework and Remembering pp. 149–150 **Going Further** Activity Card 5-5 Coins Math Journals

123 Use Math Talk today!

Keeping Skills Sharp

Quick Practice ⏱ 5 MINUTES	Daily Routines
Goal: Fluency with zeros patterns. **Zeros Patterns** Select four **Student Leaders** to go to the board and write three products involving two non-zero digits. The first product should have no zeros in the factors, the second product should have a zero in one factor, and the third product should have a zero in both factors (see the example below). See Lesson 4.	**Homework Review** Ask a student volunteer to share a word problem. Invite several students to solve it at the board, while the others work at their seats. **Estimate** A large box of cereal holds about 19 servings. A community center orders 5 large boxes of the cereal. About how many servings will that provide? about 100 servings

Problem	Class Response	Student Leader Writes
6 × 7	"42 ones equals forty-two."	= 42
6 × 70	"42 tens equals four hundred twenty."	= 420
60 × 70	"42 hundreds equals four thousand, two hundred."	= 4,200

Teaching the Lesson

Multiplication Methods

 25 MINUTES

Goal: Relate the area model for multiplication to numeric methods for multiplication.

Materials: Student Activity Book or Hardcover Book p. 231

✓ **NCTM Standards:**
Number and Operations
Representation
Communication

Teaching Note

Math Background This lesson uses the concept of place values and of breaking numbers into parts. The area model shows each place-value product as a rectangle. Each part of this area model needs to be related to the new numerical methods for today: Expanded Notation and Algebraic Notation. These methods just organize the writing of the 2 multiplications differently.

English Language Learners

Write 36 × 4 on the board. Draw a rectangle showing 36 = 30 + 6 along the base of the rectangle and 4 for height. Write *area model*.

• **Beginning** Say: We use the area model to find the areas. Then we add the areas together. Write and say: **4 × 30 = 120. 4 × 6 = 24. 120 + 24 = 144.**

• **Intermediate and Advanced** Ask: What do we use to find the areas? area model What is 4 × 30? 120 What is 4 × 6? 24 What is 120 + 24? 144

▶ **Numeric Multiplication Methods** WHOLE CLASS

Create Word Problems for the Problem Write the problem 9 × 28 on the board. Ask the class to create word problems for these numbers. Tell them that they can use any kind of multiplication problem, not just areas. Emphasize that the area rectangle model can be used to solve any kind of multiplication situation.

Then tell students that you are going to show them 2 methods of multiplication that Grade 4 students find easy to understand and to do. Their job is to understand each method. Later they can choose which method they use, including any method they invent or already know as long as they can explain it.

Expanded Notation Method Demonstrate how to use the Expanded Notation Method to solve 9 × 28. Be sure students can relate each numerical step to a part of the drawing.

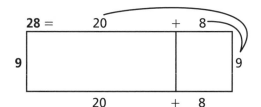

Algebraic Notation Method Now demonstrate the Algebraic Notation Method. Be sure that students can connect each step of the Algebraic Notation Method to the corresponding part of the drawing.

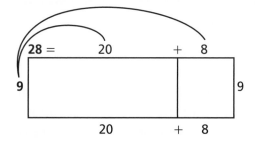

Tell students that we will call the method of drawing an *area model* and adding the areas of the sections the Rectangle Sections Method. Point out that students now know three multiplication methods—the Rectangle Sections Method, the Expanded Notation Method, and the Algebraic Notation Method.

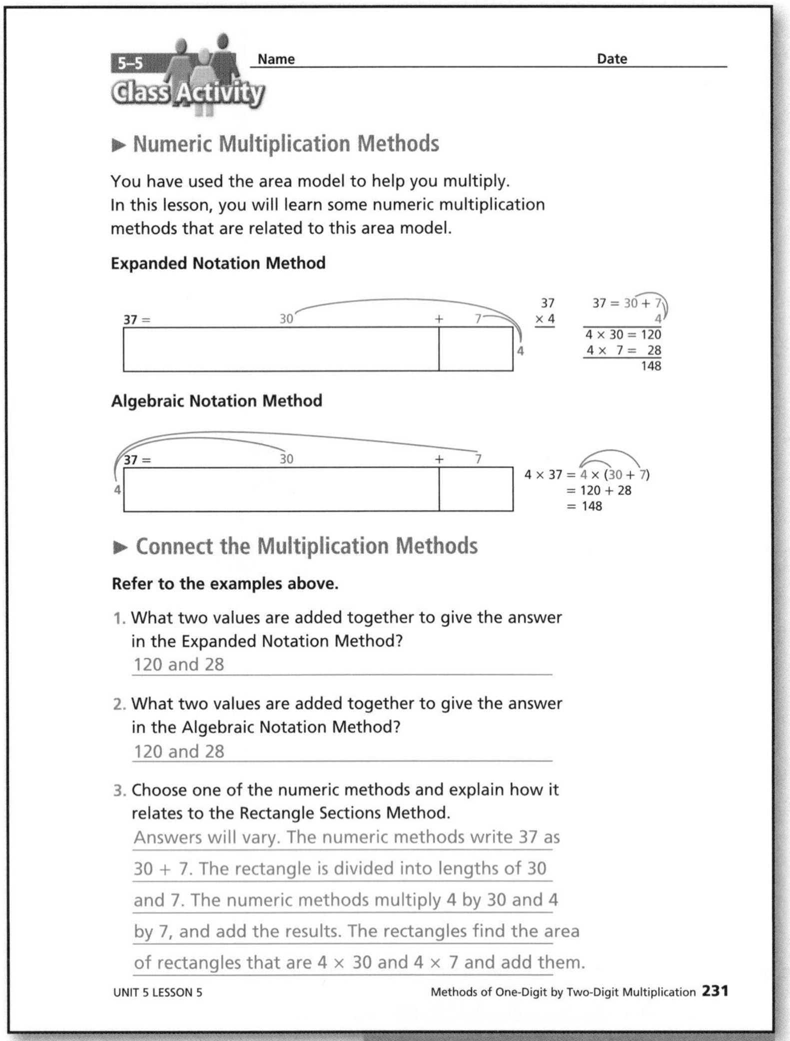
5-5 Class Activity

Name Date

▶ Numeric Multiplication Methods

You have used the area model to help you multiply. In this lesson, you will learn some numeric multiplication methods that are related to this area model.

Expanded Notation Method

37 = 30 + 7

$$\begin{array}{r} 37 \\ \times\ 4 \\ \hline \end{array} \qquad \begin{array}{r} 37 = 30 + 7 \\ 4 \\ \hline 4 \times 30 = 120 \\ 4 \times 7 = \underline{28} \\ 148 \end{array}$$

Algebraic Notation Method

37 = 30 + 7

$4 \times 37 = 4 \times (30 + 7)$
$= 120 + 28$
$= 148$

▶ Connect the Multiplication Methods

Refer to the examples above.

1. What two values are added together to give the answer in the Expanded Notation Method?
   120 and 28
2. What two values are added together to give the answer in the Algebraic Notation Method?
   120 and 28
3. Choose one of the numeric methods and explain how it relates to the Rectangle Sections Method.
   Answers will vary. The numeric methods write 37 as 30 + 7. The rectangle is divided into lengths of 30 and 7. The numeric methods multiply 4 by 30 and 4 by 7, and add the results. The rectangles find the area of rectangles that are 4 × 30 and 4 × 7 and add them.

UNIT 5 LESSON 5 Methods of One-Digit by Two-Digit Multiplication **231**

Student Activity Book page 231

▶ Connect the Multiplication Methods PAIRS

Summarize the two numeric methods by discussing the examples on Student Book page 231. Then have students work in **Student Pairs** to answer exercises 1–3.

Give students an opportunity to say which method they prefer and why. Try to make sure every method is represented as a method that someone prefers. It may be interesting and informative to make a bar chart to show the number of students who prefer each method.

Teaching Note

Math Background The students are using the Distributive Property of Multiplication over Addition when they multiply each number summed in the parentheses by the number outside the parentheses. This property is often referred to simply as the Distributive Property.

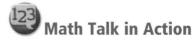

Math Talk in Action

Which method is your favorite?

Kari: I like to draw rectangles because it is easy to see how big each part is.

Maree: I prefer the Algebraic Notation Method because I like to have it all on one line.

Jordy: I prefer the Expanded Notation Method because I like to see the whole step for each part to be sure I get it right. When I show all my work in the expanded form, it is easier to see where I have made a mistake.

Activity 2

Practice Multiplication

 20 MINUTES

Goal: Use expanded or algebraic notation to multiply a one-digit number by a two-digit number.

Materials: Student Activity Book or Hardcover Book p. 232

 NCTM Standard:
Number and Operations

 Ongoing Assessment

Have the students use their favorite method to find 7 × 58.

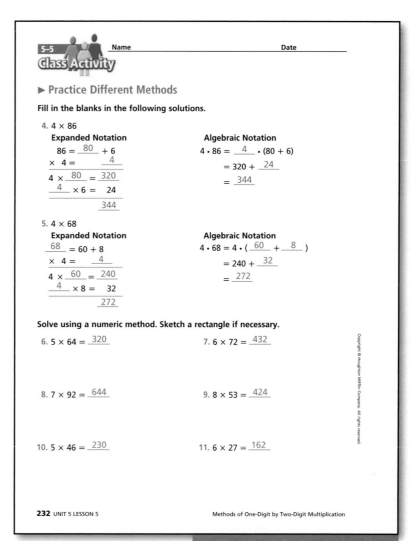

5–5
Class Activity

Name _____ Date _____

▶ **Practice Different Methods**

Fill in the blanks in the following solutions.

4. 4 × 86

Expanded Notation
86 = __80__ + 6
× 4 = ____4____
4 × __80__ = 320
__4__ × 6 = 24
_____
344

Algebraic Notation
4 • 86 = __4__ • (80 + 6)
= 320 + __24__
= __344__

5. 4 × 68

Expanded Notation
__68__ = 60 + 8
× 4 = ____4____
4 × __60__ = 240
__4__ × 8 = 32
_____
272

Algebraic Notation
4 • 68 = 4 • (__60__ + __8__)
= 240 + __32__
= __272__

Solve using a numeric method. Sketch a rectangle if necessary.

6. 5 × 64 = __320__   7. 6 × 72 = __432__

8. 7 × 92 = __644__   9. 8 × 53 = __424__

10. 5 × 46 = __230__   11. 6 × 27 = __162__

232 UNIT 5 LESSON 5   Methods of One-Digit by Two-Digit Multiplication

Student Activity Book page 232

▶ Practice Different Methods INDIVIDUALS

Have the students practice the Expanded Notation Method and Algebraic Notation Method by solving exercises 4 and 5 on page 232 of the Student Book. Then let them choose the numeric method that works best for them to find the products in exercises 6–11.

Students who are having difficulty with the new numeric methods, Expanded Notation and Algebraic Notation, should be encouraged to find the product using the Rectangle Sections Method. This numeric method organizes the multiplication and is sufficient for Grade 4. More advanced students may want to practice using both methods on page 232. They could choose one method for the even-numbered exercises and the other method for the odd-numbered exercises.

② Going Further

Intervention — Activity Card 5-5

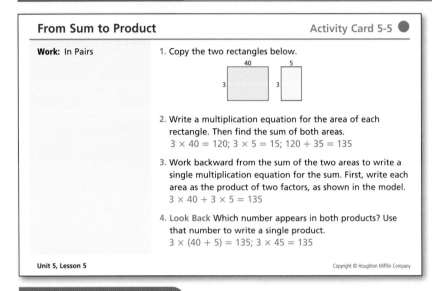

From Sum to Product — Activity Card 5-5 ●

Work: In Pairs

1. Copy the two rectangles below.

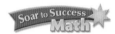

2. Write a multiplication equation for the area of each rectangle. Then find the sum of both areas.
$3 \times 40 = 120$; $3 \times 5 = 15$; $120 + 35 = 135$

3. Work backward from the sum of the two areas to write a single multiplication equation for the sum. First, write each area as the product of two factors, as shown in the model.
$3 \times 40 + 3 \times 5 = 135$

4. **Look Back** Which number appears in both products? Use that number to write a single product.
$3 \times (40 + 5) = 135$; $3 \times 45 = 135$

Unit 5, Lesson 5 — Copyright © Houghton Mifflin Company

Activity Note Review the Distributive Property before students begin this activity.

✎ Math Writing Prompt

Explain Your Thinking Explain how to use the Expanded Notation Method to solve 3×27.

Soar to Success Math ★ Software Support

Use *Soar to Success* for instruction of students needing targeted support for underlying skills.

▲ On Level — Activity Card 5-5

Notation Game — Activity Card 5-5 ▲

Work: In Pairs

Use:
• 1 coin

1. One partner writes a one-digit by two-digit multiplication.

2. The other partner flips a coin to choose the method for solving the problem. For heads, use the Expanded Notation Method. For tails, use the Algebraic Notation Method. Find the product.

 3×27

3. Exchange roles and repeat the activity twice.

4. **Math Talk** Discuss each method. Which method do you prefer? Why?

Unit 5, Lesson 5 — Copyright © Houghton Mifflin Company

Activity Note To check answers, have the partner who created the problem solve it with the alternative method. Students can then compare answers and discuss.

✎ Math Writing Prompt

Make Connections Draw an area model that represents the Algebraic Notation Method of finding the product 3×42.

MegaMath Grades K-6 Software Support

Use *MegaMath* for review and reinforcement of the concepts and skills presented in this lesson.

■ Challenge — Activity Card 5-5

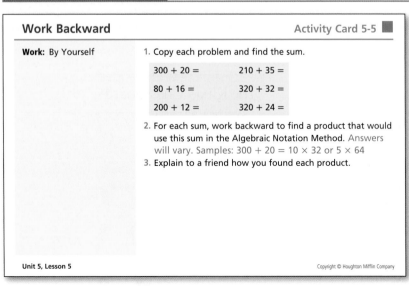

Work Backward — Activity Card 5-5 ■

Work: By Yourself

1. Copy each problem and find the sum.

$300 + 20 =$	$210 + 35 =$
$80 + 16 =$	$320 + 32 =$
$200 + 12 =$	$320 + 24 =$

2. For each sum, work backward to find a product that would use this sum in the Algebraic Notation Method. Answers will vary. Samples: $300 + 20 = 10 \times 32$ or 5×64

3. Explain to a friend how you found each product.

Unit 5, Lesson 5 — Copyright © Houghton Mifflin Company

Activity Note Challenge students to write as many products as they can for each sum, within a given time period.

✎ Math Writing Prompt

Compare Methods Describe the differences between the Expanded Notation Method and the Algebraic Notation Method.

✷ DESTINATION Math· Software Support

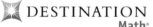

Use *Destination Math* to take students beyond the concepts and skills presented in this lesson.

③ Homework and Spiral Review

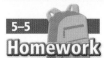

Homework **Goal:** Additional Practice

✔ Include students' work for page 149 as part of their portfolios.

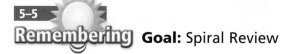

5–5
Remembering **Goal:** Spiral Review

This Remembering activity would be appropriate anytime after today's lesson.

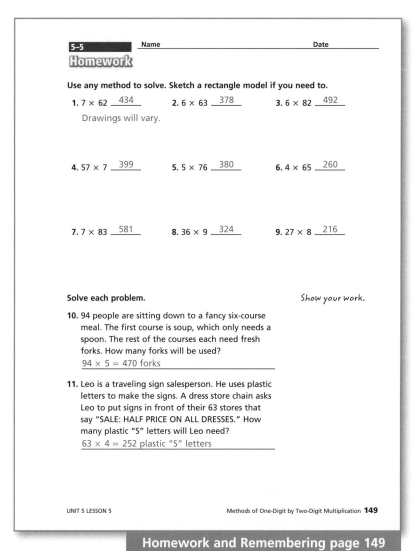

5–5 Name _____ Date _____
Homework

Use any method to solve. Sketch a rectangle model if you need to.

1. 7 × 62 __434__   2. 6 × 63 __378__   3. 6 × 82 __492__

Drawings will vary.

4. 57 × 7 __399__   5. 5 × 76 __380__   6. 4 × 65 __260__

7. 7 × 83 __581__   8. 36 × 9 __324__   9. 27 × 8 __216__

Solve each problem.   *Show your work.*

10. 94 people are sitting down to a fancy six-course meal. The first course is soup, which only needs a spoon. The rest of the courses each need fresh forks. How many forks will be used?
94 × 5 = 470 forks

11. Leo is a traveling sign salesperson. He uses plastic letters to make the signs. A dress store chain asks Leo to put signs in front of their 63 stores that say "SALE: HALF PRICE ON ALL DRESSES." How many plastic "S" letters will Leo need?
63 × 4 = 252 plastic "S" letters

UNIT 5 LESSON 5   Methods of One-Digit by Two-Digit Multiplication **149**

Homework and Remembering page 149

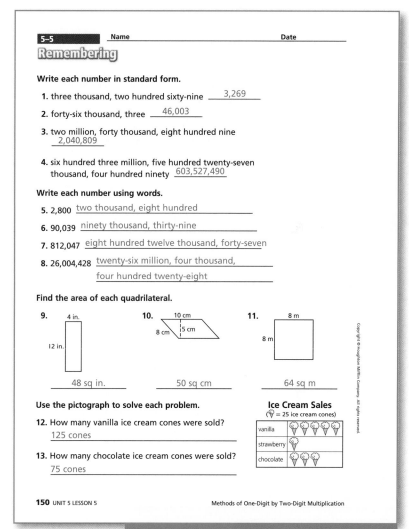

5–5 Name _____ Date _____
Remembering

Write each number in standard form.

1. three thousand, two hundred sixty-nine ___3,269___
2. forty-six thousand, three ___46,003___
3. two million, forty thousand, eight hundred nine
2,040,809
4. six hundred three million, five hundred twenty-seven thousand, four hundred ninety 603,527,490

Write each number using words.

5. 2,800 two thousand, eight hundred
6. 90,039 ninety thousand, thirty-nine
7. 812,047 eight hundred twelve thousand, forty-seven
8. 26,004,428 twenty-six million, four thousand, four hundred twenty-eight

Find the area of each quadrilateral.

9. 4 in. 12 in. — 48 sq in.
10. 10 cm 8 cm 5 cm — 50 sq cm
11. 8 m 8 m — 64 sq m

Use the pictograph to solve each problem.

Ice Cream Sales
(🍦 = 25 ice cream cones)

vanilla	🍦🍦🍦🍦🍦
strawberry	🍦🍦
chocolate	🍦🍦🍦

12. How many vanilla ice cream cones were sold?
125 cones
13. How many chocolate ice cream cones were sold?
75 cones

150 UNIT 5 LESSON 5   Methods of One-Digit by Two-Digit Multiplication

Homework and Remembering page 150

Home or School Activity

 Literature Connection

The King's Chessboard Have students read the first few pages of this book written by David Birch (Puffin 1993, Illustrator Davis Grebu). Ask students to figure out on what day two-digit times one-digit multiplication is needed to find how much rice the wise man will be paid. Have students act out helping the king by finding each day's pay throughout Unit 5. You might want to have a bulletin board showing each day's payment.

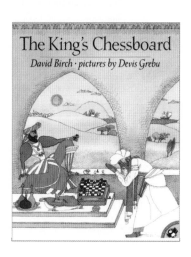

The King's Chessboard
David Birch · pictures by Devis Grebu

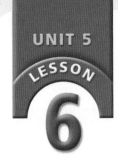

Discuss Different Methods

Lesson Objective

- **Compare and analyze methods of multiplication.**

The Day at a Glance

Today's Goals	Materials	

1 Teaching the Lesson
A1: Compare methods for multiplying a one-digit number by a two-digit number.
A2: Practice multiplying with different methods.
 	
2 Going Further
▶ Differentiated Instruction
 	
3 Homework and Spiral Review
	Lesson Activities
	Student Activity Book pp. 233–234
	  or Student Hardcover Book
	  pp. 233–234
	Homework and Remembering
	  pp. 151–152
		Going Further
		Activity Cards 5-6
		Math Journals

123 Use **Math Talk** today!

Keeping Skills Sharp

Quick Practice   ⏱ 5 MINUTES

Goal: Fluency with zeros patterns.

Zeros Patterns Select four **Student Leaders** to go to the board and write three products involving two non-zero digits. One product should have no zeros in the factors, another should have a zero in one factor, and another should have a zero in both factors (see the example below). See Lesson 4.

Problem	Class Response	Student Leader Writes
8 × 9	"72 ones equals seventy-two."	= 72
8 × 90	"72 tens equals seven hundred twenty."	= 720
80 × 90	"72 hundreds equals seven thousand, two hundred."	= 7,200

Daily Routines

Homework Review If students have difficulty with word problems, encourage them to write situation equations and then change them to solution equations.

What's Wrong? Ms. Miller measured the length of a room as 12 feet and the width of the room as 9 feet. She told a carpet salesperson that she needed 42 square feet of carpeting. What did Ms. Miller do wrong? How can she correct her measurement? She used the perimeter instead of the area (12 + 9 + 12 + 9 = 42). She should multiply 12 × 9 = 108 to find the area.

1 Teaching the Lesson

Compare Multiplication Methods

 25 MINUTES

Goal: Compare methods for multiplying a one-digit number by a two-digit number.

Materials: Student Activity Book or Hardcover Book p. 233

✓ **NCTM Standards:**
Number and Operations
Problem Solving
Communication

Teaching Note

What to Expect From Students
Comparing five methods at once is a task of greater complexity than students are used to at this level, and some students may struggle or stop working. Help students break down their comparisons into smaller parts. They may want to circle two methods at a time. Encourage students to discuss how they feel about comparing several methods at once and strategies they personally use for handling large or difficult tasks such as this one.

English Language Learners

Write *similar* and *different* on the board. Refer to the table showing methods to solve 9 × 28.

• **Beginning** Say: *Similar* means "alike." These methods give *similar* ___. answers *Different* means "not alike." The steps in these methods are ___. different
• **Intermediate and Advanced** Ask: **How are these methods similar?** answers **How are they different?** number of steps, operations used

▶ **Share Multiplication Methods** WHOLE CLASS

On the board, write 9 × 28 = ___. Then have students share any solution methods they know that have not been discussed on previous days. They should be able to relate their method to the area model.

5-6
Class Activity   Name _____ Date _____

▶ Compare Multiplication Methods

Compare these methods for solving 9 × 28.

Method A	Method B	Method C	Method D	Method E
28 = 20 + 8	28 = 20 + 8	28	28	7 28
× 9 = 9	× 9 = 9	× 9	× 9	× 9
9 × 20 = 180	180	180	72	252
9 × 8 = 72	72	72	180	
252	252	252	252	

1. How are all the methods similar? List at least two similarities.
   Answers will vary.

2. How are the methods different? List at least three differences.
   Answers will vary.

▶ Analyze the Shortcut Method

Method E can be broken down into 2 steps.

Method E:	Step 1	Step 2
	7 28	7 28
	× 9	× 9
	2	252

3. Where are the products 180 and 72 from methods A–D?
   Answers will vary. Possible answer: The 72 is shown by the rightmost 2 and the carried 7. The 180 is the 2 × 9 and is added to the carried 7 to make 25 (250).

UNIT 5 LESSON 6   Discuss Different Methods **233**

Student Activity Book page 233

▶ **Compare Multiplication Methods** WHOLE CLASS

Send five students to the board. Have each student neatly copy one of the numeric methods shown onto the board. Be sure the methods are copied in the same order as on page 233 of the Student Book. Have the students describe each step of their method. Then have the class identify the changes in each succeeding method.

● Method A is the full Expanded Notation Method, including the tens and ones equations.

- Method B shows the Expanded Notation Method without the tens and ones equations, which can be done mentally.

- Method C drops writing the step of separating the tens and ones in 28 (done mentally) but still multiplies the tens before the ones (multiplying left to right).

- Method D multiplies the tens and ones separately but starts with the ones place. (The Expanded Notation Method can be done in either order.)

- Method E adds the tens and ones multiplications together as you go and writes them in the same row. You multiply by the ones first and write the tens value above the tens column in the top factor so you can add it to the tens multiplication (9×2 tens = 18 tens, plus the 7 tens from 9×28 is 25 tens).

Discuss exercises 1–2.

▶ Analyze the Shortcut Method WHOLE CLASS

Discuss the two steps for Method E on Student Book page 233. Ask the following questions:

- **Describe step 1 with place-value language.** Possible answer: 9×8 ones = 72 ones. Write 2 in the ones column and write the 7 tens above the tens column.

- **Describe step 2 with place-value language.** Possible answer: 9×2 tens = 18 tens. Add the 7 tens from step 1 to make a total of 25 tens. Write 5 in the tens column and write 2 in the hundreds column.

Point out that the result is the same as with the Expanded Notation Method, but the Shortcut Method allows us to use fewer symbols. In step 1, we arrange the result of 9×8 differently. Before we wrote 72, but here we split 72 into 70 and 2. We place the 2 in the same position as before but the 70 gets placed as a 7 above the 2 in 28 so that it can be added to the product found in step 2. In step 2 we multiply 9×20 and add the 70 from step 1. By splitting the 72 and adding 70 to 180, we have streamlined the process.

Now have the class work in **Student Pairs** to answer exercise 3 on page 233.

Teaching Note

Math Background The Shortcut Method (Method E) is the common method currently taught in most schools in the United States. It is a complex method that is difficult for many fourth-graders, especially when multiplying a two-digit number by a two-digit number. For many students, it is a process that is memorized rather than understood. In this activity, we relate it to the Expanded Notation Method by first dropping steps and switching the order of multiplication from the highest place-value (tens in this case) to the lowest place value (ones in this case). The Shortcut Method is too difficult for many fourth-graders. It will be more of a focus in Grade 5.

Teaching Note

What to Expect from Students Less-accomplished students may continue to use an area drawing and add the products outside the rectangle. We call this the Rectangle Sections Method. It helps students organize their thinking, and it generalizes well to two-digit by two-digit problems. This makes it an acceptable method for fourth-graders.

Teaching the Lesson (continued)

Activity 2

Practice Multiplication

 20 MINUTES

Goal: Practice multiplying with different methods.

Materials: Student Activity Book or Hardcover Book p. 234

 NCTM Standard:
Number and Operations

Ongoing Assessment

Have students use a numeric method to solve:

$$\begin{array}{r} 37 \\ \times\ 4 \\ \hline \end{array}$$

The Learning Classroom

Math Talk Remind students of the **Solve and Discuss** structure of this program. Ask four or five students to go to the board and solve a problem, using any method they choose. The other students work on the same problem at their desks. Then the students at the board explain their methods. Students at their desks ask questions and assist each other in understanding the problem. Thus, students actually solve, explain, question, and justify. Usually only two or three students explain because classes do not like to sit through more explanations.

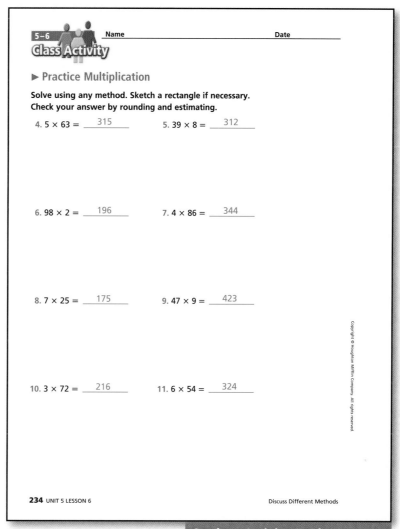

5-6 Class Activity Name _____ Date _____

▶ Practice Multiplication

Solve using any method. Sketch a rectangle if necessary. Check your answer by rounding and estimating.

4. $5 \times 63 =$ ___315___   5. $39 \times 8 =$ ___312___

6. $98 \times 2 =$ ___196___   7. $4 \times 86 =$ ___344___

8. $7 \times 25 =$ ___175___   9. $47 \times 9 =$ ___423___

10. $3 \times 72 =$ ___216___   11. $6 \times 54 =$ ___324___

234 UNIT 5 LESSON 6   Discuss Different Methods

Student Activity Book page 234

▶ Practice Multiplication PAIRS

Use **Solve and Discuss** for exercises 4–11 on Student Book page 234. Make sure a variety of solution methods are presented.

Intervention   Activity Card 5-6

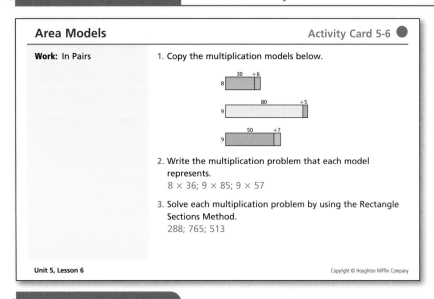

Area Models   Activity Card 5-6 ●

Work: In Pairs

1. Copy the multiplication models below.

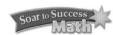

2. Write the multiplication problem that each model represents.
   8 × 36; 9 × 85; 9 × 57

3. Solve each multiplication problem by using the Rectangle Sections Method.
   288; 765; 513

Unit 5, Lesson 6   Copyright © Houghton Mifflin Company

Activity Note If time permits, repeat the activity by having students draw their own area models and then exchanging papers with a partner.

✏ Math Writing Prompt

Choose a Method If you could only use one method for multiplying one-digit numbers by two-digit numbers, which method would you choose? Explain.

Soar to Success Math ★ Software Support

Use *Soar to Success* for instruction of students needing targeted support for underlying skills.

On Level   Activity Card 5-6

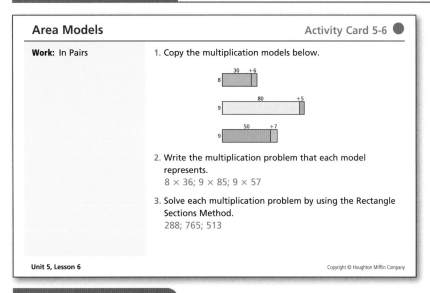

Area Models   Activity Card 5-6 ●

Work: In Pairs

1. Copy the multiplication models below.

2. Write the multiplication problem that each model represents.
   8 × 36; 9 × 85; 9 × 57

3. Solve each multiplication problem by using the Rectangle Sections Method.
   288; 765; 513

Unit 5, Lesson 6   Copyright © Houghton Mifflin Company

Activity Note If time permits, repeat the activity by having students draw their own rectangle models and then exchanging papers with another student.

✏ Math Writing Prompt

Explain Your Thinking Explain to another student how to use the Shortcut Method to solve 8 × 93.

MegaMath Grades K-6 Software Support

Use *MegaMath* for review and reinforcement of the concepts and skills presented in this lesson.

Challenge   Activity Card 5-6

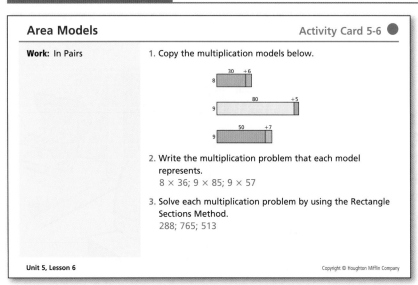

Area Models   Activity Card 5-6 ●

Work: In Pairs

1. Copy the multiplication models below.

2. Write the multiplication problem that each model represents.
   8 × 36; 9 × 85; 9 × 57

3. Solve each multiplication problem by using the Rectangle Sections Method.
   288; 765; 513

Unit 5, Lesson 6   Copyright © Houghton Mifflin Company

Activity Note To extend the activity, have students come up with other sets of products that have the same pattern.

✏ Math Writing Prompt

Your Opinion Is it helpful to learn several different methods for multiplying? Explain.

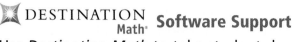

DESTINATION Math® Software Support

Use *Destination Math* to take students beyond the concepts and skills presented in this lesson.

③ Homework and Spiral Review

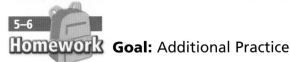 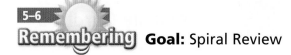

5–6
Homework **Goal:** Additional Practice

Use this Homework page to provide students with more practice multiplying, using different methods.

5–6
Remembering **Goal:** Spiral Review

This Remembering activity would be appropriate anytime after today's lesson.

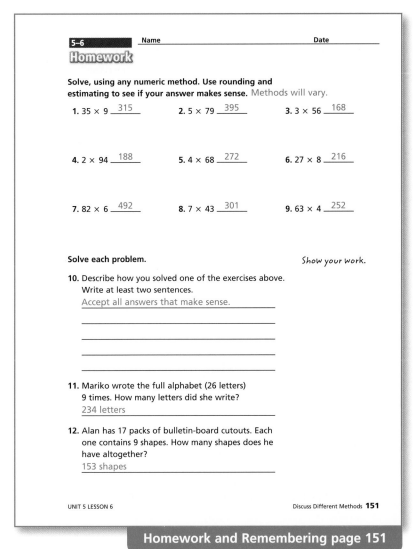

5–6
Homework
Name _____ Date _____

Solve, using any numeric method. Use rounding and estimating to see if your answer makes sense. Methods will vary.

1. 35 × 9 _315_   **2.** 5 × 79 _395_   **3.** 3 × 56 _168_

4. 2 × 94 _188_   **5.** 4 × 68 _272_   **6.** 27 × 8 _216_

7. 82 × 6 _492_   **8.** 7 × 43 _301_   **9.** 63 × 4 _252_

Solve each problem.   *Show your work.*

10. Describe how you solved one of the exercises above. Write at least two sentences.
Accept all answers that make sense.
_____
_____
_____

11. Mariko wrote the full alphabet (26 letters) 9 times. How many letters did she write?
234 letters

12. Alan has 17 packs of bulletin-board cutouts. Each one contains 9 shapes. How many shapes does he have altogether?
153 shapes

UNIT 5 LESSON 6   Discuss Different Methods **151**

Homework and Remembering page 151

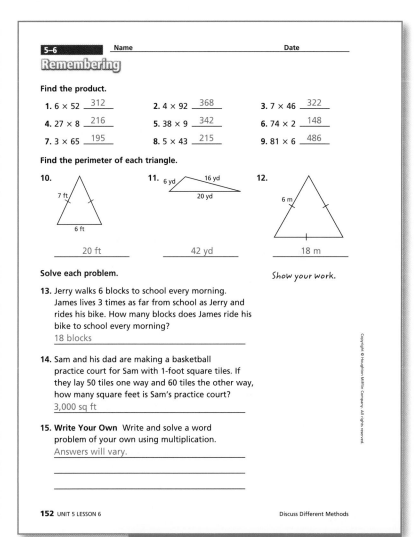

5–6
Remembering
Name _____ Date _____

Find the product.

1. 6 × 52 _312_   **2.** 4 × 92 _368_   **3.** 7 × 46 _322_

4. 27 × 8 _216_   **5.** 38 × 9 _342_   **6.** 74 × 2 _148_

7. 3 × 65 _195_   **8.** 5 × 43 _215_   **9.** 81 × 6 _486_

Find the perimeter of each triangle.

10.
7 ft
6 ft
_20 ft_

11. 6 yd   16 yd
20 yd
_42 yd_

12.
6 m
_18 m_

Solve each problem.   *Show your work.*

13. Jerry walks 6 blocks to school every morning. James lives 3 times as far from school as Jerry and rides his bike. How many blocks does James ride his bike to school every morning?
18 blocks

14. Sam and his dad are making a basketball practice court for Sam with 1-foot square tiles. If they lay 50 tiles one way and 60 tiles the other way, how many square feet is Sam's practice court?
3,000 sq ft

15. Write Your Own Write and solve a word problem of your own using multiplication.
Answers will vary.
_____
_____

152 UNIT 5 LESSON 6   Discuss Different Methods

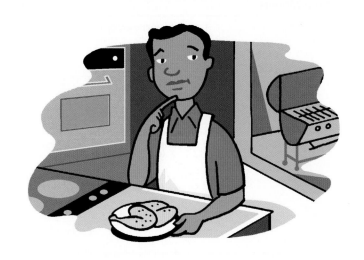

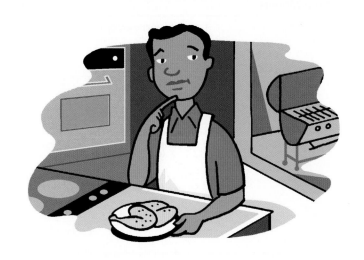

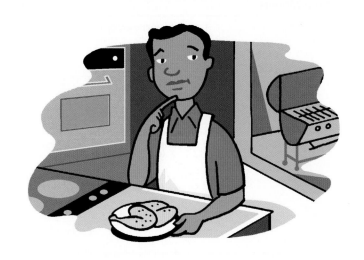

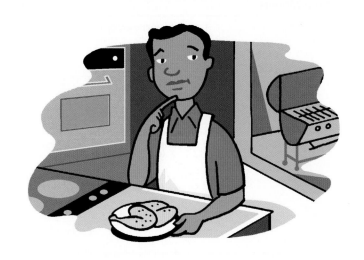

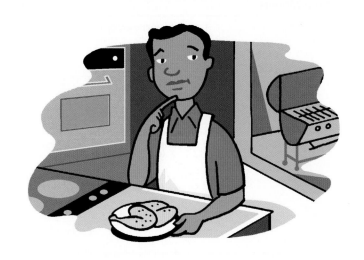

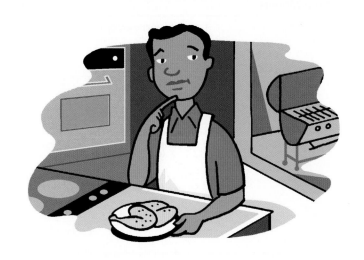

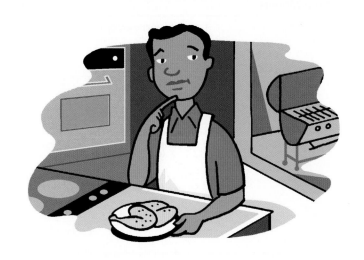

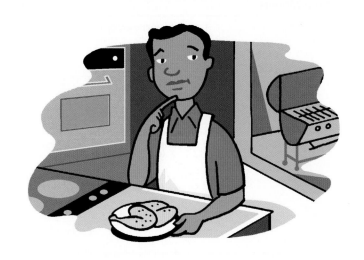

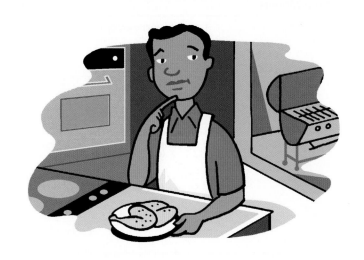

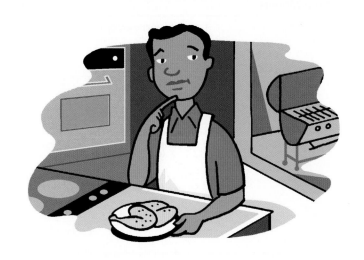

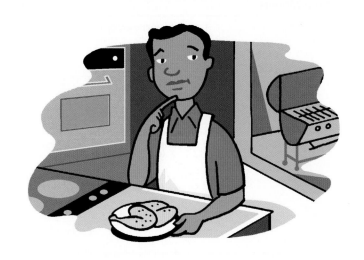

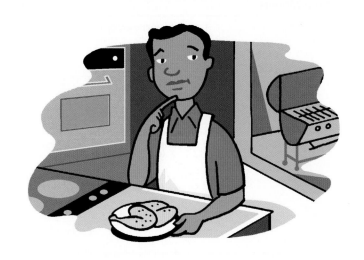

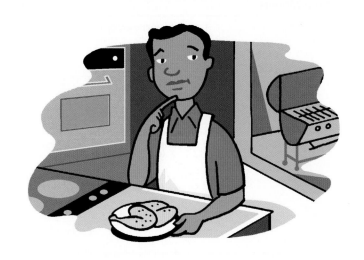

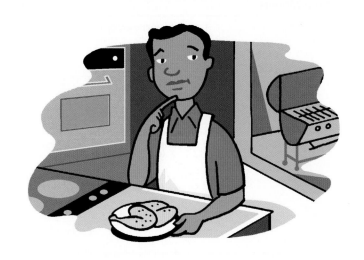

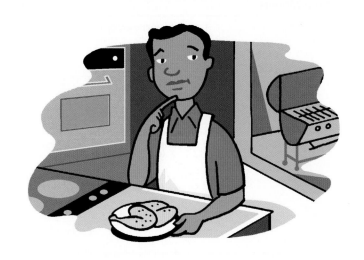

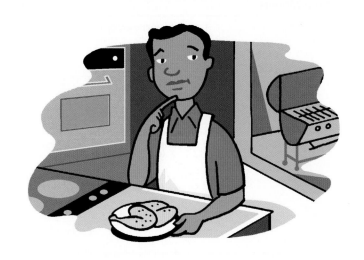

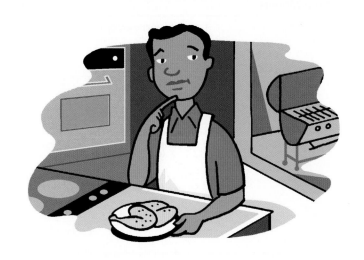

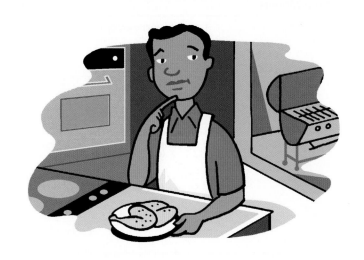

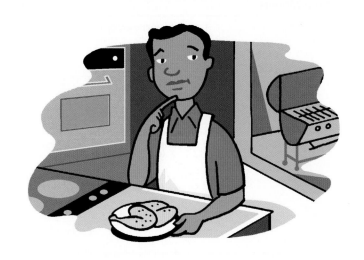

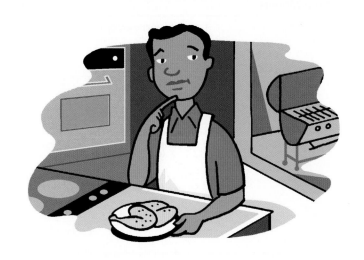

Homework and Remembering page 152

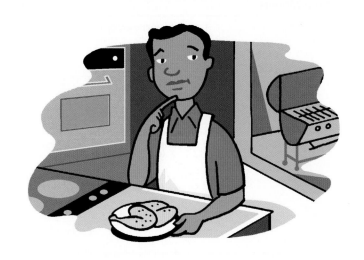

Home or School Activity

🌐 Real-World Connection

Cooking Methods Just as there are several different ways to multiply the same two numbers, there are several different ways to cook a particular food item. For example, we can heat food on a stovetop, bake it in the oven, or BBQ it on a grill. Have students identify a food that can be cooked in these three ways and have them explain why a person may choose to use each of the methods.

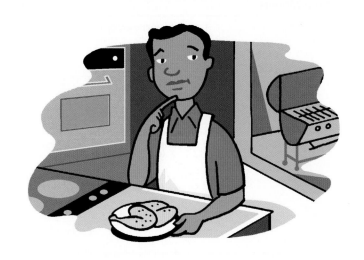

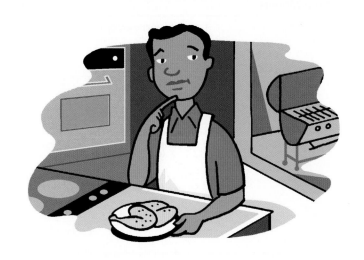

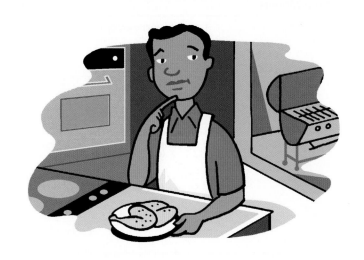

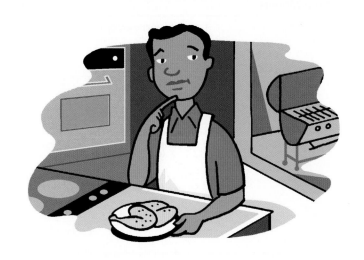

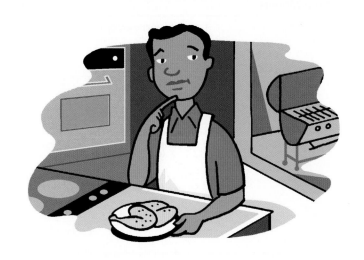

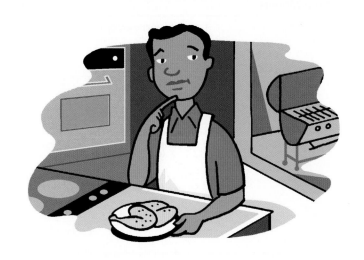

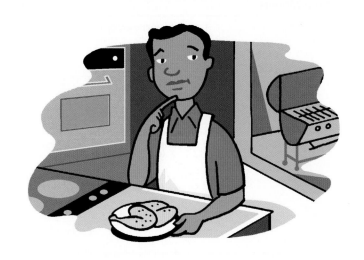

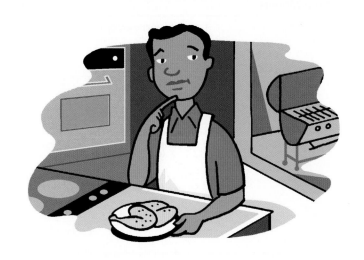

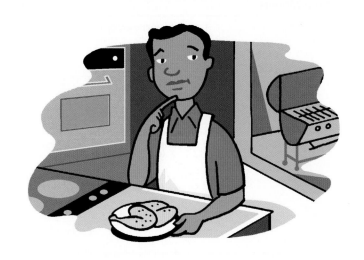

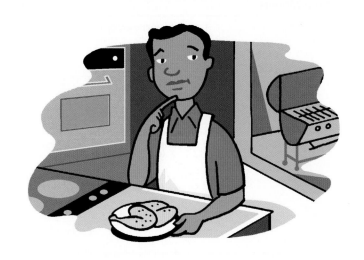

540 UNIT 5 LESSON 6

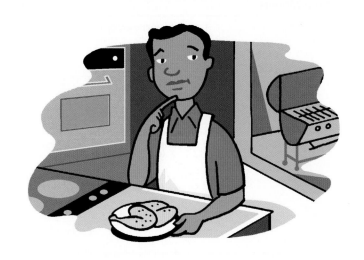

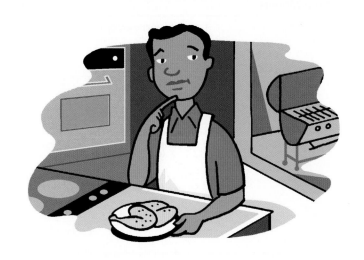

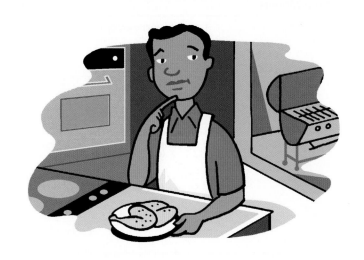

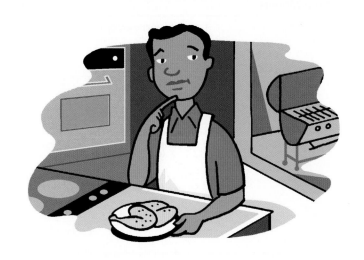

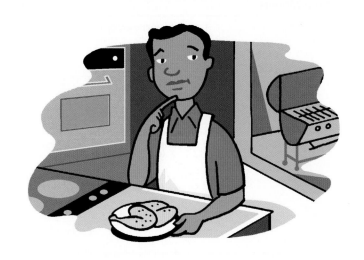

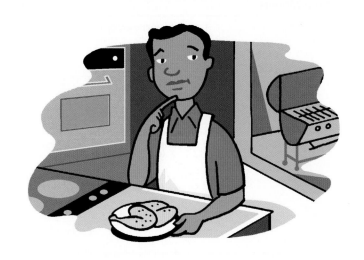

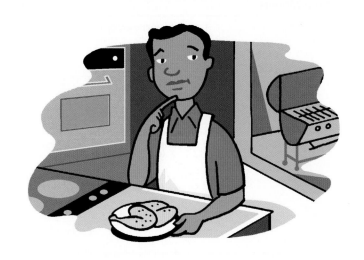

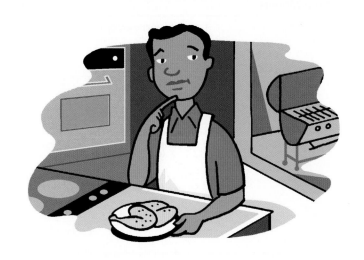

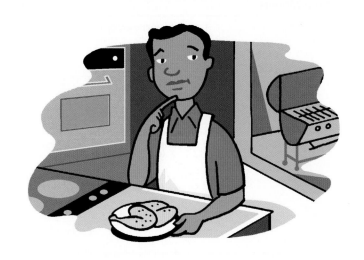

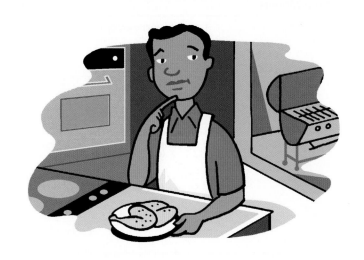

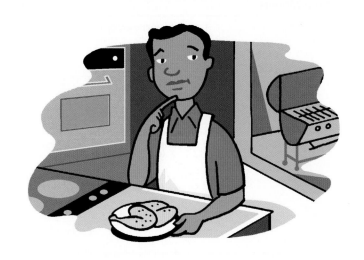

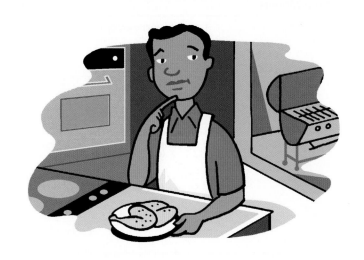

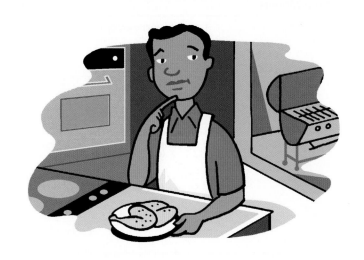

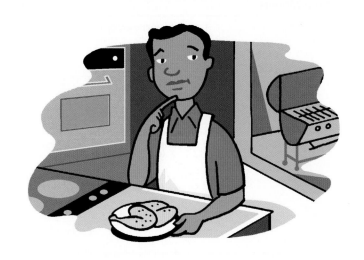

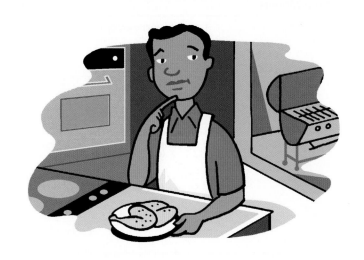

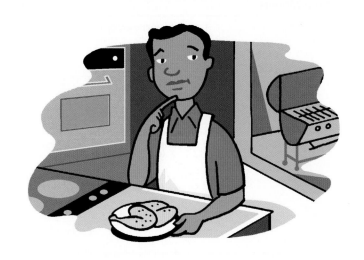

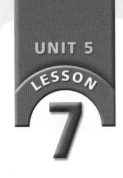

One-Digit by Three-Digit Multiplication

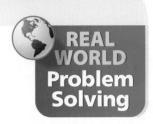

Lesson Objectives

- Draw area models to represent the product of a one-digit number and a three-digit number.
- Use numeric methods to multiply a one-digit number by a three-digit number.

The Day at a Glance

Today's Goals	Materials
① Teaching the Lesson **A1:** Model multiplication of one-digit numbers by hundreds. **A2:** Model one-digit by three-digit multiplication. **A3:** Practice multiplication of one-digit numbers by three-digit numbers. **② Going Further** ▶ Math Connection: Multiplication With Dollars and Cents ▶ Differentiated Instruction **③ Homework and Spiral Review**	**Lesson Activities** Student Activity Book p. 235 or Student Hardcover Book p. 235 Homework and Remembering pp. 153–154 MathBoard Materials Base-ten blocks (optional) **Going Further** Student Activity Book p. 236 or Student Hardcover Book p. 236 Activity Cards 5-7 Go *Fish* Game Cards (TRB M64) Scissors Math Journals

123 *Use* Math Talk *today!*

Keeping Skills Sharp

Quick Practice ⏱ 5 MINUTES

Goal: Fluency with zeros patterns.

Zeros Patterns Select four **Student Leaders** to go to the board to write three products involving two non-zero digits. A product can have no zeros in the factors, a zero in one factor, a zero in both factors, or two zeros in one factor (see the example below). See Lesson 4.

Problem	Class Response	Student Leader Writes
6×40	"24 tens equals two-hundred forty."	$= 240$
60×40	"24 hundreds equals two thousand, four hundred."	$= 2,400$
600×4	"24 hundreds equals two thousand, four hundred."	$= 2,400$

Daily Routines

Homework Review Let students work together to check their work. Initially, pair less able students with more able students. Remind students to use what they know about helping others.

Reasoning A store has 40 kites to give away. If each person gets the same number of kites, how many different ways are there to distribute the kites? 8 ways: 1 kite each to 40 people, 2 kites to 20 people, 4 kites to 10 people, 5 kites to 8 people, 8 kites to 5 people, 10 kites to 4 people, 20 kites to 2 people, 40 kites to 1 person

1 Teaching the Lesson

Activity 1

Multiply One-Digit Numbers by Hundreds

 15 MINUTES

Goal: Model multiplication of one-digit numbers by hundreds.

Materials: MathBoard Materials

 NCTM Standards:
Number and Operations
Representation
Communication

▶ Draw One-Digit by Hundreds Multiplication

WHOLE CLASS

Work on the board, as students follow along on their MathBoards. Have the students draw an area model to show 4 × 200. Instruct them to label the sides and divide their rectangles in half to show two hundreds.

$$200 = 100 + 100$$

$$4 \boxed{\qquad\qquad|\qquad\qquad} 4$$

Near their sketch, have the students write these steps for multiplying 4 × 200.

$$
\begin{aligned}
4 \times 200 &= 4 \times (2 \times 100) \\
&= (4 \times 2) \times 100 \qquad \text{Associative Property} \\
&= 8 \times 100 \\
&= 800
\end{aligned}
$$

Write the following to help students relate the product to previous patterns that they have seen:

$4 \times 2 = 4 \times 2 \times 1$	= 8 ones	= 8
$4 \times 20 = 4 \times 2 \times 10$	= 8 tens	= 80
$4 \times 200 = 4 \times 2 \times 100$	= 8 hundreds	= 800

Have students summarize how the 5s are tricky with respect to this zeros pattern. The number 5 times any even number ends in a zero, so these products do not look like they fit this pattern. But if you think about—and even underline—the 5s product, they really do fit the pattern.

Ask students for problem situations in the world where people might need to multiply 4 × 200. The class needs to be spending time on the numeric aspects of multi-digit multiplication, but we do not want this necessary numerical work to become too disconnected from real-world situations.

Use the Area Model to Multiply Hundreds

▶ Different Methods WHOLE CLASS

Explain to students that they will now solve 1-digit times 3-digit problems using each of the 3 methods they know: Rectangle Sections, Expanded Notation, and Algebraic Notation. You will be asking for volunteers to go to the board for each method. Tell students that everyone needs to draw rectangle sketches and relate each part of their sketch to each step of their numeric method. This helps everyone understand. Later, during the practice for Activity 3, students do not have to draw rectangles if they do not want to do so. At the end of the lesson, discuss any other methods students want to share.

▶ Discuss the Rectangle Sections Method

WHOLE CLASS   Math Talk

Have some student volunteers draw rectangles showing 4 × 237 on the board as everyone else sketches on their MathBoards.

237 =	200	+	30	+	7		800
4	4 × 200 = 800		4 × 30 = 120		4 × 7 = 28	4	120
							+ 28
							948

Have students find the area of each section and then add to find the total area.

Discuss solutions relating each step inside the rectangle to the products added outside the rectangle. Be sure that listeners understand the steps for finding the product of 4 × 237 by using the Rectangle Sections Method. First multiply 4 × 200 = 800, then multiply 4 × 30 = 120, then multiply 4 × 7 = 28. Add 800 + 120 + 28 = 948.

 20 MINUTES

Goal: Model one-digit by three-digit multiplication.

Materials: MathBoard Materials, Student Activity Book or Hardcover Book p. 235, base-ten blocks (optional)

 NCTM Standards:
Number and Operations
Representation
Communication

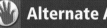 **Alternate Approach**

Base-Ten Blocks Have students model 4 × 237 using base-ten blocks.

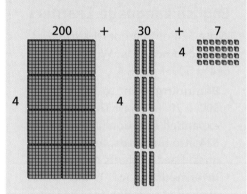

Ask students to explain how this base-ten model matches the area sketch.

Activity continued ▶

❶ Teaching the Lesson (continued)

Activity 2

Teaching Note

What to Expect from Students As students work with the area model to show different methods of multiplying a one-digit number by a three-digit number, many may realize that the only difference in the methods is in the order of the steps. Some students may arrive at the correct conclusion that, in all three methods, you multiply the ones, tens, and hundreds and then add all three products to get the final product. This realization can help students to be successful when they work with the Shortcut Method, but the notation in the Shortcut Method is too difficult for many fourth-graders.

English Language Learners

Write 524 on the board. Write *expanded notation*. Write $524 = 500 + 20 + 4$.

- **Beginning** Point to $524 = 500 + 20 + 4$. Say: **This is expanded notation. We expand 524 into hundreds, tens, and ones.** Have students repeat.
- **Intermediate** Ask: **Is this expanded notation for 524?** yes **What does expanding 524 show?** hundreds, tens, and ones in 524
- **Advanced** Have students tell the steps to write a number in expanded notation.

▶ Discuss the Expanded Notation Method

WHOLE CLASS   Math Talk

Have students go to the board to sketch a model and solve 4×237 using the Expanded Notation Method, while the other students work on their MathBoards. Have students add arcs to show the multiplications.

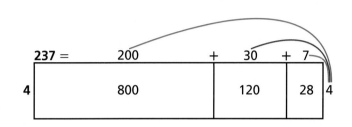

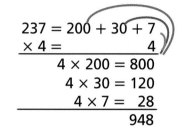

Have a student discussion of how each step in the Expanded Notation Method relates to each part of the rectangle model.

- Have someone summarize the Expanded Notation Method: What three steps are used in the Expanded Notation Method? You split 237 into hundreds, tens, and ones. Then you multiply each of the three place values by 4. Then you add the three products together.

- Then discuss as a class how the Expanded Notation Method is similar to the Rectangle Sections Method. They both use expanded notation of 237. They both multiply 4×200, 4×30, and 4×7. They both add the three products together at the end to find the final product.

▶ Discuss the Algebraic Notation Method

WHOLE CLASS   Math Talk

Invite some students to the board to sketch a model and solve 4×237 using the Algebraic Notation Method, while the rest of the class works on their MathBoards. Make sure the students add the arcs to show each multiplication. Have students explain their numeric steps and relate them to the model.

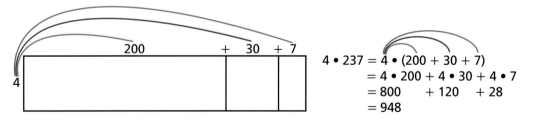

Make sure students see that 237 must again be written in expanded notation. Then, each addend is multiplied by 4. The process is the same but where things are written is different. Ask if anyone has another method they want to share and discuss it.

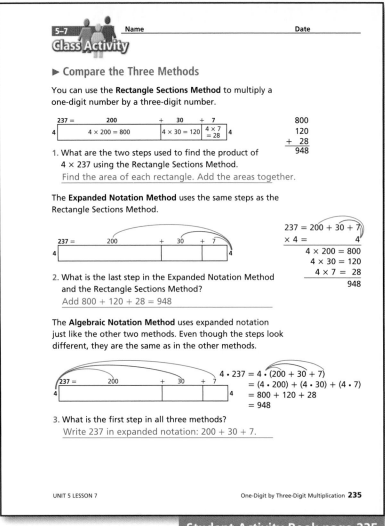

► Compare the Three Methods WHOLE CLASS

As a summary, have students answer questions 1–3 on Student Book page 235, which ask them to compare the three methods for multiplying a one-digit number by a three-digit number. See Math Talk in Action in the sidebar for a possible discussion to wrap up the activity.

Activity 2

Practice One-Digit by Three-Digit Multiplication

► Practice Multiplication PAIRS

Write the following on the board:

$6 \times 328 = 1{,}968$ $7 \times 456 = 3{,}192$

$8 \times 279 = 2{,}232$ $3 \times 725 = 2{,}175$

Have the students work in **Student Pairs** to multiply. Pair students who understand the methods with students who are struggling.

 Math Talk in Action

What do the three methods have in common?

Steve: Somewhere in each method, you have to multiply 4 times 200, 4 times 30, and 4 times 7.

Mirella: In all of the methods, you have to add 800 + 120 + 28 to get your final answer.

Ahmed: Even though one of the methods is called The Expanded Notation Method, you really do expanded notation in all of the methods. You have to split 237 into 200 + 30 + 7 for all three.

 Ongoing Assessment

As students work with the methods and models of multiplying one-digit numbers by three-digit numbers, listen in as they explain their strategies to their partners. Listen for place-value language, expanded notation, and ideas about multiplying hundreds, tens, and ones by the single-digit factor.

 20 MINUTES

Goal: Practice multiplication of one-digit numbers by three-digit numbers.

 NCTM Standards:
Number and Operations
Representation
Communication

② Going Further

Math Connection: Multiplication With Dollars and Cents

► Problem Solving With Money

WHOLE CLASS

In this activity, students will connect one-digit by three-digit multiplication with multiplication of dollars and cents.

Write this problem on the board:

$$5 \times \$1.49$$

Ask students to think of a word problem that could be solved using 5 × $1.49. Possible answer: Water bottles cost $1.49 each. How much will 5 water bottles cost?

Help the students to understand that $1.49 is a three-digit number and that the three methods learned for multiplying a one-digit number by a three-digit number can be used to multiply money. Instead of hundreds, tens, and ones, we can think of the digits as dollars, dimes, and pennies. So:

$$\$1.49 = \$1.00 + \$0.40 + \$0.09$$

$$= 1 \text{ dollar} + 4 \text{ dimes} + 9 \text{ pennies}$$

Have students use **Solve and Discuss** to find 5 × $1.49. They may choose any method to solve.

In working with money problems with amounts given in dollars and cents, some students may prefer to write all the values as cents, so there is no decimal point.

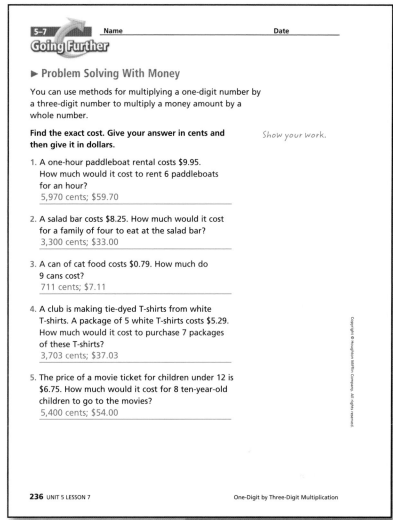

Student Activity Book page 236

Within the student activity book page:

5-7
Going Further

Name _____ Date _____

► Problem Solving With Money

You can use methods for multiplying a one-digit number by a three-digit number to multiply a money amount by a whole number.

Find the exact cost. Give your answer in cents and then give it in dollars.   *Show your work.*

1. A one-hour paddleboat rental costs $9.95. How much would it cost to rent 6 paddleboats for an hour?
5,970 cents; $59.70

2. A salad bar costs $8.25. How much would it cost for a family of four to eat at the salad bar?
3,300 cents; $33.00

3. A can of cat food costs $0.79. How much do 9 cans cost?
711 cents; $7.11

4. A club is making tie-dyed T-shirts from white T-shirts. A package of 5 white T-shirts costs $5.29. How much would it cost to purchase 7 packages of these T-shirts?
3,703 cents; $37.03

5. The price of a movie ticket for children under 12 is $6.75. How much would it cost for 8 ten-year-old children to go to the movies?
5,400 cents; $54.00

236 UNIT 5 LESSON 7   One-Digit by Three-Digit Multiplication

Make sure the students understand that the process of multiplying money is the same whether there is a decimal or not.

If there is a decimal point in the money amounts in the original problem, then students should write the final answer with a decimal point. Make sure students understand that the decimal point is always between the dollars and cents in a money amount.

$$5 \times \$1.49 = (5 \times 1.00) + (5 \times 0.40) + (5 \times 0.09)$$
$$= \quad \$5.00 \ + \ \$2.00 \ + \ \$0.45$$
$$= \quad \$7.45$$

Have students look at page 236 of the Student Book. Use **Solve and Discuss** for exercises 1–5.

Differentiated Instruction

Use Expanded Notation   Activity Card 5-7 ●

Work: By Yourself

1. Look at the model of 2 × 132 below. How many times does the model show the expanded form of 132? Twice

| 100 | 30 | 2 |
| 100 | 30 | 2 |

2. Use the model to find the product of 2 × 132. 264

3. **Analyze** How could you change the model above to find the product of 4 × 132? add two more rectangles each showing 100 + 30 + 2; 528

4. Make models for 3 × 251 and 2 × 924. Then find each product. 753; 1,848

Unit 5, Lesson 7   Copyright © Houghton Mifflin Company

Activity Note If time permits, have students draw their own Expanded Notation model and exchange papers with another student. Then have them identify the multiplication problem for the model.

 Math Writing Prompt

Place Value Use place-value language to explain why 458 and 584 represent different numbers even though they have the same digits.

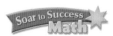 **Software Support**

Use *Soar to Success* for instruction of students needing targeted support for underlying skills.

Go Fish   Activity Card 5-7 ▲

Work: In Pairs

Use:

• *Go Fish* Game Cards (TRB M64)

• Scissors

1. Make 10 pairs of game cards. On one card, show a one-digit by three-digit multiplication. On the other card, show the matching partial sum. Exchange cards with another pair of students.

```
  125        500
×   5        100
           + 25
```

2. Shuffle the cards. Each player takes 5 cards.

3. Take turns asking for a match. If your partner has your match, set the pair down. If there is no match, end your turn by drawing another card from the deck to match, if possible. The first player to have no cards left is the winner.

Unit 5, Lesson 7   Copyright © Houghton Mifflin Company

Activity Note Extend the activity by having two pairs of students form a larger group, playing the game with 20 cards.

 Math Writing Prompt

Word Problem Write a word problem for 4 × 372. Explain how to find the answer.

 Software Support

Use *MegaMath* for review and reinforcement of the concepts and skills presented in this lesson.

Use Substitution   Activity Card 5-7 ■

Work: By Yourself

1. Look at the substitution shown below to evaluate the expression $n \times 3$ for $n = 7$.

   $n \times 3 = 7 \times 3 = 21$

2. Find the value of the product $n \times 3$ for each value of n given. 27, 135, 363, 834

   $n = 9$

   $n = 45$

   $n = 121$

   $n = 278$

3. When $w = 127$ and $p = 3$, what is $w \times p$? 381

Unit 5, Lesson 7   Copyright © Houghton Mifflin Company

Activity Note To extend the activity, have students write their own multiplication expressions and values for the variables and then exchange with partners to practice substitution.

 Math Writing Prompt

Compare Explain why 4 • (300 + 20 + 5) is the same as (4 • 300) + (4 • 20) + (4 • 5).

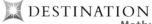 **Software Support**

Use *Destination Math* to take students beyond the concepts and skills presented in this lesson.

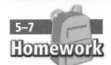Homework and Spiral Review

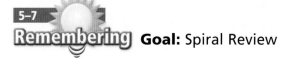

5–7 Homework **Goal:** Additional Practice

Use this Homework page to provide students with more practice with the area model and expanded notation.

5–7 Remembering **Goal:** Spiral Review

This Remembering activity would be appropriate anytime after today's lesson.

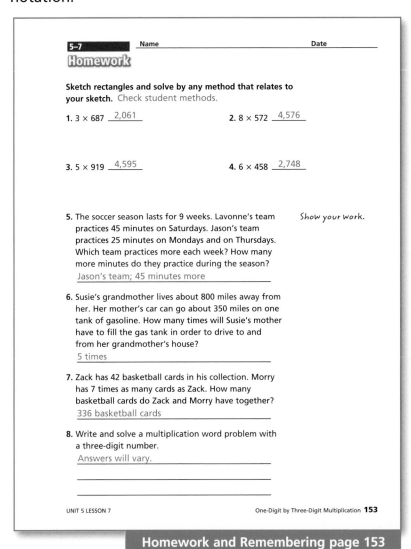

5–7 Homework

Name _____ Date _____

Sketch rectangles and solve by any method that relates to your sketch. Check student methods.

1. 3 × 687 ___2,061___

2. 8 × 572 ___4,576___

3. 5 × 919 ___4,595___

4. 6 × 458 ___2,748___

5. The soccer season lasts for 9 weeks. Lavonne's team practices 45 minutes on Saturdays. Jason's team practices 25 minutes on Mondays and on Thursdays. Which team practices more each week? How many more minutes do they practice during the season?
Show your work.
Jason's team; 45 minutes more

6. Susie's grandmother lives about 800 miles away from her. Her mother's car can go about 350 miles on one tank of gasoline. How many times will Susie's mother have to fill the gas tank in order to drive to and from her grandmother's house?
5 times

7. Zack has 42 basketball cards in his collection. Morry has 7 times as many cards as Zack. How many basketball cards do Zack and Morry have together?
336 basketball cards

8. Write and solve a multiplication word problem with a three-digit number.
Answers will vary.

UNIT 5 LESSON 7   One-Digit by Three-Digit Multiplication **153**

Homework and Remembering page 153

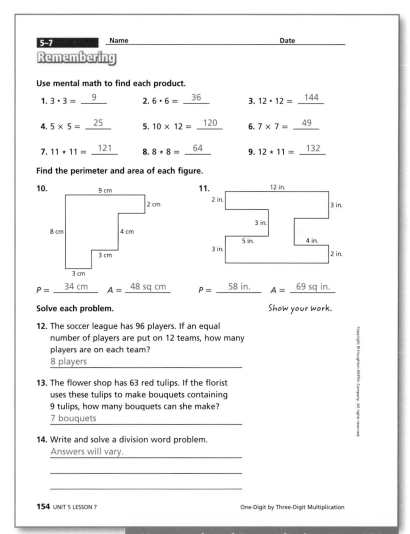

5–7 Remembering

Name _____ Date _____

Use mental math to find each product.

1. 3 · 3 = ___9___   2. 6 · 6 = ___36___   3. 12 · 12 = ___144___

4. 5 × 5 = ___25___   5. 10 × 12 = ___120___   6. 7 × 7 = ___49___

7. 11 * 11 = ___121___   8. 8 * 8 = ___64___   9. 12 * 11 = ___132___

Find the perimeter and area of each figure.

10.

P = ___34 cm___   A = ___48 sq cm___

11.

P = ___58 in.___   A = ___69 sq in.___

Solve each problem.   *Show your work.*

12. The soccer league has 96 players. If an equal number of players are put on 12 teams, how many players are on each team?
8 players

13. The flower shop has 63 red tulips. If the florist uses these tulips to make bouquets containing 9 tulips, how many bouquets can she make?
7 bouquets

14. Write and solve a division word problem.
Answers will vary.

154 UNIT 5 LESSON 7   One-Digit by Three-Digit Multiplication

Homework and Remembering page 154

Home or School Activity

 Social Studies Connection

Benjamin Banneker Benjamin Banneker was an African American scientist and mathematician who lived from 1731–1806. He was the technical assistant in the first surveying of the Federal District, which is now Washington, D.C. Surveyors determine the area of a region and the length of boundary lines.

In Washington D.C., a city block is 264 feet. Have students determine the length of seven city blocks in Washington, D.C. Have the students find the length of a block and a street in their town. Students may want to act out parts of the book.

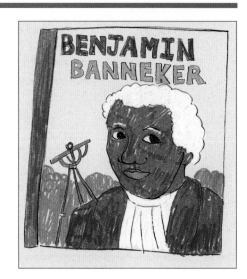

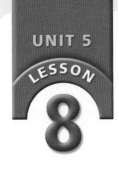

Practice One-Digit by Three-Digit Multiplication

Lesson Objectives

- Multiply one-digit numbers by three-digit numbers.
- Use the shortcut Method (the standard multiplication algorithm).
- Estimate products of one-digit and three-digit numbers.

The Day at a Glance

Today's Goals	Materials

1 Teaching the Lesson
A1: Review different methods of multiplying one-digit numbers by three-digit numbers.
A2: Use the Shortcut Method to multiply a one-digit number by a three-digit number.
A3: Round and estimate one-digit by three-digit multiplication.
 	
2 Going Further
▶ Extension: One-Digit by Four-Digit Multiplication.
▶ Differentiated Instruction
 	
3 Homework and Spiral Review
	Lesson Activities
	Student Activity Book pp. 237–239
	  or Student Hardcover Book
	  pp. 237–239
	Homework and Remembering
	  pp. 155–156
	
	Going Further
	Student Activity Book
	  p. 240 or Student
	  Hardcover Book
	  p. 240
	Activity Cards 5-8
	Math Journals
	
	123 *Use* **Math Talk** *today!*

Keeping Skills Sharp

Quick Practice ⏱ 5 MINUTES	Daily Routines
Goal: Fluency with zeros patterns. **Zeros Patterns** Select four **Student Leaders** to go to the board to write three products involving two non-zero digits. A product can have no zeros in the factors, a zero in one factor, a zero in both factors, or two zeros in one factor. See Lesson 4.	**Homework Review** Ask students to describe briefly some strategies they used in their homework. Sometimes you will find that students solve the problem correctly but use an inefficient strategy. **Money** Victoria is buying helium balloons for her gymnastics group to carry in a parade. There are 4 people in her group, and each person will carry 2 balloons. If the balloons cost \$3.12 each, how much will Victoria spend on balloons? \$24.96

Problem	Class Response	Student Leader Writes
6×30	"18 tens equals one-hundred eighty."	$= 180$
60×30	"18 hundreds equals one thousand, eight hundred."	$= 1,800$
600×3	"18 hundreds equals one thousand, eight hundred."	$= 1,800$

① Teaching the Lesson

Review Different Methods

 20 MINUTES

Goal: Review different methods of multiplying one-digit numbers by three-digit numbers.

 NCTM Standards:
Number and Operations
Algebra
Representation
Communication

Teaching Note

What to Expect from Students
These methods have been worked with extensively in previous lessons. Review the three methods only as needed by the students in your class. All students do not need to master all three methods. Each student should be proficient with at least one of the methods, although some students enjoy the challenge of mastering and explaining all three.

▶ Review Different Multiplication Methods

WHOLE CLASS

Write 435 × 9 on the board and draw the corresponding area model.

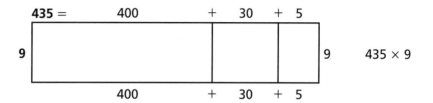

Have three students come to the board to each demonstrate one of the three methods to multiply a one-digit number by a three-digit number: Rectangle Sections Method, Expanded Notation Method, and Algebraic Notation Method.

For each method, the student should relate the numeric steps to the area model.

Rectangle Sections Method

435 =	400	+	30	+ 5	
9	9 × 400 = 3,600		9 × 30 = 270	9 × 5 = 45	9

$$\overset{1}{3{,}600}$$

$$\begin{array}{r} 3{,}600 \\ 270 \\ +\ \ 45 \\ \hline 3{,}915 \end{array}$$

Students who are watching the students at the board should ask questions to clarify their understanding of the method. For example,

● Why did you multiply 9 × 30?

● How did you get 3,915 as the final answer?

Expanded Notation Method

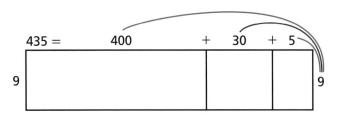

$$435 = 400 + 30 + 5$$

$$
\begin{array}{r}
435 = 400 + 30 + 5 \\
\times\, 9 = \qquad\qquad\quad 9 \\
\hline
9 \times 400 = 3{,}600 \\
9 \times 30 = \quad 270 \\
9 \times 5 = \qquad 45 \\
\hline
3{,}915
\end{array}
$$

The Algebraic Notation Method

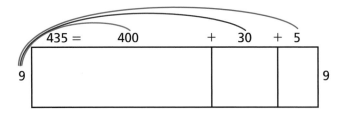

$$435 = 400 + 30 + 5$$

$$9 \bullet 435 = 9 \bullet (400 + 30 + 5)$$

$$= (9 \bullet 400) + (9 \bullet 30) + (9 \bullet 5)$$

$$= 3{,}600 + 270 + 45$$

$$= 3{,}915$$

Math Talk When all methods have been presented, have students discuss how the methods are alike and how they are different.

The Learning Classroom

Math Talk As students formulate questions to ask their fellow students about each method, they help themselves as well as other students clarify their understanding of each of the processes. They also have to use math vocabulary as they work to make their questions understood. Students who answer the questions get experience in communicating clearly in a step-by-step fashion.

Activity 2

Use the Shortcut Method

 15 MINUTES

Goal: Use the Shortcut Method to multiply a one-digit number by a three-digit number.

Materials: Student Activity Book or Hardcover Book pp. 237–238

 NCTM Standards:
Number and Operations
Representation
Communication

Teaching Note

What to Expect from Students
Because there are many different methods to multiply a one-digit number by a three-digit number, students may not realize that all the methods involve the same steps, no matter how hidden they are. Help students to see that every multiplication of a one-digit number by a three-digit number will have the same four steps:

1) Multiply ones by ones.

2) Multiply ones by tens.

3) Multiply ones by hundreds.

4) Add all of the products.

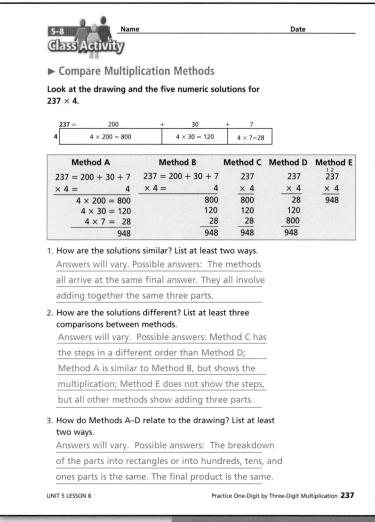

Student Activity Book page 237

▶ Compare Multiplication Methods WHOLE CLASS

Have a **Student Leader** draw a rectangle model for 4 × 237 on the board. Use **Solve and Discuss** to find the solution.

Direct the students to method A on page 237 in the Student Book. Method A is the full Expanded Notation Method, including the hundreds, tens, and ones equations. Discuss this method with the class.

● How do the equations in method A relate to the drawing? The equations and the drawing show all of the multiplying you have to do to find the final product.

● What four steps do you have to do in method A? You have to 1) multiply 4 × the hundreds, 2) multiply 4 × the tens, 3) multiply 4 × the ones, and 4) add all of those products together.

Ask students to look at method B. This is the Expanded Notation method without the hundreds, tens, and ones equations. Ask the students to notice what is different between methods A and B. In method B, we don't show the full place value equations. We just show the answers.

Have the students look at method C, which drops the step of separating 237 into hundreds, tens, and ones. Ask students to compare this method to method B. Ask the students what is not written but what is "understood" in method C. The expanded notation is not written but it is understood because $4 \times$ the 2 in the hundreds place is $4 \times 200 = 800$, $4 \times$ the 3 in the tens place is $4 \times 30 = 120$, and $4 \times$ the 7 in the ones place is 28.

Have the students look at method D, which multiplies the ones first, then the tens, then the hundreds. Ask the students to describe what has changed in method D.

Direct students' attention to method E, which is the Shortcut method. Ask the students to identify the major changes that they see between methods D and E. It looks much shorter, it has some regrouped digits at the top, there are no visible "in-between" steps like adding 28, 120, and 800 to get the final total.

After the class discussion on these solutions, have students complete exercises 1–3.

Teaching Note

Order of Steps Method D appears to be a repeat of method C but with the intermediate products appearing in a different order. This method is important because, in the Shortcut Method of multiplying a one-digit number by a three-digit number, the process begins by multiplying ones by ones in order to regroup the product easily in one step. In the Shortcut Method, unlike all of the others, the order of the multiplication matters.

Activity continued ▶

Activity 2

 Math Talk in Action

Use place-value language to describe the Shortcut Method step-by-step.

Amanda: Step 1 is ones multiplication. I would multiply 4 × 7 ones = 28 ones. Write the 8 in the ones column below the 7 ones and 4 ones. Regroup 20 ones to make 2 tens and write a 2 above the 3, which is in the tens column.

Saul: In step 2, you do tens multiplication. 4 × 3 tens = 12 tens. Add the 2 tens from the ones multiplication to make a total of 14 tens. Write 4 in the tens column below the line. Regroup the 10 tens to make one new hundred. Write a 1 above the hundreds column.

Rachel: Step 3 is hundreds multiplication. Multiply 4 × 2 hundreds = 8 hundreds. Add the 1 hundred from the tens multiplication step for a total of 9 hundreds. Write 9 in the hundreds column.

English Language Learners

Help students describe each step on Student Book page 238.

- **Beginning** Say: Step 1 shows 4 × 7. Step 2 shows 4 × 30 plus the 2 tens from 28. Step 3 shows 4 × 200 plus the 1 hundred from 140. Have students repeat.
- **Intermediate** Say: Step 1 shows ___. 4 × 7 Step 2 shows 4 × 30 plus ___. 2 tens from 28 Step 3 shows 4 × 200 plus ___. 1 hundred from 140
- **Advanced** Have students work in pairs to tell the steps. Then have volunteers share their ideas with the class.

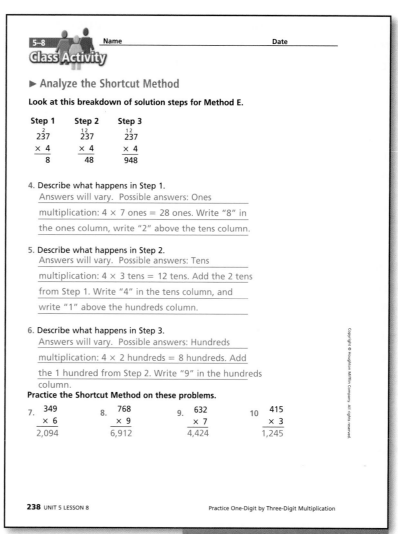

Student Activity Book page 238

▶ **Analyze the Shortcut Method** WHOLE CLASS

Page 238 of the Student Book shows the steps involved in method E, the Shortcut Method.

Exercises 4–6 ask students to explain each step. Discuss the answers as a class. See a sample of classroom dialogue in the Math Talk in Action in the sidebar.

After the discussion, have students work in **Student Pairs** to complete exercises 7–10.

Estimate Products of One-Digit and Three-Digit Numbers

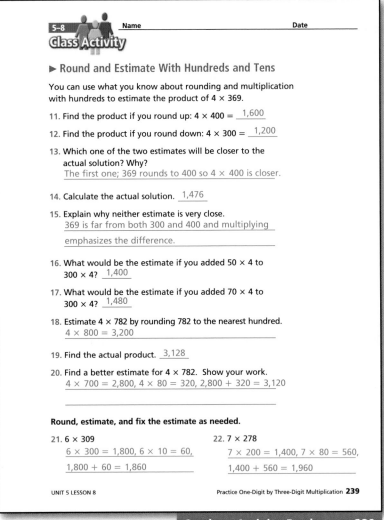

 20 MINUTES

Goal: Round and estimate one-digit by three-digit multiplication.

Materials: Student Activity Book or Hardcover Book p. 239

 NCTM Standards:
Number and Operations
Communication

Teaching Note

Math Background When estimating products, the larger the place to which one is rounding, the less accurate an estimate can be. Multiplication magnifies the difference between an actual number and a rounded number. In rounding and estimating with hundreds, adding or subtracting rounded tens can bring an estimate closer to the "real" answer. As with all rounding, numbers that are closer to their rounded estimates will have an estimate closer to the answer than will numbers that are further. For example, 4×389 versus 4×369.

▶ Round and Estimate With Hundreds and Tens

WHOLE CLASS

Write $4 \times 369 = 1,476$ on the board and have students turn to page 239 in their Student Book.

Tell students that you want to estimate the product by rounding 369 to the nearest hundred. Ask students which digit tells us whether to round up or down. Underline the 3 in 369. Have students answer exercises 11–12. Then, write the framing equations above and below the original problem as shown.

$$4 \times 400 = 1,600$$

$$4 \times \underline{3}69 = 1,476$$

$$4 \times 300 = 1,200$$

Activity continued ▶

Activity 3

Teaching Note

Properties of Multiplication

By using the Distributive Property, students can use mental math and make more accurate estimates of products. The problem 4 × 370 can be rewritten as (4 × 300) + (4 × 70) which is easy to compute mentally.

Discuss question 13.

● **Which estimate is closer to the actual solution?** 4 × 400 = 1,600

● **How do you know?** Because 369 rounds up to 400, 4 × 400 = 1,600 is closer to 4 × 369 than 4 × 300 = 1,200 is.

Have students answer exercise 14 and then determine how far the actual answer is from each of the estimates. 1,600 − 1,476 = 124; 1,476 − 1,200 = 276; 1,600 is closer to 1,476.

● **Why is neither estimate very close?** 369 is not very close to either 300 or 400 and when you multiply 300 or 400 by 4 you are magnifying this difference four times.

Have students answer exercise 16. Point out that it is a closer estimate.

● **Why did this give us a better estimate?** This estimate was found by finding (4 × 50) + (4 × 300) = 4 × 350. It is better because 369 is closer to 350 than it is to 300.

Have students answer exercise 17. Have students discuss why (4 × 70) + (4 × 300) is an even better estimate than 4 × 350. 369 is only 1 away from 370 so the estimate is very close to the actual answer.

Review the steps for finding an accurate estimate of 4 × 369 with students.

1. Round to the lower hundred. 369 rounds down to 300

2. Multiply to estimate. 4 × 300 = 1,200

3. Round the tens in the original factor. 69 rounds to 70

4. Multiply the tens estimate. 4 × 70 = 280

5. Add the two estimates. 1,200 + 280 = 1,480

1,480 is much closer to the actual product of 1,476 than our earlier frames.

Problems 18–20 ask students to use this method to estimate 4 × 782. Work through these problems as a class.

Use **Solve and Discuss** for problems 21–22. Make sure different estimation methods are presented.

Step 1 may be confusing to some students because they would round 369 up to 400 when rounding to the nearest hundred. Emphasize that when you are doing a closer 2-step estimate, you round down but then add to that first estimate to get it closer. This 2-step estimating is difficult for many students. Do not spend time on it unless it is an important mastery goal for your state or district.

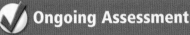
Ongoing Assessment

Have each student multiply 8 × 637, using their favorite method. Then have students round, estimate a product, and fix the estimate so that it is close to the actual product.

②Going Further

Extension: One-Digit by Four-Digit Multiplication

Goal: Multiply a one-digit number by a four-digit number.

Materials: Student Activity Book or Hardcover Book p. 240

✓ **NCTM Standards:**
Number and Operations
Communication
Representation

▶ One-Digit by Four-Digit Multiplication | WHOLE CLASS |

Write 8 × 3,248 on the board.

Tell students that the four multiplication methods they have learned can be used to multiply a one-digit number by a four-digit number.

Have the students look at page 240 in their Student Book. Direct them to look at the area model for 8 × 3,248 and the Rectangle Sections Method equations below the model.

Ask the students what is different about multiplying a one-digit number by a four-digit number compared to multiplying a one-digit number by a three-digit number. You have to multiply the one-digit factor by thousands. There is one more multiplication and one more number to add.

Have the students look at the Expanded Notation Method. Have them again tell you what changes have been made to multiply a one-digit number by a four-digit number compared to multiplying by a three-digit number. Just like in the Rectangle Sections Method, you have to multiply the one-digit number by the thousands and then add all four of the products.

Have the students now look at the Algebraic Notation Method. Ask the students how many multiplication problems must be solved to find the final product. 1) Ones times the thousands, 2) ones times the hundreds, 3) ones times the tens, and 4) ones times the ones.

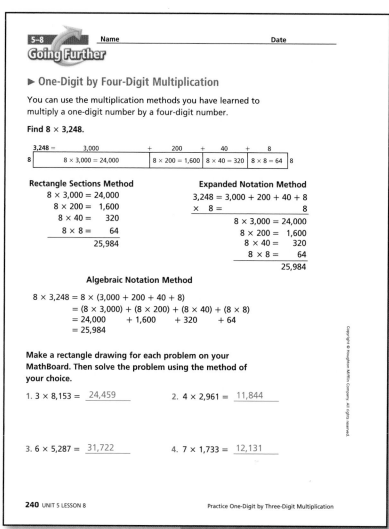

Student Activity Book page 240

Have a volunteer show how to use the Shortcut Method to find 8 × 3,248.

$$\begin{array}{r} {\scriptstyle 1\ 3\ 6} \\ 3{,}248 \\ \times\quad 8 \\ \hline 25{,}984 \end{array}$$

Have the students work in **Student Pairs** to complete exercises 1–4.

Differentiated Instruction

● Intervention — Activity Card 5-8

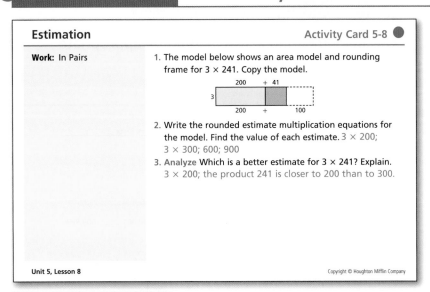

Estimation — Activity Card 5-8 ●

Work: In Pairs

1. The model below shows an area model and rounding frame for 3 × 241. Copy the model.

2. Write the rounded estimate multiplication equations for the model. Find the value of each estimate. 3 × 200; 3 × 300; 600; 900

3. Analyze Which is a better estimate for 3 × 241? Explain. 3 × 200; the product 241 is closer to 200 than to 300.

Unit 5, Lesson 8   Copyright © Houghton Mifflin Company

Activity Note Students should calculate the actual product and then compare estimates. The closer estimate is better. Point out that 241 is less than 250, and so it is rounded down for a closer estimate.

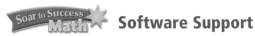

Math Writing Prompt

Explain Rounding Explain how to determine whether to round the number 681 up to 700 or down to 600.

Soar to Success Math — Software Support

Use *Soar to Success* for instruction of students needing targeted support for underlying skills.

▲ On Level — Activity Card 5-8

Partial Products — Activity Card 5-8 ▲

Work: By Yourself

1. Copy the missing-digit puzzle below.

2. Each blank represents a missing digit. Complete the puzzle.

3. Explain What strategies did you use to find the missing digits?

4. Create your own missing-digits puzzle, and exchange it with another student to solve.

Unit 5, Lesson 8   Copyright © Houghton Mifflin Company

Activity Note To extend the activity, have students create their own missing-digit puzzle and exchange it with another student.

Math Writing Prompt

Choose Your Method Describe the multiplication method that makes the most sense to you. Explain why.

MegaMath — Software Support

Use *MegaMath* for review and reinforcement of the concepts and skills presented in this lesson.

■ Challenge — Activity Card 5-8

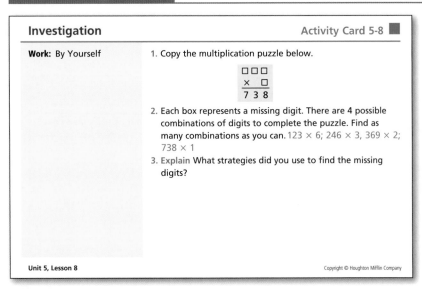

Investigation — Activity Card 5-8 ■

Work: By Yourself

1. Copy the multiplication puzzle below.

2. Each box represents a missing digit. There are 4 possible combinations of digits to complete the puzzle. Find as many combinations as you can. 123 × 6; 246 × 3, 369 × 2; 738 × 1

3. Explain What strategies did you use to find the missing digits?

Unit 5, Lesson 8   Copyright © Houghton Mifflin Company

Activity Note Have students discuss any patterns they see in the four solutions. Then have them make up their own multiplication puzzle with four solutions for other students to solve.

Math Writing Prompt

Regrouping Explain why a 2 might be written above the tens column in a multiplication problem.

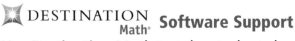

DESTINATION Math — Software Support

Use *Destination Math* to take students beyond the concepts and skills presented in this lesson.

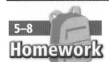# ③ Homework and Spiral Review

5-8
Homework **Goal:** Additional Practice

✓ Include students' work for page 155 as part of their portolios.

5-8
Remembering **Goal:** Spiral Review

This Remembering activity would be appropriate anytime after today's lesson.

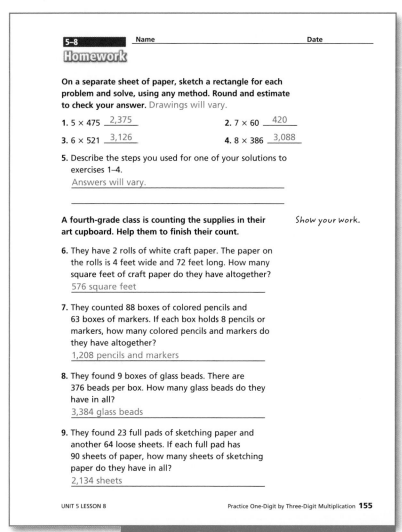

5-8	Name		Date

Homework

On a separate sheet of paper, sketch a rectangle for each problem and solve, using any method. Round and estimate to check your answer. Drawings will vary.

1. 5×475 ___2,375___   2. 7×60 ___420___

3. 6×521 ___3,126___   4. 8×386 ___3,088___

5. Describe the steps you used for one of your solutions to exercises 1–4.
   Answers will vary.

A fourth-grade class is counting the supplies in their art cupboard. Help them to finish their count.   *Show your work.*

6. They have 2 rolls of white craft paper. The paper on the rolls is 4 feet wide and 72 feet long. How many square feet of craft paper do they have altogether?
   576 square feet

7. They counted 88 boxes of colored pencils and 63 boxes of markers. If each box holds 8 pencils or markers, how many colored pencils and markers do they have altogether?
   1,208 pencils and markers

8. They found 9 boxes of glass beads. There are 376 beads per box. How many glass beads do they have in all?
   3,384 glass beads

9. They found 23 full pads of sketching paper and another 64 loose sheets. If each full pad has 90 sheets of paper, how many sheets of sketching paper do they have in all?
   2,134 sheets

UNIT 5 LESSON 8   Practice One-Digit by Three-Digit Multiplication **155**

Homework and Remembering page 155

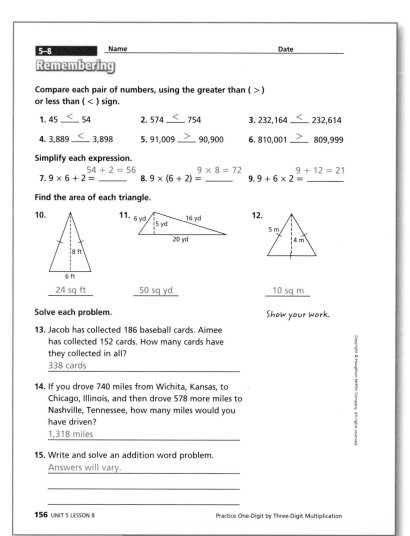

5-8	Name		Date

Remembering

Compare each pair of numbers, using the greater than (>) or less than (<) sign.

1. $45 \underline{<} 54$ 2. $574 \underline{<} 754$ 3. $232,164 \underline{<} 232,614$

4. $3,889 \underline{<} 3,898$ 5. $91,009 \underline{>} 90,900$ 6. $810,001 \underline{>} 809,999$

Simplify each expression.

7. $9 \times 6 + 2 = \underline{54 + 2 = 56}$ 8. $9 \times (6 + 2) = \underline{9 \times 8 = 72}$ 9. $9 + 6 \times 2 = \underline{9 + 12 = 21}$

Find the area of each triangle.

10. [triangle: 8 ft height, 6 ft base]   11. [triangle: 6 yd, 5 yd, 16 yd, 20 yd]   12. [triangle: 5 m, 4 m]

24 sq ft   50 sq yd   10 sq m

Solve each problem.   *Show your work.*

13. Jacob has collected 186 baseball cards. Aimee has collected 152 cards. How many cards have they collected in all?
    338 cards

14. If you drove 740 miles from Wichita, Kansas, to Chicago, Illinois, and then drove 578 more miles to Nashville, Tennessee, how many miles would you have driven?
    1,318 miles

15. Write and solve an addition word problem.
    Answers will vary.

156 UNIT 5 LESSON 8   Practice One-Digit by Three-Digit Multiplication

Homework and Remembering page 156

Home or School Activity

🌐 Real-World Connection

Exact or Estimate Math is used in many different ways during the course of a day. Students can research by asking family members or friends when they use math. Have the students put their findings into two columns: *When an Exact Answer is Needed* and *When an Estimate Works*.

Then have them use their research to give a general description of when exact answers are needed and when estimates work.

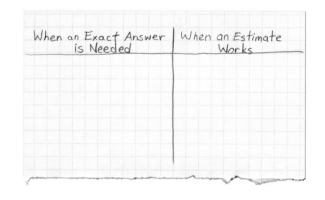

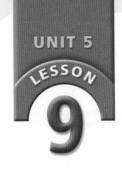

UNIT 5

LESSON 9

Too Much or Too Little Information

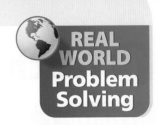

REAL WORLD Problem Solving

Lesson Objective

• Determine what information is needed to solve a word problem.

The Day at a Glance

Today's Goals	Materials
1 Teaching the Lesson **A1:** Identify extra information in word problems. **A2:** Identify missing information in word problems. **2 Going Further** ▶ Differentiated Instruction **3 Homework and Spiral Review**	**Lesson Activities** Student Activity Book pp. 241–242 or Student Hardcover Book 241–242 Homework and Remembering pp. 157–158	**Going Further** Activity Cards 5-9 Number cubes Math Journals

123 *Use* **Math Talk** *today!*

Keeping Skills Sharp

Quick Practice ⏱ 5 MINUTES	Daily Routines

Goal: Fluency with zeros patterns.

Zeros Patterns Select four **Student Leaders** to go to the board to write three products involving two non-zero digits. Let two of the students choose any pair of non-zero digits. For the other two students, *specify that one of their digits must be 5 and the other must be an even number.* Have them write their products so that one has no zeros in the factors, another has a zero in one factor, and another has a zero in both factors (see the example below). See Lesson 4.

Problem	Class Response	Student Leader Writes
5 × 4	"20 ones equals twenty."	= 20
5 × 40	"20 tens equals two hundred."	= 200
50 × 40	"20 hundreds equals two thousand."	= 2,000

Homework Review If students give incorrect answers, have them explain how they found the answers. This can help you determine whether the error is conceptual or procedural.

Reasoning Suppose 20 students play soccer and 15 students play baseball. Four students play both soccer and baseball. Use a Venn diagram to show how many people play one or both sports? 31 students: 16 play only soccer, 11 play only baseball, and 4 play both soccer and baseball.

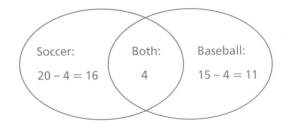

Soccer: 20 − 4 = 16   Both: 4   Baseball: 15 − 4 = 11

① Teaching the Lesson

Numeric Information in a Word Problem

 30 MINUTES

Goal: Identify extra information in word problems.

Materials: Student Activity Book or Hardcover Book p. 241

 NCTM Standards:
Problem Solving
Number and Operations

English Language Learners

Write the donation problem on the board. Underline the word *donate*.

- **Beginning** Say: *Donate* means "to give." A student who donates $6 to the school gives $6 to the school. Have students repeat.
- **Intermediate** Ask: What does *donate* mean? to give What is a student who donates $6 to the school doing? giving $6 to the school
- **Advanced** Have students name items that people donate to others.

▶ Just the Needed Information WHOLE CLASS

This lesson focuses on identifying what information is necessary for solving a problem. Begin by discussing a problem that contains only the necessary numeric information.

Write the following problem on the board:

> A school with 237 students is raising money for new gym equipment. If every student donates $6, how much money is donated?

Read the problem. Give students a minute or two to solve it, and then discuss the solution.

- How many numbers are in this word problem? two

- What question is the problem asking? How much money would be donated by the students?

- How can we figure out how much money was donated? Multiply the amount donated by each student by the number of students.

- How many numbers are needed to solve this problem? two

Point out that in this word problem, we are given two numbers and we need both numbers to solve the word problem. The problem contains only the numeric information needed to solve the problem.

▶ Too Much Information WHOLE CLASS

Write the following problem on the board:

> Ms. Sanchez's class had a cake sale to raise money for gym equipment. The class sold 43 cakes for $7.00 each. In all, 132 people came to the sale. How much money did the class raise?

Read the problem. Give students a minute or two to solve it, and then discuss the solution.

- How can we figure out how much the class raised? Multiply the number of cakes sold by the price of each cake.

- What numerical information is not needed to solve the problem? 132

- Why is it not needed? The number of people who came to the bake sale does not help us find how much the class raised.

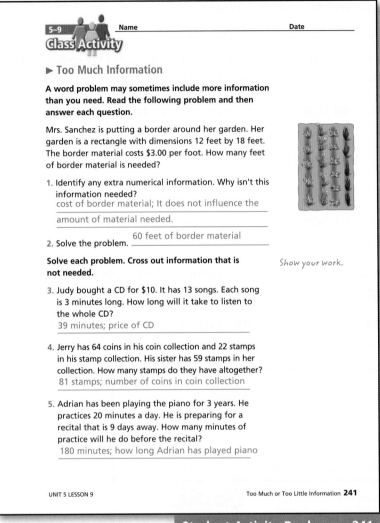

Student Activity Book page 241

The content of Student Activity Book page 241:

5–9
Class Activity

Name _____ Date _____

▶ **Too Much Information**

A word problem may sometimes include more information than you need. Read the following problem and then answer each question.

Mrs. Sanchez is putting a border around her garden. Her garden is a rectangle with dimensions 12 feet by 18 feet. The border material costs $3.00 per foot. How many feet of border material is needed?

1. Identify any extra numerical information. Why isn't this information needed?
   cost of border material; It does not influence the
   amount of material needed.

2. Solve the problem. _____60 feet of border material_____

Solve each problem. Cross out information that is not needed.

Show your work.

3. Judy bought a CD for $10. It has 13 songs. Each song is 3 minutes long. How long will it take to listen to the whole CD?
   39 minutes; price of CD

4. Jerry has 64 coins in his coin collection and 22 stamps in his stamp collection. His sister has 59 stamps in her collection. How many stamps do they have altogether?
   81 stamps; number of coins in coin collection

5. Adrian has been playing the piano for 3 years. He practices 20 minutes a day. He is preparing for a recital that is 9 days away. How many minutes of practice will he do before the recital?
   180 minutes; how long Adrian has played piano

UNIT 5 LESSON 9   Too Much or Too Little Information **241**

Have students use **Solve and Discuss** for problems 1–2 on Student Book page 241. Ask several students to tell how they know what information is not needed. See the side column for a sample discussion of problem 1.

Some students may find it easier to recognize information that is critical to solving the problem, while others may find it easier to eliminate the unnecessary information. Encourage students to use both strategies by circling information they think is necessary and crossing out information they believe is not needed.

• What information is necessary for finding the amount of border material that is needed around a rectangular garden? the length and width of the garden

Use **Solve and Discuss** for problems 3–5.

Differentiated Instruction

Extra Help Before students start their work in the Student Book, suggest that they make and label a drawing to help them understand the problem.

 Math Talk in Action

How did you know that the cost of the material was not needed?

Evan: The cost of the material does not have anything to do with the length of the border. You would need the same amount of material no matter how much it cost.

Karen: To find the amount, you only need to know the length and width of the garden, so I know I don't need to know the cost of the material.

Too Much or Too Little Information **563**

Activity 2

Missing Information in a Word Problem

 20 MINUTES

Goal: Identify missing information in word problems.

Materials: Student Activity Book or Hardcover Book p. 242

 NCTM Standards:
Problem Solving
Number and Operations

✔ Ongoing Assessment

Have students list the information that is needed to solve the following problem:

Eric starts reading a book today. He plans to read the same number of pages each day. How many days until he is done?

Teaching Note

Language and Vocabulary Make sure students understand the meaning of the words in the word problems. In the example discussed at the top of the page, a *lap* is not what one creates by sitting down, but rather, one circuit of a racetrack or other circular course. Or it can be one length of a straight course, such as the length of a swimming pool.

▶ Too Little Information WHOLE CLASS

Write the following problem on the board:

Mr. Schwartz's class had a 50-lap walk-a-thon to raise money for gym equipment. Each student in the class found a business to sponsor them at $2 per lap. How much money did the class raise?

Read the problem. Give students a minute or two to try to solve it, and then discuss it.

● Can this problem be solved? no

● Why not? We don't know how many students are in the class.

Ask the class to suggest how the problem can be revised so it can be solved. Revise the problem as a class and find the answer as a class.

Have students use **Solve and Discuss** to complete exercises 6–10 on Student Book page 242.

For problem 10, have several students share their revised problems, and discuss as a class how to solve each one.

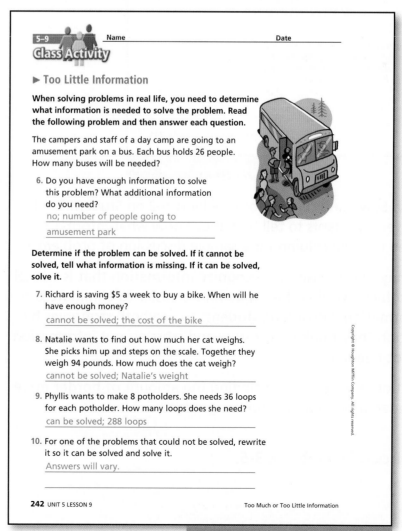

Student Activity Book page 242

② Going Further

Differentiated Instruction

Intervention Activity Card 5-9

Identify Extra Information Activity Card 5-9

Work: By Yourself

1. Read and copy the problem below.

> Four friends are going to see a movie that is 115 minutes long. The tickets are $6 per person. What is the total cost of the movie for the friends?

2. What information is the question asking? total cost

3. On your paper, circle the numbers (in digits or words) that relate to solving the problem. four; 6

4. Draw an X over any number (in digits or words) that is not needed to solve the problem. 115

5. Solve the problem. $24

Unit 5, Lesson 9 Copyright © Houghton Mifflin Company

Activity Note Check that students correctly identify "four" as one of the numbers in the problem and realize they have enough information to solve it.

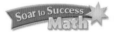 **Math Writing Prompt**

Compare Is it easier to recognize that you do not have enough information to solve a word problem or to eliminate extra information? Explain.

Soar to Success Math **Software Support**

Use *Soar to Success* for instruction of students needing targeted support for underlying skills.

On Level Activity Card 5-9

Identify Information Needed Activity Card 5-9 ▲

Work: In Pairs

1. The table below shows some types of problems and the information needed to solve them.

Type of Problem	Information Needed
area multiplication	length and width
array multiplication	number of rows and columns
change plus	starting amount, change

2. Think What other types of word problems have you seen? Copy the table and work together to add other types of problems to the table.

3. Compare your list with those of other students.

Unit 5, Lesson 9 Copyright © Houghton Mifflin Company

Activity Note To extend the activity, have students select one of the problem types and write two word problems—one with too much information and one with not enough information—to exchange and solve.

 Math Writing Prompt

Explain How do you determine if a word problem has all the necessary information?

MegaMath Grades K-6 **Software Support**

Use *MegaMath* for review and reinforcement of the concepts and skills presented in this lesson.

Challenge Activity Card 5-9

Round-Robin Word Problems Activity Card 5-9 ■

Work: In Small Groups

Use:
• Number cube, labeled 1–6

1. Work Together Write and solve a word problem. One student rolls the number cube. Use the table below to determine what type of problem to write.

Number on Cube	Type of Problem
1, 2	Just the right amount of information
3, 4	Too much information
5, 6	Too little information

2. Take turns writing the problem, one line at a time. Each student adds new information to the problem.

3. Once the problem is complete, work together to solve it, if possible.

Unit 5, Lesson 9 Copyright © Houghton Mifflin Company

Activity Note Have students identify any missing or extra information in their problem. Then have them discuss how to change a problem that could not be solved to make it possible to find a solution.

 Math Writing Prompt

Critical Thinking How do you write a multistep word problem?

 DESTINATION Math **Software Support**

Use *Destination Math* to take students beyond the concepts and skills presented in this lesson.

③ Homework and Spiral Review

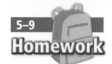

Homework Goal: Additional Practice

Use this Homework page to provide students with more practice identifying the information that is needed to solve a problem.

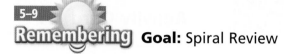

Remembering Goal: Spiral Review

This Remembering activity would be appropriate anytime after today's lesson.

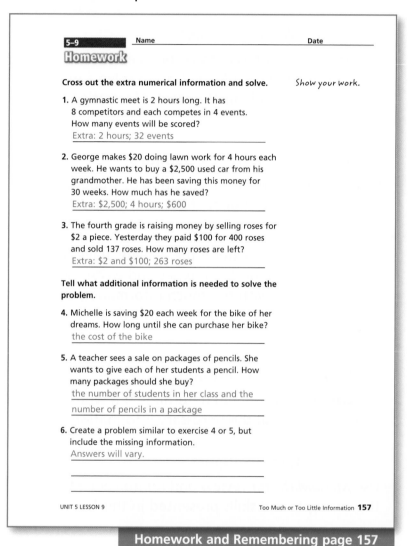

5–9 Name _____ Date _____
Homework

Cross out the extra numerical information and solve.   *Show your work.*

1. A gymnastic meet is 2 hours long. It has 8 competitors and each competes in 4 events. How many events will be scored?
   Extra: 2 hours; 32 events

2. George makes $20 doing lawn work for 4 hours each week. He wants to buy a $2,500 used car from his grandmother. He has been saving this money for 30 weeks. How much has he saved?
   Extra: $2,500; 4 hours; $600

3. The fourth grade is raising money by selling roses for $2 a piece. Yesterday they paid $100 for 400 roses and sold 137 roses. How many roses are left?
   Extra: $2 and $100; 263 roses

Tell what additional information is needed to solve the problem.

4. Michelle is saving $20 each week for the bike of her dreams. How long until she can purchase her bike?
   the cost of the bike

5. A teacher sees a sale on packages of pencils. She wants to give each of her students a pencil. How many packages should she buy?
   the number of students in her class and the number of pencils in a package

6. Create a problem similar to exercise 4 or 5, but include the missing information.
   Answers will vary.

UNIT 5 LESSON 9   Too Much or Too Little Information **157**

Homework and Remembering page 157

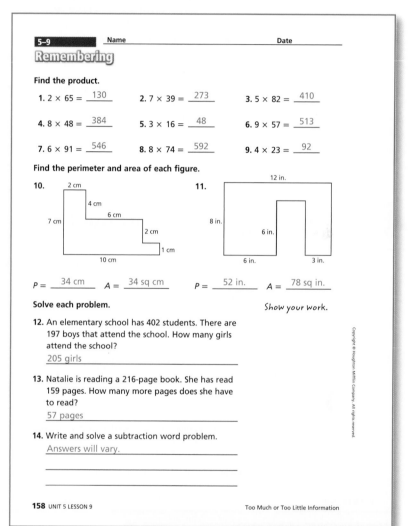

5–9 Name _____ Date _____
Remembering

Find the product.

1. 2 × 65 = _130_   2. 7 × 39 = _273_   3. 5 × 82 = _410_

4. 8 × 48 = _384_   5. 3 × 16 = _48_   6. 9 × 57 = _513_

7. 6 × 91 = _546_   8. 8 × 74 = _592_   9. 4 × 23 = _92_

Find the perimeter and area of each figure.

10. 2 cm / 4 cm / 6 cm / 7 cm / 2 cm / 10 cm / 1 cm

11. 12 in. / 8 in. / 6 in. / 6 in. / 3 in.

P = _34 cm_   A = _34 sq cm_   P = _52 in._   A = _78 sq in._

Solve each problem.   *Show your work.*

12. An elementary school has 402 students. There are 197 boys that attend the school. How many girls attend the school?
    205 girls

13. Natalie is reading a 216-page book. She has read 159 pages. How many more pages does she have to read?
    57 pages

14. Write and solve a subtraction word problem.
    Answers will vary.

158 UNIT 5 LESSON 9   Too Much or Too Little Information

Homework and Remembering page 158

Home or School Activity

 Real-World Connection

Decisions Have students describe a situation in which they have to make a decision. Then have them list information that would help them make an informed decision.

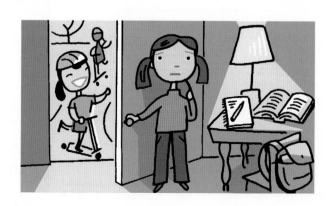

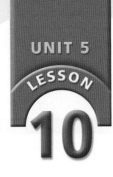

Solve Multistep Word Problems

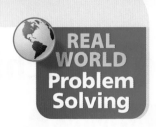
Lesson Objective

● **Solve multistep word problems.**

The Day at a Glance

Today's Goals	Materials
① Teaching the Lesson **A1:** Explore hidden questions in multistep word problems. **A2:** Solve multistep word problems **② Going Further** ▶ Differentiated Instruction **③ Homework and Spiral Review**	**Lesson Activities** Student Activity Book pp. 243–244 or Student Hardcover Book pp. 243–244 Homework and Remembering pp. 159–160 Quick Quiz 2 (Assessment Guide)

	Going Further
	Activity Cards 5-10 Student Book p. 244 Homework p. 159 Math Journals

123 *Use*
Math Talk
today!

Keeping Skills Sharp

Quick Practice 🕐 5 MINUTES	**Daily Routines**
Goal: Fluency with zeros patterns. **Zeros Patterns** Select four **Student Leaders** to go to the board to write three products involving two non-zero digits and up to two zeros. That is, a product can have no zeros in the factors, a zero in one factor, a zero in both factors, or two zeros in one factor (see the example below). See Lesson 4.	**Homework Review** Have students discuss the problems from their homework. Encourage students to help each other resolve any misunderstandings. **Too Much or Too Little Information** Only 1,500 people are allowed in an auditorium at one time. Exactly 1,436 people attend a band concert in the auditorium on Friday. The attendance at a band concert in the auditorium on Saturday is 1,475. How many people in all attend the concert on Friday and Saturday? Was any information not needed? 2,911 people; 1,500 people allowed in the auditorium was not needed.

Problem	Class Response	Student Leader Writes
7×900	"63 hundreds equal six thousand, three hundred."	$= 6,300$
7×90	"63 tens equals six hundred thirty."	$= 630$
70×90	"63 hundreds equals six thousand, three hundred."	$= 6,300$

Teaching the Lesson

Identify Hidden Questions

 20 MINUTES

Goal: Explore hidden questions in multistep word problems.

Materials: Student Activity Book or Hardcover Book p. 243

✔ **NCTM Standards:**
Problem Solving
Number and Operations

Teaching Note

Math Background Multistep word problems may be difficult for some children. Learning to identify the questions that were not asked is an important step in learning to solve such problems. Students have different ways of approaching such problems. Math drawings with numbers can often help in solving. Many multistep problems are difficult to put into one equation, so this should not be emphasized. Some students may need to fully master one-step problems before spending a lot of time on multistep problems.

English Language Learners

Show a cube in your hand. Close your hand around the cube. Write the word *hidden*.

- **Beginning** Say: **I hid the cube. It is hidden.** Have students repeat. Say: **Some math problems have hidden questions.**
- **Intermediate** Say: **The cube is hidden. We cannot ___.** see it Ask: **Are there hidden questions in some math problems?** yes
- **Advanced** Have students tell what hidden questions are in math problems.

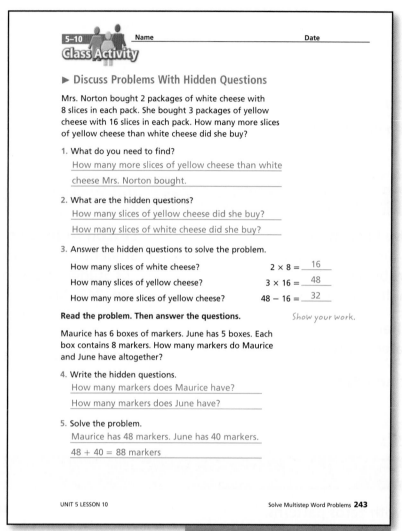

Student Activity Book page 243

▶ Discuss Problems With Hidden Questions

WHOLE CLASS

This lesson focuses on solving multistep problems that have implied or hidden questions.

Read the Problem Ask a student to read the problem at the top of Student Book page 243 or read it together.

- What is the problem about? packages of cheese

- What question is the problem asking? How many more slices of yellow cheese did she buy?

- How can we figure out how many slices of yellow cheese Mrs. Norton bought? Multiply 3 × 16.

Discuss Possible Solutions Give the students time to think about how they find the answer. Once students come up with an answer, such as 48, ask them if that is the answer to the question. Discuss that 48 slices does not answer the question because the question asks how many **more** slices of yellow cheese than slices of white cheese Mrs. Norton bought, **not** how many slices of yellow cheese she bought.

Focus on the Hidden Question Help students identify the hidden question "How many slices of yellow cheese did Mrs. Norton buy?" Have students write this question on their student pages.

● What other hidden question is there? How many slices of white cheese did she buy? Have students write this question on their student pages and then work through answering the questions in exercise 3.

● How can we find the number of slices of white cheese? We need to multiply 8 by 2.

● Do we have the answer to the question now? No. We need to subtract 16 from 48 or add up from 16 to 48.

Have students explain why they need to subtract 16 from 48 instead of adding 48 and 16.

Recognize Hidden Questions Have students read the next word problem and exercise 4. Have them discuss the questions they need to answer in order to solve the problem. Then have students complete exercise 5.

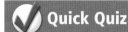 **Math Talk** When students finish this section, have volunteers show their work and explain. Encourage questioning by the other students to clarify different strategies.

After this introductory day, you may wish to spend a day or so with students working in **Student Pairs** or groups solving problems in their present learning zone. Advanced students can solve multistep problems, help other students, and write multistep problems for other students to solve.

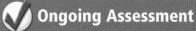

Activity 2

Solve Multistep Problems

 30 MINUTES

Goal: Solve multistep word problems.

Materials: Student Activity Book or Hardcover Book p. 244

 NCTM Standards:
Problem Solving
Communication

Class Management

Suggested Groups You may want to divide the class into groups and have each group solve only one problem. Then have each group report on their thinking strategies and final solution to the rest of the class.

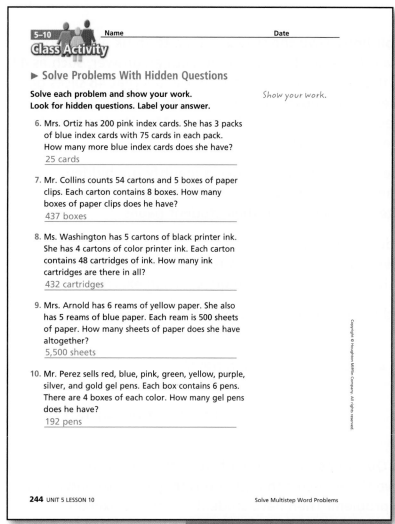

> 5–10
> **Class Activity**
> Name _____ Date _____
>
> ▶ Solve Problems With Hidden Questions
>
> Solve each problem and show your work.
> Look for hidden questions. Label your answer.
>
> *Show your work.*
>
> 6. Mrs. Ortiz has 200 pink index cards. She has 3 packs of blue index cards with 75 cards in each pack. How many more blue index cards does she have?
> 25 cards
>
> 7. Mr. Collins counts 54 cartons and 5 boxes of paper clips. Each carton contains 8 boxes. How many boxes of paper clips does he have?
> 437 boxes
>
> 8. Ms. Washington has 5 cartons of black printer ink. She has 4 cartons of color printer ink. Each carton contains 48 cartridges of ink. How many ink cartridges are there in all?
> 432 cartridges
>
> 9. Mrs. Arnold has 6 reams of yellow paper. She also has 5 reams of blue paper. Each ream is 500 sheets of paper. How many sheets of paper does she have altogether?
> 5,500 sheets
>
> 10. Mr. Perez sells red, blue, pink, green, yellow, purple, silver, and gold gel pens. Each box contains 6 pens. There are 4 boxes of each color. How many gel pens does he have?
> 192 pens
>
> **244** UNIT 5 LESSON 10   Solve Multistep Word Problems

Student Activity Book page 244

Teaching Note

Watch For! Some students write the wrong label for their answers.

Ask them to explain why they chose that label.

7. Boxes, **not** cartons

8. Cartridges, **not** cartons

9. Sheets, **not** reams

10. Pens, **not** boxes

▶ **Solve Problems With Hidden Questions** WHOLE CLASS

Have students solve word problems 6–10 on Student Book page 244. Allow time for students to talk about their solutions.

 Math Talk When students are finished, have volunteers explain their solutions to the class. Encourage questioning by other students to include or clarify other methods.

② Going Further

Differentiated Instruction

Use Hidden Questions
Activity Card 5-10 ●

Work: By Yourself

Use:
• Homework page 159

1. Read each question below.

    A. How many parking spaces are on Main Street?

    B. How many pieces of paper are needed for 1 room?

    C. How many sides are on the building?

2. Each question is a hidden question for one of the three lesson homework problems.

3. **Analyze** What hidden question goes with each homework problem. A.-3.; B.-1.; C.-2.

4. Answer each of the questions above. A. 204 spaces; B. 70 pieces; C. 4 sides

Unit 5, Lesson 10
Copyright © Houghton Mifflin Company

Activity Note Check that students correctly match each hidden question with a problem and then identify the needed information to answer the question.

 Math Writing Prompt

Explain Each Step Look at problem 8 on Student Book page 244. Explain the hidden question and the solution.

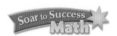 **Software Support**

Use *Soar to Success* for instruction of students needing targeted support for underlying skills.

Write Multistep Problems
Activity Card 5-10 ▲

Work: In Pairs

1. Look at the answers below. On your own, write a two-step word problem that goes with each answer.

    26 muffins

    36 days

    74 pages

2. Exchange problems with your partner. Check that the solution to each question requires two steps and that the answer is given above.

3. **Math Talk** What operations did you use for each word problem? Is there another way to solve each of the problems?

Unit 5, Lesson 10
Copyright © Houghton Mifflin Company

Activity Note Suggest that students write a numeric expression with two operations that equals each solution. If they have the operations in mind, it will be easier to write the two-step word problem.

 Math Writing Prompt

Explain Your Strategy Write a word problem with a hidden question, and then describe a method for solving it.

 Software Support

Use *MegaMath* for review and reinforcement of the concepts and skills presented in this lesson.

Write a Problem for an Equation
Activity Card 5-10 ■

Work: In Pairs

1. **Work Together** Write a word problem that can be represented by the three-step equation below.

$$(4 \times 23) + (5 \times 35) = n$$

2. Solve the problem. $n = 267$

3. On your own, write a three-step equation to exchange with your partner. Then write a word problem for your partner's equation.

4. **Discuss** Is there a hidden question in your problem? If not, how can you rewrite the problem to include a hidden question?

Unit 5, Lesson 10
Copyright © Houghton Mifflin Company

Activity Note Challenge students to write four-step equations and word problems and then exchange them to solve.

 Math Writing Prompt

Investigate Math Write an equation that involves all four operations. Then write a word problem for it.

 Software Support

Use *Destination Math* to take students beyond the concepts and skills presented in this lesson.

③ Homework and Spiral Review

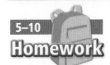

Homework **Goal:** Additional Practice

✓ Include students' work for page 159 as part of their portfolios.

Remembering **Goal:** Spiral Review

This Remembering activity would be appropriate anytime after today's lesson.

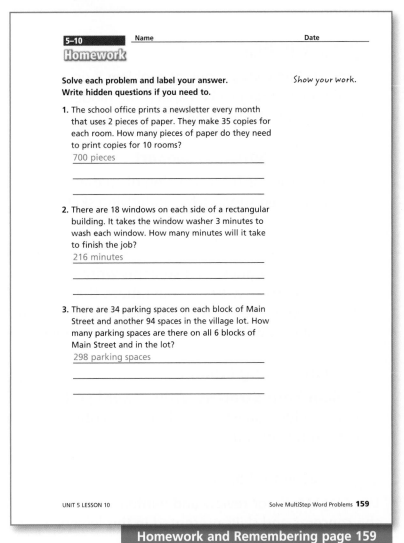

5–10	Name	Date

Homework

Solve each problem and label your answer. *Show your work.*
Write hidden questions if you need to.

1. The school office prints a newsletter every month that uses 2 pieces of paper. They make 35 copies for each room. How many pieces of paper do they need to print copies for 10 rooms?
   700 pieces

2. There are 18 windows on each side of a rectangular building. It takes the window washer 3 minutes to wash each window. How many minutes will it take to finish the job?
   216 minutes

3. There are 34 parking spaces on each block of Main Street and another 94 spaces in the village lot. How many parking spaces are there on all 6 blocks of Main Street and in the lot?
   298 parking spaces

UNIT 5 LESSON 10   Solve MultiStep Word Problems **159**

Homework and Remembering page 159

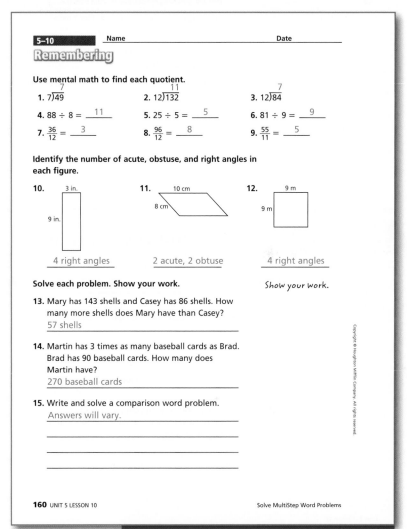

5–10	Name	Date

Remembering

Use mental math to find each quotient.
1. $7\overline{)49}$ → 7
2. $12\overline{)132}$ → 11
3. $12\overline{)84}$ → 7
4. $88 \div 8 =$ 11
5. $25 \div 5 =$ 5
6. $81 \div 9 =$ 9
7. $\frac{36}{12} =$ 3
8. $\frac{96}{12} =$ 8
9. $\frac{55}{11} =$ 5

Identify the number of acute, obstuse, and right angles in each figure.

10. 3 in. / 9 in. rectangle
    4 right angles
11. 10 cm / 8 cm parallelogram
    2 acute, 2 obtuse
12. 9 m / 9 m square
    4 right angles

Solve each problem. Show your work. *Show your work.*

13. Mary has 143 shells and Casey has 86 shells. How many more shells does Mary have than Casey?
    57 shells

14. Martin has 3 times as many baseball cards as Brad. Brad has 90 baseball cards. How many does Martin have?
    270 baseball cards

15. Write and solve a comparison word problem.
    Answers will vary.

160 UNIT 5 LESSON 10   Solve MultiStep Word Problems

Homework and Remembering page 160

Home or School Activity

Social Studies Connection

Age Puzzle Students can do research to get the information they need to solve the following word problem.

On Jordan's great-grandfather's birthday, Jordan was trying to guess his great-grandfather's age. His great-grandfather gave him this clue.

"My age is the difference between the number of U.S. Senators and the number of states that border the Great Lakes."

How old is Jordan's great-grandfather? $100 - 8 = 92$ years old

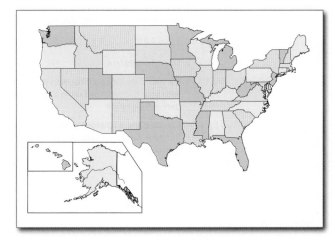

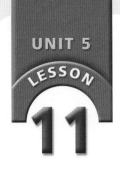

Two-Digit by Two-Digit Multiplication

Lesson Objective

● **Represent two-digit by two-digit multiplication, using area models.**

The Day at a Glance

Today's Goals	Materials

1 Teaching the Lesson
  A1: Understand two-digit by two-digit
  multiplication.
  A2: Practice two-digit by two-digit
  multiplication.
 	
2 Going Further
  ▶ Differentiated Instruction
 	
3 Homework and Spiral Review
	Lesson Activities
	Student Activity Book pp. 245–246
	  or Student Hardcover Book
	  pp. 245–246
	Homework and Remembering
	  pp. 161–162
	MathBoard Materials
	
	Going Further
	Activity Cards 5-11
	Math Journals
	
	123 *Use* **Math Talk** *today!*

Keeping Skills Sharp

Quick Practice ⏱ 5 MINUTES	Daily Routines
Goal: Fluency with zeros patterns. **Zeros Patterns** Select four **Student Leaders** to go to the board to write three products involving two non-zero digits and up to two zeros. That is, a product can have no zeros in the factors, a zero in one factor, a zero in both factors, or two zeros in one factor (see the example below). See Lesson 4.	**Homework Review** Ask students if they had difficulty with any part of the homework. Plan to set aside some time to work with students needing extra help. **Place Value** Name a number that is 10,000 less than each number below.

Problem	Class Response	Student Leader Writes
8×600	"48 hundreds equals four thousand, eight hundred."	$= 4,800$
80×60	"48 hundreds equals four thousand, eight hundred."	$= 4,800$
8×60	"48 tens equals four hundred eighty."	$= 480$

94,582 84,582   20,173 19,173

418,500 408,500   671,436 661,436

① Teaching the Lesson

Represent Multiplication

 20 MINUTES

Goal: Understand two-digit by two-digit multiplication.

Materials: MathBoard Materials, Student Activity Book or Hardcover Book p. 245

 NCTM Standards:
Number and Operations
Representation
Communication

▶ **Draw the Rectangle Model** WHOLE CLASS

Have students work on the dot side of their MathBoards as you work on the Class MathBoard. Have them draw a rectangle that measures 24 units down and 37 units across and label all four sides.

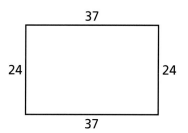

Ask one student how he or she can show the tens and ones in 37. I can draw a vertical line and write 30 + 7 across the top and bottom.

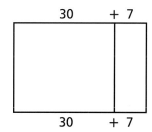

Have another student show the tens and ones in 24 by drawing a horizontal line and writing 20 + 4 on both sides.

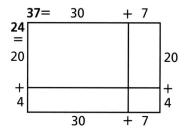

Ask students to describe what each section represents.

● The top left section shows the *tens* times the *tens* = 20 × 30.

● The top right section shows the *tens* in 24 times the *ones* in 37 = 20 × 7.

● The bottom left section shows the *ones* in 24 times the *tens* in 37 = 4 × 30.

● The bottom right section shows the *ones* times the *ones* = 4 × 7.

Have students record the equation for each area on their MathBoards.

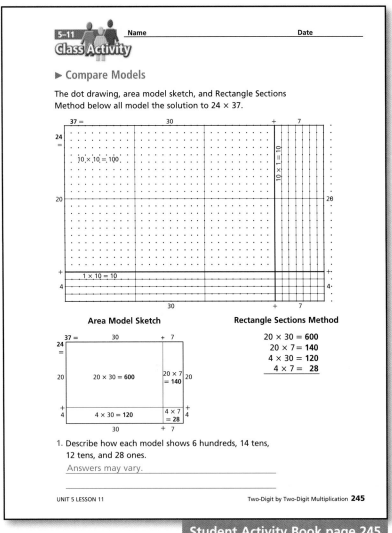

Student Activity Book page 245

Student Activity Book page 245

 Math Talk in Action

How are sections in the area sketch shown in the dot drawing?

Cheri: In the dot drawing there are six 10 × 10 squares. Each square is made up of 100 little squares, so there are 600 little squares. This is the same as 20 × 30 in the area sketch.

Pablo: I'm looking at the 20 × 7 = 140 section of the area sketch. This is the same as the section with 14 rectangles whose sides are 10 and 1. The area of each rectangle is 10 so 14 × 10 = 140.

Sara: The bottom rectangle on the left represents 120 on each picture.

Luke: In the area sketch, the bottom right corner has an area of 4 × 7 = 28. This is shown as 28 unit squares in the dot drawing.

► **Compare Models** | WHOLE CLASS |

Have students look at page 245 of the Student Book.

● See how the drawing at the top shows what we just drew on our MathBoards, but it shows some details we did not draw. What do you see in that drawing? (See Math Talk in Action in side column for sample dialogue.)

Have students relate the dot drawing, area model sketch, and the numeric Rectangle Sections Method. After the class discussion, have students answer problem 1 on page 245.

Ask students to look at the area model sketch and the sketches they drew on their MathBoards. Ask them what part of the problem looks like problems they have been solving 4 × 37 and what part is new. 20 × 37 So now they will be able to use their knowledge about multiplying by tens when they are multiplying these 2-digit by 2-digit problems. Page 246, discussed next, reviews this knowledge.

Teaching the Lesson (continued)

Activity 2

Practice Multiplication

 20 MINUTES

Goal: Practice two-digit by two-digit multiplication.

Materials: Student Activity Book or Hardcover Book p. 246

✔ **NCTM Standards:**
Number and Operations
Problem Solving
Communication

English Language Learners

Write 20 × 30 on the board. Write the word *tens*. Have students find the tens in 20 × 30.

- **Beginning** Say: There are 2 tens in 20 and 3 tens in 30. There are 2 × 3 tens in 20 × 30. Ask: **What is 2 × 3?** 6
- **Intermediate** Ask: **How many tens in 20?** 2 **In 30?** 3 **In 20 × 30?** 2 × 3, 6
- **Advanced** Have students tell how to find the number of tens in 20 × 30.

 Ongoing Assessment

Ask students questions such as:

▶ How many tens are in 20 × 30?

▶ How would you find the product of 26 × 48?

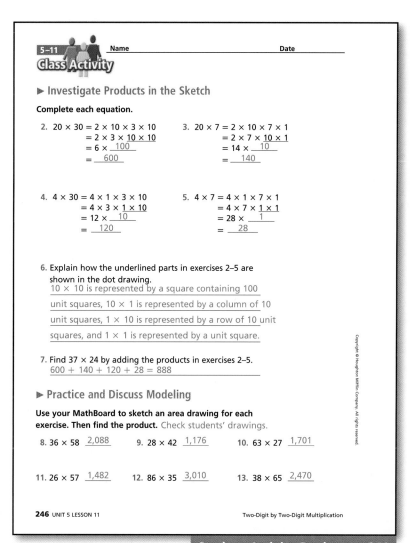

Student Activity Book page 246

▶ **Investigate Products in the Sketch** | WHOLE CLASS |

Have students complete exercises 2–7 on page 246 of the Student Book. Relate the equations to the parts of the dot drawing. For example 2 × 3 × 10 × 10 is represented by the 2 × 3 array of 10 × 10 squares.

▶ **Practice and Discuss Modeling**

| INDIVIDUALS | **Math Talk**

Use **Solve and Discuss** for exercises 8 through 13 (you may need to assign some for homework). Ask for a volunteer to solve and explain exercise 8, using each method (Rectangle Sections, Expanded Notation, and Algebraic Notation). Continue with more problems with volunteers explaining each of the three lessons.

576 UNIT 5 LESSON 11

② Going Further

Differentiated Instruction

Intervention   Activity Card 5-11

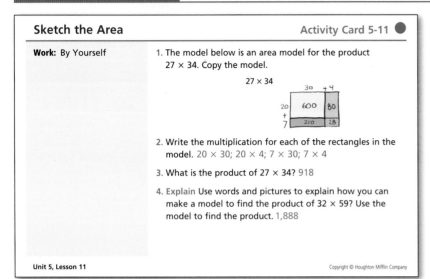

Sketch the Area   Activity Card 5-11 ●

Work: By Yourself

1. The model below is an area model for the product 27 × 34. Copy the model.

27 × 34

2. Write the multiplication for each of the rectangles in the model. 20 × 30; 20 × 4; 7 × 30; 7 × 4

3. What is the product of 27 × 34? 918

4. Explain Use words and pictures to explain how you can make a model to find the product of 32 × 59? Use the model to find the product. 1,888

Unit 5, Lesson 11   Copyright © Houghton Mifflin Company

Activity Note Students may need to use strips of paper to cover up parts of the factors in order to see which factors are contributing to the area of each part of the model.

✎ Math Writing Prompt

Explain Your Thinking Explain how to determine the product of 40 and 20 by using an area model.

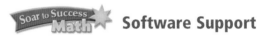 **Software Support**

Use *Soar to Success* for instruction of students needing targeted support for underlying skills.

▲ On Level   Activity Card 5-11

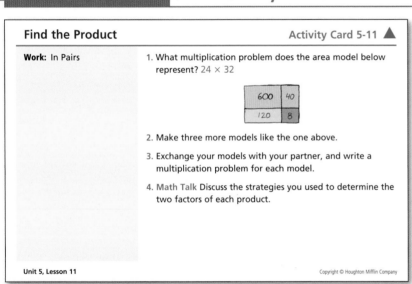

Find the Product   Activity Card 5-11 ▲

Work: In Pairs

1. What multiplication problem does the area model below represent? 24 × 32

2. Make three more models like the one above.

3. Exchange your models with your partner, and write a multiplication problem for each model.

4. Math Talk Discuss the strategies you used to determine the two factors of each product.

Unit 5, Lesson 11   Copyright © Houghton Mifflin Company

Activity Note Remind students to draw models so that the parts of each factor are a multiple of 10 and a single digit (for example, 24 is broken into 20 and 4, not 10 and 14 or 16 and 8.)

✎ Math Writing Prompt

Area Rectangle Model Explain how to find the area of each section of a rectangle model for the product of 2 two-digit numbers.

MEGAMATH **Software Support**

Use *MegaMath* for review and reinforcement of the concepts and skills presented in this lesson.

■ Challenge   Activity Card 5-11

Fill In the Area   Activity Card 5-11 ■

Work: By Yourself

1. Look at the partial area model below. The total area of the model is 462. What pair of numbers is missing from the model? What pair of numbers does the model show as having the product 462? 20 and 40; 21 × 22

2. There is another possible rectangle model for the product 462. Draw the model. Then write another pair of numbers that have the product 462. The model shows (10 + 1) × (40 + 2); 11 × 42

3. What strategy did you use to find the second pair of numbers for the product 462?

Unit 5, Lesson 11   Copyright © Houghton Mifflin Company

Activity Note Extend the activity by having students write their own products and models for the solutions of 325 and 768. 5 × 65, 25 × 13; 16 × 48, 8 × 96

✎ Math Writing Prompt

Comparing Methods Describe the differences between a dot drawing and an area model. Explain which method you prefer and why.

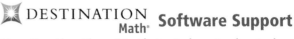 **Software Support**

Use *Destination Math* to take students beyond the concepts and skills presented in this lesson.

Two-Digit by Two-Digit Multiplication   **577**

③ Homework and Spiral Review

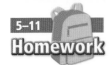 **Homework** **Goal:** Additional Practice

Use this Homework page to provide students with more practice with multiplication models.

5–11
Homework Name _____ Date _____

Sketch an area model for each exercise. Then find the product. Check student methods.

1. 74 × 92 _6,808_ 2. 65 × 37 _2,405_

3. 55 × 84 _4,620_ 4. 49 × 63 _3,087_

5. 34 × 52 _1,768_ 6. 24 × 91 _2,184_

7. Write a word problem for one exercise above.
Answers will vary.
_____
_____
_____
_____
_____
_____
_____
_____
_____
_____

UNIT 5 LESSON 11   Two-Digit by Two-Digit Multiplication **161**

Homework and Remembering page 161

Remembering **Goal:** Spiral Review

This Remembering activity would be appropriate anytime after today's lesson.

5–11
Remembering Name _____ Date _____

Add. Show your work. Check to make sure your answer makes sense.

1. 23,856 + 3,479
```
  1 1 1
  23,856
+  3,479
  27,335
```

2. 12,463 + 186,749
```
    1 11
  186,749
+  12,463
  199,212
```

3. 23,825 − 6,048
```
  23,825
−  6,048
  17,777
```

4. 91,028 − 24,683
```
  91,028
− 24,683
  66,345
```

Find the perimeter and area of each figure.

5.

6.

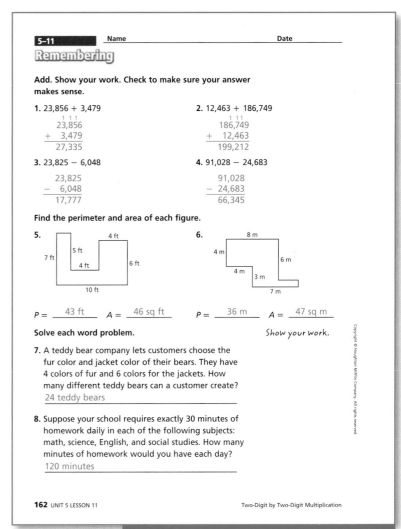

$P =$ _43 ft_ $A =$ _46 sq ft_ $P =$ _36 m_ $A =$ _47 sq m_

Solve each word problem.   _Show your work._

7. A teddy bear company lets customers choose the fur color and jacket color of their bears. They have 4 colors of fur and 6 colors for the jackets. How many different teddy bears can a customer create?
24 teddy bears

8. Suppose your school requires exactly 30 minutes of homework daily in each of the following subjects: math, science, English, and social studies. How many minutes of homework would you have each day?
120 minutes

162 UNIT 5 LESSON 11   Two-Digit by Two-Digit Multiplication

Homework and Remembering page 162

Home or School Activity

 Sports Connection

Field Area Have students look up the field dimensions for several sports, such as volleyball, tennis, and racquetball. Then have students find the area for each type of field by multiplying the field length by its width.

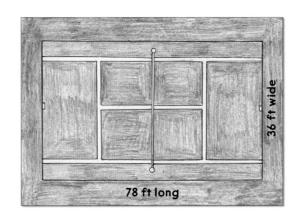

36 ft wide

78 ft long

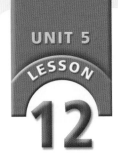

Different Methods for Two-Digit Multiplication

Lesson Objectives

● Use different methods of two-digit by two-digit multiplication.

● Explore the Shortcut Method for two-digit by two-digit multiplication.

The Day at a Glance

Today's Goals	Materials	
1 **Teaching the Lesson** **A1:** Use different methods to multiply two-digit numbers. **A2:** Introduce the Shortcut Method of multiplying two-digit numbers. **2** **Going Further** ▶ Differentiated Instruction **3** **Homework and Spiral Review**	**Lesson Activities** Student Activity Book pp. 247–248 or Student Hardcover Book pp. 247–248 Homework and Remembering pp. 163–164 MathBoard Materials	**Going Further** Activity Cards 5-12 Multiplication Methods Cards (TRB M65) Multiplication Puzzle (TRB M66) Colored pencils or crayons Index cards Scissors Math Journals

123 *Use* **Math Talk** *today!*

Keeping Skills Sharp

Quick Practice 🕐 5 MINUTES	Daily Routines
Goal: Prepare for long division with remainders. **Division With Remainders** On the board, have **Student Leaders** each write five division problems that have nonzero remainders. The leaders use pointers to point to each of the problems on their lists. The class holds up their fingers to show the factor and then, at a hand signal from the Student Leader, says the amount extra, the remainder. Problem Response 11 ÷ 4 "Each student holds up 2 fingers (*hand signal from leader*) "3 extra."	**Homework Review** Ask several students to share the problems they wrote for homework. Have the class ask clarifying questions about each problem. If necessary, model asking questions. **Elapsed Time** Thomas Jefferson, the third President of the United States, was born on April 13, 1743. The country bought the Louisiana Purchase in 1803 during Jefferson's presidency. How old was Jefferson when the Louisiana Purchase was made? 60 years old

① Teaching the Lesson

Multiply Two-Digit Numbers

 20 MINUTES

Goal: Use different methods to multiply two-digit numbers.

Materials: MathBoard Materials, Student Activity Book or Hardcover Book p. 247

✓ **NCTM Standards:**
Algebra
Number and Operations
Representation
Communication

 Math Talk Ask students to suggest word problems for 43 × 67. Elicit one problem of each of the following types: area, array, equal groups, comparison, and combination.

Area: A school field is 43 feet wide and 67 feet long. What is the area of the field?

Array: An apple orchard has 43 rows of trees. Each row has 67 trees. How many apple trees are there in the orchard in all?

Equal Groups: A bag of peanuts contains 67 peanuts. How many peanuts are there in 43 bags?

Comparison: Jen and her sister earn points for helping out. One month Jen earned 67 points and her sister earned 43 times as many points as Jen. How many points did Jen's sister earn?

Combination: The balloon store sells 43 different printed balloons. It has 67 different colors of ribbon ties. How many different combinations of balloons and ties can the store make?

▶ **Compare Multiplication Methods** [WHOLE CLASS]

Write 43 × 67 on the board. Ask students to give word problems for these numbers. Ask them to give at least one problem of each type (see Math Talk in the left column).

Explain to students that now they will discuss again how to multiply 43 × 67, using each of the three methods they know: Rectangle Sections Method, Expanded Notation Method, and Algebraic Notation Method. Then they will compare these methods. In the **Solve and Discuss** sessions below, send a neat and accurate student to the board for Rectangle Sections and have that student work at the far left of the board. Leave that problem on the board for the later comparison of methods. Have a neat and accurate student use the Expanded Notation method to the right of the Rectangle Sections problems and leave that problem on the board also. Repeat with the Algebraic Notation Method to the right so that you have all 3 problems on the board, each with their rectangle drawing and numerical method. Be sure that these students all write the problem with 67 on the top and make the same rectangle (with 43 on the left and 67 at the top (see Student Book page 247). This lesson is written so that multiple students solve, using each method, but you can just send these three students to the board all at the same time while students use the method of their choice at their seats.

Rectangle Sections Method Using **Solve and Discuss**, have students multiply 43 × 67, using the Rectangle Sections Methods and then discuss it.

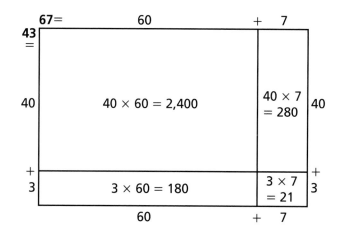

Have a **Student Leader** sketch a large copy of the area model on the board.

Expanded Notation Method Using **Solve and Discuss**, have students multiply 43 × 67 with the Expanded Notation Method. Several students can work on the board while the others work on their MathBoards.

Using colors if possible, draw arcs on one of the solutions on the board to show that you must multiply 40 × 60 *and* 40 × 7 *and* 3 × 60 *and* 3 × 7.

$$
\begin{array}{r}
67 = (60 + 7) \\
\times\ 43 = 40 + 3 \\
\hline
40 \times 60 = \ \ 2{,}400 \\
40 \times\ \ 7 = \ \ \ \ 280 \\
3 \times 60 = \ \ \ \ 180 \\
3 \times\ \ 7 = \ \ \ \ \ \ 21 \\
\hline
= \ \ 2{,}881
\end{array}
$$

Ask students to connect each numeric step to a part of the area model.

Be sure that the students notice that the four bottom equations in the Expanded Notation Method match the equations in the Rectangle Sections Method.

Algebraic Notation Method Using **Solve and Discuss**, have students multiply 67 × 43 with the Algebraic Notation Method. Each student should begin with the equation:

$$43 \times 67 = (40 + 3) \times (60 + 7)$$

Have a student draw arcs showing that you must multiply 40 × 60, 40 × 7, 3 × 60, and 3 × 7. (See Student Book page 247.) Connect the numeric steps to the model.

(123) **Math Talk Discuss All Three Methods** Using the example of each method on the board, discuss what is alike about all three methods.

● All of the methods can be represented by a rectangle.

● The areas of the same four rectangles are added to get the total.

● You are multiplying tens by tens, tens by ones, ones by tens, and ones by ones in all three methods.

Discuss what is different about the three methods.

● They are different in what is multiplied first, second, and so on.

● They are different in how they show the area of each smaller rectangle in the area model.

● They are different in how they show the addition of all of the products.

Finally, discuss with students which method they like best and why.

Repeat the discussion after students have had a chance to study the drawings and problems on Student Book page 247. Call on different students to articulate the points.

Activity continued ▶

Teaching Note

Order of Factors Students, parents, and teachers confuse the rules for writing multiplication horizontally and vertically because these rules differ in different countries. They are not as important as other order of writing rules, so you do not need to insist on them. But be aware of them because these differences mean that students' rectangles and numerical problems will differ even with the same method.

The rule is to write 43 × 67, but then write 67 at the top vertically. The *Math Expressions* examples write the top tens (60) first because it is the biggest number. The partial products will then start with the greatest factor and continue to the least factor. It will be easier for students to add the partial products in this order.

Teaching Note

Drawing Arcs Some students find that drawing arcs to mark what combinations are to be multiplied is helpful. Other students may not need them to understand the process or find that arcs clutter a model or equation and make it more difficult to understand. Because of these learning differences, using arcs in the equations and models should be optional.

Teaching Note

Watch For! As students **Solve and Discuss** to justify the Algebraic Notation Method, make sure that they show how each part of 67 is multiplied by each part of 43. This is the main concept in each of the methods shown in this lesson.

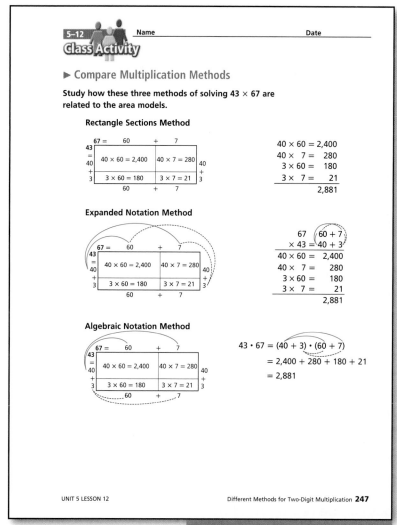

Students' drawings may vary depending upon which factor they write on top. Also, students may write the products in any order as long as they have a regular method and are sure to include all of them.

The Shortcut Multiplication Method

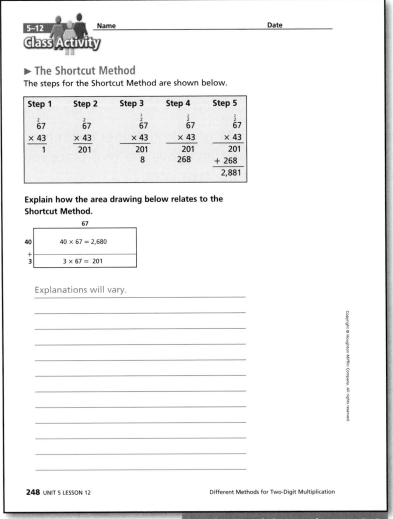

Student Activity Book page 248

 25 MINUTES

Goal: Introduce the Shortcut Method of multiplying two-digit numbers.

Materials: Student Activity Book or Hardcover Book p. 248

 NCTM Standards:
Number and Operations
Algebra
Representation
Communication

Teaching Note

Crucial Consolidation This lesson may take 2 or 3 days to complete. You must: review and compare the 3 methods, discuss the Shortcut Method and relate it to the 3 methods that find 4 products, and practice solving problems using a method of choice. These are crucial experiences for multi-digit multiplication so take the time that is necessary. Lessons 13 and 14 continue practice and discussion of the methods, so you can move on after you have solved and discussed each method during this lesson and students have solved 3 or 4 problems.

► The Shortcut Method ⬛ WHOLE CLASS

Draw the following model on the board.

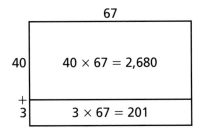

```
         67
   ┌──────────────────┐
40 │  40 × 67 = 2,680  │
   ├──────────────────┤
 + │                  │
 3 │   3 × 67 = 201    │
   └──────────────────┘
```

Point to the 2 rows in the rectangle and explain that the Shortcut Method only has 2 numeric rows. Each row is one row of the rectangle.

Explain that this model shows another way to multiply 67 × 43. Have a student who can do the Shortcut Method come to the board to work on the problem and explain each step as it is performed. Ones are commonly multiplied first although students may successfully begin by multiplying tens. The student may need your help to extend to this 2-digit case.

Activity continued ►

❶ Teaching the Lesson (continued)

Activity 2

Teaching Note

What to Expect from Students
The Shortcut Method may be familiar to the parents or older siblings of some students but its embedded steps make it more difficult for many fourth-graders. Using any of the four methods taught in this lesson is acceptable for fourth-graders.

Direct the students' attention to Student Book page 248 and walk through the steps together as a class.

$$\begin{array}{r} \overset{2}{6}7 \\ \times\ 43 \\ \hline 1 \end{array}$$

Step 1

Ask students what is being multiplied in Step 1. 3×7

Have someone explain that the 1 from 21 goes in the ones column of the first solution row. The 2 tens are written above the tens place (over the 6 in 67) to be added to the rest of the tens later.

$$\begin{array}{r} \overset{2}{6}7 \\ \times\ 43 \\ \hline 201 \end{array}$$

Step 2

Ask students what is multiplied in Step 2. 3×60

This gives 180, or 18 tens. We add the 2 new tens from Step 1 to get 20 tens. We write 20 tens, or 2 hundreds and 0 tens, in those columns of the first solution row.

Ask students what part of the model on the board represents Steps 1 and 2. The smaller bottom section of the rectangle.

$$\begin{array}{r} \overset{2}{\overset{2}{6}}7 \\ \times\ 43 \\ \hline 201 \\ 8 \end{array}$$

Step 3

Direct the students to look at Step 3. Have someone explain that this step shows 40×7, which is 280, or 2 hundreds and 8 tens. The 8 tens are written in the tens place of the second solution row.

The 2 hundreds are written above the 6 to be added in the next step when 40 is multiplying 60.

Step 4

$$
\begin{array}{r}
\overset{\scriptstyle 2}{\overset{\scriptstyle 2}{6}}7 \\
\times\ 43 \\
\hline
201 \\
268
\end{array}
$$

Ask what is multiplied in Step 4. 40 × 60 The product is 2,400 or 24 hundreds. Adding the 2 hundreds from the previous step gives 26 hundreds or 2 thousands and 6 hundreds. The 2 is written in the thousands column of the second solution row, and the 6 is written in the hundreds column.

Ask students what part of the model on the board represents Steps 3 and 4. The larger top section of the rectangle.

Step 5

$$
\begin{array}{r}
\overset{\scriptstyle 2}{\overset{\scriptstyle 2}{6}}7 \\
\times\ 43 \\
\hline
201 \\
+268 \\
\hline
2,881
\end{array}
$$

Have the students look at Step 5.

What is the last step in all four methods of multiplying two-digit numbers? Add all of the section products together.

Teaching Note

Watch For! A very common error in multiplication of two-digit numbers using the Shortcut Method is not understanding you are multiplying by tens and so misaligning the second row. Using place-value language can reinforce the concept that some numbers are multiplied by tens while others are multiplied by ones. Students see this in the Expanded Notation Method. Some people represent the product of numbers multiplied by tens by first putting a zero in the ones place. This aligns the second row properly: the product of 4 tens × 67 = 2,680.

$$
\begin{array}{r}
\overset{\scriptstyle 2}{\overset{\scriptstyle 2}{6}}7 \\
\times\ 43 \\
\hline
201 \\
+\ 2,680
\end{array}
$$

Activity continued ▶

Teaching the Lesson (continued)

Activity 2

English Language Learners

Write 36 × 74 on the board. Help students describe the shortcut method and other methods.

- **Beginning** Say: The methods are similar because they give the same ___. answer The methods are different because they have a different number of ___. parts/ steps
- **Intermediate** Ask: How are the methods similar? They give the same answer. How are the methods different? They have a different number of parts.
- **Advanced** Have students work in pairs to tell the similarities and differences. Ask volunteers to share their ideas with the class.

Ongoing Assessment

Ask students to use any of the four methods of multiplication to find 36 × 74. Make sure that four multiplications and one addition are performed. With the Shortcut Method, the multiplication steps are embedded and are less obvious.

Ask the students to tell what is alike and different about the Shortcut Method of multiplying two-digit numbers compared with the Rectangle Sections Method, the Expanded Notation Method, and the Algebraic Notation Method.

- The methods all give the same answer, use addition as a last step, and require multiplying the value of each digit of one factor by the value of each digit of the other factor.

- The area model for the Shortcut Method is different from the other three methods because it has only two sections; the other methods' models have four parts. In the Shortcut Method, you add just two numbers at the end. In the other methods, you add four numbers to get the product.

Direct the students to look at the drawing on page 248 of their Student Books. In **Student Pairs**, have them discuss the drawing and how it relates to the Shortcut Method. Students will then write their ideas about the model. It relates to the Shortcut Method because it shows that you must multiply 40 × 67 and 3 × 67 in order to get the product of 43 × 67.

②Going Further

● Intervention · Activity Card 5-12

Rectangle Models
Activity Card 5-12 ●

Work: By Yourself

Use:
- Colored pencils or crayons

1. The model below is an area model for the product 34 × 52. Copy the model, using different colors for each small rectangle.

	50	2
30	50 × 30 = 1,500	2 × 30 = 60
4	50 × 4 = 200	2 × 4 = 8

2. Write an expression for the partial sums shown in the model. 1,500 + 200 + 60 + 8

3. What is the product of 34 × 52? 1,768

4. Make and label a model to find the product 26 × 41. 1,066

Unit 5, Lesson 12   Copyright © Houghton Mifflin Company

Activity Note Students should see that four products need to be completed in order to multiply two-digit numbers using this rectangular model.

✎ Math Writing Prompt

Explain a Method Explain how finding 28 × 63 with the Expanded Notation Method involves finding four products.

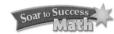 Software Support

Use *Soar to Success* for instruction of students needing targeted support for underlying skills.

▲ On Level · Activity Card 5-12

Multiplication Methods
Activity Card 5-12 ▲

Work: In Small Groups

Use:
- Multiplication Methods Cards (TRB M65)
- Index cards
- Scissors

1. **Work Together** Cut out and shuffle the four methods cards. Place them in a stack face down.

2. Write several multiplication problems, each on one index card. Then shuffle the cards and place them face down. One student chooses a multiplication problem card to place face up.

Rectangle Sections	Shortcut Method	Expanded Notation	Algebraic Notation

3. Each student takes a methods card from the stack and solves the problem by using that method. Repeat the activity until all the multiplication problems have been solved. Collect and reshuffle the methods cards for each round.

Unit 5, Lesson 12   Copyright © Houghton Mifflin Company

Activity Note Students should compare answers and check one another's work. Have them discuss which method they prefer.

✎ Math Writing Prompt

Write Your Own Write an equal-groups word problem for 27 × 32. Explain how you would solve the problem.

Software Support

Use *MegaMath* for review and reinforcement of the concepts and skills presented in this lesson.

■ Challenge · Activity Card 5-12

Multiplication Puzzle
Activity Card 5-12 ■

Work: In Pairs

Use:
- Multiplication Puzzle (TRB M66)
- Index cards

1. Look at the partial multiplication puzzle below. Expressions that share a side must have the same value.

2. **Work Together** Use all the pieces of the puzzle to complete it.

3. Put 12 index cards into a 3-by-4 array, and make your own math puzzle.

4. Shuffle the cards, and trade them with another pair to solve.

Unit 5, Lesson 12   Copyright © Houghton Mifflin Company

Activity Note Have students discuss what strategies they used to solve the puzzles.

✎ Math Writing Prompt

Write Your Own Write a word problem that requires multiplication of two-digit numbers and has an answer of 375 flowers.

✦ DESTINATION Math· Software Support

Use *Destination Math* to take students beyond the concepts and skills presented in this lesson.

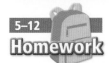 **Homework and Spiral Review**

Homework and Spiral Review

5-12 Homework Goal: Additional Practice

Use this Homework page to provide students with more practice with two-digit by two-digit multiplication.

5-12 Remembering Goal: Spiral Review

This Remembering activity would be appropriate anytime after today's lesson.

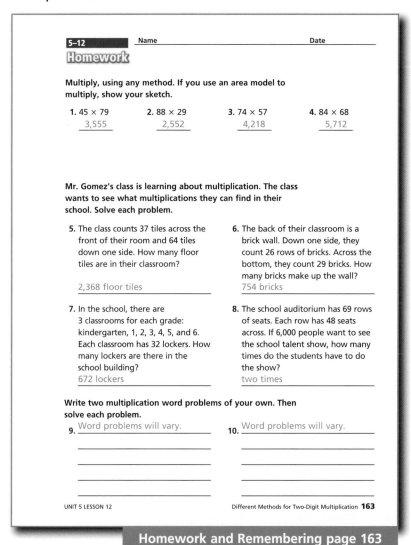

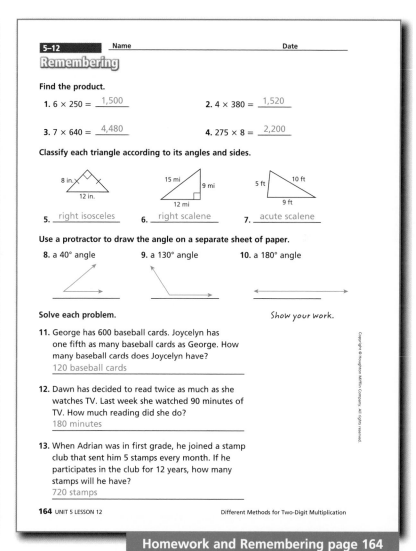

Homework and Remembering page 163

Homework and Remembering page 164

Home or School Activity

 ### Language Arts Connection

Choices In real life, people have to make choices every day. Pose a situation where someone might have to choose one method over another, such as being asked to write a book report with the choice of printing it in ink, writing it in cursive with a pencil, or typing it. Based on the three choices to accomplish the same task, have the students describe the pros and cons of each method and choose their favorite method. Ask the students to support their choice by referring to their list of pros and cons.

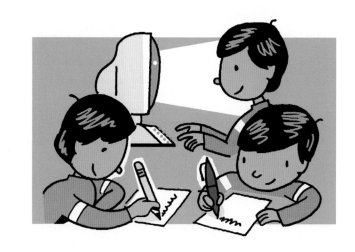

588 UNIT 5 LESSON 12

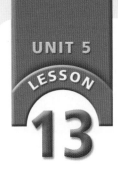

UNIT 5

LESSON

13

Check Products of Two-Digit Numbers

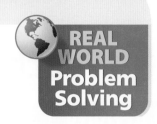

REAL WORLD Problem Solving

Lesson Objectives

● Compare numerical methods of two-digit by two-digit multiplication.

● Estimate products of two-digit numbers.

Vocabulary

estimate
round

The Day at a Glance

Today's Goals	Materials	

① Teaching the Lesson
A1: Compare multiplication methods.
A2: Estimate products of two-digit numbers.
A3: Practice two-digit by two-digit multiplication.
	Lesson Activities
	Student Activity Book p. 249 or
	  Student Hardcover Book p. 249
	Homework and Remembering
	  pp. 165–166
	MathBoard Materials
		Going Further
		Student Activity Book
		  p. 250 or Student
		  Hardcover Book
		  p. 250
		Activity Cards 5-13
		Math Journals

② Going Further ▶ Problem Solving: Estimate With Money ▶ Differentiated Instruction		
③ Homework and Spiral Review		

123 Use Math Talk today!

Keeping Skills Sharp

Quick Practice ⏱ 5 MINUTES

Goal: Prepare for long division with remainders.

Division With Remainders Have four **Student Leaders** go to the board. Each student should write five division problems with remainders. The leaders use pointers to point to each of the problems on their lists. The class holds up fingers to show the factor and then, at a hand signal from the Student Leader, says the amount extra, the remainder.

Problem	Response
25 ÷ 3	Each student holds up 8 fingers. *(hand signal from leader)* "1 extra"
19 ÷ 4	Each student holds up 4 fingers. *(hand signal from leader)* "3 extra"

Daily Routines

Homework Review Ask a student volunteer to share a word problem. Invite several students to solve it at the board, while the others work at their seats.

Estimation At a street fair, a fruit stand sells 105 pears. It sells four times as many oranges as pears, and two times as many apples as oranges. To the nearest hundred, how many of each fruit is sold? 100 pears, 400 oranges, and 800 apples

① Teaching the Lesson

Compare Methods

 15 MINUTES

Goal: Compare multiplication methods.

Materials: MathBoard Materials

 NCTM Standards:
Number and Operations
Representation

 Math Talk in Action

How are the methods alike?

Hannah: All four methods use addition as a last step.

Brett: All four methods give the same answer.

Jean: The value of each digit in the first number is multiplied by the value of each digit in the second number.

How are the methods different?

Vincent: The Shortcut Method has only two numbers added together at the end.

Is the area model for the Shortcut Method different in any way?

Patty: It only has two parts and the others have four parts.

▶ **Draw Without Dots** WHOLE CLASS

Use **Solve and Discuss** to find the product of 68 × 84. Have four volunteers go to the classroom board to solve the problem using:

> Rectangle Sections Method
> Expanded Notation Method
> Algebraic Notation Method
> Shortcut Method

Ask seated students to use the white side of their MathBoards to make a sketch (without dots). Assign **Helping Partners** to any students who might need help.

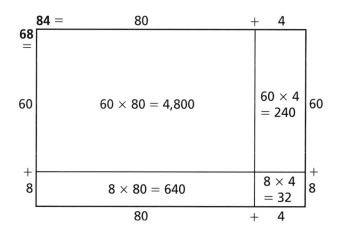

Ask each student at the board to explain the method they used. Then briefly discuss how the methods are alike and how they are different.

▶ **Real-World Connections** WHOLE CLASS

Ask students to give a variety of word problems for 68 × 84. Ask them to consider area, array, equal-groups, comparison, and combination problems.

Estimate Products of Two-Digit Numbers

▶ Estimate a Product WHOLE CLASS

Present students with the following problem:

- Joshua and Sue plan to buy rubber tiles that are 1 foot by 1 foot to cover their new backyard play area. How many tiles should they buy if the play area is 42 feet by 27 feet?

Sketch the play area on the board. Have the students use the dimensions of the yard to write an expression for the area. Then discuss how they could round the dimensions to estimate this product. Write another multiplication problem using the rounded factors next to the original expression.

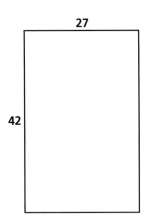

50 ㉚
42 × 27   40 × 30
㊵ 20

Using a different color marker, draw the rounding frame for the problem on top of the original rectangle. That is, draw the rectangle with the rounded factors as its dimensions.

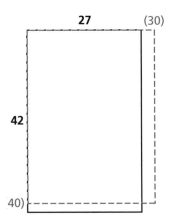

Discuss whether or not it is safe for Joshua and Sue to use their rounded estimate to buy their tiles. The model shows that rounding 27 up to 30 adds 40 × 3 = 120 more tiles, and rounding 42 down to 40 removes 2 × 27 = 54 tiles. Since 120 > 54, rounding is safe in this case.

Activity continued ▶

Activity continued ▶

---

 20 MINUTES

Goal: Estimate products of two-digit numbers.

 NCTM Standards:
Number and Operations
Representation

Teaching Note

Math Background This lesson continues the use of estimation to solve real-world problems. Estimation is used to quickly understand the value of a number or solution to a problem.

Depending on the situation, it is sometimes necessary to round up when it is important to have enough of something.

English Language Learners

Write *rounding up* and *rounding down* on the board. Discuss the tile problem on this page.

- **Beginning** Say: **Sometimes rounding up is better, in order to have enough of something.** Have students repeat.
- **Intermediate** Ask: **When is rounding up better than rounding down?** when you need to have enough of something
- **Advanced** Have students tell when rounding up or rounding down is better.

Activity 2

Teaching Note

Overestimate or Underestimate
On the board, write 68 × 84 = 5,712. Ask students to round to estimate the product: 70 × 80 = 5,600. Point out that the estimate is less than the calculated solution (5,600 < 5,712). This is a problem in some estimation situations. Sometimes it is best to overestimate and round both numbers up: 70 × 90 = 6,300. Point out that if you round both numbers down, you always will underestimate the product: 60 × 80 = 4,800. Review the word problems students suggested in the Real-World Connections on page 590. Have students identify problems where it is best to overestimate the product.

The Learning Classroom

Math Talk Encourage students to participate in the discussion of estimation and multiplication by contributing their own real-world scenarios. Start the discussion by asking students how long it takes them to get to school and how much time they allow.

Ask the students if they could use a rounded estimate for a play area that is 42 feet by 29 feet. No. Rounding up to 30 would add 1 × 40 = 40 tiles, and rounding 42 down to 40 would take away 2 × 29 = 58 tiles. 40 < 58, so they would not buy enough tiles to finish the play area.

▶ Round to Estimate ⟦WHOLE CLASS⟧

On the board, write 68 × 84 = 5,712.

Have the students give situations where a rounded solution might create a problem. Point out that for 68 × 84, the estimate is less than the calculated solution (5,600 < 5,712). It would be a problem for any situation where it is important to have enough of something. If students have trouble coming up with examples, you might suggest these situations.

- Su-Lin needs to buy 68 notebooks for her after school club. Each notebook costs $0.84. How should she round to be sure to have enough money when she gets to the checkout? In this case, it would be better to round $0.84 up to $0.90 so Su-Lin will have enough money at the checkout, especially if tax is added.

- Sam is building 68 bookshelves for the school library. He will need 84 screws to put together each bookshelf. Should Sam round up or down to be sure he buys enough screws to build all of the bookshelves? Sam should round up. It would be very frustrating to run out of screws before the project was complete! Construction materials almost always need to be overestimated.

▶ Discuss Estimation Situations ⟦WHOLE CLASS⟧ Math Talk

Discuss other real-world situations in which people estimate products. Ask students to share their ideas and their personal experiences with estimation. Here are some ideas you might bring up yourself.

- *How much time will be needed?* When grading papers, I often estimate how long it will take by estimating how long one paper will take and then multiplying by the number of students in our class.

- *How much money will be needed?* Suppose I am going on a two-week road trip this summer and need to estimate the amount of money I will need for gasoline. I can estimate the mileage of the trip, the miles my car gets for each gallon, and the cost of a gallon of gas. A close estimate is difficult in this case since the price of gasoline changes daily and a car's miles per gallon varies depending on driving conditions. Because I want to be sure that I do not run out of gas money, I should estimate the mileage on the high side, estimate the miles per gallon on the low side, and estimate the cost per gallon on the high side.

Activity 3

Practice Multiplication

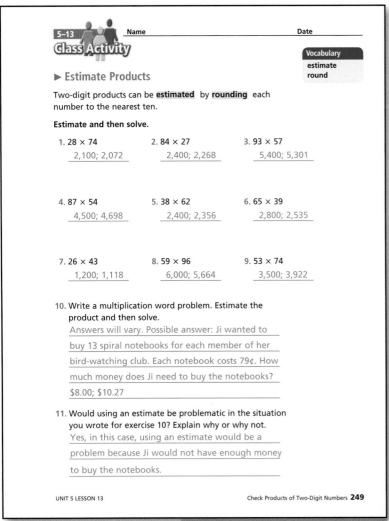

Student Activity Book page 249

  20 MINUTES

Goal: Practice two-digit by two-digit multiplication.

Materials: Student Activity Book or Hardcover Book p. 249

  NCTM Standard:
Number and Operations

Differentiated Instruction

Advanced Learners You may want to ask advanced students how they can improve their estimates when both factors have been rounded down. For instance, the estimated product for 24 × 93 is 20 × 90 = 1,800. A better estimate would also add a value for 4 × 90 = 360. Because we are rounding to the nearest hundred, we would round 360 to 400 and add this amount to 1,800 for an estimate of 2,200.

Ongoing Assessment

Have students estimate the product by rounding and then find the exact product.

▶ 22 × 13

▶ 12 × 43

▶ Estimate Products WHOLE CLASS

Use **Solve and Discuss** for exercises 1–9 on page 249 of the Student Book. When discussing problems 1 and 2, take the opportunity to review methods of multiplication.

Range of Estimates When discussing problem 4, students might want to find a range of estimates. To find the range of the products, first round both numbers up to the next multiple of 10, 90 × 60. Then round both numbers down to the lower multiple of 10, 80 × 50. 87 × 54 is between 80 × 50 and 90 × 60, or between the products 4,000 and 5,400.

Underestimate or Overestimate When discussing problems 8 and 9, write on the board:

8. 60 × 100 = 6,000   **9.** 50 × 70 = 3,500

Discuss why the first estimate is an overestimate and the second is an underestimate. 8. rounds both numbers up, 9. rounds both numbers down

Going Further

Problem Solving: Estimate With Money

Goal: Estimate products involving money.

Materials: Student Activity Book or Hardcover Book p. 250

✔ **NCTM Standards:**
Number and Operations
Communication
Representation
Problem Solving

▶ Multiplication and Money PAIRS

On Student Book page 250, read the first problem to the class. Discuss ways to estimate the answer. For instance, the number of balloons could be rounded to the nearest ten and the cost could be rounded to the nearest dollar. That would result in the product of 40×1, or $40.

Another way to estimate this answer would be to round the number of balloons to the nearest ten and the cost to the nearest ten cents. That would result in the product of 40×80, or 3,200 cents, which is $32.00.

Finally, have **Student Pairs** show the area model for the estimate and the exact amount.

Use **Solve and Discuss** for problems 2–5.

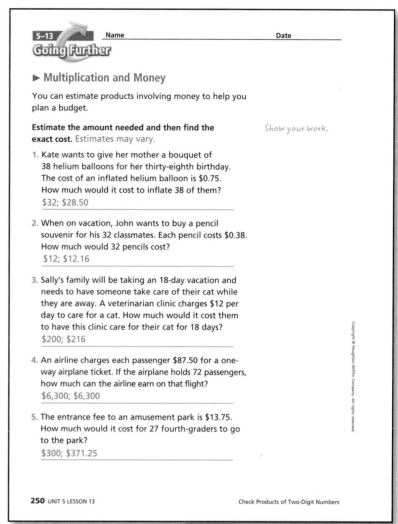

5-13
Going Further   Name _____ Date _____

▶ **Multiplication and Money**

You can estimate products involving money to help you plan a budget.

Estimate the amount needed and then find the exact cost. Estimates may vary.   *Show your work.*

1. Kate wants to give her mother a bouquet of 38 helium balloons for her thirty-eighth birthday. The cost of an inflated helium balloon is $0.75. How much would it cost to inflate 38 of them?
   $32; $28.50

2. When on vacation, John wants to buy a pencil souvenir for his 32 classmates. Each pencil costs $0.38. How much would 32 pencils cost?
   $12; $12.16

3. Sally's family will be taking an 18-day vacation and needs to have someone take care of their cat while they are away. A veterinarian clinic charges $12 per day to care for a cat. How much would it cost them to have this clinic care for their cat for 18 days?
   $200; $216

4. An airline charges each passenger $87.50 for a one-way airplane ticket. If the airplane holds 72 passengers, how much can the airline earn on that flight?
   $6,300; $6,300

5. The entrance fee to an amusement park is $13.75. How much would it cost for 27 fourth-graders to go to the park?
   $300; $371.25

250 UNIT 5 LESSON 13   Check Products of Two-Digit Numbers

Student Activity Book page 250

Differentiated Instruction

Intervention — Activity Card 5-13

Same Estimate Activity Card 5-13

Work: By Yourself

1. Estimate each of the products below. 800; 800; 800
   20 × 37   23 × 40   23 × 37

2. What rounded factors did you use for each estimated product? 20 × 40

3. List 10 other pairs of factors that would use the same rounded factors to estimate the product.

4. **Explain** How did you choose other pairs of factors? What was the least factor you used? What was the greatest factor you used? Answers will vary, but first factor must range from 15 to 24 and second factor will range from 35 to 44.

Unit 5, Lesson 13 Copyright © Houghton Mifflin Company

Activity Note If students are having difficulty finding the rounded factors, ask them to identify the range of numbers that round to 20 and the range that round to 40.

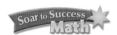 **Math Writing Prompt**

Estimation Needed Describe a situation in which you would need to estimate a product.

Soar to Success Math ★ Software Support

Use *Soar to Success* for instruction of students needing targeted support for underlying skills.

On Level — Activity Card 5-13

Build Rectangles Activity Card 5-13 ▲

Work: In Pairs

1. The area model below uses the numbers 30, 80, 5, and 2. Estimate the product. Then calculate the exact product. 2,720

   80 + 5
   30 +
   2

2. **Work Together** to create a different model that uses the same set of numbers (30, 80, 5, and 2). The model will show (30 + 5) × (80 + 2).

3. Estimate the product of the second model. Then calculate the exact product. 2,870

4. On your own, write four numbers and exchange with your partner. Draw two area models for each set. Estimate and calculate each product.

Unit 5, Lesson 13 Copyright © Houghton Mifflin Company

Activity Note If students are having difficulty identifying the second model for the first set of numbers, remind them that they can reverse the pairing of the multiple of ten and the single digit.

 Math Writing Prompt

Better to Overestimate Describe a situation in which you would need to overestimate a product.

MegaMath Grades K-6 Software Support

Use *MegaMath* for review and reinforcement of the concepts and skills presented in this lesson.

Challenge — Activity Card 5-13

Investigate Fives Activity Card 5-13 ■

Work: By Yourself

1. Follow the directions to make four estimates of the product 75 × 85.
   - Round both factors down. 5,600
   - Round both factors up. 7,200
   - Round the greater factor up and the lesser factor down. 6,300
   - Round the lesser factor up and the greater factor down. 6,400

2. Calculate the actual product. 6,375

3. **Analyze** Which method gives the best estimate? the fourth method

Unit 5, Lesson 13 Copyright © Houghton Mifflin Company

Activity Note Students can test other combinations of two-digit numbers ending in 5 to see if the fourth method of estimating always produces the best estimate.

 Math Writing Prompt

Better to Underestimate Describe a situation in which you would need to underestimate a product.

 DESTINATION Math· Software Support

Use *Destination Math* to take students beyond the concepts and skills presented in this lesson.

③ Homework and Spiral Review

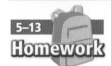

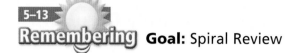

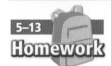 Homework **Goal:** Additional Practice

Use this Homework page to provide students with more practice with two-digit by two-digit multiplication.

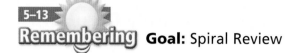 Remembering **Goal:** Spiral Review

This Remembering activity would be appropriate anytime after today's lesson.

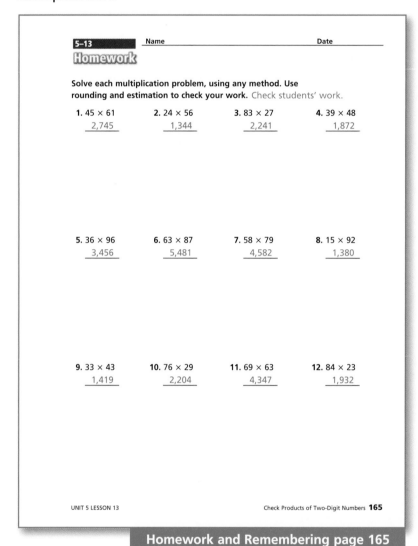

5–13 Name _____ Date _____
Homework

Solve each multiplication problem, using any method. Use rounding and estimation to check your work. Check students' work.

1. 45 × 61
2,745

2. 24 × 56
1,344

3. 83 × 27
2,241

4. 39 × 48
1,872

5. 36 × 96
3,456

6. 63 × 87
5,481

7. 58 × 79
4,582

8. 15 × 92
1,380

9. 33 × 43
1,419

10. 76 × 29
2,204

11. 69 × 63
4,347

12. 84 × 23
1,932

UNIT 5 LESSON 13   Check Products of Two-Digit Numbers **165**

Homework and Remembering page 165

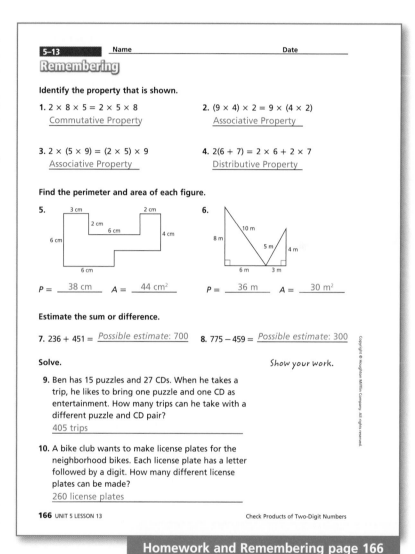

5–13 Name _____ Date _____
Remembering

Identify the property that is shown.

1. 2 × 8 × 5 = 2 × 5 × 8
Commutative Property

2. (9 × 4) × 2 = 9 × (4 × 2)
Associative Property

3. 2 × (5 × 9) = (2 × 5) × 9
Associative Property

4. 2(6 + 7) = 2 × 6 + 2 × 7
Distributive Property

Find the perimeter and area of each figure.

5.

6.

P = ___38 cm___   A = ___44 cm²___

P = ___36 m___   A = ___30 m²___

Estimate the sum or difference.

7. 236 + 451 = _Possible estimate: 700_

8. 775 − 459 = _Possible estimate: 300_

Solve.   *Show your work.*

9. Ben has 15 puzzles and 27 CDs. When he takes a trip, he likes to bring one puzzle and one CD as entertainment. How many trips can he take with a different puzzle and CD pair?
405 trips

10. A bike club wants to make license plates for the neighborhood bikes. Each license plate has a letter followed by a digit. How many different license plates can be made?
260 license plates

166 UNIT 5 LESSON 13   Check Products of Two-Digit Numbers

Homework and Remembering page 166

Home or School Connection

 ### Science Connection

Counting Cells When using a microscope, a lab technician can use a special grid to estimate the number of cells in a sample. She counts the number of cells in one square of the grid, and then multiplies that number by the total number of squares on the grid. Have students solve the following problem: If a lab technician counts 92 cells in one square of the grid sand there are 16 squares on the grid, about how many cells are in the sample?

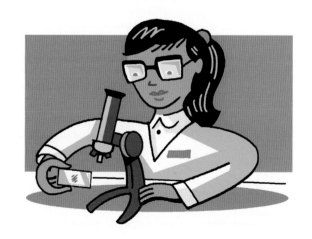

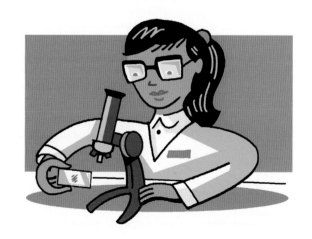

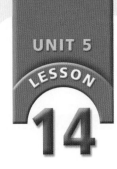

Practice Multiplication

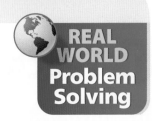
Lesson Objective

● **Practice two-digit by two-digit multiplication.**

The Day at a Glance

Today's Goals	Materials

1 Teaching the Lesson
 A1: Multiply with fewer written steps.
 A2: Practice computing and problem solving.
 	
 2 Going Further
 ▶ Math Connection: Lattice Multiplication
 ▶ Differentiated Instruction
 	
 3 Homework and Spiral Review
	Lesson Activities
	 Student Activity Book p. 251 or
	   Student Hardcover Book p. 251
	 Homework and Remembering
	   pp. 167–168
	 Quick Quiz 3 (Assessment Guide)
	
	 Going Further
	 Student Activity Book
	   p. 252 or Student
	   Hardcover Book
	   p. 252
	 Lattice Multiplication
	   Grids (TRB M67)
	 Activity Cards 5-14
	 Number cubes
	 Math Journals
	
	 123 *Use* **Math Talk** *today!*

Keeping Skills Sharp

Quick Practice ⏱ 5 MINUTES	**Daily Routines**
Goal: Prepare for long division with remainders. **Division With Remainders** Have four **Student Leaders** go to the board. Each student should write five division problems with remainders. The leaders use pointers to point to each of the problems on their lists. The class holds up fingers to show the factor and then, at a hand signal from the Student Leader, says the amount extra, the remainder.	**Homework Review** Let students work together to check their work. Initially, pair less able students with more able students. Remind students to use what they know about helping others. **Strategy Problem** How many triangles can you make by drawing diagonals inside a regular hexagon? Use grid paper to help you decide. Six equilateral triangles can be drawn inside a regular hexagon.

Problem	Response
22 ÷ 4	Each student holds up 5 fingers. *(hand signal from leader)* "2 extra"
22 ÷ 7	Each student holds up 3 fingers. *(hand signal from leader)* "1 extra"

Teaching the Lesson

Write Fewer Steps

 25 MINUTES

Goal: Multiply with fewer written steps.

✔ **NCTM Standards:**
Number and Operations
Representation

▶ **Drop Written Steps** [WHOLE CLASS]

Point out to students that when they use the Expanded Notation Method, they do not have to write all of the steps all of the time.

Invite several students to solve 43 × 67 on the classroom board. Ask one of the students to draw an area model and another to write out the complete Expanded Notation Method. Ask the remaining volunteers to drop one or more written steps from their solutions. Here are some of the solutions that may be on the board.

Expanded Notation

$$
\begin{array}{r}
67 = 60 + 7 \\
\times\ \ 43 = 40 + 3 \\
\hline
40 \times 60 = 2{,}400 \\
40 \times 7 = 280 \\
3 \times 60 = 180 \\
3 \times 7 = +\ \ 21 \\
\hline
2{,}881
\end{array}
$$

No Expanded Factors

$$
\begin{array}{r}
67 \\
\times\ \ 43 \\
\hline
40 \times 60 = 2{,}400 \\
40 \times 7 = 280 \\
3 \times 60 = 180 \\
3 \times 7 = +\ \ 21 \\
\hline
2{,}881
\end{array}
$$

Factor Equations Not Written

$$
\begin{array}{r}
67 \\
\times\ \ 43 \\
\hline
2{,}400 \\
280 \\
180 \\
+\ \ \ 21 \\
\hline
2{,}881
\end{array}
$$

Discuss the different solutions. Encourage student volunteers to explain how to do the steps mentally without writing them out.

Be sure that students see that these methods are the same except that some steps are done mentally rather than writing them out.

▶ Compare the Shortened Expanded Notation and Shortcut Methods [WHOLE CLASS]

Have students discuss the similarities and differences between the Shortened Expanded Notation Method and the Shortcut Method.

Expanded Notation

```
       67
    ×  43
    2,400 ⎤
          ⎦ 2,680
      280 ⎤
      180 ⎤
          ⎦ 201
    +  21 ⎦
    2,881
```

Shortcut Method
(starting with ones)

```
       2
       2
       67
    ×  43
      201
  + 2,680
    2,881
```

Discuss how the numbers added in the Expanded Notation Method relate to the numbers added in the Shortcut Method.

- The top two rows added in the Expanded Notation Method show 40 × 60 and 40 × 7, so they relate to the second row in the Shortcut Method, 40 × 67.

- The bottom two rows added in the Expanded Notation Method show 3 × 60 and 3 × 7, so they relate to the first row in the Shortcut Method, 3 × 67.

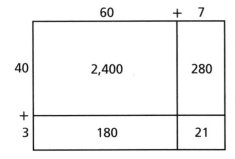

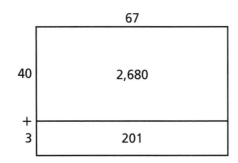

Ask students to describe how the main difference in these 2 methods appears in the rectangle model. Then quickly sketch these on the board and summarize: there are 4 products for Expanded Notation because you multiply each tens and ones in the 67 by each tens and ones in the 43 and you start with the tens. For the Shortcut Method, you start with ones and multiply the whole 67 so you only get 2 rows in the rectangle and 2 products in the numerical problem.

Activity continued ▶

Activity 1

▶ **Variations of the Multiplication Methods** WHOLE CLASS

When multiplying a two-digit number by a two-digit number, the convention when using the Expanded Notation Method is to start with the tens place, and the convention when using the Shortcut Method is to start with the ones place. These are only conventions and both can be done starting with the other place-value.

Expanded Notation (starting with ones)	Shortcut Method (starting with tens)

Expanded Notation:
$$
\begin{array}{r}
67 \\
\times\ 43 \\
\hline
21 \\
180 \\
280 \\
+\ \ 2{,}400 \\
\hline
2{,}881
\end{array}
$$
with 21 and 180 bracketed as 201, and 280 and $2{,}400$ bracketed as $2{,}680$.

Shortcut Method:
$$
\begin{array}{r}
\overset{2}{\overset{2}{67}} \\
\times\ 43 \\
\hline
2{,}680 \\
+\ \ \ \ 201 \\
\hline
2{,}881
\end{array}
$$

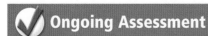 **Math Talk** Have students tell why they prefer one method over another. This conversation will help students see the advantages of certain methods.

Encourage all students to use whichever method works best for them.

▶ **Estimate Products** PAIRS

Have **Student Pairs** use any method to estimate the product of 67 × 43. Discuss the different methods and why some are more accurate than others.

Round	Range of Estimates	Overestimate
70 × 40 = 2,800	60 × 40 = 2,400 70 × 50 = 3,500	70 × 50 = 3,500

Point out that rounding one number up and one number down often gives an estimate closer to the exact answer.

Computation and Problem Solving

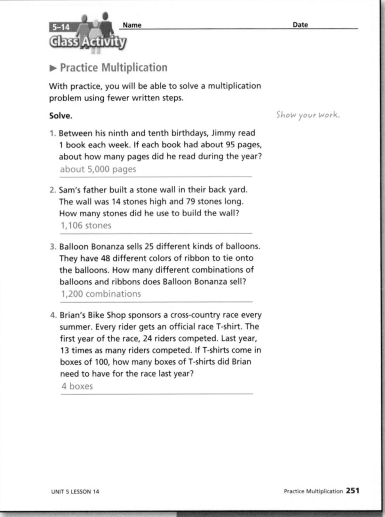

▶ Practice Multiplication SMALL GROUPS

On Student Book page 251, use **Solve and Discuss** for problems 1–4 to give students practice with computation and problem solving. Encourage students to discuss each problem and decide whether an estimate is a sufficient answer or if they need to calculate a precise answer.

Tell students to use the numeric method that works best for them. Ask them to use rounding to check that their answers make sense. Students should be able to explain the numeric method that they are using to solve the problems.

 20 MINUTES

Goal: Practice computing and problem solving.

Materials: Student Activity Book or Hardcover Book p. 251

 NCTM Standards:
Number and Operations
Problem Solving

 Math Talk in Action

Would rounding make Brian short on shirts in problem 4?

Mario: Yes. If Brian rounded 24 and 13 down to estimate the number of shirts, he would think that he needs about $20 \times 10 = 200$ shirts. Since the shirts come in packages of 100, he might figure that he better get 3 packages, since he knows he needs more than 200 shirts. But even 300 shirts is too few ($24 \times 13 = 312$).

English Language Learners

Have students tell which steps are needed to solve problem 1 on Student Book page 251.

• **Beginning** Say: **Round 52 down to 50. Round 95 up to 100. 50 × 100 = about 5,000 pages.** Have students repeat.

• **Intermediate** Ask: **How do you round 52?** down to 50 **How do you round 95?** up to100 **What is 50 × 100?** about 5,000 pages

• **Advanced** Have students tell how to round numbers and use them to solve.

 Quick Quiz

See Assessment Guide for Unit 5 Quick Quiz 3.

Going Further

Math Connection: Lattice Multiplication

Goal: Use lattice multiplication.

Materials: Student Activity Book or Hardcover Book p. 252, Lattice Multiplication Grids (TRB M67)

✔ **NCTM Standards:**
Number and Operations
Communication
Representation

► Lattice Multiplication PAIRS

In this activity, students connect two-digit by two-digit multiplication with the lattice multiplication method.

How It Works Lattice Multiplication is included here for historical interest and because some other math programs teach it. But some students do not understand why it works. The focus here is on understanding that the diagonals of the lattice organize all of the products into their correct place values. You, therefore, can read off the answer by starting at the top left and moving down and across the ones place. A tricky part of the method is that when you are adding the diagonals and get a 2-digit total (see Step 5), you need to put the tens part of that number in the next left column. In Step 5, 8 tens + 2 tens + 8 tens = 18 tens, so 8 is written outside the lattice in the tens place and the 1 in the 18 is written inside the hundreds diagonal waiting to be added with the hundreds.

Using the Lattice Use Student Book page 252 as **Student Pairs** work through the steps of the method, and connect these steps to the rectangle model (see that the lattice has the 2-digit products in the same locations as in the rectangle (24 then 28 and down left 18 and then 21). But the lattice method does not show place values by using zeros. Have a **Student Pair** or **Small Group** explain how the lattice method works and how it organizes the place values.

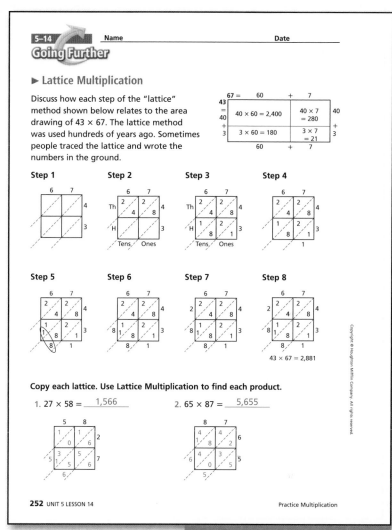

Student Activity Book page 252

Differentiated Instruction

● Intervention — Activity Card 5-14

Missing Parts — Activity Card 5-14

Work: In Pairs

1. **Work Together** Copy the missing-parts multiplication problems below. Work together to complete each problem. 312; 2,346

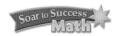

$$24 = \underline{20} + 4$$
$$\times 13 = 10 + \underline{3}$$
$$10 \times 20 = \underline{200}$$
$$10 \times \underline{4} = 40$$
$$\underline{20} \times 3 = 60$$
$$3 \times 4 = \underline{12}$$
$$\underline{312}$$

$$46 = \underline{40} + 6$$
$$\times 51 = \underline{50} + 1$$
$$50 \times 40 = \underline{2,000}$$
$$\underline{50 \times 6} = 300$$
$$\underline{40 \times 1} = 40$$
$$1 \times 6 = \underline{6}$$
$$\underline{2,346}$$

2. On your own, write a missing-parts multiplication problem. Exchange with your partner to solve.

Unit 5, Lesson 14 — Copyright © Houghton Mifflin Company

Activity Note Have students discuss what strategies they used to find the missing parts. Some students may want to draw a rectangle model to help with identifying the factors and partial sums.

Math Writing Prompt

Missing Steps Explain how some of the steps in the Expanded Notation Method can be left out and done mentally instead.

Soar to Success Math — Software Support

Use *Soar to Success* for instruction of students needing targeted support for underlying skills.

▲ On Level — Activity Card 5-14

Rolling Problems — Activity Card 5-14 ▲

Work: In Pairs

Use:
- 8 number cubes, labeled 1–6

1. Each student rolls four number cubes.

2. On your own, use the digits on the cubes to write a multiplication problem with 2 two-digit numbers. Then calculate the product. A possible problem for the digits above is 51 × 13.

3. After each roll, the player with the greater product earns one point.

4. The first player to win 5 points wins the game.

5. **Math Talk** What strategies did you use to write the greatest possible product? Which do you think worked the best?

Unit 5, Lesson 14 — Copyright © Houghton Mifflin Company

Activity Note Remind students that they can arrange the digits from the number cubes in any order to form 2 two-digit numbers.

Math Writing Prompt

Explain the Process Some students write small numbers above the tens column in multiplication. Write a problem where this occurs and explain what these numbers mean.

MegaMath — Software Support

Use *MegaMath* for review and reinforcement of the concepts and skills presented in this lesson.

■ Challenge — Activity Card 5-14

Multiplication Patterns — Activity Card 5-14 ■

Work: By Yourself

1. Compute each pair of products below.

    21 × 13 and 12 × 31   273; 372

    11 × 31 and 13 × 11   341; 143

2. Identify any patterns that you see in the pairs of products. When the digits of each factor are reversed, the digits in the product are reversed.

3. Find two other pairs of products that follow the same pattern.

Unit 5, Lesson 14 — Copyright © Houghton Mifflin Company

Activity Note To help students find numeric patterns, have them draw rectangular models for the pairs of numbers.

Math Writing Prompt

Describe Advantages Describe one advantage of finding products by using an area model and one advantage of finding products by using the Shortcut Method.

DESTINATION Math® — Software Support

Use *Destination Math* to take students beyond the concepts and skills presented in this lesson.

③ Homework and Spiral Review

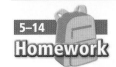

5-14

Homework **Goal:** Additional Practice

Use this Homework page to provide students with more multiplication practice.

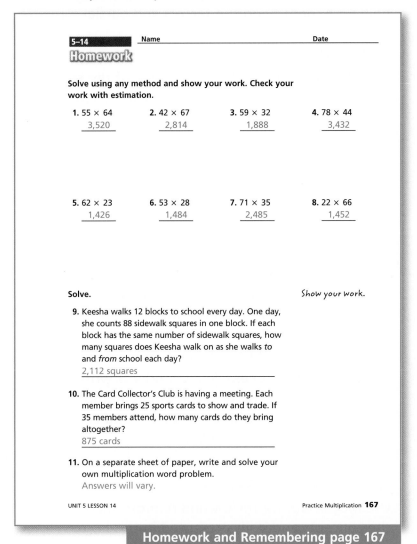

5-14 Name _____ Date _____
Homework

Solve using any method and show your work. Check your work with estimation.

1. 55 × 64
3,520

2. 42 × 67
2,814

3. 59 × 32
1,888

4. 78 × 44
3,432

5. 62 × 23
1,426

6. 53 × 28
1,484

7. 71 × 35
2,485

8. 22 × 66
1,452

Solve.   *Show your work.*

9. Keesha walks 12 blocks to school every day. One day, she counts 88 sidewalk squares in one block. If each block has the same number of sidewalk squares, how many squares does Keesha walk on as she walks *to* and *from* school each day?
2,112 squares

10. The Card Collector's Club is having a meeting. Each member brings 25 sports cards to show and trade. If 35 members attend, how many cards do they bring altogether?
875 cards

11. On a separate sheet of paper, write and solve your own multiplication word problem.
Answers will vary.

UNIT 5 LESSON 14   Practice Multiplication **167**

Homework and Remembering page 167

5-14

Remembering **Goal:** Spiral Review

This Remembering activity would be appropriate anytime after today's lesson.

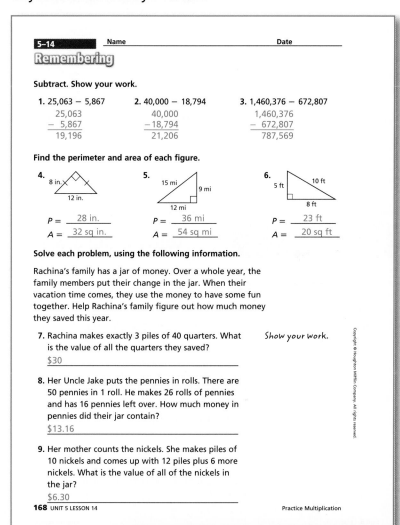

5-14 Name _____ Date _____
Remembering

Subtract. Show your work.

1. 25,063 − 5,867
   25,063
 − 5,867
   19,196

2. 40,000 − 18,794
   40,000
 − 18,794
   21,206

3. 1,460,376 − 672,807
   1,460,376
 − 672,807
     787,569

Find the perimeter and area of each figure.

4. 8 in. / 12 in.
P = 28 in.
A = 32 sq in.

5. 15 mi / 9 mi / 12 mi
P = 36 mi
A = 54 sq mi

6. 5 ft / 10 ft / 8 ft
P = 23 ft
A = 20 sq ft

Solve each problem, using the following information.

Rachina's family has a jar of money. Over a whole year, the family members put their change in the jar. When their vacation time comes, they use the money to have some fun together. Help Rachina's family figure out how much money they saved this year.

7. Rachina makes exactly 3 piles of 40 quarters. What is the value of all the quarters they saved?   *Show your work.*
$30

8. Her Uncle Jake puts the pennies in rolls. There are 50 pennies in 1 roll. He makes 26 rolls of pennies and has 16 pennies left over. How much money in pennies did their jar contain?
$13.16

9. Her mother counts the nickels. She makes piles of 10 nickels and comes up with 12 piles plus 6 more nickels. What is the value of all of the nickels in the jar?
$6.30

168 UNIT 5 LESSON 14   Practice Multiplication

Homework and Remembering page 168

Home or School Activity

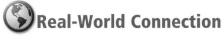

Real-World Connection

Farming Have students research farming techniques to find how a farmer lays out the seeds for a crop. Have them describe what information they would need to estimate the number of stalks of corn that a farmer has planted.

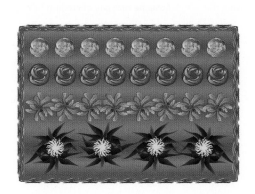

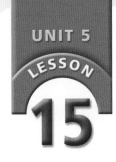

Multiplication With Hundreds

Lesson Objectives

● Use an area model to represent multiplication of hundreds.

● Explore and use different methods to multiply hundreds.

The Day at a Glance

Today's Goals	Materials	

1 Teaching the Lesson
A1: Use different methods to multiply hundreds.
A2: Practice multiplication with hundreds.
	Lesson Activities
	Student Activity Book pp. 253–254
	  or Student Hardcover Book
	  pp. 253–254
	Homework and Remembering
	  pp. 169–170
	MathBoard Materials
		Going Further
		Activity Cards 5-15
		Index cards
		Math Journals

2 Going Further ▶ Differentiated Instruction		
3 Homework and Spiral Review		

123 Use Math Talk today!

Keeping Skills Sharp

Quick Practice ⏱ 5 MINUTES	Daily Routines
Goal: Practice division with remainders. **Division With Remainders** Have four **Student Leaders** go to the board. Each student should write five division problems with remainders. The leaders use pointers to point to each of the problems on their lists. The class holds up fingers to show the factor and then, at a hand signal from the Student Leader, says the amount extra, or the remainder.	**Homework Review** Send students to the board to show their solutions for problems 9–10. Have each student at the board explain his/her solution. Encourage the rest of the class to ask clarifying questions and make comments. **Reasoning** Write the following problem on the board. Have students make up the missing information and then solve the problem. Mr. Canfield sells between 100 and 150 tickets to a charity dinner. Mrs. Nakagawa sells three times as many tickets as Mr. Canfield sells. How many tickets could Mrs. Nakagawa sell? How did you find your answer? Multiply $3 \times 100 = 300$ and $3 \times 150 = 450$. Mrs. Nakagawa could sell between 300 and 450 tickets.

Problem	Response
$3)\overline{17}$	Each student holds up 5 fingers. (*hand signal from leader*) "2 extra"
$6)\overline{27}$	Each student holds up 4 fingers. (*hand signal from leader*) "3 extra"

① Teaching the Lesson

Different Methods to Multiply Hundreds

 30 MINUTES

Goal: Use different methods to multiply hundreds.

Materials: MathBoard Materials, Student Activity Book or Hardcover Book pp. 253–254

 NCTM Standards:
Algebra
Number and Operations
Representation
Communication

Teaching Note

Math Background In previous lessons the students used area models to show multiplication of ones and tens. They will now use area models to represent multiplication with hundreds. Such models are too large to draw on the dot side of the MathBoard, so students will need to make sketches on the white side of the board. Emphasize that it is *not* necessary for the lengths in their drawing to be to scale.

English Language Learners

Write 5 × 700 on the board. Have students tell how to use 5 × 7 to help solve the problem.

• **Beginning** Say: **There are 7 hundreds in 700. 7 hundreds × 5 = 35 hundreds.** Have students repeat.
• **Intermediate** Ask: **How many hundreds in 700?** 7 What is 7 hundreds × 5? 35 hundreds
• **Advanced** Have students work in pairs. One partner writes an expression using a one-digit number × 800. The other tells how to solve it.

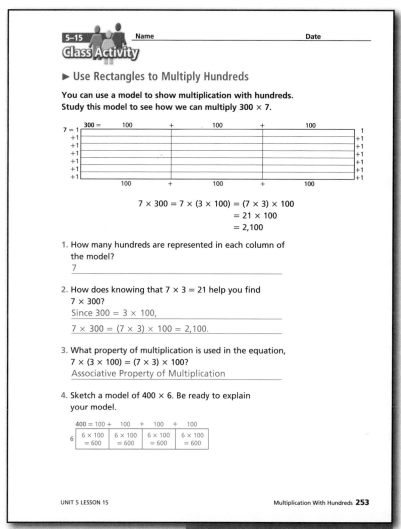

Student Activity Book page 253

▶ Use Rectangles to Multiply Hundreds ‖WHOLE CLASS‖

Use **Solve and Discuss** for 7 × 300.

Direct students to the area model at the top of page 253 of the Student Book. Have students explain what each part of the model represents.

● Each 1 × 100 rectangle represents 100.

● There are 3 hundreds in each row.

● There are 7 hundreds in each column.

Direct students to look at the multiplication below the model. Have students discuss mathematical properties as they relate each of the steps to the model.

● 7 × (3 × 100) is shown by 7 rows with 3 hundreds in each row.

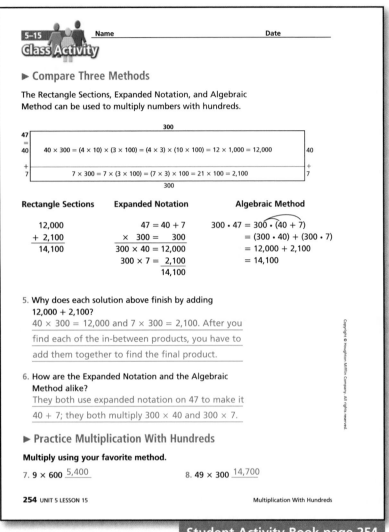

Student Activity Book page 254

Content from the Student Activity Book page:

▶ **Compare Three Methods**

The Rectangle Sections, Expanded Notation, and Algebraic Method can be used to multiply numbers with hundreds.

300

47
=
40 | $40 \times 300 = (4 \times 10) \times (3 \times 100) = (4 \times 3) \times (10 \times 100) = 12 \times 1,000 = 12,000$ | 40
+
7 | $7 \times 300 = 7 \times (3 \times 100) = (7 \times 3) \times 100 = 21 \times 100 = 2,100$ | +
7

300

Rectangle Sections	Expanded Notation	Algebraic Method
12,000	$47 = 40 + 7$	$300 \cdot 47 = 300 \cdot (40 + 7)$
$+\ 2,100$	$\times\quad 300 =\quad 300$	$= (300 \cdot 40) + (300 \cdot 7)$
14,100	$300 \times 40 = 12,000$	$= 12,000 + 2,100$
	$300 \times 7 =\ \underline{2,100}$	$= 14,100$
	14,100	

5. Why does each solution above finish by adding 12,000 + 2,100?
   $40 \times 300 = 12,000$ and $7 \times 300 = 2,100$. After you find each of the in-between products, you have to add them together to find the final product.

6. How are the Expanded Notation and the Algebraic Method alike?
   They both use expanded notation on 47 to make it 40 + 7; they both multiply 300 × 40 and 300 × 7.

▶ **Practice Multiplication With Hundreds**

Multiply using your favorite method.

7. 9 × 600 __5,400__   8. 49 × 300 __14,700__

254 UNIT 5 LESSON 15   Multiplication With Hundreds

The Learning Classroom

Building Concepts Using different methods to solve multiplication of hundreds puts the properties of multiplication to work. The properties that are emphasized in this lesson should be reviewed by writing them on the board and discussing them. They are:

Commutative Property of Multiplication
$a \times b = b \times a$

Associative Property of Multiplication
$a \times (b \times c) = (a \times b) \times c$

Distributive Property of Multiplication
$a \times (b + c) = a \times b + a \times c$

Class Management

Looking Ahead You may wish to collect Student Book page 254 once the lesson is completed. Students will need this page in the next activity and in Lesson 16.

● $(7 \times 3) \times 100$ is shown as the 7-by-3 array of hundreds.

● 21×100 shows there are a total of 21 hundreds.

Discuss questions 1–4.

▶ **Compare Three Methods** WHOLE CLASS

Have students **Solve and Discuss** for 47 × 300.

Direct the students' attention to the description and the rectangle drawing at the top of Student Book page 254.

Ask questions to promote discussion:

● What is similar about this drawing and the drawing for 300 × 7 on page 253? They both use rectangles to represent multiplication.

Activity continued ▶

Teaching the Lesson *(continued)*

Activity 1

 Math Talk in Action

Compare and contrast the three methods: Rectangle Sections, Expanded Notation, and Algebraic Method.

Anna: All three methods work with 47 as 40 + 7. They have 40 × 300 and 7 × 300 as parts of their solutions.

Dmitri: They all end by adding 12,000 plus 2,100.

Mai: Rectangle Sections is the easiest to write because you only add the totals, but you do not need to draw the rectangle.

● **What is different about the two drawings?** There are no small rectangles to represent hundreds, 47 is shown along the side as 40 + 7, 300 is shown as one large rectangle instead of three separate columns, and so on.

● **What multiplications do the two rectangular sections show?** 40 × 300 and 7 × 300

Direct the students to look at the multiplications for 40 × 300 and 7 × 300 inside the area model on page 254. Have the students discuss the equations in each of the rectangles in the model. Emphasize that they do not need to write all of these equations for new problems. They are written for this first problem so we see what the patterns are for the larger multiplications.

Discuss and relate the solution methods shown. See a sample dialogue in Math Talk in Action in the sidebar. Discuss questions 5–6.

Activity 2

Practice Hundreds Multiplication

 25 MINUTES

Goal: Practice multiplication with hundreds.

Materials: Student Activity Book or Hardcover Book p. 254

 NCTM Standards:
Number and Operations
Algebra

Ongoing Assessment

Observe how effectively students work with the multipliers as they **Solve and Discuss** each equation. See that they are able to use expanded notation, group factors to multiply, and record their process step by step.

▶ **Practice Multiplication With Hundreds** WHOLE CLASS

Use **Solve and Discuss** to solve problems 7 and 8 on Student Book page 254.

If time permits, have the students use **Solve and Discuss** for some of the problems below. Remind the students, if necessary, that "5 × even number" problems appear to have an extra zero because the 5s product ends with zero.

6 × 400 = 2,400	700 × 9 = 6,300
58 × 300 = 17,400	500 × 27 = 13,500
34 × 800 = 27,200	400 × 87 = 34,800
23 × 600 = 13,800	500 × 37 = 18,500
49 × 600 = 29,400	500 × 6 = 3,000
700 × 61 = 42,700	500 × 60 = 30,000

② Going Further

Differentiated Instruction

Intervention · Activity Card 5-15

Tens and Hundreds · Activity Card 5-15

Work: In Pairs

Use:
• Index cards

1. On your own, find each product below.

6 × 10 60	6 × 20 120
6 × 100 600	6 × 200 1200
6 × 30 180	6 × 40 240
6 × 300 1800	6 × 400 2400

2. **Explain** What strategies did you use to find each of the products?

3. **Work Together** Make flashcards with similar problems, as shown.

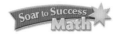

5 × 200	1,000
Front	Back

4. Practice multiplying, using the flash cards.

Unit 5, Lesson 15   Copyright © Houghton Mifflin Company

Activity Note Have students identify patterns in the products. Check that students are using and correctly explaining appropriate strategies.

✐ Math Writing Prompt

Explain Your Thinking Explain to a student who just joined your class how to multiply 8 × 400.

Soar to Success Math ★ Software Support

Use *Soar to Success* for instruction of students needing targeted support for underlying skills.

On Level · Activity Card 5-15

Memory Game · Activity Card 5-15 ▲

Work: In Pairs

Use:
• 20 Index cards

1. Make 10 pairs of game cards. One card in each pair shows a multiplication problem with hundreds, and the other shows the product.

31 × 200	6,200

2. Shuffle the cards, and arrange them face down in a 4-by-5 array.

3. Take turns flipping over two cards. If the cards match, pick them up. If the cards do not match, turn them back over.

4. Continue taking turns until all the cards are matched. The player with more cards is the winner of the memory game.

Unit 5, Lesson 15   Copyright © Houghton Mifflin Company

Activity Note To make the game more challenging, have students make and use more cards, or have four students work together to increase the possible number of matches.

✐ Math Writing Prompt

Area Models Explain how the area model for the product 30 × 200 compares to the area model for 36 × 200.

MegaMath Grades K-6 Software Support

Use *MegaMath* for review and reinforcement of the concepts and skills presented in this lesson.

Challenge · Activity Card 5-15

Look for Patterns · Activity Card 5-15 ■

Work: By Yourself

1. Find each product below.

4 × 4 16	11 × 11 121
4 × 44 176	11 × 11 1121
4 × 444 1,776	11 × 111 1221

2. Identify any patterns you see in the two groups. See below.

3. Write the next problem and its product for each group.
4 × 4,444 = 17,776; 11 × 1,111 = 12,221

2. The two digits of the first product are the first and last digit of each of the other products. Each time a digit is added to a factor, the sum of the digits in the first product is written as a middle digit of the new product.

Unit 5, Lesson 15   Copyright © Houghton Mifflin Company

Activity Note To extend the activity, have students look for and describe other multiplication number patterns.

✐ Math Writing Prompt

Compare Strategies Consider the methods you know for multiplying 52 × 400. Describe the method you think is easiest to use, and explain why you think so.

✸ DESTINATION Math® Software Support

Use *Destination Math* to take students beyond the concepts and skills presented in this lesson.

Multiplication With Hundreds **609**

③ Homework and Spiral Review

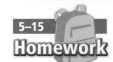

Homework **Goal:** Additional Practice

Use this Homework page to give students more practice multiplying hundreds and solving word problems using multiplication with hundreds.

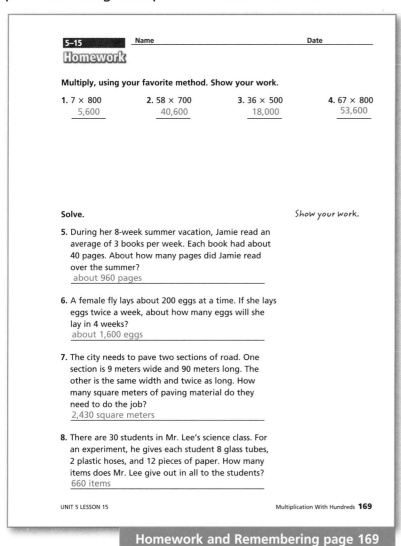

5–15	Name	Date

Homework

Multiply, using your favorite method. Show your work.

1. 7 × 800	2. 58 × 700	3. 36 × 500	4. 67 × 800
5,600	40,600	18,000	53,600

Solve.   *Show your work.*

5. During her 8-week summer vacation, Jamie read an average of 3 books per week. Each book had about 40 pages. About how many pages did Jamie read over the summer?
about 960 pages

6. A female fly lays about 200 eggs at a time. If she lays eggs twice a week, about how many eggs will she lay in 4 weeks?
about 1,600 eggs

7. The city needs to pave two sections of road. One section is 9 meters wide and 90 meters long. The other is the same width and twice as long. How many square meters of paving material do they need to do the job?
2,430 square meters

8. There are 30 students in Mr. Lee's science class. For an experiment, he gives each student 8 glass tubes, 2 plastic hoses, and 12 pieces of paper. How many items does Mr. Lee give out in all to the students?
660 items

UNIT 5 LESSON 15   Multiplication With Hundreds **169**

Homework and Remembering page 169

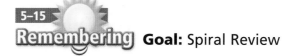

Remembering **Goal:** Spiral Review

This Remembering activity would be appropriate anytime after today's lesson.

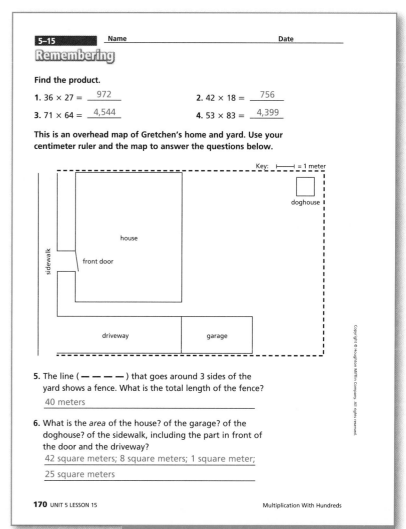

5–15	Name	Date

Remembering

Find the product.

1. 36 × 27 = 972   2. 42 × 18 = 756
3. 71 × 64 = 4,544   4. 53 × 83 = 4,399

This is an overhead map of Gretchen's home and yard. Use your centimeter ruler and the map to answer the questions below.

Key: ├——┤ = 1 meter

doghouse

house

sidewalk

front door

driveway   garage

5. The line (— — —) that goes around 3 sides of the yard shows a fence. What is the total length of the fence?
40 meters

6. What is the *area* of the house? of the garage? of the doghouse? of the sidewalk, including the part in front of the door and the driveway?
42 square meters; 8 square meters; 1 square meter;
25 square meters

170 UNIT 5 LESSON 15   Multiplication With Hundreds

Homework and Remembering page 170

Home or School Activity

Real-World Connection

Food Drive Have students pretend that they are helping organizers of a food drive determine the number of ounces of food a school must collect to be given an award. Tell them that the committee has set a goal of 32 ounces per student. Have them set school goals for schools with an enrollment of 100 students, 200 students, and 300 students.

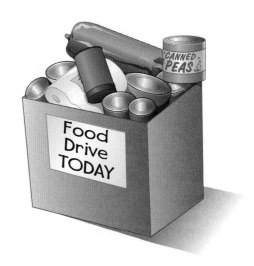

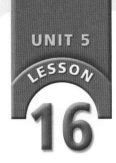

UNIT 5
LESSON
16

Multiplication With Thousands

Lesson Objectives

- Use an area model to represent multiplication with thousands.
- Use several methods to multiply with thousands.

The Day at a Glance

Today's Goals	Materials

① Teaching the Lesson
A1: Model multiplication with thousands.
A2: Multiply with thousands, using several methods
 	
② Going Further
▶ Differentiated Instruction
 	
③ Homework and Spiral Review
	Lesson Activities
	Student Activity Book pp. 255–256
	  or Student Hardcover Book
	  pp. 255–256
	Homework and Remembering
	  pp. 171–172
	MathBoard Materials
	Base-ten blocks (optional)
	Quick Quiz 4 (Assessment Guide)
	
	Going Further
	Activity Cards 5-16
	Product Search
	  (TRB M68)
	Math Journals

123 Use Math Talk today!

Keeping Skills Sharp

Quick Practice 🕐 5 MINUTES

Goal: Practice division with remainders.

Division With Remainders Have four **Student Leaders** go to the board. Each student should write five division problems with remainders. The leaders use pointers to point to each of the problems on their lists. The class holds up fingers to show the factor and then, at a hand signal from the Student Leader, says the amount extra, the remainder.

Problem	Response
4)‾17	Each student holds up 4 fingers. *(hand signal from leader)* "1 extra"
8)‾27	Each student holds up 3 fingers. *(hand signal from leader)* "3 extra"

Daily Routines

Homework Review Ask students if they had difficulty with estimation in the homework. Plan to set aside some time to work with students needing extra help.

Logic Have students use the words *always, sometimes,* or *never* to complete these sentences.

1) If you draw one diagonal line from one corner to another in a rectangle, you will _____ form two triangles. always

2) You can _____ draw three lines of symmetry in an isosceles triangle. sometimes, if the isosceles triangle is also equilateral

① Teaching the Lesson

Model Thousands Multiplication

 30 MINUTES

Goal: Model multiplication with thousands.

Materials: MathBoard Materials, Student Activity Book or Hardcover Book p. 255, base-ten blocks (optional)

 NCTM Standards:
Algebra
Number and Operations
Representation
Communication

 Alternate Approach

Base-ten blocks Use base-ten blocks to show the building of 1 hundred with 10 tens. Then lay out 10 hundred flats to show 1 thousand.

10 tens = one hundred block

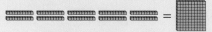

10 hundreds blocks = one thousand

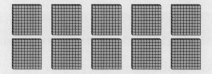

You can stack 10 hundred flats to show a 1 thousand block.

Write on the classroom board:
7 × 3,000

Have students describe how they would use base-ten blocks to model 7 × 3,000.

You would need two more groups of 10 hundred flats to make 3,000. Then you would need seven groups of 3,000.

▶ Visualize Thousands WHOLE CLASS

Write on the classroom board:

7 × 3,000   47 × 3,000

Have the students discuss how these relate to:

7 × 300   47 × 300

The products are 10 times bigger because 3,000 is 10 times bigger than 300.

Ask students to draw an area model of 7 × 3,000 on their MathBoards.

Discuss students' drawings:

● **How is your drawing similar to the rectangle for 7 × 300 that we saw yesterday?** The models should be very similar. They use the same rectangles to represent hundreds and thousands.

● **Does a model for 7 × 3,000 need to be larger than one for 7 × 300?** No, because it is a model that just represents larger numbers.

● **How are the models different?** They are different only in labeling. Thousands are labeled instead of hundreds.

Have a brief discussion with students to compare the length of 100 with 1,000 so that they understand that these really are quite different but that our drawings of these two amounts look similar because we don't want to use up all the paper necessary to really draw 100 or 1,000. Put 2 student MathBoards side by side lengthwise up at the front. Ask students how many squares across the MathBoards are together. There are 50 dots across each MathBoard, so there will be 49 squares on each MathBoard, so there will be 98 squares across. Draw 2 more squares on one of the MathBoards so that there are now 100 squares. This gives one visualization of a length of 100.

Now ask how long 1,000 squares would be. 1,000 would look like ten such pairs of MathBoards overlapping so that the 100 squares were adjacent to each other. Estimate how long ten such pairs are (for example, the width of the classroom). So if we made *actual* drawings of 1 x 1,000 the drawings would be only 1 square tall and the length of the 1,000 just described. This is why our drawings are much different than the real 1 x 1,000 rectangles would be. The drawings are meant to help students think about which numbers they are multiplying and why.

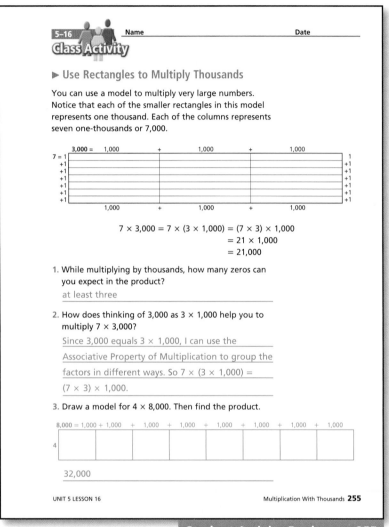

Student Activity Book page 255

▶ Use Rectangles to Multiply Thousands ‖WHOLE CLASS‖

Using **Solve and Discuss**, have students multiply 7 × 3,000.

Direct students' attention to page 255 of the Student Book. Have students compare their models and multiplication with the model and equation at the top of the page.

● How is your model like the model on the page?

● How are your multiplication steps similar to or different from what is shown?

Have students discuss questions 1 and 2. For question 1, discuss the fact that there will be at least three zeros and sometimes four if the product of non-zero digits ends in a zero (for example, 5 × 4,000 = 20,000).

Have students solve problem 3 and then discuss the answers.

❶ Teaching the Lesson (continued)

Multiply Thousands, Using Different Methods

 35 MINUTES

Goal: Multiply with thousands, using several methods.

Materials: Student Activity Book or Hardcover Book p. 256, students' work on Student Book page 254 from Lesson 15

 NCTM Standard:
Number and Operations

 Ongoing Assessment

Use the equation, 62 × 5,000 to check for understanding. Ask individual students to use their preferred method of finding the product. Check to make sure they understand that
62 × 5,000 =
(60 × 5,000) + (2 × 5,000).

 Quick Quiz

See Assessment Guide for Unit 5 Quick Quiz 4.

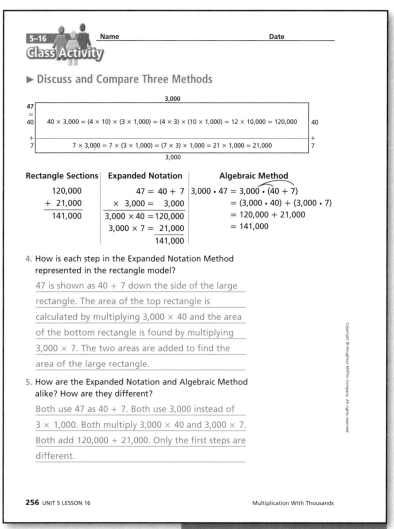

Student Activity Book page 256

► Discuss and Compare Three Methods

WHOLE CLASS   Math Talk

Have students look at the model at the top of Student Book page 256 and compare it with the model showing 47 × 300 on page 254. The students might notice that the large rectangle is split into two smaller rectangles to show 40 and 7 times the number above in both models. However, the numbers being multiplied are different (300 and 3,000). Discuss and compare the three methods used to multiply 47 × 3,000. Have students answer questions 4 and 5 and then share their ideas.

► Practice Multiplication With Thousands WHOLE CLASS

Use **Solve and Discuss** for the exercises below.

6 × 4,000	23 × 6,000	5,000 × 37	58 × 3,000
49 × 6,000	5,000 × 6	7,000 × 61	5,000 × 60

② Going Further

Differentiated Instruction

Intervention   Activity Card 5-16

More Zeros   Activity Card 5-16 ●

Work: By Yourself

1. Look at the area model for 41 × 30 below. Write the partial sums and find the product, using the model.

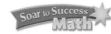

	30
40	40 × 30 = 1,200
+ 1	1 × 30 = 30

2. Draw your own models for the products 41 × 300 and 41 × 3,000.

3. **Analyze** Describe what is the same and what is different about the three products. The non-zero digits are the same, but there are a different number of zeros.

4. Use what you have observed to find the products for 53 × 20, 53 × 200, and 53 × 2,000. 1,060; 10,600; 106,000

Unit 5, Lesson 16   Copyright © Houghton Mifflin Company

Activity Note Check that students are able to follow the pattern in the models when finding the products for the problems with the factor 53.

 Math Writing Prompt

Explain Your Thinking Explain how the products of 5 × 40, 5 × 400, and 5 × 4,000 are related.

Soar to Success Math **Software Support**

Use *Soar to Success* for instruction of students needing targeted support for underlying skills.

On Level   Activity Card 5-16

Product Search   Activity Card 5-16 ▲

Work: By Yourself
Use:
• Product Search (TRB M68)

1. Compute each of the products below, and circle it on the Product Search array. Answers read from left to right and from top to bottom.

5 × 3,000	15 × 2,000	6,000 × 43
29 × 5,000	36 × 7,000	1,000 × 10
89 × 4,000	6 × 2,000	49 × 2,000

5	0	1	2	0	0	0	0
0	1	4	5	0	0	0	3
0	5	0	8	0	0	1	5
0	0	0	0	5	1	9	6
8	0	7	0	6	0	0	0
3	0	0	0	0	0	5	0
1	9	8	0	0	0	4	0
3	4	2	5	2	0	0	0

2. Write two more products that you can find in the array.

Unit 5, Lesson 16   Copyright © Houghton Mifflin Company

Activity Note To extend the activity, students can create their own puzzle array and 9 multiplication problems to exchange with a partner to solve.

 Math Writing Prompt

Make Connections Explain how the product 62 × 400 can be used to solve the problem 62 × 4,000.

MegaMath Grades K-6 **Software Support**

Use *MegaMath* for review and reinforcement of the concepts and skills presented in this lesson.

Challenge   Activity Card 5-16

Multiplication Patterns   Activity Card 5-16 ■

Work: In Pairs

1. Find each pair of products below.
   23 × 2,000 46,000   32 × 2,000 64,000
   12 × 3,000 36,000   21 × 3,000 63,000

2. Identify any patterns you see in the pairs. See below.

3. Find as many other factor pairs as you can that follow this same pattern.

   2. The tens and the ones digits are reversed in the first factor and the ten thousands and thousands place of the product.

Unit 5, Lesson 16   Copyright © Houghton Mifflin Company

Activity Note Challenge students to explain the conditions under which the pattern will occur. All single-digit products of the factors must be less than 10.

 Math Writing Prompt

Write Your Own Write and solve a word problem that can be solved with the product 34 × 6,000.

✻ DESTINATION Math **Software Support**

Use *Destination Math* to take students beyond the concepts and skills presented in this lesson.

③ Homework and Spiral Review

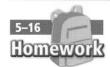

Homework **Goal:** Additional Practice

Use this Homework page to provide students with more practice with multiplying thousands and finding patterns in multiplication.

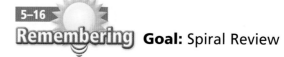

Remembering **Goal:** Spiral Review

This Remembering activity would be appropriate anytime after today's lesson.

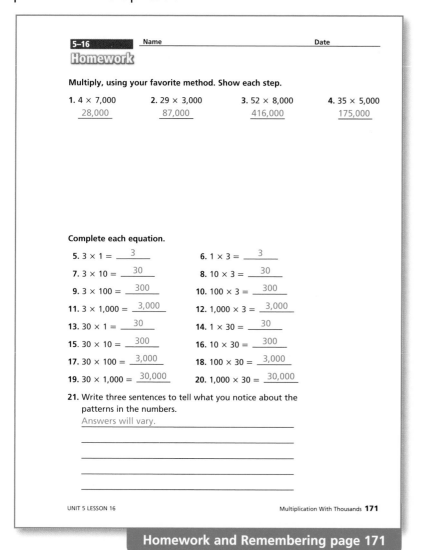

5–16 Name _____ Date _____
Homework

Multiply, using your favorite method. Show each step.

1. 4 × 7,000
28,000

2. 29 × 3,000
87,000

3. 52 × 8,000
416,000

4. 35 × 5,000
175,000

Complete each equation.

5. 3 × 1 = __3__   6. 1 × 3 = __3__

7. 3 × 10 = __30__   8. 10 × 3 = __30__

9. 3 × 100 = __300__   10. 100 × 3 = __300__

11. 3 × 1,000 = __3,000__   12. 1,000 × 3 = __3,000__

13. 30 × 1 = __30__   14. 1 × 30 = __30__

15. 30 × 10 = __300__   16. 10 × 30 = __300__

17. 30 × 100 = __3,000__   18. 100 × 30 = __3,000__

19. 30 × 1,000 = __30,000__   20. 1,000 × 30 = __30,000__

21. Write three sentences to tell what you notice about the patterns in the numbers.
Answers will vary.

UNIT 5 LESSON 16   Multiplication With Thousands **171**

Homework and Remembering page 171

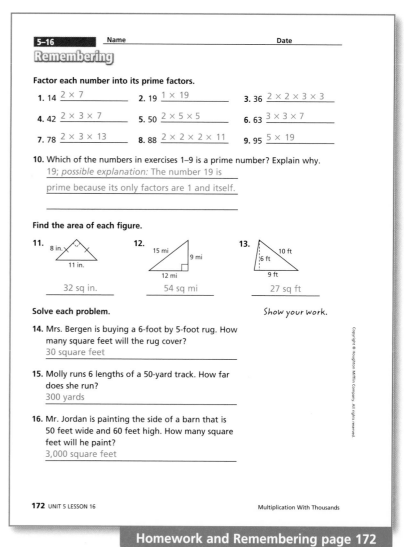

5–16 Name _____ Date _____
Remembering

Factor each number into its prime factors.

1. 14 _2 × 7_   2. 19 _1 × 19_   3. 36 _2 × 2 × 3 × 3_

4. 42 _2 × 3 × 7_   5. 50 _2 × 5 × 5_   6. 63 _3 × 3 × 7_

7. 78 _2 × 3 × 13_   8. 88 _2 × 2 × 2 × 11_   9. 95 _5 × 19_

10. Which of the numbers in exercises 1–9 is a prime number? Explain why.
19; *possible explanation:* The number 19 is prime because its only factors are 1 and itself.

Find the area of each figure.

11. 8 in. / 11 in.
32 sq in.

12. 15 mi / 9 mi / 12 mi
54 sq mi

13. 10 ft / 6 ft / 9 ft
27 sq ft

Solve each problem.   *Show your work.*

14. Mrs. Bergen is buying a 6-foot by 5-foot rug. How many square feet will the rug cover?
30 square feet

15. Molly runs 6 lengths of a 50-yard track. How far does she run?
300 yards

16. Mr. Jordan is painting the side of a barn that is 50 feet wide and 60 feet high. How many square feet will he paint?
3,000 square feet

172 UNIT 5 LESSON 16   Multiplication With Thousands

Homework and Remembering page 172

Home or School Activity

 Real-World Connection

How much does garbage cost? Students can research how much the local garbage company charges for trash pickup for each household in their community. After the data have been collected for each household, students can determine the cost of garbage pickup for 5,000 households. How many groups of 5,000 households are there in the community? What is the real cost of garbage pickup?

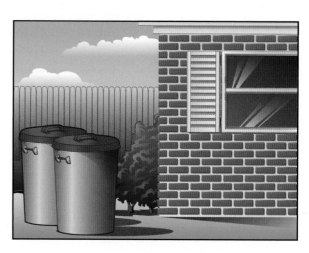

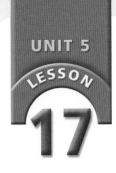

Use Mathematical Processes

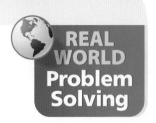

Lesson Objectives

● Solve a variety of problems, using mathematical concepts and skills.

● Use the mathematical processes of problem solving, connections, reasoning and proof, communication, and representation.

The Day at a Glance

Today's Goals	Materials	
1 Teaching the Lesson **A1:** Social Studies Connection Use and make a timeline. **A2:** Reasoning and Proof Use a clue to find the number of pencils in a box. **A3:** Representation Show two ways to cut a square into 8 identical pieces. **A4:** Communication Explain how to use the rectangle method for two-digit by two-digit multiplication. **A5:** Problem Solving Make a decision based on data in a double bar graph.	**Lesson Activities** Student Activity Book or Student Hardcover Book pp. 257–258 Homework and Remembering, pp. 173–174	**Going Further** MathBoard Dot Array (TRB M47) Number cubes Math Journals
2 Going Further ▶ Differentiated Instruction		
3 Homework and Spiral Review		

123 Use Math Talk today!

Keeping Skills Sharp

Quick Practice/Daily Routines	
No Quick Practice or Daily Routines are recommended. If you choose to do some, use activities that meet the needs of your class.	**Class Management** Use this lesson to provide more understanding of the NCTM process standards. Depending upon how you choose to carry out the activities, this lesson may take two or more days of teaching.

1 Teaching the Lesson

Math and Social Studies

🕐 **45 MINUTES**

Goal: Use and make a timeline.

Materials: Student Activity Book or Hardcover Book p. 257

✓ **NCTM Standards:**
Connections   Problem Solving   Representation

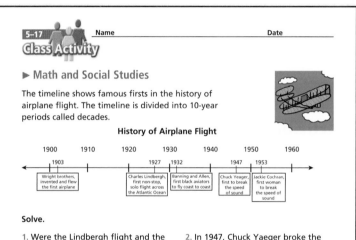

5–17
Class Activity
Name _____ Date _____

▶ Math and Social Studies

The timeline shows famous firsts in the history of airplane flight. The timeline is divided into 10-year periods called decades.

History of Airplane Flight

1900 1910 1920 1930 1940 1950 1960
1903   1927 1932   1947 1953

Wright brothers, invented and flew the first airplane | Charles Lindbergh, first non-stop, solo flight across the Atlantic Ocean | Banning and Allen, first black aviators to fly coast to coast | Chuck Yeager, first to break the speed of sound | Jackie Cochran, first woman to break the speed of sound

Solve.

1. Were the Lindbergh flight and the Banning and Allen flight in the same decade? Explain.
   No, the Lindbergh flight was in the 1920s, the Banning in the 1930s

2. In 1947, Chuck Yeager broke the speed of sound. About how many years before that did Lindbergh make his solo flight?
   about 20 years

3. Before airplanes, people flew in hot-air balloons. On a separate piece of paper, make a timeline to show the events in the table shown.

Event	Year
First hot-air balloon flight	1783
First hot-air balloon flight by a women	1784
First hot-air balloon flight in the United States	1793

4. How many years elapsed between the first hot-air balloon flight and the first airplane flight?
   120 years

5. Write an elapsed-time question that uses data from both timelines. Show the solution to the question.

UNIT 5 LESSON 17   Use Mathematical Processes **257**

Student Activity Book page 257

English Language Learners

Write *decade* and *elapsed* on the board. Draw a timeline 1920–1960. Mark off a decade with an arch. Say: **This is 1 decade.**

• **Beginning** Ask: How many years passed from 1920 to 1930? 10 Say: **10 years elapsed. A decade is 10 years.**
• **Intermediate and Advanced** Ask: How many decades elapsed from 1920 to 1960? 4

▶ **History-of-Airplane-Flight Timeline**   Math Talk 123

Task 1 Ask students when they think people first flew in airplanes. Then have students look at the timeline on Student Book page 257. Discuss the timeline, and be certain students understand that the points on the timeline show the events in the boxes below them.

▶ What does this timeline tell us about the history of flight? Have students share different things they can learn by looking at the timeline.

Give students time to answer questions 1 and 2. Have students share their answers and explain their thought processes.

▶ Create a Hot-Air Balloon Timeline

Task 2 Review question 3 and the table shown. Ask **Student Pairs** to work together to place the information in the table on a timeline. Then have students share their timelines.

▶ Explain how you set your time line up. Some students may have only shown the years from 1780 to 1800; discuss showing every year verses using the scale shown on the History-of-Airplane-Flight scale.

▶ Compare Events on a Timeline

Task 3 Elapsed Time Remind students that *elapsed time* refers to the difference between two time periods. As a class, find the number of years that elapsed between the Wright brothers' flight and today. current year − 1903 = elapsed time

Have students work individually on questions 4 and 5. Then have students share the questions they wrote with the class.

What's in the Salad?

45 MINUTES

Goal: Make a decision based on data in a double bar graph.

Materials: Student Activity Book or Hardcover Book p. 258

 NCTM Standards:
Problem Solving
Communication

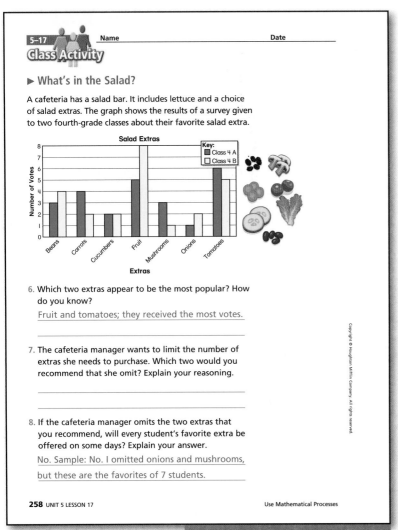

Teaching Note

Salad Bar Data Have students collect data for two groups of people, such as teens and fourth-graders, about what extras they would like in a salad. Ask them to graph the data on a double bar graph or on two single bar graphs. Then have students draw conclusions about the preferences of each group.

▶ Discuss the Bar Graph

Task 1 Begin with a whole-class discussion about the double bar graph.

▶ What do the two bars represent? The opinions of two fourth-grade classes.

▶ Is there another way the data could be presented? If so, what is an advantage of the double bar graph? table, two single bar graphs

Be sure that students understand how to read the graph before they answer question 1 on their own. As a class, review students' answers and rationales.

▶ Make a Decision   Math Talk

Task 2 Defend Your Decision Discuss the situation presented in question 2. Have volunteers explain the meaning of "wants to limit the number of extras she needs to purchase." Talk about some different ways one might decide which salad extras to stop purchasing, based on student preferences. Then have **Student Pairs** work together to answer question 2. When students have completed the question, ask volunteers to share their decisions.

▶ Which ingredients would you omit? Defend your decision.

▶ What Does the Decision Mean?

Task 3 Review question 3, and then have students answer it individually. Discuss the answer.

▶ What additional information might help the cafeteria manager make a decision that would be agreeable to everyone? Sample: She could do a second survey and ask students to choose their second favorite ingredient.

Activity 3

How Many Pencils?

 15 MINUTES

Goal: Use a clue to find the number of pencils in a box.

✔ **NCTM Standards:**
Reasoning and Proof   Problem Solving

A pencil box contains 24 pencils. Some of the pencils have an eraser on them. The box contains 4 more pencils with erasers than without erasers. How many pencils have erasers? **A.** 2 **B.** 6 **C.** 10 **D.** 14

Reasoning and Proof

Ask students to use a strategy to choose the correct answer. First, help students understand that:

total number of pencils (24) = pencils without erasers + (pencils without erasers + 4)

Then discuss how to find the answer.

▶ Which answer did you eliminate first? Why?

▶ Which answer did you eliminate next?

As a class, prove that 14 is the correct answer. $24 = (10 + 4) + 10$; $24 = 14 + 10$; $24 = 24$

Activity 4

Identical Pieces

 15 MINUTES

Goal: Show two ways to cut a square into equal pieces.

✔ **NCTM Standards:**
Representation   Problem Solving

Chan has a 4-foot square board. He will cut it into 8 identical pieces. Show two ways he can cut the board.

Representation

Discuss the problem with the class. Be certain the students understand that *identical* means that each of the 8 pieces will be congruent.

Ask students to go to the board and draw their solutions.

▶ Are there any other ways he can cut the board?

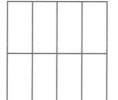 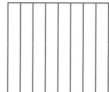 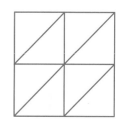

Activity 5

The Rectangle Method of Multiplying

 15 MINUTES

Goal: Explain how to use the rectangle method for two-digit by two-digit multiplication.

✔ **NCTM Standards:**
Communication   Representation

Explain how to use the rectangle method to find the product of 34 × 28.

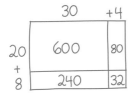

Communication

Have students work with a **Helping Partner** to write an explanation.

Hold a whole-class discussion about the rectangle method. Draw the large rectangle on the board and label it.

▶ What does this represent? the multiplication

▶ How will we divide the numbers 34 and 28? into tens and ones; 30 + 4, 20 + 8

Have volunteers draw and label the smaller rectangles.

▶ Why does the rectangle method work? The sum of the smaller products is equal to the entire product.

② Going Further

Differentiated Instruction

Intervention — Activity Card 5-17

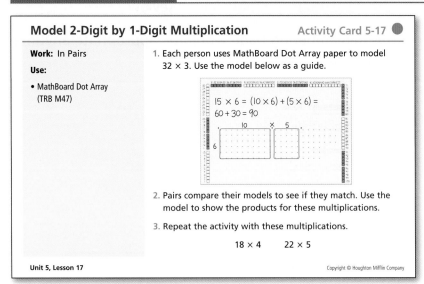

Model 2-Digit by 1-Digit Multiplication   Activity Card 5-17 ●

Work: In Pairs

Use:
- MathBoard Dot Array (TRB M47)

1. Each person uses MathBoard Dot Array paper to model 32 × 3. Use the model below as a guide.

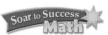

$15 \times 6 = (10 \times 6) + (5 \times 6) =$
$60 + 30 = 90$

2. Pairs compare their models to see if they match. Use the model to show the products for these multiplications.

3. Repeat the activity with these multiplications.

18 × 4   22 × 5

Unit 5, Lesson 17   Copyright © Houghton Mifflin Company

Activity Note It may be helpful to go over the model shown before students start the activity.

✎ Math Writing Prompt

Explain Your Thinking A student represented 23 as 20 + 3. Is this correct? Explain why or why not.

Soar to Success Math **Software Support**

Use *Soar to Success* for instruction of students needing targeted support for underlying skills.

On Level — Activity Card 5-17

Roll a Multiplication   Activity Card 5-17 ▲

Work: In Pairs

Use:
- 2 Number cubes, labeled 1–6

1. Each partner rolls the number cubes once and records the numbers rolled.

First Roll	Second Roll	Multiplication
3, 5	4, 1	15 × 34

2. Use the four numbers, in any combination, to write a two-digit by two-digit multiplication.

3. Each partner uses a different method to calculate the product. Then partners compare their answers.

4. Combine the digits in as many different ways as possible to find other products.

Unit 5, Lesson 17   Copyright © Houghton Mifflin Company

Activity Note Be certain students understand that the numbers rolled can be combined in any manner, not necessarily in the order rolled.

✎ Math Writing Prompt

Write a Word Problem Ask students to choose one of the multiplication problems they wrote and use it to write a word problem.

MegaMath **Software Support**

Use *MegaMath* for review and reinforcement of the concepts and skills presented in this lesson.

Challenge — Activity Card 5-17

Multiply Thousands   Activity Card 5-17 ■

Work: In Pairs

Use:
- 3 Number cubes, labeled 1–6

1. One partner rolls the numbers cubes. The other partner records the numbers rolled.

2. One partner chooses one of the numbers to use for thousands.

3. The other partner uses the other two numbers to make a two-digit multiplier, as shown in the sample.

Numbers rolled: 4, 2, 6
Multiplication: 2,000 × 46

4. Partners use any method to find the product, and then they compare their answers.

Unit 5, Lesson 17   Copyright © Houghton Mifflin Company

Activity Note Check to be sure that students understand how to use the numbers they roll to produce two factors.

✎ Math Writing Prompt

Use a Model Have students draw an area model that shows 5,000 × 4. Then students write an explanation of the model as if they were teaching it to someone.

 DESTINATION Math **Software Support**

Use *Destination Math* to take students beyond the concepts and skills presented in this lesson.

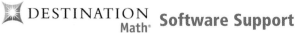
Use Mathematical Processes   **621**

③ Homework and Spiral Review

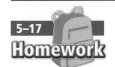

Homework Goal: Additional Practice

✓ Include students' completed Homework page 173 as part of their portfolios.

Remembering Goal: Spiral Review

This Remembering page would be appropriate anytime after today's lesson.

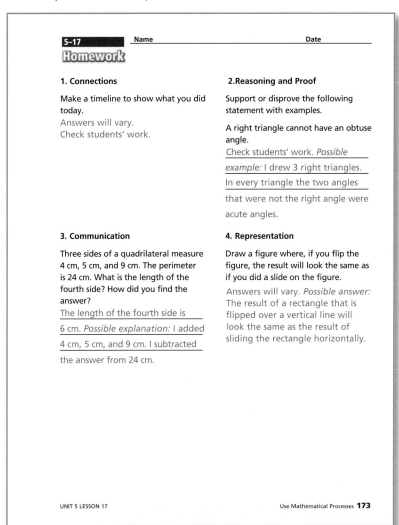

5–17   Name   Date

Homework

1. Connections

Make a timeline to show what you did today.
Answers will vary.
Check students' work.

2. Reasoning and Proof

Support or disprove the following statement with examples.

A right triangle cannot have an obtuse angle.

Check students' work. *Possible example:* I drew 3 right triangles. In every triangle the two angles that were not the right angle were acute angles.

3. Communication

Three sides of a quadrilateral measure 4 cm, 5 cm, and 9 cm. The perimeter is 24 cm. What is the length of the fourth side? How did you find the answer?

The length of the fourth side is 6 cm. *Possible explanation:* I added 4 cm, 5 cm, and 9 cm. I subtracted the answer from 24 cm.

4. Representation

Draw a figure where, if you flip the figure, the result will look the same as if you did a slide on the figure.

Answers will vary. *Possible answer:* The result of a rectangle that is flipped over a vertical line will look the same as the result of sliding the rectangle horizontally.

UNIT 5 LESSON 17   Use Mathematical Processes **173**

Homework and Remembering page 173

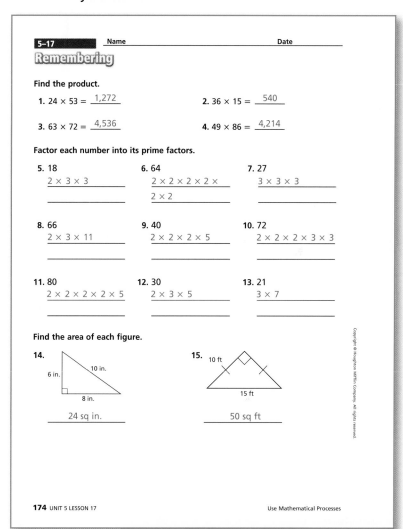

5–17   Name   Date

Remembering

Find the product.

1. $24 \times 53 =$ 1,272   2. $36 \times 15 =$ 540

3. $63 \times 72 =$ 4,536   4. $49 \times 86 =$ 4,214

Factor each number into its prime factors.

5. 18 $2 \times 3 \times 3$

6. 64 $2 \times 2 \times 2 \times 2 \times 2 \times 2$

7. 27 $3 \times 3 \times 3$

8. 66 $2 \times 3 \times 11$

9. 40 $2 \times 2 \times 2 \times 5$

10. 72 $2 \times 2 \times 2 \times 3 \times 3$

11. 80 $2 \times 2 \times 2 \times 2 \times 5$

12. 30 $2 \times 3 \times 5$

13. 21 3×7

Find the area of each figure.

14.

6 in.   10 in.   8 in.

24 sq in.

15.

10 ft   15 ft

50 sq ft

174 UNIT 5 LESSON 17   Use Mathematical Processes

Homework and Remembering page 174

Home or School Activity

 ## Social Studies Connection

Make a Timeline Have students do research about their community, their school, or their family to identify years when significant events occurred. Have them create a timeline to show the sequence of these events.

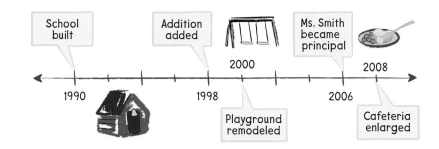

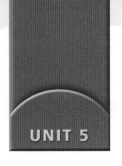

Unit Review and Test

Lesson Objective

● Assess student progress on unit objectives.

The Day at a Glance

Today's Goals	Materials
1 Assessing the Unit ▸ Assess student progress on unit objectives. ▸ Use activities from unit lessons to reteach content. **2 Extending the Assessment** ▸ Use remediation for common errors. There is no homework assignment on a test day.	Unit 5 Test, Student Activity Book or Student Hardcover Book pp. 259–260 Unit 5 Test, Form A or B, Assessment Guide (optional) Unit 5 Performance Assessment, Assessment Guide (optional)

Keeping Skills Sharp

Quick Practice ⏱ 5 MINUTES	
Goal: Review any skills you choose to meet the needs of your class. If you are doing a unit review day, use any of the Quick Practice activities that provide support for your class. If this is a test day, omit Quick Practice.	**Review and Test Day** You may want to choose a quiet game or other activity (reading a book or working on homework for another subject) for students who finish early.

Assessing the Unit

Assess Unit Objectives

🕐 **45 MINUTES** (more if schedule permits)

Goal: Assess student progress on unit objectives.

Materials: Student Activity Book or Hardcover Book pp. 259–260; Assessment Guide (optional)

▶ Review and Assessment

If your students are ready for assessment on the unit objectives, you may use either the test on the Student Book pages or one of the forms of the Unit 5 Test in the Assessment Guide to assess student progress.

If you feel that students need some review first, you may use the test on the Student Book pages as a review of unit content, and then use one of the forms of the Unit 5 Test in the Assessment Guide to assess student progress.

To assign a numerical score for all of these test forms, use 10 points for each question.

You may also choose to use the Unit 5 Performance Assessment. Scoring for that assessment can be found in its rubric in the Assessment Guide.

▶ Reteach Resources

The chart at the right lists the test items, the unit objectives they cover, and the lesson activities in which the objective is covered in this unit. You may revisit these activities with students who do not show mastery of the objectives.

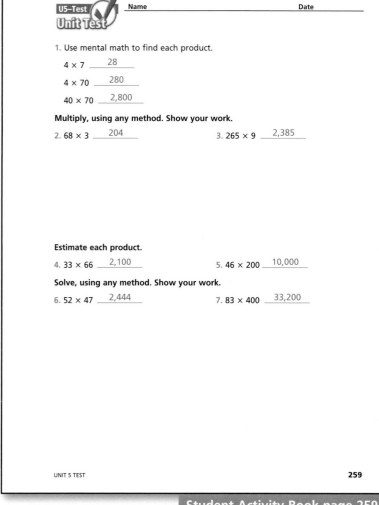

U5–Test ✓ **Unit Test**

Name _____ Date _____

1. Use mental math to find each product.

    4 × 7 ____28____

    4 × 70 ____280____

    40 × 70 ____2,800____

Multiply, using any method. Show your work.

2. 68 × 3 ____204____   3. 265 × 9 ____2,385____

Estimate each product.

4. 33 × 66 ____2,100____   5. 46 × 200 ____10,000____

Solve, using any method. Show your work.

6. 52 × 47 ____2,444____   7. 83 × 400 ____33,200____

UNIT 5 TEST   259

Student Activity Book page 259

Unit Test Items	Unit Objectives Tested	Activities to Use for Reteaching
1	**5.1** Solve multiplication problems, using mental math.	Lesson 2, Activity 1
2–3	**5.2** Multiply by a one-digit number.	Lesson 3, Activities 1–2 Lesson 5, Activities 1–2 Lesson 6, Activity 1 Lesson 7, Activity 1 Lesson 8, Activity 1
4–5	**5.3** Estimate products.	Lesson 4, Activity 1 Lesson 8, Activity 3 Lesson 13, Activity 2

Student Activity Book page 260

The worksheet shows:

U5–Test
Unit Test

Name _____ Date _____

Solve each problem. List any extra numerical information.

Show your work.

8. The fourth grade is collecting cans for a recycling center. There are 28 students in one class and 25 in another. Each student is asked to collect 15 cans. How many cans will these two classes collect in all?

   795 cans, no extra information

9. A family spent 7 hours at the zoo. They bought 2 adult tickets for $20 each and 3 child tickets for $10 each. They bought lunch for $23. How much did the tickets cost?

   $70; extra information: 7 hours, $23

10. **Extended Response** Sketch an area model for the product 23 × 6.

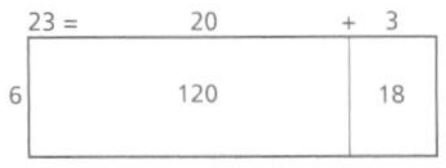

23 =	20	+ 3
6	120	18

    Explain how the area model you drew helps you to solve the multiplication problem 23 × 6.

    6 × 20 = 120; 6 × 3 = 18; 120 + 18 = 138

    _____
    _____
    _____
    _____
    _____

    * Item 10 also assesses the process skills of Representation, Connections, and Communication.

260 UNIT 5 TEST

Unit Test Items	Unit Objectives Tested	Activities to Use for Reteaching
6–7, 10	**5.4** Multiply by a two-digit number.	Lesson 11, Activities 1–2 Lesson 12, Activities 1–2 Lesson 15, Activity 1 Lesson 17, Activity 5
8–9	**5.5** Solve multistep word problems and problems with too much information.	Lesson 9, Activity 1 Lesson 10, Activity 1

▶ Assessment Resources

Free Response Tests
Unit 5 Test, Student Activity Book or Hardcover Book pp. 259–260
Unit 5 Test, Form A, Assessment Guide

Extended Response Item
The last item in the Student Book test and in the Form A test will require an extended response as an answer.

Multiple Choice Test
Unit 5 Test, Form B, Assessment Guide

Performance Assessment
Unit 5 Performance Assessment, Assessment Guide
Unit 5 Performance Assessment Rubric, Assessment Guide

▶ Portfolio Assessment

Teacher-selected Items for Student Portfolios:

- Homework, Lessons 3, 5, 8, 10, and 17
- Class Activity work, Lessons 4 and 12.

Student-selected Items for Student Portfolios

- Favorite Home or School Activity that shows critical thinking or research
- Best Writing Prompt

② Extending the Assessment

Unit Objective 5.1
Solve multiplication problems, using mental math.

Common Error: Always Uses Paper and Pencil

Students do not try to look for patterns.

Remediation: Give students oral practice multiplying numbers such as 4 × 6, 4 × 60, and 4 × 600.

Unit Objective 5.2
Multiply by a one-digit number.

Common Error: Forgets to Use Regrouping

For example, in the product 54 × 7, the product of 4 × 7 is 28, or 2 tens and 8 ones. Students may write the 8 in the answer and then multiply 5 × 7 and get 358 for an answer instead of 378. They may forget to regroup 28.

Remediation: This error is more likely when students are using the Shortcut Method. Ask them to choose another method (Rectangle Sections is often viewed by students as the easiest) in which they write the full product each time.

Common Error: Does Not Multiply Every Digit of the Multiplicand by the Multiplier

For example, students may multiply by the ones and hundreds, but neglect to multiply by the tens.

Remediation: Rewrite the product

in Algebraic Notation and draw arrows showing that the number outside the parentheses must be multiplied by each number inside the parentheses.

Unit Objective 5.3
Estimate products.

Common Error: Makes Rounding Errors Before Multiplying

Students may not round up when the last digit is equal to or greater than 5.

Remediation: Draw rectangles on dot paper and draw rounding frames. Ask students whether the length of the rectangle is closer to the length of the smaller or larger rounding frame.

Common Error: Finds an Exact Answer and Rounds the Answer

Instead of estimating by rounding the factors and multiplying the rounded factors, students find the exact answer and then round the product.

Remediation: Ask students to round each factor and write the estimate next to the factor. Then have them use the rounded numbers to multiply.

Unit Objective 5.4
Multiply by a two-digit number.

Common Error: Does Not Align Steps in Shortcut Method Correctly

When students use the Shortcut Method, they may write each product directly under the previous product.

Remediation: Show students the Rectangle Sections Method so that they understand that each product they write represents a section of the area of the rectangle. If students understand the area model, the Shortcut Method should make more sense to them, and incorrect attempts at using the method should be lessened. Some students should wait until Grade 5 or later to use the Shortcut Method because of its complexity.

Unit Objective 5.5
Solve multistep word problems and problems with too much information.

Common Error: Unable to Identify Relevant Information

Students may not be able to identify which information is needed to answer the question.

Remediation: Have students first identify what they need to find. Then have them go back to the beginning of the problem and circle the information they need, and cross out the information they don't need.

Common Error: Difficulty With Multistep Problems

Students may not be able to figure out how to start solving the problem.

Remediation: Have students act out the problem, make a math drawing, or write some new number they can find from the information in the problem.

The Metric Measurement System

UNIT 6 BUILDS on students' understanding of the base-ten structure of the place-value system to help them understand the metric system of measurement. This system of measurement is an important focus, as it is the system of measurement used in the sciences. It is also the everyday system of measurement used in almost all other countries in the world. Frequent exposure to metric units will help students think about measurement in the metric system.

Skills Trace

Grade 3	Grade 4	Grade 5
• Convert among metric units of length, capacity and mass.	• Convert among metric measures of length, capacity, and mass.	• Convert among metric measures of length, capacity, and mass.
• Choose the appropriate measurement.	• Choose the appropriate unit of metric measure.	• Choose the appropriate unit of metric measure.
• Solve problems involving metric measurements.	• Solve problems involving metric measurements.	• Solve problems involving metric measurements.
	• Explore metric units of volume.	• Relate length, area, and volume.

Unit 6   Contents

Big Idea **Base-Ten Relationships Among Metric Units**

REAL WORLD Problem Solving

Unit 6 Assessment

✓ Unit Objectives Tested	Unit Test Items	Lessons
6.1 Convert between metric measures	5–6	1, 2, 3, 4
6.2 Solve problems involving metric measurements.	9–10	1, 2, 3, 4, 5
6.3 Choose the appropriate unit of metric measure. (length, capacity, mass, temperature, volume)	1–4	1, 5

Assessment and Review Resources

Formal Assessment

Student Activity Book
- Unit Review and Test (pp. 277–278)

Assessment Guide
- Quick Quiz
- Test A–Open Response
- Test B–Multiple Choice
- Performance Assessment

Test Generator CD–ROM
- Open Response Test
- Multiple Choice Test
- Test Bank Items

Informal Assessment

Teacher Edition
- Ongoing Assessment (in every lesson)
- Quick Practice (in every lesson)
- Math Talk (in every lesson)
- Portfolio Suggestions (pp. 642, 650, 662)

(123) **Math Talk**
- ▸ The Learning Classroom (pp. 640, 645)
- ▸ Math Talk in Action (p. 644)
- ▸ Activities (pp. 629, 631, 639, 646, 653, 658, 659)
- ▸ Solve and Discuss (p. 658)
- ▸ Student Pairs (pp. 637, 640, 644, 658)
- ▸ Small Groups (pp. 647, 648, 652, 654, 658, 659, 660)
- ▸ Scenarios (p. 640)

Review Opportunities

Homework and Remembering
- Review of recently taught topics
- Cumulative Review

Teacher Edition
- Unit Review and Test (pp. 663–666)

Test Generator CD-ROM
- Custom review sheets

Planning Unit 6

NCTM Standards Key: 1. Number and Operations 2. Algebra 3. Geometry
4. Measurement 5. Data Analysis and Probability 6. Problem Solving
7. Reasoning and Proof 8. Communication 9. Connections 10. Representation

Lesson/NCTM Standards	Resources	Materials for Lesson Activities	Materials for Other Activities
6–1 **Measure Length and Distance** NCTM Standards: 3, 4, 7, 10	TE pp. 627–634 SAB pp. 261–266 H&R pp. 175–176 AC 6-1	Make a Meter (TRB M69) Scissors Tape or glue stick Pen, new pencil, and short crayon Metric rulers (optional) Overhead projector Geometry and Measurement Poster (optional)	Metric Cards (TRB M70) Meter strips (from Activity 1) or metric rulers Scissors Math Journals
6–2 **Measure Area** NCTM Standards: 4, 6	TE pp. 635–642 SAB pp. 267–270 H&R pp. 177–178 AC 6-2	Centimeter-Grid Paper (TRB M60) Meter strips (from Lesson 1) or metric rulers Sheet protectors, dry-erase markers String (optional)	Centimeter-Grid Paper (TRB M60) Meter strips (from Lesson 1) Yardsticks Newspapers, tape, scissors Math Journals
6–3 **Measure Volume and Capacity** NCTM Standard: 4	TE pp. 643–650 SAB pp. 271–272 H&R pp. 179–180 AC 6-3	Centimeter-Grid Paper (TRB M60) Make a Cubic Centimeter (TRB M71) (optional) Centimeter cubes Scissors Clear tape or glue Metric strips (from Lesson 1) or metric rulers Half-gallon milk or juice carton (optional) 1-L soda or water bottle	Centimeter cubes Meter strips (from Lesson 1) Scissors Box-shaped objects Math Journals
6–4 **Measure Mass** NCTM Standards: 4, 5	TE pp. 651–656 SAB pp. 273–274 H&R pp. 181–182 AC 6-4	Balance scales Metric weights or common objects with a mass of about one gram Meter strips from Lesson 1 or metric rulers	Metric Mass Unit Cards (TRB M72) Balance scales Quart or liter bottle of liquid Various classroom objects Math Journals
6–5 **Measure Temperature** NCTM Standard: 4	TE pp. 657–662 SAB pp. 275–276 H&R pp. 183–184 AG Quick Quiz AC 6-5	Transparency of Celsius and Fahrenheit Temperatures (TRB M73) Temperature Pairs (TRB M74) Calculators (optional) Sheet protectors, dry-erase markers	Temperature Pairs (TRB M74) Scissors Calculators Math Journals
Unit Review and Test	TE pp. 663–666 SAB pp. 277–278 AG: Unit 6 tests		

Resources/Materials Key: TE: Teacher Edition SAB: Student Activity Book H&R: Homework and Remembering
AC: Activity Cards MCC: Math Center Challenge AG: Assessment Guide ✓: Grade 4 Kits TRB: Teacher's Resource Book

Hardcover Student Book

Together, the hardcover student book and its companion Activity Workbook contain all the pages in the consumable Student Activity Workbook.

Manipulatives and Materials

- Essential materials for teaching Math Expressions are available in the Grade 4 Kit. These materials are indicated by a ✓ in these lists. At the front of this Teacher Edition is more information about kit contents, alternatives for the materials, and use of the materials.

Differentiated Instruction

Individualizing Instruction

	Level	Frequency
Activities	• Intervention • On Level • Challenge	All 3 in every lesson
	Level	Frequency
Math Writing Prompts	• Intervention • On Level • Challenge	All 3 in every lesson
Math Center Challenges	For advanced students	
	4 in every unit	

Reaching All Learners

	Lessons	Pages
English Language Learners	1, 2, 3, 4, 5	627, 635, 643, 651, 657
Extra Help	Lesson	Page
	1	628
Special Needs	Lesson	Page
	2	637
Advanced Learners	Lessons	Pages
	2, 5	638, 660

Strategies for English Language Learners

Present this problem to all students. Offer the different levels of support to meet students' levels of language proficiency.

Objective Identify measurement tools and what they are used for.

Problem Draw a ruler, a scale, and a thermometer on the board. Ask: **What are these?** Label each as students name them. Ask: **Which do I use to measure?** *Possible answers:* Measure my height, my weight, or how warm it is outside.

Newcomer

• Point to the measurement tools. Say: **Let's name the measurement tools.** Provide measurement tool names as needed.

Beginning

• Point to the measurement tools and name them. Say: **We use a ruler to measure length. We use a scale to measure weight or mass. We use a thermometer to measure temperature.** Have students repeat.

Intermediate

• Point to the measurement tools. Ask: **Which do I use to measure my height?** ruler **Which do I use to measure my weight?** scale **Which do I use to find out how warm it is outside?** thermometer

Advanced

• Have students give their own example of what they could measure using each of the measurement tools.

Connections

Science Connection
Lesson 4, page 656

Social Studies Connections
Lesson 2, page 642
Lesson 5, page 662

Real-World Connection
Lesson 3, page 650

Independent Learning Activities

Ready-Made Math Challenge Centers

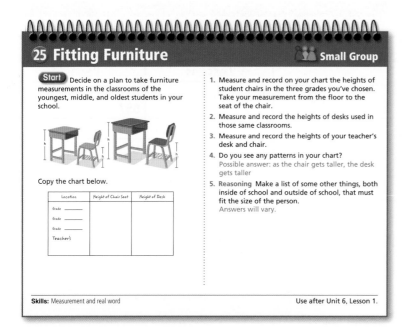

25 Fitting Furniture — Small Group

Start Decide on a plan to take furniture measurements in the classrooms of the youngest, middle, and oldest students in your school.

Copy the chart below.

Location	Height of Chair Seat	Height of Desk
Grade ____		
Grade ____		
Grade ____		
Teacher's		

1. Measure and record on your chart the heights of student chairs in the three grades you've chosen. Take your measurement from the floor to the seat of the chair.
2. Measure and record the heights of desks used in those same classrooms.
3. Measure and record the heights of your teacher's desk and chair.
4. Do you see any patterns in your chart? Possible answer: as the chair gets taller, the desk gets taller
5. **Reasoning** Make a list of some other things, both inside of school and outside of school, that must fit the size of the person. Answers will vary.

Skills: Measurement and real word — Use after Unit 6, Lesson 1.

Grouping Small Groups

Materials Meter sticks, measuring tapes

Objective Students compare measurements to begin to form ideas about proportion.

Connections Measurement and Real World

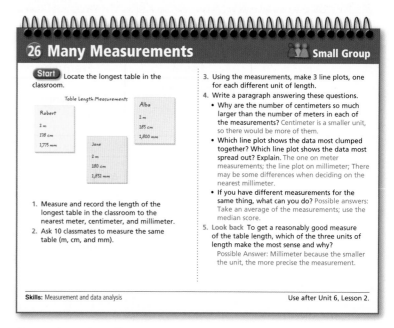

26 Many Measurements — Small Group

Start Locate the longest table in the classroom.

Table Length Measurements

Robert
2 m
178 cm
1,775 mm

Alba
2 m
185 cm
1,800 mm

Jane
2 m
180 cm
1,852 mm

1. Measure and record the length of the longest table in the classroom to the nearest meter, centimeter, and millimeter.
2. Ask 10 classmates to measure the same table (m, cm, and mm).
3. Using the measurements, make 3 line plots, one for each different unit of length.
4. Write a paragraph answering these questions.
   • Why are the number of centimeters so much larger than the number of meters in each of the measurements? Centimeter is a smaller unit, so there would be more of them.
   • Which line plot shows the data most clumped together? Which line plot shows the data most spread out? Explain. The one on meter measurements; the line plot on millimeter; There may be some differences when deciding on the nearest millimeter.
   • If you have different measurements for the same thing, what can you do? Possible answers: Take an average of the measurements; use the median score.
5. **Look back** To get a reasonably good measure of the table length, which of the three units of length make the most sense and why? Possible Answer: Millimeter because the smaller the unit, the more precise the measurement.

Skills: Measurement and data analysis — Use after Unit 6, Lesson 2.

Grouping Small Groups

Materials Rulers, meter sticks, m/cm/mm tape measures

Objective Students learn that the more precise a measurement, the more deviation in the results.

Connections Measurement and Data

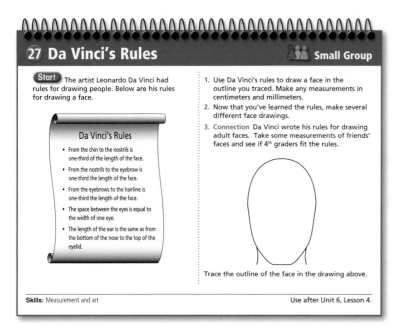

27 Da Vinci's Rules — Small Group

Start The artist Leonardo Da Vinci had rules for drawing people. Below are his rules for drawing a face.

Da Vinci's Rules
• From the chin to the nostrils is one-third of the length of the face.
• From the nostrils to the eyebrow is one-third the length of the face.
• From the eyebrows to the hairline is one-third the length of the face.
• The space between the eyes is equal to the width of one eye.
• The length of the ear is the same as from the bottom of the nose to the top of the eyelid.

1. Use Da Vinci's rules to draw a face in the outline you traced. Make any measurements in centimeters and millimeters.
2. Now that you've learned the rules, make several different face drawings.
3. **Connection** Da Vinci wrote his rules for drawing adult faces. Take some measurements of friends' faces and see if 4th graders fit the rules.

Trace the outline of the face in the drawing above.

Skills: Measurement and art — Use after Unit 6, Lesson 4.

Grouping Small Groups

Materials Tracing paper

Objective Students use measurement proportions for drawing the human face.

Connections Measurement and Art

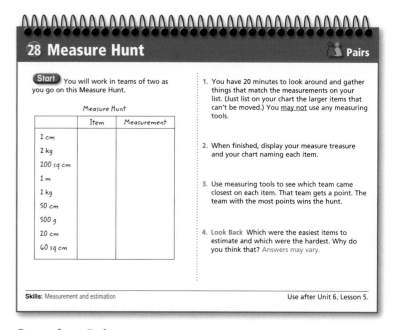

28 Measure Hunt — Pairs

Start You will work in teams of two as you go on this Measure Hunt.

Measure Hunt

Item	Measurement
1 cm	
2 kg	
200 sq cm	
1 m	
1 kg	
50 cm	
500 g	
20 cm	
60 sq cm	

1. You have 20 minutes to look around and gather things that match the measurements on your list. (Just list on your chart the larger items that can't be moved.) You may not use any measuring tools.
2. When finished, display your measure treasure and your chart naming each item.
3. Use measuring tools to see which team came closest on each item. That team gets a point. The team with the most points wins the hunt.
4. **Look Back** Which were the easiest items to estimate and which were the hardest. Why do you think that? Answers may vary.

Skills: Measurement and estimation — Use after Unit 6, Lesson 5.

Grouping Pairs

Materials Classroom objects

Objective Students use their knowledge of linear and mass measurement to estimate common objects.

Connections Measurement and Estimation

Ready-Made Math Resources

Technology — Tutorials, Practice, and Intervention

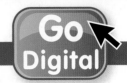

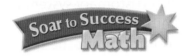

Use activity masters and online, individualized intervention and support to bring students to proficiency.

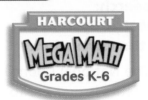

Help students practice skills and apply concepts through exciting math adventures.

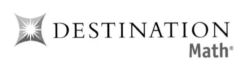

Extend and enrich students' understanding of skills and concepts through engaging, interactive lessons and activities.

Visit **Education Place**®
www.eduplace.com

Visit www.eduplace.com/mx2t/ and find family, teacher, and student materials, activities, games, and more.

Literature Links

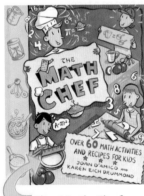

The Math Chef

The Math Chef
Children will learn about metric and customary measurement in this book of recipes written by Joan D'Amico and Karen Eich Drummond. The recipes include everything from cherry-baked apples to tortilla 'n' cheese fiesta salad! Included in the math activities that follow each recipe.

Math Background

Putting Research into Practice for Unit 6

From Current Research:
The Role of the Metric System of Measurement in the Curriculum

In March of 2000, The National Council of Teachers of Mathematics issued the following position statement on Metrication.

Position

The National Council of Teachers of Mathematics recommends the use of the metric system as the primary measurement system in mathematics instruction.

Background and Rationale

Measurement is a common daily activity performed throughout the world and in all sectors of society. As a well-conceived, logical system of units, the metric system provides models that reinforce concepts and skills involving numeration, decimal relationships, and estimation, connecting mathematics to the rest of the pre-K–12 curriculum. For example:

- Conversion between metric units is facilitated by the decimal nature and consistent prefixes of the system, which lead to a high degree of accuracy in measurements.
- Units for volume, capacity, and mass are interrelated (for example, one cubic decimeter of water, which is one liter, has a mass of one kilogram).

On an international level in the scientific and industrial worlds, the metric system is the standard system of measurement. Canada adopted the metric system long ago and immediately mandated that all school curricula use the metric system exclusively. To compete in a world that already functions with this system, our students also need to be competent with the metric system.

Recommendations

- Given that the English customary system is well established in the United States and that the metric system is used throughout the rest of the world, the pre-K–12 curriculum should include both systems.
- For all teachers to become proficient with the metric system, professional development and support will be necessary and should be provided.
- All mathematics educators should assume responsibility for providing leadership and direction in metrication by integrating it into the entire curriculum at every grade level.

Other Useful References:
Metric Measurement

National Council of Teachers of Mathematics. *Principles and Standards for School Mathematics* (Measurement Standard for Grades 3–5). Reston: NCTM, 2000.

Van de Walle, John A. "Measuring Area." *Elementary and Middle School Mathematics: Teaching Developmentally.* 4th ed. New York: Addison, 2001. pp. 284–287.

Van de Walle, John A. "Measuring Volume and Capacity." *Elementary and Middle School Mathematics: Teaching Developmentally.* 4th ed. New York: Addison, 2001. pp. 287–288.

Van de Walle, John A. "Measuring Weight and Mass." *Elementary and Middle School Mathematics: Teaching Developmentally.* 4th ed. New York: Addison, 2001. pp. 288–289.

Getting Ready to Teach Unit 6

Metric Units of Measurement

Do as much of this unit as is necessary to meet important state and district goals. You may choose to just focus on a few core concepts like metric length and area.

Base Units of Measurement

Metric units are derived from the base units: meters, liters, and grams. Prefixes are used to name bigger and smaller units. Emphasis is placed on the metric units that are most commonly used in everyday life around the world and units with which students may already be familiar. For example, students may know about 2-L bottles or 10-km Olympic races or outdoor thermometers that display temperatures in Celsius degrees.

Units of Length or Distance and Derived Units

Lessons 1 and 2

Common benchmarks can help students have a feel for the sizes of metric units. One meter is a little more than one yard. Things that are typically measured in yards, such as lengths of rope and heights of mountains, are also measured in meters. Bigger lengths, such as distances between cities, are measured in kilometers. Smaller lengths, such as the length of a pencil, are measured in centimeters, and very small lengths are measured in millimeters.

Just as area can be measured in square inches, square feet, square yards, and square miles, area in the metric system can be measured in square centimeters, square meters, and square kilometers. Volume in the metric system is measured in cubic units, such as cubic centimeters or cubic meters.

Math Expressions Vocabulary

As you teach this unit, emphasize understanding of these terms.

- Celsius
- cubic unit
- metric system
- millimeter
- volume

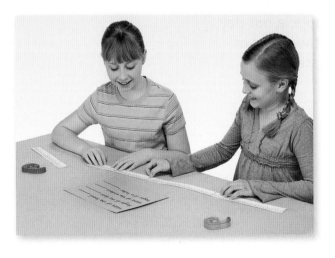

Units of Capacity

Lesson 3

Capacity is a measure of volume usually associated with liquids or with containers that hold liquids. One liter is a little more than one quart. Bottled water, juices, and carbonated drinks often come in one-liter or two-liter containers. Smaller quantities of liquids are typically labeled in milliliters. Milliliters and grams are used in this country for prescriptions.

Units of Mass (or Weight)

Lesson 4

Weight is dependent on the effects of gravity, but mass is a measurement independent of gravity. A person who weighs 150 pounds on Earth weighs less on the moon, but still has the same mass. Because we all live on Earth, we sometimes talk in everyday terms about something "weighing 100 grams." One gram is a very small unit. A paper clip or peanut has a mass of about one gram.

The metric system unifies all of these units. One milliliter of water has a mass of one gram and occupies a volume of one cubic centimeter.

Units of Temperature

Lesson 5

By definition, water boils at 100°C and freezes at 0°C. There are conversion equations for changing Fahrenheit temperatures to Celsius and vice versa. However, they are not easy to calculate mentally. A rough estimate can be made by multiplying a Celsius temperature by two and adding 30.

The best way for students to become comfortable with both scales is to relate them to common experiences. For example, a hot day of about 95°F is about 35°C. Sweater or light jacket weather of about 60°F is about 16°C. Snow is likely to fall and stay on the ground at about 25°F or –4°C.

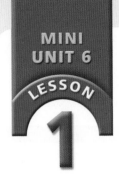

Measure Length and Distance

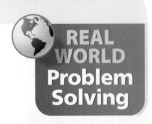
Vocabulary

millimeter
centimeter
decimeter
meter
kilometer
prefixes
metric system

Lesson Objectives

● Explore the system of metric units of length or distance.

● Estimate and measure length and distance, using metric units.

● Choose appropriate units for measuring.

The Day at a Glance

Today's Goals	Materials
1 **Teaching the Lesson** **A1:** Explore and relate the basic units of length in the metric system. **A2:** Identify and relate metric measurement prefixes. **A3:** Estimate and measure length and distance, using appropriate units. **2** **Going Further** ▶ Differentiated Instruction **3** **Homework and Spiral Review**	**Lesson Activities** Student Activity Book pp. 261–266 or Student Hardcover Book pp. 261–266 and Activity Workbook pp. 90–91 (includes Family Letters) Homework and Remembering pp. 175–176 Make a Meter (TRB M69) Scissors Tape or glue stick Pen, new pencil, and short crayon Metric rulers (optional) Overhead Projector Geometry and Measurement Poster (optional)	**Going Further** Activity Cards 6-1 Metric Cards (TRB M70) Meter strips from Activity 1 or metric rulers Scissors Math Journals

123 *Use* **Math Talk** *today!*

Keeping Skills Sharp

Daily Routines	English Language Learners

Place Value Read aloud the following numbers. Have students write a number that is 1,000 less than the given number.

63,468	48,217
62,468	47,217
79,340	10,798
78,340	9,798

Write *meter strip* on the board. Have students use a meter strip to find the number of decimeters, centimeters, and millimeters in 1 meter.

● **Beginning** Say: **The meter strip shows parts of a meter. There are 10 decimeters in 1 meter. There are 100 centimeters in 1 meter. There are 1,000 millimeters in 1 meter.** Have students repeat.

● **Intermediate** Ask: **What does the meter strip show?** parts of a meter **How many decimeters in 1 meter?** 10 **How many centimeters in 1 meter?** 100 **How many millimeters in 1 meter?** 1,000

● **Advanced** Have students tell how meters, decimeters, centimeters, and millimeters are related. Ask: **Which unit is the largest?** meters **Which is the smallest?** millimeters

Teaching the Lesson

Explore the Meter

 20 MINUTES

Goal: Explore and relate the basic units of length in the metric system.

Materials: Make a Meter (TRB M69), scissors, tape or glue stick, Student Activity Book or Hardcover Book p. 261, pen, new pencil, short crayon, overhead projector, Geometry and Measurement Poster (optional)

✓ **NCTM Standards:**
Measurement
Representation

▶ Make a Meter Strip WHOLE CLASS

Give each student TRB M69 and have all students cut on the dotted lines to create the pieces for their meter strip.

They join the first two parts of the meter strip by placing the 255-mm mark at the end of the first part over the 255-mm mark at the beginning of the second part, aligning the tops, and taping or pasting the parts together. Have students complete their meter strips in the same fashion with the remaining two pieces.

mm													
	190	200	210	220	230	240	250	260	270	280	290	300	310	320	330
cm	19	20	21	22	23	24	25	26	27	28	29	30	31	32	33
dm		2											3			

▶ Parts of a Meter WHOLE CLASS

Write on the board:

mm = millimeter
cm = centimeter
dm = decimeter
m = meter

Ask students to look at their meter strips, especially at the beginning and end, and discuss what the vertical lines at the top represent. Then have students describe what each set of markings represents, starting with the meter marking at the bottom of the strip.

mm	10	20	30	40	50	60	70	80	90	100	960	970	980	990	1000
cm	1	2	3	4	5	6	7	8	9	10	96	97	98	99	100
dm										1					10
m															1

● What does the *m* stand for at the beginning? meter How many meters are in your strip? 1 meter How do you know? the number 1 printed at the end

● What does *dm* stand for? decimeter How many decimeters are in your strip and how do you know? 10 dm; printed at the end How does the word *decimeter* help you remember that there are 10 decimeters in 1 meter? The prefix deci makes me think of 10, as in decimal numbers.

● What does *cm* stand for? centimeter How many centimeters are in your strip and how do you know? 100 cm; printed at the end How can you remember that there are 100 centimeters in 1 meter? Centi-sounds like cent, and there are 100 cents in 1 dollar.

● What does *mm* stand for? millimeter How many millimeters are in your strip? 1,000 mm Why are all of the millimeter numbers not printed on the strip? There is no room.

Have the students discuss questions 1–5 on Student Book page 261 and connect each unit with its length on their meter strips.

Invite students to practice finding millimeters on their strips.

Differentiated Instruction

Extra Help If students have difficulty overlapping the ends to make their meter strips, have them cut off the ends and butt each part to the next.

Class Management

You may want to display the Geometry and Measurement Poster while students study this unit.

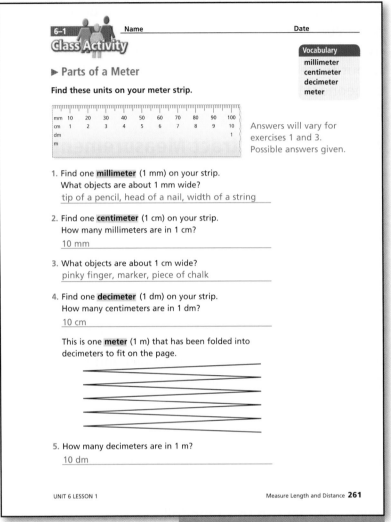

6-1 Class Activity

Name Date

Vocabulary
millimeter
centimeter
decimeter
meter

▶ **Parts of a Meter**

Find these units on your meter strip.

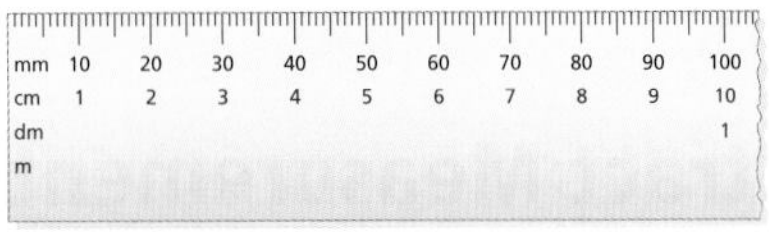

Answers will vary for exercises 1 and 3. Possible answers given.

1. Find one **millimeter** (1 mm) on your strip. What objects are about 1 mm wide?
 tip of a pencil, head of a nail, width of a string
2. Find one **centimeter** (1 cm) on your strip. How many millimeters are in 1 cm?
 10 mm
3. What objects are about 1 cm wide?
 pinky finger, marker, piece of chalk
4. Find one **decimeter** (1 dm) on your strip. How many centimeters are in 1 dm?
 10 cm

 This is one **meter** (1 m) that has been folded into decimeters to fit on the page.

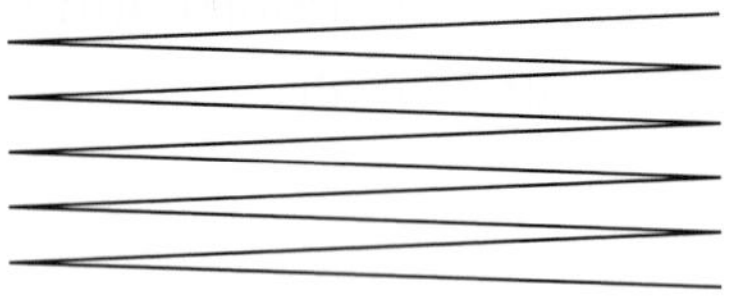

5. How many decimeters are in 1 m?
 10 dm

UNIT 6 LESSON 1 Measure Length and Distance **261**

Student Activity Book page 261

Rounding On Homework page 175 students are asked to round millimeter measurements to the nearest centimeter. Do a few such exercises now while students are looking at their paper meters.

- Find 462 millimeters. Is that closer to 46 cm or 47 cm? Why? 46 cm because 462 is closer to 460 than to 470
- Find 847 millimeters. What cm is it between? 84 cm and 85 cm To which is it closer and why? 85 cm because 7 is more than half-way to the next higher cm

Class Management

Looking Ahead Students will need their meter strips for Activity 2 and in Lessons 2 and 3.

▶ Discuss Measurement Concepts

WHOLE CLASS **Math Talk**

Have students look at their meter strips as you informally discuss these measurement concepts:

Iteration For measurement, any measuring tool has units that repeat.

- Describe the repeating units on your meter strip. millimeters, centimeters, and decimeters

Partitioning Any measuring tool has large units divided into a smaller units that are the same size.

- How are the units on your meter strip the same? Students should understand that the units on their measuring strip are the same size. Any ruler has same-sized units that repeat.

Compensatory Principle More smaller units than larger units are needed to measure any distance.

Give students an estimate of the classroom width in centimeters, such as 1000 centimeters.

- If you measured the width of our classroom using meters, would the number of meters be greater or less than 1000? Explain how you know. Less, 1000 cm = 10 m; students should generalize that the smaller the unit used to measure a distance, the greater the number of units needed, and vice versa.

Transitivity This concept involves the relationship of three elements. For example, if Object A is longer than Object B and Object B is longer than Object C, then Object A is longer than Object C. Demonstrate this concept by placing a new pencil and a pen on the overhead.

- Is the pencil longer or shorter than the pen? longer

Replace the pencil with a short crayon.

- Is the pen longer or shorter than the crayon? longer
- Without directly comparing them, is the pencil longer or shorter than the crayon? How do you know? longer; since the pencil is longer than the pen and the pen is longer than the crayon, then the pencil must be longer than the crayon.

Teaching the Lesson (continued)

Activity 2

Convert Measurements

 20 MINUTES

Goal: Identify and relate metric measurement prefixes.

Materials: meter strips made in Activity 1 or metric rulers, Student Activity Book or Hardcover Book p. 262

✔ **NCTM Standards:**
Geometry
Reasoning and Proof

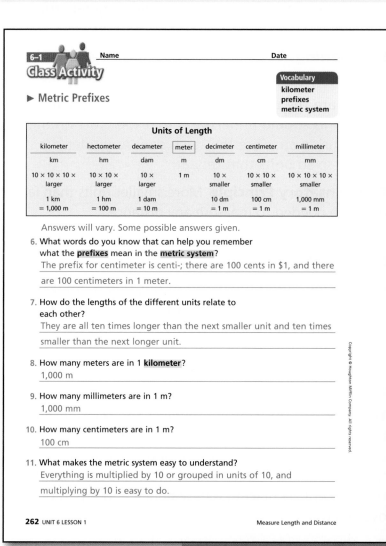

Student Activity Book page 262

 Ongoing Assessment

Ask students to explain the relationship between millimeters, centimeters, decimeters, meters, and kilometers.

▶ Metric Prefixes [WHOLE CLASS]

As a class, focus on the chart on Student Book page 262. Discuss the prefixes *deca-*, *hecto-*, and *kilo-*. Invite students to share anything they already know about these units. For example, some may know someone who runs in 5-km or 10-km races. Together, answer questions 6–11.

▶ Add and Subtract Measurements
[WHOLE CLASS]

Give students an opportunity to use their meter strips or centimeter rulers to measure the length and width of a sheet of paper in centimeters and millimeters. For example, the length is 27 cm 5 mm and the width is 21 cm 3 mm.

● If you place two sheets of paper end-to-end, how can you use addition to find the total length?

Invite a student to work at the board and explain the procedure for finding the answer.

$$\begin{array}{r} 27 \text{ cm } 5 \text{ mm} \\ + 27 \text{ cm } 5 \text{ mm} \\ \hline 55 \text{ cm } 0 \text{ mm} \end{array}$$

● Why isn't 54 cm 10 mm the correct answer? We regroup 10 mm as 1 cm because 10 mm = 1 cm.

Invite a student to solve the following subtraction at the board and explain the procedure.

$$\begin{array}{r} 23 \text{ cm } 5 \text{ mm} \\ - 17 \text{ cm } 8 \text{ mm} \\ \hline 5 \text{ cm } 7 \text{ mm} \end{array}$$

● Explain how we can subtract 8 mm from 5 mm. Since 1 cm = 10 mm, we ungroup 1 cm into 10 mm.

Generalize Discuss the similarities between adding and subtracting metric measures and whole numbers. Lead students to generalize that when we subtract whole numbers, we ungroup tens to subtract ones (1 ten = 10 ones), and we ungroup centimeters to subtract millimeters (1 cm = 10 mm). When we add whole numbers we regroup 10 ones as 1 ten, and we regroup 10 mm as 1 cm.

Emphasize that we group and ungroup the same way because both our numeration system and the Metric System of Measurement are base-ten systems.

Precision and Measurement

 20 MINUTES

Goal: Estimate and measure length and distance, using appropriate units.

Materials: meter strips made in Activity 1 or metric rulers, Student Activity Book or Hardcover Book pp. 263–264

 NCTM Standards:
Measurement
Representation

▶ Discuss Precision

WHOLE CLASS   **Math Talk**

Write on the board: Mount Everest, the tallest mountain in the world, is 8,848 meters high.

Also write the word *precise* on the board.

● What does *precise* mean? exact; definite; accurate

● Which unit—meter, centimeter, or millimeter—will result in the most precise measurement? Why? Millimeter is a very small unit and it gives the most accurate measurements.

Lead a class discussion about precise and estimated measurements.

● The height of Mount Everest is 8,848 meters. Is that an exact height or an estimate? Tell why. An estimate; it is very difficult to measure large objects exactly.

● Why is the height of Mount Everest reported in meters, and not in decimeters or centimeters? A measurement of the mountain in centimeters or decimeters would be in very large numbers which would make the measurement more difficult to visualize and understand.

● How do we decide how precise our measurements need to be? We have to judge how we will use the measurement. Geologists need to know how high mountains are, but meters are good enough for their purposes.

● When do we need more precision in measurement? When precision affects how we use the measurement; for example, if measurements aren't precise in building a house, the walls and floors may be crooked.

Ask for Ideas Write the terms *length, capacity,* and *mass* on the board and give students an opportunity to brainstorm situations in which a precise measurement of length, capacity, or mass is necessary.

length shoes for proper fit; carpentry, architecture, planning a trip for the space shuttle

capacity some recipes; liquid prescriptions; chemical solutions; capacity of a scuba diving air tank

mass launching a satellite; the dose of a liquid medication; a quantity used in an experiment

▶ Estimation and Measurements

WHOLE CLASS

Write on the board:

> Nancy needs three boards. Each board must be exactly 31 cm long, but she can buy boards only in full meter lengths. How many meters of boards does she need to buy?

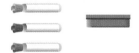

Ask for Ideas Invite students to name different situations in which people estimate rather than measure precisely.

● What does Nancy need to know? Why? Can she estimate? Exactly how many centimeters she needs and what the next higher whole meter is; so she will have enough; she can't estimate or she might not have enough.

Activity continued ▶

① Teaching the Lesson (continued)

Activity 3

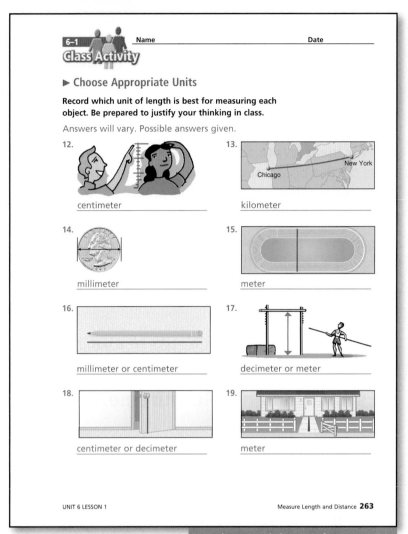

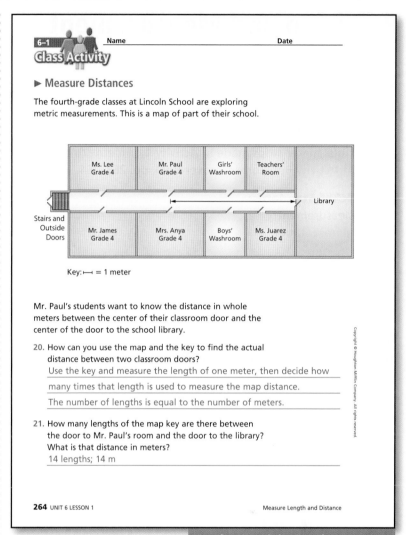

▶ Choose Appropriate Units INDIVIDUALS

Have students look at the picture in exercise 12 on Student Book page 263.

● Which metric length unit would you use to measure your height? centimeter

● Why not whole meters? The height of almost everyone would be the same number of meters; you couldn't use the measurements to compare heights.

● Why not millimeters? You could, but you'd have to be very precise and the numbers would be large.

● Why not decimeters? You could, but it would be less precise than centimeters, and people don't use decimeters much.

Ask students to complete exercises 13–19 and to share their answers and reasoning with the class.

▶ Measure Distances INDIVIDUALS

As a class, discuss the map of the school on Student Book page 264. Point out that the length of the key is 5 mm or 0.5 cm but it represents 1 m. Invite students to complete exercises 20 and 21; discuss their responses as a class.

Measuring Real Objects Invite students to use their meter strips (or other metric rulers that you may have available) to measure objects and distances in and around the classroom to the nerarest mm and the nearest cm. They should estimate each distance before measuring to help develop their intuitive understanding of metric units. You might ask:

● Estimate the perimeter of the top of your desk.

● Name the perimeter. Use your meter strip.

● How close was your estimate to the actual perimeter?

② Going Further

Intervention — Activity Card 6-1

Use Metric Benchmarks
Activity Card 6-1

Work: By Yourself

Use:
• Metric ruler or Make a Meter (TRB M69)

1. Choose the metric unit that is about equal to each of the following:
   • The length of your arm m
   • The width of your finger cm
   • The width of your palm dm
   • The thickness of a button mm

2. Estimate the width and length of your Student Book. Use your finger width and palm width to help you estimate.

3. Now measure the Student Book with a ruler or meter strip. Compare your estimate to the actual measure.

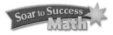

Unit 6, Lesson 1   Copyright © Houghton Mifflin Company

Activity Note If students are having difficulty identifying the metric measures, give them the following list: millimeter, centimeter, decimeter, meter, and kilometer.

Math Writing Prompt

Choose Appropriate Units Explain why you would not use kilometers or millimeters to measure the size of a room.

Soar to Success Math — Software Support

Use *Soar to Success* for instruction of students needing targeted support for underlying skills.

On Level — Activity Card 6-1

Make Metric Equations
Activity Card 6-1 ▲

Work: By Yourself

Use:
• Metric Cards (TRB M70)
• Scissors

1. Cut out the metric cards and arrange them to make four correct equations like the one below.

| 1 | meter | = | 100 | centi | meters |

2. Record each equation.

3. Describe a situation when you might need to use one of the equations that you made.

Unit 6, Lesson 1   Copyright © Houghton Mifflin Company

Activity Note Challenge students to make additional number cards that are related by powers of 10, such as 2, 20, and 200, and to use them to write more metric equations.

Math Writing Prompt

Explain Your Thinking When might you use different units to measure the same thing? For example, when would you use centimeters to measure a ribbon? When might you use meters?

MegaMath Grades K-6 — Software Support

Use *MegaMath* for review and reinforcement of the concepts and skills presented in this lesson.

Challenge — Activity Card 6-1

Estimate Lengths
Activity Card 6-1 ■

Work: In Pairs

Use:
• Metric ruler or Make a Meter (TRB M69)

1. Estimate the metric lengths of each of 10 different objects in your classroom.

2. Then use the ruler or meter strip to find the actual measure.

3. **Discuss** How do your estimates compare with the actual measures? How could you make more accurate estimates?

Unit 6, Lesson 1   Copyright © Houghton Mifflin Company

Activity Note To extend the activity, have students estimate and measure each object, using centimeters and decimeters.

Math Writing Prompt

Investigate Math Describe how to change a metric measurement to another unit. For example, 16 centimeters is equal to how many millimeters?

DESTINATION Math® — Software Support

Use *Destination Math* to take students beyond the concepts and skills presented in this lesson.

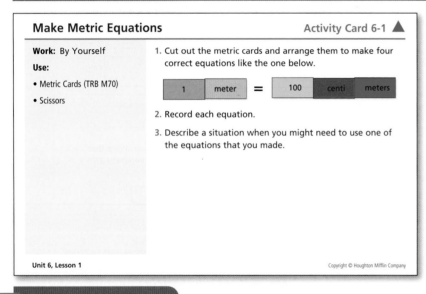
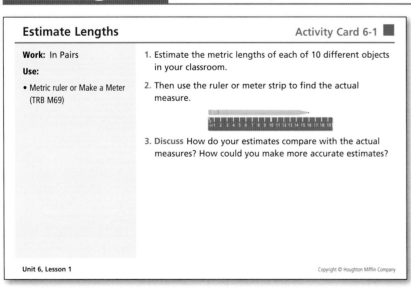

Measure Length and Distance   **633**

③ Homework and Spiral Review

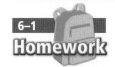

For homework, students continue to work with metric units of length.

This Remembering activity would be appropriate anytime after today's lesson.

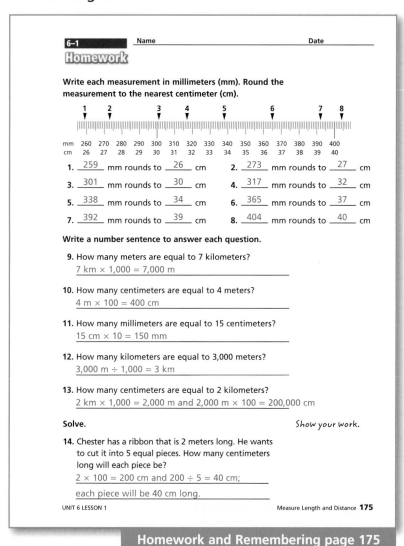

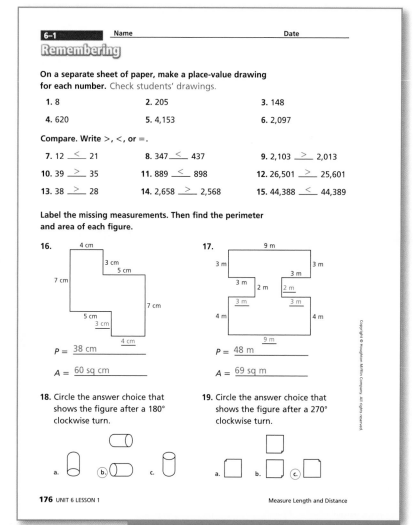

Homework and Remembering page 175

Homework and Remembering page 176

Home and School Connection

Family Letter Have students take home the Family Letter on Student Book page 265 or Activity Workbook page 90. This letter explains how the concept of measuring length and distance is developed in *Math Expressions*. It gives parents and guardians a better understanding of the learning that goes on in math class and creates a bridge between school and home. A Spanish translation of this letter is on page 266 in the Student Book and page 91 in the Activity Workbook.

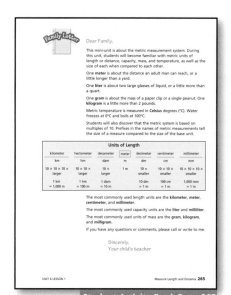

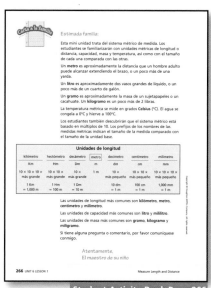

Student Activity Book Page 265

Student Activity Book Page 266

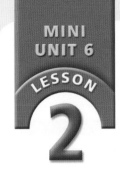

Measure Area

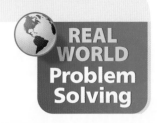
Vocabulary

square unit
square meter
square centimeter
square millimeter
square decimeter
square kilometer

Lesson Objective

• Identify and use metric units of area.

The Day at a Glance

Today's Goals	Materials	
1 **Teaching the Lesson** A1: Identify metric units of area. A2: Measure area in metric units. A3: Convert among metric units of area. **2** **Going Further** ▶ Problem Solving Strategy: Use a Simpler Problem ▶ Differentiated Instruction **3** **Homework and Spiral Review**	**Lesson Activities** Student Activity Book pp. 267–269 or Student Hardcover Book pp. 267–269 Homework and Remembering pp. 177–178 Centimeter-Grid Paper (TRB M60) Meter strips (from Lesson 1) or metric rulers Sheet protectors Dry-erase markers Overhead projector (optional) String (optional)	**Going Further** Student Activity Book p. 270 or Student Hardcover Book p. 270 Activity Cards 6-2 Centimeter-Grid Paper (TRB M60) Meter strips (from Lesson 1) Yardsticks Newspapers Tape Scissors Math Journals

123 Use
Math Talk
today!

Keeping Skills Sharp

Daily Routines	English Language Learners
Homework Review Ask students if they had difficulty with any part of the homework. Plan to set aside some time to work with students needing extra help. **Skip Count** Have students skip count ▶ by 5s from 725 to 775. ▶ by 10s from 462 to 522.	Write *area* and *square units* on the board. Draw a 3 × 2 rectangle, showing the square units inside the rectangle. Write *Units* to the right of rectangle. List *meter* and *centimeter* underneath. • **Beginning** Say: **The area of the figure is 6 square units. If each unit is a meter, the area is 6 square meters.** Continue with centimeters. • **Intermediate** Ask: **What is the *area* of the rectangle in square units?** 6 square units **If each unit is a meter, what is the area?** 6 square meters **If each unit is a centimeter, what is the area?** 6 square centimeters • **Advanced** Have students tell how the area label of the rectangle would change if each unit was a meter or centimeter.

① Teaching the Lesson

Measure Area in Metric Units

 20 MINUTES

Goal: Identify metric units of area.

Materials: Student Activity or Hardcover Book p. 267, meter strips from Lesson 1 or metric rulers, string (optional)

 NCTM Standard:
Measurement

▶ Metric Units of Area (optional)

WHOLE CLASS

Discuss exercises 1–4 on Student Book page 267.

● What is the length of each side of a square centimeter in millimeters? 10 mm

● What is its area in square millimeters?
10 mm × 10 mm = 100 sq mm

● What is the length of each side of the square decimeter in centimeters? 10 cm

● What is its area in square centimeters?
10 cm × 10 cm = 100 sq cm

Before discussing exercises 5 and 6, have the students use meter strips to make a one-meter square on the classroom floor.

● How many decimeters are in one meter? 10 dm

● What is the length of each side of a one-meter square in decimeters? 10 dm

● What is the area of a one-meter square in square decimeters? 10 dm × 10 dm = 100 sq dm

---

6–2

Class Activity

Name _____ Date _____

Vocabulary
square unit
square meter
square centimeter
square millimeter
square decimeter

▶ Metric Units of Area

Area is measured in **square units**, such as **square meters**.
This is one **square centimeter** (sq cm): ☐

1. Why is it called a square unit?
   Each side of the square is the same length
   and is one unit long.

This square centimeter is divided into **square millimeters** (sq mm): ▦

2. How many sq mm are in 1 sq cm?
   100 sq mm

This array of square centimeters is one **square decimeter** (sq dm).

3. How many square centimeters are in 1 sq dm?
   100 sq cm

4. How many square millimeters are in 1 sq dm?
   10,000 sq mm

5. How many square decimeters are in 1 sq m? Explain.
   100 sq dm;
   each side is 10 dm;
   10 × 10 = 100 sq dm

6. How many square centimeters are in 1 sq m? How do you know?
   10,000 sq cm; each side is 1 meter or 100 centimeters;
   a square that is 100 cm by 100 cm has 10,000 sq cm in it.

UNIT 6 LESSON 2   Measure Area **267**

Student Activity Book page 267

▶ Perimeter and Area of Real Objects

PAIRS

Give students an opportunity to work in **Student Pairs** and use their meter strips (or other metric rulers that you may have available) to measure real objects in the classroom, and determine the perimeter and the area of one or more faces of those objects.

Make sure students understand that perimeter is a measure of distance around and area is a measure of the number of square units that are needed to cover a surface.

Share Measurements Students can identify the classroom object that they have measured and name the perimeter and area that was computed.

▶ Estimate Length, Perimeter, and Area

Students can estimate, using a benchmark or personal referent. For example:

Length or Perimeter One type of personal referent that can be used to estimate is the length of a foot or the width of a hand. Have students measure the width of one of their hands or the length of their partner's foot and then use these referents (or use them proportionally, such as "*Three of my shoe length is* about the *same as 1 meter*") to make estimates of length, perimeter, and area.

Area Students can estimate the area of one of their hands; a typical estimate is 130 sq cm. Then students can estimate the area of their desktop by estimating the number of hands that could be placed on the desktop without overlap, and then multiply that number by 130 sq cm to estimate the area of the entire desktop.

You might choose to have students estimate the area of one of their footprints, then walk heel-to-toe for the entire length and width of the classroom. Multiplication and addition can then be used to estimate the area of the entire floor.

Differentiated Instruction

Special Needs If students have difficulty measuring objects, let them work in groups of three. One student holds a ruler to the width of the object, while another holds a ruler to the length. A third student records the measurements.

 ### Alternate Approach

Using String Estimates of perimeter and area can also be made using string. For example, a long length of string can be placed around the perimeter of a shape and the string can then be placed against a meter stick to estimate the perimeter, or estimates can be made by first cutting a 50- or 100-cm length of string and using that length repeatedly to measure.

Challenge interested students to make estimates of perimeter and area, using one or both of these methods.

Teaching Note

Math Background Note the difference between a one-meter square and a measurement of one square meter. A one-meter square is a square with sides one meter long. One square meter is an area measurement of a figure that doesn't have to be square. A one-meter square can be rearranged to form other figures (triangle, rectangle, and so on) and still have an area of one square meter.

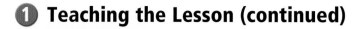

① Teaching the Lesson (continued)

Activity 2

Calculate Area

 20 MINUTES

Goal: Measure area in metric units.

Materials: Student Activity Book or Hardcover Book p. 268; Centimeter-Grid Paper (TRB M60), sheet protectors, dry-erase markers, overhead projector (optional); meter strips from Lesson 1 or metric rulers

 NCTM Standard:
Measurement

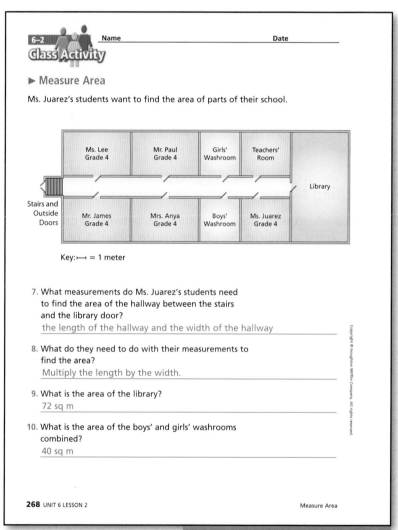

6-2 Class Activity

Name _____ Date _____

▶ Measure Area

Ms. Juarez's students want to find the area of parts of their school.

|Ms. Lee Grade 4|Mr. Paul Grade 4|Girls' Washroom|Teachers' Room| |
|Stairs and Outside Doors|Mr. James Grade 4|Mrs. Anya Grade 4|Boys' Washroom|Ms. Juarez Grade 4|Library|

Key: ⊢—⊣ = 1 meter

7. What measurements do Ms. Juarez's students need to find the area of the hallway between the stairs and the library door?
   the length of the hallway and the width of the hallway

8. What do they need to do with their measurements to find the area?
   Multiply the length by the width.

9. What is the area of the library?
   72 sq m

10. What is the area of the boys' and girls' washrooms combined?
    40 sq m

268 UNIT 6 LESSON 2   Measure Area

Student Activity Book page 268

▶ **Measure Area** | WHOLE CLASS |

Have the students discuss ways to find the area of the hallway on the school map on Student Book page 268. Review the use of the key as needed.

● How can you use the key to make a ruler to measure the drawing? Use the edge of a piece of paper and mark units along the edge.

Have students complete exercises 7–10.

If you think your students need more practice calculating area in square centimeters, use TRB M60. Have students use a plastic sheet protector so that they can draw on the sheet multiple times. You can also use TRB M60 with an overhead projector.

Differentiated Instruction

Advanced Learners Ask students to suppose that they want to cover the classroom floor with carpet tiles that measure 2 feet on each side. How many carpet tiles will they need? Remind students that they may need partial tiles for some places, but the tiles can only be ordered as whole tiles.

Ongoing Assessment

Ask students to record the area of one square meter in square millimeters, square centimeters, and square decimeters.

Compare Metric Units of Length and Area

 20 MINUTES

Goal: Convert among metric units of area.

Materials: Student Activity Book or Hardcover Book p. 269

 NCTM Standard:
Measurement

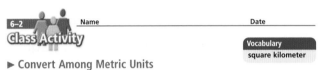

Name _____ Date _____

Vocabulary
square kilometer

▶ **Convert Among Metric Units**

Compare units of length or distance with units of area.

Units of Area

square kilometer	hectare	are	square meter	square decimeter	square centimeter	square millimeter
sq km	ha	a	sq m	sq dm	sq cm	sq mm
100 × 100 × 100 larger	100 × 100 × larger	100 × larger	1 sq m	100 × smaller	100 × 100 × smaller	100 × 100 × 100 × smaller
1 sq km = 1,000,000 sq m	1 ha = 10,000 sq m	1 a = 100 sq m		100 sq dm = 1 sq m	10,000 sq cm = 1 sq m	1,000,000 sq mm = 1 sq m

Solve.

11. How many meters long is each side of a square that has an area of 4 square meters (sq m)?
    2 m

12. How many one-meter squares cover a square that has an area of 4 square meters (sq m)?
    4 one-meter squares

13. How many meters long is each side of a square that has an area of 4 **square kilometers** (sq km)?
    2,000 m

14. How many one-meter squares cover a square that has an area of 4 sq km?
    4,000,000 one-meter squares

15. How is a square measurement unit like a square number in multiplication?
    A square measurement unit is the product of a number of units
    multiplied by itself, just as a square number is the product of a
    number multiplied by itself.

UNIT 6 LESSON 2   Measure Area **269**

Student Activity Book page 269

▶ **Convert Among Metric Units**

WHOLE CLASS

As a class, focus on the chart on Student Book page 269. Discuss the metric prefixes as well as the difference between measuring length and measuring area in the metric system.

● What is the base metric unit for measuring distance? the meter

● What is the base metric unit for measuring area? the square meter

● Which unit names for measuring distance and measuring area are similar? meter and square meter, decimeter and square decimeter, centimeter and square centimeter, millimeter and square millimeter, kilometer and square kilometer

● Why is each unit of area 100 times larger or smaller than the unit beside it? because there are 10 × 10 units of area inside each bigger unit, and it takes 10 × 10 smaller units to make up each bigger unit

123 Math Talk Invite students to complete questions 11–15, and encourage discussion about the results.

Teaching Note

Language and Vocabulary The *hectare* is commonly used to measure land area. It is a square hectometer, the same area as a 100-meter square. The measurement unit *square decameter* (or *are*) is rarely used and is given here to show the relationships among metric units. Neither a *hectare* nor an *are* will be used in measurement problems.

② Going Further

Problem Solving Strategy: Use a Simpler Problem

Goal: Use the results from a simpler problem to solve a more difficult problem.

Materials: Student Activity Book or Hardcover Book p. 270

✔ **NCTM Standards:**
Measurement
Problem Solving

6-2
Going Further

Name _____ Date _____

▶ Use a Simpler Problem

To solve a more difficult problem, sometimes you can think about a simpler problem.

1. Manuel cuts a length of rug into pieces of equal area. He cuts 8 square pieces like the one shown.

2 m | 16 m

What is the area of each piece of rug? 4 sq m

Hint: What would the answer be if he made just one cut? two cuts?

2. Adita used square tiles to make a design. The sides of her tiles are 5 centimeters. She made a square design, using 36 of the tiles. What was the perimeter of her design? 120 cm

5 cm

Hint: What would the perimeter be if she used one-centimeter square tiles?

3. Adita used red and yellow tiles for her design in problem 2. She used one yellow tile for every three red tiles. How many of each color did she use? 27 red tiles, 9 yellow tiles

4. Challenge How many different ways can you name a line segment, using any 2 of the first 8 letters of the alphabet? 56 ways

A ———————— B

270 UNIT 6 LESSON 2   Measure Area

Student Activity Book page 270

▶ Act It Out   WHOLE CLASS

Use the **Scenario** structure to help students solve a difficult problem by solving a simpler version of it.

● If eight students all shake hands with each other, how many handshakes will take place?

Invite eight students to act out the problem as you record together the number of handshakes.

Have students act out the handshake problem again, this time with two students, then three students, then four students, and so on.

● What pattern can you see? 1, 3, 6, 10, and so on; Add 2, then 3, then 4, and so on.

1	3	6	10	15	21	28
+2	+3	+4	+5	+6	+7	

28 handshakes

▶ Use a Simpler Problem   PAIRS

As a class, discuss problem 1 on Student page 270.

● After 1 cut, how many pieces will there be? 2

● After 2 cuts, how many pieces will there be? 3

● After 3 cuts? 4

● What is the pattern? The number of pieces is one more than the number of cuts.

● After 8 cuts, how many pieces will there be? 9

● What operation will you use to find the area of each piece? division

Have **Student Pairs** complete problem 1 and continue with problems 2–4.

● In problem 2, you found the perimeter of the square of 36 one-centimeter tiles to be 24 cm. How can you find the perimeter with 5-cm tiles? Multiply 5 by 24.

● In problem 3, there are four tiles in the diagram. What do you have to multiply 4 by to get 36 tiles? 9

● There were three red tiles, so what do you multiply 3 by to get the total number of red tiles? 9

● In problem 4, try joining two dots, then a set of three dots, then four dots, and so on. What problem have you seen that is like this one? The handshake problem.

The Learning Classroom

Scenario Using a scenario demonstrates mathematical relationships in a visual and memorable way. A group of students act out a situation. Scenarios create meaningful contexts in which students relate math to their lives.

Differentiated Instruction

Intervention — Activity Card 6-2

Make a Chart — Activity Card 6-2

Work: In Pairs

1. Copy each table below.

Length Units		
Prefix		
deci-	1 m =	10 dm
centi-	1 m =	100 cm
milli-	1 m =	1,000 mm

Area Units		
Prefix		
deci-	1 sq m =	100 sq dm
centi-	1 sq m =	10,000 sq cm
milli-	1 sq m =	1,000,000 sq mm

2. Complete the tables to show equivalent metric measures for 1 meter in the length table and 1 square meter in the area table.

Unit 6, Lesson 2 — Copyright © Houghton Mifflin Company

Activity Note Students may wish to use the metric length equivalencies to sketch the subdivisions of a square meter before completing the area units. Ask students to identify any patterns they see.

Math Writing Prompt

Explain Your Thinking Explain why an area of 1,000 sq cm is the same as an area of 10 sq dm.

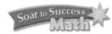 **Software Support**

Use *Soar to Success* for instruction of students needing targeted support for underlying skills.

On Level — Activity Card 6-2

Estimate Area in Square Centimeters — Activity Card 6-2 ▲

Work: In Pairs

Use:
• Centimeter-Grid Paper (TRB M60)

1. Draw a large irregular figure on centimeter-grid paper.

2. Record the following information.
   • whole square centimeters inside the figure
   • partial square centimeters inside the figure
   • estimated area of the figure

Unit 6, Lesson 2 — Copyright © Houghton Mifflin Company

Activity Note Students should decide how to keep track of each category of squares as they count. They need to recall that 1 square decimeter equals 100 square centimeters to rewrite the estimate.

Math Writing Prompt

Investigate Math Explain what happens to the area of a square when you multiply both dimensions by two.

 Software Support

Use *MegaMath* for review and reinforcement of the concepts and skills presented in this lesson.

Challenge — Activity Card 6-2

Compare Areas — Activity Card 6-2 ■

Work: In Pairs

Use:
• Make a Meter (TRB M69), 4 copies
• 4 yardsticks
• Whole newspaper pages
• Tape
• Scissors

1. Cut and tape newspaper pages to show one square meter.

2. Cut and tape newspaper pages to show one square yard.

3. Align two corners of the squares. Which area is greater—a square meter or a square yard? square meter

4. **Analyze** How can you use the newspaper models to estimate the size of a square yard in square centimeters?
   Measure the rectangles in square centimeters that represent the difference between the square meter and square yard. Subtract that amount from 10,000 square centimeters; possible answer: about 8,200 sq cm.

Unit 6, Lesson 2 — Copyright © Houghton Mifflin Company

Activity Note Pair students who find cutting and taping easy with students who find it more challenging.

Math Writing Prompt

Use Reasoning Explain what happens to the area of a 1-mm square when you multiply both dimensions by 10, by 100, and by 1,000.

 Software Support

Use *Destination Math* to take students beyond the concepts and skills presented in this lesson.

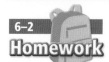

③ Homework and Spiral Review

6-2
Homework **Goal:** Additional Practice

✓ Include students' work for page 177 as part of their portfolios.

6-2 Name _____ Date _____
Homework

Solve the word problem. *Show your work.*

1. A room is 5 m wide and 7 m long. What is the area of the floor?
   35 sq m

2. A farm is 1 km wide and 2 km long. What is its area in square kilometers?
   2 sq km

3. Write and solve two metric-area word problems.
   Word problems will vary.

UNIT 6 LESSON 2   Measure Area **177**

Homework and Remembering page 177

6-2
Remembering **Goal:** Spiral Review

This Remembering activity would be appropriate anytime after today's lesson.

6-2 Name _____ Date _____
Remembering

Write the number for the word name.

1. one thousand, forty ___1,040___
2. six thousand, thirty-seven ___6,037___
3. nine thousand, four hundred sixty-three ___9,463___
4. one hundred fifty thousand, two ___150,002___

Write the word name for the number.

5. 204 two hundred four
6. 4,827 four thousand, eight hundred twenty-seven
7. 11,005 eleven thousand, five
8. 56,000,789 fifty-six million, seven hundred eighty-nine

Round each number to the nearest ten, hundred, and thousand.

	Ten	Hundred	Thousand
9. 1,748	1,750	1,700	2,000
10. 50,637	50,640	50,600	51,000
11. 739	740	700	1,000
12. 2,009,584	2,009,580	2,009,600	2,010,000

Solve. *Show your work.*

13. Augusto had four cards each, measuring 3 in. by 5 in. He taped them together to make one larger card. Draw the new arrangement of cards and name its perimeter.
    Arrangements will vary. A possible perimeter is 32 in.

178 UNIT 6 LESSON 2   Measure Area

Homework and Remembering page 178

Home or School Activity

 Social Studies Connection

The Area of Your State Have students find the area of their state in square kilometers. Ask them: which U.S. state has the greatest area? Which has the smallest area?

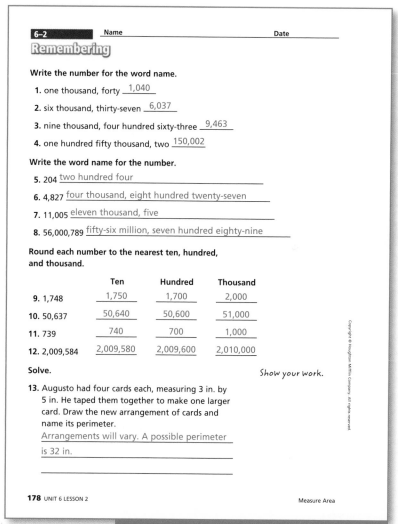

←220 km→

430 km

Indianapolis

Indiana

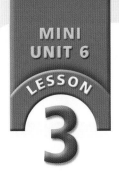

Measure Volume and Capacity

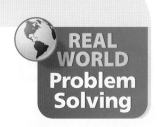

REAL WORLD **Problem Solving**

Vocabulary

cubic centimeter	kiloliter
cubic decimeter	milliliter
cubic meter	volume
cubic millimeter	capacity
liter	

Lesson Objectives

- Explore metric units of volume and capacity.
- Measure volume and capacity, using metric units.

The Day at a Glance

Today's Goals	Materials	
1 Teaching the Lesson **A1:** Explore volume; use cubic centimeters to create a cubic decimeter. **A2:** Calculate volume, using the formula *length × width × height*. **A3:** Discuss the difference between measuring volume and measuring capacity; recognize and relate metric units of capacity. **2 Going Further** ▶ Differentiated Instruction **3 Homework and Spiral Review**	**Lesson Activities** Student Activity Book pp. 271–272 or Student Hardcover Book pp. 271–272 Homework and Remembering pp. 179–180 Centimeter-Grid Paper (TRB M60) Make a Cubic Centimeter (TRB M71) (optional) Centimeter cubes Scissors Clear tape or glue Meter strips (from Lesson 1) or metric rulers Half-gallon milk or juice carton (optional) 1-L soda or water bottle	**Going Further** Activity Cards 6-3 Centimeter cubes Meter strips (from Lesson 1) Scissors Box-shaped objects Math Journals

123 *Use* **Math Talk** *today!*

Keeping Skills Sharp

Daily Routines	English Language Learners
Homework Review Ask several students to share the problems they wrote for homework. Have the class ask clarifying questions about each problem. If necessary, model asking questions. **Strategy Problem** How many boxes of spaghetti do you need to stack in a pyramid shape with five boxes in the bottom row and one box in the top row? Draw a picture to show your answer. 15 boxes	Write *volume* and *cubic units* on the board. Draw 2 × 3 × 4 rectangular prism. Write *Units* to the right, and list *millimeter* and *decimeter* underneath. • **Beginning** Say: **The volume of the figure is 24 cubic units. If each unit is a millimeter, the volume is 24 cubic millimeters.** Continue with decimeters. • **Intermediate** Say: **The volume of the figure is 24 cubic units. If each unit is a millimeter, what is the volume?** 24 cubic millimeters **If each unit is a decimeter, what is the volume?** 24 cubic decimeters • **Advanced** Have students tell how the volume label of the figure would change if each unit was a millimeter or decimeter.

① Teaching the Lesson

Volume

 25 MINUTES

Goal: Explore volume; use cubic centimeters to create a cubic decimeter.

Materials: centimeter cubes (100 per pair or group), Centimeter-Grid Paper (TRB M60), scissors, clear tape or glue, meter strips from Lesson 1 or metric rulers, Make a Cubic Centimeter (TRB M71) (optional), half-gallon milk or juice carton (1 per group) (optional)

 NCTM Standard:
Measurement

▶ Cubic Units WHOLE CLASS

Give each student a centimeter cube and invite students to measure the dimensions of the cube, using their meter strip or metric ruler.

● What are the dimensions? All sides are 1 cm.

● What is the area of any face? 1 sq cm

● Why does a square centimeter represent one unit of **area?** Its area is one square unit because its length is 1 cm and its width is 1 cm, and length times width equals area.

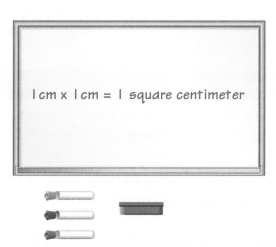

I cm x I cm = I square centimeter

● The whole cube is called a *cubic centimeter*. It represents one unit of volume. Why might that be so? Its volume is one cubic unit because its length is 1 cm, its width is 1 cm, and its height is 1 cm, and length times width times height equals volume.

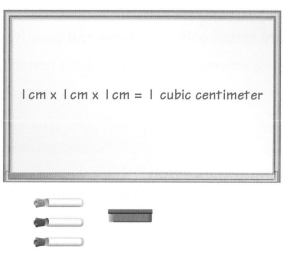

I cm x I cm x I cm = I cubic centimeter

Explain that we measure volume in cubic units, and that cubic units can be different sizes. We choose a convenient unit, smaller or larger, depending on the size of the object we are measuring.

✋ Alternate Approach

Make a Cubic Centimeter To gain a better understanding of what 1 cubic centimeter represents, students can cut TRB M71, then use folds and tape or glue to form one or more cubic centimeters.

▶ Build an Array of Cubic Centimeters
PAIRS

Explain to students that each **Student Pair** or group will make an array of cubic centimeters to create a square decimeter. Have students determine how many cubic centimeters they will need in order to make their arrays. A sample dialogue follows.

123 Math Talk in Action

How many cubic centimeters will you need for the square decimeter?

Afnan: One decimeter equals 10 centimeters, so one side of the square will be 10 centimeters.

Luc: And it's a square, so all sides are equal.

Right. And how do we find the area of a square?

Hisako: By multiplying length times width, so 10 × 10. That's 100 cubic centimeters for our array.

Class Management

If possible, each pair of students should make a 10 × 10 array of centimeter cubes to make a square decimeter. If you don't have enough cubes, have more students work together.

When they construct a cubic decimeter, students will need to build ten arrays (1,000 cubes total). This will be a strong visual aid to help them understand cubic volume.

Ask each pair of students to cut out two strips from TRB M60. (If they will be using glue instead of tape, students need to leave a "tail" at one end of the paper strip for the glue.)

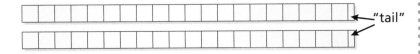
"tail"

Students tape or glue the ends of the two strips together to make a continuous loop. Starting a square or two away from any joined edges, they make a fold after every ten squares to create a four-sided "corral" of paper.

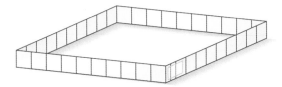

Ask students to make a square array by placing handfuls of centimeter cubes into the corral and arranging them in rows and columns.

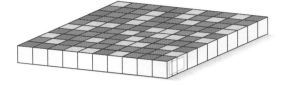

Once the last cube is in place, have students completely cover one side of their array with strips of clear tape so that the array stays together. For additional stability, students can turn over the array and tape the other side.

Ask the students about their arrays.
- What are the dimensions of each array? 10 cubes across and 10 cubes deep

- How many cubes are in each array altogether? 10 cubes × 10 cubes = 100 cubes

Teaching Note

Math Background The Greek mathematician Archimedes estimated the volume of the universe by figuring out how many grains of sand would fill it. First, he estimated how many grains of sand would fit in a poppy seed, then how many poppy seeds would fit in his finger, then how many fingers would fit in a stadium, and finally, how many stadiums would fit in the universe.

The Learning Classroom

Math Talk Always start new topics by eliciting as much from students as possible. Students often know some things about new topics. This builds feelings of competence and confidence and helps create the classroom community where everyone is a teacher and a learner. So even where the directions for a lesson are directing you to do the talking, remember to always ask for students' own ideas first.

Activity continued ▶

Activity 1

▶ Build a Cubic Decimeter WHOLE CLASS

Explain that students will work together to create a cubic decimeter. Invite them to estimate how many cubic centimeters they will need.

● How many of our arrays do we need to make a cubic decimeter? 10

Invite small groups to stack their arrays to make a large cube. Have the students measure each side with their meter strip to verify that each measures one decimeter. (The tape may cause the measurement to be slightly greater than one decimeter, but it should be close.)

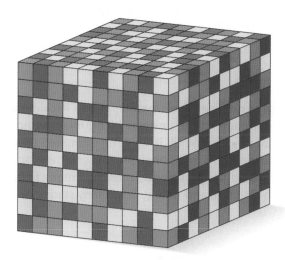

 Math Talk Discuss the dimensions and size of the large cube with the class. Lead them to understand that one cubic decimeter is equal to 1,000 cubic centimeters.

● How many centimeter cubes across is the bigger cube? 10

● How many centimeter cubes deep is it? 10

● How many high? 10

● What larger metric unit does each face of the bigger cube represent? 1 sq dm

● What is the name of the metric unit for the whole bigger cube? 1 cu dm

● How can we discover how many cubic centimeters are in one cubic decimeter?

100 + 100 + 100 + 100 + 100 + 100 + 100 + 100 + 100 + 100
or   100 × 10   or   10 × 10 × 10

✋ Alternate Approach

Use Real-World Materials Students can also explore a cubic decimeter, using a half-gallon milk or juice carton. These cartons typically measure a little less than 10 cm across and deep. If you cut off the top of the carton about 10 cm from the bottom, you have an open container that is about 1 cubic decimeter.

Activity 2

Metric Units of Volume

 15 MINUTES

Goal: Calculate volume, using the formula *length × width × height.*

Materials: Student Activity Book or Hardcover Book p. 271, metric rulers

✓ **NCTM Standard:**
Measurement

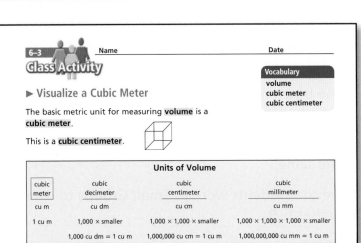

6-3
Class Activity

Name _____ Date _____

Vocabulary
volume
cubic meter
cubic centimeter

▶ Visualize a Cubic Meter

The basic metric unit for measuring **volume** is a **cubic meter**.

This is a **cubic centimeter**.

Units of Volume			
cubic meter	cubic decimeter	cubic centimeter	cubic millimeter
cu m	cu dm	cu cm	cu mm
1 cu m	1,000 × smaller	1,000 × 1,000 × smaller	1,000 × 1,000 × 1,000 × smaller
	1,000 cu dm = 1 cu m	1,000,000 cu cm = 1 cu m	1,000,000,000 cu mm = 1 cu m

1. How many centimeters are equal to one meter? __100 cm__

2. How many cubic centimeters do you think you will need for a cubic meter?
   100 × 100 × 100 or, 1,000,000 cu cm

3. What pattern do you see in the metric units of volume in the chart?
   Each cubic unit is 1,000 times smaller than the one to its left.

▶ Measure Volume

Each student at Lincoln School has a coat locker. Each locker is 1 meter high, 3 decimeters deep, and 5 decimeters across.

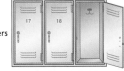

4. How can you find the total space inside a student locker?
   Convert all measurements to the same unit and then multiply the height, depth, and width.

5. What is the volume of each locker? __150 cu dm__

UNIT 6 LESSON 3   Measure Volume and Capacity **271**

Student Activity Book page 271

▶ **Visualize a Cubic Meter** SMALL GROUPS

Invite students to share suggestions for ways to make one cubic meter. Encourage them to think about how they used cubic centimeters to make a cubic decimeter.

● How many cubic decimeters do you need to have to make one cubic meter? 10 cu dm across, 10 cu dm deep, 10 cu dm high, for a total of 1,000 cu dm

● How can you find out how many cubic centimeters are in 1 cubic meter? 100 × 100 × 100 = 1,000,000 cu cm

Have students work in **Small Groups** to complete exercises 1–3 on Student Book page 271.

▶ **Measure Volume** SMALL GROUPS

Have students look at the chart on Student Book page 271. Use the chart as a tool for discussing and relating metric units of volume.

● How do the names for metric units of volume relate to the names for metric units of length? The names are the same but include the word *cubic.*

Invite students to work together in **Small Groups** to discuss and solve exercises 4–5.

Measure the Volume of a Classroom Object
Again working in their **Small Groups**, students find a classroom object that is shaped like a rectangular prism, measure it, and determine its volume. Invite students to share their work with the rest of the class.

✓ Ongoing Assessment

As the groups measure and find the volume of a classroom object, engage them in conversations about the units and the calculations.

▶ What unit did you use for the length measurements?

▶ What unit will you use for volume?

▶ How do you calculate volume?

Watch for students who seem to be struggling with the multiplication and follow up with extra help.

Activity 3

Metric Units of Liquid Volume

 15 MINUTES

Goal: Discuss the difference between measuring volume and measuring capacity; recognize and relate metric units of capacity.

Materials: empty 1-L soda or water bottle, Student Activity Book or Hardcover Book p. 272

 NCTM Standard:
Measurement

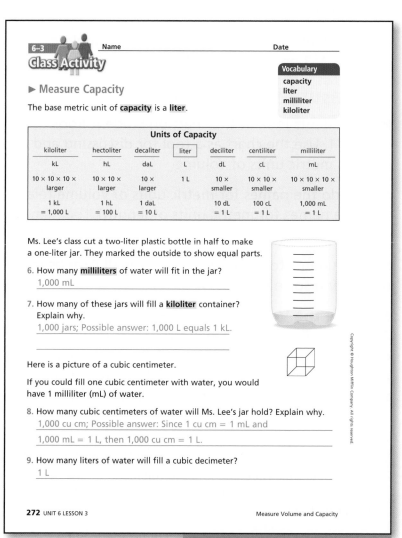

▶ **Measure Capacity** SMALL GROUPS

Give the students a chance to see and handle an empty 1-L soda or water bottle so they can get a sense of how big one liter is.

Explain that capacity is a measure of how much a container can hold, and it is used to describe the volume of a liquid.

Have students examine the chart on Student Book page 272. Together, discuss the names of units of capacity and compare units of capacity to those of volume and length. Be sure students recognize that:

● the base unit is different from that of volume or length, but the prefixes remain the same.

● the relationship between neighboring units remains the same.

Have the students work in **Small Groups** to complete exercises 6–9.

▶ **Estimate Capacity** WHOLE CLASS

Bring a variety of empty plastic containers from home and display them in the classroom. Provide students with a benchmark (such as "This container has a capacity of 100 milliliters."), and ask them to use the benchmark to estimate the capacity of the other containers.

Students can also use a familiar benchmark, such as an empty plastic 12-ounce water bottle, to make estimates. The metric equivalent of such a bottle is about 350 mL. Students can estimate the capacity of the other containers in milliliters.

If water is available, students could pour water to check the reasonableness of their estimates.

②Going Further

Differentiated Instruction

Intervention — Activity Card 6-3

Count Cubes — Activity Card 6-3 ●

Work: In Pairs

Use:
• Centimeter cubes (about 150)

1. One partner uses the centimeter cubes to make a rectangular prism.

2. The other partner records the dimensions of the prism. Then count the cubes to find the volume.

3. **Work Together** Use the formula for the volume of a rectangular prism to calculate the volume.

   Volume = length × width × height

4. Exchange roles and repeat the activity.

Unit 6, Lesson 3   Copyright © Houghton Mifflin Company

Activity Note Have students use the same number of cubes to make a second prism and repeat the activity. Discuss why the volumes are equal.

✎ Math Writing Prompt

Investigate Math Explain how to find the volume of a rectangular prism built from centimeter cubes without counting the cubes. Why might this method be useful for very large prisms?

Soar to Success Math ★ Software Support

Use *Soar to Success* for instruction of students needing targeted support for underlying skills.

On Level — Activity Card 6-3

Match Game — Activity Card 6-3 ▲

Work: In Pairs

Use:
• Make a Meter (TRB M69) or centimeter ruler
• Scissors
• Several box-shaped objects

1. One partner chooses an object. The other chooses another object with about the same volume.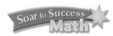

2. On your own, measure the dimensions of your object, and calculate the volume. Compare results with your partner, and check each other's work.

3. The first partner earns one point if the difference in volumes is greater than 10 cubic centimeters. The second partner earns one point if the difference in volumes is less than 10 cubic centimeters.

4. Exchange roles and repeat the activity. The first player to earn 5 points wins.

Unit 6, Lesson 3   Copyright © Houghton Mifflin Company

Activity Note Before beginning the activity, remind students of metric benchmarks that can help them estimate. Have students discuss any particular strategies they use to select the second object.

✎ Math Writing Prompt

Summarize Information Describe how the metric system works by describing the prefixes and base units.

MegaMath Software Support

Use *MegaMath* for review and reinforcement of the concepts and skills presented in this lesson.

Challenge — Activity Card 6-3

More Than One Solution — Activity Card 6-3 ■

Work: By Yourself

1. A rectangular sink holds 6 L of water when the water in the sink is 5 cm deep. What could be the length and width of the sink?

2. Use what you know about finding volume to find 3 possible solutions for the length and width of the sink. The information below will help you. Possible solutions: Any set of dimensions for a 1,200 sq cm rectangle.

   6 L = 6,000 mL
   6,000 mL = 6,000 cu cm

3. **Explain** What strategy did you use to solve the problem? Why did you choose that strategy?

Unit 6, Lesson 3   Copyright © Houghton Mifflin Company

Activity Note Remind students that the formula for volume is
volume (v) = length (l) × width (w) × height (h).

✎ Math Writing Prompt

Explain Your Thinking About how many 2-liter bottles of water are equivalent to one gallon? Explain how you know.

✦ DESTINATION Math· Software Support

Use *Destination Math* to take students beyond the concepts and skills presented in this lesson.

③ Homework and Spiral Review

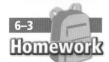
Homework **Goal:** Additional Practice

✓ Include students' work for page 179 as part of their portfolios.

6–3 Name _____ Date _____
Homework

Complete.

1. How many milliliters are equal to 3 L?
3,000 mL

2. How many milliliters are equal to 35 L?
35,000 mL

3. How many liters are equal to 5,000 milliliters?
5 L

4. How many kiloliters are equal to 5,000 liters?
5 kL

Solve.   *Show your work.*

5. Every morning for breakfast, Mika drinks 200 mL of orange juice. How many liters of orange juice does she drink in 10 days?
2 L of orange juice

6. Steven's crayon box is 7 cm wide, 2 dm long, and 4 cm deep. What is the volume of Steven's crayon box in cubic centimeters?
560 cu cm

7. Write and solve a metric-volume word problem and a metric-capacity word problem.
Word problems will vary.
_____
_____
_____
_____
_____

UNIT 6 LESSON 3   Measure Volume and Capacity **179**

Homework and Remembering page 179

6–3 Name _____ Date _____
Remembering

Use each digit once. Write the greatest number and the least number you can make.

	Greatest	Least
1. 9, 4, 8, 1, 2, 4, 0, 7	98,744,210	10,244,789
2. 6, 4, 1, 9, 2, 1, 3, 0	96,432,110	10,123,469
3. 7, 0, 6, 3, 0, 5, 8	8,765,300	3,005,678
4. 5, 3, 7, 0, 4, 2, 6	7,654,320	2,034,567

Compare. Write >, <, or =.

5. $8,135 < 8,153$ **6.** $67,280 < 68,720$ **7.** $153,609 < 156,390$

8. $2,409 < 2,904$ **9.** $92,416 > 91,426$ **10.** $502,147 < 520,147$

11. $6,711 > 6,171$ **12.** $89,735 > 83,597$ **13.** $620,793 > 620,739$

Write the value of the underlined digit.

14. 5,6̲73 600   **15.** 1̲9,357 9,000   **16.** 4̲7,678 40,000

17. 6̲78,924 600,000   **18.** 1,8̲39,155 30,000   **19.** 8,08̲4,576 0

Solve.   *Show your work.*

20. Mr. Okutani is decorating a bulletin board that is 5 dm high and 7 dm wide. He has 2 packages of border that each contain 125 cm of border. Does he have enough border to go all around the outside of the bulletin board? Explain.
Bulletin board: 50 + 50 + 70 + 70 = 240 cm
Border: 125 + 125 = 250 cm
Yes; the amount of border is greater than the
perimeter of the bulletin board.

180 UNIT 6 LESSON 3   Measure Volume and Capacity

Homework and Remembering page 180

Home or School Activity

 Real-World Connection

Unusual Units of Volume Estimate the volume of a bathtub.

- How many tennis balls would fit in a bowling ball?
- How many bowling balls would fit in a beach ball?
- How many beach balls would fit in your bathtub?

1 bathtub = _____ tennis balls

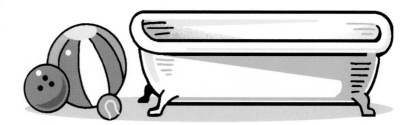

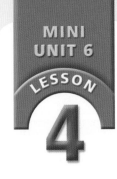

MINI UNIT 6

LESSON

4

Measure Mass

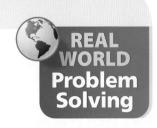

REAL WORLD Problem Solving

Lesson Objectives

- Recognize metric units of mass.
- Measure the mass of objects, using metric units.

Vocabulary

mass	milligram
gram	tonne
kilogram	

The Day at a Glance

Today's Goals	Materials	
1 Teaching the Lesson **A1:** Identify and relate metric units of mass. **A2:** Compare and describe data about mass measured in metric units. **A3:** Measure the mass of real-world objects in metric units; display data in a bar graph. **2 Going Further** ▶ Differentiated Instruction **3 Homework and Spiral Review**	**Lesson Activities** Student Activity Book pp. 273–274 or Student Hardcover Book pp. 273–274 Homework and Remembering pp. 181–182 Balance scales Metric weights or common objects with a mass of about one gram Meter strips from Lesson 1 or metric rulers	**Going Further** Activity Cards 6-4 Metric Mass Unit Cards (TRB M72) Balance scales Quart or liter bottle of liquid Various classroom objects 123 *Use* Math Talk *today!*

Keeping Skills Sharp

Daily Routines	English Language Learners
Homework Review Ask a student volunteer to share a word problem. Invite several students to solve it at the board, while the others work at their seats. **Strategy Problem** The Yoo family's entertainment center is in four sections that stand side by side. The sections are two drawer units of the same size, a bookcase, and a TV cabinet. The TV cabinet is as wide as the bookcase and the drawer units together. One drawer unit is 15 inches wide and is ½ the width of the bookcase. How wide is the entire entertainment center? 120 inches, or 10 feet	Draw an elephant, a cat, and an ant on the board. Have students tell which is the largest, smallest, heaviest, and lightest. Write *matter*. Say: **Everything is made of matter. The elephant is the biggest. It has the most matter.** Write the word *mass*. Say: **Mass is the amount of matter in an object.** • **Beginning** Say: **The elephant has the most ___.** matter **It has the greatest mass. The ant has the least mass.** Have students repeat. • **Intermediate** Ask: **Which of these animals has the most matter?** the elephant **Does the elephant have the greatest mass?** yes **Which animal has the least matter?** the ant **Does it have the least mass?** yes • **Advanced** Ask: **Which animal has more matter and a greater mass than you?** the elephant Have students identify animals that have less matter and a smaller mass than themselves.

1 Teaching the Lesson

Activity 1

Mass

 15 MINUTES

Goal: Identify and relate metric units of mass.

Materials: one or more balance scales with metric weights, or common objects with a mass of about one gram (small metal paper clips, centimeter cubes); Student Activity Book or Hardcover Book p. 273

 NCTM Standard:
Measurement

▶ What a Gram Feels Like WHOLE CLASS

If you have access to a balance scale with metric weights, give the students a chance to hold the gram weight and to balance a few lightweight objects on the scale.

Alternatively, use a common object with a mass of one gram, such as a small metal paper clip, to give the students an approximate benchmark. Some manufactured centimeter cubes have a mass of one gram.

Teaching Note

Math Background *Mass* is the amount of matter in an object. Mass is constant. A mass of one gram is the same on Earth or on the Moon. Scientists like to measure mass rather than weight because it is constant.

Weight is the effect of gravity on matter. Because the force of gravity is not the same everywhere in the universe, weight varies. For example, a person weighs less on the Moon than he or she does on Earth because the force of gravity is less on the Moon.

▶ Measure Mass WHOLE CLASS

As a class, discuss the chart at the top of Student Book page 273.

● What is the base metric unit for measuring mass? the gram

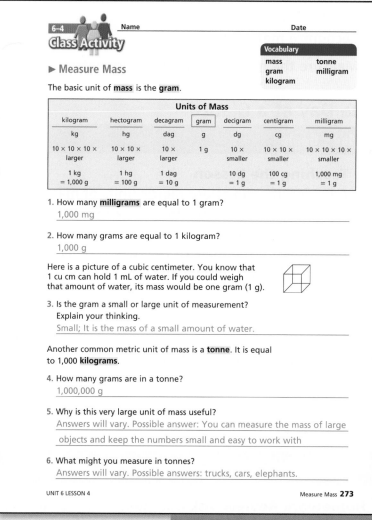

Student Activity Book page 273

● How are the names of the units that measure mass alike? They all have *gram* in them.

● Which units are larger than a gram? kilogram, hectogram, decagram

● Which units are smaller? decigram, centigram, milligram

● What do you notice about the prefixes? They are the same as those for other metric measuring units.

Invite the students to work in **Small Groups** to complete exercises 1–6.

Activity 2

Compare Mass

 20 MINUTES

Goal: Compare and describe data about mass measured in metric units.

Materials: Student Activity Book or Hardcover Book p. 274

 NCTM Standards:
Measurement
Data Analysis and Probability

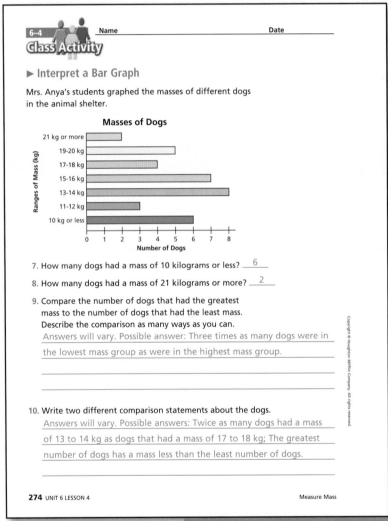

6-4
Class Activity

Name _____ Date _____

▶ **Interpret a Bar Graph**

Mrs. Anya's students graphed the masses of different dogs in the animal shelter.

Masses of Dogs

Ranges of Mass (kg): 21 kg or more, 19-20 kg, 17-18 kg, 15-16 kg, 13-14 kg, 11-12 kg, 10 kg or less

Number of Dogs: 0 1 2 3 4 5 6 7 8

7. How many dogs had a mass of 10 kilograms or less? __6__

8. How many dogs had a mass of 21 kilograms or more? __2__

9. Compare the number of dogs that had the greatest mass to the number of dogs that had the least mass. Describe the comparison as many ways as you can.
   Answers will vary. Possible answer: Three times as many dogs were in the lowest mass group as were in the highest mass group.

10. Write two different comparison statements about the dogs.
    Answers will vary. Possible answers: Twice as many dogs had a mass of 13 to 14 kg as dogs that had a mass of 17 to 18 kg; The greatest number of dogs has a mass less than the least number of dogs.

274 UNIT 6 LESSON 4   Measure Mass

Copyright © Houghton Mifflin Company. All rights reserved.

Student Activity Book page 274

▶ **Interpret a Bar Graph** WHOLE CLASS

Have the students discuss the graph. Review the parts of a bar graph (title, axes, scales) and what the bars show.

● A graph is a good way to summarize and present data. Why is it important to have a title for your graph? The title tells you what the graph is all about. Without a title you wouldn't know how to interpret the data.

● What else on the graph helps you understand what the graph is showing? Each bar shows the mass of a dog.

● What do the bars show us? They show the number of dogs in each mass range.

● How can you use a bar graph to make comparisons? You can look at the bars and quickly see which one is longer. You can also see how much longer each bar is than another. If you need to know the exact numbers, you can look at the axes and figure it out.

 Math Talk Ask the students to complete exercises 7–10. Encourage them to use the language of mathematics to compare the information. For example:

● Four more dogs had a mass of 10 kg or less than had a mass of 21 kg or more.

● Four fewer dogs had a mass of 21 kg or more than had a mass of 10 kg or less.

● Three times as many dogs had a mass of 10 kg or less than had a mass of 21 kg or more.

● One third as many dogs had a mass of 21 kg or more than had a mass of 10 kg or less.

✓ Ongoing Assessment

It's estimated that each person in the United States consumed about 122 kg of meat during the year 2000. Ask students to write the equivalent of 122 kg in hectograms, decagrams, grams, decigrams, centigrams, and milligrams.

Activity 3

Find Mass

 20 MINUTES

Goal: Measure the mass of real-world objects in metric units; display data in a bar graph.

Materials: balance scales with metric weights, meter strips from Lesson 1 or metric rulers

 NCTM Standards:
Measurement
Data Analysis and Probability

▶ Find the Mass of Real-World Objects

SMALL GROUPS

Ask students to work in **Small Groups** to find the mass of several objects in the classroom. Have them make a bar graph of their data and then write comparison statements to summarize their data.

Invite each group to present its data and comparisons to the rest of the class.

Encourage students to state their comparisons in a variety of ways. For example:

● You found that there are twice as many objects with a mass from 10 g to 11 g than a mass from 4 g to 5 g. How else can you say that? There were half as many objects with a mass from 4 g to 5 g as a mass from 10 g to 11 g.

● Four more objects were between 5 g and 6 g than were between 6 g and 7 g. What's another way to say that? Four fewer objects were between 6 g and 7 g than were between 5 g and 6 g.

 Alternate Approach

Use Volume to Determine Mass If you do not have access to balance scales, have students use volume to determine mass. Students use their meter strips from Lesson 1 to measure the volume of various objects in the classroom. Remind students that one cubic centimeter holds one milliliter of water that has a mass of one gram. Have students calculate what the mass of each object would be if it were made of water, and then continue the lesson as described.

▶ Estimate Mass WHOLE CLASS

Bring a variety of items from home that have metric measures of mass, such as a small cereal box, a box of baking soda, a bag of oatmeal, and so on. Use a piece of masking tape to cover the mass description that appears on each item. Make sure the tape can be lifted to read the original mass or weight.

Provide students with a benchmark (such as "This product has a mass of 500 grams.") and ask them to use the benchmark to estimate the mass of the other items. One way for students to make an estimate is to hold the benchmark item in one hand and another item in the other hand. "If this box is 500 grams, then this item is about 100 grams."

If a scale is available, students could use metric weights and the containers to check their estimates.

 Class Management

As the groups work through the task, ensure that they are thinking about the title, axes, labels, and scale for their bar graph.

② Going Further

● Intervention   Activity Card 6-4

Match Game   Activity Card 6-4 ●

Work: In Pairs

Use:
- Metric Mass Unit Cards (TRB M72)
- Scissors

1. **Work Together** Cut out the cards and shuffle them. Place them face down without overlapping.

2. Take turns turning over two cards at a time. If the cards show a unit and its abbreviation, keep the cards. If not, turn the cards back over.

3. Continue playing until all the cards are matched. The player with more cards at the end of the game wins.

Unit 6, Lesson 4   Copyright © Houghton Mifflin Company

Activity Note To extend the activity, have students refer to the Units of Mass chart on Student Book page 273 and name an object for each unit of mass.

Math Writing Prompt

Use Reasoning Why does it make more sense to measure the mass of your body in kilograms than in milligrams? What things might you measure in milligrams?

Soar to Success Math Software Support

Use *Soar to Success* for instruction of students needing targeted support for underlying skills.

▲ On Level   Activity Card 6-4

Use a Benchmark   Activity Card 6-4 ▲

Work: In Pairs

Use:
- Balance scale
- Quart or liter of liquid
- Classroom objects

1. A benchmark is a common item that you can use as a close estimate for a unit of measure. A liter or quart carton of milk is a good benchmark for a one-kilogram mass.

2. Choose 6 objects in the room, each with a different mass. Predict whether each object has a mass greater than or less than a liter carton of milk. Record each prediction.

3. Check your predictions by using the milk carton and a balance scale.

4. **Discuss** Were your predictions accurate? How could you make more accurate predictions?

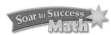

Unit 6, Lesson 4   Copyright © Houghton Mifflin Company

Activity Note One way to increase the accuracy of predictions is to identify additional benchmarks to compare with items to measure. Have students estimate the mass of a pint and a gallon.

Math Writing Prompt

Investigate Math Choose two metric units of mass, and explain how those units are related by multiplication and by division.

MegaMath Grades K-6 Software Support

Use *MegaMath* for review and reinforcement of the concepts and skills presented in this lesson.

■ Challenge   Activity Card 6-4

Equations and Measures   Activity Card 6-4 ■

Work: In Pairs

Use:
- Abbreviation cards from Metric Mass Unit Cards (TRB M72)
- Scissors

1. Cut out the abbreviation cards. Shuffle them and place them face down.

2. Select one pair of cards at a time and write an equation to show how the units are related.

3. For the seventh card, draw an object that can be measured by using that unit.

4. Shuffle the cards and place them face down again. Repeat the activity to write new equations.

Unit 6, Lesson 4   Copyright © Houghton Mifflin Company

Activity Note Students may wish to make a Units of Mass chart before beginning this activity to make it easier to relate the different units.

Math Writing Prompt

Explain Your Thinking How is the metric system of measurement the same as our place-value system, and how is it different?

DESTINATION Math Software Support

Use *Destination Math* to take students beyond the concepts and skills presented in this lesson.

③ Homework and Spiral Review

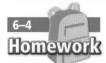

6–4 Homework Goal: Additional Practice

For homework, students work with metric units of mass and weight.

6–4 Remembering Goal: Spiral Review

This Remembering activity would be appropriate anytime after today's lesson.

6–4 Homework Name _____ Date _____

Complete.

1. How many grams are in 4 kg? _4,000 g_
2. How many grams are in 40 kg? _40,000 g_
3. How many grams are in 400 kg? _400,000 g_
4. How many grams are in 5,000 kg? _5,000,000 g_
5. How many grams are in 50,000 kg? _50,000,000 g_
6. How many grams are in 500,000 kg? _500,000,000 g_

Solve.   *Show your work.*

7. Angie's puppy weighed 3 kg when she first got it. Two years later, it weighed 9 kg. How many grams of weight did the puppy gain?
   _6,000 g_

8. Mr. Silverstein bought 3 packages of rice at the store. The big package contained 1 kg. Each of the 2 smaller packages contained 450 grams. How many grams of rice did he buy in all?
   _1,900 g_

9. Write and solve two metric-mass or metric-weight word problems.
   Word problems will vary.
   _____
   _____
   _____
   _____
   _____

UNIT 6 LESSON 4   Measure Mass **181**

Homework and Remembering page 181

6–4 Remembering Name _____ Date _____

Add or subtract. Round and estimate the addition or subtraction to see if your answer makes sense.

1. 37,496 + 1,530	2. 165,309 + 31,284	3. 488,531 − 48,260
39,026	196,593	440,271

4. 195,307 + 40,682	5. 514,736 + 278,093	6. 694,301 − 250,682
235,989	792,829	443,619

7. 6,830 + 270,915	8. 5,750,813 − 41,978	9. 9,835,061 − 784,255
277,745	5,708,835	9,050,806

Solve.   *Show your work.*

10. Every year, Edith runs 5K (5 km) races each month for 6 months. The other 6 months she runs 10K races. How many kilometers does she run in races each year?
    _90 km_

11. The floor of Rachel's bedroom is 16 sq m. Reggie's bedroom is 4 m wide and 5 m long. Whose bedroom is bigger? Explain your thinking.
    Reggie's bedroom: 4 × 5 = 20 sq m
    20 sq m is larger than 16 sq m, so Reggie's
    bedroom is bigger.

182 UNIT 6 LESSON 4   Measure Mass

Homework and Remembering page 182

Home or School Activity

 Science Connection

Animal Data The mass of an adult African elephant is about 7,000 kg, or 7,000,000 g. An adult polar bear has a mass of about 600 kg, or 600,000 g. Have students investigate the mass of other animals and display their data in a table showing both grams and kilograms.

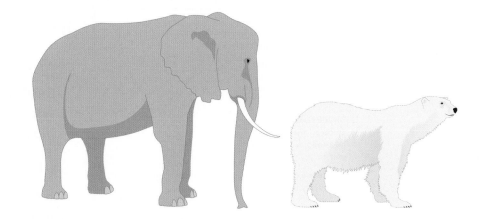

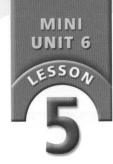

Measure Temperature

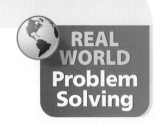
Lesson Objectives

- Demonstrate understanding of the metric temperature scale.
- Relate the metric temperature scale to everyday experiences.

Vocabulary

Celsius
Fahrenheit

The Day at a Glance

Today's Goals	Materials
1 **Teaching the Lesson** **A1:** Explore and identify temperatures, using the Celsius scale. **A2:** Relate Celsius temperatures to real-world situations. **A3:** Choose an appropriate metric measurement and explain the choice. **2** **Going Further** ▶ Differentiated Instruction **3** **Homework and Spiral Review**	**Lesson Activities** Student Activity Book pp. 275–276 or Student Hardcover Book pp. 275–276 Homework and Remembering pp. 183–184 Quick Quiz (Assessment Guide) Transparency of Celsius and Fahrenheit Temperatures (TRB M73) Temperature Pairs (TRB M74) Overhead projector (optional) Calculators (optional) Sheet protectors Dry-erase markers **Going Further** Activity Cards 6-5 Student Activity Book p. 275 or Student Hardcover Book p. 275 Temperature Pairs (TRB M74) Scissors Calculators Math Journals

123 Use Math Talk today!

Keeping Skills Sharp

Daily Routines	English Language Learners
Homework Review Ask students to describe briefly some strategies they used in their homework. Sometimes you will find that students solve the problem correctly but use an inefficient strategy. **Reasoning** A rectangle has side lengths of 4 feet and 8 feet. How can you change the side lengths so the rectangle will have half the area? 4 ft × 4 ft one fourth the area? 4 ft × 2 ft Explain your thinking.	Draw a thermometer on the board and label it *thermometer*. Have students name things that the thermometer can be used for. Write *temperature scale* and list *Fahrenheit* and *Celsius* underneath. • **Beginning** Say: **A thermometer is a measurement tool. We use it to measure temperature.** Have students repeat. Say: **The common temperature scale in the U.S. is called** *Fahrenheit*. **The metric temperature scale is called** *Celsius*. Have students repeat. • **Intermediate** Say: **What kind of measurement tool is this?** a thermometer **What does a thermometer measure?** temperature **What is the common temperature scale in the U.S.?** Fahrenheit **What is the metric temperature scale?** Celsius • **Advanced** Have students tell what they use thermometer for and what is the difference between the Fahrenheit and Celsius temperature scales.

1 Teaching the Lesson

Activity 1

The Celsius Scale

 20 MINUTES

Goal: Explore and identify temperatures, using the Celsius scale.

Materials: Student Activity Book or Hardcover Book pp. 275–276; transparency of Celsius and Fahrenheit Temperatures (TRB M73) and overhead projector (optional); calculator (optional)

 NCTM Standard:
Measurement

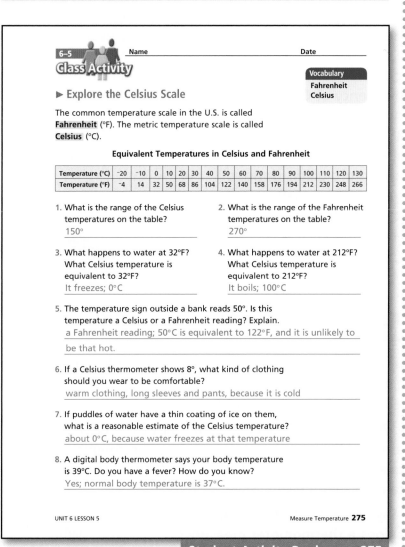

Student Activity Book page 275

▶ Explore the Celsius Scale

| WHOLE CLASS | | Math Talk |

Invite students to discuss what they already know about the Celsius temperature scale. Use the chart on Student Book page 275 as a tool for discussion. Relate temperatures in the chart to those the students are familiar with, such as today's indoor or outdoor temperature or other recent temperatures. You can use TRB M73 on an overhead projector to help the students better understand the Celsius scale. Use **Solve and Discuss** for exercises 1–8.

▶ Write Equivalent Temperatures | PAIRS |

After the discussion, have the students work in **Student Pairs** or **Small Groups** to complete exercises 9–14 on Student Book page 276.

Teaching Note

Math Background Anders Celsius was a Swedish astronomer who lived from 1701 to 1744. He devised a temperature scale where 0° was the freezing point of water and 100° was the boiling point of water. He called it the "centigrade scale" because it had 100 degrees. Later, it became known as the Celsius scale.

 Alternate Approach

Use a Calculator to Convert Temperature Although students need to understand Celsius temperature by relating it to everyday experiences, they can also practice using mathematical formulas on a calculator to convert between Fahrenheit and Celsius temperatures.

$$°C = (°F - 32) ÷ 1.8$$

$$°F = (°C × 1.8) + 32$$

Write the formulas on the board. Choose some Fahrenheit temperatures and some Celsius temperatures from the chart on Student Book page 275, and ask students to convert them. This will help students gain confidence with the formulas. Students can then practice converting temperatures that do not appear in the chart.

Celsius Temperatures

 20 MINUTES

Goal: Relate Celsius temperatures to real-world situations.

Materials: Temperature Pairs (TRB M74), sheet protector, dry-erase markers, Student Activity Book or Hardcover Book p. 276

✔ **NCTM Standard:**
Measurement

▶ Relate Celsius Temperatures to Everyday Experiences [INDIVIDUALS]

Give each student TRB M74 and a sheet protector. Present students with a temperature situation, and have them use a dry-erase marker to mark the Celsius thermometer with an appropriate temperature or temperature range for each situation. Situations and answers might include:

- a comfortable bath or shower warm but not hot, about 25°C

- a summer drink cool but not frozen, about 8°C

- cooking a hot dog in water boiling hot, 100°C

- a snow cone freezing or just above freezing, 0° to 3°C

- normal body temperature, 37°C

Invite students to show their work, share their suggestions, and explain their thinking. If there is time, have students suggest other temperature situations while their classmates mark the temperature range and explain their answers.

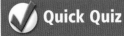 **Quick Quiz**

See Assessment Guide for Unit 6 Quick Quiz.

6–5
Class Activity

Name _____ Date _____

▶ **Write Equivalent Temperatures**

Write an equivalent temperature. Use the chart on the previous page. Estimates may vary.

9. 40°F 5°C   10. 75°F 24°C   11. 0°F ⁻18°C

12. 15°C 59°F   13. 35°C 95°F   14. ⁻15°C 5°F

▶ **Relate Celsius Temperatures to Everyday Experiences**

Each day of the school year, Mr. James's students measure the outside temperature in degrees Celsius (°C). They made a table of their results. This table shows four sample weeks from different times of the year.

Days	Week A					Week B					Week C					Week D				
	M	T	W	Th	F	M	T	W	Th	F	M	T	W	Th	F	M	T	W	Th	F
Temp. (°C)	⁻20	⁻19	⁻18	⁻4	⁻8	6	5	8	4	9	13	15	18	21	18	28	31	27	25	29

15. How is the temperature during Week A different from the temperature in Week D?
much colder during Week A than Week D
_____
_____

16. In your city, what month or months of the year could each week represent? Explain your thinking.
Answers will vary.
_____
_____

276 UNIT 6 LESSON 5   Measure Temperature

Student Activity Book page 276

---

(123) **Math Talk** Have the students look at Student Book page 276. Together, discuss the temperatures in the table that accompanies exercises 15 and 16.

- What might you want to drink if you were playing outside during week A? Possible answer: hot chocolate

- What might you want to drink if you were playing outside during week D? Possible answer: lemonade

- Do you think week D could be the week that comes after week A? No. The temperatures for week A are very different from the temperatures in week D. I don't think the temperatures would change that quickly.

Ask students to work together in **Small Groups** to complete exercises 15 and 16.

Activity 3

Measurement Units and Tools

 15 MINUTES

Goal: Choose an appropriate metric measurement and explain the choice.

 NCTM Standard:
Measurement

▶ Choose an Appropriate Measurement Unit WHOLE CLASS

Ask students what metric units they would use to

- describe the distance between two cities. kilometers
- measure the mass of a dog. kilograms
- describe the amount of juice in a bottle. milliliters or centiliters
- decide whether to wear a jacket to school. degrees Celsius
- describe the volume of a box. cubic centimeters or cubic decimeters

Invite a volunteer to suggest a measurement task; have the class choose an appropriate metric unit for that measurement. They should be able to explain their thinking. For example:

- What is a possible measurement situation? find the length of a pencil
- The situation you named is about finding length. What is the base unit of length in the metric system? the meter
- What prefix might you choose to go with the meter? Why? I would choose *centi-*. Decimeters would be too big because I think the length of a pencil would be just a bit more than one decimeter.
- Would another prefix make sense, too? *Milli-* would work, too. With millimeters, the number would be bigger, but it wouldn't be too big.

▶ Choose the Appropriate Measurement Tool SMALL GROUPS

List the following tools on the board:

- centimeter ruler
- meter stick
- protractor
- cup
- scale
- thermometer
- clock
- square units
- cubic units

Ask for Ideas Invite students to work in **Small Groups** to suggest the names of other tools that are used to measure, and add those names to the list.

Make a List Then have students make a list of three situations for which each tool is used to measure.

Share Ideas After the lists have been compiled, invite a volunteer from each group to read their list aloud.

Differentiated Instruction

Advanced Learners Have students track temperatures in degrees Celsius one day a week for the rest of the year. Every week, a different student can record TV or radio reports, or research on the Internet for official weather bureau reports.

✓ Ongoing Assessment

Ask students to explain how to identify the base unit of a metric measurement from reading the name of the unit. Then ask them how to identify the number of base units in the name of a metric unit.

②Going Further

Intervention — Activity Card 6-5

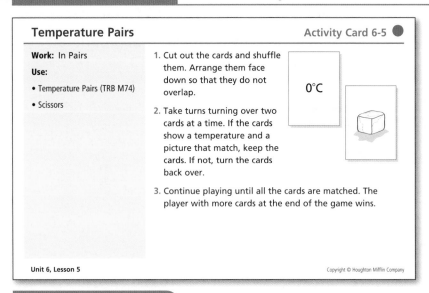

Temperature Pairs   Activity Card 6-5 ●

Work: In Pairs

Use:
- Temperature Pairs (TRB M74)
- Scissors

1. Cut out the cards and shuffle them. Arrange them face down so that they do not overlap.

0°C

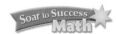

2. Take turns turning over two cards at a time. If the cards show a temperature and a picture that match, keep the cards. If not, turn the cards back over.

3. Continue playing until all the cards are matched. The player with more cards at the end of the game wins.

Unit 6, Lesson 5   Copyright © Houghton Mifflin Company

Activity Note After students have finished the game, discuss other possible situations that match each temperature.

✎ Math Writing Prompt

Use Reasoning Describe the difference in the clothing you might wear for temperatures of 30°F and 30°C.

Soar to Success Math — Software Support

Use *Soar to Success* for instruction of students needing targeted support for underlying skills.

On Level — Activity Card 6-5

Show What You Know   Activity Card 6-5 ▲

Work: In Pairs

1. On your own, write about a situation that is weather or temperature related.

2. Exchange your paper with your partner. Write a reasonable temperature range in degrees Celsius to match the situation.

3. **Discuss** How did you decide your response to the given situation?

4. Repeat the activity for a new situation.

Unit 6, Lesson 5   Copyright © Houghton Mifflin Company

Activity Note Suggest that students use benchmarks to help them determine the range for each situation and to justify responses.

✎ Math Writing Prompt

Estimate Explain how the Celsius scale makes it easy to remember the freezing point and boiling point of water. How does this help you estimate temperatures on the Celsius scale?

MegaMath Grades K-6 — Software Support

Use *MegaMath* for review and reinforcement of the concepts and skills presented in this lesson.

Challenge — Activity Card 6-5

Predict and Verify   Activity Card 6-5 ■

Work: By Yourself

Use:
- Temperature chart on Student Book page 275
- Calculator

1. Select 10 temperatures in degrees Fahrenheit that do not appear in the temperature chart on Student Book page 275.

2. Use the chart to estimate each temperature in degrees Celsius.

$$°C = (°F - 32) ÷ 1.8$$

$$°F = (°C × 1.8) + 32$$

3. Use a calculator and the formulas above to check your predictions.

4. **Explain** What strategies did you use to make your predictions?

Unit 6, Lesson 5   Copyright © Houghton Mifflin Company

Activity Note Remind students to be careful about how they enter numbers and operations into the calculator so that it performs the operations in the correct order.

✎ Math Writing Prompt

Explain Your Thinking Will the number value of a measure in degrees Celsius always be less than the number value for the equivalent degrees Fahrenheit? Explain how you know.

✳ DESTINATION Math — Software Support

Use *Destination Math* to take students beyond the concepts and skills presented in this lesson.

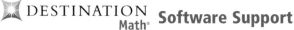

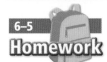 # Homework and Spiral Review

Homework Goal: Additional Practice

✓ Include students' work for page 183 as part of their portfolios.

Remembering Goal: Spiral Review

This Remembering activity would be appropriate anytime after today's lesson.

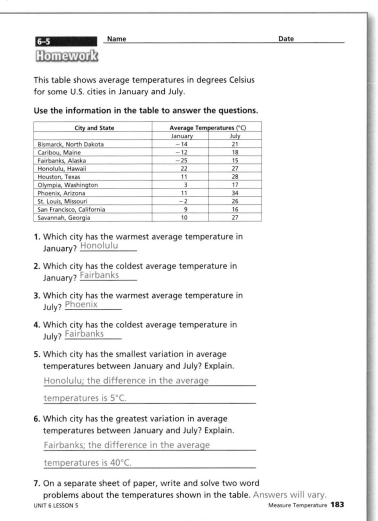

6–5   Name   Date

Homework

This table shows average temperatures in degrees Celsius for some U.S. cities in January and July.

Use the information in the table to answer the questions.

City and State	Average Temperatures (°C)	
	January	July
Bismarck, North Dakota	−14	21
Caribou, Maine	−12	18
Fairbanks, Alaska	−25	15
Honolulu, Hawaii	22	27
Houston, Texas	11	28
Olympia, Washington	3	17
Phoenix, Arizona	11	34
St. Louis, Missouri	−2	26
San Francisco, California	9	16
Savannah, Georgia	10	27

1. Which city has the warmest average temperature in January? Honolulu

2. Which city has the coldest average temperature in January? Fairbanks

3. Which city has the warmest average temperature in July? Phoenix

4. Which city has the coldest average temperature in July? Fairbanks

5. Which city has the smallest variation in average temperatures between January and July? Explain.
   Honolulu; the difference in the average
   temperatures is 5°C.

6. Which city has the greatest variation in average temperatures between January and July? Explain.
   Fairbanks; the difference in the average
   temperatures is 40°C.

7. On a separate sheet of paper, write and solve two word problems about the temperatures shown in the table. Answers will vary.

UNIT 6 LESSON 5   Measure Temperature **183**

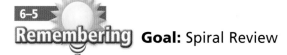

6–5   Name   Date

Remembering

Multiply.

1. 67	2. 98	3. 35	4. 26	5. 44	6. 59
× 3	× 7	× 8	× 13	× 37	× 82
201	686	280	338	1,628	4,838

Write the metric unit that you think best measures each amount or distance. Explain your thinking. Units and explanations may vary.

7. the distance between two cities
   kilometers

8. the amount of water in a glass
   milliliters

9. the height of a building
   meters

10. the width of a piece of paper
    centimeters

Solve.

11. Melba has a 2-liter bottle of water. She and 2 friends each drink 250 mL of the water. Together, did they drink more than or less than half of the bottle of water? Explain your thinking.
    2,000 − 250 − 250 − 250 = 1,250 mL
    Half of 2,000 mL is 1,000 mL. There are 1,250 mL left, so they drank less than half of the bottle of water together.

12. Two bottles of apple juice cost the same amount of money. One contains 1 L and the other contains 1,200 mL. Which bottle is the better buy?
    1 L = 1,000 mL
    The second bottle, containing 1,200 mL, is the better buy because there is more apple juice in it.

184 UNIT 6 LESSON 5   Measure Temperature

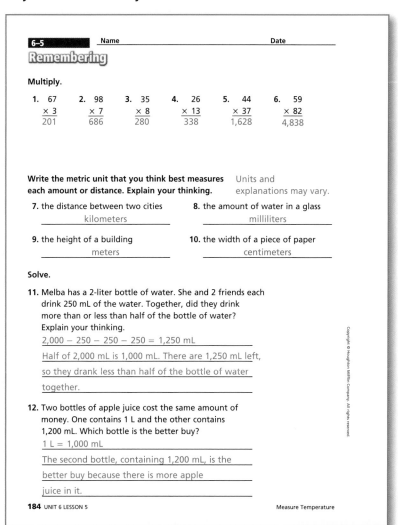

Homework and Remembering page 183

Homework and Remembering page 184

Home or School Activity

 ### Social Studies Connection

World Temperatures Students choose a place they would like to visit. Invite them to research the average high and low monthly temperatures in degrees Celsius for that place, and then to create a bar graph to display their results. Resources might include reference books, the Internet, or travel brochures.

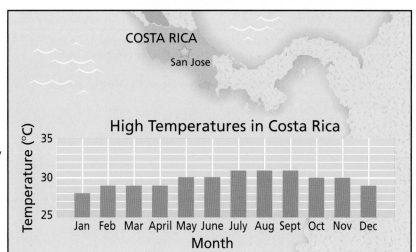

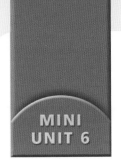

Unit Review and Test

Lesson Objective

● **Assess student progress on unit objectives.**

The Day at a Glance

Today's Goals	Materials
1 **Assessing the Unit** ▸ Assess student progress on unit objectives. ▸ Use activities from unit lessons to reteach content. **2** **Extending the Assessment** ▸ Use remediation for common errors. There is no homework assignment on a test day.	Unit 6 Test, Student Activity Book or Student Hardcover Book pp. 277–278 Unit 6 Test, Form A or B, Assessment Guide (optional) Unit 6 Performance Assessment, Assessment Guide (optional)

Keeping Skills Sharp

Daily Routines 🕐 5 MINUTES	
If you are doing a unit review day, go over the homework. If this is a test day, omit the homework review.	**Review and Test Day** You may want to choose a quiet game or other activity (reading a book or working on homework for another subject) for students who finish early.

Assessing the Unit

Assess Unit Objectives

⏱ **45 MINUTES** (more if schedule permits)

Goal: Assess student progress on unit objectives.

Materials: Student Activity Book or Hardcover Book pp. 277–278; Assessment Guide (optional)

▶ Review and Assessment

If your students are ready for assessment on the unit objectives, you may use either the test on the Student Book pages or one of the forms of the Unit 6 Test in the Assessment Guide to assess student progress.

If you feel that students need some review first, you may use the test on the Student Book pages as a review of unit content, and then use one of the forms of the Unit 6 Test in the Assessment Guide to assess student progress.

To assign a numerical score for all of these test forms, use 10 points for each question.

You may also choose to use the Unit 6 Performance Assessment. Scoring for that assessment can be found in its rubric in the Assessment Guide.

▶ Reteaching Resources

The chart lists the test items, the unit objectives they cover, and the lesson activities in which the objective is covered in this unit. You may revisit these activities with students who do not show mastery of the objectives.

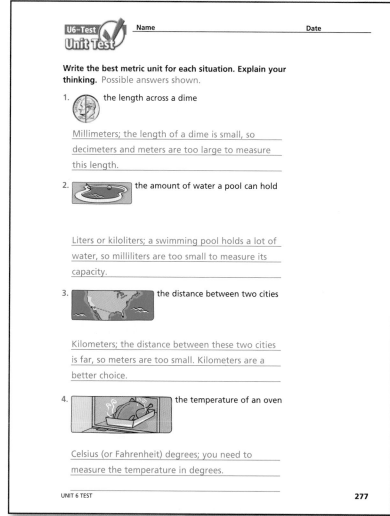

Student Activity Book page 277

Unit Test Items	Unit Objectives Tested	Activities to Use for Reteaching
5–6	**6.1** Convert between metric measures.	Lesson 1, Activities 1–2 Lesson 2, Activities 1, 3 Lesson 3, Activities 1–3 Lesson 4, Activity 1
9–10	**6.2** Solve problems involving metric measurements.	Lesson 1, Activity 3 Lesson 2, Activity 2 Lesson 3, Activity 2 Lesson 4, Activity 2 Lesson 5, Activity 2

U6–Test

Unit Test ✓

Name _____ Date _____

Write the correct metric unit to complete the equation.

5. 1 meter = 100 _centimeters_

6. 1,000 millimeters = 1 _meter_

7. 10 liters = 10,000 _milliliters_

8. 1,000 grams = 1 _kilogram_

Cassie entered the triple jump event at her school's field day. She made 3 attempts. Use this information to solve these word problems.

9. In her first attempt, Cassie jumped 1,210 cm in total. In her second attempt, she jumped 1,180 cm in total. How much farther, in centimeters, did she jump on the better of the two attempts?

30 cm farther

Show your work.

10. **Extended Response** In her third attempt, Cassie jumped 48 dm, 340 cm, and 4 m. What is the total distance, in centimeters, that Cassie jumped? Explain your answer.

You need to first convert the distances to the
same unit, centimeters; then add. She jumped
1,220 cm in total.

* Item 10 also assesses the process skills of Problem Solving and Communication.

278 UNIT 6 TEST

Student Activity Book page 278

Unit Test Items	Unit Objectives Tested	Activities to Use for Reteaching
1–4	**6.3** Choose the appropriate unit of measure (for length, mass, capacity, temperature, volume).	Lesson 1, Activity 3 Lesson 5, Activity 3

▶ **Assessment Resources**

Free Response Tests
Unit 6 Test, Student Activity Book or Hardcover Book pp. 277–278
Unit 6 Test, Form A, Assessment Guide

Extended Response Item
The last item in the Student Book test and in the Form A test will require an extended response as an answer.

Multiple Choice Test
Unit 6 Test, Form B, Assessment Guide

Performance Assessment
Unit 6 Performance Assessment, Assessment Guide
Unit 6 Performance Assessment Rubric, Assessment Guide

▶ **Portfolio Assessment**

Teacher-selected Items for Student Portfolios:

- Homework, Lessons 2, 3, and 5
- Class Activity work, Lessons 1, 4

Student-selected Items for Student Portfolios:

- Favorite Home or School Activity
- Best Writing Prompt

Unit Review and Test **665**

② Extending the Assessment

Unit Objective 6.1
Convert between metric measures.

Common Error: Uses Incorrect Operation When Converting

Some students may multiply when they convert from smaller units to larger units and divide when they convert from larger units to smaller units.

Remediation Have students measure a line on the floor that is 2 meters long (use masking tape). Give them measurement in both centimeters and meters. Help them to discover that the smaller the unit of measurement is, the larger the number of units is. For example, centimeters are smaller than meters; 200 is more than 2.

Unit Objective 6.2
Solve problems involving metric measurements.

Common Error: Doesn't Measure From Zero

Some students may fail to measure a length properly with their ruler.

Remediation Make sure students are measuring from the zero mark on their ruler. Rulers may vary from one manufacturer to another. On some rulers, for example, zero is positioned flush at the left end of the ruler. On others, zero is indented slightly from the left end of the ruler. Encourage students to familiarize themselves with the ruler they will be using to make measurements.

Unit Objective 6.3
Choose the appropriate unit of measure (for length, mass, capacity, temperature, volume).

Common Error: Does Not Recall the Units of Measure Used in the Metric System

Some students may not recall length, area, or volume when choosing a unit.

Remediation Have students make a poster or chart that shows the metric units used to measure length, mass, capacity, temperature, and volume.

Student Glossary

Glossary

acre A measure of land area. An acre is equal to 4,840 square yards.

acute angle An angle smaller than a right angle.

acute triangle A triangle with three acute angles.

addend One of two or more numbers added together to find a sum.

Example:

$$7 + 8 = 15$$

addend addend sum

analog clock A clock with a face and hands.

angle A figure formed by two rays with the same endpoint.

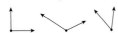

array An arrangement of objects, symbols, or numbers in rows and columns.

area The amount of surface covered or enclosed by a figure measured in square units.

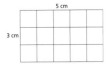

5 cm

3 cm

Associative Property of Addition Grouping the addends in different ways does not change the sum.

Example: $3 + (5 + 7) = 15$
$(3 + 5) + 7 = 15$

Associative Property of Multiplication Grouping the factors in different ways does not change the product.

Example: $3 \times (5 \times 7) = 105$
$(3 \times 5) \times 7 = 105$

Glossary (Continued)

average (mean) The size of each of n equal groups made from n data values. It is calculated by adding the values and dividing by n.

Example: 75, 84, 89, 91, 101
$75 + 84 + 89 + 91 + 101 = 440$,
then $440 \div 5 = 88$. The average is 88.

bar graph A graph that uses bars to show data. The bars may be vertical or horizontal.

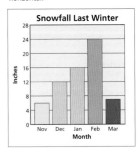

Snowfall Last Winter

Inches / Month (Nov, Dec, Jan, Feb, Mar)

base For a triangle or parallelogram, a base is any side. For a trapezoid, a base is either of the parallel sides. For a prism, a base is one of the congruent parallel faces that may not be rectangular. For a pyramid, the base is the face that does not touch the vertex of the pyramid.

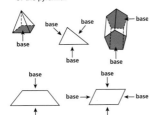

break-apart drawing A diagram that shows two addends and the sum.

81
72 9

capacity A measure of how much a container can hold.

Celsius The metric temperature scale.

---

center The point that is the same distance from every point on the circle.

center

centimeter A unit of measure in the metric system that equals one hundredth of a meter. 1 cm = 0.01 m

change minus A change situation that can be represented by subtraction. In a change minus situation, the starting number, the change, or the result will be unknown.

Example:

Unknown Start	Unknown Change	Unknown Result
$n - 2 = 3$	$5 - n = 3$	$5 - 2 = n$

change plus A change situation that can be represented by addition. In a change plus situation, the starting number, the change, or the result will be unknown.

Example:

Unknown Start	Unknown Change	Unknown Result
$n + 2 = 5$	$3 + n = 5$	$3 + 2 = n$

circle A plane figure that forms a closed path so that all the points on the path are the same distance from a point called the center.

circle graph A graph that uses parts of a circle to show data.

Example:

Favorite Fiction Books

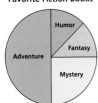

Humor, Fantasy, Mystery, Adventure

circumference The distance around a circle.

closed Having no endpoints.

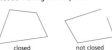

closed   not closed

collection situations Situations that involve putting together (joining) or taking apart (separating) groups.

column A part of a table or array that contains items arranged vertically.

Glossary (Continued)

combination situation A situation in which the number of possible different combinations is determined. A table can sometimes be used to show all possible combinations; multiplication can be used to calculate the number of combinations.

Example:

Different Sandwich Combinations

	peanut butter	cheese	turkey
wheat bread	peanut butter on wheat bread	cheese on wheat bread	turkey on wheat bread
white bread	peanut butter on white bread	cheese on white bread	turkey on white bread

Number of combinations = $3 \times 2 = 6$

common denominator A common multiple of two or more denominators.

Example: A common denominator of $\frac{1}{2}$ and $\frac{1}{3}$ is 6 because 6 is a multiple of 2 and 3.

Commutative Property of Addition Changing the order of addends does not change the sum.

Example: $3 + 8 = 11$
$8 + 3 = 11$

Commutative Property of Multiplication Changing the order of factors does not change the product.

Example: $3 \times 8 = 24$
$8 \times 3 = 24$

comparison bars Bars that represent the larger amount and smaller amount in a comparison situation.

For addition and subtraction:

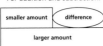

smaller amount   difference
larger amount

For multiplication and division:

smaller amount   smaller amount   smaller amount   larger amount
smaller amount

comparison situation A situation in which two amounts are compared by addition or by multiplication. An *additive comparison situation* compares by asking or telling how much more (how much less) one amount is than another. A *multiplicative comparison situation* compares by asking or telling how many times as much one amount is as another. The multiplicative comparison may also be made using fraction language. For example, you can say, "Sally has one fourth as much as Tom has," instead of saying "Tom has 4 times as much as Sally has."

complex figure A figure made by combining simple geometric figures like rectangles and triangles. The factor pairs of 18 are 1 and 18, 2 and 9, 3 and 6.

Student Glossary (Continued)

---

composite number A number greater than 1 that has more than one factor pair. Examples of composite numbers are 10 and 18. The factor pairs of 10 are 1 and 10, 2 and 5. The factor pairs of 18 are 1 and 18, 2 and 9, 3 and 6.

concave A polygon is concave if at least one diagonal is outside of the polygon.

cone A solid figure with a curved base and a single vertex.

circular cone

congruent Exactly the same size and shape.

Example: Triangles *ABC* and *PQR* are congruent.

convex A polygon is convex if all of the diagonals are inside the polygon.

cube A solid figure that has 6 faces that are congruent squares.

cubic centimeter A metric unit for measuring volume. It is the volume of a cube with one-centimeter edges.

cubic foot A unit for measuring volume. It is the volume of a cube with one-foot edges.

cubic inch A unit for measuring volume. It is the volume of a cube with one-inch edges.

cubic meter A metric unit for measuring volume. It is the volume of a cube with one-meter edges.

cubic yard A unit for measuring volume. It is the volume of a cube with one-yard edges.

cylinder A solid figure with two congruent curved bases.

circular cylinder

D

data A collection of information.

Glossary **S5**

Glossary (Continued)

decimal number A representation of a number using the numerals 0 to 9, in which each digit has a value 10 times the digit to its right. A dot or **decimal point** separates the whole-number part of the number on the left from the fractional part on the right.

Examples: 1.23 and 0.3

decimal point A symbol used to separate dollars and cents in money amounts or to separate ones and tenths in decimal numbers.

Examples:

$8.59   1.2

decimal point

decimeter A unit of measure in the metric system that equals one tenth of a meter. 1 dm = 0.1 m

denominator The number below the bar in a fraction. It shows the total number of equal parts in the fraction.

Example:

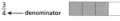

$\frac{3}{4}$ ◀— denominator

diagonal A line segment that connects vertices of a polygon, but is not a side of the polygon.

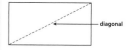

diagonal

diameter A line segment from one side of a circle to the other through the center. Also the length of that segment.

difference The result of a subtraction.

Example: 54 − 37 = 17 - difference

digit Any of the symbols 0, 1, 2, 3, 4, 5, 6, 7, 8, or 9.

digital clock A clock that shows us the hour and minutes with numbers.

 AM 9:30

Digit-by-Digit A method used to solve a division problem.

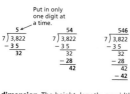

Put in only one digit at a time.

$$7\overline{)3,822}$$

dimension The height, length, or width.

Examples:
A line segment has only length, so it has *one* dimension.
A rectangle has length and width, so it has *two* dimensions.
A cube has length, width, and height, so it has *three* dimensions.

S6 Glossary

Distributive Property You can multiply a sum by a number, or multiply each addend by the number and add the products; the result is the same.

Example:

$3 \times (2 + 4) = (3 \times 2) + (3 \times 4)$

$3 \times 6 = 6 + 12$

$18 = 18$

dividend The number that is divided in division.

Example: $9\overline{)63}$, 63 is the dividend.

divisor The number you divide by in division.

Example: $9\overline{)63}$, 9 is the divisor.

dot array An arrangement of dots in rows and columns.

double bar graph Data is compared by using pairs of bars drawn next to each other.

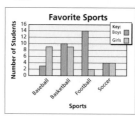

Favorite Sports

E

edge The line segment where two faces of a three-dimensional figure meet.

edge

equally likely In probability, equally likely means having the same chance of occurring.

Example: When flipping a coin, the coin is **equally likely** to land on heads or tails.

Equal-Shares Drawing A diagram that shows a number separated into equal parts.

equation A statement that two expressions are equal. It has an equals sign.

Examples: $32 + 35 = 67$

$67 = 32 + 34 + 1$

$(7 \times 8) + 1 = 57$

equilateral Having all equal sides.

Example: An equilateral triangle

equivalent fractions Two or more fractions that represent the same number.

Example: $\frac{2}{4}$ and $\frac{4}{8}$ are equivalent because they both represent one half.

Glossary **S7**

Glossary (Continued)

estimate A number close to an exact amount or to find about how many or how much.

expanded form A way of writing a number that shows the value of each of its digits.

Example: Expanded form of 835:
$800 + 30 + 5$
8 hundreds + 3 tens + 5 ones

Expanded Notation A method used to solve multiplication and division problems.

Examples:

43×67

$$\begin{array}{r} 67 = 60 + 7 \\ \times\, 43 = 40 + 3 \\ \hline 40 \times 60 = 2400 \\ 40 \times 7 = 280 \\ 3 \times 60 = 180 \\ 3 \times 7 = +21 \\ \hline 2,881 \end{array}$$

$3,822 \div 7$

$$\begin{array}{r} 6 \\ 40 \\ 500 \end{array} \Big\} 546$$

$$7\overline{)3,822}$$

expression One or more numbers, variables, or numbers and variables with one or more operations.

Examples: 4
$6x$
$6x - 5$
$7 + 4$

F

face A flat surface of a three-dimensional figure.

factor One of two or more numbers multiplied to find a product.

Example:

$4 \times 5 = 20$

factor   factor   product

Factor Fireworks Shows how a whole number can be broken down into a product of prime factors.

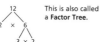

This is also called a **Factor Tree**.

factor pair A factor pair for a number is a pair of whole numbers whose product is that number.

Example:

$5 \times 7 = 35$

factor   product
pair

Factor Triangle A diagram that shows a factor pair and the product.

Example:

Fahrenheit The temperature scale used in the United States.

S8 Glossary

T2 Student Glossary

Fast Array A numerical form of an array that shows an unknown factor or unknown product.

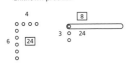

foot A U.S. customary unit of length equal to 12 inches.

fraction A number that is the sum of unit fractions, each an equal part of a set or part of a whole.

Examples: $\frac{3}{4} = \frac{1}{4} + \frac{1}{4} + \frac{1}{4}$

$\frac{5}{4} = \frac{1}{4} + \frac{1}{4} + \frac{1}{4} + \frac{1}{4} + \frac{1}{4}$

frequency table A table that shows how many times each event, item, or category occurs.

Frequency Table	
Height	Frequency
47	1
48	2
49	4
50	3
51	1
52	0
53	2
Total	13

function A set of ordered pairs of numbers such that for every first number there is only one possible second number.

Example: The relationship between yards and feet.

Yards	1	2	3	4	5	6	7
Feet	3	6	9	12	15	18	21

function table A table of ordered pairs that shows a function.

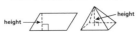

Rule: add 2		Heads	1	2	3	4
Input	Output	Legs	2	4	6	8
1	3					
2	4					
3	5					
4	6					

G

gram The basic unit of mass in the metric system.

greater than (>) A symbol used to compare two numbers. The greater number is given first below.

Example: 33 > 17
33 is greater than 17.

greatest Largest. Used to order three or more quantities or numbers.

H

height The perpendicular distance from a base of a figure to the highest point.

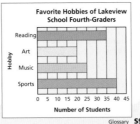

horizontal bar graph A bar graph with horizontal bars.

Favorite Hobbies of Lakeview School Fourth-Graders

(bar graph: Hobby vs. Number of Students 0 5 10 15 20 25 30 35 40 45; categories Reading, Art, Music, Sports)

---

hundredth A unit fraction representing one of one hundred parts, written as 0.01 or $\frac{1}{100}$.

7.634
↑
hundredth

one hundredth $= \frac{1}{100} = 0.01$

I

Identity Property of Multiplication The product of 1 and any number equals that number.

Example: $10 \times 1 = 10$

improper fraction A fraction that is greater than or equal to 1. The numerator is greater than or equal to the denominator.

Examples: $\frac{13}{4}$ or $\frac{4}{4}$

inch A U.S. customary unit of length.

Example: |———— 1 inch ————|

inequality A statement that two expressions are not equal.

Examples: 2 < 5
4 + 5 > 12 − 8

inverse operations Opposite or reverse operations that undo each other. Addition and subtraction are inverse operations. Multiplication and division are inverse operations.

Examples: 4 + 6 = 10 so, 10 − 6 = 4 and 10 − 4 = 6.
3 × 9 = 27 so, 27 ÷ 9 = 3 and 27 ÷ 3 = 9.

isosceles trapezoid A trapezoid with a pair of opposite congruent sides.

isosceles triangle A triangle with at least two congruent sides.

K

kilogram A unit of mass in the metric system that equals one thousand grams. 1 kg = 1,000 g

kiloliter A unit of capacity in the metric system that equals one thousand liters. 1 kL = 1,000 L

L

least Smallest. Used to order three or more quantities or numbers.

least common denominator The least common multiple of two or more denominators.

Example: The least common denominator of $\frac{1}{2}$ and $\frac{1}{3}$ is 6 because 6 is the smallest multiple of 2 and 3.

length The measure of a line segment or one side or edge of a figure.

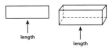

length   length

---

less than (<) A symbol used to compare two numbers. The smaller number is given first below.

Example: 54 < 78
54 is less than 78.

line A straight path that goes on forever in opposite directions.

Example: line AB

A   B

line of symmetry A line that divides a figure into two congruent parts.

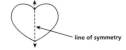
line of symmetry

line plot A diagram that shows the frequency of data on a number line.

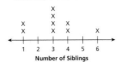
Number of Siblings

line segment Part of a line that has two endpoints.

line symmetry A figure has line symmetry if it can be folded along a line to create two halves that match exactly.

liter The basic unit of capacity in the metric system. 1 liter = 1,000 milliliters.

M

mass The measure of the amount of matter in an object.

mean (average) The size of each of n equal groups made from n data values. It is calculated by adding the values and dividing by n.

Examples: 75, 84, 89, 91, 101
75 + 84 + 89 + 91 + 101 = 440, then 440 ÷ 5 = 88. The mean is 88.

measure of central tendency The mean, median, or mode of a set of numbers.

median The middle number in a set of ordered numbers. For an even number of numbers, the median is the average of the two middle numbers.

Examples: 13 26 34 47 52
The median for this set is 34.
8 8 12 14 20 21
The median for this set is (12 + 14) ÷ 2 = 13.

meter The basic unit of length in the metric system.

mile A U.S. customary unit of length equal to 5,280 feet.

milligram A unit of mass in the metric system that equals one thousandth of a gram. 1 mg = 0.001 g

milliliter A unit of capacity in the metric system that equals one thousandth of a liter. 1 mL = 0.001 L

millimeter A unit of length in the metric system that equals one thousandth of a meter. 1 mm = 0.001 m

---

misleading language Language in a comparing sentence that may cause you to do the wrong operation.

Example: John's age is 3 more than Jessica's. If John is 12, how old is Jessica?

mixed number A number that can be represented by a whole number and a fraction.

Example: $4\frac{1}{2} = 4 + \frac{1}{2}$

mode The number that appears most frequently in a set of numbers.

Example: 2, 4, 4, 5, 7, 7
4 is the mode in this set of numbers.

N

net A flat pattern that can be folded to make a solid figure.

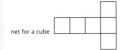
net for a cube

number sentence A mathematical statement that uses =, <, or > to show how numbers or expressions are related. The types of number sentences are equations and inequalities.

Example: 25 + 25 = 50
13 > 8 + 2

numerator The number above the bar in a fraction. It shows the number of equal parts.

Example:

$\frac{3}{4}$ ← numerator $\frac{3}{4} = \frac{1}{4} + \frac{1}{4} + \frac{1}{4}$

obtuse angle An angle greater than a right angle and less than a straight angle.

obtuse triangle A triangle with one obtuse angle.

Order of Operations A set of rules that state the order in which operations should be done.

STEPS: -Compute inside parentheses first.
-Multiply and divide from left to right.
-Add and subtract from left to right.

ounce A unit of weight equal to one sixteenth of a pound. A unit of capacity equal to one eighth of a cup (also called a fluid ounce).

P

parallel Lines in the same plane that never intersect are parallel. Line segments and rays that are part of parallel lines are also parallel.

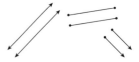

Student Glossary (Continued)

Glossary S13

parallelogram A quadrilateral with both pairs of opposite sides parallel.

Partial-Quotients Method A method used to solve division problems where the partial quotients are written next to the division problem instead of above it.

Example:
```
  8)178
 -160 | 20
   18
  -16 |  2
    2 | 22
   22 R2
```

pentagon A polygon with five sides.

perimeter The distance around a figure.

perpendicular Lines, line segments, or rays are perpendicular if they form right angles.

Example: These two line segments are perpendicular.

pi A special number equal to the circumference of a circle divided by its diameter. Pi can be represented by the symbol π and is approximately 3.14.

pictograph A graph that uses pictures or symbols to represent data.

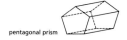

Books Checked Out of Library

Student	
Najee	
Tariq	
Celine	
Jamarcus	
Brooke	

= 5 books

place value The value assigned to the place that a digit occupies in a number.

Example: 235

The 2 is in the hundreds place, so its value is 200.

plane A flat surface that extends without end.

polygon A closed plane figure with sides made of straight line segments.

pound A unit of weight in the U.S. customary system.

prime number A number greater than 1 that has 1 and itself as the only factor pair. Examples of prime numbers are 2, 7, and 13. The only factor pair of 7 is 1 and 7.

prism A solid figure with two congruent parallel bases joined by rectangular faces. Prisms are named by the shape of their bases.

pentagonal prism

probability A number between 0 and 1 that represents the chance of an event happening.

Glossary (Continued)

S14

product The answer to a multiplication.

Example: $9 \times 7 = 63$

product

pyramid A solid with a polygon for a base whose faces meet at a point called the vertex.

Q

quadrilateral A polygon with four sides.

quotient The answer to a division problem.

Example: $9)\overline{63}$; 7 is the quotient.

R

radius A line segment that connects the center of a circle to any point on that circle. Also the length of that line segment.

range The difference between the greatest number and the least number in a set.

ray Part of a line that has one endpoint and extends without end in one direction.

rectangle A parallelogram with four right angles.

Rectangle Sections A method using rectangle drawings to solve multiplication or division problems.

reflection A transformation that flips a figure onto a congruent image. Sometimes called a *flip*.

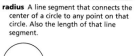

Glossary S15

regular polygon Having all sides and angles congruent.

Example: A square is a regular quadrilateral.

remainder The number left over after dividing two numbers that are not evenly divisible.

Example: $5)\overline{43}$ 8 R3 The remainder is 3.

Repeated Groups situation A multiplication situation in which all groups have the same number of objects.

rhombus A parallelogram with congruent sides.

right angle One of four congruent angles made by perpendicular lines.

right angle

right triangle A triangle with one right angle.

round To find the nearest ten, hundred, thousand, or some other place value. The usual rounding rule is to round up if the next digit to the right is 5 or more and round down if the next digit to the right is less than 5.

Examples: 463 rounded to the nearest ten is 460.
463 rounded to the nearest hundred is 500.

row A part of a table or array that contains items arranged horizontally.

S

scalene A triangle with no equal sides is a scalene triangle.

simplest form A fraction is in simplest form if there is no whole number (other than 1) that divides evenly into the numerator and denominator.

Examples: $\frac{3}{4}$ This fraction is in simplest form because no number divides evenly into 3 and 4.

Glossary S16

simplify a fraction To divide the numerator and the denominator of a fraction by the same number to make an equivalent fraction made from fewer but larger unit fractions.

Example: $\frac{5}{10} = \frac{5 \div 5}{10 \div 5} = \frac{1}{2}$

situation equation An equation that shows the action or the relationship in a problem.

Example: $35 + n = 40$

slant height The height of a triangular face of a pyramid.

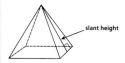

slant height

solution equation An equation that shows the operation to perform in order to solve the problem.

Examples: $n = 40 - 35$

sphere A solid figure shaped like a ball.

square array An array in which the number of rows equals the number of columns.

square centimeter A unit of area equal to the area of a square with one-centimeter sides.

square decimeter A unit of area equal to the area of a square with one-decimeter sides.

square foot A unit of area equal to the area of a square with one-foot sides.

square inch A unit of area equal to the area of a square with one-inch sides.

square kilometer A unit of area equal to the area of a square with one-kilometer sides.

square meter A unit of area equal to the area of a square with one-meter sides.

square mile A unit of area equal to the area of a square with one-mile sides.

square millimeter A unit of area equal to the area of a square with one-millimeter sides.

square number The product of a whole number and itself.

Example: $3 \times 3 = 9$
9 is a square number.

square unit A unit of area equal to the area of a square with one-unit sides.

square yard A unit of area equal to the area of a square with one-yard sides.

standard form The form of a number written using digits.

Example: 2,145

sum The answer when adding two or more addends.

Example:

$53 + 26 = 79$

addend   addend   sum

surface area The total area of the two-dimensional surfaces of a three-dimensional figure.

T

table Data arranged in rows and columns.

tally chart A chart that uses tally marks to record and organize data.

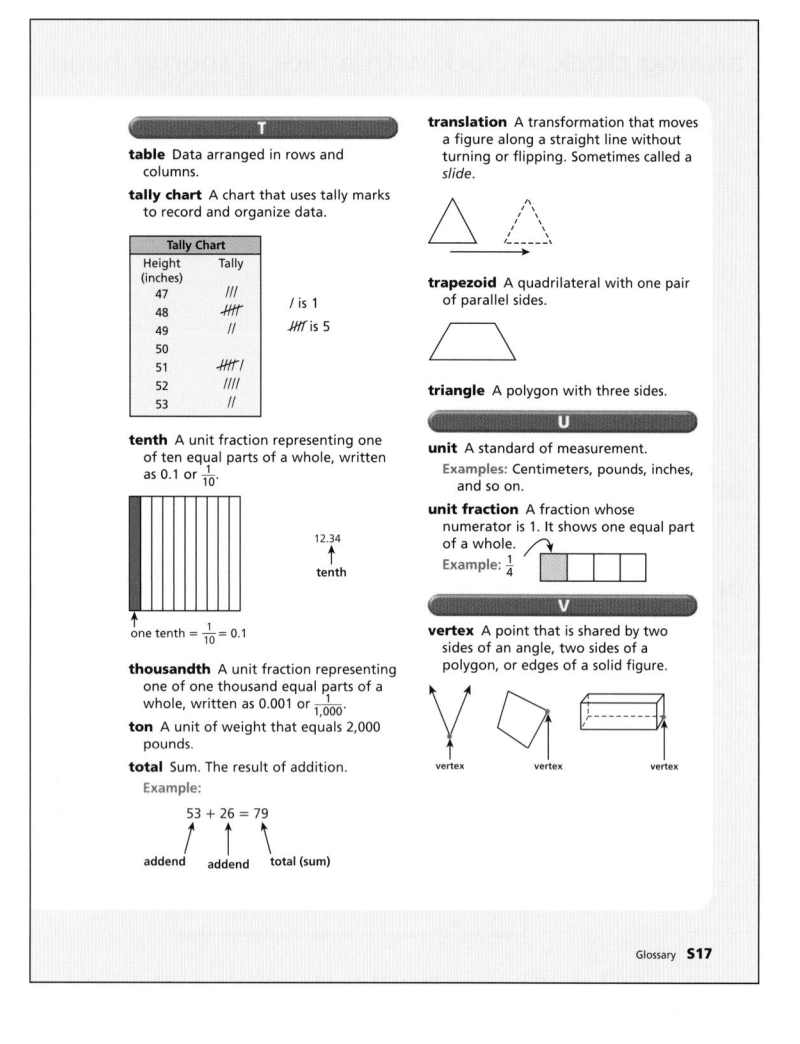

Tally Chart

Height (inches)	Tally
47	///
48	ĦĦ
49	//
50	
51	ĦĦ /
52	////
53	//

/ is 1
ĦĦ is 5

tenth A unit fraction representing one of ten equal parts of a whole, written as 0.1 or $\frac{1}{10}$.

one tenth = $\frac{1}{10}$ = 0.1

12.34
↑
tenth

thousandth A unit fraction representing one of one thousand equal parts of a whole, written as 0.001 or $\frac{1}{1,000}$.

ton A unit of weight that equals 2,000 pounds.

total Sum. The result of addition.

Example:

$$53 + 26 = 79$$

addend   addend   total (sum)

translation A transformation that moves a figure along a straight line without turning or flipping. Sometimes called a *slide*.

trapezoid A quadrilateral with one pair of parallel sides.

triangle A polygon with three sides.

U

unit A standard of measurement.
Examples: Centimeters, pounds, inches, and so on.

unit fraction A fraction whose numerator is 1. It shows one equal part of a whole.
Example: $\frac{1}{4}$

V

vertex A point that is shared by two sides of an angle, two sides of a polygon, or edges of a solid figure.

vertex   vertex   vertex

Glossary (Continued)

vertical bar graph A bar graph with vertical bars.

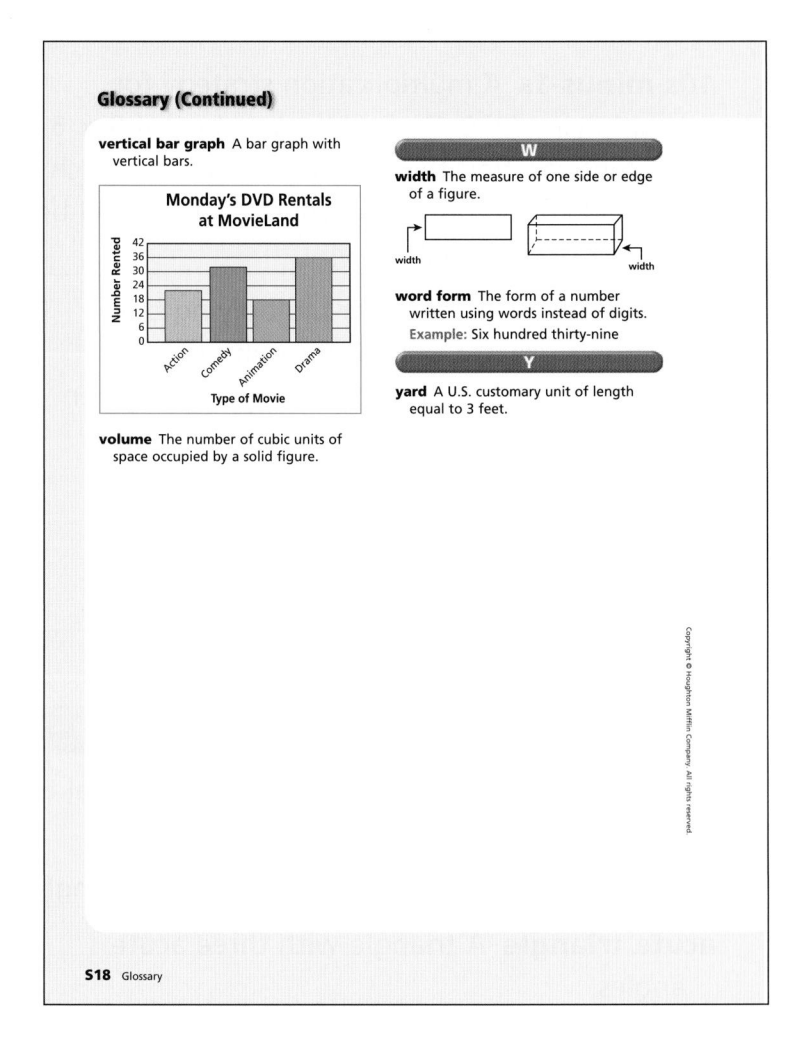

Monday's DVD Rentals at MovieLand

Number Rented / Type of Movie (Action, Comedy, Animation, Drama)

volume The number of cubic units of space occupied by a solid figure.

W

width The measure of one side or edge of a figure.

width   width

word form The form of a number written using words instead of digits.
Example: Six hundred thirty-nine

Y

yard A U.S. customary unit of length equal to 3 feet.

Teacher Glossary

10s-minus-1s A multiplication strategy for multiplying by 9. To find the product of 9 × 6, a student can find the product of 10 × 6, which is 60, and know that the product of 9 × 6 will be one six less than 60, or 54.

5s shortcut A strategy for multiplying by numbers greater than 5. To multiply 7 × 3, students think of the 5 count-bys of 15. Then they think of the additional count-bys of 3, saying 18, 21. Therefore, 7 × 3 = 21.

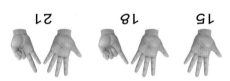

A

acre A measure of land area. An acre is equal to 4,840 square yards.

acute angle An angle smaller than a right angle.

acute triangle A triangle with three acute angles.

Add Around a Ten An addition strategy. To use this strategy to add 38 + 6, a student would think, "38 and how many more make 40? Take 2 from the 6, leaving 4, and 40 + 4 = 44."

addend One of two or more numbers added together to find a sum. In the equation $7 + 4 + 8 = \square$, the numbers 7, 4, and 8 are addends.

Algebraic Notation Method A strategy for multiplying like multiplying algebraic expressions. The multiplication exercise 9 × 28 is shown here using the Algebraic Notation Notation Method.

Example: $9 \cdot 28 = 9 \cdot (20 + 8)$
$= (9 \cdot 20) + (9 \cdot 8)$
$= 180 + 72$
$= 252$

analog clock A clock with a face, a shorter hand, and a longer hand.

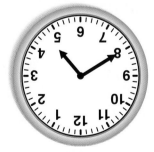

angle A figure formed by two rays or two line segments that meet at an endpoint.

area The amount of surface covered or enclosed by a figure measured in square units.

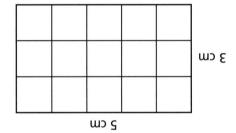

area model (for multiplication) A model of multiplication that shows each place-value product within a rectangle drawing.

Example: $9 \times 28 =$

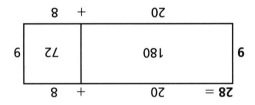

array An arrangement of objects, symbols, or numbers in columns and rows.

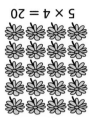
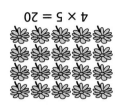

$5 \times 4 = 4 \times 5$

$5 \times 4 = 20$

$4 \times 5 = 20$

Associative Property of Addition Grouping the addends in different ways does not change the sum. For all numbers a, b, and c,
$a + (b + c) = (a + b) + c$.

Associative Property of Multiplication Grouping the factors in different ways does not change the product. For all numbers a, b, and c,
$a \times (b \times c) = (a \times b) \times c$.

average (mean) The sum of given numbers divided by the number of numbers used in computing the sum.
Example: The average (mean) of 75, 84, 89, 91, and 101 is $75 + 84 + 89 + 91 + 101 = 440$; then $440 \div 5 = 88$.

axes Reference lines from which distances are measured on a coordinate grid.

B

bar graph A graph that uses bars to show data. The bars may be vertical or horizontal.

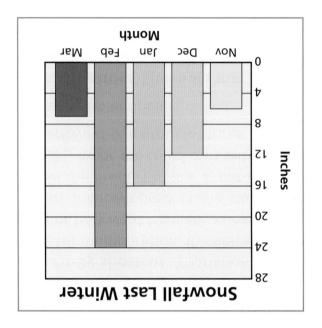

base For a triangle or parallelogram, a base is any side. For a trapezoid, a base is either of the parallel sides. For a prism, a base is one of the two congruent parallel faces. For a pyramid, the base is the face that does not touch the vertex of the pyramid.

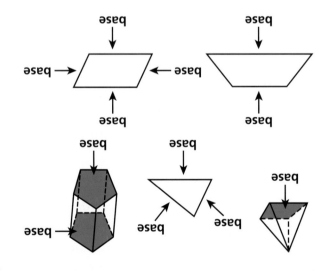

break-apart drawing A drawing that students create to show the relationship between addition and subtraction.

C

capacity A measure of how much a container can hold.

cell The rectangle in a table, where a column and row meet.

Celsius The metric temperature scale. 0°C is the freezing point of water and 100°C is the boiling point of water. To convert from Celsius to Fahrenheit, use the formula: $F = (C \times 1.8) + 32$.

Teacher Glossary (Continued)

center The point in a circle that is the same distance from every point on the circle.

centimeter (cm) A unit of measure in the metric system that equals one hundredth of a meter.
1 cm = 0.01 m

change A quantity used when solving addition or subtraction equations. A change can be an increase or a decrease. A change can be known or unknown.

Start + Change = Result
or
Start – Change = Result

change minus A change situation that can be represented by subtraction. In a change minus situation, the starting number, the change, or the result will be unknown.

Example: Unknown Unknown Unknown
Start Change Result
$n - 2 = 3$ $5 - n = 3$ $5 - 2 = n$

change plus A change situation that can be represented by addition. In a change plus situation, the starting number, the change, or the result will be unknown.

Example: Unknown Unknown Unknown
Start Change Result
$n + 2 = 5$ $3 + n = 5$ $3 + 2 = n$

Check Sheets Sheets used together with Write-On Sheets to check computation exercises. (See Write-On Sheets.)

circle A plane figure that forms a closed path so that all the points on the path are the same distance from a point called the center.

circle graph A graph that uses parts of a circle to show data. (Also called a pie graph or pie chart.)

circumference The distance around a circle.

Class Multiplication Table A poster in table form that displays the multiplication facts and their associated number sentences. Columns of the table are 1 — 9 and rows of the table are 1 — 12.

X	1	2	3	4	5	6	7	8	9
1	1·1=1	1·2=2	1·3=3	1·4=4	1·5=5	1·6=6	1·7=7	1·8=8	1·9=9
2	2·1=2	2·2=4	2·3=6	2·4=8	2·5=10	2·6=12	2·7=14	2·8=16	2·9=18
3	3·1=3	3·2=6	3·3=9	3·4=12	3·5=15	3·6=18	3·7=21	3·8=24	3·9=27
4	4·1=4	4·2=8	4·3=12	4·4=16	4·5=20	4·6=24	4·7=28	4·8=32	4·9=36
5	5·1=5	5·2=10	5·3=15	5·4=20	5·5=25	5·6=30	5·7=35	5·8=40	5·9=45
6	6·1=6	6·2=12	6·3=18	6·4=24	6·5=30	6·6=36	6·7=42	6·8=48	6·9=54
7	7·1=7	7·2=14	7·3=21	7·4=28	7·5=35	7·6=42	7·7=49	7·8=56	7·9=63
8	8·1=8	8·2=16	8·3=24	8·4=32	8·5=40	8·6=48	8·7=56	8·8=64	8·9=72
9	9·1=9	9·2=18	9·3=27	9·4=36	9·5=45	9·6=54	9·7=63	9·8=72	9·9=81
10	10·1=10	10·2=20	10·3=30	10·4=40	10·5=50	10·6=60	10·7=70	10·8=80	10·9=90
11	11·1=11	11·2=22	11·3=33	11·4=44	11·5=55	11·6=66	11·7=77	11·8=88	11·9=99
12	12·1=12	12·2=24	12·3=36	12·4=48	12·5=60	12·6=72	12·7=84	12·8=96	12·9=108

Multiplication Table

Close Count-By A known number that can be used to find an unknown product. If a student does not know the product of 8 × 3, but knows that 9 × 3 = 27, he/she could start with 27 and count backward one group of three.

Close Count-By shortcut A variation of the 5s shortcut for multiplication. It involves working forward or backward from any known product to find an unknown product. If a student does not know the product of 8 × 3, but knows that 9 × 3 = 27, he or she could start with 27 and count backward one group of three.

closed Having no endpoints.

collection situations Situations that involve putting together (joining) or taking apart (separating) groups.

column A part of a table or array that contains items arranged vertically.

combination situation A situation in which all possible different pairs are made by putting one first kind of thing with one second kind of thing. We can use a table to show all possible combinations.

Example:

Different Sandwich Combinations

	peanut butter	**cheese**	**turkey**
wheat bread	peanut butter on wheat bread	cheese on wheat bread	turkey on wheat bread
white bread	peanut butter on white bread	cheese on white bread	turkey on white bread

Commutative Property of Addition Changing the order of addends does not change the sum. For all numbers a and b, $a + b = b + a$.

Commutative Property of Multiplication Changing the order of factors does not change the product. For all numbers a and b, $a \times b = b \times a$.

comparison bars Bars that represent the larger amount and smaller amount in a comparison situation; students draw different length bars to represent each number.

For addition and subtraction:

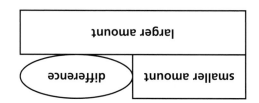

For multiplication and division:

smaller amount	smaller amount	smaller amount

smaller amount	

comparison situation A situation in which two amounts are compared by addition or by multiplication. An *additive comparison situation* compares by asking or telling how much more (or how much less) one amount is than another. A *multiplicative comparison situation* compares by asking or telling how many times as many one amount is as another. The multiplicative comparison may also be made using fraction language. For example, you can say, "Sally has one fourth as much as Tom has," instead of saying "Tom has 4 times as much as Sally has."

complex figure A figure made by combining simple geometric figures like rectangles and triangles.

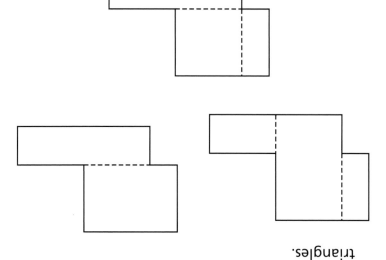

composite number A number greater than 1 that has more than two factors. Examples of composite numbers are 10 and 18. The factor pairs of 10 are: 1 and 10, 2 and 5. The factor pairs of 18 are 1 and 18, 2 and 9, 3 and 6.

concave A polygon is concave if at least one diagonal is outside of the polygon.

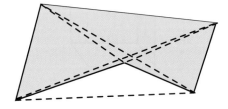

cone A solid figure with a circular base and a single vertex.

circular cone

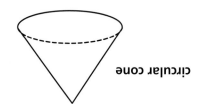

Teacher Glossary (Continued)

congruence For geometric figures, the condition of having the same size and shape.

congruent Exactly the same size and shape.

convex A polygon is convex if all the diagonals are inside the polygon.

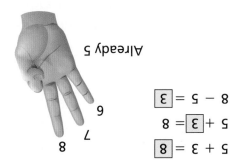

count on An addition or subtraction strategy in which students begin with one partner and count on to the total. This strategy can be used to find an unknown partner or an unknown total.

$5 + 3 = \boxed{8}$

$5 + \boxed{3} = 8$

$\boxed{3} = 5 - 8$

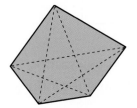

8
7
6
Already 5

count-bys Products that are found by counting-by a particular number; 5 count-bys would be 5, 10, 15, 20, 25, and so on; 3 count-bys would be 3, 6, 9, 12, and so on.

cube A solid figure with 6 faces that are congruent squares.

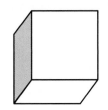

cubic centimeter A metric unit for measuring volume. It is the volume of a cube with one-centimeter edges.

cubic decimeter A metric unit for measuring volume. It is the volume of a cube with one-decimeter edges.

cubic foot A unit for measuring volume. It is the volume of a cube with one-foot edges.

cubic inch A unit for measuring volume. It is the volume of a cube with one-inch edges.

cubic meter A metric unit for measuring volume. It is the volume of a cube with one-meter edges.

cubic millimeter A metric unit for measuring volume. It is the volume of a cube with one-millimeter edges.

cubic yard A unit for measuring volume. It is the volume of a cube with one-yard edges.

cup A customary unit for measuring capacity. There are 2 cups in 1 pint.

cylinder A solid figure with two circular, congruent bases.

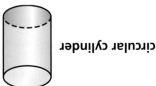

circular cylinder

D

data A collection of information.

decimeter A unit of measure in the metric system that equals one tenth of a meter. 1 dm = 0.1 m

diagonal A line segment connecting two non-adjacent vertices of a polygon.

diameter A line segment from one side of a circle to the other through the center. Also the length of that segment.

difference The result of a subtraction. In the subtraction equation, 5 − 2 = 3, 3 is the difference.

digit Any of the symbols: 0, 1, 2, 3, 4, 5, 6, 7, 8, or 9.

digital clock A clock that shows the hour and minutes with numbers.

AM 9:30

dimension A way to describe how a figure can be measured.

Examples:

A line segment has only length, so it has one dimension.

A rectangle has length and width, so it has two dimensions.

A cube has length, width, and height, so it has three dimensions.

dimensions The measurements of sides of geometric figures; the height, length, or width.

Distributive Property You can multiply a sum by a number, or multiply each addend by the number and add the products; the result is the same. For all numbers a, b, and c, $(a + b) \times c = (a \times c) + (b \times c)$.

dividend A number that is divided in division.

Example: $9\overline{)63}$ with quotient 7, 63 is the dividend.

divisor The number you divide by in division.

Example: $9\overline{)63}$ with quotient 7, 9 is the divisor.

dot array An arrangement of dots in rows and columns.

double bar graph Data is compared by using pairs of bars drawn next to each other.

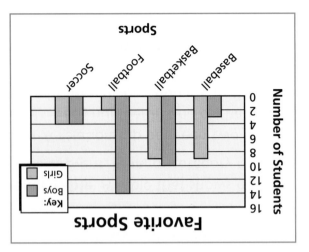

Doubles for Tens A subtraction strategy. To use this strategy for the subtraction exercise 130 − 60, a student would think, "60 + 60 = 120, so 10 more to make 130 is 70."

Down Over 10 (or 100) A subtraction strategy. To use this strategy for the subtraction exercise 15 − 9, a student would think, "15 down to 10 is 5, plus 1 more down to 9 is 6 so 15 − 9 = 6."

E

edge The line segment where two faces of a three-dimensional figure meet.

equal groups Concept used in multiplication and division situations. 5 × 6 = 30. There are 5 equal groups of 6 items.

Equal-Shares Drawing A diagram that shows a number separated into equal parts. Students draw circles with a number inside. That number tells the group size. The number of circles is the multiplier (the number of groups). The lines joining the circles point to the total, or product.

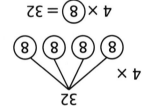

$$4 \times \circled{8} = 32$$

equation A statement that two expressions are equal.

Example: 32 + 35 = 67

67 = 32 + 34 + 1

(7 × 8) + 1 = 57

equilateral Having all equal sides.

Example: An equilateral triangle.

estimate (noun) A number close to an exact amount. An estimate tells about how much or about how many.

estimate (verb) To make a thoughtful guess or to tell about how much or about how many.

expanded form A way of writing a number that shows the value of each of its digits.

Example: Expanded form of 835:
800 + 30 + 5
8 hundreds + 3 tens + 5 ones

Expanded Notation A method used to solve multiplication and division problems.

Example: 28 = 20 + 8

$$\begin{array}{r} \times \quad 9 \ = \ 9 \\ \hline 9 \times 20 = 180 \\ 9 \times 8 \ = \ 72 \\ \hline 252 \end{array}$$

expression One or more numbers, variables, or numbers and variables with one or more operations.

Examples: 4
6x
6x − 5
7 + 4

F

---

face A flat surface of a three-dimensional figure.

Factor Fireworks Shows how a whole number can be broken down into a product of prime factors. (Also called a **Factor Tree**.)

factor One of two or more numbers multiplied to find a product.

factor pair A factor pair for a number is a pair of whole numbers whose product is that number.

Example: A factor pair for 35 is 5 and 7.

Factor Triangle A diagram that shows a factor pair and the product.

Fahrenheit The temperature scale used in the United States. 32°F is the freezing point of water and 212°F is the boiling point of water. To convert from Fahrenheit to Celsius, use the formula: $C = \dfrac{(F - 32)}{1.8}$.

Fast Array A numerical form of an array that shows a multiplication or a division problem; can have an unknown factor or unknown product.

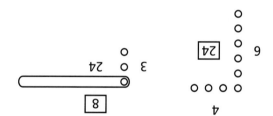

fewer *Fewer* is used to compare two quantities that can be counted. There are fewer red books than blue books. *Less* is used to compare two quantities that can be measured. There is less water than juice.

fluid ounce A U.S. customary unit of capacity equal to 2 tablespoons.

foot A U.S. customary unit of length equal to 12 inches.

frequency table A table that shows how many times each event, item, or category occurs.

function A relationship between two sets of numbers. Each number in one of the sets is paired with exactly one number in the other set.

Example: The relationship between yards and feet.

Yards	1	2	3	4	5	6	7
Feet	3	6	9	12	15	18	21

G

gallon A U.S. customary unit for measuring capacity. One gallon is equal to four quarts.

gram The basic unit of mass in the metric system.

greatest Largest. Used to compare three or more quantities or numbers.

group (verb) To combine ones to form tens, to combine tens to form hundreds, and so on. To put smaller unit fractions together into a larger one: fifteenths can be grouped into groups of five to form thirds.

H

height The perpendicular distance from a base of a figure to the highest point.

horizontal Parallel to the horizon; going straight across.

hundred box In a place-value drawing, a square box representing that 10 "quick tens" equal one hundred. A hundred box is a quick way of drawing 100.

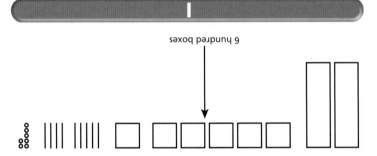

6 hundred boxes

I

Identity Property of Multiplication The product of 1 and any number equals that number.

Example: $10 \times 1 = 10$

inch A U.S. customary unit of length equal to $\frac{1}{12}$ foot.

Example:

|— 1 inch —|

inequality A statement that two expressions are not equal.

Examples: $2 < 5$

$4 + 5 > 12 - 8$

inverse operation Opposite or reverse operations that undo each other. Addition and subtraction are inverse operations. Multiplication and division are inverse operations.

Examples: $4 + 6 = 10$ so, $10 - 6 = 4$ and
$10 - 4 = 6$
$3 \times 9 = 27$, so $27 \div 9 = 3$ and $27 \div 3 = 9$

irregular Having sides of different lengths or angles of different measures.

is greater than Having a value that is more than that of another quantity or expression.

is greater than (>) Words used to define the "greater than" symbol. $6 > 5$ is read as "6 is greater than 5."

is less than Having a value that is less than that of another quantity or expression.

is less than (<) Words used to define the "less than" symbol. $5 < 6$ is read as "5 is less than 6."

isosceles trapezoid A trapezoid with a pair of opposite congruent sides.

isosceles triangle A triangle with at least two congruent sides.

K

key A part of a map, graph, or chart that explains what symbols mean.

kilogram A unit of mass in the metric system that equals one thousand grams. $1 \text{ kg} = 1,000 \text{ g}$

kiloliter A unit of capacity in the metric system that equals one thousand liters. $1 \text{ kL} = 1,000 \text{ L}$

kilometer A metric unit of length that equals one thousand meters. $1 \text{ km} = 1,000 \text{ m}$

L

leading A comparing sentence containing language that suggests which operation to use to solve the problem.

least Smallest. Used to compare three or more quantities or numbers.

length The measure of a line segment or one side or edge of a figure.

line A straight path that goes on forever in opposite directions.

line of reflection A line over which a figure is flipped to produce a mirror image of the figure. Each point of the original figure and corresponding point on the flipped figure is the same distance from the line of reflection.

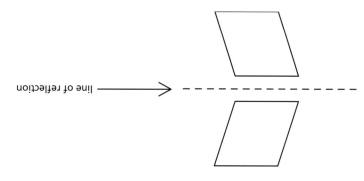

line of reflection

line of symmetry A line that divides a figure into two congruent parts.

line plot A diagram that shows the frequency of data on a number line.

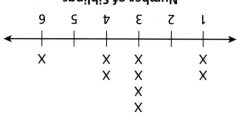

Number of Siblings

line segment Part of a line that has two endpoints.

line symmetry A figure has line symmetry if it can be folded along a line so the two halves match exactly.

liter The basic unit of capacity in the metric system. 1 liter = 1,000 milliliters.

M

Make 10 Tens A strategy for adding multi-digit numbers. To use this strategy to add 90 + 60, a student would think, "9 tens and how many more tens make 10 tens? Take 1 ten from the 6 tens, leaving 5 tens and 10 tens + 5 tens = 150."

mass The amount of matter in an object. (Mass is constant; weight varies because it is subject to the effect of gravity on matter.)

median The middle number in a set of ordered numbers. For an even number of numbers, the median is the average of the two middle numbers.

Examples: 13 26 34 47 52

The median for this set is 34.

8 8 12 14 20 21

The median for this set is
$(12 + 14) \div 2 = 13$.

meter The basic unit of length in the metric system.

mile A U.S. customary unit of length equal to 5,280 feet.

milligram A unit of mass in the metric system that equals one thousandth of a gram. 1 mg = 0.001 g

milliliter A unit of capacity in the metric system that equals one thousandth of a liter. 1 mL = 0.001 L

millimeter A unit of length in the metric system that equals one thousandth of a meter. 1 mm = 0.001 m

misleading language Language in a comparing sentence that may cause you to do the wrong thing.

Example: John's age is 3 more than Jessica's. If John is 12, how old is Jessica?

Teacher Glossary (Continued)

mode The number that appears most frequently in a set of numbers.

Example: 2, 4, 4, 4, 5, 7, 7
4 is the mode in this set of numbers.

multiple A number that is the product of a given number and any whole number. 4 is a multiple of 4 because it is the product of 4 and the whole number 1; 8 is a multiple of 4 because it is the product of 4 and the whole number 2. (See count-bys.)

multiplier One of the factors in a multiplication equation. In the 9s equations, each of the numbers that multiplies 9 is the multiplier.

N

New Groups Above Method A strategy for multi-digit addition. The new groups are placed above the existing groups. This is the common method of addition.

Example:
```
 1 1
 246
+197
 443
```

New Groups Below Method A strategy for multi-digit addition. The new groups are placed below the line waiting to be added.

Example:
```
 246
+197
 443
 1 1
```

no action A type of collection situation in which there is no action required—the addends and the total do not increase or decrease but are just described in different ways.

non-standard unit A unit of measure not commonly recognized, such as a paper clip to measure a gram. An inch and a centimeter are standard units of measure.

number sentence A mathematical statement that uses =, <, or > to show how numbers or expressions are related. Number sentences can be equations or inequalities.

Examples: 25 + 25 = 50
13 > 8 + 2

Number Path A display of the numbers from 1 through 100 in groups of five, found on the outside edge on one side of the MathBoard.

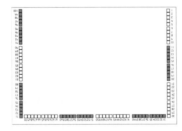

O

obtuse angle An angle greater than a right angle and less than a straight angle.

obtuse triangle A triangle with one obtuse angle.

operation A mathematical process. Addition, subtraction, multiplication, division, and raising a number to a power are operations.

Order of Operations A set of rules that state the order in which operations should be done.
STEPS: -Compute inside parentheses first.
-Multiply and divide from left to right.
-Add and subtract from left to right.

ounce A unit of weight equal to one sixteenth of a pound. A unit of capacity equal to one eighth of a cup. (It is also called a fluid ounce.)

P

parallel Lines in the same plane that never intersect are parallel. Line segments and rays that are part of parallel lines are also parallel.

parallelogram A quadrilateral with both pairs of opposite sides parallel.

Teacher Glossary (Continued)

partial products Products of the smaller products in the Rectangle Sections method of multiplying.

Partial Quotients Method A method used to solve division problems where the partial quotients are written next to the division problem instead of above it.

perimeter The distance around a figure.

perpendicular Lines, line segments, or rays are perpendicular if they form right angles.

pi (π) A special number equal to the circumference of a circle divided by its diameter. Two common approximations used for pi are $\frac{22}{7}$ and 3.14.

pictograph A graph that uses pictures or symbols to represent data.

pint A U.S. customary unit for measuring capacity. One pint is equal to two cups.

place value The value assigned to the place that a digit occupies in a number.

Example: 235
↓
The 2 is in the hundreds place, so its value is 200.

place-value drawing A drawing that represents a number. Thousands are represented by a vertical rectangle, hundreds are represented by boxes (hundred boxes), tens by vertical lines (quick tens), and ones by small circles.

Example:

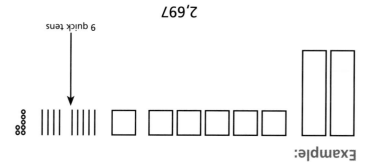

2,697

9 quick tens

plane figure A figure that has two dimensions.

point symmetry Property that pertains to a figure that can be turned less than a full turn (360°) and still look the same as it did before the turn. Also called rotational symmetry.

polygon A closed plane figure with straight line segments for its sides.

pound A unit of weight in the U.S. customary system. One pound is equal to sixteen ounces.

prime number A number greater than 1 that has 1 and itself as the only factors. Examples of prime numbers are 2, 7, and 13. The only factors of 7 are 1 and 7.

prism A three-dimensional figure that has two parallel congruent bases and parallelograms for faces. Prisms are named by the shape of their bases.

product The answer to a multiplication. In the problem 3 × 4 = 12, 12 is the product.

Product Cards Cards that display a multiplication exercise on one side and a division exercise on the other side. The multiplication and division exercises on a card involve the same factor-factor-product combination. The multiplication side shows one factor times the other factor; the division side shows the product divided by a factor from the multiplication table.

put together A type of collection situation in which groups of objects are joined.

pyramid A solid with a polygon for a base whose faces meet in a point called the vertex.

Q

quadrilateral A polygon with four sides.

quart A U.S. customary unit for measuring capacity. One quart is equal to 32 ounces.

Quick 9s A short cut for multiplying by 9 in which students bend down one finger to represent the multiplier. The remaining fingers to the left of the bent finger represent the tens digit of the product and the fingers to the right of the bent finger represent the ones digit of the product.

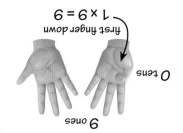

first finger down
$1 \times 9 = 9$
0 tens
9 ones

Quick Ten A vertical line students draw to represent 10.

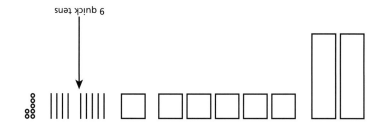

9 quick tens

quotient The answer to a division problem.

Example: $9\overline{)63}$, 7 is the quotient.

R

radius A line segment that connects the center of a circle to any point on that circle. Also the length of that line segment.

range The difference between the greatest number and the least number in a set.

ray Part of a line that has one endpoint and extends without end in one direction.

rectangle A parallelogram with four right angles.

Rectangle Sections Method A strategy for multiplying or dividing multi-digit numbers. The multiplication exercise 9×435 is shown here using the Rectangle Sections Method.

	400	+	30	+	5	
9	$9 \times 400 = 3,600$		$9 \times 30 = 270$		$9 \times 5 = 45$	9

$435 =$

$$\begin{array}{r} \overset{1}{3,600} \\ 270 \\ +\ 45 \\ \hline 3,915 \end{array}$$

reflection A transformation that moves a figure about a line to form a congruent image. Sometimes called a flip.

reflection symmetry See line symmetry.

remainder The number left over after dividing two numbers that are not evenly divisible. In the division example 32 divided by 6, the quotient is 5 with a remainder of 2. There are 5 groups of 6 and one more group that has only 2 items (the remainder).

Repeated Groups A multiplication situation in which all groups have the same number of objects.

repeated-groups problem A type of multiplication word problem in which there are several same size groups of items and the total number of items must be determined.

result An outcome of an operation. A result can be known or unknown.

Start + Change = Result

or

Start − Change = Result

rhombus A parallelogram with congruent sides.

right angle One of four congruent angles made by perpendicular lines.

right triangle A triangle with one right angle.

Teacher Glossary (Continued)

rotational symmetry See point symmetry.

round To find the nearest ten, hundred, thousand, or some other place value. The usual rounding rule is to round up if the next right digit is 5 or greater and round down if the next right digit is less than 5.
Example: 463 rounded to the nearest ten is 460. 463 rounded to the nearest hundred is 500.

row A part of a table or array that contains items arranged horizontally.

rule One or more statements that tell how to find an answer. In a pattern such as a function table or number sequence, it is what is done to the first number to get to the second number and so on. The rule *Add 3* is shown in the function table and the rule $n + 7$ is shown in the number sequence.

Rule: Add 3	
0	3
1	4
2	5
3	6

16, 23, 30, 37, 44, 51   Rule: $n + 7$

S

scale On a graph, the numbers along the axes. The numbers are arranged in order with equal intervals.

scalene triangle A triangle with no equal sides.

Secret Code Cards A page of cut-out cards used to teach place value from tens to thousands. Students write different digits in the blank spaces to "build" various numbers of up to four digits.

Shortcut Method of Multiplication A strategy for multiplying. It is the current common method in the United States.

Step 1
$$\begin{array}{r} \overset{7}{28} \\ \times\ 9 \\ \hline 2 \end{array}$$

Step 2
$$\begin{array}{r} \overset{7}{28} \\ \times\ 9 \\ \hline 252 \end{array}$$

Show Subtotals Method A strategy for adding multi-digit numbers in which students add each place value in expanded form, find a subtotal for each place value, and then add the subtotals. To use this strategy to add 879 + 754, a student would add 800 + 700 and find the subtotal 1,500, then add 70 + 50 and find the subtotal 120, and then add 9 + 4 and find the subtotal 13. The student would then add the subtotals 1,500 + 120 + 13 to find the total 1,633. (The Show Subtotals Method is convenient for numbers up to about 5 digits.)

$$\begin{array}{r} 879 \\ +\ 754 \\ \hline 1500 \\ 120 \\ 13 \\ \hline 1,633 \end{array}$$

simplify a fraction To divide the numerator and denominator of a fraction by the same number to make an equivalent fraction made from fewer but larger unit fractions.
Example: $\frac{5}{10} = \frac{5 \div 5}{10 \div 5} = \frac{1}{2}$

situation equation An equation students write to represent a word problem. It represents a literal translation of the problem. It may or may not have the unknown isolated on one side of the equals sign.

solid A figure with three dimensions.

solution equation An equation that shows the operation to perform in order to solve the problem. It is related to the operation needed to solve the problem rather than to a literal translation of the word problem.
Example: $n = 40 - 35$

sphere A solid figure that is shaped like a ball.

square A figure with four right angles and four congruent sides.

square array An array in which the number of rows equals the number of columns.

square centimeter A unit of area equal to the area of a square with one-centimeter sides.

square decimeter A unit of area equal to the area of a square with one-decimeter sides.

square foot A unit of area equal to the area of a square with one-foot sides.

square inch A unit of area equal to the area of a square with one-inch sides.

square kilometer A unit of area equal to the area of a square with one-kilometer sides.

square meter A unit of area equal to the area of a square with one-meter sides.

square mile A unit of area equal to the area of a square with one-mile sides.

square millimeter A unit of area equal to the area of a square with one-millimeter sides.

square number The product of a whole number and itself.
Example: $3 \times 3 = 9$
9 is a square number.

square unit A unit of area equal to the area of a square with one-unit sides.

square yard A unit of area equal to the area of a square with one-yard sides.

standard form The form of a number written using digits.
Example: 2,145

standard unit A recognized unit of measure, such as an inch or a centimeter. A non-standard unit of measure might be a paper clip.

start A quantity used when solving addition or subtraction equations. A start can be known or unknown.
Start + Change = Result
or
Start − Change = Result

sum The answer when adding two or more addends. In the addition equation, 3 + 2 = 5, 5 is the sum.

surface area The total area of the two-dimensional surfaces of a three-dimensional figure.

symmetry See line symmetry and point symmetry.

T

table Data arranged in rows and columns.

take apart A type of collection situation in which groups of objects are separated.

Take from 10 (or 100) A subtraction strategy. To use this strategy for the subtraction exercise 15 − 9, a student would think, "15 is made from 10 and 5. For 15, I take 9 from the 10 and have 1 to put with the 5, making 6, so 15 − 9 = 6."

tally To count and record data or the type of mark that represents an individual item of data.

Teacher Glossary (Continued)

U

ungroup To break into smaller groups in order to subtract. For example, 1 hundred can be ungrouped into 10 tens, and 1 ten can be ungrouped into 10 ones.

unit A standard of measurement. **Examples:** centimeter, inch, pound, and so on.

V

variable A letter or a symbol that represents a number in an algebraic expression.

vertex A point that is shared by two sides of an angle, two sides of a polygon, or edges of a solid figure. Also the point of a cone.

vertical Straight up and down.

volume The number of cubic units in a solid figure.

W

width The measure of one side or edge of a figure.

word form The form of a number written using words instead of digits. **Example:** 639 is six hundred thirty-nine.

Write-On Sheets Sheets students use to practice computation examples. They can be placed in sheet protectors and used repeatedly with dry-erase markers.

Y

yard A U.S. customary unit of length equal to 3 feet.

Target A transparent square used to find a product in the Multiplication Table. A product is found in a cell at the intersection of a row and column.

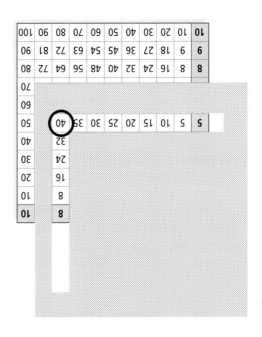

thousand bar In a place-value drawing, a bar representing that 10 hundred boxes equal one thousand. A thousand bar is a quick way of drawing one thousand.

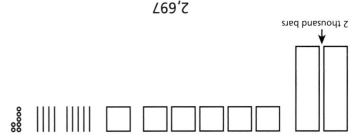

ton A unit of weight that equals 2,000 pounds.

tonne A metric unit of mass that equals 1,000 kilograms.

total Sum. The result of addition. This term is used in *Math Expressions* to refer to the sum of two partners.

triangle A polygon with three sides.

Recommended Books

Unit BFFP

Amanda Bean's Amazing Dream: A Mathematical Story, by Cindy Neuschwander, illustrated by Liza Woodruff, Math Activities by Marilyn Burns (Scholastic Press, 1998)

Unit 1

Anno's Mysterious Multiplying Jar, by Masaichiro and Mitsumasa Anno (Philomel Books, 1983)

Arithme-Tickle: An Even Number of Odd Riddle-Rhymes, by Patrick Lewis, illustrated by Frank Remkiewicz (Voyager Books, Harcourt, Inc., 2002)

Unit 2

Grandfather Tang's Story: A Tale Told with Tangrams, by Ann Tompert, illustrated by Robert Andrew Parker (Dragonfly Books, 1990)

Unit 3

Sold! A Mathematics Adventure, by Nathan Zimelman, illustrated by Bryn Barnard (Charlesbridge Publishing, 2000)

Unit 4

A Fly on the Ceiling, by Julie Glass, illustrated by Richard Walz (Random House Children's Books, 1998)

Unit 5

The King's Chessboard, by David Birch, illustrated by Davis Grebu (Puffin 1993)

Rabbits Rabbits Everywhere, a Fibonacci Tale, by Ann McCallum, illustrated by Gideon Kendall (Charlesbridge Publishing, 2007)

Unit 6

The Math Chef, by Joan D'Amico and Karen Eich Drummond, illustrated by Tina Cash-Walsh (John Wiley & Sons, Inc., 1997)

Unit 7

The Great Divide: A Mathematical Marathon, by Dayle Ann Dodds, illustrated by Tracey Mitchell (Candlewick Press, 2005)

A Remainder of One, by Elinor J. Pinczes, illustrated by Bonnie MacKain (Houghton Mifflin Company, 1995)

Unit 8

Tiger Math: Learning to Graph from a Baby Tiger by Ann Whitehead Nagda and Cindy Bickel (Henry Holt and Company, 2000)

Unit 9

Fraction Action, by Loreen Leedy (Holiday House, 1994)

The Math Chef, by Joan D'Amico and Karen Eich Drummond, illustrated by Tina Cash-Walsh (John Wiley & Sons, Inc., 1997)

Sir Cumference and the First Round Table: A Math Adventure, by Cindy Neuschwander, illustrated by Wayne Geehan (Charlesbridge Publishing, 2002)

Unit 10

Building with Shapes, by Rebecca Weber (Compass Point Books, 2005)

Unit 11

Careless at the Carnival: Junior Discovers Spending, by Dave Ramsey, illustrated by Marshall Ramsey (Lamp Press, 2003)

Pigs Will Be Pigs: Fun with Math and Money, by Amy Axelrod, illustrated by Sharon McGinley-Nally (Aladdin, 1997)

Unit 12

Hottest, Coldest, Highest, Deepest, by Steve Jenkins (Houghton Mifflin Company, 1998)

Index

Index (Continued)

Index (Continued)

Index (continued)

Index (Continued)

Index (Continued)

Q

R

Index (Continued)

T